make time for Joe.

With a little help from my friends, I find time to cozy up with an old favorite. The java is hot, fresh and flowing. And the most important meal of the day is always on the house. It's one place I always find a warm welcome. I'm with friends. **Plus, we offer AAA rates.*** **For reservations, call your AAA agent, visit hampton.com or call 1-800-HAMPTON.**

Friendly Service   Cozy Hampton Bed   100% Satisfaction Guarantee   we love having you here.*   *Hampton*

AAA Show Your Card & Save   *Subject to availability.

The Hilton Family

©2008 Hilton Hotels Corporation

Oregon
& Washington

Are we meeting your travel needs?
Send written comments to:

AAA Member Comments
1000 AAA Drive, Box 61
Heathrow, FL 32746-5063

Published by AAA Publishing
1000 AAA Drive
Heathrow, FL 32746-5063
Copyright AAA 2009
All rights reserved

Advertising Rate and Circulation Information: (407) 444-8280

Printed in the USA by
Quebecor World, Buffalo, NY

Photo Credit: (Cover & Title Page)
North of Brookings, OR
© Ed Callaert
Larry Ulrich Stock

Printed on recyclable paper.
Please recycle whenever possible.

Mixed Sources
Product group from well-managed forests and other controlled sources
www.fsc.org Cert no. SW - COC - 002550
© 1996 Forest Stewardship Council

Stock #4620

Oregon & Washington

MAPS

Featured Information

MAPS

4

Save First, Then Travel

with the lowest hotel rates from AAA.com

- **AAA.com**pare:
  67% of the time, the lowest rate on standard double occupancy rooms at partner hotels can be found at AAA.com*

- **AAA.com**plete:
  Mapping, Diamond Ratings, reviews and destination information

- **AAA.com**fort:
  Booking and service from the travel name you trust

Visit your nearest AAA office, click on AAA.com or call 1-866-AAA-SAVE.

67%
AAA.com

16% AARP℠   15% Travelocity   11% Orbitz   10% Expedia

Tips for AAA.com's

Quick tips for using TripTik® Travel Planner's enhanced features.

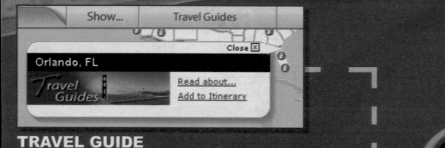

TRAVEL GUIDE
Select the 'Travel Guides' button to get AAA's exclusive travel information.

HOTEL BOOKING AT LOW RATES
Click to book partner hotels at low online rates.

CLICK AND DRAG ROUTE MODIFICATION
Click and drag the route to the roads you prefer to travel.

TripTik® Travel Planner

CUSTOM MAPS
Click to add points of interest to MyPlaces then 'Print' full color maps showing just the places you chose.

Show on Map

MyPlaces (6) (New)   Print   Clear All

Epcot
SeaWorld Orlando
Bahama Breeze
Landrys Seafood House
Orlando Premium Outlets
SpringHill Suites at The Marriott Village

- Pan/Identify/Modify Tool
- Rubberband Zoom Tool
- Identify Road Tool

TripTik Travel Planner
AAA.com's all-in-one maps,
directions and travel
information resource.

AAA
ROAD
Atlas
Travel With Someone You Trust
2009
Traveling with
Your Pet
AAA PetBook
SPIRAL GUIDES
FLORIDA
SPIRAL GUIDES
LAS VEGAS
SPIRAL GUIDES
ESSENTIAL
Canada
East
AAA

Attractions, lodgings and restaurants are listed on the basis of merit alone after careful evaluation and approval by one of AAA/CAA's full-time, professionally trained inspectors. Evaluations are unannounced to ensure that we see an establishment just as you would see it.

An establishment's decision to advertise in the TourBook guide has no bearing on its evaluation or rating. Advertising for services or products does not imply AAA endorsement.

Information in this guide was believed accurate at the time of publication. However, since changes inevitably occur between annual editions, we suggest you work with your AAA travel professional or check on AAA.com to confirm prices and schedules.

How the TourBook Guide is Organized

The TourBook guide is organized into three distinct sections.

The **Points of Interest** section helps you plan daily activities and sightseeing excursions and provides details about the city or attraction you are visiting.

The **Lodgings and Restaurants** section helps you select AAA Approved accommodations and dining facilities meeting your specific needs and expectations.

The **Reference** section provides indexes for locating information within this guide and items to aid the trip planning process.

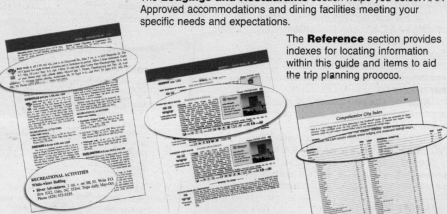

Locating the Attractions, Lodgings and Restaurants

Attractions, lodgings and restaurants are listed under the city in which they physically are located - or in some cases under the nearest recognized city. Most listings are alphabetically organized by state, province, region or island, then by city and establishment name.

A color is assigned to each state or province so that you can match the color bars at the top of the page to switch from the **Points of Interest** section to the **Lodgings and Restaurants** section.

Spotting maps help you physically locate points of interest, lodgings and restaurants in the major destinations.

The Comprehensive City Index located in the **Reference** section contains an A-to-Z list of cities.

Destination Cities and Destination Areas

Destination cities, established based on government models and local expertise, include metropolitan areas plus nearby vicinity cities. **Destination areas** are regions with broad tourist appeal; several cities will comprise the area.

If a city falls within a destination's vicinity, the city name will appear at its alphabetical location in the book, and a cross reference will give you the exact page on which listings for that city begin.

An orientation map appears at the beginning of each destination section to familiarize you with that destination.

GEM Designation

A indicates the attraction has been rated a AAA GEM, a "must see" point of interest that offers a *Great Experience for Members®*. These attractions have been judged to be of exceptional interest and quality by AAA Inspectors.

A GEM listing page with a brief description of individual GEM attractions follows the Orientation map near the beginning of each state or province Points of Interest section. Cross-references guide the reader to the attraction's listing page.

Discount Savings

The SAVE icon denotes those attractions offering AAA/CAA, AAA MasterCard, AAA VISA or international Show Your Card & Save discount cardholders a discount off the attraction's standard admission. Present your card at the attraction's admission desk.

A list of participating points of interest appears in the Reference section of this guide.

Shopping establishments preceded by a SAVE icon also provide to AAA/CAA members a discount and/or gift with purchase; present your card at the mall's customer service center to receive your benefit.

Exceptions

- Members should inquire in advance concerning the validity of the discount for special rates.

- The SAVE discount may not be used in conjunction with other discounts.

- Attractions that already provide a reduced senior or child rate may not honor the SAVE discount for those age groups.

- All offers are subject to change and may not apply during special events, particular days or seasons or for the entire validity period of the TourBook guide.

Adventure Travel

There are inherent risks with adventure travel activities like air tours, hiking, skiing and white-water rafting. For your own safety, please read and adhere to all safety instructions. Mentions of these activities are for information only and do **not** imply endorsement by AAA.

Shopping areas: Mast General Store, 630 W. King St., operates out of a 1913 building, stocked with a variety of goods includi... Swa Box Amish

RED OAK is off I-95 exit 4A, just n. to Dogw 1812 house has eight 60-foot columns and is fu 9-7, May 15-Labor Day; 9-5, Apr. 1-May 14 a of year. Hours may vary; phone ahead. Close admission 45 minutes before closing. Admission $8; MC, VI. Phone (555) 555-5555 or (800) 555-5555.

holiday... 10-18); free (on Tues.).

BOONVILLE (B-4) pop. 1,138, elev. 1,066'

RED OAK is off I-95 exit 4A, just n. to Dogwood Dr., then 2 mi. e. to 610 Magnolia St. The 1812 house has eight 60-foot columns and is furnished in period. Allow 1 hour minimum. Daily 9-7, May 15-Labor Day; 9-5, Apr. 1-May 14 and day after Labor Day-Thanksgiving; 10-4, rest of year. Hours may vary; phone ahead. Closed Jan. 1, Easter, Thanksgiving and Dec. 25. Last admission 45 minutes before closing. Admission $8; $5 (ages 6-12 and 66+); $3 (ages 0-5). AX, DS, MC, VI. Phone (555) 555-5555 or (800) 555-5555.

RECREATIONAL ACTIVITIES

White-water Rafting

- **River Adventures**, 1 mi. s. on SR 50. Write P.O Box 1012, Gale, NC 35244. Trips daily May-Oc Phone (828) 555-5555.

BREVARD (F-3) pop. 6,789, elev. 2,229'

The town is a popular summer resort at the e trance to Pisgah National Forest (*see place listing* 166). Brevard is in an area known as the "Land Waterfalls," sporting more than 250 named wa falls such as Laughing Falls and Courthouse F Brevard Music Center offers concerts nightly, weekend in June to mid-

Brevard

RECREATIONAL ACTIV

White-water Rafting

- **River Adventures**, 1 mi. s Box 1012, Gale, NC 3524 Phone (828) 555-5555.

Directions

Unless otherwise specified, directions are given from the center of town, using the following highway designations:

I=interstate highway   **US**=federal highway
SR=state route   **CR**=county road
FM=farm to market   **FR**=forest road
Mex.=Mexican highway   **Hwy.**=Canadian or Caribbean highway

Prices and Dates of Operations

Admission prices are quoted without sales tax. Children under the lowest age specified are admitted free when accompanied by an adult. Days, months and age groups written with a hyphen are inclusive.

Prices pertaining to points of interest in the United States are quoted in U.S. dollars; points of interest in Canada are quoted in Canadian dollars; prices for points of interest in Mexico and the Caribbean are quoted as an approximate U.S. dollar equivalent.

Schedules and admission rates may change throughout the validity period of this guide. Check AAA.com for the most current information.

Credit Cards Accepted

AX=American Express   **JC**=Japan Credit Bureau
CB=Carte Blanche   **MC**=MasterCard
DC=Diners Club   **VI**=VISA
DS=Discover

Bulleted Listings

Gambling establishments within hotels are presented for member information regardless of whether the lodging is AAA Approved.

Recreational activities of a participatory nature (requiring physical exertion or special skills) are not inspected.

Wineries are inspected by AAA Inspectors to ensure they meet listing requirements and offer tours.

All are presented in an abbreviated bulleted format for informational purposes.

NE — BURLINGTON, NC   125

Chamber of Commerce: P.O.
on City, NC 28713; phone (828)
...867-0246.

then 2 mi. e. to 610 Magnolia St. The
n period. Allow 1 hour minimum. Daily
ter Labor Day-Thanksgiving; 10-4, rest
Easter, Thanksgiving and Dec. 25. Last
6-12 and 66+); $3 (ages 0-5). AX, DS,

...departing
...Bryson City, combines rail and
excursions in one outing. The adventure
a scenic 2-hour train trip across Fontana
top of Nantahala Gorge. Rafts are then
r a guided 3-hour trip down the Nan-
ar. Lunch is included.
n under 60 pounds are not permitted. Al
rs minimum. Trips daily mid-Apr. to late
begin at $66; $51 (ages 3-12). DS, MC,
(828) 488-2384 or (800) 451-9972.

ATIONAL ACTIVITIES
ater Rafting

hala Outdoor Center, 26 mi. s.w. on US
Write 13077 Hwy. 19W, Bryson City, NC
. Trips daily Mar.-Oct. Phone (828)
175 or (800) 232-7238.

Raft, 12 mi. s. on US 19W. Write 11044 US
. Bryson City, NC 28713. Trips daily Mar.-
. Phone (828) 488-3316 or (800) 872-7238.

dwater Ltd., 12 mi. s.w. on US 19/74W.
te P.O. Box 309, Long Creek, SC 29658. Trips
y Apr.-Oct. Phone (828) 488-2384 or (800)
...9972.

RLINGTON (A-5) pop. 44,917, elev. 656'
urlington is a textile industry center with numer-
...outlet shops that attract bargain hunters
...es. Clothing, leather goods, towels,
...ets and furniture are popular
...as a maintenance and re-
...Carolina Railroad; the
...as a train station and

...ty Park, at South
...is a 1910 Dentzel
R 50. Write P.O. ...eir detail and intri-
s daily May-Oct. ...ls still exist world-
...s, the hand-carved
...ffe and reindeer, four
...The carousel operates
..., phone (336) 222-5030.

Understanding the Lodging Listing

Local Member Value

 or and identify hotels that offer members a rate guarantee and up to two free special amenities as part of their Official Appointment partnership with AAA. Rate guarantee: Discounted standard room rate (usually based on last standard room availability) or the lowest public rate available at time of booking for dates of stay. Free special amenity options are included in the listing and could be either: breakfast, local telephone calls, newspaper, room upgrade, preferred room, or high-speed Internet.

Diamond Rating

The number of Diamonds informs you of the overall complexity of a lodging's amenities and service. Red indicates an Official Appointment lodging. An in place of Diamonds indicates the property has not been rated but is included as an "information only" service. A detailed description of each rating level appears on page 20.

Classification

All Diamond Rated lodgings are classified using three key elements: style of operation, overall concept and service level. See pages 22-23 for details on our classifications.

Rates

The property's standard 2-person rates and effective dates are shown.

Rates are provided to AAA by each lodging and represent the publicly available rate or ranges for a standard room. Rates are rounded to the nearest dollar and do not include taxes. U.S., Mexican and Caribbean rates are in U.S. dollars; rates for Canadian lodgings are in Canadian dollars.

Information about cancellation and minimum stay policies is provided in the **Terms** section of the property's listing.

Online Reservations

This notation indicates AAA/CAA members can conveniently check room availability, validate room rates and make reservations for this property in a secure online environment at AAA.com.

Service Availability

Unit types, amenities and room features preceded by the word "Some" indicate the item is available on a limited basis, potentially within only one unit. The term "Fee" appearing to the left of an amenity icon indicates an extra charge applies.

Nationwide Member Value

The blue box in the listing identifies hotel brands that offer an everyday member benefit at all AAA Approved locations. (See page 19 for additional program benefits.)

Spotting Symbol

Black ovals with white numbers are used to locate, or "spot," lodgings on maps we provide for larger cities.

Credit Cards Accepted

AX=American Express JC=Japan Credit Bureau
CB=Carte Blanche MC=MasterCard
DC=Diners Club VI=VISA
DS=Discover

Some properties accept cash but require a credit card at registration. If you plan to pay in cash, call in advance for restrictions.

Icons

Lodging icons represent some of the member values, services and facilities offered.

Phone: (555)555-5555 75
just e on SR

Phone: 555/555-5555 11

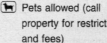

(H) Hilton
AAA Benefit:
embers save 5%
more everyday!

laundry, airport transportation, beach shuttle,
es, business center. Cards: AX, DS, MC, VI.
nternet. (See color ad p 478)
/SOME UNITS

laundry, airport transportation, beach shuttle,
es, business center. Cards: AX, DS, MC, VI.
nternet. (See color ad p 478)
/SOME UNITS

Phone: (555)555-5555 9
exit 16, just e
tional activities
room standard
nterior/exterior
-site. Terms:
, dual phone
games (fee).
oor. Leisure
ennis courts,
each cruisers,
coin laundry,
, PC, fax,
al telephone

FEE VCR

Phone: 555/555-5555
Palace: downtown; in historic district.
ed with antiques and family heirlooms; a
. Smoke free premises. 6 one-bedroom
. Bath: combo or shower only. Parking:
brary, hair dryers. Some: DVD players.
et. Business Services: meeting rooms,

Phone: 555/555-5555 18
ity: The large facility boasts spacious,
square-foot casino with a cafe, market
hower only. Parking: 2 one-bedroom suites
igh-speed internet, dual phone lines,
players. Dining: 4 restaurants, also,
ent. Pool(s): heated outdoor. Leisure
st Services: valet laundry, wireless
enter. Cards: AX, DS, MC, VI. Free
rnet.

Discounts

ASK May offer discount

Member Services

- ✈ Airport transportation
- 🐕 Pets allowed (call property for restrictions and fees)
- 🍴 Restaurant on premises
- 🍴→ Restaurant off premises (walking distance)
- 24🛎 24-hour room service
- 🍸 Full bar
- 👶 Child care
- &M Accessible features (call property for available services and amenities)

Leisure Activities

- 🎰 Full-service casino
- 🏊 Pool
- 💪 Health club on premises
- 💪 Health club off premises
- ⛹ Recreational activities

In-Room Amenities

- ⊠ Designated non-smoking rooms
- VCR VCR
- 🎬 Movies
- 🧊 Refrigerator
- Microwave
- ☕ Coffee maker
- A̸C̸ No air conditioning
- T̸V̸ No TV
- CT̸V̸ No cable TV
- ☎̸ No telephones

Safety Features

(see page 24)
(Mexico and Caribbean only)

- S Sprinklers
- D Smoke detectors

Understanding the Restaurant Listing

Official Appointment

AAA or CAA indicates Official Appointment (OA) restaurants. The OA program permits restaurants to display and advertise the AAA or CAA emblem. These establishments are highlighted in red to help you quickly identify them. The AAA or CAA Approved sign helps traveling members find restaurants that want member business.

Local Member Value

SAVE identifies restaurants that offer a Show Your Card & Save® discount to AAA/CAA members.

Diamond Rating

The number of Diamonds informs you of the overall complexity of food, presentation, service and ambience. Red indicates an Official Appointment restaurant. A detailed description of each Diamond level appears on page 21.

Cuisine Type

The cuisine type helps you select a dining facility that caters to your individual taste. AAA currently recognizes more than 120 different cuisine types.

Prices

Rates shown represent the minimum and maximum entree cost per person. Exceptions may include one-of-a-kind or special market priced items. Rates are rounded to the nearest dollar and do not include taxes. U.S., Mexican and Caribbean rates are in U.S. dollars; rates for Canadian restaurants are in Canadian dollars.

Icons

Icons provide additional information about services and facilities.

AC No air-conditioning

&M Accessible features offered

(call property for available services and amenities)

⊠ Designated smoking section available

Menus

This notation indicates AAA/CAA members can conveniently view the restaurant's menu in a secure online environment at AAA.com.

Spotting Symbol

White ovals with black numbers serve as restaurant locators and are used to locate, or "spot," restaurants on maps for larger cities.

Classifications

If applicable, a restaurant may be defined as:

Classic - renowned and/or landmark restaurant in business longer than 25 years, known for unique style and ambience.

Historic - establishments must meet one of the following criteria:

- Listed on the National Register of Historic Places
- Designated a National Historic Landmark
- Located in a National Register Historic District

Separate criteria designate historic properties in Canada, Mexico and the Caribbean.

Credit Cards Accepted

AX = American Express
CB = Carte Blanche
DC = Diners Club
DS = Discover
JC = Japan Credit Bureau
MC = MasterCard
VI = VISA

---

alls of the popular theme restaurant. **Phone:** 555/555-5555 ㊺
on the menu is a wide variety of American cuisine—from burgers
d pasta. Casual dress. **Bar:** Full bar. Live music on the weekends
I-75/85, exit 248C northbound, 0.4 mi w; exit 249A southbound.
te (fee). **Cards:** AX, DS, JC, MC, VI. **Hours:** 11 am-11 pm.

eat buffets for lunch and dinner. **Phone:** 336/547-8868
ushi and dim sum selection. Included in the buffet are a
ell as crab legs. Menu service is also available. Casual dress.
-11 pm, Sun noon-10 pm. **Address:** 4408 Landover Rd 27407

panded to this newly constructed building, **Phone:** 555/555-5555 ㊸
atmosphere is informal, yet the menu offerings are cutting
nal. Dressy casual. **Bar:** full bar. located behind a
pm-9 pm. Closed: 12/25; also Sun, Mon & **Reservations:** accepted.
ation: I-40, exit 213, 2 mi n, then just e on Hunt Club Rd; for dinner Super
g: on-site. **Cards:** AX, DC, DS, MC, VI. **Classic**

rket St,
n, then 0.8 mi w.

y upscale dining atmosphere. The menu features dishes **Phone:** 336/273-7057
uch as in stuffed rainbow trout and lamb with honey-mint
red with flair, including roasted pulled pork, fried chicken
Reservations: accepted. **Hours:** 11:30 am-9.30 pm, Fri-
also Sun. **Address:** 100-D W Washington St 27401
street. **Cards:** AX, DS, MC, VI.

ale eatery, with the focus of the cuisine on incorporating **Phone:** 336/370-0707
American fare. Casual dress. **Bar:** full bar.
Fri & Sat-11 pm, Sun 10 am-10 pm. Closed: 11/27,
Location: Wendover Ave, exit US 220 N/Westover
ds: AX, DS, MC, VI.

menu of burgers, wraps, sandwiches and hearty pub **Phone:** 336/274-1373
oor seating is offered during warm weather. Casual
. Closed: 1/1, 11/27, 12/24, 12/25. **Address:** 345 S
king: street. **Cards:** AX, DS, MC, VI.

st and is served with a smile in the comfortable, **Phone:** 336/294-5551
. **Hours:** 11 am-3:30 & 5-9:30 pm. **Address:** 4109-
stbound; exit 214 westbound, 1 mi ne, exit Spring
, MC, VI.

sh and chips, gourmet sandwiches, the signature **Phone:** 336/299-3649
gus beef. Sauces, dressings and soups are
brewery. Casual dress. **Bar:** full bar. **Hours:** 11
27, 12/25. **Address:** 714 Francis King St 27410
st w on Hunt Club Rd, then just n. **Parking:** on-

newly constructed building, located behind a **Phone:** 336/297-0950
informal, yet the menu offerings are cutting
sual. **Bar:** full bar. **Reservations:** accepted.
sed: 12/25; also Sun, Mon & for dinner Super
it 213, 2 mi n, then just e on Hunt Club Rd;
ds: AX, DC, DS, MC, VI.

AAA/CAA members can generally expect to pay no more than the maximum regular rate printed in the TourBook guide in each rate range for a standard room. On rare occasions AAA receives or inadvertently publishes incorrect rates.

Obtain current AAA/CAA member rates and make reservations at AAA.com. Rates may vary within the range, depending on season and room type. Listed rates are usually based on last standard room availability.

Discounts

Member discounts, when offered, will apply to rates quoted within the rate range and are applicable at the time of booking. Special rates used in advertising, as well as special short-term promotional rates lower than the lowest listed rate in the range, are not subject to additional member discounts.

Exceptions

Rates for properties operating as concessionaires for the U.S. National Park Service are not guaranteed due to governing regulations. Rates in the Mexico TourBook are not guaranteed and may fluctuate based on the exchange rate of the peso.

Lodgings may temporarily increase room rates, not recognize discounts or modify pricing policies during special events. Examples of special events range from Mardi Gras and the Kentucky Derby (including pre-Derby events) to college football games, holidays, holiday periods and state fairs. Although some special events are listed in AAA/CAA TourBook guides and on AAA.com, it is always wise to check in advance with AAA travel professionals for specific dates.

Get the Room You Reserved

When making your reservation, identify yourself as a AAA or CAA member and request written confirmation to guarantee: type of room, rate, dates of stay, and cancellation and refund policies. At registration, show your membership card.

When you find your room is not as specified, and you have written confirmation of reservations for a certain type of accommodation, you should be given the option of choosing a different room or finding one elsewhere. Should you choose to go elsewhere and a refund is refused or resisted, submit the matter to AAA/CAA within 30 days, along with complete documentation, including your reasons for refusing the room and copies of your written confirmation and any receipts or canceled checks associated with this problem.

If you are charged more than the maximum rate listed in the TourBook guide for a standard room, question the additional charge. If management refuses to adhere to the published rate, pay for the room and submit your receipt and membership number to AAA/CAA within 30 days. Include all pertinent information: dates of stay, rate paid, itemized paid receipts, number of persons in your party and the room number you occupied, and list any extra room equipment used. A refund of the amount paid in excess of the stated maximum will be made if our investigation indicates that unjustified charging occurred.

Deposit, Refund and Cancellation Policies

Most establishments give full deposit refunds if they have been notified at least 48 hours before the normal check-in time. Listing prose will note if more than 48 hours' notice is required for cancellation. Some properties may charge a cancellation or handling fee. When this applies, "cancellation fee imposed" will appear in the listing. If you cancel too late, you have little recourse if a refund is denied.

When an establishment requires full or partial payment in advance and your trip is cut short, a refund may not be given.

When canceling a reservation, phone the lodging immediately. Make a note of the date and time you called, the cancellation number if there is one, and the name of the person who handled the cancellation. If your AAA/CAA club made your reservation, allow them to make the cancellation for you as well, so you will have proof of cancellation.

Check-in and Check-out Times

Check-in and check-out times are shown in the lodging listings, under Terms, only if they are before 3 p.m. or after 10 a.m. respectively.

Members Save With Our Partners

These National Show Your Card & Save® partners provide the listed member benefits. Visit AAA.com/Save to discover all the great Show Your Card & Save® discounts in your area. Admission tickets that offer greater discounts may be available for purchase at the local AAA/CAA club. A maximum of six attraction tickets is available at the discount price at the gate; six discounted tickets is also the maximum for Amtrak and Gray Line.

SeaWorld, Busch Gardens, Sesame Place
AAA.com/SeaWorld, AAA.com/BuschGardens, AAA.com/SesamePlace

- Save on admission at the gate, at participating offices, or online

- Save 10% on up-close dining; visit Guest Relations for details

Six Flags AAA.com/SixFlags

- Save on admission at the gate, at participating offices, or online

- Save 10% on merchandise purchases of $15 or more at in-park stores

Universal Orlando Resort and Universal Studios Hollywood
AAA.com/Universal

- Save on admission at the gate, at participating offices, or online

- Save 10% at select food and merchandise venues in-park and at Universal CityWalk®

Restaurant Partner
Savings applies to AAA/CAA members and up to five guests.

Hard Rock Cafe

- Save 10% on food, non-alcoholic beverages and merchandise at all U.S. and select Canadian and international locations

Landry's Seafood House, The Crab House, Chart House, Muer Seafood Restaurants, and Aquarium and Downtown Aquarium Restaurants

- Save 10% on food and non-alcoholic beverages at all of the above restaurants

- Save 10% on merchandise at Aquarium and Downtown Aquarium restaurants

Tanger Outlet Centers www.tangeroutlet.com

- Save up to 20% on total purchase at select merchants with AAA/CAA coupon booklet

- Member BONUS: FREE $5 gift card for each additional Tanger Outlet Center visited after first within same calendar year

- Show membership card and register at the AAA customer service desk when you visit

Amtrak

- 10% discount on rail fare when booked at least 3 days in advance of travel date

Grand Canyon Railway

- Save up to 20% on rail fare, hotel accommodations, restaurant and gift shop purchases sold outside of Grand Canyon National Park

Gray Line AAA.com/GrayLine

- Save 10% on sightseeing tours of 1 day or less worldwide

AAA Preferred Lodging Partners

EXPECT SAVINGS, SELECTION, AND SATISFACTION

- **Best AAA/CAA member rates for your dates of stay.** Provide valid membership number when placing reservation and show your card at hotel check-in.
- **Satisfaction guarantee.** Notify the property if you are dissatisfied with any part of your stay. If the matter cannot be resolved, you may be entitled to compensation (see page 17).
- **Seasonal promotions and special member offers.** Visit AAA.com to view current offers.
- **Everyday member benefit.*** Look for the blue boxes in the TourBook listings for everyday values offered at all AAA Approved locations.

*Offer good at time of publication: Chains and offers may change without notice. Preferred Hotel Partner discounts may vary in Mexico and the Caribbean.

10% Off Best Available Rates
Best Western International

5% or more Off Best Available Rates
Conrad, Doubletree, Embassy Suites, Hampton, Hilton, Hilton Garden Inn, Hilton Grand Vacations, Homewood Suites, and Waldorf=Astoria Collection

HYATT
HOTELS & RESORTS ®

10% Off Best Available Rates
Andaz, Grand Hyatt, Hyatt Place, Hyatt Regency, Hyatt Summerfield Suites, and Park Hyatt

Marriott.
HOTELS & RESORTS

5% or more Off Best Available Rates
Courtyard, Fairfield Inn, JW Marriott, Marriott, Renaissance Hotels & Resorts, Residence Inn, SpringHill Suites, and TownePlace Suites

HOTELS & RESORTS WORLDWIDE, INC.

5-15% Off Best Available Rates
aloft, element, Four Points, Le Meridien, Sheraton, St. Regis, The Luxury Collection, Westin, and W Hotels

Understanding the Diamond Ratings

AAA/CAA inspectors have evaluated and rated each of the 58,000 lodging and restaurant establishments in the TourBook series to ensure quality travel information for our members. All properties must meet AAA's minimum requirements (for lodgings) concerning cleanliness, comfort and security - or - AAA's minimum requirements (for restaurants) pertaining to cleanliness, food preparation and service.

Eligible applicants receive an unannounced evaluation by a AAA/CAA inspector that includes two distinct components:

- **AAA Approval:** The inspector first must determine whether the property meets the criteria required to be AAA Approved. Every establishment that meets these strict guidelines offers AAA members the assurance that, regardless of the Diamond Rating, it provides acceptable quality, cleanliness, service and value.
- **AAA Diamond Rating:** Once an establishment becomes AAA Approved, it is then assigned a rating of one to five Diamonds, indicating the extensiveness of its facilities, amenities and services, from basic to moderate to luxury. These Diamond Ratings guide members in selecting establishments appropriately matched to their needs and expectations.

LODGINGS

1 Diamond

One Diamond lodgings typically appeal to the budget-minded traveler. They provide essential, no-frills accommodations and basic comfort and hospitality.

2 Diamond

Two Diamond lodgings appeal to family travelers seeking affordable yet more than the basic accommodations. Facilities, decor and amenities are modestly enhanced.

3 Diamond

Three Diamond lodgings offer a distinguished style. Properties are multi-faceted, with marked upgrades in physical attributes, amenities and guest comforts.

4 Diamond

Four Diamond lodgings are refined and stylish. Physical attributes are upscale. The fundamental hallmarks at this level include an extensive array of amenities combined with a high degree of hospitality, service and attention to detail.

5 Diamond

Five Diamond lodgings provide the ultimate in luxury and sophistication. Physical attributes are extraordinary in every manner. Service is meticulous, exceeding guest expectations and maintaining impeccable standards of excellence. Extensive personalized services and amenities provide first-class comfort.

fyi The lodging listings with **fyi** in place of Diamonds are included as an *information only* service for members. The icon indicates that a property has not been rated for one or more of the following reasons: too new to rate, under construction, under major renovation, not evaluated, may not meet all AAA requirements.

A property not meeting all AAA requirements is included for either its member value or because it may be the only accommodation available in the area. Listing prose will give insight as to why the **fyi** designation was assigned.

4 Diamond

Four Diamond restaurants provide a distinctive fine-dining experience that is typically expensive. Surroundings are highly refined with upscale enhancements throughout. Highly creative chefs use imaginative presentations to augment fresh, top-quality ingredients. A proficient service staff meets or exceeds guest expectations. A wine steward may offer menu-specific knowledge to guide selection.

5 Diamond

Five Diamond restaurants are luxurious and renowned for consistently providing a world-class experience. Highly acclaimed chefs offer artistic menu selections that are imaginative and unique, using only the finest ingredients available. A maître d' leads an expert service staff in exceeding guest expectations, attending to every detail in an effortless and unobtrusive manner.

RESTAURANTS

1 Diamond

One Diamond restaurants provide simple, familiar specialty food (such as burgers, chicken, pizza or tacos) at an economical price. Often self-service, basic surroundings complement a no-nonsense approach.

2 Diamond

Two Diamond restaurants offer a familiar, family-oriented experience. Menu selection includes home-style foods and family favorites, often cooked to order, modestly enhanced and reasonably priced. Service is accommodating yet relaxed, a perfect complement to casual surroundings.

 The restaurants with **fyi** in place of Diamonds are included as an *information only* service for members. These listings provide additional dining choices but have not yet been evaluated.

3 Diamond

Three Diamond restaurants convey an entry into fine dining and are often positioned as adult-oriented experiences. The atypical menu may feature the latest cooking trends and/or traditional cuisine. Expanded beverage offerings complement the menu. The ambience is well coordinated, comfortable and enhanced by a professional service staff.

Understanding the Lodging Classifications

To ensure that your lodging needs and preferences are met, we recommend that you consider an establishment's classification when making your travel choices. While the quality and comfort at properties with the same Diamond Rating should be consistent (regardless of the classification), there are differences in typical decor/theme elements, range of facilities and service levels.

Lodging Classifications

Bed & Breakfast

Typically smaller scale properties emphasizing a high degree of personal touches that provide guests an "at home" feeling. Guest units tend to be individually decorated. Rooms may not include some modern amenities such as televisions and telephones, and may have a shared bathroom. Usually owner-operated with a common room or parlor separate from the innkeeper's living quarters, where guests and operators can interact during evening and breakfast hours. Evening office closures are normal. A continental or full, hot breakfast is served and is included in the room rate.

1884 Paxton House Inn
Thomasville, GA

Cabin

Vacation-oriented, typically smaller scale, freestanding units of simple construction—roughly finished logs or stone—and basic design or décor. Often located in wooded, rural, or waterfront locations. As a rule, basic cleaning supplies, kitchen utensils, and complete bed and bath linens are supplied. The guest registration area may be located off site.

Greenbrier Valley Resorts
Gatlinburg, TN

Condominium

Vacation-oriented—commonly for extended-stay purposes—apartment-style accommodations of varying design or décor. Routinely available for rent through a management company, units often contain one or more bedrooms, a living room, full kitchen, and an eating area. Studio-type models combine the

Sands of Kahana
Kahana, Maui, HI

sleeping and living areas into one room. As a rule, basic cleaning supplies, kitchen utensils, and complete bed and bath linens are supplied. The guest registration area may be located off site.

Cottage

Vacation-oriented, typically smaller scale, freestanding units with home style enhancements in architectural design and interior décor. Often located in wooded, rural, or waterfront locations. Units may vary in design and décor. As a rule, basic cleaning supplies, kitchen utensils, and complete bed and bath linens are supplied. The guest registration area may be located off site.

Paradise Villas, Little Cayman Island

Country Inn

Although similar in definition to a bed and breakfast, country inns are usually larger in scale with spacious public areas and offer a dining facility that serves—at a minimum—breakfast and dinner.

Greenville Inn, Greenville, ME

Hotel

Commonly, a multistory establishment with interior room entrances offering a variety of guest unit styles. The magnitude of the public areas is determined by the overall theme, location and service level, but may include a variety of facilities such as a restaurant, shops, fitness center, spa, business center, and/or meeting rooms.

The Grand America Hotel
Salt Lake City, UT

Motel

Commonly, a one- or two-story establishment with exterior room entrances and drive up parking. Typically, guest units have one bedroom with a bathroom of similar décor and design. Public areas and facilities are often limited in size and/or availability.

Best Western Deltona Inn, Deltona, FL

Ranch

Typically a working ranch with an obvious rustic, Western theme featuring equestrian-related activities and a variety of guest unit styles.

Lost Valley Ranch, Deckers, CO

Vacation Rental House

Vacation-oriented—commonly for extended-stay purposes—typically larger scale, freestanding, and of varying design or décor. Routinely available for rent through a management company, houses often contain two or more bedrooms, a living room, full kitchen, dining room, and multiple bathrooms. As a rule, basic cleaning supplies, kitchen utensils, and complete bed and bath linens are supplied. The guest registration area may be located off site.

ResortQuest, Hilton Head Island, SC

Lodging Sub-classifications

The following are sub-classifications that may appear along with the classifications listed previously to provide a more specific description of the lodging.

Boutique

Often thematic and typically an informal, yet highly personalized experience; may have a luxurious or quirky style which is fashionable or unique.

Casino

Extensive gambling facilities are available, such as: blackjack, craps, keno, and slot machines. **Note:** This sub-classification will not appear beneath its Diamond Rating in the listing. It will be indicated by a ☙ icon and will be included in the row of icons immediately below the lodging listing.

Classic

Renowned and landmark properties, older than 50 years, well-known for their unique style and ambience.

Contemporary

Overall design and theme reflects characteristics of the present era's mainstream tastes and style.

Extended Stay

Offers a predominance of long-term accommodations with a designated full-service kitchen area within each unit.

Historic

These properties are typically over 75 years of age and exhibit many features of a historic nature with respect to architecture, design, furnishings, public record, or acclaim. Properties must meet one of the following criteria:

- Maintained the integrity of the historical nature
- Listed on the National Register of Historic Places
- National Historic Landmark or located in a National Register Historic District

Separate criteria designate historic properties in Canada, Mexico and the Caribbean.

Resort

Recreation-oriented, geared to vacation travelers seeking a specific destination experience. Travel packages, meal plans, themed entertainment, and social and recreational programs are typically available. Recreational facilities are extensive and may include spa treatments, golf, tennis, skiing, fishing, or water sports. Larger resorts may offer a variety of guest accommodations.

Retro

Overall design and theme reflect a contemporary design reinterpreting styles from a bygone era.

Vacation Rental

Typically houses, condos, cottages or cabins; these properties are a "home away from home" offering more room and greater value for the money. In general, they provide the conveniences of home, such as full kitchens and washers/dryers. Located in resort or popular destination areas within close proximity to major points of interest, attractions, or recreation areas, these properties may require a pre-arranged reservation and check-in at an off-site location. Housekeeping services may be limited or not included.

Vintage

Offers a window to the past and provides an experience reflecting a predominance of traits associated with the era of their origin.

Guest Safety

Room Security

In order to be approved for listing in AAA/CAA TourBook guides for the United States and Canada, accommodations must have dead bolt locks on all guest room entry doors and connecting room doors.

If the area outside the guest room door is not visible from inside the room through a window or door panel, viewports must be installed on all guest room entry doors. Bed and breakfast properties and country inns are not required to have viewports. Ground floor and easily accessible sliding doors must be equipped with some type of secondary security locks.

Even with those approval requirements, AAA cannot guarantee guest safety. AAA Inspectors view a percentage of rooms at each property since it is not feasible to evaluate every room in every lodging establishment. Therefore, AAA cannot guarantee that there are working locks on all doors and windows in all guest rooms.

Fire Safety

Because of the highly specialized skills needed to conduct professional fire safety inspections, AAA/CAA Inspectors cannot assess fire safety.

Properties must meet all federal, state/province and local fire codes. Each guest unit in all U.S. and Canadian lodging properties must be equipped with an operational, single-station smoke detector. A AAA/CAA Inspector has evaluated a sampling of the rooms to verify this equipment is in place.

Mexico and the Caribbean

Requirements for some features, such as door locks and smoke detectors/sprinkler systems, differ in Mexico and the Caribbean. If a property met AAA's security requirements at the time of the evaluation, the phrase "Meets AAA guest room security requirements" appears in the listing.

Service Animals

The Americans with Disabilities Act (ADA) prohibits U.S. businesses that serve the public from discriminating against persons with disabilities. Some businesses have mistakenly denied access to persons who use service animals. Businesses must permit entry to guests and their service animals, as well as allow service animals to accompany guests to all public areas of a property.

A property is permitted to ask whether the animal is a service animal or a pet, and whether the guest has a disability. The property may not, however, ask questions about the nature of the disability, the service provided by the animal, or require proof of a disability or certification that the animal is a service animal. These regulations may not apply in Canada, Mexico or the Caribbean.

No fees or deposits, even those normally charged for pets, may be charged for service animals. Service animals fulfill a critical need for their owners—they are not pets.

Frank Frand with his seeing eye dog, Cardinal.

Getting AAA discounts on hotels:
Smart.

Getting AAA discounts on everything else:
Ingenious.

If you use your AAA card only to get hotel discounts, then big benefits are passing you by. AAA is one of the biggest discount clubs around, using its clout of 51 million members to get discounts at more than 160,000 locations around the world. Use your AAA card to get discounts on everything from computers and books to clothing and prescriptions. Visit AAA.com/discounts and discover a new way to save.

Savings for all Seasons

Hertz rents Fords and other fine cars.
® REG. U.S. PAT. OFF. © HERTZ SYSTEM INC., 1999/2006-99.

No matter the season, Hertz offers AAA members exclusive discounts and benefits.

Operating in 145 countries at over 8,000 locations, Hertz makes traveling more convenient and efficient wherever and whenever you go. Hertz offers AAA members discounts up to 20% on car rentals worldwide.

To receive your exclusive AAA member discounts and benefits, mention your AAA membership card at time of reservation and present it at time of rental. **In addition**, to receive a free one car class upgrade on daily, weekly or weekend rental in the United States, Puerto Rico and Canada, mention PC# 969194 at the time of reservation. Offer is valid for vehicle pick-up on or before 12/15/09.

For reservations and program details, visit AAA.com/hertz, call your AAA Travel office or the Hertz/AAA Desk at **1-800-654-3080**.

Rent Wisely.®

Oregon

Jagged Cliffs & Pounding Waves

Agitated waters thrash against the craggy coastline

Majestic Mount Hood

Recreation abounds year-round on Oregon's highest point

Of Wine & Roses

Wineries dot western valleys; June brings the Portland Rose Festival

Charming Covered Bridges

Horse-and-buggy memories are kept alive in Oregon's central west

The Gorge

Dramatic geography adds breathtaking appeal to Columbia Gorge

International Rose Test Garden, Portland
© AAA / Denise Campbell

John Day Fossil Beds National Monument / © Larry Ulrich

Mother Nature embraces Oregon. Her touch is felt in the lush landscapes that lie west of the majestic Cascades and in the high desert country that spreads to their east.

Although the gold deposits that lured pioneers to migrate westward in the mid-1800s have long since been depleted, the state is amply blessed with other treasures. Verdant valleys yield roses and vineyard grapes. Winding rivers nurture salmon and steelhead trout. The craggy coast offers stunning vistas of the endless Pacific blue.

Had you been among the many who trekked to Oregon during the "Great Migration of 1843," you would have

come for the resources and the wealth of opportunity. Today, you're most likely to seek the serenity of nature undisturbed.

You'll find it reflected in the brilliant blue waters of Crater Lake, atop the white snow-capped peak of Mount Hood, across the vivid green pastures of the Willamette Valley.

You'll experience it as you ride through the rapids of the Rogue or hike the challenging terrain of Deschutes National Forest or cast fishing lines into the surf at Seal Rock.

It may even reveal itself more subtly during a relaxing winery tour or inside a quaint covered bridge.

The quest for peace ends in Oregon.

Clearly, this chunk of the Pacific Northwest was particularly blessed by the handiwork of nature at its most exuberantly unrestrained.

Dramatic, glacier-covered Mount Hood. Endless summer fruit orchards undulating across the Hood River Valley. Haystack Rock, the Devil's Punch Bowl and other coastal geological curiosities shaped by the pounding Pacific. The extraordinary sapphire hues of Crater Lake. The blazing fall foliage of maples in the Willamette Valley.

Oregon's people reflect a similar exuberance in their active lifestyle, social pioneering and state pride. They confidently revel in their relationship with nature. The two major state universities, for example, eschewed the common warrior and fearsome creature mascots in favor of the benign, yet indigenous, Beavers and Ducks.

Not all is placid in Oregon's people, however, and the environment is not always tranquil. Witness the extreme on the mighty Snake River thundering through Hells Canyon—a spectacle perhaps best appreciated driving the rough and winding 24-mile road from the precariously remote town of Imnaha to Hat Point Lookout, looming 5,700 feet above the river.

Before Lewis and Clark

Imagine the look on the faces of Meriwether Lewis and William Clark as they first stumbled upon Oregon's stunning landscapes. Their mission, commissioned by visionary President Thomas Jefferson, was to explore and map the vast territory secured by the Louisiana Purchase. They certainly weren't the first humans to appreciate the scenery, however; native peoples thrived for thousands of years before the white man arrived.

Geography—specifically, the mountainous barrier rising up in the form of the north-south Cascade Range—determined the lifestyle of the state's earliest residents. West of the Cascades, the living was comparatively easy. Shellfish, salmon, berries and wild game stocked tribal larders, extensive rivers aided in travel, and stands of virgin timber provided unlimited building materials.

In the climatically harsh country east of the Cascades it was another story. Semi-nomadic Indians followed animal migrations and subsisted on seeds and roots. The necessity of survival ruled out the artistic pursuits cultivated by the coast and valley tribes. But when fur traders, missionaries and especially homesteaders driven inexorably westward by the

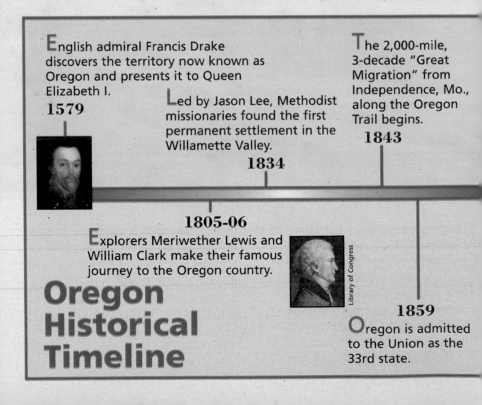

English admiral Francis Drake discovers the territory now known as Oregon and presents it to Queen Elizabeth I.
1579

Led by Jason Lee, Methodist missionaries found the first permanent settlement in the Willamette Valley.
1834

The 2,000-mile, 3-decade "Great Migration" from Independence, Mo., along the Oregon Trail begins.
1843

1805-06
Explorers Meriwether Lewis and William Clark make their famous journey to the Oregon country.

Library of Congress

Oregon Historical Timeline

1859
Oregon is admitted to the Union as the 33rd state.

doctrine of Manifest Destiny all followed in Lewis and Clark's wake, it was inevitable that ancient homelands would be usurped and government treaties would force their inhabitants onto reservations.

Some 300,000 pioneers who sought a new life at the end of a 2,000-mile trek west along the Oregon Trail found out the hard way—braving weather extremes, cholera epidemics and Indian attacks—that the journey to the promised land was no bed of roses.

Flying with their Own Wings

Hardships endured by these early settlers likely fueled the maverick spirit often associated with Oregonians. It reveals itself in the secessionist movement that has flared up several times since the early 1850s. It also is evident in the state's healthy constituency of survivalists and staunch environmentalists.

Economically, this spirit results in some offbeat ways to make a living. One of the state's faster growing industries is wild mushroom gathering. Western Oregon's mild, damp climate is fabulous for fungus, and the popularity of exotic varieties—particularly in the Japanese and European markets—has contributed to steady economic growth. While most pickers' profits aren't likely to approach the get-rich-quick dreams of 19th-century gold prospectors, mushroom hunting does score points as an environmentally friendly enterprise.

Saving a Piece of the Planet

With such spectacular land to enjoy, it's no wonder that Oregonians passionately defend it. One-time hippies drawn by the state's liberal streak have joined with activists of all stripes to lobby for progressive legislation that preserves and protects natural resources.

The length of Oregon's coast, a lavishly scenic stretch encompassing everything from placid tide pools to wave-lashed capes, is protected as public property by bills passed in 1967 and 1972. The recycling efforts that now are commonplace kicked off here in 1971 with the Bottle Bill, a first that offered refundable deposits on glass and aluminum beverage containers.

More recently, the diminutive spotted owl has been in the news. The logging industry's attempts to fell old-growth Douglas firs, the owl's natural habitat, had the bird's defenders up in arms. The controversy raised an ongoing issue in this resource-rich state—conservation versus economic livelihood.

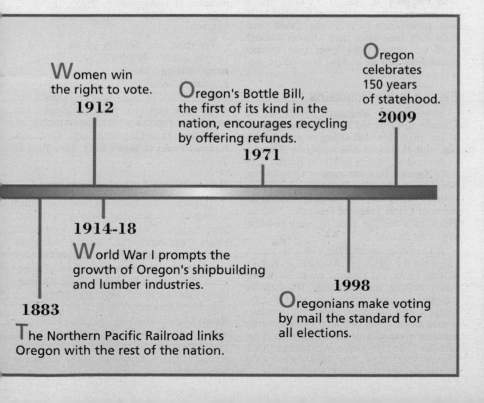

Women win the right to vote. **1912**

Oregon's Bottle Bill, the first of its kind in the nation, encourages recycling by offering refunds. **1971**

Oregon celebrates 150 years of statehood. **2009**

1914-18 World War I prompts the growth of Oregon's shipbuilding and lumber industries.

1883 The Northern Pacific Railroad links Oregon with the rest of the nation.

1998 Oregonians make voting by mail the standard for all elections.

Recreation

If it can be done outdoors, there's a good chance it can be done somewhere in Oregon. Shimmering sands and color-kissed skies accentuate the popular public beaches. Lake and mineral spring resorts are tucked away in mountain areas. The pristine natural sandbox at Oregon Dunes National Recreation Area calls out to thrill-seekers on off-road vehicles.

Wide, open grasslands along with 13 national forests provide the backdrop for exceptional **fishing** and **hunting**. Oregon waters teem with large mouth bass, catfish and coho salmon as well as brook, rainbow and steelhead trout. Serious anglers revere the Rogue River's spring and fall runs of Chinook salmon and steelhead trout. Deep-sea and surf fishing bring in halibut, salmon, sea bass and cod.

Head to the central and eastern uplands to hunt antelopes, grouse, pheasants and quails; lakes and swamps harbor ducks and geese. Bears, deer and elk roam in the mountains.

Oregonians enjoy an extensive park system. Although most areas are open year-round (weather permitting), some state parks do close in winter. More than half of the parks offer **camping** all year. A $3 entry fee is charged year-round for day-use facilities at 26 state parks. State parks charge varied overnight user fees; rates from October through April are generally $4 lower than summer prices. Fees also are charged at some national forest campgrounds.

Playing in the Mountains

Snow-centered adventures abound in the Cascade, Siskiyou and Blue mountain regions. If you enjoy **downhill skiing** or **snowboarding**, visit Hoodoo in Sisters; Mount Bachelor in Bend; or the resorts on Mount Hood. Crater Lake National Park and most of Oregon's national forests are ideal for challenging **cross-country skiing** and **snowshoeing**. Take in the sights of Crater Lake and Deschutes National Forest at a thrilling pace by **snowmobiling** across the terrain.

If you equate summer fun with river rapids, check out the Deschutes, Klamath, McKenzie, Rogue, Snake and Umpqua rivers for **whitewater rafting** and **kayaking**. **Windsurfing** adventurists hone their skills at Columbia Gorge, where the natural geography simulates a wind tunnel. Even land lovers appreciate the scene of vivid sails dotted on the river. Contact the Columbia Gorge Windsurfing Association, P.O. Box 182, Hood River, OR 97031; phone (541) 386-9225.

Huge swells make for great **surfing** in spring and winter; try Short Sands Beach, south of Cannon Beach; Pacific City; or Otter Rock. If you prefer a face-to-face rendezvous with the creatures below the surface, give an offshore **scuba diving** voyage a whirl. Start your explorations from Port Orford or the towns on Tillamook Bay.

If wet and wild is not your style, explore Oregon's landscape. Trails for **hiking** and **horseback riding** wind through nearly every park, forest and recreation area.

Adventures in Mountain Biking

The state's range of terrain lends itself to great **mountain biking**. Adults and children alike can tackle the leisurely ride at Banks/Vernonia Linear State Park near Banks; phone (800) 551-6949. For an exhilarating challenge, try Fifteenmile on Mount Hood; Larch Mountain near Corbett; or Cascade Head near Lincoln City. Riders of all abilities will find what they need at Deschutes National Forest.

To receive a free **bicycling** guide, Columbia River Gorge bicycling guide or a coastal bicycle route map, write to the Oregon Department of Transportation at 355 Capitol St. N.E., Salem, OR 97301, or phone (503) 986-3556.

For those who like fun on the wild side, Oregon doesn't disappoint. Lift off from a **hang gliding** launch at Abert Rim in Fremont-Winema National Forests or at Woodrat Mountain, 10 miles west of Medford, for a bird's-eye view of awesome geography. For an up-close experience with rugged beauty, try **rock climbing** at Columbia Gorge, Deschutes National Forest or Smith Rock State Park in Terrebonne.

Recreational Activities

Throughout the TourBook, you may notice a Recreational Activities heading with bulleted listings of recreation-oriented establishments listed underneath. Similar operations also may be mentioned in Destination City recreation sections. Since normal AAA inspection criteria cannot be applied, these establishments are presented only for information. Age, height and weight restrictions may apply. Reservations often are recommended and sometimes are required. Addresses and/or phone numbers are provided so visitors can contact the attraction for additional information.

Fast Facts

POPULATION: 3,421,399.

AREA: 97,073 square miles; ranks 10th.

CAPITAL: Salem.

HIGHEST POINT: 11,239 ft., Mount Hood.

LOWEST POINT: Sea level, Pacific Ocean.

TIME ZONE(S): Pacific/Mountain. DST.

TEEN DRIVING LAWS: No unrelated passengers under age 20 are permitted for the first 6 months of an intermediate license; maximum three unrelated passengers under age 20 for the following 6 months of an intermediate license. Driving is not permitted midnight-5 a.m. Cell phones and text messaging are banned for drivers under age 18 who hold a learner's permit or intermediate license. The minimum age for an unrestricted driver's license is 17. For more information phone (503) 945-5000.

MINIMUM AGE FOR GAMBLING: 21.

SEAT BELT/CHILD RESTRAINT LAWS: Seat belts required for driver and all passengers 16 and older and taller than 57 inches. Children weighing more than 40 lbs., but less than 57 inches tall must be in a child restraint or seat belt; child restraints required for under 40 lbs.

CELL PHONE RESTRICTIONS: See Teen Driving Laws section above.

HELMETS FOR MOTORCYCLISTS: Required for all riders.

RADAR DETECTORS: Permitted.

MOVE OVER LAW: Driver is required to slow down and vacate the lane nearest stopped police, fire and rescue vehicles using audible or flashing signals.

FIREARMS LAWS: Vary by state and/or county. Contact Oregon State Police Patrol Division, 3700 S.E. 92nd Ave., Portland, OR 97216; phone (503) 731-3020.

HOLIDAYS: Jan. 1; Martin Luther King Jr. Day, Jan. (3rd Mon.); Lincoln's Birthday, Feb. (1st Mon.); Washington's Birthday, Feb. (3rd Mon.); Memorial Day, May (last Mon.); July 4; Labor Day, Sept. (1st Mon.); Columbus Day, Oct. (2nd Mon.); Veterans Day, Nov. 11; Thanksgiving; Christmas, Dec. 25.

TAXES: Oregon has no statewide sales tax. State tax on lodgings can vary up to 5 percent. (Localities can charge tax on top of state tax; the Portland area has a lodging tax of 12.5 percent.)

INFORMATION CENTERS: State welcome centers are open Apr.-Oct. at the following locations: on I-5 south of Ashland; on US 101 at Astoria; on US 101 north of Brookings; on US 97 south of Klamath Falls; at jct. US 395/SR 40 in Lakeview; on I-84 at Ontario; across the I-5 bridge over the Columbia River at Portland; on US 101 in Seaside; and on I-82 in Umatilla. Another center, in Salem, is open year-round. Hours vary by location. In addition, 24-hour Travel Infocenter gazebos are in rest areas on I-5, I-84, US 97 and US 101.

AREA CODE REQUIRED: Whenever you make a local call within Oregon from a 503 or 971 area code, you must dial the area code as well as the seven-digit telephone number.

FURTHER INFORMATION FOR VISITORS:
Travel Oregon
670 Hawthorne Ave. S.E., Suite 240
Salem, OR 97301
(800) 547-7842

RECREATION INFORMATION:
Oregon Department of Parks and Recreation
725 Summer St. N.E., Suite C
Salem, OR 97301-1271
(503) 986-0707
(800) 551-6949 (parks information)
(800) 452-5687 (reservations)

FISHING AND HUNTING REGULATIONS:
Oregon Department of Fish and Wildlife
3406 Cherry Ave. N.E.
Salem, OR 97303
(503) 947-6000
(800) 720-6339 (24-hour information line within Oregon)

NATIONAL FOREST INFORMATION:
Bureau of Land Management
333 S.W. First Ave.
Portland, OR 97204
P.O. Box 2965
Portland, OR 97208
(503) 808-6002

Pacific Northwest Region
333 S.W. First Ave.
P.O. Box 3623
Portland, OR 97208
(503) 808-2468
(877) 444-6777 (reservations)

SPECIAL REGULATIONS: Motorists are not permitted to pump their own gas at service stations in Oregon.

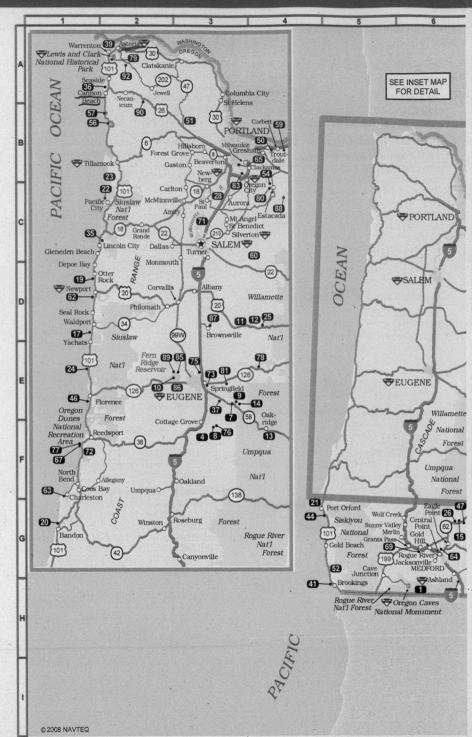

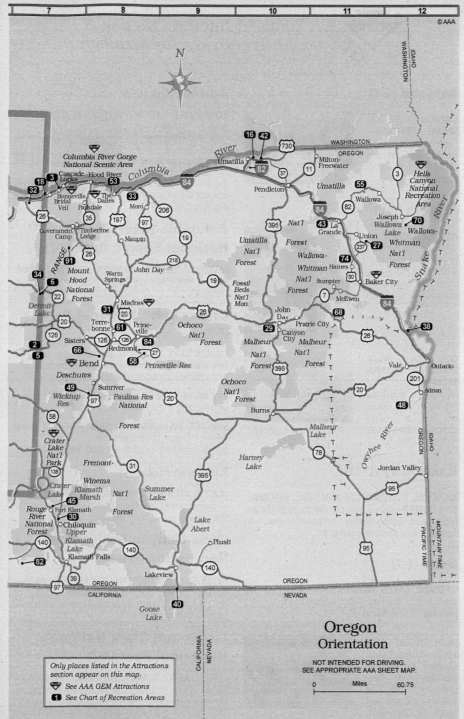

Oregon
Orientation

NOT INTENDED FOR DRIVING.
SEE APPROPRIATE AAA SHEET MAP.

Only places listed in the Attractions
section appear on this map.

See AAA GEM Attractions

See Chart of Recreation Areas

© AAA

4083-E

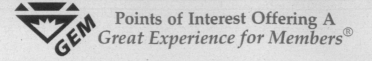

Points of Interest Offering A
Great Experience for Members®

Ashland (G-6)

OREGON SHAKE-SPEARE FESTIVAL—Experience the Bard's works at this venerable festival. See p. 48.

Astoria (A-2)

ASTORIA COLUMN—Grand views of the Pacific and surrounding area await those willing to climb the 164 stairs to the top of this monument. See p. 50.

COLUMBIA RIVER MARITIME MUSEUM—Pacific Northwest maritime history is the focus of the museum's comprehensive collections. See p. 50.

Baker City (D-11)

NATIONAL HISTORIC OREGON TRAIL INTERPRETIVE CENTER—Relive pioneer life through the exhibits and living-history demonstrations presented at this complex. See p. 51.

Bend (E-7)

CASCADE LAKES HIGHWAY—A nearly 90-mile scenic route, the highway traverses the Deschutes National Forest. See p. 52.

HIGH DESERT MUSEUM—Indoor and outdoor exhibits at this extensive complex highlight the history, flora and fauna of the West. See p. 54.

Bonneville (C-7)

BONNEVILLE LOCK AND DAM—This river management system spanning the Columbia has a visitor center featuring an underwater viewing area for watching fish. See p. 54.

Columbia River Gorge National Scenic Area (B-7)

HISTORIC COLUMBIA RIVER HIGHWAY—Awesome natural scenery abounds along this route. See p. 59.

Crater Lake National Park (F-7)

CRATER LAKE NATIONAL PARK—Crater Lake offers scenic drives, hiking trails and the brilliance of its namesake body of water. See p. 61.

RIM DRIVE—The 33-mile scenic road offers plenty of beautiful vistas. See p. 64.

SINNOTT MEMORIAL OVERLOOK—Get a good view of Crater Lake and learn about the natural and human history of the region. See p. 64.

Eugene (E-2)

HULT CENTER FOR THE PERFORMING ARTS—The center is noted for its architecture as well as for the acoustics of its two theaters. See p. 68.

Hells Canyon National Recreation Area (B-12)

HELLS CANYON NATIONAL RECREATION AREA—North America's deepest gorge is the standout of this ruggedly scenic wilderness region in northeastern Oregon. See p. 72.

Lewis and Clark National Historical Park (A-2)

LEWIS AND CLARK NATIONAL HISTORICAL PARK—Multiple sites make up this park, which includes a replica of the log fort originally built in 1805 by explorers Meriwether Lewis and William Clark. See p. 78.

Madras (D-8)

THE COVE PALISADES STATE PARK—The main attractions at the park are three canyons carved by three different rivers. See p. 79.

Newberg (B-3)

CHAMPOEG STATE HERITAGE AREA— Exploration and settlement of Oregon's Willamette Valley began here more than 150 years ago. See p. 84.

Newport (D-1)

OREGON COAST AQUARIUM—Some 500 species of sea life call this giant complex home. See p. 85.

Oregon Caves National Monument (H-5)

OREGON CAVES NATIONAL MONUMENT—Located in southwestern Oregon's Siskiyou Mountains, these caves feature impressive formations carved by Mother Nature. See p. 89.

Oregon City (B-4)

END OF THE OREGON TRAIL INTERPRETIVE CENTER—Exhibits and presentations educate modern travelers about the arduous trek that led to Oregon City. See p. 107.

Portland (B-3)

INTERNATIONAL ROSE TEST GARDEN—Thousands of beautiful roses, their perfume lingering in the air, are displayed in beds that are immaculately maintained. See p. 101.

OREGON HISTORICAL SOCIETY—The three-dimensional-looking murals on the center's facade are an invitation to explore within. See p. 100.

OREGON MUSEUM OF SCIENCE AND INDUSTRY (OMSI)—Thematic halls offer state-of-the-art exhibits, many of them hands-on. See p. 100.

OREGON ZOO—Embark on a tour of exotic animals at Portland's popular zoo. See p. 101.

PORTLAND ART MUSEUM—The collections at the Rose City's premier gallery range from works by native peoples to works by cutting-edge contemporary artists. See p. 100.

PORTLAND JAPANESE GARDEN—The meticulous arrangement of plants, trees, water and architecture forms a harmonious whole. See p. 102.

WASHINGTON PARK—This park stands out for its beauty and popular attractions. See p. 101.

Salem (C-3)

HALLIE FORD MUSEUM OF ART—The expansive building showcases a variety of artwork, including Pacific Northwest baskets and Egyptian art. See p. 115.

STATE CAPITOL—Take a tour to better appreciate the art and architecture of this building. See p. 116.

Silverton (C-3)

SILVER FALLS STATE PARK—Multiple waterfalls in this lovely setting will definitely wow you. See p. 117.

The Dalles (C-8)

COLUMBIA GORGE DISCOVERY CENTER AND MUSEUM—Visitors can explore cultural and geologic history through exhibits at the official interpretive center for the Columbia River Gorge National Scenic Area. See p. 120.

Tillamook (B-1)

TILLAMOOK AIR MUSEUM—More than 40 restored vintage flying aircraft are displayed at one of the top private collections in the United States. See p. 121

RECREATION AREAS

	MAP LOCATION	CAMPING	PICNICKING	HIKING TRAILS	BOATING	BOAT RAMP	BOAT RENTAL	FISHING	SWIMMING	PETS ON LEASH	BICYCLE TRAILS	WINTER SPORTS	VISITOR CENTER	LODGE/CABINS	FOOD SERVICE
NATIONAL PARKS *(See place listings)*															
Crater Lake (F-7) 183,224 acres on the crest of the Cascade Range off SR 62.		•	•	•					•		•	•	•	•	•
NATIONAL FORESTS *(See place listings)*															
Deschutes 1,602,609 acres in central Oregon, 6 mi. s. of Bend via US 97. Horse rental.		•	•	•	•	•	•	•	•	•		•	•	•	•
Fremont-Winema More than 2 million acres in south-central Oregon.		•	•	•	•	•	•	•	•	•		•	•		
Malheur 1,465,397 acres in eastern Oregon.		•	•	•	•	•	•		•	•		•	•		
Mount Hood 1.1 million acres in northwestern Oregon.		•	•	•	•	•	•	•	•	•		•	•	•	•
Ochoco 847,938 acres in central Oregon off US 26.		•	•	•	•	•	•	•	•	•		•			
Rogue River-Siskiyou Rogue portion 635,000 acres in southwestern Oregon off I-5 from Medford; Siskiyou portion 1,092,302 acres in southwestern Oregon.		•	•	•	•	•	•	•	•	•		•	•	•	•
Siuslaw 630,000 acres in western Oregon.		•	•	•	•	•	•	•	•	•		•			
Umatilla 1.4 million acres in northeastern Oregon. Horse rental.		•	•	•	•	•	•	•	•	•		•	•		
Umpqua 984,602 acres in southwestern Oregon, 33 mi. e. of Roseburg on SR 138.		•	•	•	•	•	•	•	•	•		•	•	•	•
Wallowa-Whitman 2,392,160 acres in northeastern Oregon. Horse rental.		•	•	•	•	•	•	•	•	•		•			
Willamette 1,675,407 acres in western Oregon.		•	•	•	•	•	•	•	•	•				•	•
NATIONAL RECREATION AREAS *(See place listings)*															
Hells Canyon (B-12) 652,977 acres off SR 82 near Joseph. Horse rental.		•	•	•	•	•	•		•		•			•	
Oregon Dunes (E-1) 32,000 acres between North Bend and Florence.		•	•	•	•	•			•	•				•	
ARMY CORPS OF ENGINEERS															
Applegate Lake (H-6) 205 acres 23 mi. s.w. of Medford via SR 238.	**1**	•	•			•		•	•	•					
Blue River Lake (E-7) 1,420 acres off SR 126 at Blue River. Water skiing.	**2**	•	•			•		•	•	•					
Bonneville Lock and Dam (C-7) 206,000 acres 40 mi. e. of Portland via I-84 exit 40. *(See Bonneville p. 54.)*	**3**	•	•	•	•	•	•	•		•			•		
Cottage Grove Reservoir (F-3) 6 mi. s. of Cottage Grove via I-5.	**4**	•	•		•			•	•	•					
Cougar Lake (E-7) 1,280 acres s.e. of Blue River off SR 126 and West Side Rd. Water skiing.	**5**	•	•		•	•		•	•	•					
Detroit Lake (D-7) 3,500 acres off SR 22 at Detroit. Water skiing.	**6**	•	•		•	•		•	•	•					
Dexter Lake (E-3) Off SR 58 at Dexter. Water skiing.	**7**		•		•	•		•		•					
Dorena Reservoir (F-3) 5 mi. e. of Cottage Grove off I-5.	**8**	•	•		•	•		•	•	•					
Fall Creek Lake (E-3) 1,820 acres 16 mi. s.e. of Springfield via Jasper Lowell Rd. Water skiing.	**9**	•	•		•	•		•	•	•					
Fern Ridge Reservoir (E-2) 9,000 acres 12 mi. w. of Eugene off SR 126. Water skiing.	**10**	•	•		•	•		•	•	•					
Foster Lake (D-3) 1,220 acres off US 20 at Sweet Home. Water skiing.	**11**	•	•		•	•		•	•	•					
Green Peter Lake (D-4) 3,720 acres n.e. of Sweet Home off Quartzville Rd. Water skiing.	**12**	•	•		•			•	•	•					
Hills Creek Lake (F-4) 2,710 acres s.e. of Oakridge off SR 58 and Rigdon Rd. Water skiing.	**13**	•	•		•			•	•	•					
Lookout Point Lake (E-4) 4,360 acres just s. of Dexter off SR 58.	**14**	•	•		•	•		•		•					
Lost Creek Lake (G-6) 3,430 acres 30 mi. n.e. of Medford via SR 62. Water skiing.	**15**	•	•	•	•	•	•	•	•	•				•	
McNary Lock and Dam (B-10) 9,718 acres 1 mi. e. of jct. I-82 and US 730 at Umatilla. Water skiing. *(See Umatilla p. 122.)*	**16**		•		•	•		•	•	•					
STATE															

RECREATION AREAS

RECREATION AREAS	MAP LOCATION	CAMPING	PICNICKING	HIKING TRAILS	BOATING	BOAT RAMP	BOAT RENTAL	FISHING	SWIMMING	PETS ON LEASH	BICYCLE TRAILS	WINTER SPORTS	VISITOR CENTER	LODGE/CABINS	FOOD SERVICE
Beachside (D-1) 17 acres 4 mi. s. of Waldport on US 101.	17	•	•	•				•		•				•	
Benson (C-7) 272 acres 30 mi. e. of Portland off I-84. Disc golf course.	18		•		•	•		•	•	•					
Beverly Beach (D-1) 130 acres 7 mi. n. of Newport on US 101. Wildlife viewing; salmon migration interpretive trail.	19	•	•	•				•		•				•	
Bullards Beach (G-1) 1,226 acres 2 mi. n. of Bandon on US 101. Horse camp. *(See Bandon p. 52.)*	20	•	•	•	•	•		•		•	•			•	
Cape Blanco (G-4) 1,880 acres 9 mi. n. of Port Orford, then 6 mi. w. off US 101. Historic. Horse camp; horseback riding, whale watching. *(See Port Orford p. 111.)*	21	•	•	•				•		•				•	
Cape Kiwanda (C-2) 185 acres 1 mi. n. of Pacific City off US 101. Scenic. Tide pools.	22		•	•				•		•					
Cape Lookout (B-2) 1,974 acres 12 mi. s.w. of Tillamook off US 101. Bird-watching; clamming; whale watching.	23	•	•	•				•		•				•	
Carl G. Washburne Memorial (E-1) 1,089 acres 14 mi. n. of Florence on US 101. Wildlife viewing; tide pools.	24	•	•	•				•		•				•	
Cascadia (D-4) 253 acres 14 mi. e. of Sweet Home on US 20.	25	•	•					•	•	•					
Casey (G-6) 80 acres 29 mi. n.e. of Medford on SR 62.	26		•			•	•	•	•	•					
Catherine Creek (C-11) 160 acres 8 mi. s.e. of Union on SR 203.	27	•	•	•				•		•					
Champoeg (O-0) 567 acres on the Willamette River 7 mi. e. of Newberg off US 99W. Historic. Wildlife viewing. *(See Newberg p. 84.)*	28	•	•	•	•			•		•			•	•	•
Clyde Holliday (D-10) 15 acres 7 mi. w. of John Day on US 26. Bird-watching, tepee camping, wildlife viewing.	29	•	•	•				•		•					
Collier Memorial (G-7) 655 acres near Chiloquin on US 97. Historic. Wildlife viewing; horse camp. *(See Chiloquin p. 58.)*	30	•	•	•				•		•			•		
The Cove Palisades (D-8) 4,130 acres 15 mi. s.w. of Madras off US 97. *(See Madras p. 79.)*	31	•	•	•	•	•	•	•	•	•			•	•	•
Dabney (C-7) 135 acres 19 mi. e. of Portland on US 30. Disc golf.	32		•	•	•	•		•	•	•					
Deschutes River (C-8) 515 acres 17 mi. e. of The Dalles off I-84. White-water rafting.	33	•	•	•	•	•		•		•	•				
Detroit Lake (D-7) 104 acres 2 mi. w. of Detroit on SR 22.	34	•	•		•	•	•	•	•	•					
Devil's Lake (C-1) 109 acres at Lincoln City on US 101.	35	•	•		•	•	•	•		•				•	
Ecola (A-1) 1,303 acres 2 mi. n. of Cannon Beach off US 101. Historic. Whale watching, wildlife interpretive site; Adirondack shelters for hiker camping, two scenic beaches. *(See Cannon Beach p. 56.)*	36	•	•	•				•		•				•	
Elijah Bristow (E-3) 848 acres 15 mi. s.e. of Eugene on SR 58. Horseback riding, wildlife viewing.	37		•	•				•		•	•				
Farewell Bend (D-12) 72 acres 4 mi. s. of Huntington off I-84. Historic.	38	•	•		•	•		•	•	•					
Fort Stevens (A-2) 3,763 acres 10 mi. w. of Hammond on US 101. Historic. Wildlife viewing. *(See Warrenton p. 125.)*	39	•	•	•	•	•		•	•	•			•	•	
Goose Lake (H-9) 64 acres 15 mi. s.w. of Lakeview off US 395.	40	•	•			•	•	•		•					
Harris Beach (H-4) 171 acres 2 mi. n. of Brookings on US 101. Whale watching, wildlife viewing; tide pool interpretation.	41	•	•	•				•		•				•	
Hat Rock (B-10) 735 acres 9 mi. e. of Umatilla off US 730.	42		•	•	•	•	•	•	•	•					
Hilgard Junction (C-11) 233 acres 8 mi. w. of La Grande off I-84. Bird-watching, rafting, wildlife viewing.	43	•	•		•			•		•					
Humbug Mountain (G-4) 1,842 acres 6 mi. s. of Port Orford on US 101. Wildlife viewing.	44	•	•	•				•		•					
Jackson F. Kimball (G-7) 19 acres 3 mi. n. of Klamath Falls off SR 232.	45	•	•					•		•					
Jessie M. Honeyman Memorial (E-1) 522 acres 2.5 mi. s. of Florence off US 101. Winter ATV dunes access.	46	•	•	•	•	•	•	•	•	•			•		•
Joseph P. Stewart (G-6) 910 acres 35 mi. n.e. of Medford off SR 62.	47	•	•	•	•	•	•	•	•	•	•				

RECREATION AREAS

	MAP LOCATION	CAMPING	PICNICKING	HIKING TRAILS	BOATING	BOAT RAMP	BOAT RENTAL	FISHING	SWIMMING	PETS ON LEASH	BICYCLE TRAILS	WINTER SPORTS	VISITOR CENTER	LODGE/CABINS	FOOD SERVICE
Lake Owyhee (E-12) 730 acres 33 mi. s.w. of Nyssa off SR 301. Tepee camping. *(See Adrian p. 48.)*	48	•	•		•	•	•	•		•					
La Pine (E-7) 2,008 acres 8.5 mi. n. of La Pine off US 97.	49	•	•	•				•		•				•	
Lewis and Clark (B-4) 56 acres 16 mi. e. of Portland off I-84.	50		•		•	•	•	•		•			•		
L.L. Stub Stewart (B-3) 1,650 acres 1 mi. n. of Buxton on SR 47. Horseback riding.	51	•	•	•						•	•	•			
Loeb (G-5) 320 acres 8 mi. n.e. of Brookings off US 101.	52	•	•					•	•					•	
Mayer (C-8) 613 acres 10 mi. w. of The Dalles off I-84. Windsurfing takeoff point.	53		•		•	•		•							
Milo McIver (B-4) 937 acres 5 mi. w. of Estacada off SR 211. Disc golf, wildlife viewing.	54	•	•	•	•	•		•		•					
Minam (C-11) 602 acres 15 mi. n.e. of Elgin off SR 82. Birdwatching, rafting, wildlife viewing.	55	•	•		•			•		•					
Nehalem Bay (B-1) 878 acres 3 mi. s. of Manzanita Junction off US 101. Horse camp.	56	•	•	•	•	•		•		•				•	
Oswald West (B-1) 2,474 acres 5 mi. n. of Manzanita on US 101. Historic. Clamming; surfboarding. Note: The campground is closed until further notice; phone for updates.	57	•	•	•				•		•					
Prineville Reservoir (E-8) 365 acres 17 mi. s.e. of Prineville off US 26.	58	•	•	•	•	•		•	•	•			•	•	
Rooster Rock (B-4) 927 acres 22 mi. e. of Portland off I-84. Off-leash pet area.	59		•	•	•	•		•	•	•					•
Silver Falls (C-4) 9,064 acres 26 mi. e. of Salem on SR 214. *(See Silverton p. 117.)*	60	•	•	•				•	•	•	•		•	•	•
Smith Rock (D-8) 623 acres 3 mi. e. of Terrebonne via US 97 following signs. Rock climbing, wildlife viewing. *(See Terrebonne p. 120.)*	61	•	•	•				•		•					
South Beach (D-1) 411 acres 2 mi. s. of Newport on US 101. Interpretive boardwalk to beach viewpoint.	62	•	•					•		•	•				
Sunset Bay (F-1) 395 acres 2 mi. s.w. of North Bend.	63	•	•	•	•	•		•	•	•					
Tou Velle (G-6) 51 acres 9 mi. n. of Medford off SR 62. Birdwatching, wildlife viewing.	64		•	•	•	•		•		•					
Tryon Creek (B-4) 627 acres 6 mi. s.w. of Portland off I-5 on Terwilliger Blvd. Horseback riding, wildlife viewing.	65		•							•	•		•		
Tumalo (E-7) 320 acres 5.5 mi. n. of Bend off US 20.	66	•	•					•	•	•				•	
Umpqua Lighthouse (F-1) 450 acres 6 mi. s. of Reedsport off US 101. *(See Reedsport p. 112.)*	67	•	•	•	•			•		•				•	
Unity Lake (D-11) 39 acres 5 mi. n. of Unity Junction on SR 7.	68	•	•		•	•		•		•					
Valley of the Rogue (G-5) 275 acres 3 mi. s. of Rogue River off I-5. Interpretive riverside trail.	69	•	•	•				•		•					
Wallowa Lake (C-12) 166 acres 6 mi. s. of Joseph on SR 82.	70	•	•	•	•	•	•	•	•	•				•	
Willamette Mission (C-3) 1,686 acres 8 mi. n. of Salem on Wheatland Ferry Rd. Historic. Horseback riding.	71		•	•	•	•		•		•	•				
William M. Tugman (F-1) 560 acres 19 mi. n. of Coos Bay on US 101.	72	•	•	•	•	•		•	•	•				•	
OTHER															
Alton Baker (E-3) 490 acres on Centennial Blvd. off Coburg Rd. in Eugene. Bird-watching, canoeing. *(See Eugene p. 67.)*	73		•	•				•		•	•				
Anthony Lakes (D-11) 28 mi. w. of North Powder off I-84.	74	•	•	•	•			•	•	•		•			
Armitage (E-3) 57 acres 5 mi. n. of Eugene on Coburg Rd. Dog park, horseshoe pits, sand volleyball court.	75	•	•	•	•			•	•	•					
Baker Bay (F-3) 88 acres at 35635 Shoreview Dr. in Dorena. Horseshoe pits, marina, sand volleyball court.	76	•			•	•		•	•	•					•
Bastendorff Beach (F-1) 91 acres 2 mi. w. of Charleston via Coos Rd. Playground. *(See Charleston p. 58.)*	77	•	•					•	•						

RECREATION AREAS

	MAP LOCATION	CAMPING	PICNICKING	HIKING TRAILS	BOATING	BOAT RAMP	BOAT RENTAL	FISHING	SWIMMING	PETS ON LEASH	BICYCLE TRAILS	WINTER SPORTS	VISITOR CENTER	LODGE/CABINS	FOOD SERVICE
Ben and Kay Dorris (E-4) 92 acres about 2 mi. e. of Vida on US 126.	78		•	•	•	•		•		•					
Cullaby Lake (A-2) 165 acres 8 mi. s. of Astoria off US 101. Playground.	79	•	•	•	•	•		•	•	•	•				
Estacada Timber Park (C-4) 55 acres 1 mi. w. of Estacada on SR 224.	80		•		•	•		•	•	•					•
Hendricks Bridge (E-3) 17 acres about 9 mi. e. of Springfield on US 126. Horseshoe pits, sand volleyball court.	81		•	•	•	•		•	•	•					
Howard Prairie Lake (G-7) 250 acres 22 mi. e. of Ashland.	82	•	•		•	•	•	•	•	•					
Mary S. Young (C-3) 133 acres on SR 43 in West Linn.	83		•	•						•	•	•			
Ochoco Lake (E-8) 10 acres 7 mi. e. of Prineville on US 26.	84	•	•		•	•		•	•	•					
Orchard Point (E-3) 49 acres 17.5 mi. n.w. of Eugene via the Prairie Rd. exit off the Beltline W., n. on Irving St., then 6.5 mi. w. on Clear Lake Rd. Windsurfing; horseshoe pits, marina, playground, sand volleyball court.	85		•		•	•		•	•	•					•
Perkins Peninsula (E-3) 39 acres 9 mi. w. of Eugene on SR 126. Ball field.	86		•		•	•		•	•	•					
Pioneer Park (D-3) 18 acres off Main St. at the end of Park Ave. in Brownsville. *(See Brownsville. p. 55.)*	87	•	•	•						•	•				
Promontory (C-4) 37 acres 7 mi. e. of Estacada via SR 224.	88	•	•	•	•	•	•	•	•	•			•		
Richardson (E-2) 157 acres 17.5 mi. n.w. of Eugene via the Prairie Rd. exit off the Beltline W., n. on Irving St., then 8 mi. w. on Clear Lake Rd. Amphitheater, horseshoe pits, marina, playground, sand volleyball court.	89		•	•	•	•		•	•	•					
Spruce Run (B-2) 128 acres on the lower Nehalem River 3 mi. s. of Elsie on FR 912.	90	•	•	•				•	•	•					
Timothy Lake (D-7) 1,400 acres 10 mi. s.e. of Mount Hood on US 26 to Skyline Rd., then 10 mi. s., following signs. *(See Mount Hood and Mount Hood National Forest p. 83.)*	91	•	•	•	•	•		•	•	•	•	•			
Young's River Falls (A-2) 10 acres 15 mi. s. of Astoria on Young's River Loop Rd.	92		•	•				•	•	•					

Oregon Temperature Averages
Maximum/Minimum
From the records of The Weather Channel Interactive, Inc.

	JAN	FEB	MAR	APR	MAY	JUNE	JULY	AUG	SEPT	OCT	NOV	DEC
Bend	40/23	44/25	51/27	57/30	65/36	73/41	81/46	81/46	72/39	62/32	46/28	40/23
Eugene	46/33	51/35	56/37	61/39	67/43	73/47	81/51	82/51	77/47	65/41	52/37	46/33
Medford	47/31	54/33	58/36	64/39	72/44	81/50	90/55	90/55	84/48	70/40	53/35	45/31
Pendleton	42/25	48/28	57/33	64/38	72/44	80/50	88/54	88/52	79/44	66/35	51/31	42/26
Portland	46/37	50/39	56/41	61/44	67/49	73/53	79/57	79/58	74/55	63/48	51/42	46/37

Exploring Oregon

For descriptions of places in bold type, see individual listings.

Central

Born of fire and in places shaped by ice, central Oregon extends from the lava fields south of **Bend** north to the Columbia River and from the Cascade summit eastward to the foothills of the Blue Mountains. The western one-fourth of the region is the east slope of the Cascades, heavily forested, studded with lakes and crowned with a gleaming succession of volcanic peaks.

The rest of central Oregon is the great central plateau, marked by juniper-peppered volcanic buttes and cinder cones, isolated ranges covered with ponderosa pine and gorges cut through lava by relentless rivers.

The primary north-south highway through the region is US 97. After leaving the Klamath Basin it crosses into the Deschutes River watershed, following the Little Deschutes through the **Deschutes National Forest**. The eastern part of the forest contains features that testify to the monumental forces that shaped central Oregon. SR 31 and several forest roads lead into the lava fields from La Pine and other points along US 97, but remember: this is forbidding country and you should check on road conditions locally before venturing off the main paved highways.

A few miles north of La Pine, Cascade Lakes National Scenic Byway heads west into the Cascades, offering (except in winter, when part of it closes) a 100-mile scenic loop through the western part of Deschutes National Forest. The drive winds around a series of large lakes and features views of snowcapped volcanic peaks like Three Sisters and Mt. Bachelor. It rejoins US 97 at Bend.

Deschutes National Forest / © Charles A. Blakeslee / age fotostock

Westward Ho!
The Splendor
of Oregon Country

At Bend US 97 intersects with cross-state US 20, which angles northwest to **Sisters.** Sisters is the gateway to two important Cascade passes, McKenzie and Santiam. The former is reached by SR 242, a summer-only, no-trailers road that ranks among the state's more scenic mountain drives. The Santiam Pass area is lower and tamer but very popular for both summer and winter recreation.

North of Bend US 97 crosses an expanse of juniper and sage en route to the geographical center of the state, **Redmond.** From here trans-state SR 126 leads east to **Prineville** and US 26, which crosses the high desert and the Ochoco Mountains into the John Day country. The rimrock area around Prineville is rich in agate, jasper, petrified wood and thunder eggs. Farther east the Painted Hills and Sheep Rock units of **John Day Fossil Beds National Monument** tell much about the Oregon of 30 million years ago.

From Redmond US 97 runs north past the head of Crooked River Gorge—there are good views into the chasm from Smith Rock State Park and Ogden Scenic Wayside, both a few miles from **Terrebonne**—and across a part of Crooked River National Grasslands to **Madras.** Nearby lakes Simtustus and Billy Chinook are favorites for boating, fishing, houseboat vacationing and water skiing. White-water outfitters abound in Madras, because below Pelton Dam the Deschutes River is a designated state scenic waterway that ranks high in adventure as well.

US 26 west of Prineville intercepts US 97 a few miles south of Madras, then continues northwest into the Warm Springs Indian Reservation. **Warm Springs** is the headquarters of the vast reserve, which extends from the Cascade summit between Mount

Jefferson and Abbot Pass eastward to the Deschutes.

From the potato and peppermint fields around Madras, US 97 traverses somewhat more open range country to a junction with US 197. US 197 continues north, crossing the Deschutes at **Maupin** and passing through such small towns as Tygh Valley (scene of the annual Pacific Northwest Championship All-Indian Rodeo) before reaching the Columbia River a few miles east of **The Dalles.** US 97 veers northeast across a high grassland punctuated by scattered ghost towns. Shaniko, with its weathered buildings and old vehicles, remembers its turn-of-the-20th-century heyday as a thriving railroad and sheep-raising center. Antelope, another once-lusty community, lies south of Shaniko off SR 218.

At Antelope SR 218 turns east toward the John Day River and the Clarno Unit of the John Day Fossil Beds National Monument. Beyond the John Day River the plateau gives way to the hills of wheat country. SR 218 ends in Fossil at SR 19,

Warm Springs Indian Reservation, Warm Springs
© Heeb Photos / eStock Photo

an important trans-grain belt link between US 26 and the Columbia River. To the north roll wheat fields; to the south lie the broken buttes and domelike hills that have lured fossil hunters and gold seekers.

Until it meets US 30/I-84 at the Columbia River, US 97 intersects with only one other major route. At Wasco SR 206 turns southeast across 42 miles to SR 19 at Condon, the seat of wheatrich Gilliam County; northwest of Wasco, it passes near the mouth of the Deschutes River en route to its terminus west of Biggs. US 97 proceeds to Biggs, where a bridge carries it across the Columbia to Maryhill, Wash. For more information about exploring central Oregon contact the Central Oregon Visitors Association, 661 S.W. Powerhouse Dr., Suite 1301, Bend, OR 97702; phone (888) 545-7442.

Coast

Among the nation's more spectacular shorelines, the Oregon coast stretches some 400 miles from the California border near **Brookings** to **Astoria** at the mouth of the broad, gray Columbia River. In between, outlined by breakers, lie beaches protected by rocky headlands, miles of sand dunes, lighthouses and more than 50 state parks and waysides. With the fir-clad Coast Range shouldering in some places to the water's edge, this sparkling marine region offers photogenic scenery at every turn.

A trip along US 101, the Oregon Coast Highway, misses very little of the shoreline: Only at **Coos Bay, Tillamook,** and from **Florence** to **Reedsport** does the highway take a somewhat inland tangent. In each case side roads

lead to the seaside at such scenic spots as Cape Arago, Cape Meares and Cape Lookout. US 101 also is a doorway to one of the nation's best white-water rivers, the Rogue, which spills into the Pacific near **Gold Beach.**

Several of Oregon's rarities are found along this corridor. In the south, deep in a wilderness reserve in the **Rogue River-Siskiyou National Forest,** grows one of the world's rarest shrubs, the kalmiopsis. Stands of myrtle are found near Coquille and Myrtle Point, and the northernmost stand of redwoods can be seen in Loeb State Park just east of Brookings. A 40-mile ribbon of sand dunes between **North Bend** and Florence is set aside in Oregon Dunes National Recreation Area, part of the **Siuslaw National Forest.** A few miles north of Florence is the only year-round sea lion rookery on the U.S. mainland.

Towns and villages that bead the coast are often part fishing port, part resort and part industrial center. Astoria began with the Lewis and Clark expedition's encampment at Fort Clatsop in 1805-06 and the founding of John Jacob Astor's fur trading post in 1811. While much of the town's charm stems from its 19th-century appearance, the treasury is supplied chiefly by canneries and the massive shipping industry.

Other venerable towns are **Seaside,** the state's oldest and largest ocean resort, and **Newport,** with its turn-of-the-20th-century waterfront and centurylong standing as a lively resort community. For more information about exploring the Oregon coast contact the Oregon Coast Visitors Association, P.O. Box 74, Newport, OR 97365; phone (541) 574-2679 or (888) 628-2101. A detailed map of the Oregon coast can be obtained by contacting your local AAA office.

The Mount Hood Scenic Loop: Portland, Mount Hood and the Columbia River Gorge National Scenic Area

Few of Oregon's touring regions pack so much diversity into

so small an area as the Portland-Mount Hood-Columbia Gorge area. The state's largest city, its highest mountain and one of its most magnificent rivers are all within 70 miles of one another, linked by the Mt. Hood National Scenic Byway.

From **Portland,** where commerce, culture, environmental stewardship and industry are equally evident, US 26 leads through acres of orchards to Mount Hood, the centerpiece of **Mount Hood National Forest.** In addition to its beauty and geo-

East of Hood River lies **The Dalles,** the true eastern gateway to the Columbia Gorge. Here began the series of rapids that marked the river's thunderous breaching of the Cascade Range, presenting a final hazard to pioneers bound for the Willamette Valley.

Dams at The Dalles and **Bonneville** temper, if not wholly tame, the river. It rolls westward between high, waterfall-laced walls, paralleled by I-84 (the low road) and the actual Historic Columbia River Highway, old US

395; the eastern boundary follows the Snake River north from **Ontario** through the continent's deepest river gorge—Hells Canyon.

The Blue Mountains extend across the region from southwest to northeast, where they spill into Washington state. East of the Blues and separated from them by the Grande Ronde and Powder River valleys, are the Wallowa Mountains. South of the Blues lie mountains of a different character, the jagged Strawberry Range. The northwestern corner of the area is the Umatilla Basin, with its wheat fields, truck farms and lively capital, **Pendleton.**

Following nearly the same trace as its wagon-cut ancestor, today's Oregon Trail, I-84, bisects the region diagonally from southeast to northwest. After leaving the Snake River Valley near Huntington—pioneers dubbed the spot Farewell Bend for just that reason—the highway runs through hilly rangeland to **Baker City** in the Powder River Valley.

In the 1860s the mountains flanking Baker City teemed with prospectors; derelict towns and abandoned diggings are scattered throughout the **Wallowa-Whitman National Forest.** The Elkhorn Drive, a 106-mile route comprising SR 7 and a network of forest service roads west of Baker City, passes mining and logging towns and the Anthony Lakes recreation area before returning to the valley near North Powder.

Mount Hood National Forest / © Craig Tuttle / Art Life Images

logical significance—Mount Hood is a dormant volcano—the peak's prime attraction is year-round skiing: historic **Timberline Lodge** and **Government Camp** are the highlights of the area.

A short distance east of the Timberline cutoff, SR 35 turns north through the Hood River Valley, one of the country's more productive fruit-growing areas. The drive is especially rewarding in April, when the orchards blossom against the backdrop of forested hills and Mount Hood's glistening snow. Panorama Point, just east of the highway a few miles before it reaches the Columbia Gorge, offers an exceptional view of the valley.

SR 35 terminates at I-84/US 30 at **Hood River.** At this point in mid-gorge the winds are ideal for windsurfing, and all summer the Columbia River dances with the gaudy sails of surfboards.

30 (the high road). Particularly along US 30, numerous waysides, overlooks and state parks permit leisurely sightseeing.

A different perspective is available from a stern-wheeler that operates from **Cascade Locks** during the summer. The two highways emerge from the gorge at the Sandy River and enter Portland, completing the loop. For more information contact Oregon's Mount Hood Territory, Zigzag Ranger District, 70220 E. US 26, Zigzag, OR 97049; phone (503) 622-3191 or (800) 424-3002.

Northeast

Roughly speaking, northeastern Oregon extends from the western foothills of the Blue Mountains to the Idaho border and from the mountains north of **Burns** to the Washington border. The western edge of the region is more or less delineated by US

East of Baker City SR 86 threads along the Wallowa foothills to Oxbow Dam and the southern gateway to **Hells Canyon National Recreation Area.**

The segment of I-84 between Baker City and Pendleton is especially scenic. After dipping into Grande Ronde Valley at **La Grande,** the highway climbs to the summit of the Blue Mountains. The view from the final grade down to Pendleton is spectacular.

La Grande also is the starting point for another of northeastern Oregon's scenic specials: The Hells Canyon Overlook at Hat

Point via **Wallowa Lake**. SR 82 runs along the Grande Ronde River to Elgin, then curves east and southeast for a breathtaking run to Enterprise; the designated scenic route then follows SR 3 northward into Washington.

SR 82 ends at **Joseph**, near the north end of the lake; a paved road goes on to Imnaha, at the boundary of Hell's Canyon National Recreation Area. The last 24 miles to Hat Point are gravel. The drive from Imnaha to Hat Point takes approximately an hour.

Along the western edge of the region between US 20 at Burns and I-84 at Pendleton, US 395 illustrates the transition from semi-arid range land to wheat country. North of Burns it traverses the Silvies and Bear valleys, passes the western shoulder of the Strawberry Mountain Wilderness in the **Malheur National Forest,** then drops into the John Day Valley. **Canyon City** and **John Day** both figured in the gold rush of 1862-64.

At John Day US 395 intersects with US 26. To the east US 26 crosses the Blue Mountains via Dixie Pass, a popular winter sports area; to the west it parallels the John Day River into central Oregon. A few miles west of John Day US 395 turns north again, traversing five mountain passes and interesting valleys en route to Pendleton. Northwest of Pendleton the highway travels through irrigated farmland around Hermiston and reaches the Columbia at **Umatilla**, where it crosses just below McNary Dam into Washington.

South

Three mountain ranges and two major river systems define southern Oregon. The region extends eastward from the Coast Range, across the valleys of the Umpqua and Rogue and over the Cascades to the lakes and pine lands of the Klamath Basin.

I-5, with its sometimes parallel, sometimes concurrent companion SR 99, traverses the Rogue and Umpqua River valleys. It is especially scenic between the California border and **Grants Pass** as it passes from the summit of the Siskiyous into Rogue River Valley, the state's chief pear-growing region. At **Ashland** I-5 runs into Renaissance England; Ashland is the home of the annual Oregon Shakespeare Festival.

Medford, the largest city and commercial hub of the valley, is the western terminus of SR 62, which arcs northeastward to **Crater Lake National Park,** then south to US 97 near **Chiloquin** in the Klamath Basin. Another facet of the Rogue valley lives in historic **Jacksonville.** Grants Pass is the starting point for the many raft trips that challenge the Rogue.

US 199, the Redwood Highway from California's redwood coast, joins I-5 at Grants Pass. The segment of US 199 between the border and O'Brien is particularly scenic. During the gold rush prospectors scoured these hills and streams for "color," with considerable success. **Cave Junction** is the access point for another treasure, **Oregon Caves National Monument.**

North of Grants Pass I-5 crosses three low passes and enters the rich Umpqua River valley, famous for fishing, logging, melon growing and wine producing. The largest town in the valley is **Roseburg,** a convenient base for visiting the local wineries and such towns as late 19th-century **Oakland**.

The 103 miles of SR 138 from Roseburg to **Crater Lake National Park** ranks among Oregon's most scenic highways. The route follows the North Fork of the Umpqua into the **Umpqua National Forest,** passes near many dramatic waterfalls and climbs to the summit of the Cascades along Diamond Lake, near the base of Mount Thielsen. At the entrance to the national park the scenic route continues south to Crater Lake; SR 138 heads due east to join US 97.

Running north-south through the central part of the state, US 97 very nearly marks the boundary between southern Oregon and the semiarid southeastern region. The chief town is sunny **Klamath Falls.**

Two highways turn west from Klamath Falls into the Cascade lake country. SR 66 meets I-5 at Ashland; SR 140 arches northwest and west, crossing the divide near Mount McLoughlin, and joins SR 62 just north of Medford. Both offer access to year-round recreation.

North of Klamath Falls, attractions at Chiloquin and **Fort Klamath** explore Oregon's logging industry and life at a frontier army post. To order an informational brochure phone the Southern Oregon Visitors Association at (800) 448-4856.

Southeast

Consisting of two of the state's largest counties and most of a third, the sparsely populated southeastern region stretches from the California border to the foothills of the Strawberry Range north of **Burns,** and from the Gearhart Mountains of the

Crater Lake National Park / © Roberto Gerometta / Lonely Planet Images

Klamath Falls / © Tobin Rogers / Alamy

Fremont-Winema National Forests eastward to the Idaho border.

Faulting, volcanism and erosion were—and are—the artists here, and they have created the setting for some of Oregon's most singular surprises: a geyser, colossal fault scarps, lava flows, lakes and canyons whose walls tell tales of unremembered time.

For all its acreage, southeastern Oregon has few major highways. Many of the most interesting features are reached only by gravel or dirt roads. Always check road and weather conditions locally before venturing off the main routes.

US 395, the north-south artery through the western part of the region, enters Oregon from California via the Goose Lake Valley. On the west a jumble of mountains and rims conceals the Gearhart Mountain Wilderness; on the east rise the commanding Warner Mountains. Goose Lake, like other lakes in the region, is a vestige of prehistoric Lake Chewaucan, whose ancient shorelines are visible on the surrounding mountainsides.

At **Lakeview,** the business center for the area, US 395 intersects the western leg of SR 140. Part of the route called the "Winnemucca to the Sea Highway," SR 140 slices along the Nevada-Oregon border, joins US 395 for

a few miles to Lakeview, then resumes its westward course across the southern Cascades to **Medford.** (From Medford, follow I-5 west to Grants Pass and US 199 southwest to Crescent City, CA, to complete the "to the sea" part.)

At Valley Falls US 395 comes to a Y. The left arm is SR 31, the Fremont Highway, named for the young army lieutenant whose expedition came this way in 1843. SR 31 passes Summer and Silver lakes and connects with US 97 at the town of La Pine.

The Y's right arm is US 395, which threads along the base of one of the highest exposed fault scarps in North America, the Abert Rim. Besides being geologically and scenically awesome, the 2,000-foot-high escarpment is a favorite site for hang gliding.

The rim separates Lake Abert from the Warner Valley, whose lakes and streams support large ranches and whose eastern wall is the massive volcanic ridge of Hart Mountain. The Warner Valley is reached by an unpaved road that cuts south from US 395 about 10 miles north of Lake Abert; it passes through **Plush,** from where another road enters the vast, game-rich Hart Mountain Refuge, then continues south to SR 140 east of Lakeview. East of the junction, off SR 140 near

Adel, is one of Oregon's two spouting geysers.

Beyond Lake Abert, US 395 crosses some 90 miles of sage plains and alkali flats to Riley, where it meets US 20. Westbound, US 20 leads to **Bend;** eastward it runs concurrently with US 395 to Burns.

Two roads head south from Burns. SR 78 skirts the state's largest lake, formed by the merger of Harney and Malheur lakes, then heads southeast to meet US 95. SR 205 runs south from Burns, passes the lake and follows the edge of the Malheur National Wildlife Refuge. Frenchglen, at the south end of the refuge, has changed little since the days of the cattle barons. Its eight-room hotel is preserved as a state historic wayside.

At Frenchglen an unimproved road loops to the summit of Steens Mountain, one of the largest fault-block mountains on the continent. On the west the mountain rises gently from the Harney Plain to the aspen-clad summit; on the east it plunges abruptly to the Alvord Desert five thousand feet below. The summit road is usually passable from mid-July through October, but not always for every kind of vehicle; and weather at 9,000 feet can deteriorate swiftly even in summer. You should stop at the Bureau of Land Management office in Burns for a map and current road information before undertaking the summit road, or consider taking one of the all-day van tours that are available in Burns.

A loop around the whole mountain follows SR 205 south from Frenchglen, then to Fields. At Fields, which once prospered on freighting borax, another gravel road turns north along the eastern base of the mountain, traverses a semiarid sagebrush plateau and intersects with SR 78 some 100 miles southeast of Burns.

US 95, running from McDermitt on the Nevada border north to Burns Junction, then east through **Jordan Valley** to Idaho, holds within its arc the dry, desolate Owyhee country. Here rises the Owyhee River, whose spring white-water potential has only recently been widely recognized. North of Rome, where river trips usually begin, the river is a designated state scenic waterway. Also near Rome are the Pillars of Rome, the dramatically sheer, layered sides of a dry canyon. Northwest of Jordan Valley lie some of the more recent lava flows in the country.

Two miles before US 95 enters Idaho, a scenic gravel road heads north, following part of an old stage route through Succor Creek Canyon. Like much of southeastern Oregon, the canyon is rich in thunder eggs, a geode containing opal and agate. The gravel road connects with SR 201, which drops into the agricultural Snake River Valley. At Owyhee a side road turns west along the Owyhee River to bass-rich Owyhee Lake; SR 201 continues north through Nyssa to **Ontario.**

Willamette Valley

In the 1800s the Willamette Valley was the end of the Oregon Trail—both the cause of and cure for the "Oregon Fever" that propelled thousands of pioneers westward. The region's excellent soils and long growing season quickly delivered on their promise of bountiful, diversified crops, which in turn attracted more and more settlers.

While retaining its agricultural importance, the valley is now home to more than 60 percent of Oregon's people and has eight of the 10 largest cities. From its headwaters, the Willamette River flows northward some 120 miles to the Columbia River; the valley, flanked by the heavily forested Cascades and Coast Range, is about 60 miles wide.

Although I-5 is the chief artery, running in an almost straight line from **Cottage Grove** to **Portland,** SR 99 (designated W or E depending on its position relative to the river) offers a closer view of the valley's charms. Among those charms is the largest concentration of covered bridges outside New England—testimony to the Yankee origins of many of Oregon's settlers. Six of the bridges are within a few miles of Cottage Grove, the southernmost major city in the valley.

The largest metropolitan area in the southern part of the valley is created by **Eugene,** home of the University of Oregon, and neighboring **Springfield,** the gateway to the McKenzie River recreation area.

Farther north lie the mid-valley cities of **Albany,** appropriately named **Corvallis** (heart of the valley), and the gracious state capital, **Salem.** The region's industries range from grass seed, mint and wood products through high-tech research and manufacturing, to education: Oregon State University is in Corvallis; Willamette University is in Salem.

In the northern part of the valley the urban aspect becomes more noticeable. This was the first part of interior Oregon to be settled; such towns as **Oregon City,** the original capital of Oregon Territory, and **Newberg** have buildings dating from the early 1800s. Complementing the commerce and industry of the cities are the fruit and nut orchards and, most recently, the vineyards. Grapes grown in the Willamette Valley's soils have produced wines that have commanded international acclaim. To order informational brochures phone Oregon Wine Country at (541) 750-0156 or (866) 548-5018.

Eugene / © Chris Luneski / Alamy

Points of Interest

ADRIAN (E-12) pop. 147, elev. 2,228'

LAKE OWYHEE STATE PARK is reached by SR 201 and a county road winding through 10 miles of erosion-sculpted canyons along the Owyhee River. The lake provides 60 miles of scenic, canyon-skirted waterway. Along the lake's eastern shore, the red-tinted cliffs of Succor Creek Canyon rise 1,000 feet above water level.

McCormack and Indian Creek campgrounds are on the Lake Owyhee Reservoir just above the dam. East of Lake Owyhee is Succor Creek State Natural Area, which is popular with rock hounds.

Please be advised that while the road to the Lake Owyhee area is scenic, it is also winding and narrow. The climb to the reservoir is moderately steep. Inquire about road conditions before entering the canyon; drive cautiously and yield to oncoming traffic. Picnic areas and boat ramps are available. Fishing is permitted. Phone (800) 551-6949. *See Recreation Chart.*

ALBANY (D-3) pop. 40,852, elev. 210'

Albany was the home of the Calapooia Indians before being settled in 1848 by two brothers from Albany, N.Y. The town changed its name in 1853 to Takenah, an American Indian word describing the depression, or large pool, created by the Calapooia River as it flows into the Willamette. Two years later the town was Albany again, because too many people insisted on translating *Takenah* as "hole in the ground."

Despite its brief identity crisis, Albany grew rapidly between 1851-1900, and its citizens erected hundreds of Victorian homes. More than 700 of the town's early structures remain, and several can be toured on select days throughout the year. Contact the Albany Visitors Association for details; phone (541) 928-0911 or (800) 526-2256.

A popular pastime is touring the area's numerous covered bridges. Oregon has the largest collection of covered bridges outside of New England; a detailed brochure outlining their locations is available from the visitors association.

Albany Visitors Association: 250 Broadalbin St. S.W., Suite 110, P.O. Box 965, Albany, OR 97321; phone (541) 928-0911 or (800) 526-2256.

Self-guiding tours: A self-guiding driving tour past many of the city's historic buildings, featuring such styles as Queen Anne, Italianate, French Second Empire and Classic Revival, is detailed on a map and brochure available from the visitors association.

ALLEGANY (F-2) elev. 37'

GOLDEN AND SILVER FALLS STATE PARK is at the end of the Coos River Hwy. in the Coast Range.

Two waterfalls, both about 100 feet high, and an old-growth myrtle forest highlight its 157 acres. Glenn Creek Road, the main road in the park, is gravel and not recommended for trailers and large motor homes. No drinking water is available. Daily dawn-dusk. Free. Phone (800) 551-6949.

AMITY (C-3) pop. 1,478, elev. 159'

Deriving its name from the peaceful resolution of a dispute in 1849, Amity was the site of one of the earliest woolen mills in Oregon.

WINERIES

• **Amity Vineyards** is at 18150 Amity Vineyards Rd. S.E.; from SR 99W take Rice Ln. .25 mi. e. to Amity Vineyards Rd., then .75 mi. n. Tasting room and self-guiding tours daily 11-6, June-Sept.; noon-5, rest of year. Closed Jan. 1, Thanksgiving and Dec. 25. Phone (503) 835-2362 or (888) 264-8966.

ASHLAND (H-6) pop. 19,522, elev. 1,868'

A crossroads for culture and outdoor activity, Ashland is home to the Oregon Shakespeare Festival *(see attraction listing).* Recreational opportunities at 100-acre Lithia Park include hiking, horseshoes, picnicking, tennis and volleyball. Numerous lakes in the region permit fishing and water sports. A scenic stretch of I-5 passes through Ashland, intersecting with SR 66.

Ashland Chamber of Commerce: 110 E. Main St., P.O. Box 1360, Ashland, OR 97520; phone (541) 482-3486.

OREGON SHAKESPEARE FESTIVAL is at 15 S. Pioneer St. One of the oldest and largest repertory theaters in the nation, the company annually presents 11 classic and contemporary plays in three theaters: the 1,200-seat outdoor Elizabethan Stage; the contemporary 600-seat Angus Bowmer Theatre; and the intimate New Theatre, which can be configured to accommodate three types of seating layouts. Before evening performances, guests can watch the Green Show, a 35-minute courtyard production by guest performers; acts change regularly.

Free summer park talks are held in Bill Patton Garden. Concerts, discussions and lectures are held in the 1923 Carpenter Hall. Preface talks are available to acquaint guests with that evening's production, and post-show discussions with actors are offered after matinees. Classes and activities also are held throughout the year.

was then. Reputed to be the antique capital of Oregon, many historic buildings house antique shops. The city is the home of the state's first National Historic District.

Shopping areas: The Aurora Colony Historic District, downtown, includes a number of specialty shops.

FIR POINT FARMS is at 14601 Arndt Rd. Visitors can enjoy the farm's produce stand, display garden, greenhouse, animal petting area, nature trail and nut house. Old growth fir trees enhance the grounds, which afford views of Mount Hood. Tours are available during spring and fall. Allow 1 hour minimum. Tues.-Sat. 9-6, Sun. 11-5, Apr.-Dec. Free. Phone (503) 678-2455.

SAVE **OLD AURORA COLONY MUSEUM** is at 15018 2nd St. N.E. at jct. Liberty St. The museum displays items from the Aurora Colony, a German Christian communal society that thrived in the 19th century. The complex includes an 1861 ox barn, an 1863 colony house, an 1876 log cabin, a wash house, a re-created tie-shed and a courtyard with an herb garden.

Allow 30 minutes minimum. Tues.-Sat. 11-4, Sun. noon-4, Feb.-Dec.; closed major holidays. Admission $6; $5 (ages 60+); $2 (students with ID); free (ages 0-5). Phone (503) 678-5754.

BAKER CITY (D-11) pop. 9,860, elev. 3,446'

The Baker Valley gave the Oregon Trail pioneers their first glimpse of the promise of the Oregon Territory. The National Historic Oregon Trail Interpretive Center (see attraction listing) at Flagstaff Hill was built to preserve and interpret the Oregon Trail heritage.

In 1861 gold was discovered in Baker County by miners searching for the mythical Blue Bucket Mine. Subsequently, several mining towns sprang up throughout the county, many of which are now ghost towns. The Armstrong gold nugget, weighing 80.4 ounces, was found here.

Many of Baker City's historic buildings are reminiscent of the ornate architecture of the early gold rush days. Baker City Historic District has more than 100 commercial and residential buildings spread over 40 acres. Among them are the 1889 Geiser Grand Hotel and the Natatorium.

In the heart of the ghost town area is Sumpter Valley Dredge State Heritage Area, the centerpiece of which is a 1,250-ton gold dredge built in 1935 and operated until 1954. More than $4.5 million in gold was extracted from the valley by the dredge. Self-guiding and interpretive tours of the dredge are available May through October; the trail surrounding it is open year-round; phone (541) 894-2486 or (800) 551-6949. Train rides are available in summer (see Sumpter Valley Railroad p. 80).

The mountains that were once the miner's El Dorado are now an easily accessible recreational retreat. The Blue Mountains to the west and the Wallowa Mountains to the east are within the boundary of the Wallowa-Whitman National Forest (see place listing p. 124). Another nearby highlight is Hells Canyon National Recreation Area (see place listing p. 72), which lies east via SR 86.

A scenic stretch of I-84 begins just south of Baker City, running 93 miles northwest to Pendleton.

Baker County Visitors Bureau: 490 Campbell St., Baker City, OR 97814; phone (541) 523-3356 or (800) 523-1235.

Self-guiding tours: Maps and brochures for self-guiding walking and driving tours are available at the visitor and convention bureau. Tours include the Baker City Historic District, gold-mining towns, the Hells Canyon National Scenic Byway and the National Elkhorn Scenic Byway. Literature for self-guiding tours of nearby ghost towns can be obtained as well.

ADLER HOUSE MUSEUM is at 2305 Main St. The turn-of-the-20th-century house was built by a prominent businessman. Guided tours are available. Allow 1 hour minimum. Fri.-Mon. 10-2, Memorial Day weekend-Labor Day. Admission $5; free (ages 0-15). Phone (541) 523-9308.

BAKER HERITAGE MUSEUM is off I-84 exit 304 to 2480 Grove St. at jct. Campbell St. Displayed is a comprehensive collection of rock, mineral and semiprecious stone specimens as well as period clothing and memorabilia dating back to the 1860s. Allow 1 hour, 30 minutes minimum. Daily 9-5, mid-Mar. to mid-Oct. Admission $5; $4.50 (ages 60+); free (ages 0-15); $18 (family, maximum six adults). Phone (541) 523-9308.

GEM **NATIONAL HISTORIC OREGON TRAIL INTERPRETIVE CENTER** is along the Hells Canyon Scenic Byway on SR 86, 5 mi. e. of I-84 exit 302. The 509-acre site includes original 1850s wagon ruts from the Oregon Trail, which cross an approximate .75-mile section on the site, as well as 1890s remains of the former Flagstaff Gold Mine. The center features artifacts, theater presentations and life-size dioramas that provide insights into exploration, settlement, American Indian culture, mining history, natural history and the development of public lands. Living-history presentations and demonstrations of pioneer skills are offered in a 150-seat theater and at an outdoor wagon encampment.

A replica of a 1920s gold stamp mill is open during summer. A 4.2-mile trail system passes scenic views and historic sites and includes interpretive panels. The Oregon Trail wagon ruts can be reached from a hiking trail starting at the interpretive center or from an easier paved trail that can be accessed from a pullout on SR 86. A stone marker was placed at the site in 1906 by mid-19th century pioneer and Oregon Trail preservation advocate Ezra Meeker.

Picnic facilities are available. Allow 2 hours minimum. Daily 9-6, Apr.-Oct.; 9-4, rest of year.

Closed Jan. 1, Thanksgiving and Dec. 25. Living-history presentations are offered spring through early fall; phone for schedule and fees. Admission Apr.-Oct. $8; $4.50 (ages 62+); free (ages 0-15). Admission rest of year $5; $3.50 (ages 62+); free (ages 0-15). Federal Passes are accepted. AX, DS, MC, VI. Phone (541) 523-1843.

USBANK is at 2000 Main St. The bank features an exhibit of native gold in all its naturally occurring forms as well as the Armstrong Nugget, an 80.4-ounce gold nugget that was discovered on June 19, 1913. Mon.-Thurs. 10-5, Fri. 10-6. Free. Phone (541) 523-7791.

BANDON (G-1) pop. 2,833, elev. 55'

Bandon is an important harbor and a popular vacation spot and artists' colony. The area's major industries focus on the export of cranberry products; many cranberry bogs can be seen north and south of town. Bandon's beaches, strewn with agates, jasper and other semiprecious stones, are very popular with rock hounds and beachcombers.

About 2 miles north on US 101 is Bandon Dunes, a golf course developed on natural rolling dunes along the Pacific, with seven holes set alongside the ocean; and Pacific Dunes, built along undisturbed bluffs. Both courses have been rated among the nation's best. A third golf course, Bandon Trails, is located inland.

Bandon Chamber of Commerce: 300 S.E. Second, P.O. Box 1515, Bandon, OR 97411; phone (541) 347-9616.

Shopping areas: Oldtown Bandon boasts art galleries and craft shops.

BANDON HISTORICAL SOCIETY MUSEUM is on US 101 at 270 Fillmore Ave. S.E. The museum features exhibits about local American Indian artifacts, dairy farming, cheese making, cranberry harvesting, the local timber/logging industry and the town's devastating fires of 1914 and 1936. A maritime room has exhibits about shipbuilding, riverboats, sailing vessels, commerce and shipwrecks.

Two pioneer rooms depict early businesses, tourism, schools and vintage clothing and feature more than 1,500 historic photos of Bandon's past. Mon.-Sat. 10-4, first Mon. in Feb.-Dec. 23; closed Thanksgiving. Admission $2; free (ages 0-12). Phone (541) 347-2164.

BULLARDS BEACH STATE PARK is 2 mi. n. on US 101. The Coquille River Lighthouse is on the north jetty. It is reached by road through the day-use area and features an exhibit and tours. Park activities include camping, hiking, kite flying, beachcombing and bicycling. A horse camp, yurts (domed tents) and wildlife viewing areas are available; interpretive programs are presented in summer. Swimming is not permitted.

Migrating gray whales can be seen from Face Rock Wayside. Day-use area open daily dawn-dusk. Lighthouse daily 10-4, Apr.-Oct. Whale sightings

are common early mornings, Mar.-May and in Dec. Free. Phone (541) 347-2209 or (800) 551-6949. *See Recreation Chart and the AAA Northwestern CampBook.*

SAVE **WEST COAST GAME PARK SAFARI** is 7 mi. s. on US 101. About 450 exotic animals representing more than 75 species roam the 20-acre park. Visitors can view or walk among numerous free-roaming animals and pet some of the selected cubs, which may include lions, tigers, cougars, leopards and bears. Llamas, deer and other animals can be fed.

Allow 1 hour minimum. Daily 9-6, June 15-Labor Day; 9-5, rest of year. Hours may vary; phone ahead. Closed Thanksgiving and Dec. 25. Admission $15; $14 (ages 60+); $8.75 (ages 7-12); $5.50 (ages 2-6). DS, MC, VI. Phone (541) 347-3106.

BEAVERTON—see Portland p. 106.

BEND (E-7) pop. 52,029, elev. 3,623'

Bordered by the Deschutes National Forest *(see place listing p. 65)* and the Cascade Mountains, Bend is surrounded by diverse recreational areas and is the hub of the region's activities. Tumalo State Park *(see Recreation Chart and the AAA Northwestern CampBook)* is 5.5 miles north and La Pine State Park *(see Recreation Chart and La Pine in the AAA Northwestern CampBook)* is 27 miles south. Drake Park, in the historic downtown along the Deschutes River, is known for its abundance of waterfowl.

The Old Mill District, just west of US 97, is a shopping, dining and entertainment destination. Timber production was once a major industry in Bend, and the area occupies the site of a former sawmill. The brick powerhouse buildings and three smokestacks remain, adding character to this mixed-use development. Les Schwab Amphitheater draws popular artists and also hosts free concerts on Sunday afternoons June through August; phone (541) 312-8510.

Central Oregon Visitors Association: 661 S.W. Powerhouse Dr., Suite 1301, Bend, OR 97702; phone (541) 389-8799 or (800) 800-8334. *See color ad p. 53.*

Shopping areas: The Old Mill District, just w. of US 97 exit 138 or 139, features nearly three dozen stores, including Aerosoles, Ann Taylor Loft, Banana Republic, Gap, Sunglass Hut and Talbots.

GEM **CASCADE LAKES HIGHWAY** begins at Bend and runs w. on SR 46 past Mount Bachelor and s. on SR 46; drivers may return to Bend by following FR 61 e. to Crescent, then n. on US 97 to Bend. The 87-mile scenic drive meanders through Deschutes National Forest *(see place listing p. 65).* Just off SR 46 are several lakes, including Cultus, Devil's, Elk, Lava, North and South Twin, Sparks and Todd as well as Crane Prairie and Wickiup reservoirs. The highway also offers views of the Three Sisters, Mount Bachelor and Broken Top.

ESCAPE.

ROUTE.

To embark on an incredible journey, you need an incredible guide. Open ours and discover a wealth of information, including vacation planning, reservations and registration for the largest amateur golf tournament in the west, the Pacific Amateur Golf Classic. For your free guide go to visitcentraloregon.com or call 1-888-545-7442.

The 100 room Inn, or our townhome rentals, are your perfect headquarters for fun. Three 18 hole golf courses, an 18 hole putting course, an indoor pool, three sports centers, a water spray park, a day spa, and miles of hiking and biking trails make Eagle Crest the perfect place to visit. Call our reservations department to find out about our current packages.

1-888-513-1079 • www.eagle-crest.com

CENTRAL OREGON'S ONLY AAA FOUR DIAMOND RESORT
Sunriver Resort offers endless recreation and unique amenities.
- 63 holes of phenomenal golf
- World-class Sage Springs Club and Spa
- One indoor/three outdoor pools
- Marina on Deschutes River
- Year-round kids programs
- Ideal base camp for Bend and surrounding area
- Condé Nast "Top 50 Ski Resort"
- Golf Magazine "Gold Medal Resort"

Call reservations for AAA discount and information on golf, spa and special packages.

1-888-547-2603 • www.sunriver-resort.com

Central **Oregon**
VISITORS ASSOCIATION

EVERYTHING UNDER THE SUN.

BEND • SUNRIVER • REDMOND • SISTERS

Recreational opportunities found along the byway include boating, camping, fishing, hiking, horseback riding, sailing, swimming and windsurfing in the summer, and alpine and Nordic skiing, ice skating and snowmobiling in the winter. The portion of the road between the Mount Bachelor Ski Resort and the Deschutes Bridge is usually closed November through May due to snowfall. Free. Phone (541) 383-5300 for the Deschutes National Forest or (541) 383-4000 for the Bend Ranger District.

DES CHUTES HISTORICAL CENTER AND MU-SEUM is at 129 N.W. Idaho Ave. A three-story, 1914 stone schoolhouse contains exhibits pertaining to the prehistory and history of Deschutes County, including homesteading, logging and U.S. Forest Service history. Photographs, a 1907 Holsman motor-buggy and a re-creation of an early 20th-century classroom are included. A research library is on the premises. Allow 30 minutes minimum. Tues.-Sat. 10-4:30; closed Thanksgiving and Dec. 25. Admission $5; $2 (ages 13-17). Phone (541) 389-1813.

HIGH DESERT MUSEUM is 3.5 mi. s. on US 97. This interactive museum has a variety of indoor and outdoor exhibits exploring the culture, history, art and wildlife of the Columbia River Plateau and Great Basin. Outdoor displays include live otter, porcupine, bobcat and birds of prey presentations. Nature trails feature trailside exhibits about forestry and settlement, including a pioneer homestead and a historic, working sawmill, both with living history interpretation.

Indoor exhibits include "Spirit of the West," with walk-through dioramas; a display about Plateau Indians contains baskets, beaded bags, rugs, blankets, dolls and jewelry. An interactive exploratory exhibit teaches children about animal homes, habitats and hideaways. A tourist information center is on the premises. Food is available. Allow 3 hours minimum. Daily 9-5; closed Jan. 1, Thanksgiving and Dec. 25. Admission $15; $12 (ages 65+); $9 (ages 5-12). MC, VI. Phone (541) 382-4754.

LAVA BUTTE AREA—
see Deschutes National Forest p. 66.

LAVA CAST FOREST GEOLOGICAL AREA—
see Deschutes National Forest p. 66.

LAVA RIVER CAVE—
see Deschutes National Forest p. 66.

NEWBERRY CRATER—
see Deschutes National Forest p. 66.

PILOT BUTTE STATE SCENIC VIEWPOINT is e. on US 20. The 101-acre park contains Pilot Butte, a lone cinder cone rising 511 feet above the city. From the summit there is a magnificent view of the Cascade Range. No drinking water is available. Daily dawn-dusk. Free. Phone (800) 551-6949.

WANDERLUST TOURS picks up passengers from various points throughout the central Oregon area. Naturalists guide half-day canoe, cave, volcano and GPS eco-challenge tours. Snowshoe,

starlight/moonlight canoe tours and evening bonfire tours also are offered. Equipment is provided. Allow 3 hours minimum. Half-day tours depart daily at 9 and 1:30; inquire about other tour times and for other evening tours. Admission $42-$110; $37-$110 (ages 0-11). MC, VI. Phone (541) 389-8359 or (800) 962-2862.

RECREATIONAL ACTIVITIES
Skiing

- **Mount Bachelor Ski Resort** is 22 mi. s.w. on the Cascade Lakes Hwy. Write P.O. Box 1000, Bend, OR 97709. Mon.-Fri. 9-4, Sat.-Sun. 8-4, mid-Nov. to mid-May. Phone (541) 382-2442 or (800) 829-2442.

White-water Rafting

- **Ouzel Outfitters** provides transportation from area locations. Write P.O. Box 817, Bend, OR 97709. Half- and full-day trips depart daily, multiday trips depart weekly, May-Oct. Phone (541) 385-5947 or (800) 788-7238.

BONNEVILLE (C-7) elev. 52'

Bonneville was named for Capt. Benjamin L.E. Bonneville, whose life as an explorer in the Rocky Mountain country was documented in Washington Irving's "The Adventures of Captain Bonneville."

The Bonneville Dam spans the Columbia River from Oregon to Washington, a distance of 3,460 feet. A scenic portion of I-84 passes through Bonneville and parallels the Columbia River from Troutdale 150 miles east to Boardman.

BONNEVILLE LOCK AND DAM is off I-84 exit 40, spanning the Columbia River. Part of a system of dams which produces power and creates a 465-mile navigable waterway, this dam is in four sections, separated by Bradford, Cascade and Robins islands.

The Bradford Island Visitor Center, features an underwater viewing room from which visitors can see fish swimming up a fish ladder. Most species can be seen March through November. Audiovisual presentations, powerhouse viewing and local history displays also are available. A navigation lock is located between the visitor center and the fish hatchery.

Access to the Washington facilities *(see North Bonneville, Wash.; p. 190)* is via the Bridge of the Gods, 4 miles east at Cascade Locks. Picnicking and fishing are permitted on the Washington side. Allow 1 hour, 30 minutes minimum. Daily 9-5; closed Jan. 1, Thanksgiving and Dec. 25. Hours may vary; phone ahead. Free. Phone (541) 374-8820. *See Recreation Chart.*

Bonneville Fish Hatchery is off I-84 exit 40, adjacent to the dam at 70543 N.E. Herman Loop. Display ponds contain sturgeon and trout. The salmon spawn late October through November. Daily 7:30-dusk. Office open Mon.-Fri. 7:30-4; closed holidays. Free. Phone (541) 374-8393.

JOHN B. YEON STATE PARK is off I-84 exit 35, then 1.75 mi. w. Trails lead to viewpoints and waterfalls. Picturesque Elowah Falls is on the McCord Creek Trail. Daily dawn-dusk. Free. Phone (800) 551-6949.

BRIDAL VEIL (C-7) elev. 56'

Bridal Veil, a former lumber mill community in a valley along the Historic Columbia River Highway (see Columbia River Gorge National Scenic Area p. 59), is surrounded by rocky cliffs and waterfalls. The Bridal Veil Post Office, near the I-84 interchange, was established July 7, 1887, and is one of the oldest post offices in Oregon.

BRIDAL VEIL FALLS STATE PARK is on scenic US 30 at Milepost 28. A .33-mile trail leads to the falls, and a .5-mile paved path ascends to the gorge overlook. Daily dawn-dusk. Free. Phone (800) 551-6949.

GUY W. TALBOT STATE PARK is 4 mi. w. on US 30 from I-84 exit 22. Contained within the park is Latourell Falls, a picturesque cataract along the Columbia River bluffs. Picnicking is permitted and hiking trails are available. Daily dawn-dusk. Free. Phone (800) 551-6949.

SHEPPERD'S DELL STATE PARK is about 3 mi. w. on US 30. A historic bridge and a waterfall accessible by a short trail are on the grounds. Parking is limited. Daily dawn-dusk. Free. Phone (800) 551-6949.

BROOKINGS (H-5) pop. 5,447, elev. 129'

Because of its unusually mild climate, Brookings is sometimes called "The Banana Belt of Oregon." Temperatures regularly reach around 70 F in winter. Flowers bloom all year—about 90 percent of the country's Easter lilies are grown locally. Commercial fishing, lumbering, wood products and tourism are Brookings' largest industries.

The only aerial attack on the mainland United States by a Japanese war plane during World War II occurred just east of town near Mount Emily.

The port of Brookings-Harbor and the Chetco and Winchuck rivers provide popular fishing areas. Nearby streams offer abundant salmon and steelhead and cutthroat trout. Harris Beach and Loeb state parks are nearby (see Recreation Chart and the AAA Northwestern CampBook). Hiking, agate seeking, beachcombing, surf perch fishing and crabbing also are popular activities.

Forest and trail maps and other recreational information about the Rogue River-Siskiyou National Forest (see place listing p. 112) are available from the Gold Beach Ranger District, 539 Chetco Ave., P.O. Box 4580, Brookings, OR 97415; phone (541) 412-6000. Goat Island, also known as Bird Island, is a migratory bird sanctuary at the north edge of town off Harris Beach.

Brookings-Harbor Chamber of Commerce: 16330 Lower Harbor Rd., P.O. Box 940, Brookings, OR 97415; phone (541) 469-3181 or (800) 535-9469.

AZALEA PARK is off US 101. More than 1,000 wild azaleas and rhododendrons bloom in late spring and early fall in this 27-acre park. An extensive play area for children called Kidtown is available. Summer concerts are presented at the outdoor "Stage Under the Stars." Picnicking is permitted. Daily dawn-dusk. Free. Phone (541) 469-3181.

THE CENTRAL BUILDING is downtown at 703 Chetco Ave. on US 101. The building once served as the administrative building for a group of lumber companies that owned and operated the mill town of Brookings; it now houses a museum, an antique mini-mall and two art galleries. Mon.-Sat. 10-5. Free. Phone (541) 469-7755.

BROWNSVILLE (D-3) pop. 1,449, elev. 358'

Settled in 1846, Brownsville retains many homes dating 1850-1900 and several historic buildings. The Moyer House, 201 Main St., is an 1881 Victorian Italianate home furnished in period; phone (541) 466-3390. Off Main Street at the end of Park Avenue, Pioneer Park (see Recreation Chart) offers camping, fishing, swimming and other recreational opportunities as well as picnic facilities mid-April to mid-October.

Over the River-Through the Woods Scenic Byway is a 66-mile route that leaves I-5 and travels up SR 228 east through South Santiam River Canyon to the junction with SR 126. The byway connects I-5 to the West Cascade and McKenzie/Santiam Pass scenic byways.

Self-guiding tours: Guide books for historical walking and driving tours are available at the Linn County Historical Museum (see attraction listing) or at the city hall on Main Street. City hall is open Mon.-Fri. 8-5; phone (541) 466-5666.

LINN COUNTY HISTORICAL MUSEUM is at 101 Park Ave. The museum displays a late 19th-century railroad depot, a wagon used to travel the Oregon Trail, an American Indian exhibit, freight cars, and artifacts and photographs depicting life from the pioneer days to the 1940s. Allow 1 hour minimum. Mon.-Sat. 11-4, Sun. 1-5; closed Jan. 1, Easter, Thanksgiving and Dec. 25. Donations. Phone (541) 466-3390.

THE LIVING ROCK MUSEUM is 3 mi. e. on SR 228 off I-5 Brownsville exit. Displays include Biblical scenes portrayed in illuminated rock, wood carvings, oil paintings of Oregon wildlife, a mineral collection and an exhibit on the history of logging in Oregon. Guided tours are available. Allow 30 minutes minimum. Tues.-Sat. 10-5; evenings by appointment. Donations. Phone (541) 466-5814.

BURNS (E-10) pop. 3,064, elev. 4,148'

Few people associate the Old West and its cowboy legends with Oregon, but Burns was once the unofficial capital of the 19th-century cattle empires that staked claim to the grasslands of this high desert plateau. Henry Miller, who acquired a million acres and more than a million head of cattle, was typical of the cattle barons who settled the region.

The junction of US 20, which roughly follows the old Central Oregon Emigrant Trail, and US 395 in Burns have made the town a transportation hub. The Burns Paiute Indian Reservation is on the north edge of town.

About 70 miles south of Burns is 30-mile-long Steens Mountain, which slopes gradually away from Malheur Lake to its 9,733-foot summit, then drops abruptly to the Alvord Desert on the east. Aspen groves, lakes and meadows stud the area.

About 50 miles west of Burns off US 20, the Glass Buttes rise some 2,000 feet above the surrounding countryside. The buttes, one of the largest known outcroppings of iridescent obsidian, furnished generations of American Indians with material for spear points and other implements. Together with the outcroppings found in Yellowstone National Park, they supplied most of the arrowheads for tribes as far east as Ohio.

Harney County Chamber of Commerce: 76 E. Washington St., Burns, OR 97720; phone (541) 573-2636.

HARNEY COUNTY HISTORICAL MUSEUM is at 18 W. D St. Visitors will find wildlife displays, Camp Harney artifacts, photographs, pioneer items, old machinery and wagons, and American Indian sandals and mats dating back 11,000 years. Allow 1 hour minimum. Mon.-Sat. 10-4, first Tues. in Apr.-Sept. 30; by appointment rest of year. Admission $4; $3 (senior citizens); $1 (ages 6-12); $6 (family, up to four people). Phone (541) 573-5618.

MALHEUR NATIONAL WILDLIFE REFUGE is about 24 mi. s. on SR 205, then 6 mi. e. on Sodhouse Ln. The 187,000-acre refuge contains marsh, ponds, lakes, meadows and uplands desert; 320 bird and 58 mammal species have been recorded. Malheur Lake, a nesting and feeding stop along the Pacific flyway, is at the northern boundary. Wildlife is visible along a 41-mile auto tour route beginning south of the refuge headquarters. A museum contains wildlife exhibits and more than 200 mounted specimens.

Refuge and museum daily dawn-dusk. Visitor center Mon.-Thurs. 8-4, Fri.-Sun. 9-3, late Feb.-Oct. 31; Mon.-Thurs. 8-3, Fri. 9-3, rest of year. Schedule may vary; phone ahead. Prime bird season is mid-Mar. to mid-June. Free. Phone (541) 493-2612.

OARD'S MUSEUM is 23 mi. e. at 42456 US 20E. The museum offers American Indian art and artifacts. Highlights include a complete costume worn by an Indian chief in 1890; antique gun, doll, horsehair pottery and Paiute Indian cradle board collections; an art gallery of American Indian works; and

more than 100 antique clocks. Allow 1 hour minimum. Mon.-Sat. 8-7, Sun. 9-6. Free. Phone (541) 493-2535 or (800) 637-0252.

CANNON BEACH (A-1) pop. 1,588

Cannon Beach was named for the cannon that washed ashore from a schooner shipwrecked in 1846. The coastline includes the world's third largest monolith, Haystack Rock.

Cannon Beach Information Center and Chamber of Commerce: 207 N. Spruce St., P.O. Box 64, Cannon Beach, OR 97110; phone (503) 436-2623.

Shopping areas: Hemlock Street has a variety of specialty shops featuring glass blowing, clothing, arts and crafts.

ECOLA STATE PARK is on the coast 2 mi. n. off US 101 and is part of Lewis and Clark National Historical Park (see place listing p. 78). The Corps of Discovery saw a beached whale south of what is now the state park, and the expedition party traded with the Tillamook Indians for blubber, meat and oil.

Sea lion and bird rookeries are on offshore rocks, and a small gang of elk roams freely. It also is a premier whale watching location; a cliff trail offers scenic views. Part of the Oregon Coast Trail (also designated as the Lewis and Clark National Historic Trail) runs through the park. There is access to two scenic beaches. Picnicking is permitted. Daily dawn-dusk. Admission $3 (per vehicle); free (pedestrians). Phone (800) 551-6949. See Recreation Chart.

CANYON CITY (E-10) pop. 669, elev. 3,194'

The discovery of gold in nearby Canyon Creek prompted the overnight settlement of a mining camp in 1862. During the height of the gold rush, supplies and mail were brought into camp three times a week from The Dalles by Pony Express, later replaced by freight service over the old Dalles Military Road. Passions ignited by the gold rush were further heightened by clashes between the pro-Union Oregon miners and the Confederate Californians.

GRANT COUNTY HISTORICAL MUSEUM is at 101 S. Canyon City Blvd., just n. of the post office. Regional relics and artifacts comprise the collection. Allow 30 minutes minimum. Mon.-Sat. 9-4:30, Sun. by appointment, May-Sept.; by appointment rest of year. Admission $4; $3.50 (ages 62+); $2 (ages 7-17). Phone (541) 575-0362.

Joaquin Miller's Cabin is next to Grant County Historical Museum at 101 S. Canyon City Blvd. This was the home of the Oregon poet and his family. Mon.-Sat. 9-4:30, Sun. by appointment, May-Sept.; by appointment rest of year. Admission included in Grant County Historical Museum ticket of $4; $3.50 (ages 62+); $2 (ages 7-17). Phone (541) 575-0362.

CANYONVILLE (G-3) pop. 1,293, elev. 785'

GAMBLING ESTABLISHMENTS
• **Seven Feathers Hotel & Casino Resort** is at 146 Chief Miwaleta Ln. Daily 24 hours. Phone (541) 839-1111 or (800) 548-8461.

CARLTON (C-2) pop. 1,514, elev. 199'

WINERIES
• **Anne Amie Vineyards** is at 6580 N.E. Mineral Springs Rd. Tours and tastings daily 10-5, Mar.-Dec.; Mon.-Fri. by appointment, Sat.-Sun. 10-5, rest of year. Closed Jan. 1, Thanksgiving and Dec. 25. Phone (503) 864-2991.

CASCADE LOCKS (C-7)
pop. 1,115, elev. 102'

The town was named for the series of locks built in 1896 on the Columbia River, once the primary artery of transportation in the state. Before the locks were built, travelers along the river had to dock and make a rocky, treacherous portage around the dangerous cascades and white-water rapids of this section of the Columbia.

The locks were submerged in 1938 by the rising backwaters of the Bonneville Lock and Dam *(see Bonneville p. 54)*. However, the upper portion remains in Marine Park and attests to the artistry of the dry masonry stonecutters of bygone days.

A scenic portion of I-84 passes near Cascade Locks, following the Columbia River from Troutdale 150 miles east to Boardman. The town also is an access point to the Pacific Crest National Scenic Trail.

PORT OF CASCADE LOCKS AND MARINE PARK is at 355 Wa-Na-Pa St. The scenic 20-acre riverfront park offers historic locks, a marina, camping, a museum, picnic shelters and a visitor center. The museum has tools, photographs and other regional artifacts. Also of interest is the state's first locomotive, "The Oregon Pony." Fishing is permitted. Visitor center open daily 9-7, May-Sept. Museum open Mon.-Fri. noon-5, Sat.-Sun. 10-5, May-Sept.; by appointment, rest of year. Donations. Phone (541) 374-8619 or (800) 224-3901.

Columbia River Adventures/Cruises, departing from within Port of Cascade Locks and Marine Park, operates the *Columbia Gorge Sternwheeler.* Narrated sightseeing cruises through the Columbia River Gorge are offered. Dinner and champagne brunch cruises also are available. Two-hour sightseeing excursions depart Mon.-Tues. and Thurs.-Fri. at 1, Sat.-Sun. at 10 and 2, May-Oct. Departure times may vary; phone ahead. Fare for sightseeing cruise $26; $16 (ages 4-12). Reservations are required for meal cruises. AX, DS, MC, VI. Phone (503) 224-3900 or (800) 224-3901.

CAVE JUNCTION (G-5)
pop. 1,363, elev. 1,325'

Cave Junction, a primary point of access to Oregon Caves National Monument *(see place listing p.*

89), was once known for its nearby rich gold fields. One prospector discovered a nugget that was worth $1,200 in the late 1850s. Most of the deserted mining camps have become overgrown by forest. Several area wineries offer guided tours and tastings.

Illinois River Valley Chamber of Commerce and Visitors Center: 201 Caves Hwy., P.O. Box 312, Cave Junction, OR 97523; phone (541) 592-3326 or (541) 592-4076.

GREAT CATS WORLD PARK is at 27919 Redwood Hwy. Visitors receive an up-close view of more than 17 species in one of the West Coast's largest and most varied collections of exotic cats. Throughout the park, staff and trainers can be observed interacting with the predators. Allow 1 hour minimum. Daily 10-6, June-Aug.; daily 11-5, Sept.-Oct.; daily 11-4, mid-Mar. through May 31; Sat.-Sun. 11-5, in Nov.; Sat.-Sun. 11-4, Feb. 1 to mid-Mar. Admission $13; $11 (ages 66+); $9 (ages 4-12). MC, VI. Phone (541) 592-2957.

KERBYVILLE MUSEUM is 2 mi. n. on US 199 at 24195 Redwood Hwy. The museum, filled with 60,000 artifacts, is in the 1880s Naucke House; rooms are furnished in period. Displays include a collection of farm and mining machinery, some of which is handmade. An annex has antique guns as well as logging, military, American Indian and pioneer artifacts. A Takelma Indian pithouse also is on site.

Guided tours are available by request. Allow 1 hour, 30 minutes minimum. Thurs.-Mon. 11-3, Apr. 1-Oct. 1. Admission $4; $3 (ages 62+); $2 (ages 6-16); $10 (family, 2 adults and 2 children). Phone (541) 592-5252.

CENTRAL POINT (G-6)
pop. 12,493, elev. 1,272'

Central Point, named for the intersection of two stagecoach routes, is the home of Jackson County Exposition Park, where county fairs, rodeos and festivals take place.

Central Point Chamber of Commerce: 150 Manzanita St., Central Point, OR 97502-0043; phone (541) 664-5301.

CRATER ROCK MUSEUM is 1.3 mi. e. on SR 99 then .4 mi. e. to 2002 Scenic Ave. The site features minerals from around the world and a large collection of petrified woods as well as rocks that are indigenous to Oregon and other parts of the United States and Mexico. Fossils, American Indian artifacts, a mid-1800s scrimshaw collection and shells also are included, and glass work by artist Dale Chihuly and his students is displayed. Guided tours are available by appointment. Allow 30 minutes minimum. Tues.-Sat. 10-4. Admission $4; $2 (students and 55+); free (ages 0-5). Phone (541) 664-6081.

DOGS FOR THE DEAF is off I-5 exit 33; take Biddle Rd. .25 mi. e. to Table Rock Rd., go 8 mi. n., w. on Wheeler Rd. at mile marker 10, then .25 mi. w.

to 10175 Wheeler Rd. This non-profit agency, which trains dogs to assist the deaf, hearing impaired and those with other special needs, offers tours and demonstrations. Training apartments are designed to look like home interiors; visitors can watch demonstrations where dogs are taught to alert their masters based on various sounds.

Tours include kennels where the dogs live during 4-6 months of intensive training and a 15-minute video is shown. A pet memorial park is on the property. Allow 1 hour minimum. Tours depart Mon.-Fri. on the hour at 10, 11, 1 and 2, May-Sept.; Mon.-Fri. at 10 and 2, rest of year. Hours may vary; phone ahead. Closed major holidays. Free. Phone (800) 990-3647 or TTY (541) 826-9220.

CHARLESTON (F-1)

Deep-sea fishing is a way of life in Charleston. Halibut, snapper, tuna and other fish as well as oysters are abundant in the waters off Coos Bay. Charter boats conduct fishing, whale-watching and scenic bay and ocean tours. Crabbing and clamming also are popular local recreational activities. The 91-acre Bastendorff Beach County Park is 2 miles west *(see Recreation Chart and the AAA Northwestern CampBook).*

SHORE ACRES STATE PARK AND BOTANICAL GARDENS is 4 mi. w. off Cape Arago Hwy. A former estate with 5 acres of formal gardens, this scenic, 743-acre park is landscaped with azaleas, roses, rhododendrons and other plants. A glass-walled shelter overlooking the ocean provides visitors with a view of seaside cliffs and possibly whales. Daily 8 a.m.-dusk. Admission $3 (per private vehicle); free (pedestrians). Phone (541) 888-3732 or (800) 551-6949.

SOUTH SLOUGH NATIONAL ESTUARINE RESEARCH RESERVE is off Cape Arago Hwy. at 61907 Seven Devils Rd. (SR 101). The 4,800-acre freshwater and saltwater reserve includes hiking and canoe trails that offer views of the area's plants, birds and various animals. An interpretive center displays exhibits about the estuarine environment and offers educational programs. Allow 1 hour minimum. Trails open daily dawn-dusk. Interpretive center open daily 10-4:30, June-Aug.; Tues.-Sat. 10-4:30, rest of year. Closed holidays. Free. Phone (541) 888-5558.

CHILOQUIN (G-7) pop. 716, elev. 4,138'

COLLIER MEMORIAL STATE PARK is 30 mi. n. of Klamath Falls on US 97. The open-air museum is one of the largest collections of logging artifacts in the nation. Also on the grounds is a pioneer log-cabin village and a 1.5-mile hiking trail. Daily dawn-dusk. Free. Phone (800) 551-6949. *See Recreation Chart and Klamath Falls in the AAA Northwestern CampBook.*

KLAMATH MARSH NATIONAL WILDLIFE REFUGE is 20 mi. n. on US 97, then 6 mi. e. on Silver Lake Rd. Refuge headquarters is 12 mi. farther e. on Silver Lake Rd. The 40,845-acre refuge harbors egrets, herons, sandhill cranes, bald eagles and other waterfowl and birds of prey. The best time to visit and view birds is May through June. A canoe area is open July-Sept. Road conditions may vary; phone ahead. Allow 1 hour minimum. Daily dawn-dusk. Free. Phone (541) 783-3380.

TRAIN MOUNTAIN RAILROAD MUSEUM is at 36941 S. Chiloquin Rd. The museum, dedicated to the preservation of area railroad heritage, displays large and hobby-style cars and provides historical information. Visitors can see what is reputedly the world's longest hobby railroad—nearly 15 miles of 7-1/2 inch gauge mainline track on 320 acres—featuring four tunnels as well as a miniature logging camp and town. Mon.-Fri. 10-4 (weather permitting). Hours may vary; call ahead. Train rides are given Sun. 10-3 (museum closed), Memorial Day-Labor Day. Museum free. Train rides by donation. Phone (541) 783-3030.

GAMBLING ESTABLISHMENTS

• **Kla-Mo-Ya Casino** is at 34333 US 97N. Daily 24 hours. Phone (541) 783-7529 or (888) 552-6692.

CLACKAMAS—see Portland p. 106.

CLATSKANIE (A-2) pop. 1,528, elev. 20'

Named for a small tribe of American Indians who once inhabited the region, Clatskanie is at the confluence of the Columbia and Clatskanie rivers. It is now a center for the processing of lumber and pulp into paper.

Clatskanie Chamber of Commerce: 155 W. Columbia River Hwy., P.O. Box 635, Clatskanie, OR 97016; phone (503) 728-2502.

[SAVE] **HISTORICAL FLIPPIN CASTLE** is at 620 S.W. Tichenor St. The restored gingerbread-style residence is crowned with twin turrets, creating the castle-like appearance. It was built 1898-1900 for prominent lumber businessman Thomas Flippin and his family. The house is furnished in period and features two Italian marble fireplaces.

Food is available (lunches are served to the public in the basement Mon.-Fri. at noon.) Allow 1 hour minimum. Tours are offered by appointment. Admission $4; $3 (ages 60+); $2 (ages 0-11). Phone (503) 728-3608.

COLUMBIA CITY (A-3) pop. 1,571, elev. 80'

CAPLES HOUSE is at 1915 First St. Built in 1870, the house now serves as a museum. On the grounds are a country store, the Pioneer Tool Shed and the Knapp Social Center. The Carriage House displays antique dolls, period clothing and toys. Allow 1 hour minimum. Fri.-Sun. and holidays 1-5, Mar.-Oct. Admission $3; $2 (ages 0-12). Phone (503) 397-5390.

COLUMBIA RIVER GORGE NATIONAL SCENIC AREA (B-7)

Following the Columbia River in both Oregon and Washington, the scenic area consists of 292,000 acres of sheer cliffs, mountainous forestland, hilly deciduous woods and grassy plains. The Oregon section extends from the Sandy River near Troutdale about 80 miles east to the Deschutes River. Rain forests and waterfalls, characteristic of the area's western end, give way east of the mountains to oak woods and grasslands.

Before settlement brought towns and dams, the rapids near The Dalles were impassable, requiring a difficult portage around the river and its enclosing cliffs. By 1913 plans were under way to create a scenic roadway similar to Charlemagne's winding roads through the Rhine Valley.

The Columbia provides a wide travel corridor and recreational playground. Through a collaboration of preservation and developmental interests, many public recreational areas have been set aside. Phone (541) 308-1700 for more details, including safety information.

COLUMBIA GORGE INTERPRETIVE CENTER—*see Stevenson, Wash., p. 271.*

HISTORIC COLUMBIA RIVER HIGHWAY is e. of Portland; for the best views of the gorge, enter the area from the w. at I-84 exit 17. Portions of the scenic highway split and become parallel roads: The upper level, old US 30, is the older, more scenic route; the lower level, I-84, is an interstate highway.

The highway provides panoramic views of the Columbia River Gorge at Crown Point State Scenic Viewpoint *(see attraction listing)* and, near Portland,

at Women's Forum State Park. East of the latter park, Larch Mountain Road runs 14 miles to a view at Sherrard Point, where a short trail accesses views of mounts Adams, Hood, Jefferson, Rainier and St. Helens.

The other 22 miles of this scenic road travel through the gorge, with 2,000-foot-tall cliffs, unusual rock formations and 11 waterfalls. The highest waterfall along the drive is 620-foot-tall Multnomah. Near the base of the falls, an interpretive center has displays of the biology, geology and history of the area. Food is available. Free. Phone (541) 308-1700.

VISTA HOUSE AT CROWN POINT STATE SCENIC VIEWPOINT is about 3 mi. e. of Corbett off I-84 exit 22. The view from Crown Point and the Vista House overlook offers a 30-mile panorama of the Columbia River Gorge from 733 feet above sea level. Vista House was built soon after the scenic highway was dedicated in 1916. Park open daily 24 hours. Vista House open daily 9-6, Apr.-Oct.; schedule varies rest of year. Donations. Phone (503) 695-2230.

COOS BAY (G-1) pop. 15,374, elev. 10′

The busy port of Coos Bay was founded in 1854 by J.C. Tolman of the Coos Bay Co. The town, originally named Marshfield after Tolman's hometown in Massachusetts, was renamed Coos Bay by referendum in 1944. Coos Bay is one of the world's largest ports for forest products. Wood chips account for a major portion of the port's export tonnage shipped to domestic and worldwide markets each year.

Coos Bay Boardwalk, on the downtown waterfront along Bayshore Drive at the foot of Anderson Avenue, features a wooden walkway overlooking

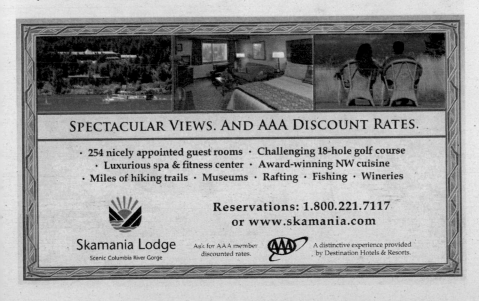

the public boat docks. Interpretive displays document the bay's natural and human history, emphasizing transportation. A covered area houses the historic wooden tug *Koos*, with interpretive panels about tugboats.

Coos Bay straddles scenic US 101, which winds past Oregon Dunes National Recreation Area *(see Siuslaw National Forest p. 118)* just north of town and continues along the Oregon coast to Florence.

Coos Bay Chamber of Commerce: 50 Central Ave., Coos Bay, OR 97420; phone (541) 269-0215 or (800) 824-8486.

Self-guiding tours: Brochures describing self-guiding hiking, biking, walking and driving tours as well as charter boat tours are available at the chamber of commerce.

COOS ART MUSEUM is at 235 Anderson Ave. Local, regional, national and touring exhibits are featured. Collections include works by Frank Boyden, Alexander Calder, Red Grooms, Tom Hardy, Roy Lichtenstein, Henk Pander, Robert Rauschenberg and Larry Rivers. Prefontaine Memorial Gallery honors former Olympian Steve Prefontaine, a native of Coos Bay. Allow 30 minutes minimum. Tues.-Fri. 10-4, Sat. 1-4; closed major holidays. Admission $5; $2 (students and senior citizens). Phone (541) 267-3901.

THE MILL CASINO HOTEL & RV PARK— *see North Bend p. 86.*

THE OREGON CONNECTION (HOUSE OF MYRTLEWOOD) is off US 101 at 1125 S. 1st St. Visitors may take self-guiding tours of a factory where myrtlewood logs are used to manufacture various products. Allow 30 minutes minimum. Mon.-Sat. 9-6, Sun. 10-5, June-Sept.; 10-5, rest of year. Closed Jan. 1, Easter, Thanksgiving and Dec. 25. Free. Phone (541) 267-7804 or (800) 255-5318.

CORBETT (B-4)

Corbett is east of the Sandy River, whose waters come from the melting glaciers on the south slope of Mount Hood. "The smelt are running in the Sandy" is a common refrain in the spring, when millions of the small, oily fish ascend the river to spawn. Impromptu anglers cast aside their poles in favor of buckets and other imaginative snares to catch the fish.

A scenic portion of US 30 passes through Corbett and Crown Point State Scenic Viewpoint *(see Historic Columbia River Highway p. 59)*. Scenic I-84 parallels the Columbia River from Troutdale 150 miles east to Boardman.

CORVALLIS (D-2) pop. 49,322, elev. 273'

Located on the Willamette River between the Coastal Mountain range to the west and the Cascades to the east, Corvallis lives up to its Latin name meaning "heart of the valley." It is one of the

state's leading centers of commerce, culture and education.

Established in 1845, Corvallis has a variety of period buildings in its historic district. Of particular interest is the 1888 Benton County Courthouse; it is one of the oldest courthouses in Oregon still in use.

Oregon State University is the source of much of the city's cultural and intellectual wealth, while such industries as agriculture, high-technology and forest products contribute to its material resources.

The 5,300-acre William L. Finley National Wildlife Refuge, 6 miles south off SR 99W, provides habitat for a large population of migratory Canada geese, ducks and swans.

Corvallis Tourism: 553 N.W. Harrison Blvd., Corvallis, OR 97330; phone (541) 757-1544 or (800) 334-8118.

Self-guiding tours: Brochures outlining driving, bicycling and walking tours of the region and highlighting local wineries, covered bridges and historic sites are available from the visitors bureau Mon.-Sat. 9-5, July-Aug., Mon.-Fri. 9-5, rest of year.

COTTAGE GROVE (F-3)
pop. 8,445, elev. 642'

Settled between two rivers, Cottage Grove is a recreation center for south Lane County. Area attractions include six covered bridges, two lakes, numerous streams, historic homes and the Bohemia gold-mining district.

Cottage Grove Area Chamber of Commerce: 700 E. Gibbs St., Suite C, Cottage Grove, OR 97424; phone (541) 942-2411.

COTTAGE GROVE MUSEUM is at jct. H St. and Birch Ave. at 147 H St. An octagonal structure built as a Roman Catholic church in 1897, the museum contains American Indian artifacts; old mining tools; a working model of an ore stamp mill; 61 original Oregon covered bridge prints; a *Titanic* display; and articles relating to pioneer domestic life, farming and industry. Allow 1 hour minimum. Wed.-Sun. 1-4, mid-June through Labor Day; Sat.-Sun. 1-4, rest of year. Donations. Phone (541) 942-2369.

CRATER LAKE NATIONAL PARK (F-7)

See map page 62.

Elevations in the park range from 4,250 ft. near the park's southern boundary to 8,929 ft. at Mount Scott. Refer to AAA maps for additional elevation information.

Crater Lake National Park is on the crest of the Cascade Range, 72 miles east of Medford off I-5 to SR 62; or, from Klamath Falls, take US 97 north 21 miles, then west on SR 62 for 29 miles. The park also can be reached from Roseburg by taking I-5 to SR 138E.

The park's centerpiece is Crater Lake, noted for its brilliant blue water. The lake is 6 miles long, 4.5 miles wide and 1,943 feet deep. Its 26-mile shoreline is encircled by lava cliffs that rise 500 to 2,000 feet. For much of the year snow covers the mountains and peaks that encircle the lake.

Until about 7,700 years ago, Mount Mazama, a 12,000-foot volcano, occupied the site of Crater Lake. Eruptions emptied the magma chamber beneath the mountain and caused the mountaintop to collapse, creating the caldera that now contains the lake. As volcanic activity slowed, springs, snow and rain began to fill the caldera, resulting in the formation of the nation's deepest lake.

Embracing three zones of vegetation, the park has about 680 species of plants and a variety of trees, including several types of hemlock, fir, pine and spruce. The park also is known for its wildflowers.

Small game is abundant; among the large mammals are black bears, elk and mule deer. More than 200 species of birds have been identified. It is forbidden to feed, tease or in any way molest bears or other wildlife, as they are potentially dangerous.

General Information and Activities

The park is open daily 24 hours (weather permitting). Except during years of very heavy snowfall, the northern entrance road opens in mid-June; Rim Drive opens in early July. Both remain open until the first heavy snowfall. Visitors to the park are advised to prepare their cars for snowy conditions from October through June.

The park has two visitor centers, each of which have natural history displays and information about conducted trips, road conditions and points of interest. All-weather roads are open to Steel Visitor Center, 4 miles north of SR 62 from the south park entrance at park headquarters; phone (541) 594-3100. It is open daily 9-5, early Apr.-early Nov.; 10-4, rest of year. Closed Dec. 25.

All-weather roads from the south entrance also are open to Rim Village, on the south side of the lake, via SR 62. Rim Village Visitor Center is open daily 9:30-5, early June-late Sept. (weather permitting). It is the focal point of park activities and the starting point of several trails.

Accommodations at Mazama Village, 7 miles south of Rim Village, and gasoline are available from mid-May to mid-October. Food is available year-round. The historic, renovated 1915 Crater Lake Lodge at Rim Village also is open mid-May to mid-October. For reservations phone (888) 774-2728.

There are more than 90 miles of maintained trails within Crater Lake National Park—snow usually blocks them from October to July. Mountain trails lead to the summits of several of the high points above the rim and down 764 feet to the lake. The Wizard Island Tail to the rim ascends richly forested slopes that rise high above a lava plateau.

Near park headquarters is Castle Crest Wildflower Trail. The 1-mile Cleetwood Trail, a trail leading to the lakeshore, begins along Rim Drive 11 miles north of Rim Village Visitor Center. The Sinnott Memorial Overlook *(see attraction listing)* provides a view of Crater Lake.

Back-country permits are required for overnight trips and are available free of charge at the visitor centers. Winter snowmobiling is allowed on the north entrance road only. No snowmobile facilities or ski tows are available. Picnicking is permitted. *See Recreation Chart and the AAA Northwestern CampBook.*

ADMISSION to the park is $10 (per private vehicle for a seven-day pass); $5 (per person per bicycle or motorcycle).

PETS must be restricted at all times, either in vehicles or by leash, and are not allowed in public buildings or on trails.

ADDRESS inquiries to the Steel Visitor Center, Crater Lake National Park, P.O. Box 7, Crater Lake, OR 97604. Phone (541) 594-3100 for visitor information and current road and weather information.

Points of Interest

CLOUDCAP is on Crater Lake's e. rim within Crater Lake National Park. The mountain affords one of the best views of the lake. Its summit, almost 1,774 feet above the lake, is reached via a .75-mile paved spur road off Rim Drive.

Park daily 24 hours (weather permitting). The northern entrance road usually opens mid-June and Rim Drive usually opens early July; both remain open until first heavy snowfall. Visitor center hours vary by location and season. Admission included in Crater Lake National Park admission of $10 (per private vehicle for a seven-day pass); $5 (per person per bicycle or motorcycle). Phone (541) 594-3100.

CRATER LAKE BOAT TOURS depart from Cleetwood Cove Dock within Crater Lake National Park. Park naturalists explain the area's geological and natural history on 1.75-hour trips. The trail from the parking area to the dock is steep and should not be attempted by those with respiratory or ambulatory problems.

Up to seven tours depart daily, usually on the hour 10-4 on a first-come, first-served basis, early July to mid-Sept. (weather permitting). The 10:00 tour includes a drop-off at Wizard Island *(see attraction listing)* and guests are picked up later after a day of fishing and hiking; length of time on island varies. Tour schedule may vary; phone ahead to confirm. Fare $26.50; $16 (ages 3-11). Wizard Island drop-off fare $36.50; $20 (ages 3-11). Phone ahead to verify fares. Guests must also pay the park admission of $10 (per private vehicle for a seven-day pass); $5 (per person per bicycle or motorcycle). AX, DS, MC, VI. Phone (541) 594-3100.

GARFIELD PEAK is reached by a 1.75-mile trail from the lodge within Crater Lake National Park.

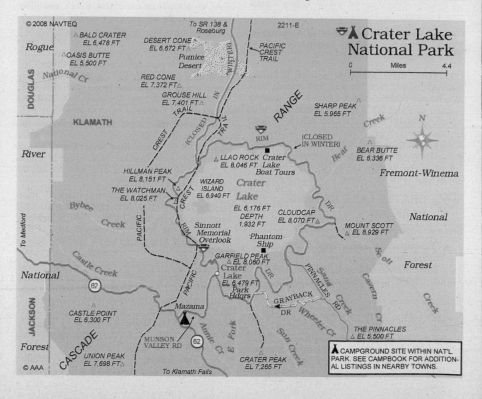

© 2008 NAVTEQ   2211-E

⚑🏕 Crater Lake National Park

To SR 138 & Roseburg

Rogue

△ BALD CRATER EL 6,478 FT

DESERT CONE EL 6,672 FT△

PACIFIC CREST TRAIL

△ OASIS BUTTE EL 5,500 FT

Pumice Desert

0   Miles   4.4

National Cr

RED CONE EL 7,372 FT△

GROUSE HILL EL 7,401 FT△

KLAMATH

SHARP PEAK EL 5,965 FT

Creek

N

RIM

(CLOSED IN WINTER)

BEAR BUTTE EL 6,336 FT

River

HILLMAN PEAK EL 8,151 FT

△ LLAO ROCK EL 8,046 FT

Crater Lake Boat Tours

Bear

Fremont-Winema

THE WATCHMAN EL 8,025 FT

WIZARD ISLAND EL 6,940 FT

Crater

Bybee

EL 6,176 FT DEPTH 1,932 FT

CLOUDCAP EL 8,070 FT△

DR

MOUNT SCOTT △ EL 8,929 FT

National

Creek

Sinnott Memorial Overlook

Lake

Phantom Ship

Forest

To Medford

GARFIELD PEAK △ EL 8,060 FT

Crater Lake Park Hdqrs

PINNACLES

Scott

Cavern Cr

National

62

Castle Creek

Mazama

GRAYBACK DR

Wheeler Cr

Sun Creek

Creek

JACKSON

△ CASTLE POINT EL 6,300 FT

🏕

MUNSON VALLEY RD

62

Annie Cr

E Fork

THE PINNACLES △ EL 5,500 FT

Forest

UNION PEAK EL 7,698 FT△

© AAA

CASCADE

To Klamath Falls

CRATER PEAK EL 7,265 FT

🏕 CAMPGROUND SITE WITHIN NAT'L PARK. SEE CAMPBOOK FOR ADDITIONAL LISTINGS IN NEARBY TOWNS.

DOUGLAS

RANGE

CREST

TRAIL

(CLOSED)

PACIFIC

RIM

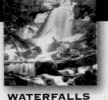

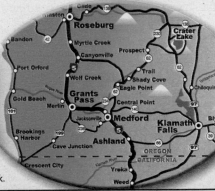

The 8,060-foot summit provides views of the surrounding area. Park daily 24 hours (weather permitting). The northern entrance road usually opens mid-June and Rim Drive usually opens early July; both remain open until first heavy snowfall. Visitor center hours vary by location and season. Admission included in Crater Lake National Park admission of $10 (per private vehicle for a seven-day pass); $5 (per person per bicycle or motorcycle). Phone (541) 594-3100.

HILLMAN PEAK is just n. of The Watchman in Crater Lake National Park. The highest point on the rim at 8,151 feet, Hillman Peak was named for the first non-American Indian to reach the rim of Crater Lake. It is a bisected cone of Mount Mazama.

Park daily 24 hours (weather permitting). The northern entrance road usually opens mid-June and Rim Drive usually opens early July; both remain open until first heavy snowfall. Visitor center hours vary by location and season. Admission included in Crater Lake National Park admission of $10 (per private vehicle for a seven-day pass); $5 (per person per bicycle or motorcycle). Phone (541) 594-3100.

LLAO ROCK is on Crater Lake's n. rim in Crater Lake National Park. This conspicuous feature is a lava flow filling an ancient explosion crater. Named for the American Indian spirit Llao, Chief of the Below World, the formation rises more than 1,850 feet above the lake.

Park daily 24 hours (weather permitting). The northern entrance road usually opens mid-June and Rim Drive usually opens early July; both remain open until first heavy snowfall. Visitor center hours vary by location and season. Admission included in Crater Lake National Park admission of $10 (per private vehicle for a seven-day pass); $5 (per person per bicycle or motorcycle). Phone (541) 594-3100.

MOUNT SCOTT is accessed by a 2.5-mile trail from Rim Drive in Crater Lake National Park. This is the highest point in the park, at 8,929 feet. The trail leads to the top; a fire lookout station offers extensive views.

Park daily 24 hours (weather permitting). The northern entrance road usually opens mid-June and Rim Drive usually opens early July; both remain open until first heavy snowfall. Visitor center hours vary by location and season. Admission included in Crater Lake National Park admission of $10 (per private vehicle for a seven-day pass); $5 (per person per bicycle or motorcycle). Phone (541) 594-3100.

PHANTOM SHIP rises about 160 feet above Crater Lake's surface within Crater Lake National Park. The remnants of lava flows from an old volcanic cone, it resembles a ship at sail. The best views are from the launches and from Kerr Notch (Phantom Ship Overlook), 8 miles east of park headquarters on Rim Drive.

Park daily 24 hours (weather permitting). The northern entrance road usually opens mid-June and Rim Drive usually opens early July; both remain

open until first heavy snowfall. Visitor center hours vary by location and season. Admission included in Crater Lake National Park admission of $10 (per private vehicle for a seven-day pass); $5 (per person per bicycle or motorcycle). Phone (541) 594-3100.

THE PINNACLES are along Wheeler Creek Canyon near the e. boundary of Crater Lake National Park. The formations are spires of fused pumice and scoria; some rise 200 feet above the canyon floor. Other spires and fluted columns eroded from soft volcanic material can be seen in Castle Creek Canyon, Godfrey Glen and Annie Creek Canyon.

Park daily 24 hours (weather permitting). The northern entrance road usually opens mid-June and Rim Drive usually opens early July; both remain open until first heavy snowfall. Visitor center hours vary by location and season. Admission included in Crater Lake National Park admission of $10 (per private vehicle for a seven-day pass); $5 (per person per bicycle or motorcycle). Phone (541) 594-3100.

 RIM DRIVE encircles the Crater Lake caldera within Crater Lake National Park. The 33-mile scenic road includes lookout points offering fine views of the area, including Vidae Falls. Towed trailers are not recommended on the east, north and south portions of Rim Drive. Parking for trailers is provided.

The road is open early July to mid-Oct. (weather permitting). Park daily 24 hours (weather permitting). Visitor center hours vary by location and season. Admission included in Crater Lake National Park admission of $10 (per private vehicle for a seven-day pass); $5 (per person per bicycle or motorcycle). Phone (541) 594-3100.

SINNOTT MEMORIAL OVERLOOK is below the Rim Village Visitor Center in Crater Lake National Park. An exhibit building has displays about geology and natural and human history. Exhibits, maps, paintings and pictures detail lake history and points of interest; the lake can be viewed from the parapet.

Exhibit building open daily 9:30-5, early July-early Oct. (weather permitting). Admission included in Crater Lake National Park admission of $10 (per private vehicle for a seven-day pass); $5 (per person per bicycle or motorcycle). Phone (541) 594-3100.

THE WATCHMAN is within Crater Lake National Park near the rim of the lake directly w. of Wizard Island and can be reached from Rim Drive by a 1-mi. trail. The peak affords a rare panorama of the park and surrounding country from more than 1,800 feet above the lake. It also is the site of a fire lookout station.

Park daily 24 hours (weather permitting). The northern entrance road usually opens mid-June and Rim Drive usually opens early July; both remain open until first heavy snowfall. Visitor center hours vary by location and season. Admission included in Crater Lake National Park admission of $10 (per private vehicle for a seven-day pass); $5 (per person per bicycle or motorcycle). Phone (541) 594-3100.

WIZARD ISLAND is in Crater Lake within Crater Lake National Park. Access is obtained from Crater Lake Boat Tours *(see attraction listing)*. The island is a cinder cone rising 760 feet above the lake's surface. According to legend, the spirit Llao was thrown into the lake by an enemy spirit; monsters devoured all except the head, leaving it to form the island. Fishing is permitted, and a 1-mile trail leads from the shore to the cone's crater. The hike is strenuous, and there are no services on the island.

The drop-off boat tour usually departs daily at 10 on a first-come, first-served basis, early July to mid-Sept. (weather permitting). A boat arrives later in the day to pick up guests; length of time on island varies, so phone to confirm. Schedule may vary; phone ahead. Wizard Island drop-off fare $36.50; $20 (ages 3-11). Phone ahead to verify fares. Guests are also responsible for the park admission of $10 (per private vehicle for a seven-day pass); $5 (per person per bicycle or motorcycle). MC, VI. Phone (541) 594-3100.

DALLAS (C-2) pop. 12,459, elev. 326'

Settled in the 1840s and incorporated in 1874, Dallas was named for George Mifflin Dallas, U.S. vice president under James K. Polk. Among the town's historic buildings is the 1899 Polk County Courthouse. The 35-acre Dallas City Park offers sightseeing and outdoor recreation opportunities; phone (503) 623-2338. The Delbert Hunter Arboretum and Botanic Garden in the park features native plants. Baskett Slough National Wildlife Refuge is just northeast off SR 22.

Dallas Area Chamber of Commerce: 119 S.W. Court St., Dallas, OR 97338; phone (503) 623-2564.

RECREATIONAL ACTIVITIES
Recreational Complex

- **Dallas Aquatic Center Recreational Complex**, e. of jct. SR 223 and Ellendale Rd., then s. to 1005 LeCreole Dr., Dallas, OR 97338. Mon., Wed. and Fri. 5:30 a.m.-8 p.m., Tues. and Thurs. 6 a.m.-9 p.m., Sat. 9-9, Sun. 1:30-5. Phone (503) 623-9715.

DEPOE BAY (D-1) pop. 1,174

Along the sea wall north of Depoe Bay's harbor, natural rock tubes are flooded by the incoming tide and spout geyserlike sprays. At times these streams arch over US 101.

Five state park or wayside areas—Boiler Bay, Depoe Bay, Devil's Punch Bowl *(see Otter Rock p. 89)*, Fogarty Creek *(see Recreation Chart)* and Rocky Creek—are near town along US 101. All offer views of the Oregon coast. Fishing (except at Boiler Bay) and picnicking are permitted. Sea lions inhabit most of the coastal area and whales often can be spotted. Whale Watching Center, downtown at 119 S.W. US 101, introduces visitors to the species of whales that can be spotted in the area as well as the best times, months and locations to see them.

Maps list the best viewing locations and schedules of volunteers that can be found along the coast to educate the public about whales and whale watching. The facility is open daily 9-5 between Memorial Day and Labor Day and Wednesday through Sunday 10-4 during the rest of the year; phone (541) 765-3304.

Depoe Bay Chamber of Commerce: 223 S.W. US 101, P.O. Box 21, Depoe Bay, OR 97341; phone (541) 765-2889.

Shopping areas: The downtown area has a number of galleries and shops.

DOCKSIDE CHARTERS is just e. of US 101 via Bay St. to 270 Coast Guard Pl. Zodiac boat tours and 1.5-hour narrated whale-watching tours are offered. From late February through March and early November to mid-December, whales are not in the area, but the whale-watching tour still offers views of other wildlife. Fishing charters also are available for 5, 6 or 8 hours.

Zodiac tours (minimum 2 passengers) depart daily on the hour 9-3 (weather permitting). Whale-watching tours (minimum 6-8 passengers) depart daily at noon, 1:30 and 3 (weather permitting). Closed Thanksgiving and Dec. 25. Whale-watching fare $20; $10 (ages 5-12). Zodiac fare $25 (1 hour); $35 (1.5 hours); $45 (2 hours). MC, VI. Phone (541) 765-2545 or (800) 733-8915 to verify passenger minimums, schedule and fares.

DESCHUTES NATIONAL FOREST

Elevations in the forest range from 2,150 ft. at Lake Billy Chinook to 10,495 ft. at Mt. Jefferson. Refer to AAA maps for additional elevation information.

Deschutes National Forest is southwest of Bend on US 97, north of Crater Lake National Park *(see*

DID YOU KNOW

Crater Lake is the deepest lake in the United States at 1,943 feet.

place listing p. 61) on the eastern slope of the Cascades. The third largest national forest in Oregon and one of the most popular, it is comprised of heavily forested land and volcanic landscapes. The forest's several areas of past volcanic activity are easily accessible from US 97.

The Newberry National Volcanic Monument area contains several volcanic features, including nearby Lava River Cave *(see attraction listing)*, one of the longest uncollapsed lava tubes in the Northwest. The cave was once the pathway of an underground stream of molten rock. Molten lava also formed the Lava Cast Forest Geological Area *(see attraction listing)* as it engulfed a forest. Lava Lands Visitor Center sits at the base of Lava Butte Cone. The 7,000-year-old cone's lava flow once dammed the Deschutes River.

To the south lies Newberry Crater *(see attraction listing)*; its two lakes, obsidian (black glass) lava flow and crater-rim waterfalls are part of a volcano that encompasses 500 square miles. The landscape of the volcano has been created over the last 500,000 years. Archeological excavations conducted in the crater led to the discovery of one of the oldest houses in the Western Hemisphere. Studies show that the inhabitants hunted bears, deer, rabbits and bison.

The area's past volcanism provides numerous recreational opportunities for hikers and climbers, and the more than 200 lakes and miles of streams challenge anglers. Diamond Peak, Mount Jefferson, Mount Washington and Three Sisters wilderness areas offer hikers terrain ranging from rugged volcanic landscapes to alpine meadows and waterfalls.

Horses for pack and saddle trips are available locally. A number of areas throughout the forest offer downhill and cross-country skiing and permit snowmobiling. A chairlift goes to the top of the 9,065-foot Mount Bachelor peak in the summer. A day-use pass for all Deschutes National Forest sites is $5 (per private vehicle). For information and permits contact the Forest Supervisor, Deschutes National Forest, 1001 S.W. Emkay Dr., Bend, OR 97702; phone (541) 383-5300. *See the Recreation Chart and the AAA Northwestern CampBook.*

 CASCADE LAKES HIGHWAY— *see Bend p. 52.*

LAVA BUTTE AREA is 11 mi. s. of Bend on US 97 within Deschutes National Forest. The 500-foot cinder cone is one of more than 400 cones in the Deschutes National Forest formed from volcanic eruptions. A road spirals to an observation lookout at the top. The lookout is closed when extreme fire danger or visible smoke is present. A .25-mile hiking trail surrounds the rim.

The Lava Lands Visitor Center offers interpretive dioramas, displays and information. Visitor center daily 9-5, July 4-Labor Day weekend; Wed.-Sun. 9-5, May 1-July 3 and day after Labor Day to mid-Oct. Day-use pass (includes all Deschutes National Forest sites) $5 (per private vehicle). Phone (541) 593-2421.

LAVA CAST FOREST GEOLOGICAL AREA is 14 mi. s. of Bend on US 97, then 11 mi. e. on FR 9720 (a rough dirt road), within Deschutes National Forest. Along a self-guiding nature trail are the molds of pine trees that were engulfed by slow-moving lava 6,000-8,000 years ago. Daily 24 hours (weather permitting). Day-use pass (includes all Deschutes National Forest sites) $5 (per private vehicle). Phone (541) 593-2421 for the Lava Lands Visitor Center (May 1 to mid-Oct.).

LAVA RIVER CAVE is 11 mi. s. of Bend on US 97 within Deschutes National Forest. Formed by lava flows, the cave is about a mile long. Lanterns are available for rental. Since the cave's temperature is 35-40 F, it is a good idea to bring warm clothing and sturdy shoes. No drinking water is available. Picnicking is permitted. Self-guiding tours are available daily 9-4, May-Oct. (weather permitting). Day-use pass (includes all Deschutes National Forest sites) $5 (per private vehicle). Lantern rental fee $3. Phone (541) 593-2421 for the Lava Lands Visitor Center.

METOLIUS RIVER RECREATION AREA is about 20 mi. n. of Sisters off US 20 and SR 126 within Deschutes National Forest. The area is a scenic region of lush mountain meadows and ponderosa pine. The Metolius River, which flows from a large spring at the base of Black Butte, is popular for fly-fishing.

Note: Unless you are an experienced rafter, a guide is recommended. Phone for more details and for safety information. Conditions vary from year to year. Daily 24 hours. Day-use pass (includes all Deschutes National Forest sites) $5 (per private vehicle). Phone (541) 383-5300.

NEWBERRY CRATER is 22 mi. s. of Bend and about 13 mi. e. of US 97 on CR 21 within Deschutes National Forest. The huge caldera is the location of Paulina and East lakes. These lakes are separated by cinder cones and a large obsidian flow of more recent geological occurrence. They are popular areas for camping, hiking and fishing.

Visitors can view Paulina Falls from an observation point off FR 21. The caldera can be accessed late Apr.-Oct. 31 (weather permitting). In winter and early spring visitors can drive 10 miles toward the caldera and then must either snowshoe, snowmobile or cross-country ski the last 3 miles to view the caldera; phone for additional information about access. Paulina Lake Visitor Center daily 9-5, July 4-Labor Day weekend; Wed.-Sun. 9-5, May 1-July 3 and day after Labor Day to mid-Oct. Phone ahead to verify schedule. Day-use pass (includes all Deschutes National Forest sites) $5 (per private vehicle). Phone (541) 536-8802, or (541) 593-2421 for the Lava Lands Visitor Center (May 1 to mid-Oct.).

EAGLE POINT (G-6) pop. 4,797, elev. 1,305'

BUTTE CREEK MILL is off SR 62 then .6 mi. e. on Linn Rd. and .3 mi. n.e. to 402 N. Royal Ave., following signs. Built in 1872, the mill is the last operating water-powered flour mill west of the Mississippi. Visitors can see the mill in action and watch a 16-minute film. Picnic spots are available along the creek. Allow 30 minutes minimum. Mon.-Sat. 9-5, Sun. 11-5. Hours vary on holidays; call ahead. Free. Phone (541) 826-3531.

ESTACADA (C-4) pop. 2,371, elev. 512'

Estacada is known as the Christmas Tree Capital of the world. In a valley at the foot of the Cascade Mountains, the town is sheltered by the forested bluffs that overhang the Clackamas River. As the gateway to the Mount Hood National Forest *(see place listing p. 82)*, the area offers abundant recreational opportunities and is the starting point of the West Cascades National Scenic Byway, which ends in Ashland. The 220-mile scenic route passes through old growth forest, along the Clackamas River and through the Western Cascade Mountains. Take SR 224 and FR 46 south from Estacada to Detroit; SR 22 and SR 126 to McKenzie Bridge; then FR 19 south to Oakridge. The best time for the drive is May through October.

Built in 1883, the Philip Foster Historical Farm, 5 miles west of downtown, was the last stop on the Oregon Trail before pioneers reached Oregon City; phone (503) 637-6324.

The Estacada Murals, which depict local activities and historical events, can be found adorning the walls of local businesses.

Estacada-Clackamas River Area Chamber of Commerce: 475 S.E. Main St., P.O. Box 298, Estacada, OR 97023; phone (503) 630-3483.

EAGLE CREEK NATIONAL FISH HATCHERY is at 34288 S.E. Rainbow Rd. Coho salmon and winter steelhead can be seen swimming up fish ladders in nearby creeks in season. Adult salmon can be seen from late September through November, and adult winter steelhead can be seen January through March. Mon.-Fri. 7:30-4. Free. Phone (503) 630-6270.

EUGENE (E-2) pop. 137,893, elev. 422'

Located at the confluence of the Willamette and McKenzie rivers at the southern end of the Willamette Valley, Eugene is the state's second largest metropolitan area and home to the University of Oregon.

Surrounded by farmlands, forest and mountains, Eugene is noted for its fine parks, including Spencer Butte Park. A coniferous forest surrounds the park's South Hills Ridgeline Trail. The park also features 2,065-foot Spencer Butte, the highest point in the Eugene area, and a wide variety of plant and animal life. Hiking and mountain bike trails are available. At Skinner Butte Park along the Willamette River,

RiverPlay Discovery Village is a highlight. This playground lets children scale a replica of Skinner Butte and dig for faux fossils in a sandy area. The park is also home to a replica of the 1846 one-room cabin where Eugene and Mary Skinner lived; in 1851 he began platting what is now the city of Eugene. The park is open daily dawn to dusk.

Miles of bicycle trails and opportunities for water sports can be found along the Willamette River. Riverfront picnic areas and meandering walkways thread through 5 acres of roses at Owen Memorial Rose Garden, along the south bank of the Willamette at N. Jefferson Street; phone (541) 484-5307.

In the east hills of Eugene is Hendricks Park Rhododendron Garden, graced by more than 6,000 rhododendrons and azaleas; phone (541) 484-5307. The Mount Pisgah Arboretum encompasses 200 acres of wooded hillsides and trails within the Lane County Howard Buford Recreation Area. Alton Baker Park *(see Recreation Chart)* offers duck ponds and various developed recreational facilities. The McKenzie River white-water area is nearby. Set against a wooded hillside, the Cascades Raptor Center houses non-releasable permanent resident birds in large outdoor enclosures; phone (541) 485-1320.

Eugene and its sister city Springfield are at the head of a series of dams constructed by the Army Corps of Engineers for flood control in the Willamette River Basin. Lookout Point, Dexter and Fall Creek lakes *(see Recreation Chart)* formed by their namesake dams 20 miles southeast on SR 58, have picnic, fishing and boating facilities. The nearby Lookout Point Powerhouse offers guided tours by appointment two weeks in advance; phone (541) 937-2131 or (541) 937-2129.

Convention and Visitors Association of Lane County Oregon: 754 Olive St., Eugene, OR 97401; phone (541) 484-5307 or (800) 547-5445.

Self-guiding tours: A brochure of the East Skinner Butte historic landmark area outlines a self-guiding walking tour of downtown focusing on several historic buildings dating 1855-1929. The landmark honors one of Eugene's founding fathers.

Maps and information can be obtained from the visitors association Mon.-Fri. 8:30-5, Sat.-Sun. 10-4, May-Sept.; Mon.-Fri. 8:30-5, Sat. 10-4, rest of year.

Shopping areas: Valley River Center on Valley River Way is a major area shopping mall. Other popular shopping areas include the Fifth Street Public Market, at Fifth and High, with its specialty shops; Oakway Center, Oakway and Coburg roads, with nearly two dozen stores, including Coldwater Creek and Pottery Barn; and the Saturday Market, downtown, where vendors sell crafts and food to the accompaniment of mimes and musicians March through December.

EXPERIENCE OREGON has varied boarding locations. These 1- to 4-day bus trips highlight Portland, Willamette Valley, central and eastern Oregon and the coast. For destinations, schedules, departure times and park-and-ride locations write 1574 Coburg Rd., #123, Eugene, OR 97401. Fares start at $25, depending on destination and tour package. Phone (541) 342-2662 or (888) 342-2662.

 HULT CENTER FOR THE PERFORMING ARTS is on Willamette St. between 6th and 7th aves.; from I-5, take exit 194B, following signs to city center. The center, noted for its fine architectural and acoustical design, has two theaters—the 2,500-seat Silva Concert Hall and the 500-seat Soreng Theater—which feature plays, concerts and other performances by international, national, regional and local talent. Changing art exhibits are displayed in the Jacobs Gallery.

Lobby and ticket office open Tues.-Fri. noon-5, Sat. 11-3. Guided tours of the center are offered Thurs. by reservation. Tours free. Phone (541) 682-5000 for ticket office, or (541) 682-5733 for tour reservations.

LANE COUNTY HISTORICAL MUSEUM is at 740 W. 13th Ave. Displays interpret Lane County history from its early settlement through present day. Exhibits feature 19th-century vehicles, logging history, period rooms and a display highlighting the Eugene Park Blocks with artifacts from the 1898 Lane County courthouse. An Oregon Trail exhibit includes an authentic Oregon Trail wagon, diary quotes, artifacts, maps and photographs. Allow 1 hour minimum. Tues.-Sat. 10-4. Admission $3; $2 (ages 61+); 75c (ages 15-17). Phone (541) 682-4242, or (541) 682-4239 for recorded message.

MAUDE KERNS ART CENTER is at 1910 E. 15th Ave., 2 blks. e. of the University of Oregon campus. Art education classes and several galleries are featured. Allow 30 minutes minimum. Mon.-Fri. 10-5:30, Sat. noon-4. Sat. hours may vary; phone ahead. Donations. Phone (541) 345-1571.

THE SCIENCE FACTORY CHILDREN'S MUSEUM AND PLANETARIUM is at 2300 Leo Harris Pkwy. s. of Autzen Stadium in Alton Baker Park. The museum features a variety of hands-on exhibits designed for all ages. Planetarium shows also are presented. Special events that include additional activities are often held on weekends. Daily 10-4, July-Aug.; Wed.-Sun.10-4, rest of year. Planetarium shows are offered Sat.-Sun. at 1 and 2. Admission to museum or planetarium $4; $3 (senior citizens); free (ages 0-2). Combined admission $7. MC, VI. Phone (541) 682-7888.

[SAVE] **SHELTON-McMURPHEY-JOHNSON HOUSE** is downtown at 303 Willamette St. on the s. side of Skinner Butte Park. A city landmark, the 1888 Queen Anne-style Victorian house is known as the "Castle on the Hill." Its location offers panoramic views of the city and surrounding hillsides. Changing historical exhibits are featured, and visitors may explore the landscaped grounds. Allow 1 hour minimum. Self-guiding and docent tours are available Tues.-Fri. 10-1, Sat.-Sun. 1-4; closed holidays. Hours may vary; call ahead. Admission $5; $2 (ages 6-12). Phone (541) 484-0808.

UNIVERSITY OF OREGON is bounded by Franklin Blvd., 11th and 18th aves., and Alder and Moss sts. Some 20,400 students attend the university. Visitors can stroll the park-like arboretum, which features 4,000 trees representing 500 varieties. Hayward Field hosts major track and field events, including the annual Prefontaine Classic. Campus guided tours depart from the first floor of Oregon Hall Mon.-Fri. at 9:30 and 12:30, Sat. at 10:30. Visitor information is available at a kiosk on 13th Ave. near Agate St. Mon.-Fri. 8-5. Free. Reservations are recommended. Phone (541) 346-3201 or (800) 232-3825.

[SAVE] **Jordan Schnitzer Museum of Art** is at 1430 Johnson Ln., near the Knight Library on the University of Oregon's west campus. Built in 1932 and renovated and expanded from 2002-05, it contains more than 13,000 objects of historic and contemporary art. The collection includes art from multiple countries, including America, China, Japan and Korea. Temporary exhibitions are presented throughout the year.

Metered parking is available on Kincaid and University, with free parking areas available on weekends. Guided tours offered by reservation. Allow 1 hour minimum. Tues.-Sun. 11-5 (also Wed. 5-8); closed major holidays. Admission $5; $3 (ages 13-18 and 63+); free (ages 0-12, students with ID, and on first Fri. of the month). MC, VI. Phone (541) 346-3027.

[SAVE] **Museum of Natural and Cultural History** is at 1680 E. 15th Ave., near Hayward Field on the University of Oregon's east campus. "Oregon—Where Past is Present" tells the story of the state's geologic past and 15,000 years of Northwest cultural history. Visitors can explore an interactive lab offering hands-on science-based activities for all ages. Also featured are changing exhibits as well as a courtyard with more than 100 species of native plants and outdoor art illustrating traditional Pacific Northwest Indian culture. Documentaries about the Northwest are shown in the museum's theater.

Parking is available with permit from museum admission desk. Allow 30 minutes minimum. Wed.-Sun. 11-5; closed major holidays. Admission $3; $2 (ages 3-18 and 63+); $8 (family, two adults and up to four youths); free (Wed.). Phone (541) 346-3024.

WINERIES

- **King Estate Winery** is off I-5 exit 182, 12.5 mi. w. on Oregon Ave., then 2.5 mi. s. on Territorial Hwy. to 80854 Territorial Rd. Daily 11-9; closed Jan. 1, Thanksgiving and Dec. 25. Phone (541) 942-9874 or (800) 884-4441.

- **Silvan Ridge-Hinman Vineyards** is 5 mi. s. on Bertleson Rd., then 2.5 mi. w. on Spencer Creek Rd. to 27012 Briggs Hill Rd. Daily noon-5; closed major holidays. Phone (541) 345-1945.

FLORENCE (E-1) pop. 7,263, elev. 11'

Between Florence and the ocean lies an extensive area of sand dunes that sometimes reach a height of 300 feet. A good view of the area is from the observation deck in nearby Harbor Vista County Park *(see the AAA Northwestern CampBook)*; phone (541) 997-3128.

Other natural highlights include the freshwater lakes, sand dunes and beach that constitute Jessie M. Honeyman Memorial State Park *(see Recreation Chart and the AAA Northwestern CampBook)* just south of the town.

A scenic section of US 101 bisects Florence; several attractions can be seen along its route. Six miles north on US 101 is Darlingtonia Botanical Wayside, a sphagnum bog noted for cobra lilies; self-guiding walkways provide access to the bog.

Heceta Head Lighthouse State Scenic Viewpoint, 13 miles north on US 101, provides access to the lighthouse by way of a short trail. The lighthouse, which houses Oregon's most powerful beacon, overlooks scenic bluffs and is popular with photographers. Tours are available April through October.

Florence Area Chamber of Commerce: 290 US 101, Florence, OR 97439; phone (541) 997-3128.

Shopping areas: Historic Old Town on Bay Street offers a variety of clothing, antique and other specialty shops and restaurants along the mouth of the Siuslaw River.

SANDLAND ADVENTURES is 1 mi. s. of Florence Bridge on US 101. The outfitter offers guided dune buggy tours of the Oregon Dunes near the Siuslaw River aboard 7-10 passenger or giant 27-passenger dune buggies. Sandland Adventures also features train rides, a go-cart track, bumper boats and miniature golf.

Dune buggy tours daily 9-5, Mar.-Dec.; extended hours June 1-Labor Day. Closed Easter, Thanksgiving and Dec. 24-25. Half-hour dune buggy tour $25. One-hour tour $45. Giant dune buggy tour $12. Reservations are recommended June 1-Labor Day. DS, MC, VI. Phone (541) 997-8087.

SEA LION CAVES are 11 mi. n. at 91560 US 101. Noted in the *Guinness World Records* as the world's largest sea cave, this area is home to wild Steller sea lions. The mammals can be observed in their natural surroundings. Bring binoculars in the spring and summer to watch for gray whales and rare sea birds. A flight of stairs and pathway leading to an elevator provide access to the 1,500-foot-long cavern. A scenic path leads to the outdoor viewing area. Information about sea lions and other coastal animals and plants is provided and a short film is shown.

Allow 30 minutes minimum. Open daily 8-6, July-Aug.; 9-5, rest of year. Closed Thanksgiving and Dec. 25. Admission $10; $9 (60+); $6 (ages 3-12). MC, VI. Phone (541) 547-3111.

SIUSLAW PIONEER MUSEUM is at the corner of Maple and Second sts. in Old Town. The museum houses displays and artifacts representing American Indians and early pioneers, while an audiovisual presentation outlines a brief history of the Florence area. A research library contains local historical and pioneer family information. Allow 30 minutes minimum. Tues.-Sun. noon-4, Feb. 1-Dec. 24; closed Easter and Thanksgiving. Admission $3; free (ages 0-17). Phone (541) 997-7884.

GAMBLING ESTABLISHMENTS

- **Three Rivers Casino** is .8 mi. e. of US 101 to 5647 SR 126. Daily 24 hours. Phone (541) 997-7529 or (877) 374-8377.

FOREST GROVE (B-2) pop. 17,708, elev. 169'

The town's founders aptly named Forest Grove for the surrounding white oak and fir forests. Nearby Pacific University, established as Tualatin Academy in 1849, is one of the oldest academic institutions in the Northwest. Five wineries and a sake brewery are in the vicinity; all offer tours and tastings.

Forest Grove Chamber of Commerce: 2417 Pacific Ave., Forest Grove, OR 97116; phone (503) 357-3006.

FORT KLAMATH (G-7) elev. 4,200'

The Fort Klamath region, now a cattle-raising district, was the scene of frequent clashes between white settlers and the Modoc Indians during the 1870s. From 1863 to 1890 Fort Klamath was the Army post from which the federal government conducted its Indian campaign.

FORT KLAMATH HISTORICAL FRONTIER POST AND MUSEUM is on SR 62. Built in 1863 to protect wagon trains from Indian attacks, the post contains exhibits that depict frontier life. American Indian artifacts and military medals are included. Living-history re-enactments are held. The graves of Captain Jack, a leader of the Modoc Indians, and three of his warriors are on the grounds. A historic post office also is on site. Allow 1 hour minimum. Thurs.-Mon. 10-6, June-Sept. Donations. Phone (541) 381-2230 or (541) 883-4208.

FREMONT-WINEMA NATIONAL FORESTS

Elevations in the forests range from 4,000 ft. at Klamath Falls to 8,454 ft. at Crane Mountain. Refer to AAA maps for additional elevation information.

Extending from the high mountain country of the Cascade Crest north and south of Crater Lake eastward through the Klamath Basin to the area known as "Oregon's Outback," the Fremont-Winema National Forests embrace more than 2 million acres. The two forests, which were administratively combined in 2002, extend over a high plateau broken by numerous faults and buttes, presenting a variety of landscapes, from sagebrush and juniper to pine forests and meadows.

So dramatic is the contrast that Lt. John Fremont in his journal of 1843 described being snowbound on a ridge in December while summer conditions prevailed in the prairie below. Fremont named these neighboring areas Winter Ridge and Summer Lake, respectively. Winter Ridge's topography is a familiar pattern—timbered slopes often rise sharply from sagebrush flatlands.

Volcanism shaped the area and left such features as Gearhart Mountain, one of the forests' highest volcanic domes. This mountain is the centerpiece of the Gearhart Wilderness Area, which is characterized by high mountain meadows, U-shaped valleys and other glacial features. The terrain of the Gearhart Wilderness makes it popular with hikers and cross-country skiers. Mountain Lakes, Sky Lakes, and Mount Thielsen wilderness areas also preserve nature in its primitive state.

Other favorite areas include forest camps and dispersed sites in the Warner Mountain Range, the Crane Mountain National Recreation Trail and the southern portion of Abert Rim, a favorite hang gliding launch site. Fremont-Winema National Forests also offers small mountain lakes, the largest of which is the Thompson Reservoir. Skiing is available at the Warner Canyon Ski Area. Historic firelookouts and cabins are available to rent and provide breathtaking views of the forests' landscape.

Part of the Pacific Crest National Scenic Trail threads along the west edge of the forests. Horseback riding, hiking and cross-country skiing are popular diversions. Resorts are at Lake of the Woods and Rocky Point.

For further information contact the Information Receptionist, Fremont-Winema National Forests, 1301 South G St., Lakeview, OR 97630; phone (541) 947-2151. *See Recreation Chart and the AAA Northwestern CampBook.*

LAKE OF THE WOODS is 36 mi. n.w. of Klamath Falls within Fremont-Winema National Forests. Near the base of 9,497-foot Mount McLoughlin, the lake is reached by a paved road and surrounded by dense woodlands at an elevation of about 5,000 feet. Snowmobiling and cross-country skiing are popular in winter. Fishing and water skiing also are permitted. Camping areas are open early June-late Sept.; phone ahead to verify. Phone (541) 885-3400.

GASTON (B-2) pop. 600, elev. 182'

WINERIES

• **Elk Cove Vineyards** is 3 mi. w. off SR 47 to 27751 N.W. Olson Rd. Daily 10-5; closed Jan. 1, Thanksgiving and Dec. 24-25. Phone (503) 985-7760 or (877) 355-2683.

GLENEDEN BEACH (C-1) elev. 46'

Gleneden Beach lies south of Siletz Bay. Beachcombing for driftwood, agates and glass net floats is a popular activity, particularly early in the day during low tide or after storms.

Shopping areas: Shops at Salishan, on US 101 on the property of Salishan Spa & Golf Resort, has a variety of galleries as well as craft, culinary and specialty shops.

GOLD BEACH (G-5) pop. 1,897, elev. 60'

Named for the placer mining prevalent until an 1861 flood swept the deposits out to sea, Gold Beach is a gateway for many activities in this popular coastal and river recreation area. The coastal vistas offer rewarding settings for photographers, especially along the 37-mile drive south to California via US 101.

Gold Beach Visitors Center: 94080 Shirley Ln., P.O. Box 375, Gold Beach, OR 97444; phone (541) 247-7526 or (800) 525-2334.

CAPE SEBASTIAN STATE SCENIC CORRIDOR is 7 mi. s. on US 101. Included is a group of park units covering 1,104 acres of open and forested land. It also is a good viewpoint for whale watching. Cape Sebastian is a towering headland rising 700 feet above sea level. Scenic views, wildflowers and hiking trails are among the park's attractions. Daily dawn-dusk. Free. Phone (800) 551-6949.

JERRY'S ROGUE RIVER JET BOATS depart from the port of Gold Beach. A 6-hour/64-mile trip, a 6-hour/80-mile round-trip and an 8-hour/104-mile round-trip are available. All trips stop at an upriver lodge for lunch or dinner. A museum provides a pictorial history of the Rogue River as well as natural history displays.

Morning (lunch) trip schedules operate daily from May 1-Oct. 15. Afternoon (dinner) trip schedules operate daily July 1-Labor Day. Fare for 64-mile trip $45; $20 (ages 4-11). Fare for 80-mile trip $61; $30 (ages 4-11). Fare for 104-mile trip $87; $40 (ages 4-11). Fare does not include meals. Admission to museum is free. Reservations are suggested, and passengers are asked to arrive 30 minutes before departure. DS, MC, VI. Phone (541) 247-4571 or (800) 451-3645.

ROGUE RIVER MAIL BOAT TRIPS & WHITE WATER TRIPS depart from the Mail Boat Dock, .25 mi. upstream from the n. end of the Rogue River Bridge. A 64-mile scenic and historic mail delivery jet boat trip as well as 80-mile and 104-mile whitewater trips are available. All trips, except the Express Delivery, stop at an upriver lodge for lunch or dinner.

The 64-mile trip departs daily at 8:30 and 2:30, July 1-Labor Day; at 8:30, May-June and day after Labor Day-Oct. 15. The 80-mile trip departs daily at 8 and 2:45, July 1-Labor Day; at 8, June 15-30 and day after Labor Day-Sept. 30. The 104-mile trip departs daily at 8, May-Oct. The 80-mile white-water Express Delivery departs daily at noon, July 1-Labor Day. Passengers should arrive 30 minutes before departure.

Fare for 64-mile trip $42; $16 (ages 4-11). Fare for either 80-mile trip $58; $26 (ages 4-11). Fare for 104-mile trip $84; $37 (ages 4-11). Fares may vary; phone ahead. Fare does not include meals. Reservations are recommended. DS, MC, VI. Phone (541) 247-7033 or (800) 458-3511.

GOLD HILL (G-6) pop. 1,073, elev. 1,085′

[SAVE] **HOUSE OF MYSTERY AT THE OREGON VORTEX** is from south, off I-5 exit 40, right for 1/4 mi., left 2 mi. on SR 234, then right 4 mi. on Sardine Creek Rd. From north, off I-5 exit 43, left 200 yards, r. on SR 234 for 1 mi., then left 4 mi. on Sardine Creek Rd. The House of Mystery, originally an assay office, is home to bizarre phenomena. Balls appear to roll uphill, short people seemingly get taller and visitors are unable to stand upright. The odd happenings are said to be attributed to a whirlpool of invisible energy.

Guided tours are available. Allow 1 hour minimum. Daily 9-5, June-Aug.; 9-4, Mar.-May and Sept.-Oct. Admission $9; $8 (ages 62+); $7 (ages 6-11). Phone (541) 855-1543.

GOVERNMENT CAMP (C-7) elev. 3,880′

The alpine resort community of Government Camp is on the south flanks of Mount Hood, surrounded by forests of fir, hemlock, cedar and pine. After federal soldiers used the site to store wagons in the winter of 1849, the area was called "the government camp in the mountains." The first settlers arrived in 1900 and a hotel opened in 1911. The highway reached the area in 1920 and was extended around the mountain to Hood River in 1926. This road now forms the Mount Hood Scenic Byway.

The Northwest's first ski area opened just east of Government Camp in 1927; the Summit Ski Area, with one rope tow and one double chair, is still operating. The Oregon Trail Kiosk, at Government Camp Loop Road and E. Little Trail, has displays about the Barlow Road, a wagon road opened in 1846, connecting the Oregon Trail at The Dalles with the Willamette Valley.

MOUNT HOOD CULTURAL CENTER AND MUSEUM is at 88900 US 26 business loop. Permanent exhibits document the human and natural history of Mount Hood. Themes include winter sports, mountain climbing, national forest history, the Civilian Conservation Corps., settlement around Oregon's largest volcano and the area's historic Steiner cabins built in the 1920s-30s. The museum also displays historical photographs and hosts changing exhibitions of local and regional artists.

Allow 30 minutes minimum. Daily 10-5, Memorial Day weekend-Labor Day; Thurs.-Sun. 10-5, rest of year. Closed Jan. 1, Thanksgiving and Dec. 25. Free. Phone (503) 272-3301.

RECREATIONAL ACTIVITIES
Skiing
• [SAVE] **Mt. Hood Skibowl** is on US 26. Write 87000 E. US 26, Government Camp, OR

97028. Mon.-Thurs. 9 a.m.-10 p.m., Fri. 9 a.m.-11 p.m., Sat. 8 a.m.-11 p.m., Sun. 8 a.m.-10 p.m., mid-Nov. to mid-Apr. Phone (503) 272-3206 or (503) 222-2695.

GRAND RONDE (C-2) pop. 271, elev. 344′

GAMBLING ESTABLISHMENTS
• **Spirit Mountain Casino** is on SR 18. Daily 24 hours. Phone (800) 760-7977.

GRANTS PASS (G-5) pop. 23,003, elev. 951′

A stopping place on the California stage route, Grants Pass was named when settlers building the main road through town heard of Gen. Ulysses S. Grant's capture of Vicksburg in 1863. The town now is a central point in the Rogue River region and the departure point for many downriver raft trips. Numerous riverside parks offer boating, camping, fishing, and swimming *(see the AAA Northwestern CampBook).*

A particularly scenic stretch of I-5 begins at the junction with US 199 in Grants Pass, running 60 miles southeast to the California line.

Hellgate Canyon, northwest of the city, marks the Rogue River's entrance into the Coast ranges. Guides can be hired for various trips along the Rogue River to Gold Beach. [SAVE] Schmidt House Museum, 508 S.W. 5th St., is a turn-of-the-20th-century structure built for the family of pioneer businessman Claus Schmidt; phone (541) 479-7827.

Grants Pass Visitors and Convention Bureau: 1995 N.W. Vine St., Grants Pass, OR 97526; phone (541) 476-5510 or (800) 547-5927. *See color ad p. 63.*

Shopping areas: The historic downtown district features antique shops and art galleries.

The Grower's Saturday Market, at 4th and F streets on the Southern Oregon lot, and the Grower's Wednesday Market, in Riverside Park, are open-air agricultural markets in Oregon. Features include seasonal fruits and vegetables, a nursery and baked goods as well as musicians, artisans and craftspeople. Grower's Saturday Market is open Saturdays 9-1, March through November; Wednesday Market is open Wednesdays 9-1, June through September. For information phone (541) 476-5375.

GRANTS PASS MUSEUM OF ART is in the historic downtown district at 229 S.W. G St. Exhibits feature local, regional and national contemporary American art. Allow 30 minutes minimum. Tues.-Sat. noon-4. Free. Phone (541) 479-3290.

ROGUE RIVER HELLGATE JETBOAT EXCURSIONS departs from the north bank of the Rogue River at 966 S.W. 6th St. Two-hour Quick & Scenic 36-mile trips and 5-hour White Water 75-mile trips through Hellgate Canyon are offered. Brunch, lunch and dinner cruises also are offered.

Scenic trip departs daily at 8:45 and 1:45, early June-late Aug.; at 8:35 and 12:45, in late Aug.; at

1:45, May 1-early June and at 12:45, Sept. 1-late Sept. White water trip departs daily at 9:45 and 3:15, May 1-early June; at 8:30 and 2:45, early June-Aug. 31. Phone ahead to verify and for other tour schedules. Scenic trip $35; $25 (ages 4-11). White water trip $60; $42 (ages 4-11). Phone ahead to verify and for other tour fares. White water trip not recommended for ages 0-3. AX, DS, MC, VI. Phone (541) 479-7204 or (800) 648-4874. *See color ad p. 63.*

WILDLIFE IMAGES REHABILITATION AND EDUCATION CENTER is at 11845 Lower River Rd. About 80 percent of the animals rehabilitated here are released back into the wild. Tour guides provide information about the center's permanent residents housed outdoors in a gated compound; visitors observe and learn about owls, bald eagles and osprey as well as mountain lions, black bears, Kodiak bears and wolves. A display of snakes, spiders and lizards is inside.

Allow 1 hour, 30 minutes minimum. Center open daily 9-5. Tours daily at 9:30, 11:30, 1:30 and 3. Closed Jan. 1, Thanksgiving and Dec. 25. Donations. Reservations are required for tours. Phone (541) 476-0222.

GRESHAM—*see Portland p. 106.*

HAINES (D-11) pop. 426, elev. 3,334'

EASTERN OREGON MUSEUM is 4 blks. off US 30. Visitors will find a reconstructed blacksmith shop, kitchen, parlor, an old saloon bar, an 1880s train depot, a doll collection and pioneer relics including household, mining and farming artifacts. A carriage wing houses surreys, buggies and gigs. Allow 30 minutes minimum. Wed.-Mon. 9:30-4:30, mid-May to mid-Sept; by appointment rest of year. Admission $2; $5 (family). Phone (541) 856-3233, or (541) 856-3380 off season.

HELLS CANYON NATIONAL RECREATION AREA (B-12)

Hells Canyon National Recreation Area is reached via SRs 82 and 86 in northeastern Oregon and US 95 in western Idaho. The 652,977-acre area straddles the Snake River Canyon and encompasses parts of national forests in both states.

Confined within steep, eroded black basalt walls, the surging Snake River has carved North America's deepest gorge, measuring 7,913 feet from He Devil Mountain to Granite Creek below. White-water rapids alternating with deep pools characterize this 72-mile free-flowing portion of the Snake River as it races north to meet the Columbia River.

The varied elevations of Hells Canyon support mixed plant communities sheltering such wildlife as bears, bobcats, bighorn sheep, cougars, elk, mule deer, mountain goats and many smaller birds, mammals and reptiles. Sturgeon, reputedly growing up to 11 feet long, inhabit the Snake River, sharing it with bass, catfish, salmon, steelhead trout and rainbow trout.

From the desertlike canyon floor to the alpine lakes of the Seven Devils region, the area presents a variety of recreational opportunities including boating, float trips and backpacking. From Pittsburg Landing, the Kirkwood Historic Ranch and Museum, once the home of Idaho governor and U.S. senator Len B. Jordan, is accessible by powerboat, float boat or pack trail.

The Rapid River originates in the Seven Devils Mountains and eventually joins the Little Salmon River. The forks of the Rapid River provide quality water for raising chinook salmon and therefore house the Rapid River Fish Hatchery.

The 214,000-acre Hells Canyon Wilderness, with its extensive trail system, protects a large portion of the canyon along the Oregon-Idaho border. If you plan to fish the lakes and the Snake River shoreline, you must acquire the appropriate state licenses *(see Fast Facts box)*; both Oregon and Idaho licenses are valid for boat fishing on the river.

Scenic Hells Canyon All American Road/SR 86 is a series of routes to and through the Hells Canyon National Recreation Area. **On the Oregon side** the best route is a two-lane paved loop that originates in Baker City. From Baker City follow SR 86 to Richland for approximately 41 miles. From Richland continue on SR 86 north for 11 miles to Halfway. From Halfway follow SR 86 for 20 miles to Oxbow.

Nine miles north of Halfway, SR 86 will intersect with FR 39N. Take FR 39N through the heart of the Wallowa Mountains, high mountain country and through the town of Joseph to Enterprise. One mile west of Enterprise on SR 82 is the Wallowa Mountain Visitors Center. Continue along SR 82 west for approximately 64 miles to arrive back on I-84 at La Grande. The entire loop will take approximately 5 hours.

Another possible route from the Oregon side to the recreation area is via SR 82 to Enterprise and Joseph. From Joseph it is possible to go to Hat Point, a 6,982-foot ridge overlooking Hells Canyon, via Imnaha. The route to Hat Point, open summer through early fall, follows FR 4240, a gravel, narrow road with steep grades.

Another route from Imnaha, FR 3955, parallels the Imnaha River as it meanders through rims and benches similar to those along the Snake River. This route connects with the Wallowa Mountain Loop (FR 39), which leads back to Joseph or Halfway. FR 3955 and FR 39 are maintained for cars and trailers. FR 39 can be followed east to FR 3965, which leads to the Hells Canyon overlook. With an elevation of 6,000 feet, the overlook provides a spectacular view of the Wallowa Mountains in Oregon and Idaho. These roads are closed in winter.

Buckhorn Springs, a scenic area overlooking the Imnaha drainage, can be reached from FR 46 off SR 3, a mostly gravel logging road.

For maps and brochures of different drives contact the Baker County Chamber and Visitors Bureau, 490 Campbell St., Baker City, OR 97814; phone (541) 523-3356 or (800) 523-1235.

On the Idaho side the best route to the canyon is SR 71. From Cambridge, Idaho, the road runs 29 miles northwest to Oxbow, crossing the Snake River near Brownlee Dam. It crosses back into Idaho at Oxbow, then follows the river north to Hells Canyon Dam. The total distance is about 55 miles. Another access point is Pittsburg Landing, 17 miles west of US 95 at White Bird via gravel FR 493.

Note: The Idaho side of the canyon is in the Mountain Time Zone, while the Oregon side observes Pacific Time. It is advisable to check with the Hells Canyon National Recreation Area regarding road conditions and construction. Some roads are gravel and caution should be exercised. Phone (541) 426-5546 or (800) 523-1235.

More than 30 outfitters provide float and jet boat trips down the Snake River from Hells Canyon Dam and jet boat trips upstream from Lewiston, Idaho, and from Asotin and Clarkston, Wash. For a list of local outfitters contact the Supervisor, Hells Canyon National Recreation Area, 2535 Riverside Dr., P.O. Box 699, Clarkston, WA 99403; phone (509) 758-0616 for information, (509) 758-1957 for float reservations, or (509) 758-0270 for powerboat reservations. *See Recreation Chart and the AAA Northwestern CampBook.*

BEAMERS HELLS CANYON TOURS— *see Clarkston, Wash., p. 162.*

HELLS CANYON ADVENTURES is on SR 86 (All American Rd.), 1 mi. n. of Hells Canyon Dam and 23 mi. n. of Oxbow, OR. Half-day jet boat tours depart at 10 (Pacific time) for a lunch trip and at 2 (no lunch served). Full-day jet boat tours depart at 9, traveling through the canyon's deepest part, navigating the largest rapids and visiting the Kirkwood Historical Ranch and Museum. One-day white-water rafting trips, overnight jet boat tours and fishing charters on the Snake River also are available.

Tours depart daily May 15-Sept. 15. Inquire about off-season tours. Admission ranges from $45 to

$300; call ahead to verify prices. Forest service fees are included, but fuel surcharges are not. Reservations are recommended. MC, VI. Phone (541) 785-3352 or (800) 422-3568. *See color ad p. 72.*

HILLSBORO—*see Portland p. 106.*

HOOD RIVER (C-8) pop. 5,831, elev. 154'

In addition to being one of Oregon's major apple-growing regions, the Hood River Valley is among the world's leading producers of winter pears. A 47-mile loop through the valley via SR 35 south to Parkdale, then north on SR 281 to Hood River, winds through the heart of fruit country.

The scenic Mt. Hood National Scenic Byway, SR 35, starts at the east edge of Hood River, off I-84 exit 64, and circles the eastern shoulder of Mount Hood *(see Mount Hood and Mount Hood National Forest p. 82).* Panorama Point, 3.5 miles south on Eastside Road, gives a sweeping view of the Hood River Valley. I-84 also provides scenic vistas from Boardman to Troutdale.

Prevailing strong winds through the Columbia River Gorge make this a world-renowned windsurfing area. The Hood River Event Site, off I-84 exit 63 at the foot of Second Street, features a beach and is the venue for local and international windsurfing events. The park also is available to amateur windsurfers and has a good vantage point for watching the sport (parking $5). For more information on windsurfing, contact the Columbia Gorge Windsurfing Association, 202 Oak St., Suite 150, P.O. Box 182, Hood River, OR 97031; phone (541) 386-9225.

Hood River County Chamber of Commerce: 720 E. Port Marina Dr., Hood River, OR 97031; phone (541) 386-2000 or (800) 366-3530.

Shopping areas: Shops downtown feature crafts and antiques as well as handmade goods from local artists. The Hood River Saturday Market, showcasing local artists and growers, operates downtown at 5th and Columbia on Saturdays 9-3 from early May to early October.

FLIGHTLINE SERVICES is at 3608 Airport Rd. The pilot points out local landmarks on the tours, which include the Hood River Valley, Columbia Gorge and a circle tour of Mount Hood. Passengers view a number of peaks in the Cascade Range, as well as mountain valleys, glaciers, waterfalls, alpine lakes, lava flows and orchards.

Allow 1 hour minimum. Daily 8-6, in summer; 8-5, rest of year (weather permitting). Closed Thanksgiving and Dec. 25. Fare $67 (per half-hour), $118 (per hour), $177 (1.5 hours). Prices are per person, 2 person minimum. AX, DS, MC, VI. Phone (541) 386-1133.

FULL SAIL BREWING COMPANY is at 506 Columbia St. The independent employee-owned business, founded in 1987, evolved from a small microbrewery to a leading craft brewer. It is one of the few manual brew houses of its size in the country and presents tours exploring the art of brewing beer, which is created using water from a spring on Mount Hood.

Guided tours are available. Under age 12 are not permitted on tour. Allow 30 minutes minimum. Brewery open 11:30 -10:30. Tours depart at 1, 2, 3 and 4; reservations are requested for groups over 10 persons. Closed Jan. 1, Thanksgiving and Dec. 25. Tours free. Phone (541) 386-2247.

THE HISTORY MUSEUM OF HOOD RIVER is in Port Marina Park; from I-84 exit 64 follow signs. The museum displays pioneer artifacts and exhibits about area history. Allow 1 hour minimum. Mon.-Sat. 10-5, Sun. 1-5, May-Sept. (also Tues. and Thurs. 5-7, July-Aug.); daily 1-5, in Apr. and Oct. Donations. Phone (541) 386-6772.

MOUNT HOOD RAILROAD departs from the Hood River Depot 1 blk. s. of I-84 exit 63. Two- and 4-hour round-trip tours through the scenic Hood River Valley are offered. Trains stop in Odell or Parkdale, at the base of Mount Hood. Visitors ride in historic 1910-20s Pullman cars along the river and through forests, meadows and pear and apple orchards. A cupola in the caboose provides excellent views. A two-level dome car is used for dinner and brunch trips.

Excursion trips depart Tues.-Sun. at 10 and 2, July-Aug.; Wed.-Sun. at 10 and 2, Apr.-June; Wed.-Sun. at 10 and 3, Sept.-Oct.; Sat.-Sun. at 10, Nov.-Dec. Dinner trips depart Sat. (and some Fri.) at 5:30, Apr.-Sept.; Sat. (and some Fri.) at 4:30, Oct.-Dec.; phone to confirm schedule. Brunch trains depart Sun. at 11, Apr.-Dec. Excursion fare $25; $23 (ages 60+); $15 (ages 2-12); add $2 for special events. Dinner train $80. Brunch train $58. AX, DS, MC, VI. Phone (541) 386-3556 or (800) 872-4661.

RECREATIONAL ACTIVITIES

Kayaking

• **Columbia Gorge Kayak School** trips depart from 6 Oak St. Guided kayak tours on the Columbia River and white-water trips with inflatable kayaks on the Klickitat River are offered. Daily May-Sept. (weather permitting). Phone (541) 806-4190.

WINERIES

• **Hood River Vineyards** is at 4693 Westwood Dr. Daily 11-5. Hours may vary during winter months; call ahead. Phone (541) 386-3772.

JACKSONVILLE (G-6)
pop. 2,235, elev. 1,640'

Founded in 1852, Jacksonville has more than 100 preserved pioneer buildings—more than 80 of which have historical markers. This collection is the result of "gold fever"; it was here that the Pacific Northwest's first gold discovery occurred. Several museums reflect pioneer life in the 1800s.

Between June and early September, the Britt Festivals take place at Britt Pavilion. During this time,

40-45 concerts are given at the outdoor amphitheater. Musical styles include blues, jazz, pop, country and folk. Classical music fans aren't left out either; the Classical Festival is held the first 3 weeks in August. Phone (541) 773-6077 or (800) 882-7488 for information and the box office.

Self-guiding tours: Walking tours past historic sites in the downtown area are detailed on brochures available at the information center at the Rogue River Valley Railway Depot/Visitors Center, next to the post office on N. Oregon and C streets; phone (541) 899-8118.

Shopping areas: California and Oregon streets feature a variety of boutiques.

BEEKMAN BANK is at 3rd and California sts. The second bank in Oregon, it closed in 1915 at the death of founder C.C. Beekman. The bank appears as it was the day Beekman died, with all of its original 1863 furnishings preserved behind glass. Daily 10-5, Memorial Day-Labor Day. Free. Phone (541) 773-6536.

CHILDREN'S MUSEUM is at 5th and D sts. Visitors can learn about the life of a pioneer child in a gold rush town 1850-1930. Hands-on activities and exhibits are presented. Allow 30 minutes minimum. Wed.-Sat. 1-4; closed Jan. 1, Thanksgiving and Dec. 25. Admission $5; $3 (ages 3-12 and 65+). Phone (541) 773-6536.

JACKSONVILLE MUSEUM is at 5th and C sts. In an 1883 Italianate-style brick courthouse, the museum portrays the history of Jacksonville and southern Oregon. Popular exhibits include "Peter Britt: The Man Beyond the Camera" and "Jackson County Milestones." Allow 30 minutes minimum. Wed.-Sat. 1-4; closed Jan. 1, Thanksgiving and Dec. 25. Admission $5; $3 (ages 3-12 and 65+). Phone (541) 773-6536.

WINERIES

• **Valley View Winery** is 8 mi. s. off SR 238 to 1000 Applegate Rd. Daily 11-5; closed Jan. 1, Thanksgiving and Dec. 25. Phone (541) 899-8468 or (800) 781-9463.

JEWELL (A-2)

JEWELL MEADOWS WILDLIFE AREA is 1.5 mi. w. on SR 202. Divided among three land parcels totaling 1,200 acres, this wildlife area affords views of Roosevelt elk and other native animals. Four marked viewpoints designate the area where the elk feed and rest. Daily 24 hours. Free. Phone (503) 755-2264 or (503) 947-6000.

JOHN DAY (D-10) pop. 1,821, elev. 3,083

John Day, for whom the town was named, was a young Virginian and scout of the Astor overland expedition of 1811. During the gold-rush years of 1862-64, mail carried by horseback passed through town from Canyon City to The Dalles.

Fish Hatcheries

The Oregon Department of Fish and Wildlife operates more than 30 hatcheries and several rearing ponds statewide. These facilities raise salmon, steelhead and several species of trout, with salmon comprising more than half the total number of fish raised. In addition to playing a vital role in maintaining healthy fish populations throughout state waters, hatcheries help to repopulate endangered species, supplement natural stocks, provide harvest opportunities for tribal and commercial fishers, and offer public angling opportunities.

Each year Oregon's hatcheries raise and release more than 50 million fish. Salmon and steelhead are usually released as smolts—measuring about 6 inches long—when they are ready to begin seaward migration. Trout are stocked in rivers, lakes and reservoirs as 2-inch fingerlings, as catchable fish measuring about 8 inches and as trophy-size trout weighing up to several pounds each.

Fall and winter are busy times at salmon and steelhead facilities. This is when adult salmon and steelhead return after spending 1 to 5 years in the ocean. Hatchery workers remove eggs from adult fish to begin the production cycle once again. Trout hatcheries operate on varying schedules, extracting eggs from adult fish held on site year-round, or from fish collected at remote trapping locations. Visitors are welcome to observe these activities.

Contact individual hatcheries for more specific information about seasonal fish-raising activities. For additional information contact the Oregon Department of Fish and Wildlife, 3406 Cherry Ave. N.E., Salem, OR 97303-4924; phone (503) 947-6201, or (800) 720-6339 (24-hour information line within Oregon).

Besides transporting mail at the rate of 50c a letter, the daring riders often carried fortunes in gold dust. Attacks by bandits and hostile Indians were among the rigors of the job. By 1864 pony express riders were replaced by pack trains and freight wagons over The Dalles Military Wagon Road.

Modern John Day is a business community and trading center. Descendants of gold miners raise cattle and log the surrounding timberlands.

Lying in a broad valley, John Day is almost surrounded by the steep hills and rugged peaks of Malheur National Forest *(see place listing p. 80)*, whose headquarters and a district office are in town. The office provides maps and other information about recreational activities in the forest.

Grant County Chamber of Commerce: 301 W. Main St., John Day, OR 97845; phone (541) 575-0547 or (800) 769-5664.

KAM WAH CHUNG STATE HERITAGE SITE is 1 blk. n. of US 26 next to the city park; the visitor center is at 125 N.W. Canton. The building, believed to be built sometime in the 1860s, was originally used as a trading post and later served as a Chinese doctor's office and store from the mid-1880s to the mid-1940s. In the early 1900s the Buddhist shrine from the town's temple was moved to a room in this building, and the site also became a religious center.

Displays include supplies, traditional Chinese medicines and herbs, business and financial records, and early western trade goods. Guided tours are available. Allow 30 minutes minimum. Daily 9-5, May-Oct. Donations. Phone (541) 575-2800 or (800) 551-6949.

JOHN DAY FOSSIL BEDS NATIONAL MONUMENT

In north-central Oregon, John Day Fossil Beds National Monument comprises 14,000 acres in three units: the Sheep Rock Unit, 7 miles northwest of Dayville on US 26; the Clarno Unit, 18 miles west of Fossil on SR 218; and the Painted Hills Unit, 9 miles northwest of Mitchell off US 26. The fossil beds contain a variety of plant and animal fossils, and each unit displays different colored geological formations.

Fossil collecting is prohibited without a research permit, but many other activities are available. Hiking and picnicking are popular, and wildlife and wildflowers are abundant throughout the park. The John Day River offers trout fishing in season. Serving as the main visitor center, the Thomas Condon Paleontology Center has a fossil museum and is 2 miles north of the junction of SR 19 and US 26 in the Sheep Rock Unit, next to monument headquarters at the James Cant Ranch; the ranch house has a museum highlighting the area's human history. Free. Phone (541) 987-2333.

JORDAN VALLEY (F-12) pop. 239

In the center of Jordan Valley stands a *pelota fronton,* or "ball court," which was built by the area's Basque settlers in 1915 for playing pelota, a game similar to American handball.

Driven by economic hardship and political oppression, thousands of Basques left their homeland in the Pyrenees in the late 1800s and settled in the western United States. Some became masons, fishermen or miners, but most became range shepherds.

The Basques, independent people believed to be the oldest surviving race in Europe, lived a nomadic life herding flocks. They traveled across western ranges in search of better pastures, accepting sheep instead of wages. A few Basque shepherds still roam the area, but most gradually assimilated into the country's urban culture.

Jordan Crater, which erupted just 2,500 years ago, is one of the youngest volcanoes in the continental United States. Antelope Reservoir, 10 miles southwest of town, offers trout fishing and boating.

JOSEPH (C-11) pop. 1,054, elev. 4,400'

The secluded town of Joseph, near Wallowa Lake State Park *(see Recreation Chart and the AAA Northwestern CampBook)* and the gateway to Hells Canyon National Recreation Area *(see place listing p. 72)*, is a popular vacation spot. Three bronze casting foundries and several art galleries specializing in bronze sculpture are in the vicinity.

Day-long pack trips, which include food, horses and guide, are available in the High Wallowas; information is available from the chamber of commerce. Downhill skiing is available nearby.

Joseph Chamber of Commerce: P.O. Box 13, Joseph, OR 97846; phone (541) 432-1015 or (800) 585-4121. A kiosk on SR 82 provides travel information.

WALLOWA COUNTY MUSEUM is on SR 82. Exhibits include historical artifacts from Wallowa County pioneer days. Displays in one room are dedicated to Nez Perce Indians. Allow 30 minutes minimum. Daily 10-5, Memorial Day weekend-third weekend in Sept.; closed Sat. of Chief Joseph Days, the last full weekend in July. Admission $2.50; free (ages 0-12). Phone (541) 432-6095.

WALLOWA LAKE TRAMWAY is at 59919 Wallowa Lake Hwy. The tram climbs about 4,000 feet to the 8,150-foot level on Mount Howard. It is among the steepest tram rides in North America—the vertical ascent is 3,700 feet from the base elevation of 4,450. From this point the peaks of the Eagle Cap Wilderness Area, the Seven Devils of Idaho and the rim of Hell's Canyon are visible. There also are 2.5 miles of trails with magnificent vistas.

Allow 1 hour minimum. The tramway departs daily 10-5, July-Aug.; 10-4, Memorial Day weekend-June 30 and in Sept., weather permitting. Fare $22; $18 (ages 12-17); $14 (ages 4-11). DS, MC, VI. Phone (541) 432-5331.

Food is available. Daily 9-5; closed Easter, Thanksgiving and Dec. 25. Closing is at 2 on Dec. 24 and 31. Guided tours are available twice daily; times vary so phone ahead to confirm. Admission (aviation or space museum) $13; $12 (ages 65+); $11 (ages 5-16). Combination ticket for aviation museum or space museum and IMAX $20; $19 (ages 65+); $18 (ages 5-16). Combination ticket for both museums $24; $22 (ages 65+); $20 (ages 5-16). Combination ticket for both museums and IMAX $30; $28 (ages 65+); $26 (ages 5-16). Phone (503) 434-4180.

IMAX Theater is 3 mi. n.e. of jct. SR 99/18 at 500 N.E. Captain Michael King Smith Way at the Evergreen Aviation & Space Museum. It houses one of the largest 3-D theater screens in the Northwest and features 3-D IMAX educational films.

Daily 11-4:30 (also Fri.-Sat. 4:30-6:30); closed Easter, Thanksgiving and Dec. 25. Admission $11; $10 (ages 65+); $9 (ages 3-17). Combination ticket with aviation museum or space museum $20; $19 (ages 65+); $18 (ages 5-16). Combination ticket with both museums $30, $28 (ages 65+); $26 (ages 3-17). Phone (503) 434-4180.

LAWRENCE GALLERY is 5 mi. w. at 19700 S.W. SR 18. The fine arts gallery is reputedly Oregon's largest and features changing exhibits of art and sculpture from more than 150 Pacific Northwest artists as well as a 3-acre outdoor sculpture garden. Allow 1 hour minimum. Daily 10-5:30; closed Jan. 1 and Dec. 25. Free. Phone (503) 843-3633 or (800) 894-4278.

MEDFORD (G-6) pop. 63,154, elev. 1,374'

Medford is a tourist and commercial center for the area's agricultural, manufacturing and lumber producing communities. Fruit growing is a primary industry.

Medford is headquarters for the Rogue River-Siskiyou National Forest *(see place listing p. 112)*, which offers opportunities for fishing, hunting and rafting. The Cole Rivers Fish Hatchery, north on SR 62 near the town of Trail, offers self-guiding and guided tours; phone (541) 878-2235, ext. 10.

A 60-mile scenic stretch of I-5, beginning in Grants Pass and running to the California state line, passes through Medford.

Medford-Jackson County Chamber of Commerce: 101 E. 8th St., Medford, OR 97501; phone (541) 779-4847 or (800) 469-6307.

HARRY AND DAVID TOURS depart from the Harry and David Country Village store at 1314 Center Dr. The 1-hour guided walking tours provide a look at the gift basket and plant packing house. Visitors get a complete view of how some of the chocolates and other snacks are made as well as the packing of pears and gifts. Free chocolate samples are provided at the end of the tour.

Comfortable clothing and shoes are recommended for the factory tour. Tours depart Mon.-Fri. at 9:15,

10:30, 12:30 and 1:45. Fee $5. Reservations are required. Phone (877) 322-8000.

SOUTHERN OREGON HISTORICAL SOCIETY HISTORICAL RESEARCH LIBRARY is at 106 N. Central Ave. The non-circulating collection in the research library is one of the largest historical repositories in the Pacific Northwest with nearly 1 million images, photographs, documents and original negatives. Allow 1 hour minimum. Wed.-Thurs. 1-4:30; closed major holidays. Fee $5; $2 (students with ID). Phone (541) 858-1724.

RECREATIONAL ACTIVITIES

White-water Rafting

- SAVE **Arrowhead River Adventures** depart from exit 30 off US 5. Write 720 Greenleaf Dr., Eagle Point, OR 97524-7770. Other activities are offered. Full-day trips depart daily at 8 a.m., half-day trips depart daily at 10 and 2, mid-May through Nov. 30. Phone (541) 830-3388 or (800) 227-7741.

MERLIN (G-5) elev. 907'

RECREATIONAL ACTIVITIES

Boating

- SAVE **Galice Resort Raft Trips** depart from Galice Resort, 11744 Galice Rd., 15 mi. w. of I-5 exit 61. Half-day trips depart daily at 9 and 1, May-Oct. Full-day trips depart daily at 9, May-Oct. Phone (541) 476-3818.

Kayaking

- **Orange Torpedo Trips** depart from 210 Merlin Rd., 3 mi. w. of I-5 exit 61. Multiple rafting trips and other activities are offered. Half-day trips depart daily at 8:30 and 11:30, May-Sept. Full-day trips depart daily at 8:30, May-Sept. Phone (800) 635-2925.

White-water Rafting

- SAVE **Ferron's Fun Trips** depart from Hog Creek Boat Landing. Write P.O. Box 585, Merlin, OR 97532. Half- and full-day trips on the Rogue River are offered daily at 9. Afternoon half-day trips begin at 12:30 from Galice. Boat rentals are available. Reservations are required. Phone (541) 474-2201 or (800) 404-2201.

- **Rogue River Raft and Fishing Trips** depart from 8500 Galice Rd.; take I-5 exit 61. Write Morrison's Rogue River Lodge, 8500 Galice Rd., Merlin, OR 97532. Other activities are offered. Rafting trips depart May-Sept. Phone (541) 476-3825 or (800) 826-1963.

MILTON-FREEWATER (B-11)
pop. 6,470, elev. 1,033'

FRAZIER FARMSTEAD MUSEUM is s.e. on 14th St. to 1403 Chestnut St. Built in 1892, the Victorian/Craftsman-style house is restored and contains antique furnishings and 19th-century household items. On the grounds are six outbuildings: two barns, a combination carriage house, milk barn and tack room; a one-room cottage; a woodshed; and a chicken house. Flower, herb and rose gardens embellish the property. Guided tours are available. Allow 30 minutes minimum. Thurs.-Sat. 11-4, Apr.-Dec. Donations. Phone (541) 938-4636.

MILWAUKIE—*see Portland p. 106.*

MONMOUTH (D-2) pop. 7,741, elev. 201'

Monmouth traces its beginnings to the mid-1850s, when pioneer settlers from Illinois set aside 640 acres for a town and Christian college, naming the site for their hometown. Established in 1856, Monmouth University was among the first institutions of higher education in the Northwest. The college was not prosperous, however, and was taken over by the state in 1882, becoming a teachers' school. Today, Monmouth remains essentially a college town, dominated by the campus of Western Oregon University.

Monmouth & Independence Chamber of Commerce: 355 Pacific Ave., Suite A, Monmouth, OR 97361; phone (503) 838-4268.

JENSEN ARCTIC MUSEUM is at 590 W. Church St. on the campus of Western Oregon University. Extensive collections of arctic art and artifacts are on display, and an exhibit presents the sights and sounds of an arctic day. Allow 1 hour minimum. Wed.-Sat. 10-4; closed Jan. 1, Thanksgiving, day after Thanksgiving and Dec. 25. Donations. Phone (503) 838-8468.

MORO (C-8) pop. 337, elev. 1,808'

In the late 1860s, homesteading started on the rolling Columbia Plateau in the area now known as Moro, Oregon's smallest county seat. The town began as a trading post established in 1879 and eventually became a trading center for one of the state's major wheat growing areas.

SHERMAN COUNTY HISTORICAL MUSEUM is at 200 Dewey St. More than 10,000 artifacts and photographs are displayed in five key exhibits: Wheat Through the Ages; A Century of Rural Living; Oregon Trails, Rails and Roads; Patriotism: Pride and Anguish; and Conservation, Cultivation and Clothespins. Allow 1 hour minimum. Daily 10-5, May-Oct. Admission $3; $1 (students). Phone (541) 565-3232.

MOUNT ANGEL (C-3) pop. 3,121, elev. 168'

Settled by German pioneers in the 1880s, the town bore several names–Frankfort, Roy and Fillmore–before Father Adelhelm Odermatt named it Mount Angel, an English derivation of Engelberg, a Swiss abbey where he received theological training. Roman Catholic institutions dominate the town, reflecting its ethnic origins. The spire of St. Mary's Church, in a modified Gothic style, is visible for miles around. The former St. Mary's College presently houses a convent of Benedictine sisters.

American Indians called the 480-foot knoll on the eastern edge of town Tapalamaho, meaning "place

of communion with the Great Spirit." Father Odermatt renamed it Mount Angel when he established Mount Angel Abbey *(see attraction listing p. 113)* on its slopes in 1882.

Mount Angel Chamber of Commerce: 5 N. Garfield St., P.O. Box 221, Mount Angel, OR 97362; phone (503) 845-9440.

MOUNT HOOD AND MOUNT HOOD NATIONAL FOREST

Elevations in the forest range from 200 ft. at the Columbia River to 11,239 ft. at Mount Hood. Refer to AAA maps for additional elevation information.

The Mount Hood National Forest reaches from the Columbia River Gorge National Scenic Area along the Cascades to Mount Jefferson and from the foothills east of Portland to the central Oregon plateau. From Portland, the forest may be entered directly from US 26. Another option is to take I-205 to SR 212/224; when the road splits take SR 212 and then pick up US 26. The Hood River entrance to the forest is off SR 35.

Majestic Mount Hood rises 11,239 feet in splendid isolation, dominating the horizon for miles around. Many living glaciers extend to near the timberline on all sides. The peak is the highlight of the Mount Hood National Forest and the highest point in the state. Alpine meadows, waterfalls, glaciers, hot springs and more than 4,000 miles of streams and 160 lakes grace the forest.

The Columbia River Gorge was formed by an ancient river of lava that also created nearby 620-foot Multnomah Falls. Columbia River Gorge National Scenic Area maintains parts of the gorge; for information write 902 Wasco Ave., Suite 200, Hood River, OR 97031; phone (541) 308-1700.

Spectacular scenic drives include the Mt. Hood National Scenic Byway *(see attraction listing)* and the Clackamas River Highway. Forested acreage consists primarily of conifers—cedar, fir, hemlock, pine and spruce. Badger Creek, Bull of the Woods, Mark O. Hatfield, Mount Hood, Salmon Huckleberry and part of the Mount Jefferson Wilderness are congressionally preserved wilderness areas comprising 192,568 acres within the forest.

Recreational activities are varied; there are picnic areas, campgrounds and a 1,200-mile network of trails. The Timberline Lodge, dedicated Sept. 28, 1937, was built using local materials and construction techniques and designed to harmonize with its natural surroundings. Much of the hand-crafted furnishings and detailed woodwork has been restored.

Several downhill skiing areas, including year-round skiing at Timberline, are in the Government Camp area; cross-country skiing and snowshoeing can be pursued in other areas. For additional information contact the Mount Hood National Forest, 16400 Champion Way, Sandy, OR 97055; phone (503) 668-1700. *See Recreation Chart and the AAA Northwestern CampBook.*

MT. HOOD NATIONAL SCENIC BYWAY encircles the mountain area of Mount Hood National Forest. The scenic drive begins in Portland on I-84 and travels east through the canyon gorge carved by the Columbia River. At Hood River, take SR 35 south to view the orchards and forested Hood River Valley, then US 26 west past Barlow Pass, which was used by pioneers traveling the Barlow Road section of the Oregon Trail from The Dalles to the Willamette Valley. The loop crosses White River. US 26 provides timberline access, travels through the Villages of Mt. Hood (Brightwood, Welches, Wemme, Zigzag and Rhododendron) and eventually rejoins I-84 outside of Portland in Troutdale.

For additional information contact Oregon's Mount Hood Territory Visitor Information Center, 1726 Washington St., Oregon City, OR 97045. Phone (800) 424-3002.

TIMOTHY LAKE is within Mount Hood National Forest, 10 mi. s.e. of Mount Hood on US 26 to Skyline Rd., then 10 mi. s., following signs. This 1,400-acre lake has six separate camping and picnic areas open from June to September, weather permitting. Four of the six—Gone Creek, Hood View, Oak Fork and Pine Point—are on the south shore of the lake. Meditation Point is near the north shore and can be reached by trail or boat. North Arm also is on the north side and is accessible by motorized vehicle. A 13-mile-long hiking trail circles the lake. *See Recreation Chart.*

NECANICUM (A-2)

SADDLE MOUNTAIN STATE NATURAL AREA is 8 mi. n.e. off US 26. The park extends around Saddle Mountain; at 3,287 feet, it is the highest point in the north end of the Coast Range. Panoramic views can be seen from the summit, reached by a 2.5-mile hiking trail. There are also native plants in the area. Park daily dawn-dusk, Mar. 1-Nov. 1. Season may be extended (weather permitting); phone to confirm. Park free; fees for camping. Phone (800) 551-6949.

NEWBERG (B-3) pop. 18,064, elev. 176'

Newberg was the first community in Oregon to hold Friends (Quaker) services. President Herbert Hoover lived in Newberg as a child and attended Friends Pacific Academy, which was the forerunner of George Fox University. Now with more than 3,000 undergraduate and graduate students, it is the largest Christian college in the state and is located near Hess Creek Canyon. Italian architect Pietro Belluschi designed the Wheeler Sports Center as well as the Centennial Tower. Memorabilia about Hoover and former United States Senator Mark Hatfield is displayed in the Herbert Hoover Academic Building. Guided tours of the campus can be arranged; phone (503) 538-8383.

Some of Oregon's older and larger wineries are in and around Newberg. Bald Peak State Park, 9 miles northwest, has picnic areas and views of the Cascade Mountains and the Coast Range.

Wineries

Nearly 200 wineries and more than 350 vineyards dot the Oregon landscape, illustrating the growth and popularity of this major statewide industry. Wineries are located throughout the state's western valleys from Ashland north to Portland and east to Hood River. The "Vintage Oregon" brochure published by the Oregon Advisory Board describes six viticultural valley regions: Applegate, Columbia, Rogue, Umpqua, Walla Walla and Willamette.

Soil, weather and gentle, sunny  slopes in Oregon enable wine grapes to ripen slowly during the summer and fall to develop exquisite flavors that have been recognized with many rewards. In the Willamette Valley, the temperate climate makes growing conditions ideal for cool-climate grapes. These include Chardonnay, Pinot Gris, Pinot Noir and Riesling. Other grapes include Cabernet Sauvignon, Merlot and Syrah, grown in the warmer southern Oregon valleys.

Most Oregon wineries are small, family-owned farms. Individual attention to producing and caring for wines is a hallmark of the dedicated Oregon winemaker. The devotion and commitment of both owners and workers is evident as they engage in the craft of producing fine wines.

Almost all of Oregon's wineries welcome visitors throughout the year for tours and tastings. Brochures for each of the eight Oregon winery regions can be ordered from the Oregon Wine Board for a $4.99 shipping/handling fee; phone (503) 228-8336, option #2.

Chehalem Valley Chamber of Commerce: 415 E. Sheridan St., Newberg, OR 97132; phone (503) 538-2014.

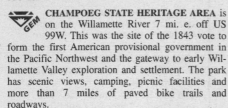 **CHAMPOEG STATE HERITAGE AREA** is on the Willamette River 7 mi. e. off US 99W. This was the site of the 1843 vote to form the first American provisional government in the Pacific Northwest and the gateway to early Willamette Valley exploration and settlement. The park has scenic views, camping, picnic facilities and more than 7 miles of paved bike trails and roadways.

More than 2 miles front the Willamette River. Trails provide wildlife viewing opportunities in meadows, wetlands and woods. Daily dawn-dusk. Admission $3 (per private vehicle). Phone (503) 678-1251. *See Recreation Chart and Aurora in the AAA Northwestern CampBook.*

Champoeg State Heritage Area Visitors' Center, 8239 Champoeg Rd. N.E., includes exhibits about Champoeg history and the 1862 Donald Manson Barn and Farmstead. Ranger-led tours are available in summer. Daily 9-5, Memorial Day weekend-Labor Day. Hours vary rest of year; phone ahead. Closed Jan. 1, Thanksgiving and Dec. 25. Free. Phone (503) 678-1251, ext. 221, or (800) 452-5687 for camping reservations.

SAVE **DAR Pioneer Mothers' Memorial Cabin Museum** is at 8035 Champoeg Rd. N.E. within Champoeg State Heritage Area. Built in 1931 as a memorial to pioneer mothers, it is furnished with pioneer artifacts to reflect the 1850s. Guided tours are available by appointment. Fri.-Sun. and holidays 1-5, Mar.-Oct. Admission $4; $3 (ages 65+); $2 (ages 0-12). Phone (503) 633-2237.

SAVE **DAR Robert Newell House Museum** is at 8089 Champoeg Rd. N.E. on a hillside west of the Champoeg State Heritage Area entrance. A reconstruction of a house built in 1852, it contains gowns that belonged to Oregon governors' wives as well as an antique quilt collection. An 1850 Butteville jail and a pioneer school are on the grounds. Guided tours are available by appointment (minimum 10 people). Fri.-Sun. and holidays 1-5, Mar.-Oct. Admission $4; $3 (ages 65+); $2 (ages 0-12). Phone (503) 678-5537.

HOOVER-MINTHORN HOUSE MUSEUM is at 115 S. River and E. Second sts. This is where President Herbert Hoover spent 4 years of his boyhood. The restored 1881 house contains original furnishings, photographs and mementos of Hoover's residency. Allow 30 minutes minimum. Wed.-Sun. 1-4, Mar.-Nov.; Sat.-Sun. 1-4, or by appointment, in Feb. and Dec. Closed Thanksgiving and Dec. 25. Admission $3; $2 (students and senior citizens); 50c (ages 0-10). Phone (503) 538-6629.

WINERIES

• **Rex Hill Vineyards** is at 30835 N. SR 99W. Daily 11-5, day after Thanksgiving-Memorial

Day; daily 10-5, rest of year. Closed Jan. 1, Easter, Memorial Day weekend, July 4, Thanksgiving weekend and Dec. 25. Phone (503) 538-0666 or (800) 739-4455.

NEWPORT (D-1) pop. 9,532, elev. 68′

Spread across a blunt, ridged peninsula between the Pacific Ocean and Yaquina Bay, Newport has been a resort community for more than 100 years. The charm of the turn-of-the-20th-century era is preserved in the historic Bay Front, a waterfront section of the town.

The Lincoln County Vietnam Commemorative Walk Memorial in Donald A. Davis Park is dedicated to war veterans. A sculpture is placed at 19 degrees northeast to cast its shadow across the granite each April 30th, a reminder of the day the Vietnam War ended.

The Newport Performing Arts Center hosts performances by local and visiting artists, including ballets, concerts and plays. For ticket and schedule information phone (541) 265-2787 or (888) 701-7123.

Newport's location at the entrance of Yaquina Bay has made fishing an important industry. Clamming, crabbing and fishing are popular recreational pursuits; charter and rental boats are available.

A number of nearby day-use areas and campgrounds are scattered along US 101, a scenic highway that bisects Newport and extends along the entire Oregon coast.

Greater Newport Chamber of Commerce: 555 S.W. Coast Hwy., Newport, OR 97365; phone (541) 265-8801 or (800) 262-7844.

Shopping areas: Sea Towne is on US 101N. The Historic Bay Front, Historic Nye Beach and Bay Boulevard, have open-air fish markets and galleries.

HATFIELD MARINE SCIENCE CENTER is at 2030 S.E. Marine Science Dr. on Yaquina Bay, which is reached by access roads from the southern end of the Yaquina Bay Bridge. This is Oregon State University's coastal campus for marine science research and education. The visitor center has aquariums, interactive exhibits, tide pools and displays about marine research. Films about whales and other marine topics are shown daily in the auditorium. Guided nature walks along the estuary are available during the summer season.

Allow 1 hour minimum. Visitor center open daily 10-5, Memorial Day-Labor Day; Thurs.-Mon. 10-4, rest of year. Donations. Phone (541) 867-0100.

MARINE DISCOVERY TOURS depart from Anchor Pier on the historic bay front at 345 S.W. Bay Blvd. The company offers a 2-hour SeaLife cruise, which explores the ocean, bay and river. Excursions feature narration by naturalist guides and include hands-on activities. Gray whales, sea lions, porpoises, seals and coastal birds may be seen. Trips depart daily 9-5, Mar.-Oct. Fare $35; $33 (ages 65+); $17 (ages 4-13). Reservations are recommended. DS, MC, VI. Phone (541) 265-6200 or (800) 903-2628.

NEWPORT VISUAL ART CENTER is at 777 N.W. Beach Dr. The center features paintings, photographs and changing exhibits. Next door, the Yaquina Art Center features the works of its members. Allow 30 minutes minimum. Newport Visual Art Center open Tues.-Sun. 11-6. Yaquina Art Center open daily 11-4. Free. Phone (541) 265-6540.

OREGON COAST AQUARIUM is just e. of US 101 at the s. end of Yaquina Bay Bridge at 2820 S.E. Ferry Slip Rd. The six-acre, 40,000-square-foot aquarium features more than 15,000 marine animals representing some 500 species. Indoor and outdoor exhibits introduce visitors to coastal sea life, including sea otters, harbor seals, California sea lions, jellyfish and giant Pacific octopuses.

The largest indoor display features sturgeon and endangered salmon, spotlighting current issues relating to salmon survival. Also included is a touch pool filled with sea stars, anemones, sea cucumbers, sea urchins and skates. Animal encounters and behind-the-scenes tours offer visitors up-close views of ocean creatures.

Sharks, skates, and other deep-sea denizens can be seen in Passages of the Deep, a 200-foot acrylic tunnel running through three ocean habitats. With large viewing windows built into the floor, visitors will enjoy nearly 360-degree views of wolf eels, bat rays and a variety of sharks. Tufted puffins and pigeon guillemots reside among the cliffs and in the pools of what are reputedly the largest outdoor seabird aviaries in North America.

Allow 2 hours minimum. Daily 9-6, Memorial Day weekend-Labor Day; 10-5, rest of year. Closed Dec. 25. Admission $14.25; $12.25 (ages 65+); $8.75 (ages 3-12). AX, DS, MC, VI. Phone (541) 867-3474.

OREGON COAST HISTORY CENTER is at 545 S.W. 9th St. The center includes the Log Cabin Museum and the Burrows House Museum. Exhibits showcase the central Oregon coast, including local American Indian tribes and the Coast Reservation, pioneer settlement, logging, tourism and maritime history. A research library also is available. Tues.-Sun. 10-5, June-Sept.; 11-4, rest of year. Closed major holidays. Donations. Phone (541) 265-7509.

RIPLEY'S BELIEVE IT OR NOT! is at 250 S.W. Bay Blvd. Bizarre and unusual mysteries of nature and technology are displayed. Allow 30 minutes minimum. Daily 9-8, July-Aug.; daily 10-6 (also Sat. 6-7 p.m.), Memorial Day weekend-June 30 and in Sept.; Mon.-Fri. 11-6, Sat. 10-7, Sun. 10-6, Apr. 1-day before Memorial Day weekend; daily 10-5 (also Sat. 5-6), in Oct.; Mon.-Fri. 11-4, Sat.-Sun. 10-5, mid-Feb. through Mar. 31; Mon. and Thurs.-Fri. 11-4, Sat.-Sun. 10-5, Nov. 1 to mid-Feb. Closed Thanksgiving and Dec. 25. Admission $9.95; $5.95 (ages 5-12). AX, DS, MC, VI. Phone (541) 265-2206.

UNDERSEA GARDENS is at 250 S.W. Bay Blvd. Visitors can see marine plants and animals in their natural habitat through large underwater windows. Scuba diving shows are presented regularly.

Allow 30 minutes minimum. Daily 9-8, July-Aug.; daily 10-6 (also Sat. 6-7 p.m.), Memorial Day weekend-June 30 and in Sept.; Mon.-Fri. 11-6, Sat. 10-7, Sun. 10-6, Apr. 1-day before Memorial Day weekend; daily 10-5 (also Sat. 5-6), in Oct.; Mon.-Fri. 11-4, Sat.-Sun. 10-5, mid-Feb. through Mar. 31; Mon. and Thurs.-Fri. 11-4, Sat.-Sun. 10-5, Nov. 1 to mid-Feb. Closed Thanksgiving and Dec. 25. Admission $9.95; $5.95 (ages 5-12). AX, DS, MC, VI. Phone (541) 265-2206.

THE WAX WORKS is at 250 S.W. Bay Blvd. Wax figures, some animated, are the focus here. A 5-minute film is presented about the 1980 eruption of Mount St. Helens.

Allow 30 minutes minimum. Daily 9-8, July-Aug.; daily 10-6 (also Sat. 6-7 p.m.), Memorial Day weekend-June 30 and in Sept.; Mon.-Fri. 11-6, Sat. 10-7, Sun. 10-6, Apr. 1-day before Memorial Day weekend; daily 10-5 (also Sat. 5-6), in Oct.; Mon.-Fri. 11-4, Sat.-Sun. 10-5, mid-Feb. through Mar. 31; Mon. and Thurs.-Fri. 11-4, Sat.-Sun. 10-5, Nov. 1 to mid-Feb. Closed Thanksgiving and Dec. 25. Admission $9.95; $5.95 (ages 5-12). AX, DS, MC, VI. Phone (541) 265-2206.

YAQUINA BAY LIGHTHOUSE is just s. on US 101 in Yaquina State Recreation Site. One of the first navigational aids built on the Pacific Northwest coast, the 1871 Cape Cod-style house contains both the lighthouse tower and light keeper's living quarters. Rumored to be haunted, it is furnished in period. Daily 11-5, June 1-Labor Day; noon-4, rest of year (weather permitting). Closed Thanksgiving and Dec. 25. Free. Phone (541) 265-5679 or (541) 867-7451.

YAQUINA HEAD OUTSTANDING NATURAL AREA is 3 mi. n. of jct. US 20 and US 101. The beautiful coastal headland offers the chance to explore tidal pools, hiking trails, an interpretive center, a rocky beach and Yaquina Head Lighthouse. Active since 1873, it was the fifth lighthouse built in Oregon and the state's tallest. Wildlife enthusiasts may spot gray whales, seals, murres, cormorants and intertidal organisms.

Allow 2 hours minimum. Natural area daily dawn-dusk. Interpretive center daily 9-5, June-Sept.; 10-4, rest of year. Lighthouse daily noon-4. Guided tours are given 9-11:30, June-Sept. Admission $7 (per vehicle). Phone (541) 574-3100.

NORTH BEND (F-1) pop. 9,544

On a peninsula jutting into the Coos Bay, North Bend thrives on a combination of timber activities, manufacturing, retail and several privately owned oyster farms. The town straddles US 101, a scenic route that runs along the Oregon Coast from California to Washington. North Bend also is the gateway to the Oregon Dunes National Recreation Area *(see Siuslaw National Forest p. 118).*

North Bend Visitor Information Center: 1380 Sherman Ave./US 101, North Bend, OR 97459; phone (541) 756-4613 or (800) 472-9176.

Self-guiding tours: Brochures describing bay, dune and whale watching tours are available at the visitor center. Artwalk, a self-guiding tour of various galleries in North Bend's historic downtown area, occurs the second Thursday of each month from 5-8 p.m. Maps are available at the public library and participating businesses.

Shopping areas: The Bayfront Crafters' Market gives local artisans and crafters an opportunity to showcase their talents every Saturday on the waterfront from May through September.

COOS HISTORICAL & MARITIME MUSEUM is on US 101 (Sherman Ave.) at the n. end of North Bend/Coos Bay. Exhibits cover the area's history beginning with American Indian life and emphasizing the cultural importance of local waterways and the ocean. Allow 30 minutes minimum. Tues.-Sat. 10-4 (also Sun. noon-4, July-Aug.). Admission $2; free (ages 0-11). Phone (541) 756-6320.

GAMBLING ESTABLISHMENTS

- **The Mill Casino Hotel & RV Park** is 1 mi. s. on US 101 at 3201 Tremont Ave. Daily 24 hours. Phone (541) 756-8800 or (800) 953-4800.

OAKLAND (F-3) pop. 954, elev. 449′

Settled in the early 1850s, Oakland takes its name from the Oregon white or Garry oaks that dot the area's rolling grasslands. Poultry farming was important here in the early 1900s, and Oakland billed itself as "Turkey Capital of the Nation." The town is renowned for its historic brick buildings from the late 19th century. This collection of more than 130 structures, many labeled with their vintage and original use, constitutes Oregon's first designated historic district.

Self-guiding tours: A brochure outlining a self-guiding walking tour of the historic district is available at Oakland Museum.

OAKLAND MUSEUM is at 130 Locust St. Displays depict early life in Oakland and the surrounding valley, historic profiles of settlers, commerce, agriculture and the local turkey industry. Allow 30 minutes minimum. Daily 12:30-3:30; closed major holidays. Donations. Phone (541) 459-3087.

OAKRIDGE (F-4) pop. 3,148, elev. 1,220′

Oakridge sits at the foothills of the Cascade Mountains. Nearby Lookout Point and Hills Creek reservoirs both provide water sports in their recreation areas. Salt Creek Falls, one of the highest waterfalls in Oregon, is 16 miles east on SR 58. Green Waters Park, located at the east end of town, has picnic facilities.

The Aufderheide Scenic Byway begins 3 miles west of Oakridge off SR 58 and continues north to SR 126. The Office Bridge, the longest covered bridge in Oregon, is in nearby Westfir. About 30 miles east via SR 58 at the Willamette Pass Resort in Crescent Lake, the Oregon Skyway offers gondola rides Friday through Sunday from late May to mid-September; phone (541) 345-7669.

Oakridge-Westfir Area Chamber of Commerce: 48362 SR 58, P.O. Box 217, Oakridge, OR 97463; phone (541) 782-4146.

OCHOCO NATIONAL FOREST

Elevations in the forest range from 3,500 ft. at the forest's boundary to 6,900 ft. atop Lookout Mountain. Refer to AAA maps for additional elevation information.

Ochoco National Forest is divided into two sections, or ranger districts, in Central Oregon and is accessible by US 26 from Prineville. The forest covers 847,938 acres of pine, fir, larch, lodgepole and juniper. Under the same administration is the Crooked River National Grassland, with 111,379 acres of juniper-dotted rangeland north of Redmond. US 26 cuts through Grassland to Madras.

Within the forest's boundaries are three designated wilderness areas: Mill Creek, Bridge Creek and Black Canyon. These areas are primarily enjoyed by visitors looking for a primitive experience through hiking and back-country camping. Opportunities for camping and fishing are available at Walton Lake, Antelope Reservoir and Haystack Reservoir. Additional camping opportunities include but are not limited to Ochoco Divide, Wildcat, Sugar Creek, Wolf Creek, Mud Springs and a horse camp at Allen Creek.

Some geological areas of interest are Steins and Twin Pillars, volcanic monoliths that jut upward through the high desert landscape. Other points of interest are the Lookout Mountain Trail, Rimrock Springs Wildlife Viewing Area, four wild and scenic

Covered Bridges

Highwaymen used them for cover while awaiting their victims; political rallies, church meetings and dances were held in them; and sweethearts secretly met in them. Oregon's covered bridges once served as more than just routes over the numerous waterways; they were part of Oregon's pioneer culture. As early as 1850 pioneers began constructing strong bridges made from Oregon's plentiful timber. Oregon's bridges were covered to protect them from the rainy weather, doubling their life span.

In the 1930s there were more than 300 covered bridges in the state of Oregon. Today there are fewer than 50 of these picturesque reminders of horse-and-buggy days. With the largest concentration of covered bridges west of the Mississippi, Oregon's many bridges vary in size, shape and design.

The longest covered bridge is Lane County's Office Bridge. Built in 1939, this 180-foot bridge, north of Oakridge on North Fork Road, originally connected with a lumber mill and office—thus its name Office Bridge.

Jackson County is home to the shortest of Oregon's covered bridges—Lost Creek Bridge. Spanning just 39 feet, Lost Creek Bridge was built in 1919.

The Chitwood Bridge, 18 miles east of Newport on Hwy. 20 in Lincoln County, was saved from demolition in 1982 and rebuilt—thus making it the newest covered bridge in Oregon.

Several counties, including Benton, Douglas, Lane, Lincoln and Linn, offer brochures outlining the bridges in their area. Contact the Willamette Valley Visitors Association to obtain a free guide; phone (866) 548-5018.

rivers and the meadows of Big Summit Prairie, known for their spectacular early summer wildflower displays.

Antelopes, elk and mule deer are some of the animals found on the forested and open land. Beneath the soil lie deposits of petrified wood; jasper; quartz; and the Oregon state rock, the thunder egg, a geode containing opal or agate. For this reason rockhounding is a popular activity.

Camping is available, although some camping areas do not have water. For further information and maps contact the Forest Supervisor, Ochoco National Forest, 3160 N.E. Third St., Prineville, OR 97754; phone (541) 416-6500. *See Recreation Chart and the AAA Northwestern CampBook.*

ONTARIO (E-12) pop. 10,985, elev. 2,153'

The Ontario area, in an agricultural belt along the Snake River, has many reservoirs with good fishing and hunting, including Bully Creek Reservoir to the west. The agate, jasper, fossils, thunder eggs and petrified wood make the region particularly popular with rock hounds. Thirty miles west of Ontario is Keeney Pass, on the main wagon train route of the Oregon Trail.

Ontario Chamber of Commerce and Visitor and Convention Bureau: 676 S.W. 5th Ave., Ontario, OR 97914; phone (541) 889-8012 or (866) 989-8012.

[SAVE] **FOUR RIVERS CULTURAL CENTER AND MUSEUM** is at 676 S.W. 5th Ave. The center celebrates the ethnic diversity of the area through displays describing the area's history and culture. The museum features an introductory video presentation along with interactive and changing exhibits. Allow 1 hour, 30 minutes minimum. Mon.-Sat. 10-4; closed major holidays. Admission $4; $3 (ages 6-17 and 65+); free (ages 0-14 on Wed. when accompanied by an adult). Phone (541) 889-8191.

OREGON CAVES NATIONAL MONUMENT (H-5)

Oregon Caves National Monument is in the Siskiyou Mountains, 20 miles east of Cave Junction on SR 46 (Caves Highway). Its access road winds through the dense forests that are southwest Oregon's trademark. Due to narrow roads and ice and snow concerns, trailers and large recreational vehicles are discouraged from traveling the Caves Highway but can park at the visitor center in Cave Junction and drive smaller tow vehicles to the caves.

Note: The 20-mile drive from Cave Junction to the monument can take 45-50 minutes. A stop at the visitor center in Cave Junction is recommended to obtain a map containing parking and cave information as well as a diagram outlining the steepness of the climb in the cave.

In the marble heart of Mount Elijah at the 4,000-foot level, nature has carved and decorated the "Marble Halls of Oregon." Pillars, stalactites and canopies of calcite line passageways and hang from the vaulted domes of the cavern's many galleries.

Paradise Lost has calcite flowstone and drapery formations on the walls of a room 60 feet high. The largest room, about 250 feet in length, was created by underground streams. A 7-foot calcite column, some large flowstone cascades and a fault line imprint resembling a whale's spine are a few of the cave's features.

There are marked trails in the park for day hikers; connecting trails lead into nearby Rogue River-Siskiyou National Forest *(see place listing p. 112).* It is best to check trail conditions with park rangers before hiking in winter and spring.

The 90-minute cave tour is mildly strenuous with more than 500 stairs; visitors must be accompanied by a guide. Comfortable walking shoes and protective clothing are recommended, as the year-round temperature inside the caves is 44 F. Pets are permitted on paved surfaces within the monument's boundaries and on adjoining forest service land. Camera tripods are allowed outside the cave.

Tours are offered at regular intervals with a maximum of 16 people. For safety reasons, children must be over 42 inches tall; they may not be carried through the cave. For families with children shorter than 42 inches, a sneak peek into the cave may be possible.

Tours depart daily 10-4, mid-Mar. through Fri. before Memorial Day and mid-Oct. through Nov. 30; 9-6, mid-June through Labor Day; 9-5, day after Labor Day to mid-Oct. and Memorial Day weekend to mid-June. Closed Thanksgiving. Admission $8.50; $6 (ages 0-16). MC, VI. Phone (541) 592-2100 ext. 262 (visitor center).

OREGON CITY—*see Portland p. 107.*

OTTER ROCK (D-2) elev. 82'

DEVIL'S PUNCH BOWL STATE PARK is just off US 101, following signs. At high tide, a bowl-shaped rock formation often fills from below with a roar. Ocean views can be seen from the park. Daily dawn-dusk. Free. Phone (800) 551-6949.

MARINE GARDENS is n. of Devil's Punch Bowl off B St. At low tide, pools and caves of the rocky area reveal sea urchins and other forms of tidal pool life. Inquire locally for current tide tables. Daily dawn-dusk. Free. Phone (800) 551-6949.

OTTER CREST STATE SCENIC VIEWPOINT is on Cape Foulweather on US 101. Otter Crest, a bold, flat-topped rock rising 453 feet above the tide, offers spectacular views of sandy beaches, surf and the rocky shore where sea otters once dwelt. It is now inhabited by seals, sea lions and birds. Gray whales can often be seen from this location. Daily dawn-dusk. Free. Phone (800) 551-6949.

PACIFIC CITY (C-2) pop. 1,027

Pacific City lies on the Nestucca River and its namesake bay, at the southern end of the Three Capes Scenic Loop. Cape Kiwanda's dramatic sandstone cliffs dominate the north end of town, rising from the beach in giant mounds of sand. The mono-lith off the north end of the beach is 327-foot Haystack Rock, not to be confused with the larger feature of the same name at Cannon Beach.

The town is a resort and fishing center, famous for its dory fleet. Rather than navigate the roundabout Nestucca Bay channel, anglers launch their dories directly into the Pacific surf around 6 a.m. and return in the afternoon. These flat-bottomed boats came into use in the 1920s, after gill net fishing was banned in the bay.

Bob Straub State Park, at the south end of town, occupies the sandpit separating Nestucca Bay from the ocean. Some of the longest waves on the Oregon coast make Pacific City a surfing center. Hang gliders congregate around Cape Kiwanda.

Pacific City-Nestucca Valley Chamber of Commerce: P.O. Box 75, 34370 US 101, Cloverdale, OR 97112; phone (503) 392-4340 or (888) 549-2632.

PARKDALE (C-8) pop. 266, elev. 1,744'

This small community on the northeast edge of Mount Hood National Forest *(see place listing p. 82)* was established in 1910 and is the southern terminus of the Mount Hood Railroad *(see Hood River p. 74)*, one of the few remaining U.S. railroads operating on a switchback, permitting the train to climb the 100-foot-tall Columbia River Gorge through Hood River Valley to Parkdale.

PENDLETON (C-10) pop. 16,354, elev. 1,068'

One of the West's prominent rodeos is the Pendleton Round-Up begun in 1910. Held the second full week in September, the 4-day event includes daily afternoon rodeos and the Happy Canyon Indian Pageant. The Westward Ho Parade features pack trains, stagecoaches and American Indians dressed in traditional regalia. A tepee village occupied by tribes from throughout the Pacific Northwest is assembled for the celebration. Beneath the arena grandstand is the Round-Up Hall of Fame *(see attraction listing).*

Downtown, visitors can view the restored 1889 Seth Thomas Clock Tower located outside the courthouse on the corner of Court Avenue and S.E. 4th Street. The 57-foot clock symbolizes the growth and prosperity of the 1880s. Visitors can view the glass-enclosed clockworks at eye level. An authentic World War II air raid siren sounds in town Monday through Friday at noon.

A scenic stretch of I-84 begins at Pendleton, intersecting with US 395 before continuing 93 miles southeast to Baker City.

Pendleton Chamber of Commerce: 501 S. Main St., Pendleton, OR 97801; phone (541) 276-7411 or (800) 547-8911.

Shopping areas: Melanie Square Shopping Center, in the downtown area as well as in the 1700 block of Court Place, has a variety of shops. Antique stores can be found on S.E. Court Avenue and throughout town.

HERITAGE STATION MUSEUM is at 108 S.W. Frazer Ave. Changing exhibits tell the story of the region's settlement and development. One exhibit explores various modes of communication, including replicas of a post office, a print shop, a train depot office, a branding scene and private collections of radios and telephones. A one-room schoolhouse and a caboose also are featured.

Allow 1 hour minimum. Tues.-Sat. 10-4; closed Jan. 1, Thanksgiving and Dec. 25. Admission $6; $2 (students with ID); $15 (family). MC, VI. Phone (541) 276-0012.

McKAY CREEK NATIONAL WILDLIFE REFUGE is 7 mi. s. off US 395. The 1,836-acre refuge harbors large numbers of waterfowl, primarily ducks and geese, in an open water reservoir surrounded by riparian and upland habitats of bunch grasses, low sage and cottonwood/willow riparian zone. Limited hunting is permitted; an opening weekend hunting permit for upland game is required. Daily 5 a.m.-1.5 hours after sunset, Mar.-Sept. Free. Phone (509) 371-9212.

PENDLETON ROUND-UP & HAPPY CANYON HALL OF FAME is at 1114 S.W. Court Ave. across the street from the Round-Up Grounds. The Hall of Fame contains exhibits showcasing more than 90 years of memorabilia, photographs, wagons, Western items and Indian artifacts associated with the rodeo and night show held during Round-Up. Allow 30 minutes minimum. Mon.-Sat. 10-4. Admission $5; $4 (senior citizens); $2 (students). Phone (541) 278-0815.

PENDLETON UNDERGROUND TOURS is at 37 S.W. Emigrant Ave., 1 blk. off Main St. The company offers a 90-minute guided walking tour through service tunnels, card rooms, a meat market, Chinese living quarters, jails and more. Tour schedule varies Mon.-Sat.; phone ahead. Fee $15; $10 (ages 6-18). Under age 6 are not permitted. Reservations are required. MC, VI. Phone (541) 276-0730.

PENDLETON WOOLEN MILLS is at 1307 S.E. Court Pl. Guided tours show how woolen products are created. Allow 30 minutes minimum. Tours depart Mon.-Fri. at 9, 11, 1:30 and 3; closed for 2 weeks in Aug. (phone to confirm dates), holidays and Dec. 25-Jan. 1. Store hours Mon.-Sat. 8-6, Sun. 9-5. Free. Phone (541) 276-6911 or (800) 568-3156.

[SAVE] **TAMASTSLIKT CULTURAL INSTITUTE** is 6 mi. e. via I-84 exit 216, then .5 mi. n. on SR 331. Situated on the historic Oregon Trail and housed in a striking wood and stone building that blends traditional and modern design elements, the institute features exhibits depicting the history and culture of the Cayuse, Umatilla and Walla Walla tribes. Multimedia displays, murals, artifacts and a living culture village illustrate the tribes' more than 10,000 years on the Columbia Plateau.

Food is available. Allow 1 hour, 30 minutes minimum. Daily 9-5, Apr.-Oct.; Mon.-Sat. 9-5, rest of

The Informed Traveler

Sales Tax: Oregon levies no sales tax. The Portland area has a lodging tax of 12.5 percent and a rental car tax of 12.5 percent.

WHOM TO CALL

Emergency: 911

Police (non-emergency): (503) 823-3333

Hospitals: Adventist Medical Center, (503) 257-2500; Legacy Emanuel Hospital and Health Center, (503) 413-2200; Legacy Good Samaritan Hospital, (503) 413-7711; OHSU Hospital, (503) 494-8311; Providence St. Vincent Medical Center, (503) 216-1234.

WHERE TO LOOK

Newspapers

Portland's daily paper is *The Oregonian*, with morning and evening editions. *The Willamette Week* is published each Wednesday, while the *Portland Tribune* is published each Tuesday and Friday.

Radio

Portland radio station KXL (750 AM) is an all-news/weather station; KOPB (91.5 FM in northern Oregon, 550 AM and 103.1 FM in southern Oregon) is a member of National Public Radio.

Visitor Information

The Travel Portland Visitor Information Center: Pioneer Courthouse Square, 701 S.W. Sixth Ave., Portland, OR 97204; phone (503) 275-8355 or (877) 678-5263.

The information center, junction Sixth Avenue and Morrison Street, offers self-guiding tour brochures, city maps and visitor assistance/recommendations Mon.-Fri. 8:30-5:30, Sat. 10-4. In summer, the center is also open Sun. 10-2.

The *Willamette Week* reports on weekly entertainment, shopping specials and current events. In addition, the weekly *Portland Guide*, available at most local hotels, has tourist information.

TRANSPORTATION

Air Travel

Portland International Airport, 9 miles east of I-5 off I-205, is served by most domestic airlines. Transportation from downtown to the airport is available from airport shuttles, which run between the airport and major downtown hotels every 30 minutes daily 5 a.m.-midnight. The public bus and light-rail system, TriMet, also serves the airport; phone (503) 238-7433 Mon.-Fri. 7:30-5:30 for schedules. Taxi fares between the airport and downtown average approximately $25-$40.

Rental Cars

Several rental car agencies serve the Portland area. Hertz, (503) 528-7900 (airport), (503) 249-5727 (downtown) or (800) 654-3080, offers discounts to AAA members.

Rail Service

The Amtrak passenger train terminal is at 800 N.W. 6th Ave.; phone (800) 872-7245.

Taxis

Cabs must be hired by phone or at taxi stations in front of major hotels, although a few will answer a hail from the street in the downtown business district. Some of the larger companies include Broadway Cab Co., (503) 227-1234, and Radio Cab, (503) 227-1212. Fares are metered. Most taxi services charge $2.50 for one person for the first mile then $2.50 for each additional mile and a $1 fee for each additional passenger.

Public Transport

Transportation by bus, streetcar or light rail is available in Portland. *See Getting Around, Public Transportation.*

along the Pacific on the west; from the east US 26 skirts Mount Hood on its approach, while US 30 parallels the Columbia River, frequently following the I-84 alignment.

Bypass routes are provided by I-405, which skirts the western downtown area, and I-205, which swings in a wider arc through the eastern environs. Both interchange with major routes and streets en route.

Getting Around

Street System

Portland is divided into five sections—S.W., S.E., N., N.W. and N.E.—with the Willamette River dividing east from west and Burnside Street separating north from south. A series of 11 bridges connects the east and west sides. Street addresses are keyed to each of the sections—121 N.E. 21st Ave., or 200 S.W. Taylor St.

The city's major thoroughfares are, from west to east, Burnside Street, Sandy Boulevard and US 26 (Powell Boulevard), and from north to south, Grand Avenue, Martin Luther King Jr. Boulevard and 82nd Street. Many minor streets, especially downtown, are one-way, with alternate streets going in opposite directions.

The speed limit within the city is 25 mph, except in the business district and school zones, where it is 20 mph. Most major thoroughfares and express boulevards have limits of 35 mph, unless otherwise posted.

Left turns on red are permitted on one-way streets only; the driver must come to a full stop and yield to traffic with the green light. Right turns on red, after coming to a full stop and yielding to traffic with the right-of-way, are permitted at all intersections unless otherwise posted.

Rush hours are 6:30-8:30 a.m. and 3:30-6 p.m. Congestion is greatest on I-5, I-84 and US 26 during these times.

Parking

Parking lots are scattered liberally throughout the downtown area; on-street parking is difficult to find any time of the day or night. Parking rates range from 95c to $4 an hour, depending on the location.

Public Transportation

The TriMet transit agency, which serves three counties, divides the city into three fare zones. Sections are designated by a colored symbol. Within Zone 1 is downtown, inner-city Portland. Fareless Square, a 300-block area bounded by Irving Street on the north, the Willamette River on the east and I-405 on the south and west, contains Old Town, several major shopping areas, including Lloyd Center and the Portland Transit Mall, which is restricted to buses and pedestrians. All rides within Fareless Square are free.

The fare for one or two zones is $2; $1.65 (ages 7-18); 80c (ages 65+ and those physically impaired); free (children under 7 with passenger). Adult all-zone rides are $2.30. Fares may vary; phone ahead

World Forestry Center Discovery Museum / © AAA / Denise Campbell

not permitted; required clothing includes pants and closed-toe shoes. Participants must sign a waiver before taking the tour. Flashlights are provided to every fourth tour participant. Refunds are not provided. Allow 1 hour, 30 minutes minimum. Tours generally run daily after 4 p.m.; call for specific departure times. Participants must arrive 10 minutes prior to tour departure. Closed Jan. 1, Thanksgiving and Dec. 24-25. Admission $13; $8 (ages 0-11). Reservations and prepayment are required. MC, VI. Phone (503) 622-4798.

(SAVE) **PORTLAND WALKING TOURS** departs from multiple locations, including downtown, the Pearl District and Old Town/Chinatown. Knowledgeable guides outline history, architecture, artwork, bridges, fountains, parks, neighborhoods and food. Allow 3 hours minimum. Daily 10-7, Apr.-Nov. Admission $19; $15 (ages 11-17 and 65+); $5 (ages 5-10). AX, DS, MC, VI. Phone (503) 774-4522.

Sports and Recreation

Portland offers a wide variety of sports, ranging from sailing to mountain climbing. The city's extensive system of parks provides jogging trails, bicycle paths, swimming pools, tennis courts and nature trails. Nearby state parks also have recreational and camping facilities.

Boating is available at many marinas on the Columbia and Willamette rivers as well as at state parks; most marinas have many types of craft for rent in the spring and summer.

Fishing opportunities abound on the Willamette River as well as in state parks and in area lakes and streams. Chinook salmon are present in the lower Willamette March through early May, while steelhead run throughout the year in the Clackamas and Sandy rivers. For more information phone the Oregon Department of Fish and Wildlife at (503) 947-6000.

White-water rafting and **float trips** are offered throughout the state, usually April through September. Rates vary depending on length of trip (full-day or multiday).

Reservations for trips can be made through the following Portland area companies: Oregon River Experiences, 18074 S. Boone Ct., Beavercreek, OR 97004, (503) 632-6836 or (800) 827-1358; Zoller's Outdoor Odysseys, 1248 SR 141, White Salmon, WA 98672, (509) 493-2641 or (800) 366-2004; River Drifters, P.O. Box 7962, Bend, OR 97708, (800) 972-0430; and River Trails Canoe and Raft Rental, 336 E. Historic Columbia River Hwy., Troutdale, OR 97060, (503) 667-1964.

Hunting opportunities abound in the mountains and forests surrounding Portland. For information about hunting and fishing areas and licenses phone the Oregon Department of Fish and Wildlife at (503) 947-6000.

Hiking and **horseback riding** enthusiasts have miles of trails to explore in nearby state parks and national forests. Forest Service maps and other details are available from the U.S. Forest Service at Mount Hood; phone (503) 668-1700.

Mountain climbing and **skiing** are possible a short distance from Portland. Mount Hood, about an hour's drive from the city, is said to be one of the most climbed mountains in the world. Information about ski resorts and conditions is available from AAA Oregon/Idaho; phone (503) 222-6700. Information about mountain climbing is available from the U.S. Forest Service at Mount Hood; phone (503) 668-1700.

Bicycle trails wind through city parks; most connect with the statewide network of paths. Maps and route information can be obtained from Portland Parks and Recreation, 1120 S.W. Fifth Ave., Suite 1302, Portland, OR; 97204 phone (503) 823-7529. The 1.5-mile-long Eastbank Esplanade, between I-5 and the Willamette River, serves as a bicycle and pedestrian corridor; it includes a 1,200-foot floating walkway.

Tennis players have the choice of the city's indoor courts or outside facilities. Indoor courts must be reserved. Phone the Portland Tennis Center at (503) 823-3189.

Golf enthusiasts can play at any of 18 public courses, including Eastmoreland at 2425 S.E. Bybee St., (503) 775-2900; Heron Lakes, 3500 N. Victory Blvd. at West Delta Park, (503) 289-1818; RedTail, 8200 S.W. Scholls Ferry Rd., (503) 646-5166; and Rose City at 2200 N.E. 71st Ave., (503) 253-4744. For the courses listed prices average about $23-$41 for 18 holes, and about $18-$23 for nine holes.

Swimming is possible early June through August at several parks in the metropolitan area, including Dishman Pool, 77 N.E. Knott St.; Grant Park, 2300 N.E. 33rd Ave.; Mount Scott Park, 5530 S.E. 72nd Ave. at Harold Street; and Sellwood Park, 7951 S.E. 7th Ave. Nominal admission fees may be charged; phone (503) 823-5130 for schedules and information.

Spectators will find there is much for them to watch. The Rose Garden Arena, at 1 N. Center Ct., hosts most of the city's sporting expositions and events. Here, the Trail Blazers plays professional **basketball** from mid-October through June. The Portland Winter Hawks play semi-professional **hockey** from October through March. For ticket information, phone (503) 231-8000 for the Trail Blazers and (503) 236-4295 for the Winter Hawks.

Next door, the Memorial Coliscum serves as a second site for spectator sports. PGE Park is home to the Beavers, the AAA **baseball** team, and the Timbers, Portland's **soccer** team. Baseball is played from April 1 through Labor Day, and soccer takes the field from late April to early Sept.; phone (503) 553-5555 for ticket information.

Auto racing can be seen in the summer at the Portland International Raceway in West Delta Park at 1940 N. Victory Blvd., (503) 823-7223. **Horse racing** with pari-mutuel betting takes place at Portland Meadows, 1001 N. Schmeer Rd., October through April; phone (503) 285-9144.

Note: Policies vary concerning admittance of children to pari-mutuel betting facilities. Phone for information.

Shopping

With the largest collection of cast-iron-fronted structures outside New York City, Portland has preserved a majority of them in two historic districts: Skidmore/Old Town and Yamhill. The two areas blend historic preservation with modern commerce, as many of these landmarks are filled with shops, galleries and restaurants.

The Skidmore/Old Town District straddles West Burnside Street between Davis and Stark streets. The area encompasses 21 blocks in the downtown/waterfront area and boasts many significant historic buildings.

From the Burnside Bridge between S.W. Front Avenue and S.W. 1st Avenue is the Portland Saturday Market, said to be the largest, continuously operated open-air market in the United States. Craftspeople, artists, entertainers, cooks and farmers come to sell their goods and/or entertain the public at more than 250 booths and a food court. Open Saturday 10-5 and Sunday 11-4:30, March through December, the market sells only handcrafted (or locally grown) items; phone (503) 222-6072.

Another notable building in this area includes the Skidmore-Fountain Building, a marketplace that has kept its late 1800s character. A few blocks south of the Skidmore/Old Town District is the smaller Yamhill District.

In stark contrast to these historic buildings are the World Trade Center Buildings I, II and III, which house businesses, restaurants and galleries.

The nearby waterfront between the Hawthorne and Marquam bridges has reverted from freeway to a pleasant strip of grass and trees, with an esplanade bordered by the shops, restaurants and residences of RiverPlace.

Before the restoration of the historic areas, many businesses had moved uptown to an area between S.W. 4th and 10th avenues. Such department stores as Meier & Frank and Nordstrom are here. One former department store has been transformed into the Galleria, 921 S.W. Morrison St. Pioneer Place offers more than 80 specialty shops, Saks Fifth Avenue and Tiffany and Co. and a large movie theater.

There are other downtown places of note. Powell's City of Books is said to be the world's largest bookstore of used and new books; it covers an entire city block and holds more than one million volumes. Nearby on the West Side is N.W. 21st and N.W. 23rd Streets, known as Nob Hill ("Northwest" by the locals), which contains an eclectic collection of 250 shops, boutiques, galleries and restaurants, some within restored Victorian houses.

Outside the downtown area are several places of interest. On the East Side, at Grand Avenue and N.E. Weidler, is one of Portland's oldest and largest urban malls, the Lloyd Center, offering an indoor ice-skating rink. To the north of downtown off I-5 at the Interstate Bridge is the Jantzen Beach SuperCenter, with more than 50 shops.

The Old Sellwood Antique Row, southeast of downtown along S.E. 13th Avenue beyond the east end of the Sellwood Bridge, features some 50 antique and craft shops in a well-preserved community where decades-old buildings are marked with signs labeling past owners and building dates.

Shopping centers in the suburbs include the Clackamas Town Center, with more than 180 stores and a library, off I-205 and S.E. Sunnyside Road; and Washington Square Mall, off I-5 south on SR 217 in Tigard. Woodburn Company Stores *(See color ad)*, about 30 miles south at 1001 Arney Rd. in Woodburn, is an outlet center with 100 stores to choose from.

Performing Arts

The Portland Center for the Performing Arts is the focal point for the city's major cultural events. Unlike many such centers, this is a decentralized complex with three buildings in separate locations. They include the Arlene Schnitzer Concert Hall, the Keller Auditorium and the New Theatre Building.

The Arlene Schnitzer Concert Hall, S.W. Broadway at Main Street, is a restored 1928 vaudeville house where the Oregon Symphony Orchestra performs. "The Schnitz" features other musical concerts, dance and touring shows.

Directly across the street from "the Schnitz" is the New Theatre Building, which encompasses two performance spaces: the 292-seat Dolores Winningstad Theater and the 924-seat Newmark Theater. These theaters are the hosts for performances by the Oregon Ballet Theatre, the Portland Center Stage and a number of choral and orchestral groups.

Several blocks away, at 222 S.W. Clay St., the Keller Auditorium showcases performances by the Portland Opera and various national touring groups. The Oregon Ballet Theatre also takes the stage here.

For ticket and schedule information for the entire complex phone (503) 248-4335. Chamber Music Northwest, (503) 223-3202, performs concerts during June and July at the Catlín Gabel School or Reed College.

Special Events

Of the several events and celebrations in the Portland area, the 🌹 Portland Rose Festival in early June tops the list. The festival lasts 3-4 weeks and includes a band competition, exhibits, one of the country's largest children's parades, the nationally televised Grand Floral Parade, the Starlight Parade, the Champ Car Grand Prix of Portland, the Tigard Festival of Balloons, an air show, a national arts festival and a traditional rose show. For information about tickets and the schedule of events, phone (503) 227-2681.

Other summer events in Portland include the Waterfront Blues Festival on 4th of July weekend, which features both international and Oregon's finest blues artists. The Portland Scottish Highland Games are held in mid-July; phone (503) 293-8501. The Multnomah County Fair, which offers agricultural and horticultural exhibits and live entertainment, is held in late July.

The Mount Hood Jazz Festival, held in early August on the campus of the Main City Community Park in Gresham, features renowned jazz musicians from all over the country; phone (503) 491-5950. In mid-August Portland's restaurants present The Bite of Oregon, a food extravaganza at Tom McCall Waterfront Park. With its large tents, German oompah-pah bands and festive atmosphere, The Oktoberfest at Oaks Park resembles the Oktoberfest celebrations in Germany. It takes place in late September.

The Portland Vicinity

BEAVERTON (B-3) pop. 76,129, elev. 188'

Named for the abundance of beaver dams in the area, Beaverton was established in 1868 as a shipping point on the Oregon Central Railroad. Now it is an electronics, light industry and research center. Complementing the city's industry are its almost 300 acres of vineyards and a variety of recreational facilities.

Washington County Visitors Association: 11000 S.W. Stratus St., Suite 170, Beaverton, OR 97008; phone (503) 644-5555 or (800) 537-3149.

Shopping areas: Beaverton Town Square, at Canyon Road and SR 217, includes more than 40 stores. Washington Square Mall, off SR 217 at 9585 S.W. Washington Square Rd. in Tigard, features five leading department stores and more than 140 specialty shops.

TUALATIN HILLS NATURE PARK AND INTERPRETIVE CENTER is at 15655 S.W. Millikan Blvd. Interpretive signs provide explanations of native flora and fauna in this 222-acre urban green space. Almost 2 miles of paved trails along with almost 3 miles of unpaved secondary paths wind past marshes, creeks, ponds, meadows and mixed oak and conifer forests. A display area and library are in the interpretive center. Educational programs and classes are available throughout the year.

Allow 30 minutes minimum. Nature park open daily dawn-dusk. Interpretive center Mon.-Fri. 8:30-5, Sat.-Sun. 9-5; closed major holidays. Free. Phone (503) 629-6350.

WINERIES

• **Ponzi Vineyards** is at 14665 S.W. Winery Ln. off Scholls Ferry Rd. Daily 10-5; closed Easter, Thanksgiving and Dec. 25. Phone (503) 628-1227.

CLACKAMAS (B-4) pop. 5,177, elev. 51'

OREGON MILITARY MUSEUM is off I-205 exit 12, e. on SR 212, then n. on S.E. 102nd St. to 10101 S.E. Clackamas Rd. This museum preserves the military history of Oregon from the mid-1800s to the present. Restored artifacts include artillery, vehicles, weapons and uniforms. Buildings include a 1911 Battery A Barn and a WWII Quonset hut. A research library containing field and technical manuals can be visited by appointment. Allow 30 minutes minimum. Fri.-Sat. 9-5 or by appointment. Donations. Phone (503) 557-5359.

GRESHAM (B-4) pop. 90,205

Gresham was founded in 1852 by pioneers who cut a trail through the wilderness as they came over Mount Hood on their way to the Willamette Valley.

Gresham is now the gateway to the Columbia River Gorge and the Mount Hood recreation area and offers abundant recreational activities including boating, fishing, hiking and skiing.

Gresham Area Chamber of Commerce: 701 N.E. Hood Ave., Gresham, OR 97030; phone (503) 665-1131.

HILLSBORO (B-3) pop. 70,186, elev. 174'

Hillsboro, founded in 1842, was home for several of the settlers who helped establish a civil government for the Oregon Territory. Twenty minutes west of Portland, the city is nestled in the Tualatin Valley halfway between the Cascade Mountains and the Pacific Ocean. Hillsboro is known as a center for high-tech industries such as computers and electronics.

The area produces thousands of gallons of berry and fruit wines annually; the climate is similar to the grape-growing region of France. Local wineries offer tastings and guided tours. Jackson Bottom Wetlands Preserve, 2600 S.W. Hillsboro Hwy., is a 725-acre urban green space with an education center and trails offering opportunities for wildlife viewing; phone (503) 681-6206.

Greater Hillsboro Chamber of Commerce: 5193 N.E. Elam Young Pkwy., Suite A, Hillsboro, OR 97124; phone (503) 648-1102.

SAVE **RICE NORTHWEST MUSEUM OF ROCKS AND MINERALS** is off US 26W exit 61N, just n. to Groveland Dr., then 1.3 mi. w. to 26385 N.W. Groveland Dr. A 9,000-square-foot exhibit space contains thousands of world-class minerals, crystals, fossils, meteorites, petrified wood and fluorescents. Visitors can see copper minerals, a variety of gems, agates and red rhodochrosite. Allow 30 minutes minimum. Wed.-Sun. 1-5; closed major holidays. Admission $7; $6 (ages 60+); $5 (ages 5-17). AX, MC, VI. Phone (503) 647-2418.

WINERIES

• **Oak Knoll Winery** is 4 mi. s. off SR 219 at 29700 S.W. Burkhalter Rd. Mon.-Fri. 11-6, Sat.-Sun. 11-5, May-Sept.; daily 11-5, rest of year. Closed Jan. 1, Easter, Thanksgiving, and Dec. 25. Phone (503) 648-8198.

MILWAUKIE (B-3) pop. 20,490, elev. 300'

SAVE **NORTH CLACKAMAS AQUATIC PARK** is off I-205 at the Sunnyside exit, then 1 mi. w. on Sunnyside Rd. to 7300 S.E. Harmony Rd. The park features a wave pool, lap pool, water slides, dive well, kiddie pool, 29-foot climbing wall and a spa. Food is available. Mon.-Fri. noon-4 (also Mon., Wed. and Fri. 7-9 p.m.), Sat.-Sun. noon-7, mid-June through Labor Day; Fri. 6 p.m.-9 p.m., Sat. noon-7, Sun. 1-5, rest of year. Admission $9.99; $6.99 (ages 9-17 and 62+); $4.99 (ages 3-8). Phone (503) 557-7873.

OREGON CITY (C-4) pop. 25,754, elev. 55'

Oregon's first capital and the end of the Oregon Trail, Oregon City is on the Willamette River's east bank where the river plunges 40 feet over a basaltic ridge at Willamette Falls. Falls Vista Viewpoint, on SR 99E near the southern entrance into town, reveals a fine view of the falls. Across the river in West Linn are the Willamette Falls Locks, which opened the upper Willamette to navigation.

The Municipal Free Elevator, Seventh Street and Railroad Avenue, lifts pedestrians 90 feet up the face of a bluff to a residential-business district. An observation deck at the top overlooks the downtown area and the falls. Mount St. Helens can be seen on a clear day.

In Mountain View Cemetery, on Hilda Street off SR 213, is the grave of Peter Skene Ogden, a British fur trader who explored much of western America in the 1820s.

Oregon City Chamber of Commerce: 1201 Washington St., Oregon City, OR 97045; phone (503) 656-1619.

Shopping areas: Oregon City Shopping Center, at McLoughlin Boulevard and I-205 bridge, and the downtown area offer a variety of popular shops.

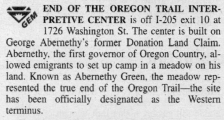 **END OF THE OREGON TRAIL INTERPRETIVE CENTER** is off I-205 exit 10 at 1726 Washington St. The center is built on George Abernethy's former Donation Land Claim. Abernethy, the first governor of Oregon Country, allowed emigrants to set up camp in a meadow on his land. Known as Abernethy Green, the meadow represented the true end of the Oregon Trail—the site has been officially designated as the Western terminus.

Changing exhibits provide information about the trail and Oregon City history. Interpreters in period attire present talks and demonstrations of activities from pioneer times. "Bound for Oregon," a 34-minute digital presentation, spotlights the experiences of pioneers as they traveled westward, American Indians and John McLoughlin, the "Father of Oregon."

Show and presentation times vary; call ahead. Allow 1 hour, 30 minutes minimum. Mon.-Sat. 9:30-5, Sun. 10:30-5, Memorial Day-Labor Day; Tues.-Sat. 11-4, rest of year. Closed Jan. 1, Thanksgiving and Dec. 25. Hours may vary; call ahead. Admission Memorial Day-Labor Day (includes entry to Museum of the Oregon Territory and Stevens-Crawford Heritage House) $9; $7 (ages 65+); $5 (ages 5-17). Admission rest of year (includes entry to Museum of the Oregon Territory and Stevens-Crawford Heritage House) $7; $5 (ages 5-17). AX, DS, MC, VI. Phone (503) 657-9336.

JOHN McLOUGHLIN HOUSE NATIONAL HISTORIC SITE, a unit of Fort Vancouver National Historic Site, is at Seventh and Center sts. The restored residence was built in 1845 by Dr. John McLoughlin, "Father of Oregon," a Hudson's Bay

The Oregon Trail

The lure of the Oregon country unleashed one of the largest peacetime migrations in the history of the world. The "Great Migration" began in 1843 when 1,000 pioneers, 120 wagons and 5,000 head of livestock left Independence, Mo.

Early pioneers, with their possessions and dreams for a new beginning, were ill-prepared for the trail's dangers: drought, blizzards, disease, wild animals and hostile American Indians. One out of 10 emigrants died along the trail, but this did not deter the mass overland migration that continued for nearly 3 decades.

AP Images / Don Ryan

The gateway to the northwest was actually several major emigrant trails starting at the Missouri River and ending in Oregon City. The Barlow Road route dropped south at The Dalles past Mt. Hood and Timberline Road. The Applegate Trail opened in 1846 and crossed the southern Oregon Cascade Mountains through Grants Pass, Medford and Klamath Falls. The Meek-Elliott-Macy route was established in 1854 after 9 years of unsuccessful attempts to find passage from the Malheur River across Oregon's desert to Eugene. In all, the trail extended 2,040 miles and stretched across six states. Traffic along this highway was so relentless, swelled by lengthy wagon trains, that ruts as deep as 6 feet scarred the fragile prairie. Many of the ruts are still visible. It is estimated that more than 200,000 people crossed the route 1840-60.

Co. representative who helped the first American pioneers who came across the Oregon Trail.

The home contains original and period furnishings. Victorian handcraft demonstrations are given the second Saturday of the month. Allow 1 hour minimum. Wed.-Sat. 10-4, Sun. 1-4, mid-Feb. to mid-Dec.; closed holidays. Free. Phone (503) 656-5146.

MUSEUM OF THE OREGON TERRITORY is .5 mi. s. on US 99E to 211 Tumwater Dr., following signs. The museum features permanent and changing exhibits about the Oregon Territory. American Indian petroglyphs from the Williamette Valley, an early 20th-century pharmacy and a research library housing county historical documents also are included.

Allow 1 hour minimum. Daily 11-4, Memorial Day-Labor Day; Tues.-Sat. 11-4, rest of year. Closed Jan. 1, Thanksgiving and Dec. 25. Hours may vary; call ahead. Admission Memorial Day-Labor Day (includes entry to End of the Oregon Trail Interpretive Center and Stevens-Crawford Heritage House) $9; $7 (ages 65+); $5 (ages 5-17). Admission rest of year (includes entry to End of the Oregon Trail Interpretive Center and Stevens-Crawford Heritage House) $7; $5 (ages 5-17). MC, VI. Phone (503) 655-5574.

STEVENS-CRAWFORD HERITAGE HOUSE is at 603 Sixth St. Guided tours lasting 45 minutes are offered of the 1907-08 home, which contains original period furnishings.

Wed.-Sat. noon-4, Feb.-Dec.; closed July 4, Thanksgiving and Dec. 25. Hours may vary; call ahead. Admission Memorial Day-Labor Day (includes entry to End of the Oregon Trail Interpretive Center and Museum of the Oregon Territory) $9; $7 (ages 65+); $5 (ages 5-17). Admission rest of year (includes entry to End of the Oregon Trail Interpretive Center and Museum of the Oregon Territory) $7; $5 (ages 5-17). MC, VI. Phone (503) 655-2866.

TROUTDALE (B-4) pop. 13,777, elev. 73'

Troutdale is the western gateway to the Columbia River Gorge. The downtown area's vintage buildings are typical of Oregon's depot towns of the early 20th century.

West Columbia Gorge Chamber of Commerce: 107 E. Historic Columbia River Hwy., P.O. Box 245, Troutdale, OR 97060; phone (503) 669-7473.

Shopping areas: Historic downtown buildings now contain antique and specialty stores and galleries. Columbia Gorge Factory Stores, off I-84 exit 17, houses such outlets as Big Dog Sportswear, Carter's, Harry and David, Levi's and Van Heusen.

WINERIES

- **Edgefield Winery** is off I-84 exit 16 at 2126 S.W. Halsey St. Daily noon-10. Phone (503) 665-2992.

Nearby Washington

BATTLE GROUND pop. 9,296, elev. 290'

In 1855 a group of American Indians being detained at Fort Vancouver escaped, and their chief was accidentally killed. A band of volunteer soldiers permitted the escapees to give their chief a traditional burial; the volunteers were later chided by soldiers at the fort for not waging a battle against the fugitives. Although there never was a "battle ground," the name nevertheless was adopted by the town that was established in 1902.

Three miles northeast of town off SR 502 is Battle Ground Lake State Park. The site is believed to be a caldera formed by the collapse of a volcanic cone *(see Recreation Chart and the AAA Northwestern CampBook).*

Battle Ground Chamber of Commerce: 1419 W. Main St., Suite 110, Battle Ground, WA 98604; phone (360) 687-1510.

RIDGEFIELD pop. 2,147, elev. 219'

Chinook Indians occupied the area when Lewis and Clark passed through in 1806. Ridgefield, established in the 1860s, was an important trading center. The Civil War veterans who settled here called the town Union Ridge. The area contains pioneer homesteads and a few orchards dating back to the turn of the 20th century, when the district specialized in prunes.

RIDGEFIELD NATIONAL WILDLIFE REFUGE is 3 mi. w. of I-5 exit 14. The Carty unit features a 2-mile self-guiding hiking trail through open fields and oak and fir tree groves. Cathlapotle Plankhouse, a full-scale replica of a Chinookan structure, houses exhibits of natural and cultural history. The River "S" Unit, south of Ridgefield, consists of ponds, fields and pasture; its 4.2-mile self-guiding auto tour route is open daily; the half-mile hiking trail is open May through September.

The refuge supports sandhill cranes, songbirds, reptiles and mammals. Canada geese, tundra swans and a variety of ducks are numerous in the winter months. Allow 2 hours minimum. Refuge open daily dawn-dusk. Plankhouse open Sat.-Sun. noon-4, Apr.-Oct. Entrance fee $3 (per vehicle). Phone (360) 887-4106.

RECREATIONAL ACTIVITIES
Kayaking
- **Ridgefield Kayak** departs from depart McCuddy's Marina at 5 Mill St. Guided and non-guided kayak trips on water trails surrounding Ridgefield National Wildlife Refuge are offered. Write P.O. Box 1325, Ridgefield, WA 98642. Reservations are required. Daily 10-6. Phone (360) 727-4520 or (503) 319-1146.

VANCOUVER pop. 143,560, elev. 42'

At the head of deepwater navigation on the Columbia River, Vancouver is the oldest city in Washington.

It was founded in 1824 as Fort Vancouver by the Hudson's Bay Co. During the 1860s the young town prospered from the gold rushes to eastern Washington and Idaho. Connections with the Northern Pacific from Kalama and increased river traffic furthered the town's development into a busy shipping center.

The Kaiser Co. shipyard, constructed in 1942 after the United States entered World War II, built about 140 vessels that were used in Pacific warfare. Today Vancouver's port accommodates both ocean and river commerce. Aluminum and high-tech industries also contribute to the city's economy.

Esther Short Park, at the corner of Columbia and W. 8th streets, was the property of the first Americans to file a land claim in the area. The park, established in 1853, has the oldest town square in the state. It includes the 1867 Slocum House, a Rhode Island-style home now used as a community theater; a massive woodcarving of an American Indian; and the Avard Fairbanks' bronze monument to the pioneer woman.

Providence Academy, 400 E. Evergreen Blvd., was the first permanent Catholic school in the Northwest. Erected in 1873 under the direction of Mother Joseph, it is constructed from about 300,000 handmade bricks. Covington Historical House, 4201 Main St., is an 1848 log cabin said to be the first schoolhouse in the Oregon Territory north of the Columbia River.

Southwest Washington Visitor Information Center: 750 Anderson St., Vancouver, WA 98660; phone (360) 750-1553, ext. 21 or (877) 600-0800, ext. 21.

Shopping areas: Westfield Shoppingtown, just west of I-205 exit 30 on SR 500, is the major shopping center for Vancouver. The largest department stores are JCPenney, Macy's, Nordstrom and Sears. Vancouver Farmer's Market, Esther Street between 6th and 8th streets, is open on weekends, early April through October.

CLARK COUNTY HISTORICAL MUSEUM, 1511 Main St., is housed in a 1909 Carnegie Library. Displays of pioneer life include an early doctor's office, a Victorian parlor, a country store and changing exhibits. The museum also houses a reference library. Allow 30 minutes minimum. Tues.-Sat. 11-4 (also first Thurs. of the month 5-9); closed holidays. Admission $4; $3 (ages 62+ and students with ID); $2 (ages 6-18); $10 (family, up to four people). Phone (360) 993-5679.

VANCOUVER NATIONAL HISTORIC RESERVE consists of nearly a dozen diverse sites; a visitor center is at 1501 E. Evergreen Blvd. in Fort Vancouver National Historic Site *(see attraction listing).* The sites represent the settlement of the area from the American Indian period to the present.

The "upper" portion of the reserve includes Fort Vancouver National Historic Site, Vancouver Barracks, Pearson Air Field and Officers Row National Historic District. The "lower" portion is made up of the Water Resources Education Center, Waterfront Park, Kaiser Shipyard Overlook, Old Apple Tree Park and a section of Discovery Trail. The Vancouver Land Bridge, designed by Maya Lin, spans SR 14 and connects the two sections of the reserve. Seven installations along its route commemorate the 1804-06 Lewis and Clark Expedition. Visitor center open daily 9-5, mid-Mar. through Oct. 31; 9-4, rest of year. Closed Jan. 1, Thanksgiving and Dec. 24-25. Phone for individual site schedules. Phone (360) 816-6230.

Fort Vancouver National Historic Site is e. on Mill Plain Blvd. off I-5 exit 1C, then s. on Ft. Vancouver Way and e. to 1001 E. 5th St., within Vancouver National Historic Reserve; the visitor center is at 1501 E. Evergreen Blvd. The 200-acre site was the center of the Hudson's Bay Co.'s fur-trading empire 1825-60. In 1849 the first U.S. military post in the Pacific Northwest was founded nearby. The Hudson's Bay Co. stockade and several buildings have been reconstructed and furnished in period. A visitor center has a museum.

Allow 1 hour minimum. Fort and visitor center open daily 9-5, mid-Mar. through Oct. 31; 9-4, rest of year. Closed Jan. 1, Thanksgiving and Dec. 24-25. Admission to reconstructed fort $3; free (ages 0-15); $5 (family). Phone (360) 816-6200.

Officer's Row National Historic District is on Officer's Row within Vancouver National Historic Reserve. The 21 Victorian homes, formerly the residences of officers at the U.S. Army post, were built 1849-1906.

The 1886 Marshall House, 1301 Officer's Row, is named for Gen. George C. Marshall, author of the post-World War II European recovery plan. A tour includes a 25-minute video about Officer's Row and the history of Vancouver since 1850. Allow 30 minutes minimum. Mon.-Fri. 9-5, selected Sat.-Sun. 11-5; closed Thanksgiving and Dec. 25. Free. Phone (360) 693-3103.

Pearson Air Museum is 1 mi. s.e. of I-5 exit 1C at 1115 E. 5th St., within Vancouver National Historic Reserve. Exhibits, photographs and relics relate the history of aviation in the Northwest and at Pearson—the country's oldest continuously operating airfield.

A monument next to the museum marks the site where three Soviet aviators completed the first trans-polar flight and the first non-stop flight from Russia to the United States in 1937. The flight took 63 hours and 16 minutes.

Guided tours are available. Allow 1 hour minimum. Tues. noon-5, Wed.-Sat. 10-5, Sun. 11-4, early June-Labor Day; Wed.-Sat. 10-5, rest of year. Closed Jan. 1, July 5, Thanksgiving and Dec. 25. Admission $6; $5 (ages 55+ and military with ID); $3 (ages 6-12). Phone (360) 694-7026.

Water Resources Education Center is at 4600 S.E. Columbia Way at the e. end of Marine Park within Vancouver National Historic Reserve. Hands-on exhibits about water usage and conservation and a 350-gallon aquarium comprise the center. Computer programs explain how water comes out of the tap and what happens after it goes down the drain. A waterfront trail is on the grounds. Allow 1 hour minimum. Mon.-Sat. 9-5; closed Jan. 1, July 4, Thanksgiving and Dec. 25. Free. Phone (360) 487-7111.

WASHOUGAL pop. 8,595, elev. 65'

Washougal straddles a peninsula between the Columbia and its namesake river. Bearing an American Indian name meaning "rushing water," Washougal is the Washington gateway to the Columbia Gorge. At Reed Island, three miles southeast, the crew of the HMS *Chatham* claimed the Columbia River for England in October 1792. The expedition's leader, William Broughton, also named Mount Hood.

Lewis and Clark camped at Cottonwood Beach on the Washougal River (then called the Seal River) in March 1806. Settlement began along the Washougal River in the late 1840s, after American possession of the Oregon Country north of the Columbia River was established in 1846. A townsite was platted in 1880 and Washougal was incorporated in 1908.

The town's woolen mills have attracted expert weavers from New England and Europe. Of historical significance is the Mount Pleasant Grange Hall, 6.5 miles east on SR 14, the oldest continuously used grange hall in the state.

Camas-Washougal Chamber of Commerce: 422 N.E. 4th Ave., P.O. Box 919, Camas, WA 98607; phone (360) 834-2472.

PENDLETON WOOLEN MILL is off SR 14 Washougal exit at 2 Pendleton Way. Tours demonstrate how raw wool is processed into fabric. No more than 2 children under age 12 are permitted per adult. Forty-five minute tours, including 1 mile of walking, depart Mon.-Fri. at 9, 10, 11 and 1:30; closed holidays. Tour not offered for 2 weeks in Aug. and Dec.; dates vary, call ahead. Store open Mon.-Fri. 8-5, Sat. 9-5, Sun. 11-5. Closed Jan. 1, Easter, Thanksgiving and Dec. 25. Free. Phone (360) 835-1118 or (800) 568-2480.

TWO RIVERS HERITAGE MUSEUM is at 1 16th St. Exhibits describe local history. Artifacts on display include Chinook Indian arrowheads, hunting tools and baskets. An extensive collection of photographs and writings outlines the lives of Camas and Washougal founders. Allow 30 minutes minimum. Tues.-Sat. 11-3; closed holidays. Admission $3; $2 (ages 61+); $1 (ages 6-18). Phone (360) 835-8742.

Portland Rose Festival / © Janis Miglavs / Danita Delimont Stock Photography

This ends listings for the Portland Vicinity.
The following page resumes the alphabetical listings of cities in Oregon.

PORT ORFORD (G-5) pop. 1,153, elev. 60′

The bluffs overlooking the Pacific Ocean were first sighted in 1792 by Capt. George Vancouver, who named the area for England's Earl of Orford. Port Orford, settled in the 1850s, became a shipping center for cedar. While lumber is still an important resource, tourism, fishing and cranberry farming are the area's primary industries.

A natural deep-water port, Port Orford is Oregon's only coastal port that required few man-made adaptations. The fishing fleet is hoisted from the water onto a dry dock and stored on rolling cradles to escape the rough seas whipped up by southwesterly winds.

Geographically speaking, the town is said to be the westernmost incorporated city in the contiguous United States. Recreational opportunities include scuba diving, whale watching, fishing and crabbing. Humbug Mountain State Park, 6 mi. s. on US 101, offers camping, picnicking, hiking and fishing; phone (800) 551-6949 *(see Recreation Chart and the AAA Northwestern CampBook).*

Port Orford & North Curry County Chamber of Commerce: P.O. Box 637, Port Orford, OR 97465; phone (541) 332-8055. A visitor center is in Historic Oceanfront Battle Rock Park on US 101.

CAPE BLANCO STATE PARK is 4 mi. n., then 3 mi. w. off US 101. The park was named by Spanish explorers for its chalky appearance due to a concentration of fossilized shells. Camping is available year-round. Park open daily 24 hours. Nearby Cape Blanco Lighthouse offers tours Tues.-Sun. 10-3:30, Apr.-Oct. Park free. Lighthouse $2; free (ages 0-15). Phone (541) 332-6774 for the park or (541) 332-2207 for the lighthouse. *See Recreation Chart and the AAA Northwestern CampBook.*

The Hughes House is 8 mi. n.w., following signs to 91814 Cape Blanco Rd., within Cape Blanco State Park. The Eastlake Victorian-style ranch house, built in 1898, contains collections of photographs and a variety of antiques. Allow 30 minutes minimum. Tues.-Sun. 10-3:30, Apr.-Oct. Donations. Phone (541) 332-0248.

PORT ORFORD LIFEBOAT STATION MUSEUM is in Port Orford Heads State Park, 1.5 mi. w. on Coast Guard Rd. Commissioned in 1934, the station provided search and rescue assistance until 1970. Now a museum, it contains a 36-foot motor lifeboat and a Lyle rescue gun as well as a dog tag machine from World War II. Port Orford Heads State Park offers walking trails with views of the ocean. Allow 30 minutes minimum. Thurs.-Mon. 10-3:30, Apr.-Oct.; by appointment rest of year. Free. Phone (541) 332-0521.

PREHISTORIC GARDENS is 10 mi. s. on US 101. Life-size replicas of dinosaurs are in a rain forest setting. Dogs are permitted. Allow 30 minutes minimum. Daily 8-dusk, Mar.-Nov.; Thurs.-Sun. 9-4, rest of year (weather permitting). Hours may vary; phone ahead. Admission $8; $7 (ages 11-17 and 65+); $6 (ages 3-10). MC, VI. Phone (541) 332-4463.

PRAIRIE CITY (D-10) pop. 1,080, elev. 3,538′

Prairie City nestles near the base of 9,000-foot Strawberry Mountain at the eastern end of the upper John Day Valley. Founded in 1868, the town became Grant County's prime shipping point in 1910 when the narrow-gauge Sumpter Valley Railroad linked it with the Union Pacific system mainline in Baker City.

Prairie City Visitor Information Center: 124 N.W. Front St., P.O. Box 217, Prairie City, OR 97869; phone (541) 820-3739.

DEWITT MUSEUM AND PRAIRIE CITY DEPOT is at Main and Bridge sts. in Depot Park. The former 1910 train depot includes the station agent's office as well as freight, baggage and waiting rooms. Antique tools and other memorabilia are displayed along with photographs depicting life along the railway. A kitchen, parlor and bedroom typical of the early 1900s contain period furnishings and mannequins. Allow 30 minutes minimum. Wed.-Sun. 10-5, May 15-Oct. 15. Admission $3; free (ages 0-8). Phone (541) 820-3330.

PRINEVILLE (D-8) pop. 7,356, elev. 2,868′

The rimrocks that almost encircle Prineville as well as the region's other unusual geological features make it a favorite place for rock hounds. The chamber of commerce has information about areas where thunder eggs, agates and petrified wood can be found.

Other recreational activities, including cross-country skiing, snowmobiling, hiking, boating and fishing, are found nearby at Prineville Reservoir as well as at Ochoco National Forest *(see place listing p. 87, Recreation Chart and the AAA Northwestern CampBook).*

Prineville-Crook County Chamber of Commerce: 390 N.E. Fairview, Prineville, OR 97754; phone (541) 447-6304.

REDMOND (E-8) pop. 13,481, elev. 3,015′

Surrounded by an abundance of juniper trees, Redmond is an oasis in central Oregon's high desert. The Redmond Air Center, a Forest Service smoke jumping, firefighting and training installation at the Redmond Airport. Arrangements can be made for a free guided tour of the facilities. Local recreational opportunities include rock climbing, fishing, hiking, white-water rafting and Nordic and alpine skiing.

Redmond Chamber of Commerce: 446 S.W. 7th St., Redmond, OR 97756; phone (541) 923-5191.

PETERSEN ROCK GARDENS are 7 mi. s.w. off US 97 at 7930 S.W. 77th St. The gardens embrace 4 colorful acres. Bridges, terraces and replicas of historic structures are built of rock and petrified wood. A museum displays rare rock specimens. Picnicking is permitted. Allow 1 hour minimum. Museum open daily 9-5. Gardens open daily 9-7, Memorial Day weekend-Labor Day; 9-dusk, rest of year. Admission $4.50; $3 (senior citizens); $2 (ages 12-16); $1 (ages 6-11). Phone (541) 382-5574.

PETER SKENE OGDEN STATE PARK is 9 mi. n. on US 97. The 86-acre park flanks the Crooked River Gorge and offers scenic viewpoints, encompassing both highway bridge approaches. Picnicking is permitted. Daily dawn-dusk. Free.

REEDSPORT (F-2) pop. 4,378

Water was once the bane of existence for Reedsport, built on marshy tideland filled in with clay taken from the hills behind town. Flooding was so frequent that most of the town's early buildings and sidewalks had to be elevated 3 to 8 feet above ground. A devastating flood in 1964 resulted in the construction of a dike to protect the lower part of town.

Reedsport's watery surroundings evoke images of the salmon, steelhead trout and striped bass that abound. Adjacent Winchester Bay, at the mouth of the Umpqua River, is among Oregon's most productive sport-fishing harbors.

US 101 is a scenic highway that passes through Reedsport and stretches along the Oregon coast. It features such nearby scenic areas as Oregon Dunes National Recreation Area *(see Siuslaw National Forest p. 118)* along its route. SR 38 from I-5 to US 101 parallels the scenic Umpqua River valley. Dean Creek Elk Viewing Area offers more spectacular scenery 3 miles east of Reedsport. Hiking, camping, beachcombing and whale watching are popular activities near town.

Reedsport-Winchester Bay Chamber of Commerce: 855 S. US 101, P.O. Box 11, Reedsport, OR 97467; phone (541) 271-3495 or (800) 247-2155.

UMPQUA DISCOVERY CENTER is at 409 Riverfront Way, along the Umpqua riverfront boardwalk area. The interpretive center houses interactive exhibits about the Lower Umpqua area and the Oregon coast. Hands-on exhibits, displays, murals and video presentations portray the region's natural and cultural history. "Tidewaters & Time" traces events from the days of the Kuuich Indians in the 1700s to a 1900s tidewater town, while "Pathways to Discovery" takes visitors on a historical journey via a simulated indoor trail, including a slide into a bear cave.

Allow 1 hour minimum. Daily 9-5, June-Sept.; 10-4, rest of year. Closed Jan. 1, Thanksgiving and Dec. 25. Admission $8; $7 (ages 65+); $4 (ages 6-15); $20 (family). MC, VI. Phone (541) 271-4816.

UMPQUA LIGHTHOUSE STATE PARK is 6 mi. s. off US 101. The park is bordered by the Oregon Dunes National Recreation Area, which has sand dunes reaching heights up to 500 feet. Just around the corner on Lighthouse Road is the Umpqua Lighthouse–its beam of red and white light is visible for 19 miles.

Park open daily dawn-dusk. Guided lighthouse tours daily 10-4, May-Oct.; by appointment, rest of year. Park free. Lighthouse tour $3; $2 (ages 6-15). Phone (541) 271-4631 for tour information. *See Recreation Chart and the AAA Northwestern CampBook.*

ROGUE RIVER (G-6) pop. 1,847

PALMERTON ARBORETUM is off I-5 Rogue River city exit 58, following signs. Featured is a variety of labeled plants, shrubs and trees as well as a duck pond, playground and picnic area. The Skevington Crossing footbridge connects to the Anna Classick Bicentennial Park. Allow 30 minutes minimum. Daily 8-dusk. Free. Phone (541) 582-4401.

ROGUE RIVER–SISKIYOU NATIONAL FOREST

> Elevations in the forest range from 200 ft. near the Pacific Ocean to 9,495 ft. at Mount McLoughlin. Refer to AAA maps for additional elevation information.

The main entrance for the Rogue River section of the approximately 1.8-million-acre Rogue River-Siskiyou National Forest is from the south via I-5 from Medford, while the entrance for the Siskiyou section is on Oregon's southern coast and may be accessed on the east by US 199, on the west by US 101 and on the north and south by I-5.

From the Cascades to the coast, the forest spans three mountain ranges within four distinct geologic provinces. Seven isolated wilderness areas feature more than 324,000 pristine acres. The forest also contains hundreds of miles of free-flowing water in 11 major rivers teeming with wild strains of salmon and steelhead.

The Rogue River section encompasses two separate units in southwestern Oregon. The western unit includes 7,535-foot Mount Ashland, the highest point in the Siskiyou Mountain Range, and the headwaters of the Applegate River. Its many environs include open woodlands, conifer forests and rocky ridgetops with many botanical specimens.

The eastern unit contains the upper reaches of the Rogue River and Mount McLoughlin, a 9,495-foot volcanic cone. The Upper Rogue is generally too difficult for float trips, but it is still popular for other recreational pursuits and for its scenery in the volcanic terrain of the Cascade Range. The area's forest of Douglas fir, ponderosa pine and other conifers is enhanced by meadows, lakes and streams.

The Rogue River section is the western gateway to Crater Lake National Park *(see place listing p 61)*. Two fascinating geological interpretive sites, Natural Bridge and Rogue Gorge, are located along Crater Lake Highway. Developed campgrounds and opportunities for snowmobiling, sledding and cross-country skiing are available.

The Pacific Crest National Scenic Trail follows the southern Oregon Cascades and Siskiyou Mountains from Crater Lake into California. This and other forest trails provide access for hiking or pack-and-saddle trips.

Within the Applegate Valley region is Dutchman's Peak Lookout, with an elevation of 7,410 feet; it was built in 1927. It is one of the last cupola-topped lookout buildings still in use to detect forest fires. The lookout, 33 miles from Ashland via I-5 and SR 238, affords a panoramic view.

Also in the gold-rich Applegate Valley are remnants of hydraulic mining operations carried out by Chinese miners in the mid-19th century; one such site is along the Gin Lin Trail near the popular recreation facilities at Applegate Lake.

The Siskiyou section has rugged scenery and varied recreational facilities. Known as the "Botanist's Paradise," Siskiyou contains large numbers of plant species, including Brewer/weeping spruce and Port Orford cedar.

The Rogue River-Siskiyou National Forest and Medford District Bureau of Land Management jointly manage the Rogue National Wild and Scenic River. The river traverses the area, and is famous for catches of salmon and cutthroat and steelhead trout, in addition to its challenging white-water rafting. Hiking and backpacking are popular in the spring and fall, but high temperatures in late summer may discourage some hikers from hiking the entire 40-mile Rogue River Trail.

The Wild Rogue Wilderness is along the Rogue River between Mule Creek and Watson Creek; the area is accessible only by river or by foot trail. Boat trips are available up the Rogue River from Gold Beach (see place listing p. 70) and downriver from Grants Pass (see place listing p. 71).

Kalmiopsis Wilderness covers 180,000 acres, with shallow, rocky canyons and mountain streams. It is accessible only by foot or by horseback. This is the principal range of the rare Port Orford cedar and the Brewer, or weeping, spruce. The *Kalmiopsis lea-chiana*, a small plant similar to the rhododendron considered to be one of the world's rarest shrubs, also can be found in the wilderness.

The 17,200-acre Grassy Knob Wilderness lies in steep, rugged tree-covered canyons 7 miles east of Port Orford. Two roads provide access to the area and offer vistas of the wilderness and the Pacific.

The Red Buttes Wilderness, 3,414 acres southeast of Cave Junction, extends north from the California border. Eleven miles of trails, including the Boundary National Recreation Trail, are within the small wilderness area, which ranges in elevation from 3,600 to 6,300 feet. Wildflowers and open ridge-top meadows characterize the sub-alpine wilderness.

The Bear Camp Road (Forest Road # 23) is not advisable for winter travel. It also is not recommended for travel trailers or larger recreational vehicles. SR 199 (the Redwood Highway) is the most preferable route to travel, especially for recreational vehicles, vehicles towing trailers, or for those unaccustomed to driving on winding mountain roads with one lane.

For further information contact Rogue River-Siskiyou National Forest, 3040 Biddle Rd., P.O. Box 520, Medford, OR 97504; phone (541) 618-2200. *See Recreation Chart and the AAA Northwestern CampBook.*

ROSEBURG (G-3) pop. 20,017, elev. 479′

Once known for its rich timber industry, Roseburg is a recreation seeker's delight. Centrally located, Roseburg is 70 miles from the ocean and 70 miles from snow-capped mountains. East of Roseburg, SR 138 has been designated a national scenic byway and leads to recreational activities at Diamond Lake and Crater Lake National Park (see place listing p. 61).

Visitors seeking information about area wineries can contact the Umpqua Valley Winegrowers Association for information; phone (541) 673-5323.

Roseburg Visitors Center: 410 S.E. Spruce St., P.O. Box 1262, Roseburg, OR 97470; phone (541) 672-9731 or (800) 444-9584. *See color ad p. 63.*

(SAVE) **DOUGLAS COUNTY MUSEUM OF CULTURAL AND NATURAL HISTORY** is off I-5 exit 123 to 123 Museum Dr. Exhibits depict the history of the Umpqua Valley, from the Cascade Mountains to the Oregon coast. The museum reputedly has the state's largest display of natural history specimens, dioramas and more than 20,000 historic photographs, all relating to the history, natural environs and growth of Douglas County. A research library is accessible.

Allow 1 hour minimum. Museum open Mon.-Fri. 9-5, Sat. 10-5, Sun. noon-5; closed major holidays. Library open Mon.-Fri. 1-4:30. Admission $4; $3 (55+); $2 (ages 4-17 and college students). MC, VI. Phone (541) 957-7007.

WINERIES

- **Hillcrest Vineyard** is 10 mi. n.w. of I-5 Garden Valley Ave. exit 125, w. on Melrose Rd., w. on Doerner Rd. (CR 90), then n. on Elgarose Rd. to 240 Vineyard Ln. Daily 11-5, Mar.-Dec.; closed major holidays. Phone (541) 673-3709.

- **Spangler Vineyards** is at 491 Winery Ln. Daily 11-5; closed major holidays. Phone (541) 679-9654.

ST. BENEDICT (C-3)

MOUNT ANGEL ABBEY is off I-5 exit 271, s. on SR 214 to Mount Angel, then 1 mi. e. on College Rd. to 1 Abbey Dr. Founded in 1882 by Benedictine monks, the abbey rests on a hilltop providing sweeping views of the Willamette Valley and snow-capped Cascade volcanoes. A self-guiding walking tour includes the Retreat House, hilltop garden, library, monastery, statues, a museum and church. The library, one of only two buildings in the nation designed by renowned Finnish architect Alvar Aalto, contains rare books and religious articles. The bell tower, which stands more than 120 feet high, houses 8 bells that ring five times a day.

Allow 30 minutes minimum. Abbey daily 8:30-5. Library Mon.-Fri. 9-4, Sat. 1-4. Closed religious holidays. Call in advance to confirm hours. Free. Phone (503) 845-3030.

ST. HELENS (B-3) pop. 10,019, elev. 98′

On the Oregon side of the Columbia River, St. Helens lies 18 miles southwest of Mount St. Helens. From its inception, the town's deepwater position on the river made it a port. Olde Towne, the city's waterfront area, includes many historic properties, shops and a riverfront park.

South Columbia County Chamber of Commerce: 2194 Columbia Blvd., St. Helens, OR 97051; phone (503) 397-0685.

Shopping areas: Shops can be found along the waterfront in Old Towne.

ST. PAUL (C-3) pop. 354, elev. 170′

French-Canadian trappers who settled in the area in the 1830s called the nearby plains the French Prairie. In 1839, Archbishop Francis Norbert Blanchet established St. Paul Mission, from which the town, now a National Historic District, received its name.

HEIRLOOM ROSE GARDENS is off I-5 exit 278, 7 mi. w. on Ehlen Rd., then n. on Hwy. 219 to Champoeg Rd. and 2 mi. e. to 24062 Riverside Dr. N.E. Five acres of English-style gardens contain some 3,000 varieties of hybrid tea, English Legend, old garden, ground cover, hybrid musk, hybrid perpetual, shrub, climber, miniature and David Austin English roses. A 100-foot-long pergola has 50 rambler rose varieties.

The flowers bloom from May to November, reaching their peak in mid-June. Allow 30 minutes minimum. Daily 9-5, May-Sept.; 9-4, rest of year. Closed Jan. 1, Easter, Thanksgiving and Dec. 25. Free. Phone (503) 538-1576.

SALEM (C-3) pop. 136,924, elev. 171′

Salem is the capital of Oregon and the state's third largest city. The city was founded in 1841 by Methodist missionary Jason Lee, whose goal was to gather American Indians together and "teach them to cultivate the ground and live more comfortably than they could by hunting, and as they do this, teach them religion."

After limited success, Lee became discouraged. He decided to lay out a town and sell lots to finance the Oregon Institute, which developed into the present-day Willamette University, the oldest institution of higher learning west of Missouri.

Salem had only one house when it was plotted, and the Calapooya Indian name *Chemeketa*, or "place of rest," was proposed for the town's name. Missionaries, however, preferred the Biblical word *salem*, which means "peace."

The landscaped grounds of the Civic Center on Liberty Street contain foot and bike trails, fountains, Austrian black swans and sculptures. Schreiner's Iris Gardens on Quinaby Road N.E. offers a spectacle of blooming irises in the spring.

Other facets of the city include an antique woolen mill, historic homes, a missionary settlement and Corban College.

Travel Salem: Salem Travel Café, 181 High St., Salem, OR 97301-3641; phone (503) 581-4325 or (800) 874-7012. Satellite visitor centers are at 3301 Market St. N.E. in the Red Lion Hotel and at 3125 Ryan Dr. S.E. at the Best Western Mill Creek Inn.

Shopping areas: Lancaster Mall, off I-5 at Market Street and Lancaster Drive, has department stores such as Macy's. Downtown, the Salem Center Mall, connected with sidewalks to JCPenney, Kohl's, Macy's and Nordstrom, has specialty shops and restaurants.

BUSH'S PASTURE PARK is at 890 Mission St. S.E. The 90-acre city park is planted with several varieties of rare trees, shrubs and roses. Baseball, picnicking and tennis facilities are available. Daily 5 a.m.-midnight. Free. Phone (503) 588-6336.

Bush Barn Art Center (Salem Art Association) is at 600 Mission St. S.E., next to the Bush House Museum in Bush's Pasture Park. Monthly exhibitions and a gallery are featured. Tues.-Fri. 10-5, Sat.-Sun. noon-5. Free. Phone (503) 581-2228.

Bush Conservatory is on the grounds of the Bush House at 600 Mission St. S.E. within Bush's Pasture Park. The greenhouse, said to be the oldest west of the Mississippi, was built in 1882 and has been restored. Daily 7:30-3:30. Free. Phone (503) 588-6336.

SAVE **Bush House Museum** is at 600 Mission St. S.E. in Bush's Pasture Park. The Italianate home was built circa 1877 by Asahel Bush, pioneer banker and newspaper publisher. It contains most of its original furnishings, gas fixtures (wired for electricity in the 1890s), elaborate Japanese wallpapers, 10 Italian marble fireplaces and a collection of 19th-century artwork. Tues.-Sun. noon-5, May-Sept.; Tues.-Sun. 1-4, Oct.-Dec. and Mar.-Apr.; phone for hours rest of year. Admission $4; $3 (students with ID and senior citizens); $2 (ages 6-12). Phone (503) 363-4714.

SAVE **Deepwood Estate** is at 1116 Mission St. S.E. at 12th St., within Bush's Pasture Park; parking is available on 12th St. The 1894 Queen Anne Victorian is set on 4.5 acres of English-style gardens and nature trails. Lord & Schryver, said to be the Northwest's first female landscape architecture firm, designed sections of the gardens using fences, hedges and arbors. The residence features fine oak woodwork, stained-glass windows and a multi-gabled carriage house.

Allow 1 hour minimum. Gardens open daily dawn-dusk. Guided tours are offered on the hour Sun.-Fri. 2-4, mid-May to mid-Sept.; Wed.-Thurs. and Sat. 11-3, or by appointment, rest of year. Garden admission free. Tour $4; $3 (students with ID and senior citizens); $2 (ages 6-12). Phone (503) 363-1825.

HALLIE FORD MUSEUM OF ART is e. of city center at 700 State St. The 27,000-square-foot, three-story museum is comprised of four galleries containing permanent collections and two galleries for temporary exhibits. Works by American artist John Wesley Jarvis and French artist Jean-Baptiste Camille Corot are featured as well as pieces from Asia, Egypt, Europe, the Middle East and Pakistan. During April and May the museum displays paintings, sculpture, prints, drawings and photography by Willamette University students.

The Native American Gallery presents Northwestern basketry and contemporary and traditional artwork. Allow 1 hour minimum. Tues.-Sat. 10-5, Sun. 1-5; closed holidays. Admission $3; $2 (ages 63+ and students with ID); free (ages 0-12). AX, MC, VI. Phone (503) 370-6855.

MARION COUNTY HISTORICAL SOCIETY MUSEUM & ARCHIVE is on the grounds of the Mission Mill Museum and accessible from 1313 Mill St. S.E. The "Doorways to Marion County History" exhibit provides visitors with a guide to the county's history and existing heritage sites. A growing research library-archive also is available. Allow 30 minutes minimum. Tues.-Sat. noon-4; closed major holidays. Admission $4; $3.50 (ages 55+); $2.50 (students). Phone (503) 364-2128.

MISSION MILL MUSEUM-SALEM'S AMERICAN TREASURE is at 1313 Mill St. S.E. The 5.5-acre historic park features three historic homes, a church and eight buildings from the Thomas Kay Woolen Mill, founded in 1889. A millrace which passes through the grounds was the sole power source for the mill for most of its active years. Tours of the buildings explore the architecture and lifestyles of the Northwest's early 19th-century settlers and turn-of-the-20th-century industrial beginnings.

Food is available. Allow 2 hours minimum. Mon.-Sat. 10-5; closed Jan. 1, Thanksgiving and Dec. 25. Admission $8; $7 (ages 55+ and students); $4 (ages 6-12); $24 (family). DS, MC, VI. Phone (503) 585-7012.

Jason Lee House, the Parsonage, John D. Boon House and Pleasant Grove Church are on the grounds of Mission Mill Museum-Salem's American Treasure at 1313 Mill St. S.E. The buildings are restored and furnished in period. Lee House and Parsonage (1841) are said to be the oldest remaining frame houses in the Pacific Northwest and were part of a Methodist mission that settled in the Salem area. The John D. Boon house (1847) was built by an early Oregon politician. The Pleasant Grove Church is said to be the oldest Presbyterian church in the state.

Allow 1 hour minimum. Guided tours Mon.-Sat. at 11, 1 and 3; phone ahead to verify times. Tour (includes admission to all Mission Mill Museum-Salem's American Treasure sites) $8; $7 (ages 55+ and students); $4 (ages 6-12); $24 (family). Phone (503) 585-7012.

Thomas Kay Woolen Mill is on the grounds of Mission Mill Museum-Salem's American Treasure at 1313 Mill St. S.E. The mill includes a restored, operating water-power turbine, operating loom and machine shop. Established in 1889, the mill demonstrates the process of converting fleece into woolen fabric and the importance of the mill to the community.

Allow 1 hour minimum. Self-guiding tours are offered Mon.-Sat. 10-4; call ahead to verify times. Mill tour (includes admission to all Mission Mill Museum-Salem's American Treasure sites) $8; $7 (ages 55+ and students); $4 (ages 6-12); $24 (family). DS, MC, VI. Phone (503) 585-7012.

PREWITT-ALLEN ARCHAEOLOGICAL MUSEUM is on the Corban College campus at 5000 Deer Park Dr. S.E. Exhibits contain Middle Eastern and Biblical artifacts, including replicas of the Rosetta Stone, the Code of Hammurabi of Babylon, and the Black Obelisk of Shalmanser. Other exhibits include falcon mummies and New Testament manuscripts. Mon.-Thurs. 7:45 a.m.-11 p.m., Fri. 7:45-6, Sat. 11-6, Sun. 3-11, Sept.-Apr.; Mon.-Fri. 8-5, rest of year. Free. Phone (503) 375-7016.

RIVERFRONT PARK is on the western edge of downtown along Front St., between Union and Ferry sts. The 23-acre park, formerly occupied by warehouses and industrial activities, features rolling, grassy lawns and paved paths. A bluff overlooks the Willamette River and Willamette Slough. At the southern end stands Eco Earth Globe, which used to be used by the Boise Cascade paper mill to hold acids that turned wood chips into pulp. The industrial relic's spherical surface is now decorated with nearly 86,000 colorful tiles to depict a globe. Salem's Riverfront Carousel features 42 brightly painted hand-carved horses, two wagons, a carousel band and a brass ring.

There also is an amphitheater, a covered pavilion, a children's play area and a boat dock. Picnicking is permitted. Food is available. Allow 1 hour minimum. Park daily 5 a.m.-midnight. Carousel Mon.-Thurs. 10-7, Fri.-Sat. 10-9, Sun. 11-6, June-Aug.; Mon.-Thurs. 10-6, Fri.-Sun. 11-5, rest of year. Carousel closed Thanksgiving. Park free. Carousel $1.50 (per ride). Phone (503) 588-6336 or (503) 540-0374 for the carousel.

A.C. Gilbert's Discovery Village is downtown at 116 Marion St. N.E., within Riverfront Park. The children's museum is housed in three historic homes and includes a 20,000-square-foot outdoor discovery center. All exhibits are hands-on with an emphasis on science, arts and humanities. Allow 2 hours minimum. Mon.-Sat. 10-5, Sun. noon-5; closed Jan. 1, Easter, Thanksgiving and Dec. 25. Admission $5.50; $4 (ages 60+); $2.50 (ages 1-2). Phone (503) 371-3631.

Willamette Queen departs from the public boat dock in Riverfront Park. One-hour Willamette River sightseeing excursions are offered on the 87-foot stern-wheeler, which is a smaller version of the types of boats that once operated on the Mississippi and Yukon rivers. Lunch, dinner and Sunday brunch cruises also are offered.

Departures require a minimum of 10 passengers. Sightseeing excursions depart Tues.-Sat. at 2, Sun. at 3:30. Phone ahead to verify schedule and for lunch, dinner and Sunday brunch cruise schedules. Sightseeing excursion fare $12; $6 (ages 4-10). Phone for lunch, dinner and Sunday brunch cruise fares. Reservations are required for all cruises. MC, VI. Phone (503) 371-1103.

STATE CAPITOL is between Court and State sts. The modern Greek marble structure was dedicated in 1938 and expanded in 1977. In addition to the Governor's Suite and the House and Senate chambers, the capitol is home to exhibits about history, rocks and minerals as well as art. The building's rotunda features four large Depression Era murals depicting significant events in the state's history. The bronze state seal in the floor of the rotunda lies 106 feet below the dome.

The building is topped with a 23-foot statue symbolic of the Oregon pioneers, and an elevated viewing platform offering views of the city sits at the base. The 30-minute Gold Pioneer tower tour includes a 121-step climb on a circular staircase around the inside of the rotunda.

Building open Mon.-Fri. 8-5 (also Sat. 9-4, July-Aug. and in Dec.). Guided 45-minute tours depart Mon.-Fri. on the hour 9-4, June-Sept.; reservation rest of year. Tower tours depart Mon.-Fri. on the hour 9-4, third week in Mar.-Sept. 30. Self-guiding walking tours are available year-round. Free. Phone (503) 986-1388.

WINERIES

- **Bethel Heights Vineyard** is at 6060 Bethel Heights Rd. N.W. Tues.-Sun. 11-5, May-Oct.; Sat.-Sun. 11-5, Mar.-Apr. and Nov.-Dec. Closed Easter, Thanksgiving and Dec. 25. Phone (503) 581-2262.

- **Honeywood Winery** is at 1350 Hines St. S.E. Mon.-Fri. 9-5, Sat. 10-5, Sun. 1-5; closed Jan. 1, Easter, Thanksgiving and Dec. 25. Phone (503) 362-4111 or (800) 726-4101.

SEAL ROCK (D-1) elev. 7'

Nearby Seal Rock Wayside State Park offers clamming, surf fishing, beachcombing, picnicking and an interpretive display at the scenic viewpoint.

Shopping areas: The small community of Seal Rock is known for craft shops that carry such wares as jewelry, ceramics, antiques and large chain saw-carved wood sculptures.

SEASIDE (A-1) pop. 5,900, elev. 15'

The state's oldest ocean resort community, Seaside has attracted vacationers since its first guest house was completed in the 1850s. The highlight is the Promenade, referred to locally as "The Prom."

The concrete structure was built in 1920 to replace a wooden boardwalk. Walkers, joggers and bicyclists make good use of the 1.8-mile path that parallels the Pacific Ocean. The sights include beach grass and dunes as well as nearby Tillamook Head and Tillamook Rock Lighthouse in the distance. Benches and coin-operated telescopes along the way invite you to take your time while absorbing the coastal views. Broadway, the town's main street, ends at the Prom's historic automobile turnaround.

The Prom offers access to the 3-mile beach, where you're likely to find more walkers, beachcombers, volleyball games and people flying kites than swimmers because the water temperature averages a chilly 55-65 F. At receding tides, beachcombers can find wonderful treasures; tide tables can be picked up from the Seaside Visitors Bureau and other area businesses. The Cove is a good spot for surfing, though. If you do brave the cold water for a dip or to surf, a wet suit is a must.

Bikers can pedal the Oregon Coast Bike Route, which follows scenic US 101 for the most part, offering views of the ocean as it traverses hills and temperate rain forests. The trail should be ridden north to south May through October due to strong northwesterly winds. The visitors bureau has brochures about the route. Canoeing, kayaking and paddleboating are possible on the Necanicum and Neawanna rivers. Quatat and Cartwright parks have boat ramps, and canoes, kayaks and paddleboats can be rented at Quatat Park. Other recreational opportunities include bird-watching, clamming, crabbing and fishing. For fishing license, season and limit information, phone the Oregon Department of Fish and Wildlife at (503) 947-6000. If you're up for a moderately difficult hike, head to the end of Sunset Boulevard to begin the 6-mile Tillamook Head National Recreation Trail (also part of Lewis and Clark National Historic Trail and the Oregon Coast Trail) between Seaside and Ecola State Park. It's a great place for bird-watching and whale watching. Whales inhabit the area all year, but from mid-March to mid-April and in December, additional migrating whales may be spotted.

Seaside and the local vicinity encompass the destination that Lewis and Clark and their Corps of Discovery were after on their 1804-06 westward journey, and the role this area played in their travels is kept alive. The expedition party wintered at nearby Fort Clatsop, and during that time several of the men were sent to build a salt cairn so they could boil the water from the ocean to extract salt for use in flavoring meat and preserving it through the winter and for their return trip. The site they selected is in Seaside, and a replica of what the stone fireplace structure is believed to have looked like is open year-round at the Salt Works, located just off the Prom at Lewis and Clark Way. The Salt Works site is part of Lewis and Clark National Historical Park *(see place listing p. 78)*. During a weekend in mid-August, reenactments are performed. Tillamook Head also factored into their stay that winter when Capt. Clark, Sacagawea and several others from the party traveled it to reach a beached whale to obtain meat and blubber. A bronze statue of Lewis and Clark and Lewis' dog Seaman stands at the center of the Prom's turnaround to commemorate the explorers' journey.

Seaside Visitors Bureau: 7 N. Roosevelt Dr., Seaside, OR 97138; phone (503) 738-3097 or (888) 306-2326.

Shopping areas: Broadway has a variety of specialty shops offering such items as apparel; crafts; kites; souvenirs; Northwest seafood; and candies, including chocolates, fudge and saltwater taffy. Seaside Antique Mall, at Broadway and Holladay streets, has nearly 90 dealers. Seaside Factory Outlet Center, on US 101, has more than 20 stores.

SEASIDE AQUARIUM is on 2nd Ave. at the Promenade. Exhibits feature marine life from the Oregon coast. Visitors can feed the seals and dip their hands in the touch tanks. Allow 30 minutes minimum. Open daily at 9; closing times vary, so call ahead. Admission $7; $5.75 (senior citizens); $3.50 (ages 6-13); $23 (family, up to six people). MC, VI. Phone (503) 738-6211.

SEASIDE MUSEUM AND HISTORICAL SOCIETY is at 570 Necanicum Dr., 4 blks. n. of 1st. Ave. Displays depict the history of Seaside and include Clatsop Indian items, Lewis & Clark salt makers, logging memorabilia and a working 1920s Linotype. The restored Butterfield Cottage adjacent to the museum depicts a 1912 beach cottage and rooming house. Mon.-Sat. 10-4, Sun. noon-3, May-Oct.; daily noon-3, rest of year. Closed major holidays. Admission $3; $2 (ages 62+); $1 (ages 7-18). Phone (503) 738-7065.

SILVERTON (C-3) pop. 7,414, elev. 249'

Silverton is nestled at the edge of the Silver Falls State Park *(see attraction listing)*, where its namesake Silver Creek makes its way to the Willamette Valley. Founded in 1854 as a saw milling town, Silverton is an important supply center for the surrounding farmland. Cooley's Gardens, 2 miles west on SR 213, is said to be one of the world's largest commercial iris growers; some 250 acres bloom in May and June.

Silverton Area Chamber of Commerce: 426 S. Water St., P.O. Box 257, Silverton, OR 97381; phone (503) 873-5615.

SAVE **FRANK LLOYD WRIGHT'S GORDON HOUSE,** 879 W. Main St., was designed in 1957 and built 1963-64; it was moved to Silverton in 2001 from nearby Wilsonville. It is the state's only building designed by Frank Lloyd Wright and the only one open to the public in the Pacific Northwest. The Usonian-style home has been restored and preserved as Wright designed it. Guided tours depart daily on the hour noon-4. Admission $5. Reservations are recommended (walk-in guests are only accepted if a tour has already been scheduled). MC, VI. Phone (503) 874-6006.

OREGON GARDEN is at 879 W. Main St.; from I-5 exit 260, 8 mi. e. on Chemawa Rd., 1.2 mi. s. on Howell Prairie Rd., 4.7 mi. e. on Silverton Rd., 5 mi. s. on Westfield Rd., then just s.w. to Main St. The 80-acre botanical display garden will eventually encompass 240 acres. Included are sensory, conifer, rose, children's, home demonstration and Northwest gardens in addition to wetlands, water features and an oak grove. A tram escorts guests around the grounds.

Food is available. Allow 2 hours minimum. Daily 10-6 (also Wed. and Sat. 7 a.m.-10 a.m.), May-Sept.; daily 10-4, rest of year. Admission (May-Sept.) $10; $9 (ages 60+); $8 (ages 8-17). Admission (Apr. and Oct.) $8; $7 (ages 60+); $6 (ages 8-17). Admission rest of year $5; $4 (ages 8-17 and 60+). AX, MC, VI. Phone (503) 874-8100 or (877) 674-2733.

GEM **SILVER FALLS STATE PARK** is 14 mi. s.e. on SR 214. Comprising 9,064 acres, this is Oregon's largest state park. The north and south forks of Silver Creek tumble over ancient basalt lava flows, forming a cluster of accessible waterfalls in a lush temperate rain forest setting. The 8.7-mile Trail of Ten Falls/Canyon Trail forms a loop passing each of the park's waterfalls. The trail leads behind four: the 177-foot South Falls, 93-foot Lower South Falls, the 106-foot Middle North Falls and the 136-foot North Falls. There are more than 25 miles of recreational trails for hiking, mountain biking and equestrian use, but not all the trails can accommodate all activities, so inquire before heading out.

The park's natural vegetation includes Douglas fir, western hemlock and bigleaf maple with an understory of salal, sword fern and Oregon grape. Pacific blacktail deer and 95 bird species inhabit the forest. Black bears, cougars and coyotes live in the park's remote reaches. South Falls Lodge, built by the Civilian Conservation Corps in the 1930s, contains furnishings crafted from only two Oregon myrtle trees.

Picnicking is permitted. Food is available. Allow 2 hours minimum. Daily dawn-dusk. Admission $3 (per private vehicle). Phone (503) 873-8681, ext. 31. *See Recreation Chart and the AAA Northwestern CampBook.*

SISTERS (E-7) pop. 959

The area around Sisters was a crossroads for American Indian travelers long before settlers from the Midwest and East arrived in the 19th century. John C. Frémont, guided by Kit Carson, passed through the region in 1843.

The snowcapped Three Sisters Peaks, originally called Faith, Hope and Charity, form the backdrop for the town of Sisters and the Deschutes National Forest *(see place listing p. 65)*. Western facades provide a frontier town flavor. The Hotel Sisters, one of the few original buildings still standing, has been restored and serves as a Western-style saloon and restaurant.

Sisters reputedly has the largest concentration of llamas in North America. Elk can be viewed at Patterson Ranch, on the west end of town, and llamas can be seen at Hinterland Ranch, east of town.

On the edge of the high desert, the community is at the major recreational crossroads of US 20 and SRs 126 and 242 connecting the Willamette Valley and central Oregon. The McKenzie Pass Scenic Highway *(see Willamette National Forest p. 125)* begins just west of town off US 20/SR 126. The road, open from early July through early October, offers panoramic views of the Cascades and nearby lava fields.

Sisters Area Chamber of Commerce: 291 E. Main Ave., Sisters, OR 97759; phone (541) 549-0251.

RECREATIONAL ACTIVITIES
Skiing

- **Hoodoo Ski Area** is 22 mi. w. on US 20, then just s. on access road, following signs. Write US 20, Box 20, Sisters, OR 97759. Sun.-Tues. and Thurs. 9-4, Fri.-Sat. 9-9, Thanksgiving-Easter (weather permitting). Phone (541) 822-3799, or (541) 822-3337 for snow information.

SIUSLAW NATIONAL FOREST

Elevations in the forest range from sea level at the Pacific Ocean to 4,097 ft. at Mary's Peak. Refer to AAA maps for additional elevation information.

Stretching from Tillamook to Coos Bay, the timbered slopes of the 630,000-acre Siuslaw National Forest meet the ocean and extend in sections along Oregon's shore. Beachcombing and fishing are allowed on 46 miles of public beach, and there are lakes and streams in the wooded areas. Hunting, boating, camping and picnicking are favorite pastimes. Day-use pass $5. *See Recreation Chart and the AAA Northwestern CampBook.*

If planning a multiple-day visit, an Oregon Coast Pacific Passport is recommended. For additional information contact the Forest Supervisor, Siuslaw National Forest, 4077 Research Way, Corvallis, OR 97333; phone (541) 750-7000.

CAPE PERPETUA VISITORS CENTER is 3 mi. s. of Yachats off US 101 within Siuslaw National Forest. A movie describes the natural forces that shaped the Oregon coast. Displays interpret the ecology and history of the area.

Nearby are the Devil's Churn and Cook's Chasm. Cape Perpetua Overlook, 2 miles off US 101, the highest point on the Oregon coast accessible by vehicle, provides an excellent view of the coast. The

giant spruce tree located on the Giant Spruce Trail has been designated as an Oregon Heritage Tree. Camping is available at Cape Perpetua from mid-May through September. Allow 30 minutes minimum. Interpretive center open daily 10-5:30, Memorial Day-Labor Day; 10-4, rest of year. Closed Thanksgiving and Dec. 25. Admission $5 (per private vehicle). Phone (541) 547-3289.

OREGON DUNES NATIONAL RECREATION AREA is between North Bend and Florence within Siuslaw National Forest. The 32,000-acre dunes encompass 40 miles of sand and average 250 feet in height. At its widest point the area extends inland about 2.5 miles. The Oregon Dunes day use area between Reedsport and Florence leads to observation platforms and hiking trails. Freshwater lakes are accessible from the area.

The visitors center, jct. US 1 and SR 38 in Reedsport, has displays and a movie about sand dunes. Picnicking is permitted. Day use area daily 7 a.m.-9 p.m., spring-fall; 7-7, during winter months. Visitor center daily 8-4:30, Memorial Day-Labor Day; Mon.-Fri., 8-4:30, rest of year. Day pass $5. Phone (541) 271-6000. *See Recreation Chart.*

SPRINGFIELD (E-3) pop. 52,864, elev. 472'

Springfield, separated from its sister city of Eugene by the Willamette River, has a diversified economy, including forest products, technology and medical services. It also is an access point to the McKenzie River, which offers fishing and whitewater rafting amid striking scenery. Island Park on the Willamette River and Willamalane Park are popular picnicking spots.

Shopping areas: The Gateway Mall, off I-5 at Harlow and Gateway streets, offers more than 80 stores, including Kohl's and Sears.

SPRINGFIELD MUSEUM is at 590 Main St. The museum is housed in a 1911 Oregon Power Co. substation. Changing art and antiques are exhibited in the Kathleen Jensen Gallery. An interpretive exhibit explores local history, logging, agriculture and contains photographs, tools and household items from the turn of the 20th century. Allow 30 minutes minimum. Tues.-Fri. 10-4, Sat. noon-4; closed major holidays and Dec. 24-Jan. 2. Admission $2; free (ages 0-18). Phone (541) 726-2300.

RECREATIONAL ACTIVITIES

White-water Rafting

• **Oregon Whitewater Adventures** is at 39620 Deerhorn Rd.; departure locations vary. Half-day, full-day and multiday guided paddle-raft trips are available on several rivers, including the McKenzie and North Umpqua. Trips are offered Apr.-Oct.; departure times vary. Phone (541) 746-5422 or (800) 820-7238.

SUNNY VALLEY (G-5) elev. 1,273'

SAVE **APPLEGATE TRAIL INTERPRETIVE CENTER** is off I-5 exit 71, then just e. to 500 Sunny Valley Loop (before the covered bridge). The

5,400-square-foot facility contains displays about the Applegate Trail (blazed as an alternate route to the more dangerous Oregon Trail), and the impact the Gold Rush, stage lines and railroad had on the area. Historical re-enactments take place in a 3-screen theater. A one-room log building, kiosks and grave sites are located near the Grave Creek Covered Bridge.

Allow 1 hour minimum. Daily 10-5, May 1-Nov. 1; Thurs.-Sun. 10-5, rest of year. Admission $5.95; $4.95 (ages 13-18 and 65+). AX, DS, MC, VI. Phone (541) 472-8545 or (888) 411-1846.

SUNRIVER (E-8)

Sunriver is a planned resort and residential community built among the pinewoods and meadows beside the Deschutes River. Development began in 1968 on the site of Camp Abbott, a World War II-era Army Corps of Engineers training facility. The 3,300-acre complex now has approximately 2,800 homes and more than 850 condominiums. There are visitors year-round, but in summer the population can grow to nearly 20,000.

The lone vestige of Sunriver's military legacy is the Great Hall, built in 1943 as a Corps of Engineers officers' club. It features native logs and stone and is an architectural showcase of Oregon's forest products heritage. Recently remodeled, the hall is now used for business meetings, corporate retreats and conventions.

Sunriver offers recreation activities for all tastes and capabilities. Golf is a big draw in summer. There are more than 35 miles of paved bike trails and many more for mountain bikes and hiking. Other summer activities include tennis (31 courts), horseback riding, river float trips, canoeing and kayaking. Fishing opportunities abound along the Deschutes River. Winter attracts cross-country skiers, and visitors can also enjoy snowmobiling, tobogganing, ice fishing and ice-skating.

Sunriver Area Chamber of Commerce: P.O. Box 3246, Sunriver, OR 97707; phone (541) 593-8149. The visitor center is in Village at Sunriver Building #5 at 57100 Beaver Dr.

SUNRIVER NATURE CENTER & OBSERVATORY is off Circle 3 at 57245 River Rd. Situated on 8 acres between Lake Aspen and the Deschutes River, the museum features exhibits describing the natural history of central Oregon, including a meteorite exhibit. A botanical garden contains more than 100 plant species, and a nature trail encounters birds of prey; signs identify native plants and wildlife. The observatory is available for solar viewing and nighttime star gazing.

Allow 30 minutes minimum. Nature center daily 9-5, Memorial Day weekend-Labor Day; Tues.-Sat. 10-4, rest of year. Phone for observatory schedule. Closed Jan. 1, Thanksgiving and Dec. 25. Admission to nature center (Memorial Day weekend-Labor Day) $3; $2 (ages 0-12). Admission (rest of year) $2; $1 (ages 0-12). Observatory programs $6; $4 (ages 0-12). Phone (541) 593-4394.

RECREATIONAL ACTIVITIES
Horseback Riding

- **Sunriver Stables** guided trail rides depart from 57215 River Rd. Rides last from 30 minutes to 8 hours. Other activities also are offered. Write P.O. Box 4220, Sunriver, OR 97707. Reservations are required. Daily 9-3, Mar.-Nov. (weather permitting). Phone (541) 593-6995.

RECREATIONAL ACTIVITIES
White-water Rafting

- **Sun Country Raft Tours** trips on the Upper Deschutes River depart from Village at Sunriver Building #10. Write 531 S.W. 13th St., Bend, OR 97702. Daily, May-Sept. Phone (541) 382-6277 or (800) 770-2161.

TERREBONNE (D-8) pop. 1,469, elev. 2,860′

SMITH ROCK STATE PARK is 3 mi. e. off US 97. The park offers scenic views of colorful cliffs above the Crooked River. Rock climbing, hiking and picnicking are popular activities. Daily dawn-dusk. Day-use permit $3. Phone (541) 548-7501 or (800) 551-6949. *See Recreation Chart.*

THE DALLES (C-8) pop. 12,156, elev. 96′

Lying on a great crescent bend of the Columbia River, The Dalles was an outgrowth of its location. The river narrows and once spilled over a series of rapids, which the French voyageurs christened *les dalles,* or "the trough."

American Indians and later fur traders found this natural break in navigation a convenient place for trade, a fact Lewis and Clark mentioned when describing it as "the great Indian mart of all this country."

Until 1845, when a wagon road was built, emigrants on the Oregon Trail could continue their journey only by floating their wagons down the treacherous Columbia. The rapids have since been submerged by the backwater of The Dalles Dam. A marker in City Park at 6th and Union streets commemorates the area where the overland route of the Oregon Trail ended 1843-46.

Much of The Dalles' past lingers in its many 19th-century homes and churches and in its museums. Scenic drives include a section of Historic Highway 30 between Mosier and The Dalles, and scenic I-84 bordering the Columbia from Troutdale to Boardman.

Recreational activities are available at nearby Deschutes River State Park *(see Recreation Chart and the AAA Northwestern CampBook),* where whitewater rafting and fishing are popular. The Columbia at The Dalles is a favorite area for sailboarding and fishing.

The Dalles Area Chamber of Commerce: 404 W. 2nd St., The Dalles, OR 97058; phone (541) 296-2231 or (800) 255-3385.

Self-guiding tours: Maps detailing a 45- to 60-minute self-guiding walking tour through historic downtown and residential areas are available from the chamber of commerce.

COLUMBIA GORGE DISCOVERY CENTER AND MUSEUM is off I-84 exit 82; take US 30 (Historic Columbia River Hwy.) 1.5 mi. n. to Discovery Dr., then n.e. This official interpretive center for the Columbia River Gorge National Scenic Area contains permanent exhibits illustrating the geologic creation of the Columbia Gorge and the varieties of wildlife and vegetation. The Wasco County Historical Museum details the county's history.

One exhibit demonstrates the amount, categorization and use of the nearly 30 tons of goods and equipment carried by the Lewis and Clark expedition. An Ice Age exhibit features a life-size 13-foot Columbian mammoth as well as interpretation about the role the Ice Age played in the population of the Americas. The Kids Explorer Room provides a hands-on learning experience. Wildlife can be seen year-round, and wildflowers are in bloom April through June.

The grounds offer paved trails, scenic overlooks and picnic areas. Food is available. Allow 1 hour minimum. Daily 9-5; closed Jan. 1, Thanksgiving and Dec. 25. Admission $8; $7 (senior citizens); $4 (ages 6-16). Grounds free. MC, VI. Phone (541) 296-8600.

FORT DALLES MUSEUM is at 500 W. 15th St. at Garrison St. Pioneer history exhibits are displayed in one of the last two remaining buildings of the fort, established in 1850. Three Swedish log buildings and a historic vehicle collection are on site. Allow 30 minutes minimum. Daily 10-5, Memorial Day weekend-Labor Day; otherwise varies. Admission $5; $4 (ages 55+); $1 (ages 7-17). Phone (541) 296-4547.

OLD ST. PETER'S LANDMARK is at W. 3rd and Lincoln sts. The 1897 red-brick Gothic church features a 170-foot-tall steeple topped by a 6-foot-tall rooster weather vane. Architectural highlights include 36 Povey Brothers stained-glass windows, a Madonna statue carved from the keel of an 1850s sailing ship and unusual lion's head water spouts. Carved Italian Carrara marble altars and pressed tin ceilings adorn the inside. The church's Kilgen pipe organ, installed in 1925, is made of rare tiger wood. Allow 30 minutes minimum. Tues.-Fri. 11-3, Sat.-Sun. 1-3, Feb.-Dec.; closed major holidays. Donations. Phone (541) 296-5686.

ORIGINAL WASCO COUNTY COURTHOUSE is at 410 W. 2nd Pl. Films are presented about the history of Wasco County, the Columbia Gorge and attractions in The Dalles area. Self-guiding walking tours of the downtown area begin at the 1859 building. Allow 30 minutes minimum. Wed.-Sat. 11-3, June-Aug.; guided tours by appointment year-round. Donations. Phone (541) 296-4798 for the courthouse or (541) 296-3359 for guided tours.

THE DALLES ART CENTER is at 220 E. 4th St. Formerly the Carnegie Library, the 1910 building contains changing exhibits and the work of local artists. Trees, brick paths, planters and benches adorn the grounds around the building. Allow 30 minutes minimum. Tues.-Sat. 11-5; closed Jan. 1, July 4, Thanksgiving and Dec. 25. Free. Phone (541) 296-4759.

THE DALLES DAM VISITOR CENTER is n. of I-84 exit 87 on US 197, then e. on Lonepine Rd. The differing opinions that industry, farmers, recreationists, fishers and American Indians have about The Dalles Dam and Lock are presented with recorded comments. There are interactive displays and a 7-minute video about the dam as well as a live camera view of the fish ladder. There also is a turn-of-the-20th-century rose garden on the grounds. Picnicking is permitted. Daily 9-5, May-Sept. Guided 30-minute tours are available by request. Free. Phone (541) 296-9778.

TILLAMOOK (B-1) pop. 4,352, elev. 22'

Tillamook's lush grasses, nurtured by 72-90 inches of rain a year, sustain the herds that compose Oregon's dairy industry. Much of the county's annual milk production of 25 million gallons is made into natural cheddar cheese.

In addition to its agricultural importance, Tillamook is a major recreation center. Charter boats for crabbing and deep-sea fishing are available 10 miles north in Garibaldi. Beachcombing, clamming, and jetty, river and surf fishing are popular activities at the beach areas 9 miles west of town. Hiking, hang gliding, scuba diving, windsurfing, kayaking and canoeing also are among the area's recreational opportunities.

A scenic section of US 101 passes through Tillamook and connects with SR 6, which runs through the Tillamook State Forest from Portland.

Tillamook Area Chamber of Commerce: 3705 N. US 101, Tillamook, OR 97141; phone (503) 842-7525.

LATIMER QUILT AND TEXTILE CENTER is 1 mi. n. of jct. SR 6 and US 101 at 2105 Wilson River Loop Rd. This 1930s converted schoolhouse features a textile gallery with changing exhibits, a research library with out-of-print patterns and books, a quilting room, a spinning and weaving room, and handcrafted gifts. Visitors can view artists at work. Allow 30 minutes minimum. Daily 10-5, May-Sept.; Tues.-Fri. 10-4, Sat. and some Sun. noon-4, rest of year. Admission $3; free (ages 0-5). Phone (503) 842-8622.

THREE CAPES ROAD is a 38.5-mile drive running w. to the ocean, then s. along the coast, rejoining US 101 s. of Cloverdale. The road passes the towns of Capes Meares, Oceanside, Netarts, Cape Lookout, Tierra del Mar, Cape Kiwanda and Pacific City. The Cape Meares Lighthouse and the Octopus Tree, a large Sitka spruce used by American Indians as a burial tree, are along the route at Cape Meares.

TILLAMOOK AIR MUSEUM is at 6030 Hangar Rd. The museum features one of the country's top private collections of more than 40 World War II aircraft. It is home to a former blimp hangar that served as a U.S. Navy air station for Lighter-Than-Air (LTA) anti-submarine activities during World War II. The planes are housed in one of the world's largest clear span wood buildings. An exhibit hall contains photographs of the hangar construction, wartime memorabilia as well as rare aviation artifacts, including a World War II Luftwaffe flight jacket and remains from the German airship *Hindenburg*.

Certain aircraft are occasionally used in air shows or require maintenance, and during these times they are not available for viewing. Allow 1 hour minimum. Daily 9-5; closed Thanksgiving and Dec. 25. Admission $11.50; $10.50 (ages 65+); $7 (ages 6-17). MC, VI. Phone (503) 842-1130.

TILLAMOOK COUNTY CREAMERY ASSOCIATION (TILLAMOOK CHEESE) is 2 mi. n. on US 101. A self-guiding tour includes interactive kiosks, video presentations, an observation area and historical displays. Food is available. Allow 1 hour minimum. Daily 8-8, mid-June through Labor Day; 8-6, rest of year. Free. Phone (503) 815-1300 or (800) 542-7290.

TILLAMOOK COUNTY PIONEER MUSEUM is at 2nd St. and Pacific Ave. (US 101). Three floors of exhibits, housed within a former 1905 courthouse, include wildlife dioramas, a mineral room, a logging display, a doll collection, a blacksmith shop, a Victorian bedroom and items relating to pioneer, American Indian, military and natural history. A steam donkey, a large steam engine used for logging operations, also is on the grounds. The museum also has a research library with genealogical information.

Allow 1 hour, 30 minutes minimum. Tues.-Sat. 9-5, Sun. 11-5; closed major holidays. Admission $3; $2 (ages 63+); 50c (ages 12-17); $7 (family). Phone (503) 842-4553.

TILLAMOOK FOREST CENTER, 45500 Wilson River Hwy., educates visitors about the Tillamook Forest's history. Displays include a well-preserved steam donkey machine used for hauling logs and replicas of a homesteader's cabin, a train station, a stage coach stop and a logging camp. The Tillamook Burn Theater demonstrates the power of a forest fire. Naturalists present interactive talks and guided walks on a variety of forest topics, which feature a 250-foot-long suspension bridge and a fire tower.

Allow 1 hour, 30 minutes minimum. Daily 10-5, Memorial Day-Labor Day; Wed.-Sun. 10-4, rest of year. Hours may vary; call ahead. Free. Phone (503) 815-6800 or (866) 930-4646.

TIMBERLINE LODGE (C-7) elev. 6,060'

Timberline Lodge is a recreation and resort center on the southern flank of Mount Hood. Its name describes the transition zone where alpine forests of spruce, fir and pine yield to alpine meadows and treeless rock and talus slopes. The namesake alpine resort hotel, built in the mid-1930s, has Cascadian-style architecture featuring local stone and wood with intricate American Indian and pioneer motifs. In clear weather the view extends southward more than 120 miles to Mount Jefferson, the Three Sisters and beyond.

Mount Hood is the country's most-climbed glacier peak. Climbers typically set out for the 8-hour round trip from Timberline Lodge. Climbing equipment and special precautions are necessary. The required free wilderness permit is available at Timberline's Wy'East Day Lodge. Check with the Forest Service for more information; phone (503) 668-1700 or (503) 622-3191.

Timberline receives between 500 and 600 inches of snow in an average year and is the only place in North America where alpine skiing is practiced year round.

RECREATIONAL ACTIVITIES

Skiing

• SAVE **Timberline Ski Resort** is at US 26 and Timberline Rd. Write Timberline Lodge, OR 97028. Daily 9-4, Sept. 1-late Mar.; 7-2, rest of year. Schedule may vary; call ahead. Phone (503) 622-7979, or (503) 222-2211 for weather updates.

TROUTDALE—*see Portland p. 108.*

TURNER (C-3) pop. 1,199

SAVE **ENCHANTED FOREST** is off I-5 exit 248 at 8462 Enchanted Way S.E. Rides and storybook characters are featured in a wooded setting. A re-created early mining town, Old World village, bobsleds, a log flume ride, a roller coaster, interactive target shooting, a haunted house, summer comedy theater and a water/light show also are included.

Allow 2 hours minimum. Daily 10-5, mid-Mar. through Mar. 31 and May 1-Labor Day; Sat.-Sun. 10-6, day after Labor Day-Sept. 30 and in Apr. Hours may vary; call ahead. Last admission 30 minutes before closing. Admission $9.75; $8.75 (ages 62+ and ages 3-12). Additional fee for ride tickets. DS, MC, VI. Phone (503) 363-3060 or (503) 371-4242.

WINERIES

• **Willamette Valley Vineyards** is off I-5 exit 248 at 8800 Enchanted Way S.E. Tours by appointment daily 11-6; closed Jan. 1, Thanksgiving and Dec. 25. Phone (503) 588-9463 or (800) 344-9463.

UMATILLA (B-9) pop. 4,978, elev. 294'

Founded as Umatilla Landing in 1864, Umatilla sprang up virtually overnight as an important trade and shipping center during the gold rush. This was primarily due to its key location at the confluence of the Umatilla and Columbia rivers. Local records report that at one time during the rush, 13 buildings were erected within 4 days. Just 6 months after its founding, Umatilla had more than 100 buildings, 25 stores and two hotels. The town remained a major shipping center until the 1880s, when the construction of the Oregon Railway and Navigation Line diverted traffic and trade.

Umatilla Chamber of Commerce: 1530 6th St., P.O. Box 67, Umatilla, OR 97882; phone (541) 922-4825.

MCNARY LOCK AND DAM is 1 mi. e. of jct. I-82 and US 730. The dam is part of the vast inland waterway system of the Columbia and Snake rivers. Of interest are the Pacific Salmon Visitor Information Center, locks, fish ladder, fish viewing room and nature trail. A boat ramp is available; fishing is permitted. The visitor center offers audiovisual programs and talks on salmon and hydropower.

Self-guiding tours of the grounds can be taken daily dawn-dusk. Visitor center and Pacific Salmon Visitor Information Center daily 9-5. Free. Phone (541) 922-2268. *See Recreation Chart.*

UMATILLA NATIONAL WILDLIFE REFUGE is reached via US 730 (between the towns of Irrigon and Boardman), then n. 2 mi. on Paterson Ferry Rd. The refuge's 25,347 acres of wetlands, open waters, uplands and croplands attract large concentrations of birds, including waterfowl and bald eagles. A large herd of mule deer is among the resident wildlife. Allow 1 hour minimum. Daily 5 a.m.-dusk. Free. Phone (509) 546-8300.

UMATILLA NATIONAL FOREST

Elevations in the forest range from 1,600 ft. in Troy to 8,131 ft. at Vinegar Hill. Refer to AAA maps for additional elevation information.

Extending from northeast Oregon into the southeastern corner of Washington, Umatilla National Forest encompasses 1.4 million acres in four ranger districts. Its name is derived from an American Indian word meaning "water rippling over sand." The highest point in the forest, at 8,131 feet, lies within the Vinegar Hill/Indian Rock Scenic Area. A drive to Indian Rock Lookout offers a view of the subalpine area.

Trips along the summit of the Blue Mountains on the primitive Kendall-Skyline, the paved Blue Mountain National Scenic Byway and the gravel Summit Road offer panoramic views. More than 2,000 miles of other forest roads offer wildlife viewing opportunities for visitors. Although these roads provide roadside viewpoints into the wilderness, travel within the wilderness areas is served by many trails and can be toured only by foot or horseback.

There are ample opportunities for winter sports as well as fishing, hunting, hiking and pack-and-saddle trips. Many picnic and camping areas are provided.

The Wenaha-Tucannon Wilderness, 177,465 acres astride the Oregon-Washington border in the northern Blue Mountains, is characterized by rugged basaltic ridges and deep canyons. Two additional wilderness areas are the North Fork Umatilla

Wilderness encompassing 20,144 acres, and the North Fork John Day Wilderness, which stretches over 121,800 acres.

For further information or to obtain a permit contact Umatilla National Forest, 2517 S.W. Hailey Ave., Pendleton, OR 97801; phone (541) 278-3716. *See Recreation Chart and the AAA Northwestern CampBook.*

UMPQUA (F-2)

WINERIES

- **Henry Estate Winery** is off I-5 exit 136, following signs to 687 Hubbard Creek Rd. Daily 11-5; closed holidays and last Sun. in Jan. Phone (541) 459-5120 or (800) 782-2686.

UMPQUA NATIONAL FOREST

Elevations in the forest range from 1,120 ft. where the North Umpqua River leaves the forest to 9,182 ft. at Mount Thielsen. Refer to AAA maps for additional elevation information.

Umpqua National Forest is 33 miles east of Roseburg on SR 138, stretching from Cottage Grove in the north to Tiller in the south. Offering something for nearly every outdoor enthusiast, the 984,602-acre forest has miles of trails winding through hills and valleys covered with Douglas fir and western hemlock. The Pacific Crest National Scenic Trail runs from Windigo Pass to Crater Lake. The 79-mile North Umpqua Trail winds from the High Cascades to Glide.

The Diamond Lake Recreation Area is dominated by Diamond Lake, flanked to the east by Mount Thielsen and to the west by Mount Bailey. The Rogue Umpqua National Scenic Byway (SR 138), called the Highway of Waterfalls, parallels the North Umpqua River, providing a 172-mile scenic drive from Roseburg to Diamond Lake.

The three wilderness areas in the forest are Boulder Creek Wilderness, a 19,100-acre area important as an old-growth, timbered watershed of the North Umpqua River; the Rogue-Umpqua Divide Wilderness, a 26,350-acre area noted for its interesting geologic formations and extensive trail system; and the Mount Thielsen Wilderness, part of the Oregon Cascade Recreation Area totaling 21,593 acres.

Fishing for steelhead trout is popular in the forest's many streams and rivers. Saddle trips can be taken. Cross-country skiing and snowmobiling trails are open in the winter. For further information contact Umpqua National Forest, 2900 N.W. Stewart Pkwy., Roseburg, OR, 97470; phone (541) 672-6601, or TTY (541) 957-3459. *See Recreation Chart and the AAA Northwestern CampBook.*

UNION (C-11) pop. 1,926, elev. 2,717'

Many Victorian homes have been preserved in Union, including Wildwood, an 1869 Gothic mansion at Main and Bryan streets. Several 19th-century red-brick buildings line Main Street.

SAVE **UNION COUNTY MUSEUM** is at 33 S. Main St. Permanent exhibits include the Cowboys Then & Now collection, which highlights the history of cowboys and cattle in North America. Other displays describe the natural and cultural history of the county. A living room, bedroom, kitchen and school room are furnished in period. Mon.-Sat. 10-4, Mother's Day to mid-Oct. Admission $4; $3 (ages 60+); $2 (students with ID); free (ages 0-5). Phone (541) 562-6003.

VALE (E-12) pop. 1,976, elev. 2,400'

STONE HOUSE MUSEUM is at 255 Main St. The impressive sandstone building served as a significant stop along the Oregon Trail. Originally a hotel, it opened in 1873 and later became a stagecoach station. Restored, it now contains period relics and interpretive exhibits about the Oregon Trail and the development of Malheur County. Allow 30 minutes minimum. Tues.-Sat. noon-4, May 1 (weather permitting) to mid-Oct. Donations. Phone (541) 473-2070.

WALDPORT (D-1) pop. 2,050

At the mouth of the Alsea River, Waldport is popular with saltwater and freshwater anglers. The coastline on both sides of Alsea Bay varies from smooth sandy beaches to rugged rocky formations.

Several nearby state parks offer hiking, agate hunting, clamming and crabbing. Many of these parks can be found along the scenic stretch of US 101, which travels along the Pacific Coast from California into Washington. Just east of Waldport is Drift Creek Wilderness Area, which offers untouched old-growth forest for hikers.

The Alsea Bay Interpretive Center, 620 N.W. Spring St., offers exhibits outlining the history and development of various bridges connecting the Oregon coastline; phone (541) 563-2002.

Waldport Chamber of Commerce: 620 N.W. Spring St., P.O. Box 669, Waldport, OR 97394; phone (541) 563-2133.

WALLOWA (C-11) pop. 869

EAGLE CAP EXCURSION TRAIN is at E. 4th and N. Storie sts. Passengers ride in restored train cars on leisurely trips through Northeastern Oregon. Excursions pass through rugged canyons, along scenic rivers and across the Wallowa Valley. An additional train travels from Elgin to Minam along the Grande Ronde and Wallowa rivers.

Allow 4 hours minimum. Departures on Sat., May-Oct. Departure time depends on excursion selected; phone ahead. Seasonal tours also are available. Admission (varies by excursion type) $45-$65; $40-$55 (ages 60+); $20 (ages 3-16). Reservations are recommended. Phone (800) 323-7330 for reservations.

WALLOWA LAKE (C-11)

Rich in American Indian lore and legend, beautiful Wallowa Lake is at the foothills of the steep, forested mountains at the upper end of Wallowa Valley. Near the north end of the lake is the grave of Chief Joseph, leader of the Nez Perce, whose son Joseph battled the U.S. Army after the elder Joseph's death.

The 4-mile-long lake is the center of a popular recreational region. Horseback pack trips in the High Wallowas can be arranged. At the lake's southern tip is Wallowa Lake State Park *(see Recreation Chart and Joseph in the AAA Northwestern CampBook)*.

WALLOWA LAKE TRAMWAY—*see Joseph p. 76.*

WALLOWA-WHITMAN NATIONAL FOREST

Elevations in the forest range from 800 ft. at Hell's Canyon along the Snake River to 9,838 ft. at Sacajawea Peak. Refer to AAA maps for additional elevation information.

Extending from the Blue Mountains in the southwest to the Grande Ronde and Powder rivers, over the Wallowa Mountains to the Snake River and over the Seven Devils Mountains in western Idaho, Wallowa-Whitman National Forest encompasses 2,392,160 acres.

Varied scenery characterizes the area, which contains snowcapped peaks, rushing mountain streams, timbered slopes and canyons. Travel in the Eagle Cap Wilderness Area, 358,461 acres of rugged beauty, is limited to foot or horseback. The Hells Canyon National Recreation Area *(see place listing p. 72)* is within the forest.

Skiing, snowmobiling, fishing, boating, hunting, camping and picnicking opportunities are available. Horse rentals and commercial guided tours are available from Forest Service permitted outfitters. For further information contact the Forest Supervisor, Wallowa-Whitman National Forest, 3285 11th St., P.O. Box 907, Baker City, OR 97814; phone (541) 523-4476. *See Recreation Chart and the AAA Northwestern CampBook.*

WARM SPRINGS (D-8)
pop. 2,431, elev. 1,574'

Warm Springs is on SR 26 in the Warm Springs Indian Reservation. The 640,000 acres of the reservation are occupied by the Warm Springs, Wasco and Paiute tribes. Self-guiding tours of the Warm Springs National Fish Hatchery, 13 miles northwest on SR 3, are available.

[SAVE] **THE MUSEUM AT WARM SPRINGS** is at 2189 SR 26. Exhibits from the Warm Springs, Wasco and Paiute Indian tribes include ceremonial clothing, drums, tools, murals, reconstructed mat houses and an art gallery featuring indigenous art. Allow 1 hour minimum. Daily 9-5, Mar.-Oct.; Wed.-Sun. 9-5, rest of year. Closed Jan. 1, Thanksgiving and Dec. 25. Admission $7; $6 (ages 60+); $3 (ages 5-12). DS, MC, VI. Phone (541) 553-3331.

WARRENTON (A-1) pop. 4,096, elev. 7'

Platted in 1891 through the efforts of founder Daniel Knight Warren, Warrenton was built mostly on tidal flats. A system of dikes constructed by Chinese laborers in 1878-79 keeps the town dry. Many boats moored nearby offer charter fishing trips and tours of the Columbia River.

Shopping areas: Specialty retail and gift shops can be found at Youngs Bay Shopping Center near US 101 and Harbor Road.

FORT STEVENS STATE PARK is off US 101 at 100 Peter Iredale Rd., following signs. The park is part of Lewis and Clark National Historical Park *(see place listing p. 78)*. The coastal campground park is near the mouth of the Columbia River. Fort Stevens protected the entrance to the Columbia River from the Civil War through World War II. The *Peter Iredale*, a British Bark that shipwrecked in 1906, is visible at low tide. Clamming is permitted in season; state license required.

Daily dawn-dusk. Day-use fee $3 (per private vehicle). Phone (503) 861-1671 or (800) 551-6949, or (800) 452-5687 for reservations. *See Recreation Chart.*

Fort Stevens Historical Area and Military Museum is off US 101 at 100 Peter Iredale Rd., within Fort Stevens State Park. The museum includes a war games building, gun batteries and a guardhouse. During the summer guided tours of the installation are offered in a military truck; underground bunker tours also are available.

Allow 1 hour, 30 minutes minimum. Daily 10-6, June-Sept.; 10-4, rest of year. Museum accepts donations. Underground bunker tour $4; $2 (ages 3-12). Military truck tour $4; $2 (ages 3-12). Parking $3. Phone (503) 861-2000.

WILLAMETTE NATIONAL FOREST

Elevations in the forest range from 1,155 ft. at Winberry Creek to 10,358 ft. at South Sister Peak. Refer to AAA maps for additional elevation information.

In western Oregon, Willamette National Forest covers 1,675,407 acres of high mountain country. The forest is known for its outstanding natural features and diverse outdoor recreation opportunities. Access is limited to horse or foot travel in some parts, including the Mount Jefferson, Mount Washington, Three Sisters, Middle Santiam, Waldo Lake, Menagerie, Bull of the Woods and Diamond Peak wildernesses.

With more than 1,400 miles of trails and over 80 campgrounds, the forest provides ample recreational opportunities, including hiking and camping. The forest is open to hunting and fishing in regular seasons. Big game animals include elk, bears and deer; fishing enthusiasts can find several varieties of trout in the many lakes and streams.

Four wilderness areas have extensive volcanic formations. The Pacific Crest National Scenic Trail winds along the summit of the Cascades through wilderness areas, offering scenic vistas of waterfalls and mountain lakes.

Self-guiding tour cassette tapes of the Aufderheide Scenic Byway are available free of charge from the Middle Fork ranger district office on SR 58, (541) 782-2283, and the McKenzie River ranger district office on McKenzie Highway, (541) 822-3381. The drive is about 70 miles in length. Visitors should call the office before beginning their trip as weather and snow conditions at high elevations may be different from those on the valley floor.

The Hoodoo and Willamette Pass ski areas provide many skiing opportunities, and snowmobile areas are located near Willamette Pass on Waldo Lake Road and near Big Lake just off Santiam Pass on Highway 20. For further information contact the Forest Supervisor, Willamette National Forest, 3110 Pierce Pkwy., Springfield, OR 97477; phone (541) 225-6300. *See Recreation Chart and the AAA Northwestern CampBook.*

McKENZIE PASS SCENIC HIGHWAY (SR 242) traverses between Belknap Springs and Sisters. The road snakes across 5,324-foot McKenzie Pass. Excellent views of the Three Sisters, Mount Washington, Mount Jefferson and other volcanic formations can be seen from Dee Wright Observatory, at the summit.

Lava fields at the summit constitute one of the larger, more recent flows in the country. The .5-mile, marked Lava River Interpretive Trail explains the geological phenomena of the area. The highway is not suitable for trailers. Phone ahead before beginning your trip as weather and snow conditions at high elevations may be different from those found on the valley floor. Open early July early Oct. Free. Phone (541) 822-3381.

McKENZIE RIVER AREA is e. of Springfield. The river is noted by anglers for its rainbow trout. About 1.5 miles east of McKenzie Bridge is the 26-mile McKenzie River National Recreation Trail, accessed from SR 126. From McKenzie Bridge, SR 126 veers northward at Belknap Springs and follows the Upper McKenzie River to its headwaters at Clear Lake. At its north end is a submerged forest, inundated more than a millennium ago when a lava flow dammed the canyon. Boat rentals (motors prohibited) and campsites are available.

Note: Only very experienced rafters should attempt to raft the river without the assistance of a guide. A voluntary registration system is in place for those who attempt to navigate the river on their own. Phone (541) 822-3381 for more details and additional safety information.

WALDO LAKE RECREATION AREA is 70 mi. e. of Eugene, with access via a 12-mile paved road from SR 58. The 6,420-acre lake has three campgrounds on the east shore. Waldo Lake Wilderness Area, 37,157 acres, is to the north, west and south of the lake. Gas-powered boats are permitted. The area is normally accessible July-Oct. (weather permitting). Phone (541) 782-2283.

WINEMA NATIONAL FOREST—
see Fremont-Winema National Forests p. 69.

WINSTON (G-2) pop. 4,613, elev. 528'

SAVE **WILDLIFE SAFARI**, 1790 Safari Rd., is a 600-acre drive-through zoological park featuring exotic animals roaming freely in natural surroundings. Live animal programs as well as elephant and train rides are featured seasonally. Safari Village offers a small petting zoo; food is available. More than a dozen animal encounter activities, including animal feedings and elephant bathings, are offered for additional fees.

No convertibles are permitted in the bear drive-through. Pet kennels are available. Food is available. Allow 1 hour, 30 minutes minimum. Park daily 9-5, early Mar. through Nov. 1; daily 10-4, rest of year. Closed Dec. 25. Phone ahead to confirm schedule. Admission (Memorial Day weekend-Labor Day) $17.99; $14.99 (ages 60+); $11.99 (ages 4-12). Admission (rest of year) $14.99; $11.99 (ages 60+); $8.99 (ages 4-12). Phone ahead to verify rates. AX, DS, MC, VI. Phone (541) 679-6761.

WOLF CREEK (G-5) elev. 1,293′

WOLF CREEK INN is off I-5 exit 76 in the center of town at 100 Front St. The inn has been in almost continuous operation since it was built as a stagecoach inn on the Oregon Territorial Road in the early 1880s. The classical revival-style building has been restored and furnished in different periods to reflect the changing character of the inn over the decades. Guided tours are available by request. Food is available Thurs.-Sun. Allow 30 minutes minimum. Self-guiding tours Thurs.-Sun. 9:30-5, Mon.-Wed. 9:30-noon. Free. Phone (541) 866-2474.

YACHATS (D-1) pop. 617

Yachats (YAH-hahts) is a small village nestled between lush forested mountains and dramatic Pacific surf. Uncrowded beaches are ideal for agate hunting, beachcombing, fishing, picnicking or strolling. The area offers a diverse selection of trails for hikers and mountain bikers of all levels; trails range from difficult to wheelchair accessible. Along the oceanfront, visitors can discover rocky promontories and observe dramatic surf, especially during winter storms occurring December through February.

The nearby Yachats River is a popular spot for salmon and steelhead fishing. Just south of town is Cape Perpetua *(see Siuslaw National Forest p. 118)*, the highest point on the Oregon coast. It offers a dramatic ocean view from its 800-foot-high stone lookout. The U.S. Forest Service operates an interpretive center and campground at Cape Perpetua and maintains 26 miles of hiking trails that lead past old-growth temperate rain forest, tide pools and the beach.

Yachats Visitors Center & Chamber of Commerce: 241 US 101, P.O. Box 728, Yachats, OR 97498; phone (541) 547-3530 or (800) 929-0477.

LITTLE LOG CHURCH & MUSEUM is 1 blk. w. of US 101 at the corner of W. Third and Pontiac sts. The church, constructed 1929-30, is on the original site. The structure contains the original windows, pews, organ and carved pulpit. An annex houses historic exhibits and works of local artists and writers. Allow 30 minutes minimum. Fri.-Wed. noon-3. Donations. Phone (541) 547-3976.

Washington

The Evergreen State

Firs, pines and hemlocks bedeck the slopes of Washington's hills

Take Your Umbrella

Some of the areas in the Olympic Peninsula are among the rainiest places on Earth

Two for the Price of One

In Washington you can enjoy ocean coastlines as well as mountain peaks

Northwestern Cuisine

The state is well-known for its salmon, but don't forget Washington's apples and wines

Parks and Forests

Three national parks and six national forests lie completely within Washington's borders

Mount Vernon
© William Neill
Larry Ulrich Stock

Mount Rainier National Park / © SIME s.a.s. / eStock Photo

Washington: The Evergreen State.

The nickname derives from an abundance of forestland, but there's a good chance that your neighbors will be "ever green" as they envy your exploration of this awe-inspiring state.

Venture underground to pass through lava tubes and limestone caves or climb high above the horizon line on the face of a majestic mountain.

Check out the breathtaking view of the Pacific Ocean and Tatoosh Island from the scenic overlook at Cape Flattery near Neah Bay.

Observe impressive specimens: Puget Sound octopuses that weigh upwards of 300 pounds, Pacific Giant salamanders

that grow to more than a foot in length, a Douglas fir that exceeds 200 feet in height at Queets Rain Forest in Olympic National Park.

Drive along the hard sandy beach at Long Beach Peninsula or across the world's longest floating bridge, Evergreen Point, which spans Lake Washington in Seattle.

Hike up the trailhead west of White River Campground near Sunrise to view the enormous Emmons Glacier, one of 26 that extend down Mount Rainier. Schuss down the runs at ski areas in Wenatchee National Forest.

Whatever activities fill your plate, Washington will satisfy your appetite for adventure.

Washington is a book that refuses to be confined by the definition of a single genre. It incorporates history, drama and romance while dabbling in mystery and adventure. Compelling and sharp, it appeals to a broad audience.

An American Indian heritage dates back thousands of years. Many cities share their names with tribes: Chinook, Colville, Nooksack, Okanogan, Puyallup, Quinault, Spokane, Walla Walla and Yakima.

The Indian influence lingers in reservations in Marysville, Neah Bay, Taholah and Toppenish. Petroglyphs near Clarkston, Dallesport, Snoqualmie, Spokane and Yakima depict the natives' experiences.

The state's modern history hinges on a single event: the Klondike gold rush of 1897. Washington's role as a gateway to the north did two things. First, it forged a harmonious relationship between Canada and the United States. The Peace Arch, on I-5 at the border near Blaine, commemorates this amity. Second, it introduced legions of fortune seekers to the state's scenic appeal.

Although few hit the proverbial mother lode in Alaska and the Great White North, they did find a genuine treasure in the ruggedly handsome Evergreen State.

The dramatic snowcapped peaks of the mighty Cascades pierce clouds as they stretch high into the sky. The petrified wood of ginkgo trees, dating back 15 million years, is a sight to behold at Ginkgo Petrified Forest State Park in Vantage.

Subterranean exploration comes in two categories: lava and limestone. Tubes tunnel through massive lava flows at Ape Cave Geologic Site. Limestone stalagmites and stalactites are the predominant features at Gardner Cave in Crawford State Park in the state's northeast corner.

Massive dams—Bonneville, Grand Coulee, Rocky Reach—harness the power of the Columbia River, along which photographers perch to snap colorful pictures of windsurfers' vibrant sails dotted across the water's surface.

In the Mood for Love

Wine and roses provide a hint of romance. Vineyards proliferate in the Yakima and Walla Walla valleys. The delicate fragrance of rosebuds in bloom penetrates the atmosphere at Woodland Park Rose Garden in Seattle and Point Defiance Park in Tacoma.

Contemporary couples may find that certain *je ne sais quoi* in a variation on that

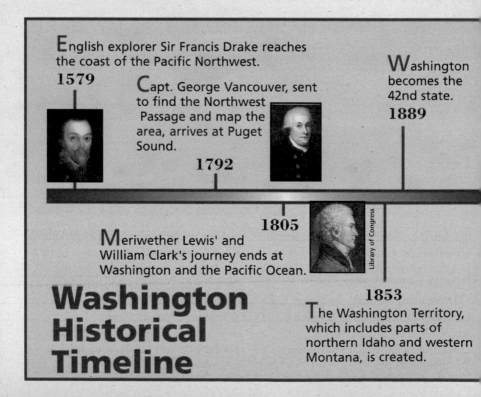

English explorer Sir Francis Drake reaches the coast of the Pacific Northwest.

1579

Capt. George Vancouver, sent to find the Northwest Passage and map the area, arrives at Puget Sound.

1792

Washington becomes the 42nd state.

1889

1805

Meriwether Lewis' and William Clark's journey ends at Washington and the Pacific Ocean.

Library of Congress

Washington Historical Timeline

1853

The Washington Territory, which includes parts of northern Idaho and western Montana, is created.

theme: breweries and bulb flowers. You can sample varieties of beer and ale at breweries in Woodinville and Seattle. Displays of daffodils, tulips and hyacinths blanket Roozengaarde in Mount Vernon and Van Lierop Bulb Farm in Puyallup.

There are other ways to capture that warm, fuzzy feeling. Feel the sand between your toes as you admire a technicolor sunset on the beaches of the Long Beach Peninsula or Ocean Shores. Paddle a raft down the Skagit River and admire soaring bald eagles. Cruise the San Juan Islands to catch a glimpse of orca and minke whales, porpoises and harbor seals.

Full of Fascinating Secrets

Washington has its share of intriguing mysteries. Although Mount St. Helens has been quiet since a turbulent 1980 awakening, subtle occurrences suggest that it's napping with one eye open.

Two petroglyphs found in the Columbia River Gorge—each of which shows a figure in an elaborate headdress with a feisty dog at his side—are believed to be of Peruvian Moche warriors. How the artist and subject would have met baffles researchers.

The name given to Mystery Bay Recreation Area is fitting. During Prohibition alcohol smugglers dodged U.S. Coast Guard ships by ducking their shallow draft boats beneath overhanging trees in the bay's north end. Puzzled by the smugglers' disappearances, Coast Guard members gave the harbor its apropos appellation.

A curious flame at Flaming Geyser State Park in Auburn once generated enough interest to warrant a feature on "Ripley's Believe It or Not!" The 8-inch flame—produced when methane gas rising from an old coal test hole is ignited—once burned several feet high.

If adventure fuels your fire, you're in the right place. Explore Gifford Pinchot National Forest via a llama pack trek, fly over magnificent Mount Rainier, or let your financial well-being hinge on the whim of a casino's one-armed bandit.

Indeed, there is a lot to love about Washington, the only state named for a president. Much like a literary classic, once it's in your grasp, you'll have a hard time letting go.

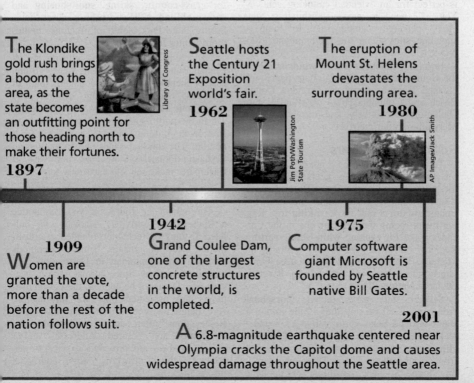

The Klondike gold rush brings a boom to the area, as the state becomes an outfitting point for those heading north to make their fortunes.
1897

Library of Congress

Seattle hosts the Century 21 Exposition world's fair.
1962

Jim Poth/Washington State Tourism

The eruption of Mount St. Helens devastates the surrounding area.
1980

AP Images/Jack Smith

1909
Women are granted the vote, more than a decade before the rest of the nation follows suit.

1942
Grand Coulee Dam, one of the largest concrete structures in the world, is completed.

1975
Computer software giant Microsoft is founded by Seattle native Bill Gates.

2001
A 6.8-magnitude earthquake centered near Olympia cracks the Capitol dome and causes widespread damage throughout the Seattle area.

Recreation

There isn't much you *can't* do in a state that has as much acreage set aside for parks and wilderness areas as Washington does. Whether you play in the sea, on the shore, in the rain, in the snow, on the ground or in the air, you'll have a smorgasbord of recreational options in the Evergreen State.

Come face to face with denizens of the deep while **scuba diving** or **snorkeling** offshore in the Pacific. Both sports also draw legions of water lovers to the San Juan Islands and Puget Sound; you'll find underwater state parks at Blake Island, northwest of Vashon Heights; Fort Worden, north of Port Townsend; and Kopachuck, southwest of Gig Harbor.

Although boat traffic is heavy in the Juan de Fuca Strait and in Puget Sound, there are quieter spots where you can enjoy a **sailing** day. Sequim Bay, east of Sequim, is one of them. While sailing around the San Juan Islands, drop anchor at one of the many small islands that can be accessed only by boat. Here you can enjoy hiking, primitive camping and picnicking—often in blissful solitude.

The 150-mile Cascadia Marine Trail, extending from Olympia north to Point Roberts, is perfect for an extended **canoeing** getaway. You will need to pay a Washington State Parks' per-night camping fee to camp at shoreline sites along the route; phone (206) 545-9161.

Hop on a sailboard and go **windsurfing** on the Columbia River. Several state parks—including Daroga, north of Orondo; Doug's Beach and Columbia Hills, west and east of Dallesport, respectively; and Maryhill, east of Maryhill—border the river.

Rolling on the Rivers

Turn the excitement up a notch and explore the rapids. Experienced paddlers can put in at the upstream end of the Green River gorge in Kanaskat-Palmer State Park, northeast of Enumclaw, for a raucous **kayaking** trip. Raging rivers racing through canyons in the Cascades make for exciting **white-water rafting.** Regional outfitters head to such rivers as the Methow, Skykomish and Wenatchee. For a tamer ride, check out the Elwha River in Olympic National Park.

Several state parks include **horseback riding** trails. Take on the 5-mile route at Battle Ground Lake, north of Battle Ground.

Experience trestles and tunnels while **bicycling** along the 66-mile trail that parallels I-90 from Cedar Falls to Thorp. The rugged terrain on Mount Spokane, northeast of Spokane,

makes for particularly challenging mountain biking.

You'll experience beautiful vistas while **hiking** at Wallace Falls State Park, north of Gold Bar; Larrabee State Park, on the west side of Chuckanut Mountain south of Bellingham; and Lake Chelan State Park, west of Chelan. Weaving through four national forests and two national parks, the Pacific Crest National Scenic Trail offers excellent sightseeing.

Awakening to Adventure

Set up camp for the night at Deception Pass State Park, north of Oak Harbor, and in the morning you can decide whether to sail, scuba dive, swim, fish, hike, bike, picnic or explore the interpretive center. Most other state parks also offer **camping** facilities; phone (360) 902-8844.

Abundant precipitation makes for unparalleled **downhill skiing** and **snowboarding** in the Pacific Northwest. The back country at Crystal Mountain entices experts with its woods, chutes and steep bowls. Stevens Pass near Skykomish beckons to snowboarders. Many national forests boast of ample acreage for **cross-country skiing, snowshoeing** and **snowmobiling.** A lighted **tubing** run at Fields Spring State Park, south of Anatone, invites more winter fun.

Launching sites for **hang gliding** are at Chelan Butte, south of Chelan; Steptoe Butte, east of Steptoe; and Tiger Mountain, south of Issaquah. Superb **climbing** awaits you throughout the Cascades, from Mount Shuksan in the north, southeast of Mount Baker, to Beacon Rock in the south, west of North Bonneville. The unusual sandstone formations at Peshastin Pinnacles State Park, northwest of Cashmere, make the site especially appealing.

Recreational Activities

Throughout the TourBook, you may notice a Recreational Activities heading with bulleted listings of recreation-oriented establishments listed underneath. Similar operations also may be mentioned in Destination City recreation sections. Since normal AAA inspection criteria cannot be applied, these establishments are presented only for information. Age, height and weight restrictions may apply. Reservations often are recommended and sometimes are required. Addresses and/or phone numbers are provided so visitors can contact the attraction for additional information.

Fast Facts

POPULATION: 5,894,121.

AREA: 66,511 square miles; ranks 20th.

CAPITAL: Olympia.

HIGHEST POINT: 14,411 ft., Mount Rainier.

LOWEST POINT: 5 ft. below sea level, Ebey Island, Snohomish County.

TIME ZONE(S): Pacific. DST.

TEEN DRIVING LAWS: No unrelated passengers under age 20 are permitted for the first 6 months; a maximum of three unrelated passengers are permitted for the following 6 months. Nighttime restrictions: 1 a.m.-5 a.m. Restrictions are lifted at age 18. For more information phone (360) 902-3900.

MINIMUM AGE FOR GAMBLING: 18.

SEAT BELT/CHILD RESTRAINT LAWS: Seat belts required for driver and all passengers 16 and older. Children ages 8 through 15 and taller than 4'9" must use a child restraint or seat belt. Child restraints are required for children ages 4 through 7 and less than 4'9" tall. Children under 13 must be in rear seat if passenger airbag is present.

HELMETS FOR MOTORCYCLISTS: Required for all riders.

RADAR DETECTORS: Permitted.

MOVE OVER LAW: Driver is required to slow down and vacate the lane nearest police, fire and rescue vehicles stopped on the side of the road and using audible or flashing signals.

CELL PHONE RESTRICTIONS: All drivers are prohibited from texting or using a hand-held cell phone while driving.

FIREARMS LAWS: Vary by state and/or county. Contact Department of Licensing, Firearms Program, P.O. Box 9649, Olympia, WA 98507; phone (360) 664-6616.

HOLIDAYS: Jan. 1; Martin Luther King Jr. Day, Jan. (3rd Mon.); Lincoln's Birthday, Feb. 12; Washington's Birthday, Feb. (3rd Mon.); Memorial Day, May (last Mon.); July 4; Labor Day, Sept. (1st Mon.); Election Day; Veterans Day, Nov. 11; Thanksgiving, Nov. (4th Thurs.); Christmas, Dec. 25.

TAXES: Washington's statewide sales tax is 6.5 percent, with cities and counties each allowed to add increments. Cities and counties may levy lodgings taxes of up to 2.6 percent except in Seattle and the rest of King County, where lodgings taxes are higher.

INFORMATION CENTERS: State welcome centers at Custer, Oroville, Megler and Maryhill are open May through September. The Vancouver information center, at the northbound I-5 Gee Creek Rest Area, and the Seattle-Tacoma International Airport information center are open throughout the year.

FURTHER INFORMATION FOR VISITORS:

Washington State Tourism
Department of Community, Trade and
 Economic Development
128 Tenth Ave. S.W.
P.O. Box 42525
Olympia, WA 98504-2525
(800) 544-1800

RECREATION INFORMATION:

State Parks and Recreation Commission
7150 Cleanwater Dr. S.W.
P.O. Box 42650
Olympia, WA 98504-2650
(360) 902-8844
(888) 226-7688 (reservations)

FISHING AND HUNTING REGULATIONS:

Department of Fish and Wildlife
600 Capitol Way N.
Olympia, WA 98501-1091
(360) 902-2200

NATIONAL FOREST INFORMATION:

Outdoor Recreation Information Center
222 Yale Ave. N.
Seattle, WA 98109
(206) 470-4060
(877) 444-6777 (national forest
 reservations)
TTY (877) 833-6777

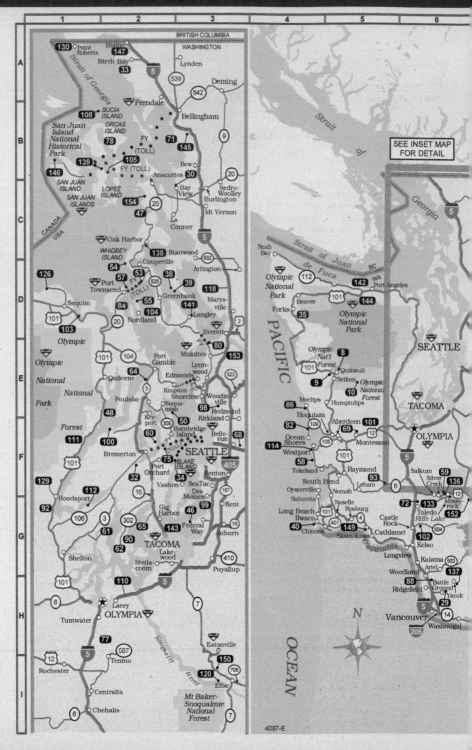

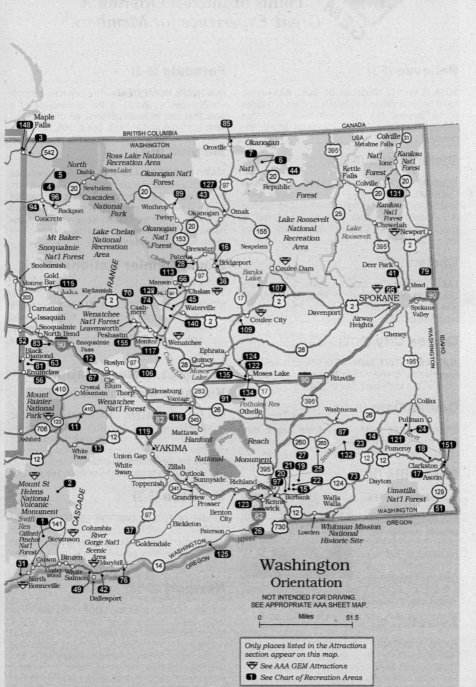

7　8　9　10　11　12

© AAA

Maple Falls

BRITISH COLUMBIA

WASHINGTON

CANADA

USA

Colville

Metaline Falls

Oroville

Okanogan

Nat'l

Ione

Kaniksu Nat'l Forest

North Diablo

Ross Lake National Recreation Area

Ross Lake

Republic

Kettle Falls

Nat'l

Forest

Newhalem

Okanogan Nat'l Forest

Colville

Kaniksu Nat'l Forest

Concrete

Rockport

Cascades National Park

Winthrop

Okanogan

Omak

Lake Roosevelt National Recreation Area

Chewelah

Newport

Twisp

Okanogan Nat'l Forest

Lake Chelan National Recreation Area

Lake Chelan

Brewster

Nespelem

Lake Roosevelt

Deer Park

Mt Baker-Snoqualmie Nat'l Forest

Pateros

Bridgeport

Coulee Dam

Mead

Snohomish

Manson

Banks Lake

SPOKANE

Gold Bar

Monroe

Chelan

Spokane Valley

Skykomish

Waterville

Wenatchee Nat'l Forest

Cashmere

Davenport

Airway Heights

Carnation

Leavenworth

Coulee City

Cheney

Issaquah

Peshastin

Snoqualmie

North Bend

Wenatchee

WASHINGTON

IDAHO

Black Diamond

Snoqualmie Pass

Monitor

Ephrata

Enumclaw

Roslyn

Quincy

Moses Lake

Ritzville

Crystal Mountain

Cle Elum Thorp

Columbia

Moses Lake

Mount Rainier National Park

Wenatchee Nat'l Forest

Ellensburg

Vantage

Potholes Res

Othello

Washtucna

Colfax

Ashford

Mattawa

Pullman

Hanford

Reach

White Pass

YAKIMA

Snake

Pomeroy

Clarkston

Mount St Helens National Volcanic Monument

Union Gap

White Swan

Zillah

Outlook

Sunnyside

Richland

National

Monument

Pasco

Burbank

Dayton

Asotin

Umatilla Nat'l Forest

Toppenish

Grandview

Prosser

Kennewick

Walla Walla

Swift Res

Gifford Pinchot Nat'l Forest

Stevenson

Columbia River Gorge Nat'l Scenic Area

Bickleton

Benton City

Paterson

Lowden

Whitman Mission National Historic Site

WASHINGTON

OREGON

Carson

Bingen

Underwood

White Salmon

Goldendale

WASHINGTON

River

North Bonneville

Maryhill

OREGON

Dallesport

Washington

Orientation

NOT INTENDED FOR DRIVING.
SEE APPROPRIATE AAA SHEET MAP.

0　Miles　51.5

Only places listed in the Attractions section appear on this map.

See AAA GEM Attractions

See Chart of Recreation Areas

© 2008 NAVTEQ

Points of Interest Offering A
Great Experience for Members®

Bellevue (F-3)

ROSALIE WHYEL MUSEUM OF DOLL ART—From handmade porcelain baby dolls to mass-produced plastic Barbies, this museum's huge collection highlights doll making as a form of artistic expression. See p. 245.

Blake Island (F-3)

TILLICUM VILLAGE NORTHWEST COAST INDIAN CULTURAL CENTER—Take a 1-hour cruise from Seattle to enjoy the traditional baked salmon dinner and interpretive program presented at this Northwest Coast American Indian village longhouse. See p. 245.

Chelan (D-9)

LAKE CHELAN—This clear blue lake, part of Lake Chelan National Recreation Area, is said to be one of the most beautiful in the Pacific Northwest. See p. 160.

Coulee City (E-10)

SUN LAKES STATE PARK—The site of a now dry waterfall far grander than Niagara is the centerpiece of this state park. See p. 164.

Coulee Dam (D-10)

GRAND COULEE DAM—One of the largest concrete structures in the world, the dam provides irrigation, power and flood control. See p. 164.

Eatonville (H-3)

NORTHWEST TREK WILDLIFE PARK— This park's 723 acres provide natural settings for its animal residents, all natives of the Northwest; a tram tour guided by naturalists allows close-up encounters with moose, elk, caribou and bison. See p. 167.

Everett (E-3)

FLYING HERITAGE COLLECTION—Thunderbolt, Hellcat, Mustang, Zero, Spitfire and Hurricane? These aircraft are all part of an outstanding collection of fighter planes and related World War II-era artifacts on display at Paine Field. See p. 247.

Ferndale (B-2)

HOVANDER HOMESTEAD—The restored turn-of-the-20th-century house is the centerpiece of a park that also includes gardens, an orchard, and farm buildings and animals. See p. 168.

Maryhill (H-8)

MARYHILL MUSEUM OF ART—In the chateaulike home of a wealthy entrepreneur, the art museum has an extensive collection of works by Auguste Rodin; American Indian artifacts; American and European paintings; Russian icons; and items donated by Queen Marie of Romania, who presided at the museum's dedication. See p. 179.

Mount Rainier National Park (F-7)

MOUNT RAINIER NATIONAL PARK—A landmark in the Pacific Northwest, ice-clad, volcanic Mount Rainier is covered by 26 glaciers; forests, meadows and ridges add to the alpine scenery. See p. 182.

Mount St. Helens National Volcanic Monument (G-7)

MOUNT ST. HELENS NATIONAL VOLCANIC MONUMENT—The monument's 110,000 acres encompass the volcano and the area devastated by its 1980 eruption; from Johnston Ridge visitors can see the destruction a volcano is capable of as well as Nature's recuperative powers. See p. 185.

Mukilteo (E-3)

FUTURE OF FLIGHT AVIATION CENTER & BOEING TOUR—View exhibits touting next-generation aircraft then board a bus to Boeing's production facility to see how passenger jets are built. See p. 253.

Newport (D-12)

INTERNATIONAL SELKIRK LOOP—This exhilaratingly scenic driving route traverses the Selkirk Mountains, a wilderness region that encompasses northeastern Washington, northern Idaho and southeastern British Columbia. Rivers, lakes and wildflower-dotted meadows offer year-round recreational opportunities from canoeing to hiking to ice fishing, all against a backdrop of mountain vistas. See p. 189.

North Bonneville (H-7)

BONNEVILLE DAM—WASHINGTON SHORE VISI-TOR CENTER—Check out the underwater windows in the fish viewing building as well as the power generators and turbines on your self-guiding tour of this hydroelectric facility. See p. 190.

Oak Harbor (C-2)

DECEPTION PASS STATE PARK—Named for the channel that separates Whidbey and Fidalgo islands, the park contains beaches, an interpretive center, more than 38 miles of hiking trails, lakes, marshes, sand dunes and rocky cliffs. See p. 191.

Olympia (H-2)

THE CAPITOL CAMPUS—The state's legislative, judicial and administrative offices are clustered on 30 landscaped acres; several of the buildings can be toured. See p. 194.

STATE CAPITAL MUSEUM—The museum, in a 32-room California mission-style mansion, contains displays about state government and history, an art gallery and gardens. See p. 194.

Olympic National Park (E-1, D-5)

HOH RAIN FOREST—Self-guiding nature trails lead to areas of intense green growth—trees, mosses, lichens and ferns thrive in the rain forest's moist environment. See p. 197.

HURRICANE RIDGE—Bring your camera and take advantage of the spectacular views of the Strait of Juan de Fuca and the glacier-covered Olympic Mountains; nature trails are accessible. See p. 197.

OLYMPIC NATIONAL PARK—Glacier-topped mountains, temperate rain forests and Pacific Ocean shores are the diverse elements that make up this national park, most of which is protected as wilderness. See p. 195.

Port Townsend (D-2)

FORT WORDEN STATE PARK & CONFERENCE CENTER—Built as one of a series of coastal fortresses guarding the Puget Sound area during the 1890s, the fort retains its parade grounds and restored Victorian houses; a museum and a science center also are part of the park. See p. 201.

PORT TOWNSEND—One of the state's oldest cities, the historic seaport of Port Townsend is known for its eclectic architecture. See p. 201.

San Juan Islands (C-1)

MORAN STATE PARK—Even in a state blessed with scenic riches, the views at this park are sublime. Climb to the top of Mt. Constitution for a sweeping panorama that takes in water, islands and rugged mountain ranges. See p. 208.

SAN JUAN ISLANDS—In the northwesternmost part of Washington, these 172 picturesque islands, reachable by ferry from Anacortes and Bellingham, are popular getaways due to their moderate climate and tranquil nature. See p. 208.

Seattle (C-6, F-3)

EXPERIENCE MUSIC PROJECT (EMP)—Filled with high-tech interactive exhibits and housed in a head-turning, contoured metal building designed to look like a smashed guitar, this tribute to American popular culture allows visitors to appreciate, celebrate and even create music. See p. 231.

LAKE WASHINGTON SHIP CANAL AND HIRAM M. CHITTENDEN LOCKS—The canal and busy navigational locks connect saltwater Puget Sound with freshwater Lake Washington; a salmon fish ladder, botanical gardens and a visitor center are part of the site. See p. 224.

THE MUSEUM OF FLIGHT—The evolution of aviation is portrayed through historical aircraft displayed in the restored Red Barn, the original manufacturing plant of The Boeing Co., and in the Great Gallery, where more than 40 planes seem ready to take off. See p. 225.

OLYMPIC SCULPTURE PARK—This urban park is an inspiring combination of engineering ingenuity, man-made art and nature's beauty. And it's a lovely place for a waterside stroll. See p. 226.

PIKE PLACE MARKET—Originally a farmers' market, Pike Place has diversified to include arts and crafts, street performers, shops and restaurants in addition to fish markets and produce stands. See p. 227.

PIONEER SQUARE HISTORIC DISTRICT—Rebuilt after the 1889 fire, Pioneer Square's 30 blocks contain restored buildings that now house art galleries, boutiques, antique shops and restaurants; a pedestrian mall, Waterfall Park, and Smith Tower are other landmarks. See p. 228.

SCIENCE FICTION MUSEUM AND HALL OF FAME—Travel to other planets without leaving terra firma at this museum that showcases such pop culture gems as Capt. Kirk's chair from "Star Trek" as well as out-of-this-world props from movies like "Star Wars," "Blade Runner," and "The Terminator." See p. 231.

SEATTLE ART MUSEUM

DOWNTOWN—The museum's permanent collections of Asian, African and Northwest Coast Indian art are renowned. See p. 229.

SEATTLE ASIAN ART MUSEUM—In Volunteer Park, the museum's six galleries contain one of the nation's top collections of Asian art. See p. 230.

SEATTLE CENTER—Formerly the site of the 1962 World's Fair, the center's 74 acres are now occupied by gardens, fountains, sculptures, a children's museum, an amusement park and a science center. See p. 230.

SPACE NEEDLE—This structure that symbolizes Seattle served as the focal point for the 1962 World's Fair; an observation deck offers panoramic views. See p. 231.

TEATRO ZINZANNI—Where can you see a show that combines comedy, cabaret and Cirque-style spectacle while indulging in an expertly prepared multi-course dinner? At Teatro ZinZanni, that's where. See p. 232.

UNDERGROUND TOUR—The underground city beneath Pioneer Square, created as a result of the 1889 Great Fire, is humorously explored. See p. 236.

WASHINGTON PARK ARBORETUM—Seattle is a city rich in urban green spaces, and the arboretum is one of the most rewarding—a constantly evolving classroom not only for horticultural students and gardeners but for anyone who is entranced by the simple beauty of nature. See p. 233.

WOODLAND PARK ZOO—More than 300 species of animals from around the world live at this zoo; rain forest, tropical Asia and African savanna are some of the habitats. See p. 234.

Spokane (D-11)

MANITO PARK—Gardens of all types—Japanese, perennial, rose, lilac and formal—grace the grounds of this park; a conservatory continues the floral theme. See p. 269.

RIVERFRONT PARK—This city park retains many of the features developed for Expo '74, including a carousel, an aerial gondola ride and an IMAX theater; the Spokane River cascades through the park. See p. 269.

Stevenson (H-7)

COLUMBIA GORGE INTERPRETIVE CENTER—The region's natural and cultural history is depicted at this museum in a scenic setting with Table Mountain in the background. See p. 271.

Tacoma (G-2)

THE HAROLD E. LeMAY MUSEUM—Explore the evolving world of wheels on a tour of this world-class motor vehicle collection. Ford, Chevy, Packard, Pierce-Arrow, Tucker: They're all here and then some. See p. 260.

MUSEUM OF GLASS—An eye-catching, stainless steel-clad conical tower distinguishes the exterior of this modern art museum, which emphasizes creations made of glass. See p. 260.

POINT DEFIANCE PARK—One of the nation's largest urban parks, Point Defiance has such diverse offerings as gardens, hiking trails, a historic fort, a zoo and aquarium, a logging museum and a marina. See p. 261.

POINT DEFIANCE ZOO AND AQUARIUM—Animals native to the Pacific Rim are exhibited here in natural habitats; two aquariums offer glimpses of sea life common to Puget Sound and the South Pacific. See p. 261.

WASHINGTON STATE HISTORY MUSEUM—As its name implies, this museum is where to go for anything pertaining to Washington history; interactive exhibits and dioramas depict the people, events and cultures that have shaped the state. See p. 262.

Wenatchee (E-9)

ROCKY REACH DAM—In addition to a visitor center, this Z-shaped dam also has galleries devoted to river history and railroads; a fish ladder and a garden are other highlights. See p. 277.

Washington Temperature Averages
Maximum/Minimum
From the records of The Weather Channel Interactive, Inc.

	JAN	FEB	MAR	APR	MAY	JUNE	JULY	AUG	SEPT	OCT	NOV	DEC
Seattle	46 / 36	50 / 37	53 / 39	58 / 42	64 / 47	70 / 52	75 / 55	76 / 56	70 / 52	60 / 46	51 / 40	46 / 36
Spokane	33 / 22	39 / 26	49 / 30	58 / 36	66 / 43	74 / 49	82 / 55	83 / 55	73 / 46	59 / 36	41 / 29	33 / 22
Walla Walla	41 / 29	47 / 33	56 / 37	64 / 41	72 / 48	80 / 54	91 / 61	89 / 61	79 / 53	66 / 44	50 / 36	41 / 29
Yakima	38 / 21	46 / 25	56 / 29	64 / 33	72 / 40	80 / 46	87 / 51	86 / 50	78 / 42	64 / 33	48 / 26	37 / 20

RECREATION AREAS

	MAP LOCATION	CAMPING	PICNICKING	HIKING TRAILS	BOATING	BOAT RAMP	BOAT RENTAL	FISHING	SWIMMING	PETS ON LEASH	BICYCLE TRAILS	WINTER SPORTS	VISITOR CENTER	LODGE/CABINS	FOOD SERVICE
NATIONAL PARKS (See place listings)															
Mount Rainier (F-7) 378 square miles.		●	●	●				●				●	●	●	●
North Cascades (C-7, C-8) 505,000 acres.		●		●				●					●		
Olympic (D-4, D-5) 923,000 acres.		●	●	●	●	●	●	●	●	●					
NATIONAL FORESTS (See place listings)															
Colville (B-4, C-5) 1,100,000 acres. Northeastern Washington.		●	●	●	●	●		●	●	●		●			
Gifford Pinchot (B-4, C-5) 1,312,000 acres. Southwestern Washington. Mountain climbing; horse rental.		●	●	●	●	●	●	●	●	●		●	●	●	●
Goose Lake (G-7) 7 acres 13 mi. w. of Trout Lake via SR 141, FR 24 and FR 60.	**1**	●	●		●	●		●	●	●					
Takhlakh Lake (G-7) 32 mi. s.e. of Randle via SR 131, FR 23 and FR 2329. Mountain views.	**2**	●	●	●	●	●		●	●	●					
Mount Baker-Snoqualmie (E-7) 1,700,000 acres. Northwestern Washington.		●	●	●	●	●	●	●	●	●		●	●	●	●
Douglas Fir (B-7) 2 mi. e. of Glacier on SR 542.	**3**	●	●	●		●		●		●					
Horseshoe Cove (C-7) 14 mi. n. of Concrete on Baker Lake.	**4**	●		●	●	●		●	●	●					
Shannon Creek (C-7) 24 mi. n. of Concrete on Baker Lake. Water skiing.	**5**	●		●	●	●		●		●					
Okanogan (A-7) 1,706,000 acres. North-central Washington.		●	●	●	●	●		●	●	●		●			
Bonaparte Lake (C-10) 16 acres 7 mi. n.w. of Wauconda via SR 20 and CR 4953. Nature trails.	**6**	●	●		●	●		●	●	●					
Lost Lake (C-10) 23 acres 17 mi. n.w. of Wauconda via SR 20, CR 4953, FR 32 and FR 33. Nature trails.	**7**	●	●	●	●			●	●	●					
Olympic (B-10) 632,324 acres. Northwestern Washington.		●	●	●	●	●		●	●	●		●	●	●	●
Falls Creek (E-5) 3 acres 3 mi. e. of US 101 on Quinault Lake. Water skiing; nature trails.	**8**	●	●	●	●	●		●	●	●					
Willaby (E-4) 7 acres 2 mi. e. of US 101 on Quinault Lake. Nature trail.	**9**	●	●	●	●	●		●	●	●					
Wynoochee Lake-Coho (E-5) 2,777 acres 1 mi. w. of Montesano on US 12, then 37 mi. n. on FR 22 (Old Wynoochee Valley Rd.).	**10**	●	●	●	●	●		●	●	●					
Wenatchee (D-5) 2,200,000 acres. Central Washington.		●	●	●	●	●	●	●	●	●		●	●	●	●
Bumping Lake (F-7) 19 acres 3 mi. s. of Gooseprairie.	**11**	●	●		●	●		●	●	●					
Kachess (E-8) 92 acres 15 mi. n. of Easton via I-90 and FR 49. Nature trails.	**12**	●	●	●	●	●		●	●	●	●				
Rimrock Lake Area (F-8) at Rimrock off US 12. Water skiing.	**13**	●	●		●	●		●	●	●					
NATIONAL RECREATION AREAS (See place listings)															
Lake Chelan (B-8) 62,000 acres. North central Washington. Horse rental, houseboat rental.			●	●	●		●	●	●				●	●	●
Lake Roosevelt (C-10) 100,059 acres. Northeastern Washington. Water skiing; houseboat rental.		●	●		●	●	●	●	●	●				●	●
Ross Lake (A-8) 118,000 acres. Northwestern Washington.		●	●		●	●	●	●					●	●	●
ARMY CORPS OF ENGINEERS															
Central Ferry (F-11) 185 acres 22 mi. n.w. of Pomeroy on SR 127. Water skiing.	**14**	●	●		●	●		●	●	●				●	
Charbonneau Park (G-10) 244 acres 8 mi. e. of Burbank on SR 124, then 2 mi. n. on Sun Harbor Dr.	**15**	●	●			●		●	●	●					
Chief Joseph Dam (D-9) 864 acres off SR 17 in Bridgeport. (See Bridgeport p. 158)	**16**		●		●	●		●					●		
Chief Looking Glass (G-12) 5 mi. s. of Clarkston on SR 129.	**17**		●	●		●		●		●					
Chief Timothy (F-12) 282 acres 8 mi. w. of Clarkston on US 12. Water skiing.	**18**	●	●			●		●	●	●			●	●	●
Fishhook Park (G-10) 46 acres 15 mi. e. of Burbank on SR 124, then 4 mi. n. on Page Rd.	**19**	●	●		●	●		●	●	●					

RECREATION AREAS

	MAP LOCATION	CAMPING	PICNICKING	HIKING TRAILS	BOATING	BOAT RAMP	BOAT RENTAL	FISHING	SWIMMING	PETS ON LEASH	BICYCLE TRAILS	WINTER SPORTS	VISITOR CENTER	LODGE/CABINS	FOOD SERVICE
Hood Park (G-10) 99 acres 3 mi. s. of Pasco on US 12/395 at SR 124.	20	•	•		•	•		•	•	•					
Ice Harbor Lock and Dam (G-10) 524 acres 12 mi. e. of Pasco off US 12/395, then 5.5 mi. e. on SR 124 and 2.5 mi. n. on Ice Harbor Dam Rd.	21	•	•	•	•	•		•	•				•		
Levey Park (G-11) 50 acres 10.5 mi. e. of Pasco on Pasco-Kahlotus Rd., then 1 mi. s. on Levey Rd.	22		•		•	•		•	•	•					
Little Goose Lock and Dam (F-11) 16,364 acres 8 mi. n.e. of Starbuck off US 12 on Little Goose Dam Rd.	23		•		•	•		•	•				•		
Lower Granite Lock and Dam (F-12) 14,863 acres 27 mi. w. of Pullman on SR 194.	24		•		•	•		•	•	•					
Lower Monumental Lock and Dam (G-11) 14,726 acres 7 mi. s. of Kahlotus on Devil's Canyon Rd.	25		•		•	•		•		•					
McNary Lock and Dam (G-10) 17 acres 1.5 mi. e. of Umatilla, Ore., on US 730, then 1 mi. n. on McNary Dam Rd.	26		•		•	•		•					•		
Windust Park (F-10) 54 acres 10 mi. n.e. of Pasco on Pasco-Kahlotus Rd., then 5 mi. s.e. on Burr Canyon Rd.	27	•	•		•	•		•	•						
STATE															
Alta Lake (D-9) 182 acres 2 mi. s.w. of Pateros off SR 164. Scuba diving, snowmobiling, water skiing	28	•	•	•	•	•		•	•	•		•			
Battle Ground Lake (H-6) 280 acres 3 mi. n.e. of Battle Ground off SR 502. *(See Battle Ground in Portland p. 108)*	29	•	•	•	•	•		•	•	•	•		•		•
Bay View (B-3) 25 acres 7 mi. w. of Burlington via SR 20. Scuba diving.	30	•	•		•			•		•					
Beacon Rock (H-7) 4,482 acres 35 mi. e. of Vancouver via SR 14. Rock climbing, mountain biking.	31	•	•	•	•	•		•		•	•				
Belfair (F-2) 63 acres 3 mi. w. of Belfair on SR 30. Crabbing.	32	•	•					•	•	•					
Birch Bay (A-2) 193 acres 1 mi. s. of Birch Bay off SR 548. Scuba diving, water skiing. *(See Birch Bay p. 156)*	33	•	•		•			•		•					
Blake Island (F-3) 476 acres 4 mi. w. of Seattle via boat. Clamming, scuba diving, water skiing. *(See Blake Island in Seattle p. 245)*	34	•	•	•		•		•					•	•	•
Bogachiel (D-4) 123 acres 6 mi. s. of Forks at Bogachiel on US 101.	35	•	•	•	•			•	•	•					
Bridgeport (D-9) 824 acres .75 mi. n. of Bridgeport via SR 17. Golf, water skiing.	36	•	•		•	•		•	•	•					•
Brooks Memorial (G-8) 700 acres 12 mi. n.e. of Goldendale off US 97. Snowmobiling.	37	•	•	•				•		•		•	•		
Cama Beach (D-2) 433 acres 14 mi. s.w. of Stanwood on Camano Island. Bird-watching, clamming, crabbing.	38	•	•	•				•		•				•	
Camano Island (D-3) 134 acres 14 mi. s.w. of Stanwood on Camano Island. Scuba diving.	39	•	•	•	•	•		•	•	•				•	
Cape Disappointment (G-4) 1,882 acres 3 mi. s.w. of Ilwaco via SR 100. Historic. Lewis and Clark Interpretive Center. *(See Ilwaco p. 172)*	40	•	•	•		•		•		•			•	•	•
Centennial Trail (D-12) 372 acres along the Spokane River between Nine Mile Falls and the Idaho state line. Mountain biking, snowshoeing.	41		•					•	•	•		•			
Columbia Hills (H-8) 3,338 acres 17 mi. e. of White Salmon off SR 14. Rock climbing, windsurfing; Indian petroglyphs.	42	•	•	•	•	•		•		•					
Conconully (C-9) 80 acres 18 mi. n.w. of Omak off US 97. Snowmobiling, water skiing.	43	•	•		•	•		•		•			•	•	•
Curlew Lake (C-10) 123 acres 10 mi. n.e. of Republic on SR 21. Snowmobiling, water skiing.	44	•	•	•	•	•		•	•	•					
Daroga (D-9) 90 acres 6 mi. n. of Orondo. Tennis, water skiing; ballpark.	45	•	•	•	•	•		•	•	•			•		
Dash Point (G-3) 397 acres 5 mi. n.e. of Tacoma on SR 509.	46	•	•	•				•		•					

RECREATION AREAS

	MAP LOCATION	CAMPING	PICNICKING	HIKING TRAILS	BOATING	BOAT RAMP	BOAT RENTAL	FISHING	SWIMMING	PETS ON LEASH	BICYCLE TRAILS	WINTER SPORTS	VISITOR CENTER	LODGE/CABINS	FOOD SERVICE
Deception Pass (C-2) 4,129 acres 9 mi. n. of Oak Harbor on Whidbey Island. Scuba diving. *(See Oak Harbor p. 191)*	47	•	•	•	•	•	•	•	•	•			•		•
Dosewallips (E-2) 425 acres at Brinnon off US 101.	48	•	•	•	•			•		•	•				
Dougs Beach (H-7) 400 acres 2 mi. e. of Lyle. Kayaking, windsurfing.	49							•	•	•					
Fay Bainbridge (F-3) 17 acres 4 mi. n. of Bainbridge Island on SR 305. Scuba diving.	50	•	•		•	•		•		•					
Fields Spring (G-12) 793 acres 5 mi. s. of Anatone off SR 129. Sledding, snowmobiling.	51	•	•	•						•		•			
Flaming Geyser (E-7) 480 acres 1.75 mi. s. of Black Diamond on SR 169, then 2.75 mi. w. on S.E. Green Valley Rd. *(See Auburn p. 242)*	52		•	•				•		•					
Fort Casey (D-2) 411 acres 3 mi. s. of Coupeville off SR 20. Scuba diving. *(See Whidbey Island p. 278)*	53	•	•	•	•	•		•		•			•		
Fort Ebey (D-2) 645 acres 3 mi. w. of Coupeville off SR 20. Scuba diving.	54	•	•	•				•		•					
Fort Flagler (D-2) 783 acres 11 mi. n.e. of Port Hadlock on Marrowstone Island. Historic. Scuba diving. *(See Nordland p. 190)*	55	•	•	•	•	•		•		•	•			•	
Fort Ward (E-7) 137 acres 4 mi. s.w. of Bainbridge Island on Pleasant Beach Dr. Historic. Crabbing, scuba diving.	56		•	•		•		•		•					
Fort Worden (D-2) 443 acres 1 mi. n. of Port Townsend via Cherry St. Historic. Scuba diving. *(See Port Townsend p. 201)*	57	•	•	•	•	•		•		•	•		•	•	•
Grayland Beach (F-4) 411 acres on SR 105 in Grayland.	58	•		•				•		•	•				
Ike Kinswa (F-6) 454 acres 5 mi. n.w. of Mossyrock via US 12. Water skiing.	59	•	•	•	•	•		•	•	•		•			•
Illahee (F-2) 75 acres 3 mi. n.e. of Bremerton on SR 306. Scuba diving, water skiing.	60	•	•	•	•	•		•		•					
Jarrell Cove (G-2) 43 acres 15 mi. n.e. of Shelton off SR 3 on Hartstene Island. Scuba diving.	61	•	•		•	•		•		•					
Joemma Beach (G-2) 122 acres 4 mi. s.w. of Lakebay on Case Inlet. Scuba diving, water skiing.	62	•	•		•	•		•		•					
Kanaskat-Palmer (E-7) 297 acres 11 mi. n.e. of Enumclaw. Kayaking, rafting.	63	•	•	•				•		•					
Kitsap Memorial (E-2) 58 acres 6 mi. n. of Poulsbo off SR 3. Scuba diving.	64	•	•	•				•		•				•	
Kopachuck (G-2) 109 acres 7 mi. w. of Gig Harbor via Rosedale St. and Kopachuck Rd. Scuba diving, water skiing.	65	•	•	•	•	•		•		•					
Lake Chelan (D-9) 127 acres 9 mi. w. of Chelan off US 97 Alt. Scuba diving, water skiing. *(See Chelan p. 160)*	66	•	•	•	•	•		•	•	•			•		
Lake Easton (E-8) 516 acres at Easton off I-90. Snowmobiling.	67	•	•	•	•	•		•	•	•		•			
Lake Sammamish (F-3) 507 acres 2 mi. n.w. of Issaquah via I-90. Water skiing.	68		•	•	•	•		•	•	•					•
Lake Sylvia (F-5) 234 acres 1 mi. n. of Montesano off US 12. *(See Montesano p. 181)*	69	•	•	•	•	•	•	•	•	•					•
Lake Wenatchee (D-8) 489 acres 22 mi. n. of Leavenworth off SR 207. Skiing, snowmobiling; horse rental.	70	•	•	•	•	•	•	•	•	•		•			•
Larrabee (B-2) 2,683 acres 7 mi. s. of Bellingham on SR 11. Scuba diving, water skiing.	71	•	•	•	•	•		•		•					
Lewis and Clark (G-6) 620 acres 12 mi. s.e. of Chehalis off I-5 exit 68.	72	•	•	•				•		•					
Lewis and Clark Trail (G-11) 37 acres 4 mi. w. of Dayton on US 12. Historic.	73	•	•	•				•		•		•			
Lincoln Rock (D-8) 80 acres 6 mi. n.e. of Wenatchee via US 2. Cross-country skiing, water skiing.	74	•	•	•	•	•		•	•	•		•			
Manchester (F-2) 111 acres 6 mi. n.e. of Port Orchard via Beach Dr. Scuba diving.	75	•	•	•	•			•		•					

RECREATION AREAS

	MAP LOCATION	CAMPING	PICNICKING	HIKING TRAILS	BOATING	BOAT RAMP	BOAT RENTAL	FISHING	SWIMMING	PETS ON LEASH	BICYCLE TRAILS	WINTER SPORTS	VISITOR CENTER	LODGE/CABINS	FOOD SERVICE
Maryhill (H-8) 98 acres 12 mi. s. of Goldendale on US 97. Water skiing, windsurfing.	76	•	•	•	•			•	•	•					
Millersylvania (H-2) 841 acres 10 mi. s. of Olympia off I-5 exit 95.	77	•	•	•	•			•	•	•					
Moran (B-2) 5,252 acres on Orcas Island, reached by ferry from Anacortes. *(See Orcas Island p. 208).*	78	•	•	•	•	•	•	•	•	•				•	
Mount Spokane (D-12) 13,643 acres 30 mi. n.e. of Spokane via US 2 and SR 206. Mountain biking, skiing, snowmobiling.	79	•	•	•						•		•	•		
Mukilteo (E-3) 18 acres at Mukilteo. Scuba diving.	80		•		•	•		•		•					
Nolte (E-7) 117 acres 6 mi. n.e. of Enumclaw off SR 169.	81		•	•	•			•	•	•					
Ocean City (F-4) 170 acres at the s. edge of Ocean City off SR 109. Scuba diving.	82	•	•					•		•			•		
Olallie (E-7) 521 acres 6 mi. e. of North Bend via I-90. Mountain biking, rock climbing.	83		•	•				•		•					
Old Fort Townsend (D-2) 377 acres 3 mi. s. of Port Townsend off SR 20. Historic. *(See Port Townsend p. 201)*	84	•	•	•				•		•					
Osoyoos Lake (B-9) 46 acres 1 mi. n. of Oroville on US 97. Ice skating, water skiing.	85	•	•		•	•		•	•	•					•
Pacific Beach (E-4) 10 acres in Pacific Beach. Clamming, kayaking, surfing.	86	•	•					•	•	•					
Palouse Falls (F-11) 83 acres 17 mi. s.e. of Washtucna off SR 261.	87	•	•	•						•					
Paradise Point (H-6) 88 acres 19 mi. n. of Vancouver off I-5 exit 16.	88	•	•	•	•	•		•		•					
Pearrygin Lake (C-9) 578 acres 5 mi. n.e. of Winthrop off SR 20. Snowmobiling.	89	•	•	•	•	•		•	•	•			•		
Penrose Point (G-2) 152 acres 1 mi. e. of Lakebay off SR 302. Clamming.	90	•	•	•				•		•					
Potholes (F-9) 640 acres 10 mi. s.e. of Moses Lake on SR 17, then 14 mi. w. on SR 262.	91	•	•		•			•		•					
Potlatch (G-1) 57 acres n. of Shelton off US 101. Scuba diving, water skiing.	92	•	•	•	•	•	○	•		•					•
Rainbow Falls (F-5) 850 acres 18 mi. w. of Chehalis on SR 6. Kayaking.	93	•	•	•				•		•					
Rasar (C-7) 169 acres 19 mi. e. of Burlington on SR 20.	94	•	•	•				•							
Riverside (D-12) 10,000 acres 6 mi. n.w. of Spokane off SR 291. Historic. Scenic. Bird-watching, kayaking, rock climbing, snowmobiling, water skiing, wildlife viewing; horse trails, petroglyphs. *(See Spokane p. 270)*	95	•	•	•	•	•		•	•	•		•	•	•	
Rockport (C-7) 457 acres w. of Rockport off SR 20.	96	•	•	•											
Sacajawea (G-10) 284 acres 3 mi. s.e. of Pasco off US 12. Historic. Water skiing. *(See Pasco p. 198)*	97		•		•	•		•	•	•			•	•	
Saint Edward (E-3) 316 acres 2 mi. s. of Kenmore on Juanita Dr. N.E. Historic. Bird-watching, horseback riding, mountain biking, water skiing.	98		•	•				•	•	•			•		
Saltwater (G-3) 88 acres 2 mi. s. of downtown Des Moines off Marine View Dr. Clamming, scuba diving.	99	•	•	•				•	•	•					•
Scenic Beach (F-2) 88 acres 12 mi. n.w. of Bremerton at Seabeck. Scuba diving.	100	•	•	•				•		•					
Schafer (F-5) 119 acres 8 mi. n. of Satsop on the Satsop River. Rafting.	101	•	•	•				•		•					
Seaquest (G-6) 475 acres 5 mi. e. of Castle Rock off I-5 exit 49.	102	•	•	•				•		•					
Sequim Bay (D-1) 92 acres 7 mi. s.e. of Sequim off US 101. Scuba diving.	103	•	•	•	•	•		•		•					
South Whidbey (D-2) 347 acres 10 mi. s. of Coupeville on Whidbey Island. Clamming, scuba diving.	104	•	•	•				•		•					
Spencer Spit (B-2) 130 acres on the e. side of Lopez Island. Clamming, scuba diving.	105	•	•	•	•			•		•					

RECREATION AREAS

	MAP LOCATION	CAMPING	PICNICKING	HIKING TRAILS	BOATING	BOAT RAMP	BOAT RENTAL	FISHING	SWIMMING	PETS ON LEASH	BICYCLE TRAILS	WINTER SPORTS	VISITOR CENTER	LODGE/CABINS	FOOD SERVICE
Squilchuck (E-8) 288 acres 7 mi. s. of Wenatchee on Squilchuck Canyon Rd. Snow skiing.	106	•	•	•						•		•			
Steamboat Rock (D-10) 3,523 acres 11 mi. s. of Grand Coulee on SR 155. Scuba diving, water skiing.	107	•	•	•	•	•	•	•	•	•					•
Sucia Island (B-1) 564 acres 2.5 mi. n. of Orcas Island. Accessible only by boat.	108	•	•	•				•	•						
Sun Lakes (E-10) 4,024 acres 4 mi. s.w. of Coulee City off SR 17. Golf; horse rental. *(See Coulee City p. 164)*	109	•	•	•	•	•	•	•	•	•				•	•
Tolmie (H-2) 106 acres 8 mi. n.e. of Olympia off I-5 exit 111. Scuba diving; underwater park.	110		•	•				•	•	•					
Triton Cove (F-1) 29 acres 5 mi. n. of Eldon on US 101 on Hood Canal.	111		•		•	•		•	•						
Twanoh (F-1) 182 acres 5 mi. e. of Union on SR 106. Water skiing.	112	•	•	•	•	•		•	•	•					•
Twenty-five Mile Creek (D-9) 235 acres 25 mi. w. of Chelan on 25 Mile Creek Rd.	113	•	•	•	•	•	•	•	•						•
Twin Harbors (F-4) 172 acres 3 mi. s. of Westport on SR 105. Clamming.	114	•	•	•				•	•						
Wallace Falls (D-7) 1,422 acres 2 mi. n.e. of Gold Bar off US 2. *(See Gold Bar p. 170)*	115	•	•	•				•	•						
Wanapum (F-9) 451 acres 3 mi. s. of Vantage on the Columbia River. Water skiing.	116	•	•	•	•	•		•	•	•			•		
Wenatchee Confluence (E-8) 197 acres 3 mi. n. of Wenatchee. Tennis, water skiing, windsurfing; ballparks.	117	•	•	•	•	•		•	•	•	•				
Wenberg (D-3) 46 acres 4 mi. n. of Marysville via I-5, then 8 mi. w. off SR 531. Water skiing.	118	•	•	•	•	•		•	•	•					•
Yakima Sportsman (F-8) 247 acres 1 mi. e. of Yakima off I-82 exit 34.	119	•	•	•				•		•					

OTHER

	MAP LOCATION	CAMPING	PICNICKING	HIKING TRAILS	BOATING	BOAT RAMP	BOAT RENTAL	FISHING	SWIMMING	PETS ON LEASH	BICYCLE TRAILS	WINTER SPORTS	VISITOR CENTER	LODGE/CABINS	FOOD SERVICE
Alder Lake Park (I-3) 385 acres 5.5 mi. s.w. of Elbe off SR 7 on Pleasant Valley Rd.	120	•	•		•	•		•	•	•					
Boyer Park (F-12) 56 acres 23 mi. w. of Pullman via SR 194.	121	•	•		•	•		•	•	•				•	•
Cascade Park (E-10) On Valley Rd. near Moses Lake. Water skiing; playground.	122	•	•		•	•		•	•						
Columbia Park (G-10) 434 acres at Kennewick along Lake Wallula. Archery, golf, tennis; ballpark.	123	•	•	•	•	•	•	•	•	•	•				
Connelly Park (E-10) 5 mi. n. of Moses Lake, w. of SR 17 on McConihe Rd. Playground.	124		•					•	•	•					
Crow Butte (H-9) 1,312 acres 13 mi. w. of Paterson on SR 14. Water skiing, windsurfing.	125	•	•		•	•		•	•	•					
Dungeness (D-1) 5 mi. w. of Sequim on US 101, then 4 mi. n. on Kitchen Rd. Horse trails.	126	•	•	•				•	•						
Eastside Park (C-9) 73 acres .25 mi. w. of Main St. on Omak Ave. in Omak.	127	•	•		•			•	•				•		
Entiat Park (D-8) On US 97A in Entiat.	128	•	•		•	•		•	•						
Lake Cushman (F-1) 603 acres 7 mi. n.w. of Hoodsport via SR 119. Water skiing.	129	•	•	•	•	•		•	•	•					
Lighthouse Marine Park (A-1) 22 acres on s.w. corner of Point Roberts at 811 Marine Dr. Clamming, whale watching; boardwalk, observation tower.	130	•	•					•		•					
Little Pend Oreille (C-12) 40,198 acres 25 mi. e. of Colville via SR 20. *(See Colville p. 163)*	131	•	•	•	•	•		•	•	•					
Lyon's Ferry (F-11) 1,282 acres 20 mi. s.e. of Washtucna off SR 261. Historic. Water skiing.	132	•	•		•	•		•	•	•	•				
Mayfield Lake (G-6) 51 acres 3 mi. w. of Mossyrock on US 12.	133	•	•					•	•						•
Montlake Park (F-10) Beaumont and Linden aves. in Moses Lake. Water skiing.	134		•	•	•	•		•	•				•		

RECREATION AREAS

	MAP LOCATION	CAMPING	PICNICKING	HIKING TRAILS	BOATING	BOAT RAMP	BOAT RENTAL	FISHING	SWIMMING	PETS ON LEASH	BICYCLE TRAILS	WINTER SPORTS	VISITOR CENTER	LODGE/CABINS	FOOD SERVICE
Moses Lake (E-9) 78 acres 5 mi. w. of Moses Lake off I-90 exits 174 and 175. Scuba diving, water skiing.	135		•		•	•		•	•	•					•
Mossyrock Park (F-6) 272 acres 3 mi. e. of Mossyrock via Aljune and Swofford rds.	136	•	•	•	•	•		•	•	•					•
Moulton Falls County Park (G-6) 388 acres 3 mi. s. of Yacolt on CR 16.	137		•	•				•	•						
Oak Harbor Beach Park (C-2) 40 acres .25 mi. e. of SR 20 in Oak Harbor on Whidbey Island.	138	•	•		•	•		•	•						
Odlin County Park (B-1) 80 acres on n. side of Lopez Island. Bird-watching, clamming.	139	•	•	•	•	•		•	•	•					
Orondo River Park (E-9) 6 acres 2 mi. n. of Orondo. Water skiing.	140	•	•		•	•			•	•					
Phil Simon Park (D-3) In Langley on Whidbey Island.	141		•		•	•		•	•						
Pillar Point County Park (D-5) 4 acres 35 mi. w. of Port Angeles off SR 112. Clamming.	142	•	•		•	•		•							
Point Defiance Park (G-2) 698 acres in Tacoma off Pearl St. Scuba diving, tennis. *(See Tacoma in Seattle p. 261)*	143		•	•	•	•	•	•	•		•				•
Salt Creek County Park (D-5) 196 acres 15 mi. w. of Port Angeles off SR 112.	144	•	•	•				•	•						
Samish Park (B-3) 39 acres 10 mi. s. of Bellingham off I-5 exit 246 on North Lake Samish Dr. Canoeing.	145		•	•	•			•	•	•					
San Juan County Park (B-1) 15 acres on w. side of San Juan Island. Scuba diving.	146	•	•	•	•	•		•	•	•					
Semiahmoo County Park (A-2) 300 acres at the entrance to Semiahmoo Spit on the w. side of Drayton Harbor in Blaine. Clamming, sailing, water skiing. *(See Blaine p. 157)*	147		•					•	•				•		
Silver Lake County Park (B-7) 411 acres 4 mi. n. of Maple Falls off SR 542. Horse rental.	148	•	•	•	•	•	•	•	•			•	•	•	
Skamokawa Vista Park (G-5) 28 acres .5 mi. w. of Skamokawa on SR 4. Baseball, basketball, tennis.	149	•	•		•	•		•							
Sunny Beach Point (I-3) 9 acres on Alder Lake off SR 7. Water skiing.	150		•		•			•	•						
Swallows Park (F-12) 1 mi. s. of Clarkston on SR 129.	151		•	•	•			•	•	•					
Taidnapam Park (G-6) 5 mi. e. of Morton on US 12, s. on Kosmos Rd., then 4 mi. e. on Champion Haul Rd.	152	•	•		•	•		•	•	•					
Thornton A. Sullivan Park (E-3) 27 acres 5 mi. s. of Everett on 112th St., S.E. Nature trails.	153		•		•		•	•	•	•					
Washington Park (C-2) 220 acres 4 mi. w. of Anacortes on Anacortes Sunset Ave. Scenic drive.	154	•	•	•	•			•	•						
Wenatchee River County Park (E-8) 10 acres 10 mi. n.w. of Wenatchee on US 2/97. White-water rafting; ballparks.	155	•	•		•	•		•		•					

Exploring Washington

For descriptions of places in bold type see individual listings.

Columbia River Gorge

Rimmed by sheer cliffs separating Washington and Oregon, the Columbia River Gorge is hailed as one of the most scenic areas in the state. Tamed by hydroelectric projects, the once rogue river now provides a wide corridor for tourism and trade. The gorge runs from the moist forests near **Washougal,** through the Cascades, and out into drier, more open country east of **Bingen** and **White Salmon.**

A journey along 150-mile-long SR 14 from **Vancouver** to Plymouth parallels the river, covering a spectrum of changes in topography and vegetation. Bridges cross the river near **Stevenson,** Bingen, Dallesport, **Maryhill** and Plymouth. The Columbia River Gorge National Scenic Area covers 253,500 acres on both the Washington and Oregon banks between Washougal and Maryhill.

Beacon Rock State Park, 5 miles west of Stevenson, provides a sweeping view of the gorge. Bonneville Dam has bridled the Columbia's waters since 1938, providing a wider waterway for lumber and port towns like nearby Stevenson. **Carson,** 5 miles east of Stevenson, and Underwood, 5 miles west of Bingen, provide easy access to the **Gifford Pinchot National Forest.** Bingen, a logging town, also is known for its wineries. Doug's Beach State Park, just east of Lyle, is a windsurfing mecca.

Some 20 miles east of Bingen, US 197 turns south across the river to **The Dalles, Ore.** A few miles past the junction is The Dalles Dam; its impoundment extends to the US 97/SR 14 intersection in Maryhill. The next 80 miles to Plymouth are typical of the dry, hilly country sandwiched between the Cascades and the Blue Mountains.

Lake Chelan, Chelan / Sunny Walter / Washington State Tourism

Wandering through Washington

Between Whitcomb and **Paterson** SR 14 parallels the northern edge of the Umatilla National Wildlife Refuge, which occupies wetlands and arid grasslands on both sides of the river. SR 14 ends at I-82 just outside Plymouth. McNary Dam is nearby.

North-Central

To put it simply, north-central Washington is the northern Cascades. Bounded on the west by the Puget Sound Basin, on the east by the Columbia and Okanogan rivers, on the north by Canada and on the south by I-90, this is the roughest part of the range. It is a welter of peaks, crags and ridges, scored by deep ravines and crowned by two snowy volcanoes: sporadically restive Mount Baker, at the northwestern edge of the range, and dormant Glacier Peak, in the center.

Most of the region lies within the **Mount Baker-Snoqualmie, Okanogan** and **Wenatchee national forests, North Cascades National Park** and two national recreation areas, **Ross Lake** and **Lake Chelan.**

Three routes link the west and east slopes, and all three are designated scenic highways. The one north-south route, negotiable only by horses and hikers, is the Pacific Crest National Scenic Trail.

The 100-mile section of I-90 from Seattle to **Ellensburg** is designated the Mountains to Sound Greenway, part of America's National Scenic Byway System. Snoqualmie Pass is the conduit for heavily traveled transcontinental I-90; at 3,022 feet the lowest Cascades pass, it is the first to be plowed after a snowfall. It is the state's busiest winter sports development, with four ski areas at the summit. The scenic section begins near **North Bend,** tops the summit and coasts along the Yakima River to **Cle Elum** and Ellensburg. Another scenic drive, SR 903, goes deeper into the summit country via **Roslyn** and Cle Elum Lake; it is reached from Cle Elum or via SR 10 from Ellensburg.

US 2 crosses the center of the region through dramatic 4,061-foot Stevens Pass, also kept open—for the most part—in winter. The route enters the Cascades foothills at Startup—named, incidentally, for a settler named Startup, not because it is where visitors start up into the mountains. Beginning at **Gold Bar,** the scenic segment twists east, skirting such picturesque towns as **Index** and **Skykomish.**

After cresting the pass and its adjoining ski area, the route runs through several small resort communities and the cutoff to Wenatchee Lake, then penetrates the dramatic Tumwater Canyon. A few miles east of Bavarian-style **Leavenworth** US 2 is joined by US 97 the rest of the way through **Cashmere** to **Wenatchee,** traversing the Wenatchee Valley, one of the nation's prime apple growing regions.

The northernmost cross-Cascades route is SR 20, crossing 4,860-foot Rainy Pass and 5,477-foot Washington Pass through North Cascades National Park. Designated as scenic all the way from the Puget Sound Basin, the route travels the length of the Skagit Valley before entering the summit country east of Diablo. From December into April, winter snows usually close the road between Diablo and Mazama.

From Mazama SR 20 follows the Methow River through **Winthrop** to **Twisp.** There it bears east over 30 townless, mountainous miles to US 97 at **Okanogan,** while SR 153 continues along the Methow to meet US 97 at **Pateros.**

There is one more way to reach the heart of the northern Cascades: by boat, up fiordlike Lake Chelan between **Chelan** and Stehekin.

Northeast

From the Okanogan Valley eastward to the Idaho border, and from the Canadian border south to I-90, northeastern Washington presents variety on a grand scale. The northern part is the Okanogan Highlands; its mountains, the Kettle River Range and the Selkirks are an extension of the northern Rockies.

In the south spreads the vast basaltic plateau, formed by lava flows and scoured by the rushing meltwaters of the last ice age. The most prominent feature, however, is the mighty Columbia River, which curves down from Canada and furnishes irrigation, power and recreation to much of eastern Washington.

Except between **Ellensburg** and **Wenatchee,** US 97 delineates the western edge of the region as it snakes northward between the Columbia and the Cascades foothills. Basalt cliffs keep the river in bounds, as do the Rock Island and Rocky Reach dams, both near Wenatchee. The landscape to the east opens out as the highway nears Entiat, but the hills crowd close on the west all the way to **Chelan.**

Art Wolfe / Getty Images

After passing another dam at Azwell, the highway continues along the west bank of the Columbia to Pateros, where SR 153 turns northwest into the Methow Valley. A few miles east of **Brewster,** US 97 forsakes the Columbia and heads north along the Okanogan River Valley; SR 17 branches south, leading to Chief Joseph Dam at **Bridgeport,** and thence into coulee country.

The deep, steep-walled coulees were ancient channels of the Columbia before melting ice allowed it to resume its original course. Some again contain water, thanks to dams; Grand Coulee Dam and **Lake Roosevelt**

National Recreation Area are reached from SR 17 via SR 174.

The dam is the northern end of a particularly scenic route through this dramatic area. SR 155 passes the Grand Coulee Dam. At **Coulee City** US 2, which spans the farming country between Wenatchee and **Spokane,** carries the scenic route west to a junction with SR 17. In turn SR 17 heads south past Dry Falls, once three times the size of Niagara. The coulees and channeled scablands of this region were carved more than 15,000 years ago by a series of cataclysms known as the Ice Age Floods. The highway passes many lakes and huge farms en route to Soap Lake, where the road branches onto SR 28 to **Ephrata.** SR 17 continues south to meet I-90 at **Moses Lake.**

When it turns north into the Okanogan, US 97 enters Washington's Old West. The route parallels the Cariboo Trail, which funneled cattle between **Pasco** and Canada in the 1860s and was a highway for goldseekers later in the century. The valley is still largely devoted to ranching.

Running along the western edge of the Colville Indian Reservation, the route passes **Okanogan** and **Omak.** At the former, SR 20 from **Twisp** joins US 97 and runs concurrently with it to Tonasket. At Tonasket US 97 proceeds north to **Oroville** and the Canadian border, but SR 20 turns east, embarking on one of the state's least known scenic mountain drives.

Passing through the **Okanogan** and **Colville national forests,** it crosses the highest pass in the state highway system—5,575-foot Sherman Pass—and descends to the Columbia River and US 395 near **Kettle Falls.** At this point, US 395 heads north to the Canadian border and south toward Spokane; the scenic route follows it south to **Colville,** then branches east through the Selkirks.

At the Pend Oreille River SR 31 turns north toward **Metaline Falls** and Canada, and SR 20 bears south through slightly less scenic but still interesting mining country. SR 20 ends at US 2 at Newport, northeast of Spokane on the Idaho border.

I-90 is the main corridor across Washington. It leaves the Cascades at Ellensburg, leaps the Columbia at **Vantage,** then climbs the cliffs to George. It then runs virtually curveless to Ritzville, intersecting en route with SR 283/28 to Ephrata and SR 17 at Moses Lake. At Ritzville US 395 joins I-90 for another nearly straight run to Spokane. Throughout, the route traverses the productive cropland that is the essence of the Inland Empire.

Olympic Peninsula

Contrasts and extremes distinguish the Olympic Peninsula. The Olympic Mountain Range divides it into two distinct worlds: the wild, sparsely populated western side, with its wave-wracked coast, ancient glaciers and the largest temperate zone rain forests in the world, and the sheltered eastern side, with its irrigated plains, picturesque mill towns and the Kitsap Peninsula's mosaic of islands, peninsulas and bays.

Making a loop along the Olympic Peninsula's edge, US 101 connects these disparate realms and provides access into **Olympic National Park** and the **Olympic National Forest.**

From **Olympia,** at the southern tip of Puget Sound, US 101 passes shallow Oyster Bay en route to the old logging town of **Shelton,** where SR 3 begins its trek along the Kitsap Peninsula's spine. Bounded by Hood Canal on the west and Puget Sound on the east, the peninsula is marked by such towns as **Bremerton,** home to a major Navy shipyard, and Poulsbo, noted for its Norwegian character.

SR 106 provides a scenic alternate route back to US 101, which borders oyster- and clam-rich Hood Canal. Inland, side roads lead into the high country of the Olympic National Forest. Meadows, woodlands and banks of rhododendron straddle US 101 as it continues north to the SR 20

junction to historic **Port Townsend.**

US 101 then turns westward along the Strait of Juan de Fuca. The only sizable towns on this narrow, remote coast are **Sequim** and **Port Angeles;** the latter offers one of the best approaches into the lofty heights of Olympic National Park. Such viewpoints as Hurricane Ridge and Deer Park offer panoramas of the park's jagged peaks, lowland lakes and wildflower meadows. Mountain goats, bears, elk, marmots and chipmunks are but a few of the animals that can be seen; the Elwha River, just west, is noted for steelhead trout.

From Port Angeles SR 112, a National Scenic Byway, continues the coastal route and links towns and resorts geared to sport fishing. The busiest, **Neah Bay,** at the end of SR 112, boasts fishing resorts run by the Makah Tribe. The beaches next to these salmon ports yield agates and driftwood. Cape Flattery, the very northwestern tip of the peninsula, presents spectacular cliffs bounded by wave-battered offshore rocks.

The offshore waters along 135 miles of shoreline between Cape Flattery and Copalis Beach form the Olympic Coast National Marine Sanctuary. The reserve extends 35 to 40 miles out to sea. Within the sanctuary lie the wild beaches of Olympic National Park, most of which can be approached only by muddy hiking trails through forests and small meadows. Over the centuries dozens of ships have wrecked along this stretch of coast.

By contrast, few trails penetrate the dense rain forests on the inland side of US 101. In the Hoh, Queets and Quinault river valleys, Sitka spruce and Douglas fir with 8-foot trunks grow to

Olympic National Park
© Charles A. Blakeslee / age fotostock

heights of 275 feet, and mosses and ferns carpet the forest floor. Roads off US 101 venture into all three valleys and lead to highcountry trails and campgrounds of the national park.

At Ruby Beach, a scenic section of US 101 rejoins a tamer coast, known for sandy beaches, driftwood, razor clams and smelt runs. Turning inland again, the highway borders the Quinault Indian Reservation en route to Lake Quinault, one of the park's most developed recreational areas. US 101 runs south to **Aberdeen.** At **Hoquiam** SR 109 heads west to the seashore resort towns north of Grays Harbor.

US 12/SR 8, the final leg of the loop, affords views of the least rugged, yet most remote, side of the Olympics as it returns to Olympia.

Puget Sound and San Juan Islands

Puget Sound cleaves southward from the Strait of Juan de Fuca nearly two-thirds of the way through the state. In a direct line, the sound is about 140 miles long, but its indented eastern shore wriggles much farther than that between **Olympia** and the Canadian border.

One of the world's great embayments, the sound shelters in its many harbors not only fishing fleets and countless pleasure craft, but also, at such ports as **Bellingham, Everett,** Olympia, **Seattle** and **Tacoma,** the giant vessels of the international tradeways. **Whidbey Island** and the **San Juan Islands,** in the northern half of the sound, remain in many ways a world apart.

On the narrow belt separating the sound and the Cascades foothills, 55 percent of the state's population lives and works in a sprawling conurbation that includes five of Washington's largest cities and its heaviest concen-

to **Enumclaw,** east of which it provides a scenic drive to Sunrise in the eastern side of the park.

Development, industry and traffic increase as I-5 continues north through Seattle. Glimpses of Lake Washington and the sound, with their respective mountain backdrops, intersperse views of the hilly city. I-405 bypasses downtown by skirting the eastern shore of Lake Washington; it connects with I-90, the scenic Snoqualmie Pass highway, then continues through **Bellevue** to rejoin I-5 between Seattle and Everett.

North of Everett towns become farther apart as I-5 traverses farming and dairy country. There are often views of the

Lummi Island is west of Bellingham. Boat charters, available at harbors all along the sound, allow exploration of the waterways off the ferry lanes.

Between Everett and Burlington I-5 connects with several highways that become designated scenic routes as they enter the Cascades. US 2 runs east from Everett, through the Skykomish Valley and over Stevens Pass; its scenic segment begins at **Gold Bar.** The Mountain Loop Highway, a route comprising SR 92, several county and forest service roads (one unpaved segment is closed in winter) and part of SR 530, loops east from Everett and returns to I-5 near **Arlington.**

At Burlington SR 20 turns east through **Sedro-Woolley** to **North Cascades National Park.** Leading east from Bellingham the scenic Mount Baker Highway (SR 542) follows the Nooksack River into the high Cascades between Mount Baker and Mount Shuksan; the final 2 miles climbing up to the viewpoint at Artist Point are open only in the summer.

Burlington also is the southern terminus of SR 11, the Chuckanut Drive, which hugs a bluff high above Samish Bay all the way to Bellingham. North of the city I-5 travels through farming country before entering Canada at **Blaine.**

South-Central

Rolling northward from the Columbia River Gorge to I-90 and eastward from the western slopes of the Cascades to the Columbia River, the mountains and valleys of south-central Washington present a variegated picture indeed. The region has three of the state's great isolated volcanoes. Mount St. Helens, a less benign presence since its eruption in 1980, is the westernmost; it is the focus of **Mount St. Helens National Volcanic Monument.**

Some 35 miles due east of St. Helens, glacier-girt Mount Adams sits amid the broad, lake-strewn meadows of the Cascade crest. In the north, looming some 8,000 feet above its forested foothills in **Mount Rainier National Park,**

Johnston Ridge, Mount St. Helens National Volcanic Monument / Jim Poth
Washington State Tourism

tration of business and industry.

The chief corridor through this busy area is I-5. It reaches the sound at Olympia, the state capital, then speeds northeast toward Tacoma; a side road leads to venerable **Steilacoom,** the oldest incorporated town in the state.

Just south of Tacoma I-5 intersects with SR 512 which, with SR 167, forms an inland route to Seattle via the increasingly industrial Green River Valley. Near **Puyallup** SR 161 branches south along a high ridge that offers stunning views of Mount Rainier. Beyond the old farming and logging town of Graham, SR 161 is part of the scenic route to Paradise in **Mount Rainier National Park.** Another road, SR 410, leaves SR 167 at Sumner; it leads

Cascades, which become increasingly rugged as they roll north. Mount Baker, the northernmost of Washington's volcanoes, shimmers above forest peaks in the **Mount Baker-Snoqualmie National Forest.**

A few miles west of Everett is **Mukilteo,** the mainland slip for the ferry to Whidbey Island. SR 525/20 along the island's spine earns its scenic designation when clear weather permits views of the sound, wooded islands, the Olympic Mountains and the Cascades. SR 20 leaps Deception Pass to reach the mainland between **Anacortes** and **Mount Vernon.**

Anacortes and **Bellingham** are the ferry ports for the San Juan Islands. State ferries call at **Lopez, Shaw, Orcas** and **San Juan;**

is the mighty peak that Washingtonians simply call The Mountain. Almost all of the southern Cascades are within the **Gifford Pinchot National Forest.**

The mountains in the eastern part of the region are different. The forested granite peaks of the Cascades blend into the more rounded, bare ridges and basalt outcrops of the Simcoe Mountains, Rattlesnake Hills and Horse Heaven Hills.

The third major feature of the area is the rich Yakima Valley, a wide streak of green and gold slicing southeastward between the dun hills to the Columbia River. The valley is widest around **Yakima,** its largest city and chief commercial center.

Other than I-90 *(see North-Central),* there is only one all-year highway through the Cascades—US 12. A designated scenic route from Morton through the Cowlitz River Valley, over 4,500-foot White Pass to Naches, it is doubly important since it connects with every other major highway in the region. It also links with a network of forest roads that rambles through the back country to the Columbia Gorge. Scenic highlights of the route include the Palisades and Clear Creek Falls bracketing White Pass and Rimrock Lake.

Several miles north of Packwood US 12 junctions with scenic SR 123, which runs north through the eastern edge of Mount Rainier National Park to SR 410 (closed in winter), thus creating a scenic loop highway around all but the west side of the mountain. The Stevens Canyon Road (closed in winter) in the southern portion of the park meets SR 123 a few miles above the US 12 junction.

SR 410, the northern arc of the loop, begins at **Enumclaw;** after intersecting with SR 123 it twists over 5,440-foot Chinook Pass and descends the eastern slope, ending at US 12 west of Naches. The Mather Memorial Parkway, an 85-mile stretch of SR 410 between Enumclaw and Naches, is designated an All American Road. Both Chinook Pass and 4,694-foot Cayuse Pass at the

junction of SRs 410 and 123 are closed in winter.

At Yakima US 12 is joined by I-82/US 97 from **Ellensburg** on I-90. SR 821 offers a 27-mile alternate through the scenic Yakima Canyon. US 12 and I-82 run concurrently along the north bank of the Yakima River, through **Zillah, Sunnyside, Grandview** and **Prosser.** The vineyards of this area make it Washington's largest wine producing district. US 97 follows the south bank of the river to **Toppenish,** then turns south on a scenic trip over 3,107-foot Satus Pass to **Goldendale** and **Maryhill.**

Prosser, on I-82/US 12, is the northern end of an important shortcut to Pendleton. SR 221 climbs south into the Horse Heaven Hills, where vineyards and wheatfields have supplanted mustangs, then follows SR 14 to Plymouth and McNary Dam. Just west of **Richland** I-82 also veers south toward McNary Dam. US 12 continues through the Tri-Cities area to southeastern Washington.

Southeast

Southeastern Washington seems to contain a little of everything. From the Columbia River it extends eastward across lava plateau and productive valleys, over the Palouse wheat country and the rugged northern end of the Blue Mountains to the Idaho border. The Oregon state line marks the southern boundary; I-90 delineates the northern. The Snake River, having emerged from Hells Canyon *(see Oregon p. 72),* arches westward to meet the Columbia at **Pasco.**

Two primary highways cross the region south to north: US 395 through the center and US 195 along the eastern edge. Besides I-90, west-to-east routes are US

Manito Park, Spokane
Sunny Walter / Washington State Tourism

12 in the south and SR 26 across the middle. There are numerous connecting routes as well, some of them especially scenic.

From Pasco, the smallest of the Tri-Cities (the other two being **Kennewick** and **Richland),** US 395 speeds northeast across miles of farmland toward Ritzville, where it joins I-90 for the remainder of the distance to **Spokane.** En route it intersects with SR 17, which heads north toward the Pothole Lakes country and I-90 at **Moses Lake,** and SR 26.

US 12 turns south from Pasco along the Columbia, then veers east along the Walla Walla River. The valley is rich in both crops and history: Acres of sweet onions and vineyards bring the Walla Walla name to tables throughout the west; **Whitman Mission National Historic Site** commemorates the culmination of some unhappy circumstances in 1847. At **Walla Walla** US 12 begins its winding course between the Snake River and the foothills of the Blue Mountains; Waitsburg, **Dayton** and Pomeroy are the largest towns the route meets before it descends to **Clarkston.**

From Clarkston scenic SR 129 follows the Snake to **Asotin,** then heads toward Oregon's Wallowa Mountains, joining scenic SR 3 in Oregon.

US 195 actually branches north into Washington from Clarkston's Idaho sibling, Lewiston. It travels into the Palouse country, closely bypassing **Pullman.** At **Colfax** the highway connects with SR 26, an important corridor through the heart of eastern Washington's granary. Buttes rise to the east of US 195; Steptoe, offering panoramic views, is reached via SR 271, which leaves US 195 north of Colfax and rejoins it near Rosalia. The rest of the way to Spokane the route traverses farming and grazing lands.

Vantage, on the Columbia River, is the starting point of two of the major routes across the region—I-90 *(see Northeast)* and SR 26—as well as for SR 243. SR 26 arrows almost due east, reaching the Palouse country and US 195 by way of **Othello** and a few other widely separated towns. SR 243 follows the east bank of the river past Wanapum and Priest Rapids dams; the section between Vantage and Beverly is scenic, hugging the clifflined Columbia River.

Southwest

The southwest corner of Washington is a green, rainy land extending from the Pacific shore across the coastal mountains and the inland valleys to Mount St. Helens and the foothills of the Cascades. The Columbia River is the southern boundary; the northern is marked by SR 8/US 12 between **Olympia** and the Grays Harbor cities of **Aberdeen** and **Hoquiam.** With its long beaches and excellent clamming and fishing, the coast is the chief vacation area; elsewhere farming, logging and dairying prevail.

Coastal US 101 and inland I-5 funnel traffic between western Oregon and Puget Sound. Only three paved highways link these arteries: SR 4, SR 6 and US 12.

US 101 merits the scenic designation that applies from the Columbia to **Raymond.** It threads between the river and the Willapa Hills to the stem of the Long Beach Peninsula, then veers north along Willapa Bay. Oysters farmed in the bay as well as cranberries and the recreation offered by **Ilwaco,** Seaview, **Long Beach** and other resort villages on the peninsula sustain the area's economy.

After bridging the Naselle River, SR 4 leaves US 101, branching southeast for a scenic drive through **Grays River, Skamokawa** and **Cathlamet** to I-5 at **Kelso.** US 101 continues north to **South Bend** and Raymond.

At Raymond US 101 proceeds north across woods and farmlands toward Aberdeen. SR 105 ends at Aberdeen too, but only after making a long loop along the bay and ocean shores to the fishing center of **Westport.** Raymond also is the western end of SR 6, which rambles through two towns with interesting names—**Lebam** and Pe Ell—and meets I-5 at **Chehalis.**

I-5 begins its beeline northward through Washington at **Vancouver,** the state's oldest settlement. North of Vancouver, I-5 passes **Kalama** and **Woodland** before turning away from the river at the twin cities of **Longview** and Kelso. Pretty farms and such busy little cities as **Toledo,** Chehalis and **Centralia** fall behind as the highway speeds toward Puget Sound.

One constant presence, though it can be seen from only a few places along I-5, is the burly hulk of Mount St. Helens, centerpiece of **Mount St. Helens National Volcanic Monument.** Two scenic roads approach the area. SR 503 leaves I-5 at Woodland and follows the Lewis River through **Ariel** and Cougar to the southern edge of the monument.

The 52-mile extension of the Spirit Lake Memorial Highway (SR 504) leads from I-5 at **Castle Rock** to Johnston Ridge in Mount St. Helens National Volcanic Monument.

Whitman Mission National Historic Site / © Brent Bergherm / age fotostock

Points of Interest

ABERDEEN (F-5) pop. 16,461, elev. 10'

Named for the Scottish city, Aberdeen wraps around the head of expansive Grays Harbor at the mouths of the Chehalis and Wishkah rivers. The settlement grew up around a sawmill established in 1884. By 1910 dozens of lumber and shingle mills lined the harbor and the population rose to 17,000.

Handsome Victorian and Craftsman-style homes grace Aberdeen's hillside residential district north of downtown. Samuel Benn Park, E. 9th and N. I streets, offers tennis courts, a playground, a rose garden and a network of pathways through landscaped rolling hills.

Grays Harbor Chamber of Commerce—Aberdeen: 506 Duffy St., Aberdeen, WA 98520; phone (360) 532-1924 or (800) 321-1924.

Shopping areas: South Shore Mall, 1.2 miles south on SR 105 (S. Boone Street), features JCPenney and Sears.

ABERDEEN MUSEUM OF HISTORY is at 111 E. 3rd St. The museum uses period furnishings to recreate scenes from the town's pioneer days. Of particular note are photographs, a slide show, a mural depicting an old-growth forest and a collection of antique firefighting equipment. Allow 1 hour minimum. Tues.-Sat. 10-5, Sun. noon-4; closed Jan. 1, July 4 and Dec. 25. Donations. Phone (360) 533-1976.

LAKE ABERDEEN FISH HATCHERY is 3 mi. e. on US 12, then .7 mi. n. on Lake Aberdeen Rd. More than 1 million fish are artificially spawned and raised at the hatchery annually. The summer steelhead run is June through September; the winter steelhead run is January through March. Guided tours are available by appointment. Daily 8-5. Free. Phone (360) 533-1663.

AIRWAY HEIGHTS (E-11)
pop. 4,500, elev. 1,400'

Established in 1942 to house personnel stationed at nearby Fairchild Army Base, Airway Heights is only 8 miles from downtown Spokane. A roadside monument 2 miles west on US 2 commemorates the Spokane Plains Battlefield where in 1858 U.S. Army troops clashed with and ultimately defeated American Indians from half a dozen Columbia Plateau bands.

GAMBLING ESTABLISHMENTS

- **Northern Quest Casino** is at 100 N. Hayford Rd. Sun.-Thurs. 9 a.m.-5 a.m., Fri.-Sat. 24 hours. Phone (509) 242-7000 or (888) 603-7051 in Wash.

ANACORTES (B-2) pop. 14,557, elev. 75'

Anacortes occupies the northern end of hilly Fidalgo Island, which is linked by bridges to Whidbey Island to the south and the mainland to the east. Settled in the 1860s, the town was first called Ship Harbor, but in 1876 town promoter Amos Bowman had it changed to a Spanish-sounding version of "Anna Curtis," his wife's maiden name.

The Depot Arts Center at 7th St. & R Ave. features changing art exhibits by various regional artists. The center is housed in a former Great Northern Railway depot built in 1911.

From the 1,270-foot summit of Mount Erie, 5 miles south via Heart Lake and Mt. Erie roads, views extend to the Cascades, Olympics and San Juan Islands. Campbell Lake, at the base of the mountain, is unusual; not only is it on an island, but it has an island inside of it as well. Washington Park *(see Recreation Chart)*, 4 miles west on wooded Fidalgo Head, offers beaches and hiking trails.

Washington State Ferries offers daily car ferry service to the San Juan Islands and Sidney, British Columbia. Reservations for vehicles on the Anacortes-to-Sidney ferry are highly recommended. A $10 per day maximum fee ($25 for 3 days, $40 for 7 days) is charged for parking at the ferry terminal May to mid-October. For ferry information phone (206) 464-6400 or (888) 808-7977 in Wash. Skagit County maintains a toll car ferry service from the foot of "I" Avenue to Guemes Island; phone (360) 293-6356.

Anacortes Chamber of Commerce: 819 Commercial Ave., Suite A, Anacortes, WA 98221; phone (360) 293-3832.

ANACORTES MUSEUM is at 1305 8th St. Inside the 1911 Carnegie Library building, the museum includes maritime and local history exhibits and a research library. Allow 30 minutes minimum. Mon. Tues. and Thurs.-Sat. 10-4, Sun. 11-4; closed Jan. 1, Easter, Thanksgiving and Dec. 25. Donations. Phone (360) 293-1915.

W.T. Preston is at 7th St. and R Ave. The *Preston* was the last stern-wheeler to operate on Puget Sound. Retired in 1981, the stern-wheeler is now a maritime museum showing the vessel's mechanism. The rooms and cabins feature original furnishings. The adjacent Snagboat Heritage Center chronicles the role of snagboats in keeping navigation channels clear. Allow 30 minutes minimum. Mon.-Tues. and Thurs.-Sat. 10-4, Sun. 11-4, Memorial Day-Aug. 31 Sat. 10-4, Sun. 11-4, Apr. 1-day before Memorial Day and Sept.-Oct.; by appointment rest of year. Admission $3; $2 (ages 65+); $1 (ages 8-16).

ISLAND ADVENTURES WHALE WATCHING is at 1801 Commercial Ave. Conducting tours among the

San Juan Islands, Island Adventures focuses mainly on the area's resident killer whales and guarantees a whale sighting on each trip. Passengers may also see gray, minke and humpback whales along with porpoises, seals, sea lions, bald eagles and a variety of seabirds.

Allow 5 hours minimum. Trips depart twice daily June 15-Labor Day; once daily Mar. 10-June 14 and day after Labor Day-Dec. 31. Fare mid-June through Labor Day $79; $74 (ages 65+, and students and active military with ID); $49 (ages 3-12). Fare rest of season $69; $64 (ages 65+ and students and active military with ID); $49 (ages 3-12). Reservations are recommended. MC, VI. Phone (360) 293-2428 or (800) 465-4604.

GAMBLING ESTABLISHMENTS

Swinomish Casino is 3 mi. e. on SR 20. Sun.-Thurs. 9 a.m.-4 a.m., Fri.-Sat. 24 hours; closed Dec. 25. Phone (360) 293-2691.

RECREATIONAL ACTIVITIES
Kayaking

SAVE **Anacortes Kayak Tours** departs from 1801 Commercial Ave., Anacortes, WA 98221. Trips of varying duration available Mar.-Oct. Phone (360) 588 1117 or (800) 992 1801.

ARIEL (G-6)

Ariel is most commonly associated with Merwin Dam, one in a string of huge power development units on the Lewis River. It forms crescent-shaped Lake Merwin, which offers excellent fishing, boating and swimming. Merwin Park Recreation Area, half a mile south on Merwin Village Road, offers day-use recreational facilities on the north shore of Yale Lake.

SPEELYAI STATE HATCHERY is at 11001 Lewis River Rd. The hatchery uses mature fish trapped in the Lewis River to spawn and raise nearly 1 million coho and 1 million chinook salmon per year. Best salmon viewing season is May-Oct. Daily 8-5. Free. Phone (360) 231-4210.

ARLINGTON—see Seattle p. 242.

ASHFORD (F-7) pop. 267, elev. 1,770'

Located just outside the Nisqually entrance to Mount Rainier National Park, Ashford was settled in the 1880s. Initially a sawmill settlement, it became the main gateway to the park when the Tacoma Eastern Railway reached town in 1904. In the early days most park visitors came by rail; passenger train service continued until 1926, the same year the road leading to the park was paved. Today, Ashford has a collection of comfortable lodgings and bed & breakfast properties. The Recycled Spirits of Iron Sculpture Park is 3 miles west on SR 706.

Mt. Rainier Visitor Association: 30027 E. SR 706, P.O. Box 214, Ashford, WA 98304; phone (360) 569-0910 or (877) 617-9950.

RECREATIONAL ACTIVITIES
Skiing (cross-country)

- **Mount Tahoma Trails** offers 50 miles of trails for cross-country skiing. Trailhead .5 mi. w. on SR 706. Other activities are available. Write P.O. Box 206, Ashford, WA 98304. Phone (360) 569-2451.

ASOTIN (G-12) pop. 1,095, elev. 760'

Originally named Has-Hu-Tin (meaning eel), the town of Asotin got its present spelling by an act of the legislature in 1886. Because of its mild climate, Asotin, at the confluence of the Snake River and Asotin Creek, is part of the banana belt of eastern Washington.

The town is at the southern end of the Clearwater and Snake River National Recreation Trail, a 16-mile paved route following the river shoreline north through the Clarkston-Lewiston area. The Snake River Road continues 21 miles south to the mouth of the Grande Ronde River at the northern entrance to Hells Canyon.

Asotin Chamber of Commerce: P.O. Box 574, Asotin, WA 99402; phone (509) 243-4242.

AARDVARK'S SNAKE RIVER, USA departs from 7357 Snake River Rd. This river outfitter offers guided jet boat tours on the Snake River to Hells Canyon and the Salmon River Canyon. Boat and kayak rentals and guided hunting trips also are available. Allow 4 hours minimum. Daily 9-6. Half-day tour $480 for entire boat (up to five people); fuel surcharge may apply. DS, MC, VI. Phone (509) 243-9404 or (800) 564-9737.

ASOTIN COUNTY MUSEUM is at 215 Filmore St. The museum depicts early Western life through American Indian and pioneer artifacts, a Salmon River barge, preserved log cabin, pole frame barn, schoolhouse, blacksmith shop, Colvill windmill and shepherd's cabin. Allow 30 minutes minimum. Tues.-Sat. noon-4, Apr.-Oct.; Sat. 1-4 or by appointment rest of year. Donations. Phone (509) 243-4659.

AUBURN—see Seattle p. 242.

BAINBRIDGE ISLAND—see Seattle p. 242.

BATTLE GROUND—
see Portland in Oregon p. 108.

BAY VIEW (C-3) pop. 334, elev. 98'

This peaceful community overlooking Padilla Bay was platted in 1884. Just north of town is Bay View State Park, a popular recreation area since the late 19th century. The park offers beach access and camping (see Recreation Chart).

PADILLA BAY NATIONAL ESTUARINE RESEARCH RESERVE AND INTERPRETIVE CENTER is .2 mi. n. of Bay View State Park at 10441 Bay View-Edison Rd. This 10,600-acre reserve protects habitats ranging from open marine waters, tideflats, marshes and beaches to wooded uplands and open fields. It is home to a variety of fish, mammals and birds, including nearly 250 visiting bird species. An interpretive center has interactive learning modules about estuaries and watersheds. More than 3 miles of trails lead to beach, shoreline and upland areas.

Educational programs are presented periodically. Allow 1 hour, 30 minutes minimum. Center open Wed.-Sun. 10-5; closed holidays. Trails open daily dawn-dusk. Donations. Phone (360) 428-1558.

BEAVER (D-4) elev. 390'

Beaver was settled in 1891 at the southern end of Lake Pleasant in the Soleduck Valley. After rail lines were built into the woods, the town became a booming logging camp.

SOL DUC HATCHERY INTERPRETIVE CENTER is 4 mi. w. on US 101, then 1 mi. s.w. on Mary Clark and Pavel rds. The center depicts the life cycle, production and harvest of salmon. Also of interest are the salmon trap and pen. Allow 30 minutes minimum. Daily 8-4:30. Free. Phone (360) 327-3246.

BELLEVUE—see Seattle p. 243.

BELLINGHAM (B-3) pop. 67,171, elev. 60'

Formed in 1903 by the consolidation of four adjacent communities—Fairhaven, Bellingham (originally called Unionville), New Whatcom (Sehome) and Whatcom—Bellingham took its name from the bay it overlooks. The bay in turn was named by Capt. George Vancouver's 1792 expedition in honor of Sir William Bellingham, a controller in the British Navy who had personally checked Vancouver's supplies prior to embarkation from England. The city's complex street system is the result of these separate towns being pieced together.

Bellingham's central business district rises behind the docks at the head of the bay. Among the sights is the Mount Baker Theatre, 104 N. Commercial St., a 1927 movie palace with an Art Deco-Moorish interior and the original pipe organ that provided accompaniment to silent films. The wooded campus of Western Washington University, established in 1893, crowns the heights just south of downtown. Bellingham has an impressive collection of Victorian and craftsman-style homes, particularly in the residential neighborhoods to the south and north of the downtown area. Eldridge, on the near-north side, is a historic district noted for its concentration of stately mansions.

The southern section of the city was once the separate and thriving municipality of Fairhaven, founded in 1883. Its substantial brick buildings now house shops, boutiques and cafes giving the district an early 20th-century ambience.

The Bellingham Cruise Terminal, at the foot of Harris Avenue, is the southern terminus of the Alaska Marine Highway's weekly ferry service to Ketchikan, Juneau and other ports in the Alaska panhandle; for information phone (800) 642-0066.

Bellingham/Whatcom County Convention and Visitors Bureau: 904 Potter St., Bellingham, WA 98229; phone (360) 671-3990 or (800) 487-2032.

Shopping areas: Fairhaven, the restored business district centered on 12th Street and Harris Avenue features a variety of specialty shops, boutiques, galleries and restaurants. A farmer's market sets up at the Village Green on Wednesdays, April through October. A cluster of antique and second-hand stores is on Holly Street between Commercial Street and Central Avenue. Bellis Fair, at I-5 exit 256, has more than 125 stores, including JCPenney, Kohl's, Macy's and Sears. The Bellingham Farmer's Market is held Saturdays April through December at the corner of Railroad Avenue and East Chestnut Street.

AMERICAN MUSEUM OF RADIO AND ELECTRICITY is at 1312 Bay St. Dedicated to the history of electricity and radio, the museum's collection covers four centuries of human achievement beginning in 1580. Among the many great inventors documented are Thomas Edison, Benjamin Franklin and Guglielmo Marconi. A library features schematics, rare books and magazines from radio's Golden Age. One exhibit consists of a full-scale replica of the *Titanic's* radio room. Guided tours are available. Allow 1 hour minimum. Wed.-Sat. 11-4 or by appointment; closed Jan. 1, Thanksgiving and Dec. 25. Admission $5; $2 (ages 6-12). Phone (360) 738-3886.

[SAVE] **BELLINGHAM RAILWAY MUSEUM** is at 1320 Commercial St. The museum documents the railroad, logging and mining heritage of Whatcom and Skagit counties from 1883 to the present. Displays include historic photos, timetables and several model railroad layouts, including some in G and O scales that visitors are welcome to touch and help operate. A computer-based train simulator and children's play area also are available. Allow 30 minutes minimum. Thurs.-Sat. and Tues. noon-5; closed major holidays. Admission $4; $2 (ages 3-16); $6 (family, up to four members). Phone (360) 393-7540.

CHUCKANUT DRIVE is 3 mi. s. on I-5 to exit 250, then 1 mi. w. on SR 11. This scenic highway winds for 8 miles along the rocky shore of Samish Bay at the base of 1,900-foot Chuckanut Mountain. Magnificent views extend out across the bay to the San Juan Islands. In places a dense forest canopy arches over the roadway and in autumn maples and alders blaze with color. Established in 1915 Larrabee State Park, near the north end of the drive, is Washington's oldest *(see Recreation Chart).*

GLEN ECHO GARDEN is 6 mi. e. of I-5 exit 22 on SR 542, then .75 mi. s.e. on Y Rd. Nestled in a glen of western red cedars, the 3-acre garden strikingly incorporates giant stumps into its design. Theme areas include begonias and fuchsias, roses and an English garden. The Blue Garden features plants with blue and purple flowers arranged around a blue fountain. Allow 30 minutes minimum. Open

Mon.-Sat. 10-6, mid-May through Sept. 30. Admission $7.50; $6 (ages 13-18 and 60+); $3 (ages 6-12). Phone (360) 592-5380.

MARITIME HERITAGE PARK is at 514 W. Holly St. On the site of an 1852 sawmill, the heritage center includes a seven-station interpretive path that explores the life cycle of salmon. Some 3 million pink, coho and chum salmon are released every spring. The best viewing time is mid-October to mid-December. A native plant garden features interpretive signs and a hand-carved Salmon Woman totem pole. Picnic facilities are available. Allow 1 hour minimum. Daily dawn-dusk. Free. Phone (360) 676-6806.

MINDPORT is at 210 W. Holly St. This museum combines fine art with interactive art displays that encourage quiet contemplation. Visitors also learn about science through humorous exhibits that include optical illusions and brain teasers. A gallery features work by Washington artists. Allow 30 minutes minimum. Wed.-Fri. noon-6, Sat. 10-5, Sun. noon-4; closed holidays. Admission $2. Phone (360) 647-5614.

ROEDER HOME is at 2600 Sunset Dr. Containing a cultural arts center, the 1908 house features interior oak paneling, hand-painted murals and a state-of-the-art built-in vacuum cleaning system. A gallery displays changing exhibits of regional arts. Tours of the house are available on request. Allow 30 minutes minimum. Mon.-Thurs. 9-4, otherwise by appointment; closed holidays. Donations. Phone (360) 733-6897.

SEHOME HILL ARBORETUM is on a wooded ridge that is accessible by footpath from the Western Washington University campus or by automobile from the Bill McDonald Pkwy. Six miles of trails lead through the 180-acre reserve that features native flora. Panoramic views from the observation tower include the city, Bellingham Bay, the San Juan Islands, Mount Baker and the mountains of southern British Columbia. Daily 6 a.m.-dusk. Free.

SQUALICUM HARBOR is 1 mi. n.w. on Roeder Ave. One of the largest marinas on Puget Sound, Squalicum Harbor features promenades, a 2,500-gallon marine life tank and a variety of shops and restaurants. A boat launch and visitor moorage are available for a fee. Daily dawn-dusk. Free. Phone (360) 676-2542 or (360) 676-2500.

Island Mariner Cruises departs from 5 Harbor Loop at Squalicum Harbor. This tour company offers 6-hour narrated whale-search and nature cruises through the San Juan Islands. Orca, gray and minke whales, porpoises, harbor seals, bald eagles and various sea birds are some of the wildlife that can be seen on the 70- to 90-mile island tour. A 2.5-hour sunset cruise of Bellingham Bay features a narrated history of the area.

Whale-watch cruises depart daily at 10, spring-fall; phone ahead for schedule information. Sunset cruises depart Thurs. (also some Tues.) at 6:30 p.m., late June through Aug. Whale-watch cruise $75. Sunset cruise $25. Reservations are recommended. MC, VI. Phone (360) 734-8866 or (877) 734-8866.

Marine Life Center is at 1801 Roeder Ave. The center is an open-air, covered exhibit featuring marine animals from the waters of Washington. The touch pool allows visitors to touch live specimens of sea stars, hermit crabs, anemones and sea cucumbers. The main observation pool holds 1,500 gallons of sea water; it includes rockfish, perch, sea stars and sculpins. One aquarium is home to a giant Pacific octopus. Daily 10-6, June-Aug.; 11-5, rest of year. Admission $1; 50c (children). Phone (360) 671-2431.

[SAVE] **VICTORIA/SAN JUAN CRUISES** departs from the Bellingham Cruise Terminal at 355 Harris Ave. The tour company offers narrated passenger boat service to Victoria, British Columbia, and the San Juan Islands. Tours depart daily at 9 (Victoria) and 9:30 (Friday Harbor), mid-May to early Oct. Round-trip fare to Victoria (includes dinner) $129; $79 (ages 13-20); $49 (ages 3-12). Round-trip fare to Friday Harbor in the San Juan Islands $59; $39 (ages 6-12). MC, VI. Phone (360) 738-8099, (800) 443-4552, or (888) 734-8180 from Friday Harbor.

WESTERN GALLERY AND OUTDOOR SCULPTURE COLLECTION is on the Western Washington University campus, 1 mi. w. via I-5 exit 252, then s.w. on Bill McDonald Pkwy. to the visitor information center in the Campus Services building. Visitors to the outdoor sculpture collection will find 29 works by regional, national and international artists focusing on various themes. Representing the period 1960-present, the sculptures are displayed throughout the campus. A self-guiding tour brochure is available from the visitor center. The Western Gallery, in the Fine Arts Complex, features changing contemporary art exhibitions.

Allow 1 hour minimum. Gallery open Mon.-Fri. 10-4 (also Wed. 4-8), Sat. noon-4, late Sept. to mid-June; closed between school sessions. Visitor information center open Mon.-Fri. 7 a.m.-8 p.m., mid-Sept. to mid-June; 7-5, rest of year. Outdoor sculpture collection accessible daily 24 hours. Free. Parking $2 (per hour); $7 (all day). Phone (360) 650-3900.

WHATCOM CHILDREN'S MUSEUM is at 227 Prospect St. Providing educational experiences through interactive exhibits and displays, the museum contains hands-on activities geared toward children ages 2-8. **Note:** In summer 2009, the museum will move into the new Whatcom Art and Children's Museum at 216 Grand St. Allow 1 hour minimum. Thurs.-Sat. 10-5, Tues.-Wed. and Sun. noon-5. Admission $3.50. Phone (360) 733-8769.

WHATCOM MUSEUM is at 121 Prospect St. Housed in an 1892 Victorian building once used as city hall, the museum features regional history displays and contemporary art. Changing art displays are offered at the Arco Exhibition Gallery annex across the street.

Note: In summer 2009, the museum will relocate its art exhibits to the Whatcom Art and Children's Museum at 216 Grand St. Allow 1 hour minimum. Tues.-Sun. noon-5; closed Jan. 1, July 4, Thanksgiving, day after Thanksgiving and Dec. 25. Donations. Phone (360) 676-6981.

BENTON CITY (G-9) pop. 2,624, elev. 499′

Though it lies in the Eastern Washington arid terrain, Benton City is cradled by the arable bend of the Yakima River. Irrigation canals developed in the early 1900s bring precious water to this parched land, allowing the desert to flourish with pastures, orchards and vineyards. The Red Mountain area, east of Benton City on SR 224, is a premium red wine-producing region.

Benton City Chamber of Commerce: P.O. Box 401, Benton City, WA 99320; phone (509) 588-4984.

WINERIES

• **Chandler Reach Winery** is 1 mi. e. of I-82 exit 93, following signs to 9506 Chandler Rd. This Tuscan-style winery overlooks the lower Yakima Valley and Red Mountain. Tours are given by advance reservation. Thurs.-Sun. 11-5, early Mar. to mid-Dec.; call for hours rest of year. Closed major holidays. Phone (509) 588-8800.

• **Kiona Vineyards and Winery** is off I-82 exit 96, .75 mi. n.e. on SR 224, then 3.4 mi. n. to 44612 Sunset Rd. Daily noon-5; closed Jan. 1, Thanksgiving and Dec. 25. Phone (509) 588-6716.

• **Seth Ryan Winery** is off I-82 exit 96, .75 mi. n.e. on SR 224, just n. to 35306 Sunset Rd. Daily noon-5, Apr.-Oct.; Tues.-Sun. noon-5, rest of year. Closed Dec. 25-Jan. 1. Phone (509) 588-6780.

• **Terra Blanca Winery and Estate Vineyard** is .25 mi. e. of I-82 exit 96 on SR 224, then .5 mi. n. to 34715 N. DeMoss Rd. Daily 11-6; closed Easter, Thanksgiving and Dec. 25. Phone (509) 588-6082.

BICKLETON (G-9) pop. 113

Surrounded by wheat fields near the base of the Horse Heaven Hills, Bickleton bills itself as the "Bluebird Capital of the World." The mountain bluebird and the Western bluebird both nest in the area, and since the 1960s more than 2,000 blue and white nest boxes have been built, mostly on fenceposts along county roads. These migratory species are residents from February through October, but the best viewing time is during the April-July nesting season. A large bluebird house beside the town post office honors a local couple who put up the first nest boxes.

ALDER CREEK PIONEER MUSEUM is on the w. edge of town at 4 E. Market St. The museum's centerpiece is a vintage Armitage Herschell/Herschell

Spillman two-track portable carousel featuring 2 horses, four carriages, a steam engine and a band organ. Additional changing exhibits showcase the history of eastern Klickitat County. Allow 30 minute minimum. Open Thurs.-Sat. 10-3, Sun. noon-4, Apr. 1 to early Oct., or by appointment; closed holidays. Admission $4; $1 (ages 0-11); $10 (family rate, two adults plus children). Phone (509) 896-2007.

BINGEN (H-7) pop. 672, elev. 1,131′

The neighboring communities of Bingen and White Salmon, opposite Hood River, Oregon, overlook the Columbia River south of Mount Adams. Bingen's Germanic architectural motifs reflect the town's sister city relationship with its namesake on the Rhine River in Germany. Orchards on the terraced land above the river produce peaches, apples, cherries and pears. Several wineries in the vicinity offer tastings.

THE GORGE HERITAGE MUSEUM is at 202 E. Humboldt St. Located in a 1912 former church, the museum houses a country store replica, historical photographs, pioneer clothing, farm tools, medical equipment and American Indian artifacts. Videos illustrate contemporary American Indian affairs. Allow 30 minutes minimum. Thurs.-Sun. and holidays 11:30-4:30, mid-May through Sept. 30; or by appointment. Donations. Phone (509) 493-3228.

BIRCH BAY (A-2) pop. 4,961, elev. 20′

Known to the area's American Indians as Tsarwuch, the crescent-shaped bay was named Ensenada de Garzón by the Spanish expedition of Galiano and Valdés in 1792. Capt. George Vancouver's visit late that same year gave the bay its present name, a reference to the prevalence of the western paper birch.

Today Birch Bay is a waterfront resort community near the British Columbia border, Birch Bay particularly popular with summer vacationers. Birch Bay State Park (see Recreation Chart) is 1 mile south on the coast.

Birch Bay Chamber of Commerce Visitor Center: 4880 Beachcomber Dr., Suite C, Birch Bay, WA 98230; phone (360) 371-5004.

BIRCH BAY WATER SLIDES is 5 mi. w. of I-5 exit 270 at 4874 Birch Bay-Lynden Rd. The park features four 400-foot warm-water flumes that descend in loops and curves to receiving pools. Also featured are three children's flumes and one ramp slide, inner tube rides, a 60-foot-high hydrocliff slide, an activity pool, a whirlpool, a volleyball court, picnic facilities and beach areas.

Food is available. Daily 10-6, late June-Labor Day; Sat.-Sun. and holidays 11-6, Memorial Day weekend-late June. Admission $16; $11 (ages 3- and 60+). Admission after 3 p.m. $11; $9 (ages 3- and 60+). MC, VI. Phone (360) 371-7500.

BLACK DIAMOND (E-7)
pop. 3,970, elev. 628′

Black Diamond is named for the Black Diamond Coal Co. of California, which by 1895 was the primary developer of a major vein found in the region years earlier. Among the area's natural assets is the Green River Gorge State Park Conservation Area, which includes Nolte, Flaming Geyser and Kanaskat-Palmer state parks *(see Recreation Chart)*. Three miles south SR 169 spans the gorge 200 feet above the river.

BLACK DIAMOND HISTORICAL MUSEUM is at 32627 Railroad Ave. at the corner of Baker St. The museum is in an 1883 Columbia-Puget Sound Line depot. Exhibits of 19th-century Americana include coal machinery, a Western jail, a country store and replicas of a country doctor's office, a coal mine entrance, a coal car, a caboose, a fire hose house and a miner's wash house.

Guided tours are available; reservations should be made at least 2 weeks in advance. Allow 30 minutes minimum. Thurs. 9-4, Sat.-Sun. noon-4, June-Aug.; Sat.-Sun. noon-3, rest of year. Closed holidays. Donations. Phone (360) 886-2142, or (253) 852-6763 for tour reservations.

BLAINE (A-2) pop. 3,770, elev. 77'

Blaine is a port of entry on Drayton Harbor just south of the British Columbia border. First settled in 1856, it enjoyed a fleeting boom during the Fraser River gold rush. After the Homestead Act began attracting farmers to the area about 1870, Blaine became a dairy supply center and fishing port.

Semiahmoo County Park, across the harbor, contains three 19th-century bunkhouse buildings. The tideflats offer beachcombing and bird-watching opportunities *(see Recreation Chart)*.

Peace Arch State and Provincial Park, on I-5 at the international border, commemorates more than 100 years of harmony between the United States and Canada. The inscriptions on the arch, erected in 1921, read "Children of a Common Mother" and "Brethren Dwelling Together in Unity."

Occupying a former 19th-century fishing fleet bunkhouse at 9261 Semiahmoo Parkway, the Semiahmoo Park Maritime Museum houses an exhibit describing the Alaska Packers Semiahmoo Cannery, which operated 1890-1985. The museum also features a scale model fish trap and a restored Bristol Bay fishing boat along with photos and paintings depicting local historic scenes. Phone (360) 383-2900. The museum is in Semiahmoo County Park. The park's tideflats offer beachcombing and bird-watching opportunities *(see Recreation Chart)*.

The 1946 passenger ferry MV *Plover*, which used to transport cannery workers across Drayton Harbor between Blaine and Semiahmoo Spit, now transports tourists and residents along the same route. The 11-minute westbound trip departs from the Blaine Visitor's Dock and offers views of the harbor, Semiahmoo Bay and Mount Baker. The 23-minute eastbound trip affords sightings of harbor seals and shorebirds as well as harbor views. The ferry operates Fri.-Sun., Memorial Day weekend to Labor Day. Fare $2; free (ages 0-12). For information phone the visitor information center.

Blaine Visitor Information Center: 728 Peace Portal Dr., Blaine, WA 98230; phone (360) 332-4544 or (800) 624-3555.

BLAKE ISLAND—*see Seattle p. 245.*

BOTHELL—*see Seattle p. 245.*

BOW (B-3) elev. 12'

Located on the North Samish River near the base of Chuckanut Mountain, Bow was first called Brownsville after pioneer settler William Brown, who established a sawmill here in the late 19th century. After a post office opened in 1901, Brown suggested the town's present name, which he took from a district and train station in London, England.

GAMBLING ESTABLISHMENTS

- **Skagit Valley Casino Resort** is off I-5 exit 236, then e. to 5984 Darrk Ln. E. Sun.-Thurs. 9 a.m.-3 a.m., Fri.-Sat. 9 a.m.-5 a.m. Phone (360) 724-7777 or (877) 275-2448.

BREMERTON—*see Seattle p. 246.*

BREWSTER (D-9) pop. 2,189, elev. 820'

In 1896 a Columbia River steamboat company built a ferry landing at the homestead of John Bruster. By the time the town was officially established in 1910, the spelling had been changed to Brewster by the post office. Today the town stands on the shores of Lake Pateros, the reservoir behind Wells Dam, which is 14 miles downstream. The region around the town is known for its many apple orchards.

Brewster Chamber of Commerce: 105 S. Third St., P.O. Box 1087, Brewster, WA 98812; phone (509) 689-3464.

FORT OKANOGAN STATE PARK & INTERPRETIVE CENTER is 5 mi. e. on US 97, then .5 mi. e. on SR 17, then s. on Fort Okanogan Rd. to park entrance. Dedicated to the history of Fort Okanogan, an early 19th-century fur trading post, the interpretive center overlooks the fort's original site and explains the fur trade through displays of artifacts, dioramas and a video presentation. John Jacob Astor's Pacific Fur Co. established the fort in 1811, and it is considered to be the state's first settlement. The fort was acquired by the Hudson's Bay Co. in 1821.

Special presentations are offered on selected weekends. Allow 30 minutes minimum. Daily 9-5, mid-May to mid-Oct. Free. Phone (509) 689-6665.

BRIDGEPORT (D-9) pop. 2,059, elev. 829'

On the Columbia River several miles above its confluence with the Okanogan, Bridgeport began as a wheat shipping point in the late 1800s. Apples are now the area's prime agricultural product. Massive Chief Joseph Dam *(see attraction listing)* impounds the Columbia just east of town. Bridgeport State

Park, northeast of town, offers water-based activities on Rufus Woods Lake, camping and golf *(see Recreation Chart)*.

Bridgeport Chamber of Commerce: P.O. Box 395, Bridgeport, WA 98813; phone (509) 686-5656.

CHIEF JOSEPH DAM is just n. off SR 17. Second only to Grand Coulee Dam *(see attraction listing p. 164)* in the production of hydropower, Chief Joseph Dam is more than a mile long and 236 feet high. Named for the Nez Perce chief, the dam spans the Columbia River and features several viewpoints and picnic areas. The visitor center, at the base of the dam, offers exhibits and a 10-minute audiovisual presentation about the dam's construction. *See Recreation Chart.*

Note: A photo ID is required for admittance. Backpacks are not permitted. Guided tours are available. Allow 1 hour minimum. Daily 9-4, May-Oct.; by appointment rest of year. Guided tours are given at 10 and 2, Memorial Day-Labor Day. Free. Phone (509) 686-5501 or (509) 686-3545.

BURBANK (G-10) pop. 3,303, elev. 365'

Located at the point where the Snake River empties into the Columbia, Burbank started out as a ferry crossing. Early 20th-century attempts at irrigation failed until the federally financed Columbia Basin Project of the 1950s.

McNARY NATIONAL WILDLIFE REFUGE is at 64 Maple St. The refuge covers more than 15,000 acres of wetlands, river islands, riparian woodlands, upland and farmland along the Columbia, Snake and Walla Walla rivers. One in a chain of refuges along the Pacific flyway, this is an important resting and feeding place for thousands of migrating waterfowl. The refuge offers an environmental learning center, a 1.9-mile interpretive trail and a bird watching blind. Daily dawn-dusk. Free. Phone (509) 546-8300 or (509) 546-8356.

BURLINGTON (C-3) pop. 6,757

Founded as a logging camp in the 1880s, Burlington became an important rail junction served by both the Great Northern and Northern Pacific lines. Named for the city in Vermont, the town serves as a commercial center for the surrounding farms that produce peas, cauliflower, seed crops and flower bulbs.

Burlington Chamber of Commerce: 111 S. Cherry St., Burlington, WA 98233; phone (360) 757-0994.

Shopping areas: Cascade Mall, off I-5 exit 229, offers 75 stores including JCPenney, Macy's and Sears. Adjacent to the Cascade Mall is The Outlet Shoppes at Burlington, with more than 50 stores.

CHILDREN'S MUSEUM OF SKAGIT COUNTY is .5 mi. s. of SR 20 on S. Burlington Blvd. to Cascade Mall. Interactive theme areas, including a boat, crane, farmers market, science zone and art studio,

plus participation in drama and reading, encourag children to experiment, create and learn throug play. Allow 1 hour minimum. Tues.-Fri. 10-7, Sa 10-6, Sun. 11-6; closed Jan. 1, Easter, Memori Day, July 4, Labor Day, Thanksgiving and Dec. 2. Admission $5; free (under 1). MC, VI. Phone (36(757-8888.

CARNATION—*see Seattle p. 246.*

CARSON (H-7) elev. 242'

Carson is located on its namesake creek at the e trance to the Wind River Valley, just above its co fluence with the Columbia River. When Lewis an Clark passed through the area in 1805, they encou tered their first ash trees in the Northwest, namin the creek for the tree. Later it was called Katsner, (which Carson is supposedly a corruption.

The Wind River Valley has hot springs and wide variety of outdoor recreation. Forest Road 3 leads north into the southern Washington Cascade and the eastern side of Mount St. Helens Nationa Volcanic Monument *(see place listing p. 185)*.

CARSON NATIONAL FISH HATCHERY is 14 m n. at 14041 Wind River Hwy. Built by the Civilia Conservation Corps, the hatchery began operation i 1937. The hatchery's ponds and incubation building are spring-fed and maintain a constant temperatu of 42 F. Year-round viewing of chinook salmon available, though the best time to see the large, adu fish is May through August. Spawning takes plac in August, and the young fry are marked with code wire tags in May. Allow 30 minutes minimun Daily 7:30-4. Free. Phone (509) 427-5905.

CASHMERE (E-8) pop. 2,965, elev. 795'

Named for south Asia's fabled Vale of Kashmi Cashmere, in the heart of Wenatchee Valley, is su rounded by fruit orchards. The town's roots can t traced back to a Roman Catholic mission establishe in 1863. The central business district has an Earl American look with its lampposts and covered sid walks. The sandstone towers of Peshastin Pinnacl State Park, 2 miles northwest on US 2/97, are popular rock climbing area.

Cashmere Chamber of Commerce: 204 Cotta, Ave., P.O. Box 834, Cashmere, WA 98815; phor (509) 782-7404.

Shopping areas: Cashmere has two large antiqu malls, Antique Mall of Cashmere, 603 Cotlets Wi near Cashmere Pioneer Village & Museum; ar Apple Annie Antique Gallery, at the junction of U 2 and Eels Way.

ARRASTRA is 10 mi. s. of US 2 on US 97. Ident fied by a roadside historic interpretive marker, th unusual 1861 water-powered ore grinding device of Spanish design. The machine ground gol bearing ore to powder until the 1880s.

CASHMERE PIONEER VILLAGE & MUSEUM is at 600 Cotlets Way. This museum re-creates the history of the Columbia River Indians before the arrival of the pioneers. Its collection of artifacts is considered among the best in the Northwest.

The village comprises 20 authentic pioneer structures, including a smithy, assay office, school, hotel, general store, saddle shop, doctor and dentist office, saloon, jail and railroad buildings. A working water wheel is on the bank of the Wenatchee River.

Allow 1 hour minimum. Daily 9:30-4:30, Mar.-Oct.; Fri.-Sun. 10:30-3:30, Nov. 15-Dec. 21. Admission $4.50; $3.50 (ages 13-18 and 62+); $2.50 (ages 5-12); $10 (family). Phone (509) 782-3230.

LIBERTY ORCHARDS CO. INC. is at 117 Mission Ave. The company offers 20-minute tours through its candy factory, including the kitchen and packaging area. The company produces fruit and nut confections covered with powdered sugar; free samples are offered. Tours do not always coincide with production times. Allow 30 minutes minimum. Mon.-Fri. 8-5:30, Sat.-Sun. 10-4, Apr.-Dec.; Mon.-Fri. 8:30-4:30, rest of year. Free. Phone (509) 782-4088.

CASTLE ROCK (G-5) pop. 2,130, elev. 59′

The town's namesake, a 150-foot-high rock, was a landmark for Cowlitz Indians and Hudson's Bay Co. traders as early as 1832. Castle Rock prospered as a Cowlitz River steamboat port and trading center for valley farms. A local sawmill was the first to produce cedar shingles from the Western red cedar that grows in abundance in the region.

Castle Rock marks the beginning of the Spirit Lake Memorial Highway (SR 504), a scenic route that leads past the areas affected by the eruption of Mount St. Helens in 1980. The Mount St. Helens Silver Lake Visitor Center (*see attraction listing p. 187*) is 5 miles east of I-5 exit 49.

Castle Rock Chamber of Commerce Visitor Center: 147 Front Ave. NW, Castle Rock, WA 98611; phone (360) 274-6603.

EXHIBIT HALL is at 147 Front Ave. N.W. The hall features displays that convey the impact of the Mount St. Helens eruptions on the area. Recordings of 911 phone calls when the mountain erupted offer oral histories. Other exhibits include logging equipment and historical photographs. The historic 1907 city jail is adjacent; tours are available. Quilt shows are held in February. Allow 30 minutes minimum. Daily 9-5, May-Sept.; Wed.-Sat. 10-2, rest of year. Closed Thanksgiving and Dec. 25. Donations. Phone (360) 274-6603.

CATHLAMET (G-5) pop. 565, elev. 53′

Cathlamet is a picturesque riverside settlement linked with rural Puget Island and known as Little Norway for its largely Scandinavian population. Of interest is the 1895 Pioneer Church, built into a rock outcropping that overlooks the village. The last remaining ferry service on the lower Columbia River operates between Puget Island—accessible by bridge

from town—and Westport, Ore. Phone (360) 795-3301 for ferry information.

A once endangered population of white-tailed deer, thought to be extinct in the 1930s, lives within the Julia Butler Hansen National Wildlife Refuge. The refuge covers 4,757 acres on the mainland and several islands in the Columbia River below Cathlamet. Wildlife often can be seen from Steamboat Slough and Brooks Slough roads, especially in the morning and evening when the deer feed in the pastures. Motorists should watch for animals in or near roadways.

WAHKIAKUM COUNTY HISTORICAL MUSEUM is at 65 River St. The museum has displays from the county, including farm implements, artifacts from various Northwest Indian tribes, guns and logging equipment. Allow 1 hour minimum. Tues.-Sun. 11-4, June-Sept.; Thurs.-Sun. 1-4, rest of year. Admission $3; $1.50 (ages 55+); free (ages 0-12). Phone (360) 795-3954.

RECREATIONAL ACTIVITIES

Kayaking

- **Columbia River Kayaking** trips depart from various locations on the Lower Columbia River, including Slow Boat Farm on Puget Island, 2 mi. s. on SR 409, then 1.9 mi. s.e. to 422 E. Birnie Slough Rd. Reservations are required. Trips depart year-round. Phone (360) 849-4016.

CENTRALIA (I-2) pop. 14,742, elev. 188′

Along with neighboring Chehalis, Centralia forms the commercial center of the rich Chehalis Valley farmland and nearby timberlands. More than a dozen outdoor murals depicting 19th-century Centralia grace downtown buildings.

Fort Borst Park, off Belmont Road, includes an arboretum, small rhododendron gardens and recreational facilities. The Borst Family Homestead, built around 1860, is off Johnson Road in the southern part of the park. Because the wood and joints were hardened and dipped in white lead for waterproofing, the house is well preserved. It features original furnishings. The 1855 Borst Granary Blockhouse housed the pioneer family and briefly served as a military post during a period of conflict with American Indians.

Lewis County Convention & Visitors Bureau: 500 NW Chamber Way, Chehalis, WA 98532; phone (360) 748-8885 or (800) 525-3323.

Shopping areas: The Centralia Factory Outlet Center, on both sides of I-5 exit 82, has more than 50 stores. Downtown's Tower Avenue between Locust and Maple streets features more than a dozen antique stores and more than 300 dealers. The Centralia Square Antique Mall, 201 S. Pearl St., features some 135 antique dealers.

CHEHALIS (I-1) pop. 7,057, elev. 196′

Chehalis was formed in 1873 when the Lewis County seat was moved from Claquato. First named

Saundersville, the town's name was changed to Chehalis in 1879. The historic neighborhood on Pennsylvania Avenue features a variety of architectural styles. Claquato Church on Stern Road is one of the oldest churches in the state. The 1858 structure functioned for a time as Claquato Academy; the bronze bell in the belfry was cast in Boston in 1857 and shipped around Cape Horn.

Lewis County Convention & Visitors Bureau: 500 NW Chamber Way, Chehalis, WA 98532; phone (360) 748-8885 or (800) 525-3323.

SAVE **CHEHALIS-CENTRALIA RAILROAD** is w. of I-5 exit 77 on SR 6, then s. on Riverside Rd. The railroad offers steam train excursions through the Chehalis Valley to Millburn and Ruth. Dinner trains and special seasonal trips also are available; phone for schedule. Allow 2 hours minimum. Trips to Millburn depart Sat.-Sun. at 1 and 3, Memorial Day weekend-Sept. 30. Trips to Ruth depart Sat. at 5, Memorial Day weekend-Sept. 30. Ruth round-trip $13; $12 (ages 65+); $10 (ages 4-15). Millburn round-trip $10; $9 (ages 65+); $7 (ages 4-15). MC, VI. Phone (360) 748-9593.

JOHN R. JACKSON HOUSE HISTORIC SITE is 3 mi. e. of I-5 exit 68, then .2 mi. s. on Jackson Hwy. The site features one of the oldest pioneer structures north of the Columbia River. An important meeting place during the organization of the Washington Territory, the small 1845 log cabin also was a stopover for pioneer travelers. The structure, which served as the Jackson Courthouse, is in a small park on Jackson's Prairie. Its sparsely furnished interior can be viewed through the windows. Daily 8 a.m.-dusk. Log cabin open by appointment. Free. Phone (360) 864-2643.

LEWIS COUNTY HISTORICAL MUSEUM is at 599 N.W. Front Way. In the historic 1912 Northern Pacific Depot, the museum features a blacksmith shop, saw filing shop, general store, pioneer kitchen, Chehalis Indian artifacts and a model railroad exhibit. There also is an extensive research library focusing on genealogy and Lewis County history as well as a hands-on area for children.

Allow 30 minutes minimum. Tues.-Sat. 10-5, Sun. 1-5, Memorial Day weekend-Labor Day; Tues.-Sat. 10-5, rest of year. Closed holidays. Admission $4; $3 (ages 60+); $2 (ages 4-16). Phone (360) 748-0831.

VETERANS MEMORIAL MUSEUM is at 100 S.W. Veterans Way. Dedicated to America's veterans, the museum houses displays of military memorabilia from wars as early as the American Revolution. Small arms, a variety of uniforms, cavalry-era saddles and even a 1942 Stuart tank are exhibited. Visitors can watch videos of veterans recounting their experiences. A 30-foot by 60-foot American flag covering one wall was donated by the crew of the USS *Abraham Lincoln*.

Guided tours are available. Allow 1 hour minimum. Tues.-Sat. 10-5, Sun. 1-5, June-Sept.; Tues.-Sat. 10-5, rest of year. Closed major holidays. Admission $5; $3 (ages 6-18). Phone (360) 740-8875.

CHELAN (D-9) pop. 3,522, elev. 1,238'

Chelan, set amid orchards and vineyards at the southern end of its 55-mile-long namesake lake, has been a resort since the beginning of the 20th century. Dry, warm summers draw crowds to its three public beaches. Recreational activities include swimming, boating, water skiing and parasailing. Hang gliding and paragliding are popular at Chelan Sky Park, south of town via Chelan Butte Rd.

More than a dozen colorful murals decorate the exteriors of many downtown buildings. The Chelan Riverwalk offers a paved 1-mile loop along the Chelan River. Area scenic drives include SR 150 northwest to Manson, and the road along the lake's south shore to Twenty-five Mile Creek State Park *(see Recreation Chart)*. The sunny hillsides flanking the lake have become an emerging grape growing region, and wine touring is increasingly popular.

Lake Chelan Chamber of Commerce—Chelan: 102 E. Johnson Ave., P.O. Box 216, Chelan, WA 98816; phone (509) 682-3503 or (800) 424-3526.

CHELAN AIRWAYS is at 1328 W. Woodin Ave., 1 mi. w. on US 97 Alt. This airline offers seaplane sightseeing tours and air taxi service to Stehekin at the upper end of Lake Chelan or to points beyond in the Cascade Mountains. Passengers must check in at least 30 minutes prior to departure. Flights depart daily 8-5; closed Dec. 25. Round-trip fares to Stehekin from $165. Sightseeing tours from $85. Reservations are required. MC, VI. Phone (509) 682-5555 or (509) 682-5065.

GEM **LAKE CHELAN** is in a glacier-carved trough on the eastern flank of the Cascade Range. One of the most scenic areas in the Pacific Northwest, the 55-mile-long lake extends from the semi-arid orchards and benchlands near the Columbia River northwestward into the alpine heart of the North Cascades. At 1,500 feet deep, the lake is one of the continent's deepest; in places its bottom lies 400 feet below sea level.

Snowcapped peaks flank the lake's upper reaches, towering more than 8,000 feet above its surface. Roads lead along both banks of the lake's lower reaches. Two state parks are on the south shore. Lake Chelan State Park *(see Recreation Chart)* is 9 miles west off US 97 Alt. and SR 971. Nine miles farther up S. Lakeshore Drive is Twenty-five Mile Creek State Park *(see Recreation Chart)*. Phone (509) 687-3710 for Lake Chelan State Park or (509) 687-3610 for Twenty-five Mile Creek State Park.

Lake Chelan Boat Co. departs from the dock at 1418 W. Woodin Ave. The company has been carrying passengers on the lake since the 1890s. Service is offered on the *Lady of the Lake II* and the *Lady Express* year-round between Chelan and Stehekin, in Lake Chelan National Recreation Area *(see place listing p. 175)*. Stops, which vary depending on the trip, are made at Fields Point Landing, Prince Creek, Lucerne and Moore Point.

Pets must be transported in approved kennels, which can be rented at the dock. Round-trips depart daily at 8:30, May 1-Oct. 15; daily at 10, Mar. 15-Apr. 30 and Oct. 16-31; Sun.-Mon., Wed. and Fri. at 10, rest of year. Closed Dec. 25. Fare $39-$59; $19.50-$29.50 (ages 2-11); fuel surcharge may apply. Reservations are recommended. Phone (509) 682-4584 or (888) 682-4584 for reservations; (509) 682-2224 for a recorded schedule.

LAKE CHELAN MUSEUM is at Woodin Ave. and Emerson St. The museum displays natural and historical items relating to American Indian culture and pioneer life. Of interest is a firefighting exhibit and historic photos from the early 1900s. Allow 30 minutes minimum. Mon.-Sat. 10-4, June 1-Oct. 1; by appointment rest of year. Admission $2; $1 (ages 6-18 and 62+); $5 (family). Phone (509) 682-5644.

SLIDEWATERS is .4 mi. w. on E. Woodin Ave., .1 mi. s. on S. Lake St., then e. to 102 Waterslide Dr. Water park thrill rides include Downhill Racer; Thunder Rapids river ride; the 400-foot-long Tube Blaster with two 360-degree turns; and Purple Haze, a 420-foot-long enclosed tube. The park also contains two intermediate slides, two kiddie slides, a play area for small children, a pool and an arcade. Food is available. Picnicking is permitted. Allow 1 hour minimum. Daily 10-7, mid-June through Labor Day; 10-6, Memorial Day weekend through mid-June. Admission $17; $14 (ages 3 to under 48 inches tall). Admission 3 hours before closing to closing $14; $11 (ages 3 to under 48 inches tall). AX, DS, MC, VI. Phone (509) 682-5751.

WINERIES

- **Lake Chelan Winery** is 5 mi. n.w. at 3519 SR 150. Daily 11-8, May-Oct.; 11-5, rest of year. Closed Thanksgiving and Dec. 25. Phone (509) 687-9463.

- **Tsillan Cellars** is 3 mi. w. at 3875 US 97A. Daily 11-7, May-Oct.; Wed.-Sun. noon-5, rest of year. Closed Jan. 1, Thanksgiving and Dec. 25. Phone (509) 682-9463 or (877) 682-8463.

CHENEY (E-12) pop. 8,832, elev. 2,373′

Rolling grasslands dotted with lakes and pine woods surround (CHEE-nee), which sprang up with the arrival of the railroad from Spokane in 1881. First called Willow Springs, then Depot Springs, the town's present name honors the director of the Northern Pacific Railroad. Impressed by this, Benjamin P. Cheney donated $10,000 toward the founding of an academy in 1882; this school became the nucleus of Eastern Washington University.

Among Cheney's most interesting architectural sites are the 1907 Interurban Railway Depot at Second Street and College Avenue, and a collection of Victorian homes at Third and F streets that includes an elaborate Queen Anne-style residence built in 1904.

The 23-mile-long Columbia Plateau Trail follows an abandoned rail line through a scenic landscape of pine forest, grasslands and lakes that includes Turnbull National Wildlife Refuge. The northernmost 4 miles of the trail are paved; the remainder is crushed rock. The north trailhead is at Fish Lake, 4 miles east on SR 904.

West Plains Chamber of Commerce: 201 First St., P.O. Box 65, Cheney, WA 99004; phone (509) 235-8480 or (509) 299-8480.

TURNBULL NATIONAL WILDLIFE REFUGE is w. on SR 904, then 4.5 mi. s. on Cheney Plaza Rd. to Smith Rd. The 15,468-acre refuge is an important breeding area for numerous species of waterfowl; tundra swans can be seen occasionally in spring. A public use area includes a self-guiding driving tour. Daily dawn-dusk. Admission $3 per private vehicle. Phone (509) 235-4723.

CHEWELAH (D-12) pop. 2,186, elev. 1,671′

Missionaries, both Protestant and Roman Catholic, were active in the area in the mid-19th century. A plaque at Chewelah's First Congregational Church, Park and Webster streets, commemorates the first Protestant sermon in the Pacific Northwest.

An Indian agency was established in 1873, and the agency's original hand-hewn log cabin is located at 309 Third St. The Spokane Falls & Northern Railway reached Chewelah in 1889, after which the town prospered as a supply center for the surrounding mining district.

Chewelah Chamber of Commerce: 214 E. Main St., P.O. Box 94, Chewelah, WA 99109; phone (509) 935-8595.

GAMBLING ESTABLISHMENTS

- **Chewelah Casino** is at 2555 Smith Rd. Sun.-Thurs. 9 a.m.-2 a.m., Fri.-Sat. open 24 hours. Phone (509) 935-6167 or (800) 322-2788.

RECREATIONAL ACTIVITIES

Skiing

- **49 Degrees North** is 10 mi. e. on Flowery Trail Rd., P.O. Box 166, Chewelah, WA 99109. Fri.-Tues. 9-4, late Nov.-early Apr. Phone (509) 935-6649 or (866) 376-4949.

CHINOOK (G-4) pop. 457

On May 12, 1792, thousands of American Indians witnessed Capt. Robert Gray's dramatic entrance into the mouth of the Columbia River in his great winged ship, the *Columbia Rediviva*. The historic landing established a strong U.S. claim to all country drained by the Columbia River. Chinook's past also is distinguished by Meriwether Lewis and William Clark, who camped just east of town with members of their expedition in November 1805, just prior to the culmination of their 2.5-year transcontinental journey.

Before fixed gear was outlawed in Washington waters in 1934, Chinook's fishing industry brought such prosperity that the town enjoyed the highest per capita wealth of any settlement of its size in the country.

FORT COLUMBIA STATE PARK is 1.7 mi. e. on US 101. Part of Lewis and Clark National Historical Park, this site is one of three military posts established at the mouth of the Columbia River during the Spanish-American War. The 600-acre area encompasses 12 old structures, including bunkers, lookouts, searchlight stations, 8-inch gun batteries and a commanding officer's house with period antiques. An interpretive center features historical displays.

Picnic facilities are available. Park open daily dawn-dusk. Commanders House open daily 11-4, July 1-Labor Day; by appointment rest of year. Interpretive center open daily 10-5, July 1-Labor Day; by appointment rest of year. Free. Phone (360) 777-8221.

CLARKSTON (G-12) pop. 7,337

In 1902, after several name changes, the townspeople named their city Clarkston after William Clark, just as their neighbors in Lewiston, Idaho, named their town for Meriwether Lewis. The noted explorers spent time at the confluence of the Snake and Clearwater rivers where they were assisted by the Nez Perce. Six-thousand-year-old petroglyphs are accessible from River Road. Directions are available at the chamber of commerce.

A series of dams on the Snake River has made Clarkston a shipping center. The town's once barren landscape now offers a variety of recreational opportunities, including boating, camping, fishing and swimming. The Clearwater and Snake River National Recreation Trail offers a paved hiking and biking trail along 16 miles of river shoreline in the Clarkston-Lewiston area.

Several companies offer 1- and 2-day jet boat excursions and 3- and 5-day river float trips through Hells Canyon. Reservation information is available from the chamber of commerce.

Clarkston Chamber of Commerce: 502 Bridge St., Clarkston, WA 99403; phone (509) 758-7712 or (800) 933-2128.

BEAMERS HELLS CANYON TOURS departs from the Beamers Tour Dock behind the Quality Inn at 700 Port Dr. This tour company offers jet boat excursions through Hells Canyon—North America's deepest river gorge. The 1-day Snake River trip provides opportunities to view three mountain ranges, three states and three rivers. Half-day and other excursions also are available. One-day trip daily, May-Sept.; Sat. Sun., Mar. Apr. and in Oct. Fare $119; $59.50 (ages 6-12). Half-day trips $69; $34.50 (ages 6-12). DS, MC, VI. Phone (509) 758-4800 or (800) 522-6966.

SNAKE DANCER EXCURSIONS departs from the Hells Canyon Resort & Marina on US 12 at 1550 Port Dr. This tour company offers a variety of jet boat excursions along the Snake River. Allow 4 hours minimum. Daily 7-6. Fare $90-$195; free (ages 0-5). Reservations are recommended. AX, DS, MC, VI. Phone (509) 758-8927 or (800) 234-1941.

TROPICAL OASIS WATERPARK is at the Asotin County Family Aquatic Center, 1.2 mi. s. on 6th St. (becomes SR 129), 1.2 mi. w. on Fleshman Way, .1 mi. s. on SR 128, then .1 mi. w. to 1603 Dustan Loop. The park features a wave pool, a 210-foot-long inner tube slide, a 158-foot-long enclosed body flume, a 155-foot-long open flume slide, a zero-depth entry activities pool and a sand play area.

Picknicking is permitted. Daily 11:30-6 (also Tues. and Thurs. 6-8 p.m.), early June to mid-Aug. Admission $7.25; $6.75 (students and military with ID); $6.25 (ages 4-17 and 60+). MC, VI. Phone (509) 758-0110.

CLE ELUM (E-8) pop. 1,755, elev. 1,905'

Meaning "swift water" in the Kittitas Indian tongue, Cle Elum aptly describes its namesake river, which tumbles down from Lake Cle Elum 8 miles to the northwest. The town originated as a gold claim in 1883. Three years later coal was discovered and Cle Elum gained a sawmill, a school and a stop on the Northern Pacific Railroad. Coal mining in Cle Elum ended in 1963.

The town is known as the entrance to a vast recreation area: the Wenatchee and Mount Baker-Snoqualmie national forests (*see place listings p. 277 and p. 182*). Nearly every conceivable sport can be enjoyed in the forests. A popular local activity is a 3- to 4-hour raft trip down the 16-mile stretch of the Yakima between Cle Elum and Thorp.

Cle Elum-Roslyn Chamber of Commerce: 401 W. 1st St., Cle Elum, WA 98922; phone (509) 674-5958.

CARPENTER MUSEUM is 3 blks. n. of 1st St. on Billings Ave. (at the corner of 3rd St.). Built in 1914, the restored, 3-story white frame building was the home of Frank Carpenter, the area's first successful banker. Original furnishings depict the lifestyle of a prosperous early 20th-century businessman and his family. The third floor features a ballroom, while another section houses an art gallery. Allow 30 minutes minimum. Fri.-Sun. noon-4, May-Sept.; closed holidays. Donations. Phone (509) 674-5958.

CLE ELUM HATCHERY is .3 mi. s. of W. 1st St. on S. Cle Elum Way, then .8 mi. w. on Charter Rd., then 4 mi s on Spring Chinook Rd., following signs to 800 Spring Chinook Way. This multiagency supplemental and research facility is helping rebuild salmon runs on the Yakima River. Utilizing an ecosystem approach, hatchery scientists experiment with different fish-rearing techniques. Interpretive panels describe natural and human history and explain the decline of salmon and the role of the hatchery.

Picnicking is permitted. Guided 30-minute tours available on request. Daily 9-3:30, May to late Sept. Free. Phone (509) 674-3704.

IRON HORSE STATE PARK can be accessed at the corner of 6th St. and Milwaukee Ave. The park encompasses 100 miles of the John Wayne Pioneer Trail, which follows a historic railway line along the scenic Yakima River and over the Cascades into western Washington. The trail winds through fir and pine forests, rolling farmlands and steep canyons, running atop lofty railroad trestles and even into tunnels along the way. Cross-country skiing is popular in winter. Picnicking is permitted. Daily 6:30 a.m.-9 p.m., Memorial Day weekend-Labor Day; 8-5, rest of year. Free. Phone (509) 656-2230.

COLFAX (F-12) pop. 2,844, elev. 1,974'

Settled in 1870, Colfax lies at the heart of The Palouse, a hilly region renowned for its fertile soils. The town is the seat of Whitman County, one of the nation's most productive wheat, barley, dry pea and lentil growing areas. In the late 1890s, Eastern Washington communities sponsored an immigrant bureau in Chicago, and chartered special trains to carry homesteaders to the area. The handsome, turn-of-the-20th-century brick and stone buildings lining Main Street attest to the prosperity of the period.

The Perkins House, 623 N. Perkins Ave., built in 1884 by town founder James Perkins, features period furnishings and memorabilia. The adjacent log cabin was built in 1870. For information phone the chamber of commerce.

Colfax Chamber of Commerce: 109 E. Wall St., Colfax, WA 99111; phone (509) 397-3712.

STEPTOE BUTTE STATE PARK is 6 mi. n. on US 195, then 4 mi. n.e. on Old State Hwy., then 1 mi. n.e. on Hume Rd., and then 3 mi. w. on Steptoe Butte Rd., following signs. Within its 150 acres, the park includes the 3,612-foot butte first known as Pyramid Peak. In 1858 Lt. Col. Edward J. Steptoe and 156 men suffered one of the worst defeats of the regular Army near the butte that now bears his name when they encountered a contingent of Nez Perce, Coeur d'Alene and Spokane Indians.

Steptoe Butte is accessible by road and affords a 70- to 80-mile view in all directions. Parking and picnic facilities are available, but drinking water is not. Daily 6-6. Free. Phone (360) 902-8844.

COLUMBIA RIVER GORGE NATIONAL SCENIC AREA—

see place listing in Oregon p. 59.

COLVILLE (B-11) pop. 4,988, elev. 1,917'

Fort Colvile, built at Kettle Falls in 1825, served as the chief center of trade in the northwest for the Hudson's Bay Co. The company moved to Canada in 1853 and a military post was built just northeast of the present townsite. However, in 1882 the fort was abandoned and the town of Colville soon was

established in its place. Fort Colvile Monument on SR 20 commemorates the military post.

Little Pend Oreille National Wildlife Refuge, 13 mi. e. on Bear Creek Rd., has a string of lakes offering recreational facilities including fishing, hunting, camping, hiking and biking. For information phone (509) 684-8384. *See Recreation Chart.*

Colville Chamber of Commerce: 121 E. Astor, Colville, WA 99114; phone (509) 684-5973.

KELLER HERITAGE CENTER is at 700 N. Wynne St. in Keller Park. The center comprises an early-20th-century residence, a museum of American Indian and pioneer items, Colville's first schoolhouse, a farmstead cabin, a trapper's cabin, a lookout tower, a smithy, a sawmill and a machinery building with antique farming equipment and tools. A mining exhibit also is available. Museum open Mon.-Thurs. 10-4, Fri.-Sun. 1-4, June-Aug.; daily 1-4 in May and Sept.; by appointment rest of year. Admission $5; $3 (ages 60+ and persons with permanent disabilities); $2 (ages 5-17); $10 (family). Phone (509) 684-5968.

COLVILLE NATIONAL FOREST

Elevations in the forest range from 1,289 ft. at the Columbia River Dam to 7,309 ft. at Gypsy Peak. Refer to AAA maps for additional elevation information.

In northeastern Washington, Colville National Forest covers about 1,100,000 acres and possesses varied attractions. In the center of the forest is Roosevelt Lake; Grand Coulee Dam *(see p. 164)* is to the south. Through the middle of the forest courses the Columbia River. Gardner Cave, in the forest's eastern half, offers tours of its stalagmite and stalactite formations.

In the northeast corner of the forest, east of Metaline Falls, is the 41,000-acre Salmo-Priest Wilderness Area. To preserve this wilderness, no motorized vehicles are permitted. However, FRs 22, 20 and 270 and Sullivan Creek Road, south of Metaline Falls off SR 31, lead to trailheads where visitors can continue into the wilderness area on foot. The roads are closed due to weather from mid-November to early or mid-June.

Recreation information as well as brochures and maps outlining several of the forest's self-guiding automobile and hiking tours are available at ranger stations in Kettle Falls, Metaline Falls, Newport and Republic, and at the Forest Supervisor's office, 765 S. Main St., Colville, WA 99114; phone (509) 684-7000. *See Recreation Chart and the AAA Northwestern CampBook.*

CONCRETE (C-7) pop. 790, elev. 435'

Clay and limestone from this area were deemed to be of high enough quality to induce two companies to open cement plants here in the 1890s. To demonstrate the durability of their product, most of the central business district was rebuilt with concrete following a 1921 fire. A 1916 bridge was erected using reinforced concrete, despite an engineer's recommendation; the Thompson Bridge still stands at the east end of town. The town's namesake industry closed in 1968.

Concrete Chamber of Commerce: Main St., P.O. Box 743, Concrete, WA 98237; phone (360) 853-7042.

PUGET SOUND ENERGY PLANT AND VISITORS CENTER is at 46110 E. Main St. The center contains replicas of the Upper and Lower Baker dams and area relief maps as well as mounted native fish and an outdoor fish trap used in the center's stocking program. The best viewing time is June through September. Allow 1 hour minimum. Mon.-Fri. 7-3:30, Sat.-Sun. 9-5:30, late June-Labor Day; Mon.-Fri. 7-3:30, rest of year. Closed federal holidays. Free. Phone (360) 853-8341.

COULEE CITY (E-10) pop. 600, elev. 1,584'

Coulee City is the former junction of railroad and stagecoach lines running along the Columbia River. According to Guy Waring, a 19th-century pioneer and author, the trains and coaches were deliberately scheduled *not* to connect with each other, forcing passengers to spend the night in town. Coulee City still gets many passers-through; it is the only place between Soap Lake and Coulee Dam where east-west travelers can cross the Grand Coulee. Dramatic rock cliffs flank the coulee north and south of town.

Coulee City Chamber of Commerce: P.O. Box 896, Coulee City, WA 99115; phone (509) 632-5043.

SUN LAKES STATE PARK is 4 mi. s.w. off SR 17. Huge floods rushing across eastern Washington during the last ice age carved a network of gashes, the largest of which is Grand Coulee. Dry Falls, Grand Coulee's central feature, was once a 3.5-mile-wide cataract over which water plunged about 400 feet. For those not

---

DID YOU KNOW

Sonora Louise Smart Dodd of Spokane was the originator of Father's Day.

---

wishing to attempt the moderately rough road through the park, Dry Falls is visible from both SR 17 and the interpretive center. *See Recreation Chart.*

Allow 1 hour minimum. Park open daily 6:30 a.m.-dusk. Interpretive center open Thurs.-Mon. 9-6, Tues.-Wed. 9-4:30, May 1-Labor Day; daily 9-4:30, rest of year. Free. Phone (509) 632-5214.

COULEE DAM (D-10) pop. 1,044, elev. 1,145'

Coulee Dam, as well as the adjacent communities of Electric City, Elmer City and Grand Coulee, sprang from the desert in 1933 to house workers on Grand Coulee Dam. More than 8,000 workers labored on the project which was completed in 1942. The dam was built on the site of Seaton's Ferry, a remote crossing of the Columbia River; the ferry operated 1920-34.

The town still reflects its original dichotomy: Engineers Town, at the west end of the dam, features the comfortable homes built for project engineers and managers, while Mason City, at the east end, housed contractors and workers. Historical murals and buildings give insight into the construction era. Crown Point, 2 miles west on SR 174, offers a panoramic view of the dam from a vantage point 626 feet above the Columbia. Bicentennial Park, adjacent to North Dam Park on SR 155, features the Gehrke Windmills, a collection of more than 50 windmills constructed of colorfully painted pieces of castaway iron.

Grand Coulee Dam Area Chamber of Commerce: 306 Midway Ave., P.O. Box 760, Grand Coulee, WA 99133-0760; phone (509) 633-3074 or (800) 268-5332.

GRAND COULEE DAM is off SR 155. The dam harnesses the Columbia River for irrigation, power and flood control. Said to be one of the largest concrete structures in the world, it is 550 feet high, 500 feet wide at its base, 5,223 feet long and contains nearly 12 million cubic yards of concrete. Behind the dam Roosevelt Lake extends 151 miles upstream to the Canadian border. Six giant pumps lift water from this reservoir to Banks Lake.

The dam's massive face is illuminated by a 36-minute laser light show presented during the summer. Good viewpoints are found below the dam on both banks, at Douglas Park and at Crown Point. The Visitor Arrival Center, on SR 155 on the west bank below the dam, features displays and a film about the construction of the multi-purpose dam. Guided 45-minute tours of the Third Powerhouse are available.

Allow 2 hours minimum. Visitor center open daily 9 a.m.-11 p.m., Memorial Day weekend-July; 9 a.m.-10:30 p.m., in Aug.; 9 a.m.-9:30 p.m., in Sept.; 9-5, rest of year. Closed Jan. 1, Thanksgiving and Dec. 25. Third Powerhouse tours are given daily 10-5, Feb.-Nov. Laser light show presented nightly at 10, Memorial Day weekend-July 31; at 9:30, in Aug.; at 8:30, in Sept. Free. Phone (509) 633-9265.

LAKE ROOSEVELT NATIONAL RECREATION AREA—*see place listing p. 176.*

GAMBLING ESTABLISHMENTS

• **Coulee Dam Casino** is at 515 Birch St. Sun.-Thurs. 9 a.m.-2 a.m., Fri.-Sat. 24 hours. Phone (509) 633-0766 or (800) 556-7492.

COUPEVILLE (D-2) pop. 1,723, elev. 2'

Coupeville, on Whidbey Island *(see place listing p. 278)*, was established in 1853, making it one of the oldest cities in the state. Several of its homes date back to the mid-19th century. Three old blockhouses built to defend Puget Sound and settlers' homes from the Coast Salish Indians can be visited. West of town is Madrona Way, a 4-mile scenic route that winds along the shore of Penn Cove. The drive is named for the Pacific madrona, a dark evergreen tree with shaggy cinnamon-colored bark.

Central Whidbey Chamber Visitor Information Center: 107 S. Main St., Bldg. E, Coupeville, WA 98239; phone (360) 678-5434 or (360) 678-5664.

Shopping areas: Antique shops, art galleries, crafts stores and souvenir shops line Front Street between Alexander and Center streets downtown.

SAVE **ISLAND COUNTY HISTORICAL MUSEUM** is .25 mi. n. of SR 20 at Alexander and Front sts. The museum's exhibits portray the history of the island's towns and the maritime industry. Mon.-Sat. 10-5, Sun. 11-5, July-Sept.; Mon.-Sat. 10-4, Sun. 11-4, rest of year. Admission $3; $2.50 (ages 65+, students and military with ID); free (ages 0-3); $6 (family). Phone (360) 678-3310.

CRYSTAL MOUNTAIN (F-7) elev. 4,380'

Northeast of Mount Rainier, Crystal Mountain is a resort community offering winter recreation.

Crystal Mountain Visitor Information Center: 33914 Crystal Mountain Blvd., Crystal Mountain, WA 98022; phone (360) 663-2265.

RECREATIONAL ACTIVITIES

Skiing

• **Crystal Mountain** is s.e. on SR 410. Write 33914 Crystal Mountain Blvd., Crystal Mountain, WA 98022. Other activities are offered. Daily 9-4, mid-Nov. to mid-Apr. Phone (360) 663-2265 or (888) 754-6199.

DALLESPORT (G-8) pop. 1,185, elev. 213'

First called Rockport, later Grand Dalles and then North Dalles, Dallesport was once an important trading town and served as the seat of Klickitat County until that governmental function shifted to nearby Goldendale. Located on a bench, or shoreline terrace, directly opposite The Dalles, Dallesport was linked with its larger Oregon neighbor by ferry until a bridge opened in 1953.

COLUMBIA HILLS STATE PARK is 2 mi. e. of the US 197 jct. on SR 14, at milepost 84. This 3,338-acre park encompasses multiple ancient basalt lava flows shaped by Ice Age floods. Horsethief Lake and the Columbia River offer opportunities for swimming, boating and windsurfing. The lake is excellent for beginning windsurfers. Horsethief Butte is a popular rock climbing area *(see Recreation Chart).*

The park is renowned for its rock art, created by American Indians 200 to upwards of 3,000 years ago—perhaps the greatest concentration in the Pacific Northwest. An interpretive display overlooks rock art relocated from Petroglyph Canyon, which was flooded by the reservoir behind The Dalles Dam in 1956. Free guided 90-minute tours of rock art sites on the Temani Pesh-wa Trail are offered by reservation Fri.-Sat. at 10, Apr.-Oct. (the trail is not ADA accessible). Allow 1 hour minimum. Park open daily dawn-dusk. Free. Phone (509) 767-1159.

DAVENPORT (E-11) pop. 1,730, elev. 2,430'

Freshwater springs enticed Montana-bound gold prospectors to camp here in the 1860s. Homesteading started around 1880, and a town, first called Cottonwood Springs, developed as the Northern Pacific Railroad built a line across the coulee scablands. Davenport remains an important trading center for the surrounding wheat farms.

Davenport Visitor Information Center & Chamber of Commerce: 600 Seventh St., Davenport, WA 99122; phone (509) 725-6711.

LINCOLN COUNTY HISTORICAL MUSEUM is at 600 Seventh St. The museum contains Spokane Indian artifacts, extensive photographs and farm equipment as well as pioneer furniture, clothing and tools. Allow 1 hour minimum. Mon.-Sat. 9-5, May-Sept.; by appointment rest of year. Closed holidays. Donations. Phone (509) 725-6711 or (509) 725-2221.

DAYTON (G-11) pop. 2,655, elev. 1,606'

Dayton, founded in 1871, nestles beside the Touchet (TOO-she) River. Flour milling was the first industry, and the town prospered as a trading center for surrounding farms, ranches and timberlands. The town includes three historic districts. Visitors can see a sampling of Dayton's historic homes by driving along First, Second and Third streets south of Main.

Dayton Chamber of Commerce: 166 E. Main, P.O. Box 22, Dayton, WA 99328; phone (509) 382-4825 or (800) 882-6299.

Self-guiding tours: The depot and chamber of commerce have walking-tour maps describing Dayton's historic districts; phone (509) 382-2026.

COLUMBIA COUNTY COURTHOUSE is at 341 E. Main St. This restored 1887 Italianate courthouse is reported to be the oldest working courthouse in the state. Exhibits include historical photographs and maps. A 22-foot lantern caps the building. Allow 15 minutes minimum. Mon.-Fri. 8:30-4:30; closed holidays. Free. Phone (800) 882-6299.

HISTORIC DAYTON DEPOT is at 222 E. Commercial St. Built by the Oregon Railroad and Navigation Co. in 1881, the restored two-story, wood-frame depot is said to be Washington's oldest. The second floor, formerly the stationmaster's living quarters, now houses rotating displays of historical items. Guided tours are available. Allow 30 minutes minimum. Wed.-Sat. 10-noon and 1-5, Sun. 1-4, May-Oct.; Wed.-Sat. 11-4, rest of year. Closed some holidays. Admission $5; free (ages 0-12). MC, VI. Phone (509) 382-2026.

RECREATIONAL ACTIVITIES

Skiing

- **Bluewood** is 23 mi. s.e. of Dayton on North Fork Touchet River Rd. Write: P.O. Box 88, Dayton, WA 99328. Wed.-Sun. and holidays 9-4, late Nov.-late Mar.; daily 9-4, mid-Dec. to Jan. 1. Phone (509) 382-4725, or (509) 522-4110 for snow updates.

DEER PARK (D-11) pop. 3,017, elev. 2,123′

The forested environs and a plentitude of whitetail deer prompted railroad workers to describe the area as a "deer park." New Yorker William Hopkins Short settled here in 1889, establishing a sawmill to supply lumber to the railroad. Deer Park was platted in 1899 and incorporated in 1908. The town's lakes offer swimming, fishing and boating.

Deer Park Chamber of Commerce: 316 E. Crawford Ave., Suite A, P.O. Box 518, Deer Park, WA 99006; phone (509) 276-5900.

NORTH SPOKANE FARM MUSEUM is .5 mi. w. on W. Crawford St. (becomes W. Monroe Rd.), 7 mi. s. on W. Monroe Rd., then .1 mi. w. to 6223 W. Ridgeway Rd. The museum is located on a 10-acre working grain farm on Wildrose Prairie, which was homesteaded in 1916.

Among the collection's farming paraphernalia from 1850-1950 are walk-behind plows, tractors, a reaper and wooden and metal combines. An upstairs gallery contains nearly 5,000 pieces of English Ironstone china. Historical photos and period household items round out the collection. Allow 1 hour minimum. Wed.-Sun. 9-4, Apr.-Oct.; by appointment rest of year. Donations. Phone (509) 466-2744.

DEMING (A-3) pop. 210, elev. 207′

The Salish-speaking Nooksack people have lived in this area for thousands of years. European settlement began in the 1880s, and the town was named for George Deming, owner of the land development company.

Local specialty crops include raspberries, strawberries and Christmas trees. Deming Homestead

Eagle Park, 3 miles east on SR 542, then south on Truck Road, offers a good vantage for watching bald eagles feeding on spawned-out salmon from December into February.

GAMBLING ESTABLISHMENTS

- **Nooksack River Casino** is at 5048 Mount Baker Hwy. Mon.-Thurs. 8 a.m.-3 a.m., Fri.-Sun. 24 hours. Phone (360) 592-5472 or (877) 935-9300.

WINERIES

- **Mount Baker Vineyards** is on SR 542 at 4298 Mount Baker Hwy. Daily 11-5. Phone (360) 592-2300.

DES MOINES—see Seattle p. 246.

EATONVILLE (H-3) pop. 2,012, elev. 810′

Founded in 1889, Eatonville was named for pioneer settler Thomas C. Van Eaton. Large-scale milling began after the railroad arrived in 1904, and the town became an important lumbering center.

Greater Eatonville Chamber of Commerce Visitor's Center: 105 Carter St., P.O. Box 845, Eatonville, WA 98328; phone (360) 832-4000.

 NORTHWEST TREK WILDLIFE PARK is 6 mi. n. on SR 161. This 723-acre park features animals native to the Northwest. A guided tram tour through the free-roaming area allows visitors to see moose, caribou, elk, bison and other animals in their natural habitats. Highlights include a grizzly habitat and several walk-through animal exhibits, a children's nature discovery center and a theater. A picnic pavilion is available.

Allow 3 hours minimum. Park opens daily at 9:30, mid-Feb. to Oct.; Fri.-Sun. at 9:30, rest of year. Closing times vary. Tours depart daily on the hour Apr.-Oct.; at 10:30, noon, 1:30 and 3, rest of year. Closed Thanksgiving and Dec. 25. Admission $15; $13.50 (ages 65+); $10 (ages 5-12); $7 (ages 3-4). DS, MC, VI. Phone (360) 832-6117.

PIONEER FARM MUSEUM AND OHOP INDIAN VILLAGE is 2 mi. n. on SR 161, then 1.5 mi. w. on Ohop Valley Rd. E. The 1880s farm offers guided tours with such hands-on activities as milking and other household and farm chores similar to those the pioneers performed some 100 years ago. Horse or buggy rides are offered. Guides conduct 1.5-hour tours and explain pioneer life. Hour-long guided tours of the Ohop Indian Village also are available.

Allow 2 hours minimum. Daily 11-4, Father's Day-Labor Day; Sat.-Sun. 11-4, Mar. 15-day before Father's Day and day after Labor Day-day before Thanksgiving. Ohop Indian Village tours are conducted Fri.-Sun. at 1 and 2:30, Father's Day-Labor Day. Museum admission $7.50; $6.50 (ages 3-18 and 62+). Indian village tour $7; $6 (ages 3-18 and 62+). Combination pioneer museum/Ohop Indian village tour $13.50; $11.50 (ages 3-18 and 62+). AX, DS, MC, VI. Phone (360) 832-6300.

EDMONDS—see Seattle p. 247.

ELBE (I-3) pop. 21, elev. 1,211′

First called Browns Junction, the town's name was changed to honor pioneer settler Henry Lutkens' birthplace, the Elbe Valley in Germany. The diminutive Little White Church on SR 7 was built in 1906 for the German-speaking Lutheran congregation.

MOUNT RAINIER SCENIC RAILROAD is 3.5 mi. s. on SR 7, then 1.5 mi. e. on Mineral Creek Rd. in Mineral. The railroad consists of a steam-powered excursion train that travels 12 miles through tall timber and over high bridges from Elbe to Divide. Trains feature restored coaches and open cars. Seasonal and theme trips are offered. For more information contact Mount Rainier Scenic Railroad, P.O. Box 250, Mineral, WA 98355.

Allow 1 hour, 30 minutes minimum. Sightseeing departures Thurs. at 2, Sat. at 10:30 and 2:30, Sun. at 2, late May-late Sept. Sightseeing fare $20; $18 (ages 62+ and military with ID); $15 (ages 4-12). Reservations are recommended. DS, MC, VI. Phone (360) 492-5588 or (888) 783-2611.

ELLENSBURG (F-8) pop. 15,414, elev. 1,577′

Ellensburg, situated in the middle of the Kittitas Valley, is noted for its cattle ranches and farms raising hay, corn and other crops. The valley once was a neutral area in which the mutually hostile Wenatchee, Nez Perce and Yakama Indians hunted and fished together in peace. European settlement of the area dates back to the 1860s when the town grew from a trading post known as Robber's Roost.

After the Northern Pacific Railroad built its transcontinental line through the valley in 1886, farming expanded and the town boomed. Ellensburg became so prosperous that in 1889 it was a serious contender to become the state capital.

Ellensburg's downtown, rebuilt after a fire in 1889, features numerous brick and stone buildings. On the north side of town,Central Washington University is home to a Japanese garden and the Chimpanzee and Human Communications Institute. Rockhounds visit in search of blue agates, which are found only in the area. The Yakima River is a popular rafting stream May-September both above and below Ellensburg.

Ellensburg Chamber of Commerce: 609 N. Main St., Ellensburg, WA 98926; phone (509) 925-3138, (509) 925-2002 or (888) 925-2204.

CHILDREN'S ACTIVITY MUSEUM is at 400 N. Main St. The museum offers hands-on activities, changing exhibits and summer art programs. There also is a play area for children ages 0-1. Allow 30 minutes minimum. Wed.-Sat. 10-5 (also first Fri. of the month 5-6); closed holidays. Admission $4.25; free (ages 0-12 months); $14.50 (family). Phone (509) 925-6789.

CLYMER MUSEUM is at 416 N. Pearl St. Exhibiting the works of Western artist John Ford Clymer, the collection includes cover illustrations for the *Saturday Evening Post* and oils depicting wildlife and Western themes. The museum also features changing exhibits. Allow 30 minutes minimum. Mon.-Fri. 10-5, Sat. 10-4, Sun. noon-4, May-Dec.; Mon.-Fri. 10-5, Sat. noon-4, rest of year. Closed Jan. 1, Easter, Memorial Day, July 4, Labor Day, Thanksgiving and Dec. 25. Free. Phone (509) 962-6416.

KITTITAS COUNTY HISTORICAL MUSEUM is at 114 E. 3rd Ave. The museum is in the 1889 Cadwell building, which has unusual horseshoe-shaped windows. Among the exhibits are American Indian artifacts and pioneer tools and articles as well as a display of petrified wood, antiques, dolls, a printing press, telephone equipment, seven antique vehicles and the Rollinger Rock and Mineral Collection. Mon.-Sat. 10-4; closed holidays. Donations. Phone (509) 925-3778.

OLMSTEAD PLACE STATE PARK is 3 mi. e. on Mountain View Ave., then s. on N. Ferguson Rd. This 217-acre park preserves the legacy of a pioneer family farm. Settled in 1875, it was one of the first homesteads in Kittitas Valley. Historic farm buildings include a log cabin, granary, barns, sheds and the residence, built in 1908 and containing period furnishings. The site features a carefully restored historic garden and dozens of pieces of early farm equipment. The three-quarter-mile Altapes Creek Interpretive Trail links a red barn and the reconstructed Seaton Cabin School.

Allow 1 hour minimum. Park open daily 6:30-dusk, Apr.-Sept.; 8-dusk, rest of year. Guided 1-hour tours given Sat.-Sun. noon-4, Memorial Day weekend-Labor Day. Free. Phone (509) 925-1943.

ENUMCLAW (E-7) pop. 11,116, elev. 742'

After encountering a severe thunderstorm in the area, Duwamish Indians referred to a nearby mountain as Enumclaw or "thundering mountain." The town, established in 1885, was named for the mountain.

The pastureland surrounding Enumclaw is a noted horse raising area, producing more than 20 breeds, including Thoroughbreds, Morgans, paso finos and paints. January through June are the best months to see foals romping in their paddocks.

Enumclaw Area Chamber of Commerce: 1421 Cole St., Enumclaw, WA 98022; phone (360) 825-7666.

FEDERATION FOREST STATE PARK is 18 mi. e. on SR 410. The park consists of 619 acres of old growth forest with nature trails and picnic areas. Exhibits at the Catherine Montgomery Interpretive Center illustrate the state's seven contrasting life zones. Park open daily 8 a.m.-dusk, early Apr. to early Nov. Interpretive center open Wed.-Sun. 9-4, May-Sept.; Sat.-Sun. 9-4, in Apr.; by appointment rest of year. Free. Phone (360) 663-2207.

MUD MOUNTAIN DAM is 5.5 mi. e. on SR 410, then 2.5 mi. s. on Mud Mountain Rd. A viewing platform with interpretive panels overlooks the dam, built in the 1940s to control flooding on the White River. A park includes overlooks, a children's wading pool, hiking trails, a picnic area and a playground. Daily 9-dusk, Apr. to mid-Nov.; Mon.-Fri. 9-4, rest of year. Free. Phone (360) 825-3211.

EPHRATA (E-9) pop. 6,808, elev. 1,277'

The natural springs west of Ephrata have attracted people for thousands of years. Farmers came after the Great Northern Railroad laid their transcontinental mainline through this area in 1892. The town's Biblical name was bestowed upon it by railway officials for the wells of Ephrath, an ancient name for Bethlehem.

Ephrata became seat of Grant County in 1909, and the 1917 County Courthouse is still heated by geothermal waters. Cattle ranching and wheat farming dominated the region until 1950 when the Columbia Basin Project began supplying water through its network of canals. Over the next 3 decades this irrigation project transformed the desert into a patchwork of cropland.

Ephrata Chamber of Commerce: 1 Basin St. S.W., P.O. Box 275, Ephrata, WA 98823; phone (509) 754-4656.

GRANT COUNTY HISTORICAL MUSEUM AND VILLAGE is at 742 Basin St. N.W. The museum contains a collection of historic pictures, tools, farm equipment, rocks, Wanapum and Sinkiuse Indian artifacts, cowboy paraphernalia, clothing and household furnishings from the homestead era. Exhibits are arranged chronologically from prehistoric times to the start of the Columbia Basin project. Visitors can also walk through a 36-building village made up of historic structures. Allow 2 hours minimum. Mon.-Tues. and Thurs.-Sat. 10-5, Sun. 1-4, early May-Sept. 30. Admission $3.50; $2.50 (ages 6-15). Phone (509) 754-3334.

EVERETT — *see Seattle p. 247.*

FEDERAL WAY — *see Seattle p. 248.*

FERNDALE (B-2) pop. 8,758, elev. 30'

Ferndale, in the northwest corner of the state, was so named in 1872 when the area's first schoolteacher noticed clumps of ferns surrounding the schoolhouse. The town is now a trade center for area farms.

Ferndale Chamber of Commerce: 5683 Second Ave., Ferndale, WA 98248; phone (360) 384-3042.

HOVANDER HOMESTEAD is 1 mi. s. via Hovander Rd. The 1903 restored house is part of a large park encompassing an interpretive center, barn, milkhouse, children's farm zoo, wildlife viewing, gardens and picnic sites. The house and barn are furnished with antiques and vintage equipment.

Allow 1 hour minimum. Grounds open daily 8 a.m.-dusk. House open Thurs.-Sun. noon-4:30, early June-Labor Day; Sat.-Sun. noon-4:30, in May. House $1; 50c (ages 5-12). Phone (360) 384-3444.

PIONEER PARK is at 1st and Cherry sts. Buildings dating 1870-95 form a pioneer village of 11 log structures, including a post office, barn, church, granary, schoolhouse, stagecoach inn, veteran's museum, jail and homesteads. Relics illustrate life during the pioneer era, and costumed guides conduct tours. Allow 1 hour minimum. Park open Mon.-Fri. 9-5, Sat.-Sun. 9-dusk. Guided and self-guiding tours are available Tues.-Sun. 11:30-4:30, May 15-Sept. 15. Tour fee $3; $2 (ages 6-12 and 55+). Phone (360) 384-6461 or (360) 384-4302.

TENNANT LAKE NATURAL HISTORY INTERPRETIVE CENTER is 1 mi. s. via Hovander Rd. The center offers displays interpreting the seasons as well as a nature walk and a boardwalk trail around a marshy wetland. The Fragrance Garden is specially designed for the visually impaired—plants have singular smells and textures and are signed in braille.

Grounds open daily 8 a.m.-dusk. Center open Thurs.-Sun. noon-4, mid-June through Labor Day. Hours vary rest of year; phone ahead. Free. Phone (360) 384-3064.

GAMBLING ESTABLISHMENTS

- **Silver Reef Casino**, off I-5 exit 260, 3.5 mi. w. on Slater Rd. to 4876 Haxton Way. Daily 24 hours. Phone (360) 383-0777 or (866) 383-0777.

FORKS (D-4) pop. 3,120, elev. 375′

This important Olympic Peninsula logging community takes its name from the forks of the three nearby rivers: the Bogachiel, Calawah and Sol Duc. Forks began in the late 1870s as an agricultural community; commercial logging followed a decade later. In addition to providing the town's name, area rivers support spectacular runs of steelhead trout during the summer and winter, attracting anglers.

Forks Chamber of Commerce: 1411 S. Forks Ave., P.O. Box 1249, Forks, WA 98331; phone (360) 374-2531 or (800) 443-6757.

FORKS TIMBER MUSEUM is .75 mi. s. on US 101 across from the airport. The museum has a variety of items from the 1870s to the 1950s. Displays include a pioneer kitchen, farm equipment and a logger's memorial. Logging equipment and a fire lookout tower document Forks' role as an important logging community. Nature trails and picnic areas are available. Guided tours are available by appointment. Allow 1 hour minimum. Tues.-Sat. 10-4, June to mid-Oct.; Fri.-Sat. 10-4, in May; by appointment rest of year. Donations. Phone (360) 374-9663.

RECREATIONAL ACTIVITIES
Fishing

- **All-Ways Fishing** offers guided fishing trips for salmon, steelhead and trout on several Olympic Peninsula rivers including the Sol Duc. P.O. Box 184, Forks, WA 98331. Other activities are offered. Trips depart year-round. Phone (360) 374-2052.

GIFFORD PINCHOT NATIONAL FOREST

Elevations in the forest range from 80 ft. at an island in the Columbia River to 12,276 ft. at Mount Adams. Refer to AAA maps for additional elevation information.

Straddling the Cascade Range from Mount Rainier to the Columbia River, Gifford Pinchot National Forest covers 1,312,000 acres of mountains, meadows, caves, canyons and streams. On opposite edges of the forest, restless 8,364-foot Mount St. Helens and glacier-clad 12,276-foot Mount Adams tower above the lesser peaks; the fields of wild huckleberries scattered through the forest and surrounding Mount Adams lure thousands of pickers in late summer.

Forest roads are usually open from late May through November; however, many are narrow and winding and should be traveled with care. Check current road and weather conditions carefully. For information about Mount St. Helens contact the Forest Supervisor's office or Mount St. Helens National Volcanic Monument (see place listing p. 185) at (360) 449-7800.

Of the forest's seven wilderness areas, Goat Rocks and Mount Adams are the largest. Permits are required to enter the Indian Heaven, Mount Adams, Goat Rocks, Trapper Creek, Tatoosh and Glacier View wilderness areas. The forest is home to many species of animals; common birds are ducks, grouse, ravens and Steller and Canada jays. Salmon and trout inhabit the many streams.

Of particular interest are the Big Lava Beds 14 miles west of Trout Lake on FR 60. The unusual formations originated from a 500-foot-deep crater in the northern part of the lava bed. Ice Cave, 6 miles southwest of Trout Lake on SR 141, is one of numerous lava tubes in an area known as the Big Trench Cave System. Ice usually remains in the 400-foot cave until late summer.

Another interesting volcanic feature is the Palisades, which is visible from US 12, 2.5 miles east of the SR 123 junction. The Clear Fork of the Cowlitz River has cut a deep gorge into an ancient lava flow, exposing an impressive 486-foot-high cliff of columnar basalt. Trails can be followed on foot or horseback.

The Pacific Crest National Scenic Trail traverses the forest on its passage from Mexico to Canada. Canoes and boats with small motors are permitted on some lakes; watch for speed restrictions. Snowmobiling, snowshoeing and cross-country skiing are popular winter pastimes. Fishing and hunting are permitted in season. Downhill skiing is available late November to early April at White Pass, east of Packwood on US 12.

A Northwest Forest Pass, available at ranger stations, is required for parking at most trailheads in the forest. A day pass costs $5 per vehicle; an annual pass costs $30. Recreation information is available at ranger stations in Amboy, Carson, Randle and Trout Lake, or by writing the Forest Supervisor's Office, Gifford Pinchot National Forest, 10600 N.E. 51st Cir., Vancouver, WA 98682; phone (360) 891-5000. *See Recreation Chart and the AAA Northwestern CampBook.*

GIG HARBOR—*see Seattle p. 248.*

GOLD BAR (D-7) pop. 2,014, elev. 204'

A former prospector's camp, Gold Bar is a logging headquarters that also serves the needs of small farms in the region. During construction of the Great Northern Railroad, anti-Chinese sentiment in this area was so strong that Chinese laborers were forced to flee the camp hidden in hastily built coffins.

WALLACE FALLS STATE PARK is 2 mi. n.e. off US 2. This 4,735-acre park features a 2.5-mile trail that ascends 880 feet through wooded parkland to the crest of 265-foot Wallace Falls. Excellent views of the Skykomish Valley can be had from the top of the falls. *See Recreation Chart.* Picnic and limited tent camping facilities are available. RV camping or parking is not permitted. Daily 8 a.m.-dusk. Free. Phone (360) 793-0420.

GOLDENDALE (H-8) pop. 3,760, elev. 1,509'

Settled in 1872, Goldendale stands in a broad upland valley commanding panoramas of the Cascade volcanoes of Mount Hood and Mount Adams. Pioneer ranchers raised sheep and cattle, but after the arrival of the railroad in 1903, wheat farming prevailed. The many Victorian houses surrounding the central business district reflect the town's early prosperity.

Greater Goldendale Area Chamber of Commerce: 903 E. Broadway, P.O. Box 524, Goldendale, WA 98620; phone (509) 773-3400.

GOLDENDALE OBSERVATORY STATE PARK is 1.5 mi. n. of Main St. on Columbus Ave. The observatory has a 24.5-inch Cassegrain reflecting telescope, one of the largest of its kind in the country available for public use. There also are a 10-inch Mead telescope for viewing the sun and various small telescopes available. Wed.-Sun. 2-5 and 8-midnight, Apr.-Sept.; Fri.-Sun. 2-5 and 7-10, rest of year. Guided programs begin five minutes after each opening. Free. Phone (509) 773-3141.

PRESBY MUSEUM is at 127 W. Broadway. The museum occupies the 1902 Winthrop B. Presby Mansion. Displays of household items include a large coffee mill collection, and a pioneer exhibit features branding irons and brands. Also on display are a newspaper office, carriage house and one-room

school. Allow 30 minutes minimum. Daily 9-5, mid-Apr. to mid-Oct.; by appointment rest of year. Admission $4.50; $1 (ages 6-12). Phone (509) 773-4303.

▼ GRAND COULEE DAM—
see Coulee Dam p. 164.

GRANDVIEW (G-9) pop. 8,377, elev. 790'

Grandview, in the lower Yakima Valley, takes its name from the spectacular westward view of Mount Rainier and Mount Adams. The fertile soil of the valley enhances the bounty of such local crops as apples, asparagus, corn, hops, grapes, peaches and cherries.

Grandview Chamber of Commerce: 107 Division St., Grandview, WA 98930; phone (509) 882-2100.

GRANDVIEW ROSE GARDEN is at W. 2nd St. and Avenue G in Westside Park. Earthen paths crisscross this garden containing nearly 1,000 rose bushes in raised beds bordered by lava rock. Roses bloom late May to early fall. Allow 30 minutes minimum. Daily dawn-dusk. Free. Phone (509) 882-9200.

RAY E. POWELL MUSEUM is 3 blks. s. of Main St. on S. Division St., at the corner of E. 4th St. The museum features local history exhibits, including veterans' memorabilia, weapons, Native American artifacts and early household utensils and furnishings. A 1902 Kiblinger automobile is said to be one of only two in existence. A 1921 contractor's roadway stamp from the original Yellowstone Trail highway is outside the museum entrance.

Allow 30 minutes minimum. Tues.-Sun. 2-4, mid-Mar. to mid-Oct.; closed holidays. Donations. Phone (509) 882-9238.

GREENBANK (D-3) elev. 158'

Overlooking the entrance to Holmes Harbor, this Whidbey Island village is named for Green Bank, Delaware, the boyhood home of one of its early settlers.

MEERKERK RHODODENDRON GARDENS is 1.5 mi. s. on SR 525, then .2 mi. e. on Resort Rd. The gardens contain 10 acres of more than 2,000 rhododendrons scattered throughout a 53-acre woodland preserve. Allow 1 hour minimum. Daily 9-4. Admission $8; free (ages 0-15 with an adult). Phone (360) 678-1912.

WINERIES

- **Greenbank Farm** is .2 mi. n. on SR 525, then e. on Wonn Rd. Daily 10-5, June-Sept.; Mon.-Fri. 11-5, Sat.-Sun. 10-5, in May; Mon.-Fri. 11-4, Sat.-Sun. 10-5, rest of year. Closed Jan. 1, Thanksgiving and Dec. 25. Phone (360) 678-7700.

HANFORD REACH NATIONAL MONUMENT (F-9)

Established by presidential proclamation in June 2000, Hanford Reach National Monument embraces 195,000 acres of federal lands on two sides of the Hanford Reservation in south-central Washington. The monument protects the Hanford Reach, the last free-flowing stretch of the Columbia River in the United States above Bonneville Dam. With summer temperatures routinely reaching 100 degrees Fahrenheit and annual rainfall less than 7 inches, this is the hottest and driest part of the state. The area supports a unique community of plants and animals.

Hanford Reach comprises two separate sections. The 120,000-acre northeast portion preserves the left bank of the Columbia River, including Saddle Mountain National Wildlife Area and the Wahluke Slope and White Bluffs area. The gravel bars along this stretch of river harbor spawning grounds for the largest surviving population of wild salmon in the Columbia basin. The 60,000-acre Wahluke Unit is open to the public. A boat launch, several hiking trails and an overlook are available, but no camping is permitted.

The other segment of the monument lies southwest of SR 240. It constitutes the Fitzner Eberhardt Arid Lands Ecology Reserve, Washington's largest remaining shrub-steppe landscape. Due to its sensitive nature, this section is closed to the public.

Hanford Reach National Monument is administered by the U.S. Fish and Wildlife Service. Information is available from their Tri-Cities office at 3250 Port of Benton Blvd., Richland, WA 99354; phone (509) 371-1801.

HOODSPORT (G-1) elev. 70′

First settled in 1880, Hoodsport lies at the base of the Olympic Mountains on the shore of Hood Canal, the westernmost arm of Puget Sound. Clams, oysters and shrimp are harvested from area waters. SR 119 leads west to Lake Cushman, a popular recreation area in the southeast corner of Olympic National Park *(see place listing p. 195)*.

WINERIES

- **Hoodsport Winery** is at N. 23501 US 101. Daily 9-6; closed Thanksgiving and Dec. 25. Phone (360) 877-9894.

HOQUIAM (E-4) pop. 9,097, elev. 10′

Forest products have been a staple of Hoquiam's economy since its first sawmill opened in 1882. The city's name derives from the Chehalis Indian word Ho-qui-umpts, meaning "hungry for wood." Grays Harbor is a natural outlet for the area's prime export.

The Seventh Street Theatre, 313 7th St., was built 1927-28 and was the first theater in the state to show talking motion pictures. The tideflats lining the harbor west of town shelter migrating shorebirds in spring and fall.

Grays Harbor Chamber of Commerce-Hoquiam: 506 Duffy St., Aberdeen, WA 98520; phone (360) 532-1924 or (800) 321-1924.

GRAYS HARBOR NATIONAL WILDLIFE REFUGE is 1.5 mi. w. on SR 109, .5 mi. s. on Paulson Rd., then .5 mi. w. to 1400 Airport Way. The refuge is one of North America's four major shorebird staging areas. Several hundred thousand birds gather on the refuge's muddy tide flats from late April through early May to prepare for the continuation of their northbound journey to the Arctic.

A 1-mile trail provides viewing access. The best time to view the shorebirds is from 2 hours before to 2 hours after high tide. Allow 1 hour minimum. Daily dawn-dusk. Free. Phone (360) 753-9467.

HOQUIAM'S CASTLE is at 515 Chenault Ave. Built in 1897 as the home of lumber industry magnate Robert Lytle and restored in 1999, the turreted 20-room mansion contains antique furnishings and chandeliers. Allow 30 minutes minimum. Tours are given Wed.-Sat. 1-4, Memorial Day weekend-Labor Day weekend. Admission $5. Reservations are required. Phone (360) 533-2005.

SAVE **POLSON MUSEUM** is on US 101 at 1611 Riverside Ave. The 26-room mansion belonged to timber heir Arnold Polson. The museum provides a pictorial history of the Grays Harbor communities as well as special exhibits throughout the year. A rose garden is featured in the park. Wed.-Sat. 11-4, Sun. noon-4, Apr.-late Dec.; Sat.-Sun. noon-4, rest of year. Admission $4; $2 (students with ID); $1 (ages 0-11); $10 (family). Phone (360) 533-5862.

HUMPTULIPS (E-5) pop. 216, elev. 131′

Humptulips, a farming community above the Humptulips River, once served as the logging outlet for the largest stand of Douglas fir in the Northwest. The stand was so dense that loggers had little choice but to fell all timber in the same direction. The town's unusual name is derived from an American Indian term meaning either "chilly region" or "hard to pole," a reference to the river.

HUMPTULIPS FISH HATCHERY is 1.5 mi. w. of US 101 on Kirkpatrick Rd. The hatchery raises winter-run steelhead and chinook and coho salmon. Self-guiding tours are available. Daily 8-4. Free. Phone (360) 987-2215.

ILWACO (G-4) pop. 950, elev. 11′

Protected by tall headlands to the west, Ilwaco lies northeast of Cape Disappointment just inside the mouth of the Columbia River, location of one of the most treacherous river bars in the world. Over the course of two centuries, the hazardous conditions at the Columbia bar and along the nearby coast claimed hundreds of vessels, earning area waters the nickname, "Graveyard of the Pacific."

Cape Disappointment Coast Guard Station and Lighthouse, 3.7 miles southeast off US 101, is the home of one of the largest search and rescue facilities in the state; it also houses the Coast Guard's only heavy-weather Motor Lifeboat School.

Ilwaco is a popular sport fishing port especially during the prime fishing season, which is May through October. Charter operators specialize in guided fishing trips for salmon, halibut, tuna, bottom fish or sturgeon. A Washington fishing license, available from charter operators, is required.

CAPE DISAPPOINTMENT STATE PARK is 3 mi. s.w. off US 101. Captain Meares named this headland in 1788, describing his feelings upon not discovering the fabled Northwest Passage. The park is part of Lewis and Clark National Historical Park, and within its boundaries is 1852 Fort Canby, which guarded the entrance to the Columbia River and was Washington's first military installation. The Cape Disappointment Lighthouse, commissioned in 1856, is the oldest lighthouse in the state. *See Recreation Chart.* Daily 6:30 a.m.-dusk. Free. Phone (360) 642-3078.

Lewis and Clark Interpretive Center, within Cape Disappointment State Park, traces the 2.5-year, 8,000-mile trek led by Meriwether Lewis and William Clark. The exhibits portray medical treatment, food, entertainment, discipline and the contributions of the Chinook and other tribes toward the trip's success.

Sketches by the explorers and artifacts collected on the expedition are displayed and a multimedia presentation depicts the highlights of the journey. There is a 200-yard uphill walk to the center; a shuttle is available July 1-Labor Day. Allow 1 hour minimum. Daily 10-5; closed Thanksgiving and Dec. 25. Admission $5; $2.50 (ages 7-17). Phone (360) 642-3029.

North Head Lighthouse, within Cape Disappointment State Park, was built in 1898 and crowns its namesake promontory overlooking the Pacific. In 1853 the sailing ship *Vandalia* foundered on the rocks just north of the light on Beards Hollow. Tours of the lighthouse are offered. **Note:** Children are not permitted on lighthouse stairs. Daily 10-5:30, May 1-Labor Day; Sat.-Sun. 11-3 and by appointment rest of year. Hours may vary; phone ahead. Admission $2.50. Phone (360) 642-3078 or (360) 642-3029.

COLUMBIA PACIFIC HERITAGE MUSEUM is just s.e. of US 101 at 115 S.E. Lake St. The museum depicts frontier life in southwest Washington. Exhibits include Chinook Indian and pioneer artifacts as well as a model of an early 20th-century seaside town, a working replica of a narrow gauge railway, a fully refurbished 19th-century passenger railcar and a model of the Columbia estuary. Other exhibits portray the Lewis and Clark expedition, area shipwrecks and horse seine fishing.

Mon.-Sat. 10-4, Sun. noon-4; closed Thanksgiving and Dec. 25. Admission $5; $4 (ages 55+); $2.50 (ages 12-17 and students with ID). Phone (360) 642-3446.

WILLAPA NATIONAL WILDLIFE REFUGE has its headquarters 8.5 mi. n. of jct. US 101 and US 101 Alt. The refuge encompasses 14,000 acres of marshland, upland forests, pastures and tidal estuaries. Long Island has a stand of 1,000-year-old red cedars and tidal marshes that support deer, bears, elks, coyotes, and beavers. More than 180 species of migratory birds have been sighted among the salt marshes and shifting dunes of Leadbetter Point at the entrance to Willapa Bay. The refuge also includes the adjoining tidal flats at the southern tip of Willapa Bay.

Camping is permitted on the Long Island Unit, but it is accessible by private boat only. Allow 4 hours minimum. Daily dawn-dusk. Free. Phone (360) 484-3482.

INDEX (D-7) pop. 157, elev. 532'

Surrounded by high peaks, Index enjoys a dramatic setting on the rushing North Fork Skykomish River. The town takes its name from Mount Index, a 6,000-foot granite spire dominating the southern horizon. Several frame buildings date from the town's early years as a railroad and miner's supply center including the 1898 Bush House and the 1903 Red Men's Wigwam. A giant saw on display in the town park was used to quarry local granite for the steps of the state capitol in Olympia.

RECREATIONAL ACTIVITIES
White-water Rafting

- **Alpine Adventures** leaves from various points on the Skykomish and North Fork Skykomish rivers. Write P.O. Box 373, Gold Bar, WA 98251. Rafting trips depart Mar.-Aug. Phone (360) 863-6505 or (800) 723-8386.

- **Wave Trek** offers rafting on the Skykomish and North Fork Skykomish rivers. Write 444 Avenue A, P.O. Box 63, Index, WA 98256. Rafting trips depart Apr.-Aug. Phone (360) 793-1705 or (800) 543-7971.

IONE (C-12) pop. 479, elev. 2,090'

Ione has always been a timber town. Pend Oreille River steamboats linked Washington's northeastern corner with the outside world from the late 1880s until the railroad arrived in 1909. A sawmill built by the Panhandle Lumber Co. opened in this small community in 1901 and by 1909 employed 700 workers; a smaller mill continues to operate on the site. The era of river transportation is fondly recalled during Down River Days the last full weekend in July. The festivities include a parade, a cowboy breakfast and snowmobile races on the water.

The Lions Club Excursion Train offers sightseeing trips along the scenic Pend Oreille on six selected weekends from late July to mid-October. The 20-mile round trip aboard three classic railroad coaches and three open-air cars converted from rolling stock runs along the north end of the Pend Oreille Valley Railroad between Ione and Metaline Falls. The track snakes along cliffs rising up from the river far below and negotiates a series of low wooden trestles as well as the mighty Box Canyon Bridge, with one splendid view after another. Reservations are required; phone (509) 442-5466.

No road can provide comparable vistas, but if you can't take the train ride Box Canyon Viewpoint, 4 miles north of Ione on SR 31, offers a gander at the rugged canyon scenery; it overlooks a narrow, rocky gorge spanned by a railroad bridge.

BOX CANYON DAM is 4 mi. n. on SR 31. It was built in 1955 and backs up the Pend Oreille River for 56 miles to Aleni Falls Dam, east of Oldtown, Idaho. The overlook just south of the dam surveys the gorge. The visitor center has displays about the dam's construction, and there are picnic grounds and a fishing pond for kids at an adjacent park. Food is available. Guided 45-minute tours of the site, including the powerhouse, are given by request Memorial Day weekend-Labor Day. Visitor center open daily 9-5:30, Memorial Day weekend-Labor Day; Mon-Fri. 9-1, rest of year. Closed holidays. Free. Phone (509) 442-4103.

ISSAQUAH—*see Seattle p. 249.*

KALAMA (G-6) pop. 1,783, elev. 210′

Founded in the 1840s, Kalama is named for Hawaiian native John Kalama, who settled in the area after marrying the daughter of a Nisqually chief. In addition to being a busy shipping center, Kalama claims two superlatives: a 149-foot single-tree totem pole, in Marine Park, and the first fish hatchery in the state. The latter has been replaced by two newer hatcheries. Nearly 100 antique dealers are in malls and individual shops on N. 1st Street.

Kalama Chamber of Commerce: P.O. Box 824, Kalama, WA 98625; phone (360) 673-6299.

KELSO (G-6) pop. 11,895, elev. 26′

The dramatic and much lauded run of smelt up the Cowlitz River in January and February has earned Kelso the title Smelt Capital of the World. Also plentiful are steelhead trout and sturgeon, making Kelso an important fishing and canning center.

Kelso Visitor Information Center: 105 Minor Rd., Kelso, WA 98626; phone (360) 577-8058.

Shopping areas: Kelso's major shopping center is Three Rivers Mall, just west of I-5 exit 39 at Allen Street and SR 4. The mall contains JCPenney, Macy's and Sears.

COWLITZ COUNTY HISTORICAL MUSEUM is at 405 Allen St. The museum recounts local history including an exhibit portraying settlement and transportation from the period prior to European settlement to the present. Other exhibits include portions of a loggers' bunkhouse, a railroad depot, historical photographs, a reassembled log cabin with period furnishings, a canoe and other Cowlitz Indian artifacts. Allow 30 minutes minimum. Tues.-Sat. 9-5,

Sun. 1-5; closed holidays. Donations. Phone (360) 577-3119.

KENNEWICK (G-10) pop. 54,693, elev. 362′

Meaning "winter paradise" in the Yakama Indian tongue, Kennewick was surrounded by bunch grass until the late 1800s, when the first of a series of irrigation projects began to convert the sagebrush into farmland. Favored with a brief winter season, the fertile land became the best grape producing area in the state. The 1957 Kennewick Highland irrigation project supplies water to 20,500 acres of alfalfa, corn and beans.

Reinforced by the huge hydroelectric dams harnessing the lower bend of the Columbia River, Kennewick's economy also is supported by chemical and agricultural processing. Kennewick, Pasco and Richland *(see place listings p. 198 and p. 205)* form the urban Tri-Cities area.

Near the confluence of the Columbia, Snake and Yakima rivers, Kennewick is the departure point for various scenic and recreational cruises on the Columbia River. Lake Wallula features developed recreational facilities at Columbia Park *(see Recreation Chart).*

Tri-Cities Visitor and Convention Bureau— Kennewick: 6951 W. Grandridge Blvd., Kennewick, WA 99336; phone (509) 735-8486 or (800) 254-5824.

Shopping areas: Kennewick's major shopping mall is Columbia Center, 3 miles north of I-82 exit 109 on Badger Road. Stores include JCPenney, Macy's and Sears.

DEMONSTRATION GARDEN is .75 mi. s. of US 395 on W. 19th Ave., then 2 blocks n. to 1620 S. Union St. Twenty-three themed areas include rock, herb, Japanese, children's, bird and butterfly, xeriscape, water, rose, vegetable, native plant and small tree gardens. Allow 30 minutes minimum. Daily dawn-dusk. Free. Phone (509) 735-3551.

EAST BENTON COUNTY HISTORICAL SOCIETY MUSEUM is at 205 Keewaydin Dr. The museum contains historical photographs and displays illustrating the area's beginnings in agriculture, business and education. A diorama depicts the 9,000-year-old Kennewick Man discovered on the banks of the Columbia River in 1996. Allow 30 minutes minimum. Tues.-Sat. noon-4; closed major holidays. Admission $4; $3 (ages 60+); $2 (ages 5-18). Phone (509) 582-7704.

KENMORE—*see Seattle p. 249.*

KENT—*see Seattle p. 250.*

KETTLE FALLS (C-11)
pop. 1,527, elev. 1,625′

American Indians formerly gathered in great numbers to fish for salmon at the Kettle Falls cataract on the Columbia River, now beneath the waters of Lake Roosevelt. In 1825, the Hudson's Bay Company established a gristmill at nearby Myers Falls, making this the first European settlement in Washington east of the Cascades. The town was relocated to its present site in the 1930s as the reservoir formed behind Grand Coulee Dam.

Kettle Falls Area Chamber of Commerce: P.O. Box 119, Kettle Falls, WA 99141; phone (509) 738-2300.

KETTLE FALLS HISTORICAL CENTER, 3 mi. w. at US 395 and St. Paul's Mission Rd., documents 9,000 years of human habitation in the area. Dioramas depict the American Indian way of life prior to European contact, as well as the trading post and pioneer periods. St. Paul's Mission is a log church restored to its 1847 appearance. An interpretive hiking trail leads from the mission to an overlook of the falls now submerged by Lake Roosevelt; the trail is not plowed in winter. Wed.-Mon. 11-5, mid-May to mid-Sept.; closed holidays. Donations. Phone (509) 738-6964.

KEYPORT—*see Seattle p. 250.*

KINGSTON—*see Seattle p. 250.*

KIRKLAND—*see Seattle p. 250.*

KLONDIKE GOLD RUSH NATIONAL HISTORICAL PARK—*see Seattle p. 223.*

LACEY (H-2) pop. 31,226, elev. 185′

Lacey, a suburban community just east of Olympia, was first called Woodland, honoring pioneer Isaac Woods who settled there in 1852. By the 1890s Lacey boasted a sawmill, resort hotel and the region's major horse racing track. To avoid confusion with a namesake town in southern Washington, the name was changed to Lacey.

Tudor style buildings dominate the campus of St. Martins University, founded in 1895 by the Order of St. Benedict. Tolmie State Park *(see Recreation Chart),* 4.5 miles west of I-5 exit 111, features 1,800 feet of shoreline on Puget Sound, a saltwater marsh and a 2.5-mile nature trail. The near-shore waters are popular with scuba divers.

The Chehalis Western Trail is a recreation trail following the route of a logging railroad that operated from 1926 into the mid-1980s. The 5.2-mile gravel north segment, suitable for horseback riding, connects Martin Way and Lindsley Lane S.E. with Puget Sound at Woodard Bay. Offering walkers, runners, bikers and rollerbladers views of Mount Rainier, the 14-mile paved south segment connects 14th Avenue S.E. at Chambers Lake with SR 507, 2 miles west of Rainier, where it connects with the 14.5-mile Yelm-Tenino Trail.

Lacey Thurston County Chamber of Commerce: 8300 Quinault Dr. NE, Suite A, Lacey, WA 98503; phone (360) 491-4141.

Shopping areas: The Lacey Farmer's Market, off College Street at 7th Avenue, is open Sat.-Sun. 10-3, mid-June to mid-Aug.; phone (360) 491-3214.

LACEY MUSEUM is at 829½ Lacey St. Occupying a house that has served as a private residence, fire station and the first city hall, the museum features photographs and artifacts depicting the history of the community. Allow 30 minutes minimum. Thurs.-Fri. 11-3, Sat. 9-5; closed major holidays. Donations. Phone (360) 438-0209.

NISQUALLY NATIONAL WILDLIFE REFUGE is 7 mi. e. to I-5 exit 114, then .5 mi. n. on Brown Farm Rd. Protecting the Nisqually delta, the refuge encompasses saltwater and freshwater marshes, tideflats, forests, grasslands and streams that provide habitats for a variety of birds, mammals and reptiles. The refuge can only be reached by foot trail; 6.5 miles of trails wind through the refuge. An observation platform, fishing facilities and visitor center are available.

Pets and bicycles are not permitted. Daily dawn-dusk. Visitor center Wed.-Sun. 9-4; closed Jan. 1, Thanksgiving and Dec. 25. $3 (family). Phone (360) 753-9467.

GAMBLING ESTABLISHMENTS

- **Red Wind Casino** is at 12819 Yelm Hwy. Sun.-Wed. 9 a.m.-5 a.m., Thurs.-Sat. 24 hours. Phone (360) 412-5000 or (866) 946-2444.

LA CONNER (C-3) pop. 761, elev. 50′

This picturesque fishing port dates back to the founding of a trading post in 1868. J.S. Conner purchased the store in 1870 and named the settlement for his wife, Louisa Anne, or L.A. Conner. In the late 19th century dikes and drainage works transformed the boggy marshlands of the nearby Skagit Flats into fertile farmland. Hops and oats were early boom crops that made La Conner an important trading center and port; today flower bulbs are an important crop.

Streets in the town's compact business district along the Swinomish Channel offer dozens of interesting shops, boutiques and galleries. Some of the buildings date back to the late 1800s. The 1869 Magnus Anderson Cabin is the oldest; it stands at the corner of 2nd and Commercial streets.

The west bank of the channel is part of the Swinomish Indian Reservation, established in 1855. Boats for fishing and sightseeing charters are available at the La Conner Marina at the town's northern edge.

La Conner Chamber of Commerce: P.O. Box 1610, La Conner, WA 98257; phone (360) 466-4778 or (888) 642-9284.

Shopping areas: Clothing stores, art galleries and a variety of specialty shops can be found on 1st Street between Morris and Douglas streets.

LA CONNER QUILT & TEXTILE MUSEUM is at 703 S. 2nd St. The museum features turn-of-the-20th-century decor on the first floor, and changing exhibits of textile art and well-displayed quilts from around the United States and the world on the second and third floors. Built in 1891, the Victorian mansion was completely renovated after being damaged by a 1973 fire. Allow 1 hour minimum. Wed.-Sun. 11-5, May-Mar.; daily 10-5, in Apr. Closed Jan. 1-16, Easter, July 4, Thanksgiving, and Dec. 25 and 31. Admission $5; free (ages 0-11). Phone (360) 466-4288.

MUSEUM OF NORTHWEST ART is at 121 S. 1st St. Focusing on the visual art of the Pacific Northwest, the museum displays collections of paintings, glass and sculpture. Allow 1 hour minimum. Daily 10-5; closed Thanksgiving and Dec. 25. Admission $5; $4 (ages 66+); $2 (students with ID); free (ages 0-11). AX, MC, VI. Phone (360) 466-4446.

SKAGIT COUNTY HISTORICAL MUSEUM is on top of the hill at 501 S. 4th St. The museum features three large galleries of Skagit history—from American Indian basketry and logging saws to tiny lead soldiers and china dolls. Hands-on family activities can be found throughout the museum, and visitors can enjoy panoramic views from the museum's observation deck. Allow 1 hour minimum. Tues.-Sun. 11-5; closed major holidays. Admission $4; $3 (ages 6-12 and 66+); $8 (family). Phone (360) 466-3365.

LAKE CHELAN NATIONAL RECREATION AREA (D-8)

Forming the southern tip of the North Cascades National Park Service complex, Lake Chelan National Recreation Area is accessible only by trail, boat or charter float plane from Chelan (see place listing p. 160). The approximately 62,000-acre area is at the northern end of Lake Chelan, one of the deepest lakes in the country and one of Washington's largest inland bodies of fresh water.

Deer, bears and marmots are among the animals that live in the mountains surrounding the Stehekin Valley. The only town within the recreation area is remote Stehekin, whose name means "the way through" in the Chelan Indian tongue. Free camping permits and recreation information are available at the historic Golden West Visitor Center and ranger station daily 8:30-5, mid-Mar. to mid-Oct.; hours vary rest of year. Phone (360) 854-7365, ext. 14.

Park rangers lead naturalist walks and conduct a variety of educational programs. Recreational opportunities range from short day hikes to overnight camping to strenuous mountain climbing; boating and fishing are popular in Lake Chelan and nearby streams.

Several trails traverse the area; most follow the creeks that flow into the Stehekin River. A particularly spectacular site is Rainbow Falls; raft trips,

kayak tours and trail rides are offered by Cascade Corrals, 3 blocks from Stehekin Landing.

Shuttle bus service operates from Stehekin to various trailheads late May to early October. For information about trail conditions, transportation and recreation opportunities contact Lake Chelan National, Recreation Area, 428 W. Woodin Ave., Chelan, WA 98816; phone (509) 682-2549. *See Recreation Chart.*

LAKE ROOSEVELT NATIONAL RECREATION AREA (C-10)

Stretching from the Grand Coulee Dam along Franklin D. Roosevelt Lake toward the Canadian border in northeastern Washington, this area encompasses 100,059 acres. Geologic formations in much of the region are the result of intense volcanic activity followed by cataclysmic ice age floods. Natural vegetation ranges from sage to pine forests. Numerous wildflowers grace the southern lava flows and terraces along the lake. Deer are common; beavers and muskrats frequent the shores.

Franklin D. Roosevelt Lake is a popular recreation area. Activities include boating, swimming, water skiing, camping, fishing and hunting. A state license is required for fishing or hunting; jet skis have been banned from the lake. The park contains 34 developed recreation sites. Houseboat rentals are available at nearby marinas.

Points of interest in the recreation area include St. Paul's Mission *(see Kettle Falls p. 173)* and Fort Spokane *(see attraction listing).* For more information contact Lake Roosevelt National Recreation Area, 1008 Crest Dr., Coulee Dam, WA 99116-1259; phone (509) 633-9441. *See Recreation Chart and the AAA Northwestern CampBook.*

FORT SPOKANE is 25 mi. n. of Davenport on SR 25. This 19th-century military outpost was built to ensure peaceful relations between Colville and Spokane Indians and white settlers. A visitor center and museum are in the brick guardhouse, one of four remaining outpost buildings. A self-guiding trail follows the old parade grounds. Historical interpretive programs are offered in the summer.

Allow 1 hour, 30 minutes minimum. Grounds open daily dawn-dusk. Museum open daily 10-5:30, mid-June through Labor Day. Free. Phone (509) 725-2715, ext. 43, mid-June through Labor Day or (509) 633-9441, ext. 130, rest of year.

LAKEWOOD—*see Seattle p. 252.*

LANGLEY (D-3) pop. 959, elev. 80'

Picturesque Langley perches on a bluff overlooking Saratoga Passage. German immigrant Jacob Anthes founded the town, which was named for Seattle judge and fellow developer J.W. Langley, in 1890.

Langley Chamber of Commerce: 208 Anthes Ave., P.O. Box 403, Langley, WA 98260; phone (360) 221-6765.

Shopping areas: Antique shops, art galleries and specialty stores cluster along First Street.

RECREATIONAL ACTIVITIES

Kayaking

- **Whidbey Island Kayaking** departs from the Langley Marina and four other locations in the area. Write 2724 Evening Glory Ct., Clinton, WA 98236. The outfitter offers sea kayaking tours. Daily Mar.-Oct. (weather permitting). Phone (800) 233-4319.

LEAVENWORTH (E-8)
pop. 2,074, elev. 1,164'

Leavenworth is at the base of the Cascade Mountains near the western end of the Wenatchee Valley. Established in 1890, it prospered as a logging and fruit packing center. By the early 1960s community leaders decided to promote Leavenworth as a tourist destination by capitalizing on its scenic setting. Gradually the town was remodeled to look like a Bavarian village complete with alpine architecture and flower-filled window boxes and hanging baskets.

Leavenworth Carriage Company offers horse-drawn carriage rides; phone (509) 421-0679. Art displays are featured in City Park on weekends from May to October. A bridge in Waterfront Park leads to nature trails on 15-acre Blackbird Island.

Area recreational opportunities include hiking, fishing, swimming, horseback riding, white-water rafting, snowmobiling and skiing. The Wenatchee River between Leavenworth and Monitor is one of Washington's most popular white-water rafting streams, with relatively calm stretches alternating with class III and IV rapids. The rafting season extends from May through September.

A mile northwest of Leavenworth, US 2 parallels the Wenatchee River through the scenic Tumwater Canyon, which blazes with color in the fall.

Leavenworth Chamber of Commerce: 940 US 2, P.O. Box 327, Leavenworth, WA 98826; phone (509) 548-5807.

Shopping areas: Dozens of specialty shops line Front Street in downtown Leavenworth.

LEAVENWORTH NATIONAL FISH HATCHERY is 2 mi. s. on Icicle Rd. The hatchery is part of the Grand Coulee Dam project. More than 1.7 million chinook salmon are raised at the hatchery annually. A visitors center illustrates the life history of salmon. The hatchery holds a salmon festival in late September. Allow 30 minutes minimum. Daily 8-4. Donations. Phone (509) 548-7641.

NUTCRACKER MUSEUM is downtown at 735 Front St. A 14-minute video introduces the history of nutcrackers and the museum. The collection includes more than 5,000 nutcrackers from some 40 countries; the oldest date from the 1300s. Four-thousand-year-old nutting stones also are on display.

Allow 1 hour minimum. Daily 2-5, May-Oct.; Sat.-Sun. 2-5, rest of year; other times by appointment. Closed Easter, Thanksgiving and Dec. 25. Admission $2.50; $1 (ages 6-16). MC, VI. Phone (509) 548-4573 or (509) 548-4708.

RED-TAIL CANYON FARM is 2 mi. n. on Chumstick Hwy. from jct. US 2 to 11780 Freund Canyon Rd. Hay rides (in summer) and sleigh rides (in winter) through timbered woods are offered at this 120-acre working draft horse ranch. Allow 1 hour minimum. Daily 9-4; closed Dec. 25. Fare $16; $8 (ages 2-12). Reservations are required. MC, VI. Phone (509) 548-4512 or (800) 678-4512.

RECREATIONAL ACTIVITIES
Horseback Riding

- **Eagle Creek Ranch** is 2.25 mi. n. on Chumstick Rd., then 5.5 mi. e. on Eagle Creek Rd. Write P.O. Box 719, Leavenworth, WA 98826. Other activities are offered. Daily Apr.-Oct. Phone (509) 548-7798 or (800) 221-7433.

- **Icicle Outfitters & Guides** departs from stables 2.5 mi. w. on Icicle Rd. Write P.O. Box 322, Leavenworth, WA 98826. Daily 9-5, mid-May to late Sept. Phone (509) 669-1518 or (800) 497-3912.

White-water Rafting

- **Alpine Adventures** departs from a point on the Wenatchee River off US 2. Write P.O. Box 373, Gold Bar, WA 98251. Daily 9-5, Apr.-Sept. Phone (509) 470-7014 or (800) 723-8386.

- **Enchanted Water Tours** departs from a put-in point on the Wenatchee River 2 mi. e. on US 2. Write P.O. Box 611, Leavenworth, WA 98826. Other activities are offered. Daily 8-6, Apr.-Aug. Phone (509) 548-5031 or (888) 723-8987.

- **Leavenworth Outfitters, Inc.** departs from 220 US 2. Write 325 Division St., Leavenworth, WA 98826. The company offers rafting trips on the Wenatchee River and Icicle Creek. Other activities are offered. Daily Apr.-Oct. Phone (509) 548-0368.

- **Orion River Expeditions, Inc.** offers trips on the Wenatchee River. Write 12681 Wilson St., Leavenworth, WA 98826. Apr. 1-Aug. 1. Phone (509) 548-1401 or (800) 553-7466.

- **Osprey Rafting Company** departs from various points on the Wenatchee River. Write P.O. Box 668, Leavenworth, WA 98826. Daily 8-6, Apr.-Aug. Phone (509) 548-6800 or (800) 743-6269.

- **Riverrider.com** departs from various points on the Wenatchee River. Write P.O. Box 666, Leavenworth, WA 98826. Daily 9-6, Apr.-Aug.); otherwise varies rest of year. Phone (509) 548-4575 or (800) 448-7238.

LEBAM (F-5) pop. 176, elev. 190′

Just east of the Willapa Hills and the Willapa River, the former logging town of Lebam got its name from founder J.W. Goodell, who simply took his daughter Mabel's name and spelled it backward.

FORKS CREEK SALMON HATCHERY is 2 mi. w. on SR 6. The hatchery raises more than 2 million chinook salmon, 700,000 coho salmon and 100,000 steelhead trout a year. Especially interesting is a trap for adult fish, open September through February, and the incubation facilities, open November through April. Allow 30 minutes minimum. Daily 8-4:30. Free. Phone (360) 934-5457.

LONG BEACH (G-4) pop. 1,283, elev. 10′

A popular oyster farming and vacation center, Long Beach is at the southern end of Long Beach Peninsula, known for 25 miles of hard sand beach. Area sports include surf fishing, swimming, boating and deep-sea fishing. Among the peninsula's scenic viewpoints are Cape Disappointment and North Head lighthouses (see Ilwaco p. 171), North Jetty and Beard's Hollow. About 230 ships have been wrecked near Cape Disappointment.

The Long Beach Dunes Trail includes a 12-foot-wide elevated boardwalk extending along 2,300 feet of beachfront. It has three observation platforms with interpretive displays of natural history, including a restored skeleton of a 38-foot gray whale. The main access point is at the foot of Bolstad Street, off SR 103.

Long Beach Peninsula Visitors Bureau: 3914 Pacific Way (jct. US 101 and SR 103), Seaview, WA 98644; phone (360) 642-2400 or (800) 451-2542.

PACIFIC COAST CRANBERRY RESEARCH FOUNDATION MUSEUM is 1 mi. n. on SR 103, then .7 mi. e. on Pioneer Rd. The museum details the procedures used in the planting and harvesting of cranberries. Old and new machinery is displayed. Guided tours of the museum and a cranberry bog are available. Self-guiding tour brochures of the farm are available. Allow 30 minutes minimum. Daily 10-5, Apr. 1 to mid-Dec.; closed July 4. Free. Phone (360) 642-5553.

WORLD KITE MUSEUM & HALL OF FAME is 3 blks. w. of SR 103 at 303 Sid Snyder Dr. S.W. The museum displays hundreds of kites from around the world and throughout history. Exhibits change regularly. Allow 30 minutes minimum. Daily 11-5, May-Sept.; Fri.-Tues. 11-5, rest of year. Closed Dec. 25. Admission $5; $4 (ages 60+); $3 (ages 3-15). Phone (360) 642-4020.

RECREATIONAL ACTIVITIES
Horseback Riding

- **Back Country Wilderness Outfitters** offers beach rides from its corral at the corner of Sid Snyder Dr. and Shoreview Dr. P.O. Box 327, Seaview, WA 98644. Other activities are offered. Rides depart daily (weather permitting). Phone (360) 642-2576 or (503) 338-2954

- **Skippers Equestrian Center** offers guided 1- and 2-hour beach rides from its corral 3 blks. west of

SR 103 on Sid Snyder Dr. Write P.O. Box 621, Long Beach, WA 98631. Rides depart daily (weather permitting). Phone (360) 642-3676.

LONG BEACH PENINSULA—
see Ilwaco, Long Beach, Nahcotta and Oysterville.

LONGVIEW (G-5) pop. 34,660, elev. 13'

Founded in 1923 on the site of an abandoned settlement known as Monticello, Longview was named for timber entrepreneur R.A. Long, who selected the riverside location for a deepwater port and forest products complex. The city, one of the largest planned communities in the country, was designed with a distinctive curving grid of streets interspersed with parks. R.A. Long Park (the Civic Center) is flanked by many of the city's earliest buildings, most built in the Georgian style, including the 1926 library and the 1923 Monticello Hotel.

Across from the hotel, at 18th and Olympia, is a memorial to a group of settlers who met here in 1852 to petition the U.S. Congress to create a territory north of the Columbia River separate from Oregon. Calling themselves the Monticello Convention, the settlers saw their wish granted the following year with the creation of Washington Territory. Visitors will find another historic site south of town at the mouth of the Cowlitz River; Lewis and Clark's Corps of Discovery camped here in 1805.

Just north of Long Park, spanning Olympia Way at Civic Center, is Nutty Narrows, said to be the world's only bridge for squirrels. A local resident built the bridge in 1963 to provide the critters with safe passage over the busy thoroughfare.

Kelso-Longview Chamber of Commerce: 1563 Olympia Way, Longview, WA 98632; phone (360) 423-8400.

LOPEZ ISLAND—
see San Juan Islands p. 208.

LOWDEN (G-10) elev. 492'

Vineyards, wheat fields and row crops surround little Lowden, first called Frenchtown due to the many French Canadians who settled in the Walla Walla Valley during the early 19th century. The present name salutes pioneer homesteader Francis M. Lowden Sr.

WINERIES
• **L'Ecole No. 41** is 4.4 mi. e. on US 12, just n. to 41 Lowden School Rd. in Lowden. Daily 10-5; closed Jan. 1, Easter, July 4, Thanksgiving and Dec. 25. Phone (509) 525-0940.

LYNDEN (A-3) pop. 9,020, elev. 103'

First settled in the 1860s, Lynden became home to miners returning from the gold rush of 1858. Other homesteaders followed, and together they turned the valley into fertile farmland. Many Dutch immigrants arrived at the beginning of the 20th century, and Lynden evolved into a prosperous agricultural region and one of the largest dairy centers in

the nation. Other important crops include berries, potatoes and peas.

A 72-foot tall working windmill greets visitors to Fort Street in the historic downtown area, where a four-block stretch has a bit of turn-of-the-20th-century Amsterdam flavor.

Lynden Chamber of Commerce: 518 Front St., Lynden, WA 98264; phone (360) 354-5995.

Shopping areas: Dutch Village Mall, 655 Front St., offers 18 shops specializing in Dutch imports.

BERTHUSEN PARK is 1.7 mi. n. on SR 539, then 1 mi. w. on W. Badger Rd., then s. 2 blks. to 8837 Berthusen Rd. This 236-acre former homestead features a nature trail, a fishing stream and a barn containing antique farm equipment. Picnicking is permitted. Allow 30 minutes minimum. Daily 8 a.m.-dusk. Free. Phone (360) 354-6717.

LYNDEN PIONEER MUSEUM is at 217 Front St. The museum focuses on early 20th-century life. A pioneer street features 26 full-scale representations of early Lynden businesses, including a railroad depot, hotel, drugstore, barn, barnyard and farmhouse with period furnishings. Other displays include antique automobiles, more than 40 buggies, tractors and other farm equipment and Coast Salish Indian artifacts. Allow 1 hour minimum. Mon.-Sat. 10-4, Sun. 1-4; closed holidays. Admission $7; $4 (ages 6-14, 65+ and students with ID). Phone (360) 354-3675.

GAMBLING ESTABLISHMENTS
• **Nooksack Northwood Casino** is 4 mi. e. of SR 539 on SR 544, then 2 mi. n. on Northwood Rd. Sun.-Thurs. 8 a.m.-3 a.m., Fri.-Sat. 8 a.m.-4 a.m. Phone (360) 734-5101 or (877) 777-9847.

LYNNWOOD—*see Seattle p. 253.*

MANSON (D-9) elev. 1,160'

Named for the president of a local land development company, Manson is located on the east bank of Lake Chelan. Logs were once rafted down the lake to a sawmill that formed the nucleus of the settlement. The surrounding hillsides are covered with orchards. The Lake Chelan Boat Co. offers passenger-only boat service to points along the lake (*see attraction listing p. 160*).

Lake Chelan Chamber of Commerce—Manson: 102 E. Johnson Ave., P.O. Box 216, Chelan, WA 98816; phone (509) 682-3503 or (800) 424-3526.

GAMBLING ESTABLISHMENTS
• **Mill Bay Casino** is off SR 150 at 455 Wapato Lake Rd. Sun.-Thurs. 8 a.m.-4 a.m., Fri.-Sat. 24 hours; closed Dec. 25. Phone (509) 687-2102 or (800) 648-2946.

MAPLE FALLS (B-7) pop. 277, elev. 646'

Established beside Maple Creek in 1901, the town took the name of a nearby waterfall. Silver

Lake County Park, 4 miles north of Maple Falls, nestles between high mountains beside its namesake lake. The park has 3 miles of trails and a historic house featuring early logging displays *(see Recreation Chart)*. Hang gliding is popular off 4,990-foot Black Mountain, which is east of the park.

RECREATIONAL ACTIVITIES

Skiing

- **Mount Baker Ski Area** is 28 mi. e. on SR 542. Write 1019 Iowa St., Bellingham, WA 98229. Daily 9-3:30, late Nov.-Mar. 31; Sat.-Sun. 9-3:30, Apr. 1-early May. Phone (360) 734-6771, or (360) 671-0211 for snow information.

White-water Rafting

- **River Recreation, Inc.** departs from various points on the Nooksack River. Write P.O. Box 2124, Bothell, WA 98041. July-Aug. Phone (425) 741-5901 or (800) 464-5899.

MARYHILL (H-8) pop. 98, elev. 180'

Maryhill was founded in 1907 by Samuel Hill, who thought the sunny site had the makings of an agricultural utopia. An eccentric lawyer and pacifist Quaker, Hill also was a talented road and monument builder; his works include the Peace Arch State and Provincial Park in Blaine *(see place listing p. 157)* and the Columbia River Scenic Highway on the Oregon side of the Columbia River Gorge.

In 1913 Hill also built the 3.6-mile Loops Road, just east of the junction of US 97 and SR 14. The twisting byway was the first to be paved in Washington and is now open to pedestrians and bicyclists.

MARYHILL MUSEUM OF ART is on SR 14, 2.7 mi. w. of US 97. The museum is in a chateaulike mansion built by Northwest entrepreneur Samuel Hill. Although it was dedicated by Queen Marie of Romania in 1926, the museum did not open until 1940. European and American paintings are complemented by a collection of Auguste Rodin sculptures and watercolors and 18th-century Russian icons.

Other highlights include Hill photographs and memorabilia, American Indian basketry and artifacts, the 1945 Théâtre de la Mode French fashion mannequin gallery, international chess sets and personal items donated by Queen Marie, including items by Fabergé. The works displayed in the Special Exhibitions Gallery are changed during the season. The grounds include an outdoor sculpture garden and a Lewis & Clark overlook with interpretive panels. Picnicking is permitted. Food is available. Allow 1 hour minimum. Daily 9-5, Mar. 15-Nov. 15. Admission $7; $6 (ages 65+); $2 (ages 6-16). AX, DS, MC, VI. Phone (509) 773-3733.

STONEHENGE is 1 mi. e. of jct. US 97 and SR 14, then .7 mi. s. On a cliff overlooking the Columbia River, this 1918 concrete replica of the 4,000-year-old Stonehenge in Wiltshire, England, is a memorial to the men of Klickitat County killed in World War I. Built 40 years before the position of Stonehenge was decoded for astronomical measurement, the reproduction is not exact. The crypt of the monument's builder, Maryhill founder Samuel Hill, is a short walk southwest of the replica. Daily 7 a m - dusk. Free.

WINERIES

- **Maryhill Winery** is 5 mi. w. of US 97 on SR 14. The winery is set on a spectacular bluff overlooking the vineyards, the Columbia River and Mount Hood. Live music takes place Sat.-Sun. 1-5, June-Sept. Guided 1-hour tours are given by reservation. Tastings daily 10-6; closed Jan. 1, Thanksgiving, and Dec. 24-25 and 31. Phone (509) 773-1976, ext. 308, or (877) 627-9445, ext. 308.

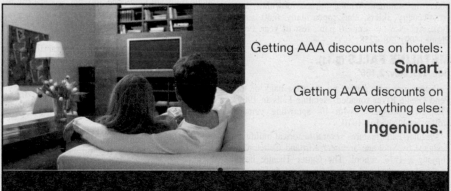

MARYSVILLE—see Seattle p. 253.

MATTAWA (F-9) pop. 2,609, elev. 777′

Priest Rapids and Wanapum (see Vantage p. 274) dams, two major hydroelectric dams built on the Columbia River in the 1950s, created Priest Rapids and Wanapum lakes. Both reservoirs feature several public recreation areas.

PRIEST RAPIDS DAM is 5.5 mi. s. on SR 243, then 1.5 mi. w. Completed in 1959, the dam can generate more than 955,000 kilowatts of power. Picnicking is permitted. Free.

McNARY LOCK AND DAM—

see Umatilla, Ore., p. 122.

MEAD (D-12) elev. 1,906′

[SAVE] **CAT TALES ZOOLOGICAL PARK** is at 17020 N. Newport Hwy. (US 2). This haven for endangered and exotic felines features specimens ranging from North American bobcats to Bengal tigers and includes rare leopards and a large collection of panthers. Visitors ages 8+ can feed a lion or tiger with the help of a zookeeper. Allow 1 hour minimum. Tues.-Sun. 10-6, May-Sept.; 10-4, rest of year. Closed Thanksgiving and Dec. 25. Admission $8; $6 (ages 55+ and students with ID); $5 (ages 0-12); free (ages 55+ on Sun. and the physically impaired). AX, DS, MC, VI. Phone (509) 238-4126.

MOUNT SPOKANE is 15 mi. n.e. in Mount Spokane State Park (see Recreation Chart). An improved road leads to the 5,878-foot summit where, in clear weather, sweeping views encompass portions of Washington, Idaho, Montana and British Columbia. A Civilian Conservation Corps-built shelter, known as Vista House, crowns the summit. Washington's largest state park features more than 100 miles of trails, which draw hikers and mountain bikers in summer. Winter attracts downhill and cross-country skiers. Park open daily 6:30 a.m.-dusk, Apr.-Nov.; 8 a.m.-10 p.m., rest of year. Free. Phone (509) 238-4258.

METALINE FALLS (B-11)
pop. 223, elev. 2,100′

Prospectors who settled on the west bank of the Pend Oreille River founded Metaline Falls in 1909. The town prospered with its sprawling cement works, established in 1910.

Metaline Falls features several historical buildings designed by Spokane architect Kirtland Cutter. Occupying a 1912 school, The Cutter Theatre hosts live performances and showcases an art gallery and the Historic Schools Display. A viewpoint 2 miles west of SR 31 north of town overlooks the narrow, rugged gorge of Z Canyon. Just east of town is the Colville National Forest's Salmo-Priest Wilderness Area.

Metalines Chamber of Commerce: P.O. Box 388, Metaline Falls, WA 99153; phone (509) 446-3683.

BOUNDARY DAM is 11.5 mi. n. of the town of Metaline via CR 62 to Boundary Dam Rd., on the w. side of Z Canyon. This 340-foot-tall dam features a visitors gallery within a limestone cavern. **Note:** For security reasons, a photo ID is required for all adults. Allow 1 hour minimum. Visitors gallery open Thurs.-Mon. 10:30-4:30, Memorial Day weekend-Labor Day. Guided tours are given on request. Free. Phone (509) 446-3083. ·

Boundary Dam Vista House is 11 mi. n. on SR 31 to the access road at Crescent Lake, then 2 mi. w. The Vista House is perched on the east side of Z Canyon, overlooking Boundary Dam. Exhibits include the hydroelectric project, indigenous wildlife and the border patrol. A trail loops down to an overlook, cantilevered over the edge of the canyon high above the dam; the view is spectacular. Picnicking is permitted. Allow 1 hour minimum. Daily dawn-dusk, Memorial Day weekend-Sept. 30. Free. Phone (509) 446-3083.

GARDNER CAVE is 11 mi. n. of Metaline on Boundary Dam Rd. in Crawford State Park. With 1,055 feet of passageway, it is reputed to be the third longest limestone cavern in the state. Picnic facilities are available. Allow 1 hour minimum. Open Thurs.-Mon. 9-6, late Apr.-Labor Day. Guided tours are given daily at 10, noon, 2 and 4 (weather permitting). Free. Phone (509) 446-4065 or (509) 238-4258.

MOCLIPS (E-4) pop. 615, elev. 43′

Moclips is the northernmost of a string of beach towns along the Pacific between Point Grenville and Ocean Shores. The Northern Pacific Railroad opened its North Beach line in 1905, serving shingle mills and small beach resorts. The queen of these resorts was the 300-room Moclips Beach Hotel, built on pilings at the edge of the sea. Storm waves destroyed the hotel and much of the town in 1911. The shingle mills are long gone, too, but Moclips still remains as a popular beach getaway.

The beach south of the mouth of the Moclips River was formerly called Moonstone for its once-plentiful agate beds. North of the river the beach curves to the rocky headland of Point Grenville. A Spanish expedition commanded by Bruno Heceta landed here on July 14, 1775, claiming the land in the name of King Carlos III. The Quinault Indian Reservation begins at the northern edge of town. Access to beaches within the reservation is restricted; to obtain a beach pass stop by the main Tribal Administration Building in Taholah, 9 miles north of Moclips on SR 109, on weekdays. For additional information phone (360) 276-8215, ext. 208 or 309.

MUSEUM OF THE NORTH BEACH is just s. of town on SR 109. Historical photographs, maps and other artifacts chronicle the history of the beach communities from Ocean Shores to Taholah. There are displays about the Northern Pacific Railroad, logging and early resort hotels, a general store exhibit, a re-created Flying-A gasoline station and a collection of Quinault Indian baskets.

Allow 30 minutes minimum. Thurs.-Mon. 11-4, May-Sept.; Sat.-Sun. 11-4, rest of year. Closed Jan. 1 and Dec. 25. Donations. Phone (360) 276-4441.

MONITOR (E-8) elev. 710'

The main industry here is obvious—stacks of apple boxes stand outside packing sheds and storage warehouses that line the railroad tracks. The community was first called Browns Flats when it was founded in the late 1880s. The present name was adopted in 1902 to commemorate the Civil War-era ironclad.

The Wenatchee River above Monitor is one of Washington's most popular white-water rafting streams. Most outfitters start near Leavenworth and end at Wenatchee River County Park, just downstream from Monitor. The rafting season extends from May into September, although the river is at its highest and most exciting in late spring.

RECREATIONAL ACTIVITIES
White-water Rafting

• **River Recreation, Inc.** departs from 3133 Main St., off US 2/97. Write P.O. Box 2124, Bothell, WA 98041. Daily, Apr.-Aug. Phone (425) 741-5901 or (800) 464-5899.

MONROE—*See Seattle p. 253*

MONTESANO (F-5) pop. 3,312, elev. 66'

Founded in the 1850s near the confluence of the Chehalis and Wynoochee rivers, Montesano is a trading center for regional farming and lumber businesses. The Grays Harbor County Court House's indoor murals depict area history, including Capt. Robert Gray's discovery of Grays Harbor in 1792. Saturday and Sunday afternoons the Chehalis Valley Historical Museum, 7 blocks w. of Main St. at 703 W. Pioneer Ave., documents the role of the area's forest products industry; phone (360) 249-5800.

Montesano is known as the origin of commercial forestry's tree-farm system. Weyerhaeuser established the Clemons Tree Farm in 1941; today the farm sprawls over 200,000 acres. Lake Sylvia State Park *(see Recreation Chart)*, 1 mile north of town off US 12 exit 104, is the site of the county's first sawmill. Along the park's 2-mile Sylvia Creek Forestry Trail, 15 interpretive markers describe management of a working forest.

Montesano Chamber of Commerce: 117 Fleet St. S., P.O. Box 688, Montesano, WA 98563; phone (360) 249-5522.

MOSES LAKE (E-10) pop. 14,953, elev. 1,060'

Eighteen-mile-long Moses Lake consists of three main arms with 120 miles of shoreline. Recreational activities here include fishing, swimming, water skiing and boating.

The lake, and in turn the city, takes its name from Chief Moses, whose tribe inhabited the area for generations. Chief Moses traveled to Washington, D.C., to speak with President Rutherford B. Hayes and was one of the Northwest's most influential American Indian leaders.

Cattle ranching was introduced into the area at the turn of the 20th century. Established beside the lake in 1910, the town of Neppel was named for the wife of a Milwaukee-based German language newspaper that promoted the new settlement.

When the community incorporated in 1938, it took a new name: Moses Lake. World War II brought an army air force base to the area and an influx of Japanese American families that had been forced to relocate inland in 1942. After 1950, the irrigation works of the Columbia Basin Project initiated the area's agricultural transformation.

The former Larson Air Force Base, maintained to protect Grand Coulee Dam and the Hanford Atomic Energy Commission site, features a 13,500-foot runway, one of the nation's longest. Boeing, the U.S. military, Japan Airlines and other air carriers use the facility for heavy jet testing and training.

Moses Lake Chamber of Commerce: 324 S. Pioneer Way, Moses Lake, WA 98837; phone (509) 765-7888 or (800) 992-6234.

MOSES LAKE MUSEUM AND ART CENTER is at 228 W. 3rd Ave. The museum contains American Indian artifacts and exhibits that highlight local history. Art exhibits are displayed in the gallery. Tues.-Sat. 11-5. Donations. Phone (509) 766-9395.

SURF 'N SLIDE WATER PARK is at 401 W. Fourth Ave. in McCosh Park. The park features two 2,000-foot water slides, a lazy river, beach, the double-chute Flow Rider and a swimming pool. Other facilities include a sand volleyball court and children's activity area. Food is available. Picnicking is permitted. Mon.-Thurs. 11-6:30, Fri.-Sun. 11-7, mid-June to late Aug.; Mon.-Fri. 4-8, Sat.-Sun. 11-7, Memorial Day weekend to mid-June and late Aug.-Labor Day. Admission $8; $7 (ages 13-17); $6 (ages 5-12 and 64+). MC, VI. Phone (509) 766-9246.

MOSSYROCK (F-6) pop. 486, elev. 698'

Settlement began here at the east end of Klickitat Prairie in the early 1850s. Today, area farmers raise flower bulbs on the rich prairie soil. Just east of town, US 12 spans a 255-foot-deep gorge through which the Cowlitz River flows.

MOSSYROCK DAM is 3 mi. e. on US 12. Built in 1968, Mossyrock Dam, the tallest in Washington, rises 606 feet and forms 23-mile-long Riffe Lake. Hydrovista offers an overlook and interpretive displays of the hydroelectric project. Mossyrock Park *(see Recreation Chart)* is on the southwest corner of the lake. Picnicking is permitted. Daily 24 hours. Free.

MOUNT BAKER-SNOQUALMIE NATIONAL FOREST

Elevations in the forest range from 280 ft. along the Skykomish River east of Gold Bar to 10,778 ft. at the summit of Mount Baker. Refer to AAA maps for additional elevation information.

The Mount Baker-Snoqualmie National Forest covers the western slopes of the Cascades from the Canadian border to the northern boundary of Mount Rainier National Park.

Some of the state's most primitive regions are within the 1,700,000-acre forest. Mount Baker, at 10,778 feet, dominates the northern section and is the site of Sherman Crater's thermal activity that began in 1975. The Mount Baker Wilderness surrounds the volcano. Glacier Peak, at 10,568 feet, towers over the central part of the forest; the Glacier Peak Wilderness lies between Stevens Pass and North Cascades National Park. In the high country between Snoqualmie Pass and Stevens Pass is Alpine Lakes Wilderness.

Four east-west highways provide scenic drives— I-90, US 2, SR 20 and SR 410. National Scenic Byways include the Mount Baker Highway (SR 542) from Glacier to Artist Point, and the Stevens Pass Highway (US 2) east from Gold Bar to Leavenworth. Mountain Loop Highway also is a National Scenic Byway leading into the heart of the western Cascades. From Granite Falls it parallels the South Fork of the Stillaguamish River past Mount Pilchuck, numerous forest service campgrounds and old mine sites.

Silverton, 22 miles east, is a former gold and silver mining center. Four miles past Silverton a 1-mile trail leads to the Big Four Ice Caves. **Note:** Due to a 2006 storm, the trail to the ice caves is closed indefinitely. The road beyond is closed from November until April or May.

From Barlow Pass the partly gravel road, which is subject to closure due to washouts, leads north to Darrington. The former road to Monte Cristo, an important 1890s gold mining town, is closed indefinitely due to washouts but is accessible to hikers. Check road and trail conditions at Darrington Ranger Station; phone (360) 436-1155.

Wildlife abounds and fish are plentiful. Pack trips and hiking are popular, particularly along the Pacific Crest National Scenic Trail. The Washington portion of the trail runs along the north-south crest of the Cascades for more than 500 miles from the Columbia River to the British Columbia border. Camping and winter sports also are available.

Skiing is available at Snoqualmie Pass Summit on I-90 (see Snoqualmie Pass p. 266), at Mount Baker on SR 542 (see Maple Falls p. 178) and at Stevens Pass on US 2 (see Skykomish p. 266). Visitor information is available at ranger stations in Darrington, Enumclaw, North Bend, Sedro-Woolley and Skykomish; public services centers at Glacier and Verlot and a visitors center at Snoqualmie Pass are open late May to late September. The Heather Meadows Visitor Center is open from late July to early October, depending on snow conditions.

A Northwest Forest Pass, available at ranger stations, is required for parking at most trailheads in the forest. A day pass costs $5 per vehicle; an annual pass costs $30. For recreation information contact the Outdoor Recreation Information Center, 222 Yale Ave. N., Seattle, WA 98109; phone (206) 470-4060. For further information contact the Forest Supervisor's Office, Mount Baker-Snoqualmie National Forest, 2930 Wetmore Ave., Everett, WA 98201; phone (425) 783-6000 or (800) 627-0062, ext. 0. *See Recreation Chart and the AAA Northwestern CampBook.*

▼ MOUNT RAINIER NATIONAL PARK (F-7)

Elevations in the park range from 1,610 ft. at the Carbon River entrance station to 14,411 ft. at the summit of Mount Rainier. Refer to AAA maps for additional elevation information.

Mount Rainier National Park has four entrances: the Nisqually, off SR 706 in the southwest; the Carbon River, on Carbon River Road in the northwest (which is closed indefinitely due to flood damage); the White River, on White River Road off SR 410 in the northeast; and the Stevens Canyon Road entrance in the southeast.

Mount Rainier, a towering, ice-clad volcano rising 14,411 feet, is a striking landmark in the Pacific Northwest. The cap of glacial ice that conceals all but a few crags and ridges makes it doubly impressive. Although Mount Rainier currently is dormant, it is not extinct. It belongs to the class of exploding volcanoes, much like recently awakened Mount St. Helens, and quite conceivably could one day erupt in a similar manner.

Although mere remnants of their former size, Rainier's 35 square miles of glaciers constitute the largest single-peak glacial system in the contiguous United States: 26 glaciers extend down the mountainside. Six of them—Nisqually, Ingraham, Emmons, Winthrop, Kautz and Tahoma—originate in the summit ice cap. Many other major glaciers are born of snows in valley heads, or cirques, between 10,000 and 12,000 feet; the most notable of these are Cowlitz, Carbon, Russell, North and South Mowich and Puyallup glaciers.

Forests cover the mountainsides up to 5,000 feet, where alpine meadows of wildflowers and grass contrast with masses of ice at higher elevations. The timberline is at about 6,500 feet. Deer, bears and mountain goats inhabit the forests, meadows and ridges. Park animals, either large and small, should not be fed; all food should be locked up or out of the reach of wildlife.

Flowers in the high meadows bloom from late June to mid-August. Huckleberries, vine maple and mountain ash grow throughout the park; fall colors are at their best from late September to early October.

General Information and Activities

The park is open daily. Only the Nisqually (southwest) entrance and Nisqually-Paradise Road are open all year, unless storms or avalanches threaten passage. All other roads are closed from late October or the first snowfall, whichever comes first, to somewhere between late April and early July, depending upon the occurrence of snowfalls. Cayuse Pass, between the northern boundary on SR 410 to Ohanapecosh, is usually closed from early December to early May. The road between Chinook Pass and Cayuse Pass is closed from mid-November to late May.

Naturalists conduct free guided and illustrated talks from late June through Labor Day at Longmire, Paradise, Sunrise, Carbon River and Ohanapecosh; schedules are posted at visitor centers. Snowshoe walks are conducted at Paradise from late December to early April. Self-guiding nature trails and wayside exhibits are found throughout the park. Hiker information centers are at Longmire, White River and at park visitor centers.

Permits are required for overnight backpacking. Sightseeing flights can be arranged through private operators in Morton and Puyallup as well as at nearby airports. Information concerning roads, camps and programs can be obtained by contacting the Park Superintendent's office. For information about the park's inns write Mount Rainier Guest Services, 55106 Kernahan Rd. E., Ashford, WA 98304; phone (360) 569-2400.

Special regulations apply to climbers; details are available from the Park Superintendent. Rainier Mountaineering Inc., at Ashford, conducts climbing schools and seminars as well as guided climbs. For details contact Rainier Mountaineering Inc., 30027 SR 706 E., P.O. Box Q, Ashford, WA 98304; phone (360) 569-2227 or (888) 892-5462.

Trout fishing is permitted without a license; check at a ranger station for special regulations. Hunting is prohibited. Winter sports and a snow

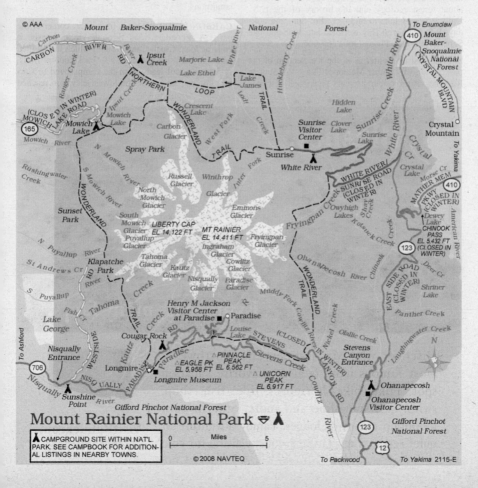

play area are available at Paradise from late December into late March or early April (weather permitting). Snowmobiles are permitted only on designated roads. *See Recreation Chart and the AAA Northwestern CampBook.*

VISITOR CENTERS are throughout the park. They offer a variety of free information and exhibits. *See color ad.*

Henry M. Jackson Visitor Center at Paradise is 18 mi. e. of the Nisqually park entrance via Paradise Rd. The visitor center has exhibits, audiovisual programs and an observation deck. Daily 10-6, May-Sept.; Sat.-Sun. and holidays 10-5, rest of year. Phone (360) 569-6036.

Longmire Museum is 6 mi. e. of the Nisqually park entrance via Paradise Rd. The museum has interesting geology, flora and fauna, history and transportation exhibits. Daily 9-5, May 1-early Sept.; 9-4, rest of year. Phone (360) 569-2211, ext. 3314.

Ohanapecosh Visitor Center is in the s.e. corner of the park off SR 123. The visitor center has exhibits about forest ecology and the history of the park. Daily 9-5, mid-June to mid-Oct.; Fri.-Sun. and holidays 9-5, Memorial Day weekend-late June and late Sept. to mid-Oct. Phone (360) 569-6046.

Sunrise Visitor Center is in the n.e. section of the park 16 mi. off Mather Memorial Pkwy. via Sunrise Rd. The visitor center presents geological displays.

Daily 9-6, mid-June to mid-Sept. Phone (360) 663-2425.

ADMISSION to the park is by weekly pass that costs $15 per private vehicle or $5 per person on foot or bicycle. Annual passes, valid for 1 year, cost $30. Campground fees are $12-$15 per private vehicle.

PETS are permitted only if they are on a leash or are otherwise physically restrained at all times. Dogs and cats are not permitted on the trails or in buildings.

ADDRESS general inquiries to the Superintendent, Mount Rainier National Park, 55210 238th Ave. E., Ashford, WA 98304; phone (360) 569-2211.

Points of Interest

More than 140 miles of roads and 300 miles of trails are open to the public. Trail maps are available at all visitor centers. Permits are required for back-country camping. Road opening and closing dates vary from year to year depending on snow conditions.

CARBON RIVER ROAD is in the n.w. corner of the park. A secondary road through virgin forests, it ends at Ipsut Creek Campground, which has limited camping facilities and access to back-country trails. A 3.5-mile trail leads from the campground to Carbon Glacier, said to be the lowest elevation reached

by a glacier in the 48 states. **Note:** The road is closed indefinitely to motor vehicles at the park boundary due to flood damage; the route is open to hikers and bicyclists.

EAST SIDE ROAD (SR 123) extends across the eastern section of the park from Ohanapecosh to SR 410 at Cayuse Pass. The Stevens Canyon Road intersection is 2 miles north of Ohanapecosh. Tipsoo Lake and Chinook Pass are 5 miles east of Cayuse Pass on SR 410; excellent panoramas of Mount Rainier, Governors Ridge, the Pacific Crest National Scenic Trail and the high country of the Cascade Mountains are available from this site.

MOWICH LAKE ROAD is accessible via the SR 165 entrance in the park's n.w. corner. Although this dirt and gravel surfaced byway is not a through road, it serves as a trailhead for those taking trips into the park's back country. Camping is permitted at a designated campsite along the lake, but campfires are prohibited. The road is open mid-July to mid-Oct. (weather permitting).

NISQUALLY-PARADISE ROAD from the s.w. entrance, connects with West Side Rd., 1 mi. from the park entrance. On the way to Paradise Valley are the Kautz Mudflow area, a museum at Longmire; Christine Falls; the trail to 320-foot Comet Falls, accessible only in summer; and 168-foot Narada Falls. The road is open all year, but chains may be required in winter months.

NORTHERN LOOP TRAIL runs 17.5 mi. from Carbon River to Sunrise. It climbs through rugged Windy Gap, intersects with a trail leading to Natural Bridge and passes Lake James, Grand and Berkeley parks and Frozen Lake. By combining the section of the Wonderland Trail from Sunrise past Mystic Lake and the Winthrop Glacier, this trail can be extended to a 36-mile loop back to Carbon River. The trail is free of snow only from late July to mid-September.

STEVENS CANYON ROAD leaves Nisqually-Paradise Rd. about 1 mi. beyond Narada Falls. The road furnishes an east-west connection in the park. The effects of glacial and water erosion are apparent at the Box Canyon of the Cowlitz River. Picnicking is permitted a half-mile west.

There are excellent views of Mount Rainier, Mount Adams and the Tatoosh Range along this route, which intersects East Side Road 2 miles above Ohanapecosh; the best views are westbound. The road is usually open Memorial Day weekend to mid-Oct. (weather permitting).

WEST SIDE ROAD leaves Nisqually-Paradise Rd. 1 mile from the park entrance. The road, improved but not surfaced, provides access to the west side trailheads. The road is closed indefinitely at Milepost 3; beyond that point the right of way is accessible to hikers. It is not a through road and is often closed due to bad weather or high water damage. Check for conditions.

WHITE RIVER/SUNRISE ROAD runs from the n.e. entrance to the Sunrise area. It passes Fryingpan Creek; White River Campground and the trail to the Emmons Glacier moraine; and Sunrise Point, offering a panorama stretching from Mount Baker in the north to Mount Hood in the south. Branching out from Sunrise Visitor Center, a variety of trails pass through alpine scenery with views of Mount Rainier's glaciers. The meadows are known for their summer alpine wildflower displays. Road open early July-late Oct. (weather permitting).

WONDERLAND TRAIL encircles Mount Rainier. It is divided into different portions. The 30-mile section from Paradise to Sunrise passes lakes, falls and Box Canyon, which is noted as one of the most unusual river canyons in America. From Sunrise to Carbon River—16.5 miles—hikers enter the primitive area of the park to see Winthrop Glacier, Mystic Lake and Carbon Glacier.

From Carbon River to Longmire, a 39-mile stretch, the trail passes Mowich Lake, Golden Lakes, Sunset Park, Klapatche Park, Indian Henry's Hunting Ground and other points of interest. The 6.5-mile section from Longmire to Paradise passes Carter, Madcap and Narada falls. Travel on the Wonderland Trail is recommended only from mid-July to mid-Sept.

◥ MOUNT ST. HELENS NATIONAL VOLCANIC MONUMENT (G-7)

In southwestern Washington, Mount St. Helens National Volcanic Monument contains the volcano and the surrounding area devastated by the 1980 eruption. Access to the 110,000-acre monument is limited; local roads only skirt the region, ending in overlooks providing scenic views. Southeast of the crater FR 25 branches off from FR 90 and continues north, becoming SR 131, then meets US 12 at Randle. Northeast of the volcano FR 99 branches west off FR 25, ending at the Windy Ridge viewpoint from which Mount St. Helens crater and Spirit Lake can be seen.

The roads are open from late May or mid-June to late October (weather permitting). The Spirit Lake Memorial Highway (SR 504) extends 50 miles from I-5 at Castle Rock to Johnston Ridge. Except for the section between Coldwater Ridge and Johnston Ridge, this road is kept open year-round; however, chains or winter traction devices may be necessary.

Until May 18, 1980, Mount St. Helens was one of Washington's snowcapped crown jewels. Spirit Lake, at its northern base, was a primary recreation center. The surrounding hills of the Gifford Pinchot National Forest *(see place listing p. 169)* beckoned hikers and outdoors enthusiasts as well as loggers whose livelihoods its timber provided.

At 8:32 a.m. an explosion of incredible force blew the top 1,313 feet and much of the bulging north face off Mount St. Helens, shot a dense plume of smoke and ash 80,000 feet into the air and released a mile-wide avalanche that raised Spirit Lake by more than 200 feet and laid over forests as if they had been combed. Mud and logs surged down the Toutle and Cowlitz rivers, temporarily clogging the Columbia River shipping lanes with silt. The pall of ash turned morning into midnight as it fell, halting traffic for a hundred miles and covering parts of three states with a fine gray powder.

The cataclysm was not wholly unexpected. Since the initial puff of steam and ash appeared on Mar. 27, signaling the end of the mountain's 123-year-long sleep and announcing the first volcanic activity in the contiguous 48 states since the eruption of California's Mount Lassen 1914-21, Mount St. Helens had become one of the world's most closely monitored volcanoes.

Weeks before the great explosion, increasing seismic phenomena, heat and the swelling north slope had changed "*if* the mountain blows" to "*when* the mountain blows." Despite the renewal of life in the area since the 1980 blast, the watch continues as subsequent, but subtle, episodes suggest that the volcano might not yet be ready for another nap.

General Information and Activities

If you are planning to travel in southwestern Washington, you might wish to check with your home AAA club for the latest highway and recreation area information, then update that information by checking with clubs once you arrive in the Pacific Northwest. Many roads within the Gifford Pinchot National Forest are usually closed from November until April or May; you should check at Forest Service offices before driving on these roads.

More information about the volcanic area can be obtained from the Mount St. Helens National Volcanic Monument Headquarters, 42218 N.E. Yale Bridge Rd., Amboy, WA 98601; phone (360) 449-7800.

Sightseeing helicopter flights are available from several locations along SR 504. Flights also leave daily from Seattle's Boeing Field. Helicopter rides are available at Hoffstadt Bluffs Visitor Center (*see attraction listing*).

A growing network of hiking trails is becoming accessible around the volcano. It is possible to climb

the southern flank of Mount St. Helens, allowing about 7-12 hours for the rigorous trek to the summit and back; a $15 permit is required to climb April through October. For permit and reservation information about the summit climb and information about the hiking trails contact monument headquarters. The Mount St. Helens climbing information line is (360) 449-7861. **Note:** Climbing may be suspended periodically due to volcanic activity.

A pass is required at developed sites and visitor centers. A Monument Pass, valid for one day at Johnston Ridge Observatory costs $8; free (ages 0-15). The America the Beautiful – National Parks and Federal Recreational Lands Passes (Annual Pass, Senior Pass, Access Pass) also are accepted at this visitor center. A Northwest Forest Pass costing $5 per vehicle for a day pass or $30 for an annual pass is required at sites on the east and south sides of the monument.

Points of Interest

APE CAVE GEOLOGIC SITE is on FR 8303, 1 mi. w. of FR 83. Thought to be the longest lava tube in the Western Hemisphere, the 12,810-foot tunnel was found within a massive lava flow that oozed from the volcano almost 2,000 years ago. Flowing downhill, the stream of lava cooled and formed a hard crust. In time the lava drained and left an intricate, winding lava cave behind. The cave was first explored in 1946 by the St. Helens Apes—the local Boy Scout troop for whom the cave is named.

Visitors should have three light sources, sturdy shoes and a jacket; the temperature is a constant 42 degrees Fahrenheit. The Ape Cave Information Station is open Wed.-Sun. 10-5, late June-Labor Day. Guided tours are available daily 11-3, late June-Labor Day. A Northwest Forest Pass is required, which is $5 per vehicle; an annual pass costs $30. Phone (360) 449-7800.

FOREST LEARNING CENTER AT MOUNT ST. HELENS is off I-5 exit 49, then 33 mi. e. on SR 504 (Spirit Lake Memorial Hwy.) to Milepost 33. The center offers displays highlighting the eruption of Mount St. Helens and the recovery and reforestation efforts currently underway. Visitors can sit inside the cockpit of a helicopter and take a video-taped tour of Mount St. Helens. Many hands-on

displays also are featured, and platforms offer a panorama of the mountain. Allow 30 minutes minimum. Daily 10-6, June-Aug.; 10-5, May 15-31 and Sept. 1 to mid-Oct. Free. Phone (360) 414-3439.

HOFFSTADT BLUFFS VISITOR CENTER is off I-5 exit 49, then 27 mi. e. on SR 504 (Spirit Lake Memorial Hwy.) to Milepost 27. The center overlooks the panoramic Toutle River and the valley leading to Mount St. Helens. Helicopter rides are offered late May through September 30 (weather permitting). Visitors can watch glassblowers at work daily May through October. Food and picnic facilities are available. Daily 9-7, Memorial Day weekend-Labor Day; 10-6, Mar. 1-day before Memorial Day weekend and in Nov.; 11-4, rest of year. Free. Helicopter rides $165 per person. Phone (360) 274-7750.

JOHNSTON RIDGE OBSERVATORY is on SR 504 at Milepost 53. The observatory is the closest to the crater and lava dome and offers panoramic views. The facility is named for a volcanologist, on duty at the time of the eruption, who was one of the 57 people who lost their lives during this catastrophic event. Interpretive exhibits explain the series of events leading to the eruption of the volcano and the resulting change to the landscape. A 16-minute video presentation re-creates the eruption. An interpretive trail is available.

Allow 1 hour minimum. Daily 10-6, May-Oct. (weather permitting). Monument Pass $8; free (ages 0-15). MC, VI. Phone (360) 274-2140.

MOUNT ST. HELENS SILVER LAKE VISITOR CENTER is on the shore of Silver Lake, 5 mi. e. of I-5 exit 49 on SR 504. A walk-in model of the volcano illustrates its composition; pictorial and interpretive material and a film highlight the May 18, 1980, eruption. A .13-mile trail outside the center leads to a viewpoint overlooking Silver Lake and, 34 miles east, Mount St. Helens.

Allow 30 minutes minimum. Daily 9-5, May-Sept.; 9-4, rest of year. Admission $3; $1 (ages 7-17). Phone (360) 274-0962.

SCENIC DRIVES are provided by a network of state and forest roads connecting with I-5 and US 12. Mount St. Helens is visible on clear days from Chehalis to Salem, Ore. A series of Forest Service roads forms a 60-mile link between Cougar and Randle, the principal western and northern gateways into the forest. FR 90, along the southern edge of the volcanic area east of Cougar, is paved as far as its intersection with FR 25, a paved road extending north to Randle.

A number of paved and gravel forest service roads branch off FRs 90 and 25, with viewpoints within the volcanic area. Many forest service roads are closed from October through June, depending on snow conditions. A concession stand and portable toilets are available at Cascade Viewpoint on FR 99. Groceries are available at the east end of Swift Reservoir.

Roads, some unpaved, leading into the volcanic area include Cougar Creek Road (FR 8303) from FR 83 to Ape Cave, which crosses a 1,900-year-old lava field with numerous caves and tubes as well as the first 10 miles of FR 81 from Cougar, which passes Merrill Lake and Kalama Falls.

A particularly scenic road is the Spirit Lake Memorial Highway (SR 504), which follows the north fork of the Toutle River to the Johnston Ridge Observatory *(see attraction listing p. 187).* Overlooks along the highway provide views of the crater and northwest lava dome, the blast zone, Castle Lake and Coldwater Lake. The road ends 7 miles beyond Coldwater Ridge at Johnston Ridge.

FR 99 branches off FR 25 and travels west past Meta Lake to within 5 miles of the volcano at Windy Ridge. There, at the road's end, visitors have a fine view of the devastation stretching from Mount St. Helens' crater to Spirit Lake. For other viewpoint locations contact the monument headquarters. Phone (360) 449-7800.

MOUNT VERNON (C-3)
pop. 26,232, elev. 23′

Named for President George Washington's Potomac River home, Mount Vernon dates back to a trading post established on the banks of the Skagit River in 1870.

West of Mount Vernon is one of the nation's largest commercial bulb growing regions. Bulb farms cluster along county roads branching north and south from SR 20; follow SR 536 west from I-5 exit 226.

Daffodils bloom from mid-March to early April, tulips during the first half of April and irises in early May. Maps pinpointing the location of various flower fields and dates of festival events are available from the chamber of commerce. The chamber also houses a visitor information center.

Tulip season coincides with April's ⬧ Skagit Valley Tulip Festival, a month-long event celebrated throughout the Skagit Valley with display gardens, exhibits, food, fairs and shows. Among the largest display gardens are those at Tulip Town-Skagit Valley Bulb Farm, Roozengaarde and Lefeber Bulb Co.

Mount Vernon Chamber of Commerce: 105 E. Kincaid St., Suite 101, P.O. Box 1007, Mount Vernon, WA 98273; phone (360) 428-8547.

LA CONNER FLATS DISPLAY GARDENS is .5 mi. w. on Division St. (SR 536), 1 blk. s. on Wall St., 5.5 mi. w., then .5 mi. s. on Best Rd. Perennials, rhododendrons, roses, vegetables and alpine plants are among the variety found in this 11-acre English-style garden. Daily 10-6. Donations. Phone (360) 466-3190.

ROOZENGAARDE is .5 mi. w. on Division St. (SR 536), 1 blk. s. on Wall St., 3 mi. w. on McLean Rd., then s. on Beaver Marsh Rd. The 3-acre display garden is filled with tulips, irises, daffodils and other flowering bulbs. Roozengaarde is a division of the Washington Bulb Co., one of the world's largest growers of tulips, daffodils and irises. The main blooming season is late March-early May. Picnic facilities are available. Mon.-Sat. 9-6, Sun. 11-4. Admission in Apr. $3; free (ages 0-4). Free rest of year. Phone (360) 424-8531.

TULIP TOWN is s. of SR 20 at 15002 Bradshaw Rd. Open only for the month of April, this show garden of the Skagit Valley Bulb Farm features indoor and outdoor displays of 60 tulip varieties. In recognition of the tulip's status as the "World's Peace Flower," a special exhibit contains varieties from 17 peace gardens around the world. Visitors can walk through the fields or take a tractor trolley ride. Garden paths may be muddy; all-weather shoes are recommended. Allow 30 minutes minimum. Daily 9-5:30, in Apr. Admission $5; free (ages 0-16). Phone (360) 424-8152.

W.S.U. DISCOVERY GARDEN is 4 mi. w. of I-5 exit 226 via SR 536. It showcases thousands of varieties of plants that do well in western Washington. Color borders, Japanese, evergreen, ornamental grass, cottage, fuchsias, ground covers, iris, heather, herbs, roses, and children's and native plants are among the themed areas. Picnicking is permitted. Allow 30 minutes minimum. Daily dawn-dusk. Free. Phone (360) 428-4278.

RECREATIONAL ACTIVITIES

Bicycling

• **Tulip Country Bike Tours** depart from the tour center at 13391 Avon Allen Rd. (from I-5 exit 230, take SR 20 w. to Avon Allen Road, then s. to the tour center). Guided 4- to 6-hour bike trips are offered Apr.-Sept. Phone (360) 424-7461.

MUKILTEO—see Seattle p. 253.

NAHCOTTA (G-4) elev. 19′

On the Willapa Bay shore of the Long Beach Peninsula, Nahcotta is an important oyster center. Oyster dredging on the bay dates back to the mid-19th century and huge mounds of oyster shells line the bayfront. Established in 1888 as the terminus of a narrow-gauge railroad linking the bay with Ilwaco on the Columbia River, its name commemorates a Chinook chief who befriended early settlers.

WILLAPA BAY INTERPRETIVE CENTER is on the jetty just e. of SR 103 at 4000 273rd St. The center traces the history of oyster commerce on the bay. Exhibits include an oysterman's shack, a tide clock and pioneer and American Indian oyster harvesting tools. An 8.5-minute videotape about the oyster industry is shown. Allow 30 minutes minimum. Fri.-Sun. and holidays 10-3, Memorial Day weekend-late Sept. Donations. Phone (360) 665-4547.

NASELLE (G-5) pop. 377, elev. 12′

Pioneers found the area's lush landscape perfect for dairy farming. In the late 1800s many settlers came from Finland, and today their descendents form a large portion of the local population. The town's name is derived from the Nisal, a local American Indian tribe.

NASELLE HATCHERY is 1.7 mi. e. of SR 4 on North Valley Rd. The hatchery offers informative displays and self-guiding tours of its coho and chinook salmon and steelhead trout facility. It is most interesting during spawning season, October through November. Daily 8-5. Free. Phone (360) 484-7716.

NEAH BAY (C-4) pop. 794, elev. 50′

Washington's first European settlers, the Spanish, landed in Neah Bay, which they called Núñez Gaona, in 1791. They established a fort that lasted 5 months.

Panoramas of Neah Bay Harbor, Vancouver Island and the Strait of Juan de Fuca extend from Koitlah Point, 3 miles west of Neah Bay off SR 112. Farther west off SR 112 at the tip of the peninsula is Cape Flattery, where a 30-minute hike takes visitors to the most northwestern point in the contiguous United States.

Neah Bay's American Indian heritage is preserved at the Makah Indian Reservation and headquarters. Seasonal wildlife viewing opportunities abound on the reservation: Eagles, falcons and hawks migrate across the area in March; gray whales migrate along the Pacific coast in April and May; and trumpeter swans appear in November. Charters for fishing and wildlife viewing are available.

Of particular interest are Shi-Shi Beach, the Cape Flattery Trail, and other Pacific Ocean and Strait of Juan de Fuca trails. No alcohol is permitted. Visitors are welcome on the tribe's beaches but shellfish and shell gathering are restricted to tribal members.

A $10-per-vehicle recreational use permit is required for visitors wanting to hike, boat, camp or park at various trailheads. Permits, valid for a calendar year, can be purchased at the Makah Cultural and Research Center *(see attraction listing)*, the tribal headquarters and at most businesses in town.

MAKAH CULTURAL AND RESEARCH CENTER is on SR 112. The center contains exhibits pertaining to Makah history and culture. Some items are 500-year-old finds from the Makah's ancestral village of Ozette, part of which was buried in a catastrophic mudslide. Replicas of a 60-foot cedar longhouse and oceangoing canoes are displayed.

Allow 1 hour minimum. Daily 10-5; closed Jan. 1, Thanksgiving and Dec. 25. Admission $5; $4 (ages 62+, full-time students with ID and military in uniform); free (ages 0-5). MC, VI. Phone (360) 645-2711.

NEILTON (E-5) pop. 345, elev. 483′

The town was first called Jonesville for early settler Neil A. Jones, but in 1910 the name was switched to Neilton to avoid confusion with a like-named community in Klickitat County.

QUINAULT NATIONAL FISH HATCHERY is 3 mi. s. on US 101, then 5 mi. w. on Moclips Hwy. The hatchery was built to restore fish populations reduced by logging. More than 3 million salmon and trout are spawned and raised at the hatchery annually. An interpretive center explains the operation of the hatchery. Travel within the Quinault Indian Reservation is limited to designated roads. Allow 30 minutes minimum. Daily 7-3:30. Free. Phone (360) 288-2508.

NEMAH (F-5)

NEMAH SALMON HATCHERY is 2.5 mi. e. on N. Nemah Rd. The hatchery releases more than 3 million chinook, coho and chum salmon. Heavy runs are between October and December, when mature fish are diverted into holding ponds. Allow 30 minutes minimum. Daily 8-4:30. Free. Phone (360) 875-6147.

NESPELEM (D-10) pop. 212, elev. 350′

Nespelem is the headquarters of the Confederate Tribes of Colville. Established in 1872, the reservation encompasses more than 1.4 million acres and includes members of the Colville, Entiat/Chelan, Lake, Methow, Moses Columbia, Nespelem, Nez Perce, Okanogan, Palouse, Sanpoil, Senijextee, Skitwish and Wenatchee tribes.

Chief Joseph, legendary leader of the Nez Perce, is buried on a hillside northeast of town. Visitors to the area may drive in the reservation; picnicking, camping, hunting and rock and plant collecting are prohibited.

Colville Confederated Tribes: P.O. Box 150, Nespelem, WA 99155; phone (509) 634-2200.

NEWHALEM (C-8) elev. 525′

Derived from an American Indian word meaning goat snare, Newhalem is a company town of frame houses and well-tended yards built to house employees of the Skagit River Hydroelectric Complex. A visitor center on SR 20 has displays and interpretive material on the Skagit River project and area recreational opportunities.

Nearby is a 1926 Baldwin steam locomotive that operated on the Seattle City Light Railway. Also of interest are the Trail of Cedars nature walk and Ladder Creek Falls and Rock Garden, where summer evening illumination makes for a pleasant stroll.

SKAGIT TOURS—SEATTLE CITY LIGHT can be reached by following signs on SR 20 to the tour center. The Diablo Lake Adventure Tour focuses on the hydroelectric facilities around SR 20.

Highlights of the 2.5-hour tour include a boat trip on remote Diablo Lake and motor coach access to historic Diablo Dam. The 4-hour Diablo Dam Good Dinner Tour featuring an all-you-can eat, sit-down meal is available on Monday and Thursday. For reservations write Skagit Tours, Seattle City Light, 500 Newhalem St., Rockport, WA 98283.

Diablo Lake Adventure Tours depart Fri.-Sun. at 12:30, July-Aug.; Sat.-Sun. at 12:30 in June and Sept. Diablo Dam Good Dinner Tour departs Mon. and Thurs. at 12:30, July-Aug. Hours may vary; phone ahead. Adventure tour fare $25; $20 (ages 63+); $12 (ages 6-12). Dinner tour fare $55; $50 (ages 63+); $45 (ages 13-19); $40 (ages 6-12). A fuel surcharge may apply, call for details. Reservations are recommended. MC, VI. Phone (206) 684-3030, or (206) 233-2709 June-Sept.

RECREATIONAL ACTIVITIES
White-water Rafting

- **Osprey River Adventures** departs from Goodell Campground off SR 20 on the Skagit River, P.O. Box 1305, Twisp, WA 98856. July-Oct. Phone (509) 997-4116 or (800) 997-4116.

NEWPORT (D-12) pop. 1,921, elev. 2,142′

Newport faces the Idaho border at the point where the Pend Oreille River enters Washington. A store opened on the Idaho side in 1889, and in 1890 a post office was established with the name Newport, in the hopes that the town would attract river traffic. In 1892 the Great Northern Railroad built a depot on the Washington side of the border and the community shifted west, thriving as an outfitting center for nearby mines.

The original settlement is now Oldtown, Idaho *(see place listing in the Idaho, Montana & Wyoming TourBook)*, separated from Newport by State Avenue. Newport also is the Washington entryway to the International Selkirk Loop *(see attraction listing)*.

Newport-Oldtown Chamber of Commerce: 325 W. 4th St., Newport, WA 99156; phone (509) 447-5812 or (877) 818-1008.

INTERNATIONAL SELKIRK LOOP is a 280-mile scenic byway in northeastern Washington, northern Idaho and adjoining British Columbia. Starting at Newport, the 74-mile Washington segment follows SR 20 north to Tiger, then SR 31 north to the Canadian border through a sparsely settled part of the state known as "Washington's forgotten corner."

Between Newport and Metaline Falls the route parallels the Pend Oreille River, where dense forests of aspen, fir, cedar and pine alternate with patches of farmland. Practically the entire loop follows either a river or a lakeshore, waterways that historically were used for transportation in this remote area. Rising up on both sides of the river, the Selkirk Mountains ascend to heights of 5,000 feet in the south and more then 7,000 feet in the north.

Watch for ospreys and eagles fishing the waters and soaring the skies; large bundles of sticks high in the trees mark their nesting sites. Big horn sheep also inhabit the Selkirks, and winter foraging brings them down to river level. Moose, deer and elk are other wilderness dwellers that might be spotted during the winter months as they search out tender vegetation hiding beneath a blanket of snow.

North of Ione the valley narrows to form Box Canyon; an excursion train ride between Ione and Metaline Falls takes you through parts of the canyon not accessible by road. For a more exhilarating adventure, embark on a guided kayak trip that negotiates spectacular Z Canyon. Or take your pick of recreational pursuits—golf, fishing, boating, swimming, mountain biking and horseback riding all can be enjoyed. Summer, when wildflowers are in full bloom, is a great time to hike the hundreds of miles of trails crisscrossing the rugged, lavishly scenic terrain of the Selkirk wilderness region.

Towns with attraction listings located on the Washington portion of the route are Ione, Metaline Falls and Newport. Chambers of commerce and visitor centers along the loop provide maps and information, or write Selkirk International Loop, P.O. Box 920, Bonners Ferry, ID; phone (208) 267-0822 or (888) 823-2626.

PEND OREILLE COUNTY HISTORICAL MUSEUM is at the s. end of downtown at 402 S. Washington Ave. This former Milwaukee Road train depot displays an interesting hodgepodge of historical photographs, objects from the pioneer era and Newport memorabilia. On the grounds are a caboose, a pioneer school house and church, a fire lookout, a settler's cabin, a hunter's cabin, a logging bunkhouse and displays of farm equipment and Native American artifacts. Allow 30 minutes minimum. Daily 10-4, May 1 to mid-Oct.; by appointment rest of year. Closed holidays. Free. Phone (509) 447-5388 or (509) 447-2770 (mid-Oct. through Apr. 30).

NORDLAND (D-2)

Located on Marrowstone Island, the village of Nordland is named for pioneer landowner Peter F. Nordby who platted the town site on the small cove of Mystery Bay in 1892. The cove was first called Nicholls Bay for James Nicholls who farmed here in 1871. Its present name came into popular usage during Prohibition because bootleggers had a habit of hiding their boats here.

Just north of town, Mystery Bay State Park caters primarily to boaters, but also offers nearly 700 feet of tidewater shoreline and a view west to the Olympics. State Road 116 connects Marrowstone Island to the mainland.

FORT FLAGLER STATE PARK is at the northern tip of Marrowstone Island 4 mi. n. on SR 116. The fort was established in 1899 as a part of the strategic coastal defense known as the "Triangle of Fire." It possessed 6- and 10-inch disappearing guns; trails connect the gun batteries. The park contains historical displays and offers scenic views of Puget Sound and the Cascade Mountains. *See Recreation Chart.* Daily 6:30 a.m.-dusk, mid-Apr. through Sept. 30; 8 a.m.-dusk, rest of year. Free. Phone (360) 385-1259 or (360) 385-3701.

NORTH BEND—see Seattle p. 254.

NORTH BONNEVILLE (H-7)
pop. 593, elev. 74'

North Bonneville is named for Capt. Benjamin Louis Eulalie Bonneville, a French-born American army officer who explored a large portion of the Northwest in the early 1830s. Bonneville's travels were chronicled in Washington Irving's book "Adventures of Captain Bonneville, U.S.A., in the Rocky Mountains and the Far West," published in 1837.

The town was established in 1933 to house construction workers on the Bonneville Dam. It was relocated to its present site in 1976 to make way for a new powerhouse.

BEACON ROCK is in Beacon Rock State Park *(see Recreation Chart)*. Believed to be the core of an extinct volcano, it is one of the largest geological formations of its kind in the world. A 1-mile trail with many switchbacks and bridges winds to the top of the 848-foot monolith. The summit affords an excellent view of the Columbia Gorge. Park open daily 8 a.m.-dusk. The summit trail is open year-round (weather permitting). Free. Phone (509) 427-8265.

BONNEVILLE DAM—WASHINGTON SHORE VISITOR CENTER is at the n. end of the dam off SR 14. The center offers self-guiding tours of the massive hydroelectric facility on the Columbia River. The orientation building contains a staffed information center and access to Bonneville Dam's second powerhouse. The fish viewing building contains underwater windows and regional history displays that cover such topics as early history, development of the fishing industry and fish life cycles.

The power generators and turbines also are noteworthy. Access to the Oregon facilities is via the Bridge of the Gods, about 2 miles east. **Note:** Due to security concerns, access to some areas may be restricted. Allow 1 hour minimum. Daily 9-5; closed Jan. 1, Thanksgiving and Dec. 25. Free. Phone (509) 427-4281 or (503) 374-8820.

NORTH CASCADES NATIONAL PARK (C-7, C-8)

Elevations in the park range from 400 ft. at the western entrance of the park to 9,127 ft. at the summit of Mount Shuksan. Refer to AAA maps for additional elevation information.

North Cascades National Park can be reached via trails off the North Cascades Highway (SR 20), from Marblemount on the western side and from Mazama through Okanogan National Forest on the eastern side. The highway is closed between Diablo Lake and Mazama from the first major snowfall until April or May. From Marblemount, Cascade River Road leads east for 22 miles and is the only accessible road into the park. The park also can be reached by boat via Lake Chelan or from Canada via Ross Lake.

The park embraces 505,000 acres in north-central Washington. Its northern and southern sections, separated by Ross Lake National Recreation Area *(see place listing p. 207)*, are bordered by Okanogan National Forest *(see place listing p. 193)* to the east, Lake Chelan National Recreation Area *(see place listing p. 175)* to the southeast, Wenatchee National Forest *(see place listing p. 277)* to the south and Mount Baker-Snoqualmie National Forest to the west *(see place listing p. 182)*.

Park terrain is the result of glaciation; more than 315 glaciers remain active. Jagged peaks, sheer canyons and many rivers and lakes characterize the landscape.

Mountain goats, deer and black and grizzly bears are among the most common animals in the park. Rarely visible but present are cougars and wolverines. Smaller mammals and a host of birds, including white-tailed ptarmigans, also inhabit the area. Hunting is prohibited. Several varieties of trout live in park waters.

General Information and Activities

North Cascades National Park is open daily 24 hours year-round. Highway access is non-existent in winter; however, SR 20 is passable from mid-April to mid-November (weather permitting).

Hiking access and roadside views of the northwest corner of the park are offered from SR 542 east from Bellingham. A passenger ferry provides round-trip service between Stehekin, in Lake Chelan National Recreation Area *(see place listing p. 175)*, and Chelan, at the southern end of Lake Chelan *(see Chelan p. 160)*. Shuttle bus service transports visitors from Stehekin to High Bridge and Cottonwood in the remote southeast portion of the park, late May through early October.

Trails suitable for hiking and climbing wind through the back country. Primitive campsites are available by free permit issued at most ranger stations; the most developed sites are off SR 20 in the Ross Lake National Recreation Area *(see place listing p. 207)*. Summer naturalist activities, including evening programs and guided walks, are featured at campgrounds in both recreation areas.

An information center adjoining SR 20 in Sedro-Woolley is open daily 8-4:30, Memorial Day-Columbus Day; Mon.-Fri. 8-4:30, rest of year. Weather forecasts, trail conditions and free permits for back-country camping are available at the Chelan, Marblemount, Newhalem and Stehekin ranger stations; phone (509) 682-2549 in Chelan, (360) 854-7245 in Marblemount, or (206) 386-4495, ext. 11 in Newhalem for details. *See Recreation Chart and the AAA Northwestern CampBook.*

ADMISSION to the park is free.

PETS are permitted in the Lake Chelan and Ross Lake national recreation areas only if they are on a leash or otherwise restricted at all times. Dogs and cats are not permitted on the trails or in buildings.

ADDRESS inquiries to the Park Superintendent's Office, North Cascades National Park, 810 SR 20, Sedro-Woolley, WA 98284; phone (360) 854-7200.

OAK HARBOR (C-2) pop. 19,795, elev. 84'

The largest town on Whidbey Island *(see place listing p. 278)*, Oak Harbor takes its name from the white oak trees in the area. Many of the first settlers were Dutch; as a result, Holland Gardens in Holland Park, with its windmill and flower beds, and the Dutch windmill in Oak Harbor Beach Park are reflections of the Dutch influence that can be found throughout town.

North of Oak Harbor is Whidbey Island Naval Air Station, home to the Navy's electronic warfare squadrons and Pacific Meteorology and Oceanographic Detachment.

Greater Oak Harbor Chamber of Commerce: 32630 SR 20, Oak Harbor, WA 98277; phone (360) 675-3755.

DECEPTION PASS STATE PARK is 9 mi. n. on SR 20. Capt. George Vancouver named the cliff-lined channel that separates Whidbey and Fidalgo islands in 1792. Within the park's 4,200 acres are freshwater lakes, tracts of forest, marshland, sand dunes, offshore islands and almost 15 miles of saltwater shoreline. The coastal landscape includes cliffs, rocky shores, beaches of gravel and sand, tide flats and hidden coves.

A roadside viewpoint at the southern end of Deception Pass Bridge offers a panorama of the channel between Whidbey and Fidalgo islands. More than 38 miles of hiking trails meander through the park. *See Recreation Chart.* Daily 6:30-dusk, Apr.-Sept.; 8-dusk, rest of year. Free. Phone (360) 675-2417.

DID YOU KNOW

The area around Mt. Vernon, Washington, claims to grow more tulips than Holland.

Civilian Conservation Corps Interpretive Center is 1 mi. n. of the Deception Pass Bridge at Bowman Bay. The center documents the story of the Civilian Conservation Corps—a federal program that helped support the newly established state park system in the 1930s by building picnic shelters, residences, restrooms and hiking trails in state parks. Daily 10-6, Apr. 1-Labor Day; by appointment rest of year. Free. Phone (360) 675-2417.

OCEAN SHORES (F-4) pop. 3,836, elev. 43'

Occupying a sandy peninsula separating Grays Harbor from the Pacific Ocean, Ocean Shores is a popular resort area. Built in the 1960s, this planned community features over 6 miles of sandy ocean beach and a network of 23 miles of freshwater lakes and canals. Recreational activities include swimming, fishing, clamming, kayaking, horseback riding and golf. Charter fishing trips are available from Ocean Shores Marina, while Damon Point, at the southern tip of the peninsula, is one of the Northwest's premier sites for bird-watching.

A daily passenger ferry service runs from the marina to Westport late June-Labor Day; the service is available weekends early May to late June and day after Labor Day to late September. **Note:** The ferry service is temporarily discontinued, and there is no scheduled date for resuming operation; for further information phone (360) 289-3386.

Ocean Shores Visitors and Information Center: 120 W. Chance-a-la-Mer St., P.O. Box 1447, Ocean Shores, WA 98569; phone (360) 289-9586 or (800) 762-3224. *See color ad.*

OCEAN SHORES INTERPRETIVE CENTER is at 1033 Catala Ave. S.E. The center offers hands-on nature exhibits as well as displays describing indigenous peoples, early pioneers, shipwrecks and such natural phenomena as tsunamis. Video presentations educate visitors about beach safety, erosion, birds, wetlands and area geology. Allow 30 minutes minimum. Daily 11-4, Apr.-Sept.; Sat.-Sun. 11-4, rest of year. Free. Phone (360) 289-4617.

GAMBLING ESTABLISHMENTS

- **Quinault Beach Resort & Ocean Shores Casino** is at 78 SR 115. Mon.-Thurs. 9 a.m.-2 a.m., Fri.-Sat. 9 a.m.-5 a.m., Sun. 9 a.m.-3 a.m. Phone (360) 289-7777.

RECREATIONAL ACTIVITIES

Horseback Riding

- **Chenois Creek Horse Rentals** departs from the beach end of Damon Rd., just north of the entrance to Ocean Shores. Write 620 Ocean Beach Rd., Hoquiam, WA 98550. Daily 10-5, late June-Labor Day; Sat.-Sun. 10-4, rest of year (weather permitting). Phone (360) 533-5591.

OKANOGAN (C-9) pop. 2,484, elev. 860'

While exploring the Pacific Northwest in 1883, Gen. G.W. Goethals, a military man and chief engineer of the Panama Canal, camped in what is now one of Okanogan's two city parks. The town itself was established as Alma in 1888; it was renamed Pogue in 1905, and finally dubbed Okanogan in 1907. Its commercial growth was thwarted by the fact that the Okanogan River was only deep enough for steamboats to reach the town during May and June.

An irrigation system in 1906 attracted new settlers and businesses; a few years later a railroad line and a bridge over the river gave the town an added boost. Its primary industries are agriculture and cattle ranching. Apple orchards extend along the Okanogan River from the Canadian border to the Columbia River.

Okanogan Chamber of Commerce: P.O. Box 1125, Okanogan, WA 98840; phone (509) 422-2283.

OKANOGAN COUNTY HISTORICAL MUSEUM is at 1410 Second Ave. N. The museum exhibits items pertaining to local history, including a reproduction of a 19th-century Main Street and a replica of the town's 1910 fire station. Daily 10-4, Memorial Day weekend-Labor Day. Admission $2; free (ages 0-11). Phone (509) 422-4272.

GAMBLING ESTABLISHMENTS

• **Okanogan Bingo and Casino** is at 41 Appleway Rd. Sun.-Thurs. 9 a.m.-2 a.m.; Fri.-Sat. 24 hours. Phone (509) 422-4646 or (800) 559-4643.

OKANOGAN NATIONAL FOREST

Elevations in the forest range from 778 ft. at Pateros to 8,105 ft. at the summit of Jack Mountain in the Pasayten Wilderness. Refer to AAA maps for additional elevation information.

In a rough triangle formed by the Canadian border, the Cascade Range and the Columbia and Okanogan rivers, the forest covers 1,706,000 acres. Smaller sections are east of Oroville and Tonasket. Farther to the north is Pasayten Wilderness, containing 529,607 acres. Trails include 63 miles of the Pacific Crest National Scenic Trail. The Lake Chelan-Sawtooth Wilderness contains 145,667 acres.

One of the great scenic attractions in this area is the North Cascades Highway (SR 20), which connects Winthrop and Marblemount and is open late April through early November (weather permitting). The Washington Pass Scenic Overlook, 32 miles west of Winthrop at an elevation of 5,500 feet, offers a short loop trail to an overlook, picnic sites and a visitor information center.

Also on the North Cascades Highway is the Rainy Lake Trail at Rainy Pass. The 1-mile trail is paved and is open July through September.

A narrow gravel road leads to Slate Peak, 19 miles northwest of Mazama. Reaching an elevation of 7,400 feet, the road offers a panorama of the North Cascades. The road, leading to the highest elevation in the state accessible by automobile, is open from July until the first snowfall; it is not suitable for trailers.

Reached from the north and south by US 2 and US 97 and from the east and west by scenic North Cascades Highway (SR 20), the national forest offers winter sports, hunting and fishing. Rock hunting also is popular. Ranger stations are in Tonasket and Winthrop *(see place listing p. 280).*

A Northwest Forest Pass, available at ranger stations, is required for parking at most trailheads in the forest west of the Okanogan River. Day passes cost $5 per vehicle; an annual pass costs $30 per vehicle. Information about any of the forest's areas can be obtained by writing the Okanogan Valley Office, Okanogan and Wenatchee National Forests, 1240 Second Ave. S., Okanogan, WA 98840; phone (509) 826-3275. *See Recreation Chart and the AAA Northwestern CampBook.*

OLYMPIA (H-2) pop. 42,514, elev. 36'

Settlers first arrived at Budd Inlet at the southern end of Puget Sound in the 1840s. Their community, Smithfield, became the site of the first U.S. customhouse in the Northwest and was renamed Olympia for the magnificent mountains to the northwest. The town flourished; it is capital of the state and an important commercial center.

Olympia is the starting point of the Olympic Highway (US 101), which circles the Olympic Peninsula and continues along the coast into northern California. Passing many beach and lake resorts, this highway provides access to Olympic National Park and Olympic National Forest *(see place listings p. 195 and 194).*

The well known Olympia oyster is taken from Puget Sound in this vicinity. The best beds are found west of town in Mud, Oyster and Big and Little Skookum bays.

In September and October salmon can be observed from the Fifth Street Bridge as they go into Capitol Lake; the fish also can be seen going up the fish ladders on the Deschutes River in Tumwater Falls Park. Olympia's Japanese Garden, on Plum Street north of Union Avenue, commemorates the sister city relationship with Yashiro, Japan.

Olympia-Lacey-Tumwater Visitor and Convention Bureau: 809 Legion Way S.E., P.O. Box 7338, Olympia, WA 98501; phone (360) 704-7544 or (877) 704-7500.

Self-guiding tours: More than 80 works of art may be seen on a self-guiding walking tour of downtown's public art. Visitors also may take a self-guiding tour of the downtown historic district. Brochures and maps are available at the visitor and convention bureau.

Shopping areas: Westfield Shoppingtown Capital, 2 miles west on Black Lake Boulevard off US 101, is the area's major shopping center. Stores include

JCPenney and Macy's. The Olympia Farmers Market, 700 N. Capitol Way, is open Thurs.-Sun. 10-3, Apr.-Oct.; Sat.-Sun. 10-3, Nov.-Dec.; phone (360) 352-9096.

The Capitol Campus is on a hill south of downtown. The State Capitol Visitor Information Center is at jct. Sid Snyder Ave. and Capitol Way. The campus includes buildings housing the legislative, judicial and administrative offices in a landscaped setting. A stroll around the grounds reveals imposing monuments and a Tivoli Fountain replica.

The legislative building, the capitol, dominates the campus. Completed in 1928, the 287-foot masonry dome is one of the largest in the world. Louis Comfort Tiffany designed the chandelier that hangs in the rotunda. Guided tours are available. Information about a self-guiding tour of the grounds and the Temple of Justice is available at the visitor center. The 1908 Georgian-style Governor's Mansion, furnished with fine antiques, is the oldest building on the campus.

Guided tours of the capitol depart on the hour daily 10-3. Governor's Mansion tours are available most Wed. Visitor center open Mon.-Fri. 8-5, Sat.-Sun. 10-4, Memorial Day weekend to mid-Sept.; Mon.-Fri. 8-5, rest of year. Capitol Conservatory open Mon.-Fri. 8-4. Visitor center and Capitol Conservatory closed Jan. 1, Thanksgiving and Dec. 25. Free. Reservations are required for Governor's Mansion tour.

Phone (360) 586-3460 for the visitor center or (360) 902-8880 for tour information.

HANDS ON CHILDREN'S MUSEUM is at 106 11th Ave. S.W. The museum features activities and interactive displays that encourage learning through hands-on play. The Good For You Gallery promotes healthy eating habits and exercise. Backyard Wilderness teaches children about the environment, and in Build It they can build houses and ships. An Early Development Center for toddlers and a child-oriented art studio also are available.

Allow 1 hour minimum. Mon.-Sat. 10-5 (also first Fri. of the month 5-9 p.m.), Sun. noon-5; closed holidays. Admission $7.95; $6.95 (ages 55+); $4.95 (ages 13-23 months). MC, VI. Phone (360) 956-0818.

MIMA MOUNDS NATURAL AREA PRESERVE is 10 mi. s. off I-5 exit 95; take Maytown Rd. 4 mi. w. to Waddell Creek Rd., then .7 mi. n.w. to park entrance. This preserve's 637 acres encompasses a curious topography of regularly spaced hills approximately 7 feet high.

An interpretive center details the natural history of the area and presents the various theories of the mounds' origins. Self-guiding trails traverse the open prairie and forests; wildflowers are at their peak April through June. Daily 8-dusk. Free. Phone (360) 577-2025.

OLD STATE CAPITOL is downtown at 600 Washington St. Originally built as the Thurston County courthouse, this 1892 Romanesque Revival building served as the state capitol 1903-27 while the present building was under construction. Damaged by fire in 1928 and earthquake in 1949, the building has been renovated and currently houses the offices of the state's Superintendent of Public Instruction. Brochures outlining a self-guiding tour are available. Allow 30 minutes minimum. Mon.-Fri. 8-5; closed holidays. Free. Phone (360) 902-8880.

OLYMPIC FLIGHT MUSEUM is at the Olympia Regional Airport, 7637-A Old Hwy. 99 S.E. Visitors to this museum dedicated to aviation history can see a supersonic jet, Vietnam-era helicopters and vintage biplanes. There are also aviation-themed artworks, piston and jet engine displays and more than 300 scale models. Changing displays from the museum's collection of meticulously restored aircraft include a P-51D Mustang, a A6M2 Zero replica, a F-104A Starfighter and an AH-1 Cobra helicopter.

Allow 30 minutes minimum. Daily 11-5, Memorial Day weekend-Labor Day; Tues.-Sun. 11-5, rest of year. Closed major holidays. Admission $7; $5 (ages 7-12). AX, MC, VI. Phone (360) 705-3925.

STATE CAPITAL MUSEUM is at 211 21st Ave. S.W. A California mission-style mansion that was originally the home of Olympia banker Clarence Lord, the 32-room house has photographs and historic documents pertaining to Washington territorial and state governments, pioneer settlement and Northwest Coast Indians. A gallery displays changing exhibits of art and history. Outdoor highlights include the Pioneer Herb Garden and the Delbert McBride Ethnobotanical Garden.

Allow 30 minutes minimum. Wed.-Sat. 11-3; closed major holidays. Admission $2; $1.75 (ages 60+); $1 (ages 6-18); $5 (family). Phone (360) 753-2580.

OLYMPIC NATIONAL FOREST

Elevations in the forest range from sea level at Hood Canal to 6,988 ft. at Buckhorn Mountain. Refer to AAA maps for additional elevation information.

On the Olympic Peninsula, the 632,324-acre Olympic National Forest is noted for its rugged mountain terrain, lush rain forests and glacial streams. Deer and bears are plentiful, and the Roosevelt elk population is the largest anywhere. Douglas fir, Western red cedar, Western hemlock, bigleaf maple, rhododendron and wildflowers are among the forest's prominent flora.

More than 200 miles of trails wind through the forest, with some overlapping into Olympic National Park. Pets are permitted on forest trails. Trout fishing is popular; hunting is permitted in season. Most recreation sites are open May through October. Evidence of early mining activities, railroad logging and exploration remains.

Of special interest is the Quinault Rain Forest. Two loop trails into the rain forest begin at the nature trail parking lot off South Shore Road, 2 miles off US 101 at Lake Quinault. Five wilderness areas encompass thousands of acres; Buckhorn is the largest. Permits are not needed to enter the wilderness areas; however, motorized vehicles' are not permitted.

The Steel Bridge, in the southeast portion of the forest, stands 420 feet above the basalt-lined canyon of Vance Creek. Built by Simpson Timber Co. in 1929 for its logging railway, the span was opened to vehicle use in 1964. The bridge is 8 miles west of US 101 on Skokomish Valley Road, then 2.4 miles north on the gravel FR 2340.

Panoramas of the Olympics, Hood Canal and Puget Sound can be had from Mount Walker viewpoint, reached by a gravel road off US 101 south of Quilcene. Also especially . scenic is Seal Rock Beach, along the Hood Canal 2 miles north of Brinnon. *For descriptions of areas near the national forest, see Olympia p. 193 and Olympic National Park p. 195.*

A Northwest Forest Pass, available at ranger stations, is required for parking at most trailheads in the forest. A day pass costs $5 per vehicle; an annual pass costs $30 per vehicle. Ranger stations are located at Forks, Quilcene and Quinault. For further information contact the Olympic National Forest Supervisor's Office, 1835 Black Lake Blvd. S.W., Suite A, Olympia, WA 98512-5623; phone (360) 956-2402. *See Recreation Chart.*

▼ OLYMPIC NATIONAL PARK
(E-1, D-5)

Elevations in the park range from sea level along 60 miles of beach to 7,965 ft. at Mount Olympus. Refer to AAA maps for additional elevation information.

US 101 forms an inverted U shape around the park and the adjacent Olympic National Forest. Paved entrance roads include Hurricane Ridge Road, off Race Street in Port Angeles; Elwha Road, 8 miles southwest of Port Angeles; Sol Duc Road, west of Lake Crescent; Hoh Road, 13 miles south of Forks; and North and South Shore roads, along Lake Quinault.

Unpaved roads off US 101 include Deer Park Road, east of Port Angeles, not for use by trailers or recreational vehicles; Queets Road, east of Queets; Staircase Road, west of Hoodsport; and Dosewallips Road, west of Brinnon. All of these roads end fewer than 20 miles into the park; to preserve the wilderness, no roads pass through the park's interior.

Olympic National Park is a scenic wilderness of 923,000 acres extending from glacier-clad mountains to ocean shore. Ranging between these borders are coniferous rain forests, glaciers, lakes and streams as well as 57 miles of unspoiled coastline. The wilderness area encompasses the interior of the Olympic Peninsula, between Hood Canal on the east and the Pacific Ocean on the west.

Mount Olympus, at 7,965 feet, is the highest of the park's mountains, which rise within 35 miles of the sea. The range is extremely rugged, with spectacular cliffs and crags and deep, forested valleys. On the upper slopes are glaciers unusual for their formation at such a relatively low elevation and latitude.

Magnificent stands of Sitka spruce, Douglas fir, Western hemlock and Western red cedar cover the lower mountainsides. On the upper slopes near the timberline, Alaska cedar, mountain hemlock and subalpine fir intermingle with alpine meadows. More than 600 miles of trails run through virgin forests and along stream banks in narrow valleys to ridgetops and mountain passes.

Snowfall might make passage on some trails difficult; check with the visitor centers and ranger stations in the park. Only experienced mountain climbers should attempt to scale the park's challenging peaks. The Olympic high country can be reached by automobile only from the north side where roads lead to subalpine meadows at Deer Park and Hurricane Ridge. .

Rainfall averaging 140 inches nourishes a lush temperate rain forest in the western valleys of the park. The most interesting of the centuries-old forests are found in the valleys of the Hoh, Quinault, Bogachiel and Queets rivers.

The area teems with wildlife. Of the 6,500 elk estimated to inhabit the peninsula, 5,000 are in the park, chiefly on the western slope of the mountains. Blacktail deer and many smaller mammals are common throughout the park. Hunting is prohibited. Among the great variety of birds in the park is the bald eagle.

General Information and Activities

Though the park is open all year, parts of the high country are usually closed by snow from early fall until July. The streams of the Olympic Mountains offer fine fishing; salmon fishing is excellent in the Strait of Juan de Fuca and the ocean. No license is required for fishing within the park boundaries, but steelhead trout and salmon punch cards are required in season. Sol Duc Hot Springs is in the Sol Duc Valley, 12 miles southeast of US 101 *(see attraction listing p. 197).*

A number of self-guiding nature trails have been developed throughout the park. Rangers/naturalists give interpretive talks late June through Labor Day; check with the visitor centers for schedules. Visitor centers are open all year at Port Angeles and the Hoh Rain Forest. The Kalaloch center is open daily Memorial Day weekend through September. The Storm King (Lake Crescent) center is open mid-June to early September; phone for schedule. The Hurricane Ridge Center is open daily mid-June through late September, and when the Hurricane Ridge Road is open, rest of year. Road conditions prohibit the passage of trailers in some areas of the park. *See Recreation Chart and the AAA Northwestern Camp-Book.*

ADMISSION of $15 per vehicle, good for 7 days anywhere in the park, is charged at Elwha, Heart o' the Hills, Hoh, Staircase and Sol Duc entrances. An entrance fee of $5 is charged for individuals and bicyclists except in winter. An Olympic Park Annual Pass costs $30. Camping fees range from $10-$18. A permit fee of $5 per group plus $2 per person per night is charged to camp overnight in the park's back-country wilderness.

PETS are permitted in developed areas only. Pets must be leashed and may not be left unattended or tied to a stationary object. Leashed pets are permitted only during daylight hours on beaches from Rialto Beach north to Ellen Creek and the beaches between the Hoh and Quinault Indian reservations.

ADDRESS inquiries to the Park Superintendent's Office, Olympic National Park, 600 E. Park Ave., Port Angeles, WA 98362; phone (360) 565-3130, or (360) 565-3131 for recorded information.

Points of Interest

DEER PARK can be reached via a 17-mi., mountainous, mostly unpaved road 5 mi. e. of Port Angeles; the road is not recommended for trailers. The park is a subalpine meadow featuring endemic plants. A short trail leads to the summit of 6,007-foot Blue Mountain, which affords views of the Dungeness Valley, Olympic Mountains, Strait of Juan de Fuca, Vancouver Island and the San Juan Islands. Daily 24 hours. The access road is usually closed Oct. to mid-June; check for conditions. Free.

ELWHA RIVER VALLEY is accessible via a paved road off US 101, 8 mi. w. of Port Angeles. The valley is 40 miles long from the river's headwaters

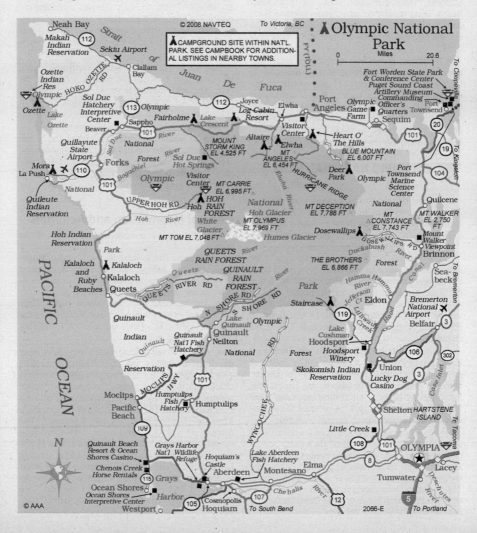

near Mount Olympus to its outlet into the Strait of Juan de Fuca. After 5 miles the road reaches impounded Lake Mills, then climbs to an observation point and continues along tributary Boulder Creek. At the road's end a 2-mile trail leads to primitive Olympic Hot Springs. Park entrance fee $15 per vehicle.

 HOH RAIN FOREST can be reached via a 18-mi. paved road off US 101, 13 mi. s. of Forks. A visitor center features informative displays and serves as a departure point for several self-guiding nature trails, including the frequently photographed Hall of Mosses Trail. Allow 1 hour minimum. Daily 9-4, June 1-Labor Day; otherwise varies rest of year. Visitor center free. Park entrance fee $15 per vehicle. Phone (360) 374-6925.

HURRICANE RIDGE can be reached from Port Angeles via Hurricane Ridge Rd., a 7-percent-grade highway. More than 5,200 feet above sea level, Hurricane Ridge features a lodge, open for day use only, that provides striking views of the Olympic Mountains, the Strait of Juan de Fuca and Vancouver Island. Nature trails wind through the meadows, where wildflowers bloom from late June through October. A narrow, gravel road leads 8 miles east along the crest to Obstruction Peak.

Naturalist programs are held daily July 1 through Labor Day. During the ski season rentals and rope tow service are available on weekends (weather permitting). The winter use area also features cross-country ski and snowshoe trails. Park entrance fee $15 per vehicle. Phone (360) 565-3131 for road conditions, weather information and activities.

KALALOCH AND RUBY BEACHES can be reached by short trails off US 101 n. of Queets. These are two of the park's most accessible beach areas. Kalaloch, southernmost of the two, has a campground and offers clifftop views of the coast. Ruby Beach, with its sea arches and offshore islands, is more of a wilderness beach. Smaller beaches in the vicinity are designated by numbers. Free.

LAKE CRESCENT is 17 mi. w. of Port Angeles on US 101. This deep freshwater lake is named for its shape. Surrounded by high mountains, including 4,534-foot Storm King Mountain, the lake is 10 miles long and 624 feet deep. Near the midpoint along US 101 is the trailhead for a 1-mile trail that leads to 90-foot Marymere Falls. Free.

LAKE QUINAULT is in the s.w. corner of the park accessible by US 101. The Quinault River rises in the peninsula's interior and flows into 3-mile-long Lake Quinault at an elevation of less than 200 feet above sea level with peaks rising to 4,000 feet surrounding the valley.

The North Shore Road runs east from US 101 along the lake to the Quinault Ranger Station where the .5 mile Maple Glade Rain Forest Trail loops through the woodlands. Free. Phone (360) 288-2444.

OLYMPIC NATIONAL PARK VISITOR CENTER is s. of US 101 via Race St., at 3002 Mount Angeles Rd. The visitor center provides park information and presents a slide program. Museum displays relate to wildlife, plants, geology and Northwest Coast Indian culture. A nature trail, accessible to the physically impaired, is available. Daily 9-4:30, May 1-Labor Day; otherwise varies. Free. Phone (360) 565-3130.

SOL DUC HOT SPRINGS is in the Sol Duc Valley, 30 mi. w. of Port Angeles and 12 mi. s.e. of US 101. Natural mineral water flows from the springs at a temperature of 128 F and is piped into three large outdoor swimming pools ranging in temperature from 99 F to 104 F. Lodging, campsites, RV facilities and food are available. The pools are open daily at 9, late Mar.-late Oct. Closing times vary; phone ahead. Admission $11; $8 (ages 4-12, 62+, military with ID and the physically impaired). Admission $8 (2 hours before closing). AX, DS, MC, VI. Phone (360) 327-3583 or (866) 476-5382.

RECREATIONAL ACTIVITIES

White-water Rafting

- **Olympic Raft & Kayak** provides trips on the Elwah and Hoh rivers in and around Olympic National Park. Write 123 Lake Aldwell Rd., Port Angeles, WA 98363. Rafting and sea kayaking trips are offered daily year-round. Phone (360) 452-1443 or (888) 452-1443.

OMAK (C-10) pop. 4,721, elev. 837'

A sister city to Okanogan *(see place listing p. 193)*, Omak derives its name from the Salish word *omache*, meaning "good medicine." Apple orchards are a prime business, as is the growing of baby's breath, a florist industry staple.

Eastside Park *(see Recreation Chart)* is a quarter-mile west of Main Street on Omak Avenue. Nearby attractions reminiscent of the past include several ghost towns that harken back to the gold rush days.

Omak Chamber of Commerce: 401 Omak Ave., P.O. Box 3100, Omak, WA 98841; phone (509) 826-4218 or (800) 225-6625.

ST. MARY'S MISSION is 4 mi. e. via SR 155, then 1.5 mi. s. Father Etienne de Rougé founded this Jesuit mission in 1886 to minister to the 12 bands of the Colville Federation. The present church dates from 1910. The adjacent Paschal Sherman Indian School, the state's only American Indian boarding school, is managed by the Colville Confederated Tribes. The church and grounds are open daily 24 hours. Visitors should register at the main office when school is in session. Free. Phone (509) 422-7581.

ORCAS ISLAND—

see San Juan Islands p. 208.

OROVILLE (C-9) pop. 1,653, elev. 913'

Set in a deep valley flanked by high ridges, Oroville takes its name from the Spanish word for gold for good reason: A strike found near the mouth of the Similkameen River in 1861 resulted in the establishment of the boom town. The arrival of the railroad in 1914 and the construction of irrigation works eventually turned the town's economic focus to commercial orchards, the first of which was planted in 1858 by prospector Hiram Smith. Most of the town's wealth is now found in the form of locally grown apples.

The Old Oroville Depot Museum, a 1907 Great Northern depot at 1210 Ironwood St., contains exhibits about Oroville's history; phone (509) 476-2476. Nearby Osoyoos Lake State Park (see Recreation Chart) offers several recreational facilities.

Oroville Visitor Welcome Center: 1730 Main St., P.O. Box 2140, Oroville, WA 98844; phone (509) 476-2739.

OLD MOLSON MUSEUM is 10 mi. e. on Oroville-Chesaw Rd., then 5 mi. n. on Molson Rd. A town site founded as a mining venture in 1900, the museum features a collection of early-20th-century buildings including a bank, an assay office and two homestead cabins. A church, relocated here in 1922, is 1 block north. Allow 1 hour minimum. Daily dawn-dusk, Apr.-Nov. Donations. Phone (509) 485-3292.

Molson School Museum is 2 blks. n. of Old Molson Museum. The school museum contains several schoolrooms, a library and displays of various pioneer household articles and tools. Food is available. Allow 1 hour minimum. Daily 10-5, Memorial Day weekend-Labor Day. Donations.

OTHELLO (F-10) pop. 5,847, elev. 1,038′

Founded on a Northern Pacific branch rail line in 1902, Othello was named for the Shakespeare play. The town, which is located in the heart of the Columbia Basin Project, boomed in the 1950s as irrigation waters transformed the surrounding desert into a productive farming region. Today the district is known for its high potato yields.

Greater Othello Chamber of Commerce: 33 E. Larch St., P.O. Box 2813, Othello, WA 99344; phone (509) 488-2683 or (866) 684-3556.

COLUMBIA NATIONAL WILDLIFE REFUGE is w. on Main. St. to Broadway, then 5 mi. n. to the first paved road and on to park entrance, following signs. This 23,100-acre refuge is a nesting area for numerous species of wildlife. Blue-winged and cinnamon teal, redhead, ruddy and mallard ducks nest in the summer. Ledges and cracks in the cliffs provide a nesting habitat for red-tailed hawks, swallows, ravens, and great horned and barn owls. Visitor information is available from the refuge's offices at 735 E. Main St. Allow 1 hour, 30 minutes minimum. Mon.-Thurs. 7-4:30, Fri. 7-3:30. Free. Phone (509) 488-2668.

OLD HOTEL ART GALLERY is at 33 E. Larch St. The gallery displays folk art and handicrafts produced by Northwestern artists. Paintings, sculpture and other works are exhibited in the rooms of a former railroad era boarding house built in 1912. Outside, a restored Milwaukee Road caboose has displays about the railroad. Tues.-Sat. 10-5; closed holidays. Free. Phone (509) 488-5936.

OUTLOOK (G-9) elev. 784′

WINERIES

• **Tefft Cellars** is off I-82 exit 63, 1 mi. w. on Yakima Valley Hwy., 3 mi. n. on N. Outlook Rd., then .5 mi. w. to 1320 Independence Rd. Daily 10-5; closed Jan. 1, Thanksgiving and Dec. 25. Phone (509) 837-7651 or (888) 549-7244.

OYSTERVILLE (F-4) elev. 10′

Oysterville, settled in 1854, is one of the oldest towns in Washington. Its early prosperity derived from its namesake bivalve, which was a sought after delicacy in San Francisco where a plate of them fetched about $50 in gold. The town served as the seat of Pacific County 1855-93. It boasts a number of homes dating back to the late 19th century, many of which have been restored. The entire community constitutes a historic district. Red Cottage, built 1863-64, is the oldest surviving building.

PASCO (G-10) pop. 32,066, elev. 380′

Its location at the confluence of the Yakima, Snake and Columbia rivers has made Pasco a transportation center since its founding in the late 1800s. With its sister cities, Kennewick and Richland, Pasco dominates commercial development at the southern entrance to the Columbia River Basin.

Tri-Cities Visitor and Convention Bureau—Pasco: 6951 W. Grandridge Blvd., Kennewick, WA 99336; phone (509) 735-8486 or (800) 254-5824.

Shopping areas: Broadmoor Square, I-182 exit 7, offers discount shopping at more than a dozen stores.

THREE RIVERS CHILDREN'S MUSEUM is at 5274 Outlet Dr. in the Broadmoor Square Mall. The museum offers a variety of hands-on educational activities for children ages 2-12. Changing thematic exhibits are featured. Allow 1 hour minimum. Wed.-Fri. 10-5, Sat. noon-5; closed holidays. Admission $3; free (ages 0-12 months). DS, MC, VI. Phone (509) 543-7866.

FRANKLIN COUNTY HISTORICAL MUSEUM is at 305 N. Fourth Ave. The museum presents displays relating to agriculture, railroading, river and air transportation and local history. Also featured are American Indian artifacts. Tues.-Fri. noon-4. Donations. Phone (509) 547-3714.

ICE HARBOR DAM is 12 mi. e. on SR 124. The dam is one of four dams on the lower Snake River extending river barge navigation from the Pacific Ocean to Lewiston, Idaho. Lake Sacajawea, formed by the dam, covers 9,200 acres. A visitor center has a fish viewing room and a display about the dam. A 12-minute slide show and a videotape program about salmon can be seen as well. Note: The road crossing the dam is closed due to security concerns. Allow 1 hour minimum. Visitor center open daily 9-5, Apr.-Oct. Free. Phone (509) 547-7781.

SACAJAWEA STATE PARK is .5 mi. n. on N. 4th Ave., 4.4 mi. e. on US 12, then 2 mi. s. to 2503 Sacajawea Park Rd. The 284-acre park features shorelines at the confluence of the Snake and Columbia rivers. The park is named for the Shoshone woman guide of the Lewis and Clark expedition, which camped here in October 1805.

The Sacajawea Interpretive Center has interactive displays about Sacajawea and the Lewis and Clark expedition; it also showcases bone and stone tools up to 12,000 years old. See Recreation Chart. Picnicking is permitted. Allow 45 minutes minimum. Park open daily 6:30 a.m.-dusk, late Mar.-Oct. 31. Interpretive center open 10-5, late Mar.-Oct. 31. Free. Phone (509) 545-2361.

WINERIES

• **Preston Premium Wines** is 5 mi. n. on US 395. Daily 10-5:30; closed Jan. 1, Easter, Thanksgiving and Dec. 25. Phone (509) 545-1990.

PATEROS (D-9) pop. 643, elev. 776'

Located on the Columbia River just above the confluence with the Methow River, Pateros was founded in 1895. First called Ives Landing, the name was changed in 1900 to honor a town in the Philippines where a pioneer settler had served during the Spanish-American War. It prospered as a fruit growing center after the railroad arrived in 1914.

Pateros was relocated in 1968 when the pool behind Wells Dam flooded the original site. Alta Lake State Park, 3 miles southwest of town, is a popular recreation area (see Recreation Chart).

PATERSON (G-9) elev. 377'

WINERIES

• **Columbia Crest Winery** is 1 mi. n. of SR 14 on SR 221. Daily 10-4:30; closed major holidays. Phone (509) 875-2061 or (888) 309-9463.

PESHASTIN (E-8) elev. 1,033'

Peshastin was established with the 1892 arrival of the Great Northern railroad. Its name derives from the Indian term pish-pish-astin, which means broadbottom canyon.

WINERIES

• **Icicle Ridge Winery** is 1 mi. n. of US 2 at jct. Main St. and 8977 North Rd. Daily noon-5; closed holidays. Phone (509) 548-7019.

POINT ROBERTS (A-1)

In the northwest corner of the state, Point Roberts was named in 1792 by Captain George Vancouver for his friend and fellow captain, Henry Roberts. The Oregon Treaty of 1846 established the international boundary at the 49th parallel, making the southern half of the point American territory. To reach the outlier of Washington by road involves a 23-mile drive through British Columbia.

Boundary Marker Number 1, the last remaining original marker from the 1857-62 survey, stands in a park at the west end of Roosevelt Road. Lighthouse Marine Park (see Recreation Chart), on Marine Drive at the southwest end of the point, features a 600-foot boardwalk and an observation deck offering views across the Strait of Georgia to Vancouver Island and the Gulf Islands.

Point Roberts Chamber of Commerce: P.O. Box 128, Point Roberts, WA 98281; phone (360) 945-2313.

POMEROY (F-12) pop. 1,517, elev. 1,877'

Located along Pataha Creek amid the rolling, fertile Palouse upland, Pomeroy is the only county seat in the country designated by an act of Congress. As the area was being settled in the 1880s, a bitter rivalry developed between Pomeroy and nearby Pataha City over the location of the county government. After lawsuits and an inadvertent omission from the Territorial Enabling Act failed to resolve the dispute, Congress passed its own act in 1884 that, among other stipulations, proclaimed Pomeroy the Garfield County seat.

The blocks lining Main Street form a historic district of one-, two- and three-story brick structures erected in the late 19th and early 20th centuries. Two interesting buildings are the Revere Hotel at Main and 7th streets, which counts two presidents among its guests, and the Seeley Theater on 7th Street. The 1901 Garfield County Courthouse is unusual in that the statue of Justice atop its tower is not blindfolded—one of only 20 "unblind" justices in the country. The 1878 Pataha Flour Mill, 3 miles east on US 12, is now a museum of intact milling machinery; phone (509) 843-3925.

GARFIELD COUNTY MUSEUM is 1 blk. s. of Main St. (US 12) on 7th St. to 708 Columbia St. Themed areas filled with donated items portray the area's early settlement and include a parlor, dining room, kitchen and bedroom, country store, drug store, post office, doctor's office, blacksmith shop, school and chapel. Allow 30 minutes minimum. Tues.-Fri. noon-5, May-Sept.; Fri. noon-5, rest of year. Open by appointment other times. Closed holidays. Donations. Phone (509) 843-3925.

PORT ANGELES (D-5) pop. 18,397, elev. 20'

In 1791 Spanish captain Francisco Eliza sailed into the natural harbor of what is now Port Angeles and became the first European to see this area. He named the site Puerto de Nuestra Señora de los Angeles, "Port of Our Lady of the Angels," from which the current name is derived. The 4.5-mile sandbar that forms the harbor is called Ediz Hook, which offers a panorama of the city and the Olympic Mountains.

Black Ball Transport operates passenger and automobile ferry service daily between Port Angeles and Victoria, 18 miles across the Strait of Juan de Fuca; phone (360) 457-4491. Victoria Express offers daily passenger fast-ferry service to Victoria late May through late September and to Friday Harbor from mid-June to early September; phone (360) 452-8088.

Port Angeles Visitor Information Center: 121 E. Railroad Ave., Port Angeles, WA 98362; phone (360) 452-2363, ext. 0.

ARTHUR D. FEIRO MARINE LIFE CENTER is on the city pier at the foot of Lincoln St. The center presents displays and a large touch tank of local intertidal marine flora and fauna. Tues.-Sun. 10-5, Memorial Day weekend-early Sept. Off-season hours may vary; phone ahead. Admission $3; $2 (ages 56+); $1 (ages 4-17). Phone (360) 417-6254.

MUSEUM AT THE CARNEGIE is at Second and Lincoln sts. Housed in the town's renovated 1919 Carnegie Library building, the museum showcases Clallam County history using displays of donated memorabilia and thousands of historic photos. Permanent and changing exhibits describe the county's four American Indian tribes, the arrival of the early explorers, the northern Olympic peninsula's shipbuilding industry and the creation of Olympic National Park. Allow 30 minutes minimum. Wed.-Sat. 1-4; closed major holidays. Donations. Phone (360) 452-6779.

OLYMPIC COAST DISCOVERY CENTER is at 115 E. Railroad Ave. On the Port Angeles waterfront, the center introduces visitors to the nearby 3,300-square-mile Olympic Coast National Marine Sanctuary, which extends several miles into the Pacific off the northwestern Washington coast. The center orients visitors to the sanctuary's diverse habitats and geological features using interactive kiosks, displays, models and video presentations narrated by researchers.

Guided tours are available. Food is available. Allow 30 minutes minimum. Wed.-Sun. 11-5, Memorial Day weekend-Labor Day; otherwise varies rest of year. Closed Dec. 25. Free. Phone (360) 457-6622.

PORT ANGELES FINE ARTS CENTER is .2 mi. e. of Race St. on E. Lauridsen Blvd. The center features changing exhibits of contemporary paintings, sculpture, photographs, drawings and other media. The center also holds lectures, concerts and other performances. The 5-acre grounds have walking trails and Webster's Woods, an outdoor art park featuring sculptures and site works by Northwest artists. The grounds also offer a panorama of the city, harbor and Strait of Juan de Fuca.

Allow 30 minutes minimum. Wed.-Sun. 11-5, Mar.-Oct.; Wed.-Sun. 10-4, rest of year. Grounds open daily dawn-dusk. Closed Jan. 1, July 4, Thanksgiving, day after Thanksgiving and Dec. 24-25 and 31. Donations. Phone (360) 417-4590.

RECREATIONAL ACTIVITIES

Kayaking

- **Adventures Through Kayaking** is at 4821 S. Dry Creek Rd., Port Angeles, WA 98363. Freshwater and sea kayaking tours are offered year-round. Phone (360) 417-3015 or (888) 900-3015.

WINERIES

- **Olympic Cellars** is 6 mi. e. at 255410 US 101. Daily 11-6, May-Sept.; Mon.-Sat. 11-5, Sun. noon-5, rest of year. Closed Jan. 1, Easter, Thanksgiving and Dec. 25. Phone (360) 452-0160.

PORT GAMBLE (E-2) elev. 40'

In 1853, the same year Washington Territory was created, a group of Maine lumbermen established a sawmill in Port Gamble. The company town that grew up around the mill featured the architectural style typical of the New England they left behind.

The village is now a historic district characterized by Victorian frame houses behind picket fences, street corners lit by gas lamps, and expanses of

common lawns that recall the village greens of New England settlements. Even many of the ornamental trees were imported from the Northeast.

One of the longest continuously operating mills in North America, the Pope and Talbot mill on Port Gamble's waterfront closed in 1995. The Hood Canal Nursery and Research Center, west of town on SR 3, grows seedlings for reforestation. Self-guiding tours around the facility are available on weekdays.

PORT GAMBLE HISTORIC MUSEUM is in the lower level of Port Gamble General Store, on SR 104. Exhibits trace the development of the town's lumber industry 1853-present. Allow 30 minutes minimum. Daily 9:30-5, May-Oct.; Fri.-Sun. 9:30-5, rest of year. Admission $4; $3 (ages 66+ and students with ID); free (ages 0-6). Phone (360) 297-8074.

PORT ORCHARD—*see Seattle p. 254.*

PORT TOWNSEND (D-2)
pop. 8,334, elev. 120′

Founded in the early 1850s, Port Townsend was one of the leading cities on Puget Sound in the late 19th century. The first settlers arrived here in 1851, and by 1853 the customs house was relocated here from Olympia, making it the official point of entry. The port offered safe moorage for the large sailing vessels of the time, and the economy prospered, first from providing supplies to gold seekers bound for British Columbia, then later from speculating on the prospects of attracting a transcontinental railroad line.

The city boasted consulates, banks, large hotels, a streetcar line, shipyards and all manner of commercial establishments. Its expansive layout reflects the hope that Port Townsend would become the region's major port and trading center. The population reached 7,000, but when plans for a railroad fizzled in 1895, a long period of decline set in.

Much of the city's charm stems from its impressive collection of Victorian-era architecture. The entire central portion is a historic district with homes sporting turrets, pergolas, towers, gingerbread trim and Carpenter Gothic details. Only a few are open to the public, including the Rothschild House *(see listing p. 202)* and a number of bed and breakfasts.

Water Street forms the main business district. Its brick buildings, mostly dating from the late 1800s, contain hotels, restaurants, bars, coffee houses, stores and antique shops. An excellent example of the town's architectural eclecticism is the Jefferson County Courthouse on Walker Street. Built in 1892, it combines Romanesque and Gothic motifs as well as elements of a fairytale castle.

St. Paul's Church, Tyler and Jefferson streets, was built in 1865, making it the oldest Episcopal church in the diocese of Olympia. The bell in the tower was donated by a cutter captain on the condition that it be rung on foggy days to help guide sailing vessels into the bay.

The 1893 Customs House, Washington and Van Buren streets, presently houses the post office; its lobby features historic photographs. Haller Fountain, at Washington and Taylor, was originally built for the Mexican exhibit at the 1893 Chicago World's Exhibition. The structure at the top of the bluff above Taylor Street is the old Fire Bell Tower, built in 1885.

Nearby Old Fort Townsend State Park *(see Recreation Chart)* includes the site of a U.S. Army post built in 1856 to protect settlers. The fort was abandoned in 1895 after it was destroyed by fire. The site is now a wildlife sanctuary.

Washington State Ferries offers daily service from Port Townsend to Keystone on Whidbey Island; phone (888) 808-7977 in Wash. Puget Sound Express provides daily passenger service to the San Juan Islands from late March to early October; phone (360) 385-5288.

The Port Townsend Chamber Music Festival is a major summertime event in a town that has long been home to artists and musicians. World-renowned ensembles like the Tokyo String Quartet play the music of Brahms, Mozart, Schubert and other classical masters at the Joseph F. Wheeler Theater at Fort Worden. Two public concerts are given in late June; for ticket information phone (360) 385-3102 or (800) 733-3608.

Port Townsend Visitor Information Center: 2437 E. Sims Way, Port Townsend, WA 98368; phone (360) 385-2722 or (888) 365-6978.

Shopping areas: Lining the bay along Water Street, former saloons distinguished by handsome facades are now occupied by antique shops, restaurants, art galleries and specialty shops. Port Townsend Antique Mall, 802 Washington St., has more than 50 shops.

FORT WORDEN STATE PARK & CONFERENCE CENTER is 1 mi. n. via Cherry St. The fort within this 443-acre park was part of an important system of coastal fortresses guarding the entrance to Puget Sound established in the 1890s. The large, grassy parade ground remains, and the handsome Victorian houses along Officers' Row have been restored. The rhododendron garden contains more than 1,100 plants. *See Recreation Chart.*

Centrum, a non-profit center for the arts and creative education, offers a year-round program of events. For information and tickets contact Centrum, P.O. Box 1158, Port Townsend, WA 98368. Park open daily 6:30 a.m.-dusk. Free. Phone (360) 385-4730 or (360) 344-4400 for the park.

Commanding Officer's Quarters is in the park. Built in 1904 in the Jeffersonian style, this nearly 6,000-square-foot house features a slate roof and decorated boxed cornices. It has been restored and contains period late Victorian and Edwardian furnishings, providing a glimpse into the lives of a U.S. Army colonel and his family in the first decade of the 20th century. Guided tours are available by appointment.

Allow 30 minutes minimum. Daily 10-5, Memorial Day weekend-Labor Day; Sat.-Sun. noon-4, Mar. 1-day before Memorial Day weekend and day after Labor Day-Oct. 31. Admission $2; free (ages 0-11). Phone (360) 344-4452 or (360) 344-4400.

Port Townsend Marine Science Center is in Fort Worden State Park. The center features two exhibit buildings and touch pools displaying local marine life. The Natural History exhibit showcases beach rocks, marine animal fossils and sand from around the world; the Washington Geo-Puzzle illustrates land-forming processes. Daily guided walks and interpretive programs are offered in the summer.

A 3-hour nature and birding boat trip around Protection Island National Wildlife Refuge is offered in April, July and October; phone for details. Wed.-Mon. 11-5, mid-June through Labor Day; Fri.-Sun. noon-4, early Apr. to mid-June and day after Labor Day-Oct. 31; by appointment rest of year. Natural History exhibit Fri.-Sun. noon-4, Feb.-Mar. and Nov.-Dec. Admission $5; $3 (ages 6-17). Phone (360) 385-5582 or (800) 566-3932.

Puget Sound Coast Artillery Museum is 1 mi. n. via Cherry St. at the eastern edge of the park. The museum describes the coastal defense system's history with exhibits of uniforms, guns and historic photographs. Allow 30 minutes minimum. Sun.-Fri. 11-4, Sat. 10-5, July-Aug.; daily 11-4, rest of year. Admission $2; $1 (ages 6-12); $5 (family). Phone (360) 385-0373.

JEFFERSON COUNTY HISTORICAL SOCIETY MUSEUM is in the restored 1891 city hall building at Madison and Water sts. The museum exhibits Northwest Coast American Indian artifacts, maritime memorabilia and highlights the Victorian heritage of the city.

Allow 30 minutes minimum. Daily 11-4, Mar.-Dec.; Sat.-Sun. 11-4, rest of year. Closed Jan. 1, Thanksgiving and Dec. 25. Admission $4; $1 (ages 3-12). Phone (360) 385-1003.

PUGET SOUND EXPRESS departs from 227 Jackson St. Offering tours of the Strait of Juan de Fuca, Puget Sound Express makes a 2-hour stop in the small fishing community of Friday Harbor. A naturalist explains the different types of wildlife indigenous to the San Juan archipelago that can be viewed, including bald eagles, seals and orcas.

Allow 9 hours minimum. Tours depart daily at 9, late Mar.-early Oct. Round-trip fare $68.50-$78.50; $48.50-$53.50 (ages 2-10). One-way fare $49 50-$52.50; $34.50-$42.50 (ages 2-10). A fuel surcharge may apply; call for details. Reservations are recommended. MC, VI. Phone (360) 385-5288.

ROTHSCHILD HOUSE is at Jefferson and Taylor sts. This fully restored 1868 Greek Revival house features original period furnishings, an herb garden and a flower garden with many early varieties of

roses, peonies and lilacs. Daily 11-4, May-Sept. Admission $4; $1 (ages 5-11). Phone (360) 379-8076.

SAVE **SIDEWALK TOURS** departs from various downtown locations. The waterfront tour provides an overview of the town's history through anecdotes and an informative narrative. The homes tour visits two of the town's historic houses. Allow 1 hour minimum. Daily 9-7. Waterfront tour $10. Homes tour $12. Reservations are required. Phone (360) 385-1967.

POULSBO—see Seattle p. 254.

PROSSER (G-9) pop. 4,838, elev. 662'

Part of the Yakima Valley's fruit growing district, Prosser also is a shipping point for cattle and sheep. The treeless Horse Heaven Hills, where wild horses once roamed, rise to the south. Horse Heaven Vista, 2.5 miles southeast via SR 221, offers a panorama of the lower Yakima Valley, the Cascades and the Yakima River.

Vineyards are plentiful in the area; their harvest period is generally the last 2 weeks in September. More than a dozen wineries offer tastings; for a list, contact the chamber of commerce.

Prosser Visitor Information Center: 1230 Bennett Ave., Prosser, WA 99350; phone (509) 786-3177 or (800) 408-1517.

BENTON COUNTY HISTORICAL MUSEUM is in the city park at Seventh St. and Paterson Ave. The museum has more than 20,000 items, including pioneer and American Indian artifacts, a natural history diorama, Edison phonographs, a cut glass and porcelain collection, 37 oversized hand-carved model cars and reconstructions of a Victorian parlor and an early homestead. A collection of gowns dates 1843-1920. Allow 1 hour minimum. Tues.-Sat. 10-4, Sun. 1:30-4:30; closed Jan. 1, Easter, Thanksgiving and Dec. 25. Admission $2; $1 (ages 0-17). Phone (509) 786-3842.

WINERIES

• **Alexandria Nicole Cellars** is e. of I-82 exit 82 via Wine Country Rd., left on Benitz Rd., then right on Lee Rd. Off-site, 1-hour vineyard tours available by advance reservation. Tasting room open daily 11-5; closed holidays. Phone (509) 786-3497, or (509) 832-3497 for tour reservations.

• **Desert Wind Winery** is w. of I-82 exit 82 at 2258 Wine Country Rd. Daily 10-5, Apr.-Oct; 11-5, rest of year. Tours given by appointment Sept.-Oct. Phone (509) 786-7277 or (866) 921-7277.

• **Hinzerling Winery** is 1.5 mi. from I-82 at jct. Wine Country Rd. and Sheridan Ave. Mon.-Sat. 11-5, Sun. 11-4, Mar. 1-late Dec.; Mon.-Sat. 11-5, rest of year. Closed Jan. 1, Easter, Thanksgiving and Dec. 25. Phone (509) 786-2163 or (800) 727-6702.

• **Kestrel Vintners** is e. of I-82 exit 82 via Wine Country Rd., left on Benitz Rd., then right on Lee

Rd. Daily 10-5; closed Thanksgiving and Dec. 25. Tours given by appointment. Phone (509) 786-2675 or (888) 343-2675.

- **The Winemaker's Loft**, just s. of I-82 exit 80, then .8 mi. e. on Merlot Dr. to 357 Port Ave., is a Tuscan-style building housing seven studio wineries. Tastings available daily; tours are given by advance reservation. Daily 11-6; closed Thanksgiving and Dec. 25. Phone (509) 786-2705.

PULLMAN (F-12) pop. 24,675, elev. 2,500'

Settled in 1876 among fertile rolling hills perfect for wheat cultivation, Pullman was originally known as Three Forks because of its location at the confluence of three streams. The town was renamed in 1884 to honor railroad sleeping car manufacturer George Pullman in a futile attempt to attract an endowment. In 1890, when townspeople learned that state officials would arrive in Pullman searching for a site for the state's new land grant college, they dressed in their finest clothes and congregated on the main street to create a sense of prosperity and bustle. The tactic worked, and the Washington Agricultural College opened its doors in 1892.

The Bill Chapman Palouse Trail is a 7-mile paved path following SR 270 between Pullman and Moscow. Interpretive panels depict area geology, settlement and agriculture.

Pullman Chamber of Commerce: 415 N. Grand Ave., Pullman, WA 99163; phone (509) 334-3565 or (800) 365-6948.

PALOUSE DISCOVERY SCIENCE CENTER is 1.5 mi. n. on SR 27, e. on Terre View Dr., then e. on Hopkins Ct. to 950 N.E. Nelson Ct., following signs. Exhibits and activities emphasizing hands-on learning promote science, math and technology literacy. Theme areas include Animal Hall, Mammoth Site, Little Learner's Lab and Brain Power. Make sure you stop at the very popular Lentil Pit. Allow 30 minutes minimum. Tues.-Sat. 10-3; closed holidays. Admission $6; $5 (ages 55+); $4 (ages 2-11). MC, VI. Phone (509) 332-6869.

WASHINGTON STATE UNIVERSITY occupies a hilly, 600-acre site on the e. side of Pullman. Authorized in 1890 as the Washington Agricultural College, WSU has grown to become one of the most important universities in the West, renowned for its research and curriculum in agriculture. The attractive campus of red-brick buildings is set against a backdrop of trees and rolling green lawns.

A number of facilities are open to the public. The Holland Library contains several historical collections. The exhibits in the Museum of Anthropology trace the evolution of man and depict ways of life in past and present societies; phone (509) 335-3441. The Cougars play Pac-10 football in 40,000-seat Martin Stadium; basketball is played at Beasley Coliseum. Both are located on Stadium Way.

A 90-minute campus walking tour, offered Mon.-Fri. at 9 and 1, starts at the Lighty Student Services Building, Stadium Way and Wilson Road; phone (509) 335-7345 or (888) 468-6978. Visitor parking permits can be purchased at the WSU Visitor Center, located off-campus at 225 N. Grand Ave. in the former Union Pacific Depot in downtown Pullman. Visitor center open Mon.-Fri. 7-4; call for weekend hours. Phone (509) 335-8633.

Charles R. Conner Natural History Museum is on the first floor of Abelson Hall. Three galleries display more than 700 mounted birds, mammals, reptiles and amphibians. The museum's research collection numbers more than 65,000 specimens, including displays that were part of Washington state's exhibits at the 1893 Chicago World's Fair. Allow 30

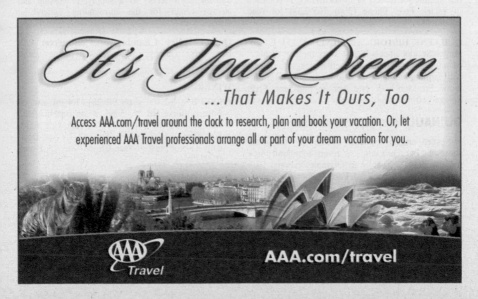

minutes minimum. Daily 8-5; closed holidays. Free. Phone (509) 335-3553

Culver Memorial is in Room 124 of the Webster Physical Sciences Building. The gallery displays hundreds of rock and mineral samples from around the world. A booth showcases fluorescent minerals, and the Jacklin Collection includes more than 2,000 cut and polished specimens of petrified wood. Allow 30 minutes minimum. Mon.-Fri. 8-5; closed holidays. Free. Phone (509) 335-1228.

Museum of Art/WSU is in the Fine Arts Center at Wilson Rd. and Stadium Way. It features changing exhibitions of regional, national and international art and artists. Lectures and guided tours complement the exhibitions. Allow 30 minutes minimum. Mon.-Sat. 10-5 (also Thurs. 5-7), late Aug.-Apr. 30; Tues.-Sat. noon-4, May-July. Closed most holidays and 2 weeks in early Aug. Free. Phone (509) 335-1910.

PUYALLUP—*see Seattle p. 255.*

QUILCENE (E-2) pop. 591, elev. 20'

Quilcene, at the head of Quilcene Bay off Hood Canal, is known for oysters. The Quilcene National Fish Hatchery, 2 miles south of town, raises many varieties of salmon.

Quilcene and Brinnon Chamber of Commerce: P.O. Box 774, Quilcene, WA 98376; phone (360) 765-4999.

MOUNT WALKER VIEWPOINT is 5 mi. s. on US 101, then 4 mi. e. via a gravel road. The viewpoint offers panoramas of Puget Sound, the Olympics and the Cascades from its 2,804-foot summit. A 2-mile hiking trail to the summit begins a quarter-mile from the beginning of the gravel road. The access road is not suitable for trailers or motor homes; it is closed in winter. Free. Phone (360) 765-2200 for road conditions.

QUILCENE HISTORICAL MUSEUM, 151 E. Columbia St., documents local history through displays of military memorabilia as well as logging, mining and farming equipment. Allow 30 minutes minimum. Fri.-Mon. 1-5, late Apr. to mid-Sept. Free. Phone (360) 765-4848.

QUINAULT (E-5) pop. 450, elev. 305'

Nestled among towering conifers on the south shore of Lake Quinault, this resort community is a popular stop for visitors to Olympic National Park and the Olympic National Forest. The area's mild, humid climate supports a lush temperate rain forest; six conifer specimens in the "Valley of the Rain Forest Giants" are recognized as champions by the National Register of Big Trees. A .3-mile walking trail branching off South Shore Road at the east edge of town leads to the world's largest Sitka spruce *(Picea sitchensis);* this 191-foot-tall monarch measures nearly 59 feet in circumference and is estimated to be around 1,000 years old.

The Rain Forest Nature Trail, off South Shore Road at the west end of town, is a half-mile interpretive loop through an old-growth forest of Douglas fir, western hemlock, western red cedar and Sitka spruce. Moss drapes the giant trees and carpets the forest floor, which is crowded with dense growths of sword fern. For information about other area hiking trails and recreational activities contact the Quinault office of the Pacific Ranger District, 353 South Shore Rd., P.O. Box 9, Quinault, WA 98575; phone (360) 288-2525.

LAKE QUINAULT MUSEUM is at 354 South Shore Rd. Displayed in the former Quinault post office are historical photographs from the 1920s to the '60s. Other exhibits include American Indian baskets and two 24-foot cedar dugout racing canoes. Allow 30 minutes minimum. Tues.-Sun. noon-5, July 1-Labor Day weekend; Sat.-Sun. noon-5, in June. Open other times by appointment. Closed Jan. 1, Thanksgiving and Dec. 25. Donations. Phone (360) 288-2583 or (360) 288-2317.

QUINCY (E-9) pop. 5,044, elev. 1,302'

The so-called Quincy Basin, a 25-square-mile ancient lake bed, was first settled by cattle ranchers in the late 1800s. The Great Northern Railroad opened its main line through here in 1892, though the main station was 8 miles west in Trinidad. Quincy incorporated in 1907, and hundreds of families homesteaded in the area, hoping to find ways of bringing water to revive the desert.

Recurring droughts in 1920-21 dried up most of the wells and forced many residents off the land. In 1933 the federal government announced the colossal Grand Coulee Dam project and the promise of irrigation. Water began flowing through the West Canal in 1951, sparking significant population growth. Today the town serves as a supply, processing and storage center for the surrounding agricultural district.

Quincy Valley Chamber of Commerce: P.O. Box 668, Quincy, WA 98848; phone (509) 787-2140.

WINERIES

- **Cave B** is 8.2 mi. s. on SR 281, 1.4 mi. s.w. on Beverly Burke Rd. N., 5 mi. w. on Baseline Rd., then .3 mi. n. to 344 Silica Rd., following signs. Sun.-Thurs. 11-5:30, Fri.-Sat. 11-7, Apr.-Dec.; daily 11-5:30, rest of year. Closed Dec. 25. Phone (509) 785-3500.

RAYMOND (F-5) pop. 2,975, elev. 14'

Raymond was founded in 1904 at the head of navigation on the Willapa River. With two railroads serving the tidewater site, the local logging industry boomed. Although most of the riverfront industrial sites have been abandoned, forest products remain a mainstay of the local economy.

Lining US 101 and SR 6 approaching Raymond is the Wildlife Heritage Sculpture Corridor featuring cast iron figures of local wildlife. The 5-mile Willapa River Trail, a paved walking and biking route, follows a former railroad right-of-way to South Bend.

Willapa Harbor Chamber of Commerce—Raymond: P.O. Box 1249, South Bend, WA 98586; phone (360) 942-5419.

SAVE NORTHWEST CARRIAGE MUSEUM is at 314 Alder St. The museum features 22 restored horse-drawn carriages, buggies and sleighs dating to the late 1800s. Visitors can see a Shelburne Landau used in the movies "Gone With The Wind" and "Jezebel" along with a road coach once used for mail delivery and a hearse with ornately carved panels. Signs describe interesting design features of each vehicle and what type of person might have used it. Allow 1 hour minimum. Mon.-Sat. 10-4, Sun. noon-4, Apr.-Sept.; Wed.-Sat. 10-4, rest of year. Admission $3; $1 (ages 6-14). MC, VI. Phone (360) 942-4150.

WILLAPA SEAPORT MUSEUM is at 310 Alder St. The museum, housed inside a warehouselike structure on the edge of town, is filled with shipping and logging memorabilia. Many of the displays are complemented by documents that provide personal insight about the items, including descriptions of their use and relevant time period. Allow 1 hour minimum. Wed.-Sat. noon-4; other times by appointment. Closed holidays. Donations. Phone (360) 942-4149 or (360) 942-2855.

REDMOND—see Seattle p. 255.

RENTON—see Seattle p. 255.

REPUBLIC (C-10) pop. 954

Nestled in the Kettle River Range, Republic was incorporated in 1900 and named after the Republic Mine—the major gold claim in the area. For decades the town was one of the nation's largest gold producers. The town's economy relies on agriculture, lumber, mining and outdoor recreation.

Republic Area Chamber of Commerce: 65 N. Clark St., P.O. Box 502, Republic, WA 99166; phone (509) 775-2704.

STONEROSE INTERPRETIVE CENTER is at 15 N. Kean St. The center provides a look at life on Earth 50 million years ago. Fossils of plants, insects and fish discovered at a nearby site are displayed. Visitors are encouraged to tour the site and dig for and keep some fossils; a fossil hunting permit can be obtained at the center. Chisels and hammers are recommended for digging; tools are available for a fee.

Daily 8-noon and 1-5, Memorial Day weekend-Labor Day; Wed.-Sun. 8-noon and 1-5, May 1-day before Memorial Day weekend and day after Labor Day-Oct. 31. Fossil site closes 1 hour before rest of center. Admission $5; $3 (ages 6-18 and 63+). Phone (509) 775-2295.

RICHLAND (G-10) pop. 38,708

Prior to World War II, Richland was a tranquil ranching settlement of approximately 200 people. The government picked the vast, almost-empty sage plains north of here as one of its development sites for the top-secret Manhattan Project, which attracted tens of thousands of workers and scientists. After the war, many remained in this planned community. Over the years, "Atomic City," as Richland has been called, was transformed into a major center of technological industries.

Richland also has been involved in less venturous pursuits. Irrigation from the Grand Coulee Dam helped develop the area's lush vineyards, fields and orchards.

Tri-Cities Visitor and Convention Bureau—Richland: 6951 W. Grandridge Blvd., Kennewick, WA 99336; phone (509) 735-8486 or (800) 254-5824.

SAVE COLUMBIA RIVER EXHIBITION OF HISTORY, SCIENCE AND TECHNOLOGY is at 95 Lee Blvd. The museum has displays, interactive exhibits and videotapes focusing on regional history and science. The Hanford Atomic Site exhibits include scale models of nuclear reactors and robotic, interactive manipulator arms connected to simulated hot cells used to handle radioactive materials. Earlier history also is included, ranging from Lewis and Clark to historic photographs. A geology exhibit depicts the region's origins and has touchable rocks.

Allow 1 hour minimum. Mon.-Sat. 10-5, Sun. noon-5; closed Jan. 1, Easter, Thanksgiving and Dec. 25. Admission $4; $3 (ages 62+ and students with ID); free (ages 0-6 with an adult). Phone (509) 943-9000.

COLUMBIA RIVER JOURNEYS depart from the dock in Howard Amon Park near Lee Blvd. and Amon Park Dr. This company offers narrated jet boat tours of Hanford Reach National Monument, which preserves the last free-flowing section of the Columbia River. Home to abundant wildlife, the reach is characterized by scenic river bluffs surrounded by prairie. During the excursion, passengers may see coyotes, mule deer, white pelicans and more. Allow 4 hours, 30 minutes minimum. Daily 8-12:30, May-Sept.; 1-5:30, in Oct. Fare $64; $49 (ages 4-11). Reservations are required. AX, DS, MC, VI. Phone (509) 734-9941 or (888) 486-9119.

RECREATIONAL ACTIVITIES

Kayaking

- **Columbia Kayak Adventures** departs from various points along the Columbia River. Write 710D George Washington Way, Richland, WA 99352. The outfitter offers half-day, all-day and multi-day guided trips on the Columbia River. Mar.-Oct. Phone (509) 947-5901.

RIDGEFIELD—see Portland in Oregon p. 108.

RITZVILLE (E-11) pop. 1,736, elev. 1,818'

Located in the heart of Washington's wheat growing region, Ritzville is named for Philip Ritz, who homesteaded here in 1878. The town was platted in 1880 and by 1904 had become a major wheat transshipment point, billing itself as the "breadbasket of the world." The downtown business district and adjoining residential area contain over two dozen historical buildings and homes from the late 1800s and early 1900s.

North of Ritzville are the channeled scablands, a landscape of erosional features formed by cataclysmic floods during the last Ice Age.

Ritzville Chamber of Commerce: 111 W. Main Ave., P.O. Box 122, Ritzville, WA 99169-0122; phone (509) 659-1936.

FRANK R. BURROUGHS HOME is at 408 W. Main St. Built 1889-90 and remodeled in 1902, the Victorian mansion was the local physician's residence. The home has been restored to period, featuring some original wallpaper, fixtures and furnishings and numerous donated historical artifacts. Highlights found in the study include original medical instruments and records and the doctor's camera collection. Also on display are period clothing, a recliner chair, a sewing machine and a phonograph.

Guided tours are available. Allow 30 minutes minimum. Tues.-Sat. 11-3 or by appointment, Memorial Day weekend-Labor Day; by appointment rest of year. Closed Jan. 1, Thanksgiving and Dec. 25. Free. Phone (509) 659-1656.

RAILROAD DEPOT MUSEUM is at jct. W. Railroad Ave. and N. Washington St. at 201 W. Railroad Ave. Featuring its original interior and fixtures, the museum occupies the red brick 1910 Northern Pacific depot. Highlights include a working Western Union telegraph, a telephone switchboard, an 1893 horsedrawn hearse, a restored Northern Pacific caboose and farm equipment.

Guided tours are given on request. Allow 30 minutes minimum. Tues.-Sat. 11-3 or by appointment, Memorial Day weekend-Labor Day; by appointment rest of year. Free. Phone (609) 659-1656.

ROCHESTER (I-1) pop. 1,829, elev. 149'

Originally a pioneer Russian settler called the community Moscow, but the town's first post office in 1890 carried the name Key. Its current name, used since 1904, honors a city in England. In the early 1900s Rochester became a trading and lumbering center with three sawmills.

A historical marker just southeast of town on Sargent Road S.W. indicates the site of Fort Henness, a U.S. Army post built on Grand Mound Prairie in 1855 to protect pioneer settlers from a perceived American Indian threat. An interpretive panel describes the fort, which once housed more than 200 people. Visitors can see chimney remains along with a pioneer cemetery on the opposite side of Sargent Road.

GAMBLING ESTABLISHMENTS

- **Lucky Eagle Casino** is 3 mi. w. on SR 12, then .8 mi. s. on Anderson Rd. to 188th Ave. S.W. Fri.-Sat. 9 a.m.-6 a.m., Sun.-Thurs. 9 a.m.-4 a.m. Phone (360) 273-2000 or (800) 720-1788.

ROCKPORT (C-7) pop. 102, elev. 275'

Rockport stands near the confluence of the Skagit and Sauk rivers. Each winter one of the largest seasonal concentrations of bald eagles in the U.S. outside of Alaska congregates along these streams to feed on the carcasses of spawned out salmon. They start arriving in late November, and their numbers build slowly in December, reaching their peak in January. Many eagles linger well into February.

The Washington State Wildlife Department has set aside a stretch of the Skagit River from Rockport to just upstream from Marblemount as a bald eagle sanctuary. The birds and their feeding habits can be observed from several roadside pullouts along SR 20. Designated sites include Howard Miller Steelhead Park in Rockport; Washington Eddy, 1 mile east of town on SR 20; and Sutter Creek, 1.3 miles farther east. Morning hours offer the best viewing opportunities.

RECREATIONAL ACTIVITIES

White-water Rafting

- **Alpine Adventures** departs from various points on the Skagit and Sauk rivers. Write P.O. Box 373, Gold Bar, WA 98251. Other activities are offered. June-Sept. Phone (360) 863-6505 or (800) 723-8386.

- **River Recreation, Inc.** departs from various points on the Skagit River. P.O. Box 2124, Bothell, WA 98041. Other activities are offered. Dec.-Feb. Phone (425) 741-5901 or (800) 464-5899.

ROSBURG (G-5) elev. 23'

GRAYS RIVER COVERED BRIDGE is 3.5 mi. e. on SR 4, then just s. on Loop Rd. Built in 1905, the 158-foot span is considered the oldest remaining covered bridge in the Northwest, and the only one of its kind in the state.

ROSLYN (E-8) pop. 1,017, elev. 2,266'

Roslyn, founded in 1886, at one time contained some of the most extensive coal fields on the West Coast. Although the last of the coal mines closed in the mid-1960s, Roslyn retains vestiges of its 1920s heyday when the population peaked at 4,000. The town served as the fictitious Cicely, Alaska, on the television series "Northern Exposure." The Roslyn Cemeteries, half a mile west of town, is a 15-acre site with 25 separate cemeteries reflecting the town's ethnic diversity.

Cle Elum-Roslyn Chamber of Commerce: 401 W. First St., Cle Elum, WA 98922; phone (509) 674-5958.

ROSLYN MUSEUM is at the w. end of downtown at 203 Pennsylvania Ave. Historic documents, photographs, mining equipment and pioneer items help tell the town's story. Allow 1 hour minimum. Mon.-Sat. 1-5, Sun. 11-3, May-Sept.; call for hours rest of year. Closed holidays. Donations. Phone (509) 649-2355.

ROSS LAKE NATIONAL RECREATION AREA (C-8)

Between the north and south sections of North Cascades National Park *(see place listing p. 190)*, Ross Lake National Recreation Area is shaped like a backward L. For access from the east, west and south, SR 20 parallels the Skagit River through the southern half of the area, continuing southeast into Okanogan National Forest *(see place listing p. 193)*. This road is normally closed east of Diablo Lake from mid-November to mid-April. Access from the north is possible only through Canada via a secondary road that begins in Hope, British Columbia.

Ross, Diablo and Gorge lakes are formed by Ross, Diablo and Gorge dams on the Skagit River. The dams are part of a hydroelectric project that supplies Seattle with electricity; a tour center is in Newhalem *(see place listing p. 189)*. The 3.5-mile Diablo Lake Trail, beginning near Diablo Lake Resort, leads to Ross Dam. From the south, access to Ross Lake is limited to trail and water routes. Seven major trails lead outward from Ross Lake into the back country.

Surrounding the lakes are 118,000 acres of glaciers, mountain peaks and forested valleys that provide habitat for a variety of wildlife. Fishing season for Ross Lake, one of the few remaining large lakes in Washington not artificially stocked, is mid-June to late October; state fishing regulations apply and a license is required. Ranger stations are on SR 20 at Marblemount, phone (360) 854-7245, and Newhalem, phone (206) 386-4495, ext 11.

For further information write the Park Superintendent's Office, North Cascades National Park, 810 SR 20, Sedro-Woolley, WA 98284-1239; phone (360) 854-7200. *See Recreation Chart and the AAA Northwestern CampBook.*

SALKUM (F-6) elev. 562'

Salkum, derived from an Indian name meaning "boiling up" in reference to the nearby waterfalls on Mill Creek, was a busy logging town with two sawmills. The mills closed after the resource was depleted in the 1930s.

COWLITZ SALMON HATCHERY is off US 12, 1 mi. s. on Fuller Rd., then e. on Spencer Rd. N. Facilities for raising chinook and coho salmon include incubation equipment, salmon sorting and fish loading machinery, a fish ladder and a barrier dam. About 10 million salmon are released annually to

accommodate the spring and fall runs. Visitors can view spawning salmon from September to mid-January. Hatchery open daily 8-5. Free. Phone (360) 985-2655.

SAN JUAN ISLAND—
see San Juan Islands p. 210.

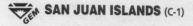 **SAN JUAN ISLANDS** (C-1)

The glaciers that covered northwest Washington approximately 15 million years ago created the San Juan Archipelago between the mainland and Vancouver Island. As part of this archipelago, the San Juan Islands consist of 172 islands ranging in size from small rocky islets to Orcas Island, with its 57 square miles of picturesque bays and steep, forested ridges.

Spanish captain Francisco Eliza charted and named the islands in 1791, 16 years after a previous expedition discovered them. In 1792 Capt. George Vancouver claimed the islands for Britain, and in 1841 Capt. Charles Wilkes declared them part of America.

The ensuing dispute over ownership of the islands nearly brought the two nations to blows during the infamous Pig War of 1859, in which a stray British pig was shot in an American potato patch. The opposing sides occupied the islands for the next 13 years, but the conflict was solved peacefully through arbitration by German Kaiser Wilhelm I, who ruled in favor of the United States. What remains of the British and American forts are now part of San Juan Island National Historical Park *(see attraction listing).*

Fidalgo, Lopez, Orcas and San Juan islands are the largest and most populated. San Juan Islands National Wildlife Refuge comprises 48 of the remaining rocks and islands, and all but Matia and Turn islands are closed to the public. The San Juan Islands contain more bald eagles than any other region in the 48 contiguous states. Great horned owls, tufted puffins and a variety of other birds and mammals inhabit the islands; salmon, seals, dolphins and orcas thrive in the waters.

Recreational opportunities abound: Boating, kayaking, swimming, scuba diving, fishing, hiking, bicycling and camping are among the main activities.

State ferries provide daily service between the ports of Friday Harbor, Anacortes, Lopez, Shaw and Orcas as well as to Sidney, British Columbia, north of Victoria; phone (888) 808-7977 in Wash. Seasonal passenger ferry service is available from Friday Harbor to Port Townsend via Puget Sound Express, (360) 385-5288; to Seattle via Clipper Navigation, (800) 888-2535; to Victoria via Victoria Express, (360) 452-8088; and to Bellingham and Victoria via Victoria/San Juan Cruises, (888) 734-8180.

Sightseeing flights are available from San Juan Air Tours in Friday Harbor; phone (360) 378-7717. Scheduled air service is available from Bellingham, Seattle-Lake Union or Seattle-Boeing Field. For further information contact AAA Washington or the San Juan Islands Visitors Bureau.

San Juan Islands Visitors Bureau: P.O. Box 1330, Friday Harbor, WA 98250; phone (888) 468-3701.

Lopez Island (C-2)

One of the least visited of the major San Juan Islands, Lopez Island offers miles of back roads leading through farms and rolling woodlands and a rugged coast marked with steep cliffs and isolated coves. Mackeye Harbor was the site of the town of Richardson, a bustling fishing port at the turn of the 20th century.

The flat and rolling landscape has made the island particularly popular with cyclists. Camping and beach access is available at Odlin County Park and Spencer Spit State Park; Agate Beach County Park also provides beach access.

LOPEZ ISLAND HISTORICAL MUSEUM is 4 mi. s. of ferry dock on Weeks Rd. to 28 Washburn Pl. in Lopez Village. The museum chronicles pioneer life on the island. Maritime exhibits include reef net boats, a captain's gig, a fish trap and steamboat models. Among the pioneer displays are kitchen utensils, horse-drawn farm machinery and what is believed to be the first automobile in San Juan County. American Indian artifacts also are featured and include three dugout canoes. Wed.-Sun. noon-4, May-Sept. Donations. Phone (360) 468-2049.

RECREATIONAL ACTIVITIES
Kayaking

• **Cascadia Kayak Tours** offers full-day and multi-day tours departing from various locations on Lopez Island. Write 441 Sweetbrier Ln., Lopez Island, WA 98261. Tours depart daily Apr.-Nov. Phone (360) 468-3008.

Orcas Island (B-2)

The largest and most rugged of the San Juan Islands, Orcas Island covers 57 square miles. Ferries dock at the Orcas village on the southern shore. Eastsound, at the head of Orcas' largest bay, is the island's major settlement. Historic buildings now house local commercial enterprises, including the Outlook Inn, which incorporates parts of a fur trappers cottage built in 1838. The Emmanuel Episcopal Church dates from 1886.

The 1,578-acre Turtleback Mountain Preserve lies on the west side of Orcas Island and comprises grasslands, oak woodlands, conifer forests and wetlands. The preserve's high elevation allows for spectacular views of the Canadian Gulf and San Juan Islands. Visitors can hike on two trails and bird-watching is a popular activity. Phone (360) 378-4402 for more information.

MORAN STATE PARK, 13 mi. n.e. of Orcas Island via Horseshoe Hwy., is one of Washington's scenic gems. Former Seattle mayor and shipbuilder Robert Moran donated land for the nucleus of the 5,252-acre park in 1920. Cloaked in a forest of Douglas fir, western red cedar and western hemlock, the park features five freshwater lakes, waterfalls and 2,409-foot Mount Constitution, the highest peak in the San Juan Islands. Paved roads connect the major sites and a network of 38 miles of trails, most built by the Civilian Conservation Corps (CCC) in the 1930s, serves hikers, mountain bikers and horseback riders.

The day-use area at Cascade Lake has a short interpretive trail and paddleboat and kayak rentals Memorial Day weekend to Labor Day. An easy 2.7-mile trail encircles the lake. Mt. Constitution Road leads to the top of its namesake peak, passing other attractions en route. Cascade Falls is accessible by a 0.2-mile trail. The 100-foot drop, set in an amphitheater of mossy woods, is the highest in the San Juans. Three other waterfalls are within a 0.6-mile hike. Mountain Lake, the park's largest, contains four small islands. An easy 3.9-mile loop trail follows its shoreline.

Beyond Mountain Lake the road ascends the steep flank of Mt. Constitution via a series of six switchbacks. The upper switchbacks offer sweeping views. This narrow roadway is open daylight hours only and is not recommended for trailers or motorhomes; it is occasionally closed in winter due to snow.

At the road's end a short trail leads through a forest of lodgepole pine to one of the Northwest's iconic views. Here at the summit the CCC erected a 50-foot observation tower out of native sandstone. Modeled after a 12th-century watchtower in the Caucasus Mountains of southern Russia, its upper levels offer a 360-degree panorama encompassing islands, saltwater channels, the Cascades and the Olympic mountains. The lower two levels contain historical displays about the park, the establishment of the park, the CCC's labors and the area's natural history. See Recreation Chart.

Food is available. Picnicking is permitted. Allow 2 hours minimum. Daily 6:30-dusk, May-Sept.; 8-dusk, rest of year. Free. Phone (360) 376-2326.

ORCAS ISLAND ECLIPSE CHARTERS AND WHALE WATCH TOURS meets adjacent to the Orcas ferry dock. The MV Orcas Express tracks whales around the San Juan Islands. Other possible sights include eagles, harbor seals, minke whales, porpoises and seabirds. Monthly lighthouse tours also are available. Allow 3 hours, 30 minutes minimum. Cruises depart daily; phone for departure times. Fare $64; $42 (ages 0-12). Reservations are required. Phone (360) 376-6566 or (800) 376-6566.

ORCAS ISLAND HISTORICAL MUSEUM is in the village of Eastsound at 181 North Beach Rd. The museum features six homestead cabins built 1870-1900. The cabins and non-historic connecting rooms display items from the American Indian and early settlement periods. The 1888 one-room Crow Valley School, on Crow Valley Road, has historical displays. Tues.-Sun. 11-4, Memorial Day weekend-late Sept. School open Wed. and Sat. noon-4; by appointment rest of year. Admission $3; $2 (ages 63+ and students with ID); $1 (ages 6-12); $10 (family). Phone (360) 376-4849.

RECREATIONAL ACTIVITIES
Kayaking
- **Shearwater Adventures** offers 3-hour, half-day and full-day guided tours from various locations on Orcas Island. Write P.O. Box 787, Eastsound,

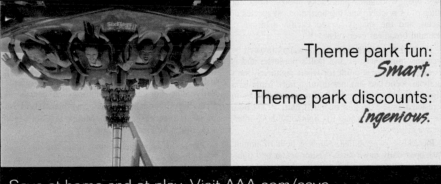

WA 98245. Tours depart daily Apr.-Oct. Reservations are required. Phone (360) 376-4699.

San Juan Island (C-1)

Westernmost of the major islands, San Juan Island covers 55 square miles. Rolling hills accented with small farms and patches of forest in the east give way to rugged terrain in the west, where Mount Dallas rises to 1,000 feet. Friday Harbor, the island's largest town and a bustling port, is a port of call for ferries and other boats.

On the island's northwest corner is Roche Harbor, a resort town and popular yachting destination. In a peaceful glen nearby is the Afterglow Vista Mausoleum, which commemorates John S. McMillan, founder of the local limeworks, which was once the largest west of the Mississippi.

San Juan Island Transit provides regular shuttle service around the island. Narrated tours are available on a limited basis by reservation; phone (360) 378-8887 or (800) 887-8387.

ISLAND MUSEUM OF ART is at 314 Spring St. in downtown Friday Harbor, 3 blks. w. of the ferry building. Visitors enter the museum courtyard beneath an arbor arch formed by a century-old camperdown elm. The gallery and courtyard contain changing displays of art by local and regional artists. Allow 30 minutes minimum. Tues.-Sun. 11-5, June-Aug.; Tues.-Sat. 11-5, Apr.-May and Sept.-Dec. Closed Thanksgiving and Dec. 25. Free. Phone (360) 370-5050.

LIME KILN POINT STATE PARK is 10 mi. w. of Friday Harbor via Beaverton Valley Rd., West Valley Rd. and Mitchell Bay Rd. to 1567 Westside Rd. Covering 36 acres, Lime Kiln is a living museum of natural and cultural history. Its name derives from the vicinity's former lime kiln operations. A .8-mile hiking trail loops through the park, traversing meadows, open woodlands and rocky shores. Look for outcrops of prickly pear, the northernmost species of cactus, and the shaggy-barked Pacific madrone, a beautiful broadleaf evergreen.

The trail overlooks Haro Strait, waters favored by orca and minke whales and Dall's porpoise, and is an excellent vantage point for whale sightings (most likely to occur late summer through fall). Lime Kiln Lighthouse was built in 1919. The trail continues to a restored lime kiln that operated until 1923. Both the park visitor center and the lighthouse have interpretive displays.

Picnicking is permitted. Allow 1 hour minimum. Park open daily dawn-dusk. Visitor center and lighthouse usually open daily 11-6, Memorial Day weekend-Labor Day. Free. Phone (360) 378-2044.

[SAVE] **MAYA'S WESTSIDE CHARTERS** departs from Friday Harbor's Snug Harbor Marina at 1997 Mitchell Bay Rd. The tour provider offers narrated whale-watch excursions aboard a small, six-passenger boat. Guides describe San Juan Island's history and various types of local wildlife, including the orcas passengers are likely to see. Allow 3 hours

minimum. Tours depart two to three times daily June-Sept.; twice daily Mar.-May and in Oct.; otherwise varies rest of year. Fare $75; $65 (ages 0-12). Reservations are required. Phone (360) 378-7996.

SAN JUAN EXCURSIONS WHALE WATCHING departs from Spring Street Landing, .5 blk. from the ferry dock. San Juan Excursions offers 3.5- to 4.5-hour whale-watch/wildlife tours in the San Juan and Canadian Gulf islands narrated by two certified naturalists. Passengers see orca whales on most trips. Bald eagles, harbor seals and many other marine mammals and birds can be seen on every trip. Allow 4 hours minimum. Daily 9-5, May-Sept. Fare $69; $62.10 (ages 65+, students, teachers and military with ID); $49 (ages 2-12). Reservations are recommended. MC, VI. Phone (360) 378-6636 or (800) 809-4253.

[SAVE] **SAN JUAN HISTORICAL MUSEUM** is at 405 Price St. in Friday Harbor. The museum consists of several historic buildings, each of which houses items relevant to its original use. An 1894 Victorian farmhouse is furnished in period and features photographs and memorabilia of island pioneers. A second building served as the San Juan County Jail 1895-1971. A resource center contains rotating exhibits describing area history. Allow 30 minutes minimum. Wed.-Sat. 10-4, Sun. 1-4, June-Sept.; by appointment rest of year. Admission $5; $4 (ages 60+); $3 (ages 6-18). Phone (360) 378-3949.

SAN JUAN ISLAND NATIONAL HISTORICAL PARK is on San Juan Island. The park commemorates the British and American struggle for possession of the San Juans—a dispute that culminated in the Pig War of 1859. The lone casualty of the war was a stray pig, and in 1872 arbitration sustained the American claim to the San Juans and set the boundary between the United States and Canada.

Ranger programs are offered weekly in summer. American Camp Visitor Center open daily 8:30-5, early June-Sept. 30; daily 8:30-4:30, Mar. 1-Memorial Day and in Oct.; Wed.-Sun. 8:30-4:30, rest of year. Closed week after Memorial Day. English Camp Visitor Center open daily 9-5, early June-early Sept. For additional information contact the Park Superintendent's Office, San Juan Island National Historical Park, 650 Mullis St., Suite 100, P.O. Box 429, Friday Harbor, WA 98250.

Picnic areas, beaches and trails are available; hunting and camping are not permitted. The grounds are open daily dawn-11 p.m. Rangers are at the sites daily. Free. Phone (360) 378-2902.

[SAVE] **SAN JUAN SAFARIS** departs from the Friday Harbor marina. Providing 3- to 4-hour guided whale-watching/wildlife tours, San Juan Safaris offers visitors the chance to view bald eagles, great blue herons, sea lions, seals, otters and orca, gray and humpback whales.

Allow 3 hours, 30 minutes minimum. Tours depart daily at 1 and 5:30, mid-June to mid-Aug.; at 1, mid-Apr. to mid-June and mid-Aug. through early Nov. Tours $69; $49 (ages 2-12). A fuel surcharge may apply; call for details. MC, VI. Phone (360) 378-1323 or (800) 450-6858.

WESTCOTT BAY SCULPTURE PARK is 10 mi. n.w. of Friday Harbor on Roche Harbor Rd., at the entrance to the village of Roche Harbor. Paths loop through this 19-acre outdoor sculpture park, which contains more than 100 works displayed in meadow, forest, pond and saltwater shoreline settings. Picnicking is permitted. Allow 1 hour minimum. Daily dawn-dusk. Admission $5. Phone (360) 370-5050.

WESTERN PRINCE **WHALE & WILDLIFE TOURS** departs from Port of Friday Harbor; the office is at 1 Spring St., adjacent to the ferry dock. The company conducts half-day naturalist-guided whale-search/wildlife excursions in the San Juan Islands and Canadian Gulf Islands aboard a 30-passenger biodiesel-powered boat. Whales are sighted during the vast majority of trips while marine mammals and bald eagles are seen on all trips.

Allow 4 hours minimum. Trips depart daily in the afternoon, Apr.-Oct. (also Sat.-Sun. at noon, in Apr. and Oct.). Fare $69; $49 (ages 0-12). AX, DS, MC, VI. Phone (360) 378-5315 or (800) 757-6722.

SAVE **WHALE MUSEUM** is 3 blks. n.w. of the ferry landing at 62 First St. N. in Friday Harbor. The museum occupies one of the island's oldest buildings. Exhibits depict the biology, behavior and sounds of whales. Included are a display comparing the skeletons of a human, a river otter and a dolphin; a genealogy exhibit of local resident killer whales; and two movies. Complete skeletons of a baby gray whale and an adult killer whale also are displayed. A children's activity room plus carvings, paintings, lithographs and photographs highlight other whale-related exhibits.

Allow 1 hour minimum. Daily 9-6, mid-Feb. through Dec. 31; closed Thanksgiving and Dec. 25. Admission $6; $5 (ages 65+); $3 (ages 5-18 and students with ID). AX, MC, VI. Phone (360) 378-4710.

RECREATIONAL ACTIVITIES

Kayaking

- **Outdoor Odysseys** offers 1- to 5-day sea kayaking trips departing from San Juan County Park near Friday Harbor. Write 12003 23rd Ave. N.E., Seattle, WA 98125. Other activities are offered. Daily mid-May to mid-Sept. Phone (206) 361-0717 or (800) 647-4621.

SEATAC—
see Seattle p. 255.

Seattle

City Population: 563,374   Elevation: 350 ft.

Editor's Picks:

Pike Place Market.................(see p. 227)

Pioneer Square Historic
    District............................(see p. 228)

Space Needle.......................(see p. 231)

Find more AAA top picks at AAA.com

Space Needle / © Steve Vidler / eStock Photo

It's time for a quick quiz. Which U.S. city:

Was originally named Duwamps?

Has the world's longest floating pontoon bridge?

Ranks 44th among U.S. cities in average annual rainfall?

Claims the highest percentage of people who bike to work?

Contains some 6,200 acres of parks?

Is the site of the first revolving restaurant?

Is home to the nation's oldest continuously operated farmers market?

Brewed what grew to be the world's biggest coffee chain?

Was the first in the country to play a Beatles song on the radio?

Of course we've already told you (there *is* that big headline above). But if you knew the answers maybe you have already discovered (and most likely fallen in love with) the singular allure of the Emerald City—a nickname that has a connection to the mythical land in "The Wizard of Oz," since visitors who first behold the magnificent surroundings framing this Northwestern metropolis often share Dorothy's sense of wonderment as she gazed upon Oz for the first time across that sea of poppies.

A bit of history to start. Archeological evidence suggests that the region around present-day Seattle has known human habitation for as long as 12,000 years; the Duwamish, Suquamish and Coast Salish peoples all occupied coastal areas stretching from southern Alaska to Oregon, fishing and surviving on the bounty of the land. Pioneers who settled along the protected eastern shore of Elliott Bay made friends with Sealth, an amiable Duwamish and Suquamish leader who negotiated a treaty relinquishing tribal land rights in much of northwestern Washington. The settlers in turn named their community in his honor—with a spelling change that made it more pronounceable.

Evergreen Point Floating Bridge's 7,578 feet span Lake Washington, one of several bodies of water that give Seattle its distinctive backdrop. Geography plays a large part in the natural beauty so abundantly on display. Puget Sound, a deepwater inlet punctuating the northwest Washington coast, not only provides scenic allure; its indentations create several fine harbors that contributed to the area's early growth. West of Puget Sound is the Olympic Peninsula, a wilderness area encompassing snow-capped mountains and lush coniferous forests. To the southeast lies towering, ice-clad Mount Rainier, a massive yet ethereal feature on the southern horizon (as long as it's a clear day). These are just three reasons why Seattle's reputation as a city of spectacular views is fully justified.

Given another, more infamous, city reputation—month after month after month of unrelentingly rainy weather—it may surprise you to find out that Seattle receives an average of about 37 inches of

$\mathcal{G}$etting $\mathcal{T}$here — *starting on p. 218*

$\mathcal{G}$etting $\mathcal{A}$round — *starting on p. 218*

$\mathcal{W}$hat $\mathcal{T}$o $\mathcal{S}$ee — *starting on p. 219*

$\mathcal{W}$hat $\mathcal{T}$o $\mathcal{D}$o — *starting on p. 234*

$\mathcal{W}$here $\mathcal{T}$o $\mathcal{S}$tay — *starting on p. 629*

$\mathcal{W}$here $\mathcal{T}$o $\mathcal{D}$ine — *starting on p. 645*

$\mathcal{E}$ssential $\mathcal{E}$xperiences — *visit AAA.com*

$\mathcal{E}$ditor's $\mathcal{E}$vent $\mathcal{P}$icks — *visit AAA.com*

precipitation a year. That's less than Boston, New York City, Philadelphia, Atlanta, Houston and St. Louis, just to name a few. Yes, it can be gloomy (Seattleites will tell you that summer finally arrives on July 4). Yes, it can be rainy (the kind of light but persistent rain that seems like it's never going to stop). But the reward for putting up with this is sweet indeed: the azure blue skies, warm sun and low humidity that characterize the glorious days of midsummer and early fall.

Besides, all that dampness is good for the garden. This is a remarkably green and flowery city, and uniformly mild weather keep is it green practically all year. You haven't really seen beauty until you've experienced extravagant clusters of pink, white, yellow, orange, lavender and red rhododendron blooms. April and May are the glory months for rhodies as well as flowering cherry and crabapple trees, lilacs and dogwoods. The height of summer brings lavish displays of roses. Japanese maples turn blazing red in autumn. Even the cedars and spruces growing along I-5 are lovely. Is it any wonder, then, that so many residents take the opportunity to enjoy the great outdoors on their way to the office?

And practically everywhere you turn there's a park. Seattle's urban green spaces are many and delightful. Imagine, for instance, happening on Kinnear Park, a little stretch of green hugging the southwest slope of Queen Anne Hill. A path winds beneath tall, stately trees. Benches invite you to stop and sit for a spell. And there are pretty views of the Elliott Bay waterfront. It's a perfect spot to just relax and enjoy nature for a few minutes.

Then you could hike up 5th Avenue W. (which helpfully becomes stairs for part of the way) to W. Highland Street and Kerry Park (see attraction listing p. 223), where the vista of downtown and the

Pike Place Market / Washington State Tourism

bay is stunning. Or head to pint-size, exceedingly picturesque Green Lake. Once around the paved, tree-lined path is 2.8 miles, perfect for an early morning jog, a bracing afternoon walk or a leisurely stroll at any time.

The Space Needle-Sky City Restaurant (See color ad p. 232), which revolves a full 360 degrees, is at the top of Seattle's instantly identifiable landmark. Opened in 1962, the needle's futuristic Jetsons-like profile remains unmistakable, although five skyscrapers to date have surpassed its 605-foot height. A trip up to the observation deck to take in the breathtaking 360-degree panorama of lakes, urban neighborhoods, the Seattle skyline and the Cascade and Olympic mountains is the No. 1 thing on many a tourist's "don't miss" list, so by all means do it.

That is, after you've done Pike Place Market. It's another definite don't miss. The market, which celebrated its centennial in 2007, started as a way to bring regional farmers and consumers together, and that remains its underlying purpose despite all sorts

Destination Seattle

*F*rom its early days as a lumbering center, Seattle has evolved into an exciting, progressive metropolitan area.

*T*he soul of the city still resides in its downtown area, however, where modern museums and landmarks are interspersed with historic areas, markets, espresso stands and shopping and entertainment districts.

© The Museum of Flight

The Museum of Flight, Seattle.
The Museum of Flight boasts a world-class and century-spanning collection of aircraft, from fighter planes like the World War I-era Sopwith Pup to today's sleek, technologically advanced passenger airliners. (See listing page 225)

Jim Poth / Washington State Tourism

Fort Nisqually Living History Museum, Tacoma.
Fur trading was one of Washington state's first entrepreneurial activities. That wild and woolly era is revisited at this living history museum in Point Defiance Park. (See listing page 261)

Suquamish •

Keyport •

Bainbridge Island •

Bremerton •

Port Orchard •   Blake Island

(16)

Gig Harbor •

Lakewood •

Steilacoom •

(5)

*P*laces included in this AAA Destination City:

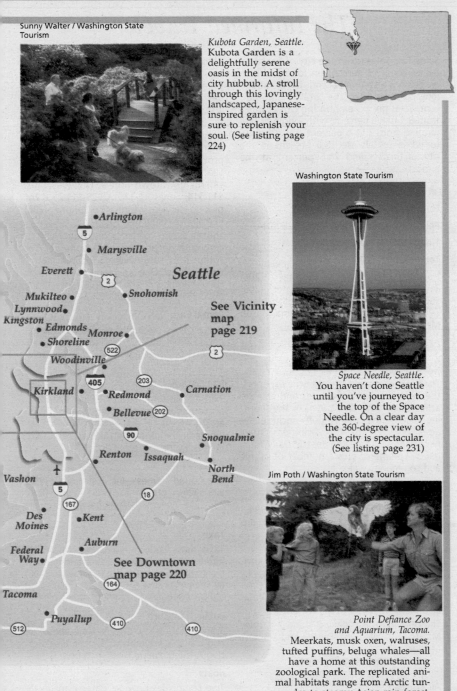

Sunny Walter / Washington State Tourism

Kubota Garden, Seattle.
Kubota Garden is a delightfully serene oasis in the midst of city hubbub. A stroll through this lovingly landscaped, Japanese-inspired garden is sure to replenish your soul. (See listing page 224)

Washington State Tourism

Space Needle, Seattle.
You haven't done Seattle until you've journeyed to the top of the Space Needle. On a clear day the 360-degree view of the city is spectacular. (See listing page 231)

Jim Poth / Washington State Tourism

Point Defiance Zoo and Aquarium, Tacoma.
Meerkats, musk oxen, walruses, tufted puffins, beluga whales—all have a home at this outstanding zoological park. The replicated animal habitats range from Arctic tundra to steamy Asian rain forest. (See listing page 261)

Seattle

See Vicinity map page 219

See Downtown map page 220

Arlington
Marysville
Everett
Mukilteo
Lynnwood
Kingston
Edmonds
Shoreline
Monroe
Snohomish
Woodinville
Kirkland
Redmond
Carnation
Bellevue
Snoqualmie
Renton
Issaquah
North Bend
Vashon
Des Moines
Kent
Auburn
Federal Way
Tacoma
Puyallup

The Informed Traveler

Sales Tax: Sales tax in the city of Seattle is 8.8 percent (9.3 percent on food and beverages in restaurants and bars); added lodging taxes bring the total to 15.6 percent. Sales tax in neighboring cities ranges from 8.5 to 8.9 percent, with lodging taxes ranging from 2 to 5 percent. Taxes on automobile rentals are 18.5 percent in the city of Seattle and 28.5 percent at the airport.

WHOM TO CALL

Emergency: 911

Police (non-emergency): (206) 625-5011

Time: (206) 361-8463

Temperature: (206) 361-8463

Hospitals: Northwest Hospital, (206) 364-0500; Swedish Medical Center, (206) 386-6000; University of Washington Medical Center, (206) 598-3300; Virginia Mason Medical Center, (206) 223-6600.

WHERE TO LOOK

Newspapers
The Seattle area has two daily newspapers, the *Seattle Post-Intelligencer* and the *Seattle Times*, both distributed in the morning. Alternative publications include *Seattle Weekly* and *The Stranger*. Other newspapers include the *Seattle Daily Journal of Commerce* plus a number of ethnic and community weeklies.

Radio
Seattle radio station KOMO (1000 AM) is an all-news/weather station; KUOW (94.9 FM) and Tacoma's KPLU (88.5 FM) are members of National Public Radio.

Visitor Information
Seattle-King County Convention and Visitors Bureau: 701 Pike St., Suite 800 (next to the escalators inside the Convention Center), Seattle, WA 98101; phone (206) 461-5840.
The bureau is open daily 9-1 and 2-5, mid-May to mid-Oct.; Mon.-Fri. 9-1 and 2-5, rest of year.

TRANSPORTATION

Air Travel
Seattle-Tacoma (Sea-Tac) International Airport is midway between Seattle and Tacoma on SR 99; most scheduled services use Sea-Tac. For Sea-Tac information phone the Skyline, (206) 431-4444 or (800) 544-1965. Boeing Field, south of the city, is a smaller airport used by private and charter planes and some regional carriers.

Gray Line's Downtown Airporter operates express buses every 30 minutes, from approximately 5:30 a.m. to 11 p.m., between Seattle-Tacoma International Airport and various downtown hotels. One-way fares $11-$14; ages 2-12, $8.25-$11.25. For pick-up service information phone (206) 624-5077 or (800) 426-7532.

Shuttle Express offers door-to-door van or limousine service to and from Sea-Tac within the Seattle-Everett-Tacoma metropolitan area. One-way fares start at $29. For information and reservations phone (425) 981-7000, or (800) 487-7433 in Wash.

Rental Cars
Hertz offers discounts to AAA members; phone (206) 903-6260 or (800) 654-3080. For lists of other agencies check the telephone directory.

Rail Service
Amtrak passenger trains, (800) 872-7245, arrive and depart the King Street Station at 3rd Avenue S. and S. King Street. Elsewhere in the area, Amtrak also serves Edmonds, Everett, Tacoma and Tukwila.

Buses
Greyhound Lines Inc. station, (206) 628-5526, (206) 628-5555 or (800) 231-2222, is at 8th Avenue and Stewart Street.

Taxis
Taxis must be ordered by telephone or hired while stopped at cab stands. Major companies are Farwest Taxi, (206) 622-1717; Orange Cab, (206) 522-8800; and Yellow Cabs, (206) 622-6500.

Public Transport
Transportation by bus, trolley, monorail and trains is available in Seattle. *See Getting Around, Public Transportation.*

Boats
Two companies provide water transportation within the greater Seattle area and to British Columbia. *See Approaches, By Boat.*

of commercial diversification. There's no better place to be early in the morning, cradling hot coffee, nibbling on a pastry and wandering among the produce, seafood, flower and craft vendors as they set up shop for another busy day. The soul of the city is right here.

In addition to fresh fish, locally grown fruits and veggies and awesome baked goods, Pike Place Market is the location of the very first Starbucks (at 1912 Pike Place). From its humble 1971 beginnings as a local coffee bean roaster and retailer Starbucks has become a global purveyor of everything from organic shade-grown beans for that perfect espresso to brewing equipment, grinders, teapots, mugs, CDs and gift cards. But Starbucks isn't the city's only corporate powerhouse; among the major companies headquartered in the greater Seattle area are Amazon.com, AT&T Wireless, Expedia, Inc. and Microsoft.

And as far as playing an early role in launching the Fab Four juggernaut, let's just say that Seattle is no slouch as far as pop culture credentials go. This is, after all, the birthplace of '60s guitarist extraordinaire and visionary rock musician Jimi Hendrix. Seattle also was the epicenter of the early 1990s alternative rock scene ("grunge" to the uninitiated) that spawned Nirvana, Pearl Jam and other bands revered by armies of disenfranchised youth.

Among Seattle's more idiosyncratic cultural institutions are Dick's Drive-In (just "Dick's" to Seattleites), a fast-food chain with five locations and the simplest of menus: burger, fries and shakes (nary a chai tea or salad of organic field greens in sight); and The Lusty Lady, an adult entertainment establishment with an impudent pink marquee in plain view of the considerably more highbrow Seattle Art Museum.

And a newsstand at the corner of Pike Street and 3rd Avenue has quietly and over time become an institution of its own. The tiny blue metal kiosk—one of the few survivors of a dying breed phased out by vending machines, home delivery and online information access—has free publications like the *Seattle Weekly* and sells local newspapers as well as copies of the Constitution and the Declaration of Independence (the real money-makers). Although the stand has occupied the same corner for almost 90 years, the current owner is facing a shutdown by the city unless the dilapidated structure is refurbished; stay tuned.

Any random episode of two popular TV hits also will offer a keenly observed take on this city's essence. "Frasier," the "Cheers" spinoff about a psychiatrist who returns from Boston to his hometown and a new gig as a radio talk show host, wasn't filmed on location—but when urbane Frasier Crane and his equally urbane brother Niles meet at Café Nervosa to discuss opera, ballet and the finer points of a good sherry, you know *exactly* what city you're in.

The same thing can be said of "Grey's Anatomy," a much-lauded drama about the trials and tribulations of a group of doctors toiling at Seattle Grace Hospital. It isn't filmed on location either (although Fisher Plaza on 4th Avenue N., a

Point Defiance Park / Tacoma Regional Convention & Visitor Bureau

stone's throw from the Space Needle, is used for some exterior shots). But flashes of the monorail and other local landmarks—and all those scenes where rain is a backdrop—say "Seattle" in no uncertain terms.

Getting There

By Car

The major north-south route is I-5 from the Canadian border through Seattle to Portland and California. East-west traffic generally follows I-90, which crosses the Cascade Mountains and approaches Seattle over Lake Washington from Spokane and the East. Additional freeway lanes on sections of I-5 and I-90 operate as reversible roadways, inbound during morning hours and outbound afternoons and evenings.

SR 520, which becomes the Evergreen Point Floating Bridge, runs east-west from I-5 in Seattle to I-405 in Bellevue. I-405 also runs north-south around Lake Washington and connects to I-5, which runs through the city.

By Boat

Washington State Ferries, Colman Dock (Pier 52) at the foot of Marion Street, link Seattle with the Olympic Peninsula via Bremerton and Bainbridge Island; passenger-only ferries link Colman · Dock (Pier 50) with Vashon Island. State ferries also leave Fauntleroy Pier in West Seattle for Vashon Island and Southworth. State ferry service also is available from Edmonds to Kingston and from Point Defiance (Tacoma) to Tahlequah (Vashon Island). Phone (206) 464-6400, or (888) 808-7977 in Wash.

Clipper Navigation provides daily round-trip passenger catamaran service between Seattle's Pier 69 and Victoria, British Columbia, and seasonal service to Friday Harbor in the San Juan Islands. For schedule information write Clipper Navigation, 2701 Alaskan Way, Seattle, WA 98121. Phone (206) 448-5000 or (800) 888-2535.

Seattle is a popular departure point for cruise ships. The ocean-going vessels dock at Pier 66 at Bell Street Pier, downtown on the waterfront and at Terminal 91 at the north end of the waterfront.

Getting Around

Street System

Seattle's avenues run north and south; they are designated by both numbers and names. Streets, also both numbered and named, run east and west. Most addresses also have area designations—N., S., E., W., NE., NW., SE. or S.W. that are important in determining correct locations. The downtown section south of Denny Way, north of Yesler Way and west of Melrose Avenue and Broadway, has avenues running parallel to Elliott Bay and streets going perpendicular to it.

Many downtown streets are one way. Synchronized traffic lights on northbound 4th Avenue and southbound 2nd Avenue make crossing the city easier. The speed limit is 30 mph or as posted. Right turns are permitted at red lights after a complete stop, unless signs indicate otherwise. Rush hours, 7-9 a.m. and 4-6 p.m., should be avoided if possible.

Portions of I-5 and I-90 have express lanes that change traffic flow during certain times; be aware of highway signs indicating times and directions.

Parking

On-street parking in downtown Seattle costs 25c for 10 minutes; $1.50 for 1 hour Mon.-Sat. 8-6. Curbside pay stations have replaced parking meters. During rush hours, however, parking is prohibited on certain streets. There are off-street parking lots throughout the downtown area. Parking garages can be found at Pacific Place (on 6th Avenue between Pine and Olive streets), on Steward Street between 2nd and 3rd avenues, on 6th Avenue between Union and Pike streets, on Pike Street between 5th and 6th avenues and on 5th Avenue between Seneca and Spring streets. Garage rates range from $3-$9 for an hour to $20-$28 for a full day.

Public Transportation

Metro Transit operates a full schedule of bus and trolley service within Seattle and King County. Passengers must have the exact fare: $1.50. These fares increase to $1.75 and $2.25, respectively, during rush hours. Passengers pay as they board on inbound and crosstown services and as they exit on outbound routes.

Free bus service is provided weekdays from 6 a.m. to 7 p.m. within the downtown area bordered by Battery Street on the north, Jackson Street on the south, 6th Avenue on the east and the waterfront on the west. For route information phone (206) 553-3000.

A 1.3-mile transit tunnel beneath Pine Street and 3rd Avenue offers fast Metro Transit and Sound Transit bus service through the downtown area. Station entrances are at Convention Place (9th Avenue and Pine Street), Westlake, University Street, Pioneer Square and the International District (5th Avenue S. and S. King Street). The transit tunnel is open Mon.-Fri. 5 a.m.-7 p.m.

South Lake Union Streetcar service operates Mon.-Fri. 6 a.m.-9 p.m., Sat. 6 a.m.-11 p.m., Sun. 10-7 between Westlake Center downtown and South Lake Union (Fairview Avenue N.) via Westlake Avenue/Terry Avenue N. and Valley Street. For information contact Metro Transit; phone (206) 553-3000.

The Monorail, which whisks passengers from its Westlake Center terminal at 5th Avenue and Pine Street to Seattle Center in 95 seconds, operates daily 9-11. The fare is $2; $1 (ages 65+ and the physically impaired); 75c (ages 5-12). For information phone (206) 905-2620.

Sound Transit provides express bus service throughout the Seattle-Tacoma-Everett-Bellevue metropolitan region. Sounder commuter trains operate Mon.-Fri. 6-9 a.m. and 4-7 p.m. between Seattle, Tacoma and Everett.

Sound Transit's Link light rail line is scheduled to start service between downtown Seattle and Seattle-Tacoma International Airport in late 2009. For information phone (206) 398-5000 or (800) 201-4900.

What To See

COAST GUARD MUSEUM NORTHWEST is at Pier 36 at 1519 Alaskan Way S. The museum displays nautical items, ship models, Coast Guard memorabilia and more than 15,000 photographs dating from the mid-1800s. Other highlights include pieces of wood from the USS *Constitution* and HMS *Bounty*. Allow 30 minutes minimum. Mon., Wed. and Fri. 9-3. Free. Phone (206) 217-6993.

COLUMBIA CENTER is downtown at 701 5th Ave., jct. Columbia St. Rising 967 feet, this 76-story building is among the tallest on the West Coast. The six-sided tower consists of alternating straight and concave facades with setbacks on the 43rd and 61st floors. Sky View, a public observation area on the 73rd floor, offers a panoramic view. Plaques at the windows identify landmarks and wall photos show the building's construction.

Note: From the 5th Ave. lobby, take an elevator to the 40th floor, then take another elevator to the 73rd floor. Allow 30 minutes minimum. Sky View open Mon.-Fri. 8:30-4:30; closed holidays. Admission $6; $4 (ages 6-12 and 55+). Pay at 5th Ave. lobby security desk mid-Sept. through Apr. 30; pay at Sky View entrance rest of year. Phone (206) 386-5151.

DISCOVERY PARK is entered via Gilman Ave. W./W. Government Way at 36th Ave. W. Named after British explorer George Vancouver's ship the *Discovery,* this 534-acre urban wilderness and wildlife sanctuary is ideal for getting away from it all—if only for an afternoon. Seattle's largest park was formerly the site of Fort Lawton, which never became a major military installation despite the fact

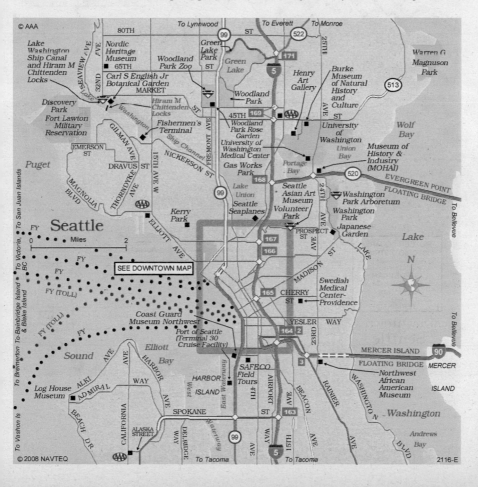

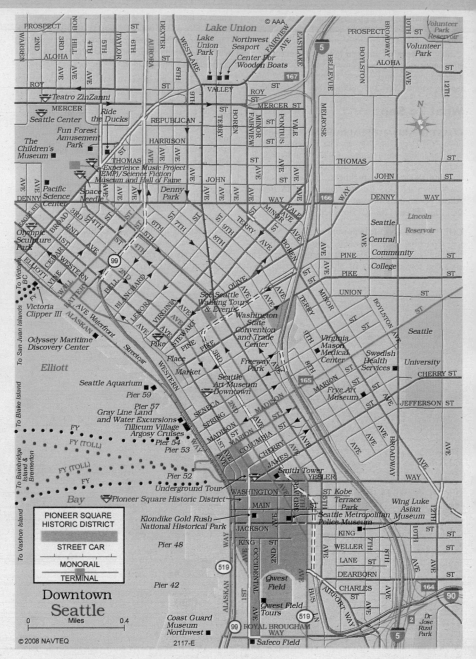

that more than a million troops passed through during World War II and some 200 buildings were built to accommodate them.

The natural setting is impressive—Magnolia Bluff overlooks Puget Sound, with (in clear weather) views of the Cascade and Olympic mountain ranges. There are cool, shady forest groves, soaring seaside cliffs, 2 miles of protected tidal beaches, sand dunes, open meadows and quiet ponds. Hiking is the best way to enjoy Discovery Park, and many visitors opt for the 2.8-mile Loop Trail that passes through lush stands of Douglas fir, western red cedar and big-leaf maple.

If you're not up for that much walking, the half-mile Wolf Tree Nature Trail is an easy jaunt through woods and wetland areas. Side trails also lead down to rocky North and sandy South beaches, distinctly different saltwater habitats that can be explored at low tide.

West Point Lighthouse, built in 1881, stands at the park's westernmost tip; the Cape Cod-style structure offers a panoramic view of the sound. The lighthouse grounds are open to the public but parking is limited; check at the visitor center for availability. The Daybreak Star Indian Cultural Center has several exhibits of Native American art. Guided bird walks are given during the spring and fall migration seasons; the park's wide variety of habitats shelter more than 230 resident and migrant species.

Picnicking is permitted. Allow 2 hours minimum. Park open daily 6 a.m.-11 p.m. Visitor center open Tues.-Sun. 8:30-5; closed holidays. Cultural center open daily 10-5. Guided, 90-minute nature and bird walks depart from the visitor center on Saturdays; reservations are required. Free. Phone (206) 386-4236 for the park or (206) 285-4425 for the cultural center.

EVERGREEN POINT FLOATING BRIDGE crosses Lake Washington between Seattle and Bellevue. The world's longest floating bridge, it consists of 33 separate pontoon units and has a total length of 7,578 feet.

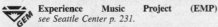 **Experience Music Project (EMP)** see Seattle Center p. 231.

FISHERMEN'S TERMINAL is off 15th Ave. W. (Emerson/Nickerson exit) at 3919 18th Ave. W. The terminal is home port to the North Pacific fishing fleet. There are many fishing vessels and a harbor-front plaza with a 30-foot-tall bronze and concrete memorial to fishermen lost at sea. Daily 24 hours. Free. Phone (206) 728-3395.

FREEWAY PARK spans Seattle's eight-lane freeway (I-5) and connects downtown to First Hill and the Washington State Convention and Trade Center. Dotted with greenery and water cascades, the park, also known as Ellis Park, is a 5-acre plaza commemorating the Bicentennial. A distinctive feature is the Narramore Fountain, a towerlike arrangement of bronze by George Tsutakawa. Daily 6 a.m.-10 p.m. Free.

CityPass and Go Seattle Card

Seattle CityPass provides Seattle visitors an opportunity to save almost 50 percent off the admission prices of five popular area attractions. CityPass ticket booklets can be purchased at any of the participating attractions: Argosy Cruises Harbor Tours, The Museum of Flight or the Experience Music Project (EMP) and Science Fiction Museum and Hall of Fame, the Pacific Science Center, the Seattle Aquarium and the Woodland Park Zoo. Tickets, which are valid for 9 days from first date of use, are $49; ages 4-12, $34. Rates are valid through Mar. 31, 2010. For further information phone (888) 330-5008. *See color ad p. 222.*

Go Seattle Card is an all-access attraction pass that offers admission to more than 30 Seattle attractions, including the Space Needle, Experience Music Project (EMP), Future of Flight Aviation Center & Boeing Tour, Woodland Park Zoo, Pacific Science Center, Argosy Cruises and more. The card is priced as low as $19.99 per day (based on a 7-day card). Go Seattle Card is available at the Experience Music Project, Argosy Cruises and the concierge desk at Pacific Place Mall; phone (800) 887-9103. *See color ad p. 223.*

FRYE ART MUSEUM is at 704 Terry Ave. The museum displays 19th- and 20th-century European and American paintings and changing exhibits of traditional and contemporary realist art. The museum also features an education wing offering art workshops. Guided tours are available. Food is available. Allow 1 hour minimum. Tues.-Sat. 10-4:30 (also Thurs. 5-7:30), Sun. noon-4:30. Guided tours Wed.-Sun. at 1:30. Closed Jan. 1, July 4, Thanksgiving and Dec. 25. Donations. Guided tours free. Phone (206) 622-9250.

GAS WORKS PARK is at 2101 N. Northlake Way; from I-5, take the 45th St. exit, go w. on N.E. 45th St. to Meridian Ave. N., turn left and proceed s. on Meridian Ave. N. to Northlake Way, then turn right (the parking lot is on the left). A plant to manufacture gas from coal was built in 1906 on this 20-acre expanse along the north shore of Lake Union. By the 1950s natural gas importation had rendered it obsolete, but the machinery still stands and presents a curious sight, looking simultaneously antiquated and futuristic.

While the generator towers remain in ruins, two older wooden structures—the boiler house and the pump house—were restored and converted into a picnic shelter and a children's "play barn." A grassy artificial hill created from construction rubble covered with topsoil is a popular spot for flying kites and watching fireworks; the sundial at its summit was created by two local artists. From this elevated

perspective the view south across the lake to the downtown skyline—flanked on the left by Capitol Hill and on the right by Queen Anne Hill—is splendid.

Picnicking is permitted. Allow 30 minutes minimum. Daily 4 a.m.-11 p.m. Free. Phone (206) 684-4075.

GREEN LAKE PARK is at 7201 E. Green Lake Dr. N.; from I-5 northbound take exit 171 to N.E. 71st St., then w. to E. Green Lake Dr. N. and the main parking lot. This urban green space is a favorite destination for walkers and joggers. The lake, carved by a glacial ice sheet, and its banks are a natural preserve for numerous tree and plant species, birds and waterfowl. Two paths—one for ambulatory users and one for cyclists and skaters—encircle the lake. Once around is 2.8 miles, just the right distance for a nice walk. Cedars, weeping willows, lush vegetation and attractive residential homes frame the water views at every turn.

The Green Lake Small Craft Center, at the lake's southwest end, has rowing, canoeing, kayaking and sailing classes, and rowing teams often use the lake for practice. The center doesn't rent boats; you can rent a canoe, paddle boat or row boat from Green Lake Boat Rental, on the northeast side of the lake. The park also is a lovely spot for a lakeside picnic. Allow 1 hour minimum. Park open daily 24 hours. Free. Phone (206) 684-4075, or (206) 527-0171 for Green Lake Boat Rental.

INTERNATIONAL DISTRICT, or ID, encompasses the blocks from Yesler Way s. to S. Dearborn St. and from 4th Ave. S E. to 12th Ave. S. Seattle's Chinatown actually is a mix of Asian communities adjoining Pioneer Square. The unofficial entry into this bustling neighborhood is through the Chinatown Gate, an archway painted lucky red that straddles S. King Street at 5th Avenue S. The orb that sits atop the gate is a fireball from heaven, a symbol of good luck.

Dragons coiled around light posts give the ID character. Serene parks—like the little nook with a flow fountain and polished stone benches in front of Starbucks, in the pedestrian plaza next to the light rail station along 5th Avenue S.—invite you to stop, relax and achieve a zen state of mind. Hing Hay Park, at the corner of S. King Street and Maynard Avenue S., is a brick-paved urban space with a lovely pagoda right in the middle and a very cool dragon mural that covers the wall of a building. It's a local gathering place where people eat lunch or take a tai chi class.

Kobe Terrace, which you can reach by walking up 7th Avenue S., is a bit of a climb but worth the effort as you gaze down at the neighborhood below from your elevated perch on the terraced hillside. Shady paths wind through the park, passing a community garden, cherry trees and a 200-year-old stone lantern on the hilltop, a gift from Kobe, Japan.

The Great Hall at Union Station, 401 S. Jackson St., was built in 1911 and restored in 1999. It features antique floor tiles, pilasters accented by a series of archways and a very impressive barrel-vaulted ceiling. These days the interior is used for weddings, high school graduation celebrations and public events. And as far as shopping goes, everyone heads to Uwajimaya, a combination grocery and department store with a food court that offers everything from burgers to *banh mi*, a Vietnamese sandwich of beef, cilantro, onions and pickled peppers served on a baguette.

Little Saigon extends from the eastern edge of the International District to Rainier Ave. S. Starting in the late 1980s, Vietnamese-Americans began opening businesses along S. Jackson Street east of I-5. Today this commercial district, a bit shabby in appearance but with its own distinct character, is filled with grocers, beauty salons, law offices, pho houses, photography studios and other small, family-owned businesses catering to the city's sizable Vietnamese-American community. Stand at the intersection of S. Jackson Street and 12th Avenue S., the heart of Little Saigon, and look around you; every storefront sports a brightly colored sign in Vietnamese.

KERRY PARK is 2 blks. w. of Queen Anne Ave. N. at the corner of W. Highland Dr. and 2nd Ave. W. Situated on the south slope of Queen Anne Hill, what this pocket park lacks in size—it's just a square of grass, a couple of benches and the abstract sculpture "Changing Form"—it makes up for with a sweeping panoramic view of downtown Seattle and Elliott Bay. This is a favorite spot for shutterbugs, particularly at sunset when city lights begin twinkling.

Stairs lead from the viewpoint down to a children's play area and a tennis court. The park is in a residential neighborhood full of gracious old homes. Residential street parking is available. A coin-operated telescope is provided. Allow 30 minutes minimum. Daily 24 hours. Free. Phone (206) 684-4075.

Marshall Park is at 7th Ave. W. and W. Highland Dr., 5 blks. w. of Kerry Park. Even smaller than Kerry Park, this tiny little grassy oasis has a few benches, a cherry tree and a delightful view overlooking Salmon Bay (part of Puget Sound), with the Magnolia Bluff neighborhood farther in the distance. Works by Pacific Northwest artists are cast in the sidewalk.

Across the street is Parsons Gardens; the Reginald H. Parsons family garden was bequeathed to the city by his children in 1956. A paved path encircles a manicured green lawn planted with flowering trees, rhododendrons and perennials. This shady little hideaway is an absolutely lovely spot for a picnic.

Residential street parking is available. Picnicking is permitted in Parsons Gardens. Allow 30 minutes minimum. Park open daily 4 a.m.-11:30 p.m.; gardens open daily 6 a.m.-9 p.m. Park and gardens free. Phone (206) 684-4075.

KLONDIKE GOLD RUSH NATIONAL HISTORICAL PARK is at 319 2nd Ave. S. in Pioneer Square Historic District. The museum commemorates the city's role in the Klondike gold rush. The Hotel Cadillac building houses a visitor center that contains photographic murals, a videotape and slide show of old-time photographs, and displays of hardware, clothing and mining relics from the gold rush era. Audiovisual programs depicting the era are shown.

Allow 2 hours minimum. Park and visitor center open daily 9-5; closed Jan. 1, Thanksgiving and Dec. 25. Gold panning demonstrations take place daily at 10 and 3, mid-June through Labor Day and by request rest of year, staffing permitting. A guided walking tour of the Pioneer Square Historic District is offered daily at 2, mid-June through Labor Day. Free. Phone (206) 220-4240.

KUBOTA GARDEN is in South Seattle's Rainier Beach neighborhood at Renton Ave. S. and S. 55th Ave. In 1927 Japanese emigrant Fujitaro Kubota bought 5 acres of logged-off swampland and created a family garden that was for many years a center for social and cultural activities in Seattle's Japanese community. This 20-acre site is now a city historical landmark and a serene haven open to the public.

Gravel paths wind among the immaculately maintained landscape of conifers, rhododendrons, Japanese red maples, various shrubs and flowering perennials. The Tom Kubota Stroll Garden has places to sit and admire a striking Weeping Blue Atlas Cedar with powdery silver-blue needles on gracefully drooping branches. The Mountainside, built by the Kubota family to celebrate the 1962 Seattle World's Fair, features waterfalls, carved stones and carefully arranged plantings. Daily dawn-dusk. Free. Phone (206) 684-4584.

LAKE UNION PARK is off Valley St. at the foot of Terry Ave. N.; take I-5 exit 167 (Mercer St./Seattle Center) to Fairview Ave. N. and turn right, turn left onto Valley St. and then right into the park via Terry Ave. N. An urban green space that highlights the maritime history of the Pacific Northwest, this 12-acre park lies at the southern end of Lake Union. A restored shoreline and beach for boat launching are currently under development; waterfront steps and a pedestrian bridge spanning the western waterway are already open to the public. Ongoing park improvements are expected to be completed by 2010.

The South Lake Union Historic Ships Wharf provides moorage for several time-honored vessels. At the water's edge is the 1941 Naval Reserve Building—locally referred to as the "Armory"—a popular location for weddings, graduation parties and other large events. But first and foremost, Lake Union Park is a great spot to enjoy breezy water views on a sunny summer day. Naval Reserve Building open Mon.-Fri. 8:30-5:30. Phone (206) 684-7254.

Center For Wooden Boats is at 1010 Valley St. The center displays more than 100 wooden vessels ranging from replicas to boats more than 100 years old. The collection includes dugout canoes from American Indian and Polynesian cultures. A Wooden Boat Festival is held the first weekend in July. The center also offers free skippered rides in their steamboat and one of their larger sailboats.

Boat rentals are available. Allow 30 minutes minimum. Daily 10-8, Memorial Day weekend-Labor Day; Tues.-Sun. 10-5, rest of year. Boat rides depart Sun. at 2 (weather permitting). Closed Jan. 1, Thanksgiving and Dec. 25. Donations. Boat rides free. Space is limited; sign-ups begin at 10 a.m. on the day of the ride. Phone (206) 382-2628.

Northwest Seaport is at 1002 Valley St. The seaport features a collection of landmark vessels moored at the end of South Lake Union Historic Ships Wharf. They include the 1904 Coast Guard lightship *Swiftsure*, which once guided commercial

and cruise ships entering and leaving the Pacific Ocean; the 1933 salmon troller *Twilight*, a type of commercial fishing boat that pulls lines hung from long poles slowly through the water; and the 1897 Pacific schooner *Wawona*, one of two surviving vessels that constituted the Pacific Northwest's once-immense commercial sailing fleet.

Hands-on "Engineer For a Day" experiences, a children's story hour and other education programs take place aboard the 1889 tugboat *Arthur Foss*. Stem-to-stern tours of the 120-foot tug also are given; reservations are necessary.

Allow 1 hour minimum. Grounds open daily 10-6, June-Sept.; hours vary rest of year. Closed Jan. 1 and Dec. 25. Donations. Phone (206) 447-9800 for tugboat tour reservations and educational program schedules.

LAKE WASHINGTON SHIP CANAL AND HIRAM M. CHITTENDEN LOCKS is in the n.w. part of the city, 4 mi. w. of I-5 exit 169. The canal connects saltwater Puget Sound with the large freshwater harbor comprising Salmon Bay, Lake Union and Lake Washington. The locks are among the busiest in the Americas and are complemented by 7 acres of botanical gardens.

The visitor center explains the history and operation of the canal and locks with historical photographs and exhibits. Also featured is a 12-minute audiovisual presentation about the canal, which is shown every 30 minutes. Summer concerts are offered most weekends at 2.

The Administration Building displays historical photographs showcasing the construction of the locks and some of the more unusual vessels that have passed through them.

Windows allow visitors to see salmon fish ladders. The heaviest salmon runs occur mid- to late June through September. A 1-hour guided tour of the locks, gardens and fish ladder is available. Allow 1 hour minimum. Lock operations can be viewed daily 7 a.m.-9 p.m. Administration Building open Mon.-Fri. 7:30-4; closed holidays. Visitor center open daily 10-6, May-Sept.; rest of year. Guided tours depart Mon.-Fri. at 1 and 3, Sat.-Sun. at 11, 1 and 3, May-Sept.; Thurs.-Mon. at 2, Mar.-Apr. and Oct.-Nov. Closed Jan. 1, Thanksgiving and Dec. 25. All facilities free. Parking $1.50 per hour. Phone (206) 783-7059.

Carl S. English Jr. Botanical Garden is adjacent to the Hiram M. Chittenden Locks, 3015 N.W. 54th St. The garden features more than 500 species of trees, shrubs and plants. Exotic species from around the world have been combined with plants indigenous to the Pacific Northwest. These include magnolias, crabapples, flowering cherries, rhododendrons, evergreen oaks, pines, palms and camellias.

A brochure outlining a self-guiding walking tour is available at the visitor center. A 1-hour guided tour includes the gardens, locks and fish ladder. Allow 30 minutes minimum. Daily 7 a.m.-9 p.m. Free. Phone (206) 783-7059.

LOG HOUSE MUSEUM is at 3003 61st Ave. S.W. The museum is in a renovated turn-of-the-20th-century log building at Alki Point, known as the "birthplace of Seattle." The museum chronicles the history of the area and features changing exhibits. Allow 30 minutes minimum. Thurs.-Sun. noon-4; closed holidays. Donations. Phone (206) 938-5293.

MERCER ISLAND FLOATING BRIDGES span Lake Washington. The bridges carry I-90 traffic over Lake Washington between Seattle and Mercer Island. The south span opened in 1940, but was destroyed by a storm in 1990. It reopened in 1993. The north span, one of the world's largest floating bridges, opened to traffic in 1989. A walkway along the north side of the north span is open to pedestrians and bicycles.

THE MUSEUM OF FLIGHT is .5 mi. n.w. of I-5 exit 158 at 9404 E. Marginal Way S. The museum chronicles the history of aerospace technology and its pioneers. Exhibits in the restored Red Barn, Boeing's first manufacturing facility, include displays of original Wright Co. documents and Boeing memorabilia 1916-58.

The Great Gallery displays 43 historic aircraft, including a replica of the 1903 Wright Flyer and a rare M/D-21 Blackbird spy plane. The Personal Courage Wing showcases 28 fighter aircraft from World Wars I and II. In the Flight Zone children learn the basics of flight through hands-on activities.

The Rendezvous in Space exhibit documents America's manned space program and the life of astronaut Charles "Pete" Conrad. The exhibit Highlights of Space: Exploring the New Frontier includes The Birth of Rocketry, Sputnik and the Space Race, and a replica of the International Space Station's laboratory.

Guided tours are available. Food is available. Allow 3 hours minimum. Daily 10-5 (also first Thurs. of the month 5-9); closed Thanksgiving and Dec. 25. Admission $14; $13 (ages 65+); $7.50 (ages 5-17); free (first Thurs. of the month 5-9). AX, DS, MC, VI. Phone (206) 764-5720. *See color ad below and on p. 222.*

MUSEUM OF HISTORY & INDUSTRY (MOHAI) is .25 mi. n. of SR 520 at 2700 24th Ave. E. in Mc-Curdy Park on Lake Washington. The museum's core exhibit, Essential Seattle, traces the 150-year history of the city with compelling artifacts, images, films and oral histories. From a basket belonging to Princess Angeline, daughter of Chief Seattle, to a WTO turtle, MOHAI has a host of items that echo the stories of the region. Traveling exhibits, lectures, classes, family events and educational programs compliment its offerings.

Daily 10-5 (also first Thurs. of the month 5-8); closed Thanksgiving and Dec. 25. Admission $8; $7 (62+ and military with ID); $6 (ages 5-17); free (first Thurs. of the month). AX, DS, MC, VI. Phone (206) 324-1126.

A Market's First Century

In August 2007 the "heart and soul of Seattle" celebrated its centennial. What better reason, then, to make a pilgrimage to Pike Place Market? Whether it's your first or your 100th visit doesn't matter; there's always something new in store at this true city institution.

The market owes its existence to consumer outrage over the high cost of produce. In 1906 the price of onions increased tenfold, and in response city councilman Thomas Revelle proposed the creation of a public street market that would bring together customers and King County's farmers. On the

© AAA / Greg Weekes

morning of Aug. 17, 1907, eight piled-high wagons pulled up to the corner of 1st Avenue and Pike Place. Everything was sold by noon, and the first market building opened for business that November.

Exploring is more fun without a planned itinerary; just follow your eyes (and nose). Three useful tips: First, the few angled parking spaces are more precious than gold; walk, take public transportation or use the Pike Place Garage at 1531 Western Ave. (one hour for free, or $5 for all-day parking if you arrive before 9:30). Second, come early (by 8 a.m.) for the best selection and to avoid crowds; lunchtime is good if you just want to be part of the wandering hordes. Third, there are restrooms on the downstairs level at the south end of the Main Arcade.

SAVE **NORDIC HERITAGE MUSEUM** is at 3014 N.W. 67th St. The museum focuses on Scandinavian cultural contributions to life in the Pacific Northwest from the 19th century to the present. Displays trace immigrants' journeys from Europe to America. Large galleries re-create the immigrants' small town settlements, the lumber and fishing industries and contributions from each of the five Nordic groups. Exhibits include handicrafts, textiles, personal effects and changing art exhibits from Scandinavia.

Allow 1 hour minimum. Tues.-Sat. 10-4, Sun. noon-4; closed Jan. 1, Thanksgiving and Dec. 24-25 and 31. Admission $6; $5 (ages 63+); $4 (students with ID). Phone (206) 789-5707.

NORTHWEST AFRICAN AMERICAN MUSEUM, 2300 S. Massachusetts St., is housed on the ground floor of the former Colman School. Displays at this small museum tell the experience of African Americans in the Pacific Northwest region (Idaho, Oregon, Washington and British Columbia). The Journey Gallery features a timeline from the present back to the pioneer era that highlights significant events and individuals. The Northwest Gallery presents changing art exhibits.

Food is available. Allow 30 minutes minimum. Wed.-Fri. 11-4:30 (also Thurs. 4:30-7), Sat. 11-4, Sun. noon-4; closed holidays. Admission $6; $4 (ages 6-17 and 61+); free (first Thurs. of the month). AX, MC, VI. Phone (206) 518-6000.

ODYSSEY MARITIME DISCOVERY CENTER is on the waterfront at Bell Street Pier (Pier 66) at 2205 Alaskan Way. The center has four galleries with more than 40 interactive exhibits that allow visitors to explore Seattle's waterfront heritage. Each gallery focuses on a different aspect of Seattle's maritime connections. An outdoor observation deck on the building's fifth floor provides panoramic views of Elliott Bay, the waterfront and the Seattle skyline.

Allow 1 hour, 30 minutes minimum. Tues.-Thurs. 10-3, Fri. 10-4, Sat.-Sun. 11-5, May-Sept.; Wed.-Thurs. 10-3, Fri. 10-4, Sat.-Sun. 11-5, rest of year. Closed Jan. 1, day before Thanksgiving, Thanksgiving and Dec. 24-25. Admission $7; $5 (ages 5-18, 62+ and military with ID); $2 (ages 2-4). AX, MC, VI. Phone (206) 374-4000.

OLYMPIC SCULPTURE PARK is on Broad St. between Western Ave. and Alaskan Way. Part of the Seattle Art Museum, this 9-acre green space—carved from a 40-foot slope with a train track and a four-lane thoroughfare running through it—is designed so that visitors can experience sculpture in an outdoor urban setting. From an elevated vantage point, the main Z-shaped path zigzags 2,200 feet down to the Elliott Bay waterfront past miniature meadow and forest grove environments that are naturally landscaped with native trees, plants and flowers.

The mostly contemporary works, a mix of permanent and on-loan installations, include "Eagle," a soaring Alexander Calder steel abstract painted a vivid orange; "Split," a stainless steel tree; and the whimsical "Typewriter Eraser, Scale X," an ordinary object rendered on a massive scale. Perhaps the most provocative work is the "Father and Son" fountain. Nude figures of a man and boy reaching out toward each other are alternately revealed and obscured by gushing water, artist Louise Bourgeois' statement on the vulnerability of familial relationships.

The glass-walled, architecturally intriguing PAC-CAR Pavilion not only provides refuge on a rainy day but has a second-story landing from which to gaze out on the expansive view of the bay and the distant Olympic Mountains. Paid parking is available beneath the pavilion; enter at Broad St. and Western Ave. Food is available. Allow 1 hour minimum.

Park open daily 30 minutes before dawn-30 minutes after dusk. Pavilion open Tues.-Sun. 10-5, May 1-Labor Day; 10-4, rest of year. Pavilion closed Jan. 1, Columbus Day, Thanksgiving, and Dec. 24-25 and 31. Park free. Pavilion parking fee $6 (0-2 hours), $12 (2-4 hours). Phone (206) 654-3100.

PIER 59 is on Alaskan Way at the foot of Pike St. A highlight of Seattle's waterfront development, the pier can be reached via a terraced walkway from Pike Place Market.

Seattle Aquarium is at 1483 Alaskan Way. The aquarium features more than 380 species of birds, fish, invertebrates and marine mammals. Highlights include the 400,000-gallon Underwater Dome, Pacific coral reef, a tide pool exhibit and discovery lab and sea otters. The Sound to Mountains Watershed features a 15-foot waterfall, salmon streams and a children's play area. Window on Washington Waters replicates the rocky, kelp-filled underwater terrain that characterizes Neah Bay, inhabited by salmon, rockfish, sea anemones and other native marine life. Educational activities include whale- and eagle-watching trips.

Food is available. Allow 1 hour, 30 minutes minimum. Daily 9:30-6. Last admission 1 hour before closing. Admission $15; $10 (ages 4-12). A combination ticket with Argosy Cruises is available. AX, MC, VI. Phone (206) 386-4300. *See color ad p. 222.*

PIKE PLACE MARKET spreads out from the corner of Pike St. and 1st Ave. Where else in Seattle can you wander among stall after stall of luscious produce, briny fresh seafood, beautiful cut flowers, savory cheeses, delectable baked goods, handicrafts galore and restaurants aplenty? Pike Place Market is the city's heart and soul, a market that opened in 1907 as an experiment in bringing together local farmers and consumers.

First-time visitors may find the sheer scope a little overwhelming, but all you really have to do is follow your eyes—or your nose. The Main Arcade stretches along Pike Place between Pike and Virginia streets. This is where many of the produce

A Market's First Century (continued)

The market is perhaps best known for its fresh produce, fishmongers and bakeries. A good location to dive in is the Main Arcade's south entrance right off Pike Place; look for Rachel, a bronze piggybank and the market's unofficial mascot, standing beneath the landmark neon "Public Market Center" sign and clock.

At Pike Place Bakery you can drool over cinnamon buns, coconut cream pies and slices of Black Forest cake before admiring the rainbow-colored displays of fruits and vegetables at the produce stands. A few steps from the bakery the guys at the Pike Place Fish Market regale shoppers with a steady stream of wisecracks while flinging whole king salmon and other fish with abandon. And speaking of entertainment, musicians, magicians and street buskers all do their performance thing on busy street corners and quiet spots under the arcades.

Following are some of our favorite Pike places; you'll no doubt discover a few of your own.

• Browse the flower tables in the Main Arcade, where dewy fresh bouquets are wrapped in crepe paper and cut flowers stand in buckets of water. Depending on the season there are tulips, irises, sunflowers, day lilies and gladiolas, to name a few. Many flower sellers are Laotian women, and you'll hear them chatting in the native Hmong language.

A Market's First Century (continued)

• If nothing else, Pike Place Market will stimulate your appetite. For a quick hunger fix, pick up a bag at the Daily Dozen Doughnut Co., 93 Pike St. These made-to-order mini delights, dusted with cinnamon or powdered sugar, dipped in chocolate or showered with candy sprinkles, are irresistible. Almost as much fun as devouring them is the loud popping sound the paper bag makes when one of the staff snaps it open with a flourish.

• Breakfast and lunch at the Sound View Cafe come with a glorious view. The window tables look out over Elliott Bay and Duwamish Head, the northern tip of the Alki Peninsula, to the distant Olympic Mountains. On a rainy day, have a warming bowl of clam chowder and a couple of pieces of ciabatta bread (to sop up every last bit) while watching fog banks roll on the water.

• The Crumpet Shop, 1503 1st Ave., specializes in the venerable English snack. Similar to an English muffin (it's also round), a crumpet is softer and spongier textured, and its porous top begs to be slathered with butter, strawberry jam or orange marmalade. Pair your crumpet with one of the shop's pre-steeped tea selections.

• Belly up to the teeny-tiny counter at Three Girls Bakery, 1514 Pike Pl., where you can get an awesome meatloaf or pastrami and corned beef sandwich. Then get in line at the equally tiny window and order to-go cookies, pastries, loaves, croissants and one of the bakery's specialties—German-style, oven-baked pretzels.

• Explore DownUnder, the three-level maze below the Main Arcade. Shops sell everything from incense, jewelry, books and antiques to vintage comics, magic paraphernalia and old travel posters.

vendors, flower sellers and specialty food retailers are located.

The fishmongers at Pike Place Fish, at the south end of the Main Arcade (near Rachel, a beloved bronze pig and the market's unofficial mascot), never fail to draw a crowd with their boisterous banter and penchant for casually tossing a whole salmon or two. Across from Pike Place Fish are the yummy cakes, croissants, cinnamon buns and other goodies sold at Pike Place Bakery. An equally tempting array is on display at Three Girls Bakery, just across Pike Place from the Main Arcade; they also have a tiny lunch counter that serves a killer meatloaf sandwich on your choice of fresh-baked bread. But after a couple of visits you'll no doubt find your own favorite market place.

Post Alley, between Pike Place and Pine Street, is a narrow pedestrian-only nook frequented by street musicians. Also on the alley is Pike Place Chowder, known for its award-winning clam chowder. DownUnder, below the Main Arcade, is a warren of specialty shops selling everything from jewelry to collectibles to toys to vintage comics. Ethnic groceries, bookstores, meat sellers and small mom 'n pop businesses also are part of the market fabric. A Starbucks branch—the very first one, on Pike Place near Stewart Street—is the lone national retailer.

If you're interested in history, the Heritage Center, on Western Avenue behind the market, has narrative panels and interactive touch-screen computers that tell the Pike Place story. The 169 steps of the Pike Street Hillclimb connect Western Avenue and Pier 59 below; waterfront access was crucial during the market's early days, since many farmers and vendors arrived by boat. Descending this flight of stairs is easy, but trudging up to the market from the waterfront is another matter, although several shops along the way can help ease the pain. (When you reach Western Avenue an elevator will take you up to the Main Arcade.)

Public parking is available in the garage at 1531 Western Ave. (behind the market), which is linked to both the Main Arcade and the waterfront by elevator. Most vendor stalls open Mon.-Sat. 10-6, Sun. 11-5; most DownUnder stores open daily 11-5. Individual business hours may vary. Produce and flower sellers, fishmongers and bakeries frequently open by 8 a.m., while restaurants stay open until 10 or 11 p.m. Heritage Center open daily 10-6. Many businesses are closed Jan. 1, Thanksgiving and Dec. 25. Free. Phone (206) 682-7453.

PIONEER SQUARE HISTORIC DISTRICT covers a 30-block area from Columbia St. s. to S. King St. and from Alaskan Way e. to 4th Ave, S. This section of Seattle has a checkered past. The site of an Indian village in the early 1850s, it developed into the young city's first downtown before disaster struck in 1889: A fire ignited by a painter's boiled-over glue pot burned out of control, leveling scores of mostly wooden buildings.

As a new downtown rose to the north, Pioneer Square seemed to be left behind, deteriorating into a motley collection of brothels, speakeasies and flop-houses. During the Depression Yesler Way became known as the first Skid Row; the expression—a derivative of Skid Road, itself a reference to logs that were literally skidded down to the waterfront from a nearby lumber mill—came to refer to any seedy area that had fallen on hard times. But by 1970 Pioneer Square had been designated a national historic district, setting the stage for its revitalization.

The original Pioneer Square was a triangle between 1st Avenue and James Street. Today this is a shady little park featuring a replica of a totem pole carved by Tlingit Indians and a statue of Suquamish and Duwamish tribal leader Chief Sealth (better known as Chief Seattle), for whom the city is named. The Pioneer Building, on 1st Avenue facing the park, is representative of the decorative Romanesque-style buildings—many of them designed by architect Elmer H. Fisher—that line the streets. The iron pergola is a replica; the 1909 original was destroyed when an 18-wheeler crashed into it in 2001.

Extending between S. Washington and S. Jackson streets is Occidental Park, a brick-paved pedestrian mall. Stop for a moment to gaze upon the life-size bronze sculptures that comprise the Fallen Firefighter's Memorial, a tribute to four Seattle firefighters who lost their lives battling a downtown warehouse fire in 1995, and to the 31 others who have died in the line of duty since 1889.

Secluded Waterfall Garden, at 2nd and S. Main streets, has water cascading down rocks, plants and outdoor seating that makes it a popular lunch spot for nearby workers and a lovely break for sightseers. The garden also marks the location of the 1907 birthplace of UPS, established in the basement of a building that formerly stood on the site.

There are shops and galleries to explore at the Grand Central Arcade, a vaulted brick arcade opening onto Occidental Park. The Elliott Bay Book Co., at the corner of 1st Avenue and S. Main Street, is a Pioneer Square institution and a great place to browse for a new purchase, linger over coffee or both. And nightlife is decidedly lively, with plenty of restaurants, bars and live music clubs.

QWEST FIELD TOURS is at 800 Occidental Ave. S. Conducted by knowledgeable guides, the tours offer a behind-the-scenes look at this state-of-the-art, 72,000-seat football stadium, home of the Seattle Seahawks. Among the areas normally off-limits that are included on the tour are the press box, playing field, visiting team locker room and a luxury suite.

Comfortable walking shoes are recommended. Allow 2 hours minimum. Tours are given daily at 12:30 and 2:30, June-Aug.; Fri.-Sat. at 12:30 and 2:30, rest of year, except during game days and special events. Admission $7; $5 (ages 3-12 and 66+). AX, DS, MC, VI. Phone (206) 381-7582.

Public Art at Qwest Field is at 800 Occidental Ave. S. Arranged mostly outside Qwest Field, this collection of fine art includes paintings, photographs, sculpture, bas-reliefs and a video installation. A pamphlet is available for self-guiding tours. Daily 24 hours. Free. Phone (206) 381-7555.

SAFECO FIELD TOURS is at jct. 1st Ave. S. and S. Royal Brougham Way at 1250 1st Ave. S. Tours explore the 20-acre, 46,500-seat home of the Seattle Mariners. The 1.25-hour tour visits the field's Mariners Hall of Fame and the Northwest Baseball Museum, plus areas typically off limits to the public, including the press box, luxury suites, dugouts and the visiting teams' clubhouse.

Comfortable walking shoes are recommended. Allow 1 hour, 30 minutes minimum. Tours depart daily at 10:30, 12:30 and 2:30, Apr.-Oct.; Tues.-Sun. at 12:30 and 2:30, rest of year. Times vary on game day; phone for schedule. Admission $8; $6 (ages 65+); $5 (ages 3-12). AX, CB, DC, DS, MC, VI. Phone (206) 346-4241 or (206) 346-4246.

SCIENCE FICTION MUSEUM AND HALL OF FAME—
see Seattle Center p. 231.

SEATTLE ART MUSEUM DOWNTOWN (SAM) is at 1300 1st Ave. (enter on 1st Ave. at the corner of Union St.). Jonathan Borofsky's 48-foot-tall, kinetic steel sculpture "Hammering Man" greets visitors outside the entrance. SAM's superbly eclectic collection encompasses American, European, African, Native American and ancient Mediterranean art. The three floors of exhibits are arranged thematically and conceptually rather than chronologically. Paintings, sculpture, furniture, wall hangings, found objects and other media are intriguingly juxtaposed in the museum's 35 galleries, challenging visitors to discover the common threads between them.

Albert Bierstadt's "Puget Sound on the Pacific Coast" is a heroically idealized 19th-century landscape painting, while "Some/One" is a sculpture comprising 40,000 stainless steel dog tags. The treasures in the Wyckoff Porcelain Room are arranged by color, shape and artistic theme. Visitors will see painted wood screens created by Tlingit Indians, 18th-century tapestries depicting mythical animals and a coffin in the shape of a Mercedes Benz. Some of the pieces feature videos about their creators. Noteworthy special exhibitions are scheduled throughout the year.

Food is available. Guided tours are available. An audio guide to the permanent collection is free with admission. Fee parking is available at the WaMu parking garage beneath the museum; enter on Union Street between 1st and 2nd avenues. Allow 2 hours minimum. Tues.-Sun. 10-5 (also Thurs.-Fri. 5-9); closed Jan. 1, Columbus Day, Thanksgiving, and Dec. 24-25 and 31.

Admission $13; $10 (ages 62+); $7 (ages 13-17 and students with ID); free to all (first Thurs. of the month); free (ages 62+ first Fri. of the month); free (ages 13-19 second Fri. of the month 5-9). Special exhibition fee $20; $17 (ages 62+); $14 (ages 13-17 and students with ID). AX, DS, MC, VI. Phone (206) 654-3100 or TTY (206) 654-3137.

SEATTLE ASIAN ART MUSEUM is at 1400 E. Prospect St. in Volunteer Park. This 40,000-square-foot museum houses one of the top seven collections of Asian art in the country. The collection encompasses a range of Chinese art, with more than 7,000 works including paintings, sculpture, calligraphy, jades, bronzes, textiles, lacquers and ceramics.

Japanese art ranges from prehistory to the present, and includes screens, ceramics, textiles and extensive archeological materials. Korean art includes large Buddhist paintings, folk art, porcelains and tomb pieces. Other galleries display works from India, the Himalayas and Southeast Asia. The Garden Court features stone sculptures.

Allow 1 hour minimum. Tues.-Sun. 10-5 (also Thurs. 5-9); closed Jan. 1, Thanksgiving and Dec. 25. Admission $5; $3 (ages 62+ and students with ID); free (ages 0-12, and first Thurs. and first Sat. of the month); free (ages 62+ first Fri. of the month). AX, MC, VI. Phone (206) 654-3100, or TTY (206) 654-3137.

SEATTLE CENTER is on the northern edge of downtown. This 74-acre campus occupies the site of Century 21 Exposition, the 1962 World's Fair. Many of the buildings now

house civic and cultural attractions. The landscaped grounds include gardens, plazas, fountains, sculpture and topiaries. Each year the campus hosts major festivals and cultural events. Phone (206) 684-7200.

The Children's Museum is in Center House, lower level. The museum encourages children and adults to participate in hands-on, innovative and educational activities. Interactive exhibits invite children to climb a mountain, explore a marmot hole, build something bigger then they are and discover new cultures. Interpretive workshops complement the exhibits.

Allow 1 hour minimum. Mon.-Fri. 10-5, Sat.-Sun. 10-6; closed Jan. 1, Thanksgiving and Dec. 25. Admission $7.50; $6.50 (ages 56+ and grandparents); free (ages 0-12 months). AX, DS, MC, VI. Phone (206) 441-1768.

Experience Music Project (EMP) is at 325 Fifth Ave. N. The museum explores the history of American popular music through state-of-the-art interactive exhibits and an extensive collection of music memorabilia. Upon entering the unusual Frank O. Gehry-designed building, visitors receive an MEG (Museum Exhibit Guide), a device with earphones that provides narration, music and text for the museum's exhibits.

The Sky Church houses a gigantic video screen that constantly pulses with music videos and performances. The Guitar Gallery follows the evolution of the favorite rock 'n' roll instrument, while an exhibit titled Northwest Passage traces the development of the Northwest music scene. Visitors can make their own music in the Sound Lab using a variety of instruments and high-tech musical gear and become a rock star in On Stage.

Food is available. Allow 4 hours minimum. Daily 10-7, Memorial Day-Labor Day; 10-5, rest of year. Admission (includes Science Fiction Museum and Hall of Fame) $15; $12 (ages 5-17, 65+, students and military with ID). AX, DC, DS, JC, MC, VI. Phone (206) 367-5483 or (877) 367-7361.

Fun Forest Amusement Park is near the base of the Space Needle at 305 Harrison St. The park features 21 thrill rides and kiddie rides including a carousel, a Ferris wheel and a roller coaster. The Entertainment Pavilion contains a 25-foot climbing wall, a laser tag area, a motion simulator, an inflatable castle, mini-golf and games.

Sun.-Thurs. noon-10, Fri.-Sat. noon-11, mid-June through Labor Day; Sat. noon-10, Sun. noon-7, Mar. 1 to mid-June and day after Labor Day-Oct. 31 (weather permitting). Entertainment pavilion open daily at 11; closing times vary. Each ride requires two or more tickets. Tickets $1. Unlimited ride pass (valid for 9 hours) $23 Mon.-Fri., mid-June through Labor Day. Phone (206) 728-1585 or (206) 728-1586.

Pacific Science Center is at 200 2nd Ave. N. The center presents science as a discovery experience rather than a subject. Exhibits include the Tropical Butterfly House and Insect Village; Kids' Works, an interactive exhibit area focusing on

sound, video and other subjects; scale model dinosaurs set in a Mesozoic environment; and an interactive planetarium. Laser light shows and two IMAX theaters, including one with 3-D capability, are among the highlights.

Allow 3 hours minimum. Daily 10-6, Memorial Day weekend-Labor Day; 10-5, rest of year. Closed Thanksgiving and Dec. 25. Exhibits admission $11; $9.50 (ages 65+); $8 (ages 6-12); $6 (ages 3-5). Combination exhibits admission and IMAX or laser matinee $15; $13.50 (ages 65+); $12 (ages 6-12); $10 (ages 3-5). Evening laser shows Thurs. $5; $8 (Fri.-Sat.). MC, VI. Phone (206) 443-2001 for general information, (206) 443-2850 for laser show schedule or (206) 443-4629 for IMAX film schedule. *See color ad p. 222.*

Science Fiction Museum and Hall of Fame shares the building with the Experience Music Project (EMP) at 325 Fifth Ave. N. Within an eye-catching Frank O. Gehry-designed structure, the museum explores the science fiction genre within a series of five exhibit galleries. The Homeworld gallery includes the Hall of Fame honoring individuals, mostly authors, for their contributions to science fiction.

Within Fantastic Voyages is Spacedock, which creates the illusion of looking through a curved window on a space station as various spaceships arrive and depart. A similar screen in the Brave New Worlds gallery offers dramatic views of visionary cityscapes from film and television. Monsters, robots and aliens occupy the Them! gallery.

Food is available. Allow 3 hours minimum. Daily 10-8, Memorial Day weekend-Labor Day; Wed.-Mon. 10-5, rest of year. Admission (includes Experience Music Project) $15; $12 (ages 5-17, 65+, students and military with ID). AX, DC, DS, JC, MC, VI. Phone (206) 367-5483 or (877) 367-7361.

Space Needle is at 219 4th Ave. N. Reaching to a height of 605 feet, the Space Needle has been Seattle's signature structure since it was built as the centerpiece for the 1962 World's Fair. An observation deck at the 520-foot level provides panoramas of the city, Puget Sound and the Cascade and Olympic mountains. An orientation exhibit offers information on major points visible from the observation deck. Telescopes are available on the outside deck walkway. A restaurant atop the needle slowly revolves full circle, providing awesome views.

Allow 1 hour minimum. Daily 9 a.m.-midnight. Elevator $16; $14 (ages 65+); $8 (ages 4-13). Single-day, two-visit ticket $20; $18 (ages 65+); $12 (ages 4-13); free to restaurant patrons. AX, DC, DS, MC, VI. Phone (206) 905-2100. *See color ad p. 232.*

SEATTLE METROPOLITAN POLICE MUSEUM is in Pioneer Square at 317 Third Ave. S. The museum recounts the history of law enforcement in Seattle beginning with the first appointed marshal in 1861 to the present. Police memorabilia on display include uniforms, weapons, photographs and various

space needle

"Live the View"

Take a journey to SkyCity, our world-famous revolving restaurant, where we serve the finest in Pacific Northwest cuisine. Or, soar a little higher to the Observation Deck, 520 feet above ground, where you'll discover breathtaking indoor and outdoor viewing. At the base you'll find our new glass-enclosed pavilion and gift shop SpaceBase, which features hundreds of items made specifically for the Space Needle.

For Reservations and Information call 1-800-937-9582, or visit www.spaceneedle.com

Photo courtesy of: Chris Eden - Callison Architecture, Inc.

other items. An actual jail cell and the city's original 911 call center from 1970 are exhibited. One area of the museum features uniforms children can try on.

Allow 30 minutes minimum. Tues.-Sat. and holidays 11-4; closed Jan. 1, Thanksgiving and Dec. 25. Admission $3; $2.70 (ages 66+); $1.50 (ages 0-12). Phone (206) 748-9991.

SEWARD PARK is at 5902 Lake Washington Blvd. S. This 300-acre park occupies all of the Bailey Peninsula, a forested finger of land jutting out from the southwestern shore of Lake Washington. The city bought the peninsula in 1911 for $322,000 and named it after William H. Seward, the former U.S. secretary of state responsible for the Alaska Purchase. The peninsula was an island before the Montlake cut of the Lake Washington Ship Canal was completed in 1916, which lowered the lake level by about 9 feet.

There are nearly 6 miles of trails. The flat, 2.4-mile paved loop trail that follows the shoreline is popular with walkers and cyclists. The northern two-thirds of the peninsula is cloaked with old growth forest of Douglas fir, western red cedar, western hemlock, big-leaf maple and madrona; forest trails provide occasionally rugged but beautifully serene hiking opportunities. Also on the park grounds are a native plant garden, an amphitheater, an art studio and a playground.

Picnicking is permitted. Allow 1 hour minimum. Daily 6 a.m.-11 p.m. (parking lot daily 6 a.m.-10 p.m.). Free. Phone (206) 684-4396.

(SAVE) **SMITH TOWER** is on 2nd Ave. and Yesler Way. This 38-story building was the tallest west of the Mississippi River when it was built in 1914. Of interest is the Chinese Room, where intricately carved Chinese characters tell the story of the Puget Sound area. An observation floor offers views of Seattle, the Olympics, Mount Rainier and the Cascades. Observation level open daily 10-8, Apr. through Oct. 31; Sat.-Sun. 10-4, rest of year. Hours may vary; phone ahead. Admission $7.50; $6 (ages 60+ and students with ID); $5 (ages 6-12). Phone (206) 622-4004.

SPACE NEEDLE— see Seattle Center p. 231.

TEATRO ZINZANNI is near Seattle Center at the corner of 3rd and Mercer sts. Many people dress up for this energetic, fun-filled evening of comedy, Cirque du Soleil-style entertainment, live music, theater, improv and dance. The 3-hour production includes a five-course meal of seasonal delights (anyone for figs and fresh goat cheese drizzled with olive oil and honey, followed by grilled albacore tuna with a smoked paprika crust?). The changing menu is overseen by celebrity chef Tom Douglas of Seattle's trendy Dahlia Lounge restaurant.

Guests are seated within a circular cabaret tent imported from Belgium. The ever-evolving show—no two performances are quite the same—is illed with a revolving cast of talented players. Zin-Zanni's wait staff are practically a show unto themselves, continually interacting with theatergoers, and if you're lucky you'll end up being a part of the proceedings. The folks who produce the show also are responsible for Bumbershoot, the city's big, end-of-summer music festival.

Although all ages are welcome, this is a long evening and much of the humor will be lost on young children. Performances begin at 6:30 Wed.-Sat., 5:30 Sun. The lounge opens for creatively prepared cocktails an hour prior to showtime. Performances $104 Wed.-Fri. and Sun., $120 Sat. Rates are higher for premium seating and on holidays. Reservations are required; tickets normally can be purchased up to 8 weeks in advance. Metered street parking and pay garages are nearby. AX, MC, VI. Phone (206) 802-0015 for the box office.

UNIVERSITY OF WASHINGTON occupies a 639-acre campus on 15th Ave. N.E. between Portage Bay and N.E. 45th St. With more than 35,000 students, UW is one of the country's largest single-campus schools. Established in downtown Seattle as the Territorial University of Washington in 1861, it relocated to its present site in 1895. In 1909 the university hosted the Alaska-Yukon-Pacific Exposition; its legacy is today's beautifully landscaped campus. The Rainier Vista promenade, centered on Drumheller Fountain, is aligned to provide a perspective of Mt. Rainier and recalls the exposition's grand scale.

Red Square, named for its brick pavement, is the heart of the campus. Extending northeast from this square is Pierce Lane, formerly known as The Quad, a shaded promenade flanked by Collegiate Gothic-style brick buildings. The dramatic facade of Suzzalo Library forms the square's east flank. It's the largest of UW's more than two dozen libraries, which collectively contain more than 6.5 million volumes and 7.5 million microforms.

The University of Washington Information and Visitor Center is on the west side of Odegaard Undergraduate Library. Free, 90-minute campus tours depart from Schmitz Hall, third floor Admissions Office lobby, at 1410 N.E. Campus Pkwy. Tours given Mon.-Fri. at 10:30 and 2:30, Sat. at 10:30 (Sat. tours meet at the George Washington Statue in front of the visitor center). Visitor center open Mon.-Fri. 8:30-5. Phone (206) 543-9198 for the visitor center, (206) 543-9686 for campus tour information.

Burke Museum of Natural History and Culture is at the 17th Ave. and N.E. 45th St. entrance to the campus. The museum focuses on the natural and cultural history of the Pacific Rim. Displays draw from a permanent collection numbering more than 5 million natural specimens, while diverse special exhibits portray this part of the world's natural and cultural stories. Family and children's events are scheduled year-round.

Food is available. Allow 30 minutes minimum. Daily 10-5 (also first Thurs. of the month 5-8);

closed Jan. 1, July 4, Thanksgiving and Dec. 25. Admission $8; $6.50 (ages 62+); $5 (ages 5-18 and students with ID); free (first Thurs. of the month). Phone (206) 543-5590.

Henry Art Gallery is on 15th Ave. N.E. at N.E. 41st St. The gallery presents changing exhibits of contemporary art. Tues.-Sun. 11-5 (also Thurs. 5-8); closed holidays. Admission $10; $6 (ages 62+); free (ages 0-12 and students with ID); donations (Thurs.). MC, VI. Phone (206) 543-2280.

VOLUNTEER PARK is entered at E. Galer St. and 15th Ave. E. and E. Prospect and 14th Ave. E. The park encompasses 44.5 acres of formal gardens and extensive lawns on Capitol Hill. The park was designed in 1912 by the renowned Olmstead Brothers architectural firm. The Conservatory has a large collection of cactuses, succulents, orchids and tropical and subtropical plants. A spiral stairway leads to the top of the 75-foot Water Tower for an excellent view of the city, its lakes and nearby mountains.

Park open daily 6 a.m.-11 p.m. Conservatory open daily 10-6, Memorial Day weekend-Labor Day; 10-4, rest of year. Admission $3. Phone (206) 684-4743.

WASHINGTON PARK ARBORETUM encompasses 230 acres extending from 40th Ave. E. and E. Madison St. n. to SR 520 and Lake Washington. In a city blessed with a preponderance of urban green spaces, Washington Park Arboretum is one of the loveliest. It contains more than 5,500 different kinds of plants from around the world—including many species native to the Pacific Northwest—that lend the overall impression of a natural but meticulously manicured woodland.

There are notable collections of conifers, maples, rhododendrons, camellias, hollies and magnolias. The sheer variety of trees and shrubs makes this an all-year destination; there is always something visually pleasing to see among the different types of plants concentrated in the main landscape areas. Spring, of course, is a highlight, exemplified by the azaleas, dogwoods and flowering cherry trees that grace Azalea Way, a promenade three-quarters of a mile long.

Rhododendron Glen, planted on a hillside valley off Arboretum Drive E., has varieties from dwarfs to tree forms and is ablaze with color from April into June. In fall Japanese maples turn a vivid array of reds and purples, and the bright yellow blooms of witch hazel in the Joseph A. Witt Winter Garden reveal that not all plants go into cold-season hibernation.

Allow 1 hour, 30 minutes minimum. Lake Washington Boulevard E., which runs through the arboretum, is open daily 24 hours. Arboretum open daily dawn-dusk; gates at the north and south end of Arboretum Drive E. are closed during non-open hours. Graham Visitors Center open daily 10-4; closed holidays. Free 60- to 90-minute guided tours depart from the visitors center first and third Sun. of the month at 1, Jan.-Nov. Free. Phone (206) 543-8800.

Japanese Garden is within the arboretum, just off Lake Washington Blvd. E. and just n. of Madison St. Designed by a team of landscape architects under the supervision of celebrated Japanese garden designer Juki Iida, this is a world of forests, lakes, mountains and a village compressed into a serene 3.5-acre space. Conifers, maples, flowering cherry trees, rhododendrons, camellias, Japanese irises, ferns and water lilies are among the plants growing in harmony with rocks and water. A copper-shingled tea house, a lake spanned by earthen and plank bridges, an 11-tiered pagoda and an *azumaya*, or sheltered resting place, are integral parts of the garden.

Daily 10-8, May 1 to mid-Aug.; 10-7, mid-Aug. to mid-Sept.; opens Tues.-Sun. at 10 (closing time varies), Mar.-Apr. and mid-Sept through Nov. 26. Forty five-minute presentations of Chado, a ritual Japanese tea ceremony, take place on select Saturdays, Sundays and Mondays at times ranging from 11 to 2:30, mid-Apr. to late June. Admission $5; $3 (ages 6-17, 65+, college students with ID and the physically impaired). Chado tickets $10. Phone (206) 684-4725.

WING LUKE ASIAN MUSEUM is at 719 S. King St. The museum presents a variety of cultural exhibits contributed by Asian-Pacific communities in the Northwest. Examples of contemporary art, historical items and changing exhibits are displayed. The museum commemorates Seattle's first Asian-American city councilman, who was active in the city's International District. Walking tours are offered (*see Walking Tours p. 236*).

Allow 30 minutes minimum. Tues.-Sun. 10-5 (also 5-8 first Thurs. and third Sat. of the month); closed holidays. Admission $8; $6 (ages 13-18 and 62+); $5 (ages 5-12); free (first Thurs. and third Sat. of the month). MC, VI. Phone (206) 623-5124.

WOODLAND PARK ZOO is at 601 N. 59th St. The 92-acre zoological garden is home to more than 300 animal species representing various worldwide ecosystems. The Tropical Rain Forest features 700 plant species along with jaguar and gorilla exhibits, while Tropical Asia offers the Elephant Forest. The Adaptations Building is home to the world's largest lizards, endangered Komodo dragons native to Indonesia.

The Trail of Vines features endangered orangutans, lion-tailed macaques and siamangs. The African Savanna has hippopotamuses, giraffes, monkeys, oryxes, zebras, African wild dogs and lions. The Northern Trail habitat features grizzly bears, river otters, gray wolves, mountain goats and bald eagles. The Temperate Forest is a wetlands exhibit that includes waterfowl, and Bug World features cockroaches, walking sticks and tarantulas. A new flamingo exhibit debuted in 2008 and a penguin exhibit is slated for a summer 2009 opening.

Allow 2 hours minimum. Daily 9:30-6, May 1-Sept. 30; 9:30-4, rest of year. Closed Dec. 25. Animal contact area open Memorial Day weekend-Labor Day. Admission May-Sept. $15; $13 (ages 65+ and the physically impaired); $10 (ages 3-12) Admission rest of year $11; $9 (ages 65+ and the physically impaired); $8 (ages 3-12). Carousel rides $2. Parking $4.50. AX, MC, VI. Phone (206) 684-4800 or TTY (206) 684-4026. *See color ad p. 222.*

Woodland Park Rose Garden is adjacent to Woodland Park Zoo. A 2.5-acre cultivated area with more than 5,000 plants representing 290 varieties of roses, the garden also features a lily pool and topiary shrubbery. Prime bloom season extends from June through October. Daily 7 a.m.-dusk. Free. Parking $4 during zoo hours. Phone (206) 684-4863.

What To Do

Sightseeing

Visitors can tour Seattle's eye-catching, glass-and-steel Seattle Central Library, at the corner of Fourth Avenue and Madison Street. Opened in May 2004, the futuristic building designed by Rem Koolhaas features stunning glass curtain walls supported by a diamond-shaped grid, cantilevered platforms jutting from a central structure and a soaring nine-level atrium.

Architectural and general interest tours of the library are available on a first-come, first-served basis by signing in at the Information Desk on Level 3; reservations are not accepted. Phone (206) 386-4636.

Boat Tours

ARGOSY CRUISES departs from piers 55/56 at the foot of Seneca St. and Lake Union. The company offers a 1-hour narrated Harbor Cruise along the waterfront and past the shipyards and a 2.5-hour Locks Cruise through the Hiram Chittenden Locks to Lake Union. The 2-hour Lakes Seattle Cruise includes Lake Union and Lake Washington and departs from AGC Marina on South Lake Union. Lunch and dinner cruises also are available aboard the Royal Argosy from Pier 56.

The 1-hour Harbor Cruise departs daily at 11, 12:15, 1:30, 2:45, 4 and 5:15, early June-late Sept.; at 12:15, 1:30, 2:45 and 4, mid-Mar. to early June and late Sept. to late Oct.; Mon.-Fri. at 1:30, Sat.-Sun. at 1:30 and 2:45, rest of year. Closed Thanksgiving and Dec. 25. The 2.5-hour Locks Cruise departs daily at 10, 1, 3:30 and 6:30, early June-early Sept.; at noon and 3:30, late Mar.-early June and mid-Sept. to late Oct.; at 1, rest of year. Closed Thanksgiving and Dec. 25. The 2-hour Lakes Seattle Cruise departs daily at 11, 1:15 and 3:30, early June-early Sept.; Mon.-Fri. at 1, Sat.-Sun. at 1 and 3:30, late Apr.-early June and early Sept. to mid-Oct.; Fri.-Sun. at 1, late Mar.-late Apr. and mid-Oct. through Dec. 31; Sat.-Sun. at 1, rest of year. Closed Dec. 25.

Harbor Cruise fare Apr.-Sept. $21; $8.50 (ages 5-12). Harbor Cruise fare rest of year $17; $8.50 (ages 5-12). Locks Cruise fare Apr.-Sept. $39; $13 (ages 5-12). Locks Cruise fare rest of year $32.50; $11 (ages 5-12). Lakes Seattle Cruise fare Apr.-Sept.

$31.50; $10 (ages 5-12). Lake Cruise–Seattle fare rest of year $25.50; $9 (ages 5-12). A fuel surcharge may apply. Reservations are recommended. AX, DC, DS, JC, MC, VI. Phone (206) 623-1445 or (800) 642-7816. *See color ad p. 222.*

SAVE GRAY LINE LAND AND WATER EXCURSIONS departs from the Sheraton Seattle Hotel at 1400 6th Ave., with pickups offered from most downtown hotels. The approximately 6-hour narrated City Sights/Cruise the Locks Combo tour combines Argosy's Locks Cruise *(see attraction listing)* with Gray Line's Seattle City Tour by motor coach. Tour departs daily at 9, Mar.-Oct. Fare $61; $30.50 (ages 2-12). AX, MC, VI. Phone (206) 624-5077 or (800) 426-7532.

RIDE THE DUCKS departs from the n.e. corner of 5th and Broad St. near the Space Needle. These whimsical tours (sing-alongs are encouraged) are conducted in World War II-era amphibious vehicles that operate on both land and water. The tour includes downtown Seattle highlights as well as sightseeing on Lake Union.

Allow 1 hour, 30 minutes minimum. Departures daily 10-5, Apr.-Oct.; otherwise varies rest of year. Fare $23; $13 (ages 0-12). Reservations are recommended. MC, VI. Phone (206) 441-3825 or (800) 817-1116.

TILLICUM VILLAGE tour boats depart from Pier 55 on Alaskan Way at the foot of Seneca St. Cruises cross Elliott Bay and Puget Sound to Blake Island State Park, where passengers can visit the Tillicum Village Northwest Coast Indian Cultural Center *(see attraction listing p. 245)* and enjoy displays of regional American Indian art, a traditional baked salmon dinner and an interpretive stage show.

Allow 4 hours minimum. Tours depart Seattle daily at 11:30 and 4:30, mid-July to mid-Aug.; daily

schedule varies rest of year. Round-trip fare (transportation only) $40; $37 (ages 60+); $12 (ages 5-12). Round-trip fare (including salmon dinner and stage show) $79; $72 (ages 60+); $30 (ages 5-12). All fares include tax; a fuel surcharge may apply. Reservations are recommended. AX, DS, MC, VI. Phone (206) 933-8600 or (800) 426-1205.

VICTORIA CLIPPER III departs from Pier 69 at 2701 Alaskan Way. The high-speed passenger vessel travels north through scenic Deception Pass to Friday Harbor in the San Juan Islands, arriving at 11:15. Passengers may disembark or, from late June to early September, stay aboard for a 2.5-hour sea life and orca whale-watching excursion complete with onboard naturalist. Whales are sighted more than 90 percent of the time. The trip back to Seattle departs at 4:30, arriving at 7:15 p.m.

Passengers should inquire about payment policy and where to park. Allow a full day. Boarding daily at 7:45, mid-May to early Sept.; Sat.-Sun. at 7:45, early-late Sept. Whale watch fare late June to early Sept. $100 (Fri.-Sun.); $85 (Mon.-Thurs.). Fare mid-May through late June and early-late Sept. $70. One child ages 0-11 free with each paying adult; otherwise half price. Listed fares require a minimum 1-day advance purchase. AX, MC, VI. Phone (206) 448-5000 or (800) 888-2535.

Bus and Trolley Tours

SAVE Gray Line Tours conducts bus trips through Seattle and its environs, including Mount Rainier and Mukilteo's Future of Flight Aviation Center & Boeing Tour. Day trips to Victoria, British Columbia, also are available. Contact Gray Line of Seattle for further information; phone (206) 626-5208 or (800) 426-7532.

SAVE Gray Line's Double Decker Tours offers narrated loop trips through the downtown area and Seattle Center in a double-decker motorcoach. The

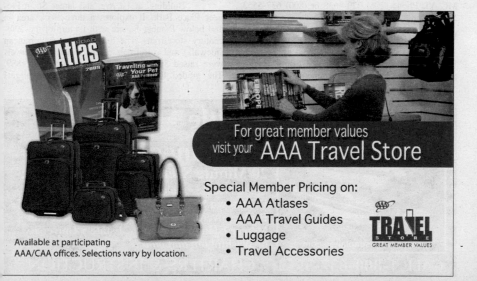

coaches make seven scheduled stops at 30-minute intervals daily 9-6, May-Sept. Tickets can be purchased from the driver. A consecutive-day pass good for 2 days is $21; $10.50 (ages 2-11). Phone (206) 624-5077 or (800) 426-7532.

Seattle Tours offers 3-hour narrated, interactive mini-coach tours of the city's highlights, including the waterfront, Pioneer Square, Ballard Locks and various neighborhoods. Door-to-door service is provided from downtown Seattle, Bellevue, SeaTac and Tukwila hotels. Tour size is limited to 24 people.

The same company operates Mount Rainier Tours. The guided mini-coach excursions to Mount Rainier National Park and the surrounding farmlands and meadows include stops at waterfalls, scenic overlooks, old-growth forests and interpretive centers, allowing opportunities for wildlife viewing, hiking and walking. For more information about either tour or to make reservations, phone (206) 768-1234 or (888) 293-1404.

Plane Tours

Seaplane sightseeing flights over the Seattle area depart daily from Kenmore Air at downtown Seattle's Lake Union. Flights last approximately 20 minutes. Daily scheduled departures to San Juan Island and Victoria, BC, also are available. Phone [SAVE] Kenmore Air, (425) 486-1257 or (800) 543-9595. Several companies also offer sightseeing flights of the area departing from Renton at the south end of Lake Washington.

SEATTLE SEAPLANES is off I-5 exit 167 to 1325 Fairview Ave. E. Departing from Lake Union, Seattle Seaplanes offers 20-minute tours highlighting the greater Seattle area. Scenic flights also are available to Mount Rainier and Mount St. Helens. Daily 8-dusk. Fare $67.50; a fuel surcharge may apply. MC, VI. Phone (206) 329-9638 or (800) 637-5553. *See color ad.*

Walking Tours

Chinatown Discovery Tours, offered by the Wing Luke Asian Museum *(see attraction listing p. 234),* provides an Asian cultural experience including a program and a leisurely guided walking tour of Seattle's Chinatown/International District. For information and reservations phone (206) 623-5124.

[SAVE] Seattle Food Tours offers guided 2.5-hour culinary and cultural walking tours of the Belltown and Pike Place Market neighborhoods, exploring cuisine, history, architecture and public art as well as shopping and entertainment venues along the way. Phone (206) 334-7119 for information or (800) 979-3370 for reservations.

If you want to focus on Pike Place Market itself, Taste Pike Place offers three different tasting tours: a morning Breakfast Bites tour, a Lunch Sampler and an afternoon Food & Wine tour. In addition to enjoying a variety of mouth-watering market goodies you'll find out how to select fresh fish and when seasonal produce is at its best. Phone (206) 725-4483 for information and reservations.

SEE SEATTLE WALKING TOURS & EVENTS leaves from Westlake Plaza at 4th and Pine sts.; meet at the Starbucks outside seating area. These comfortably paced guided walking tours offer a street-level overview of downtown Seattle, its art, architecture and history. Pike Place Market, the waterfront and the Pioneer Square Historic District are among the highlights. A stop for lunch is scheduled. Periodically other walking tours and scavenger hunts are offered.

Standard tour departs Mon.-Sat. at 10 (arrive 5 minutes prior to departure) and ends at about 4. Closed major holidays. Fee $20. Departures require a minimum of 6 people. A fee is charged for the Smith Tower Observatory. Tour prices do not include lunch. Confirmed reservations are required. Phone (425) 226-7641.

UNDERGROUND TOUR departs from Doc Maynard's Public House in the Pioneer Building, at 1st Ave. and James St. in Pioneer Place Park. It explores a three-block area in and below Pioneer Square with its turn-of-the-20th-century storefronts. The tour includes subterranean sidewalks and storefronts created when street levels were raised 8 to 35 feet following a fire in 1889. The guided tour, humorously narrated, highlights

Seattle's history in the aftermath of the fire that destroyed 30 blocks of downtown Seattle as well as 10 piers on the wharf.

Comfortable walking shoes and weather-appropriate clothing are recommended. Allow 1 hour, 30 minutes minimum. Daily departure times vary. Visitors should arrive at the departure point at least 30 minutes before their desired tour time. Fee $15; $12 (ages 13-17, 60+ and college students with ID); $7 (ages 7-12). Prices may vary. Phone (206) 682-4646.

Sports and Recreation

Seattle offers sports from skin diving to mountain climbing; its residents boast that its location and climate make it possible to sail in the morning and ski that afternoon. The extensive city park system includes more than 5,000 acres of parkland and boulevards. The many state parks in the vicinity provide recreational and camping facilities.

A variety of local outdoor recreation books and maps are sold in the Travel Store at AAA Washington offices in the metropolitan area.

Spectator sports run the gamut in Seattle. There is **automobile racing** at two major raceways in the area: Pacific Raceways in Kent, (253) 639-5927, and Evergreen Speedway in Monroe, (360) 805-6100. Racing schedules vary.

The NFL's Seattle Seahawks play **football** at Qwest Field at 800 Occidental Ave. S. Major league **baseball** is represented by the Mariners, who play at Safeco Field; the 47,116-seat stadium with a retractable roof is at First Avenue S. and S. Atlantic St.

The Seattle Storm plays WNBA **basketball** in KeyArena at Seattle Center. The Seattle Thunderbirds **hockey** team takes to the ice at Kent Events Center in Kent. Area college teams participate in all major sports.

During the August Seafair, Lake Washington provides a course for **hydroplane races. Boating** is available on freshwater Lake Washington, saltwater Puget Sound or both, thanks to the locks and canal connecting the two. A multitude of marinas provides moorage facilities. Any type of craft can be rented, from small sailboats or canoes to large seagoing yachts.

Golf courses, both municipal and commercial, are plentiful, as are driving ranges and pitch and putt courses. Some private clubs extend reciprocal privileges to visitors who are members of certain out-of-town golf clubs. The Seattle Parks and Recreation Department owns three 18-hole courses operated by Premier Golf Centers; phone (206) 285-2200 for information.

Hiking and **horseback riding** enthusiasts will find miles of forest trails in nearby areas and mountains. The U.S. Forest Service and Park Service, phone (206) 470-4060, can provide information about trails. The telephone directories contain listings of stables and academies.

Fishing opportunities are plentiful. Freshwater fishing is available from piers at Green Lake and Lake Washington, in county parks and in area lakes and streams. The Washington State Department of Fish and Wildlife, phone (425) 775-1311, is the best source for freshwater license requirements and information.

Spot Tail Salmon Guides offers private salmon fishing and saltwater fly-fishing trips daily; phone (206) 283-6680. Piers 57 and 86 are public fishing piers on Elliott Bay. Charters for Puget Sound or deep-sea fishing off the coast can be arranged; consult the telephone directories.

White-water rafting, float trips and bald eagle sightseeing tours are offered on rivers in the Cascades and Olympics. The season for white-water rafting is April through September; bald eagle sightseeing tours take place December through February. Rates for such trips are commensurate with offerings, but the average fee for a full-day excursion is $60-$90.

Reservations for trips can be made through the following agencies: Downstream River Runners, (206) 906-9227; River Recreation, Inc., (425) 741-5901 or (800) 464-5899; Riverrider.com, (206) 448-7238 or (800) 448-7238; and [SAVE] Rivers Inc., (425) 822-5296. Most agencies' offices are open weekdays during working hours.

Kayaking is available on area lakes including Lake Union. Rentals and tours are available from Northwest Outdoor Center on Lake Union, (206) 281-9694 or (800) 683-0637; and Moss Bay Rowing & Kayak Center, (206) 682-2031. Alki Kayak Tours offers guided sea kayaking trips, (206) 953-0237. **Parasailing** on Elliott Bay is offered during the summer months; contact Pier 57 at Bell Street Harbor at (206) 622-5757.

Mountain climbing and **skiing** are possible at many challenging spots in the Seattle area. Guided trips to the summit of Mount Rainier as well as instructions in climbing techniques are available *(see Mount Rainier National Park p. 182)*. Major ski areas within a short drive of the city are noted under the listings for Snoqualmie Pass, Skykomish and Crystal Mountain *(see place listings p. 266, p. 266 and p. 165).*

Swimming and **scuba diving** are favorite summer sports. There are saltwater beaches at Alki and Golden gardens and freshwater beaches on Lake Washington and Green Lake as well as several public swimming pools within the city. The telephone directory provides information about scuba diving instruction and equipment rental.

Since the 1890s **bicycling** has been a popular sport in Seattle. The city has 90 miles of signed bike routes and 30 miles of bike-pedestrian trails. The free Seattle Bicycling Guide Map details the city's extensive network of bicycle lanes, bicycle trails and streets commonly used by bicyclists. The map is available at area bicycle shops, branches of the public library and from the City Transportation Department; phone (206) 684-7583.

The Burke-Gilman Trail, designed for bicycling and hiking, extends 15.5 miles from 8th Ave. N.W. and Leary Way to Tracy Owen Station Park at 61st Avenue and SR 522. The trail skirts the University of Washington campus and offers good views of the area. North of Lake Washington it connects with the Sammamish River Trail, which then continues another 12 miles to Marymoor Park *(see Redmond p. 255)*.

One of Seattle's most popular bicycle paths is the 3-mile paved trail bordering Green Lake in the park of the same name. Many other routes connect with the city parks; others are along the waterfront.

Bike rentals are available at Bikestation Seattle, 311 Third Ave. S., phone (206) 332-9795; and at Gregg's Greenlake Cycle, 7007 Woodlawn Ave. N.E., phone (206) 523-1822.

Facilities for **tennis** and other sports also are available. The city park department maintains nearly 100 public courts, some of which are lighted for night matches; several private tennis clubs extend reciprocal privileges to travelers. Commercial ranges for **rifle** and **skeet shooting** are listed in the telephone directory. City parks have facilities for both **jogging** and **lawn bowling.** For further information phone (206) 684-4075.

Shopping

Seattle is one of those cities where a ho-hum mall is one of the *least* enticing shopping choices. Oh, there are plenty of them—it's just that there are so many other interesting places to browse and spend your hard-earned money.

Starting with Pike Place Market *(see attraction listing p. 227)*. Let's get the small caveats out of the way. Yes, it's touristy. Yes, it can get crowded (especially on Saturday and most other days beginning around 11 a.m. until 2 or 3). Yes, street parking is practically nonexistent (the Pike Place Market Parking Garage at 1531 Western Ave. is your best bet if driving). Yes, it helps to know where the restrooms are (on the downstairs level at the north and south ends of the Main Arcade).

But these are minor inconveniences in the face of bountiful pleasures. Those in the know—among them Seattleites who do their regular food shopping here—go early on a weekday morning when the vendors are setting up. Fruit, vegetables and flowers are market mainstays, and locally grown so they change with the seasons. Grab some crisp apples, a golden peach or a perfect little bunch of grapes. Select a mixed bouquet of vibrantly colorful blooms. Then head to one of the market bakeries (Pike Place Bakery and Three Girls Bakery are both divine) for a cinnamon and sugar-glazed apple fritter or a flaky almond croissant. Pick up a paper sack full of hot, fresh mini doughnuts from Daily Dozen Donuts and try not to eat every single one.

In other words, Pike Place Market is browser's heaven. The sights, the smells, the sidewalk musicians, the seafood-tossing fishmongers and the ambling crowds all make it a sensory experience of the highest order. And don't forget to explore the warren of art, craft and clothing shops "DownUnder," where you'll find everything from nag champa and incense burners (Taj Mahal Emporium) to rings, bracelets and necklaces (House of Jade) to squirt pens, fart bombs and joy buzzers (The Magic Shop).

And we haven't even mentioned Post Alley (in front of the Main Arcade), the 1st Avenue Buildings (between Stewart and Virginia streets) and the Pine to Stewart Block.

You could easily spend the whole day here, but there's lots more shopping to be done. The Pioneer Square Historic District (see attraction listing p. 228) has plenty of window-shopping potential. Poke around Pioneer Square Antique Mall (602 1st Avenue at James Street) for vintage jewelry, collectibles, clocks and toys. Laguna Vintage Pottery (116 S. Washington St.) is packed with things like ceramic plates and hand-painted vases. Men who aren't afraid to wear kilts will find exactly what they're looking for at Utilikilts (620 1st Ave.). Elliott Bay Book Co. (101 S. Main St. at 1st Avenue) is the perfect place to look for a new tome and then leaf through it in their cozy downstairs cafe over coffee and a tasty organic veggie sandwich. This bookstore is a Pioneer Square institution.

The neighboring International District (see attraction listing p. 222) is fun to explore. The Yummy House Bakery (522 6th Ave. S.; look for the yellow sign) has all kinds of "Hong Kong-style" cakes and pastries, including squares of feather-light sponge cake—usually sitting on a tray on top of the order counter—egg tarts and a variety of bubble teas. For a one-stop Asian shopping immersion experience, the place to go is Uwajimaya (600 5th Ave. S.). It's a combination grocery, gift and housewares emporium with lots of unusual items.

Seattle's downtown retail core is between 3rd and 7th avenues and Pine and University streets. This is where you'll find major department stores like Macy's and Nordstrom, familiar names like Old Navy, The Gap and Borders, and a couple of upscale shopping complexes. The four levels at Pacific Place (6th Avenue and Pine Street) offer the usual mix of men's and women's apparel, shoe, jewelry, gift and electronics retailers, plus restaurants and an 11-screen multiplex.

There are more stores, specialty shops and eateries at Westlake Center (Pine Street between 4th and 5th avenues) and City Centre (1420 5th Ave. at Pike Street). For shopping toward the luxury end of the scale—Brooks Brothers, Louis Vuitton and so forth—try Rainier Square (5th Avenue and University Street).

It stands to reason that there would be an REI in outdoor recreation-minded Seattle. If it has anything to do with camping, hiking, climbing, cycling, paddling, skiing or snowboarding, Recreational Equipment Inc. (at Eastlake Avenue and John Street) has it. This flagship store isn't just a place to repair your skis or try on backpacks—there's a mountain bike test trail, a 65-foot climbing pinnacle and stations where you can try out all kinds of recreational gear. The hiker's trail to the entrance winds past trees and waterfalls. Street parking is scarce, so take advantage of the store's parking garage; the first hour is free.

Sometimes you just want to give in to a good old-fashioned tourist trap, and Ye Olde Curiosity Shop (1001 Alaskan Way at Pier 54) will definitely satisfy the urge. This place bills itself as a museum, but shrunken heads, prehistoric elephant tusks and the Lord's Prayer engraved on a grain of rice all play second fiddle to the merchandise: a hodgepodge of gag gifts, tchotchkes, Native American art and nautically themed collectibles. Don't miss the multiple rows of butterflies and insects in display cases on the wall above the main checkout counter.

Two Seattle neighborhoods—Capitol Hill and Fremont—are funky shopping destinations. The shops along Broadway reflect Capitol Hill's friendly but edgy vibe: Vintage clothing, lots of leather, fishnets and outrageous footwear (think snakeskin platform boots) are what you'll find at places like Broadway Boutique (113 Broadway E.), Metro Clothing Co. (231 Broadway E.) and the Red Light, 312 Broadway E. (their display window has mannequins decked out in all manner of punk attire). Massai (between Olive Way and Thomas Street) has flowing scarves, exotic gifts and a very cool collection of African masks.

Compact Fremont is ideal for strolling and has an eclectic assortment of shops. Frank and Dunya (3418 Fremont Ave. N.) sells "functional, fun and fine art" created by Northwest artists. If you're looking for something just a bit racy, go no further than Bellefleur Lingerie (720 N. 35th St.). In addition to carnivorous plants and other greenhouse tropicals, The Indoor Sun Shoppe (160 N. Canal St. at Phinney Avenue N.) stocks a full range of therapy lighting to combat those gloomy Seattle winters. After your shopping spree, kick back with a cup of java at Caffe Ladro (452 N. 36th St.). This popular Seattle chain offers organic coffee and yummy baked goods made on the premises.

And if you don't consider a shopping trip complete without hitting at least one mall, make it University Village (N.E. 45th Street and 25th Avenue E.), especially on a sunny day. This outdoor shopping plaza, sprinkled with fountains and animal sculptures, offers a familiar lineup of chain retailers that includes Pottery Barn, Banana Republic, Williams-Sonoma and Restoration Hardware.

Nightlife

Maybe it's all that caffeine that helps rev up a night out in Seattle. Or perhaps the often gloomy weather makes people *really* determined to have fun. Whatever the reason, there's something for everybody after dark, from laid-back neighborhood hangouts to oh-so-hip clubs to elegant lounges.

Pioneer Square has long been a magnet for evening entertainment. The bars here are no frills, the music is mostly raucous rock or blues, and the crowds of frat boys and other partiers can be on the drunk and disorderly side. If you're up for a rowdy old time, try The Central Saloon (207 1st Ave.), where bands play nightly. The Last Supper Club

(124 S. Washington St.) has three strobe-lit floors, state-of-the-art sound, resident DJs and theme nights: Latin Night on Wednesdays, techno on Thursdays, hip-hop and house on Fridays, DJ sets on Saturdays and rock bands on Sundays. Things are a bit more sedate at the New Orleans Creole Restaurant (114 1st Ave. S.), where the live jazz and blues Monday through Thursday evenings winds down by the civilized hour of 10 p.m.

Although the vendors at nearby Pike Place Market close up shop at the end of the day, you never know when a street busker might still be hanging out, regaling passers-by with a sea chantey or an impassioned Bob Dylan folk tune. Several Pike Place restaurants and bars also offer live music. Kells Irish Restaurant & Pub, tucked above the market at 1916 Post Alley, has a jolly atmosphere, an outdoor patio and live Irish music nightly beginning around 9. A few doors away at 1919 Post Alley, The Pink Door offers cabaret entertainment every night but Monday, including a burlesque show on Saturday (cover charge is $12).

The Triple Door, downtown on Union Street across from Benaroya Hall, is another restaurant that also features live music (mainly jazz and blues) in its Musicquarium Lounge and the Mainstage, a sleek, snazzy 300-seat theater. Dimitriou's Jazz Alley (6th Avenue and Lenora Street) is the city's premier showcase. One of the top jazz clubs on the West Coast, it books big-name acts like the Count Basie Orchestra and Eartha Kitt. You can have a swell dinner here, too. Reservations are recommended; phone (206) 441-9729.

Seattle's music scene is an enormously influential one (remember alternative rock?), and there are plenty of clubs where you can catch local up and comers like the Fleet Foxes as well as the latest buzz bands. Well-known rockers and hip-hoppers play at the Showbox, 1st Avenue and Pike Street across from Pike Place Market. Indie bands not yet big enough to fill the Showbox take the stage at Neumo's, in Capitol Hill on Pike Street (a block east of Broadway). Another Capitol Hill club is Chop Suey (1325 E. Madison St.), where a free-wheeling mix of indie, hip-hop and electro acts—mostly local but with a sprinkling of national and international names thrown in—draws a young, musically hip crowd.

Gay-friendly, punked-out Capitol Hill also has some of Seattle's coolest bars. The Cha Cha Lounge (1013 E. Pike St., a block east of Broadway) has great atmosphere: red lighting, sombreros hanging from the ceiling, disco balls and flashy *lucha libre* (Mexican wrestling) paraphernalia everywhere. It's in the basement of Bimbo's Bitchin' Burrito Kitchen; just take the stairs down. The Comet Tavern, 922 E. Pike St., is a classic dive bar favored by beer drinkers who come for rowdy shows headlined by punk, garage and stoner rock bands.

Ballard, a neighborhood that has diversified from its beginnings as a Scandinavian fishing community, has its own highly regarded watering holes. If you lean toward the twangy side of rock, head on down to the Tractor Tavern (5213 Ballard Ave. N.W.). The atmosphere is bare bones and the beer comes in plastic cups; this is first and foremost a place to watch live bands, with a good view of the stage from every spot in the room. The Sunset Tavern (5433 Ballard Ave. N.W.) is a bit more unruly: you're cramped and crowded but close to the action, and the bands rock out more. Don't come here if you're looking for a mellow evening.

In Fremont, the High Dive (513 N. 36th St.) is yet another club with shows practically every night—mostly local bands looking to establish themselves. They have live music happy hours three Saturdays a month. The cover charge is almost always under $10, so an evening here won't dent your wallet. If you just want to sit and chat in a quieter atmosphere stop by Fremont Coffee (459 N. 36th St.), in a rambling old house with a wraparound porch and several rooms filled with comfy chairs. In addition to frothy lattes and imported beers they sell locally made, organic-vegan Mighty-O Donuts (try the chocolate raspberry).

Fremont also has its own summer tradition: drive-in movies. On Saturday nights from late June to early September a mix of popcorn blockbusters and family films are shown in the parking lot at N. 35th Street and Phinney Ave. N. The schedule includes three "Twisted Flicks"—cheesy B-movie groaners with the original soundtrack replaced by dialogue, sound effects and music courtesy of Jet City Improv cast members. Bring your own chairs; local vendors provide hot dogs and popcorn. The movie starts at dusk, but there are games and entertainment before the show. Tickets are $5; for more details phone (206) 781-4230.

Equally fun, although much more expensive, is an evening at Teatro ZinZanni (*see attraction listing p. 232*). This combination of music, dance, comedy and exotic Cirque du Soleil-inspired acrobatics and illusions is half cabaret, half vaudeville and takes place above, around and right alongside as you dine in multi-course splendor. Another reason to go: Tom Douglas, the celebrity chef behind Seattle's trendy Dahlia Lounge restaurant, is in charge of the changing menu. Advance reservations are highly recommended. A reminder: The show lasts 3 hours and the humor is sophisticated, so leave little kids at home.

And what if you just want peace, quiet and a beautiful setting? Watching the sun drop behind distant mountains at Olympic Sculpture Park is a simple yet deeply rewarding pleasure. Or claim a spot at dusk along the wall in little Kerry Park (on W. Highland Drive at 2nd Avenue W.) and marvel as the Seattle skyline starts to light up while an illuminated ferry glides across Elliott Bay. It's free. And it's magical.

Note: Use common sense when it comes to staying safe after dark. Downtown areas like Pioneer Square and Belltown can be dicey to wander around late at night; if in doubt, take a cab.

Performing Arts

Seattle Center (*see attraction listing p. 230*) is the cultural focus of metropolitan Seattle. Its Marion

Oliver McCaw Hall is the headquarters of the Seattle Opera Association, which presents several full-scale operatic productions during its August through May season; phone (206) 389-7676 or (800) 426-1619.

The Seattle Symphony plays at Benaroya Hall, on 2nd Avenue between Union and University streets. Nearly 200 concerts take place between September and July. Family concerts, recitals and other musical events also are offered. Tours of the building are given Tues. and Fri. at noon and 1; phone (206) 215-4747, (866) 833-4747 or for tour information (206) 215-4856.

Bagley Wright Theatre at Seattle Center houses the nationally acclaimed Seattle Repertory Theatre Company, which presents six plays from early September through early May; for curtain times phone (206) 443-2222 or (877) 900-9285.

Broadway shows are the attraction at the Fifth Avenue Theatre, 1308 5th Ave.; phone (206) 625-1900. Traveling shows, comics and popular recording artists (everything from teen pop to hard rock) take the stage at the Paramount Theatre, downtown at 911 Pine St., and the Moore Theatre, 1932 2nd Ave.; phone (206) 682-1414.

Popular with summer playgoers are A Contemporary Theater (ACT) at 700 Union St., phone (206) 292-7676; and the Intiman at the Seattle Center Playhouse, phone (206) 269-1900. Summer brings open-air concerts to the Woodland Park Zoo, Chateau Ste. Michelle Winery in Woodinville and Marymoor Park in Redmond. Check the newspapers for full listings.

Special Events

Seattle holds a wide variety of festivals and programs throughout the year. The city celebrates the coming of spring with the opening day of yachting season on the first Saturday in May, when a parade of boats sails from Lake Union to Lake Washington. Festivities continue through mid-May with street fairs held in the University District. Norwegian Constitution Day is celebrated May 17 in the city's Ballard district.

The Northwest Folklife Festival, held over Memorial Day weekend, is a showcase of traditional and folk arts of more than 100 countries. Music, dancing, crafts exhibits and demonstrations are among the activities, some of which are participatory. The Fremont Fair, featuring crafts, ethnic food, live music and a parade, is in mid-June.

Seattle Center hosts the Bite of Seattle food festival in mid-July. The 23-day Seattle Seafair, held from mid-July to early August, heads the summer schedule with street parades and hydroplane races on Lake Washington. Bumbershoot, a festival of the arts, takes place at Seattle Center on Labor Day weekend. The Christmas Cruise, noted for its fleet of colorfully illuminated boats, takes place in early December.

The Seattle Vicinity

ARLINGTON (D-3) pop. 11,713, elev. 120′

Arlington stands just below the confluence of the north and south forks of the Stillaguamish River. Settlers homesteaded on the rich valley soils in the early 1860s. Railroads arrived in the 1880s, and a station was established here under the name of Haller City. An adjacent town site was platted as Arlington, named for the national cemetery near Washington, D.C., and in 1903 residents voted to consolidate the two settlements under that name. The town prospered as a lumbering center and once ranked among the nation's top producers of shingles.

Arlington-Smokey Point Chamber of Commerce: 3710 168th St. N.E., Suite C-101, Arlington, WA 98223; phone (360) 659-5453.

GAMBLING ESTABLISHMENTS

• **Angel of the Winds Casino** is off I-5 exit 210, 1.5 mi. e. on 236th St. N.E., then .5 mi. n. on 35th Ave. N.E. to 3438 Stoluckquamish Ln. Daily 8 a.m.-4 a.m. Phone (360) 474-9740.

RECREATIONAL ACTIVITIES
White-water Rafting

• **North Cascades River Expeditions** offers white-water rafting trips on various area waterways, including the Sauk and Skagit rivers. P.O. Box 116, Arlington, WA 98223. Mar.-Oct. Phone (360) 435-9548 or (800) 634-8433.

AUBURN (G-3) pop. 40,314, elev. 79′

Originally named Slaughter after Lt. William A. Slaughter who was killed in an American Indian skirmish, the town of Auburn acquired its new name in 1893, honoring the New York town.

Auburn began as a hops farming community and turned to dairy and vegetable farming in 1900. In 1912 the Northern Pacific Railroad made Auburn its western freight terminus and many large locomotive shops opened in the area. By 1970 many shops closed, and today's major employers are Boeing and the federal government's General Services Administration.

Emerald Downs, .5 miles east of SR 167 on 15th St. N.W., offers Thoroughbred racing mid-April through early October; free stable tours are available Saturday mornings by appointment. Phone (253) 288-7000 or (888) 931-8400, or (253) 288-7711 for tours.

Note: Policies concerning admittance of children to pari-mutuel betting facilities vary. Phone for information.

Auburn Area Chamber of Commerce: 108 S. Division, Suite B, Auburn, WA 98001; phone (253) 833-0700.

Shopping areas: The Supermall of the Great Northwest, junction SRs 18 and 167, offers more than 160 stores, including Ann Taylor Loft, Burlington Coat Factory, Marshalls, Nordstrom Rack and Old Navy.

FLAMING GEYSER STATE PARK is 1.7 mi. s. on SR 169, then 2.75 mi. w. on S.E. Green Valley Rd. The park is named for an old coal test hole that has an 8-inch methane flame. The Steelhead Trout Imprinting Project holds young fish in a series of ponds to instill the habit of homing. *See Recreation Chart.* A playground is available. Daily 8-dusk. Free. Phone (253) 931-3930.

SAVE **WHITE RIVER VALLEY MUSEUM** is at 918 H St. S.E. The museum features exhibits depicting area history, including the Northern Pacific Railroad, a 1920s caboose, a pioneer cabin and a life-size exhibit representing Auburn's downtown in the 1920s. Allow 30 minutes minimum. Wed.-Sun. noon-4; closed Easter, Mother's Day, Thanksgiving and Dec. 25. Admission $2; $1 (ages 0-17 and 63+); free (Wed.). Phone (253) 288-7433.

GAMBLING ESTABLISHMENTS

• **Muckleshoot Casino** is at 2402 Auburn Way S. Daily 24 hours. Phone (253) 939-7484 or (800) 804-4944.

RECREATIONAL ACTIVITIES
White-water Rafting

• **Riverrider.com** departs from Flaming Geyser State Park on the Green River, P.O. Box 666, Leavenworth, WA 98826. Apr.-May (also Oct.-Nov. after heavy rains). Phone (206) 448-7238 or (800) 448-7238.

BAINBRIDGE ISLAND (F-2) pop. 20,308

The Bainbridge Island community of Winslow, consolidated with Bainbridge Island in 1991, traces its beginnings to the late 19th century when it was a shipbuilding center for schooners. Eagle Harbor still hums with the activities of the Washington State Ferries maintenance yard; daily ferries connect the community to nearby Seattle.

The Walkabout, a mile-long foot path, parallels the Winslow waterfront. A footbridge leads to Eagle Harbor Waterfront Park and a fishing pier. Seven miles north is Fay Bainbridge State Park (*see Recreation Chart*), a well-known Puget Sound recreation area. The entire island is popular with bicyclists, despite its hilly terrain.

Bainbridge Island Chamber of Commerce: 590 Winslow Way E., Bainbridge Island, WA 98110; phone (206) 842-3700.

Shopping areas: Downtown Winslow, Winslow Way and Madison Avenue, offers a variety of shops, galleries and eateries.

BAINBRIDGE ISLAND HISTORICAL MUSEUM is at 215 Ericksen Ave. N.E. Housed in a 1908 one-room schoolhouse, the museum features documents, memorabilia and photographs describing Bainbridge Island's history from 1854 to the present. Wed.-Mon. 1-4 (also Sat. 10-1); closed Jan. 1, Easter, July 4, Thanksgiving, Dec. 25 and 31. Admission $2.50; $1.50 (ages 65+ and students with ID); free (ages 0-4); $5 (family). Phone (206) 842-2773.

BLOEDEL RESERVE is 6.5 mi. n.w. of the ferry dock on SR 305, then .25 mi. n. on Agatewood Rd. N.E., then .5 mi. e. to 7571 N.E. Dolphin Dr. This 150-acre former private estate with a bird marsh, formal gardens, moss garden, reflection pool, Japanese garden and woodlands displays the influence of different cultures and styles on Northwest garden design. Self-guiding tours are available. Picnicking and pets are prohibited. Allow 1 hour, 30 minutes minimum. Wed.-Sun. 10-4; closed holidays. Admission $12; $8 (ages 65+); $6 (ages 5-12). Reservations are required. Phone (206) 842-7631.

WINERIES

• **Bainbridge Island Vineyards & Winery** is 4 mi. n. of the ferry dock on SR 305, then .5 mi. e. on E. Day Rd. Tastings Fri.-Sun. 11-5; other times by appointment. Tours Sun. at 2. Phone (206) 842-9463.

BELLEVUE (F-3) pop. 109,569, elev. 100'

Boy, has Bellevue grown up. The traditional role of this Eastside community—scenically wedged between lakes Washington and Sammamish—has been that of Seattle's younger, unassuming sibling. Less than 3 decades ago Bellevue was a suburban town, a bedroom community for Seattleites who wanted a little peace and quiet. No more. Washington's fifth-largest city has definitely come of age. Now there are not one but two impressive downtown skylines within spitting distance of Puget Sound.

Bellevue's first high-rise rose in 1983. More went up in the 1990s. Today a small (at least by Seattle standards) but growing forest of skyscrapers defines the city's profile. Take a walk around downtown Bellevue these days, and what you really notice is the remarkable degree of new construction. There are almost as many cranes as there are tall buildings. Steel-and-glass skeletons in progress—like the twin 42-story luxury condominium development Bellevue Towers and Avalon Meydenbauer, an upscale high-rise apartment complex—are sprouting like vertical mushrooms from a particularly fertile forest floor.

Many people migrating to downtown Bellevue already live on the Eastside. They're flocking here to take advantage of what not so long ago was an unknown concept: urban living on Lake Washington's *eastern* side. And many of the new arrivals fall into the bracket of "young professional," which makes sense, since lately Bellevue has become high-tech central: Yahoo, Expedia, Microsoft and Google all have big offices here.

Elegant urbanity—the type of atmosphere once found only in Seattle's more rarified downtown districts—is on full display at places like Lincoln Square, which opened in December 2006. This mixed-use development is representative of downtown Bellevue's new construction. It includes The Westin Bellevue, which itself is a hybrid; the lower half is a hotel, while the upper half consists of residential units. There's also a 16-screen luxury cinema, a bowling "lounge" and upscale billiard parlor, and a handful of chic shops and eateries.

Everything about Lincoln Square is sleek, from the post-modern interior design (lots of gleaming stainless steel) to the water that glides in shimmering sheets down a 65-foot vertical glass shaft to a pool bristling with sinuous emerald-green glass tubes ("Lincoln Square Fiori," the work of Dale Chihuly). Another Chihuly piece, the spectacular, three-tiered "End of the Day Chandelier," hangs above the Lincoln Way entrance and is strikingly illuminated at night. Even the seating area in the Tully's Coffee outlet (on the first level) is gussied up with Oriental rugs, artwork on the walls and fresh orchid arrangements that provide a home-away-from-home atmosphere for patrons tapping busily away on their laptops.

Downtown Park, just west of Bellevue Way N.E. between N.E. 4th and N.E. 8th streets, is an expansive greensward in the heart of downtown with a 240-foot-wide waterfall spilling into a reflecting pond. The big, open lawn is great for kite flying and a nice spot for a picnic, and the park also has a half-mile promenade shaded by a double row of trees, just the place for a leisurely stroll.

There also are tucked-away little nooks where you can enjoy the Northwest's robust natural beauty. A prime example is little Meydenbauer Beach Park, perched on the shore of Meydenbauer Bay. It's just a couple of blocks west of Downtown Park; take 98th Avenue N.E. off Lake Washington Boulevard N.E. (Don't let the green directional signs leading away from Lake Washington Boulevard and the bay fool you; just follow them and you'll get to the parking lot.) From there it's just a short jaunt down to the waterfront via a paved walkway that passes beneath lush tall trees.

There's a little slip of a beach that looks out over Meydenbauer Bay, an indentation along the Lake Washington shoreline. A whaling company was based here until the 1940s; it's been supplanted by the expensive craft moored at the adjacent Meydenbauer Bay Yacht Club. Tony homes climb the wooded hillsides above the bay. This pretty, well-kept park has a fishing dock, a picnic area and restrooms.

The Bellevue Farmers Market sets up Thursday afternoons from mid-May through early October in the parking lot of the First Presbyterian Church at 1717 Bellevue Way N.E. It supports small local family farms, which means browsers have their pick of blueberries, hazelnuts, organic fruit and produce, honey, fresh seafood, homemade baked goods and other yummy stuff. Events at the market include chef demos, hands-on activities for kids and fiddle and banjo hoedowns.

There are two cool public art installations at the Bellevue Transit Center, downtown at 10850 N.E. 6th St. "High Road" comprises three spherical shapes that appear to be walking on stilts; "Windswept" is an illuminated-from-within aluminum sculpture mounted atop an elevated platform that also serves as a bench. Bellevue's public transportation nerve center is a convenient base from which you can board Sound Transit express buses for travel throughout the Seattle-Tacoma-Everett-Bellevue metro area. For schedule and fare information phone (206) 398-5000 or (800) 201-4900.

Bellevue Chamber of Commerce: 302 Bellevue Sq., Bellevue, WA 98004; phone (425) 454-2464.

Shopping areas: The "Bellevue Collection," which consists of three separate complexes, anchors downtown shopping. Lincoln Square, on Bellevue Way N.E. between N.E. 6th and N.E. 8th streets, has stores devoted to upscale home furnishings and accessories and a couple of specialty retailers. A similar lineup of shops is at the adjacent Bellevue Place, inside the Hyatt Regency Bellevue at 900 Bellevue Way N.E. An elevated pedestrian walkway connects Lincoln Square to Bellevue Square across the street. In addition to anchor stores JCPenney, Macy's and Nordstrom, this destination mall has some 200 shops and restaurants.

Similarly upscale is the new Safeway at 300 Bellevue Way N.E. that opened across the street from the old Safeway, a downtown Bellevue fixture for 48 years. Wood floors, a fireplace and subdued mood lighting lend that urban elegant touch, with affluent shoppers lured by a nut bar, a gelato bar, a seafood bar featuring delicacies like whole octopus and Chilean sea bass, and a glass-enclosed wine cellar complete with steward on hand.

Two blocks east of Bellevue Way N.E. at 106th Avenue N.E. and N.E. 4th Street is the Bellevue Galleria, a mini mall with a handful of stores and a movie multiplex. After pampering yourself at the Gene Juarez Salon & Spa, hit the Rock Bottom Brewery for dinner. The on-premises brew masters

at this popular restaurant and evening hangout whip up a premium selection of beers, lagers and specialty ales.

Just south of the Bellevue Collection is Old Bellevue, a stretch of Main Street that was shopping central in quieter times. Some of the quaintness remains, although Old Bellevue is changing as shiny new condos and commercial buildings sprout up all around. Shopping here is more of a stroll-along-the-sidewalk-and-browse affair. The mix of shops and boutiques runs the gamut from quaint to trendy. Posh on Main carries women's designer footwear that would fit snugly into a "Sex and the City" episode, while Belle Pastry has a reputation for oh-so-fresh-baked baguettes, brioches and croissants.

Market Place@Factoria, just southeast of the I-90/I-405 junction, is where locals go when they're in an outlet mall frame of mind. The usual suspects are here, from T.J. Maxx to OshKosh B'Gosh, plus Nordstrom Rack, Old Navy; a couple of fast-food joints and—when you gotta have that java jolt—a Seattle's Best Coffee branch.

SAVE BELLEVUE ARTS MUSEUM is at 510 Bellevue Way N.E. The museum features changing exhibitions highlighting the work of regional artists, designers and crafts people. Allow 1 hour minimum. Tues.-Sat. 10-5:30 (also Fri. 5:30-9), Sun. 11-5:30; closed Jan. 1, July 4, Thanksgiving and Dec. 25. Guided tours are offered at 1. Admission $7; $5 (ages 56+ and students with ID); free (ages 0-6 and first Fri. of the month). AX, MC, VI. Phone (425) 519-0770.

BELLEVUE BOTANICAL GARDEN is at 12001 Main St. in Wilburton Hill Park. A .5-mile nature trail winds through this 53-acre tract of rolling hills, native woodlands, meadows and bogs. Gardens illustrate the use of ground covers, alpine plants, perennials, drought tolerant plants, ferns and Northwest native plants. A Japanese-influenced garden honors Yao, Bellevue's sister city in Japan.

Allow 1 hour, 30 minutes minimum. Garden open daily 7:30-dusk. Visitor center daily 9-4. Guided 90-minute tours are available weekends at 2, Apr.-Oct. Free. Phone (425) 452-2750.

F.W. WINTERS HOUSE, 2102 Bellevue Way S.E., is a 1929 Spanish eclectic-style house. Featuring period decor, it is now used as a cultural and natural interpretive center and is also the home of the Eastside Heritage Center. The grounds retain many plants representative of the nursery and bulb gardens operated by the original owners. Nature trails lead into the surrounding park. Guided tours are available. Mon.-Fri. 10-4, Sat. 10-2; closed federal holidays. Free. Phone (425) 452-2752.

LAKE HILLS GREENBELT, 15416 S.E. 16th St., is a 150-acre wildlife corridor and park featuring two lakes, 3 miles of hiking trails, agricultural areas and demonstration gardens. The ranger station has displays of native animals and plants; it also showcases sustainable building products. Grounds open daily dawn-dusk; closed holidays. Ranger station open Tues.-Thurs. noon-4. Free. Phone (425) 452-7225.

ROSALIE WHYEL MUSEUM OF DOLL ART is at 1116 108th Ave. N.E. The museum traces the history of dolls and doll making with displays of dolls from the 1680s to the present and including several from the Victorian era. One-of-a-kind dolls, doll houses, teddy bears, toys and miniatures also are on display. An English garden is on the premises. Allow 1 hour minimum. Mon.-Sat. 10-5, Sun. 1-5; closed Jan. 1, Easter, July 4, Thanksgiving and Dec. 25. Admission $8; $7 (ages 65+); $4 (ages 5-17); $28 (family). AX, MC, VI. Phone (425) 455-1116. *See color ad p. 244.*

BLAKE ISLAND (F-3)

BLAKE ISLAND STATE PARK is 8 mi. from Seattle's downtown waterfront; tour boats depart from Pier 55 in Seattle. The 475-acre park offers 15.5 miles of hiking trails, beach access and panoramic views of the Seattle skyline and surrounding mountains *(see Recreation Chart).* Deer and bald eagles are among the wildlife found in the park, which also contains Tillicum Village Northwest Coast Indian Cultural Center *(see attraction listing).*

The park is accessible only by private boat or tour boat. Park open daily 6:30 a.m.-dusk, Memorial Day-Labor Day; 8-dusk, rest of year. Tillicum Village offers "Blake Island Experience," a round-trip passenger-only boat service, for $40; $37 (ages 60+); $12 (ages 5-12). Phone (360) 731-8330 for park information, or (206) 933-8600 or (800) 426-1205 for boat reservations.

TILLICUM VILLAGE NORTHWEST COAST INDIAN CULTURAL CENTER is on the northeast shore of Blake Island State Park and is accessible by private boat or tour boat. The village features a Northwest Coast American Indian cedar longhouse where regional Indian art and artifacts are displayed. The village also offers an interpretive stage show and a traditional baked salmon dinner. Tillicum Village provides scheduled passenger-only boat tours to the island from downtown Seattle *(see attraction listing p. 235).*

Longhouse open daily 12:30-8:30, early July-early Sept.; otherwise varies rest of year. Longhouse admission free. Salmon dinner and stage show $39.95; $35.95 (ages 60+); $18 (ages 5-12). Combined dinner, stage show and tour from Seattle's Pier 55 $79.95; $72.95 (ages 60+); $30 (ages 5-12). All prices include tax. Reservations are recommended. AX, DS, MC, VI. Phone (206) 933-8600 or (800) 426-1205.

BOTHELL (E-3) elev. 27'

Named for pioneer David Bothell, this greater Seattle suburb began its existence as a settlement on the banks of the Sammamish River in the early 1870s, initially prospering as a lumbering and agricultural center. Bothell's Canyon Park district, along I-405 north of the city, is a center for high-tech businesses.

The Chase House, on the Bothell campus of the University of Washington/Cascadia Community College (off Beardsley Boulevard on 110th Avenue N.E.), dates from 1889 and was the home of the community's first physician, Dr. Reuben Chase. The campus also encompasses a wetlands area crisscrossed with several miles of paved trails. Visitors can walk along an elevated section of boardwalk where native species have been planted; signs and photographs describe the restoration process. The Town-Gown Loop, a 2.7-mile trail featuring 20 interpretive plaques, links the campus with downtown Bothell.

Greater Bothell Chamber of Commerce: 10017 N.E. 185th St., Bothell, WA 98041; phone (425) 485-4353.

Shopping areas: Country Village, 1.5 miles north via SR 527, has 45 specialty shops and galleries in an outdoor setting of landscaped gardens, ponds and shady pathways where you can feed wandering chickens.

Downtown Bothell's Main Street earns the adjective "quaint," with a plentiful selection of small shops and restaurants along a two-block stretch spruced up with pretty landscaping and colorful banners. On a scale of one to 10, the browsing potential ranks high at Bothell Jewelers & Collectibles, 10130 Main St. This establishment has everything from rhinestone brooches and vintage belt buckles to Hummel and Goebel collector plates, antique leather postcards and Beatles memorabilia. Grab a bite to eat at the Kozy Corner Cafe, 10137 Main St., a cheery, down-home diner that serves a steady stream of locals.

PARK AT BOTHELL LANDING is off SR 522 at 9919 N.E. 180th St. The city's major recreation facility fronts the Sammamish River. A pedestrian bridge spans the shallow river (more a stream at this point) and connects with the Sammamish River Trail, a 10-mile paved path running south to Redmond, on the opposite bank. Walkers, joggers and cyclists share the stretch of trail with chickens and ducks.

The park has several historical sites. The Beckstrom Log Cabin, a hand-hewn log structure dating back to 1884, once housed a family of 10 and contains pioneer-era tools. The 1893 William Hannan House contains the Bothell Historical Museum, which is filled with period furniture. Just behind the museum is Bothell's First Schoolhouse; the single room, complete with vintage desks and a pot-bellied stove, served grades 1-8. The school's bell tower stands nearby.

Picnicking is permitted. Allow 30 minutes minimum. Park open daily dawn-dusk. Museum open Sun. 1-4, May-Sept. (also first two Sundays in Dec.); closed Mother's Day. Park and museum free. Phone (425) 486-7430, or (425) 486-1889 for the museum.

BREMERTON (F-2) pop. 37,259, elev. 10′

Named for Seattle real estate entrepreneur William Bremer, Bremerton is on a hilly site indented with bays and inlets. When Bremer heard of the Navy's plan to build a station here, he purchased land surrounding the proposed facility and platted the town. The Puget Sound Naval Base is the northern home of the Pacific Fleet. Within the base is the city's largest industry—the Puget Sound Naval Shipyard.

Harborside Fountain Park, just south of the ferry terminal on First Street, overlooks the waterfront. It features five copper-plated fountains shaped like submarine sails. North of the ferry terminal, Bremerton Boardwalk offers a shoreside promenade.

Daily toll ferry service connects Bremerton with Seattle; phone (888) 808-7977 in Wash. A passenger toll ferry also links Bremerton and Annapolis to Port Orchard; phone (360) 373-2877.

Bremerton Area Chamber of Commerce: 286 Fourth St., Bremerton, WA 98337; phone (360) 479-3579.

Shopping areas: Kitsap Mall, 9 mi. n. in Silverdale, features 120 stores, including JCPenney, Kohl's, Macy's and Sears.

AURORA VALENTINETTI PUPPET MUSEUM is downtown at 257 Fourth St. The museum's collection of more than 600 puppets features original, single-strand marionettes; Indonesian shadow puppets; intricately carved rod puppets from Java; Thai animal marionettes; Edgar Bergen ventriloquist dummies; and Chinese puppets. Approximately 100 puppets are on display at a time.

Allow 30 minutes minimum. Wed.-Sat. 11-4; closed major holidays. Free. Phone (360) 373-2992.

ELANDAN GARDENS is at 3050 W. SR 16. Located beside Sinclair Inlet, the gardens feature hundreds of bonsai trees set amid giant rhododendrons, Japanese maples and stone sculptures. Some of the bonsai specimens are more than 1,000 years old. Bald eagles and great blue herons are common visitors. Allow 30 minutes minimum. Tues.-Sun. 10-5, Apr.-Oct.; Fri.-Sun. 10-5, rest of year. Closed Thanksgiving and Dec. 25. Admission $8; $1 (ages 0-12). AX, DS, MC, VI. Phone (360) 373-8260.

KITSAP COUNTY HISTORICAL SOCIETY MUSEUM is at 280 Fourth St. This museum uses dioramas, historic photographs and interactive exhibits in a timeline of county history that highlights logging, the area's first major industry. A walk-through street display of store windows with merchandise reflects commerce and architecture 1860-1940. Allow 30 minutes minimum. Tues.-Sat. 10-5 (also first Fri. of the month 5-8); closed holidays. Admission $2; $1 (ages 7-17); $5 (family); free (first Fri. of the month). Phone (360) 479-6226.

PUGET SOUND NAVY MUSEUM is at 251 First St. The museum is housed in the shipyard's original administrative office, built in 1896. Its exhibits portray the history of the shipyard and the Navy in Puget Sound. Allow 1 hour minimum. Mon.-Sat. 10-4, Sun. 1-4; closed Jan. 1, Thanksgiving and Dec. 25. Donations. Phone (360) 479-7447.

SAVE **USS *TURNER JOY* (DD-951) NAVAL MEMORIAL MUSEUM SHIP** is n. of the ferry terminal on the Bremerton Waterfront at 300 Washington Beach Ave. The ship serves as an educational facility and as an exhibit honoring the US. Navy. The *Turner Joy*, a Forrest Sherman Class destroyer commissioned in 1959, saw action in the Gulf of Tonkin incident of 1964, earning nine battle stars. Decommissioned in November 1982, the ship remains close to its original configuration. A self-guiding tour provides access to most of the ship.

Allow 1 hour minimum. Daily 10-5, May 1-Oct. 1; Mon.-Fri. 10-4, rest of year. Closed Jan. 1, Thanksgiving and Dec. 25. Admission $10; $8 (ages 63+); $6 (ages 5-12); free (military in uniform). AX, DS, MC, VI. Phone (360) 792-2457.

CARNATION (E-7) pop. 1,893, elev. 75′

Settled in 1865 by Scandinavian farmers, Carnation took the name of a neighboring dairy farm that was famous for its superior dairy herds. The daily activities of a working farm can be observed mid-May through October at Remlinger Farms, half a mile south on SR 203, then a quarter of a mile east on N.E. 32nd Street. Other highlights include animal viewing and petting, seasonal festivals and entertainment as well as puppet shows and pony and miniature steam train rides; phone (425) 333-4135.

Visitors can experience the daily life of a 14th-century English town at Camlann Medieval Village, 10320 Kelly Rd. N.E. During most weekends from late April through September 30, costumed "villagers" conduct 2-hour tours of the replica village and demonstrate blacksmithing, weaving, cooking and gardening as these tasks were performed in the era of Geoffrey Chaucer—the late 1300s. Banquets and festivals are held periodically. Phone (425) 788-8624.

DES MOINES (G-3) pop. 29,267

On the eastern shore of Puget Sound, Des Moines was settled in 1867. The city was named for the Des Moines City Improvement Co. and prospered as a major sawmill center in the late 1800s.

The Des Moines Marina, west of SR 509 at 22307 Dock Ave. S., has a 670-foot public fishing pier. Guest moorage, boat launch facilities and gasoline are available; phone (206) 824-5700. Two miles south of downtown on Marine View Dr. S. is the popular Saltwater State Park, with a 1,500-foot beach and a deep, forested ravine, offering opportunities to camp, picnic, hike and scuba dive *(see Recreation Chart and the AAA Northwestern CampBook)*.

DES MOINES BEACH PARK, 4 blks. w. of SR 509 via S. 223rd St., is a 20-acre park with meadows, woodlands, hiking trails, 635 feet of saltwater beach and a salmon-bearing stream that empties into Puget Sound. The park includes the Covenant Beach Historic District—that operated as a church retreat 1931-87. The rustic camp reflects its Swedish architectural heritage. Picnicking is permitted. Daily dawn-dusk. Free. Phone (206) 870-6527.

EDMONDS (E-3) pop. 39,515, elev. 120'

Legend has it that when logger George Brackett petitioned to establish the town of Edmonds in 1890, he added the names of his two oxen to the list to achieve the required number of petitioners. He named the town for Vermont Sen. George Franklin Edmunds but misspelled the name.

Edmonds' Puget Sound waterfront has beaches, a marina and a public fishing pier; the Olympic Mountains can be seen in the distance. Brackett's Landing Beach, just north of the ferry dock, includes Edmonds Underwater Park for scuba diving. Washington State Ferries provide frequent daily service to Kingston; phone (888) 808-7977 in Wash.

Edmonds Visitors Center: 120 5th Ave. N., P.O. Box 146, Edmonds, WA 98020; phone (425) 776-6711.

Shopping areas: Art galleries, antique shops, specialty stores and restaurants cluster along Main Street in the central business core.

EDMONDS HISTORICAL MUSEUM, 118 N. 5th Ave., chronicles the settlement and growth of Edmonds and southern Snohomish County. Special exhibits include a working model of a shingle mill and a marine room displaying the city's maritime heritage. The museum occupies the former 1910 Carnegie Library/City Hall and offers changing regional history exhibits. Allow 1 hour minimum. Wed.-Sun. 1-4; closed holidays. Donations. Phone (425) 774-0900.

EVERETT (E-3) pop. 91,488, elev. 21'

Eastern capitalists selected Everett's deepwater port as the site for a major industrial center in the early 1890s. The Panic of 1893 dashed their dreams, but by 1900 Minnesota timber entrepreneur Frederick Weyerhaeuser had established a sawmill on the fledgling town's waterfront, and within a decade the mill was among the world's largest. Timber was king in early Everett, with over a dozen lumber and shingle mills operating. Labor disputes plagued the city in the early days, however, culminating in the Everett Massacre in 1916, when seven men were shot and an unknown number drowned.

Everett's economy, once dependent on forest products, is today dominated by service industries, aerospace and the military. Boeing selected an abandoned air force base south of the city as the site for its 747 manufacturing plant in the mid-1960s, and the Everett Naval Station was established on the downtown waterfront in the early 1990s.

Many of the city's neighborhoods overlook Port Gardner, the Olympics and the Cascades. Quite a few of the mansions lining Rucker and Grand avenues north of downtown were formerly owned by timber barons. Grand Avenue Park, on Grand between 16th and 19th, contains a plaque commemorating the 1792 landing of Captain George Vancouver on the shoreline below.

Jetty Island lies off the northern end of Everett's waterfront at the channel entrance of the Snohomish River. The man-made island is 2 miles long by 200 yards wide and is home to 45 species of birds and a herd of California sea lions from October to June. The island is accessible by private boat year-round. Free ferry service is available Wed.-Mon., early July through the Sunday before Labor Day, from the 10th Street boat launch off W. Marine View Drive. Phone (425) 257-8304 or (425) 257-8300.

Snohomish County Tourism Bureau: 909 S.E. Everett Mall Way, Everett, WA 98208; phone (425) 348-5802 or (888) 338-0976.

Shopping areas: Everett Mall, 5 miles south on S.E. Everett Mall Way, has Macy's and Sears. Everett Marina Village, on the waterfront at the foot of 18th Street, is a renovated portion of the waterfront district that resembles an 1890s village.

FLYING HERITAGE COLLECTION is at the s.e. corner of Paine Field. From I-5 southbound take exit 189, go w. on SR 526, s. on Airport Rd., w. on 112th St. S.W., then n. on 30th St. W. to 109th St., following signs; from I-5 northbound take exit 186, go w. on 128th St. S.W. to Airport Rd., w. on 112th St S.W., then n. on 30th St. W. to 109th St., following signs.

The collection includes 15 meticulously restored, rare World War II-era fighter planes from the United States, the United Kingdom, Germany, Japan and the former Soviet Union. Each plane represents a technological advancement in manned flight; many are the last examples of their type known to exist, and most are in flying condition. A highlight is the Messerschmitt 163B Komet, the world's first rocket-powered fighter.

Fly days, scheduled noon to 1 on alternating Saturdays from June to early October (weather permitting), offer an opportunity to see two of these historic fighter craft take to the sky. Flights can be observed from an observation area adjacent to the runway. Guided tours are available by reservation.

Allow 1 hour minimum. Daily 10-5, Memorial Day-Labor Day; Tues.-Sat. 10-5, rest of year. Closed Thanksgiving and Dec. 25. Admission $12; $10 (ages 65+, veterans and military with ID); $8 (ages 6-15). AX, MC, VI. Phone (877) 342-3404.

FOREST PARK is 1 mi. w. of I-5 exit 192 on Mukilteo Blvd. The 111-acre park is one of the city's largest and oldest. It includes a heated pool, a children's petting farm and recreational facilities. Centennial Water Playground features 16 interactive fountains. Park open daily 6 a.m.-10 p.m. Animal farm open daily 10-4, early June to mid-Aug. Donations. Phone (425) 257-8300.

 **FUTURE OF FLIGHT AVIATION CENTER & BOEING TOUR—**
see Mukilteo p. 253.

SAVE **IMAGINE CHILDREN'S MUSEUM** is at 1502 Wall St. The museum's three floors of hands-on exhibit areas include a horizontal climbing wall, an actual walk-in bank vault and drive-up teller window, a wild animal clinic where kids can play veterinarian and a rooftop climbing structure with slides as well as a research fossil dig area. Other popular features include the mountain lookout with its panoramic views of Puget Sound and surrounding mountains.

Allow 1 hour minimum. Thurs.-Fri. 10-5:30; Tues.-Wed. and Sat. 10-4, Sun. 11-5; closed Jan. 1, Easter, Thanksgiving and Dec. 25. Admission $7; free (ages 0-12 months). MC, VI. Phone (425) 258-1006.

LEGION MEMORIAL PARK, 145 Alverson Blvd., is a recreation area featuring the 2.4-acre Evergreen Area Arboretum and Gardens, with a collection of native and exotic plants. Specialty areas include woodland and shade gardens, perennial and white borders, Japanese maples and "water-wise" plants. Daily 6 a.m.-10 p.m. Free. Phone (425) 257-8300.

MUSEUM OF FLIGHT RESTORATION CENTER is at 2909 100th St. S.W. This 23,000-square-foot working restoration facility features up to 15 historic planes at a time. Aircraft being restored include a de Havilland Comet—the first passenger jet—and the Chance Vought XF8U-1 Crusader prototype, which was the Navy's first supersonic jet fighter. Visitors also can see the completed 1933 Boeing 247D, the first modern passenger craft and the result of a 14-year restoration effort. Allow 30 minutes minimum. Tues.-Thurs. 8-4, Sat. 9-5. Donations. Phone (425) 745-5150.

FEDERAL WAY (G-3) pop. 83,259, elev. 500'

The large suburban community of Federal Way, part of the Seattle-Tacoma metropolitan area, covers a series of wooded ridges above Puget Sound. Its name comes from the federal highway built through the area in 1929. West Hylebos Wetlands Park, 4th Avenue S. off S. 348th Street, features a 1-mile self-guiding nature trail through a forest and a bog.

Federal Way Chamber of Commerce: 1230 S. 336th St., Suite F, P.O. Box 3440, Federal Way, WA 98063; phone (253) 838-2605.

Shopping areas: The Commons at Federal Way, 1 mile west of I-5 exit 143 at the southeast corner of SR 99 and S. 320th Street, contains Macy's and Sears.

PACIFIC RIM BONSAI COLLECTION is .7 mi. e. of northbound I-5 exit 142A or southbound I-5 exit 142B via SR 18, then .5 mi. n. on Weyerhaeuser Way S. This 1-acre facility was established as a symbol of the importance of trading relationships with Pacific Rim countries. The collection includes more than 50 bonsai trees from the United States, Canada, Japan, Korea, China and Taiwan. Several of the trees are more than 500 years old. Allow 30 minutes minimum. Fri.-Wed. 10-4, Mar.-Sept.; Sat.-Wed. 11-4, rest of year. Closed Jan. 1 and Dec. 24-25. Free. Phone (253) 924-5206.

RHODODENDRON SPECIES BOTANICAL GARDEN is .7 mi. e. of northbound I-5 exit 142A or southbound I-5 exit 142B via SR 18, then .5 mi. n. on Weyerhaeuser Way S. This 24-acre garden features more than 2,000 varieties of rhododendron from around the world. The alpine garden displays rhododendrons and other plants adapted to survive the harsh growing conditions of high altitudes, while a study garden arrays species of rhododendron for comparison.

Allow 1 hour minimum. Fri.-Wed. 10-4, Mar.-Sept.; Sat.-Wed. 11-4, rest of year. Admission Mar.-Oct. $5; $3 (ages 66+ and students with ID); free (ages 0-11). Free rest of year. Phone (253) 661-9377.

WILD WAVES THEME PARK is w. of I-5 exit 142B to SR 161, then s. to 36201 Enchanted Pkwy. S. This 50-acre family amusement park features 32 rides including Timberhawk, the state's largest wooden roller coaster; a double corkscrew, single inversion roller coaster; a 124-foot sky dive; and a 1906 carousel. The park also has 10 waterslides, a 24,000-square-foot wave pool, two speed slides and a raging river ride.

Food is available. Opens daily at 10, mid-June through Labor Day; closing time varies. Admission $34.99; $29.99 (under 48 inches tall); free (ages 0-2). Parking $10 (cash only). Pricing is subject to change without notice; phone ahead for details. AX, MC, VI. Phone (253) 661-8000.

GIG HARBOR (G-2) pop. 6,465, elev. 60'

On a small bay, Gig Harbor's bayfront business district retains the flavor of a fishing village. The bay was discovered by chance by members of the 1841 Wilkes expedition seeking refuge from a storm. They named the bay for their gig, a type of boat.

Five miles northwest of Tacoma over the Narrows Bridge, Gig Harbor still provides shelter—not for explorers, but for commercial fishing boats and pleasure craft. Charter skippered sailboat outings as well as rentals of power pleasure and fishing boats, sailboats, sea kayaks, paddle boats and jet skis are available. Jerisich Dock and Skansie Brothers Park, at Harborview Drive and Rosedale Road, provide public access to the bay. The park also is a venue for outdoor summer concerts. A fishermen's memorial stands at the dock.

Gig Harbor/Peninsula Area Chamber of Commerce: 3311 Harborview Dr., Suite 101, Gig Harbor, WA 98332; phone (253) 851-6865 or (800) 359-8804.

Shopping areas: Downtown along the waterfront, Harborview Drive and Finholm's Market Place feature several dozen specialty shops and art galleries. The Kimball Business District, on Kimball Drive just off Pioneer, features several dozen shops and galleries. Two farmers markets are in business from April through October: Saturdays at Kimball Park and Ride and Wednesdays at Skansie Brothers Park in downtown Gig Harbor.

[SAVE] **GIG HARBOR PENINSULA HISTORICAL SOCIETY & MUSEUM,** 1 mi. n.w. at 4218 Harborview Dr., traces local history from the American Indian era through exploration and pioneer settlements to the present. Included are interactive exhibits and displays about fishing, timber, farming and bridging the Tacoma Narrows. **Note:** The museum is currently closed and will reopen in new, larger quarters just down the road in March 2009; hours and pricing may change. Allow 30 minutes minimum. Tues.-Sat. 10-4; closed Jan. 1, July 4, Thanksgiving and Dec. 25. Admission $5; $2 (ages 3-18 and 60+). Phone (253) 858-6722.

ISSAQUAH (E-7) pop. 11,212, elev. 98′

The Seattle Pacific and Lakeshore Railroad's extension to nearby Squak Mountain in the late 1800s triggered a major coal mining boom and the settlement of the community of Gilman. The town's name was changed to Issaquah, a Coast Salish Indian word meaning "sound of waterfowl," in 1899.

Greater Issaquah Chamber of Commerce: 155 N.W. Gilman Blvd., Issaquah, WA 98027; phone (425) 392-7024.

Self-guiding tours: A map outlining a walking tour of historic downtown Issaquah is available at the Gilman Town Hall Museum and Issaquah Depot Museum (see attraction listings) and the chamber of commerce.

Shopping areas: Gilman Village, south of I-90 exit 17 at Gilman Boulevard and Juniper Street, is a complex of restored pioneer houses that contains restaurants and specialty shops. Hand-dipped chocolates are made at Boehm's Chocolate Factory, 255 N.E. Gilman Blvd. Pickering Place, north of I-90 exit 15, offers discount shopping venues.

COUGAR MOUNTAIN ZOO, at 19525 S.E. 54th St. on Cougar Mountain, is a 14-acre facility that focuses on exotic and endangered species including cougars, reindeer, cranes, tigers, macaws, emus, lemurs and alpacas. Wed.-Sun. 9-5, Jan.-Nov.; daily 10-4:30, in Dec. Closed Jan. 1, Thanksgiving and Dec. 24-25. Admission $10.50; $9.50 (ages 63+); $8 (ages 2-12). MC, VI. Phone (425) 391-5508 or (425) 392-6278.

GILMAN TOWN HALL MUSEUM is at 165 S.E. Andrews St. Constructed as a public hall in 1888, this structure served as the city hall 1898-1930. The building now houses displays describing pioneer life and the area's coal mining, timber and dairy industries. Exhibits include family heirlooms, pioneer photos and vintage household items. A 1914 concrete structure that was once used as the city jail stands behind the museum. Allow 30 minutes minimum. Thurs.-Sat. 11-3, Tues. 4-8, June-Aug.; Thurs.-Sat. 11-3, rest of year. Closed federal holidays. Donations. Phone (425) 392-3500.

ISSAQUAH DEPOT MUSEUM is at 50 Rainier Blvd. N. Located in a restored 1889 railroad depot, the museum contains exhibits detailing the history of the local railway and the development of Issaquah. In addition to railroad memorabilia, there is a model railroad layout and an exhibit on telegraphy. Visitors can board an old army railroad car and a vintage caboose. Allow 30 minutes minimum, Fri.-Sun. 11-3, Thurs. 4-8, June-Aug.; Fri.-Sun. 11-3, rest of year. Closed federal holidays. Donations. Phone (425) 392-3500.

ISSAQUAH STATE SALMON HATCHERY, 125 W. Sunset Way, raises 5 to 6 million chinook and coho salmon each year. Adult salmon return to the hatchery in fall. Self-guiding tours are offered. Grounds open daily dawn-dusk. Lobby exhibits open daily 8-4. Guided tours are available by appointment late Aug.-Oct. 31. Free. Phone (425) 391-9094, or (425) 427-0259 for tours.

KENMORE (E-3) pop. 18,678, elev. 31′

Kenmore lies at the north end of Lake Washington. Kenmore Air Harbor is one of the nation's largest commercial seaplane airports. Nearby Tracy Owen Station Park, off SR 522, has lake access. The Burke Gilman Trail also passes through the area, offering a paved recreational path to Seattle and Redmond.

Bastyr University, adjacent to St. Edward State Park, is one of the world's leading academic centers for advancing knowledge in the natural health sciences, and one of only four naturopathic schools in the nation.

Visitor Information, City of Kenmore: 6700 N.E. 181st St., Kenmore, WA 98028; phone (425) 398-8900.

ST. EDWARD STATE PARK, 1.5 mi. s. of SR 522 via 99th Ave. and Juanita Dr., occupies a wooded and hilly 316-acre site beside Lake Washington. Native Americans once used the area for fishing. From 1931 to 1976 the Roman Catholic Sulpician Order operated a seminary here, and the brick buildings set amid expansive lawns are an architectural highlight. The Grotto, a secluded garden alcove, is a serene spot to relax.

Thirteen trails lace the park, several of them leading through a forest of firs, cedars and moss-draped maples down to the 3,000-foot lakefront, the longest undeveloped shoreline on Lake Washington. Raccoons, squirrels, otters, muskrats, ducks, eagles, herons, jays, owls and woodpeckers are among the resident wildlife. One of the best hiking spots in the greater Seattle area, St. Edwards also is very popular with mountain bikers. Trail maps can be picked up at the park ranger station in the former seminary gymnasium.

Picnicking is permitted. Allow 1 hour minimum. Daily 8 a.m.-dusk. Free. Phone (425) 823-2992.

KENT (G-3) pop. 79,524

Settled in the 1880s, Kent was first called Titusville—named for its first mayor James Titus. Hops were the area's major crop, and in 1890 the town was renamed for Kent County, the English hop growing center. Dairying emerged as the prime industry after disease decimated the hop yards in 1895.

Boeing opened a plant here in 1965, and today Kent is a major wholesale distribution and light manufacturing center. Pacific Raceways, 31001 144th Ave. S.E., offers NHRA drag, road and motocross racing on its 2.25-mile track; phone (253) 639-5927. The brand-new Kent Events Center, Fifth Ave. N. and W. James St., is the home ice for the Seattle Thunderbirds hockey team; for ticket information phone (206) 448-7825 or (800) 743-9122.

Kent Chamber of Commerce: 524 W. Meeker St., Suite 1, P.O. Box 128, Kent, WA 98035-0128; phone (253) 854-1770.

GREATER KENT HISTORICAL SOCIETY MUSEUM, .3 mi. e. of SR 516 at 855 E. Smith St., is in the three-story, 1908 Craftsman-style Bereiter house. E.W. Bereiter was a prosperous businessman and served as mayor of Kent. Furnished in period, the museum has changing exhibits of local historical artifacts. Allow 30 minutes minimum. Wed.-Sat. noon-4 or by appointment; closed major holidays. Donations. Phone (253) 854-4330.

HYDROPLANE AND RACEBOAT MUSEUM is at 5917 S. 196th St.; take I-5 exit 152 e. via Orillia Rd. and S. 200th St., which curves into S. 196th St. This fascinating collection of artifacts from the sport of powerboat racing includes seven restored, operational hydroplanes dating from the 1940s to the 1980s. Other displays showcase books, trophies and race memorabilia. Visitors also can see the powerboat restoration area and engine room.

Guided tours are available. Allow 1 hour minimum. Tues.-Fri. 10-5 (also Tues. and Thurs. 5-8), May-Sept.; Tues. and Thurs. 10-8, Sat. 10-4, rest of year. Closed holidays. Admission $10; $5 (ages 6-15 and 62+). Guided tour free; audio tour fee $5. AX, DS, MC, VI. Phone (206) 764-9453.

KEYPORT (F-2) elev. 43'

Billed as "Torpedo Town USA," Keyport is home to the Naval Undersea Warfare Center. The Navy chose this site in 1910 and has been developing, storing, repairing and testing torpedoes here since 1914. The small town adjoining the base was settled in 1896. Citizens picked the town's name from the New Jersey page of an atlas in the hopes that their community would become the "key port" on Liberty Bay.

NAVAL UNDERSEA MUSEUM is 3 mi. e. of SR 3 on SR 308 to the main access road to Naval Undersea Warfare Center. The museum uses audio and visual effects to simulate an undersea atmosphere. A timeline illustrates the history of sea exploration. Exhibits focus on mines and torpedoes, submarines in the World War II Pacific Theater and the physics of the undersea world.

Outdoor exhibits include the deep-sea submersibles *Trieste II* and *DeepQuest* as well as the sail from the submarine USS *Sturgeon*. Daily 10-4, June-Sept.; Wed.-Mon. 10-4, rest of year. Closed Jan. 1, Easter, Thanksgiving and Dec. 25. Free. Phone (360) 396-4148.

KINGSTON (E-2) pop. 1,611, elev. 80'

Nestled on Appletree Cove, Kingston was one of the first ports on Puget Sound. The 1841 Wilkes expedition named this small bay for the prevalence of wild apple trees along the shore. The village took its name from William P. Kingston, who started a lumber operation here in 1888.

The town became an important port for the Mosquito Fleet, a network of small boats that crisscrossed the sound. Today Kingston is primarily a bedroom community for ferry commuters who work in Snohomish and King counties. Washington State Ferries provides frequent car ferry service across the sound to Edmonds; phone (888) 808-7977 in Wash.

Greater Kingston Community Chamber of Commerce: 11212 SR 104, P.O. Box 78, Kingston, WA 98346; phone (360) 297-3813.

GAMBLING ESTABLISHMENTS

• **The Point Casino** is 3 mi. w. on SR 104, then 2 mi. n. on Hansville Rd. to 7989 Salish Ln. N.E. Daily 24 hours. Phone (360) 297-0070 or (866) 547-6468.

KIRKLAND (F-3) pop. 45,054, elev. 100'

There aren't too many towns that can boast a lovely lakefront setting *and* a downtown that's pedestrian-friendly in the best sense of the term. And happily, Kirkland has both. No other place in the greater Seattle area has as many waterfront parks as this city on Lake Washington's northeastern shore. On a clear day you can see downtown Seattle across the lake, with the distant Olympic Mountains beyond.

In fact, exploring the waterfront—which stretches for several miles from Juanita Bay south to Yarrow

Point—is one of the most popular pastimes here. There are public beaches, woodlands and wetlands for hiking, and nesting habitats for shorebirds and eagles. Sunsets are notable regardless of the season, whether it's the blue skies and pink colors of summer or the austere slate grays of winter (and fall and spring, but Northwesterners are used to it).

Visit on a sunny summer day to take full advantage of the parks. Marina Park is just a few steps off Lake Street and downtown. It has a sandy beach and an open-air pavilion as well as a marina, and the lake views are outstanding. Celebrate the opening day of boating season in early May, or catch a music performance in July and August. A short distance north of Marina Park is Waverly Beach Park (take Central Way west to Market Street, turn right, go north a block to Waverly Way, turn left and continue to the end of the street). It has a bigger beach, a designated swimming area enclosed by a U-shaped dock (good for sunbathing on warm days), and a sweeping view of Lake Washington's northern reaches.

Juanita Bay Park (from downtown, take Market Street/98th Avenue north) encompasses 110 acres of wooded wetland, meadow and marsh areas. It's a good spot for bird watchers to roam around. The diversity of vegetation in this urban wildlife habitat area can be seen from the boardwalk nature trails that wind along the shoreline. South of downtown, Houghton Beach Park, 5811 Lake Washington Blvd. N.E., is ideal for families; there's a shallow swimming area for kids, a playground, picnic tables, beach volleyball and a public dock for fishing.

You can hardly turn around in Kirkland without bumping into a bronze sculpture or two. There's a bevy of them along the waterfront. At the Marina Park dock, "Coming Home" depicts an embracing family; nearby, along Lakeshore Plaza Drive, "Puddle Jumpers" depicts six hand-holding, leaping kids—including two with feet suspended in mid-air. This one is pure poetry in motion. Three more youngsters play "Leap Frog" at Marsh Park, just off Lake Washington Boulevard N.E.

There are plenty more sculptures on Kirkland's downtown streets. "Cow and Coyote" near the corner of Central Way and Lake Street is just what the name says: a coyote rakishly perched atop the hind end of a seemingly oblivious cow. Across the street, two bronze bunnies make for "Close Quarters" as they cuddle together in the middle of a sidewalk garden. Or take a seat next to "Betty Lou"; she's the nonchalant gal sitting on a bench at the corner of Kirkland Avenue and Main Street.

If you're strolling along the lakefront on a nice day, stop for a bite to eat at The Slip, a little slip of a restaurant on Kirkland Avenue, just steps from the water (look for the blue door, blue shutters and the stone statue of a bearded seafarer wearing a cap). On warm summer evenings folks gather on The Slip's outdoor patio deck, sipping plum mojitos and sampling menu items like their signature peanut butter bacon burger. This is casual dining Kirkland style—with a water view.

It wouldn't be Seattle—or its environs—without a place to get some excellent coffee, and Kahili Coffee, 105 S. Lake St., is the place to get it. Whether it's an espresso, Americano, latte, cappuccino or mocha, the Kona beans they use come straight from a Hawaiian farm. They also have teas and fruit smoothies as well as the usual muffins and scones. It's an inviting, airy space with plenty of comfy chairs. Free Wi-Fi access—plus occasional live music—will encourage you to stick around for awhile.

The Kirkland Wednesday Market sets up from May through October on Park Lane between Main and 3rd streets. Produce vendors offer a bounty of seasonal, locally grown fruits and veggies—sweet corn, baby lettuces, summer squash, heirloom tomatoes, blackberries, gooseberries, nectarines and more—plus flowers, jam, baked goods and crafts.

Get into the artistic spirit on Kirkland Second Thursdays, which take place the second Thursday of the month from 6 to 8 p.m. This is when downtown galleries spotlight new artists and new works. Meet them and pick up some tips on art selection, framing and presentation; for more information phone (425) 889-8212. Downtown restaurants and venues feature jazz and other live music on Kirkland Jazz Nights, which also take place the second Thursday of the month (April through December); phone (425) 893-8766. Obviously, Thursday is a good night to hit town.

The focus of Kirkland Uncorked, held in mid-July, is fine Washington food and wine. This 3-day "festival of style and taste" is the city's signature summer event. A tasting garden highlights the products of Washington wineries, paired with gourmet nibbles. The festivities also include live jazz and light classical performances, luxury boats that can be toured and a "cover dog" contest for pooches, with proceeds going to a shelter for homeless animals. It all takes place at Marina Park.

You'll be lucky to find on-street parking downtown in summer, but it's free. There are parking lots with both free and metered spaces at Marina Park, on Lake Street S. and on Main Street. You can park free for 4 hours in the municipal parking garage beneath the Kirkland Library (entrances are on 3rd Street and Kirkland Avenue), or all day for $5.

Greater Kirkland Chamber of Commerce: 401 Parkplace, Suite 102, Kirkland, WA 98033; phone (425) 822-7066.

Shopping areas: As you would expect in a town dedicated to the arts, there are more than a few art galleries to browse, most of them concentrated in an easily walkable area downtown. The Howard/Mandville Gallery, 120 Park Ln., is one of the largest, with paintings, sculpture and prints by regional and nationally known artists. Emerging as well as established contemporary Northwest artists exhibit at the Park Lane Gallery, 130 Park Ln.

Handcrafted jewelry and glass, clay, wood and metal pieces are on display at the Lakeshore Gallery, 107 Park Ln. The Gunnar Nordstrom Gallery,

127 Lake St. S., is an intimate space that displays contemporary fine art. Regional artist Bill Braun's works are huge favorites here. His *trompe l'oeil* paintings are incredibly realistic: simply rendered montages of flowers, houses and butterflies that look just like a child's construction paper art project. You won't believe your eyes.

Interspersed among the galleries are a slew of specialty shops and boutiques; just wander until you find one that appeals to you. Bella Bambini (3 Lake St.) has cute baby items. Skateboarders will find everything they need at Trickwood (114 Lake St.). Fashionistas will approve of Promesse (128 Central Way) and Via Lago (129 Lake St.).

Kirkland Parkplace, on Central Way about half a mile west of I-405 exit 18, has specialty stores like Ravenna Gardens and Tim's Seafood; restaurants, bakeries and (naturally) a Starbucks; and a six-screen cinema.

Nightlife: The Wilde Rover Irish Pub & Restaurant, 111 Central Way, is named after Irish playwright, novelist and poet Oscar Wilde. It offers a full menu of evening entertainment, from live music on "Celtic Mondays" to open mic nights and a trivia contest on Wednesdays. Hoist a Guinness Stout and offer the traditional Irish drinking toast: "Sláinte!" (Pronounce it "slanj" and you'll be in the ballpark.)

The Kirkland Avenue Pub (205 Kirkland Ave.) is a casual hangout where you can shoot pool or watch the ball game while grabbing a bite to eat. The Central Club (124 Kirkland Ave.) is another popular gathering spot for everybody from bikers to Microsoft geeks. There's live music here on Wednesday and Sunday nights.

A bit rowdier is the Shark Club (52 Lakeshore Plaza at Marina Park). This is where young, trendy 20-somethings congregate for loud music, drink specials, dance nights and general revelry. There's a nominal cover charge, and it's packed on weekends. The scene is similar at Tiki Joe's Wet Bar (108 Kirkland Ave.), which has live and DJ music, karaoke, a hopping happy hour, more drink specials and no cover charge.

SAVE ARGOSY CRUISES departs from Kirkland Marina Park, 1.2 mi. w. off I-405 exit 18. The 1.5-hour narrated Lakes Cruise Kirkland follows the Lake Washington shoreline, offering a glimpse of luxurious waterfront homes and mountain scenery. Cruises depart daily at 11:30, 1:30 and 3:30, early June-Labor Day; Mon.-Fri. at 1:30, Sat.-Sun. at 1:30 and 3:30, early May-early June and day after Labor Day to mid-Oct.; Fri.-Sun. at 1:30, mid-Oct. to late Nov.; Sat.-Sun. at 1:30, early Apr.-early May. Fare $29; $9 (ages 5-12). A fuel surcharge may apply; phone for details. AX, DC, DS, JC, MC, VI. Phone (206) 623-4252 or (800) 642-7816.

KIRKLAND ARTS CENTER is .2 mi. n. at 620 Market St. Housed in the Peter Kirk Building, built in 1891, the center's art gallery displays a variety of works by artists from across the country with a focus on Northwest art. Mon.-Fri. 11-6, Sat. 11-5; closed holidays. Free. Phone (425) 822-7161.

LAKEWOOD (G-2) pop. 58,211, elev. 260'

The Tacoma suburban city of Lakewood takes its name from the more than one dozen lakes and ponds within the town's boundaries.

McChord Air Force Base and the U.S. Army's Fort Lewis, two of the country's largest armed forces installations, adjoin Lakewood on the south. Fort Steilacoom, on Steilacoom Boulevard at the western edge of town, was established in 1849 on land rented from the Hudson's Bay Co. The army vacated the fort in 1868. Two years later an insane asylum, later a state mental hospital, was established in its place. All that remains of the military post are four 1858 houses, a cemetery and the parade ground. The former fort is now Lakewood's largest recreation area.

Lakewood Area Chamber of Commerce: 4650 Steilacoom Blvd. S.W., Bldg. 19, Suite 109, Lakewood, WA 98499; phone (253) 582-9400.

FORT LEWIS MILITARY MUSEUM is off I-5 exit 120, n. on 41st Division Dr., following signs. Located at one of the Army's largest permanent posts—Fort Lewis—the museum features galleries displaying weapons, uniforms and vehicles relevant to the military history of the Pacific Northwest. The fort was the first military installation created as the result of a gift of land by private citizens to the federal government. Visitors must obtain a pass at the main gate, south of I-5 exit 120. Allow 1 hour minimum. Wed.-Sun. noon-4; closed holidays. Donations. Phone (253) 967-7206.

SAVE LAKEWOLD GARDENS is 9 mi. s. on I-5 to exit 124, then 1 mi. w. to 12317 Gravelly Lake Dr. S.W. Garden highlights of this 10-acre former private estate include formal parterres and topiaries, Japanese maples and rhododendrons, a giant Douglas fir that creates its own shade garden, an 18th-century sculptured lion fountain and a medieval Knot Garden with unusual plants. The Georgian-style manor also is open to visitors.

Wed.-Sun. 10-4, Apr.-Sept.; hours vary rest of year. Admission $5; $3 (ages 63+, students and military with ID); free (ages 0-11). Reservations are required for guided tours. MC, VI. Phone (253) 584-4106.

LAKEWOOD HISTORY MUSEUM is in the town center at 6211 Mt. Tacoma Dr. S.W. A timeline traces Lakewood's development from the 1840s to the present. Permanent exhibits include maps, historic documents, a pioneer cabin, an early post office and a business office circa 1935-45. Temporary exhibits are mounted as well. Guided tours are available by appointment. Allow 30 minutes minimum. Tues.-Sat. 10-4; closed holidays. Donations. Phone (253) 682-3480.

LYNNWOOD (E-3) pop. 33,847, elev. 370'

The area's tall, virgin timber attracted loggers in the early 1900s. Later the Seattle-Everett interurban trolley line provided a reliable transportation link, and by 1917 the Puget Mill Co. was marketing 5- and 10-acre plots on their logged lands as far away as Chicago. Part of their marketing effort was the 32-acre Alderwood Manor Demonstration Farm, which offered would-be farmers hands-on experience in rural life, featuring a fish hatchery, gardens and a hotel.

Scriber Lake Park, at 196th Street S.W. and 52nd Avenue W., offers winding paths, native vegetation and an unusual floating walkway. The 13-mile paved Interurban Trail links Lynnwood with Everett.

Snohomish County Visitor Information Center—Lynnwood: 19921 Poplar Way, Lynnwood, WA 98036; phone (425) 776-3977.

Shopping areas: Alderwood Mall, 3000 184th St. S.W., has more than 200 stores, including JCPenney, Macy's, Nordstrom and Sears.

HERITAGE PARK is east of I-5 exit 181 at 19921 Poplar Way. The park features historic buildings including the 1919 Wickers Building, the first general store for the community that was then called Alderwood Manor. Inside is the visitor information center and displays of historic photographs showcasing the interurban railway. An adjacent structure houses the restored Interurban Trolley Car 55, which provided daily service between Seattle and Everett 1910-1939. Allow 30 minutes minimum. Park open daily dawn-dusk. Visitor center Fri.-Sat., Mon. and Wed. 9-5; Sun., Tues. and Thurs. 9-3. Free. Phone (425) 744-6478.

MARYSVILLE (D-3) pop. 25,315, elev. 15'

In 1877 James P. Comeford built a trading post on Ebey Slough and thus founded the town of Marysville. The town's industries have included boat building and woodworking; one of the earliest logging locomotives was built in Marysville in 1883. Today the town's main businesses include dairy products, agriculture and light industry. The Tulalip Indian Reservation, established in 1855, is the site of the oldest Roman Catholic mission on Puget Sound.

Greater Marysville-Tulalip Chamber of Commerce: 8825 34th Ave. N.E., Suite C, Marysville, WA 98271; phone (360) 659-7700.

Shopping areas: Seattle Premium Outlets, west of I-5 exit 202, features more than 100 stores including Ann Taylor, Banana Republic, Burberry, Gap Outlet and Tommy Hilfiger.

GAMBLING ESTABLISHMENTS

• **Tulalip Casino**, 10200 Quil Ceda Blvd. Daily 24 hours. Phone (360) 651-1111 or (888) 272-1111.

MONROE (D-7) pop. 13,795, elev. 72'

The earliest homesteaders settled the rich river bottomlands along the Snohomish and Skykomish rivers in 1858. Originally called Park Place, the town was renamed for President James Monroe in 1889. It prospered first as a logging center, then later as a farming community. The scenic Stevens Pass Highway (US 2) follows the Skykomish River east into the Cascade Range.

Evergreen Speedway, located at the Evergreen State Fairgrounds, 1 mi. w. of Monroe on US 2, offers racing and NASCAR-sanctioned events Saturdays from April to September; phone (360) 805-6100.

Monroe Chamber of Commerce: 111 W. Main St., Monroe, WA 98272; phone (360) 794-5488.

WASHINGTON SERPENTARIUM is 2 mi. e. of jct. SR 203 at 22715 US 2. The serpentarium displays more than 50 snakes, including rattlesnakes, pythons, cobras and mambas. The collection also features turtles, tortoises and lizards. Highlights include 10 of the world's deadliest snakes and an albino alligator. Allow 45 minutes minimum. Daily 10-6. Admission $6; $5 (ages 3-17). AX, MC, VI. Phone (360) 805-5300.

MUKILTEO (E-3) pop. 18,019, elev. 12'

Mukilteo, named for the Suquamish word meaning "good camping ground," was the site of the Point Elliott Treaty of 1855. The document, signed by the leaders of 22 local tribes, relinquished land claims to white settlers. A lighthouse built in 1905 is open to visitors on weekends and holidays Apr.-Sept.; phone (425) 513-9602. Toll ferry service connects the mainland with Clinton on Whidbey Island; phone (888) 808-7977 in Wash.

FUTURE OF FLIGHT AVIATION CENTER & BOEING TOUR is off I-5 exit 189, then 4.5 mi. w. on SR 526, following signs to 8415 Paine Field Blvd. The center features several learning zones with interactive computer stations that let visitors design and test their own aircraft using software similar to that used by Boeing engineers.

A four-story-high tail section from a 747 Jumbo Jet is one of the most impressive items visitors can see. Changing displays show off the latest technology and materials from various aerospace companies. Tours of Boeing's commercial jet assembly plant depart from the aviation center and allow visitors to watch airplanes—including 747s, 767s, 777s and, in the near future, 787s—being manufactured and tested.

Purses, backpacks and such electronic devices as cell phones, pagers and cameras are not permitted on the tour. Food is available. Future of Flight Aviation Center open daily 8:30-5:30. Tours are given on the hour 9-3 (last tour at 11, Dec. 24 and 31); closed Jan. 1, Thanksgiving and Dec. 25. Tour (includes gallery admission) $15; $14 (ages 65+ and military with ID); $8 (ages 0-15). Admission (gallery only)

$9; $4 (ages 6-15). Children must be at least 4 feet tall to take the tour. Reservations are recommended for the tour; a $2.50 fee is charged for advance bookings. MC, VI. Phone (425) 438-8100 or (800) 464-1476.

NORTH BEND (E-7) pop. 4,746, elev. 445'

The chief agricultural center for the upper Snoqualmie Valley, North Bend straddles the South Fork of the Snoqualmie River. The town's proximity to Snoqualmie Pass and the western slopes of the Cascade Range make it a good starting point for trips to both areas.

Mountains have influenced local architecture, much of which sports an alpine motif. Nearby Mount Si (SIGH) reaches an elevation of 4,167 feet; a 4-mile trail to the summit ascends 3,500 feet and affords spectacular views. Linking with the 2-mile Rattlesnake Ledge Trail, the 8.8-mile Rattlesnake Mountain Trail provides views of Mount Si, North Bend and the Snoqualmie River Valley. The early 1990s television series "Twin Peaks" was filmed in North Bend and neighboring Snoqualmie.

Snoqualmie Valley Chamber of Commerce: North Bend Way, P.O. Box 357, North Bend, WA 98045; phone (425) 888-4440.

Shopping areas: Factory Stores at North Bend, I-90 exit 31, offers discount shopping in more than 50 stores.

CEDAR RIVER WATERSHED EDUCATION CENTER is at 19901 Cedar Falls Rd. S.E. The center features interpretive exhibits, interactive displays and multimedia presentations about the more than 92,000-acre Cedar River Watershed, which is owned and maintained by Seattle as a source of drinking water for nearly 1.3 million people. Access to the watershed is limited to maintain water quality, but guided nature tours are offered on summer weekends. Other special programs are offered.

Allow 30 minutes minimum. Tues.-Sun. 10-5, Apr.-Oct.; Tues.-Fri. 10-4, rest of year. Closed most holidays. Free. Guided tours $10; $5 (ages 55+ and students with ID). Ages 0-5 are not permitted. Reservations are required. Phone (206) 733-9421.

SNOQUALMIE VALLEY HISTORICAL MUSEUM, off I-90 exit 31, then .5 mi. n. to 320 Bendigo Blvd. S., contains Snoqualmie Indian artifacts and pioneer memorabilia and furnishings, including a vintage 1910 kitchen and parlor. Highlights include a 28-foot cedar dugout canoe, a farm shed with antique farming equipment and historical photographs. A diorama depicts the beginnings of the logging industry. Guided tours are available by appointment. Allow 30 minutes minimum. Thurs.-Sun. 1-5, Apr.-Oct.; closed Easter, Mother's Day and Father's Day. Donations. Phone (425) 888-3200.

SNOQUALMIE VALLEY RAILROAD— see Snoqualmie p. 256.

PORT ORCHARD (F-2) pop. 7,693, elev. 13'

The first settlers in the area built houses on the wooded shores of Sinclair Inlet in 1854 and named their community Sidney. Sawmills and shipyards formed a sound base for the town's economy, and in 1903 Sidney was renamed Port Orchard and made the seat of Kitsap County.

Antique and specialty shops operate near the marina, and the waterfront park is the scene of a farmers market and outdoor concerts in summer. The Log Cabin Museum, 416 Sidney Ave., features an early 20th-century log house with period furnishings; phone (360) 876-3693. Daily passenger ferry service links Port Orchard and Annapolis to nearby Bremerton; phone (360) 373-2877 for schedule.

Port Orchard Chamber of Commerce: 1014 Bay St., Suite 8, Port Orchard, WA 98366; phone (360) 876-3505 or (800) 982-8139.

Shopping areas: Antique shopping is popular in Port Orchard. Olde Central Antique Mall, 801 Bay St., has more than 40 dealers.

SIDNEY ART GALLERY AND MUSEUM is at 202 Sidney Ave. The museum is housed on the upper level of a 1908 Masonic Temple. Displays include a pioneer post office, doctor's office, schoolhouse, mercantile, a hardware store and exhibits about early-day logging. Downstairs galleries feature pottery and paintings by Northwest artists. Allow 30 minutes minimum. Tues.-Sat. 11-4, Sun. 1-4; closed major holidays. Free. Phone (360) 876-3693.

POULSBO (E-2) pop. 6,813

Set on hillsides overlooking Liberty Bay, Poulsbo is a picturesque port with a strong Scandinavian heritage. The first postmaster called it Paulsbo, meaning "Paul's Place" in Norwegian, but a postal service misspelling ultimately prevailed.

In the 1880s Norwegians comprised 90 percent of the town's population, and Norwegian was commonly heard on city streets well into the 1920s. Today evidence of Poulsbo's heritage can be seen in the Norwegian banners decorating Front Street, cafes that offer Scandinavian delicacies and streets bearing the names of Norwegian royalty. Many buildings feature the decorative architectural motif known as rosemaling, which often incorporates floral designs.

Greater Poulsbo Chamber of Commerce: 19351 8th Ave., Suite 108, Poulsbo, WA 98370; phone (360) 779-4848 or (877) 768-5726.

POULSBO MARINE SCIENCE CENTER is .4 mi. s. of SR 305 via Lincoln Dr. to 18743 Front St. N.E. Puget Sound's fresh and saltwater environments are on display in six aquarium tanks that re-create such areas as estuaries, intertidal zones, the vicinity of wharves and pilings and the muddy sea floor. You also can watch videos about marine life. Allow 30 minutes minimum. Thurs.-Sun. 11-4. Free; donations are accepted. Phone (360) 598-4460.

PUYALLUP (G-3) pop. 33,011, elev. 48'

After crossing the plains in a covered wagon, Ezra Meeker arrived at a site just east of what is now Tacoma *(see place listing p. 257)* and named it for the Puyallup tribe; the name means "generous people." Puyallup is the home of a lucrative flower bulb industry based on the irises, daffodils and tulips that thrive in the area's soil and climate.

Puyallup/Sumner Chamber of Commerce: 323 N. Meridian, P.O. Box 1298, Puyallup, WA 98371; phone (253) 845-6755.

Shopping areas: South Hill Mall, .25 mile south of SR 512 on Meridian Street E., features JCPenney, Macy's and Sears. Downtown Puyallup has a dozen antique and secondhand shops, most on Meridian Street.

MEEKER MANSION, 312 Spring St., is a 17-room Italianate Victorian house that was the home of Ezra Meeker, an entrepreneur and Puyallup's first mayor. Guided tours of the 1890 mansion reveal ceiling art, handcrafted fireplaces, leaded glass windows and period furnishings. A variety of events are held at the mansion throughout the year.

Allow 30 minutes minimum. Wed.-Sun. noon-4, closed Jan. 1, Easter, Thanksgiving and Dec. 25. Admission $4; $3 (ages 12-18 and 62+); $2 (ages 0-11). Admission half price on Thurs. Phone (253) 848-1770.

VAN LIEROP BULB FARM is 1.5 mi. e. of SR 512/161; take E. Pioneer Ave. exit to 13407 80th St. E. A 1-acre spring display garden with a variety of daffodils, tulips and hyacinths is in bloom March through April. Allow 30 minutes minimum. Mon.-Fri. 8:30-5:30, Sat.-Sun. 9-5, Jan. 15 to mid-May. Free. Phone (253) 848-7272.

REDMOND (E-3) pop. 45,256, elev. 50'

First called Salmonberg for the abundance of salmon in the Sammamish River, Redmond was renamed to honor pioneer settler and first postmaster Luke McRedmond. Today the local economy is based on light industries and electronics. Redmond is headquarters of such well-known companies as Microsoft, Nintendo of America and Eddie Bauer.

The city offers miles of bike trails; the paved Sammamish River Trail connects the city with Woodinville, Bothell and Seattle. Other recreation areas include Lake Sammamish State Park *(see Recreation Chart)* and Farrel-McWhirter Park.

Greater Redmond Chamber of Commerce: 16210 N.E. 80th St., P.O. Box 628, Redmond, WA 98073-0625; phone (425) 885-4014.

Shopping areas: Redmond Town Center, on Redmond Way, offers more than 100 shopping venues, including Macy's, Borders Books and Music, Eddie Bauer and REI.

MARYMOOR PARK, .5 mi. s. on W. Lake Sammamish Pkwy. N.E., is a 642-acre recreation area on the site of Seattle banker James Clise's estate. The park provides facilities for picnicking, tennis, soccer, rugby, lacrosse, rock climbing, horseback riding, softball and bicycling; the velodrome is the scene of international-class bicycling events. The park also has a radio-controlled model airplane field. Daily 8-dusk. Free. Phone (206) 205-3661.

MICROSOFT VISITOR CENTER is at 4420 148th Ave., N.E., Building 127, adjacent to Microsoft's corporate headquarters. The visitor center recounts the software giant's history along with the history of personal computing through a 30-foot-long timeline that includes a large collection of computer memorabilia. Interactive, hands-on product displays showcase current technology and explore possibilities for future Microsoft products. Allow 1 hour minimum. Mon.-Fri. 9-7. Free. Phone (425) 703-6214.

RENTON (F-3) pop. 50,052, elev. 45'

Originally a Duwamish Indian encampment, Renton has evolved into a manufacturing city at the southern end of Lake Washington, and production of jet aircraft is the main heavy industry. Boeing rolled out its first commercial jet, the 707, at its Renton plant, which now produces 737 aircraft.

Gene L. Coulon Memorial Beach Park, 2 miles north on Lake Washington Boulevard, offers freshwater fishing, swimming, boating and a nature trail. Renton River Days, held in August, features arts and crafts, entertainment, rides, games and athletic events. Greenwood Memorial Park Cemetery, N.E. 4th St. and Monroe Ave. N.E., contains a memorial to Seattle-born rock legend Jimi Hendrix.

Renton Chamber of Commerce: 300 Rainier Ave. N., Renton, WA 98057; phone (425) 226-4560.

RENTON HISTORY MUSEUM, 235 Mill Ave. S., features exhibits tracing the city's growth from a Duwamish Indian camp through its 19th-century coal mining and lumber producing days to its current status as a manufacturing center. Displays focus on Boeing's Renton plant, pioneer lifestyles and Renton soldiers who fought in World Wars I and II.

The collection includes a World War I flight simulator and a vintage neon movie theater sign. Allow 30 minutes minimum. Tues.-Sat. 10-4; closed holidays. Admission $3; $1 (ages 8-16). Phone (425) 255-2330.

SEATAC (F-3) pop. 25,496, elev. 371'

SeaTac takes its name from Seattle-Tacoma International Airport, which opened in 1947. International Boulevard (SR 99), with its dozens of hotels, restaurants, long-term parking lots, car rental agencies and other businesses catering to air travelers, is the main thoroughfare of this suburban community. Two-hour guided tours of the airport are offered Tuesday, Wednesday and Thursday at 10 a.m., September through June. Advance reservations are required; phone (206) 433-5386.

HIGHLINE SEATAC BOTANICAL GARDEN is at 13735 24th Ave. S. This 10.5-acre site encompasses display gardens, wooded areas and walking trails. Elda Behm's Paradise Garden, relocated in 2000-01 for an airport runway expansion project, has a recirculating water feature with a stream, four waterfalls and pools. Themed areas include a Japanese garden and seasonal plantings showcasing day lilies, iris and roses. A sensory garden is adjacent to the nearby senior center.

Picnicking is permitted. Allow 30 minutes minimum. Daily 7 a.m.-dusk. Free. Phone (206) 391-4003.

SHORELINE (E-2) pop. 53,025, elev. 475'

Just north of Seattle, Shoreline is primarily a residential community. Richmond Beach, 3 miles west of SR 99 via N. 185th Street and Richmond Beach Road, offers one of the largest sand beaches on Puget Sound.

Shoreline Chamber of Commerce: 18560 First Ave. N.E., Shoreline, WA 98155; phone (206) 361-2260.

SHORELINE HISTORICAL MUSEUM, 749 N. 175th St., is housed in a 1912 elementary school. Exhibits include a schoolroom, blacksmith shop, general store, farmhouse and community history room. The museum also features a collection of vintage 1900-1950 radios. Tues.-Sat. 10-4; closed holidays. Donations. Phone (206) 542-7111.

SNOHOMISH (D-7) pop. 8,494, elev. 64'

Founded in 1859 at the confluence of the Pilchuck and Snohomish rivers, Snohomish's rich history is reflected in its homes and commercial buildings. The residential area north of 2nd Street has some substantial Victorians, and a number of 19th-century buildings along 1st Street and the riverbank have been restored. The Snohomish Visitor Information Center, a replica of a turn-of-the-20th-century railroad station, provides an interpretive exhibit and a 10-minute video about the town's history. In keeping with its Victorian-era atmosphere, Snohomish bills itself the antique capital of the Northwest.

The Blackman House Museum, 118 Ave. B, was built in 1878 by Snohomish's first mayor, Hyrcanus Blackman. Subsequently enlarged and remodeled in 1895, the house and its furnishings have been restored to reflect the Victorian period. Phone (360) 568-5235.

The 16-mile Centennial Trail, a paved path for pedestrians and bicyclists, was built on the abandoned Burlington Northern Railroad right-of-way.

Snohomish Visitor Information Center: 1301 First St., Snohomish, WA 98290; phone (360) 862-9609.

Self-guiding tours: Driving or walking tour maps of Snohomish are available from the visitor information center.

Shopping areas: Snohomish's historic business district, on 1st Street between Cedar Avenue and Avenue D, contains some 20 malls providing space for

more than 450 antique dealers. Restored buildings house restaurants and specialty shops.

RECREATIONAL ACTIVITIES

Hot Air Ballooning

• **Airial Balloon Co.** departs from a site near Harvey Field airport, 10123 Airport Way, Snohomish, WA 98296. Flights daily after dawn and before dusk (weather permitting). Phone (360) 568-3025.

SNOQUALMIE (E-7) pop. 1,631, elev. 423'

Snoqualmie Falls Park, on SR 202 between Snoqualmie and Fall City, is at the site of an underground power plant to which water from the falls is sometimes diverted. An observation platform overlooks the 268-foot falls; a trail leads down to the river at the base of the falls.

NORTHWEST RAILWAY MUSEUM, on SR 202 and King St., occupies the former 1890 Northern Pacific Snoqualmie Depot. A collection of railway rolling stock, including antique steam locomotives and diesel engines, stands west of the station. Allow 30 minutes minimum. Daily 10-5; closed Jan. 1, Thanksgiving and Dec. 25. Donations. Phone (425) 888-3030.

SAVE **Snoqualmie Valley Railroad,** departing from Snoqualmie Depot as well as from North Bend, offers a scenic 11-mile round-trip excursion through Snoqualmie, North Bend and Snoqualmie Falls. Trains depart Snoqualmie Depot Sat.-Sun. at 11, 12:30, 2 and 3:30; July-Aug.; noon, 1:30 and 3, Apr.-June and Sept.-Oct. Fare 10; 9 (ages 62+); 7 (ages 2-12). AX, MC, VI. Phone (425) 888-3030.

STEILACOOM (G-2) pop. 6,049, elev. 50'

Steilacoom, founded in 1854, is Washington's oldest incorporated town and the site of the state's first library, courthouse and territorial jail. Many other structures in the town are more than a century old, including the first Protestant church in the state. The Roman Catholic Immaculate Conception Church, dating from 1856, is one of the oldest churches still in use in the state. Car ferry service is available to Anderson and Ketron islands; phone (253) 798-2766.

Steilacoom Chamber of Commerce: P.O. Box 88585, Steilacoom, WA 98388; phone (253) 582-4204.

Self-guiding tours: Maps outlining a walking tour of Steilacoom's historic attractions can be obtained at Steilacoom Historical Museum (see attraction listing)

STEILACOOM HISTORICAL MUSEUM, 1801 Rainier St., features exhibits that focus on regional pioneers. Displays include historical photographs, pioneer furnishings and original volumes from Washington Territory's first library. Adjacent to the museum are the restored 1857 Nathaniel Orr Home, which features original furnishings, and a pioneer orchard planted in the early 1900s. A wagon shed displays original tools. Allow 30 minutes minimum. Sat.-Sun. 11-3; closed holidays. Donations (museum). Nathaniel Orr Home $2; $1 (ages 0-12). Phone (253) 584-4133.

SUQUAMISH (E-2) pop. 3,510, elev. 202'

Suquamish Memorial Cemetery is the burial site of one of the most important American Indian leaders of the Northwest—Chief Sealth, who is better known today as Chief Seattle. Sealth's father, Schweabe, was a Suquamish chief; his mother was the daughter of a Duwamish chief.

As a young man Sealth gained renown as a warrior and leader, controlling regional tribes—but he also maintained friendly relations with early American and European settlers and protected them from Indian attacks. The chief also formed a personal friendship with local entrepreneur David Swinson "Doc" Maynard. Chief Sealth died in 1866 at the age of 80. In honor of their friendship, Maynard urged other settlers to name in his honor the fledgling community that later became the city and seaport of Seattle.

An interpretive marker at the west end of Agate Pass off SR 305 marks the former site of The Old Man House, which once housed eight Indian chiefs and their families.

SAVE SUQUAMISH MUSEUM, 2 mi. s. on SR 305 at the w. end of Agate Pass Bridge at 15838 Sandy Hook Rd., portrays the lifestyle of the Puget Sound Indians before and after the coming of nonnative settlers. Features include photographs, artifacts and recorded interviews. Guided tours are available with 48 hours notice.

Allow 30 minutes minimum. Daily 10-5, May-Sept.; Fri.-Sun. 11-4, rest of year. Holiday hours vary; phone ahead. Admission $4; $3 (ages 55+); $2 (ages 0-12). Phone (360) 598-3311, ext. 422.

GAMBLING ESTABLISHMENTS

• **Suquamish Clearwater Casino**, off SR 305 at 15347 Suquamish Way N.E. Fri.-Sun. 24 hours, Mon.-Thurs. 9 a.m.-5 a.m. Phone (360) 598-8700 or (800) 375-6073.

TACOMA (G-2) pop. 193,556, elev. 87'

See map page 258.

Tacoma is defined in part by a nickname: "The City of Destiny." Early settlers coined the name in hopes that their community—established in 1852 when a Swedish immigrant built a water-powered sawmill on a creek near the head of Commencement Bay—would rise to greatness by being designated the end of the line for the Northern Pacific Railroad. The bay was indeed chosen as the western terminus in 1873, but the company built its depot on a spot 2 miles south, dubbing it "New Tacoma." By the time the transcontinental link finally came through in 1887 the two towns had merged to become one Tacoma.

"The aroma of Tacoma" is another sobriquet. The Tacoma copper smelter operated by the American Smelting and Refining Company (ASARCO) was finally shut down in 1985 due to its controversial arsenic emissions (the site is being cleaned up for redevelopment), but the paper mills that are still a defining part of the downtown waterfront continue to provide olfactory proof. "Diamond in the rough," however, best describes Tacoma today, since it's often overlooked by travelers who are more familiar with the Space Needle, Pike Place Market and Pioneer Square than the Bridge of Glass, the Spanish Steps and Bôb's Java Jive.

For one thing, the transformation over the last 20 years of downtown's former warehouse district along Pacific Avenue has been dramatic. Now known as the Museum District, this is where you'll find the Museum of Glass, the Washington State History Museum and the Tacoma Art Museum *(see attraction listings)*, plus the University of Washington-Tacoma campus.

Glass sculptor extraordinaire Dale Chihuly is a Tacoma native. His abstract blown-glass creations—explosions of color and shape inspired in part by the plants and flowers in his mother's garden—are exhibited in museums, galleries and public spaces around the world. Although the artist lives and works in a studio on Seattle's Lake Union he maintains close ties with his hometown, and the city thus boasts a bevy of Chihuly installations that can be explored on a self-guiding walking excursion. If you want to learn a little more about the man and his art, take the "Ear for Art" cell phone tour, which features audio commentary at 12 tour stops (enter the three-digit number listed on the Ear for Art label at each stop). To begin the tour, dial (888) 411-4220.

Union Station *(see attraction listing)* was built in 1911 and functioned as a train station until the early 1980s. This copper-domed brick building currently serves as a federal courthouse, but inside there are five Chihuly installations. In particular, check out the orange glass flowers adorning the half moon-shaped Monarch Window on the second floor and the chandelier hanging from the skylight in the dome, which resembles a mass of writhing, multicolored snakes.

The Bridge of Glass passes over I-705, connecting the waterfront and Pacific Avenue. This pedestrian walkway is a must for Chihuly lovers. The display pieces individually showcased along the Venetian Wall conjure up everything from vases to decanters to Martian life forms, all rendered exquisitely in colored glass.

Take a break at Cutter Point Coffee, located in the McDonald-Smith Artists Lofts Building at 1936 Pacific Ave. Savor your fresh-roasted organic blend at this cozy spot with a bit of seafaring atmosphere that complements the works by local artists on display. And it gets bonus points for free Wi-Fi access.

Tacoma is a great theater town, and the Theater District, centered along—aptly enough—Broadway, spotlights two grandly restored dames and a newer, state-of-the-art facility.

The Pantages Theater (S. 9th Street and Broadway) was built in 1918, part of the nationwide theater empire created by impresario Alexander Pantages. Modeled after the lavishly opulent theater in the Palace of Versailles in France, the Pantages welcomed W.C. Fields, Mae West and other luminaries of the day. Restored in 1983, it is home to the Tacoma Opera, the Tacoma City Ballet, the Tacoma Philharmonic and the Tacoma Symphony.

The Rialto Theater (a block up from the Pantages at S. 9th and Market streets), also restored, is a Beaux Arts jewel box of a building and former movie palace that presents performances by the Northwest Sinfonietta chamber orchestra and the Tacoma Youth Symphony, among others. The intimate Theatre on the Square, next to the Pantages, mounts an annual schedule of dramas, comedies and musicals by the Tacoma Actors Guild. Close-to-the-stage seating, a come-as-you-are atmosphere and such events as "brew pub previews" all aim to make theatergoing an accessible experience here. Contact the Broadway Center for the Performing

Arts for schedule and ticket information; phone (253) 591-5894 or (800) 291-7593.

Another artsy touch in the Theater District is the masks that are installed on the outside walls of surrounding buildings. The Woolworth Windows (on Broadway near the corner of S. 11th Street) houses cool art installations in a former Woolworth's five-and-dime store. The Tollbooth Gallery (corner of Broadway and S. 11th Street) is a street kiosk that provides a tiny space for offbeat, mixed-media installations.

Downtown Tacoma has reminders of the past, too. The Elks Temple at 565 Broadway is a throwback to those pre-TV and Internet days when fraternal organizations such as the Elks, the Odd Fellows and the Knights of Pythias were important social outlets. This imposing Beaux Arts building was built in 1916 but has been vacant since 1965 and has acquired a somewhat grimy appearance; it was recently purchased by a developer.

The Spanish Steps, the stairway that connects Broadway with Commerce Street below, were intended to be used as a fire escape. Designed after

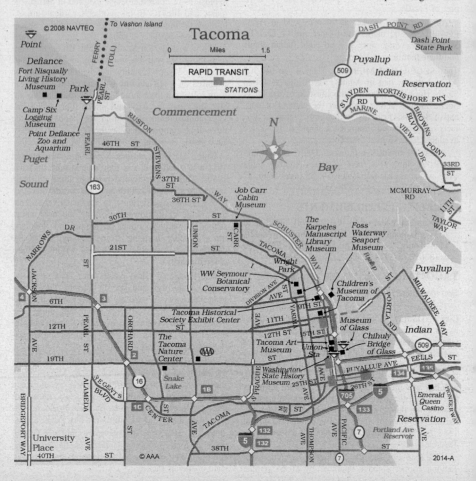

the Spanish Steps in Rome that climb from the Piazza di Spagna up to the Trinità dei Monti church, Tacoma's stairway was adorned with flowers and landscaping during its heyday, but time and city soot have been similarly unkind. The good news is that the steps will receive a makeover, with construction work due to begin in the spring of 2009. The tall, ancient-looking evergreen growing at the top of the steps is a Monkey Puzzle tree *(Araucaria araucana)*, an ornamental native to Chile and Argentina.

Stadium High School, 111 N. E St. (between 1st Street and Division Avenue), was built in 1906 and was originally going to be a luxury hotel. The turreted brick walls and narrow windows give "the castle on the hill" a decidedly Gothic look. The sunken football stadium is where Heath Ledger serenaded Julia Stiles in the 1999 movie "10 Things I Hate About You," a remake of Shakespeare's "The Taming of the Shrew" set in a contemporary high school. And the vista looking out over Commencement Bay from the top of the bleachers is spectacular.

Take advantage of Sound Transit's Tacoma Link light-rail system to explore the city. Link trains connect the Tacoma Dome station on E. 25th Street—a regional hub for bus and commuter train service—with stops at Union Station, the Convention Center and the Theater District—a convenient way to navigate downtown without driving. They run every 10 minutes Mon.-Fri. 5:20 a.m.-10 p.m. and Sat. 8 a.m. 10 p.m., and every 10 to 20 minutes Sun. and holidays 10-6. Link trains are free. For more information phone (206) 398-5000 or (800) 201-4900.

Tacoma isn't all about urban renewal and cultural enlightenment, though. It has a gritty side that's celebrated by such local institutions as Bob's Java Jive (2102 S. Tacoma Way). Rather than a tempest in a teapot, Bob's is a teapot plunked down in a rather grimy industrial neighborhood on the south side of town—which makes its offbeat charm stand out all the more. It's hard to find, but you can't miss this round white edifice complete with red spout and handle.

Above the door are the words "world famous," and Bob's certainly does have an intriguing past. It began life in 1927 as the Coffee Pot, a restaurant that during the Prohibition years had a little back room, accessed through a secret door, where patrons partook of liquor and gambling. A local businessman bought the restaurant in 1955 and renamed it the Java Jive after a popular jukebox selection by vocal group the Ink Spots. Granny Go-Go was a go-go dancing fixture here for nearly 3 decades. Java and Jive, a pair of monkeys, took up residence in a double glass cage behind the bar. Among the punks and new wavers who hung out at the Jive was Krist Novoselic, a future member of iconic Seattle grunge band Nirvana.

The Jive was shut down in 2007 for fire code violations, but supporters rallied to bring the venerable building, which is on the city's register of historic places, back up to code. It opens at 8 p.m., and for a mere $5 cover you get pool, pinball, darts, karaoke, a "jungle room" (a jungle mural painted around an addition added to the back of the teapot), beer and rowdy rock'n'roll.

Another local landmark is Frisko Freeze, a walk-up hamburger stand on N. Division Avenue (3 blocks west of Wright Park). You can't miss the classic '50s-era neon sign sitting atop a candy-cane pole. It opened in 1950—and little has changed since, from the time-honored menu of burgers, fries, onion rings and "fish wiches" to milkshakes so thick a spoon stands up with absolutely no problem. There are Seattleites who will drive 45 minutes out of their way for one of these shakes.

Since there's nary an outdoor seat at Frisko Freeze, you'll have to eat in your car. Better yet, get a milkshake to go and head down Division Avenue to Wright Park *(see attraction listing),* a lovely green rectangle shaded by beautiful old trees. Amble along the paths and listen to the kids playing; this is the sort of genteel urban scene developers were aiming for when land donated to the city in 1886 was developed into a public park modeled after the classic English design.

Other parks take advantage of the city's scenic setting. Fireman's Park, at S. 8th and A streets, overlooks Commencement Bay and the Port of Tacoma. The park's 105-foot totem (82 feet stand above ground) was carved out of red cedar by Alaskan Indians. For more panoramic views of the bay, head to Ruston Way Park, where a 2-mile-long paved walkway runs along the waterfront between Point Defiance and the North Tacoma neighborhood. On clear days you can see Vashon Island and the Olympic Mountains. Anglers can drop their lines at Les Davis Pier and the Old Town Dock.

Spectator sports? You can choose between professional baseball and ice hockey. The Tacoma Rainiers play class AAA Pacific Coast League baseball at Cheney Stadium; phone (253) 752-7700. For information about other events phone the Tacoma Dome ticket office at (253) 572-3663.

The dominant geographical feature on the Tacoma horizon is, of course, Mount Rainier. At 14,412 feet, it is not only the loftiest peak in the Cascade Range but Washington's highest point. It's also a volcano, although a dormant one; the last recorded eruption was more than 150 years ago. Rainier has three individual summit points (Columbia Crest, Point Success and Liberty Cap) that are separated by a large crater. Simultaneously built up by lava flows and torn down by erosion and eruptions over millions of years, with flanks clad in uncountable tons of snow and glacial ice, it is indeed something to behold.

Although Tacoma has long dwelled in Seattle's formidable shadow, it does trump its bigger sibling in at least one respect: the view of Rainier. It's a prominent feature of the southern landscape in most of metro Seattle, but even on a clear day it has a surreal, somewhat ethereal presence, looking rather like a ghostly painting that has somehow been pasted into place. But here there's no mistaking the mountain; it soars majestically above the City of Destiny, a definitive visual backdrop.

Tacoma Regional Convention and Visitor Bureau Visitor Information Center: 1516 Pacific Ave., Tacoma, WA 98402; phone (253) 627-2836 or (800) 272-2662.

Shopping areas: Antique Row is a concentration of more than a dozen shops along Broadway and St. Helens Avenue between S. 7th and S. 9th streets. Old Town, the original business district at McCarver Street and Ruston Way, has shops and restaurants. Tacoma Mall, west of I-5 exits 130 and 131 on Tacoma Mall Boulevard, is the area's major shopping center. JCPenney, Macy's, Nordstrom and Sears are the major department stores.

The Proctor District, on N. Proctor and N. 26th streets, features more than 60 shops and restaurants. Freighthouse Square, 1 block north of the Tacoma Dome at 25th and East D streets, is a public market that features restaurants, specialty stores and a full calendar of events.

[SAVE] **CHILDREN'S MUSEUM OF TACOMA,** 936 Broadway, features hands-on displays and programs about literature, the arts and creative play. Changing interactive exhibits also are featured. Allow 1 hour minimum. Mon.-Sat. 10-5, Sun. noon-5; closed Jan. 1, Easter, Memorial Day, July 4, Labor Day, Thanksgiving and Dec. 24-25. Admission $6; free (ages 0-12 months). Phone (253) 627-6031.

FOSS WATERWAY SEAPORT MUSEUM is at 705 Dock St. Housed in a former wheat warehouse built in 1900, the museum is dedicated to preserving the area's maritime history, including the humble 19th-century origins of the Foss Maritime Co. An activity center has a toy boatbuilding area for children and revolving, hands-on exhibits with nautical themes. A variety of boats are on display, and visitors can watch craftsmen build new vessels that will ply the waters of Tacoma's harbor.

Mon.-Fri. 10-5, Sat.-Sun. noon-5. Admission $6; $3 (ages 6-16, 55+ and military and college students with ID). MC, VI. Phone (253) 272-2750.

[GEM] **THE HAROLD E. LeMAY MUSEUM** is at 325 152nd St. E. Tacoma businessman Harold LeMay certainly loved cars, as he [SAVE] managed to amass more than 3,000 automobiles, trucks and motorcycles as well as countless items of vehicle-related memorabilia over a 40-year period. Said to be the largest privately owned collection in the world, this treasure trove is housed in several buildings on the 80-acre grounds of historic Marymount Academy.

The museum's guided tour takes you on a ride through a century of American motor vehicles, from vintage models like the 1930 Duesenberg J to the muscle cars of the 1970s to such whimsical one-off designs as the Flintmobile George Barris Kustom, which mimics the foot-powered conveyance from the old cartoon series and appeared in the 1994 live-action tribute movie "The Flintstones."

Note: The museum is scheduled to move to a new home sometime in 2010. The site, adjacent to the Tacoma Dome, will be dominated by a titanium-and-glass exhibition pavilion with sweeping curves emulating classic automobile design, and will incorporate technologically innovative exhibits that spotlight the cultural impact of cars over the years.

Layered clothing and comfortable walking shoes are recommended for the guided tour. Allow 2 hours minimum. Tues.-Sat. 10-5, Sun. noon-5, June-Aug; Tues.-Sat. 10-5, rest of year. Closed most holidays. Last tour begins at 3. Admission $15; $13.50 (ages 62+); $5 (ages 6-12). Reservations are strongly recommended. MC, VI. Phone (253) 536-2885 or (877) 902-8490.

JOB CARR CABIN MUSEUM is at 2350 N. 30th St. within Old Town Park. Considered the birthplace of Tacoma, this reconstructed log cabin was the home of the first permanent Euro-American settler to the area. The cabin is furnished in period and houses Carr family photos, original diaries, interactive displays and items from other early Tacoma settlers. Mr. Carr later became the town's first postmaster and its first mayor. Allow 30 minutes minimum. Wed.-Sat. noon-4, mid-June to Labor Day. Free. Phone (253) 627-5405.

THE KARPELES MANUSCRIPT LIBRARY MUSEUM, 407 S. G St., preserves original handwritten documents and manuscripts created by noted historical figures. Exhibits change every 3 months. Tues.-Sun. 10-4; closed major holidays. Free. Phone (253) 383-2575.

[GEM] **MUSEUM OF GLASS** is at 1801 E. Dock St. Housed in a striking building distinguished by its 90-foot-high cone sheathed in diamond-shaped stainless steel tiles, this contemporary art museum features 13,000 square feet of exhibition space dedicated mainly to changing exhibitions of contemporary and edgy works executed in glass.

Within the cone is Jane's Hot Shop, an amphitheater in which visitors can watch artists work with molten glass. Outside, winding around the cone, a broad staircase leads to the rooftop where three outdoor plazas feature reflecting pools and art installations. From Pacific Avenue, pedestrians may access the museum via the 500-foot-long Chihuly Bridge of Glass.

Food is available. Allow 1 hour minimum. Mon.-Sat. 10-5 (also third Thurs. of the month 5-8), Sun. noon-5, Memorial Day weekend-Labor Day; Wed.-Sat. 10-5 (also third Thurs. of the month 5-8), Sun. noon-5, rest of year. Closed Jan. 1, July 4, Thanksgiving and Dec. 25. Admission $10; $8 (ages 62+, students and military with ID); $4 (ages 6-12); $30 (family, two adults and four children); free (third Thurs. of the month 5-8). AX, DS, MC, VI. Phone (253) 284-4750 or (866) 468-7386.

Chihuly Bridge of Glass spans I-705 between the Museum of Glass and Union Station. This footbridge features three installations of Dale Chihuly's glass art. The ceiling of the Seaform Pavilion suspends more than 2,300 colorful glass objects above the heads of pedestrians. The two translucent, ice-blue Crystal Towers rise 40 feet above the bridge's midpoint. Farther along, the Venetian Wall show-cases 109 delicate Chihuly sculptures. Daily 24 hours. Free. Phone (253) 284-4750.

 POINT DEFIANCE PARK, 5400 N. Pearl St., has miles of woodland trails through old growth forest and landscaped areas, scenic views and a waterfront. The park features a Japanese Garden with a Shinto Shrine commemorating Kitakyushu, Tacoma's sister city.

The Northwest Native Garden showcases indigenous plants. Other gardens are dedicated to herbs, irises, rhododendrons, roses and dahlias. Never Never Land is a children's recreation space featuring storybook and nursery rhyme characters. Recreational facilities include a public fishing pier and picnic area. Rental boats and fishing gear are available at the boathouse. *See Recreation Chart.* Daily dawn-dusk. Free.

Camp Six Logging Museum is in Point Defiance Park at 5400 N. Pearl St. A replica of an early-20th-century logging camp, the museum contains relics and historic photographs of early logging in the Grays Harbor area.

Grounds open daily dawn-dusk. Museum open Wed.-Fri. 10-4, Sat.-Sun. and holidays 10-6, Memorial Day weekend through Sept. 30; Wed.-Sun. 10-4, Apr. 1-day before Memorial Day weekend; Sat.-Sun. 10-4, rest of year. Closed July 4. Logging train rides depart every 30 minutes Sat.-Sun. and noon-6:30 Mon. holidays, Memorial Day weekend to late Sept.; Sat.-Sun. noon-4, Apr. 1 to mid-May. Free. Logging train ride $4; $3 (ages 55+); $2.50 (ages 3-12); free (ages 0-2 and 100+). Phone (253) 752-0047.

 Fort Nisqually Living History Museum is in Point Defiance Park at 5400 N. Pearl St. The museum, the site of the first outpost of the Hudson's Bay Co. on Puget Sound, features one of the oldest standing structures in the state. Changing exhibits describe Washington's fur trading era. Daily 11-5, Memorial Day weekend-Labor Day; Wed.-Sun. 11-5, Apr. 1-day before Memorial Day weekend; Wed.-Sun. 11-4, rest of year. Admission daily May 1-Labor Day, Sat.-Sun. rest of year $4; $3 (ages 13-18 and 62+); $2 (ages 5-12); free (Mon.-Fri., rest of year). Phone (253) 591-5339.

Point Defiance Zoo and Aquarium, 5400 N. Pearl St., features animals from the Pacific Rim area, including Asian elephants, beluga whales, a Pacific walrus, polar bears, sea otters, sharks and snow leopards. Habitats feature the Arctic's tundra, Puget Sound's rocky shores and the tropics of the South Pacific.

The Asian Forest Sanctuary provides a lush habitat for its denizens, which include Sumatran tigers, siamangs and Asian elephants. The North Pacific Aquarium offers a glimpse of Puget Sound's marine life along with a sea horse exhibit. The Discovery Reef Aquarium displays tropical fish and sharks. Kid's Zone is a play area for children.

The Wild Wonders Outdoor Theater features animal shows. December evenings bring the Zoolights

display, with more than 500,000 lights arranged in life-size replicas of zoo animals.

Allow 2 hours minimum. Daily 9:30-6, Memorial Day-Labor Day; 9:30-5, Apr. 1-day before Memorial Day and day after Labor Day-Sept. 30; 9:30-4, rest of year. Closed third Fri. in July, Thanksgiving and Dec. 25. Admission $13; $10 (ages 65+); $9 (ages 5-12); $5 (ages 3-4). MC, VI. Phone (253) 591-5337.

TACOMA ART MUSEUM is downtown at 1701 Pacific Ave. The museum presents rotating art exhibitions. A large collection of local artist Dale Chihuly's glass art is on view. The Open Art Studio allows visitors of all ages to create their own art. Food is available. Allow 1 hour minimum. Mon.-Sat. 10-5 (also third Thurs. of the month 5-8), Sun. noon-5, Memorial Day weekend-Labor Day; Tues.-Sat. 10-5 (also third Thurs. of the month 5-8), Sun. noon-5, rest of year. Closed Jan. 1, July 4, Thanksgiving and Dec. 25. Admission $7.50; $6.50 (ages 65+, students and military with ID); free (ages 0-5 and third Thurs. of the month); $25 (family, two adults and up to four children ages 0-17). AX, MC, VI. Phone (253) 272-4258.

TACOMA HISTORICAL SOCIETY EXHIBIT CENTER, 747 Broadway, is in the Old City Hall Historic district at the n. end of downtown. Themed exhibits chronicle the changing faces of the "City of Destiny." Allow 30 minutes minimum. Wed.-Fri. noon-5; closed holidays. Donations. Phone (253) 472-3738.

TACOMA NARROWS BRIDGE is where SR 16 crosses over Tacoma Narrows, connecting Tacoma with Gig Harbor. The bridge, one of the largest suspension bridges in the world, has a center span that is 188 feet high and 2,800 feet long. The present bridge opened in 1950, replacing "Galloping Gertie," a design failure nicknamed for the way it swayed in the wind. It broke apart in a windstorm 4 months and 7 days after it opened in 1940.

A second parallel span just south of the bridge opened in July 2007. Narrows Park, south of the west end of the bridge via Lucille Parkway N.W., offers a view of the channel and the two spans.

THE TACOMA NATURE CENTER is at 1919 S. Tyler St. This 70-acre urban nature preserve is home to a variety of reptiles and amphibians as well as 20 species of mammals and roughly 100 species of birds. Visitors can follow 2.6 miles of interpretive trails that meander through woods and wetlands and along the shore of 17-acre Snake Lake. A visitor center features exhibits describing the area's plant and animal life. Allow 1 hour minimum. Daily dawn-dusk. Visitor Center open Tues.-Fri. 8-5, Sat. 10-4. Donations. Phone (253) 591-6439.

UNION STATION, 1717 Pacific Ave., is a restored 1911 railway station built by the Great Northern, Northern Pacific and Union Pacific railways. The Beaux Arts-style building features some noteworthy

Chihuly glass installations. Allow 30 minutes minimum. Station open Mon.-Fri. 8-5. Closed government holidays. Guided tours are offered Tues. and Fri. at 1 or by appointment. Free. Phone (253) 572-9310.

WASHINGTON STATE HISTORY MUSEUM, 1911 Pacific Ave., offers an overview of the Evergreen State's past and present. Hands-on exhibits, walk-through settings and interactive computers depict the state's natural setting, the lifestyle and culture of the first inhabitants, exploration and settlement of the region, and the people and events that helped shape the state.

Highlights include walking through a traditional Coast Salish plank house, safely touching a 52-foot electrical tower, riding down the Columbia River courtesy of a large-screen video and viewing one of the largest permanent model train layouts in the state. The outdoor plaza overlooks the Thea Foss Waterway, the historic red brick Warehouse District, the adjacent Union Station and Mount Rainier.

Allow 1 hour minimum. Mon.-Sat. 10-5 (also Thurs. 5-8), Sun. noon-5, Memorial Day-Labor Day; Tues.-Sat. 10-5 (also Thurs. 5-8), Sun. noon-5, rest of year. Closed Jan. 1, July 4, Thanksgiving and Dec. 25. Admission $8; $7 (ages 60+); $6 (ages 6-17 and military); $25 (family); free (Thurs. 5-8). MC, VI. Phone (253) 272-3500 or (888) 238-4373.

WRIGHT PARK is bounded by Division and 6th aves. and I and G sts. The land for the park was donated to the city in 1886. Designed in the classic tradition of a pastoral English public park, this is a delightful urban green space with rolling green lawns shaded by horse chestnut, maple, pine and Pacific madrona trees, blue spruces and deodar cedars.

Wright Park has some interesting statues. The twin Greek maidens flanking the Division Avenue entrance are reproductions of attendants to Ceres, Greek goddess of agriculture; sometimes a thoughtful passerby might place flowers in the crook of one maiden's arm. A bronze bust of Henrik Ibsen was dedicated May 17, 1913, the 99th anniversary of Norway's independence. The sculpture "Trilogy" stands on an island in the middle of a small duck pond; it depicts three youngsters romping hand in hand, just like their real-life running, swinging and playing counterparts.

Park open daily dawn-dusk. Free. Phone (253) 591-5330.

W.W. Seymour Botanical Conservatory is in Wright Park at 316 S. G St. This small glass conservatory has a distinctive 12-sided central dome and contains unusual tropical plants, orchids and seasonal flower displays. Cyclamen, tulips and hyacinths brighten the winter months; hydrangeas, cascading fuchsias in hanging pots and fragrant lilies celebrate spring; petunias, coleus and other annuals provide summer color; chrysanthemums and asters put on a fall show; and the holidays bring vivid poinsettias. Wander among the flowers for half an hour and you're bound to walk out smiling.

Tues.-Sun. 10-4:30; closed Jan. 1, Thanksgiving, Nov. 27-30 and Dec. 25. Free. Phone (253) 591-5339.

GAMBLING ESTABLISHMENTS

• **Emerald Queen Casino**, 2024 E. 29th St. Fri.-Mon. 24 hours, Tues.-Thurs. 10 a.m.-6 a.m. Phone (888) 831-7655.

VASHON (F-2) pop. 10,123

Ice age glaciers shaped the topography of Vashon Island, today a mosaic of woodland, small farms and settlements. Its first inhabitants were Shomamish Indians who visited the 12-mile by 5-mile island on hunting and gathering forays. In 1792 Capt. George Vancouver named the island for his friend James Vashon, an admiral in the British Navy. Homesteading began in the mid-19th century; farming, fishing, logging, brick making and shipbuilding flourished.

In the 1890s the town of Dockton grew up around a large drydock. Several structures including a general store, hotel and row of company houses remain from this period. Point Robinson, at the eastern tip of adjacent Maury Island, features beach access and a 38-foot lighthouse built in 1915.

Washington State Ferries links Vashon with Southworth and Fauntleroy in west Seattle. Another route links Tahlequah on south Vashon with Point Defiance in Tacoma. Passenger-only ferries connect the island with downtown Seattle. For information phone (888) 808-7977 in Wash.

Recreational opportunities abound and include hiking, bicycling, boating, fishing, kayaking, swimming and scuba diving.

Vashon Island Chamber of Commerce: 19021 Vashon Hwy. S.W., P.O. Box 1035, Vashon Island, WA 98070; phone (206) 463-6217.

RECREATIONAL ACTIVITIES

Kayaking

• **Vashon Island Kayak Co.** is 4 mi. s. on Vashon Hwy S.W., 3 mi. e. on S.W. Burton Dr., .7 mi. e. on 97th Ave. S.W. (becomes S.W. Bayview Dr.) to 8900 S.W. Harbor Dr. Trips depart from Jensen Point Boathouse in Burton Acres Park. Write P.O. Box 2957, Vashon, WA 98070. Fri.-Sun. 10-5, Memorial Day weekend-Labor Day; Sat.-Sun. 10-5, day after Labor Day to mid-Sept. Reservations are required. Phone (206) 463-9257.

WOODINVILLE (E-3) pop. 9,194, elev. 39'

Located on the Sammamish River, Woodinville takes its name from pioneer Ira Woodin who settled here in 1871. The area is noted for its wineries and one of the largest nurseries in the state: Molbak's, 13625 N.E. 175th St., which has a conservatory of tropical plants. The 12-mile Sammamish River Trail, a popular bicycling route, links Woodinville with Lake Washington and Redmond.

Woodinville Chamber of Commerce: 14421 Woodinville-Redmond Rd. N.E., Woodinville, WA 98072; phone (425) 481-8300.

RED HOOK ALE BREWERY, I-405 exit 23 to 14300 N.E. 145th St., offers 45-minute tours explaining the brewing and bottling processes, including tastings and a souvenir glass. Tours Mon.-Fri. at 1, 3 and 5, Sat.-Sun. on the hour noon-5, Memorial Day weekend-Labor Day; Mon.-Fri. at 2 and 4; Sat.-Sun. at 1, 3 and 5, rest of year. Closed Jan. 1, Thanksgiving and Dec. 25. Admission $1. Ages 0-20 are not permitted in the pub during live music performances. Phone (425) 483-3232.

RECREATIONAL ACTIVITIES

Hot Air Ballooning

• **Over the Rainbow Balloon Flights** meets passengers at 14481 Woodinville-Redmond Rd. P.O. Box 2772, Woodinville, WA 98072. Flights twice daily May-Sept. (weather permitting). Reservations are required. Phone (425) 861-8611 or (206) 364-0995.

WINERIES

• **Chateau Ste. Michelle,** 2 mi. s. on SR 202 at 14111 N.E. 145th St. Daily 10-5; closed Jan. 1, Easter, Thanksgiving and Dec. 25. Tours are given 10:30-4:30. Phone (425) 415-3300.

• **Columbia Winery,** 14030 N.E. 145th St. Daily 10-6. Phone (425) 488-2776 or (800) 488-2347.

• **Silver Lake Winery,** 15029 Woodinville Redmond Rd. Daily 11-5; closed Jan. 1, Easter, Thanksgiving and Dec. 25. Phone (425) 485-2437.

Museum of Glass / Tacoma Regional Convention & Visitor Bureau

This ends listings for the Seattle Vicinity.
The following page resumes the alphabetical listings of cities in Washington.

SEDRO-WOOLLEY (C-3)
pop. 8,658, elev. 55′

Thick stands of cedar trees covering the Skagit River valley attracted logging interests to Sedro in the late 1800s. Prospectors soon followed on their way to the Mount Baker area during the gold rush. After developing into the head of navigation on the Skagit River, Sedro merged with the town of Woolley, a junction for the Great Northern and Northern Pacific railroads. Farmland has replaced the valley's forests, although lumber remains important.

Sedro-Woolley Chamber of Commerce: 714B Metcalf St., Sedro-Woolley, WA 98284; phone (360) 855-1841 or (888) 225-8365.

SEDRO-WOOLLEY MUSEUM is at jct. Woodworth St. at 725 Murdock St. The museum depicts the town's history with displays featuring logging equipment, military uniforms, appliances, period clothing, vintage cameras and typewriters, a model railroad and schoolhouse furnishings. The Main Street area contains a general store, jail, city hall, post office, bank and smithy. A garage holds two Model T's, a 1930 Pontiac and a 1926 Seagrave fire truck.

Allow 30 minutes minimum. Wed.-Thurs. noon-4, Sat. 9-4, Sun. 1:30-4:30; closed Jan. 1, Easter, Mother's Day, Father's Day, Thanksgiving and Dec. 25. Admission $1.50; $1 (ages 55+ and students with ID). Phone (360) 855-2390.

SEQUIM (D-1) pop. 4,334, elev. 183′

Sequim (SKWIM), a Klallam Indian word meaning "calm waters," is a popular retirement area, with its relatively dry, sunny climate and varied recreational opportunities. Developed facilities are found at Sequim Bay State Park (see Recreation Chart). Dungeness Recreation Area (see Recreation Chart) in Clallam County Park, 5 miles northwest, provides camping facilities as well as access to Dungeness National Wildlife Refuge (see attraction listing). The John Wayne Marina occupies land donated by the legendary actor to allow others to enjoy his favorite fishing spot.

Lavender, which blooms from July through August, is an important local crop. Some 40 lavender farms are in the area, and many are open to the public. For more information, contact the chamber of commerce.

Sequim-Dungeness Chamber of Commerce: 1192 E. Washington, P.O. Box 907, Sequim, WA 98382; phone (360) 683-6197 or (800) 737-8462.

DUNGENESS NATIONAL WILDLIFE REFUGE is 4.5 mi. w. on US 101, then 3 mi. n. on Kitchen Dick Rd. The refuge contains one of the longest natural sandspits in the world. Dungeness Spit is about 6 miles long—and growing—and juts into the Strait of Juan de Fuca. It forms a saltwater lagoon that is used as a rest stop by thousands of migratory waterfowl. The 63-foot-high New Dungeness Lighthouse near the end of the spit offers free guided tours.

Refuge regulations prohibit fires, pets, bicycles, guns and camping. Other restrictions apply; see the refuge manager. No vehicles are allowed; visitors must park near the refuge entrance and hike in. Daily dawn-dusk. Lighthouse tours are given daily 9 a.m. until 3 hours before dusk. $3 (family). Phone (360) 457-8451 for refuge or (360) 683-9166 for lighthouse information.

DUNGENESS RIVER AUDUBON CENTER is 1.25 mi. n. of US 101 on Sequim Ave., then 3 mi. w. to 2151 W. Hendrickson Rd. in Railroad Bridge Park. Exhibits illustrate the area's natural history and emphasize the importance of environmental protection. A native plant garden and nature trails are available. Allow 30 minutes minimum. Tues.-Sat. 10-4, Sun. noon-4, May-Oct.; Tues.-Fri. 10-4, Sat. noon-4, rest of year. Closed holidays. Guided bird walks are given Wed. at 8:30 a.m. Admission $2. Phone (360) 681-4076.

MUSEUM AND ART CENTER IN THE SEQUIM-DUNGENESS VALLEY, 1 blk. n. off Washington St. at 175 W. Cedar St., has exhibits about natural and human history, farming, Coast Salish Indian and pioneer life, and works by local artists. Highlights include specimens from the Manis mastodon site. Allow 30 minutes minimum. Tues.-Sat. 9-3:30; closed holidays. Donations. Phone (360) 683-8110.

OLYMPIC GAME FARM is 5.5 mi. n. of US 101 via Sequim Ave., then 2 mi. w. on Woodcock Rd., then 1.5 mi. n. on Ward Rd. to the entrance. The farm is a 90-acre preserve that is home for a variety of animals. Visitors can drive two loop roads through large fields roamed by cougars, bears, bison, deer, elk, llamas, rhinoceroses and yaks. Such predators as lions, tigers and wolves are separated from their natural prey and can be seen in the central compound.

Food is available. Picnicking is permitted. Farm opens daily at 9; closing time varies. Closed Jan. 1, Thanksgiving and Dec. 25. Driving tour $10; $9 (ages 6-14 and 55+). DS, MC, VI. Phone (360) 683-4295 or (800) 778-4295.

GAMBLING ESTABLISHMENTS
• **Seven Cedars Casino,** 5 mi. e. on US 101. Sun.-Thurs. 10 a.m.-3 a.m., Fri.-Sat. 10 a.m.-4 a.m., Memorial Day weekend-Labor Day; Sun.-Thurs. 10 a.m.-2 a.m., Fri.-Sat. 10 a.m.-3 a.m., rest of year. Closed Dec. 24-25. Phone (360) 683-7777 or (800) 458-2597.

SHELTON (G-1) pop. 8,442, elev. 41′

Shelton, on an inlet of South Puget Sound, is known for Christmas trees and oysters. Between November and mid-December, 3 million Christmas trees are cut, packed and shipped from this area. "Tollie," a 90-ton Shay locomotive that operated in the woods near Shelton 1924-58, is displayed at Railroad Avenue and Third Street. Its caboose houses a visitor center. The Simpson Timber Co. operates one of North America's remaining logging railroads. The line extends 31 miles west.

Shelton-Mason County Chamber of Commerce: 221 W. Railroad Ave., P.O. Box 2389, Shelton, WA 98584; phone (360) 426-2021 or (800) 576-2021.

MASON COUNTY HISTORICAL SOCIETY MUSEUM, 5th St. and Railroad Ave., offers a scale replica of Grisdale, said to be the last live-in logging camp in the 48 states and the first in which chain saws were used. Other highlights are a 19th-century schoolroom and exhibits focusing on area industries: logging, farming and oyster production. Allow 1 hour minimum. Tues.-Fri. 11-5, Sat. 11-4; closed Jan. 1, Thanksgiving and Dec. 25. Donations. Phone (360) 426-1020.

SQUAXIN ISLAND MUSEUM is 6 mi. s. on SR 101 to SR 108 exit, then 1 mi. e. on Old Olympic Hwy., following signs. The museum relates the natural and cultural history of the Squaxin Island people with displays of traditional hunting, fishing and cooking tools, projectile points, basketry and beadwork, leather pouches and contemporary art work. Cultural presentations take place in the Talking Circle.

Allow 30 minutes minimum. Wed.-Sat. 9-5, Sun. 1-5; closed Memorial Day, Father's Day, July 4, Labor Day, Thanksgiving, Dec. 25 and tribal holidays. Admission $5; $4 (ages 55+); $2 (ages 5-12). Phone (360) 432-3839.

GAMBLING ESTABLISHMENTS

- **Little Creek**, 4 mi. s. on US 101 at jct. SR 108. Sun.-Thurs. 9 a.m.-4 a.m., Fri.-Sat. 9 a.m.-5 a.m. Phone (360) 427-7711 or (800) 667-7711.

- **Lucky Dog Casino** is at 19330 N. Hwy. 101. Sun.-Thurs. 9 a.m.-midnight, Fri.-Sat. 9 a.m.-2 a.m.; closed Dec. 25. Phone (360) 877-5656.

SHORELINE—*see Seattle p. 256.*

SILVER CREEK (F-6) elev. 679′

MAYFIELD DAM is .5 mi. s.e. on US 12, then 1.3 mi. s. on Gershick Rd. The dam crosses a gorge along the Cowlitz River to form 13-mile-long Mayfield Lake. An overlook offers fine views. Mayfield Lake County Park and Ike Kinswa State Park *(see Recreation Chart)* border the lake.

SKAMOKAWA (G-5) elev. 26′

Settled in 1844, Skamokawa (skah-MOCK-away) is among the best preserved of the river boat communities along the lower Columbia River. Houses dating from the late 19th century line the sloughs and creeks, recalling the era when waterways formed the lanes of commerce and communication. The town's name honors a Wahkiakum chief whose name translates to "smoke on the water," a reference to the area's early morning fogs.

Skamokawa Vista Park *(see Recreation Chart)*, west of town on SR 4, offers a good vantage point for watching giant freighters navigate the Columbia River shipping channel. Beachcombers may find pumice from the eruption of Mount St. Helens.

RIVER LIFE INTERPRETIVE CENTER AT REDMEN HALL, 1394 W. Ocean Beach Hwy. (SR 4), contains displays depicting the 1894 building's past as a pioneer schoolhouse and a fraternal lodge. Historic photographs and artifacts document life along the lower Columbia River 1850-1930. A bell tower provides vistas of the river. Allow 30 minutes minimum. Thurs.-Sun. noon-4; closed major holidays. Donations. Phone (360) 795-3007.

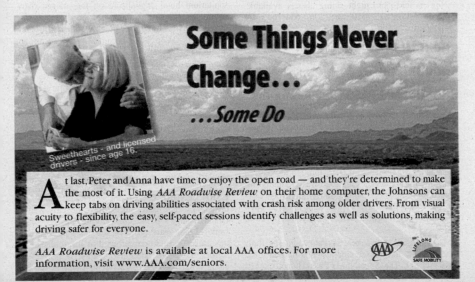

SKYKOMISH (D-8) pop. 214, elev. 931'

The Great Northern Railway built its transcontinental line through this area in the early 1890s, and after the town was platted in 1899 it became an important railway division point. The 7.8-mile Cascade Tunnel beneath Stevens Pass east of Skykomish is said to be the second longest railroad tunnel in the Western Hemisphere. One of the area's scenic highlights is Deception Falls, 6.5 miles east on US 2.

Skykomish Chamber of Commerce: 333 River Dr. E., P.O. Box 397, Skykomish, WA 98288; phone (360) 677-2261.

IRON GOAT INTERPRETIVE SITE is 10 mi. e. on US 2. Interpretive kiosks tell the story of travel over Stevens Pass, the Great Northern Railway and the railroad and resort town of Scenic, and chronicle the history of avalanches in the region. A 29-ton, 1951 Great Northern caboose also is on display. The site provides access to Iron Goat Trail, which follows 9 miles of former Great Northern rights of way on the west side of Stevens Pass. In addition to the beauty of a forest dense with ferns, alders and evergreens, hikers will see tunnels, remnants of show sheds and abandoned townsites.

Guided 3- to 6-hour heritage walks are conducted in season. Picnicking is permitted. Allow 1 hour minimum. Site open daily 24 hours, Mar.-Nov. Iron Goat Trail generally accessible July-Oct., conditions permitting. Free. Phone (206) 517-3019 for interpretive site and heritage walk schedule, or (360) 677-2414 for trail information.

RECREATIONAL ACTIVITIES
Skiing

• **Stevens Pass Ski Area**, 17 mi. e. on US 2, P.O. Box 98, Skykomish, WA 98288. Daily 9-4, late Nov. to mid-Apr.; night skiing also is available. Phone (206) 812-4510, or (206) 634-1645 for snow information.

SNOHOMISH—*see Seattle p. 256.*

SNOQUALMIE—*see Seattle p. 256.*

SNOQUALMIE PASS (E-7) elev. 3,000'

Snoqualmie Pass is a popular recreation area at the crest of the Cascade Range. American Indians used the pass to travel between western and eastern Washington. In 1868 pioneer settlers opened the Snoqualmie Wagon Road. The first automobiles negotiated the single-lane dirt track through the pass in 1915. In ensuing decades the road was gradually upgraded, becoming US 10, the Sunset Highway. During the winter of 1932-33 crews kept the road open all year for the first time. The highway was paved in 1934.

The Chicago, Milwaukee, St. Paul & Pacific Railroad opened its transcontinental line through the pass in 1909. The Snoqualmie Pass Tunnel opened in 1915; the 2.3-mile-long tunnel, abandoned by the railroad in 1980, is now part of Iron Horse State Park in Cle Elum *(see attraction listing p. 163)* and is one of the nation's longest tunnels open to hikers. Accessible from I-90 exit 54, the tunnel is open May through October; bring a light source and warm clothing. A $5 Northwest Forest Pass is required to park at the trailhead lot.

Several ski areas clustered around the pass make Snoqualmie Pass one of the state's premier winter sports complexes. The first downhill ski area in the state was opened just east of the pass in 1934.

The U.S. Forest Service has a visitor information center off I-90 exit 53 offering information about outdoor recreation in the area. The center is open Thurs.-Mon. 8:30-3:30, Memorial Day weekend-Labor Day; Fri.-Sun. 8:30-3:30, Jan.-Mar. Phone (425) 434-6111.

RECREATIONAL ACTIVITIES
Skiing

• **The Summit at Snoqualmie**, accessible from I-90 exits 52, 53 and 54. Write P.O. Box 1068, Snoqualmie Pass, WA 98068. Daily 9 a.m.-10 p.m., Thanksgiving-early Apr. Phone (425) 434-7669 or (206) 236-1600 (snow line).

SOAP LAKE (E-9) pop. 1,733, elev. 1,074'

Native Americans called Soap Lake *Smokiam,* meaning "healing waters." The 2-mile-long lake stands at the southern entrance to cliff-lined Grand Coulee. Its waters are highly mineralized; early maps labeled it Alkali Lake. The present name refers to the fringe of suds that occasionally forms along the shoreline in windy weather.

Settlers moved into this region with the coming of the Great Northern Railroad in the mid-1880s. A sanitarium hotel capitalizing on the alleged therapeutic benefits of bathing in the lake's waters opened in 1905, and was quickly followed by several others. Soap Lake became a busy resort and health spa that attracted people from around the country—especially those with skin ailments, arthritis and rheumatism. Medical advances made these resorts less popular by the mid-20th century, and irrigation water seeping into the lake over time has altered its mineral content. East Beach Park on SR 17 provides public access to Soap Lake.

Soap Lake Chamber of Commerce: P.O. Box 433, Soap Lake, WA 98851; phone (509) 246-1821. A visitor center on SR 17 at East Beach Park is staffed Fri.-Sun., mid-Apr. through Sept. 30.

LAKE LENORE CAVES are 9 mi. n. of Soap Lake on SR 17. The caves formed on the east wall of Grand Coulee's basalt cliffs during Ice Age floods some 12,000 years ago. The site has 3 miles of hiking trails; an interpretive board at the trailhead describes the caves and their history. A gravel trail along a ledge leads to a series of caves in the cliff face, which provide nesting niches for swallows and swifts. From the upper trail a sweeping view extends across Lake Lenore to the west wall of Grand Coulee.

Archeologists have found small scrapers used to prepare animal skins, evidence that Native Americans once used the caves as temporary shelters. Hikers should be alert for rattlesnakes from late spring into fall. Picnicking is permitted. Allow 30 minutes minimum. Open daily during daylight hours. Free. Phone (509) 632-5583.

SOUTH BEND (F-4) pop. 1,807, elev. 11'

The development of rich timberland established South Bend as the key point in the water and stagecoach transportation system of Washington Territory in the late 1800s. After the arrival of the railroad in 1893, the town became an important transshipment point for oysters to the eastern market. Oyster processing has been important here since the 1930s.

A descriptive marker 7.7 miles west on US 101 defines the site of Bruceville, settled in 1851 by the crew of the oyster schooner *Robert Bruce*, which burned near the site. Bruceville, later called Bruceport, was one of the pioneering oyster communities on Willapa Bay.

Willapa Harbor Chamber of Commerce— South Bend: P.O. Box 1249, South Bend, WA 98586; phone (360) 942-5419.

PACIFIC COUNTY COURTHOUSE is 2 blks. s. of US 101 on Memorial Dr. Once described as a gilded palace of extravagance, the 1911 courthouse is an excellent example of Second Renaissance Revival architecture. The rotunda is lit by a stained-glass dome 35 feet in diameter. Waterfalls and a duck pond are on the grounds. Mon.-Fri. 8-5. Free. Phone (360) 875-9337.

PACIFIC COUNTY HISTORICAL SOCIETY MUSEUM, 1008 W. Robert Bush Dr. (US 101), displays Chinook Indian crafts and artworks, photographs, local historical relics and items depicting the lumber, oyster and fishing industries of the area. The museum also is a tourist information center for southwest Washington. Daily 11-4; closed Thanksgiving and Dec. 25. Donations. Phone (360) 875-5224.

SPOKANE (D-11) pop. 195,629, elev. 1,898'

See map page 268.

Early settlers quickly spread the word that a trip to Spokane (spo-CAN) House meant warm hospitality as well as profitable business dealings. The active little trading post was the first non-Indian habitation of the Pacific Northwest. Spokane has since grown into the state's second largest city without losing its pioneering spirit.

The Northwest Fur Co. operation, established in 1810 soon after the Lewis and Clark expedition, was actually alongside the Little Spokane River about 10 miles from the present city. It was not until 1872 that the nucleus of today's Spokane was established at Spokane Falls. Grain and lumber mills replaced fur trading as the major business; the appearance of railroads coincided with a gold rush to the Coeur d'Alene district.

After fire destroyed more than 30 city blocks in 1889, the burst of rebuilding spurred development that has continued unabated. One of Spokane's most convenient features is its system of enclosed skywalks that allows pedestrians to visit many downtown establishments without having to brave the winter cold.

Historic inner-city residential neighborhoods, such as Browne's Addition, just west of downtown, and South Hill, south of I-90, feature dozens of grand mansions from the late 19th and early 20th centuries, including half a dozen designed by renowned Spokane architect Kirtland Kelsey Cutter.

Spokane Falls thunder through downtown during the spring and early summer runoff periods. The 130-foot-high series of cascades can be seen from various observation points in Riverfront Park *(see attraction listing)* as well as from the sidewalk along Spokane Falls Boulevard just west of City Hall and from the walkway on the Monroe Street Bridge.

Skiing and snowboarding are popular at Mount Spokane in Mount Spokane State Park, which is 29 miles northeast of the city. Six local wineries offer tours and tastings; contact the convention and visitors bureau for more information.

American Indian petroglyphs northwest of town near Rutter Bridge can be seen by following SR 291 (Francis Avenue) 2 miles west off US 395 (Division Street) and turning north onto Indian Trail Road for 4 miles.

Spokane Regional Convention and Visitors Bureau/Visitor Center: 201 W. Main St., Spokane, WA 99201; phone (509) 747-3230 or (888) 776-5263.

Self-guiding tours: A description of the 32-mile City Tour is available from the visitor center. Distinctive brown-and-white arrowhead signs are posted along the route, which loops through the southern and western parts of Spokane.

Shopping areas: Northtown Mall, 4 miles north of I-90 on US 2/395 at Wellesley and Division, contains JCPenney, Kohl's, Macy's and Sears. Specialty items can be found in the Flour Mill, downtown at 621 W. Mallon.

Fifteen blocks of downtown Spokane are connected by enclosed skywalks, providing climate-controlled access to stores in the city center. Major department stores so reached include Macy's and Nordstrom at River Park Square.

The Hillyard District, a former railroad town, features a collection of antique and secondhand shops, mostly on Market, between Wellesley and Francis. Antiques also can be found in the Monroe Street Antique District, which extends from Bridge Avenue north to Cleveland Avenue.

CATHEDRAL OF ST. JOHN THE EVANGELIST (Episcopal), 12th St. and Grand Blvd., is an outstanding example of Gothic architecture. The carillon's 49 bells range in weight from 17 to 5,000 pounds. Concerts are occasionally given. Guided tours are available. Allow 30 minutes minimum. Self-guiding tours daily 8:30-4:30. Hours may vary; phone ahead. Guided tours are given Wed. and Fri.-Sat. 11-2, Sun. following morning services. Free. Phone (509) 838-4277.

CAT TALES ZOOLOGICAL PARK— *see Mead p. 180.*

GONZAGA UNIVERSITY, on E. Boone Ave. 4 blks. e. of US 2/395, occupies a 131-acre landscaped campus along the Spokane River on the northeast edge of downtown. The university traces its origins to 1883, when Father Joseph M. Cataldo established a Native American boarding school for boys at the site. Named for the 16th-century Italian Jesuit saint Aloysius Gonzaga, patron of youth, it is the largest institute of private learning in the inland Northwest. Gonzaga's law school in one of only three in Washington.

Twin-steepled St. Aloysius Church is a campus landmark. The interior features oak woodwork, Italian marble, stained-glass windows and a true pipe organ with 37 ranks of keys. Just east of the church is College Hall, a four-story brick building erected in 1898. The Foley Center Library's Cowles Rare Book Room contains a collection of tomes up to 500 years old.

St. Aloysius Church is open for self-guiding tours daily during daylight hours. Phone (509) 328-4220 for campus information, (509) 313-7006 for St. Aloysius Church or (509) 313-6532 for the Foley Center Library.

The Bing Crosby Collection is on campus in the Crosby Student Center. The center's Crosbyana Room features more than 150 items relating to crooner Bing Crosby's life, including his Oscar, gold and platinum records, photographs and trophies. Crosby attended Gonzaga University and was awarded an honorary doctorate in 1937. His boyhood home also is on campus and houses displays. Allow 1 hour minimum. Mon.-Thurs. 7:30 a.m.-midnight, Fri. 7:30 a.m.-8 p.m., Sat.-Sun. 11-8, Sept.-May; Mon.-Fri. 8:30-4, rest of year. House open Mon.-Fri. 8-4:30. Free. Phone (509) 313-4097.

Jundt Art Museum is at the corner of N. Pearl St. and E. Desmet Ave. The museum features a 2,800-square-foot main gallery that houses traveling exhibits as well as rotating displays from the museum's

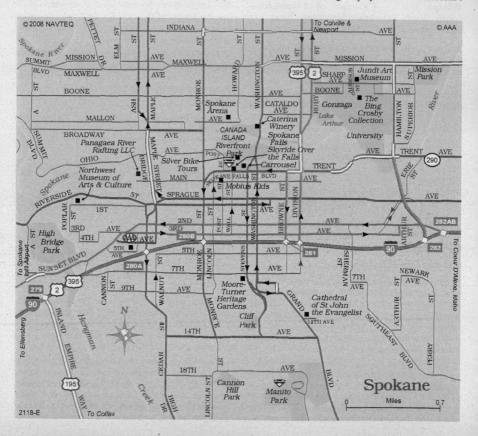

permanent collection. The permanent collection includes glass art by Dale Chihuly and bronze sculpture by Auguste Rodin along with paintings, prints, ceramics, photographs and tapestries. Suspended within the museum's spire is Dale Chihuly's work "The Gonzaga Red Chandelier."

Guided tours are available. Allow 1 hour minimum. Mon.-Fri. 10-4, Sat. noon-4, Sept.-May; Tues.-Sat. 10-4, rest of year. Closed federal and university holidays. Free. Phone (509) 313-6611.

JOHN A. FINCH ARBORETUM, w. on 2nd Ave., then s.w. on Sunset Blvd. to 3404 Woodland Blvd., cultivates a diverse collection of shrubs and trees on 57 acres along Garden Springs Creek. Highlights include a rhododendron glen, a maple section, a conifer section and a nature trail with interpretive signs in print and in Braille. Allow 2 hours minimum. Daily dawn-dusk. Free. Phone (509) 625-6200.

MANITO PARK is on Grand Blvd. between 17th and 25th aves. The 90-acre park, established in 1904, features a conservatory, Japanese garden, perennial garden, rose garden and lilac garden. The Duncan Garden, which has a fountain and gazebo, is a formal garden for the display of bedding plants. Flowering season for the formal and perennial gardens is May through October; the rose garden blooms June through September.

Allow 2 hours minimum. Park open daily 6 a.m.-11 p.m., Apr. 1-late Oct.; 6 a.m.-10 p.m., rest of year. Conservatory open daily 8-7, Memorial Day weekend-Labor Day; 8-6, early Apr.-day before Memorial Day weekend; 8-5, day after Labor Day-late Oct.; 8-3:30, rest of year. Japanese Garden open 8 a.m. to half hour before dusk, Apr. 1-Nov. 1. Free. Phone (509) 625-6622.

MOBIUS KIDS is in the lower level of Riverpark Square at 808 W. Main St. The children's museum offers a variety of creative learning and play activities. Exhibits include Geotopia, showcasing earth sciences; Bayanihan, a Filipino village featuring shopping and rice husking; The Globe Theater, where kids can perform in a stage show; Cooper's Corner, which teaches safety; and The Enchanted Forest, a play area for toddlers.

Mon.-Sat. 10-5, Sun. 11-5; closed Jan. 1, Easter, Thanksgiving and Dec. 25. Admission $5.75; $4.75 (ages 55+ and active military with ID); free (ages 0-1). MC, VI. Phone (509) 624-5437.

MOORE-TURNER HERITAGE GARDENS is at 507 W. 7th Ave.; from downtown, take Stevens St. s., then 7th Ave. w.; the gardens are in Pioneer Park, adjacent to the Corbin Art Center. Established in 1889 and maintained until 1932 as residential gardens, this north-facing hillside reverted back to nature after the house occupied by the Moore and later the Turner family was demolished in 1940. Rediscovered following cleanup after an ice storm in 1996, it has been restored to its early 20th-century appearance.

Mature deciduous trees form a green backdrop for rose and perennial gardens. Lilac bushes are among the only plants surviving from the original garden. Other features that have been reconstructed include a tea house and pergola. **Note:** The gardens are situated on a terraced hillside, with vertical paths punctuated by rough stone steps. There are some steep climbs up and down the hillside, numerous steps to negotiate and inclines without handrails.

Guided tours are available by appointment. Picnicking is permitted. Allow 30 minutes minimum. Wed.-Sun. 10-7, Memorial Day-Aug. 31; Sat.-Sun. 10-4:30, May 16-day before Memorial Day and in Sept. Free. Guided tour fee $5; $2 (ages 5-12). Phone (509) 625-6677.

[SAVE] **NORTHWEST MUSEUM OF ARTS & CULTURE** is at 2316 W. 1st Ave. in the historic Browne's Addition neighborhood. The museum displays visual art within its five underground galleries along with exhibits pertaining to regional history and American Indian and other cultures. The restored Campbell House, adjacent to the museum, is representative of Spokane's turn-of-the-20th-century "Age of Elegance."

Food is available. Allow 2 hours minimum. Tues.-Sun. 11-5; closed major holidays. Admission $7; $5 (ages 63+ and students with ID); free (ages 0-5). Phone (509) 456-3931.

RIVERFRONT PARK is off I-90 at the northern edge of downtown. Centerpiece of the 100-acre park is the Spokane River, [SAVE] which forms a series of rapids before plunging over Spokane Falls. Prior to 1974, industrial activities and rail yards dominated the site, which was cleared and redeveloped for Expo '74. Many features and attractions remain from the world's fair.

A network of walkways links all parts of the park. Pedestrian bridges lead to Havermale Island, featuring the U.S. Pavilion, an IMAX Theatre with a five-story screen and a Clock Tower, part of the former Great Northern Depot. Other attractions include a 1909 Looff Carrousel, Spokane Falls Skyride, an interactive fountain and the Spokane Sculpture Walk. Seasonal attractions include amusement rides, a Park Tour Train and an outdoor winter Ice Palace offering seasonal ice skating.

Allow 2 hours minimum. Park grounds open daily 5 a.m.-midnight. Pavilion amusement rides and Park Tour Train operate Sun.-Thurs. 11-7, Fri.-Sat. 11-9, mid-June through Labor Day. Ice Palace open Mon.-Sat. 11-5 and 7-8:30 p.m. (also Fri.-Sat. 8:30-10 p.m.), Sun. 11-5, Oct.-Mar.

Admission to park grounds free. IMAX Theatre $8.25; $7.25 (ages 13-18 and 63+); $5.75 (ages 3-12). Ice Palace $4.25; $3.25 (ages 3-17). Pavilion ride tickets vary. Park Tour Train $4.50. MC, VI. Phone (509) 625-6600, (509) 625-6687 for Ice Palace, or (800) 336-7275 in Idaho, Ore., Mont., Wash., Alberta or British Columbia.

Carrousel, on the s. side of the park, is a hand-carved antique built in 1909 by Charles Looff, who made the first carousel for Coney Island in New

York. Sun.-Thurs. 11-8, Fri.-Sat. 11-10, late May-Labor Day; daily 11-6, early Mar.-late May and day after Labor Day-early Oct.; daily noon-5, early Oct.-Dec. 31. Fare $2; $1 (ages 3-12 and 63+).

Spokane Falls Skyride Over the Falls leaves from the w. edge of the park and carries visitors over the Spokane River and falls within enclosed six-person gondolas. Sun.-Thurs. 11-8, Fri.-Sat. 11-10, late May-Labor Day; daily 11-6, early Mar.-late May and day after Labor Day-early Oct.; daily noon-5, early Oct.-Feb. 28. Fare $7; $6 (ages 13-18, 63+ and military with ID); $4 (ages 3-12). Phone (509) 625-6600.

RIVERSIDE STATE PARK is .3 mi. w. on W. Maxwell Ave. (becomes N. Pettet Dr.), .8 mi. n.w. on N. Pettet Dr. (becomes W. Downriver Dr.), 1.3 mi. w. on W. Downriver Dr., then .9 mi. n. to 4427 N. Aubrey L. White Pkwy. The park embraces over 10,000 acres along 9 miles of the Spokane River and offers 50 miles of multiuse trails as well as a 600-acre off-road vehicle area.

Highlights include the Bowl and Pitcher, a series of basalt monoliths lining the river; Deep Creek Canyon Overlook; Indian Painted Rocks, which contains ancient petroglyphs; and the riparian habitat of Little Spokane River Natural Area. *See Recreation Chart.* Allow 1 hour minimum. Daily 6:30 a.m.-dusk, Apr.-Sept.; 8 a.m.-dusk, rest of year. Free. Phone (509) 465-5064.

Spokane House Interpretive Center is in Riverside State Park. The center is on the site of a trading post that was the first structure built in the Northwest by non-natives. Displays trace the development of the site. Allow 1 hour minimum. Sat.-Sun. 10-4, Memorial Day weekend-Labor Day. Free. Phone (509) 456-5064.

RECREATIONAL ACTIVITIES

Bicycling

- **Silver Bike Tours** offers fully supported half-day, full-day and multi-day trips on area bike trails. P.O. Box 28131, Spokane, WA 99228. Trips depart June 1 to mid-Oct. Phone (877) 808-0913.

White-water Rafting

- (SAVE) **Pangaea River Rafting LLC** departs from various locations on the Spokane River. Write 18 S. Fork Nemote Creek Rd., Superior, MT 59872. Other activities are available. Daily 8-8, mid-Apr. to mid-Aug. Phone (877) 239-2392.

WINERIES

- **Arbor Crest Wine Cellars** is on Fruithill Rd.; from I-90 exit 287, go n. 1.75 mi. on Argonne Rd., then 1.1 mi. e. on Upriver Rd., then 1 mi. n.e. on Fruithill Rd., following signs. The 75-acre estate features beautifully landscaped grounds and the historic Cliff House, perched atop a bluff overlooking Spokane. Under 21 are not permitted. Open for wine tasting and 90-minute tours daily noon-5; closed Jan. 1, Thanksgiving and Dec. 25. Tastings free, $7 or $12, depending on wine

sampled; tours $12, $18 or $28, depending on offerings. Reservations are required. AX, MC, VI. Phone (509) 927-9463.

- **Caterina Winery** is at 905 N. Washington St. Located in the historic brick 1910 Broadview Dairy building, the winery offers tastings and tours on request. Daily noon-5; closed Jan. 1, Thanksgiving and Dec. 25. Tours free, tastings $5. Phone (509) 328-5069.

SPOKANE VALLEY (E-12)
pop. 80,700, elev. 2,020'

The eastern suburbs of Spokane, including the communities of Opportunity, Dishman, Greenacres and Veradale, formed the city of Spokane Valley in 2003. The paved Centennial Trail passes through the city, and float trips on the Spokane River are popular in summer.

Greater Spokane Valley Chamber of Commerce: 9507 E. Sprague Ave., Spokane Valley, WA 99206; phone (509) 924-4994 or (866) 475-1436.

Shopping areas: Valley Mall, I-90 exit 291, features JCPenney, Macy's and Sears.

SPLASHDOWN FAMILY WATERPARK is off I-90 exit 289, then s. to Mission Ave. in Valley Mission Park. Nine water slides help visitors of all ages beat the heat; two hot tubs also are available. Food is available. Mon.-Sat. 11-6 (also Tues. 6-8 p.m.), Sun. noon-6, Memorial Day weekend-Labor Day. Admission $15.99; $12.99 (under 49 inches); free (ages 65+ with photo ID); a $7 fee is charged for spectators. MC, VI. Phone (509) 924-3079.

SPOKANE VALLEY HERITAGE MUSEUM is 1.2 mi. s. of I-90 exit 289 on Pines Rd., then 1 blk. w. to 12114 E. Sprague Ave. The museum—housed in the 1912 Opportunity Township Hall building—presents rotating exhibits focusing on events that have shaped the landscape and economy of Spokane Valley, from Ice Age floods and American Indian hunters and gatherers to agricultural, industrial and commercial activities. Allow 30 minutes minimum. Tues.-Wed. and Fri. 11-4, Sat. noon-5; closed Jan. 1, Thanksgiving and Dec. 25. Admission $5; $4 (ages 55+); $3 (ages 0-18). Phone (509) 922-4570.

WINERIES

- **Latah Creek Wine Cellars** is 1 blk. n. of I-90 exit 289 on Pines Rd., then half a mile e. on Indiana Ave. Guided 15-minute tours of the production facility are given on request. Wine tasting daily 9-5; closed Jan. 1, Easter, July 4, Thanksgiving and Dec. 25. Tours and tastings free. Phone (509) 926-0164.

STANWOOD (C-3) pop. 3,923, elev. 5'

Norwegian immigrants established the first permanent settlement here in the 1870s. Initially a logging town, Stanwood became a farm trading center after the adjacent floodplain was drained and diked.

The town developed two business districts after the Great Northern Railroad bypassed the original site in the 1880s and the community of East Stanwood developed around the station. Business leaders financed a 7/8-mile narrow gauge railroad to link East Stanwood with the original town center. It was known as "the world's shortest railroad" until it ceased operation in 1938.

Stanwood Chamber of Commerce: 8725 271st Street N.W., P.O. Box 641, Stanwood, WA 98292; phone (360) 629-0562.

D.O. PEARSON HOUSE & THE STANWOOD AREA HISTORY MUSEUM is at 27108 102nd Ave. N.W. Former home of Stanwood's first mayor, the Pearson House is a three-story Second Empire Victorian built in 1890 and furnished with period pieces donated by local families. A second building behind the house features changing exhibits of photography. Allow 30 minutes minimum. Wed., Fri. and Sun. 1-4; other days by appointment. Donations. Phone (360) 629-6110.

STEILACOOM—see Seattle p. 256.

STEVENSON (H-7) pop. 1,200, elev. 103'

The Upper Cascades of the Columbia River, 2 miles west of Stevenson, were the site of a portage where pioneers reassembled their wagons after rafting down the river from The Dalles, Ore. After steamboats began to ply the upper river, the town of Upper Cascades served as the transfer point from steamboat to portage for all traffic between Portland and the Inland Empire.

Skamania County Chamber of Commerce: 167 N.W. 2nd St., P.O. Box 1037, Stevenson, WA 98648; phone (509) 427-8911.

COLUMBIA GORGE INTERPRETIVE CENTER, 990 S.W. Rock Creek Dr., features displays about the natural and cultural history of the region (see Columbia River Gorge National Scenic Area in Oregon p. 59). Exhibits depict American Indian lifestyles, the fur trading era and the harnessing of the resources of the gorge.

Highlights include a 37-foot-high, full-scale replica of a 19th-century fish wheel, a restored 1893 Corliss steam engine that served as the power source for sawmills, a collection of rosaries said to be the world's largest and a diorama of an American Indian dip-net fisher. "Cedar Trees," an outdoor installation, features three 30-foot-high totems by American Indian artist Dudley Carver. "Forged Through Time" is a 15-minute video documenting the Ice Age Floods.

Allow 1 hour minimum. Daily 10-5; closed Jan. 1, Thanksgiving and Dec. 25. Admission $7; $6 (ages 60+ and students with ID); $5 (ages 6-12). MC, VI. Phone (509) 427-8211 or (800) 991-2338.

SUNNYSIDE (G-9) pop. 13,905, elev. 743'

Boasting one of the state's first irrigation projects of more than 100,000 acres, Sunnyside is known as the asparagus capital of the Northwest. Local farms and orchards produce more than 50 other crops, including grapes processed in area wineries. Settlement by the Christian Cooperative Movement has contributed to Sunnyside's growth into a busy trade center for the lower Yakima Valley.

Local attractions include the 1859 Ben Snipes Cabin, reputedly the oldest homestead in the Yakima Valley; and the Sunnyside Wildlife Recreation Area, a haven for waterbirds and shorebirds, which is south of the city along the Yakima River.

Sunnyside Chamber of Commerce: 230 E. Edison St., P.O. Box 360, Sunnyside, WA 98944; phone (509) 837-5939 or (800) 457-8089.

DARIGOLD DAIRY FAIR is at I-82 exit 67, .3 mi. s. on Midvale Rd., then .2 mi. e. on Alexander Rd. Dairy equipment is on display. The cheese making process is described on videotape monitors and signs and can be observed through five large windows. Food is available. Allow 30 minutes minimum. Mon.-Sat. 8-6 (also 6-7 p.m., June-Aug.), Sun. 10-6; closed Easter, Thanksgiving and Dec. 25. Free. Phone (509) 837-4321.

SUNNYSIDE HISTORICAL MUSEUM is at 704 S. 4th Ave. The museum features displays of Yakama Indian artifacts and local items from the town's pioneer past including re-creations of period rooms along with collections of antiques and memorabilia. Allow 30 minutes minimum. Thurs.-Sun. 1-4, Apr. 1 to early Dec. Donations. Phone (509) 837-6010.

WINERIES

• **Tucker Cellars,** 1 mi. s. on Yakima Valley Hwy. at 70 Ray Rd. Daily 10-5. Phone (509) 837-8701.

SUQUAMISH—see Seattle p. 257.

TACOMA—see Seattle p. 257.

TENINO (I-2) pop. 1,447, elev. 290'

In the 1930s Tenino gained national attention when it issued wooden dollars after a local bank failed. This unusual solution worked and the dollars have since become collectors' items. A more durable local resource is the sandstone quarried nearby, which has been used in public buildings throughout the region, as well as in many of Tenino's commercial and residential structures.

The Tenino Depot Museum, 2 blks. s. of Sussex St. at 399 W. Park St., is housed in a 1914 railroad depot. Displays include sandstone and wooden money exhibits, a 1920s doctor's office and a logging exhibit. Phone (360) 264-4321.

Tenino Chamber of Commerce: P.O. Box 506, Tenino, WA 98589; phone (360) 264-5075.

WOLF HAVEN INTERNATIONAL, 3.2 mi. n. on Old Highway 99 S.E. and e. on Offut Lake Rd., is a sanctuary for more than 60 wolves, an endangered species. Narrated tours describe the wolf's role in the wild. The organization offers Howl-ins—programs that include music, children's games, arts and crafts, storytelling and live entertainment on an outdoor stage—along with other special events.

Allow 1 hour minimum. Tours are given on the hour Wed.-Sat. and Mon. 10-3, Sun. noon-3, Apr.-Sept.; Sat. 10-3, Sun. noon-3, Mar. and Oct.-Jan. Last tour begins 1 hour before closing. Admission $8; $7 (ages 13-18 and 62+); $6 (ages 3-12). Howl-ins $15; $12 (ages 62+); $8 (ages 3-12). Reservations are required for all events; phone for schedule. AX, DS, MC, VI. Phone (360) 264-4695 or (800) 448-9653.

THORP (E-8) pop. 273, elev. 1,635'

THORP MILL, on Thorp Hwy. 2 mi. n.w. of I-90 exit 101, preserves a pioneer industrial site built in 1883. An 8-minute video provides background on the milling process and the high level of automation at the mill, which operated until 1946. Original turn-of-the-20th-century machinery is on display. An interpretive trail loops around the site and mill pond. Picnicking facilities are available. Allow 30 minutes minimum. Grounds open daily 24 hours. Mill site open Thurs.-Sun. 10:30-2:30, Memorial Day weekend-Labor Day weekend; closed holidays. Free. Phone (509) 964-9640.

RECREATIONAL ACTIVITIES
White-water Rafting

• **Rill Adventures** departs from a point 3.25 mi. n. of I-90 exit 101 on Thorp Hwy. P.O. Box 102, Thorp, WA 98946. The outfitter offers leisure rafting trips on the Class I Yakima River. Daily, May 1-early Oct. (weather permitting). Phone (509) 964-2520 or (888) 281-1561.

TOKELAND (F-4) pop. 194, elev. 15'

A former fishing port and summer resort, Tokeland is perched on Toke Point, a 3-mile-long sand spit named for an American Indian chief renowned for his skills as a canoeist and guide. The town's weatherworn Tokeland Hotel dates back to 1885. Cape Shoalwater, 4 miles west, marks the northern entrance to Willapa Bay, first charted by Capt. John Meares in 1788. The cape is prone to erosion, and since the early 1900s sections of the highway, farms and the original lighthouse have been lost to the waves. The present lighthouse was moved to higher ground in 1952.

GAMBLING ESTABLISHMENTS

• **Shoalwater Bay Casino,** jct SR 105 and Old Tokeland Rd. Sun.-Thurs. 10 a.m.-midnight, Fri.-Sat. 10 a.m.-2 a.m. Phone (360) 267-2048.

TOLEDO (G-6) pop. 653, elev. 118'

Toledo was founded in 1879 at the head of 19th-century steamboat navigation on the Cowlitz River and named for the first paddlewheel steamboat to provide regular service. During the 1880s the town

prospered as a hop-growing center, but by 1900 most farmers had switched to dairying.

Two miles downstream is the site of Cowlitz Landing, identified by a marker off I-5 exit 59. In the 1850s the landing provided a safe place where Hudson's Bay Company traders could exchange canoes, which they used to travel north from Fort Vancouver, for horses, which were ridden on to Fort Langley on the Fraser River.

ST. FRANCIS XAVIER MISSION, 2 mi. n.e. on Jackson Hwy., then .2 mi. s. at 139 Spencer Rd., was founded in 1838 by fathers Blanchet and Demers. It is the site of the first Catholic church in the state and one of the oldest missions in the Northwest. The original building burned in the late 1890s, but a historic cemetery is on the grounds. A replica of a 19th-century Catholic ladder, a totem-like teaching tool, is displayed near the cemetery. Daily dawn-dusk. Donations. Phone (360) 864-4126.

TOPPENISH (G-8) pop. 8,946, elev. 757'

Toppenish is the headquarters of the Yakama Indian Nation, which covers more than a million acres. Toppenish is known as the City of Historical Murals. Artists have transformed the outside walls of many buildings with 70 colorful scenes depicting pioneer life in the area. A new mural is dedicated annually on the first Saturday in June. Horse-drawn vehicle tours are available May through September; phone (509) 697-8995.

Toppenish Chamber of Commerce: 5A S. Toppenish Ave., P.O. Box 28, Toppenish, WA 98948; phone (509) 865-3262 or (800) 863-6375.

Self-guiding tours: For information about the historical murals and a self-guiding walking tour brochure, contact the chamber of commerce.

AMERICAN HOP MUSEUM is at 22 S. B St. Housed in a building with a trompe l'oeil exterior, the museum contains exhibits tracing the history of the hop industry from its international commercial beginning in New York in the 17th century to the present in the Yakima Valley. Displays include historic photographs, publications, antique and modern hop equipment and memorabilia. Wed.-Sat. 10-4, Sun. 11-4 and by appointment, May-Sept.; by appointment rest of year. Admission $3; $2 (students with ID); free (ages 0-4); $7 (family). Phone (509) 865-4677.

NORTHERN PACIFIC RAILWAY MUSEUM is at 10 E. Asotin Ave. Housed in a 1911 brick passenger terminal, the museum features tools, uniforms, passenger amenities, historic photographs and other railway-related memorabilia. Museum highlights include a restored Pullman berth from the late 1800s, a steam locomotive and a re-creation of a Northern Pacific observation car with original chairs. Hand cars used to inspect tracks also are on display. Allow 30 minutes minimum. Tues.-Sat. 10-4, Sun. noon-4, May-Oct.; by appointment rest of year. Admission $5; $3 (ages 0-12). Phone (509) 865-1911.

TOPPENISH NATIONAL WILDLIFE REFUGE, 6 mi. s. on US 97, then 1 mi. w. on Pump House Rd., is in the lower Yakima Valley. Nearly 250 species of birds have been sighted on the refuge. An observation area featuring interpretive panels overlooks the wetland habitat. Refuge open daily 5 a.m.-dusk. Free. Phone (509) 865-2405.

YAKAMA NATION CULTURAL HERITAGE CENTER, .5 mi. n. on US 97 at 100 Spiel-yi Loop, includes a winter lodge/meeting hall, museum, theater, library and research center. The 76-foot-high lodge, a stylized version of the ancient Yakama winter lodge, dominates the center. Dioramas and exhibits in the 12,000-square-foot museum chronicle the history of the Yakama Indians.

Food is available. Allow 1 hour minimum. Mon.-Fri. 8-5, Sat.-Sun. 9-5; closed Jan. 1, Thanksgiving and Dec. 25. Admission $5; $3 (ages 11-18, ages 55+ and military with ID); $1 (ages 0-10). Phone (509) 865-2800.

GAMBLING ESTABLISHMENTS

- **Legends Casino,** .5 mi. w. of US 97 at 580 Fort Rd. Sun.-Thurs. 9 a.m.-4 a.m., Fri.-Sat. 9 a.m.-5 a.m. Phone (509) 865-8800 or (877) 726-6311.

TUMWATER (H-1) pop. 12,698, elev. 115'

Founded in 1845, Tumwater was the first American settlement north of Fort Vancouver. Waterpower harnessed from the Deschutes River for a brewery, mills and other industries was the key to Tumwater's prosperity in the early 1900s. The original townsite, off Deschutes Way at the foot of Grant Street, is now Tumwater Falls Historical Park, which includes the 1858 Crosby House, built by Bing Crosby's grandparents, and the 1905 Henderson House.

Tumwater Area Chamber of Commerce: 5304 Littlerock Rd. S.W., Tumwater, WA 98512; phone (360) 357-5153.

TWISP (C-9) pop. 938, elev. 1,590'

Twisp is in the Methow Valley, at the junction of the Twisp and Methow rivers. The valley had a mining boom in the 1890s, but most economic efforts now center on logging, apple production and farming. West of Twisp the North Cascades Highway (SR 20) begins its climb into scenic Okanogan National Forest and North Cascades National Park *(see place listings p. 193 and p. 190).*

Twisp Chamber of Commerce: 201 S. Methow Valley Hwy., P.O. Box 686, Twisp, WA 98856; phone (509) 997-2020.

RECREATIONAL ACTIVITIES
White-water Rafting

- **Osprey River Adventures** offers trips for various skill levels on the Methow River. Write P.O. Box 1305, Twisp, WA 98856. Trips depart Apr.-Aug. Phone (509) 997-4116 or (800) 997-4116.

UMATILLA NATIONAL FOREST—
see place listing in Oregon p. 122.

UNDERWOOD (H-7) elev. 110'

The Broughton Log Flume, the last operating log flume in the country, floated lumber from Willard down to the mill at Underwood, a drop of 1,000 feet. Visible from SR 14, the 9-mile flume closed in 1987.

SPRING CREEK NATIONAL FISH HATCHERY is 4 mi. w. of Hood River-White Salmon Bridge on SR 14. One of the oldest salmon hatcheries on the Columbia River, it was established in 1901 and has a visitor center, rearing ponds and a fish ladder. Mature chinook salmon can be seen in September; fingerlings are released in spring. Allow 30 minutes minimum. Daily 7:30-4, late Aug.-early Oct. and Dec. 1 to mid-May; Mon.-Fri. 7:30-4, mid-May to late Aug. Closed major holidays. Free. Phone (509) 493-1730.

UNION GAP (F-8) pop. 5,621, elev. 980'

Union Gap takes its name from the natural pass or gap that the Yakima River has carved through high, barren hills. The gap divides the Yakima Valley into its upper and lower portions. Yakima City was established here in 1861. In 1884 the Northern Pacific Railroad persuaded most of the town's businesses to relocate to its proposed station site 4 miles north. These relocated businesses formed the nucleus of the new town of North Yakima. In 1918 the state legislature dropped North from the new town's name and renamed old Yakima to Union Gap.

CENTRAL WASHINGTON AGRICULTURAL MUSEUM, 4508 Main St. in Fulbright Park, features 21 display buildings containing farm machinery and equipment. The museum also houses the Magness Hand Tool collection of more than 6,000 items. Of interest is a restored 1917 log cabin and a railroad boxcar with displays. Allow 2 hours minimum. Wed.-Sat. 9-5, Sun. 1-4, Tues. 9-3, Apr.-Oct.; Thurs.-Sun. 1-4, Tues. 9-3, rest of year. Donations. Phone (509) 457-8735.

VANCOUVER—*see Portland in Oregon p. 108.*

VANTAGE (F-9) pop. 70, elev. 625'

A town grew up around a ferry service that transported travelers across the Columbia River until a highway bridge was built in the 1930s. The town was relocated to higher ground when the reservoir behind Wanapum Dam flooded its site.

Several recreation areas, including Wanapum *(see Recreation Chart)* and Ginkgo state parks, border Wanapum Lake, which was formed by the dam in 1959. The monumental sculpture "Grandfather Cuts Loose the Horses" stands on a mesa overlooking the Columbia. The sculpture is best viewed from the Wanapum Vista viewpoint on eastbound I-90, 3 miles east of Vantage.

Wineries

Washington, located astride the same latitudes as the great wine regions of France, is the nation's third largest producer of wine. Leading red varietals include Merlot, Cabernet Sauvignon and Syrah; principal whites are Chardonnay, Riesling and Sauvignon Blanc.

Washington's more than 500 wineries produce vintages within nine grape growing regions (American Viticultural Areas, or AVAs). East of the Cascade Range, where summers are hot and average rainfall low, vineyards are clustered in the Yakima Valley. Adjoining, smaller AVAs include Red Mountain, Rattlesnake Hills and Horse Heaven Hills. The Walla Walla Valley is a distinct AVA specializing in Cabernet Sauvignon, Merlot and Chardonnay.

Columbia Valley, Washington's largest wine growing region, stretches from Lake Roosevelt along its namesake river to the Columbia Gorge, a distinct AVA at the Cascades' eastern edge. Wahluke Slope is a small AVA nested within the Columbia Valley. West of the Cascades, the sprawling Puget Sound AVA has a wetter, more temperate climate nurturing such varietals as Madeleine Angevine, Siegerebbe and Muller-Thurgau.

GINKGO PETRIFIED FOREST STATE PARK is .7 mi. n. of I-90 exit 136 on Vantage Hwy., then .5 mi. e. on Ginkgo Ave. The park includes 7,500 acres of fossilized ginkgo trees dating back some 10-17 million years. Unlike most other petrified forests, the trees were entombed in lava. The museum in the interpretive center contains exhibits.

Three miles of hiking trails and a .75-mile interpretive trail are 2 miles from the interpretive center; another trail leads from the interpretive center to rocks with petroglyphs. Picnic facilities are available. Allow 1 hour minimum. Park open daily 6:30 a.m.-dusk, late Mar.-early Nov.; Sat.-Sun. and holidays 8 a.m.-dusk, rest of year. Interpretive center hours vary; phone ahead. Free. Phone (509) 856-2700.

WANAPUM DAM HERITAGE CENTER is off I-90 exit 137, then 5 mi. s. on SR 243. The center offers exhibits depicting the culture of the Wanapum Indians and life along the Columbia River from prehistoric times to the construction of Priest Rapids and Wanapum dams in the 1950s. Mon.-Fri. 8:30-4:30, Sat.-Sun. 9-5; closed Jan. 1, Thanksgiving and Dec. 25. Free. Phone (509) 932-3571, ext. 2571.

VASHON—see Seattle p. 262.

WALLA WALLA (G-11)
pop. 29,686, elev. 949'

In 1836 Dr. Marcus Whitman and his wife, Narcissa, established the first permanent settlers' home in the Pacific Northwest in the valley. The town, first known as Steptoeville, traces its founding to Fort Walla Walla in 1856. The name came from the Walla Walla Indians who inhabited the valley; it means "many waters" or "small rapid stream."

During the 1860s the town prospered as outfitter for the central Idaho gold rush and served as western terminus of the pioneer Mullan Road to Fort Benton on the upper Missouri River in Montana. Wheat ranching began in the 1870s, but after 1883 Walla Walla lost preeminence to Spokane, which had attracted Northern Pacific's transcontinental rail line.

Early settlers planted an abundance of ornamental trees on city streets to remind them of their Eastern and Midwestern hometowns. The downtown core, particularly Main Street, contains dozens of preserved late 19th- and early 20th-century buildings.

The valley is noted for its rich agricultural productivity. Specialty crops include grapes and onions. The famous Walla Walla sweet—a large, round hybrid of an Italian sweet onion—is coveted for its taste. Commercial wine production began in 1977, and today there are more than 60 wineries in the area. Most specialize in red wines, such as Cabernet Sauvignon, Merlot, Sangiovese, Syrah and various blends.

Pioneer Park, Division and Alder streets, is a 47-acre recreation area with a duck pond, bandstand, rose garden, playground, swimming pool, tennis courts and an aviary of exotic birds.

Walla Walla Valley Chamber of Commerce: 29 E. Sumach St., P.O. Box 644, Walla Walla, WA 99362; phone (509) 525-0850 or (877) 998-4748.

CARNEGIE ART CENTER is at at 109 S. Palouse St. (at Alder St.). The center presents temporary exhibits by local and regional artists in a 1904 former Carnegie library. The building is on the National Register of Historic Places and is appointed with leaded-glass windows, fireplaces, oak-beamed ceilings, chandeliers and antiques. Allow 30 minutes minimum. Tues.-Sat. 11-4:30; closed major holidays. Free. Phone (509) 525-4270.

CHILDREN'S MUSEUM OF WALLA WALLA is at 77 Wainwright Dr. The museum features educational, hands-on, interactive exhibits designed to engage children 10 and under. Kids can play in a mock-up of a grocery store, a life-size fire truck and a child-size representation of the town called Wee Walla Walla. Changing science exhibits and a play area for toddlers also are offered. Thurs.-Sun. 10-5; closed holidays. Admission $4; free (ages 0-12 months). MC, VI. Phone (509) 526-7529.

[SAVE] **FORT WALLA WALLA MUSEUM,** 755 Myra Rd. at the s. end of town off SR 125, features 17 buildings depicting pioneer life, a diorama of Lewis and Clark and an extensive exhibit of American Indian artifacts and regalia. Horse-era farming, pioneer settlement and the fort's military history are displayed in five exhibit buildings. Special events take place in summer. Allow 1 hour minimum. Daily 10-5, Apr.-Oct. Admission $7; $6 (ages 62+ and students with ID); $3 (ages 6-12). DS, MC, VI. Phone (509) 525-7703.

KIRKMAN HOUSE MUSEUM is at 214 N. Colville St. Built in the 1870s by cattle rancher and businessman William Kirkman, this restored, 12-room Victorian mansion has lavish details like Corinthian columns, Greek figureheads over the upstairs windows and intricate parquet floors. The house is filled with original family furnishings, among them a box piano presented to Kirkman's eldest daughter. Historic clothing also is on display. Guided tours are available. Allow 30 minutes minimum. Wed.-Sat. 10-4, Sun. 1-4. Donations. Phone (509) 529-4373.

WHITMAN MISSION NATIONAL HISTORIC SITE—see place listing p. 280.

WINERIES

- **Forgeron Cellars** is on the southern edge of downtown at the corner of S. Third and W. Birch sts. The historic building originally housed a blacksmith. Guided tours are offered by appointment. Open for tastings daily 11-4; closed Jan. 1, Memorial Day, July 4, Labor Day, Thanksgiving and Dec. 25. Phone (509) 522-9463.

- **Northstar Winery** is 3.5 mi. s. on SR 125, .25 mi. e. on Old Milton Hwy., 1.25 mi. s. on Peppers Bridge Rd., then .75 mi. e., following signs to 1736 J.B. George Rd. Mon.-Sat. 10-4, Sun. 11-4;

Wineries (continued)

Wine touring is popular in these areas. Although there are some large wineries, most are small, boutique or family-run operations. The majority of Washington's wineries are open to the public for tastings; some offer tours.

The Washington Wine Commission publishes "Touring Washington Wine Country," a guide listing the state's wineries along with locator maps and hours of operation. Copies are available from the Washington Wine Center, 1000 Second Ave., Suite 1700, Seattle, WA 98104-3621; phone (206) 667-9463, ext. 2030.

Washington Wine Center

closed Jan. 1, Thanksgiving and Dec. 25. Phone (509) 525-6100 or (866) 486-7828.

- **Three Rivers Winery** is 6 mi. w. at 5641 US 12. Daily 10-6; closed Jan. 1, Thanksgiving and Dec. 25. Phone (509) 526-9463.

WASHOUGAL—*see Portland in Oregon p. 110.*

WASHTUCNA (F-11) pop. 260, elev. 1,024′

The farming town of Washtucna, named for a Palouse Indian chief, nestles in the swale of Washtucna Coulee, an ancient river course. Natural springs attracted the first permanent settlers in 1878. In the 1890s and early 1900s the area was the scene of several speculative irrigation schemes.

PALOUSE FALLS STATE PARK is 17 mi. s.e. on SR 260/261, then 2 mi. e. on a gravel road, following signs. In sharp contrast with the arid surroundings, massive amounts of water plummet nearly 200 feet into a deep pool at Palouse Falls, the centerpiece of this 105-acre state park. The flow peaks in spring and early summer. Layers of basalt lavas typical of the region have been exposed in the canyon below the falls. *See Recreation Chart.* Allow 30 minutes minimum. Daily dawn-dusk. Free. Phone (360) 902-8561.

WATERVILLE (E-9) pop. 1,163, elev. 2,622′

Waterville lies near the base of Badger Mountain on a plateau where wheat is grown. The town's compact business district contains 17 historic brick buildings dating to the late 1800s. Glacial erratics, or haystack rocks, are geological oddities that were deposited during the last ice age; they can be seen 26 miles northeast of town along SR 172.

DOUGLAS COUNTY HISTORICAL MUSEUM is at 124 W. Walnut St. The museum displays pioneer

---

DID YOU KNOW

Like Rome, Seattle was built on seven hills.

---

household utensils, furnishings, farm implements and the former Withrow Post Office and Mansfield State Bank. Sinkiuse Indian exhibits include baskets, tools and arrowheads. The Schluenz Rock Collection includes gems, minerals, petrified wood, meteorites and thundereggs (spherical geological formations about the size of a baseball). The 73.25-pound iron and nickel Waterville Meteorite, discovered in 1917, was the first recovered in the state.

Allow 1 hour minimum. Tues.-Sun. and holidays 11-5, Memorial Day weekend-early Oct. Donations. Phone (509) 745-8435.

WENATCHEE (E-9) pop. 27,856, elev. 651′

Wenatchee spreads along the Columbia River just below the confluence with its namesake stream. Despite its rich volcanic soil, the Wenatchee Valley was too arid for farming until the Highline Canal was built in 1903. Once irrigated, the land was planted with apple trees, and Wenatchee emerged as one of the world's largest producers of the fruit.

Wenatchee's proximity to the Wenatchee National Forest *(see place listing p. 277)* makes it a prime area for outdoor recreation, including skiing. Wenatchee Riverfront Park, at the foot of Orondo Avenue, features the Apple Capital Recreation Loop Trail, an 11-mile paved circuit linked by bridges to the east bank of the Columbia River. The trail, lighted until midnight on the Wenatchee side, is popular with pedestrians, bicyclists and roller skaters. A visitors guide is available from the visitor and convention bureau.

Wenatchee Valley Convention & Visitors Bureau: 25 N. Wenatchee Ave., Suite C111, Wenatchee, WA 98801; phone (509) 663-3723 or (800) 572-7753. *See color ad p. 277.*

Shopping areas: Wenatchee Mall, Wenatchee Avenue and Miller Street, features JCPenney. Shoppers will find specialty stores at Victorian Village, half a mile south of downtown at 611 S. Mission St. The major local shopping center is Wenatchee Valley Mall in East Wenatchee; stores include Macy's and Sears. A cluster of antique shops and boutiques can be found on Wenatchee Avenue between Kittitas and 2nd streets.

OHME GARDENS COUNTY PARK, 1 mi. n. at jct. US 2 and US 97 Alt., consists of 9 acres of alpine-type gardens built on a rocky bluff overlooking the Wenatchee Valley and Columbia River. Evergreen trees and low-growing plants blend with rugged rock formations to create effects ranging from the lush growth of a rain forest to the variegated patterns of an alpine meadow. Stone pathways connect the garden levels, leading to such features as fern-bordered pools, rustic shelters, a wishing well and a lookout at the park's highest point.

Allow 1 hour minimum. Daily 9-7, day after Memorial Day-Labor Day; 9-6, mid-Apr. through Memorial Day and day after Labor Day to mid-Oct. Admission $7; $3.50 (ages 6-17). MC, VI. Phone (509) 662-5785.

ROCKY REACH DAM, 7 mi. n. on US 97 Alt., is a Z-shaped structure 2,860 feet long. A viewpoint enables visitors to watch migrating fish ascend the mile-long juvenile fish bypass. In the powerhouse is the Museum of the Columbia, which traces life along the river beginning 10,000 years ago as well as the history of local railroads.

The information center has history exhibits displays about dam building. Gardens and a playground are on the grounds. Guided tours are given June through August. Food is available. Picnicking is permitted. Allow 30 minutes minimum. Information center open daily 8:30-5:30, May-Aug.; 9-4, mid-Mar. to Apr. 30 and Sept.-Oct. Museum open daily 8:30-5, May-Aug.; 9-3:30, mid-Mar. to Apr. 30 and Sept.-Oct. Free. Phone (509) 663-7522.

WENATCHEE VALLEY MUSEUM & CULTURAL CENTER is at 127 S. Mission St. The museum showcases regional history, natural sciences and the arts. An operating model of the Great Northern Railway is on view, as well as exhibits about aviation, the apple industry and Main Street 1910. Silent movies accompanied by a 1919 Wurlitzer pipe organ, children's enrichment programs, art shows and an annual environmental film festival are all offered.

Guided tours are available by appointment. Tues.-Sat. 10-4; closed Jan. 1, July 4, Labor Day, Thanksgiving and Dec. 25. Admission $5; $4 (ages 66+); $2 (ages 6-12); free (first Fri. of the month). Phone (509) 888-6240.

RECREATIONAL ACTIVITIES
Skiing
- **Mission Ridge** is 12 mi. s. Write 7500 Mission Ridge Rd., P.O. Box 1668, Wenatchee, WA 98807. Thurs.-Mon. and holidays 9-4, late Nov.-early Apr. Phone (509) 663-6543, or (509) 663-3200 for ski report.

WINERIES
- **Chateau Faire Le Pont Winery** is 3 mi. n. on SR 285 to Easy St. exit, 1.4 mi. n. on Easy St., .25 mi. e. on Penny Rd. to Technology Center Way, following signs to 1 Vineyard Way. Thurs.-Sat. 11-9, Sun.-Wed. 11-6. Phone (509) 667-9463 or (888) 874-9463.

WENATCHEE NATIONAL FOREST

Elevations in the forest range from 1,000 ft. in Swakane Canyon to 9,511 ft. at Bonanza Peak. Refer to AAA maps for additional elevation information.

Extending from the Cascades' peaks to the Columbia River Basin and from North Cascades National Park and Lake Chelan National Recreation Area to the Yakama Indian Reservation, Wenatchee National Forest occupies 2,200,000 acres. US 2 over Stevens Pass and US 97 over Blewett Pass are the main routes. The Pacific Crest National Scenic Trail generally follows the western boundary line.

Parts of seven wilderness areas lie within the forest: Glacier Peak and Lake Chelan-Sawtooth in the north; Alpine Lakes and Henry M. Jackson in the central portion; and Norse Peak, William O. Douglas and Goat Rocks in the south. Permits are required to enter the Enchantments area of the Alpine Lakes Wilderness.

The Summit at Snoqualmie consists of a cluster of four ski areas off I-90 on both sides of Snoqualmie Pass (see place listing p. 266). Mission Ridge Ski Area is 13 miles southwest of Wenatchee (see place listing p. 277); and White Pass ski area, off US 12, is 50 miles west of Yakima. The forest has 2,500 miles of recreation trails for hiking, horseback riding and bicycling. Popular recreation areas include Lake Wenatchee north of US 2, 20 miles north of Leavenworth; lakes Cle Elum, Kachess and Keechelus, near I-90 west of Cle Elum; Bumping Lake, off SR 410 and Rimrock Lake on US 12.

A trail pass, available at ranger stations, is required for parking at most trailheads in the forest. A day pass costs $5 per vehicle; an annual pass costs $30 per vehicle. Ranger stations are at Chelan, Cle Elum, Entiat, Lake Wenatchee, Leavenworth and Naches. For information write Wenatchee National Forest, 215 Melody Ln., Wenatchee, WA 98801-5933; phone (509) 664-9200. *See Recreation Chart and the AAA Northwestern CampBook.*

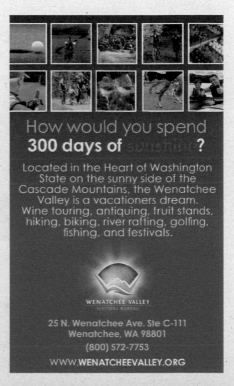

WESTPORT (F-4) pop. 2,137, elev. 12′

Westport is at the north end of an 18-mile-long beach popular for surf fishing, clam digging, crabbing or just wading. Surfers ride the waves on both sides of the Westport jetty. The town is renowned for saltwater fishing—particularly salmon, halibut and tuna—and its marina is base to a large sport fishing fleet. Nearly a dozen charter operators provide guided fishing trips; for information contact the chamber of commerce.

An 1,800-foot walk and bridge enables anglers to fish from the breakwater area as well as from the jetties. The Lighthouse Trail extends 1.5 miles south from the jetty along the beach.

Passenger-only ferry service to Ocean Shores (see place listing p. 192) is available daily late June-Labor Day; Sat.-Sun. early May-late June and day after Labor Day-late Sept. **Note:** The ferry may not run in 2009; call ahead. For further information phone (360) 268-0047.

South of Westport near Grayland, cranberry bogs bloom in mid-June and are harvested in mid-October. Grayland also is noted for its beaches.

Westport-Grayland Chamber of Commerce: 2985 S. Montesano Ave., P.O. Box 306, Westport, WA 98595-0306; phone (360) 268-9422 or (800) 345-6223.

GRAYS HARBOR LIGHT STATION is .5 mi. w. of Montesano St. at 1020 Ocean Ave. The 107-foot-tall lighthouse, commissioned in 1898, is the tallest in Washington and still an active aid to navigation. Visitors may climb the circular, 135-step iron staircase to the top of the tower to observe the Third-Order clam shell Fresnel lens and the current optic.

Guided tours are available. Allow 30 minutes minimum. Daily 10-4, Apr.-Sept.; Fri.-Mon. noon-4, Feb.-Mar. and Oct.-Nov. Grounds and lighthouse base free. Fee to climb the tower $4 (under 6 or less than 40 inches tall are not permitted; children ages 6-9 must be accompanied by an adult). Phone (360) 268-0078 or (360) 268-6214.

WESTPORT MARITIME MUSEUM is at 2201 Westhaven Dr. Housed in a former 1930s Coast Guard lifeboat station, the museum features displays of marine mammal skeletons as well as exhibits about life in a fishing port. Coast Guard and shipwreck history and a children's discovery room also are featured. A separate building houses a lens from the Destruction Island lighthouse. Eight rooms of displays cover such topics as ecology, shellfish, logging and cranberries.

Allow 30 minutes minimum. Daily 10-4, Apr.-Sept.; Fri.-Mon. and holidays noon-4, rest of year. Admission $4; $2 (ages 5-14). Phone (360) 268-0078.

WHIDBEY ISLAND (C-2)

The largest island in Puget Sound, Whidbey Island contains extensive tracts of farmland and forest,

scenic shoreline vistas and parks. Its numerous bays and coves are popular with boaters and fishermen. Capt. George Vancouver discovered the island in 1792, naming it after Joseph Whidbey, his sailing master. Whidbey proved the island was not a peninsula by navigating Deception Pass.

Deception Pass Bridge and ferries from Mukilteo and Port Townsend give access to Whidbey Island; for ferry information phone (888) 808-7977 in Wash. Whidbey Island has several notable towns, including Coupeville, one of the oldest towns in the state, Greenbank and Langley, a picturesque town that retains a historic atmosphere *(see place listings p. 165, p. 170 and p. 176)*. Oak Harbor *(see place listing p. 191)* is the largest town on the island.

Ebey's Landing National Historical Reserve, which encompasses 17,500 acres in central Whidbey, protects a variety of natural and historic sites. SR 20, SR 525 and county roads link eight major areas: Coupeville, Smith Prairie, Crockett Lake and Uplands, Ebey's Landing, Grassers Hill and Lagoon, Monroe Landing, and Fort Casey and Fort Ebey state parks *(see Recreation Chart)*. A self-guiding driving tour map is available at the Island County Historical Museum in Coupeville *(see place listing p. 165)*.

The preserved buildings, farms, parks, scenic drives and military fortifications present a historical record of the area's exploration and settlement. For further information phone (360) 678-6084.

Fort Casey State Park, 3 miles south of Coupeville off SR 20, features late 19th-century fortifications. The two 10-inch disappearing guns on display are thought to be the only ones of their size still in existence.

The park's red-roofed Admiralty Head Lighthouse was built in 1903, replacing a wooden Civil War-era structure. It remained a working lighthouse until 1922, when most ships were steam powered and the Admiralty Inlet route favored by sailing ships was no longer heavily used. The park is open daily 8-dusk. The lighthouse is open daily June through August; varies rest of year. Phone (360) 678-4519, or (360) 240-5584 for the lighthouse. *See Recreation Chart.*

Island County Tourism: P.O. Box 189, Clinton, WA 98236; phone (888) 747-7777.

WHITE PASS (F-7) elev. 4,720'

The community of White Pass straddles the crest of the Cascades a dozen miles southeast of Mount Rainier National Park. The highway through the pass opened in 1951 and is kept open during the snowy winter months. Hiking, fishing, backpacking and a full range of winter sports are popular pursuits here. The Clear Creek Overlook, 2.5 mi. e. on US 12, provides a spectacular view of 300-foot Clear Creek Falls.

RECREATIONAL ACTIVITIES
Skiing

• **White Pass Ski Area** is accessible from US 12. P.O. Box 3030, White Pass, WA 98937. Fri.-Sat.

and holidays 8:45 a.m.-10 p.m., Sun.-Thurs. 8:45-4, Dec. 26-early Mar.; daily 8:45-4, late Nov.-Dec. 25 and early Mar.-early Apr. Phone (509) 672-3101 or (509) 672-3100 for snow conditions.

WHITE SALMON (H-7) pop. 2,193, elev. 640'

Modeled after a Bavarian village, White Salmon is said to have the only glockenspiel in the U.S. west of the Mississippi. The town's location on benchlands above the Columbia offers panoramic views across the river to the Hood River Valley and snowcapped Mt. Hood.

Mt. Adams Chamber of Commerce: 1 Heritage Plaza, P.O. Box 449, White Salmon, WA 98672; phone (509) 493-3630 or (866) 493-3630.

RECREATIONAL ACTIVITIES
Fishing

• **KD Guide Service** offers guided boat fishing trips for salmon, steelhead, sturgeon and walleye on the Columbia River. P.O. Box 166, White Salmon, WA 98672. Daily year-round. Phone (509) 493-3167 or (541) 490-8397.

Horseback Riding

• **Northwestern Lake Riding Stables** offers guided 1- to 4-hour rides departing from Little Buck Creek Rd. Write 126 Little Buck Creek Rd., White Salmon, WA 98672. Daily 8-dusk. Phone (509) 493-4965.

White-water Rafting

• [SAVE] **All Adventures Rafting** departs from a location 12 mi. n. on SR 141. The outfitter offers half-day trips on the White Salmon River. Other activities are offered. Write 20 Forrest Ln., White Salmon, WA 98672. Mar.-Oct. Phone (509) 493-3926 or (800) 743-5628.

• [SAVE] **Zoller's Outdoor Odysseys** departs from a location 10 mi. n. on SR 141. The outfitter offers half-day trips on the White Salmon River and full-day trips on the Klickitat River. Write 1248 SR 141, White Salmon, WA 98672. Excursions depart daily, year-round. Phone (509) 493-2641 or (800) 366-2004.

WHITE SWAN (G-8) pop. 3,033, elev. 973'

Named for a Yakama Indian chief, White Swan lies in the western end of the Yakima Valley.

FORT SIMCOE STATE PARK, 7 mi. w., was one of two interior Washington Territory army posts established as a result of hostilities between the settlers and Yakama Indians in the fall of 1856. Two blockhouses, a guardhouse and barracks have been replicated. Officer's Row includes four original houses and a blockhouse. For further information contact the Park Supervisor's Office, Fort Simcoe State Park, 5150 Fort Simcoe Rd., White Swan, WA 98952.

Picnic facilities are available. Park open daily 6:30 a.m.-dusk, Apr.-Sept.; Sat.-Sun. and holidays 8 a.m.-dusk, rest of year. Museum and interpretive center open Wed.-Sun. 9:30-4:30, Apr.-Sept.; by appointment rest of year. Free. Phone (509) 874-2372.

WHITMAN MISSION NATIONAL HISTORIC SITE (G-11)

Seven miles west of Walla Walla off US 12, the 98-acre Whitman Mission National Historic Site memorializes a mission established in 1836 by Dr. Marcus Whitman and his wife. Called Waiilatpu, "place of the people of the rye grass," this was one of the first mission stations of its kind in the old Oregon country. It operated until 1847 when deepening cultural differences and an outbreak of measles resulted in the Indians killing the Whitmans and 11 others.

The area has been excavated and the sites of the early buildings, which were burned after the massacre, have been outlined. The visitor center contains a museum. A 10-minute slide presentation is shown on request. In summer, ranger programs are offered daily at 11:15. Demonstrations of such pioneer-era tasks as butter churning, trail cookery, candle dipping and wool dyeing, as well as American Indian crafts like cornhusk finger weaving and tulle mat construction, are given on weekends.

A 1-mile paved self-guiding trail leads to the former building sites, restored millpond, apple orchard, irrigation ditch, a portion of the Oregon Trail, the Whitman Memorial Shaft and the Great Grave. Audio stations explain the significance of the area. Picnic facilities are available.

Allow 1 hour minimum. Daily 8-6, June-Aug.; 8-4:30, rest of year. Closed Jan. 1, Thanksgiving and Dec. 25. Admission $3; free (ages 0-16); $5 (family). Phone (509) 522-6360.

WINTHROP (C-9) pop. 349, elev. 1,765'

Winthrop manages to recapture the spirit of the Old West with a colorful main street that has rows of false-fronted buildings, wooden sidewalks and old-fashioned streetlights. It's all reminiscent of the 1890s, when a mining boom brought many new settlers to the area. Poet and author Owen Wister lived in Winthrop in the early 1900s and described some of the town's sites and citizens in his novel "The Virginian."

Winthrop Chamber of Commerce: 202 SR 20, P.O. Box 39, Winthrop, WA 98862; phone (509) 996-2125 or (888) 463-8469.

NORTH CASCADE SMOKEJUMPER BASE is 4 mi. s.e. on Castle Ave. and Twisp-Winthrop Eastside Rd., then w. to 23 Intercity Airport Rd. Visitors can take 30- to 60-minute guided tours of the facility for airborne firefighters, including the parachute loft and aircraft. Jumps can be watched during training sessions, usually held in early June. Daily 9-5, July-Sept.; 8-5, May-June and in early Oct.; by appointment rest of year. Free. Phone (509) 997-9750.

SHAFER MUSEUM is off SR 20 at 285 Castle Ave. The museum includes several pioneer structures.

The log cabin built by town founder Guy Waring in 1897 contains period furnishings.

The collection includes a schoolhouse, a settler's cabin, an outdoor display of early 1900s mining and farm equipment, a 1914 Model T touring car and a rare Rickenbacker car. Of the 80 Rickenbackers produced, only 30 survive. Allow 1 hour minimum. Wed.-Mon. 10-5, Memorial Day weekend-Labor Day. Donations. Phone (509) 996-2712.

WINTHROP NATIONAL FISH HATCHERY, 1 mi. s. at 453-A Twin Lakes Rd., annually raises 600,000 spring chinook salmon, 250,000 coho salmon and 100,000 summer steelheads. A feeding pond is available. Spring release occurs in April and May. Large adult fish are at the hatchery from June through November. Allow 30 minutes minimum. Daily 7:30-4. Free. Phone (509) 996-2424.

RECREATIONAL ACTIVITIES

Hot Air Ballooning

- **Morning Glory Balloon Tours** offers morning champagne flights over the Methow Valley. Trips depart from 960 SR 20 daily, Mar.-Nov. (weather permitting); reservations are required. Write 429 Eastside County Rd., Winthrop, WA 98862, or phone (509) 997-1700.

WOODINVILLE—*see Seattle p. 262.*

WOODLAND (G-6) pop. 3,780, elev. 25'

Settled in the mid 1800s, Woodland soon developed into a bustling center for the surrounding farming, dairying and poultry raising area. Logging was a major industry in the early 20th century. An interpretive marker on Finn Hall Road describes the Old Finn Hall, a community center built in 1916 by Finnish immigrants.

Woodland Chamber of Commerce: 900 Goerig St., Woodland, WA 98674; phone (360) 225-9552.

HULDA KLAGER LILAC GARDENS is 1.5 mi. w. off I-5 exit 21 at 115 S. Pekin Rd. This 4.5-acre garden was the former estate of the renowned hybridizer Hulda Klager, whose work with lilacs brought her acclaim. A variety of plants, trees and shrubs grow in the gardens. Lilacs bloom from approximately mid-April to mid-May.

Self-guiding tours of the 1889 pioneer Victorian farmhouse are offered during the lilac blooming period. Allow 30 minutes minimum. Gardens open daily 10-4. House open daily 10-4, mid-Apr. to mid-May. Admission $2. Phone (360) 225-8996.

LEWIS RIVER HATCHERY is at 4404 Lewis River Rd. Mature coho and chinook salmon are captured and artificially spawned in the fall; their young are then incubated and raised at the facility. Daily 8-4:30. Free. Phone (360) 225-7413.

YACOLT (H-6) pop. 1,055, elev. 709'

Yacolt is situated in a small prairie cupped by the foothills of the Cascades. The name derives from a

Native American word meaning "haunted place" and recalls the mysterious disappearance of five Indian children who were gathering huckleberries on the prairie in the early 1800s. It also is immortalized in the Yacolt Burn, a series of forest fires in September 1902 that devastated 238,000 acres in this region and claimed 38 lives. The disaster encouraged the development of coordinated fire fighting efforts, including a fire lookout system.

The Chelatchie Prairie Railroad offers excursion train trips departing from the Yacolt Depot on selected weekends from February through December; phone (360) 686-3559. The nearby Cedar Creek Grist Mill dates from 1874, the oldest structure of its kind in Washington; the adjacent covered bridge was built in 1995 on the site of an earlier span.

POMEROY LIVING HISTORY FARM is 7 mi. e. of SR 503 via Rock Creek Rd. and Lucia Falls Rd., following signs. Continuously occupied by descendants of the Pomeroy family since 1910, the farm depicts rural life in the 1920s. Guided 20-minute tours of a restored 1920 log house include five second-floor bedrooms, each showcasing a different decade. The grounds include historic vegetable and herb gardens. A series of special event weekends and festivals take place May through October.

Picnicking is permitted. Allow 30 minutes minimum. Grounds open Tues.-Sun. 10-5. Tours given Wed.-Sat. 11-4, Sun. 1-4, mid-June to Aug. 31. Closed Jan. 1, Easter, Thanksgiving and Dec. 25. Admission during special event weekends $6; $3 (ages 3-11). Tour fee $3; $2 (ages 3-11). MC, VI. Phone (360) 686-3537.

YAKIMA (F-9) pop. 71,845, elev. 1,065'

Yakima (YACK-i-mah) occupies the west bank of its namesake river. The townsite developed around a Northern Pacific Railroad depot established in 1884. Originally called North Yakima, the state legislature dropped North from the town's name in 1918. The valley's irrigated fields provide a verdant contrast to the surrounding arid foothills. Fruit warehouses and packing sheds lining the railroad tracks west of First Street attest to Yakima's importance as a food processing and shipping center.

With more than 50 wineries, Yakima is the northern gateway to the Yakima Valley wine country. Wine Yakima Valley has information about area wineries; phone (800) 258-7270.

Yakima Canyon, north to I-82 exit 26, then north on SR 821, is popular with rockhounds and offers fine trout fishing along the Yakima River. About 6 miles north the Fred G. Redmon Memorial Bridge, one of the longest concrete arch spans in the nation, carries I-82 over the Selah Creek Canyon. Adjacent viewpoints offer a panorama of the 330-foot-deep gorge and distant views of Mount Rainier and Mount Adams.

The Yakima Greenway, which extends 10 miles along the Yakima and Naches rivers, features a 9-mile paved walking and bicycling path stretching from Selah Gap on the north to Union Gap on the south. A spur of the trail extends west to 40th Ave.; phone (509) 453-8280.

Capitol Theatre, a restored vaudeville house, is the venue for varied cultural performances; phone (509) 853-8000, or (877) 330-2787 for tickets. Guided tours of the theater are available.

Spectator sports teams in Yakima include the Yakima Bears, who play class A Northwest League baseball mid-June to early September at Yakima County Stadium; phone (509) 457-5151.

Yakima Valley Visitor Information Center: 101 N. Fair Ave., Yakima, WA 98901; phone (509) 573-3388 or (800) 221-0751.

Shopping areas: Track 29 features shops in railroad cars. The major local shopping center is Valley Mall, 3 miles south of downtown via S. 1st Street, featuring Gottschalks, Macy's and Sears. Yesterday's Village, 15 W. Yakima Ave., has dozens of specialty and craft shops. Today's Yesteryear, 509 W. Yakima Ave., is an antique mall with 40 dealers, and a historic district on N. Front Street houses specialty shops. Glenwood Square, S. 51st Avenue and Tieton Drive, houses shops and restaurants in a former apple warehouse.

McALLISTER MUSEUM OF AVIATION is at 2008 S. 16th Ave. Housed in a former flight school

founded in 1926, the museum features exhibits chronicling the history of aviation in eastern Washington. At any given time at least one historic or significant aircraft is on display in the hangar. Model and remote-controlled aircraft also are on display as well as various pieces of avionic equipment. Allow 30 minutes minimum. Thurs.-Fri. 10-4, Sat. 9-4; other times by appointment. Closed holidays. Donations. Phone (509) 457-4933.

YAKIMA AREA ARBORETUM, 3 mi. s.e. on Nob Hill Blvd. to 1401 Arboretum Dr., is a 46-acre reserve containing more than 2,000 species of native and non-native plants and vegetation. The flowering tree collection is at its peak in April and May. Daily dawn-dusk. Jewett Interpretive Center open Tues.-Sat. 9-4; closed holidays. Free. Phone (509) 248-7337.

SAVE **YAKIMA VALLEY MUSEUM,** 2 mi. w. at 2105 Tieton Dr. next to Franklin Park, features a large collection of carriages, coaches and wagons. Other exhibits include Yakama Indian artifacts, agricultural equipment, a working soda fountain and a hands-on children's center. The William O. Douglas Memorial Exhibit includes the United States justice's Supreme Court office. Children's Underground provides children with hands-on activities. The Gilbert House, on the other side of the park at 2109 W. Yakima Ave., is a furnished 1890s farmhouse.

Allow 1 hour minimum. Tues.-Sat. 10-5, Sun. 11-5, Memorial Day-Labor Day; Tues.-Sun. 11-5, rest of year. Closed major holidays. Admission $5; $3 (ages 61+ and students with ID); free (ages 0-5); $12 (family). Phone (509) 248-0747.

YAKIMA VALLEY TROLLEYS (YVT), S. 3rd Ave. and W. Pine St., preserves an early 20th-century interurban railroad that is the last of its kind. At its peak YVT operated 44 miles of track. The 1910 stone car barn and substation house vintage power generating equipment, antique streetcars and electric locomotives, and belt-driven shop machinery.

Allow 1 hour minimum. Car barn and substation open Sat.-Sun. and holidays 10-4. Thirty-minute trolley rides depart Sat.-Sun. and holidays on the hour 10-3, Memorial Day weekend-Labor Day; 90-minute round-trip rides to Selah depart at 10, noon and 2 (call to confirm the Selah trip). Exhibits free. Thirty-minute trolley rides $4; $3 (ages 6-12 and 60+). Ninety-minute rides $6; $4 (ages 6-12 and 60+). Phone (509) 249-5962.

ZILLAH (G-9) pop. 2,198, elev. 821'

Zillah, incorporated in 1911 and named for the daughter of the president of the Northern Pacific Railroad, is in the heart of the Yakima Valley's orchard and vineyard district. The Rattlesnake Hills Wine Trail links 14 area wineries; phone (800) 882-8939. The Fruit Loop is another winery and farm itinerary; contact the chamber of commerce for information.

An architectural oddity in Zillah is the Teapot Dome gas station, off I-82 exit 54, which was built to parody the Wyoming oil lease scandal of the early 1920s.

Zillah Chamber of Commerce: 605 1st Ave., P.O. Box 1294, Zillah, WA 98953; phone (509) 829-5055.

WINERIES

- **Bonair** is at 500 S. Bonair Rd. Daily 10-5; closed holidays. Phone (509) 829-6027.

- **Horizons Edge,** 4530 E. Zillah Dr. Thurs.-Mon. 11-5, Mar.-Nov. Phone (509) 829-6401.

- **Hyatt Vineyards,** 2020 Gilbert Rd. Daily 11-5, Feb.-Dec.; by appointment rest of year. Phone (509) 829-6333.

- **Silver Lake Winery,** 5 mi. n.e. on Vintage Rd. via Cheyne Rd. and Highland Dr. Daily 10-5, Apr.-Nov.; 11-4, rest of year. Phone (509) 829-6235.

At 60 mph, if you reach down to change the radio station you can travel the length of a football field.

Stay Focused
Keep your mind on the road.

America on the Move is made possible by generous support from General Motors Corporation, AAA, State Farm Companies Foundation, The History Channel, United States Congress, U.S. Department of Transportation, Exxon Mobil, American Public Transportation Association, American Road & Transportation Builders Association, Association of American Railroads, National Asphalt Pavement Association, The UPS Foundation.

Years from now, he'll say this

There's so much in life worth celebrating. So starting January 2009, the *Disneyland*® Resort will make it easy for you to magnify those moments in wonderful Disney style! This is the year to gather all the people who make you the happiest and celebrate at The Place Where Dreams Come True. The only thing for you to decide is, "What will you celebrate?"

was the best birthday ever.

What will you celebrate?
Disneyland
Where dreams come true

Don't Take a Vacation From Your Car Seat

Vacations should be fun and hassle-free.
If you can't bring your car seat with you, talk to your
AAA or Hertz travel counselor about special offers.

Oregon

International Rose Test
Garden, Portland
© AAA / Denise Campbell

ALBANY pop. 40,852

―――― WHERE TO STAY ――――

BEST WESTERN ALBANY INN

Phone: (541)928-6322

Hotel
$65-$149 All Year

Address: 315 Airport Rd SE **Location:** I-5, exit 234B southbound; exit 234 northbound, just sw. **Facility:** 70 one-bedroom standard units. 2 stories (no elevator), exterior corridors. **Parking:** on-site. **Terms:** cancellation fee imposed. **Amenities:** high-speed Internet, voice mail, irons, hair dryers. **Pool(s):** heated outdoor. **Leisure Activities:** whirlpool, exercise room. **Guest Services:** valet and coin laundry, wireless Internet. **Business Services:** meeting rooms, PC. **Cards:** AX, CB, DC, DS, JC, MC, VI. **Free Special Amenities: full breakfast and high-speed Internet.**

AAA Benefit:
Members save up to 20%, plus 10% bonus points with rewards program.

COMFORT SUITES

Book great rates at AAA.com

Phone: (541)928-2053

Hotel
$99-$159 3/1-10/1
$89-$139 10/2-2/28

Address: 100 Opal Ct NE **Location:** I-5, exit 234A southbound; exit 234 northbound, just se. Located adjacent to fairgrounds and expo center. **Facility:** Smoke free premises. 86 units. 80 one-bedroom standard units. 6 one-bedroom suites, some with whirlpools. 3 stories, interior corridors. *Bath:* combo or shower only. **Parking:** on-site. **Amenities:** high-speed Internet, voice mail, irons, hair dryers. **Pool(s):** heated indoor. **Leisure Activities:** sauna, whirlpool, exercise room. **Guest Services:** valet and coin laundry, wireless Internet. **Business Services:** meeting rooms, PC. **Cards:** AX, CB, DC, DS, JC, MC, VI. **Free Special Amenities: expanded continental breakfast and high-speed Internet.**

ECONO LODGE

Book great rates at AAA.com

Phone: (541)926-0170

Motel
$54-$95 All Year

Address: 1212 SE Price Rd **Location:** I-5, exit 233, just e on Santiam Hwy (US 20), then just n. **Facility:** 76 one-bedroom standard units. 2 stories (no elevator), exterior corridors. *Bath:* combo or shower only. **Parking:** on-site. **Amenities:** high-speed Internet. **Guest Services:** coin laundry, wireless Internet. **Cards:** AX, DS, MC, VI.

HOLIDAY INN EXPRESS HOTEL & SUITES   *Book great rates at AAA.com*   Phone: (541)928-8820

(AAA) [SAVE]

▼▼▼

Hotel
$109-$179 3/1-10/1
$99-$149 10/2-2/28

Address: 105 Opal Ct NE **Location:** I-5, exit 234A southbound; exit 234 northbound, just se. Located adjacent to fairgrounds and expo center. **Facility:** Smoke free premises. 71 units. 69 one-bedroom standard units. 2 one-bedroom suites with whirlpools. 3 stories, interior corridors. *Bath:* combo or shower only. **Parking:** on-site. **Amenities:** high-speed Internet, voice mail, irons, hair dryers. **Pool(s):** heated indoor. **Leisure Activities:** sauna, whirlpool, exercise room. **Guest Services:** valet and coin laundry, wireless Internet. **Business Services:** meeting rooms, business center. **Cards:** AX, CB, DC, DS, JC, MC, VI. **Free Special Amenities:** expanded continental breakfast and high-speed Internet.

[¶¶] CALL [&M] [🛏] [✕] [✕] [🎬] [🖥] [🖥] [🖥] / SOME UNITS FEE [🐕]

LA QUINTA INN ALBANY   *Book great rates at AAA.com*   Phone: (541)928-0921

▼▼

Hotel
$65-$115 All Year

Address: 251 Airport Rd SE **Location:** I-5, exit 234B southbound; exit 234 northbound, just sw. **Facility:** 62 units. 49 one-bedroom standard units, some with whirlpools. 13 one-bedroom suites, some with efficiencies or kitchens. 3 stories, interior corridors. **Parking:** on-site. **Amenities:** high-speed Internet, voice mail, irons, hair dryers. **Pool(s):** heated indoor. **Leisure Activities:** sauna, whirlpool, exercise room. **Guest Services:** valet and coin laundry, wireless Internet. **Business Services:** PC. **Cards:** AX, DS, JC, MC, VI.

[ASK] [¶¶] [🛏] [✕] [🎬] [🖥] [🖥] [🖥] / SOME UNITS [🐕] [✕] [VCR]

MOTEL 6 #4124   *Book great rates at AAA.com*   Phone: (541)926-4233

(AAA) [SAVE]

▼

Motel
$62-$75 All Year

Address: 2735 E Pacific Blvd **Location:** I-5, exit 234B southbound; exit 234 northbound, 0.5 mi w. **Facility:** 42 one-bedroom standard units. 2 stories (no elevator), exterior corridors. *Bath:* combo or shower only. **Parking:** on-site. **Amenities:** high-speed Internet. **Guest Services:** coin laundry. **Cards:** AX, CB, DC, DS, JC, MC, VI.

[🎬] [🖥] [🖥] / SOME UNITS [🐕] [✕]

PHOENIX INN SUITES-ALBANY   *Book great rates at AAA.com*   Phone: (541)926-5696

(AAA) [SAVE]

▼▼▼

Hotel
$79-$139 All Year

Address: 3410 Spicer Rd SE **Location:** I-5, exit 233, just se. **Facility:** 93 units. 90 one-bedroom standard units, some with whirlpools. 3 one-bedroom suites. 4 stories, interior corridors. *Bath:* combo or shower only. **Parking:** on-site. **Terms:** check-in 4 pm, cancellation fee imposed. **Amenities:** high-speed Internet, dual phone lines, voice mail, irons, hair dryers. *Some:* DVD players. **Pool(s):** heated indoor. **Leisure Activities:** whirlpool, exercise room. **Guest Services:** valet and coin laundry, airport transportation-Albany Airport, wireless Internet. **Business Services:** meeting rooms, PC. **Cards:** AX, CB, DC, DS, JC, MC, VI. **Free Special Amenities:** expanded continental breakfast and high-speed Internet. *(See color ad p 440 & below)*

[➕] [¶¶] [🛏] [🎬] [🖥] [🖥] [🖥] / SOME UNITS FFF [🐕] [✕] [VCR]

QUALITY INN   *Book great rates at AAA.com*   Phone: (541)928-5050

(AAA) [SAVE]

▼▼▼

Hotel
$59-$150 All Year

Address: 1100 Price Rd SE **Location:** I-5, exit 233, just e on Santiam Hwy (US 20), then just n. Located adjacent to Timber-Linn Park. **Facility:** 74 one-bedroom standard units, some with whirlpools. 3 stories, interior corridors. *Bath:* combo or shower only. **Parking:** on-site. **Amenities:** high-speed Internet, voice mail, irons, hair dryers. **Pool(s):** heated indoor. **Leisure Activities:** whirlpool, exercise room. **Guest Services:** valet and coin laundry, wireless Internet. **Business Services:** meeting rooms, PC (fee). **Cards:** AX, DS, MC, VI. **Free Special Amenities:** continental breakfast and high-speed Internet. *(See color ad p 292)*

[¶¶] CALL [&M] [🛏] [✕] [🎬] [🖥] [🖥] [🖥] / SOME UNITS FEE [🐕] [✕]

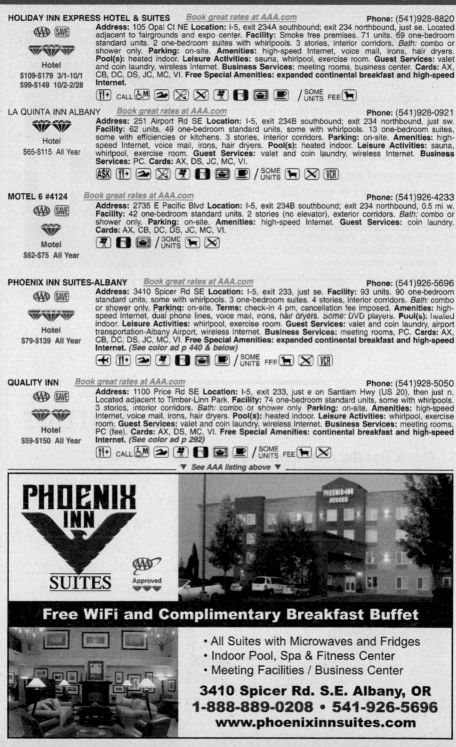

▼ See AAA listing p 291 ▼

-------- **WHERE TO DINE** --------

BURGERVILLE

American
$2-$8

Phone: 541/926-0669
First-timers shouldn't let the fast food exterior fool them, as the burgers and chicken here adhere to a higher standard. Northwest ingredients come into play in the sandwiches. Casual dress. **Hours:** 7 am-10 pm. Closed: 11/26, 12/25. **Address:** 2310 Santiam Hwy **Location:** I-5, exit 233, 0.7 mi e on US 20 (Santiam Hwy). **Parking:** on-site. **Cards:** DS, MC, VI.

THE DEPOT CAFE

Seafood
$8-$19

Phone: 541/926-7326
A longtime favorite for locals seeking a relaxing, classic seafood meal, the restaurant offers comfy booths surrounded by wood and lots of old advertising signs on the walls. The casual spot is great for enjoying calamari rings, shrimp salad, a bowl of chowder or some fish and chips. Casual dress. **Bar:** Beer & wine. **Reservations:** not accepted. **Hours:** 11 am-9 pm, Fri & Sat-10 pm, Sun-8 pm. Closed: 11/26, 12/25. **Address:** 822 S Lyon **Location:** On US 20 N; corner of 8th Ave SW; downtown. **Parking:** on-site. **Cards:** MC, VI.

NOVAK'S HUNGARIAN RESTAURANT & BAKERY   *Menu on AAA.com*

Hungarian
$8-$19

Phone: 541/967-9488
Freshly prepared recipes steeped in rich flavors are the specialty at the family-owned Hungarian restaurant. An interesting appetizer is Hungarian fried bread with garlic and preserves. The signature chicken paprikash and homemade pork sausage brim with tasty spices. Combination plates satisfy those who want to sample it all. Heart-healthy entrees, dinner house specialties and light dinners also are available. Save room for a scrumptious homemade dessert. Casual dress. **Bar:** Beer & wine. **Reservations:** suggested. **Hours:** 6:30 am-9 pm. Closed major holidays. **Address:** 2306 Heritage Way SE **Location:** I-5, exit 233, 1 mi w, then just s on Geary St; in Heritage Plaza Shopping Center, next to Joe's. **Parking:** on-site. **Cards:** AX, DS, MC, VI.

SYBARIS

American
$15-$23

Phone: 541/928-8157
In historic downtown, this bistro prepares Northwest cuisine with a bit of a French influence. The emphasis is on fresh, locally grown produce, and the menu changes monthly. Desserts are made-in-house, too. Lending to the cozy, inviting atmosphere are a large, rustic wood fireplace and artwork featuring a different local artist each month. Casual dress. **Bar:** Full bar. **Reservations:** suggested. **Hours:** 5 pm-9 pm. Closed major holidays; also Sun & Mon. **Address:** 442 SW 1st Ave **Location:** At Washington St; downtown. **Parking:** street. **Cards:** AX, MC, VI.

WYATT'S EATERY & BREWHOUSE

American
$8-$19

Phone: 541/917-3727
Hearty sandwiches and burgers, along with steaks, fish salads and pasta, are served in a friendly, publike setting. The downtown cafe occupies a renovated, historic commercial building. Casual dress. **Bar:** Full bar. **Reservations:** accepted. **Hours:** 11 am-9 pm, Fri & Sat-10:30 pm. Closed major holidays; also Sun. **Address:** 211 1st Ave W **Location:** Jct Ellsworth St; downtown. **Parking:** on-site. **Cards:** AX, DS, MC, VI.

ASHLAND pop. 19,522

-------- **WHERE TO STAY** --------

ASHLAND CHANTICLEER INN

Historic Bed
& Breakfast
$155-$195 3/1-10/31
$125-$165 11/1-2/28

Phone: 541/482-1919
Address: 120 Gresham St **Location:** Just se of downtown on Main St (SR 99), then just s. Located in a residential area. **Facility:** The inn, part of a quiet neighborhood with views of the Cascade Range, is convenient to theaters, galleries and restaurants. Smoke free premises. 6 one-bedroom standard units. 2 stories (no elevator), interior corridors. **Bath:** combo or shower only. **Parking:** on-site. **Terms:** office hours 8 am-4 pm, 2 night minimum stay - seasonal and/or weekends, 31 day cancellation notice-fee imposed. **Amenities:** DVD players, high-speed Internet, hair dryers. **Guest Services:** wireless Internet. **Business Services:** PC. **Cards:** MC, VI.

ASHLAND'S LITHIA SPRINGS RESORT & GARDENS   *Book great rates at AAA.com*

Hotel
$149-$249 All Year

Phone: (541)482-7128
Address: 2165 W Jackson Rd **Location:** I-5, exit 19, 0.5 mi s on Valley View Rd, just sw on SR 99 (N Main St), then just w. **Facility:** Smoke free premises. 25 units. 5 one-bedroom standard units, some with whirlpools. 20 one-bedroom suites with whirlpools. 1-2 stories (no elevator), interior/exterior corridors. **Bath:** combo or shower only. **Parking:** on-site. **Terms:** 2-3 night minimum stay - seasonal and/or weekends, 14 day cancellation notice-fee imposed. **Amenities:** video library, CD players, high-speed Internet, irons, hair dryers. **Leisure Activities:** bike trails, croquet, library. **Guest Services:** wireless Internet. **Business Services:** meeting rooms, PC. **Cards:** AX, DS, MC, VI. **Free Special Amenities:** high-speed Internet.

ASHLAND SPRINGS HOTEL   *Book great rates at AAA.com*

Historic
Hotel
$89-$259 All Year

Phone: (541)488-1700
Address: 212 E Main St **Location:** Corner of 1st St; center. **Facility:** The European-style hotel has been elegantly restored and features good views of downtown from large windows that date back to the 1920s. Smoke free premises. 70 one-bedroom standard units. 9 stories, interior corridors. **Bath:** combo or shower only. **Parking:** on-site. **Terms:** cancellation fee imposed. **Amenities:** high-speed Internet, dual phone lines, voice mail, irons, hair dryers. **Dining:** Larks-Home Kitchen Cuisine, see separate listing. **Guest Services:** valet laundry, wireless Internet. **Business Services:** conference facilities, business center. **Cards:** AX, DC, DS, MC, VI.

BEST WESTERN BARD'S INN   *Book great rates at AAA.com*

Hotel
$90-$190 All Year

Address: 132 N Main St **Location:** Just nw on SR 99 (N Main St) from Downtown Plaza. **Facility:** Smoke free premises. 91 units. 87 one- and 4 two-bedroom standard units, some with whirlpools. 2-3 stories, interior/exterior corridors. *Bath:* combo or shower only. **Parking:** on-site. **Terms:** cancellation fee imposed. **Amenities:** high-speed Internet, dual phone lines, voice mail, irons, hair dryers. **Pool(s):** heated outdoor. **Leisure Activities:** whirlpool. **Guest Services:** wireless Internet. **Business Services:** PC. **Cards:** AX; DS, MC, VI. **Free Special Amenities: expanded continental breakfast and high-speed Internet.**

Phone: (541)482-0049

AAA Benefit:
Members save up to 20%, plus 10% bonus points with rewards program.

BEST WESTERN WINDSOR INN   *Book great rates at AAA.com*

Hotel
$99-$189 3/1-10/15
$89-$139 10/16-2/28

Address: 2520 Ashland St **Location:** I-5, exit 14, just se on Ashland St (SR 66). **Facility:** Smoke free premises. 92 units. 84 one-bedroom standard units, some with whirlpools. 8 one-bedroom suites with kitchens. 2 stories (no elevator), exterior corridors. *Bath:* combo or shower only. **Parking:** on-site. **Amenities:** high-speed Internet, irons, hair dryers. **Pool(s):** heated outdoor. **Leisure Activities:** whirlpool, exercise room. **Guest Services:** coin laundry, area transportation-Shakespearean Theatre, wireless Internet. **Business Services:** meeting rooms, PC. **Cards:** AX, DS, MC, VI.

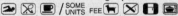

Phone: (541)488-2330

AAA Benefit:
Members save up to 20%, plus 10% bonus points with rewards program.

CEDARWOOD INN

Phone: (541)488-2000

Motel
$59-$119 All Year

Address: 1801 Siskiyou Blvd **Location:** I-5, exit 11 northbound, 2.6 mi nw; exit 14 southbound, just w on Ashland St (SR 66), 0.6 mi s on Tolman Creek Rd, then 0.6 mi w. **Facility:** 59 units. 50 one- and 7 two-bedroom standard units, some with efficiencies (no utensils). 2 one-bedroom suites with kitchens (no utensils). 2 stories (no elevator), exterior corridors. *Bath:* combo or shower only. **Parking:** on-site. **Terms:** office hours 7 am-2 am, 3 day cancellation notice. **Pool(s):** heated outdoor, heated indoor. **Leisure Activities:** sauna, steamroom, barbecue grill, picnic tables. **Guest Services:** wireless Internet. **Cards:** AX, DC, DS, MC, VI. **Free Special Amenities: continental breakfast and high-speed Internet.**

COUNTRY WILLOWS BED & BREAKFAST INN

Phone: (541)488-1590

Bed & Breakfast
$140-$255 3/1-10/31
$115-$195 11/1-2/28

Address: 1313 Clay St **Location:** I-5, exit 11 northbound, 2.3 mi nw on Siskiyou Blvd, then 0.3 mi s; exit 14 southbound; just w on Ashland St (SR 66), 0.6 mi s on Tolman Creek Rd, 0.3 mi w on Siskiyou Blvd, then 0.3 mi s. Located in a quiet country setting. **Facility:** Set against a pastoral backdrop, guest rooms in the 1896 farmhouse and in the barn are decorated in a rustic, country style. Smoke free premises. 9 units. 6 one-bedroom standard units. 2 one-bedroom suites with whirlpools. 1 cottage. 2 stories (no elevator), interior/exterior corridors. *Bath:* combo or shower only. **Parking:** on-site. **Terms:** office hours 7 am-9 pm, age restrictions may apply, 30 day cancellation notice-fee imposed. **Amenities:** video library, high-speed Internet, irons, hair dryers. *Some:* DVD players, CD players. **Pool(s):** heated outdoor. **Leisure Activities:** whirlpool, croquet, bicycles, hiking trails. **Guest Services:** wireless Internet. **Business Services:** PC. **Cards:** AX, DS, MC, VI. **Free Special Amenities: full breakfast and high-speed Internet.**

FLAGSHIP INN OF ASHLAND

Phone: (541)482-2641

Motel
$59-$119 All Year

Address: 1193 Siskiyou Blvd **Location:** I-5, exit 14, 1.3 mi w on Ashland St (SR 66), then just n. **Facility:** 63 units. 60 one- and 3 two-bedroom standard units. 2 stories (no elevator), exterior corridors. *Bath:* combo or shower only. **Parking:** on-site. **Terms:** office hours 7 am-2 am, 3 day cancellation notice. **Amenities:** high-speed Internet, irons. **Pool(s):** heated outdoor. **Leisure Activities:** barbecue & picnic area. **Guest Services:** wireless Internet. **Business Services:** meeting rooms. **Cards:** AX, DC, DS, MC, VI. **Free Special Amenities: continental breakfast and high-speed Internet.**

HOLIDAY INN EXPRESS   *Book great rates at AAA.com*

Phone: (541)201-0202

Hotel
$89-$189 All Year

Address: 565 Clover Ln **Location:** I-5, exit 14, just e on Ashland St (SR 66), then s. **Facility:** Smoke free premises. 65 one-bedroom standard units, some with efficiencies and/or whirlpools. 3 stories, interior corridors. *Bath:* combo or shower only. **Parking:** on-site. **Amenities:** high-speed Internet, dual phone lines, voice mail, irons, hair dryers. **Pool(s):** heated indoor. **Leisure Activities:** whirlpool, exercise room. **Guest Services:** valet and coin laundry, wireless Internet. **Business Services:** meeting rooms. **Cards:** AX, DC, DS, MC, VI. **Free Special Amenities: expanded continental breakfast and high-speed Internet.**

THE IRIS INN BED AND BREAKFAST

Phone: 541/488-2286

Bed & Breakfast
Rates not provided

Address: 59 Manzanita St **Location:** I-5, exit 19, 0.5 mi w, 1.7 mi s on SR 99 (N Main St), then just w. Located in a quiet residential area. **Facility:** A 1905 Victorian, this property near downtown features a hammock, deck and patio that overlook expansive gardens in a tranquil setting. Smoke free premises. 5 one-bedroom standard units. 2 stories (no elevator), interior corridors. *Bath:* combo or shower only. **Parking:** on-site. **Amenities:** high-speed Internet, hair dryers. **Guest Services:** wireless Internet. **Free Special Amenities: full breakfast and high-speed Internet.**

LA QUINTA INN & SUITES ASHLAND   *Book great rates at AAA.com*

Phone: (541)482-6932

Hotel
$69-$172 All Year

Address: 434 S Valley View Rd **Location:** I-5, exit 19, just sw. **Facility:** 71 units. 59 one-bedroom standard units, some with whirlpools. 12 one-bedroom suites with efficiencies. 4 stories, interior corridors. **Parking:** on-site. **Amenities:** video library, high-speed Internet, dual phone lines, voice mail, irons, hair dryers. **Pool(s):** heated indoor. **Leisure Activities:** whirlpool, limited exercise equipment. **Guest Services:** valet and coin laundry, wireless Internet. **Business Services:** PC. **Cards:** AX, CB, DS, MC, VI.

MCCALL HOUSE BED & BREAKFAST

Phone: (541)482-9296

Historic Bed
& Breakfast
$105-$250 3/1-1/1
$110-$160 2/1-2/28

Address: 153 Oak St **Location:** Corner of Lithia Way; center. **Facility:** This recently renovated 1883 Italianate-style Victorian home with a warm yellow exterior is a block from the theater and downtown. Smoke free premises. 10 one-bedroom standard units. 2 stories (no elevator), interior corridors. *Bath:* combo or shower only. **Parking:** on-site. **Terms:** open 3/1-1/1 & 2/1-2/28, office hours 7:30 am-10 pm, 2 night minimum stay - seasonal and/or weekends, age restrictions may apply, 30 day cancellation notice-fee imposed. **Amenities:** high-speed Internet, voice mail, irons, hair dryers. **Guest Services:** airport transportation-Ashland Airport, wireless Internet. **Business Services:** PC. **Cards:** AX, DC, DS, MC, VI.

MT ASHLAND INN

Phone: 541/482-8707

Bed & Breakfast
$180-$235 All Year

Address: 550 Mt. Ashland Rd **Location:** I-5, exit 6, just w to Mt. Ashland Rd, follow signs 5.2 mi to ski area; 8 mi s of town. Located in a secluded mountain area. **Facility:** This inn on Mount Ashland features mountain views and a rustic ambience with stained glass and stone accents. Three miles from downhill skiing. Smoke free premises. 5 one-bedroom standard units with whirlpools. 4 stories (no elevator), interior corridors. **Parking:** on-site. **Terms:** office hours 8 am-8 pm, 2 night minimum stay - seasonal and/or weekends, age restrictions may apply, 30 day cancellation notice-fee imposed. **Amenities:** CD players, high-speed Internet, hair dryers. **Leisure Activities:** sauna, whirlpool, hiking trails. **Guest Services:** wireless Internet. **Cards:** DS, MC, VI.

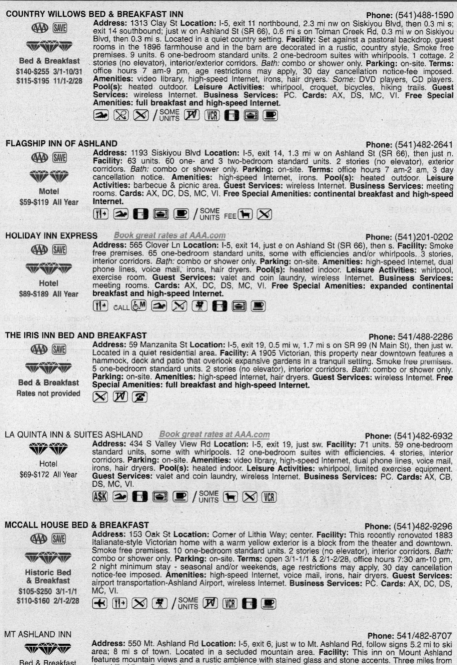

OAK HILL BED & BREAKFAST

Phone: 541/482-1554

▼▼ ▼▼

Bed & Breakfast
$155-$205 3/1-10/31
$120-$160 11/1-2/28

Address: 2190 Siskiyou Blvd **Location:** I-5, exit 11 northbound, 2.3 mi nw; exit 14 southbound, just w on Ashland St (SR 66), 0.6 mi s on Tolman Creek Rd, then 0.3 mi w. Located in a quiet area. **Facility:** Smoke free premises. 6 one-bedroom standard units. 2 stories (no elevator), interior/exterior corridors. *Bath:* combo or shower only. **Parking:** on-site. **Terms:** office hours 7 am-7 pm, 2 night minimum stay - seasonal and/or weekends, age restrictions may apply, 30 day cancellation notice-fee imposed. **Amenities:** high-speed Internet, irons, hair dryers. **Guest Services:** wireless Internet. **Business Services:** PC. **Cards:** DS, MC, VI.

PEERLESS HOTEL

Phone: 541/488-1082

▼▼ ▼▼

Historic
Country Inn
$125-$269 3/1-10/31
$90-$190 11/1-2/28

Address: 243 4th St **Location:** 3 blks n of N Main St (SR 99); center. **Facility:** Just minutes from downtown, this 1900 brick building is decorated in turn-of-the-century style with elegant fabrics and hand-painted ceilings. Smoke free premises. 6 units. 4 one-bedroom standard units, some with whirlpools. 2 one-bedroom suites, some with whirlpools. 2 stories (no elevator), interior corridors. *Bath:* combo or shower only. **Parking:** street. **Terms:** office hours 7 am-6 pm, 14 day cancellation notice-fee imposed. **Amenities:** high-speed Internet, hair dryers. **Dining:** The Peerless Restaurant, see separate listing. **Guest Services:** TV in common area, valet laundry, wireless Internet. **Cards:** AX, DS, MC, VI.

PELTON HOUSE

Phone: (541)488-7003

AAA SAVE

▼▼ ▼▼

Historic Bed
& Breakfast
$100-$185 3/1-10/31
$75-$150 11/1-2/28

Address: 228 B St **Location:** Corner of 1st St; downtown. **Facility:** The attractively renovated historical house dates back to the late 1800s and is located within walking distance of the downtown area and restaurants. Smoke free premises. 5 one-bedroom standard units. 2 stories, interior/exterior corridors. *Bath:* combo or shower only. **Parking:** on-site. **Terms:** office hours 7 am-8 pm, 14 day cancellation notice. **Amenities:** CD players, high-speed Internet, hair dryers. *Some:* DVD players, irons. **Guest Services:** wireless Internet. **Cards:** MC, VI. **Free Special Amenities: full breakfast and high-speed Internet.**

PLAZA INN & SUITES AT ASHLAND CREEK

Book great rates at AAA.com

Phone: (541)488-8900

AAA SAVE

▼▼ ▼▼

Hotel
$199-$289 3/1-10/31
$89-$149 11/1-2/28

Address: 98 Central Ave **Location:** From Downtown Plaza, just nw on N Main St (SR 99), just n on Water St, then just w. **Facility:** Smoke free premises. 91 units. 85 one-bedroom standard units, some with whirlpools. 6 one-bedroom suites. 3 stories, interior corridors. *Bath:* combo or shower only. **Parking:** on-site. **Terms:** check-in 4 pm, 2 night minimum stay - seasonal and/or weekends, cancellation fee imposed. **Amenities:** CD players, high-speed Internet, dual phone lines, voice mail, irons, hair dryers. *Some:* DVD players. **Leisure Activities:** whirlpool, sun deck, creekside patio, exercise room. **Guest Services:** valet and coin laundry, wireless Internet. **Business Services:** meeting rooms, PC. **Cards:** AX, DC, DS, MC, VI. **Free Special Amenities: expanded continental breakfast and high-speed Internet.**

ROMEO INN

Bed & Breakfast
$105-$220 All Year

Phone: (541)488-0884

Address: 295 Idaho St **Location:** I-5, exit 14, 1.1 mi w on SR 66 (Ashland St), 1.1 mi n on SR 99 (Siskiyou Blvd), 0.3 mi w on Gresham St, just s on Iowa St, then just w. **Facility:** Tall pines, gardens and a hammock accent the grounds of this Cape Cod-style house in a hilltop neighborhood. Smoke free premises. 6 units. 5 one-bedroom standard units. 1 one-bedroom suite with whirlpool. 2 stories (no elevator), interior/exterior corridors. *Bath:* combo or shower only. **Parking:** on-site. **Terms:** office hours 7 am-9 pm, 2 night minimum stay - seasonal and/or weekends, age restrictions may apply, 30 day cancellation notice-fee imposed. **Amenities:** CD players, high-speed Internet, hair dryers. *Some:* irons. **Pool(s):** heated outdoor. **Leisure Activities:** whirlpool. **Guest Services:** wireless Internet. **Cards:** DS, MC, VI.

SUPER 8 - ASHLAND

AAA SAVE

Hotel
$60-$120 All Year

Book great rates at AAA.com

Phone: (541)482-8887

Address: 2350 Ashland St **Location:** I-5, exit 14, just sw on Ashland St (SR 66). **Facility:** 68 units. 67 one-bedroom standard units. 1 one-bedroom suite with kitchen (no utensils). 3 stories (no elevator), interior corridors. **Parking:** on-site. **Amenities:** high-speed Internet, safes (fee), hair dryers. **Pool(s):** heated indoor. **Guest Services:** coin laundry, wireless Internet. **Business Services:** meeting rooms. **Cards:** AX, DC, DS, MC, VI. **Free Special Amenities: continental breakfast and high-speed Internet.**

TIMBERS MOTEL OF ASHLAND

AAA SAVE

Motel
Rates not provided

Phone: 541/482-4242

Address: 1450 Ashland St **Location:** I-5, exit 14, 1.2 mi w on Ashland St (SR 66). Located in a commercial area. **Facility:** Smoke free premises. 29 units. 27 one- and 2 two-bedroom standard units, some with kitchens. 2 stories (no elevator), exterior corridors. **Parking:** on-site. **Terms:** office hours 8:30 am-11 pm. **Amenities:** high-speed Internet. *Some:* DVD players, irons, hair dryers. **Pool(s):** heated outdoor. **Guest Services:** wireless Internet. **Free Special Amenities: local telephone calls and high-speed Internet.**

VILLAGE SUITES AT ASHLAND HILLS

AAA SAVE

Hotel
$149 3/1-10/15
$99 10/16-2/28

Book great rates at AAA.com

Phone: (541)482-8310

Address: 2525 Ashland St **Location:** I-5, exit 14, just ne on Ashland St (SR 66). **Facility:** Smoke free premises. 66 one-bedroom suites. 3 stories, interior corridors. *Bath:* combo or shower only. **Parking:** on-site. **Terms:** check-in 4 pm. **Amenities:** video library, high speed Internet, voice mail, irons, hair dryers. *Some:* DVD players. **Leisure Activities:** bike trails, bicycles, hiking trails, exercise room. **Guest Services:** valet and coin laundry, wireless Internet. **Business Services:** PC. **Cards:** AX, DS, MC, VI. **Free Special Amenities: expanded continental breakfast and high-speed Internet.**

THE WINCHESTER INN, RESTAURANT & WINE BAR

Historic
Country Inn
$135-$295 All Year

Phone: 541/488-1113

Address: 35 S 2nd St **Location:** Just s of Main St (SR 99); center. **Facility:** English tea gardens and a Victorian gazebo on the grounds enhance this country inn, which offers well-decorated guest rooms. Smoke free premises. 19 units. 16 one-bedroom standard units, some with whirlpools. 3 one-bedroom suites, some with whirlpools. 2-3 stories (no elevator), interior/exterior corridors. *Bath:* combo or shower only. **Parking:** on-site. **Terms:** office hours 7 am-11 pm, 30 day cancellation notice-fee imposed. **Amenities:** high-speed Internet, voice mail, irons, hair dryers. *Some:* DVD players, CD players. **Guest Services:** valet laundry, wireless Internet. **Business Services:** meeting rooms, PC. **Cards:** AX, DS, MC, VI.

------- **WHERE TO DINE** -------

AMUSE RESTAURANT

Regional French
$19-$32

Phone: 541/488-9000

Seasonally inspired contemporary French cuisine reflects Northwest influences. Local and organic food items play into the recipes. The atmosphere is intimate and serene in the dining room and on the seasonal patio. The wine list includes a good selection of Oregon and California choices. Dressy casual. **Bar:** Beer & wine. **Reservations:** suggested. **Hours:** 5:30 pm-9 pm. Closed: 11/26, 12/24, 12/25; also Mon. **Address:** 15 N 1st St **Location:** At N 1st and Main sts; center. **Parking:** street. **Cards:** AX, CB, DC, DS, MC, VI.

BREADBOARD RESTAURANT

American
$5-$12

Phone: 541/488-0295

Patrons can sample well-prepared breakfasts, delicious sandwiches and freshly baked goods. The bright, cheery establishment affords lovely views of the mountains and valley. Works by local artists adorn the walls. Outside seating is available in season. Casual dress. **Reservations:** not accepted. **Hours:** 7 am-2:30 pm. Closed: 7/4, 11/26, 12/25. **Address:** 744 N Main St **Location:** I-5, exit 19, 0.5 mi w, then 1.2 mi s on SR 99 (Main St). **Parking:** on-site. **Cards:** MC, VI.

CHATEAULIN

French
$18-$40

Phone: 541/482-2264

An intimate feel envelops this cozy bistro, just a skip away from the theater. Entrees—such as filet of veal roti served with a reduced white wine sauce, sauteed oyster mushrooms and roasted garlic mashed potatoes—are delicious. Triple sorbet with peach, raspberry and blueberry is an eye-catching dessert, and the Grand Marnier bombe is classically presented. Servers are knowledgeable. **Bar:** Full bar. **Reservations:** suggested. **Hours:** 5 pm-11 pm; 5:30 pm-9 pm in winter. Closed: 1/1, 11/26, 12/25; also Mon & Tues 11/1-3/31. **Address:** 50 E Main St **Location:** Center. **Parking:** street. **Cards:** AX, DS, MC, VI.

GEPPETTO'S CAFE & DINING ROOM

Italian
$6-$22

Phone: 541/482-1138

The establishment has been serving homemade Italian food for nearly three decades. Many seasonal food items come from the owner's organic farm. Casual dress. **Bar:** Full bar. **Reservations:** not accepted. **Hours:** 8 am-midnight. Closed: 11/26, 12/25. **Address:** 345 E Main St **Location:** Just s of plaza; center. **Parking:** street. **Cards:** DS, MC, VI.

LARKS-HOME KITCHEN CUISINE

American
$8-$27

Phone: 541/488-5558

Diners taste the bounty of Oregon at this restaurant, which brings the freshest produce from the farm to the table. Soothing colors and a nostalgic ambience promote a feel of casual elegance. Sidewalk dining is a seasonal option. Dressy casual. **Bar:** Full bar. **Reservations:** suggested. **Hours:** 11:30 am-2 & 5-9 pm; to 8 pm in winter; Saturday & Sunday brunch 11 am-2 pm. **Address:** 212 E Main St **Location:** Corner of 1st St; center; in Ashland Springs Hotel. **Parking:** street. **Cards:** AX, DS, MC, VI.

MONET RESTAURANT AND GARDEN   *Menu on AAA.com*

French
$17-$30

Phone: 541/482-1339

Newly renovated, the romantic dining room and lush garden reflect the color and spontaneity of Claude Monet's paintings and serve as a lovely dining setting. Cuisine hails from the chef/owner's home in the Rhone River Valley. Casual dress. **Bar:** Full bar. **Reservations:** suggested, in summer. **Hours:** Open 3/1-12/31 & 2/1-2/28; 5:30 pm-8:30 pm. Closed: 11/26, 12/25; also Sun 2/1-5/31 & 10/1-12/31 & Mon. **Address:** 36 S 2nd St **Location:** Just w from Main St; downtown. **Parking:** on-site. **Cards:** DS, MC, VI.

OMAR'S FRESH FISH & STEAKS   *Menu on AAA.com*

Steak & Seafood
$7-$20

Phone: 541/482-1281

Since 1946, the neighborhood eatery has served carefully selected, fresh seafood and hand-cut aged steaks. Daily specials feature Northwest seasonal ingredients. Entrees can be prepared to meet low-fat and low-cholesterol diets. Casual dress. **Bar:** Full bar. **Reservations:** not accepted. **Hours:** 11:30 am-2 & 5-9:30 pm, Fri & Sat-10 pm; to 9 pm, Fri & Sat-10 pm 11/1-5/1. Closed: 11/26, 12/25; also Super Bowl Sun. **Address:** 1380 Siskiyou Blvd **Location:** I-5, exit 14, 1.2 mi w. **Parking:** on-site. **Cards:** AX, CB, DC, DS, MC, VI.

OREGON CABARET THEATRE

American
$15-$20

Phone: 541/488-2902

The intimate dinner theater is housed in a 1911 church with stained-glass windows and a crystal chandelier. Seasonal specialties make up the changing menu. Dessert is served at the intermission. The dinner cost does not include the show ticket price. Casual dress. Entertainment. **Bar:** Beer & wine. **Reservations:** suggested. **Hours:** Open 3/1-12/31 & 2/1-2/28; 6:30 pm & 7 pm seating; Sunday brunch 11:30 am seating. Closed: 7/4, 11/26, 12/24, 12/25; also Tues & Wed. **Address:** 241 Hagardine St **Location:** 1 blk w of E Main St; center. **Parking:** street. **Cards:** MC, VI. **Historic**

PASTA PIATTI

Italian
$7-$15

Phone: 541/488-5493

The eatery offers a variety of homemade pastas as well as other menu items including seafood, chicken, eggplant parmigiana, grilled polenta, pizzas and panini. Casual dress. **Bar:** Beer & wine. **Hours:** 11:30 am-9 pm. Closed: 11/26, 12/25. **Address:** 358 E Main St **Location:** Downtown. **Parking:** on-site and street. **Cards:** MC, VI.

THE PEERLESS RESTAURANT

Continental
$18-$30

Phone: 541/488-6067

Seasonal Northwest cuisine is served in a contemporary, yet casual, garden atmosphere. The jungle mural on the wall and large, leafy plants add outdoor ambience to the setting. Dedicated to sustainable hormone-free cuisine, the seasonally changing menu might list such tantalizing items as herb-crusted rack of lamb, hot-alder-smoked salmon and filet mignon with black pepper and lavender crust. Casual dress. **Bar:** Full bar. **Reservations:** suggested. **Hours:** Open 3/1-12/31 & 2/1-2/28; 5:30 pm-9 pm. Closed: 11/26, 12/25; also Sun & Mon. **Address:** 265 4th St **Location:** 3 blks n of N Main St (SR 99); center; in Peerless Hotel. **Parking:** street. **Cards:** AX, DS, MC, VI.

STANDING STONE BREWING COMPANY

American
$7-$18

Phone: 541/482-2448

The full-service microbrewery offers a wide selection of ales. Menu items include a variety of meat, seafood, and chicken entrees, as well as wood-fired pizzas. Casual dress. **Bar:** Full bar. **Reservations:** accepted. **Hours:** 11:30 am-10 pm, Fri & Sat-2 am. Closed: 11/26, 12/25. **Address:** 101 Oak St **Location:** Between Main St and Lithia Way; downtown. **Parking:** street. **Cards:** MC, VI.

ASTORIA pop. 9,813

-------- WHERE TO STAY --------

ASTORIA DUNES MOTEL   *Book great rates at AAA.com*

Motel
$75-$130 5/17-2/28
$70-$125 3/1-5/16

Phone: (503)325-7111

Address: 288 W Marine Dr **Location:** Just e of Astoria Bridge on US 30. **Facility:** 58 one-bedroom standard units, some with whirlpools. 2 stories (no elevator), exterior corridors. **Parking:** on-site. **Terms:** office hours 7 am-10 pm, check-in 4 pm, cancellation fee imposed. **Amenities:** high-speed Internet. **Pool(s):** heated indoor. **Leisure Activities:** whirlpool. **Guest Services:** coin laundry, wireless Internet. **Cards:** AX, DS, MC, VI. **Free Special Amenities: continental breakfast and high-speed Internet.**

ASTORIA HOLIDAY INN EXPRESS HOTEL & SUITES   *Book at AAA.com*

Hotel
$119-$339 All Year

Phone: (503)325-6222

Address: 204 W Marine Dr **Location:** On US 30; west side of town. Located by Columbia River. **Facility:** 78 units. 63 one-bedroom standard units, some with whirlpools. 12 one- and 3 two-bedroom suites. 4 stories, interior corridors. *Bath:* combo or shower only. **Parking:** on-site. **Amenities:** video library (fee), DVD players, high-speed Internet, voice mail, irons, hair dryers. **Pool(s):** heated indoor. **Leisure Activities:** whirlpool, exercise room. *Fee:* game room. **Guest Services:** valet and coin laundry, wireless Internet. **Business Services:** meeting rooms, PC. **Cards:** AX, CB, DC, DS, JC, MC, VI.

BEST WESTERN LINCOLN INN *Book great rates at AAA.com* Phone: (503)325-2205

(AAA) **[SAVE]**

Hotel
$89-$399 3/1-9/30
$89-$199 10/1-2/28

Address: 555 Hamburg Ave **Location:** On US 101/30; at east end of Young's Bay Bridge. **Facility:** Smoke free premises. 75 units. 74 one-bedroom standard units, some with whirlpools. 1 one-bedroom suite with kitchen and whirlpool. 4 stories, interior corridors. *Bath:* combo or shower only. **Parking:** on-site. **Terms:** check-in 4 pm. **Amenities:** high-speed Internet, voice mail, irons, hair dryers. **Pool(s):** heated indoor. **Leisure Activities:** sauna, whirlpool, exercise room. **Guest Services:** coin laundry, wireless Internet. **Business Services:** meeting rooms, PC. **Cards:** AX, DC, DS, MC, VI.

AAA Benefit:
Members save up to 20%, plus 10% bonus points with rewards program.

(See color ad p 368, p 586, p 499, p 368, p 752, p 473, p 542, below, p 344, p 751, p 566 & p 500)

CLEMENTINE'S BED & BREAKFAST Phone: 503/325-2005

Historic Bed
& Breakfast
$95-$165 All Year

Address: 847 Exchange St **Location:** At 8th and Exchange sts; in historic downtown. Located in a quiet residential area. **Facility:** This 1888 Italianate-style Victorian B&B, with feathered bedding in all guest rooms, is located on a hillside within walking distance of the waterfront. Smoke free premises. 8 units. 5 one-bedroom standard units. 3 cottages. 2 stories (no elevator), interior corridors. *Bath:* combo or shower only. **Parking:** street. **Terms:** office hours 9 am-8 pm, check-in 4 pm, 2-3 night minimum stay - seasonal and/or weekends, age restrictions may apply, 7 day cancellation notice. **Amenities:** high-speed Internet, hair dryers. *Some:* DVD players, irons. **Guest Services:** wireless Internet. **Business Services:** PC. **Cards:** DS, MC, VI.

COMFORT SUITES COLUMBIA RIVER *Book great rates at AAA.com* Phone: (503)325-2000

(AAA) **[SAVE]**

Hotel
$99-$299 All Year

Address: 3420 Leif Erickson Dr **Location:** 2.5 mi e of Astoria Bridge on US 30. **Facility:** Smoke free premises. 75 units. 74 one-bedroom standard units, some with whirlpools. 1 one-bedroom suite with kitchen. 3 stories, interior corridors. *Bath:* combo or shower only. **Parking:** on-site. **Amenities:** high-speed Internet, voice mail, irons, hair dryers. **Pool(s):** heated indoor. **Leisure Activities:** sauna, whirlpool, exercise room. **Guest Services:** valet and coin laundry, wireless Internet. **Business Services:** meeting rooms, PC. **Cards:** AX, DC, DS, MC, VI. **Free Special Amenities:** expanded continental breakfast and high-speed Internet.

CREST MOTEL, P.C. Phone: 503/325-3141

(AAA) **[SAVE]**

Motel
$62-$137 All Year

Address: 5366 Leif Erickson Dr **Location:** 4 mi e of Astoria Bridge on US 30. Located in a quiet area with a panoramic view. **Facility:** 40 units. 38 one- and 2 two-bedroom standard units. 1-2 stories (no elevator), exterior corridors. *Bath:* combo or shower only. **Parking:** on-site. **Terms:** office hours 7:30 am-11 pm. **Amenities:** high-speed Internet. **Leisure Activities:** whirlpool. **Guest Services:** coin laundry, wireless Internet. **Cards:** AX, DC, DS, MC, VI.

RED LION INN ASTORIA

Book great rates at AAA.com

Phone: (503)325-7373

Motel
$99-$239 All Year

Address: 400 Industry St **Location:** Just w of Astoria Bridge on US 30, just n on Basin St (caution: do not turn onto Astoria-Megler Bridge). Located at the marina. **Facility:** 122 one-bedroom standard units. 2 stories, exterior corridors. *Bath:* combo or shower only. **Parking:** on-site. **Terms:** cancellation fee imposed. **Amenities:** high-speed Internet, voice mail, irons, hair dryers. **Leisure Activities:** exercise room. **Guest Services:** valet laundry, wireless Internet. **Cards:** AX, DC, DS, MC, VI. **Free Special Amenities:** expanded continental breakfast and high-speed Internet. *(See color ad below)*

▼ *See AAA listing above* ▼

RED LION INN
ASTORIA
Stay Comfortable

- Plush, pillowtop beds
- All rooms view Columbia River & Marina
- Microwave & refrigerator
- Close to Lewis & Clark sites & Oregon beaches
- Free wireless Internet access
- Historical trolley to downtown

AAA Member Rate
10% off
Published rates*
*Rates subject to availability. Sgl/Dbl

RED LION
R&R CLUB

400 Industry Street
Astoria, OR 97103 • (503) 325-7373

redlion.com • 800-Red Lion

Travel the world...
Save with AAA

Your AAA membership card also saves you money when you travel outside the U.S.A. and Canada. Visit AAA.com to locate Show Your Card & Save® partners around the world.

A sampling of partners throughout the world:

Entertainment and Dining
Gray Line
Hard Rock Cafe®
Paris Pass - a City Card (Europe)
Six Flags (Mexico)
The Dungeons (Europe)

Travel
Carey Limousine
Hertz®
P & O Ferries (Europe)

Lodging
Best Western International
Campanile, Kyriad & Kyriad Prestige Hotels (Europe)
Prince Hotels (Japan)
Starwood Hotels & Resorts and First Hotels

Your AAA membership card also saves you money when you travel outside the U.S.A. and Canada. Visit AAA.com to locate Show Your Card & Save® partners around the world.

Show Your Card & Save   Show your Card!

──── The following lodging was either not evaluated or did not ────
meet AAA rating requirements but is listed for your information only.

THE HOTEL ELLIOTT   **Phone:** 503/325-2222
[fyi]   Not evaluated. **Address:** 357 12th St **Location:** Between Commercial and Duane sts; downtown.
               Located in a national historic district. Facilities, services, and decor characterize an upscale property.

──── **WHERE TO DINE** ────

BAKED ALASKA   **Phone:** 503/325-7414
▼▼ ▼▼   Fresh Northwest seafood is featured at this establishment, which juts out over the Columbia River. Guests
               can request outdoor seating on the deck in season. Casual dress. **Bar:** Full bar. **Reservations:** accepted.
Regional Seafood **Hours:** 11 am-9 pm, Fri & Sat-10 pm. Closed: 12/25. **Address:** 1 12th St, Suite 1 **Location:** On waterfront;
$8-$25   downtown. **Parking:** on-site. **Cards:** AX, DC, DS, JC, MC, VI.
               [AK]

DRINA DAISY   **Phone:** 503/338-2912
▼▼ ▼▼   The hospitable restaurant focuses its menu on authentic and delicious Bosnian dishes. Casual dress. **Bar:**
               Full bar. **Reservations:** accepted. **Hours:** 11 am-10 pm. Closed: Mon & Tues. **Address:** 915 Commercial
Eastern European St **Location:** Downtown. **Parking:** street. **Cards:** AX, MC, VI.
$9-$15

FULIO'S PASTARIA & TUSCAN STEAK HOUSE   **Phone:** 503/325-9001
▼▼ ▼▼   Flavorful pasta dishes are the specialty, but delicious panini sandwiches are another option at this
               restaurant boasting a warm, relaxing atmosphere. The signature seared Caesar salad is a distinctive treat.
Italian   Choice corn-fed steaks, lamb and veal round out the menu. Casual dress. **Bar:** Full bar.
$7-$30   **Reservations:** suggested. **Hours:** 11 am-9 pm, Fri & Sat-10 pm. Closed: 11/26, 12/25; also for lunch Sun
               10/31-5/1 & Super Bowl Sun. **Address:** 1149 Commercial St **Location:** Downtown. **Parking:** street.
               Cards: AX, DS, MC, VI.

GUNDERSON'S CANNERY CAFE   **Phone:** 503/325-8642
(AAA)   At the end of a wharf facing the Columbia River's confluence with the Pacific Ocean, the laid-back
               restaurant is in an 1879 building that functioned as a salmon cannery until 1980. On a menu of mostly
▼▼ ▼▼   seafood entrees are signature dishes of Dungeness crab and shrimp cakes, sauteed lime prawns and
Regional   seafood brochette salad. Outdoor seating is available on the deck. Casual dress. **Bar:** Full bar.
Seafood   **Reservations:** accepted. **Hours:** 8 am-9 pm, Mon from 11 am. Closed major holidays. **Address:** 1 6th St
$7-$30   **Location:** On waterfront; downtown. **Parking:** on-site. **Cards:** AX, DS, MC, VI.

LINDSTROM'S DANISH MAID BAKERY   **Phone:** 503/325-3657
▼▼   A variety of Scandinavian baked goods reflective of this area are featured, as well as deli-style light lunch
               items. Casual dress. **Reservations:** not accepted. **Hours:** 4 am-5:30 pm. Closed major holidays; also Sun
Breads/Pastries **Address:** 1132 Commercial St **Location:** Downtown. **Parking:** street. **Cards:** MC, VI.
$2-$5

ROGUE ALES PUBLIC HOUSE - ASTORIA   **Phone:** 503/325-5964
▼▼ ▼▼   On Pier 39, this is a great casual place to get close to the Columbia River. After 5 pm, patrons can park in
               the warehouse that used to be a cannery. Part of the Rogue Ales chain, this place complements its
American   extensive pub menu with an abundance of made-in-house draft beers, as well as root beer and other bar
$7-$22   favorites. Casual dress. **Bar:** Full bar. **Reservations:** not accepted. **Hours:** 11 am-11 pm. **Address:** 100
               39th St, Pier 39 **Location:** 3 mi e of Astoria Bridge on US 30. **Parking:** on-site. **Cards:** AX, DS, MC, VI.
               [AK]

THE SHIP INN RESTAURANT & LOUNGE   **Phone:** 503/325-0033
▼▼ ▼▼   The popular fish and chip house, which looks out onto the river, prepares such English specialties as steak
               and kidney pie and Cornish pasty, in addition to seafood entrees available in half-, full- and dinner-size
Seafood   portions. Casual dress. **Bar:** Full bar. **Reservations:** accepted. **Hours:** 11:30 am-9 pm; to 9:30 pm in
$8-$23   summer. Closed major holidays. **Address:** 1 2nd St **Location:** 0.5 mi w, just n of US 30. **Parking:** on-site.
               Cards: AX, DS, MC, VI.

SILVER SALMON GRILLE   *Menu on AAA.com*   **Phone:** 503/338-6640
(AAA)   Beautiful fish murals and metal sculptures crafted by local artists adorn this restaurant, housed in a 1924
               building. As its name implies, salmon—prepared in several ways, including house-smoked—is at the heart
▼▼▼▼   of the menu. Guests also can try hand-cut USDA choice steaks, pasta and other Northwest seafood dishes.
               Low-carb dinners, lighter fare items and flambeed desserts are available as well as an extensive list of
Steak & Seafood house and regional wines. Stop in for daily wine tasting from 11 am-5 pm at the adjacent Silver Salmon
$10-$35   Cellars. Casual dress. **Bar:** Full bar. **Reservations:** suggested. **Hours:** 11 am-10 pm. Closed: 7/4, 11/26,
               12/25. **Address:** 1105 Commercial St **Location:** Downtown. **Parking:** street. **Cards:** AX, DC, DS, MC, VI.

T. PAUL'S URBAN CAFE   **Phone:** 503/338-5133
▼▼ ▼▼   Chic, contemporary decor complements the menu, which lists distinctive, tasty quesadillas, such as
               Caribbean jerk chicken with black bean or curry apple and chicken breast with honey-mustard sauce as well
Regional American as pasta dishes, gourmet salads, chowder and "unclassic" sandwiches. Service is efficient. Casual dress.
$7-$20   **Bar:** Beer & wine. **Hours:** 9 am-9 pm, Fri & Sat-10 pm, Sun 11 am-4 pm. Closed major holidays; also Sun
               in fall & winter. **Address:** 1119 Commercial St **Location:** Downtown. **Parking:** street. **Cards:** MC, VI.
               [AK]

───── *The following restaurant has not been evaluated by AAA* ─────
but is listed for your information only.

BRIDGEWATER BISTRO   Phone: 503/325-6777
[fyi]   Not evaluated. Down on the pier, this newer restaurant specializes in seafood and American dishes.
Address: 20 Basin St **Location:** Just s of Astoria Bridge on US 30, then just n.

BAKER CITY pop. 9,860

───── **WHERE TO STAY** ─────

ALWAYS WELCOME INN   Phone: (541)523-3431
▼▼▼ ▼▼▼   **Address:** 175 Campbell St **Location:** I-84, exit 304, just e. **Facility:** Smoke free premises. 40 one-
Motel   bedroom standard units. 2 stories (no elevator), exterior corridors. *Bath:* combo or shower only.
           Parking: on-site. **Terms:** office hours 6:30 am-midnight. **Amenities:** high-speed Internet. *Some:* irons,
$68-$76 5/1-2/28   hair dryers. **Guest Services:** wireless Internet. **Business Services:** meeting rooms. **Cards:** AX, DS,
$65-$72 3/1-4/30   MC, VI.
(ASK) [X] [□] / SOME UNITS FEE [VCR] [□] [□]

BEST WESTERN SUNRIDGE INN   *Book great rates at AAA.com*   Phone: (541)523-6444
(AAA) [SAVE]   **Address:** 1 Sunridge Ln **Location:** I-84, exit
▼▼▼ ◆◆ ▼▼▼   304, just w. **Facility:** Smoke free premises. 154
Hotel   units. 152 one-bedroom standard units. 2 one-
$85-$95 All Year   bedroom suites with whirlpools. 2 stories (no
               elevator), interior corridors. **Parking:** on-site.
               Amenities: video games (fee), high-speed   **AAA Benefit:**
               Internet, voice mail, irons, hair dryers.   Members save up to
               Pool(s): heated outdoor. **Leisure Activities:**   20%, plus 10%
               whirlpool. **Guest Services:** valet and coin   bonus points with
               laundry, area transportation, wireless Internet.   rewards program.
               Business Services: meeting rooms, PC.
               Cards: AX, CB, DC, DS, JC, MC, VI.
               (See color ad below)
[♥] [Y] [🐕] [X] [🎬] [□] / SOME UNITS FEE [🐾] FEE [□] FEE [□]

GEISER GRAND HOTEL   *Book at AAA.com*   Phone: (541)523-1889
▼▼▼ ◆ ▼▼▼   **Address:** 1996 Main St **Location:** I-84, exit 304, 0.9 mi w on Campbell St, then 0.3 mi s; downtown.
Historic   **Facility:** A restored 1889 historic hotel with many interesting features and spacious guest rooms.
Hotel   Smoke free premises. 30 one-bedroom standard units, some with whirlpools. 3 stories, interior
$89-$229 All Year   corridors. *Bath:* combo or shower only. **Parking:** on-site. **Terms:** 3 day cancellation notice.
             Amenities: video library, DVD players, CD players, high-speed Internet, voice mail, irons, hair dryers.
             Dining: Palm Court at the Geiser Grand, see separate listing. **Guest Services:** valet laundry, wireless
             Internet. **Business Services:** meeting rooms. **Cards:** AX, DS, MC, VI.
(ASK) [Y] [🔧] [X] [VCR] [🎬] / SOME UNITS FEE [🐾]

SUPER 8 BAKER CITY   *Book great rates at AAA.com*   Phone: (541)523-8282
(AAA) [SAVE]   **Address:** 250 Campbell St **Location:** I-84, exit 304, just e. **Facility:** 72 units. 71 one- and 1 two-
▼▼▼ ◆ ▼▼▼   bedroom standard units, some with whirlpools. 2 stories (no elevator), interior corridors. *Bath:* combo
Hotel   or shower only. **Parking:** on-site. **Terms:** cancellation fee imposed. **Amenities:** high-speed Internet,
$65-$80 All Year   hair dryers. **Pool(s):** heated indoor. **Leisure Activities:** whirlpool. **Guest Services:** coin laundry,
             wireless Internet. **Business Services:** PC. **Cards:** AX, DC, DS, MC, VI. **Free Special Amenities:**
             continental breakfast and high-speed Internet.
CALL [&M] [🐕] [🎬] [□] [□] [□] / SOME UNITS FEE [🐾] [X]

▼ *See AAA listing above* ▼

─── WHERE TO DINE ───

BARLEY BROWN'S BREW PUB

▽▽ ▽▽

American

$9-$15

Phone: 541/523-4266

Situated right downtown with sidewalk seating during the warm summer nights, the restaurant offers flat-iron steak from beef supplied by local ranchers as well as fresh ground burgers. Hand-crafted beers are made on site. Casual dress. **Bar:** Beer & wine. **Reservations:** accepted. **Hours:** 4 pm-10 pm. Closed major holidays. **Address:** 2190 Main St **Location:** I-84, exit 304, 0.9 mi w on Campbell St, then just s; downtown. **Parking:** street. **Cards:** MC, VI.

PALM COURT AT THE GEISER GRAND

▽▽ ▽▽

American

$4-$30

Phone: 541/523-1889

Located downtown in a restored historic hotel, the restaurant has diners sit under a large ceiling of stained glass while eating home cooked American food like clam chowder, chicken and steak. **Bar:** Full bar. **Reservations:** accepted. **Hours:** 7 am-9 pm. **Address:** 1996 Main St **Location:** I-84, exit 304, 0.9 mi w on Campbell St, then 0.3 mi s; downtown; in Geiser Grand Hotel. **Parking:** on-site. **Cards:** AX, DS, MC, VI.

SUMPTER JUNCTION

▽▽ ▽▽

American

$6-$18

Phone: 541/523-9437

A comfortable gathering spot for both locals and travelers, the restaurant is convenient to the interstate and offers friendly service and good food. The train memorabilia provides a thrill, as does the working model train that constantly circles the dining area. Casual dress. **Bar:** Beer & wine. **Reservations:** not accepted. **Hours:** 9 am-10 pm; from 6 am in summer. Closed: 11/26, 12/25. **Address:** 2 Sunridge Ln **Location:** I-84, exit 304, just w. **Parking:** on-site. **Cards:** AX, DS, MC, VI.

BANDON pop. 2,833

─── WHERE TO STAY ───

BANDON BEACH VACATION RENTALS

ⒶⒶⒶ ⑤ᴬⱽᴱ

▽▽ ▽▽

Vacation Rental House

Rates not provided

Phone: 541/347-4801

Location: 1 mi s on US 101, 0.8 mi w on Seabird Rd, then 1 mi s; registration in house behind property. **Facility:** Featuring spacious grass play areas for children, the rental property is conveniently located near several local activities. Smoke free premises. 4 houses. 1 story, exterior corridors. **Parking:** on-site. **Terms:** office hours 8 am-10 pm, check-in 4 pm. **Amenities:** video library, DVD players, high-speed Internet, irons, hair dryers. **Leisure Activities:** badminton, croquet, gas grills, picnic tables, horseshoes. **Guest Services:** complimentary laundry, wireless Internet. **Free Special Amenities: local telephone calls and high-speed Internet.**

BANDON DUNES GOLF RESORT

▽▽▽

Resort

Hotel

$200-$600 All Year

Phone: 541/347-4380

Address: 57744 Round Lake Dr **Location:** 3 mi n on US 101, just w to gate house. **Facility:** This site was chosen specifically for the terrain and weather of the southern Oregon coast, the closest thing you'll find to the golf sites in Ireland or Scotland with views of the Pacific Ocean; if you are a golf enthusiast, you can't go wrong. The clean lines and understated refinement of the rooms lend themselves to a good night's sleep so you can start all over again tomorrow. 186 units. 146 one-bedroom standard units. 21 two- and 19 three-bedroom suites. 2 stories, interior/exterior corridors. *Bath:* combo or shower only. **Parking:** on-site. **Terms:** check-in 4 pm, 21 day cancellation notice-fee imposed. **Amenities:** CD players, voice mail, irons, hair dryers. *Some: Fee:* DVD players. **Leisure Activities:** sauna, whirlpool, beach access, hiking trails, exercise room. *Fee:* golf-54 holes, massage. **Guest Services:** wireless Internet. **Business Services:** meeting rooms, business center. **Cards:** AX, DS, MC, VI.

─── ▼ *See AAA listing p 304* ▼ ───

BANDON INN

Motel
$74-$139 All Year

Phone: (541)347-4417

Address: 355 Hwy 101 **Location:** Center. **Facility:** 57 one-bedroom standard units, some with whirlpools. 3 stories (no elevator), exterior corridors. **Parking:** on-site. **Terms:** check-in 4 pm, cancellation fee imposed. **Amenities:** voice mail, irons, hair dryers. *Some:* high-speed Internet. **Guest Services:** wireless Internet. **Business Services:** fax (fee). **Cards:** AX, DC, DS, MC, VI. **Free Special Amenities:** continental breakfast and high-speed Internet. *(See color ad p 303)*

BEST WESTERN INN AT FACE ROCK

Book great rates at AAA.com

Hotel
$110-$301 All Year

Phone: (541)347-9441

Address: 3225 Beach Loop Dr **Location:** 1 mi s on US 101, 0.8 mi w on Seabird Rd, then just s. **Facility:** Smoke free premises. 74 units. 54 one-bedroom standard units. 20 one-bedroom suites, some with kitchens and/or whirlpools. 2 stories (no elevator), exterior corridors. *Bath:* combo or shower only. **Parking:** on-site. **Terms:** check-in 4 pm. **Amenities:** high-speed Internet, irons, hair dryers. **Dining:** Bandon Bill's Seafood Grill, see separate listing. **Pool(s):** heated indoor. **Leisure Activities:** sauna, whirlpool, beach access, exercise room. **Guest Services:** coin laundry, wireless Internet. **Business Services:** meeting rooms, PC, fax (fee). **Cards:** AX, CB, DC, DS, JC, MC, VI. **Free Special Amenities:** expanded continental breakfast and early check-in/late check-out.

DRIFTWOOD MOTEL

Motel
$65-$120 All Year

Phone: 541/347-9022

Address: 460 Hwy 101 **Location:** On US 101; center. Located across from Old Town. **Facility:** 22 units. 20 one-bedroom standard units. 2 one-bedroom suites with kitchens. 2 stories (no elevator), exterior corridors. **Parking:** on-site. **Terms:** cancellation fee imposed. **Amenities:** high-speed Internet, voice mail, hair dryers. **Guest Services:** wireless Internet. **Business Services:** fax. **Cards:** DS, MC, VI. **Free Special Amenities:** continental breakfast and high-speed Internet.

──── WHERE TO DINE ────

BANDON BAKING CO AND DELI

American
$3-$7

Phone: 541/347-9440

Patrons can savor homemade soups and granola, varied sandwiches and more than 70 quality bakery items, such as cookies, bars, pastries, croissants, bagels, muffins and hand-crafted breads, including cranberry bread. Coffee and espresso are fitting complements. Casual dress. **Hours:** 8 am-5 pm; to 4 pm in winter. Closed major holidays; also Sun & Mon. **Address:** 160 2nd St **Location:** US 101, exit Old Town Archway, just w. **Parking:** street.

BANDON BILL'S SEAFOOD GRILL

Seafood
$8-$30

Phone: 541/347-8151

A tiered restaurant with great views of the distant ocean and crashing waves, this place is great for a sunset dinner. The patio invites summer cocktails or catching a breeze. Menu has a nice seafood selection along with a variety of steaks, pasta, burgers and sandwiches. Casual dress. **Bar:** Full bar. **Reservations:** accepted. **Hours:** 7 am-10 pm. Closed: 11/26, 12/25. **Address:** 3225 Beach Loop Rd **Location:** 1 mi s on US 101, 0.8 mi w on Seabird Rd, then just s; in Best Western Inn at Face Rock. **Parking:** on-site. **Cards:** AX, CB, DC, DS, JC, MC, VI.

BANDON BOATWORKS RESTAURANT & JETTY CLUB LOUNGE

Menu on AAA.com

Seafood
$7-$35

Phone: 541/347-2111

The casual, rustic restaurant offers beautiful views of the jetty from every table. Although the menu includes several selections of chicken and beef, including a tasty filet mignon topped with crab, it centers on fresh seafood dishes, such as locally caught snapper and pan-fried oysters flambeed in brandy and anisette. Homemade cranberry bread is delicious. A salad bar is available. Casual dress. **Bar:** Full bar. **Reservations:** suggested. **Hours:** 11:30 am-9 pm, Sun 11 am-8:30 pm; Sunday brunch; hours extended in summer. **Address:** 275 Lincoln Ave SW **Location:** US 101, exit Old Town Archway, just n, 0.5 mi w on 1st St, 0.4 mi w on Jetty Rd, then just n. **Parking:** on-site. **Cards:** AX, DS, MC, VI.

LORD BENNETT'S RESTAURANT & LOUNGE

Menu on AAA.com

Steak & Seafood
$7-$28

Phone: 541/347-3663

Perfectly placed, this eatery looks out on the Pacific Ocean and legendary Face Rock, the rock that became so after evil spirits took the daughter of Indian Chief Siskiyou into the ocean. Lord Bennett's prides itself on using regional ingredients whenever possible in their selections of seafood and steak. Casual dress. **Bar:** Full bar. **Reservations:** suggested. **Hours:** Open 3/1-12/31 & 2/1-2/28; 11 am-2:30 & 5-9 pm, Sat & Sun from 10 am; Saturday & Sunday brunch. **Address:** 1695 Beach Loop Rd **Location:** US 101, 0.7 mi w on 11th St, 0.4 mi s. **Parking:** on-site. **Cards:** AX, DS, MC, VI.

THE WHEELHOUSE RESTAURANT　　　　　　　　　　　　　　　　　Phone: 541/347-9331

AAA
◆◆ ◆◆
Seafood
$6-$24

A nautical theme is carried out through the dining room of this restaurant near the boat basin. The emphasis is on fresh seafood, such as rock shrimp Dijon and halibut saute with hazelnuts and cranberries. Pasta, steak and chicken dishes also are served. Dressy casual. **Bar:** Full bar. **Reservations:** accepted. **Hours:** 11:30 am-9 pm; to 10 pm in summer. **Address:** 125 Chicago St **Location:** US 101, exit Old Town Archway, just w. **Parking:** street. **Cards:** AX, MC, VI.

------- *The following restaurant has not been evaluated by AAA* -------
but is listed for your information only.

ALLORO WINE BAR & RESTAURANT　　　　　　　　　　　　　　　Phone: 541/347-1850

[fyi]

Not evaluated. Diners savor freshly prepared and casually upscale Italian cuisine that incorporates Northwest ingredients wherever possible. **Address:** 375 2nd St SE **Location:** US 101, exit Old Town Archway, just w.

BEAVERTON —See Portland p. 453.

BEND pop. 52,029

------- WHERE TO STAY -------

AMERITEL INN　　*Book at AAA.com*　　　　　　　　　　　　　　Phone: (541)617-6111

◆◆◆
Hotel
$120-$170 All Year

Address: 425 SW Bluff Dr **Location:** US 97, exit 139 (Reed Market Rd), 0.3 mi w on SW Reed Market Rd, 0.3 mi n on SW Bond St, then just nw; follow signs to Old Mill District; near 3 Stacks Building. **Facility:** 96 units. 79 one-bedroom standard units, some with whirlpools. 14 one- and 3 two-bedroom suites, some with kitchens and/or whirlpools. 3 stories, interior corridors. *Bath:* combo or shower only. **Parking:** on-site. **Terms:** cancellation fee imposed. **Amenities:** video games (fee), high-speed Internet, voice mail, irons, hair dryers. **Pool(s):** heated indoor. **Leisure Activities:** whirlpool, exercise room. **Guest Services:** valet and coin laundry, wireless Internet. **Business Services:** meeting rooms, business center. **Cards:** AX, DC, DS, MC, VI.

(ASK) [icons] / SOME UNITS [X]

BEND INN & SUITES　　　　　　　　　　　　　　　　　　　　　Phone: (541)388-4114

AAA [SAVE]
◆◆◆
Hotel
$89-$149 5/16-2/28
$79-$129 3/1-5/15

Address: 15 NE Butler Market Rd **Location:** US 97, exit 136 (Butler Market Rd), just n. **Facility:** 99 one-bedroom standard units. 2 stories (no elevator), exterior corridors. **Parking:** on-site. **Terms:** check-in 4 pm. **Amenities:** high-speed Internet, voice mail, irons, hair dryers. **Pool(s):** heated outdoor. **Leisure Activities:** whirlpool. **Guest Services:** valet laundry, wireless Internet. **Business Services:** meeting rooms, PC. **Cards:** AX, DC, DS, MC, VI. **Free Special Amenities:** full breakfast and high-speed Internet.

[icons] / SOME UNITS FEE [icons] [X]

BEND RIVERSIDE MOTEL SUITES　　*Book at AAA.com*　　　　　Phone: (541)389-2363

◆◆◆
Motel
$68-$159 All Year

Address: 1565 NW Wall St **Location:** US 97, exit 137 (Revere Ave), just s. **Facility:** 84 one-bedroom standard units, some with kitchens. 1-3 stories (no elevator), exterior corridors. *Bath:* combo or shower only. **Parking:** on-site. **Amenities:** voice mail. **Pool(s):** heated indoor. **Leisure Activities:** sauna, whirlpool. **Guest Services:** coin laundry, wireless Internet. **Business Services:** meeting rooms, PC. **Cards:** AX, DS, MC, VI.

(ASK) [icons] / SOME UNITS FEE [icons]

▼ See AAA listing p 310 ▼

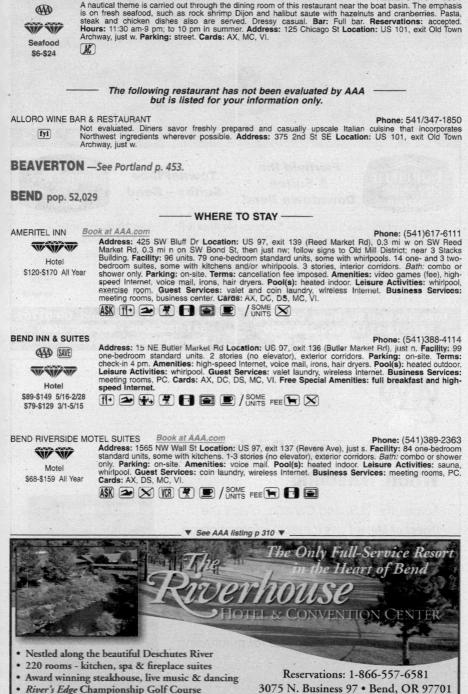

Know the Local Driving Laws When Traveling

Across the U.S. and Canada, check the *Digest of Motor Laws* for local information on automated enforcement laws, occupant protection, alcohol laws, and traffic safety. Topics also include driver licensing laws and motor vehicle fees and taxes.

Contact your local AAA club for purchasing information.

Retail price: $13.95

BEST WESTERN INN & SUITES OF BEND   *Book great rates at AAA.com*   Phone: (541)382-1515

(AAA) [SAVE]
▼▼▼ ▼▼▼
Hotel
$72-$159 All Year

Address: 721 NE 3rd St **Location:** Jct US 20 and Business Rt US 97 (NE 3rd St), just s. **Facility:** 100 units. 99 one-bedroom standard units. 1 two-bedroom suite. 2 stories (no elevator), exterior corridors. **Parking:** on-site. **Amenities:** high-speed Internet, irons, hair dryers. **Pool(s):** heated outdoor. **Leisure Activities:** whirlpool, exercise room. **Guest Services:** wireless Internet. **Business Services:** meeting rooms, PC. **Cards:** AX, DC, DS, MC, VI. **Free Special Amenities: continental breakfast and high-speed Internet.**

🏊 📷 🛏 🖥 💻 / SOME UNITS FEE 🐕 ✕

COMFORT INN & SUITES BEND   *Book at AAA.com*   Phone: 541/617-9696

▼▼▼ ▼▼▼
Hotel
Rates not provided

Address: 62065 SE 27th St **Location:** Jct US 20/97, 2 mi e on US 20, then just s. **Facility:** Smoke free premises. 64 one-bedroom standard units, some with efficiencies. 2 stories, interior corridors. *Bath:* combo or shower only. **Parking:** on-site. **Amenities:** high-speed Internet, dual phone lines, voice mail, irons, hair dryers. *Some:* DVD players. **Pool(s):** heated outdoor. **Leisure Activities:** whirlpool. **Guest Services:** valet and coin laundry, wireless Internet. **Business Services:** meeting rooms, PC.

🛗 🏊 🛎 ✕ 🖥 💻 / SOME UNITS 🛏 🖥

CRICKETWOOD COUNTRY BED & BREAKFAST   Phone: 541/330-0747

▼▼▼ ▼▼▼
Bed & Breakfast
Rates not provided

Address: 63520 Cricketwood Rd **Location:** US 97, exit 136 (NE Butler Market Rd), 3.2 mi ne on Butler Market Rd (becomes Hamehook Rd), 0.8 mi n on Hamehook Rd, just e on Repine Dr, then just n. **Facility:** Located on 10 acres in a beautiful park-like setting just five miles from historic downtown Bend. Each room is decorated in a unique garden theme. Designated smoking area. 4 units. 3 one-bedroom standard units, some with whirlpools. 1 cottage. 1-2 stories (no elevator), interior/exterior corridors. **Parking:** on-site, winter plug-ins. **Terms:** office hours 8 am-9 pm, check-in 3:30 pm, age restrictions may apply. **Amenities:** video library, DVD players, CD players, irons, hair dryers. **Leisure Activities:** whirlpool. **Guest Services:** wireless Internet. **Business Services:** PC.

✕ [VCR] 📷 💻 / SOME UNITS FEE 🐕 🅩 🛏 🖥

DAYS INN   *Book great rates at AAA.com*   Phone: 541/383-3776

(AAA) [SAVE]
▼▼▼ ▼▼▼
Hotel
Rates not provided

Address: 849 NE 3rd St **Location:** Jct US 20 and Business Rt US 97 (NE 3rd St), just s. **Facility:** 75 one-bedroom standard units. 2 stories (no elevator), exterior corridors. *Bath:* combo or shower only. **Parking:** on-site. **Amenities:** video library (fee), high-speed Internet, voice mail, irons, hair dryers. **Pool(s):** heated outdoor. **Leisure Activities:** whirlpool, picnic area, exercise room. **Guest Services:** coin laundry, wireless Internet. **Business Services:** PC. **Free Special Amenities: full breakfast and high-speed Internet.**

🏊 ✕ 📷 🛏 🖥 💻 / SOME UNITS FEE 🐕 ✕

DUNES MOTEL   Phone: (541)382-6811

(AAA) [SAVE]
▼▼▼
Motel
$49-$125 3/1-9/15
$39-$69 9/16-2/28

Address: 1515 NE 3rd St **Location:** Jct US 20 and Business Rt US 97 (NE 3rd St), just n. **Facility:** 30 one-bedroom standard units. 2 stories (no elevator), exterior corridors. **Parking:** on-site. **Terms:** office hours 7 am-11 pm. **Amenities:** high-speed Internet, hair dryers. **Guest Services:** coin laundry, wireless Internet. **Business Services:** PC. **Cards:** AX, DS, MC, VI.

🛗 📷 🛏 🖥 💻 / SOME UNITS 🐕 ✕

FAIRFIELD INN & SUITES BY MARRIOTT   *Book great rates at AAA.com*   Phone: (541)318-1747

(AAA) [SAVE]
▼▼▼ ▼▼▼
Hotel
$99-$139 All Year

Address: 1626 NW Wall St **Location:** US 97, exit 137 (Revere Ave), just s; downtown. **Facility:** Smoke free premises. 80 one-bedroom standard units, some with whirlpools. 2 stories, interior corridors. *Bath:* combo or shower only. **Parking:** on-site. **Terms:** cancellation fee imposed. **Amenities:** high-speed Internet, dual phone lines, voice mail, irons, hair dryers. *Some:* CD players. **Pool(s):** heated indoor. **Leisure Activities:** whirlpool, exercise room. **Guest Services:** valet and coin laundry, wireless Internet. **Business Services:** meeting rooms, PC. **Cards:** AX, CB, DC, DS, JC, MC, VI. *(See color ad p 306)*

CALL 🅜 🏊 ✕ 📷 💻 / SOME UNITS FEE 🐕 🛏 🖥

HOLIDAY INN EXPRESS HOTEL & SUITES   *Book great rates at AAA.com*   Phone: (541)317-8500

(AAA) [SAVE]
▼▼▼ ▼▼▼
Hotel
$99-$189 All Year

Address: 20615 Grandview Dr **Location:** On US 97; north end of town. **Facility:** 99 units. 85 one-bedroom standard units. 14 one-bedroom suites, some with whirlpools. 3 stories, interior corridors. *Bath:* combo or shower only. **Parking:** on-site. **Terms:** cancellation fee imposed. **Amenities:** voice mail, irons, hair dryers. *Some:* DVD players. **Pool(s):** heated indoor. **Leisure Activities:** whirlpool, sun deck, exercise room. **Guest Services:** valet and coin laundry, wireless Internet. **Business Services:** meeting rooms, business center. **Cards:** AX, CB, DC, DS, JC, MC, VI. **Free Special Amenities: expanded continental breakfast and high-speed Internet.**

CALL 🅜 🏊 ✕ 📷 🛏 🖥 💻 / SOME UNITS FEE 🐕 ✕

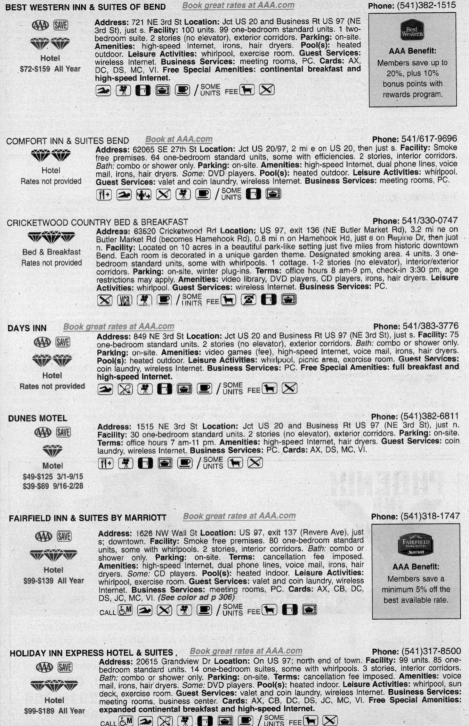

LA QUINTA INN BEND
▼▼▼
Hotel
$59-$129 All Year

Book great rates at AAA.com

Phone: (541)388-2227

Address: 61200 SE 3rd St (Business Rt US 97) **Location:** From south end jct US 97 and Business Rt US 97, just n. **Facility:** Smoke free premises. 65 one-bedroom standard units, some with whirlpools. 3 stories (no elevator), interior corridors. **Parking:** on-site. **Amenities:** high-speed Internet, voice mail, irons, hair dryers. **Pool(s):** heated indoor. **Leisure Activities:** whirlpool, limited exercise equipment. **Guest Services:** coin laundry, wireless Internet. **Business Services:** PC. **Cards:** AX, DS, MC, VI.

(ASK) ⊠ ✕ ⊡ ⊡ / SOME UNITS ⊡ ⊟ ⊟

MOUNT BACHELOR VILLAGE RESORT
▼▼▼▼
Resort Condominium
$139-$495 All Year

Book at AAA.com

Phone: (541)389-5900

Address: 19717 Mt Bachelor Dr **Location:** US 97, exit 139 (Reed Market Rd), 1.6 mi sw on Reed Market Rd, then just s. Located in a quiet area. **Facility:** On extensive grounds, this property is 18 miles from downhill skiing at Mount Bachelor; some units have river views, fireplaces and balconies. 177 units. 45 one-bedroom standard units. 62 one-, 35 two- and 25 three-bedroom suites with kitchens, some with whirlpools. 10 houses. 2 stories (no elevator), exterior corridors. **Parking:** on-site. **Terms:** office hours 7 am-11 pm, check-in 5 pm, 2 night minimum stay - seasonal and/or weekends, 14 day cancellation notice-fee imposed. **Amenities:** video library (fee), voice mail, irons, hair dryers. *Some:* DVD players. **Pool(s):** heated outdoor. **Leisure Activities:** whirlpools, fishing, 6 tennis courts, cross country skiing, bicycles, hiking trails, playground. **Guest Services:** coin laundry, wireless Internet. **Business Services:** conference facilities, business center. **Cards:** AX, DC, DS, MC, VI.

⊟ ⊠ ⊠ ⊞ ✕ ✕ (VCR) ⊟ ⊡ / SOME UNITS ⊠ ⊟

THE OXFORD HOTEL
(fyi)
Hotel

Phone: 541/749-1100

Under construction, scheduled to open June 2009. **Address:** 10 Minnesota Ave **Location:** 0.5 mi w of Business Rt US 97, exit Franklin Ave, just n on NW Bond St; downtown. **Amenities:** 59 units.

PHOENIX INN SUITES-BEND
(AAA) (SAVE)
▼▼▼
Hotel
$99-$209 All Year

Book great rates at AAA.com

Phone: (541)317-9292

Address: 300 NW Franklin Ave **Location:** US 97, exit 138 (Downtown/Mt Bachelor Dr), 0.4 mi w on NW Colorado Ave, 0.4 mi n on NW Bond St, then just e; downtown. **Facility:** Smoke free premises. 117 units. 103 one- and 5 two-bedroom standard units, some with whirlpools. 9 one-bedroom suites with whirlpools. 3 stories, interior corridors. *Bath:* combo or shower only. **Parking:** on-site. **Terms:** check-in 4 pm, cancellation fee imposed. **Amenities:** high-speed Internet, dual phone lines, voice mail, irons, hair dryers. *Some:* DVD players. **Pool(s):** heated indoor. **Leisure Activities:** whirlpool, exercise room. **Guest Services:** valet and coin laundry, wireless Internet. **Business Services:** meeting rooms, PC. **Cards:** AX, DC, DS, MC, VI. **Free Special Amenities:** expanded continental breakfast and high-speed Internet. *(See color ad p 440 & below)*

CALL ⊡M ⊠ ✕ ⊡ ⊟ ⊟ ⊡

PINE RIDGE INN
▼▼▼
Hotel
$139-$379 All Year

Phone: 541/389-6137

Address: 1200 SW Century Dr **Location:** US 97, exit 138 (Downtown/Mt Bachelor Dr), 1.5 mi sw on Colorado Ave, just s on Century Dr, then just w on Mt Bachelor Dr. **Facility:** Smoke free premises. 20 units. 13 one-bedroom standard units. 7 one-bedroom suites with whirlpools. 2 stories, interior corridors. **Parking:** on-site. **Terms:** check-in 4 pm, 2 night minimum stay - seasonal and/or weekends, 7 day cancellation notice-fee imposed. **Amenities:** video library, DVD players, irons, hair dryers. **Leisure Activities:** *Fee:* massage. **Guest Services:** valet laundry, wireless Internet. **Business Services:** business center. **Cards:** AX, DC, DS, MC, VI.

(ASK) ⊟+ CALL ⊡M FEE ⊞ ✕ ⊟ ⊡ / SOME UNITS ⊟

QUALITY INN   *Book great rates at AAA.com*   Phone: (541)318-0848

(AAA) (SAVE)

Hotel

$89-$129 All Year

Address: 20600 Grandview Dr **Location:** On US 97; north end of town. **Facility:** 51 units. 50 one-bedroom standard units, some with whirlpools. 1 one-bedroom suite with kitchen and whirlpool. 2 stories (no elevator), interior corridors. *Bath:* combo or shower only. **Parking:** on-site. **Amenities:** safes, irons, hair dryers. **Pool(s):** heated indoor. **Leisure Activities:** whirlpool. **Guest Services:** coin laundry, wireless Internet. **Business Services:** PC. **Cards:** AX, CB, DC, DS, MC, VI. **Free Special Amenities:** expanded continental breakfast and high-speed Internet.

CALL (&M) 🐾 (🏖) 🖥 (📠) (💲) / SOME UNITS FEE 🐕 🗙

RED LION HOTEL BEND   *Book great rates at AAA.com*   Phone: (541)382-7011

(AAA) (SAVE)

Hotel

$99-$196 All Year

Address: 1415 NE 3rd St **Location:** Jct US 20 and Business Rt US 97 (NE 3rd St), just n. **Facility:** Smoke free premises. 75 units. 73 one- and 2 two-bedroom standard units. 2 stories (no elevator), exterior corridors. *Bath:* combo or shower only. **Parking:** on-site. **Terms:** cancellation fee imposed. **Amenities:** video games (fee), high-speed Internet, voice mail, irons, hair dryers. **Pool(s):** heated outdoor. **Leisure Activities:** whirlpool, exercise room. **Guest Services:** valet and coin laundry, wireless Internet. **Business Services:** meeting rooms, PC. **Cards:** AX, DC, DS, MC, VI. **Free Special Amenities:** expanded continental breakfast and high-speed Internet. *(See color ad below)*

CALL (&M) 🐾 🗙 (📺) 🖥 (📠) (💲) / SOME UNITS FEE 🐕

▼ *See AAA listing above* ▼

THE RIVERHOUSE HOTEL & CONVENTION CENTER

Book great rates at AAA.com

Phone: (541)389-3111

AAA SAVE

Resort Hotel
$99-$219 All Year

Address: 3075 N Business 97 **Location:** US 97, exit 136 (Butler Market Rd) northbound, just n; exit 135B southbound. **Facility:** Many rooms overlook Deschutes River; all units with balcony or patio and some fireplaces. 220 units. 200 one-bedroom standard units, some with kitchens and/or whirlpools. 19 one- and 1 two-bedroom suites, some with kitchens and/or whirlpools. 2 stories (no elevator), interior/exterior corridors. *Bath:* combo or shower only. **Parking:** on-site. **Terms:** check-in 4 pm, 3 day cancellation notice-fee imposed. **Amenities:** video library (fee), DVD players, high-speed Internet, voice mail, irons, hair dryers. **Dining:** 2 restaurants, entertainment. **Pool(s):** heated outdoor, heated indoor. **Leisure Activities:** saunas, whirlpools, fishing, 2 lighted tennis courts, jogging, exercise room. *Fee:* golf-18 holes. **Guest Services:** valet and coin laundry, airport transportation-Redmond Airport, wireless Internet. **Business Services:** conference facilities, PC. **Cards:** AX, DC, DS, MC, VI. *(See color ad p 305)*

SEVENTH MOUNTAIN RESORT

Book great rates at AAA.com

Phone: (541)382-8711

AAA SAVE

Resort Condominium
$99-$499 All Year

Address: 18575 SW Century Dr **Location:** US 97, exit 139 (Reed Market Rd), 1.6 mi sw on Reed Market Rd, then 3.5 mi sw. **Facility:** In a quiet location convenient to Mt. Bachelor and the downtown area, the property offers some newly renovated guest rooms with a fireplace. Designated smoking area. 176 units. 29 one-bedroom standard units with kitchens. 120 one-, 17 two- and 8 three-bedroom suites with kitchens, some with whirlpools. 2 condominiums. 3 stories (no elevator), exterior corridors. **Parking:** on-site. **Terms:** check-in 4 pm, 2-4 night minimum stay - weekends, 7 day cancellation notice. **Amenities:** video library (fee), DVD players, voice mail, irons, hair dryers. **Dining:** 2 restaurants. **Pool(s):** 2 heated outdoor. **Leisure Activities:** sauna, whirlpools, fishing, miniature golf, 4 tennis courts, recreation programs, kids club, hiking trails, jogging, playground, exercise room, basketball, horseshoes, volleyball. *Fee:* canoes, rafting, guided float trips, fly fishing instruction, golf-18 holes, downhill & cross country skiing, snowmobiling, ice skating, bicycles, horseback riding, massage. **Guest Services:** valet and coin laundry, area transportation (fee)-Mt. Bachelor, wireless Internet. **Business Services:** conference facilities, business center. **Cards:** AX, DS, MC, VI. **Free Special Amenities:** preferred room (subject to availability with advance reservations) and high-speed Internet.

SHILO INN SUITES HOTEL BEND

Book great rates at AAA.com

Phone: (541)389-9600

AAA SAVE

Hotel
$112-$300 All Year

Address: 3105 OB Riley Rd **Location:** 1.5 mi n on US 97 from jct US 20 E. **Facility:** 151 one-bedroom standard units, some with kitchens and/or whirlpools. 1-3 stories (no elevator), exterior corridors. **Parking:** on-site, winter plug-ins. **Terms:** check-in 4 pm. **Amenities:** video games (fee), voice mail, irons, hair dryers. **Pool(s):** heated outdoor, heated indoor. **Leisure Activities:** sauna, whirlpools, steamroom, fishing, exercise room. **Guest Services:** valet and coin laundry, airport transportation-Redmond and Bend airports, wireless Internet. **Business Services:** meeting rooms, PC. **Cards:** AX, CB, DC, DS, JC, MC, VI. **Free Special Amenities:** expanded continental breakfast and high-speed Internet. *(See color ad below)*

TOWNEPLACE SUITES BY MARRIOTT   *Book great rates at AAA.com*   Phone: 541-382-5006

Extended Stay
Hotel
Rates not provided

Address: 755 SW 13th Pl **Location:** US 97, exit 138 (Downtown/Mt Bachelor); 1.7 mi sw on NW Colorado Ave. **Facility:** Conveniently located close to Century Drive. Smoke free premises. 71 units. 64 one-bedroom standard units with efficiencies. 7 one-bedroom suites with efficiencies. 2 stories, interior corridors. *Bath:* combo or shower only. **Parking:** on-site. **Terms:** check-in 4 pm. **Amenities:** high-speed Internet, voice mail, irons, hair dryers. *Some:* DVD players. **Pool(s):** heated outdoor. **Leisure Activities:** whirlpool, exercise room. **Guest Services:** valet and coin laundry, wireless Internet. **Business Services:** meeting rooms, PC.

AAA Benefit:
Members save a minimum 5% off the best available rate.

 / SOME UNITS FEE

The following lodging was either not evaluated or did not meet AAA rating requirements but is listed for your information only.

MCMENAMINS OLD ST. FRANCIS SCHOOL   Phone: 541/382-5174

[fyi]
Historic
Hotel

Did not meet all AAA rating requirements for viewports/peepholes in some guest rooms at time of last evaluation on 04/16/2008. **Address:** 700 NW Bond St **Location:** US 97, exit 138 (Downtown/Mt Bachelor Dr), 0.4 mi w on NW Colorado Ave, then 0.3 mi n. Facilities, services, and decor characterize a mid-scale property.

——— WHERE TO DINE ———

ANGEL THAI CUISINE   Phone: 541/388-5177

Thai
$6-$16

A great value at $6, each of the 18 authentic lunch dishes can be seasoned to the diner's taste. Any of seven desserts ends the meal on a sweet note. Casual dress. **Bar:** Full bar. **Hours:** 10:30 am-9:30 pm. Closed: Sun. **Address:** 1900 NE Division St **Location:** Just n of Revere Ave. **Parking:** on-site. **Cards:** MC, VI.

ARIANA   Phone: 541/330-5539

Mediterranean
$8-$30

The restaurant's goal is to "transport" its guests to another time and place, and it has succeeded. In addition to bold seafood offerings, such as caramelized scallops and bacon-wrapped salmon, the menu lists rosemary rack of lamb, spiced rubbed quail and cannelloni with organic spinach. Dressy casual. **Bar:** Full bar. **Reservations:** accepted. **Hours:** 11:30 am-2 & 5-10 pm, Sat-Mon from 5 pm. Closed: 11/26, 12/25. **Address:** 1304 NW Galveston St **Location:** Just o of jct 14th St. **Parking:** on-site. **Cards:** AX, MC, VI.

BLACK BEAR DINER   Phone: 541/312-8327

American
$7-$16

A homey atmosphere characterizes this family-oriented restaurant. Familiar comfort foods, such as meatloaf with mashed potatoes, are at the heart of the menu and are served in generous portions. Casual dress. **Hours:** 6 am-10 pm. **Address:** 1416 NE 3rd St **Location:** US 97, just n of jct US 20. **Parking:** on-site. **Cards:** AX, DS, MC, VI.

CAFE SINTRA   Phone: 541/382-8004

Portuguese
$6-$11

Serving breakfast and lunch, the contemporary European-style cafe prepares tasty sandwiches and a few Portuguese specialties. Casual dress. **Bar:** Beer & wine. **Reservations:** not accepted. **Hours:** 7 am-3 pm, Sun-2 pm. Closed: 11/26, 12/25. **Address:** 1024 NW Bond St **Location:** Just s of jct NE Greenwood Ave; downtown. **Parking:** street. **Cards:** MC, VI.

CORK   Phone: 541/382-6881

American
$22-$30

In the historic Old Penny Galleria, the establishment prepares upscale, eclectic cuisine. Guests can linger over French press coffee. Servers are knowledgeable. Casual dress. **Bar:** Full bar. **Reservations:** suggested. **Hours:** 5 pm-9 pm, Fri & Sat-9:30 pm. Closed major holidays; also Sun & Mon. **Address:** 150 NW Oregon Ave **Location:** Near Wall St and Oregon Ave; downtown. **Parking:** street. **Cards:** MC, VI.

ERNESTO'S   Phone: 541/389-7274

Italian
$8-$18

In a former church, the open airy restaurant boasts a cafe feel and an energetic, attentive staff. Menu offerings of chicken, veal, seafood and pasta include a tasty seafood pasta with halibut, shrimp, clams and scallops in a rich, cream sauce. Casual dress. **Bar:** Full bar. **Reservations:** accepted, Sun-Thurs. **Hours:** 11:30 am-2:30 & 4:30-9:30 pm, Fri-10 pm, Sat 4:30 pm-10 pm, Sun 4 pm-9 pm. Closed major holidays. **Address:** 1203 NE 3rd St **Location:** On Business Rt US 97. **Parking:** on-site. **Cards:** AX, DS, MC, VI.

HIGH TIDES SEAFOOD GRILL   Phone: 541/389-5244

Seafood
$7-$11

This popular, local favorite serves nicely prepared seafood as well as steaks and chicken dishes. Casual dress. **Bar:** Beer & wine. **Reservations:** accepted. **Hours:** 11 am-2:30 & 5-9 pm, Sat from 5 pm. Closed major holidays; also Sun. **Address:** 1045 NW Bond St **Location:** Just s jct of NE Greenwood Ave; downtown. **Parking:** street. **Cards:** AX, DS, MC, VI.

THE LODGE   Phone: 541/388-4998

American
$8-$15

Situated on the way to Mt. Bachelor, this eatery features a huge fireplace to warm up frozen skiers and an outdoor patio perfect for sun worshipers after a day of kayaking the nearby Deschutes River. The high-energy venue turns out items like Kobe sliders, grilled short ribs, smoked trout spinach salad and tasty desserts made just down the street. Diners can wash everything down with one of sixteen handcrafted beers on tap. Casual dress. **Bar:** Full bar. **Reservations:** not accepted. **Hours:** 11:30 am-10 pm. Closed: 11/26, 12/25. **Address:** 1441 SW Chandler Ave, Suite 100 **Location:** US 97, exit 138 (Downtown/Mt Bachelor Dr), 1.7 mi sw on NW Colorado Ave, then just w. **Parking:** on-site. **Cards:** MC, VI.

MCGRATH'S FISH HOUSE

▼▼ ▼▼

Seafood
$9-$19

Phone: 541/388-4555

The popular chain specializes in fresh Pacific Northwest seafood, including dishes grilled over a wood fire and items from the daily fresh sheet. Also on the menu are steaks, chicken, pasta and gourmet burgers. Casual dress. **Bar:** Full bar. **Hours:** 11 am-10 pm. Closed: 11/26, 12/25. **Address:** 3118 N Hwy 97 **Location:** Jct US 20 E, 1.5 mi n. **Parking:** on-site. **Cards:** AX, DC, DS, MC, VI.

MCMENAMINS

▼▼ ▼▼

American
$5-$20

Phone: 541/382-5174

The casual neighborhood eatery is where friends gather for classic pub and comfort fare, all washed down by pints of locally made beer. Large wooden booths or tables easily accommodate larger groups, and the eclectic, custom-painted walls and varied period light fixtures keep diners' eyes busy should the conversation lag. Casual dress. **Bar:** Full bar. **Hours:** 7 am-1 am. **Address:** 700 NW Bond St **Location:** US 97, exit 138 (Downtown/Mt Bachelor Dr), 0.4 mi w on NW Colorado Ave, then 0.3 mi n; in McMenamins Old St. Francis School. **Parking:** on-site. **Cards:** MC, VI.

MERENDA RESTAURANT & WINE BAR

▼▼ ▼▼

Italian
$10-$23

Phone: 541/330-2304

More than 70 wines by the glass and more than 400 by the bottle pair with Northern Italian dishes and some selections of Southern French cuisine. This place feature nightly specials from the open wood-burning rotisserie grill. Selections might include suckling pig, spring lamb and roasted shrimp. Casual dress. **Bar:** Full bar. **Reservations:** suggested. **Hours:** 11:30 am-10 pm. Closed: 11/26, 12/25. **Address:** 900 NW Wall St **Location:** At Wall and Minnesota sts; downtown. **Parking:** street. **Cards:** AX, MC, VI.

MOTHER'S JUICE CAFE

▼▼

Deli
$6-$8

Phone: 541/318-0989

Detering's Orchard owns this cafe, which should explain its outstanding fruit smoothies. Also offered here are European breakfast dishes and healthy sandwiches and salads. Casual dress. **Hours:** 7 am-5 pm, Sat & Sun from 8 am. **Address:** 1255 NW Galveston St **Location:** Just e of 14th St. **Parking:** on-site and street.

PINE TAVERN RESTAURANT   *Menu on AAA.com*

◆◆◆

▼▼ ▼▼

American
$7-$28

Phone: 541/382-5581

A local favorite for more than 70 years, the restaurant features Oregon Country beef prime rib produced by ranchers who raise steroid-free cattle. Overlooking a small lake, the tranquil garden room has a 275-year-old pine growing through its center. A garden patio is open during pleasant weather. Casual dress. **Bar:** Full bar. **Reservations:** accepted. **Hours:** 11:30 am-9:30 pm, Sun from 5 pm. **Address:** 967 NW Brooks St **Location:** At Brooks St and Oregon Ave; downtown. **Parking:** street. **Cards:** AX, DS, MC, VI. **Classic**

ROBBY J'S BISTRO AT MILL POINT

▼▼ ▼▼

Continental
$7-$26

Phone: 541/383-8220

A small bistro featuring cuisine with French and Northwest influences, Robby J's is located in the Mill Point Business Campus and is a favorite of nearby businesses. Lunch fare includes bistro sandwiches and salads as well as a few hot entrees, and dinners may feature Oregon wild salmon in a champagne mousseline sauce or cherrywood-smoked prime rib. A good selection of wines is available, and an inviting patio overlooks the bluffs and river below. Casual dress. **Bar:** Full bar. **Reservations:** suggested. **Hours:** 11 am-9 pm, Sun 9:30 am-7:30 pm. Closed major holidays. **Address:** 705 SW Bonnett Way **Location:** 0.6 mi w of jct Bond St and SW Columbia Ave (Mill Point Shopping Center) to SW Bonnett Way, just s; just s of jct SW Columbia and Colorado aves. **Parking:** on-site. **Cards:** AX, MC, VI.

STACCATO AT THE FIREHALL

▼▼ ▼▼ ▼▼

Italian
$10-$30

Phone: 541/312-3100

On the menu are fresh and contemporary Italian recipes, such as wild boar lasagna; salad with greens, prosciutto and toasted hazelnuts; and potato gnocchi with pumpkin cream, Rogue River blue cheese and toasted pumpkin seeds. The plated Sunday brunch allows for relaxed dining. Dressy casual. **Bar:** Full bar. **Reservations:** accepted. **Hours:** 5:30 pm-10 pm, Sun 10 am-1 & 5-10 pm. Closed major holidays. **Address:** 5 NW Minnesota Ave **Location:** Jct Lava St; downtown. **Parking:** street. **Cards:** AX, CB, DC, DS, JC, MC, VI.

TOOMIE'S THAI CUISINE

▼▼ ▼▼

Thai
$5-$20

Phone: 541/388-5590

Listed on the varied and extensive menu are noodle, curry, seafood, vegetarian, pork, poultry and beef dishes. Several house specials are prepared. Large windows look out onto the street. Casual dress. **Bar:** Beer & wine. **Hours:** 11:30 am-2:30 & 5:30-9:30 pm, Fri & Sat-10:30 pm. Closed: 11/26, 12/25. **Address:** 119 NW Minnesota Ave **Location:** Between Wall and Bond sts; downtown. **Parking:** street. **Cards:** AX, DC, DS, MC, VI.

TUMALO FEED COMPANY

◆◆◆

▼▼ ▼▼

American
$13-$28

Phone: 541/382-2202

The rustic dining room captures the Western mood with red-checkered tablecloths, memorabilia and lots of noise. Dishes of steak, seafood and chicken are served with delicious onion rings. The adventurous enjoy sampling the risque Rocky Mountain oysters. Casual dress. **Bar:** Full bar. **Reservations:** suggested. **Hours:** 5 pm-9 pm, Fri & Sat 4:30 pm-9:30 pm, Sun 4 pm-9 pm. Closed: 11/26, 12/24, 12/25. **Address:** 64619 W Hwy 20 **Location:** 4 mi w. **Parking:** on-site. **Cards:** MC, VI.

ZYDECO KITCHEN & COCKTAILS

▼▼ ▼▼ ▼▼

American
$12-$30

Phone: 541/312-2899

Contemporary decor colors the romantic restaurant, where two-person corner booths invite cozy conversation. The menu focuses on distinctive organic and hormone-free dishes along the lines of artichoke and corn fritters, steak salad and gemelli pasta, shrimp and andouille sausage. Dressy casual. **Bar:** Full bar. **Reservations:** suggested. **Hours:** 4:30 pm-10 pm. Closed major holidays; also Sun. **Address:** 1085 SE 3rd St **Location:** On Business Rt US 97 (3rd St); jct Reed Market Rd. **Parking:** on-site. **Cards:** MC, VI.

———— *The following restaurant has not been evaluated by AAA* ————
but is listed for your information only.

BALTAZAR'S

[fyi]

Phone: 541/382-6622

Not evaluated. **Address:** 1465 SE Knoll Ave **Location:** US 197, exit 138 (Downtown/Mt Bachelor Dr) to Colorado Ave, 1.2 mi sw on Colorado Ave to Century Dr, just n, then just w.

BLACK BUTTE RANCH

———— **WHERE TO STAY** ————

———— *The following lodging was either not evaluated or did not* ————
meet AAA rating requirements but is listed for your information only.

BLACK BUTTE RANCH
[fyi]
Not evaluated. **Address:** 13653 Hawks Beard **Location:** 8 mi w of Sisters, on US 20. Facilities, services, and decor characterize a mid-scale property.
Phone: 541/595-6211

BLUE RIVER

———— **WHERE TO STAY** ————

HARBICK'S COUNTRY INN
Motel
$70-$110 All Year
Address: 54791 McKenzie Hwy (US 126) **Location:** 6 mi e on US 126; at MM 47.5. Located in a rural area. **Facility:** 21 units. 20 one-bedroom standard units. 1 one-bedroom suite with kitchen. 1-2 stories (no elevator), exterior corridors. **Bath:** combo or shower only. **Parking:** on-site. **Terms:** office hours 8 am-11 pm. **Amenities:** DVD players. **Guest Services:** wireless Internet. **Cards:** AX, MC, VI.
Phone: 541/822-3805

BOARDMAN pop. 2,855

———— **WHERE TO STAY** ————

RIVER LODGE & GRILL   *Book great rates at AAA.com*
Hotel
$09-$129 All Year
Address: 6 Marine Dr **Location:** I-84, exit 164, 0.5 mi n on Main St, then 0.5 mi e. **Facility:** Smoke free premises. 49 units. 45 one-bedroom standard units. 4 one-bedroom suites. 2 stories, interior corridors. **Parking:** on-site. **Terms:** cancellation fee imposed. **Amenities:** voice mail, irons, hair dryers. **Dining:** restaurant, see separate listing. **Pool(s):** heated outdoor. **Leisure Activities:** saunas, whirlpool, exercise room. **Guest Services:** wireless Internet. **Business Services:** meeting rooms, PC. **Cards:** AX, DS, MC, VI. **Free Special Amenities: newspaper and high-speed Internet.**
Phone: (541)481-6800

RODEWAY INN   *Book great rates at AAA.com*
Motel
$58-$129 All Year
Address: 105 SW Front St **Location:** I-84, exit 164, just sw. **Facility:** 51 one-bedroom standard units, some with whirlpools. 1 story, exterior corridors. **Parking:** on-site. **Amenities:** high-speed Internet. *Some:* hair dryers. **Pool(s):** heated outdoor. **Guest Services:** coin laundry, wireless Internet. **Business Services:** PC. **Cards:** AX, CB, DC, DS, JC, MC, VI.
Phone: (541)481-2375

———— **WHERE TO DINE** ————

RIVER GRILL
American
$8-$24
Patrons can take in expansive views of the Columbia River while dining on a variety of tasty and innovative menu items. Casual dress. **Bar:** Beer & wine. **Reservations:** accepted. **Hours:** 6 am-10 pm. **Address:** 6 Marine Dr **Location:** I-84, exit 164, 0.5 mi n on Main St, then 0.5 mi e; in River Lodge & Grill. **Parking:** on-site. **Cards:** AX, DC, DS, MC, VI.
Phone: 541/481-6800

BRIDAL VEIL

———— **WHERE TO DINE** ————

MULTNOMAH FALLS LODGE
American
$9-$22
Nestled at the base of the 620-foot Multnomah Falls is the historic Multnomah Falls Lodge. The menu features Northwest cuisine and the historic dining rooms have cozy fireplaces with scenic views of the falls, the Columbia River gorge and the surrounding forest. Casual dress. **Bar:** Full bar. **Reservations:** accepted. **Hours:** 8 am-9 pm; Sunday brunch. Closed: 11/26, 12/25. **Address:** 55000 E Historic Columbia River Hwy **Location:** I-84, exit 31, just s. **Parking:** on-site. **Cards:** AX, DS, MC, VI.
Phone: 503/695-2376

BROOKINGS pop. 5,447

———— WHERE TO STAY ————

BEST WESTERN BEACHFRONT INN *Book great rates at AAA.com*

Phone: (541)469-7779

Hotel
$179-$295 3/1-9/30
$154-$250 10/1-2/28

Address: 16008 Boat Basin Rd **Location:** Jct US 101, 0.6 mi w on Benham Ln. **Facility:** 102 units. 99 one-bedroom standard units, some with efficiencies and/or whirlpools. 3 one-bedroom suites with kitchens and whirlpools. 3 stories, exterior corridors. **Parking:** on-site. **Amenities:** high-speed Internet, voice mail, irons, hair dryers. **Pool(s):** heated outdoor. **Leisure Activities:** whirlpool, sun deck, picnic area. **Guest Services:** coin laundry, wireless Internet. **Business Services:** meeting rooms, business center. **Cards:** AX, CB, DC, DS, MC, VI. *(See color ad below)*

AAA Benefit:
Members save up to 20%, plus 10% bonus points with rewards program.

BEST WESTERN BROOKINGS INN *Book great rates at AAA.com*

Phone: (541)469-2173

Hotel
$98-$155 All Year

Address: 1143 Chetco Ave **Location:** On US 101; north end of town. **Facility:** 68 units. 63 one- and 5 two-bedroom standard units, some with whirlpools. 2 stories (no elevator), exterior corridors. **Parking:** on-site. **Terms:** cancellation fee imposed. **Amenities:** high-speed Internet, irons, hair dryers. **Pool(s):** heated indoor. **Leisure Activities:** whirlpool. **Guest Services:** airport transportation-Brookings Airport, wireless Internet. **Business Services:** meeting rooms, PC. **Cards:** AX, CB, DC, DS, MC, VI. **Free Special Amenities:** early check-in/late check-out and high-speed Internet. *(See color ad p 315)*

AAA Benefit:
Members save up to 20%, plus 10% bonus points with rewards program.

CHETCO RIVER INN & LAVENDER FARM

Phone: (541)251-0087

Bed & Breakfast
$135-$250 All Year

Address: 21202 High Prairie Rd **Location:** Jct US 101, just e on Constitution Way, 16.6 mi ne on N Bank Chetco River Rd. Located in a quiet rustic area. **Facility:** Enjoy fishing, swimming, hiking, bird-watching or lounging on the porch; nestled along the Chetco River on 40 acres in the Siskiyou Forest. Smoke free premises. 6 units. 5 one-bedroom standard units, some with whirlpools. 1 cottage. 1-2 stories (no elevator), interior/exterior corridors. *Bath:* combo or shower only. **Parking:** on-site. **Terms:** 7 day cancellation notice. **Amenities:** high-speed Internet, hair dryers. *Some:* DVD players. **Leisure Activities:** fishing, hiking trails, horseshoes. **Guest Services:** coin laundry, wireless Internet. **Cards:** MC, VI.

▼ See AAA listing above ▼

OCEAN SUITES MOTEL

Phone: 541/469-4004

AAA [SAVE]

▼▼ ▼▼

Motel
$75-$119 All Year

Address: 16045 Lower Harbor Rd **Location:** US 101, exit Benham Ln northbound, 0.7 mi w on Benham Ln; exit Port of Brookings southbound, 0.8 mi w. **Facility:** 24 units. 2 two-bedroom standard units with kitchens. 22 one-bedroom suites with kitchens. 2 stories (no elevator), exterior corridors. **Parking:** on-site. **Terms:** office hours 7 am-10 pm. **Amenities:** video library, DVD players, high-speed Internet, voice mail, hair dryers. **Guest Services:** coin laundry. **Cards:** AX, DS, MC, VI. **Free Special Amenities:** local telephone calls and high-speed Internet.

[icons]

SOUTH COAST INN BED AND BREAKFAST

Phone: 541/469-5557

▼▼▼▼

Bed & Breakfast
$119-$159 3/1-10/1
$109-$149 10/2-2/28

Address: 516 Redwood St **Location:** Off US 101, between Oak St and Fern Ave, just e. **Facility:** Each room in this centrally located B&B is decorated in a different theme, some have large windows overlooking the ocean. Smoke free premises. 6 units. 4 one-bedroom standard units. 1 one-bedroom suite with kitchen. 1 cottage. 2 stories (no elevator), interior/exterior corridors. *Bath:* combo or shower only. **Parking:** on-site. **Terms:** age restrictions may apply, 7 day cancellation notice-fee imposed. **Amenities:** video library, CD players, hair dryers. *Some:* DVD players, irons. **Guest Services:** wireless Internet. **Business Services:** meeting rooms, PC. **Cards:** AX, DC, DS, MC, VI.

[icons] / SOME UNITS

SPINDRIFT MOTEL

Phone: 541/469-5345

AAA [SAVE]

▼▼ ▼▼

Motel
Rates not provided

Address: 1215 Chetco Ave **Location:** On US 101; north end of town. **Facility:** 35 one-bedroom standard units. 2 stories (no elevator), exterior corridors. **Parking:** on-site. **Terms:** office hours 7 am-11 pm. **Amenities:** high-speed Internet, voice mail, hair dryers. **Guest Services:** wireless Internet. **Business Services:** PC. **Free Special Amenities:** early check-in/late check-out and high-speed Internet.

[icons] / SOME UNITS

▼ See AAA listing p 314 ▼

WILD RIVERS MOTORLODGE
Phone: (541)469-5361

AAA SAVE

▼▼ ▼▼

Motel
$69-$119 3/1-9/19
$69-$99 9/20-2/28

Address: 437 Chetco Ave **Location:** On US 101, just n of Chetco River Bridge. **Facility:** 29 units. 25 one- and 4 two-bedroom standard units. 1-2 stories (no elevator), exterior corridors. *Bath:* combo or shower only. **Parking:** on-site. **Amenities:** high-speed Internet, hair dryers. **Guest Services:** wireless Internet. **Cards:** AX, DS, MC, VI. **Free Special Amenities: local telephone calls and high-speed Internet.**

⟦↑⟧ ⟦⟧ ⟦⟧ ⟦⟧ ⟦⟧ / SOME UNITS FEE ⟦⟧ ⟦✕⟧ ⟦⟧

——— WHERE TO DINE ———

BELLA ITALIA RISTORANTE
Phone: 541/469-6647

▼▼ ▼▼

Italian
$13-$35

Authentic made-in-house sauces flavor traditional Italian fare, including the highly recommended chicken rosemary ravioli. Casual dress. **Bar:** Full bar. **Reservations:** accepted. **Hours:** 4 pm-9 pm. **Address:** 1025 Chetco Ave **Location:** North end of town; in Northgate Center. **Parking:** on-site. **Cards:** MC, VI.

O'HOLLERAN'S STEAKHOUSE
Phone: 541/469-9907

▼▼ ▼▼

Steak & Seafood
$14-$25

Generous portions of grilled Chinook salmon and aged steaks hand-cut by the owner are the norm at the small, well-established restaurant. The atmosphere is warm and comfortable. Casual dress. **Bar:** Full bar. **Reservations:** suggested. **Hours:** 7 am-10 pm. Closed: 11/26, 12/25. **Address:** 1210 Chetco Ave **Location:** Just n on US 101. **Parking:** on-site. **Cards:** AX, DS, MC, VI.

SMUGGLER'S COVE
Phone: 541/469-6006

AAA

▼▼ ▼▼

Steak & Seafood
$7-$25

The eatery looks out onto the Pacific Ocean and serves simply-prepared seafood dishes. Casual dress. Entertainment. **Bar:** Full bar. **Reservations:** suggested. **Hours:** 7 am-10 pm. **Address:** 16011 Boat Basin Rd **Location:** South end on US 101, 1 mi w on Lower Harbor Rd, then just n. **Parking:** on-site. **Cards:** AX, DS, MC, VI.

BURNS pop. 3,064

——— WHERE TO STAY ———

AMERICA'S BEST INN
Book great rates at AAA.com
Phone: (541)573-1700

AAA SAVE

▼▼ ▼▼

Motel
$66-$86 3/1-10/31
$60-$72 11/1-2/28

Address: 999 Oregon Ave (US 395/20) **Location:** 1 mi w on US 395/20 from jct SR 78. **Facility:** 38 one-bedroom standard units, some with whirlpools. 2 stories (no elevator), interior/exterior corridors. **Parking:** on-site. **Terms:** office hours 6:30 am-8 pm. **Amenities:** high-speed Internet, irons, hair dryers. **Pool(s):** heated indoor. **Leisure Activities:** whirlpool. **Guest Services:** coin laundry, wireless Internet. **Business Services:** PC. **Cards:** AX, CB, DC, DS, MC, VI. **Free Special Amenities: expanded continental breakfast and high-speed Internet.**

⟦⟧ ⟦⟧ ⟦⟧ ⟦⟧ ⟦⟧ / SOME UNITS FEE ⟦⟧ ⟦✕⟧

DAYS INN BURNS
Book great rates at AAA.com
Phone: (541)573-2047

AAA SAVE

▼▼ ▼▼

Motel
$56-$80 5/1-2/28
$43-$70 3/1-4/30

Address: 577 W Monroe St **Location:** Just w on US 395/20 from jct SR 78. **Facility:** 52 units. 47 one- and 4 two-bedroom standard units. 1 one-bedroom suite. 2 stories (no elevator), exterior corridors. **Parking:** on-site, winter plug-ins. **Terms:** office hours 6 am-midnight, cancellation fee imposed. **Amenities:** hair dryers. **Pool(s):** heated outdoor. **Guest Services:** airport transportation-Burns Municipal Airport, wireless Internet. **Cards:** AX, DS, MC, VI. **Free Special Amenities: continental breakfast and high-speed Internet.**

⟦✈⟧ ⟦↑⟧ ⟦⟧ ⟦⟧ ⟦⟧ / SOME UNITS ⟦✕⟧ ⟦⟧ ⟦⟧

SAGE COUNTRY INN B & B
Phone: 541/573-7243

▼▼ ▼▼

Historic Bed
& Breakfast
$125 All Year

Address: 351 1/2 W Monroe St **Location:** Just w on US 395/20 from jct SR 78, just s on Diamond Ave or Court St. **Facility:** The 1907 Georgian Colonial home has tastefully appointed guest rooms and public areas sprinkled with antique furnishings; landscaping is attractive. Smoke free premises. 3 one-bedroom standard units. 2 stories (no elevator), interior corridors. *Bath:* shower only. **Parking:** on-site. **Amenities:** high-speed Internet, irons, hair dryers. **Guest Services:** TV in common area, wireless Internet. **Cards:** MC, VI.

⟦↑⟧ ⟦✕⟧ ⟦W⟧ ⟦⟧

SILVER SPUR MOTEL
Phone: (541)573-2077

AAA SAVE

▼▼

Motel
$47-$52 3/1-10/31
$42-$47 11/1-2/28

Address: 789 N Broadway **Location:** US 395/20; at north edge of town center. **Facility:** 26 one-bedroom standard units. 2 stories (no elevator), exterior corridors. *Bath:* combo or shower only. **Parking:** on-site. **Terms:** office hours 6:30 am-midnight. **Amenities:** high-speed Internet. **Leisure Activities:** barbecue grill. **Guest Services:** airport transportation-Burns Municipal Airport, wireless Internet. **Cards:** AX, DS, MC, VI. **Free Special Amenities: expanded continental breakfast and high-speed Internet.**

⟦⟧ ⟦⟧ ⟦⟧ ⟦⟧ ⟦⟧ ⟦⟧ / SOME UNITS FEE ⟦⟧ ⟦✕⟧

——— WHERE TO DINE ———

EL TOREO MEXICAN RESTAURANT   Phone: 541/573-1829

Mexican
$6-$19

The casual, family-run restaurant uses authentic ingredients in their extensive menu, including house-made mole sauce, house-made salsa and other sauces. Casual dress. **Bar:** Full bar. **Hours:** 11 am-9 pm, Fri & Sat-10 pm. Closed major holidays. **Address:** 239 N Broadway **Location:** Center. **Parking:** street. **Cards:** MC, VI.

MEAT HOOK STEAK HOUSE   Phone: 541/573-7698

Steak
$10-$37

This family-owned-and-operated steakhouse prepares beef offerings to satisfy any hunger. Worth a try are the rib eye, porterhouse, New York steak and burger. A good value for a hearty meal, the meal price includes soup, salad, homemade bread and an ice cream sundae. Ribbons, trophies and banners signifying three generations of cattle-showing adorn the walls of this fun spot. Casual dress. **Bar:** Full bar. **Reservations:** accepted. **Hours:** 4:30 pm-9 pm. Closed major holidays; also Sun. **Address:** 673 W Monroe St **Location:** Between Grand and Fairview aves; downtown. **Parking:** on-site. **Cards:** MC, VI.

CANBY pop. 12,790

——— WHERE TO DINE ———

BURGERVILLE   Phone: 503/266-2568

American
$2-$8

First-timers shouldn't let the fast food exterior fool them, as the burgers and chicken here adhere to a higher standard. Northwest ingredients come into play in the sandwiches. Casual dress. **Hours:** 7 am-10 pm. Closed: 11/26, 12/25. **Address:** 909 SW 1st Ave **Location:** Just sw on SR 99 E; near center of town. **Parking:** on-site. **Cards:** DS, MC, VI.

SEASONS GRILL   Phone: 503/266-3805

American
$7-$22

Contemporary country decor and charm characterize the two-story restaurant, where patrons can order daily specials, salads, sandwiches, burgers, steaks and a few fish, pasta and chicken dishes from a seasonally changing menu. In season, the deck and porch open for dining. Casual dress. **Bar:** Full bar. **Reservations:** not accepted. **Hours:** 11:30 am-10 pm, Fri-11 pm, Sat 8 am-11 pm, Sun 8 am-9 pm. Closed major holidays. **Address:** 101 N Elm St **Location:** Just n of SR 99 E; at NW 1st Ave and N Elm St; near center. **Parking:** on-site. **Cards:** AX, DS, MC, VI.

CANNON BEACH pop. 1,588

——— WHERE TO STAY ———

CANNON BEACH ECOLA CREEK LODGE   *Book at AAA.com*   Phone: (503)436-2776

Motel
$55-$230 All Year

Address: 208 5th St **Location:** 0.3 mi w of US 101 via north exit to Ecola State Park. **Facility:** Smoke free premises. 22 units. 10 one-bedroom standard units. 10 one- and 2 two-bedroom suites, some with kitchens and/or whirlpools. 2 stories (no elevator), exterior corridors. *Bath:* combo or tub only. **Parking:** on-site. **Terms:** office hours 8 am-8 pm, check-in 4 pm, 2 night minimum stay - seasonal and/or weekends, 3 day cancellation notice-fee imposed. **Amenities:** video library (fee), DVD players, high-speed Internet. *Some:* irons. **Leisure Activities:** beach access. **Guest Services:** coin laundry, wireless Internet. **Business Services:** PC. **Cards:** AX, DS, MC, VI.

ASK CALL 🔊M 🛗 ✉ 🅰 🔲 🖥 💻 / SOME UNITS FEE 🐾

INN AT CANNON BEACH   *Book at AAA.com*   Phone: 503/436-9085

Hotel
Rates not provided

Address: 3215 S Hemlock St **Location:** US 101, exit Tolovana Park, just w, then just n. **Facility:** Smoke free premises. 40 one-bedroom standard units, some with whirlpools. 2 stories (no elevator), exterior corridors. *Bath:* combo or shower only. **Parking:** on-site. **Terms:** office hours 7 am-11:30 pm, check-in 4 pm. **Amenities:** video library, DVD players, high-speed Internet, irons, hair dryers. **Guest Services:** wireless Internet. **Business Services:** meeting rooms, PC.

🅰 🛗 ✉ 🅰 VCR 🔲 🖥 💻 / SOME UNITS FEE 🐾

THE OCEAN LODGE   *Book at AAA.com*   Phone: (503)436-2241

Hotel
$199-$379 All Year

Address: 2864 S Pacific St **Location:** US 101, exit Tolovana Park, just w on Warren Way, just n on S Hemlock St, just w on W Chisana St, then just n. **Facility:** Smoke free premises. 45 units. 38 one-bedroom standard units, some with whirlpools. 7 one-bedroom suites. 2-3 stories, interior/exterior corridors. *Bath:* combo or shower only. **Parking:** on-site. **Terms:** check-in 4 pm, 2-3 night minimum stay - seasonal and/or weekends, 7 day cancellation notice. **Amenities:** video library, DVD players, high-speed Internet, voice mail, irons, hair dryers. **Leisure Activities:** beach access. **Fee:** massage. **Guest Services:** coin laundry, wireless Internet. **Cards:** AX, DC, DS, MC, VI.

🅰 🛗 ✉ 🅰 🔲 🖥 💻 / SOME UNITS FEE 🐾 🅰

SCHOONER'S COVE   Phone: 503/436-2300

Condominium
$149-$339 3/1-9/30
$129-$249 10/1-2/28

Address: 188 N Larch **Location:** Just w of jct N Hemlock St; center. **Facility:** A notable feature at this property is its beachfront lawn with grills; most units have gas fireplaces. 30 units. 4 one-bedroom standard units. 22 one- and 4 two-bedroom suites with efficiencies. 2 stories (no elevator), exterior corridors. *Bath:* combo or shower only. **Parking:** on-site. **Terms:** office hours 8 am-10 pm, check-in 4 pm, 2-3 night minimum stay - seasonal and/or weekends, 14 day cancellation notice-fee imposed. **Amenities:** video library (fee), DVD players, high-speed Internet, hair dryers. **Leisure Activities:** whirlpool, beach access. **Guest Services:** coin laundry, wireless Internet. **Business Services:** meeting rooms, PC. **Cards:** AX, DC, DS, MC, VI.

🅰 CALL 🔊M ✉ 🅰 🎥 🔲 🖥 💻

STEPHANIE INN

AAA SAVE

▼▼▼ ▼▼▼

Country Inn

$379-$619 7/1-2/28
$359-$599 3/1-6/30

Phone: (503)436-2221

Address: 2740 S Pacific St **Location:** Oceanfront. US 101, exit Tolovana Park, just w on Warren Way, just n on S Hemlock St, just w on Matanuska St, then just s. **Facility:** Enjoy an afternoon wine tasting at the beachfront inn; tastefully-appointed rooms include a fireplace and offer ocean or mountain views. Smoke free premises. 43 units. 33 one-bedroom standard units with whirlpools. 10 one-bedroom suites with whirlpools. 3 stories, interior corridors. **Parking:** on-site. **Terms:** check-in 4 pm, 2-4 night minimum stay - weekends, age restrictions may apply, 7 day cancellation notice. **Amenities:** video library, DVD players, CD players, high-speed Internet, voice mail, safes, irons, hair dryers. **Dining:** Stephanie Inn Dining Room, see separate listing. **Leisure Activities:** CD library. *Fee:* massage. **Guest Services:** airport transportation-Astoria Regional Airport, area transportation-town, wireless Internet. **Business Services:** PC. **Cards:** AX, DC, DS, MC, VI. **Free Special Amenities: full breakfast and high-speed Internet.**

✈ ▯ ➚ ✕ 🔒 🖥 / SOME UNITS 🖨

SURFSAND RESORT AT CANNON BEACH

AAA SAVE

▼▼▼ ▼▼▼

Resort
Hotel

$199-$459 7/1-2/28
$179-$439 3/1-6/30

Phone: (503)436-2274

Address: 148 W Gower St **Location:** Oceanfront. US 101, exit Cannon Beach (2nd exit); downtown. **Facility:** Newly renovated units feature upscale touches, many include a fireplace and balcony as well as views of the ocean and Haystack Rock. Smoke free premises. 97 units. 64 one-bedroom standard units, some with whirlpools. 29 one- and 4 two-bedroom suites, some with whirlpools. 2-4 stories, exterior corridors. *Bath:* combo or shower only. **Parking:** on-site. **Terms:** check-in 4 pm, 2 night minimum stay - seasonal and/or weekends, 7 day cancellation notice. **Amenities:** video library, DVD players, high-speed Internet, voice mail, safes, irons, hair dryers. **Pool(s):** heated indoor. **Leisure Activities:** saunas, whirlpool, beach access, beach cabana service, recreation programs in summer, bocci, exercise room, horseshoes, volleyball. *Fee:* massage. **Guest Services:** area transportation-within 20 mi, wireless Internet. **Business Services:** meeting rooms, PC. **Cards:** AX, DC, DS, MC, VI. **Free Special Amenities: local telephone calls and high-speed Internet.**

🍸 ➚ ✕ ✕ 🔒 🖨 🖥 / SOME UNITS FEE 🐕 🎿

TOLOVANA INN

AAA SAVE

▼▼▼ ▼▼▼

Condominium

$69-$429 All Year

Phone: (503)436-2211

Address: 3400 S Hemlock St **Location:** US 101, exit Tolovana Park, just w on Warren Way, then just s. **Facility:** Smoke free premises. 175 units. 91 one-bedroom standard units, some with kitchens. 48 one- and 36 two-bedroom suites, some with kitchens. 3 stories, exterior corridors. *Bath:* combo or shower only. **Parking:** on-site. **Terms:** check-in 4 pm, 2-3 night minimum stay - seasonal and/or weekends, 3 day cancellation notice-fee imposed. **Amenities:** video library (fee), DVD players, high-speed Internet, irons, hair dryers. **Pool(s):** heated indoor. **Leisure Activities:** sauna, whirlpool, beach access, exercise room. *Fee:* massage, game room. **Guest Services:** coin laundry, wireless Internet. **Business Services:** meeting rooms, PC. **Cards:** AX, DC, DS, MC, VI. **Free Special Amenities: newspaper and high-speed Internet.**

▯ ➚ ✕ ✕ 🎿 🔒 🖥 / SOME UNITS FEE 🐕 🖨

—— WHERE TO DINE ——

BISTRO
Phone: 503/436-2661

Continental
$15-$25

Set amid boutiques in the charming beach town, the cozy, rustic restaurant serves well-prepared fresh seafood and pasta dishes. Greek lemon soup and grilled halibut (seasonal) with rice pilaf boast interesting flavors. The menu varies seasonally. Casual dress. **Bar:** Full bar. **Reservations:** suggested. **Hours:** 4 pm-10 pm; seasonal hours vary. Closed: 11/26, 12/25; also Mon-Wed in winter. **Address:** 263 N Hemlock St **Location:** Center. **Parking:** street. **Cards:** MC, VI.

DOOGERS SEAFOOD & GRILL
Phone: 503/436-2225

Seafood
$9-$38

Popular with families, the comfortable restaurant is rustic in decor with quaint touches. On the menu are traditional preparations of primarily seafood dishes, with a handful of pasta, chicken and beef entrees. Casual dress. **Bar:** Full bar. **Hours:** 8 am-9 pm, Fri & Sat-10 pm; to 10 pm in summer. Closed: 11/26, 12/25. **Address:** 1371 S Hemlock St **Location:** US 101, exit Sunset Blvd, just s. **Parking:** on-site. **Cards:** AX, DS, MC, VI.

LAZY SUSAN CAFE
Phone: 503/436-2816

Regional American
$8-$12

For more than 27 years, the endearing cafe has served as a cozy retreat. On the menu are all-day omelets, poached egg specials, tasty homemade soups, salads, quiches and desserts. Casual dress. **Bar:** Beer & wine. **Hours:** 8 am-2:30 pm, Fri & Sat-7 pm, Sun-4 pm. Closed: 11/26, 12/25; also Tues & 12/1-12/15. **Address:** 126 N Hemlock St **Location:** Downtown; in Coaster Square. **Parking:** on-site.

LOCAL GRILL & SCOOP
Phone: 503/436-9551

American
$6-$25

The downtown cafe and soda fountain serves classic breakfasts until 11:30 am, sandwiches for lunch and steak and fish for dinner. Streetside patio seating can be requested seasonally. Casual dress. **Bar:** Beer & wine. **Reservations:** not accepted. **Hours:** 8 am-9 pm; hours may vary in winter. Closed: 11/26, 12/25. **Address:** 156 N Hemlock St **Location:** Downtown. **Parking:** on-site and street. **Cards:** MC, VI.

THE LUMBERYARD ROTISSERIE & GRILL
Phone: 503/436-0285

American
$8-$24

In what once was an old lumber-storage warehouse, this restaurant serves rotisserie sandwiches, pizza and rotisserie chicken, pork, beef and turkey entrees. A stone fireplace, Northwest timber throughout and a concrete bar enhance the decor. Outside dining is a seasonal option. Casual dress. **Bar:** Full bar. **Reservations:** not accepted. **Hours:** 11 am-9 pm; to 10 pm in summer. **Address:** 264 E 3rd St **Location:** US 101, north exit to Ecola State Park, 0.4 mi sw. **Parking:** on-site. **Cards:** AX, DC, DS, MC, VI.

MO'S RESTAURANT
Phone: 503/436-1111

Seafood
$5-$13

An area favorite, this oceanfront spot serves mostly Oregon seafood, including halibut and mollusks fresh from Mo's own oyster beds. A good choice is slumgullion: clam chowder with shrimp. The restaurant's large windows take in the view, and a patio is open in season. Casual dress. **Bar:** Full bar. **Reservations:** not accepted. **Hours:** 8 am-9 pm, Fri & Sat-10 pm; 11 am-8 pm, Fri-9 pm, Sat 8 am-9 pm, Sun 8 am-8 pm in winter. Closed: 11/26, 12/25. **Address:** 195 Warren Way **Location:** US 101, exit Tolovana Park, just w. **Parking:** on-site. **Cards:** AX, DS, MC, VI.

NEWMANS AT 988
Phone: 503/436-1151

Continental
$16-$24

French-Italian fusion dishes are well prepared at this upscale casual restaurant, which occupies a 1910 cottage. The menu changes frequently to reflect fresh seasonal ingredients. Recommended for an appetizer is the lobster ravioli, if available. Dressy casual. **Bar:** Beer & wine. **Reservations:** suggested. **Hours:** 5:30 pm-9 pm. Closed: 1/1, 12/25; also Mon. **Address:** 988 S Hemlock St **Location:** US 101, exit Sunset Blvd, just s. **Parking:** street. **Cards:** MC, VI.

STEPHANIE INN DINING ROOM
Phone: 503/436-2221

American
$59

Located in a beautiful oceanfront inn, the dining room is situated on the second floor and boasts peaceful mountain views. The prix fixe menu changes nightly, with two seating times during the busy summer season and one seating in the quieter season. Meals are based on the seasonal availability of fresh, local ingredients. Dessert is always a delectable finish to a relaxed meal. **Bar:** Full bar. **Hours:** 6 pm & 8:30 pm seatings; 7 pm seating in winter. **Address:** 2740 S Pacific **Location:** US 101, exit Tolovana Park, just w on Warren Way, just n on S Hemlock St, just w on Matanuska St, then just s; in Stephanie Inn. **Parking:** on-site. **Cards:** AX, DC, DS, MC, VI.

WAYFARER RESTAURANT   *Menu on AAA.com*
Phone: 503/436-1108

Steak & Seafood
$7-$34

Enjoy the view of Haystack Rock while dining in this upscale casual establishment. Wayfarer's offers seafood and steak, and has a fine wine list. If you arrive in the summer months, you can enjoy your meal on the outdoor patio. Casual dress. **Bar:** Full bar. **Reservations:** suggested, for dinner. **Hours:** 8 am-11 pm; to 10 pm in winter. **Address:** 1190 Pacific Dr **Location:** US 101, exit Cannon Beach (2nd exit); downtown; across from Surfsand Resort at Cannon Beach. **Parking:** on-site. **Cards:** AX, DC, DS, MC, VI.

CANYONVILLE pop. 1,293

—— WHERE TO STAY ——

BEST WESTERN CANYONVILLE INN & SUITES   *Book great rates at AAA.com*

Phone: (541)839-4200

AAA SAVE

Hotel
$80-$171 All Year

Address: 200 Creekside Dr **Location:** I-5, exit 99, just w. **Facility:** 73 one-bedroom standard units, some with whirlpools. 3 stories, interior corridors. *Bath:* combo or shower only. **Parking:** on-site. **Terms:** cancellation fee imposed. **Amenities:** high-speed Internet, voice mail, irons, hair dryers. **Pool(s):** heated indoor. **Leisure Activities:** whirlpool, exercise room. **Guest Services:** coin laundry, area transportation-casino, wireless Internet. **Business Services:** PC. **Cards:** AX, CB, DC, DS, JC, MC, VI. **Free Special Amenities: expanded continental breakfast and high-speed Internet.**

AAA Benefit:
Members save up to 20%, plus 10% bonus points with rewards program.

Enjoy a monumental vacation with AAA Travel guides.

Purchase AAA publications at participating AAA club offices, on AAA.com/BarnesAndNoble and in fine book stores.

SEVEN FEATHERS HOTEL & CASINO RESORT

Phone: (541)839-1111

Hotel
$109-$275 All Year

Address: 146 Chief Miwaleta Ln **Location:** I-5, exit 99, just e. **Facility:** The resort has impressive public areas and tastefully decorated rooms. 143 one-bedroom standard units. 4 stories, interior corridors. *Bath:* combo or shower only. **Parking:** on-site and valet. **Amenities:** high-speed Internet, voice mail, irons, hair dryers. **Dining:** The Camas Room, see separate listing. **Pool(s):** heated indoor. **Leisure Activities:** sauna, whirlpools, exercise room. *Fee:* game room. **Guest Services:** valet laundry, area transportation, wireless Internet. **Business Services:** meeting rooms, PC. **Cards:** CB, DC, DS, MC, VI.

------ **WHERE TO DINE** ------

THE CAMAS ROOM

Phone: 541/839-1111

American
$38-$55

An extensive wine list complements choices such as rack of lamb, creamy risotto and bacon-wrapped dates with braised cabbage and caramelized apples. A well-trained staff employs cart service inside the elegant dining room. Dressy casual. **Bar:** Full bar. **Reservations:** suggested. **Hours:** 5:30 pm-close; Sunday brunch. Closed: 1/1; also Mon. **Address:** 146 Chief Miwaleta Ln **Location:** I-5, exit 99, just e; in Seven Feathers Hotel & Casino Resort. **Parking:** on-site and valet. **Cards:** AX, MC, VI.

CASCADE LOCKS pop. 1,115

------ **WHERE TO STAY** ------

BEST WESTERN COLUMBIA RIVER INN   *Book great rates at AAA.com*

Phone: (541)374-8777

Hotel
$100-$180 All Year

Address: 735 WaNaPa St (US 30) **Location:** I-84, exit 44 eastbound, 0.4 mi ne; westbound, 1.4 mi nw. **Facility:** 62 one-bedroom standard units, some with whirlpools. 4 stories, interior corridors. *Bath:* combo or shower only. **Parking:** on-site. **Terms:** check-in 4 pm. **Amenities:** high-speed Internet, irons, hair dryers. **Pool(s):** heated indoor. **Leisure Activities:** whirlpool, exercise room. **Guest Services:** coin laundry, wireless Internet. **Business Services:** meeting rooms, PC. **Cards:** AX, CB, DC, DS, JC, MC, VI. **Free Special Amenities:** expanded continental breakfast and high-speed Internet. *(See color ad below)*

AAA Benefit:
Members save up to 20%, plus 10% bonus points with rewards program.

CAVE JUNCTION pop. 1,363

------ **WHERE TO STAY** ------

THE CHATEAU AT THE OREGON CAVES

Phone: (541)592-3400

Hotel
$90-$170 5/15-10/15

Address: 20000 Caves Hwy **Location:** At Oregon Caves National Monument; on SR 46. **Facility:** Smoke free premises. 23 units. 18 one- and 5 two-bedroom standard units. 3 stories (no elevator), interior corridors. *Bath:* combo, shower or tub only. **Parking:** on-site. **Terms:** open 5/15-10/15, 30 day cancellation notice-fee imposed. **Dining:** restaurant, see separate listing. **Leisure Activities:** hiking trails. **Business Services:** meeting rooms, fax. **Cards:** MC, VI.

------ **WHERE TO DINE** ------

CHATEAU AT THE OREGON CAVES

Phone: 541/592-3400

American
$10-$26

Locally grown herbs and vegetables and locally raised meat, poultry and dairy come together in dishes on the seasonal menu. Inside a historic hotel, this restaurant is sure to please the sophisticated palate. Casual dress. **Bar:** Beer & wine. **Reservations:** suggested. **Hours:** Open 5/5-10/29; 5 pm-9 pm. **Address:** 20000 Caves Hwy **Location:** At Oregon Caves National Monument; on SR 46; in The Chateau At The Oregon Caves. **Parking:** on-site. **Cards:** MC, VI.

------ ▼ *See AAA listing above* ▼ ------

THE HISTORIC CAVES DINER & SODA FOUNTAIN　　　　　**Phone: 541/592-3400**

American
$7-$12

This exciting diner serves delicious old-fashioned milk shakes and burgers. But that's not all. Servers, seating and sodas all conjure memories of another era. This spot is great for family fun. Casual dress. **Hours:** Open 5/5-10/29; 7 am-4 pm. **Address:** 20000 Caves Hwy **Location:** At Oregon Caves National Monument; on SR 46; in The Chateau At The Oregon Caves. **Parking:** on-site. **Cards:** MC, VI.

CENTRAL POINT pop. 12,493

———— WHERE TO STAY ————

FAIRFIELD INN & SUITES　　*Book great rates at AAA.com*　　　　　**Phone: (541)665-4141**

Hotel
$125-$153 All Year

Address: 1777 La Rue Dr **Location:** I-5, exit 33, just se. **Facility:** Smoke free premises. 68 one-bedroom standard units, some with whirlpools. 3 stories, interior corridors. *Bath:* combo or shower only. **Parking:** on-site. **Terms:** cancellation fee imposed. **Amenities:** high-speed Internet, voice mail, irons, hair dryers. *Some:* CD players. **Pool(s):** heated indoor. **Leisure Activities:** whirlpool, exercise room. **Guest Services:** valet and coin laundry, wireless Internet. **Business Services:** PC. **Cards:** AX, CB, DC, DS, JC, MC, VI.

AAA Benefit:
Members save a minimum 5% off the best available rate.

HOLIDAY INN EXPRESS HOTEL & SUITES　　*Book at AAA.com*　　　　**Phone: (541)423-1010**

Hotel
$109-$159 All Year

Address: 285 Penninger St **Location:** I-5, exit 33, just se. **Facility:** 84 one-bedroom standard units, some with whirlpools. 3 stories, interior corridors. *Bath:* combo or shower only. **Parking:** on-site. **Terms:** cancellation fee imposed. **Amenities:** video games (fee), high-speed Internet, voice mail, irons, hair dryers. **Pool(s):** heated indoor. **Leisure Activities:** whirlpool, exercise room. **Guest Services:** valet and coin laundry, wireless Internet. **Business Services:** meeting rooms, PC. **Cards:** AX, DC, DS, MC, VI.

SUPER 8 INN & SUITES　　*Book at AAA.com*　　　　　**Phone: (541)664-5888**

Hotel
$90-$135 All Year

Address: 4999 Biddle Rd **Location:** I-5, exit 33, 0.5 mi e. **Facility:** 78 one-bedroom standard units, some with whirlpools. 3 stories, interior corridors. *Bath:* some combo or shower only. **Parking:** on-site. **Terms:** cancellation fee imposed. **Amenities:** high-speed Internet, voice mail, hair dryers. **Pool(s):** heated outdoor. **Leisure Activities:** whirlpool, waterslide. **Guest Services:** coin laundry, wireless Internet. **Business Services:** meeting rooms. **Cards:** AX, CB, DC, DS, JC, MC, VI.

———— WHERE TO DINE ————

MAZATLAN GRILL　　　　　**Phone: 541/665-2582**

Mexican
$8-$17

Tucked in a shopping plaza, the restaurant serves a variety of Mexican dishes, as well as daily lunch specials. Colorful tiles and murals adorn the walls. Casual dress. **Bar:** Full bar. **Reservations:** accepted, except for dinner Fri & Sat. **Hours:** 11 am-9 pm, Fri & Sat-10 pm. Closed: 7/4, 11/26, 12/25. **Address:** 1350 Plaza Blvd, #E **Location:** I-5, exit 33, just w on E Pine St, just s on Freeman St, then just e; in Mountain View Plaza. **Parking:** on-site. **Cards:** AX, DS, MC, VI.

CHARLESTON

———— WHERE TO DINE ————

OYSTER COVE GRILLE & BAR　　　　　**Phone: 541/888-0703**

Regional American
$16-$30

Within walking distance of the waterfront, this restaurant offers great seafood and steaks in a pleasant setting. The staff is friendly, and those who order creme brulee get to meet the chef. Casual dress. **Bar:** Full bar. **Reservations:** accepted. **Hours:** 5 pm-9 pm; seasonal hours vary. Closed: 11/26, 12/25; also Sun & Mon. **Address:** 63346 Boat Basin Rd **Location:** Center. **Parking:** on-site. **Cards:** MC, VI.

THE PORTSIDE SEAFOOD RESTAURANT　　　　　**Phone: 541/888-5544**

Seafood
$9-$35

Greenery, soft music and tables overlooking the boat basin mingle to create a comfortable ambience at this pier restaurant. An extensive selection of fresh, local seafood items, most notably crab dishes, line the menu. A buffet is served on Friday. Casual dress. **Bar:** Full bar. **Reservations:** suggested. **Hours:** 11:30 am-11 pm; to 9 pm in winter. **Address:** 63383 Kingfisher Rd **Location:** 0.3 mi w; at Charleston Small Boat Basin. **Parking:** on-site. **Cards:** AX, CB, DC, MC, VI.

CLACKAMAS —*See Portland p. 456.*

CLATSKANIE pop. 1,528

——— WHERE TO STAY ———

CLATSKANIE RIVER INN   *Book great rates at AAA.com*   Phone: (503)728-9000

(AAA) (SAVE)   **Address:** 600 E Columbia River Hwy (US 30) **Location:** On US 30. **Facility:** 40 units. 39 one-
◆◆◆ ◆◆◆   bedroom standard units. 1 one-bedroom suite with kitchen and whirlpool. 3 stories, interior corridors.
                       Parking: on-site. **Terms:** cancellation fee imposed. **Amenities:** high-speed Internet, voice mail, irons,
Hotel   hair dryers. **Pool(s):** heated indoor. **Leisure Activities:** whirlpool. **Guest Services:** coin laundry,
$89-$149 All Year   wireless Internet. **Business Services:** meeting rooms, PC. **Cards:** AX, DC, DS, MC, VI. **Free Special**
                       Amenities: continental breakfast and high-speed Internet.

CONDON pop. 759

——— WHERE TO STAY ———

——— *The following lodging was either not evaluated or did not* ———
meet AAA rating requirements but is listed for your information only.

HOTEL CONDON   Phone: 541/384-4624
(fyi)   Not evaluated. **Address:** 202 S Main St **Location:** I-84, exit 137, 40 mi s on SR 19; downtown.
                Facilities, services, and decor characterize a mid-scale property.

COOS BAY pop. 15,374

——— WHERE TO STAY ———

BEST WESTERN HOLIDAY MOTEL   *Book great rates at AAA.com*   Phone: (541)269-5111

(AAA) (SAVE)   **Address:** 411 N Bayshore Dr **Location:** Just n of downtown on US 101.
◆◆◆ ◆◆◆   **Facility:** 83 units. 80 one- and 2 two-bedroom standard units, some with
                       kitchens and/or whirlpools. 1 one-bedroom suite with kitchen. 2 stories (no
Hotel   elevator), interior/exterior corridors. *Bath:* combo or shower only. **Parking:**   **AAA Benefit:**
$99-$159 All Year   on-site. **Amenities:** high-speed Internet, voice mail, irons, hair dryers.   Members save up to
                       Pool(s): heated indoor. **Leisure Activities:** whirlpool, exercise room.   20%, plus 10%
                       Guest Services: coin laundry, wireless Internet. **Business Services:** PC,   bonus points with
                       fax. **Cards:** AX, CB, DC, DS, JC, MC, VI. **Free Special Amenities:**   rewards program.
                       expanded continental breakfast and high-speed Internet.

RED LION HOTEL COOS BAY   *Book great rates at AAA.com*   Phone: (541)267-4141

(AAA) (SAVE)   **Address:** 1313 N Bayshore Dr **Location:** 0.5 mi n of downtown on US
◆◆◆ ◆◆◆   101. **Facility:** Smoke free premises. 145 units. 137 one- and 7 two-
                       bedroom standard units. 1 one-bedroom suite. 1-2 stories (no elevator),
Hotel   exterior corridors. *Bath:* combo or shower only. **Parking:** on-site. **Terms:**
$104-$156 All Year   cancellation fee imposed. **Amenities:** video games (fee), high-speed
                       Internet, voice mail, irons, hair dryers. *Some:* dual phone lines.
                       Pool(s): heated outdoor. **Leisure Activities:** whirlpool, exercise room.
                       Guest Services: valet and coin laundry, airport transportation-North
                       Bend Airport, wireless Internet. **Business Services:** meeting rooms.
                       Cards: AX, CB, DC, DS, MC, VI. **Free Special Amenities:** local
                       telephone calls and newspaper. *(See color ad p 324)*

▼ See AAA listing p 389 ▼

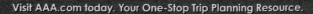

——— WHERE TO DINE ———

BENETTI'S ITALIAN RESTAURANT
Phone: 541/267-6066

The casual, comfortable family restaurant serves nightly seafood specials, homemade items and pasta imported from Italy. Casual dress. **Bar:** Full bar. **Reservations:** suggested. **Hours:** 5 pm-9 pm, Fri & Sat-10 pm; to 9:30 pm, Fri & Sat-10 pm in summer. Closed major holidays. **Address:** 260 S Broadway **Location:** On US 101; downtown. **Parking:** street. **Cards:** AX, MC, VI.

Italian
$8-$22

BLUE HERON BISTRO
Phone: 541/267-3933

Overlooking Coos Bay and its waterfront boardwalk, the restaurant presents a wide and varied menu of schnitzel, brats, warm French potato salad or seafood stew. All portions are large and a great value, and the staff is warm and fun. Casual dress. **Bar:** Full bar. **Reservations:** accepted. **Hours:** 11 am-9 pm, Sat from noon, Sun noon-8 pm. **Address:** 100 W Commercial Ave **Location:** On US 101; downtown. **Parking:** street. **Cards:** AX, MC, VI.

Regional
European
$7-$15

CITY SUBS
Phone: 541/269-9000

Guests can order from the full breakfast menu all day, except during the lunch rush. Submarine sandwiches are made on fresh bread baked daily on the premises. Fresh salads and wraps are available, too. Casual dress. **Hours:** 8 am-7 pm, Sat 10 am-4 pm. Closed major holidays; also Sun. **Address:** 149 N 4th St **Location:** Just w of US 101; downtown. **Parking:** on-site. **Cards:** AX, MC, VI.

Deli
$5-$7

COQUILLE pop. 4,184

——— WHERE TO STAY ———

MYRTLE LANE MOTEL
Phone: 541/396-2102

Address: 787 N Central Blvd **Location:** SR 42, 0.4 mi n. **Facility:** 25 units. 23 one- and 2 two-bedroom standard units, some with kitchens, 1 story, exterior corridors. *Bath:* combo or shower only. **Parking:** on-site. **Terms:** office hours 7 am-10 pm. **Leisure Activities:** basketball. **Business Services:** fax (fee).

Motel
Rates not provided

CORVALLIS pop. 49,322

——— WHERE TO STAY ———

BEST WESTERN GRAND MANOR INN & SUITES
Book great rates at AAA.com
Phone: (541)758-8571

Address: 925 NW Garfield Ave **Location:** Jct SR 34 and US 20, just w on NW Harrison Blvd, 1.4 mi n on NW 9th St, then just w. **Facility:** Smoke free premises. 55 units. 52 one-bedroom standard units. 3 one-bedroom suites. 3 stories, interior corridors. *Bath:* combo or shower only. **Parking:** on-site. **Terms:** 7 day cancellation notice-fee imposed. **Amenities:** high-speed Internet, voice mail, irons, hair dryers. **Pool(s):** heated outdoor. **Leisure Activities:** sauna, exercise room. **Guest Services:** valet and coin laundry, wireless Internet. **Business Services:** meeting rooms, PC. **Cards:** AX, CB, DC, DS, JC, MC, VI. **Free Special Amenities:** full breakfast and high-speed Internet.

Hotel
$100-$200 3/1-11/30
$90-$190 12/1-2/28

AAA Benefit:
Members save up to 20%, plus 10% bonus points with rewards program.

DAYS INN
Book great rates at AAA.com
Phone: (541)754-7474

Address: 1113 NW 9th St **Location:** Jct SR 34 and US 20, just w on NW Harrison Blvd, then 1 mi n. **Facility:** 76 one-bedroom standard units. 3 stories, interior corridors. **Parking:** on-site. **Terms:** cancellation fee imposed. **Amenities:** high-speed Internet, hair dryers. *Some:* irons. **Pool(s):** heated outdoor. **Leisure Activities:** limited exercise equipment. **Guest Services:** valet laundry, wireless Internet. **Business Services:** meeting rooms, PC. **Cards:** AX, DC, DS, JC, MC, VI. **Free Special Amenities:** expanded continental breakfast and room upgrade (subject to availability with advance reservations).

Hotel
$70-$169 3/1-9/15
$59-$145 9/16-2/28

HARRISON HOUSE BED & BREAKFAST
Phone: (541)752-6248

Address: 2310 NW Harrison Blvd **Location:** Jct SR 34 and US 20; 1 mi w of downtown. **Facility:** The restored 1939 Dutch Colonial home furnished with Williamsburg-style antiques is accented by an English cottage garden. Complimentary evening wine. Smoke free premises. 5 units. 4 one-bedroom standard units. 1 cottage. 2 stories, interior corridors. *Bath:* combo or shower only. **Parking:** on-site. **Terms:** office hours 7 am-10 pm, check-in 4 pm, 7 day cancellation notice-fee imposed. **Amenities:** video library, DVD players, high-speed Internet, irons, hair dryers. **Guest Services:** wireless Internet. **Business Services:** PC. **Cards:** AX, CB, DC, DS, JC, MC, VI.

Bed & Breakfast
$125 All Year

HILTON GARDEN INN

Book great rates at AAA.com

Phone: (541)752-5000

Hotel
$99-$219 All Year

Address: 2500 SW Western Blvd **Location:** Jct SR 34 and US 20, just w on NW Harrison Blvd, 0.6 mi s on NW 4th St, then 0.8 mi w. Located on the Oregon State University Campus. **Facility:** Smoke free premises. 153 units. 148 one-bedroom standard units. 5 one-bedroom suites, some with whirlpools. 4 stories, interior corridors. *Bath:* combo or shower only. **Parking:** on-site. **Terms:** 1-30 night minimum stay, cancellation fee imposed. **Amenities:** video games (fee), high-speed Internet, dual phone lines, voice mail, irons, hair dryers. **Pool(s):** heated indoor. **Leisure Activities:** whirlpool, exercise room. **Guest Services:** valet and coin laundry, wireless Internet. **Business Services:** meeting rooms, business center. **Cards:** AX, CB, DC, DS, JC, MC, VI.

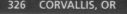
Hilton
Garden Inn

AAA Benefit:
Members save 5% or more everyday!

HOLIDAY INN EXPRESS ON THE RIVER

Book great rates at AAA.com

Phone: (541)752-0800

Hotel
$70-$209 3/1-10/31
$70-$109 11/1-2/28

Address: 781 NE 2nd St **Location:** Jct SR 34 and US 20, 0.4 mi n. **Facility:** Smoke free premises. 93 one-bedroom standard units, some with whirlpools. 3 stories, interior corridors. *Bath:* combo or shower only. **Parking:** on-site. **Terms:** cancellation fee imposed. **Amenities:** high-speed Internet, dual phone lines, voice mail, irons, hair dryers. *Some:* DVD players. **Pool(s):** heated indoor. **Leisure Activities:** whirlpool, exercise room. **Guest Services:** valet and coin laundry, wireless Internet. **Business Services:** meeting rooms, business center. **Cards:** AX, DS, MC, VI.

MOTEL 6 #4243

Book great rates at AAA.com

Phone: (541)758-9125

Hotel
$55-$99 All Year

Address: 935 NW Garfield Ave **Location:** Jct SR 34 and US 20, just w on NW Harrison Blvd, 1.4 mi n on NW 9th St, then just w. **Facility:** 61 one-bedroom standard units. 3 stories (no elevator), interior corridors. *Bath:* combo or shower only. **Parking:** on-site. **Amenities:** high-speed Internet. **Leisure Activities:** whirlpool. **Guest Services:** coin laundry, wireless Internet. **Cards:** AX, DC, DS, MC, VI. **Free Special Amenities: local telephone calls and high-speed Internet.**

SALBASGEON SUITES & CONFERENCE CENTER

Book great rates at AAA.com

Phone: (541)753-4320

Hotel
$120-$220 All Year

Address: 1730 NW 9th St **Location:** Jct SR 34 and US 20, just w on NW Harrison Blvd, then 1.4 mi n. Located across from Cinema. **Facility:** Smoke free premises. 95 units. 90 one-bedroom standard units, some with kitchens and/or whirlpools. 4 one- and 1 two-bedroom suites with kitchens and whirlpools. 3 stories, interior corridors. *Bath:* combo or shower only. **Parking:** on-site. **Amenities:** video games (fee), high-speed Internet, voice mail, irons, hair dryers. **Pool(s):** heated indoor. **Leisure Activities:** sauna, whirlpool, sun deck, exercise room. **Guest Services:** valet and coin laundry, wireless Internet. **Business Services:** conference facilities, business center. **Cards:** AX, DC, DS, MC, VI. **Free Special Amenities: expanded continental breakfast and high-speed Internet.**

SUPER 8

Book at AAA.com

Phone: 541/758-8088

Hotel
Rates not provided

Address: 407 NW 2nd St **Location:** US 20, just n of jct SR 34; downtown. **Facility:** 101 one-bedroom standard units. 3 stories, interior corridors. *Bath:* combo or shower only. **Parking:** on-site. **Amenities:** high-speed Internet, safes (fee), hair dryers. **Pool(s):** heated indoor. **Leisure Activities:** whirlpool. **Guest Services:** valet and coin laundry, wireless Internet. **Business Services:** meeting rooms, PC.

--- **WHERE TO DINE** ---

101

American
$10-$17

Phone: 541/757-0694

With an upscale lounge feel but still featuring a few strategically placed TVs for those who can't spare a minute from being tuned in to sports, this place satisfies with a wide-reaching menu. Patrons often gather after work or in the evening for appetizer "snacks," small plates and a few big entrees. Choices range from duck quesadillas, sliders, salmon corn dogs and pulled pork nachos to Dungeness crab, mac 'n' cheese and rabbit pappardelle. Casual dress. **Bar:** Full bar. **Reservations:** not accepted. **Hours:** 4:30 pm-10 pm, Thurs-Sat to midnight. Closed major holidays; also Sun. **Address:** 101 NW Jackson Ave **Location:** Jct NW 1st St; near riverfront; downtown. **Parking:** on-site. **Cards:** AX, MC, VI.

BIG RIVER RESTAURANT & BAR

American
$10-$25

Phone: 541/757-0694

Fresh fish, pasta and vegetarian entrees utilize ingredients found in the Willamette Valley and off the Oregon coast. Rustic artisan breads are baked on the premises. Daily specials and seasonal menu changes maximize the taste of the food. Casual dress. **Bar:** Full bar. **Hours:** 11 am-2 & 5-9:30 pm, Fri-11:30 pm, Sat 5 pm-11:30 pm. Closed: 12/24, 12/25; also Sun. **Address:** 101 NW Jackson Ave **Location:** Jct NW 1st St; near riverfront; downtown. **Parking:** on-site. **Cards:** AX, DC, MC, VI.

BLOCK 15 RESTAURANT & BREWERY

American
$7-$12

Phone: 541/758-2077

Located right downtown, the newest brewpub in town offers about 10 taps of fresh-made beers. The spot is popular with the college crowd and locals for "hoppy" hour, when prices are discounted on appetizers and pints. The menu includes pasta, burgers and sandwiches along with several salads thrown in for a healthy choice. Casual dress. **Bar:** Full bar. **Reservations:** not accepted. **Hours:** 11 am-11 pm, Thurs-Sat to 1 am. Closed: 11/26, 12/25. **Address:** 300 SW Jefferson Ave **Location:** Southwest corner of Jefferson Ave and 3rd St; downtown. **Parking:** street. **Cards:** AX, DS, MC, VI.

IOVINO'S RISTORANTE
Phone: 541/738-9015

Italian
$8-$28

Homemade Italian specialties are served in a casual, uptown atmosphere, which is enhanced by live music on Saturdays. Patio seating is a seasonal option. Casual dress. **Bar:** Full bar. **Reservations:** suggested. **Hours:** 11:30 am-9 pm, Sun from 5 pm. Closed major holidays. **Address:** 136 SW Washington Ave **Location:** Jct SW 1st St; near riverfront; downtown. **Parking:** street. **Cards:** AX, MC, VI.

LE BISTRO
Phone: 541/754-6680

French
$21-$28

In a 1927 building that once was a hotel, the recently renovated restaurant entices patrons with fine country French cuisine in an intimate atmosphere. On the menu are classics such as coq au vin, as well as several meat and fish entrees prepared with light, delicious sauces. Specials are offered daily. Casual dress. **Bar:** Full bar. **Reservations:** suggested. **Hours:** 5 pm-close, Sun from 4:30 pm. Closed: 1/1; 11/26, 12/25. **Address:** 150 SW Madison Ave **Location:** Just e of jct 3rd St and SW Madison Ave; downtown. **Parking:** on-site and street. **Cards:** AX, DS, MC, VI.

MCGRATH'S FISH HOUSE
Phone: 541/752-3474

Seafood
$9-$19

The popular chain specializes in fresh Pacific Northwest seafood, including dishes grilled over a wood fire and items from the daily fresh sheet. Also on the menu are steaks, chicken, pasta and gourmet burgers. Casual dress. **Bar:** Full bar. **Hours:** 11 am-10 pm. Closed: 11/26, 12/25. **Address:** 350 Circle Blvd **Location:** Just e of SR 99; north end of town. **Parking:** on-site. **Cards:** AX, DC, DS, MC, VI.

MCMENAMINS
Phone: 541/758-0080

American
$5-$20

The casual neighborhood eatery is where friends gather for classic pub and comfort fare, all washed down by pints of locally made beer. Large wooden booths or tables easily accommodate larger groups, and the eclectic, custom-painted walls and varied period light fixtures keep diners' eyes busy should the conversation lag. Casual dress. **Bar:** Full bar. **Reservations:** not accepted. **Hours:** 11 am-midnight, Wed-1 am, Thurs-Sat to 2 am, Sun noon-midnight. Closed: 11/26, 12/25. **Address:** 2001 NW Monroe Ave **Location:** Jct SR 34 and US 20, 0.8 mi w on NW Harrison Blvd, just s on NW Kings Blvd, then just w. **Parking:** street. **Cards:** MC, VI.

MCMENAMINS
Phone: 541/758-6044

American
$5-$20

The casual neighborhood eatery is where friends gather for classic pub and comfort fare, all washed down by pints of locally made beer. Large wooden booths or tables easily accommodate larger groups, and the eclectic, custom-painted walls and varied period light fixtures keep diners' eyes busy should the conversation lag. Casual dress. **Bar:** Full bar. **Hours:** 11 am-1 am, Sun noon-midnight, Mon 11 am-midnight. Closed: 11/26, 12/25. **Address:** 420 NW 3rd St **Location:** US 20, just w of jct SR 34; downtown. **Parking:** on-site. **Cards:** MC, VI.

MICHAEL'S LANDING
Phone: 541/754-6141

American
$8-$25

In what was a train station in 1909, the historic restaurant offers views of the Willamette River. The extensive menu tempts every palate, with everything from steak and seafood to chicken and creative pasta dishes. Guests can top off dinner with a delightful dessert. Casual dress. **Bar:** Full bar. **Reservations:** accepted. **Hours:** 11:30 am-9 pm, Fri & Sat-9:30 pm, Sun 10 am-8:30 pm. Closed: 12/25. **Address:** 603 NW 2nd St **Location:** On US 20, just n of jct SR 34. **Parking:** on-site. **Cards:** AX, DC, DS, MC, VI. **Historic**

NEW MORNING BAKERY
Phone: 541/754-0181

American
$5-$7

Lots of yummy baked goods, cakes, bread and desserts are prepared on site, as are salads, soups and daily special entrees, such as lasagna or quiche. Casual dress. **Bar:** Beer & wine. **Reservations:** not accepted. **Hours:** 7 am-9 pm, Fri & Sat-10 pm, Sun 8 am-8 pm. Closed major holidays. **Address:** 219 SW 2nd St **Location:** Just s of jct SW Madison Ave; downtown. **Parking:** street. **Cards:** AX, DS, MC, VI.

COTTAGE GROVE pop. 8,445

———— WHERE TO STAY ————

COMFORT INN
Book great rates at AAA.com
Phone: (541)942-9747

Hotel
$64-$150 All Year

Address: 845 Gateway Blvd **Location:** I-5, exit 174, just w. **Facility:** 64 one-bedroom standard units, some with whirlpools. 2 stories (no elevator), interior/exterior corridors. **Parking:** on-site. **Terms:** check-in 4 pm, 2 night minimum stay - seasonal and/or weekends. **Amenities:** voice mail, irons, hair dryers. *Some:* high-speed Internet. **Pool(s):** heated outdoor. **Leisure Activities:** whirlpool. **Guest Services:** coin laundry, wireless Internet. **Business Services:** meeting rooms. **Cards:** AX, DS, MC, VI. **Free Special Amenities: continental breakfast and high-speed Internet.**

HOLIDAY INN EXPRESS
Book great rates at AAA.com
Phone: (541)942-1000

Hotel
$109-$129 3/1-10/1
$99-$109 10/2-2/28

Address: 1601 Gateway Blvd **Location:** I-5, exit 174, just w. **Facility:** 41 one-bedroom standard units. 2 stories (no elevator), interior corridors. *Bath:* combo or shower only. **Parking:** on-site. **Amenities:** high-speed Internet, voice mail, irons, hair dryers. **Pool(s):** heated indoor. **Leisure Activities:** whirlpool, exercise room. **Guest Services:** coin laundry, wireless Internet. **Business Services:** business center. **Cards:** AX, CB, DC, DS, JC, MC, VI. **Free Special Amenities: expanded continental breakfast and high-speed Internet.**

COVE pop. 594

─── WHERE TO DINE ───

COVE TAVERN & STEAKHOUSE   Phone: 541/568-4716

◆◆ ◆◆

American
$5-$17

This simple eatery and bar is best known for the steak meals. Decor and service are simple, while the steaks are tender and juicy. Worth a trip off of the interstate if you're passing through this part of Oregon. Casual dress. **Bar:** Full bar. **Hours:** 11 am-9:30 pm. Closed: Mon. **Address:** 505 Main St **Location:** Downtown. **Parking:** on-site. **Cards:** MC, VI.

CRATER LAKE

─── WHERE TO STAY ───

THE CABINS AT MAZAMA VILLAGE   Phone: 541/594-2255

▼

Motel
Rates not provided

Address: 700 Mazama Village Dr **Location:** 7 mi s of Rim Village; at south entrance. **Facility:** Smoke free premises. 40 one-bedroom standard units. 1 story, exterior corridors. *Bath:* shower only. **Parking:** on-site. **Terms:** open 6/1-10/1, check-in 4 pm. **Leisure Activities:** hiking trails. **Guest Services:** coin laundry.

🍽 ✕ 🅧 🄿 🅉 💻

CRATER LAKE LODGE   Phone: 541/594-2255

▼▼ ▼▼

Classic Historic
Hotel
$125-$275   5/23-10/15

Address: 565 Rim Village Dr **Location:** At Rim Village. **Facility:** This 1915 lodge adjacent to Crater Lake has a great hall with timber supports and a stone fireplace, and many of the rooms have a view of the lake. Smoke free premises. 71 units. 68 one-bedroom standard units. 3 one-bedroom suites. 4 stories, interior corridors. *Bath:* combo or tub only. **Parking:** on-site. **Terms:** open 5/23-10/15, check-in 4 pm, cancellation fee imposed. **Amenities:** CD players. **Dining:** restaurant, see separate listing. **Leisure Activities:** hiking trails. **Cards:** AX, MC, VI.

🍽 CALL 🄻🄼 ✕ 🅧 🄿 🅉

─── WHERE TO DINE ───

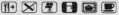

CRATER LAKE LODGE   Phone: 541/594-1184

◆◆ ◆◆

American
$9-$29

Dine at the lodge and admire the views of the lake while sampling selections from the varied menu. Casual dress. **Bar:** Full bar. **Reservations:** required, for dinner. **Hours:** Open 5/25-10/16; 7-10:30 am, 11:30-2 & 5-10 pm. **Address:** 565 Rim Village Dr **Location:** At Rim Village; in Crater Lake Lodge. **Parking:** on-site. **Cards:** AX, CB, DC, DS, JC, MC, VI.

CALL 🄻🄼 🅧

CRESCENT

─── WHERE TO STAY ───

THE WOODSMAN COUNTRY LODGE   Phone: 541/433-2710

🆎🆎 SAVE
◆◆ ◆◆

Motel
$80-$85   All Year

Address: 136740 Hwy 97 **Location:** Center. **Facility:** Smoke free premises. 15 units. 13 one-bedroom standard units. 2 one-bedroom suites, some with whirlpools. 1 story, exterior corridors. **Terms:** office hours 8 am-10 pm. **Amenities:** safes, irons, hair dryers. **Guest Services:** wireless Internet. **Cards:** AX, DS, MC, VI. Free **Special Amenities:** newspaper and high-speed Internet. *(See color ad below)*

🍽➜ ✕ 🎣 🔋 💼 💻

------ **WHERE TO DINE** ------

MOHAWK RESTAURANT & LOUNGE　　　　　　　　　　　**Phone:** 541/433-2256

American
$8-$22

In operation since the 1930s, this restaurant serves affordable home-style cooking in an informal setting. Hot and cold sandwiches, salads, burgers and steaks make up the menu. The distinctive decor incorporates a knotty pine ceiling, a glass case housing a collection of more than 1,500 bottles, and varied taxidermy mounts, including baby fawns and black bear cubs, on the walls. Casual dress. **Bar:** Full bar. **Reservations:** not accepted. **Hours:** 7 am-9 pm; to 10 pm in summer. **Address:** 136726 Hwy 97 N **Location:** Center. **Parking:** on-site. **Cards:** MC, VI.

CRESWELL pop. 3,479

------ **WHERE TO STAY** ------

SUPER 8 CRESWELL INN　　*Book great rates at AAA.com*　　　　**Phone:** (541)895-3341

Motel
$55-$80 All Year

Address: 345 E Oregon Ave **Location:** I-5, exit 182, just w. **Facility:** 70 units. 68 one-bedroom standard units, some with whirlpools. 2 one-bedroom suites with whirlpools. 2 stories (no elevator), exterior corridors. **Parking:** on-site. **Amenities:** irons, hair dryers. *Some:* high-speed Internet. **Pool(s):** outdoor. **Guest Services:** wireless Internet. **Business Services:** PC. **Cards:** AX, DS, MC, VI. **Free Special Amenities: continental breakfast and high-speed Internet.**

DALLAS pop. 12,459

------ **WHERE TO STAY** ------

BEST WESTERN DALLAS INN & SUITES　　*Book great rates at AAA.com*　　　**Phone:** (503)623-6000

Hotel
$90-$130 All Year

Address: 250 Orchard Dr **Location:** SR 223, just n. **Facility:** 42 one-bedroom standard units, some with whirlpools. 2 stories (no elevator), interior corridors. *Bath:* combo or shower only. **Parking:** on-site. **Amenities:** high-speed Internet, irons, hair dryers. **Leisure Activities:** whirlpool, exercise room. **Guest Services:** wireless Internet. **Business Services:** PC. **Cards:** AX, CB, DC, DS, JC, MC, VI.

AAA Benefit:
Members save up to
20%, plus 10%
bonus points with
rewards program.

------ **WHERE TO DINE** ------

ALTHEA'S TEA ROOM　　　　　　　　　　　　**Phone:** 503/831-4777

Specialty
$6-$16

Refined lighter fare includes sandwiches, salads and soups, in addition to such afternoon tea staples as tea sandwiches, savories and scones served with a good selection of teas. Casual dress. **Reservations:** suggested. **Hours:** 10 am-3 pm, Mon 11 am-2:30 pm. Closed major holidays; also Sun. **Address:** 184 SE Oak St **Location:** Jct SE Jefferson St; center. **Parking:** street. **Cards:** MC, VI.

MURPHY'S GRILL　　　　　　　　　　　　　**Phone:** 503/623-1211

American
$6-$22

Modestly prepared sandwiches, seafood, steak and pasta are served at the eatery. Casual dress. **Bar:** Full bar. **Reservations:** accepted. **Hours:** 10:30 am-10 pm, Sat & Sun from 7 am. Closed: 11/26, 12/25. **Address:** 288 E Ellendale Ave **Location:** Just e of jct SR 223 and E Ellendale Ave. **Parking:** on-site. **Cards:** MC, VI.

DEPOE BAY pop. 1,174

------ **WHERE TO STAY** ------

CROWN PACIFIC INN　　*Book great rates at AAA.com*　　　　**Phone:** (541)765-7773

Motel
$75-$95 All Year

Address: 50 NE Bechill St **Location:** Just n of downtown. **Facility:** 31 one-bedroom standard units, some with whirlpools. 3 stories, interior/exterior corridors. **Parking:** office hours 8 am-10 pm. **Amenities:** high-speed Internet, hair dryers. **Leisure Activities:** whirlpool. **Guest Services:** wireless Internet. **Cards:** MC, VI. **Free Special Amenities: continental breakfast and high-speed Internet.**

HARBOR LIGHTS　　　　　　　　　　　　　**Phone:** (541)765-2322

Country Inn
$109-$189 All Year

Address: 235 SE Bay View Ave **Location:** US 101, 0.3 mi se. **Facility:** Smoke free premises. 13 one-bedroom standard units, some with whirlpools. 3 stories (no elevator), interior corridors. **Parking:** on-site. **Terms:** office hours 7:30 am-8 pm, check-in 3:30 pm, 2 night minimum stay - seasonal and/or weekends, 7 day cancellation notice-fee imposed. **Amenities:** video library, DVD players, high-speed Internet, irons. **Guest Services:** wireless Internet. **Business Services:** meeting rooms. **Cards:** AX, DS, MC, VI.

SURFRIDER RESORT

 [AAA] [SAVE]

▼▼ ▼▼

Hotel

$119-$199 All Year

Phone: 541/764-2311

Address: 3115 NW US 101 **Location:** Oceanfront. 2 mi n of Depoe Bay. **Facility:** Smoke free premises. 55 units. 39 one-bedroom standard units, some with whirlpools. 8 one- and 4 two-bedroom suites, some with kitchens. 4 cottages. 3 stories (no elevator), exterior corridors. *Bath:* combo or shower only. **Parking:** on-site. **Terms:** office hours 8 am-10 pm, check-in 4 pm, 2 night minimum stay, 3 day cancellation notice-fee imposed. **Amenities:** video library (fee), DVD players, high-speed Internet, hair dryers. **Pool(s):** heated indoor. **Leisure Activities:** sauna, whirlpool, beach access, limited exercise equipment. *Fee:* game room. **Guest Services:** coin laundry, wireless Internet. **Business Services:** meeting rooms, PC. **Cards:** AX, DS, MC, VI. **Free Special Amenities:** early check-in/late check-out and high-speed Internet.

[🍴] [🍽] [🏊] [✕] [✕] [🐾] [📶] [🖥] [☕] / SOME UNITS FEE [🐕]

——— WHERE TO DINE ———

GRACIE'S SEA HAG INC

▼▼ ▼▼

Seafood

$8-$35

Phone: 541/765-2734

The landmark restaurant has remained popular with locals for 40 years. Its menu focuses mostly on seafood, such as grilled Oregon oysters, but it also dabbles in steak and sandwiches. Stained-glass windows are an attractive touch in the cozy dining room. The Friday seafood buffet lays out a great selection. Casual dress. **Bar:** Full bar. **Reservations:** not accepted. **Hours:** 8 am-10 pm; 10 am-9 pm 9/1-6/30. Closed: 12/25. **Address:** 58 E US 101 **Location:** Center. **Parking:** on-site. **Cards:** AX, DS, MC, VI.

[◥]

TIDAL RAVES

▼▼ ▼▼

Seafood

$7-$21

Phone: 541/765-2995

Some fine-dining touches and a splendid beach and ocean view are part of the attraction at the cliffside cafe. Well-prepared seafood is the specialty of the house, and a selection of fine wines is available. Casual dress. **Bar:** Beer & wine. **Reservations:** suggested. **Hours:** 11 am-9 pm. Closed: 11/26, 12/24, 12/25; also 1/1-1/14. **Address:** 279 NW US 101 **Location:** Center. **Parking:** on-site. **Cards:** AX, MC, VI.

DIAMOND

——— WHERE TO STAY ———

——— *The following lodging was either not evaluated or did not* ———
meet AAA rating requirements but is listed for your information only.

HOTEL DIAMOND

[fyi]

Phone: 541/493-1898

Not evaluated. **Address:** 10 Main St **Location:** Center. Facilities, services, and decor characterize an economy property.

DUNDEE pop. 2,598

——— WHERE TO DINE ———

THE DUNDEE BISTRO

▼▼▼▼

American

$12-$24

Phone: 503/554-1650

In the heart of Oregon's wine country, the restaurant centers its menu on the cuisine of the Willamette Valley. Organic ingredients are of the highest quality. Among regional favorites are roasted butternut squash soup and tandoor-roasted Oregon quail served with pumpkin puree, Blue Lake beans, watercress-currant vinaigrette and cherry-smoked portobello-shallot risotto. Contemporary Northwest decor marks a dining space that includes a cozy fireplace and an exhibition kitchen with a tandoor oven. Casual dress. **Bar:** Full bar. **Reservations:** suggested. **Hours:** 11:30 am-9 pm. Closed: 1/1, 11/26, 12/25. **Address:** 100-A SW Seventh St **Location:** SR 99 and Seventh St; center. **Parking:** on-site. **Cards:** AX, MC, VI.

CALL [♿M]

TINA'S RESTAURANT

▼▼▼▼

Provincial French

$11-$36

Phone: 503/538-8880

Surrounded by some of Oregon's beautiful vineyards, the recently renovated restaurant prepares fresh Northwestern foods with a country French flair. Salmon spring rolls with hazelnut sauce is a delectable appetizer. A double-sided fireplace separates the two intimate dining rooms and adds to the charm. Casual dress. **Bar:** Full bar. **Reservations:** suggested. **Hours:** 11:30 am-2 & 5-9 pm, Sat-Mon from 5 pm. Closed major holidays. **Address:** 760 Hwy 99 W **Location:** Center. **Parking:** on-site. **Cards:** AX, DS, MC, VI.

ELSIE

——— WHERE TO DINE ———

CAMP 18 RESTAURANT

▼▼ ▼▼

American

$5-$23

Phone: 503/755-1818

Travelers on their way to the Oregon coast should make the log cabin-style complex a stop on their itinerary. In the main dining room is a huge natural-rock fireplace and an awesome 85-foot ridge pole supporting the roof beams. At 25 tons, it is thought to be the largest in the country. Logger-style meals include steaks, seafood, pasta, burgers and hot and cold sandwiches. Breakfast is served until 2 pm. Restored old logging equipment is on display at the camp. Casual dress. **Bar:** Full bar. **Hours:** 7 am-8 pm, Fri & Sat-9 pm. Closed: 12/25. **Address:** 42362 US 26 **Location:** On US 26 at Milepost 18; 22 mi from Seaside/Cannon Beach. **Parking:** on-site. **Cards:** AX, DS, MC, VI.

ENTERPRISE pop. 1,895

──────── **WHERE TO STAY** ────────

BEST WESTERN RAMA INN & SUITES   *Book great rates at AAA.com*

Phone: (541)426-2000

(AAA) (SAVE)
▼▼ ▼▼
Hotel
$100-$110 3/1-9/30
$75-$85 10/1-2/28

Address: 1200 Highland Ave **Location:** 0.5 mi w on SR 82. **Facility:** 53 units. 41 one-bedroom standard units, some with whirlpools. 12 one-bedroom suites. 2 stories (no elevator), interior corridors. *Bath:* combo or shower only. **Parking:** on-site. **Terms:** cancellation fee imposed. **Amenities:** high-speed Internet, irons, hair dryers. **Pool(s):** heated indoor. **Leisure Activities:** sauna, whirlpool, exercise room. **Guest Services:** coin laundry, wireless Internet. **Business Services:** meeting rooms, PC. **Cards:** AX, DC, DS, MC, VI. **Free Special Amenities:** expanded continental breakfast and high-speed Internet.

AAA Benefit:
Members save up to 20%, plus 10% bonus points with rewards program.

🔌 ⊠ 🐾 🛢 🖨 🖥 / SOME UNITS ⊠

PONDEROSA MOTEL

Phone: (541)426-3186

▼▼ ▼▼
Motel
$56-$79 11/1-2/28
$65-$72 3/1-10/31

Address: 102 E Greenwood St **Location:** Center. Located across from the courthouse. **Facility:** 33 units. 32 one- and 1 two-bedroom standard units. 2 stories (no elevator), exterior corridors. **Parking:** on-site. **Terms:** office hours 7 am-10 pm. **Amenities:** high-speed Internet. **Guest Services:** wireless Internet. **Cards:** AX, CB, DC, DS, JC, MC, VI.

ASK 🐾 🛢 🖨 🖥 / SOME UNITS FEE 🐕 ⊠

THE WILDERNESS INN

Phone: 541/426-4535

▼▼ ▼▼
Motel
Rates not provided

Address: 301 W North St **Location:** Corner of NW 2nd St. **Facility:** 29 units. 28 one-bedroom standard units. 1 one-bedroom suite with kitchen and whirlpool. 3 stories (no elevator), exterior corridors. *Bath:* combo or shower only. **Parking:** on-site. **Terms:** office hours 7 am-10 pm. **Amenities:** high-speed Internet. **Leisure Activities:** sauna. **Guest Services:** wireless Internet. **Business Services:** meeting rooms.

🏨 🐾 🖥 / SOME UNITS FEE 🐕 ⊠ 🛢 🖨

──────── **WHERE TO DINE** ────────

LA LAGUNA FAMILY MEXICAN RESTAURANT

Phone: 541/426-3500

▼▼ ▼▼
Mexican
$6-$12

In a former home now painted a bright color, the restaurant lists among its many Mexican favorites seafood, chicken and beef dishes, along with vegetarian plates. Both small and large combinations are available. Outside seating on the covered porch or patio can be enjoyed in season. Casual dress. **Bar:** Full bar. **Reservations:** accepted. **Hours:** 11 am-9 pm, Fri-Sun to 10 pm. Closed: 4/12, 11/26, 12/25. **Address:** 307 W North St **Location:** On SR 82. **Parking:** on-site. **Cards:** MC, VI.

RIMROCK INN

Phone: 541/828-7769

▼▼ ▼▼ ▼▼
Continental
$7-$28

About 30 miles from downtown, this beautiful restaurant is on the edge of Joseph Creek Canyon. Guests can request seating in the contemporary yet rustic dining room or outside on the patio, where the mountain views are spectacular. A lighter lunch might include grilled portobello salad or a tuna and artichoke panini, followed by a piece of homemade marionberry pie. Among dinner options are pan-seared Dungeness crab cakes, wild Alaskan salmon, rib-eye and pork tenderloin. Casual dress. **Bar:** Beer & wine. **Reservations:** suggested. **Hours:** Open 5/15-10/15; 8 am-8 pm. Closed: Wed. **Address:** 83471 Lewiston Hwy (SR 3) **Location:** SR 3 (Lewiston Hwy), 35 mi n. **Parking:** on-site. **Cards:** MC, VI.

TERMINAL GRAVITY BREWING

Phone: 541/426-0158

▼▼
American
$7-$15

In season, dine outdoors at a picnic table among the willows near the small creek that runs through the property, or dine inside the Craftsman bungalow at this laid-back, popular spot. Select from salads, sandwiches and pastas, then place your order at the counter inside. Friendly service and wonderful beers brewed on the premises are also featured. Casual dress. **Bar:** Beer & wine. **Hours:** 11 am-10 pm, Sun & Mon 4 pm-9 pm; 4 pm-9 pm in winter. Closed: 11/26, 12/25; also Tues in summer; Sun-Wed in winter. **Address:** 803 SE School St **Location:** 1 blk s of SR 82; east end of town. **Parking:** on-site. **Cards:** MC, VI.

🅰🅲

EUGENE pop. 137,893—*See also SPRINGFIELD.*

──────── **WHERE TO STAY** ────────

AMERICAS BEST VALUE INN   *Book great rates at AAA.com*

Phone: (541)343-0730

(AAA) (SAVE)
▼
Motel
$49-$79 All Year

Address: 1140 W 6th Ave **Location:** I-5, exit 194B, 3 mi w on I-105, then just w on SR 99 N (6th Ave). **Facility:** 37 one-bedroom standard units, some with kitchens and/or whirlpools. 1 story, exterior corridors. **Parking:** on-site. **Terms:** office hours 7 am-midnight. **Amenities:** high-speed Internet, voice mail, irons, hair dryers. *Some:* DVD players (fee). **Leisure Activities:** exercise room. **Guest Services:** coin laundry, wireless Internet. **Business Services:** PC (fee). **Cards:** AX, CB, DC, DS, JC, MC, VI. **Free Special Amenities:** expanded continental breakfast and local telephone calls.

🐾 🛢 🖨 / SOME UNITS FEE 🐕 ⊠ FEE 📼

BEST WESTERN GREENTREE INN *Book great rates at AAA.com*

Phone: (541)485-2727

Hotel
$105-$175 All Year

Address: 1759 Franklin Blvd **Location:** I-5, exit 191 (Glenwood Blvd) southbound, 0.6 mi n, then 1.1 mi w; exit 192 northbound, 1 mi w. Located opposite University of Oregon. **Facility:** 65 units. 63 one-bedroom standard units. 1 one- and 1 two-bedroom suites. 3 stories (no elevator), interior/exterior corridors. **Parking:** on-site. **Terms:** check-in 4 pm, 3 day cancellation notice. **Amenities:** high-speed Internet, voice mail, irons, hair dryers. *Some:* DVD players. **Pool(s):** heated outdoor. **Leisure Activities:** whirlpool, exercise room. **Guest Services:** valet laundry, wireless Internet. **Business Services:** PC. **Cards:** AX, CB, DC, DS, JC, MC, VI. **Free Special Amenities:** continental breakfast and high-speed Internet. *(See color ad below)*

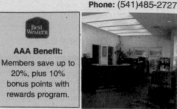

AAA Benefit:
Members save up to 20%, plus 10% bonus points with rewards program.

BEST WESTERN NEW OREGON MOTEL *Book great rates at AAA.com*

Phone: (541)683-3669

Hotel
$105-$175 All Year

Address: 1655 Franklin Blvd **Location:** I-5, exit 194B southbound to I-105, exit University of Oregon, 0.9 mi e; exit 192 northbound, 1 mi w. **Facility:** 129 units. 121 one- and 8 two-bedroom standard units. 2 stories (no elevator), interior/exterior corridors. *Bath:* combo or shower only. **Parking:** on-site. **Terms:** check-in 4 pm, 3 day cancellation notice. **Amenities:** voice mail, irons, hair dryers. *Some:* DVD players, high-speed Internet, fax. **Pool(s):** heated indoor. **Leisure Activities:** saunas, whirlpool, racquetball court, exercise room, basketball. **Guest Services:** valet and coin laundry, wireless Internet. **Business Services:** PC. **Cards:** AX, CB, DC, DS, JC, MC, VI. **Free Special Amenities:** continental breakfast and high-speed Internet. *(See color ad below)*

AAA Benefit:
Members save up to 20%, plus 10% bonus points with rewards program.

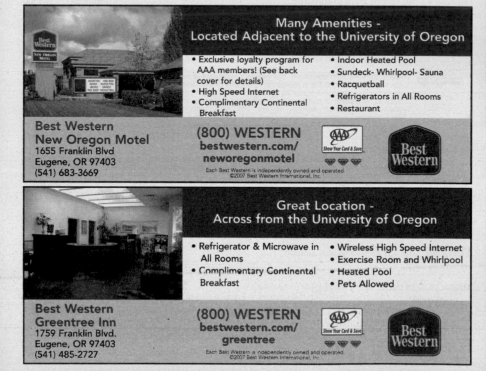

CAMPUS INN & SUITES *Book great rates at AAA.com*

Phone: 541/343-3376

AAA SAVE
▼▼ ▼▼
Motel
Rates not provided

Address: 390 E Broadway **Location:** I-5, exit 194B southbound, 1.3 mi w on I-105, exit 2 (Coburg Rd), then 1.5 mi s, follow University of Oregon signs; exit 192 northbound, 1.9 mi w. **Facility:** 59 one-bedroom standard units. 2 stories (no elevator), exterior corridors. **Parking:** on-site. **Amenities:** video library, voice mail, irons, hair dryers. *Some:* DVD players, high-speed Internet. **Leisure Activities:** whirlpool, exercise room. **Guest Services:** coin laundry, wireless Internet. **Business Services:** PC. **Free Special Amenities: continental breakfast and high-speed Internet.** *(See color ad below)*

⊞ ⊠ 📷 🛢 💻 / SOME UNITS 📷

C'EST LA VIE INN

Phone: 541/302-3014

▼▼◆▼▼
Historic Bed
& Breakfast
$130-$250 All Year

Address: 1006 Taylor St **Location:** I-5, exit 194B, 3.6 mi w on I-105 (to end of freeway), follow signs to fairgrounds, just s on Jefferson St, 0.5 mi w on W 11th Ave, just n on Polk St, then just w on 10th Ave. Located in a residential neighborhood. **Facility:** Surrounded by beautiful gardens, this 1891 inn offers upscale touches and is attractively furnished with antiques; the cottage features a fireplace. Smoke free premises. 4 units. 3 one-bedroom standard units. 1 cottage. 2 stories (no elevator), interior corridors. *Bath:* combo or shower only. **Parking:** on-site and street. **Terms:** office hours 7 am-10 pm, check-in 4 pm, age restrictions may apply, 3 day cancellation notice-fee imposed. **Amenities:** video library, DVD players, hair dryers. *Some:* irons. **Guest Services:** valet laundry, wireless Internet. **Business Services:** meeting rooms, PC. **Cards:** AX, MC, VI.

⊞ ⊠ ☎ / SOME UNITS 🛢 📷 💻

COMFORT SUITES EUGENE *Book great rates at AAA.com*

Phone: 541/343-7000

AAA SAVE
▼▼ ▼▼
Hotel
Rates not provided

Address: 3060 Brackenfern Rd **Location:** I-5, exit 191, just se on Glenwood Dr, follow signs; jct E 25th Ave. **Facility:** 66 units. 61 one- and 5 two-bedroom standard units, some with whirlpools. 1-4 stories, interior corridors. *Bath:* combo or shower only. **Parking:** on-site. **Amenities:** high-speed Internet, voice mail, irons, hair dryers. **Pool(s):** heated indoor. **Leisure Activities:** sauna, whirlpool, exercise room. **Guest Services:** valet and coin laundry, wireless Internet. **Business Services:** meeting rooms, business center. **Free Special Amenities: expanded continental breakfast and high-speed Internet.**

⊞ CALL 🔊M 🏊 ⊠ ⊠ 📷 🛢 📷 💻

COURTESY INN *Book great rates at AAA.com*

Phone: (541)345-3391

AAA SAVE
▼▼
Motel
$49-$89 All Year

Address: 345 W 6th Ave **Location:** I-5, exit 194B, 2 mi w on I-105 (to end of freeway) to 7th Ave, just e to Lincoln St, then just n: downtown. **Facility:** 33 units. 31 one- and 2 two-bedroom standard units. 1 story, exterior corridors. **Parking:** on-site. **Terms:** cancellation fee imposed. **Amenities:** voice mail, irons, hair dryers. *Some:* DVD players (fee). **Guest Services:** coin laundry, wireless Internet. **Cards:** AX, DS, MC, VI. **Free Special Amenities: continental breakfast and high-speed Internet.** *(See color ad p 334)*

⊞ 📷 🛢 📷 💻 / SOME UNITS ⊠ FEE VCR

──────── ▼ *See AAA listing above* ▼ ────────

EUGENE/SPRINGFIELD RESIDENCE INN BY MARRIOTT *Book great rates at AAA.com*

Phone: (541)342-7171

Hotel
$189-$199 All Year

Address: 25 Club Rd **Location:** I-5, exit 194B, 1.3 mi w on I-105, exit 2 (Coburg Rd), straight through jct Coburg Rd to Southwood Ln, just w, then se on Country Club Rd; follow signs for Autzen Stadium. Located across from a park and river. **Facility:** Smoke free premises. 108 units. 47 one-bedroom standard units with kitchens. 46 one- and 15 two-bedroom suites with kitchens. 3 stories, interior corridors. *Bath:* combo or shower only. **Parking:** on-site. **Terms:** cancellation fee imposed. **Amenities:** high-speed Internet, dual phone lines, voice mail, irons, hair dryers. *Some:* DVD players. **Pool(s):** heated outdoor. **Leisure Activities:** whirlpool, exercise room, sports court. **Guest Services:** valet and coin laundry, wireless Internet. **Business Services:** PC. **Cards:** AX, CB, DC, DS, JC, MC, VI.

AAA Benefit:
Members save a
minimum 5% off the
best available rate.

▼ See AAA listing p 338 ▼

541-343-7000

- Free Hi-speed Internet
- Free Deluxe Hot Breakfast
- Fresh Baked Cookies - every night • Business Center • Spa
- View Rooms • In-Room Coffee • Microwave & Refrigerator

Just off I-5, Exit 191 in Eugene •

COMFORT SUITES
BY CHOICE HOTELS

3060 E. 25th Avenue, Eugene, OR 97403

541-342-4804

UNIVERSITY INN & SUITES

Our University Inn, in Eugene, Oregon is at the hub of University athletic activity. We're within walking distance to Autzen Stadium, Mac Court, and just about any other campus event. Downtown is less than a mile away.

FEATURES: • Free Wifi Internet
• Free Deluxe Continental Breakfast
• Microwave & Refrigerators • Hair dryers & in-room coffee • Pool (sea.)

1857 Franklin Blvd, Eugene, OR 97403

▼ See AAA listing p 333 ▼

Courtesy Inn

Affordable Quality & Comfort in Downtown Eugene

- Free Continental Breakfast
- Wireless Internet Access
- Free Local Calls
- Non Smoking Rooms
- Microwave / Refrigerator
- Cable TV / HBO
- Hair Dryers / Iron & Boards
- King & Queen Size Beds
- Air Conditioning
- Guest Laundry
- Coffee Maker in Room
- Dataports

1-888-259-8481 • www.courtesyinneugene.com
345 West 6th Ave., Eugene, OR 97401

AAA Approved

EXCELSIOR INN & RISTORANTE ITALIANO

Boutique Country Inn
$99-$270 All Year

Phone: (541)342-6963
Address: 754 E 13th Ave **Location:** I-5, exit 194B southbound, 1.3 mi w on I-105, exit 2 (Coburg Rd), 1.5 mi s, follow University of Oregon signs, just e on Broadway/Franklin Blvd, just s on Patterson St, then just e; exit 192 northbound, 1.5 mi w, then just s on Alder St. Located across from a hospital complex. **Facility:** Just a few blocks from University of Oregon campus, this inn features rooms tastefully decorated in the style of the old European inns. Smoke free premises. 14 one-bedroom standard units, some with whirlpools. 3 stories, interior corridors. *Bath:* combo or shower only. **Parking:** on-site. **Terms:** office hours 7 am-11 pm, age restrictions may apply. **Amenities:** video library, CD players, high-speed Internet, voice mail, irons, hair dryers. *Some:* DVD players. **Dining:** restaurant, see separate listing. **Guest Services:** valet laundry, wireless Internet. **Business Services:** meeting rooms. **Cards:** AX, DC, DS, MC, VI.

EXPRESS INN & SUITES   *Book great rates at AAA.com*

Motel
$65-$85 All Year

Phone: (541)868-1520
Address: 990 W 6th Ave **Location:** I-5, exit 194B, 3 mi w on I-105, then just w on SR 99 N (6th Ave). **Facility:** 24 units. 23 one- and 1 two-bedroom standard units. 2 stories (no elevator), exterior corridors. **Parking:** on-site. **Terms:** office hours 7 am-11 pm, 3 day cancellation notice-fee imposed. **Amenities:** high-speed Internet, irons, hair dryers. **Guest Services:** wireless Internet. **Cards:** AX, DS, MC, VI. **Free Special Amenities:** local telephone calls and early check-in/late check-out.

HAMPTON INN   *Book great rates at AAA.com*

Hotel
$149-$199 All Year

Phone: (541)431-1225
Address: 3780 W 11th Ave **Location:** I-5, exit 195B, 9.4 mi sw on Belt Line Hwy, then 1.1 mi e. **Facility:** 61 units. 58 one-bedroom standard units. 3 one-bedroom suites. 4 stories, interior corridors. *Bath:* combo or shower only. **Parking:** on-site. **Terms:** 1-30 night minimum stay, cancellation fee imposed. **Amenities:** video games (fee), high-speed Internet, dual phone lines, voice mail, irons, hair dryers. **Pool(s):** heated indoor. **Leisure Activities:** exercise room. **Guest Services:** valet and coin laundry, wireless Internet. **Business Services:** meeting rooms, PC. **Cards:** AX, CB, DC, DS, MC, VI. **Free Special Amenities:** expanded continental breakfast and high-speed Internet. *(See color ad below)*

AAA Benefit:
Members save up to 10% everyday!

HILTON EUGENE   *Book great rates at AAA.com*

Hotel
$139-$249 All Year

Phone: (541)342-2000
Address: 66 E 6th Ave **Location:** At 6th Ave and Oak St; center. Located adjacent to Hult Center for Performing Arts. **Facility:** Smoke free premises. 269 units. 264 one-bedroom standard units. 5 one-bedroom suites. 12 stories, interior corridors. *Bath:* combo or shower only. **Parking:** on-site (fee). **Terms:** 1-30 night minimum stay, cancellation fee imposed. **Amenities:** dual phone lines, voice mail, irons, hair dryers. *Fee:* video games, high-speed Internet. *Some:* DVD players (fee). **Pool(s):** heated indoor. **Leisure Activities:** whirlpool, exercise room. **Guest Services:** valet laundry, wireless Internet. **Business Services:** conference facilities, business center. **Cards:** AX, CB, DC, DS, JC, MC, VI. *(See color ad p 337)*

AAA Benefit:
Members save 5% or more everyday!

HOLIDAY INN EXPRESS HOTEL & SUITES   *Book at AAA.com*

Hotel
$119-$179 All Year

Phone: (541)342-1243
Address: 2117 Franklin Blvd **Location:** I-5, exit 194B southbound to I-105, exit University of Oregon, 1.1 mi e; exit 192 northbound, 1 mi w. **Facility:** Smoke free premises. 80 units. 74 one-bedroom standard units. 6 one-bedroom suites with whirlpools. 4 stories, interior corridors. **Parking:** on-site. **Amenities:** high-speed Internet, voice mail, irons, hair dryers. **Pool(s):** heated indoor. **Leisure Activities:** whirlpool, exercise room. **Guest Services:** complimentary and valet laundry, wireless Internet. **Business Services:** meeting rooms, business center. **Cards:** AX, DS, MC, VI.

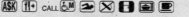
▼ See AAA listing above ▼

LA QUINTA INN & SUITES WATERFRONT   *Book great rates at AAA.com*   Phone: (541)344-8335

▼▲▼▲▼

Hotel

$99-$199 All Year

Address: 155 Day Island Rd **Location:** I-5, exit 194B, 1.3 mi w on I-105, exit 2 (Coburg Rd), straight through jct Coburg Rd to Southwood Ln, just w, then 0.5 mi se on Country Club Rd; follow signs for Autzen Stadium. Located at entrance to Alton Baker Park & river. **Facility:** 73 units. 62 one-bedroom standard units, some with whirlpools. 11 one-bedroom suites, some with efficiencies. 3 stories, interior corridors. *Bath:* combo or shower only. **Parking:** on-site. **Amenities:** video library, high-speed Internet, dual phone lines, voice mail, irons, hair dryers. *Some:* DVD players. **Pool(s):** heated indoor. **Leisure Activities:** whirlpool, exercise room. **Guest Services:** valet and coin laundry, wireless Internet. **Business Services:** meeting rooms, business center. **Cards:** AX, DS, MC, VI.

ASK �⁺⁺ ➔ ✕ ✈ 🛄 🖥 💻 / SOME UNITS 🐾 VCR

MOTEL 6 - #36   *Book at AAA.com*   Phone: (541)687-2395

▼▲▼

Motel

$55-$65 All Year

Address: 3690 Glenwood Dr **Location:** I-5, exit 191, just sw. **Facility:** 59 one-bedroom standard units. 2 stories (no elevator), exterior corridors. *Bath:* combo or shower only. **Parking:** on-site. **Amenities:** high-speed Internet (fee). **Pool(s):** heated outdoor. **Guest Services:** wireless Internet. **Cards:** AX, CB, DC, DS, MC, VI.

⁺⁺ ➔ ✈ / SOME UNITS 🐾 ✕ FEE 🛄 FEE 🖥

THE OVAL DOOR BED & BREAKFAST   Phone: (541)683-3160

▼▲▼

Bed & Breakfast

$75-$195 All Year

Address: 988 Lawrence St **Location:** I-5, exit 194B, 3.6 mi w on I-5 (to end of freeway); exit Jefferson St to 10th Ave, then e; downtown. Located in a residential neighborhood. **Facility:** Breakfast by the innkeepers, two culinary school graduates, is the specialty at this farmhouse-style home. Smoke free premises. 6 one-bedroom standard units, some with whirlpools. 3 stories (no elevator), interior corridors. *Bath:* combo or shower only. **Parking:** on-site. **Terms:** office hours 9 am-9 pm, 2 night minimum stay - weekends, 3 day cancellation notice. **Amenities:** video library, hair dryers. *Some:* CD players. **Guest Services:** wireless Internet. **Business Services:** PC. **Cards:** AX, MC, VI.

ASK ⁺⁺ FEE ➔ ✕ VCR ☎ / SOME UNITS 💻

PHOENIX INN SUITES-EUGENE   *Book great rates at AAA.com*   Phone: (541)344-0001

(AAA) (SAVE)

▼▼▼▼
Hotel
$89-$159 All Year

Address: 850 Franklin Blvd **Location:** I-5, exit 192 northbound, 1.5 mi w; exit 194B southbound to I-105, exit University of Oregon. **Facility:** Smoke free premises. 97 one-bedroom standard units, some with whirlpools. 4 stories, interior corridors. *Bath:* combo or shower only. **Parking:** on-site. **Terms:** check-in 4 pm, cancellation fee imposed. **Amenities:** high-speed Internet, dual phone lines, voice mail, irons, hair dryers. *Some:* DVD players. **Pool(s):** heated indoor. **Leisure Activities:** whirlpool, exercise room. **Guest Services:** valet and coin laundry, wireless Internet. **Business Services:** meeting rooms, PC. **Cards:** AX, DC, DS, MC, VI. **Free Special Amenities: expanded continental breakfast and high-speed Internet.** *(See color ad p 440 & p 337)*

CALL 🅱️Ⓜ️ 🛏️ ❌ 🎦 🖥️ 📶 💻 / SOME UNITS 📼

RED CARPET INN   *Book great rates at AAA.com*   Phone: (541)345-0579

(AAA) (SAVE)

▼▼▼
Motel
$55-$70 All Year

Address: 1055 6th Ave **Location:** I-5, exit 194B, 3 mi w on I-105, then just w on SR 99N (6th Ave). **Facility:** 24 units. 20 one- and 4 two-bedroom standard units. 1 story, exterior corridors. *Bath:* combo or shower only. **Parking:** on-site. **Terms:** office hours 7 am-midnight, 7 day cancellation notice-fee imposed. **Amenities:** high-speed Internet. **Guest Services:** wireless Internet. **Cards:** DS, MC, VI. **Free Special Amenities: continental breakfast and high-speed Internet.**

🎦 🖥️ 💻 / SOME UNITS FEE 🐾 ❌

RED LION HOTEL EUGENE   *Book great rates at AAA.com*   Phone: (541)342-5201

(AAA) (SAVE)

▼▼▼
Motel
$129-$199 All Year

Address: 205 Coburg Rd **Location:** I-5, exit 194B, 1.3 mi w on I-105, exit 2 (Coburg Rd), then just n. **Facility:** 137 one-bedroom standard units. 2 stories (no elevator), exterior corridors. *Bath:* combo or shower only. **Parking:** on-site. **Terms:** cancellation fee imposed. **Amenities:** high-speed Internet, voice mail, irons, hair dryers. **Pool(s):** heated outdoor. **Leisure Activities:** whirlpool, exercise room. **Guest Services:** valet and coin laundry, airport transportation-Eugene Airport, area transportation-Sacred Heart Hospital & train station, wireless Internet. **Business Services:** conference facilities, PC. **Cards:** AX, DC, DS, MC, VI. **Free Special Amenities: local telephone calls and high-speed Internet.** *(See color ad below)*

✈️ 🍴 🍸 🛏️ ❌ 🎦 🖥️ 📶 💻 / SOME UNITS FEE 🐾

UNIVERSITY INN & SUITES   *Book great rates at AAA.com*   Phone: 541/342-4804

(AAA) (SAVE)

▼▼▼
Motel
Rates not provided

Address: 1857 Franklin Blvd **Location:** I-5, exit 194B southbound to I-105, exit University of Oregon, 1 mi e; exit 192 northbound, 1.1 mi w. **Facility:** 45 one-bedroom standard units, some with whirlpools. 2 stories (no elevator), exterior corridors. *Bath:* combo or shower only. **Parking:** on-site. **Amenities:** video library (fee), high-speed Internet, irons, hair dryers. *Some:* DVD players, CD players. **Pool(s):** heated outdoor. **Guest Services:** coin laundry, wireless Internet. **Business Services:** PC. **Free Special Amenities: expanded continental breakfast and high-speed Internet.** *(See color ad p 334)*

🍴 🛏️ 🎦 🖥️ 📶 💻 / SOME UNITS FEE 🐾 ❌ 📼

VALLEY RIVER INN

Hotel
$139-$249 All Year

Phone: (541)743-1000

Address: 1000 Valley River Way **Location:** I-5, exit 194B, 2.5 mi w on I-105, exit 1, follow Valley River Center signs. Located across from Valley River Mall. **Facility:** 257 units. 248 one-bedroom standard units. 9 one-bedroom suites, some with whirlpools. 3 stories, interior corridors. *Bath:* some combo or shower only. **Parking:** on-site. **Terms:** check-in 4 pm, cancellation fee imposed. **Amenities:** high-speed Internet, voice mail, irons, hair dryers. *Some:* DVD players. **Pool(s):** heated outdoor. **Leisure Activities:** saunas, whirlpool, rental bicycles, jogging. *Fee:* massage. **Guest Services:** valet and coin laundry, area transportation, wireless Internet. **Business Services:** conference facilities, business center. **Cards:** AX, DC, DS, JC, MC, VI. *(See color ad below)*

ASK (icons) FEE (icons) / SOME UNITS (icons) FEE (icons)

▼ See AAA listing above ▼

——— WHERE TO DINE ———

ADAM'S PLACE
Phone: 541/344-6948

Regional
Continental
$22-$36

An upscale, intimate dining room with soft music awaits patrons at the popular downtown gem. The seasonal, predominantly organic menu may feature such entrees as cedar-plank-roasted Oregon halibut and Misty Isles Northwest natural beef filet mignon. Only the freshest ingredients, many of them local, are used. An extensive wine list and delectable dessert menu complement any meal. The setting is refined and cozy in the jazz lounge, where guests linger over aperitifs. Dressy casual. **Reservations:** suggested. **Hours:** 5 pm-9 pm, Fri & Sat-10 pm. Closed major holidays; also Sun & Mon. **Address:** 30 E Broadway **Location:** Jct Oak St; center. **Parking:** street. **Cards:** AX, MC, VI.

CALL &M

AMBROSIA
Phone: 541/342-4141

Italian
$9-$24

In the historic area of the city, the downtown restaurant serves as a fitting setting for intimate meals or family dining. Italian favorites such as spaghetti bolognese and ravioli are highlights, and pizzas and calzones are cooked in a wood-fired oven. Authentic wood floors and accents help create a casual atmosphere. People-watching while dining al fresco is a favorite pastime along the shop-laden avenue. Casual dress. **Bar:** full bar. **Reservations:** accepted. **Hours:** 11:30 am-10 pm, Fri-11 pm, Sat 5 pm-11 pm, Sun 5 pm-9:30 pm. Closed major holidays. **Address:** 174 E Broadway **Location:** Jct Pearl St; downtown; in Pearl Historic District. **Parking:** street. **Cards:** AX, MC, VI.

BEPPE & GIANNI'S TRATTORIA
Phone: 541/683-6661

Italian
$12-$21

The bustling villa-style neighborhood eatery specializes in homemade, traditional Italian cuisine, offered with a large selection of wines. Both the food preparations and fresh ingredients are good, and the portions are hearty. Guests can dine al fresco on the porch during warmer months. Casual dress. **Bar:** Beer & wine. **Reservations:** not accepted. **Hours:** 5 pm-9:30 pm, Fri & Sat-10 pm; to 9 pm, Fri & Sat-10 pm in winter. Closed major holidays. **Address:** 1646 E 19th Ave **Location:** I-5, exit 194B southbound, I-105, exit 2 (downtown), 2 mi s, 5.5 mi e on Franklin Blvd, 0.8 mi s on Agate St, then just e, follow signs to University of Oregon; exit 192 northbound, 1.3 mi w on Franklin Blvd, 0.8 mi s on Agate St, then just e. **Parking:** on-site. **Cards:** MC, VI.

CAFE LUCKY NOODLE
Phone: 541/484-4777

International
$8-$28

The unique and stylish restaurant skillfully blends the best of both Italian and Thai cuisines. Open long hours and conveniently located, it's a good choice at almost any time of day. The interesting menu allows combinations such as pad thai with a side of spicy peanut sauce and creamy Italian gelato for dessert. Casual dress. **Bar:** Full bar. **Reservations:** not accepted. **Hours:** 8 am-midnight, Fri & Sat-1 am. Closed: 1/1, 11/26, 12/25. **Address:** 207 E 5th Ave **Location:** At Pearl St; downtown. **Parking:** on-site and street. **Cards:** AX, MC, VI.

CAFE SORIAH
Phone: 541/342-4410

Ethnic
$8-$29

The charming bistro's intriguing mix of Mediterranean and Middle Eastern dishes includes such treats as Moroccan-style lamb over rice with dates and raisins. There's also a daily salmon special and a few flambeed entrees and desserts. Appealing wines and microbrewery beers are fitting complements. The patio is tranquil and heated. Casual dress. **Bar:** Full bar. **Reservations:** suggested. **Hours:** 11 am-2 & 5-10 pm, Fri-11 pm, Sat 5 pm-11 pm, Sun 5 pm-10 pm. Closed: 1/1, 11/26, 12/24, 12/25. **Address:** 384 W 13th Ave **Location:** Corner of Lawrence St; center. **Parking:** on-site. **Cards:** AX, MC, VI.

CAFE ZENON
Phone: 541/343-3005

Regional
International
$8-$25

The decor is trendy yet unpretentious in the friendly downtown restaurant, which serves breakfast, lunch, dinner and a great Sunday brunch. The changing menu features an eclectic mix of creative international specialties of wild game, seafood and beef. Casual dress. **Bar:** Full bar. **Reservations:** not accepted. **Hours:** 8 am-11 pm, Fri & Sat-midnight; Sunday brunch. Closed: 11/26, 12/25. **Address:** 898 Pearl St **Location:** At Broadway and Pearl St; center. **Parking:** street. **Cards:** AX, DS, MC, VI.

CHANTERELLE
Phone: 541/484-4065

Continental
$24-$33

Located downtown in the Fifth Pearl Building, Chanterelle offers intimate dining among the tranquility of soft music, tasteful decor and an attentive staff that will anticipate your every need. While the menu is not extensive, it changes on occasion offering a variety of Continental cuisine selections and daily specials. Choose from selections such as escargot and veal scallopini. Casual dress. **Bar:** Full bar. **Reservations:** suggested. **Hours:** 5 pm-10 pm. Closed major holidays; also Sun & Mon. **Address:** 207 E 5th Ave **Location:** Jct Pearl St; downtown. **Parking:** on-site. **Cards:** AX, DC, MC, VI.

EL TORITO'S GRILL
Phone: 541/683-7294

Mexican
$7-$15

Homemade Mexican favorites span from classic preparations to specialties from the country's central regions. Spicy taqueria-style tacos and carnitas michoacan (marinated pork) are tasty choices. Casual dress. **Bar:** Full bar. **Reservations:** accepted. **Hours:** 11 am-10 pm, Fri & Sat-11 pm. **Address:** 1003 Valley River Way **Location:** I-5, exit 194B southbound, 2.5 mi w on I-105, exit 1, follow Valley River Center signs; across from Valley River Mall. **Parking:** on-site. **Cards:** AX, DS, MC, VI.

EXCELSIOR INN & RISTORANTE ITALIANO
Phone: 541/342-6963

Italian
$8-$32

Patrons dine on fine cuisine and regional dishes at this charming restaurant. After a meal of American Kobe beef, a delectable dessert makes the memories linger. Late-night dining is an option in the bistro. Seating is available in the seasonal courtyard. Dressy casual. **Bar:** Full bar. **Reservations:** suggested. **Hours:** 7 am-10 & 11:30-11:30 pm, Sat 8 am-11 & 4-11:30 pm, Sun 8 am-10 & 4-11:30 pm; Sunday brunch 10 am-2 pm. Closed: 1/1, 7/4, 12/25. **Address:** 754 E 13th Ave **Location:** I-5, exit 194B southbound, 1.3 mi w on I-105, exit 2 (Coburg Rd), 1.5 mi s, follow University of Oregon signs, just e on Broadway/Franklin Blvd, just s on Patterson St, then just e; exit 192 northbound, 1.5 mi w, then just s on Alder St; in Excelsior Inn & Ristorante Italiano. **Parking:** on-site. **Cards:** AX, DC, DS, MC, VI.

MCMENAMINS
Phone: 541/345-4905

American
$5-$20

The casual neighborhood eatery is where friends gather for classic pub and comfort fare, all washed down by pints of locally made beer. Large wooden booths or tables easily accommodate larger groups, and the eclectic, custom-painted walls and varied period light fixtures keep diners' eyes busy should the conversation lag. Casual dress. **Bar:** Full bar. **Hours:** 11 am-1 am, Sun noon-midnight. Closed: 12/25. **Address:** 1243 High St **Location:** Just s of jct E 12th Ave and High St; near center. **Parking:** street. **Cards:** MC, VI.

MCMENAMINS

American
$5-$20

Phone: 541/342-4025

The casual neighborhood eatery is where friends gather for classic pub and comfort fare, all washed down by pints of locally made beer. Large wooden booths or tables easily accommodate larger groups, and the eclectic, custom-painted walls and varied period light fixtures keep diners' eyes busy should the conversation lag. Casual dress. **Bar:** Full bar. **Hours:** 11 am-1 am, Sun noon-midnight. Closed: 12/25. **Address:** 1485 E 19th Ave **Location:** I-5, exit 192 northbound, 1.3 mi w; exit 194B southbound to I-105, follow signs to University of Oregon, just s on Agate St from jct SR 126/99. **Parking:** street. **Cards:** MC, VI.

MCMENAMINS

American
$5-$20

Phone: 541/343-5622

The casual neighborhood eatery is where friends gather for classic pub and comfort fare, all washed down by pints of locally made beer. Large wooden booths or tables easily accommodate larger groups, and the eclectic, custom-painted walls and varied period light fixtures keep diners' eyes busy should the conversation lag. Casual dress. **Bar:** Full bar. **Reservations:** not accepted. **Hours:** 11 am-11 pm, Fri & Sat-midnight, Sun noon-11 pm. Closed: 11/26, 12/25. **Address:** 22 Club Rd **Location:** I-5, exit 194B southbound, 1.3 mi n on I-105, exit 2 (Coburg Rd), just ne to Southwood Ln, just sw, then just e on Country Club Rd. **Parking:** on-site. **Cards:** MC, VI.

CALL

MEKALA'S THAI RESTAURANT

Thai
$6-$18

Phone: 541/342-4872

Fresh, traditional ingredients go into the Thai dishes, which are prepared from recipes that reflect accurate renditions of such items as phad see-ew, which is prepared with tofu, chicken, beef or pork and pan-fried noodles with black soybean sauce. Thai curries, house specialties and grill and wok preparations round out the menu. An outdoor deck with a fountain is a great spot to dine in season. Casual dress. **Bar:** Full bar. **Reservations:** accepted. **Hours:** 11 am-9 pm, Fri-10 pm, Sat noon-10 pm, Sun from 4 pm. Closed major holidays. **Address:** 1769 Franklin Blvd **Location:** I-5, exit 192 northbound, 1 mi w; exit 194 southbound to I-105, follow signs to University of Oregon. **Parking:** on-site. **Cards:** MC, VI.

OREGON ELECTRIC STATION

American
$8-$28

Phone: 541/485-4444

In a turn-of-the-20th-century train station, the restaurant offers seating in antique rail cars. Among menu offerings served at this landmark spot for more than 25 years are prime rib, steak, pasta, chicken and fresh fish. Guests are encouraged to leave some space, as the dessert tray has irresistible options. Casual dress. **Bar:** Full bar. **Reservations:** accepted. **Hours:** 11:30 am-2:30 & 5-10 pm, Sat 4:30 pm-10:30 pm, Sun 4:30 pm-9:30 pm. Closed: 7/4, 12/25. **Address:** 27 E 5th Ave **Location:** Jct Williamette St; downtown. **Parking:** on-site. **Cards:** AX, MC, VI. **Historic**

RED AGAVE

Latin American
$19-$35

Phone: 541/683-2206

The popular, casual and intimate restaurant prepares inventive Latin American cuisine from the southwest United States, Mexico, Brazil and points between. Peppers—be they Anaheim, poblano, serrano or jalapeno—are definitely king here. Casual dress. **Bar:** Full bar. **Reservations:** accepted. **Hours:** 5:30 pm-9 pm, Fri & Sat-10 pm. Closed major holidays; also Sun. **Address:** 454 Willamette St **Location:** Between 4th and 5th aves; downtown. **Parking:** street. **Cards:** AX, DS, MC, VI.

RING OF FIRE

Regional Thai
$11-$19

Phone: 541/344-6475

The restaurant prepares flavorful traditional Thai offerings with a Pacific Rim twist. Fresh herbs and entrees are prepared to the diner's preferred level of spiciness. Noodles from the wok and a variety of curries mix easily with the interesting beverage creations. The popular eatery bustles both at lunch and dinner times. Casual dress. **Bar:** Full bar. **Reservations:** suggested. **Hours:** 11 am-midnight, Fri & Sat-1 am, Sun noon-midnight. Closed: 1/1, 11/26. **Address:** 1099 Chambers St **Location:** 11th Ave and Chambers St; 1.5 mi w from center; in strip mall. **Parking:** on-site. **Cards:** AX, MC, VI.

ROGUE ALES EUGENE CITY BREWERY

American
$9-$24

Phone: 541/345-4155

With 34 beers on tap, Kobe beef burgers, fish tacos, Coho salmon, build-your-own pizzas and flat iron steaks, the restaurant's menu has broad appeal. The college crowd gathers in the casual, high-energy eatery later into the evening. Casual dress. **Bar:** Full bar. **Reservations:** not accepted. **Hours:** 11 am-11 pm, Fri & Sat-midnight, Sun-10 pm. **Address:** 844 Olive St **Location:** Just s of jct Olive St and W 8th Ave. **Parking:** street. **Cards:** AX, DS, MC.

STEELHEAD BREWING COMPANY

American
$8-$17

Phone: 541/686-2739

The large establishment fills nightly for its wide selection of burgers, pizzas, steak and pasta entrees and fresh beers made in-house. Diners can watch the brewing process from behind glass walls. Casual dress. **Bar:** Full bar. **Reservations:** not accepted. **Hours:** 11:30 am-11:30 pm. Closed: 11/26, 12/25. **Address:** 100 E 5th Ave **Location:** At 5th Ave and Pearl St; downtown. **Parking:** on-site. **Cards:** AX, DS, MC, VI.

STUDIO ONE CAFE

American
$6-$10

Phone: 541/342-8596

Breakfast offerings are the draw at the bustling, college-area cafe. The menu lists four kinds of eggs Benedict, specialty salads, homemade soups, sandwiches and vegan dishes, all served in huge portions. Build-your-own breakfasts are another popular offering. Most items can be ordered in half portions. The decor speaks to the name of the place, with posters of cinema stars on the walls. Dishes also bear celebrity names. Outdoor seating is a seasonal option. Casual dress. **Reservations:** not accepted. **Hours:** 11 am-4 pm. Closed: 11/26, 12/25. **Address:** 1473 E 19th Ave **Location:** I-5, exit 194B, I-105, exit 2 (Coburg Rd), follow signs to University of Oregon, 0.5 mi s on Agate St, then just e. **Parking:** on-site. **Cards:** AX, DS, MC, VI.

SUSHI STATION JAPANESE RESTAURANT

Japanese
$8-$14

Phone: 541/484-1334

In a contemporary setting, the restaurant continually prepares fresh sushi and special rolls. Diners sit at the counter and watch the sushi being made, then grab their favorite from the rotating conveyor belt. Another option is to sit at a table with a favorite tempura, teriyaki, teppanyaki or yakisoba dish. Lunch specials also get plenty of attention. Casual dress. **Bar:** Full bar. **Reservations:** accepted. **Hours:** 11:30 am-10 pm, Sat from 4 pm. Closed: 11/26, 12/25; also Sun. **Address:** 199 E 5th Ave, #7 **Location:** Jct Pearl St; downtown. **Parking:** on-site. **Cards:** AX, DS, MC, VI.

SWEET BASIL THAI CUISINE
Phone: 541/284-2944

Thai
$9-$18

A large, festive mural decorates the high-energy restaurant, where traditional Thai dishes are served with spice levels ranging from very mild to extremely wild. The bar is popular with the after-work crowd. Casual dress. **Bar:** Full bar. **Reservations:** accepted. **Hours:** 11:30 am-3 & 5-9 pm, Fri & Sat-10 pm, Sun 5 pm-9 pm. Closed major holidays. **Address:** 941 Pearl St **Location:** Just s of jct Pearl St and Broadway; center. **Parking:** street. **Cards:** AX, MC, VI.

WATERFRONT BAR & GRILL
Phone: 541/465-4506

American
$8-$28

In a spacious setting overlooking a waterway, this restaurant prepares several food items cooked over oakwood, delicious pastas and fresh seafood. The patio is tranquil. Casual dress. **Bar:** Full bar. **Hours:** 11:30 am-2 & 5-9 pm, Fri-10 pm, Sat 5 pm-10 pm. Closed: Sun. **Address:** 2210 Martin Luther King Blvd **Location:** I-5, exit 194B, 1.3 mi w on I-105, exit 2 (Coburg Rd) just s, then e; behind the Volvo dealer. **Parking:** on-site. **Cards:** AX, MC, VI.

FLORENCE pop. 7,263

——— WHERE TO STAY ———

BEST WESTERN PIER POINT INN
Book great rates at AAA.com
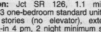
Phone: (541)997-7191

Hotel
$124-$240 3/1-9/30
$124-$190 10/1-2/28

Address: 85625 US 101 S **Location:** Jct SR 126, 1.1 mi s. **Facility:** Smoke free premises. 55 units. 53 one-bedroom standard units. 2 one-bedroom suites with kitchens. 3 stories (no elevator), exterior corridors. **Parking:** on-site. **Terms:** check-in 4 pm, 2 night minimum stay. **Amenities:** high-speed Internet, voice mail, safes (fee), irons, hair dryers. **Pool(s):** heated indoor. **Leisure Activities:** sauna, whirlpools. *Fee:* game room. **Guest Services:** wireless Internet. **Business Services:** meeting rooms, PC. **Cards:** AX, DC, DS, MC, VI. **Free Special Amenities: full breakfast and high-speed Internet.**

AAA Benefit:
Members save up to 20%, plus 10% bonus points with rewards program.

COMFORT INN
Book at AAA.com
Phone: (541)997-7797

Hotel
$89-$189 All Year

Address: 2475 US 101 N **Location:** Jct SR 126, 1 mi n. **Facility:** Smoke free premises. 52 units. 51 one-bedroom standard units. 1 one-bedroom suite with kitchen. 2 stories (no elevator), interior/exterior corridors. *Bath:* combo or shower only. **Parking:** on-site. **Terms:** check-in 4 pm, cancellation fee imposed. **Amenities:** high-speed Internet, voice mail, irons, hair dryers. **Leisure Activities:** whirlpool, exercise room. **Guest Services:** coin laundry, wireless Internet. **Business Services:** meeting rooms, PC. **Cards:** AX, DS, MC, VI.

EDWIN K BED AND BREAKFAST
Phone: 541/997-8360

Bed & Breakfast
$120-$175 All Year

Address: 1155 Bay St **Location:** Jct SR 126, 0.8 mi s on US 101, just w. Located in Old Town. **Facility:** This turn-of-the-century woodcrafter's home across the street from the Siuslaw River and sand dunes has landscaped grounds and antique furnishings. Smoke free premises. 7 units. 6 one-bedroom standard units, some with whirlpools. 1 one-bedroom suite with kitchen. 2 stories (no elevator), interior/exterior corridors. *Bath:* combo or shower only. **Parking:** on-site. **Terms:** check-in 4 pm, age restrictions may apply, 7 day cancellation notice-fee imposed. **Amenities:** high-speed Internet, hair dryers. *Some:* DVD players, CD players, irons. **Guest Services:** wireless Internet. **Business Services:** fax. **Cards:** DS, MC, VI.

LE CHATEAU MOTEL
Phone: (541)997-3481

Motel
$54-$119 All Year

Address: 1084 US 101 N **Location:** Jct SR 126, just n. **Facility:** 49 one-bedroom standard units. 2 stories (no elevator), exterior corridors. **Parking:** on-site. **Amenities:** high-speed Internet. *Some:* DVD players. **Pool(s):** heated outdoor. **Leisure Activities:** sauna, whirlpool, exercise room. **Guest Services:** coin laundry, wireless Internet. **Business Services:** PC. **Cards:** AX, DS, MC, VI. **Free Special Amenities: expanded continental breakfast and high-speed Internet.**

OCEAN BREEZE MOTEL
Phone: (541)997-2642

Motel
$59-$150 All Year

Address: 85165 US 101 S **Location:** Jct SR 126, 2 mi s. **Facility:** Smoke free premises. 13 units. 8 one- and 5 two-bedroom standard units, some with efficiencies or kitchens. 1 story, exterior corridors. *Bath:* combo or shower only. **Parking:** on-site. **Terms:** office hours 9 am-10 pm. **Amenities:** high-speed Internet, hair dryers. **Leisure Activities:** picnic tables, horseshoes. **Guest Services:** wireless Internet. **Cards:** DS, MC, VI. **Free Special Amenities: local telephone calls and high-speed Internet.**

OLD TOWN INN
Phone: (541)997-7131

Motel
$65-$99 All Year

Address: 170 US 101 S **Location:** Jct SR 126, 0.4 mi s. **Facility:** 40 one-bedroom standard units. 2 stories (no elevator), exterior corridors. **Parking:** on-site. **Terms:** office hours 7:30 am-10 pm, 2 night minimum stay - seasonal and/or weekends. **Amenities:** voice mail, hair dryers. **Guest Services:** wireless Internet. **Cards:** AX, DC, DS, MC, VI. **Free Special Amenities: local telephone calls and high-speed Internet.**

PARK MOTEL

AAA SAVE

Motel
$55-$150 All Year

Phone: (541)997-2634
Address: 85034 US 101 S **Location:** Jct SR 126, 2.2 mi s. **Facility:** Smoke free premises. 16 one-bedroom standard units, some with kitchens. 1 story, exterior corridors. *Bath:* combo or shower only. **Parking:** on-site. **Terms:** office hours 8 am-10 pm, 7 day cancellation notice. **Amenities:** high-speed Internet, hair dryers. *Some:* irons. **Leisure Activities:** horseshoes. **Guest Services:** coin laundry, wireless Internet. **Cards:** AX, DS, MC, VI. **Free Special Amenities: preferred room (subject to availability with advance reservations) and high-speed Internet.**

⊞ ⊠ Ⓚ ▤ ▦ ▣ / SOME UNITS FEE 🐾

RIVER HOUSE INN

AAA SAVE

Motel
$89-$150 All Year

Book great rates at AAA.com   Phone: (541)997-3933
Address: 1202 Bay St **Location:** Jct SR 126, 0.4 mi s on US 101, then just w. Located in Old Town. **Facility:** Smoke free premises. 40 one-bedroom standard units, some with whirlpools. 2 stories (no elevator), exterior corridors. **Parking:** on-site. **Terms:** office hours 7:30 am-10 pm. **Amenities:** high-speed Internet, hair dryers. **Guest Services:** coin laundry. **Business Services:** PC. **Cards:** AX, DC, DS, MC, VI. **Free Special Amenities: continental breakfast and high-speed Internet.**

⊠ Ⓚ ▤ ▦ ▣

—————— WHERE TO DINE ——————

BLISS HOT ROD GRILL   Phone: 541/997-6769

American
$6-$17

Guests revisit the 1950s at the friendly and fun family restaurant, which bursts with nostalgia. Memorabilia ranges from chrome counters and vinyl-covered stools to restored Ford convertibles in the dining room. Burgers, such as the Chubby Checker burger, as well as sandwiches, baskets, seafood items and thick shakes, make up much of the menu. Servers are upbeat and attentive. Casual dress. **Bar:** Full bar. **Reservations:** accepted. **Hours:** 6:30 am-9 pm, Fri & Sat-10 pm; to 8 pm, Fri & Sat-9 pm in winter. Closed major holidays. **Address:** 1179 US 101 N **Location:** Jct SR 126, 0.5 mi n. **Parking:** on-site. **Cards:** AX, DS, MC, VI.

GRAPE LEAF WINE BAR & BISTRO   Phone: 541/997-1646

International
$4-$12

Guests can try soups, salads and wrap sandwiches, as well as delicious homemade desserts at the small Old Town bistro. Wines are available by the glass, and any bottle purchased from the store may be consumed for a small corkage fee. Casual dress. **Bar:** Beer & wine. **Reservations:** accepted. **Hours:** 11 am-6 pm, Wed & Thurs-9 pm, Sun-5 pm; hours may vary in summer. Closed: 1/1, 11/26, 12/25; also Mon. **Address:** 1269 Bay St **Location:** Center; in Old Town. **Parking:** street. **Cards:** AX, DS, MC, VI.

MO'S RESTAURANT   Phone: 541/997-2185

Seafood
$8-$11

The nationally famous clam chowder and fresh Oregon seafood can be sampled in a casual dining room that overlooks the Siuslaw River and fishing boats docked nearby. Large windows afford an expansive view of the water, where the occasional seal can be seen swimming by looking for a handout or something overlooked by the fishermen. Casual dress. **Bar:** Full bar. **Hours:** 11 am-8 pm, Fri & Sat-9 pm. Closed: 11/26, 12/25. **Address:** 1436 Bay St **Location:** Center; in Old Town. **Parking:** on-site. **Cards:** AX, DS, MC, VI.

FOREST GROVE pop. 17,708

—————— WHERE TO STAY ——————

BEST WESTERN UNIVERSITY INN & SUITES   *Book great rates at AAA.com*   Phone: (503)992-8888

Hotel
$89-$199 All Year

Address: 3933 Pacific Ave **Location:** East end of town on SR 8. **Facility:** Smoke free premises. 54 units. 41 one-bedroom standard units, some with whirlpools. 13 one-bedroom suites, some with kitchens. 2 stories (no elevator), interior corridors. *Bath:* combo or shower only. **Parking:** on-site. **Terms:** check-in 4 pm, cancellation fee imposed. **Amenities:** high-speed Internet, voice mail, irons, hair dryers. **Pool(s):** heated indoor. **Leisure Activities:** sauna, whirlpool, limited exercise equipment. **Guest Services:** valet and coin laundry, wireless Internet. **Business Services:** PC. **Cards:** AX, CB, DC, DS, MC, VI. **Free Special Amenities:** expanded continental breakfast and high-speed Internet.
(See color ad p 368, p 586, p 499, p 368, p 752, p 473, p 542, p 299, below, p 751, p 566 & p 500)

AAA Benefit:
Members save up to 20%, plus 10% bonus points with rewards program.

MCMENAMINS GRAND LODGE　　　　　　　　　　　　　　Phone: 503/992-9533
(fyi)　　Not evaluated. **Address:** 3505 Pacific Ave **Location:** West end of town on SR 8. Facilities, services, and decor characterize a mid-scale property.

──────── **WHERE TO DINE** ────────

MAGGIE'S BUNS　　　　　　　　　　　　　　　　　　Phone: 503/992-2231
♦♦♦
Breads/Pastries
$4-$6
　　Oversize cinnamon buns baked fresh daily are served in a colorful, eclectic, retro and funky setting. Made-from-scratch food items include sandwiches, wraps, a few pasta dishes, chicken enchiladas and several delicious bakery items. Friendly staff are yet another reason this place is popular with breakfast and lunch diners. Breakfast is served until noon. Casual dress. **Reservations:** not accepted. **Hours:** 6:30 am-5:30 pm, Sat 7 am-2 pm. Closed major holidays; also Sun. **Address:** 2007 21st Ave **Location:** Just e of Main St; center; near Pacific University. **Parking:** street. **Cards:** AX, MC, VI.

FORT KLAMATH

──────── **WHERE TO STAY** ────────

THE ASPEN INN　　　　　　　　　　　　　　　　　　Phone: 541/381-2321
(fyi)　　Not evaluated. **Address:** 52250 Hwy 62 **Location:** 7 mi s of Crater Lake Park. Facilities, services, and decor characterize a mid-scale property.

GARIBALDI pop. 899

──────── **WHERE TO STAY** ────────

COMFORT INN　　　*Book great rates at AAA.com*　　　　　Phone: (503)322-3338
(AAA) (SAVE)
♦♦ ♦♦
Hotel
$89-$189 All Year
　　Address: 502 Garibaldi Ave **Location:** On US 101 at jct 5th St; center. Located across from the bay. **Facility:** 50 units. 49 one-bedroom standard units. 1 one-bedroom suite. 3 stories, interior corridors. *Bath:* combo or shower only. **Parking:** on-site. **Terms:** cancellation fee imposed. **Amenities:** high-speed Internet, irons, hair dryers. **Pool(s):** heated indoor. **Leisure Activities:** sauna, whirlpool, exercise room. **Guest Services:** coin laundry, wireless Internet. **Business Services:** PC. **Cards:** AX, DS, JC, MC, VI. **Free Special Amenities: expanded continental breakfast and high-speed Internet.**

[icons] / SOME UNITS FEE [icons]

──────── **WHERE TO DINE** ────────

PIRATE'S COVE　　　　　　　　　　　　　　　　　　Phone: 503/322-2092
♦♦♦
Seafood
$7-$31
　　Perched on a hill, the restaurant prepares a variety of fresh, local seafood, including clams, oysters, crab and halibut. Shellfish bouillabaisse—lobster, snow crab, crab, mussels, clams and oysters piled atop rice—is the "must-have" signature dish. Also on the menu are steak, pasta and chicken preparations. Large windows overlook the bay and the cape beyond. Casual dress. **Bar:** Full bar. **Reservations:** not accepted. **Hours:** 8 am-9 pm, Sun-8 pm. Closed: 12/25; also week prior to 12/25. **Address:** 14170 US 101 N **Location:** On US 101, 0.7 mi n. **Parking:** on-site. **Cards:** MC, VI.

GEARHART pop. 995

──────── **WHERE TO STAY** ────────

GEARHART BY THE SEA　　*Book great rates at AAA.com*　　Phone: (503)738-8331
(AAA) (SAVE)
♦♦ ♦♦
Vacation Rental
Condominium
$89-$300 All Year
　　Address: 1157 N Marion Ave **Location:** US 101, exit City Center, 1 mi w. **Facility:** Balcony units are comfortable and include either a wood stove or a fireplace. 81 units. 39 one- and 42 two-bedroom suites with kitchens. 2-5 stories, exterior corridors. **Parking:** on-site. **Terms:** check-in 4 pm, 2 night minimum stay - seasonal and/or weekends, 3 day cancellation notice-fee imposed. **Amenities:** video library (fee), DVD players, CD players, high-speed Internet, voice mail, irons, hair dryers. **Pool(s):** 2 heated indoor. **Leisure Activities:** whirlpool, beach access, clamming, exercise room. **Guest Services:** coin laundry, wireless Internet. **Business Services:** meeting rooms. **Cards:** AX, DS, MC, VI.

[icons] / SOME UNITS FEE [icons] (VCR)

──────── **WHERE TO DINE** ────────

PACIFIC WAY BAKERY & CAFE　　　　　　　　　　　　Phone: 503/738-0245
♦♦ ♦♦
American
$9-$30
　　"Typical" doesn't come to mind in describing the charming cafe's menu selections. Soups, salads and fresh bread from the adjacent bakery are innovative and flavorful. Diners are wise to indulge in a sinful dessert with a steaming cup of espresso. The dinner menu changes seasonally. Casual dress. **Bar:** Beer & wine. **Reservations:** suggested, for dinner. **Hours:** 11 am-3:30 & 5-9 pm. Closed: 11/26, 12/25; also Tues & Wed. **Address:** 601 Pacific Way **Location:** 0.4 mi w of US 101; center. **Parking:** street. **Cards:** MC, VI.

[icon]

GILCHRIST

WHERE TO DINE

GILCHRIST FAMILY RESTAURANT & LOUNGE — **Phone:** 541/433-2523

American
$7-$28

Since 1938, this modest restaurant has been serving affordable burgers, steaks, salads and pizzas, in addition to hot sandwiches, chicken and a few seafood items. A bowling alley is on the premises. Casual dress. **Bar:** Full bar. **Hours:** 7 am-9 pm. Closed: 11/26, 12/25. **Address:** 138357 Hwy 97 N **Location:** Center; in Gilchrist Mall. **Parking:** on-site. **Cards:** MC, VI.

GLADSTONE *—See Portland p. 457.*

GLIDE pop. 1,690

WHERE TO STAY

ILLAHEE INN AND RESTAURANT — **Phone:** 541/496-4870

AAA SAVE
Motel
$75-$95 All Year

Address: 170 Wild Thyme Ln **Location:** Just n to SR 138, 2.5 mi e. **Facility:** 6 one-bedroom standard units. 1 story, exterior corridors. **Parking:** on-site. **Terms:** office hours 8 am-9 pm. **Amenities:** voice mail, irons, hair dryers. **Cards:** AX, MC, VI. **Free Special Amenities: high-speed Internet.**

/ SOME UNITS FEE

STEELHEAD RUN BED & BREAKFAST AND FINE ART GALLERY — **Phone:** (541)496-0563

AAA SAVE
Bed & Breakfast
$65-$139 All Year

Address: 23049 N Umpqua Hwy (SR 138) **Location:** Just n to SR 138, 3 mi e, then just e of MM 24. **Facility:** 6 units. 3 one-bedroom standard units. 3 one-bedroom suites, some with efficiencies or kitchens. 2 stories (no elevator), interior/exterior corridors. *Bath:* combo or shower only. **Parking:** on-site. **Terms:** office hours 9 am-10 pm, 9 day cancellation notice-fee imposed. **Amenities:** video library, hair dryers. *Some:* irons. **Leisure Activities:** limited beach access, fishing, croquet, picnic area, gazebo, badminton, library, barbecue grills, table tennis, playground, horseshoes, volleyball. **Guest Services:** complimentary laundry. **Business Services:** PC. **Cards:** AX, DS, MC, VI.

CTV VCR / SOME UNITS FEE

GOLD BEACH pop. 1,897

WHERE TO STAY

AZALEA LODGE — **Phone:** 541/247-6635

AAA SAVE
Motel
Rates not provided

Address: 29481 Ellensburg Ave **Location:** On US 101; center. **Facility:** Smoke free premises. 16 units. 14 one- and 2 two-bedroom standard units. 1 story, exterior corridors. *Bath:* combo or shower only. **Parking:** on-site. **Terms:** office hours 7 am-10 pm. **Amenities:** high-speed Internet, hair dryers. **Guest Services:** wireless Internet. **Business Services:** PC. **Free Special Amenities: continental breakfast and high-speed Internet.**

AC

CLEAR SKY LODGING — **Phone:** (541)247-6456

Vacation Rental House
$120-$270 All Year

Location: On US 101, just e on 10th St. **Facility:** Comfortable, modern guest rooms are located in a quiet setting with free roaming wildlife. Smoke free premises. 7 houses. 2 stories (no elevator), exterior corridors. **Parking:** on-site. **Terms:** office hours 9 am-9 pm, 3 day cancellation notice. **Amenities:** DVD players, CD players. *Some:* high-speed Internet, hair dryers. **Leisure Activities:** sauna, whirlpool. **Guest Services:** complimentary laundry, wireless Internet. **Business Services:** meeting rooms, PC. **Cards:** AX, DS, MC, VI.

ASK VCR / SOME UNITS

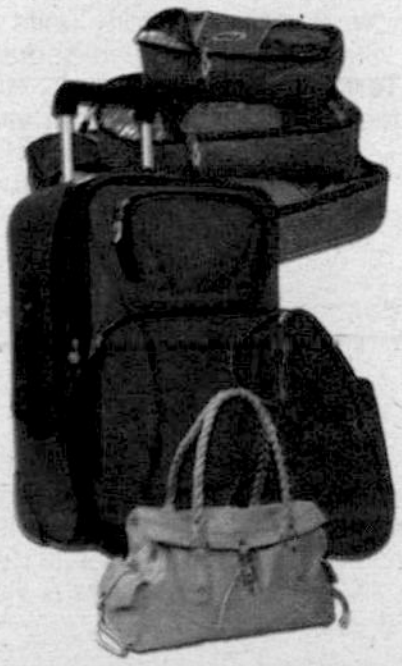

GOLD BEACH INN

AAA **SAVE**

Motel
$89-$169 All Year

Phone: 541/247-7091
Address: 29346 Ellensburg Ave **Location:** On US 101; center. **Facility:** Smoke free premises. 41 units. 40 one-bedroom standard units, some with efficiencies. 1 house. 1-4 stories (no elevator), exterior corridors. **Parking:** on-site. **Terms:** office hours 7:30 am-10 pm, cancellation fee imposed. **Amenities:** high-speed Internet. **Leisure Activities:** whirlpools, beach access. **Guest Services:** wireless Internet. **Cards:** AX, DS, MC, VI. **Free Special Amenities: expanded continental breakfast and high-speed Internet.**

GOLD BEACH RESORT AND CONDOMINIUMS

AAA **SAVE**

Hotel
$79-$185 All Year

Phone: (541)247-7066
Address: 29232 Ellensburg Ave **Location:** On US 101; south end of town. **Facility:** Smoke free premises. 55 units. 49 one-bedroom standard units, some with whirlpools. 2 one- and 4 two-bedroom suites with kitchens. 3 stories (no elevator), exterior corridors. *Bath:* combo or shower only. **Parking:** on-site. **Amenities:** high-speed Internet, voice mail, irons, hair dryers. *Some:* DVD players. **Pool(s):** heated indoor. **Leisure Activities:** whirlpool, beach access, exercise room. **Guest Services:** coin laundry, airport transportation-Gold Beach Airport, wireless Internet. **Business Services:** meeting rooms. **Cards:** AX, DS, MC, VI. *(See color ad below)*

INN OF THE BEACHCOMBER

Book great rates at AAA.com

AAA **SAVE**

Motel
$119-$184 3/1-10/31
$79-$149 11/1-2/28

Phone: (541)247-6691
Address: 29266 Ellensburg Ave **Location:** On US 101; south end of town. **Facility:** Smoke free premises. 48 one-bedroom standard units, some with whirlpools. 2 stories (no elevator), interior/exterior corridors. **Parking:** on-site. **Terms:** office hours 7 am-10 pm. **Amenities:** video library, DVD players, CD players, voice mail, hair dryers. *Some:* high-speed Internet, safes, irons. **Pool(s):** heated indoor. **Leisure Activities:** whirlpool, beach access, picnic area. **Guest Services:** wireless Internet. **Business Services:** PC. **Cards:** AX, DS, MC, VI. **Free Special Amenities: full breakfast and high-speed Internet.**

▼ See AAA listing p 348 ▼

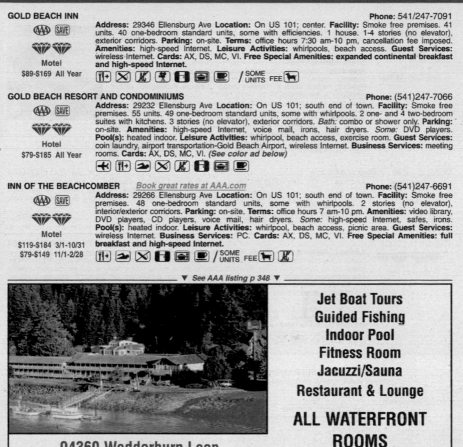
▼ See AAA listing above ▼

JOT'S RESORT

AAA SAVE

Motel
$65-$230 All Year

Phone: (541)247-6676

Address: 94360 Wedderburn Loop **Location:** Just w of US 101; north end of bridge. **Facility:** 100 units. 97 one- and 2 two-bedroom standard units, some with kitchens. 1 one-bedroom suite with kitchen. 2 stories (no elevator), exterior corridors. **Bath:** combo or shower only. **Parking:** on-site. **Terms:** check-in 4 pm, 3 day cancellation notice-fee imposed. **Amenities:** high-speed Internet, voice mail, hair dryers. *Some:* CD players, irons. **Dining:** Rod 'N Reel, see separate listing. **Pool(s):** heated outdoor, heated indoor. **Leisure Activities:** sauna, whirlpool, beach access, rental boats, fishing, pool table, exercise room. *Fee:* boat dock, river excursion boat pick-up. **Guest Services:** coin laundry, airport transportation-Gold Beach Airport, wireless Internet. **Business Services:** meeting rooms, fax (fee). **Cards:** AX, CB, DC, DS, JC, MC, VI. **Free Special Amenities:** local telephone calls and high-speed Internet. *(See color ad p 347)*

MOTEL 6 - 4047

Book at AAA.com

Motel
$61-$92 All Year

Phone: (541)247-4533

Address: 94433 Jerry's Flat Rd **Location:** Just e of jct US 101. **Facility:** 50 one-bedroom standard units, some with whirlpools. 2 stories (no elevator), exterior corridors. **Parking:** on-site. **Terms:** office hours 7 am-11 pm. **Leisure Activities:** whirlpool. **Guest Services:** coin laundry. **Business Services:** fax (fee). **Cards:** AX, DS, MC, VI.

TU TU' TUN LODGE

Country Inn
Rates not provided

Phone: 541/247-6664

Address: 96550 N Bank Rogue River Rd **Location:** Jct US 101 (north end of bridge), 6.6 mi e. Located in a quiet secluded area. **Facility:** All rooms have a balcony or patio overlooking Rogue River; complimentary morning coffee, afternoon snacks and evening hors d'oeuvres are served daily. Smoke free premises. 20 units. 16 one-bedroom standard units. 2 one-bedroom suites. 2 cottages. 2 stories (no elevator), exterior corridors. **Bath:** combo or shower only. **Parking:** on-site. **Terms:** office hours 6 am-11 pm, age restrictions may apply. **Amenities:** video library, high-speed Internet, irons, hair dryers. *Some:* DVD players, CD players. **Dining:** Tu Tu' Tun Lodge Dining Room, see separate listing. **Pool(s):** heated outdoor. **Leisure Activities:** boat dock, fishing, golf-6 holes, hiking trails, horseshoes. *Fee:* massage. **Guest Services:** complimentary and valet laundry, area transportation, wireless Internet. **Business Services:** meeting rooms, PC.

The following lodgings were either not evaluated or did not meet AAA rating requirements but are listed for your information only.

PARADISE LODGE

fyi

Phone: 541/247-6504

Not evaluated. **Address:** On Rogue River **Location:** 52 mi e of Gold Beach; accessible by river or trail only. Facilities, services, and decor characterize an economy property.

TURTLE ROCK RESORT

fyi

Phone: 541/247-9203

Not evaluated. **Address:** 28788 Hunter Creek Loop **Location:** US 101, exit Hunter Creek Loop, 0.5 mi e; between Milepost 330 and 331; south end of town. Facilities, services, and decor characterize a mid-scale property.

--- WHERE TO DINE ---

GRANT'S PANCAKE & OMELETTE HOUSE

American
$5-$13

Phone: 541/247-7208

The local favorite prepares hearty breakfasts and lunches. Guests can enjoy views of the ocean. Casual dress. **Bar:** Beer & wine. **Reservations:** accepted. **Hours:** 5:30 am-3 pm. **Address:** 29790 Ellensburg Ave **Location:** US 101; downtown. **Parking:** on-site. **Cards:** DS, MC, VI.

CALL

NOR' WESTER SEAFOOD RESTAURANT

AAA

Steak & Seafood
$18-$28

Phone: 541/247-2333

The restaurant's name says it all, as seafood is the focus of the menu. In addition to such choices as local Chinook salmon, guests can sample savory steaks and lobster. Port views are great. Casual dress. **Bar:** Full bar. **Hours:** Open 3/1-11/30 & 2/1-2/28; 5 pm-9 pm. Closed: 11/26. **Address:** 29971 Harbor Way **Location:** Just w of US 101; south end of bridge; at Port of Gold Beach. **Parking:** on-site. **Cards:** AX, MC, VI.

PATTI'S ROLLIN 'N DOUGH BISTRO, BAKERY & DELICATESSEN

American
$9-$15

Phone: 541/2474438

Guests can unwind on the seasonal deck or in the dining area of this quaint cottage across the road from the Rogue River. Just-made pastries, loaves, soups, sandwiches and even fish tacos always taste fresh. Casual dress. **Reservations:** accepted. **Hours:** 10:30 am-3 pm. Closed: Sun & Mon. **Address:** 94257 N Bank Rogue Rd **Location:** Just e of US 101; north end of bridge. **Parking:** on-site. **Cards:** MC, VI.

RIVERVIEW RESTAURANT AT ROGUE LANDING RESORT

Phone: 541/247-4276

◆◆ ◆◆
American
$13-$23

Large picture windows afford nice views at the waterside restaurant. On the menu are salads, seafood, steaks, pasta, sandwiches and pizza. Casual dress. **Bar:** Full bar. **Reservations:** accepted. **Hours:** Open 3/1-10/14 & 1/3-2/28; 4 pm-9 pm. Closed: 11/26, 12/25. **Address:** 94749 Jerry's Flat Rd **Location:** 0.8 mi e of US 101; south end of bridge. **Parking:** on-site. **Cards:** AX, MC, VI.

ROD 'N REEL

Phone: 541/247-6465

◆◆ ◆◆
Steak & Seafood
$11-$26

The established eatery is popular with the local crowd. The menu features seafood cooked in a variety of ways as well as aged beef, poultry and pasta entrees. Enjoy the spinach salad and homemade desserts. Casual dress. **Bar:** Full bar. **Reservations:** suggested. **Hours:** 3:30 pm-11 pm. Closed: 12/25. **Address:** 94321 Wedderburn Loop **Location:** Just w of US 101; north end of bridge; in Jot's Resort. **Parking:** on-site. **Cards:** AX, CB, DC, DS, MC, VI.

SPINNERS SEAFOOD, STEAK AND CHOPHOUSE

Phone: 541/247-5160

◆◆◆◆
Steak & Seafood
$14-$30

Patrons are seated in any of four rooms at this restaurant, which offers some ocean views. Menu offerings include preparations of seafood, steak, lamb, prime rib and pasta, as well as nightly specialties. If it's available, wild Oregon abalone comes highly recommended. In season, diners can request seating on the small patio. Casual dress. **Bar:** Full bar. **Reservations:** suggested. **Hours:** Open 3/1-12/31 & 2/4-2/28; 4:30 pm-9 pm; to 10 pm 7/1-10/15. **Address:** 29430 US 101 **Location:** On US 101; south side of town. **Parking:** on-site. **Cards:** AX, MC, VI.

CALL 🔅M

The following restaurant has not been evaluated by AAA but is listed for your information only.

TU TU' TUN LODGE DINING ROOM

Phone: 541/247-6664

fyi

Not evaluated. On the banks of the Rogue River, the dining room of this world-renowned lodge has a menu that changes daily, and the finest ingredients are overnighted from select vendors from around the world. Reservations are required, and dinner is exclusively a 7 pm seating with cocktails served at 6. **Address:** 96550 N Bank Rogue River Rd **Location:** Jct US 101 (north end of bridge), 6.6 mi e; in Tu Tu' Tun Lodge.

GOVERNMENT CAMP

--- WHERE TO STAY ---

MT. HOOD INN

Book great rates at AAA.com

Phone: 503/272-3205

◆◆ ◆◆
Hotel
Rates not provided

Address: 87450 E Government Camp Loop **Location:** 0.5 mi w of center. **Facility:** 57 units. 56 one-bedroom standard units, some with whirlpools. 1 one-bedroom suite. 2 stories, interior corridors. **Parking:** on-site. **Amenities:** video library (fee), DVD players, high-speed Internet, voice mail, hair dryers. **Leisure Activities:** whirlpool. **Guest Services:** coin laundry, wireless Internet. **Business Services:** meeting rooms.

The following lodgings were either not evaluated or did not meet AAA rating requirements but are listed for your information only.

COLLINS LAKE RESORT

Phone: 503/272-3051

fyi

Not evaluated. **Address:** 88149 E Creek Ridge Rd **Location:** Just w of center. Facilities, services, and decor characterize a mid-scale property.

THE LODGE AT GOVERNMENT CAMP

Phone: 503/622-7979

fyi

Not evaluated. **Address:** 30521 E Meldrum St **Location:** Just n of US 26; center. Facilities, services, and decor characterize a mid-scale property.

--- WHERE TO DINE ---

THE ICE AXE GRILL

Phone: 503/622-0724

◆◆ ◆◆
American
$7-$17

On the south slope of Mount Hood, the pub brews its eight distinctive ales with pure glacial water and regional barley and hops. The menu comprises burgers, sandwiches, pizza and such entrees as fresh rainbow trout. Casual dress. **Bar:** Beer & wine. **Reservations:** not accepted. **Hours:** 11:30 am-10 pm. **Address:** 87304 E Government Camp Loop **Location:** 0.5 mi w of center. **Parking:** on-site. **Cards:** MC, VI.

GRAND RONDE pop. 271

--- WHERE TO STAY ---

SPIRIT MOUNTAIN LODGE AND CASINO

Phone: 503/879-3764

◆◆ ◆◆
Hotel
Rates not provided

Address: 27100 SW Salmon River Hwy (SR 18) **Location:** On SR 18. **Facility:** Northwest Native American themes dominate the decor at this lodge in the middle of Oregon's coastal range; a fireplace graces the inviting lobby. 254 units. 240 one-bedroom standard units. 14 one-bedroom suites with whirlpools. 5 stories, interior corridors. **Bath:** combo or shower only. **Parking:** on-site and valet. **Amenities:** voice mail, safes, irons, hair dryers. **Fee:** video games, high-speed Internet. **Leisure Activities:** *Fee:* game room. **Guest Services:** wireless Internet. **Business Services:** conference facilities, PC.

GRANTS PASS pop. 23,003

——— WHERE TO STAY ———

BESTWAY INN   *Book great rates at AAA.com*   Phone: (541)479-2952

AAA [SAVE]

♦♦♦

Motel
$55-$75 All Year

Address: 1253 NE 6th St **Location:** I-5, exit 58, 0.9 mi s on SR 99. **Facility:** 21 one-bedroom standard units. 1 story, exterior corridors. *Bath:* combo or shower only. **Parking:** on-site. **Terms:** office hours 6 am-midnight. **Amenities:** high-speed Internet, hair dryers. *Some:* irons. **Guest Services:** wireless Internet. **Cards:** AX, DS, MC, VI. **Free Special Amenities: continental breakfast and high-speed Internet.**

[icons]

BEST WESTERN GRANTS PASS INN   *Book great rates at AAA.com*   Phone: (541)476-1117

AAA [SAVE]

♦♦♦ ♦♦♦

Hotel
$70-$142 All Year

Address: 111 NE Agness Ave **Location:** I-5, exit 55, just nw. **Facility:** 84 units. 82 one-bedroom standard units, some with whirlpools. 2 one-bedroom suites with whirlpools. 2 stories (no elevator), exterior corridors. *Bath:* combo or shower only. **Parking:** on-site. **Amenities:** high-speed Internet, irons, hair dryers. **Pool(s):** heated outdoor. **Leisure Activities:** whirlpool. **Guest Services:** valet and coin laundry, wireless Internet. **Business Services:** PC. **Cards:** AX, DC, DS, JC, MC, VI. **Free Special Amenities: continental breakfast and high-speed Internet.**
(See color ad below)

[icons]

AAA Benefit:
Members save up to 20%, plus 10% bonus points with rewards program.

BEST WESTERN INN AT THE ROGUE

Book great rates at AAA.com

Phone: (541)582-2200

AAA SAVE
◆◆◆ ◆◆◆
Hotel
$85-$110 3/1-9/15
$85-$90 9/16-2/28

Address: 8959 Rogue River Hwy **Location:** I-5, exit 48, just nw. **Facility:** Smoke free premises. 53 units. 51 one-bedroom standard units, some with whirlpools. 2 one-bedroom suites, some with whirlpools. 2 stories (no elevator), interior corridors. **Parking:** on-site. **Terms:** cancellation fee imposed. **Amenities:** high-speed Internet, irons, hair dryers. **Pool(s):** heated outdoor. **Leisure Activities:** whirlpool, exercise room. **Guest Services:** coin laundry, wireless Internet. **Business Services:** meeting rooms, PC. **Cards:** AX, CB, DC, DS, JC, MC, VI. **Free Special Amenities: expanded continental breakfast and high-speed Internet.** *(See color ad p 350)*

🍴 🏊 ⊠ 📶 🛗 📷 🖥 / SOME UNITS FEE 🐾 FEE VCR

BUONA SERA INN

Phone: 541/476-4260

◆◆◆
Motel
Rates not provided

Address: 1001 NE 6th St **Location:** I-5, exit 58, 1.1 mi s on SR 99. **Facility:** Smoke free premises. 14 units. 13 one-bedroom standard units. 1 two-bedroom suite with kitchen. 1 story, exterior corridors. *Bath:* combo or shower only. **Parking:** on-site. **Terms:** office hours 8 am-midnight. **Amenities:** high-speed Internet, hair dryers. **Guest Services:** wireless Internet.

⊠ 📶 🛗 📷 🖥 / SOME UNITS FEE 🐾

COMFORT INN

Book at AAA.com

Phone: (541)479-8301

◆◆◆ ◆◆
Hotel
$68-$130 3/1-9/18
$60-$130 9/19-2/28

Address: 1889 NE 6th St **Location:** I-5, exit 58, just s on SR 99. **Facility:** 59 one-bedroom standard units. 2 stories (no elevator), interior corridors. **Parking:** on-site. **Amenities:** high-speed Internet, irons, hair dryers. **Pool(s):** outdoor. **Guest Services:** coin laundry, wireless Internet. **Cards:** AX, DS, MC, VI.

ASK 🍴 🏊 📶 🖥 / SOME UNITS FEE 🐾 ⊠ 🛗 📷

FLERY MANOR INN

Phone: 541/476-3591

◆◆ ◆◆
Bed & Breakfast
Rates not provided

Address: 2000 Jumpoff Joe Creek Rd **Location:** I-5, exit 66, just e to Jumpoff Joe Creek Rd, then 1.7 mi s. Located in secluded countryside **Facility:** Nestled on seven acres of mountainside, this B&B offers a panoramic view of a pine forest and landscaped grounds with paths, a stream and a fountain. Smoke free premises. 4 units. 3 one- and 1 two-bedroom standard units, some with whirlpools. 2 stories (no elevator), interior corridors. **Parking:** on-site. **Terms:** check-in 4 pm, age restrictions may apply. **Amenities:** irons, hair dryers. *Some:* DVD players. **Leisure Activities:** hiking trails. **Guest Services:** TV in common area, wireless Internet. **Business Services:** meeting rooms, PC, fax.

✈ FEE 📶 ⊠ �W / SOME UNITS 🖥

HOLIDAY INN EXPRESS

Book great rates at AAA.com

Phone: (541)471-6144

AAA SAVE
◆◆◆ ◆◆◆
Hotel
$96-$169 All Year

Address: 105 NE Agness Ave **Location:** I-5, exit 55, just nw. **Facility:** 80 units. 79 one- and 1 two-bedroom standard units, some with whirlpools. 4 stories, interior corridors. *Bath:* combo or shower only. **Parking:** on-site. **Amenities:** high-speed Internet, voice mail, irons, hair dryers. **Leisure Activities:** pool & whirlpool privileges. **Guest Services:** valet and coin laundry, wireless Internet. **Business Services:** business center. **Cards:** AX, CB, DC, DS, JC, MC, VI. **Free Special Amenities: full breakfast and local telephone calls.**

🍴 FEE 📶 📶 🛗 📷 🖥 / SOME UNITS FEE 🐾 ⊠

KNIGHTS INN MOTEL

Phone: 541/479-5595

AAA SAVE
◆◆
Motel
Rates not provided

Address: 104 SE 7th St **Location:** I-5, exit 58, 1.7 mi s on SR 99, just e on G St, then just n. **Facility:** 32 one-bedroom standard units. 2 stories (no elevator), exterior corridors. *Bath:* combo or shower only. **Parking:** on-site. **Terms:** office hours 6:30 am-11 pm. **Amenities:** high-speed Internet, hair dryers. **Guest Services:** wireless Internet.

🍴 📶 🛗 📷 / SOME UNITS FEE 🐾 ⊠

LA QUINTA INN & SUITES GRANTS PASS

Book great rates at AAA.com

Phone: (541)472-1808

◆◆◆ ◆◆
Hotel
$59-$119 All Year

Address: 243 NE Morgan Ln **Location:** I-5, exit 58, 0.4 mi s on SR 99, just e on Hillcrest Dr to SR 99 N, then just n. **Facility:** 59 units. 58 one-bedroom standard units, some with efficiencies and/or whirlpools. 1 one-bedroom suite. 3 stories, interior corridors. *Bath:* combo or shower only. **Parking:** on-site. **Amenities:** high-speed Internet, dual phone lines, voice mail, irons, hair dryers. **Pool(s):** heated indoor. **Leisure Activities:** whirlpool, exercise room. **Guest Services:** valet and coin laundry, wireless Internet. **Business Services:** meeting rooms, PC. **Cards:** AX, DS, MC, VI.

ASK CALL 🅾M 🏊 📶 🛗 📷 🖥 / SOME UNITS 🐾 ⊠ VCR

THE LODGE AT RIVERSIDE

Phone: (541)955-0600

AAA SAVE
◆◆◆ ◆◆◆
Hotel
$135-$325 All Year

Address: 955 SE 7th St **Location:** I-5, exit 58, 2.5 mi s on SR 99. **Facility:** Smoke free premises. 48 units. 41 one-bedroom standard units, 7 one-bedroom suites, some with whirlpools. 2 stories, exterior corridors. **Parking:** on-site. **Terms:** office hours 7 am-11 pm, 3 day cancellation notice-fee imposed. **Amenities:** high-speed Internet, voice mail, irons, hair dryers. **Pool(s):** heated outdoor. **Leisure Activities:** whirlpool. **Guest Services:** valet laundry, wireless Internet. **Business Services:** conference facilities. **Cards:** AX, DS, MC, VI. **Free Special Amenities: expanded continental breakfast and high-speed Internet.**

🏊 FEE 📶 ⊠ 📶 🛗 🖥 / SOME UNITS FEE 📷

MOTEL 6 - #253 *Book at AAA.com*

Motel
$45-$55 All Year

Phone: (541)474-1331

Address: 1800 NE 7th St **Location:** I-5, exit 58, 0.3 mi s on SR 99. **Facility:** 122 one-bedroom standard units. 2 stories (no elevator), exterior corridors. *Bath:* shower only. **Parking:** on-site. **Pool(s):** heated outdoor. **Guest Services:** coin laundry. **Cards:** AX, CB, DC, DS, MC, VI.

REDWOOD MOTEL

Phone: 541/476-0878

Motel
$60-$352 All Year

Address: 815 NE 6th St **Location:** I-5, exit 58, 1.2 mi s on SR 99. **Facility:** Smoke free premises. 42 units. 33 one- and 3 two-bedroom standard units, some with whirlpools. 6 one-bedroom suites, some with whirlpools. 1-2 stories (no elevator), exterior corridors. *Bath:* combo or shower only. **Parking:** on-site. **Terms:** office hours 7 am-11 pm, 2 night minimum stay - seasonal, cancellation fee imposed. **Amenities:** voice mail, irons, hair dryers. *Some:* DVD players, high-speed Internet. **Pool(s):** heated outdoor. **Leisure Activities:** whirlpool, exercise room. **Guest Services:** coin laundry, wireless Internet. **Business Services:** meeting rooms, PC. **Cards:** AX, DS, MC, VI. **Free Special Amenities:** continental breakfast and local telephone calls.
(See color ad below)

RIVERSIDE INN *Book great rates at AAA.com*

Hotel
$125-$149 All Year

Phone: (541)476-6873

Address: 986 SW 6th St **Location:** I-5, exit 58, 2.5 mi s on SR 99. **Facility:** Smoke free premises. 63 one-bedroom standard units. 2-3 stories, exterior corridors. *Bath:* combo or shower only. **Parking:** on-site. **Terms:** check-in 4 pm, 3 day cancellation notice-fee imposed. **Amenities:** high-speed Internet, voice mail, irons, hair dryers. **Pool(s):** heated outdoor. **Leisure Activities:** whirlpool. **Guest Services:** valet laundry, wireless Internet. **Cards:** AX, DS, MC, VI. **Free Special Amenities:** expanded continental breakfast and high-speed Internet.

SHILO INN *Book great rates at AAA.com*

Hotel
$75-$159 All Year

Phone: (541)479-8391

Address: 1880 NW 6th St **Location:** I-5, exit 58, 0.3 mi s on SR 99. **Facility:** 70 one-bedroom standard units. 2 stories (no elevator), interior corridors. *Bath:* combo or shower only. **Parking:** on-site. **Amenities:** video games (fee), high-speed Internet, voice mail, irons, hair dryers. **Pool(s):** heated outdoor. **Leisure Activities:** sauna, steamroom. **Guest Services:** valet laundry, wireless Internet. **Business Services:** meeting rooms. **Cards:** AX, CB, DC, DS, JC, MC, VI. **Free Special Amenities:** continental breakfast and high-speed Internet.
(See color ad p 353)

SUNSET INN   *Book great rates at AAA.com*   Phone: (541)479-3305

AAA SAVE
◇◇◇◇
Motel
$55-$135 All Year

Address: 1400 NW 6th St **Location:** I-5, exit 58, 0.7 mi s on SR 99. **Facility:** 29 one-bedroom standard units. 2 stories (no elevator), exterior corridors. **Parking:** on-site. **Terms:** office hours 7 am-11 pm. **Amenities:** high-speed Internet. **Pool(s):** outdoor. **Guest Services:** wireless Internet. **Cards:** AX, DS, MC, VI. **Free Special Amenities: continental breakfast and high-speed Internet.**

SUPER 8 - GRANTS PASS   *Book great rates at AAA.com*   Phone: (541)474-0888

AAA SAVE
◇◇◇◇
Hotel
$55-$103 All Year

Address: 1949 NE 7th St **Location:** I-5, exit 58, 0.4 mi s on SR 99, just e on Hillcrest Dr to SR 99 N, then just n. **Facility:** 80 units. 79 one-bedroom standard units. 1 one-bedroom suite with kitchen (no utensils). 3 stories (no elevator), interior corridors. **Parking:** on-site. **Amenities:** high-speed Internet, safes (fee), hair dryers. **Pool(s):** heated indoor. **Leisure Activities:** whirlpool. **Guest Services:** coin laundry, wireless Internet. **Business Services:** meeting rooms, PC. **Cards:** AX, DS, MC, VI. **Free Special Amenities: continental breakfast and high-speed Internet.**

SWEET BREEZE INN   *Book great rates at AAA.com*   Phone: 541/471-4434

AAA SAVE
◇◇◇◇
Motel
Rates not provided

Address: 1627 NE 6th St **Location:** I-5, exit 58, 0.5 mi s on SR 99. **Facility:** Smoke free premises. 21 one-bedroom standard units. 2 stories (no elevator), interior/exterior corridors. *Bath:* combo or shower only. **Parking:** on-site. **Terms:** office hours 7 am-11 pm. **Amenities:** hair dryers. *Some:* high-speed Internet. **Guest Services:** wireless Internet. **Free Special Amenities: continental breakfast and preferred room (subject to availability with advance reservations).**

▼ *See AAA listing p 352* ▼

TRAVELODGE *Book at AAA.com* Phone: 541/479-6611

Motel
Rates not provided

Address: 1950 NW Vine St **Location:** I-5, exit 58, just s on SR 99. **Facility:** 61 units. 60 one-bedroom standard units. 1 one-bedroom suite. 2 stories (no elevator); exterior corridors. *Bath:* combo or shower only. **Parking:** on-site. **Amenities:** high-speed Internet, voice mail, safes (fee), hair dryers. **Pool(s):** heated outdoor. **Guest Services:** coin laundry, wireless Internet. **Business Services:** PC.

 CALL Ⓜ / SOME UNITS FEE

WEASKU INN Phone: 541/471-8000

Ⓐ SAVE

Historic
Hotel
Rates not provided

Address: 5560 Rogue River Hwy **Location:** I-5, exit 48, 3.8 mi nw on SR 99. Located in a quiet, rustic area along Rogue River. **Facility:** 1924 fishing lodge on spacious wooded landscaped grounds adjacent to the Rogue River with restored lodge units and newly constructed riverside cabins. Smoke free premises. 17 units. 5 one-bedroom standard units, some with whirlpools. 12 cabins. 2 stories (no elevator); interior/exterior corridors. **Parking:** on-site. **Terms:** office hours 7 am-11 pm. **Amenities:** video library, high-speed Internet, voice mail, irons, hair dryers. **Leisure Activities:** fishing, hiking trails. **Guest Services:** valet laundry, airport transportation-Grants Pass Airport, wireless Internet. **Business Services:** meeting rooms. **Free Special Amenities: expanded continental breakfast and high-speed Internet.**

 VCR / SOME UNITS

WHERE TO DINE

BLUE STONE BAKERY & COFFEE CAFE *Menu on AAA.com* Phone: 541/471-1922

Ⓐ

Breads/Pastries
$6-$8

The eatery is a great spot for good, light, reasonably priced food. The menu is limited to soups, salads, sandwiches, quiches and European cakes and pastries but, on the plus side, everything is made fresh from scratch with nothing but the best ingredients. Whether you're just looking for quick take-away or a comfortable place to linger over a cup of coffee and a good book, this cafe is a recommended stop. Casual dress. **Reservations:** not accepted. **Hours:** 6 am-5 pm, Sat 8 am-3 pm, Sun 9 am-3 pm. Closed major holidays. **Address:** 412 NW 6th St **Location:** I-5, exit 58, 1.6 mi s on SR 99; corner of D St. **Parking:** on-site and street. **Cards:** DS, MC, VI.

THE BREWERY Phone: 541/479-9850

Steak
$6-$25

The entrance, as well as parking space, is in back of the 1850 red brick brewery, where diners come for featured steak and seafood entrees, as well as other offerings. Casual dress. **Bar:** Full bar. **Reservations:** accepted. **Hours:** 11:30 am-2 & 4:30-8 pm, Fri & Sat-9 pm, Sun 9:30 am-1:30 & 4:30-8 pm; Sunday brunch. Closed major holidays. **Address:** 509 SW G St **Location:** At 3rd and SW G sts, 0.3 mi w of SR 99; downtown. **Parking:** on-site. **Cards:** AX, DS, MC, VI.

MATSUKAZE *Menu on AAA.com* Phone: 541/479-2961

Ⓐ

Japanese
$7-$17

Since 1984, the family-owned eatery has featured sushi and traditional Japanese dishes. Casual dress. **Bar:** Beer & wine. **Reservations:** accepted. **Hours:** 11 am-2 & 5-8:30 pm, Fri & Sat-9 pm. Closed major holidays; also Sun. **Address:** 1675 NE 7th St **Location:** I-5, exit 58, 0.4 mi s on SR 99, then just e on Hillcrest Dr. **Parking:** on-site. **Cards:** AX, DS, MC, VI.

ONE FIFTEEN BROILER Phone: 541/474-7115

Steak
$15-$30

With a classic old New York decor and a long narrow design, this steakhouse is intimate and personal. Guests can enjoy one of the best steaks in town or just a quiet cocktail. Casual dress. **Bar:** Full bar. **Reservations:** suggested. **Hours:** 11 am-3 & 5-9 pm, Fri & Sat-10 pm. Closed major holidays; also Sun & Mon. **Address:** 115 D St **Location:** I-5, exit 58, 1.6 mi s on SR 99, then just w. **Parking:** street. **Cards:** AX, DS, MC, VI.

R-HAUS Phone: 541/474-3335

American
$13-$23

River views are noteworthy from the restaurant, which serves champagne brunch on Sunday from 9:30 am-1:30 pm. An outdoor deck is open in the summer. Casual dress. **Bar:** Full bar. **Reservations:** suggested. **Hours:** 4 pm-9 pm. Closed: Jan. **Address:** 2140 Rogue River Hwy **Location:** On SR 99 S, 1.9 mi e of jct US 199 and SR 238. **Parking:** on-site. **Cards:** AX, DS, MC, VI.

RIVER'S EDGE Phone: 541/479-3938

American
$9-$40

Guests can enjoy views of the Rogue River from three tiers of seating on the large river deck. Most inside tables also afford a beautiful view. Casual dress. **Bar:** Full bar. **Reservations:** accepted. **Hours:** 11 am-3 & 4-10 pm, Fri & Sat-11 pm. Closed: 12/25. **Address:** 1936 Rogue River Hwy **Location:** On SR 99, 1.5 mi e of jct US 199 and SR 238. **Parking:** on-site. **Cards:** AX, DS, MC, VI.

WILD RIVER BREWING & PIZZA CO. Phone: 541/471-7487

American
$7-$23

A variety of in-house hand-crafted beers, stout and root beer complement wood-fired pizzas, pasta dishes, sandwiches, salad, burgers and calzones. Casual dress. **Bar:** Beer & wine. **Reservations:** accepted, except Fri & Sat. **Hours:** 10:30 am-10:30 pm, Fri & Sat-11 pm. Closed: 4/12, 11/26, 12/25. **Address:** 595 NE E St **Location:** I-5, exit 58, 1.7 mi s on SR 99. **Parking:** on-site. **Cards:** DS, MC, VI.

GRESHAM —*See Portland p. 457.*

HAINES pop. 426

WHERE TO DINE

HAINES STEAK HOUSE Phone: 541/856-3639

Steak
$8-$23

A Western frontier atmosphere with game trophies and other memorabilia sets the tone in the casual family restaurant. The "covered wagon" salad bar is a popular stop. Entrees reflect a steakhouse orientation: mostly beef with a few other choices. Casual dress. **Bar:** Full bar. **Reservations:** accepted. **Hours:** 5 pm-9 pm, Fri-10 pm, Sat 4 pm-10 pm, Sun 1 pm-9 pm. Closed: 11/26, 12/25; also Tues. **Address:** 910 Front St **Location:** 10 mi n of Baker City on US 30. **Parking:** street. **Cards:** AX, CB, DC, DS, MC, VI.

HALSEY pop. 724

——— WHERE TO STAY ———

PIONEER VILLA TRAVELODGE *Book at AAA.com*   Phone: (541)369-2804

Motel
$75-$85 3/1-9/30
$72-$82 10/1-2/28

Address: 33180 SR 228 **Location:** I-5, exit 216, just se. **Facility:** 57 one-bedroom standard units. 1 story, exterior corridors. **Parking:** on-site. **Amenities:** high-speed Internet, irons, hair dryers. **Pool(s):** outdoor. **Leisure Activities:** whirlpool. **Guest Services:** coin laundry, wireless Internet. **Business Services:** meeting rooms, PC. **Cards:** AX, CB, DC, DS, MC, VI.

ASK 🍴 🍸 🛏 🐾 🎿 🎱 🖥 💻 / SOME UNITS FEE 🐾 ✕

HERMISTON pop. 13,154

——— WHERE TO STAY ———

BEST WESTERN HERMISTON INN *Book great rates at AAA.com*   Phone: (541)564-0202

Hotel
$80-$90 All Year

Address: 2255 US 395 S **Location:** 2 mi s. **Facility:** 54 one-bedroom standard units, some with whirlpools. 2 stories (no elevator), interior corridors. *Bath:* combo or shower only. **Parking:** on-site. **Amenities:** high-speed Internet, voice mail, irons, hair dryers. **Pool(s):** heated indoor. **Leisure Activities:** exercise room. *Fee:* pool table. **Guest Services:** coin laundry, wireless Internet. **Business Services:** meeting rooms, PC. **Cards:** AX, DS, MC, VI. **Free Special Amenities: continental breakfast and high-speed Internet.**

🍴 🛏 🎿 🎱 🖥 💻 / SOME UNITS ✕ VCR

AAA Benefit:
Members save up to
20%, plus 10%
bonus points with
rewards program.

COMFORT INN & SUITES HERMISTON   *Book at AAA.com*   Phone: 541/564-5911

Hotel
Rates not provided

Address: 77514 SR 207 **Location:** I-84, exit 182, just nw. **Facility:** 65 units. 58 one-bedroom standard units. 7 one-bedroom suites. 3 stories, interior corridors. *Bath:* combo or shower only. **Parking:** on-site. **Amenities:** high-speed Internet, voice mail, irons, hair dryers. **Pool(s):** heated indoor. **Leisure Activities:** whirlpool, exercise room. **Guest Services:** coin laundry, wireless Internet. **Business Services:** PC.

CALL 🛏 🐾 🎿 🎱 🖥 💻 / SOME UNITS FEE 🐾 ✕

OAK TREE INN *Book great rates at AAA.com*   Phone: (541)567-2330

Hotel
$79-$84 3/1-9/30
$69-$79 10/1-2/28

Address: 1110 SE 4th St **Location:** 0.4 mi s on US 395, then just w. **Facility:** Smoke free premises. 62 one-bedroom standard units. 3 stories, interior corridors. *Bath:* combo or shower only. **Parking:** on-site. **Terms:** check-in 4 pm. **Amenities:** high-speed Internet. *Some:* irons, hair dryers. **Leisure Activities:** exercise room. **Guest Services:** coin laundry, wireless Internet. **Cards:** AX, DC, DS, MC, VI. **Free Special Amenities: full breakfast and high-speed Internet.**

✕ 🎿 / SOME UNITS FEE 🐾 🎱 🖥 💻

OXFORD SUITES *Book at AAA.com*   Phone: (541)564-8000

Hotel
$109-$119 All Year

Address: 1050 N 1st St **Location:** 0.5 mi n on US 395. **Facility:** 126 units. 96 one- and 10 two-bedroom standard units, some with whirlpools. 20 one-bedroom suites, some with whirlpools. 3 stories, interior corridors. *Bath:* combo or shower only. **Parking:** on-site. **Amenities:** video library (fee), high-speed Internet, voice mail, irons, hair dryers. *Some:* DVD players. **Pool(s):** heated indoor. **Leisure Activities:** whirlpool, exercise room. **Guest Services:** valet and coin laundry, wireless Internet. **Business Services:** meeting rooms, business center. **Cards:** AX, DC, DS, MC, VI.

ASK CALL 🛏 🐾 VCR 🎱 🖥 💻 / SOME UNITS FEE 🐾 ✕

——— WHERE TO DINE ———

EL CAZADOR MEXICAN GRILL & CANTINA   Phone: 541/567-2804

Mexican
$5-$14

Such traditional Mexican offerings as fajitas share menu space with chicken in mole and a few vegetarian dishes. Outside seating is a seasonal option. Casual dress. **Bar:** Full bar. **Reservations:** accepted. **Hours:** 11 am-10 pm, Fri & Sat-11 pm. Closed: 11/26, 12/25. **Address:** 1240 N 1st St **Location:** 0.3 mi n on US 395. **Parking:** on-site. **Cards:** AX, DS, MC, VI.

🔷

NOOKIE'S BISTRO & SPIRITS   Phone: 541/289-7415

American
$5-$18

Warm Southern decor welcomes guests at this downtown restaurant, where steak and seafood dishes are among contemporary and healthful choices. A good selection of cheeses and attractive list of by-the-glass wines complement the main dishes. Enhancing the appeal of the setting are an open kitchen and seasonal sheltered patio. Casual dress. **Bar:** Full bar. **Reservations:** accepted. **Hours:** 11 am- 9 pm. Closed major holidays; also Sun & Mon. **Address:** 125 N 1st St (US 395) **Location:** Jct of 1st St and W Hermiston Ave. **Parking:** on-site. **Cards:** MC, VI.

HILLSBORO —See Portland p. 460.

HINES pop. 1,623

--------- WHERE TO STAY ---------

BEST WESTERN RORY & RYAN INNS

Book great rates at AAA.com

Phone: (541)573-5050

AAA SAVE

▼▼▼▼

Hotel
$70-$145 All Year

Address: 534 US 20 N **Location:** On US 20 (Central Oregon Hwy). **Facility:** Smoke free premises. 62 one-bedroom standard units, some with whirlpools. 2 stories (no elevator), interior corridors. *Bath:* combo or shower only. **Parking:** on-site. **Terms:** 3 day cancellation notice. **Amenities:** high-speed Internet, irons, hair dryers. **Pool(s):** heated indoor. **Leisure Activities:** whirlpool. **Guest Services:** coin laundry, wireless Internet. **Business Services:** meeting rooms, PC. **Cards:** AX, DC, DS, MC, VI. **Free Special Amenities: continental breakfast and high-speed Internet.**

AAA Benefit:
Members save up to 20%, plus 10% bonus points with rewards program.

 / SOME UNITS FEE

HOOD RIVER pop. 5,831

--------- WHERE TO STAY ---------

BEST WESTERN HOOD RIVER INN

Book great rates at AAA.com

Phone: (541)386-2200

AAA SAVE

▼▼▼▼

Hotel
$95-$179 All Year

Address: 1108 E Marina Way **Location:** I-84, exit 64, just ne. **Facility:** Smoke free premises. 157 units. 147 one- and 4 two-bedroom standard units, some with whirlpools. 2 one- and 4 two-bedroom suites, some with kitchens and/or whirlpools. 2-3 stories, interior corridors. *Bath:* combo or shower only. **Parking:** on-site. **Terms:** check-in 4 pm, 3 day cancellation notice. **Amenities:** high-speed Internet, voice mail, irons, hair dryers. **Dining:** Riverside Grill, see separate listing. **Pool(s):** heated outdoor. **Leisure Activities:** whirlpool, beach access, boat dock, croquet, bicycles, exercise room, volleyball. **Guest Services:** valet and coin laundry, wireless Internet. **Business Services:** conference facilities, PC. **Cards:** AX, CB, DC, DS, MC, VI. **Free Special Amenities: full breakfast and high-speed Internet.** *(See color ad below)*

AAA Benefit:
Members save up to 20%, plus 10% bonus points with rewards program.

 / SOME UNITS FEE

COLUMBIA GORGE HOTEL

Book great rates at AAA.com

Phone: (541)386-5566

AAA SAVE

▼▼▼▼

Historic
Country Inn
$199-$399 All Year

Address: 4000 Westcliff Dr **Location:** I-84, exit 62, just sw of overpass. Located in the Columbia River Gorge National Scenic Area. **Facility:** Perched at the top of a 208-foot waterfall overlooking the Columbia River Gorge, the restored 1921 hotel features river- and garden-view guest rooms. Smoke free premises. 39 units. 35 one- and 4 two-bedroom standard units. 3 stories, interior corridors. **Parking:** on-site. **Terms:** check-in 4 pm, 14 day cancellation notice-fee imposed. **Amenities:** DVD players, CD players, high-speed Internet, voice mail, irons, hair dryers. **Dining:** restaurant, see separate listing. **Leisure Activities:** spa. **Guest Services:** valet laundry, airport transportation (fee)-Hood River Airport, area transportation-within 5 mi, wireless Internet. **Business Services:** meeting rooms, PC. **Cards:** AX, DC, DS, MC, VI. **Free Special Amenities: local telephone calls and high-speed Internet.**

FEE  / SOME UNITS FEE

COMFORT SUITES

Book great rates at AAA.com

Phone: (541)308-1000

AAA SAVE

▼▼▼▼

Hotel
$120-$250 All Year

Address: 2625 Cascade Ave **Location:** I-84, exit 62, 0.6 mi se. **Facility:** Smoke free premises. 64 units. 63 one-bedroom standard units, some with whirlpools. 1 one-bedroom suite with kitchen. 3 stories, interior corridors. *Bath:* combo or shower only. **Parking:** on-site. **Amenities:** high-speed Internet, dual phone lines, voice mail, safes (fee), irons, hair dryers. **Pool(s):** heated indoor. **Leisure Activities:** sauna, whirlpool, exercise room. **Business Services:** PC. **Cards:** AX, CB, DC, DS, MC, VI. **Free Special Amenities: expanded continental breakfast and high-speed Internet.**

▼ See AAA listing above ▼

VAGABOND LODGE

Phone: 541/386-2992

AAA SAVE

Motel
$54-$105 All Year

Address: 4070 Westcliff Dr **Location:** I-84, exit 62, 0.3 mi nw. **Facility:** 42 units. 35 one-bedroom standard units. 5 one-bedroom suites, some with kitchens. 2 cottages. 1-2 stories (no elevator), exterior corridors. *Bath:* combo or shower only. **Parking:** on-site. **Terms:** office hours 7 am-midnight. **Amenities:** high-speed Internet, voice mail. *Some:* hair dryers. **Leisure Activities:** picnic area with barbecue, playground. **Guest Services:** wireless Internet. **Cards:** AX, DC, DS, MC, VI.

⊞ 🖥 🖨 / SOME UNITS FEE 🐾 ✕ ▣

The following lodging was either not evaluated or did not meet AAA rating requirements but is listed for your information only.

HOOD RIVER HOTEL

Phone: 541/386-1900

fyi

Not evaluated. **Address:** 102 Oak St **Location:** I-84, exit 63, just s on 2nd St, then just e. Facilities, services, and decor characterize a mid-scale property.

WHERE TO DINE

CELILO RESTAURANT AND BAR

Phone: 541/386-5710

Continental
$5-$25

Set in the downtown area, this restaurant offers refined dining in a casual setting. The menu features ingredients that support local farmers of produce, beef and seafood. Begin your meal with Hood River organic figs and Bellwether Farms Crescenza cheese wrapped in prosciutto-toasted hazelnuts and saba grape musk. Then choose between free range chicken with organic dutch potato puree and wilted organic arugula and apple cider jus or the Oregon salmon with creamy polenta, organic sugar snap peas with a sauce of olives and preserved tomatoes. Make sure you save room for the Wy'East chocolate volcano cake or the Chocolate Pot de Creme Trio—a chocolate custard infused with seasonal liqueurs. Casual dress. **Bar:** Full bar. **Reservations:** suggested. **Hours:** 11:30 am-3 & 5-9:30 pm, Fri & Sat-10 pm. Closed: Sun & Mon 1/1-4/30. **Address:** 16 Oak St **Location:** Jct of 1st and Oak sts; downtown. **Parking:** street. **Cards:** AX, CB, DC, DS, JC, MC, VI.

COLUMBIA GORGE HOTEL DINING ROOM

Phone: 541/386-5566

AAA

Regional American
$9-$80

Guests can enjoy views of the Columbia River Gorge while dining. An after-dinner stroll in the magnificent gardens is a perfect end to the evening. Dressy casual. **Bar:** Full bar. **Reservations:** suggested. **Hours:** 8-10:45 am, 11-3:30 & 5-9 pm, Fri & Sat-10 pm, Sun 8 am-2 & 5-9 pm. **Address:** 4000 Westcliff Dr **Location:** I-84, exit 62, just sw of overpass; in Columbia Gorge Hotel. **Parking:** on-site. **Cards:** AX, DC, DS, MC, VI. **Historic**

CORNERSTONE CUISINE

Phone: 541/386-1900

American
$7-$25

In a historic 1913 hotel that's on the National Register of Historic Places, the restaurant infuses fine Italian cuisine with some Pacific Northwest influences. Casual dress. **Bar:** Full bar. **Reservations:** accepted. **Hours:** 7 am-9 pm, Fri & Sat-10 pm; to 8 pm, Fri & Sat-9 pm 11/2-3/31. **Address:** 102 Oak St **Location:** I-84, exit 63, just s on 2nd St, then just e; in Hood River Hotel. **Parking:** street. **Cards:** AX, CB, DC, DS, MC, VI.

DOUBLE MOUNTAIN BREWERY & TAPROOM

Phone: 541/387-0042

American
$6-$20

In the bustling downtown center, this taproom offers sandwiches, salads, pizzas and microbrewed beers to wash it all down. Seating is limited in the cozy dining room and in the outdoor area. Casual dress. **Bar:** Beer & wine. **Hours:** 4 pm-10 pm, Sat noon-11 pm, Sun noon-10 pm. Closed major holidays. **Address:** 8 4th St **Location:** Between Cascade Ave and Columbia St; downtown. **Parking:** street. **Cards:** MC, VI.

RIVERSIDE GRILL

Phone: 541/386-4410

American
$8-$30

Steaks, seafood and pasta dishes are among menu offerings at the casual riverfront restaurant. Be sure to reserve a riverview table or request outdoor seating on the deck in season. Lighter fare is served in the lounge. Casual dress. **Bar:** Full bar. **Reservations:** suggested. **Hours:** 6 am-9 pm; to 10 pm in summer. **Address:** 1108 E Marina Way **Location:** I-84, exit 64, just ne; in Best Western Hood River Inn. **Parking:** on-site. **Cards:** AX, DC, DS, MC, VI.

STONEHEDGE GARDENS

Phone: 541/386-3940

AAA

American
$12-$30

Nestled in wooded hills on private, forested acres, the 1898 country inn pleases with its markedly creative cuisine. Made-from-scratch entrees—such as roast Long Island duckling, portobello mushroom ravioli and sambuca shrimp—take design, color, texture and taste into account. Lighter bistro dishes are available. The house dessert for two is bread pudding with flaming creme brulee and bourbon caramel sauce. Seating is offered on the enclosed porch or seasonal terrace. Casual dress. **Bar:** Full bar. **Reservations:** suggested. **Hours:** 5 pm-9 pm; call for hours in winter. Closed: 11/26, 12/25. **Address:** 3405 Cascade Ave **Location:** I-84, exit 62, 1.3 mi se. **Parking:** on-site. **Cards:** AX, DS, MC, VI. **Historic**

ISLAND CITY pop. 916

WHERE TO DINE

EL ERRADERO

Phone: 541/663-1092

Mexican
$5-$12

The small, family-owned chain serves hot Mexican classics in a casual atmosphere. Casual dress. **Bar:** Full bar. **Hours:** 11 am-9 pm. Closed: 7/4, 11/26, 12/25. **Address:** 10107 1st St W **Location:** I-84, exit 261, 1.4 mi e. **Parking:** on-site. **Cards:** MC, VI.

JACKSONVILLE pop. 2,235

------ WHERE TO STAY ------

JACKSONVILLE INN

(AAA) [SAVE]

▼▼◆▼▼

Historic
Country Inn

$159-$465 All Year

Phone: (541)899-1900

Address: 175 E California St **Location:** On California St (SR 238); between 3rd and 4th sts; center. Located in the historic district. **Facility:** Western antiques lend a pioneer ambience to this mid-19th-century inn; luxuriously appointed cottages are also available near the inn. Smoke free premises. 12 units. 8 one-bedroom standard units, some with whirlpools. 4 cottages. 1-2 stories (no elevator), interior/exterior corridors. *Bath:* combo or shower only. **Parking:** on-site. **Terms:** office hours 8 am-11 pm, 3 day cancellation notice-fee imposed. **Amenities:** high-speed Internet, irons, hair dryers. *Some:* DVD players, CD players, honor bars. **Dining:** Jacksonville Inn Dinner House, see separate listing. **Leisure Activities:** bicycles. **Guest Services:** wireless Internet. **Business Services:** meeting rooms. **Cards:** AX, CB, DC, DS, MC, VI. **Free Special Amenities: full breakfast and local telephone calls.**

🍴 ☂ ✕ 🖥 / SOME UNITS 🐾 VCR 🖨 💻

JACKSONVILLE'S MAGNOLIA INN

(AAA) [SAVE]

▼▼◆▼▼

Historic Bed
& Breakfast

$95-$165 All Year

Phone: (541)899-0255

Address: 245 N 5th St **Location:** At 5th (SR 238) and D sts. Located in the historic district. **Facility:** In a quiet residential neighborhood within walking distance of shops and restaurants, this restored 1928 inn has a comfortable elegance. Smoke free premises. 9 units. 8 one- and 1 two-bedroom standard units. 2 stories (no elevator), interior corridors. *Bath:* combo or shower only. **Parking:** on-site and street. **Terms:** office hours 7 am-9:45 pm, 3 day cancellation notice-fee imposed. **Amenities:** video library, high-speed Internet, irons, hair dryers. **Guest Services:** valet laundry, airport transportation-Medford Airport, wireless Internet. **Cards:** AX, DS, MC, VI. **Free Special Amenities: expanded continental breakfast and high-speed Internet.**

🕂 CALL 🔊M ✕ VCR / SOME UNITS 🐾

MCCULLY HOUSE INN

(AAA) [SAVE]

▼▼◆▼▼

Historic Bed
& Breakfast

$135-$325 All Year

Phone: 541/899-1942

Address: 240 E California St **Location:** At E California (SR 238) and 5th sts. Located in historic district. **Facility:** The gardens at this 1860 Federal-style home contain 85 unique varieties of roses; three cottage rooms are located a block from the main inn. Smoke free premises. 7 units. 4 one-bedroom standard units. 3 cottages. 2 stories (no elevator), interior/exterior corridors. *Bath:* combo or shower only. **Parking:** street. **Terms:** office hours 8 am-5 pm, 3 day cancellation notice-fee imposed. **Amenities:** *Some:* high-speed Internet. **Guest Services:** wireless Internet. **Business Services:** meeting rooms. **Cards:** AX, MC, VI. **Free Special Amenities: expanded continental breakfast and high-speed Internet.**

✕ / SOME UNITS 📺 🖃 🖥 💻

THE STAGE LODGE

▼▼◆▼▼

Motel

$98-$175 All Year

Phone: (541)899-3953

Address: 830 N 5th St **Location:** 0.5 mi ne of downtown. **Facility:** Smoke free premises. 27 one-bedroom standard units, some with whirlpools. 2 stories (no elevator), exterior corridors. *Bath:* combo or shower only. **Parking:** on-site. **Terms:** office hours 7 am-10 pm, 7 day cancellation notice-fee imposed. **Amenities:** high-speed Internet, hair dryers. **Guest Services:** wireless Internet. **Cards:** AX, DC, DS, MC, VI.

(ASK) ✕ 🖥 / SOME UNITS FEE 🐾 🖃 💻

TOUVELLE HOUSE BED & BREAKFAST

▼▼◆▼▼

Historic Bed
& Breakfast

$149-$195 All Year

Phone: 541/899-8938

Address: 455 N Oregon St **Location:** At E and N Oregon sts; center. Located in the historic district. **Facility:** Vivid colors, dark woods, antiques, patterned wallpaper and original light fixtures carry out the period theme of this 1916 Craftsman home. Smoke free premises. 6 units. 4 one- and 2 two-bedroom standard units. 3 stories (no elevator), interior corridors. *Bath:* shower or tub only. **Parking:** on-site. **Terms:** office hours 7 am-9 pm, 1-2 night minimum stay - seasonal and/or weekends, 30 day cancellation notice-fee imposed. **Amenities:** CD players, high-speed Internet, hair dryers. **Pool(s):** heated outdoor. **Leisure Activities:** sauna. **Guest Services:** TV in common area, wireless Internet. **Business Services:** PC. **Cards:** DS, MC, VI.

🔁 ✕ 📺 🍽

------ WHERE TO DINE ------

JACKSONVILLE INN DINNER HOUSE

 *Menu on AAA.com*

(AAA)

▼▼◆▼▼

American

$9-$32

Phone: 541/899-1900

Patrons unwind in the intimate dining rooms and in the charming garden seating area. Thoughtfully prepared seafood, veal, poultry and beef entrees make up the menu. The hazelnut meringue dessert is sinful. Casual dress. **Bar:** Full bar. **Reservations:** suggested. **Hours:** 7:30-10:30 am, 11:30-2 & 4-9 pm, Mon 7:30 am-10:30 & 4-9 pm; Sun 7:30 am-2 & 4-9 pm; Sunday brunch. Closed: 11/26, 12/25. **Address:** 175 E California St **Location:** On California St (SR 238); between 3rd and 4th sts; center; in Jacksonville Inn. **Parking:** on-site. **Cards:** AX, DC, DS, MC, VI. **Historic**

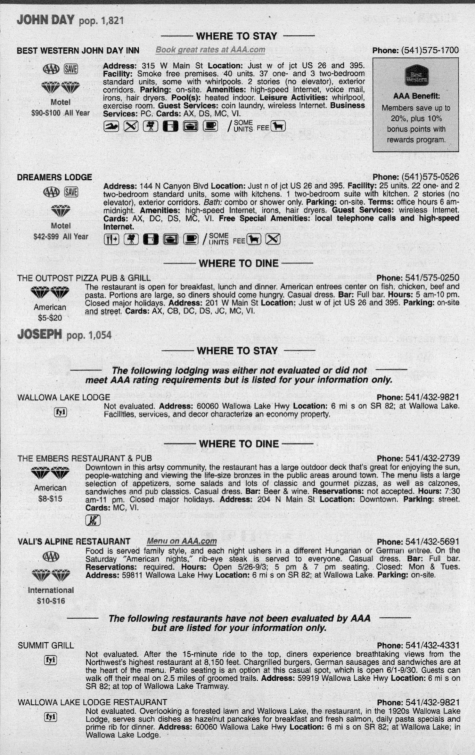

JOHN DAY pop. 1,821

------ WHERE TO STAY ------

BEST WESTERN JOHN DAY INN   *Book great rates at AAA.com*   Phone: (541)575-1700

(AAA) (SAVE)
▼▼ ▼▼
Motel
$90-$100 All Year

Address: 315 W Main St **Location:** Just w of jct US 26 and 395. **Facility:** Smoke free premises. 40 units. 37 one- and 3 two-bedroom standard units, some with whirlpools. 2 stories (no elevator), exterior corridors. **Parking:** on-site. **Amenities:** high-speed Internet, voice mail, irons, hair dryers. **Pool(s):** heated indoor. **Leisure Activities:** whirlpool, exercise room. **Guest Services:** coin laundry, wireless Internet. **Business Services:** PC. **Cards:** AX, DS, MC, VI.

AAA Benefit:
Members save up to
20%, plus 10%
bonus points with
rewards program.

⊠ ✕ 🎥 🛗 🖥 💻 / SOME UNITS FEE 🐾

DREAMERS LODGE   Phone: (541)575-0526

(AAA) (SAVE)
▼▼
Motel
$42-$99 All Year

Address: 144 N Canyon Blvd **Location:** Just n of jct US 26 and 395. **Facility:** 25 units. 22 one- and 2 two-bedroom standard units, some with kitchens. 1 two-bedroom suite with kitchen. 2 stories (no elevator), exterior corridors. *Bath:* combo or shower only. **Parking:** on-site. **Terms:** office hours 6 am-midnight. **Amenities:** high-speed Internet, irons, hair dryers. **Guest Services:** wireless Internet. **Cards:** AX, DC, DS, MC, VI. **Free Special Amenities:** local telephone calls and high-speed Internet.

🛗 🎥 🛗 🖥 💻 / SOME UNITS FEE 🐾 ✕

------ WHERE TO DINE ------

THE OUTPOST PIZZA PUB & GRILL   Phone: 541/575-0250

▼▼ ▼▼
American
$5-$20

The restaurant is open for breakfast, lunch and dinner. American entrees center on fish, chicken, beef and pasta. Portions are large, so diners should come hungry. Casual dress. **Bar:** Full bar. **Hours:** 5 am-10 pm. Closed major holidays. **Address:** 201 W Main St **Location:** Just w of jct US 26 and 395. **Parking:** on-site and street. **Cards:** AX, CB, DC, DS, JC, MC, VI.

JOSEPH pop. 1,054

------ WHERE TO STAY ------

------ *The following lodging was either not evaluated or did not* ------
meet AAA rating requirements but is listed for your information only.

WALLOWA LAKE LODGE   Phone: 541/432-9821

(fyi)

Not evaluated. **Address:** 60060 Wallowa Lake Hwy **Location:** 6 mi s on SR 82; at Wallowa Lake. Facilities, services, and decor characterize an economy property.

------ WHERE TO DINE ------

THE EMBERS RESTAURANT & PUB   Phone: 541/432-2739

▼▼ ▼▼
American
$8-$15

Downtown in this artsy community, the restaurant has a large outdoor deck that's great for enjoying the sun, people-watching and viewing the life-size bronzes in the public areas around town. The menu lists a large selection of appetizers, some salads and lots of classic and gourmet pizzas, as well as calzones, sandwiches and pub classics. Casual dress. **Bar:** Beer & wine. **Reservations:** not accepted. **Hours:** 7:30 am-11 pm. Closed major holidays. **Address:** 204 N Main St **Location:** Downtown. **Parking:** street. **Cards:** MC, VI.

🅹🅲

VALI'S ALPINE RESTAURANT   *Menu on AAA.com*   Phone: 541/432-5691

(AAA)
▼▼ ▼▼
International
$10-$16

Food is served family style, and each night ushers in a different Hungarian or German entree. On the Saturday "American nights," rib-eye steak is served to everyone. Casual dress. **Bar:** Full bar. **Reservations:** required. **Hours:** Open 5/26-9/3; 5 pm & 7 pm seating. Closed: Mon & Tues. **Address:** 59811 Wallowa Lake Hwy **Location:** 6 mi s on SR 82; at Wallowa Lake. **Parking:** on-site.

------ *The following restaurants have not been evaluated by AAA* ------
but are listed for your information only.

SUMMIT GRILL   Phone: 541/432-4331

(fyi)

Not evaluated. After the 15-minute ride to the top, diners experience breathtaking views from the Northwest's highest restaurant at 8,150 feet. Chargrilled burgers, German sausages and sandwiches are at the heart of the menu. Patio seating is an option at this casual spot, which is open 6/1-9/30. Guests can walk off their meal on 2.5 miles of groomed trails. **Address:** 59919 Wallowa Lake Hwy **Location:** 6 mi s on SR 82; at top of Wallowa Lake Tramway.

WALLOWA LAKE LODGE RESTAURANT   Phone: 541/432-9821

(fyi)

Not evaluated. Overlooking a forested lawn and Wallowa Lake, the restaurant, in the 1920s Wallowa Lake Lodge, serves such dishes as hazelnut pancakes for breakfast and fresh salmon, daily pasta specials and prime rib for dinner. **Address:** 60060 Wallowa Lake Hwy **Location:** 6 mi s on SR 82; at Wallowa Lake; in Wallowa Lake Lodge.

KEIZER pop. 32,203

──── WHERE TO STAY ────

KEIZER RENAISSANCE INN
Book great rates at AAA.com

Phone: (503)390-4733

(AAA) (SAVE)
◆◆◆◆
Hotel
$79-$99 All Year

Address: 5188 Wittenberg Ln N **Location:** I-5, exit 260B southbound; exit 260 northbound, 1.5 mi w via Chemawa Rd and Lockhaven Dr, just s on River Rd, just e on Claggett St NE, then just s. **Facility:** Smoke free premises. 86 one-bedroom standard units, some with whirlpools. 4 stories, interior corridors. *Bath:* combo or shower only. **Parking:** on-site. **Terms:** check-in 4 pm. **Amenities:** high-speed Internet, dual phone lines, voice mail, irons, hair dryers. **Pool(s):** heated indoor. **Leisure Activities:** whirlpool, exercise room. **Guest Services:** valet and coin laundry, area transportation-within 10 mi, wireless Internet. **Business Services:** conference facilities, PC. **Cards:** AX, DS, JC, MC, VI. **Free Special Amenities: expanded continental breakfast and high-speed Internet.**

KING CITY —*See Portland p. 463.*

KLAMATH FALLS pop. 19,462

──── WHERE TO STAY ────

BEST WESTERN KLAMATH INN
Book great rates at AAA.com

Phone: (541)882-1200

(AAA) (SAVE)
◆◆◆
Motel
$99-$139 3/1-10/31
$89-$129 11/1-2/28

Address: 4061 S 6th St **Location:** Just w on 6th St (SR 140) from jct SR 140 E/39 S and SR 39 N/US 97 business route. **Facility:** 52 one-bedroom standard units, some with whirlpools. 2 stories (no elevator), exterior corridors. *Bath:* combo or shower only. **Parking:** on-site. **Amenities:** high-speed Internet, voice mail, irons, hair dryers. **Pool(s):** heated indoor. **Leisure Activities:** access to bike path. **Guest Services:** wireless Internet. **Business Services:** PC. **Cards:** AX, DC, DS, MC, VI. **Free Special Amenities: continental breakfast and high-speed Internet.**

AAA Benefit:
Members save up to 20%, plus 10% bonus points with rewards program.

BEST WESTERN OLYMPIC INN
Book great rates at AAA.com

Phone: (541)882-9665

(AAA) (SAVE)
◆◆◆◆
Hotel
$120-$199 3/1-10/31
$110-$150 11/1-2/28

Address: 2627 S 6th St **Location:** 1 mi w on 6th St (SR 140) from jct SR 140 E/39 S and SR 39 N/US 97 business route. **Facility:** Smoke free premises. 92 one-bedroom standard units. 3 stories, interior corridors. **Parking:** on-site. **Terms:** check-in 4 pm, cancellation fee imposed. **Amenities:** voice mail, irons, hair dryers. *Some:* high-speed Internet. **Pool(s):** heated outdoor. **Leisure Activities:** whirlpool. **Guest Services:** valet and coin laundry, airport transportation-Klamath Falls Airport, area transportation-train station, wireless Internet. **Business Services:** meeting rooms, business center. **Cards:** AX, DC, DS, MC, VI. **Free Special Amenities: local telephone calls and high-speed Internet.** *(See color ad below)*

COMFORT INN & SUITES
Book at AAA.com

Phone: (541)882-1111

◆◆
Hotel
$99-$165 All Year

Address: 2500 S 6th St **Location:** 1.3 mi w on 6th St (SR 140) from jct SR 140 E/39 S and SR 39 N/US 97 business route. **Facility:** 57 units. 47 one-bedroom standard units, some with whirlpools. 10 one-bedroom suites, some with whirlpools. 2 stories (no elevator), interior corridors. *Bath:* combo or shower only. **Parking:** on-site. **Amenities:** high-speed Internet, voice mail, irons, hair dryers. **Pool(s):** heated indoor. **Leisure Activities:** whirlpool, limited exercise equipment. **Guest Services:** valet and coin laundry, wireless Internet. **Business Services:** meeting rooms, PC. **Cards:** AX, CB, DC, DS, MC, VI.

▼ See AAA listing above ▼

ECONO LODGE   *Book great rates at AAA.com*   Phone: (541)884-7735
Motel
$35-$110 All Year

Address: 75 Main St **Location:** US 97, exit City Center Dr, 1.3 mi s. **Facility:** 51 one-bedroom standard units. 2 stories, exterior corridors. *Bath:* combo or shower only. **Parking:** on-site. **Terms:** cancellation fee imposed. **Amenities:** high-speed Internet. **Guest Services:** wireless Internet. **Business Services:** PC. **Cards:** AX, CB, DC, DS, MC, VI. **Free Special Amenities: continental breakfast and high-speed Internet.**

GOLDEN WEST MOTEL   Phone: 541/882-1758
Motel
$42-$68 All Year

Address: 6402 S 6th St **Location:** S 6th St (SR 140) at eastern edge of town. **Facility:** 14 one-bedroom standard units, some with kitchens. 1 story, exterior corridors. *Bath:* shower only. **Parking:** on-site. **Terms:** cancellation fee imposed. **Amenities:** high-speed Internet. **Guest Services:** wireless Internet. **Cards:** AX, DS, MC, VI. **Free Special Amenities: early check-in/late check-out and high-speed Internet.**

HOLIDAY INN EXPRESS & SUITES   Phone: 541/884-9999
Hotel
$159-$239 4/1-2/28
$139-$219 3/1-3/31

Too new to rate. **Address:** 2430 S 6th St **Location:** 1.3 mi w on 6th St (SR 140) from jct SR 140 E/39 S and SR 39 N/US 97 business route. **Amenities:** 85 units, coffeemakers, microwaves, refrigerators, pool. **Cards:** AX, CB, DC, DS, JC, MC, VI.

MAJESTIC INN & SUITES   *Book great rates at AAA.com*   Phone: (541)883-7771
Motel
$35-$105 All Year

Address: 5543 S 6th St **Location:** 1 mi e on 6th St (SR 140) from jct SR 140 E/39 S and SR 39 N/US 97 business route. **Facility:** 16 one-bedroom standard units. 1 story, exterior corridors. *Bath:* shower only. **Parking:** on-site. **Terms:** cancellation fee imposed. **Amenities:** DVD players, high-speed Internet, irons, hair dryers. **Guest Services:** coin laundry, airport transportation-Klamath Falls International Airport, area transportation-train & bus stations, wireless Internet. **Business Services:** PC. **Cards:** AX, CB, DC, DS, JC, MC, VI. **Free Special Amenities: continental breakfast and high-speed Internet.**

MAVERICK MOTEL   *Book great rates at AAA.com*   Phone: (541)882-6688
Motel
$39-$109 All Year

Address: 1220 Main St **Location:** US 97 N, exit City Center, 0.3 mi e. **Facility:** 50 one-bedroom standard units. 2 stories (no elevator), exterior corridors. **Parking:** on-site. **Terms:** cancellation fee imposed. **Amenities:** irons, hair dryers. **Guest Services:** coin laundry, airport transportation-Klamath Falls International Airport, area transportation-bus shuttle, wireless Internet. **Business Services:** PC. **Cards:** AX, CB, DC, DS, JC, MC, VI. **Free Special Amenities: continental breakfast and high-speed Internet.**

MOTEL 6 - 226   *Book at AAA.com*   Phone: (541)884-2110
Motel
$45-$55 All Year

Address: 5136 S 6th St **Location:** 0.5 mi e on 6th St E (SR 140) from jct SR 39/US 97 business route. **Facility:** 62 one-bedroom standard units. 2 stories (no elevator), exterior corridors. *Bath:* shower only. **Parking:** on-site. **Pool(s):** heated outdoor. **Guest Services:** coin laundry. **Cards:** AX, CB, DC, DS, MC, VI.

OREGON 8 MOTEL   Phone: (541)883-3431
Motel
$35-$99 All Year

Address: 5225 Hwy 97 N **Location:** Between MM 270 and 271; east side of highway. **Facility:** 29 units. 23 one- and 6 two-bedroom standard units, some with kitchens and/or whirlpools. 1 story, exterior corridors. *Bath:* combo or shower only. **Parking:** on-site. **Terms:** cancellation fee imposed. **Amenities:** high-speed Internet, irons. *Some:* hair dryers. **Pool(s):** heated outdoor. **Guest Services:** coin laundry, wireless Internet. **Cards:** AX, DS, MC, VI. **Free Special Amenities: continental breakfast and high-speed Internet.**

▼ *See AAA listing p 362* ▼

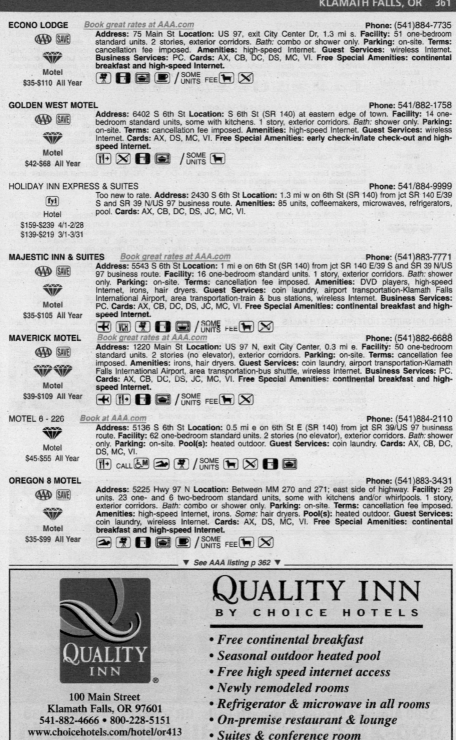

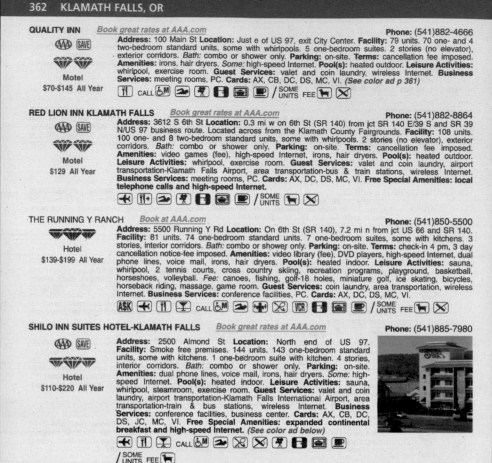

QUALITY INN   *Book great rates at AAA.com*   Phone: (541)882-4666

AAA SAVE

Motel
$70-$145 All Year

Address: 100 Main St **Location:** Just e of US 97, exit City Center. **Facility:** 79 units. 70 one- and 4 two-bedroom standard units, some with whirlpools. 5 one-bedroom suites. 2 stories (no elevator), exterior corridors. *Bath:* combo or shower only. **Parking:** on-site. **Terms:** cancellation fee imposed. **Amenities:** irons, hair dryers. *Some:* high-speed Internet. **Pool(s):** heated outdoor. **Leisure Activities:** whirlpool, exercise room. **Guest Services:** valet and coin laundry, wireless Internet. **Business Services:** meeting rooms, PC. **Cards:** AX, CB, DC, DS, MC, VI. *(See color ad p 361)*

RED LION INN KLAMATH FALLS   *Book great rates at AAA.com*   Phone: (541)882-8864

AAA SAVE

Motel
$129 All Year

Address: 3612 S 6th St **Location:** 0.3 mi w on 6th St (SR 140) from jct SR 140 E/39 S and SR 39 N/US 97 business route. Located across from the Klamath County Fairgrounds. **Facility:** 108 units. 100 one- and 8 two-bedroom standard units, some with whirlpools. 2 stories (no elevator), exterior corridors. *Bath:* combo or shower only. **Parking:** on-site. **Terms:** cancellation fee imposed. **Amenities:** video games (fee), high-speed Internet, irons, hair dryers. **Pool(s):** heated outdoor. **Leisure Activities:** whirlpool, exercise room. **Guest Services:** valet and coin laundry, airport transportation-Klamath Falls Airport, area transportation-bus & train stations, wireless Internet. **Business Services:** meeting rooms, PC. **Cards:** AX, DC, DS, MC, VI. **Free Special Amenities: local telephone calls and high-speed Internet.**

THE RUNNING Y RANCH   *Book at AAA.com*   Phone: (541)850-5500

Hotel
$139-$199 All Year

Address: 5500 Running Y Rd **Location:** On 6th St (SR 140), 7.2 mi n from jct US 66 and SR 140. **Facility:** 81 units. 74 one-bedroom standard units. 7 one-bedroom suites, some with kitchens. 3 stories, interior corridors. *Bath:* combo or shower only. **Parking:** on-site. **Terms:** check-in 4 pm, 3 day cancellation notice-fee imposed. **Amenities:** video library (fee), DVD players, high-speed Internet, dual phone lines, voice mail, irons, hair dryers. **Pool(s):** heated indoor. **Leisure Activities:** sauna, whirlpool, 2 tennis courts, cross country skiing, recreation programs, playground, basketball, horseshoes, volleyball. *Fee:* canoes, fishing, golf-18 holes, miniature golf, ice skating, bicycles, horseback riding, massage, game room. **Guest Services:** coin laundry, area transportation, wireless Internet. **Business Services:** conference facilities, PC. **Cards:** AX, DC, DS, MC, VI.

SHILO INN SUITES HOTEL-KLAMATH FALLS   *Book great rates at AAA.com*   Phone: (541)885-7980

AAA SAVE

Hotel
$110-$220 All Year

Address: 2500 Almond St **Location:** North end of US 97. **Facility:** Smoke free premises. 144 units. 143 one-bedroom standard units, some with kitchens. 1 one-bedroom suite with kitchen. 4 stories, interior corridors. *Bath:* combo or shower only. **Parking:** on-site. **Amenities:** dual phone lines, voice mail, irons, hair dryers. *Some:* high-speed Internet. **Pool(s):** heated indoor. **Leisure Activities:** sauna, whirlpool, steamroom, exercise room. **Guest Services:** valet and coin laundry, airport transportation-Klamath Falls International Airport, area transportation-train & bus stations, wireless Internet. **Business Services:** conference facilities, business center. **Cards:** AX, CB, DC, DS, JC, MC, VI. **Free Special Amenities: expanded continental breakfast and high-speed Internet.** *(See color ad below)*

▼ *See AAA listing above* ▼

SUPER 8 *Book at AAA.com*
Phone: (541)884-8880
Hotel
$74-$86 All Year

Address: 3805 Hwy 97 **Location:** On US 97, 2 mi n. **Facility:** 61 one-bedroom standard units. 3 stories (no elevator), interior corridors. **Parking:** on-site. **Amenities:** high-speed Internet, safes (fee). **Leisure Activities:** whirlpool. **Guest Services:** coin laundry, wireless Internet. **Cards:** AX, CB, DC, DS, MC, VI.

THOMPSON'S BED & BREAKFAST
Phone: 541/882-7938
Bed & Breakfast
$110-$125 All Year

Address: 1420 Wild Plum Ct **Location:** US 97, exit Lakeshore Dr, 1.5 mi w, just s on Lynnewood Blvd, just e on Vista Way, just s on Arrowhead Rd, then just e. Located in a residential area. **Facility:** Built against wooded hill with views of Upper Klamath Lake from large common room and outdoor deck. A bed and breakfast with a homey feel to it. Smoke free premises. 4 one-bedroom standard units. 2 stories (no elevator), interior corridors. *Bath:* combo or shower only. **Parking:** on-site. **Terms:** office hours 7 am-10 pm, 7 day cancellation notice-fee imposed. **Amenities:** high-speed Internet, hair dryers. **Leisure Activities:** hiking trails. **Guest Services:** complimentary laundry, wireless Internet.

——— **WHERE TO DINE** ———

BLACK BEAR DINER
Phone: 541/883-7766
American
$7-$16

A homey atmosphere characterizes this family-oriented restaurant. Familiar comfort foods, such as meatloaf with mashed potatoes, are at the heart of the menu and are served in generous portions. Casual dress. **Bar:** Beer & wine. **Hours:** 6 am-10 pm. **Address:** 5140 S 6th St **Location:** 0.5 mi e on 6th St E (SR 140) from jct SR 39/US 97 business route. **Parking:** on-site. **Cards:** AX, DS, MC, VI.

EL PALACIO
Phone: 541/882-5118
Mexican
$5-$18

Mexican cuisine makes up the small family restaurant's menu. The distinctive location in an old downtown bank building adds to the overall dining experience. Traditional dishes center on beef, chicken, pork and shrimp. Casual dress. **Bar:** Full bar. **Reservations:** accepted. **Hours:** 11 am-9 pm, Fri & Sat-10 pm. Closed: 11/26, 12/25. **Address:** 601 Main St **Location:** Northwest corner of Main and 6th (SR 140) sts. **Parking:** on-site and street. **Cards:** AX, CB, DC, DS, JC, MC, VI.

GINO'S CAFE ITALIANO
Phone: 541/884-6474
Southern Italian
$10-$20

Family owned and operated restaurant specializing in family recipes from Calabria in Southern Italy. An extensive selection of entrees are available featuring beef, chicken, veal, and of course pasta. They also offer a very good selection of pizzas, salads, and calzone. Casual dress. **Bar:** Full bar. **Reservations:** accepted. **Hours:** 5 pm-9 pm. Closed major holidays; also Sun-Wed. **Address:** 149 E Main St **Location:** 1 mi nw of jct S 6th (SR 140) and E Main sts. **Parking:** on-site. **Cards:** MC, VI.

MR. B'S STEAKHOUSE *Menu on AAA.com*
Phone: 541/883-8719
Steak
$16-$36

A cozy fireplace and candlelit tables create a warm ambience in the dining area of this former residence. The menu centers on beef, seafood, poultry, lamb and veal dishes, artfully prepared by the chef/owner since 1984. A lighter fare menu is available in the lounge and in the relaxing garden patio. Casual dress. **Bar:** Full bar. **Reservations:** accepted. **Hours:** 5 pm-close. Closed major holidays; also Sun & Mon. **Address:** 3927 S 6th St **Location:** On SR 140/39, 1.5 mi e of jct SR 140 E/39 S and N/US 97 business route. **Parking:** on-site. **Cards:** AX, DS, MC, VI.

NIBBLEY'S CAFE
Phone: 541/883-2314
American
$7-$9

This busy cafe is located in a small shopping center, and features baked goods in addition to traditional breakfast and lunch fare. One of the breakfast specialties is the oatcakes. Muffins and fresh bread of the day are also favorites. Lunch items include burgers, pitas, hot and cold sandwiches, wraps, soups and salads, a taco and a pasta of the day. Casual dress. **Bar:** Full bar. **Hours:** 6 am-4 pm, Sat from 7 am, Sun 8 am-2 pm. Closed major holidays. **Address:** 2650 Washburn Way **Location:** Jct SR 140 (SE 6th St), 0.5 mi s. **Parking:** on-site. **Cards:** AX, DS, MC, VI.

RED'S BACKWOODS BBQ
Phone: 541/883-2175
Barbecue
$8-$17

Sample a variety of different barbecue sauces to spice up your meal. The pulled and smoked meats are moist and tender. Ribs, pulled pork and chicken are the primary menu highlights. Save room for dessert; there may be a piece of buttermilk pie available. Casual dress. **Bar:** Full bar. **Hours:** 11 am-9 pm, Fri & Sat-10 pm. Closed: 11/26, 12/25. **Address:** 3435 Washburn Way **Location:** Jct SR 140 (SE 6th St), 1 mi s. **Parking:** on-site. **Cards:** AX, DS, MC, VI.

SERGIO'S DOS
Phone: 541/885-6885
Mexican
$5-$14

Colorful Mexican artwork adorns the walls of this restaurant, popular with the locals. On the menu you will find several grilled items, including "carne a la Parilla," or pieces of thin steak marinated Mexican style, then grilled. House specialties includes fajitas, crab and shrimp enchiladas and authentic Mexican seafood dishes. Casual dress. **Bar:** Full bar. **Reservations:** accepted. **Hours:** 11 am-10 pm, Sun-9 pm. Closed: 11/26, 12/25. **Address:** 4650 S 6th St **Location:** Just e on 6th St (SR 140) from jct SR 140/39. **Parking:** on-site. **Cards:** MC, VI.

LA GRANDE pop. 12,327

―――― WHERE TO STAY ――――

AMERICAS BEST VALUE SANDMAN INN

Book great rates at AAA.com

Phone: (541)963-3707

AAA [SAVE]

Hotel
$80-$85 All Year

Address: 2410 E R Ave **Location:** I-84, exit 261, just s on Island Ave, then just n. **Facility:** 63 one-bedroom standard units, some with whirlpools. 2 stories (no elevator), interior corridors. *Bath:* combo or shower only. **Parking:** on-site. **Amenities:** high-speed Internet, voice mail. *Some:* hair dryers. **Pool(s):** heated indoor. **Leisure Activities:** whirlpool, patio area with picnic table. **Guest Services:** coin laundry, wireless Internet. **Business Services:** meeting rooms, PC. **Cards:** AX, CB, DC, DS, MC, VI. **Free Special Amenities: expanded continental breakfast and local telephone calls.**

BEST WESTERN RAMA INN & SUITES

Book great rates at AAA.com

Phone: (541)963-3100

AAA [SAVE]

Hotel
$85-$200 All Year

Address: 1711 21st St **Location:** I-84, exit 261, just s on Island Ave, just e on N Albany St, then just n on R Ave. **Facility:** Smoke free premises. 65 units. 52 one-bedroom standard units, some with whirlpools. 13 one-bedroom suites. 2 stories (no elevator), interior corridors. *Bath:* combo or shower only. **Parking:** on-site. **Terms:** 3 day cancellation notice. **Amenities:** high-speed Internet, voice mail, irons, hair dryers. **Pool(s):** heated indoor. **Leisure Activities:** sauna, whirlpool, exercise room. **Guest Services:** coin laundry, wireless Internet. **Business Services:** meeting rooms, PC. **Cards:** AX, CB, DC, DS, JC, MC, VI. **Free Special Amenities: expanded continental breakfast and high-speed Internet.**

AAA Benefit:
Members save up to 20%, plus 10% bonus points with rewards program.

ROYAL MOTOR INN

Phone: (541)963-4154

AAA [SAVE]

Motel
$45-$59 3/1-11/29
$40-$50 11/30-2/28

Address: 1510 Adams Ave **Location:** I-84, exit La Grande; downtown. **Facility:** 43 one-bedroom standard units. 2 stories (no elevator), exterior corridors. **Parking:** on-site. **Terms:** office hours 7 am-11 pm. **Amenities:** high-speed Internet. **Guest Services:** wireless Internet. **Cards:** AX, DS, MC, VI. **Free Special Amenities: local telephone calls and high-speed Internet.**

STANGE MANOR INN

Phone: 541/963-2400

Historic Bed
& Breakfast
$110-$145 All Year

Address: 1612 Walnut St **Location:** I-84, exit 259 eastbound, 1 mi e on Adams Ave, then just s; exit 261 westbound, 1.1 mi w on SR 82 to Washington St, 0.8 mi w on N Ave, then n. **Facility:** In a quiet neighborhood, this 1924 Georgian colonial-style home is attractively decorated, with spacious common areas and a relaxing sunroom. Smoke free premises. 4 units. 1 one- and 2 two-bedroom standard units. 1 two-bedroom suite. 2 stories (no elevator), interior corridors. *Bath:* combo or tub only. **Parking:** on-site. **Terms:** office hours 7 am-10 pm, age restrictions may apply, 3 day cancellation notice-fee imposed. **Amenities:** video library, high-speed Internet, hair dryers. **Guest Services:** wireless Internet. **Cards:** MC, VI.

SUPER 8 LA GRANDE

Book great rates at AAA.com

Phone: (541)963-8080

AAA [SAVE]

Hotel
$65-$99 5/1-2/28
$65-$89 3/1-4/30

Address: 2407 E R Ave **Location:** I-84, exit 261, just s on Island Ave, just e on N Albany St, then just n. **Facility:** Smoke free premises. 64 one-bedroom standard units, some with whirlpools. 2 stories (no elevator), interior/exterior corridors. **Parking:** on-site. **Amenities:** high-speed Internet, hair dryers. **Pool(s):** heated indoor. **Leisure Activities:** whirlpool. **Guest Services:** coin laundry, wireless Internet. **Cards:** AX, DC, DS, MC, VI. **Free Special Amenities: continental breakfast and high-speed Internet.**

TRAVELODGE

Book at AAA.com

Phone: (541)963-7116

Motel
$55-$65 All Year

Address: 2215 Adams Ave **Location:** I-84, exit La Grande; downtown. **Facility:** 34 one-bedroom standard units. 2 stories (no elevator), exterior corridors. **Parking:** on-site. **Terms:** office hours 6:30 am-11 pm. **Amenities:** high-speed Internet, irons, hair dryers. **Guest Services:** wireless Internet. **Business Services:** PC. **Cards:** AX, DS, MC, VI.

―――― WHERE TO DINE ――――

FOLEY STATION

Menu on AAA.com

Phone: 541/963-7473

American
$8-$29

In the historic Foley Building, the popular meeting place offers an evolving menu of interesting, internationally influenced Northwest cuisine. Guests can taste local produce in season and savor the tempting aroma of freshly baked bread. Casual dress. **Bar:** Full bar. **Reservations:** suggested. **Hours:** 3 pm-10 pm, Sun from 9 am. Closed: 7/4, 11/26, 12/25. **Address:** 1114 Adams Ave **Location:** Downtown. **Parking:** on-site and street. **Cards:** DS, MC, VI.

CALL [EM]

LA PINE pop. 5,799

──── **WHERE TO STAY** ────

BEST WESTERN NEWBERRY STATION   *Book great rates at AAA.com*   Phone: (541)536-5130

Hotel
$80-$100 All Year

Address: 16515 Reed Rd **Location:** North end of town; just off SR 97. **Facility:** 40 units. 36 one-bedroom standard units. 4 one-bedroom suites. 2 stories (no elevator), interior corridors. *Bath:* combo or shower only. **Parking:** on-site. **Amenities:** irons, hair dryers. *Some:* DVD players. **Pool(s):** heated indoor. **Leisure Activities:** whirlpool. **Guest Services:** wireless Internet. **Business Services:** PC. **Cards:** AX, DS, MC, VI. **Free Special Amenities: expanded continental breakfast and high-speed Internet.**

AAA Benefit:
Members save up to 20%, plus 10% bonus points with rewards program.

LAKE OSWEGO —*See Portland p. 464.*

LAKEVIEW pop. 2,474

──── **WHERE TO STAY** ────

BEST WESTERN SKYLINE MOTOR LODGE   *Book great rates at AAA.com*   Phone: (541)947-2194

Motel
379-3129 All Year

Address: 414 N G St **Location:** Jct US 395 and SR 140. **Facility:** 38 one-bedroom standard units. 2 stories (no elevator), exterior corridors. **Parking:** on-site. **Terms:** 3 night minimum stay - seasonal, 7 day cancellation notice-fee imposed. **Amenities:** high-speed Internet, voice mail, irons, hair dryers. **Pool(s):** heated indoor. **Leisure Activities:** whirlpool. **Guest Services:** coin laundry, airport transportation-Lake County Airport, wireless Internet. **Business Services:** PC. **Cards:** AX, CB, DC, DS, MC, VI. **Free Special Amenities: continental breakfast and high-speed Internet.**

AAA Benefit:
Members save up to 20%, plus 10% bonus points with rewards program.

──── **WHERE TO DINE** ────

EL AGUILA REAL MEXICAN RESTAURANT   Phone: 541/947-5655

Mexican
$6-$15

This place is known for its pleasant, friendly atmosphere and good food, including many combination dinners, authentic made-from-scratch recipes and even some American items. Casual dress. **Bar:** Full bar. **Hours:** 11 am-9 pm, Fri & Sat-10 pm. Closed: 4/12, 11/26, 12/25. **Address:** 406 N G St **Location:** Jct SR 141; center. **Parking:** on-site. **Cards:** MC, VI.

LINCOLN BEACH pop. 2,078

──── **WHERE TO STAY** ────

CAVALIER CONDOMINIUMS   Phone: 541/764-2352

Condominium
$185-$229 All Year

Address: 325 Lancer St **Location:** 1.5 mi s on US 101, just w. Located in a secluded area. **Facility:** 20 two-bedroom suites with kitchens. 3 stories (no elevator), exterior corridors. **Parking:** on-site. **Terms:** office hours 8 am-10 pm, 2 night minimum stay - seasonal and/or weekends, 14 day cancellation notice-fee imposed. **Amenities:** DVD players, CD players, high-speed Internet, irons, hair dryers. **Pool(s):** heated indoor. **Leisure Activities:** saunas, beach access. **Guest Services:** coin laundry, wireless Internet. **Cards:** DS, MC, VI.

SALISHAN SPA & GOLF RESORT   Phone: 541/764-2371

Hotel
Rates not provided

Address: 7760 US 101 N **Location:** Just e of US 101; center. **Facility:** On a wooded hillside, this resort offers fireplace rooms with balconies overlooking a forest, golf links or Siletz Bay. Smoke free premises. 205 units. 202 one-bedroom standard units. 3 one-bedroom suites with whirlpools. 2-3 stories (no elevator), exterior corridors. *Bath:* combo or shower only. **Parking:** on-site. **Terms:** check-in 4:30 pm. **Amenities:** high-speed Internet (fee), dual phone lines, voice mail, irons, hair dryers. *Some:* CD players. *Fee:* DVD players, video games. **Dining:** 4 restaurants, also, The Dining Room At Salishan, see separate listing, entertainment. **Pool(s):** heated indoor. **Leisure Activities:** saunas, whirlpool, beach access, recreation programs, nature trails to beach, barbecue areas, bocci, hiking trails, exercise room, spa, sports court, basketball, volleyball. *Fee:* golf-18 holes, golf & tennis instructions, 3 indoor tennis courts, kids club, game room. **Guest Services:** valet laundry, airport transportation-Siletz Bay State Airport, wireless Internet. **Business Services:** conference facilities, PC. **Free Special Amenities: local telephone calls and newspaper.**

———— **WHERE TO DINE** ————

THE DINING ROOM AT SALISHAN　　　　　　　　　　　　　　　　　**Phone:** 541/764-3635

Pacific Rim
$30-$40

Contemporary Northwest decor, serene views of the Oregon coast and excellent cuisine combine to provide a pleasurable experience. Guests are almost sure to find a great vintage from the extensive wine list, which draws from a cellar of more than 10,000 bottles. Highly recommended are the decadent Dungeness crab bisque with fresh crab in a creamy bisque finished with Pernod mousseline or the local wild Chinook salmon accompanied by a huckleberry gastrique with wild mushrooms and an Oregon blue cheese souffle. Dressy casual. **Bar:** Full bar. **Reservations:** suggested. **Hours:** 5 pm-9 pm. **Address:** 7760 E US 101 N **Location:** Just e of US 101; center; in Salishan Spa & Golf Resort. **Parking:** on-site. **Cards:** AX, DC, DS, MC, VI.

SIDE DOOR CAFE　　　　　　　　　　　　　　　　　　　　　　**Phone:** 541/764-3825

Regional American
$8-$31

Refined music plays in the background in the relaxing dining room. A selection of beers and wines accompanies the sandwiches, salads and entrees, which feature seafood chicken and beef. This place is popular with locals. Casual dress. **Bar:** Full bar. **Reservations:** suggested. **Hours:** 11:30 am-8 pm, Fri & Sat-9 pm. Closed: 1/1, 11/26, 12/25; also Tues. **Address:** 6675 Gleneden Beach Loop **Location:** US 101, just w on Gleneden Beach turnoff. **Parking:** on-site. **Cards:** AX, DS, MC, VI.

LINCOLN CITY pop. 7,437

———— **WHERE TO STAY** ————

AMERICA'S BEST INN & SUITES　　*Book great rates at AAA.com*　　　　　　**Phone:** (541)994-9017

Hotel
$69-$189 3/1-10/31
$59-$159 11/1-2/28

Address: 1014 NE Hwy 101 **Location:** N of D River. **Facility:** Smoke free premises. 32 one-bedroom standard units. 2 stories (no elevator), interior corridors. **Parking:** on-site. **Terms:** cancellation fee imposed. **Amenities:** video library (fee), DVD players, high-speed Internet, irons, hair dryers. **Leisure Activities:** sauna, whirlpool. **Guest Services:** coin laundry, wireless Internet. **Cards:** AX, DC, DS, JC, MC, VI.

ASHLEY INN & SUITES　　　　　　　　　　　　　　　　　　　　**Phone:** (541)996-7500

Hotel
$69-$199 All Year

Address: 3430 NE US 101 **Location:** Just n of downtown. **Facility:** Smoke free premises. 75 units. 67 one-bedroom standard units. 8 one-bedroom suites, some with kitchens and/or whirlpools. 3 stories, interior corridors. *Bath:* combo or shower only. **Parking:** on-site. **Terms:** cancellation fee imposed. **Amenities:** video library (fee), DVD players, high-speed Internet, irons, hair dryers. **Pool(s):** heated indoor. **Leisure Activities:** sauna, whirlpool, limited exercise equipment. **Guest Services:** coin laundry, wireless Internet. **Business Services:** meeting rooms, PC. **Cards:** AX, DS, MC, VI.

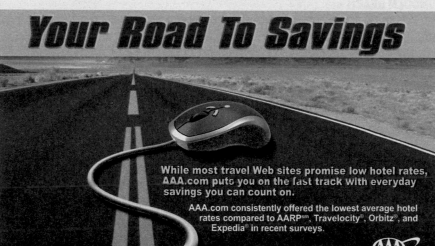

BEL-AIRE INN EXPRESS *Book at AAA.com* Phone: 541/994-2984

Hotel
Rates not provided

Address: 2945 NW Hwy 101 **Location:** North side on US 101, just s of NW 30th St. **Facility:** Smoke free premises. 62 units. 59 one- and 3 two-bedroom standard units. 3 stories, interior corridors. *Bath:* combo or shower only. **Parking:** on-site. **Terms:** check-in 4 pm. **Amenities:** video library (fee), DVD players, high-speed Internet, voice mail, hair dryers. **Pool(s):** heated indoor. **Leisure Activities:** whirlpool, limited exercise equipment. **Guest Services:** valet laundry, wireless Internet. **Business Services:** PC.

BEST WESTERN LANDMARK INN *Book great rates at AAA.com* Phone: (541)994-6060

Hotel
$107-$180 3/1-9/30
$71-$107 10/1-2/28

Address: 4430 SE Hwy 101 **Location:** South end of town. **Facility:** Smoke free premises. 62 units. 56 one-bedroom standard units, some with whirlpools. 6 one-bedroom suites. 3 stories, interior corridors. *Bath:* combo or shower only. **Parking:** on-site. **Terms:** check-in 4 pm. **Amenities:** DVD players, high-speed Internet, irons, hair dryers. *Fee:* video library, safes. **Pool(s):** heated indoor. **Leisure Activities:** sauna, whirlpool, exercise room, sun deck. **Guest Services:** coin laundry, wireless Internet. **Business Services:** meeting rooms, PC. **Cards:** AX, CB, DC, DS, JC, MC, VI. **Free Special Amenities:** full breakfast and high-speed Internet. *(See color ad below)*

AAA Benefit:
Members save up to 20%, plus 10% bonus points with rewards program.

BEST WESTERN LINCOLN SANDS SUITES *Book great rates at AAA.com* Phone: (541)994-4227

Hotel
$179-$599 3/1-9/30
$109-$399 10/1-2/28

Address: 535 NW Inlet Ave **Location:** US 101, exit NW 6th St, just w. **Facility:** Smoke free premises. 33 units. 31 one- and 2 two-bedroom suites with kitchens, some with whirlpools. 3 stories, exterior corridors. *Bath:* combo or shower only. **Parking:** on-site. **Terms:** check-in 4 pm, cancellation fee imposed. **Amenities:** video library (fee), DVD players, high-speed Internet, dual phone lines, irons, hair dryers. **Pool(s):** heated outdoor. **Leisure Activities:** sauna, whirlpool, beach access, barbecue patio with gas grills and outdoor fireplace. **Guest Services:** coin laundry, wireless Internet. **Business Services:** PC. **Cards:** AX, CB, DC, DS, MC, VI. **Free Special Amenities:** full breakfast and high-speed Internet.
(See color ad p 368, p 586, p 499, p 368, p 752, p 473, p 542, p 299, p 344, p 751, p 566 & p 500)

AAA Benefit:
Members save up to 20%, plus 10% bonus points with rewards program.

COHO INN

Motel

$65-$290 All Year

Address: 1635 NW Harbor Ave **Location:** Oceanfront. US 101, exit N 17th St, just w. **Facility:** 51 units. 30 one- and 21 two-bedroom standard units, some with efficiencies. 3 stories (no elevator), exterior corridors. *Bath:* combo or shower only. **Parking:** on-site. **Terms:** office hours 8 am-10 pm, check-in 4 pm. **Amenities:** video library (fee), DVD players, hair dryers. **Pool(s):** heated indoor. **Leisure Activities:** sauna, whirlpool, beach access, exercise room. **Guest Services:** wireless Internet. **Business Services:** meeting rooms, PC. **Cards:** AX, DS, MC, VI. **Free Special Amenities:** expanded continental breakfast and high-speed Internet.

Phone: (541)994-3684

COMFORT INN & SUITES   *Book great rates at AAA.com*

Phone: (541)994-8155

AAA SAVE
▼▼ ▼▼
Hotel
$99-$299 3/1-9/30
$89-$169 10/1-2/28

Address: 136 NE US 101 **Location:** N of D River. **Facility:** Smoke free premises. 64 units. 63 one-bedroom standard units, some with efficiencies and/or whirlpools. 1 one-bedroom suite with kitchen. 3 stories, interior corridors. *Bath:* combo or shower only. **Parking:** on-site. **Terms:** cancellation fee imposed. **Amenities:** video library (fee), high-speed Internet, voice mail, irons, hair dryers. **Guest Services:** coin laundry, wireless Internet. **Business Services:** PC. **Cards:** AX, CB, DC, DS, MC, VI. **Free Special Amenities: expanded continental breakfast and high-speed Internet.**
(See color ad p 368, p 586, p 499, p 368, p 753, p 473, p 542, p 299, p 344, p 751, p 566 & p 500)

"D" SANDS CONDOMINIUM MOTEL

Phone: 541/994-5244

▼▼ ▼▼
Motel
$94-$219 All Year

Address: 171 SW US 101 **Location:** Oceanfront. Next to D River Wayside; s of downtown. **Facility:** Smoke free premises. 63 units. 21 one-bedroom standard units with kitchens. 42 one-bedroom suites with kitchens. 3 stories (no elevator); exterior corridors. *Bath:* combo or shower only. **Parking:** on-site. **Terms:** check-in 4 pm. **Amenities:** video library (fee), DVD players, high-speed Internet, hair dryers. **Pool(s):** heated indoor. **Leisure Activities:** whirlpool, beach access. **Guest Services:** wireless Internet. **Business Services:** PC. **Cards:** AX, DS, MC, VI.

ECONO LODGE   *Book great rates at AAA.com*

Phone: (541)994-5281

AAA SAVE
▼
Hotel
$59-$229 3/1-9/30
$52-$179 10/1-2/28

Address: 1713 NW 21st St **Location:** US 101, exit NW 21st St, just w. **Facility:** 50 one-bedroom standard units. 3 stories (no elevator), interior corridors. **Parking:** on-site. **Terms:** office hours 7 am-midnight, cancellation fee imposed. **Amenities:** high-speed Internet. *Some:* DVD players, hair dryers. **Guest Services:** wireless Internet. **Cards:** AX, DS, MC, VI. **Free Special Amenities: continental breakfast and high-speed Internet.**

INN AT SPANISH HEAD   *Book great rates at AAA.com*

Phone: (541)996-2161

AAA SAVE
▼▼▼▼
Condominium
$195-$319 All Year

Address: 4009 SW US 101 **Location:** Oceanfront. South end of town. **Facility:** Set against a dramatic cliff and all guest units with spectacular oceanview. Varied guest accommodations. Smoke free premises. 120 units. 81 one-bedroom standard units, some with efficiencies. 39 one-bedroom suites with kitchens. 10 stories, interior/exterior corridors. **Parking:** on-site. **Terms:** check-in 4 pm. **Amenities:** video library (fee), DVD players, high-speed Internet, voice mail, irons, hair dryers. *Some:* CD players, dual phone lines. **Dining:** Fathoms Restaurant And Bar, see separate listing. **Pool(s):** heated outdoor. **Leisure Activities:** saunas, whirlpool, beach access, exercise room. *Fee:* recreation room. **Guest Services:** complimentary laundry, wireless Internet. **Business Services:** meeting rooms, PC (fee). **Cards:** AX, DC, DS, MC, VI. **Free Special Amenities: local telephone calls and high-speed Internet.**
(See color ad below)

LIBERTY INN

Phone: 541/994-1777

AAA SAVE
▼▼ ▼▼
Hotel
$90-$180 All Year

Address: 4990 NE Logan Rd **Location:** 0.3 mi n of US 101; north end of town. **Facility:** 76 one-bedroom standard units, some with whirlpools. 4 stories, interior corridors. *Bath:* combo or shower only. **Parking:** on-site. **Terms:** check-in 4 pm, 3 day cancellation notice-fee imposed. **Amenities:** video library (fee), DVD players, high-speed Internet, voice mail, irons, hair dryers. **Pool(s):** heated indoor. **Leisure Activities:** whirlpool, limited exercise equipment. **Guest Services:** coin laundry, wireless Internet. **Business Services:** meeting rooms, PC. **Cards:** AX, DS, MC, VI. **Free Special Amenities: expanded continental breakfast and high-speed Internet.**

▼ *See AAA listing above* ▼

LINCOLN CITY INN

(AAA) **[SAVE]**

◆◆◆

Hotel

$50-$130 All Year

Phone: (541)996-4400

Address: 1091 SE 1st St **Location:** On US 101 at D River. **Facility:** Smoke free premises. 59 one-bedroom standard units, some with whirlpools. 4 stories, interior corridors. *Bath:* combo or shower only. **Parking:** on-site. **Terms:** office hours 7:30 am-10 pm, 3 day cancellation notice. **Amenities:** video library (fee), DVD players, high-speed Internet. *Some:* hair dryers. **Leisure Activities:** whirlpool. **Guest Services:** coin laundry, wireless Internet. **Cards:** AX, DS, MC, VI. **Free Special Amenities: continental breakfast and high-speed Internet.**

⊞ ✕ 🖥 ▣ 💻 / SOME UNITS FEE 🐾

LOOKING GLASS INN

◆◆

Motel

$109-$249 3/1-9/30
$84-$189 10/1-2/28

Book at AAA.com

Phone: (541)996-3996

Address: 861 SW 51st St **Location:** US 101, exit 51st St; south end of town. **Facility:** Smoke free premises. 36 units. 21 one-bedroom standard units, some with efficiencies and/or whirlpools. 12 one- and 3 two-bedroom suites, some with efficiencies or kitchens. 3 stories (no elevator), exterior corridors. *Bath:* combo or shower only. **Parking:** on-site. **Terms:** office hours 8 am-10 pm, 2 night minimum stay - weekends, 3 day cancellation notice. **Amenities:** video library (fee), DVD players, high-speed Internet, voice mail, hair dryers. **Guest Services:** wireless Internet. **Cards:** AX, DC, DS, MC, VI.

ASK ⊞ ✕ ⚌ 🖥 ▣ 💻 / SOME UNITS FEE 🐾

MOTEL 6 - #4172

◆◆

Hotel

$46-$126 All Year

Phone: 541/996-9900

Address: 3517 NW US 101 **Location:** North end of downtown. **Facility:** 72 one-bedroom standard units. 3 stories, interior corridors. *Bath:* combo or shower only. **Parking:** on-site. **Amenities:** high-speed Internet, voice mail. **Guest Services:** coin laundry, wireless Internet. **Business Services:** meeting rooms. **Cards:** AX, CB, DC, DS, MC, VI.

CALL 🔊♿ 🎥 🖥 ▣ / SOME UNITS 🐾 ✕

NORDIC OCEANFRONT INN

(AAA) **[SAVE]**

◆◆

Motel

$69-$199 All Year

Phone: 541/994-8145

Address: 2133 NW Inlet Ave **Location:** Oceanfront. US 101, exit NW 21st St, just w. Located in a quiet residential area. **Facility:** Smoke free premises. 53 units. 46 one-bedroom standard units, some with efficiencies, kitchens and/or whirlpools. 7 one-bedroom suites, some with efficiencies or kitchens. 3 stories (no elevator), exterior corridors. **Parking:** on-site. **Terms:** office hours 8 am-10 pm, check-in 4 pm. **Amenities:** video library (fee), DVD players, high-speed Internet. **Pool(s):** heated indoor. **Leisure Activities:** saunas, whirlpool, beach access, sun deck. **Guest Services:** wireless Internet. **Cards:** AX, DS, MC, VI. **Free Special Amenities: continental breakfast and high-speed Internet.**

🏊 ✕ ⚌ VCR 🖥 ▣ 💻

THE O'DYSIUS HOTEL   *Book great rates at AAA.com*   Phone: (541)994-4121

(AAA) SAVE

▼▼▼

Hotel
$159-$365 All Year

Address: 120 NW Inlet Ave **Location:** On US 101 at D River; center. **Facility:** Smoke free premises. 29 units. 21 one-bedroom standard units, some with whirlpools. 6 one- and 2 two-bedroom suites with kitchens and whirlpools. 5 stories, interior corridors. **Parking:** on-site. **Terms:** office hours 7 am-11 pm, check-in 4 pm, age restrictions may apply. **Amenities:** video library (fee), DVD players, high-speed Internet, honor bars, irons, hair dryers. **Leisure Activities:** whirlpool, beach access. **Guest Services:** wireless Internet. **Cards:** AX, DS, MC, VI. **Free Special Amenities: continental breakfast and high-speed Internet.**

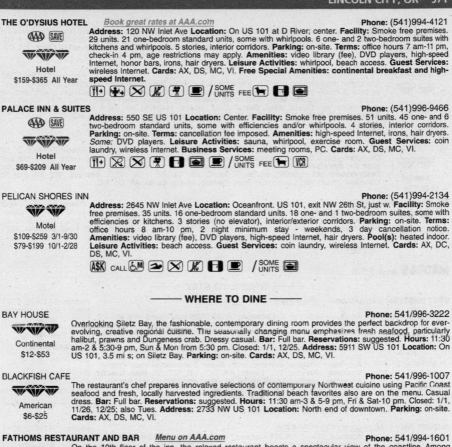

PALACE INN & SUITES   Phone: (541)996-9466

(AAA) SAVE

▼▼▼

Hotel
$69-$209 All Year

Address: 550 SE US 101 **Location:** Center. **Facility:** Smoke free premises. 51 units. 45 one- and 6 two-bedroom standard units, some with efficiencies and/or whirlpools. 4 stories, interior corridors. **Parking:** on-site. **Terms:** cancellation fee imposed. **Amenities:** high-speed Internet, irons, hair dryers. *Some:* DVD players. **Leisure Activities:** sauna, whirlpool, exercise room. **Guest Services:** coin laundry, wireless Internet. **Business Services:** meeting rooms, PC. **Cards:** AX, DS, MC, VI.

PELICAN SHORES INN   Phone: (541)994-2134

▼▼

Motel
$109-$259 3/1-9/30
$79-$199 10/1-2/28

Address: 2645 NW Inlet Ave **Location:** Oceanfront. US 101, exit NW 26th St, just w. **Facility:** Smoke free premises. 35 units. 16 one-bedroom standard units. 18 one- and 1 two-bedroom suites, some with efficiencies or kitchens. 3 stories (no elevator); interior/exterior corridors. **Parking:** on-site. **Terms:** office hours 8 am-10 pm, 2 night minimum stay - weekends, 3 day cancellation notice. **Amenities:** video library (fee), DVD players, high-speed Internet, hair dryers. **Pool(s):** heated indoor. **Leisure Activities:** beach access. **Guest Services:** coin laundry, wireless Internet. **Cards:** AX, DC, DS, MC, VI.

——— **WHERE TO DINE** ———

BAY HOUSE   Phone: 541/996-3222

▼▼▼

Continental
$12-$53

Overlooking Siletz Bay, the fashionable, contemporary dining room provides the perfect backdrop for ever-evolving, creative regional cuisine. The seasonally changing menu emphasizes fresh seafood, particularly halibut, prawns and Dungeness crab. Dressy casual. **Bar:** Full bar. **Reservations:** suggested. **Hours:** 11:30 am-2 & 5:30-9 pm, Sun & Mon from 5:30 pm. Closed: 1/1, 12/25. **Address:** 5911 SW US 101 **Location:** On US 101, 3.5 mi s; on Siletz Bay. **Parking:** on-site. **Cards:** AX, DS, MC, VI.

BLACKFISH CAFE   Phone: 541/996-1007

▼▼▼

American
$6-$25

The restaurant's chef prepares innovative selections of contemporary Northwest cuisine using Pacific Coast seafood and fresh, locally harvested ingredients. Traditional beach favorites also are on the menu. Casual dress. **Bar:** Full bar. **Reservations:** suggested. **Hours:** 11:30 am-3 & 5-9 pm, Fri & Sat-10 pm. Closed: 1/1, 11/26, 12/25; also Tues. **Address:** 2733 NW US 101 **Location:** North end of downtown. **Parking:** on-site. **Cards:** AX, DS, MC, VI.

FATHOMS RESTAURANT AND BAR   *Menu on AAA.com*   Phone: 541/994-1601

(AAA)

▼▼ ▼▼

Steak & Seafood
$6-$45

On the 10th floor of the inn, the relaxed restaurant boasts a spectacular view of the coastline. Among examples of fresh seafood are Oregon hazelnut-Parmesan-crusted Pacific snapper with charred tomato-roasted red-pepper fondue sauce, salmon in parchment paper and razor clams. Also sharing menu space are charbroiled steaks with Oregon blue cheese butter and several pasta entrees. Casual dress. **Bar:** Full bar. **Reservations:** suggested. **Hours:** 8 am-2 & 4-9 pm, Sat 8 am-9 pm; Sunday brunch. **Address:** 4009 SW US 101 **Location:** South end of town; in Inn at Spanish Head. **Parking:** on-site and valet. **Cards:** AX, CB, DC, DS, MC, VI.

KERNVILLE STEAK & SEAFOOD HOUSE   Phone: 541/994-6200

▼▼ ▼▼

Steak & Seafood
$5-$35

Many tables at this casual, friendly restaurant offer river views. Traditionally prepared steak and seafood entrees, such as filet mignon, prime rib and salmon, make up the menu. Friendly, thoughtful servers display good menu knowledge and attentive follow-up. Food is available in the lounge until midnight, and there's live music on Saturday nights. Casual dress. **Bar:** Full bar. **Reservations:** suggested. **Hours:** 11 am-9 pm. Closed major holidays; also 12/24. **Address:** 186 Siletz Hwy **Location:** 5 mi s on US 101, just e on SR 229. **Parking:** on-site. **Cards:** AX, DS, MC, VI.

KI WEST RESTAURANT & LOUNGE   Phone: 541/994-3877

▼▼ ▼▼

Seafood
$7-$25

Fresh seafood comes with an ocean view at the comfortable restaurant. Choices include Dungeness crab legs, steamer clams, grilled razor clams and pan-fried oysters. Steaks, prime rib and pasta dishes round out the menu. An early-dining menu is available daily from 4 to 6 pm. Casual dress. **Bar:** Full bar. **Reservations:** accepted. **Hours:** 8 am-10 pm. **Address:** 2945 NW Jetty Ave **Location:** 0.3 mi w of US 101 via NW 30th St. **Parking:** on-site. **Cards:** AX, MC, VI.

KYLLO'S SEAFOOD & GRILL   Phone: 541/994-3179

▼▼ ▼▼

Seafood
$8-$46

Overlooking the beachfront, the restaurant is one of the city's more popular places to dine. Guests can enjoy pasta and seafood in a contemporary beach setting while taking in the great view from the picture windows or seasonal patio. Casual dress. **Bar:** Full bar. **Hours:** 11:30 am-9 pm; hours vary in winter. Closed: 11/26, 12/25. **Address:** 1110 NW 1st Ct **Location:** US 101, exit D River, w on 1st St. **Parking:** on-site. **Cards:** AX, DS, MC, VI.

LA ROCA RESTAURANT

Phone: 541/557-1815

Regional Mexican
$5–$11

Oaxacan-style fare is served at the basic eatery. The outdoor deck is open in season. Recommended is the chicken tamale. Casual dress. **Bar:** Beer & wine. **Hours:** 11 am-7:30 pm; to 9 pm in summer. Closed: 1/1, 11/26, 12/25. **Address:** 3243 SW US 101 **Location:** South side of US 101. **Parking:** street. **Cards:** AX, DS, MC, VI.

MCMENAMINS

Phone: 541/994-7238

American
$5–$20

The casual neighborhood eatery is where friends gather for classic pub and comfort fare, all washed down by pints of locally made beer. Large wooden booths or tables easily accommodate larger groups, and the eclectic, custom-painted walls and varied period light fixtures keep diners' eyes busy should the conversation lag. Casual dress. **Bar:** Full bar. **Hours:** 11 am-11 pm, Fri & Sat-1 am. Closed: 12/25. **Address:** 4157 N Hwy 101 **Location:** North end of town. **Parking:** on-site. **Cards:** MC, VI.

MO'S RESTAURANT

Phone: 541/996-2535

Seafood
$3–$14

Overlooking Siletz Bay, the restaurant presents a menu of Oregon seafood. Clam chowder, halibut fish and chips and oysters prepared several ways are just a few of the items served. Casual dress. **Bar:** Full bar. **Reservations:** not accepted. **Hours:** 11 am-10 pm. Closed: 11/26, 12/25. **Address:** 860 SW 51st St **Location:** Off US 101; south end of town. **Parking:** on-site. **Cards:** AX, DS, MC, VI.

THE WILDFLOWER GRILL

Phone: 541/994-9663

Regional American
$9–$23

Freshly baked breads complement Northwest-influenced foods, such as seafood pasta and marionberry-hazelnut duck. The seasonal deck overlooks an estuary. Casual dress. **Bar:** Beer & wine. **Reservations:** accepted. **Hours:** 7 am-4 & 5-9 pm, Sun & Mon-4 pm. Closed: 11/26, 12/25. **Address:** 4250 NE US 101 **Location:** North end of town. **Parking:** on-site. **Cards:** DS, MC, VI.

CALL

MADRAS pop. 5,078

——— WHERE TO STAY ———

BEST WESTERN MADRAS INN   *Book great rates at AAA.com*

Phone: (541)475-6141

Motel
$110–$130 3/1-9/30
$80–$110 10/1-2/28

Address: 12 SW 4th St **Location:** On US 97/26 southbound, at B and 4th sts; downtown. **Facility:** 46 one-bedroom standard units. 2 stories (no elevator), exterior corridors. *Bath:* combo or shower only. **Parking:** on-site. **Terms:** 2 night minimum stay - seasonal and/or weekends, 3 day cancellation notice. **Amenities:** high-speed Internet, voice mail, irons, hair dryers. *Some:* DVD players (fee). **Pool(s):** heated outdoor. **Leisure Activities:** whirlpool, exercise room. **Guest Services:** wireless Internet. **Business Services:** PC. **Cards:** AX, DC, DS, MC, VI. **Free Special Amenities: expanded continental breakfast and high-speed Internet.**

/ SOME UNITS FEE   FEE VCR

AAA Benefit:

Members save up to 20%, plus 10% bonus points with rewards program.

BUDGET INN   *Book great rates at AAA.com*

Phone: (541)475-3831

Motel
$55–$99 All Year

Address: 133 NE 5th St **Location:** On US 97/26 N; downtown. **Facility:** 30 units. 28 one- and 2 two-bedroom standard units, some with efficiencies (no utensils). 1 story, exterior corridors. *Bath:* combo or shower only. **Parking:** on-site. **Amenities:** high-speed Internet, hair dryers. **Guest Services:** wireless Internet. **Business Services:** PC. **Cards:** AX, DS, MC, VI. **Free Special Amenities: local telephone calls and high-speed Internet.**

/ SOME UNITS FEE

INN AT CROSS KEYS STATION

Phone: (541)475-5800

Hotel
$76–$146 All Year

Address: 66 NW Cedar St **Location:** On US 26; north end of town. **Facility:** Smoke free premises. 72 units. 67 one- and 3 two-bedroom standard units. 2 one-bedroom suites. 3 stories, interior corridors. *Bath:* combo or shower only. **Parking:** on-site. **Amenities:** high-speed Internet, irons, hair dryers. **Pool(s):** heated indoor. **Leisure Activities:** whirlpool, exercise room. **Guest Services:** coin laundry, wireless Internet. **Business Services:** meeting rooms, business center. **Cards:** AX, MC, VI.

ASK CALL / SOME UNITS FEE

——— WHERE TO DINE ———

BLACK BEAR DINER

Phone: 541/475-6632

American
$7–$16

A homey atmosphere characterizes this family-oriented restaurant. Familiar comfort foods, such as meatloaf with mashed potatoes, are at the heart of the menu and are served in generous portions. Casual dress. **Hours:** 6 am-10 pm. **Address:** 237 SW 4th St **Location:** On US 97/26 S; downtown. **Parking:** on-site. **Cards:** AX, DS, MC, VI.

MARQUAM

——— WHERE TO DINE ———

——— *The following restaurant has not been evaluated by AAA* ———
but is listed for your information only.

MARKUM INN

Phone: 503/829-9853

[fyi]

Not evaluated. Steaks, seafood and sandwiches are available at this eatery. House specials highlight Italian food items. **Address:** 36903 S Hwy 213.

MCKENZIE BRIDGE

———— WHERE TO STAY ————

———— The following lodging was either not evaluated or did not ————
meet AAA rating requirements but is listed for your information only.

BELKNAP RESORT AND HOT SPRINGS   **Phone:** 541/822-3512
[fyi]   Not evaluated. **Address:** 59296 Belknap Springs Rd **Location:** Just e of jct SR 126 and 242; near MM
55. Facilities, services, and decor characterize an economy property.

MCMINNVILLE pop. 26,499

———— WHERE TO STAY ————

BEST WESTERN VINEYARD INN   *Book great rates at AAA.com*   **Phone:** (503)472-4900

AAA [SAVE]   **Address:** 2035 S SR 99 W **Location:** Jct SR 99 W and 18.
▼▼▼   **Facility:** Smoke free premises. 65 one-bedroom standard units, some with
whirlpools. 4 stories, interior corridors. **Parking:** on-site. **Amenities:** high-
Hotel   speed Internet, voice mail, safes, irons, hair dryers. **Pool(s):** heated indoor.
$115-$120 All Year   **Leisure Activities:** whirlpool, exercise room. **Guest Services:** valet and
coin laundry, wireless Internet. **Business Services:** PC. **Cards:** AX, DC,
DS, MC, VI. **Free Special Amenities: continental breakfast and high-
speed Internet.** *(See color ad below)*

AAA Benefit:
Members save up to
20%, plus 10%
bonus points with
rewards program.

COMFORT INN & SUITES   *Book great rates at AAA.com*   **Phone:** (503)472-1700
AAA [SAVE]   **Address:** 2520 SE Stratus Ave **Location:** Jct SR 99 W, 3.6 mi e on SR 18. Located across from
▼▼▼   Willamette Valley Medical Center. **Facility:** Smoke free premises. 66 units. 60 one-bedroom standard
units. 6 one-bedroom suites with whirlpools. 3 stories, interior corridors. *Bath:* combo or shower only.
Hotel   **Parking:** on-site. **Terms:** cancellation fee imposed. **Amenities:** high-speed Internet, voice mail, irons,
$90-$162 All Year   hair dryers. **Pool(s):** heated indoor. **Leisure Activities:** whirlpool, sun deck, exercise room. **Guest
Services:** coin laundry, wireless Internet. **Business Services:** meeting rooms, PC. **Cards:** AX, CB,
DC, DS, JC, MC, VI. **Free Special Amenities: expanded continental breakfast and high-speed
Internet.**

RED LION INN & SUITES   *Book great rates at AAA.com*   **Phone:** (503)472-1500
AAA [SAVE]   **Address:** 2535 NE Cumulus Ave **Location:** Jct SR 99 W, 2.7 mi e on
▼▼▼   SR 18. Located near Evergreen Aviation Museum. **Facility:** Smoke free
premises. 67 units. 64 one-bedroom standard units, some with
Hotel   whirlpools. 3 one-bedroom suites. 3 stories, interior corridors. *Bath:*
$94-$122 All Year   combo or shower only. **Parking:** on-site. **Amenities:** video games (fee),
high-speed Internet, voice mail, safes, irons, hair dryers. **Pool(s):** heated
indoor. **Leisure Activities:** whirlpool, exercise room. **Guest Services:**
valet and coin laundry, wireless Internet. **Business Services:** meeting
rooms, PC. **Cards:** AX, DC, DS, MC, VI. **Free Special Amenities:
continental breakfast and newspaper.** *(See color ad p 374)*

SAFARI MOTOR INN

AAA SAVE

Motel
$70-$90 All Year

Book great rates at AAA.com   **Phone:** (503)472-5187
Address: 381 NE SR 99 W **Location:** North end of SR 99 W. **Facility:** 59 one-bedroom standard units. 2 stories (no elevator), exterior corridors. **Parking:** on-site. **Terms:** cancellation fee imposed. **Amenities:** high-speed Internet, irons, hair dryers. **Leisure Activities:** patio area. **Guest Services:** wireless Internet. **Business Services:** PC. **Cards:** AX, DC, DS, MC, VI. **Free Special Amenities:** expanded continental breakfast and local telephone calls.

▼ See AAA listing p 373 ▼

RED LION INN & SUITES
MCMINNVILLE
Stay Comfortable

• Complimentary Continental breakfast
• Indoor pool, whirlpool & fitness center
• Suites available
• Free wireless Internet access
• Microwave, refrigerator & guest laundry

AAA Member Rate
10% off Published rates*
*Rates subject to availability. Sgl/Dbl

RED LION
R&R CLUB
2535 NE Cumulus Ave.
McMinnville, OR 97128 • 503-472-1500

redlion.com • 800-Red Lion

STEIGER HAUS BED & BREAKFAST INN

Phone: 503/472-0821

▼▼▼

Bed & Breakfast
$95-$150 All Year

Address: 360 SE Wilson St **Location:** SR 18, exit McMinnville, 0.5 mi nw on SE Three Mile Ln, 0.5 mi w on 1st St, then just s on Davis St; SR 99 W (NE Baker St), just e on 1st St, s on Cowls St, then just e. Located in a quiet residential area. **Facility:** Smoke free premises. 5 units. 4 one-bedroom standard units. 1 one-bedroom suite with whirlpool. 3 stories (no elevator), interior corridors. *Bath:* combo or shower only. **Parking:** on-site. **Terms:** office hours 10 am-8 pm, 2 night minimum stay - seasonal and/or weekends, age restrictions may apply, 7 day cancellation notice-fee imposed. **Amenities:** video library, CD players, high-speed Internet, hair dryers. *Some:* DVD players. **Leisure Activities:** horseshoes. **Guest Services:** wireless Internet. **Business Services:** meeting rooms, fax. **Cards:** DS, MC, VI.

YOUNGBERG HILL VINEYARDS & INN

Phone: 503/472-2727

▼▼▼

Bed & Breakfast
Rates not provided

Address: 10660 SW Youngberg Hill Rd **Location:** Jct SR 18 and 99 W, 2.3 mi sw on SR 18, 2.2 mi nw on Masonville Rd, then 0.5 mi ne. **Facility:** Scenic views of the pinot noir vineyards and beyond enhance the luxuriously-appointed guest rooms at this hilltop inn. Smoke free premises. 7 units. 4 one-bedroom standard units. 3 one-bedroom suites, some with whirlpools. 2 stories (no elevator), interior corridors. *Bath:* combo or shower only. **Parking:** on-site. **Terms:** office hours 7:45 am-6 pm. **Amenities:** irons, hair dryers. **Guest Services:** wireless Internet. **Business Services:** meeting rooms.

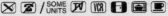

The following lodging was either not evaluated or did not meet AAA rating requirements but is listed for your information only.

MCMENAMINS HOTEL OREGON

Phone: 503/472-8427

[fyi]

Not evaluated. **Address:** 310 NE Evans St **Location:** At NE 3rd and Evans sts; downtown. Facilities, services, and decor characterize a mid-scale property.

WHERE TO DINE

THE FRESH PALATE CAFE

Phone: 503/843-1100

▼▼

American
$10-$24

A pleasant wine country lunch stop on the way to the Oregon coast, the cafe prepares delicious sandwiches, such as grilled Dungeness crab on homemade bread; pasta dishes, including alder-smoked salmon penne pasta in a caper cream sauce; crab quesadillas; and daily specials. Delectable desserts are made by hand. Works by local artists decorate the dining room. Seasonal seating is available on the deck. Casual dress. **Bar:** Beer & wine. **Reservations:** accepted. **Hours:** 11 am-3 pm, Fri & Sat-8 pm. Closed: 1/1, 11/26, 12/25. **Address:** 19706 SW Hwy 18 **Location:** Jct SR 99 W, 7.3 mi sw. **Parking:** on-site. **Cards:** AX, MC, VI.

GOLDEN VALLEY BREWERY & RESTAURANT

Phone: 503/472-2739

[AAA]

▼▼

American
$7-$38

In a 1920s warehouse, patrons can sip hand-crafted beers and wines that pair with daily specials, hand-cut steaks from cattle raised on the owner's ranch and pub staples. Foods are prepared from fresh local ingredients whenever possible. Original stained glass gives impact to the large, antique mahogany bar. Patio seating is a seasonal option. Brewery tours are available by appointment. Casual dress. **Bar:** Full bar. **Reservations:** accepted, except for dinner Fri & Sat. **Hours:** 11 am-9 pm, Fri & Sat-10 pm. Closed: 7/4, 11/26, 12/25. **Address:** 980 NE 4th St **Location:** Corner of NE Johnson and 3rd sts; downtown. **Parking:** on-site. **Cards:** AX, DS, MC, VI.

MCMENAMINS

Phone: 503/472-8427

▼▼

American
$5-$20

The casual neighborhood eatery is where friends gather for classic pub and comfort fare, all washed down by pints of locally made beer. Large wooden booths or tables easily accommodate larger groups, and the eclectic, custom-painted walls and varied period light fixtures keep diners' eyes busy should the conversation lag. Casual dress. **Bar:** Full bar. **Reservations:** not accepted. **Hours:** 7 am-11 pm, Fri & Sat-1 am. **Address:** 310 NE Evans St **Location:** At NE 3rd and Evans sts; downtown; in McMenamins Hotel Oregon. **Parking:** street. **Cards:** MC, VI.

CALL [&M]

NICK'S ITALIAN CAFE

Phone: 503/434-4471

▼▼▼

Northern Italian
$14-$42

On downtown's main street, the 28-year-old establishment occupies a 1910 building that formerly operated as a drugstore and retains the original lunch counter and stools. Diners enjoy the five-course prix fixe dinner for $42, or they may choose to order a la carte. All pasta is handmade on the premises, and a different pasta is featured each evening. Dungeness crab lasagna is delicious. Featuring wines from the Willamette Valley, the restaurant's vast wine list includes more than 100 bottles. Casual dress. **Bar:** Beer & wine. **Reservations:** suggested. **Hours:** 5:30 pm-9 pm, Fri & Sat-10 pm, Sun 5 pm-8 pm. Closed major holidays; also Mon. **Address:** 521 NE 3rd St **Location:** At Evans and 3rd sts; center. **Parking:** street. **Cards:** AX, MC, VI.

The following restaurant has not been evaluated by AAA but is listed for your information only.

RED FOX BAKERY & CAFE

Phone: 503/434-5098

[fyi]

Not evaluated. Several varieties of freshly baked breads and desserts are offered, along with tasty sandwiches. **Address:** 328 NE Evans St **Location:** At NE 3rd St; downtown; behind McMenamins Hotel Oregon.

MEDFORD pop. 63,154

Map Page	OA	✈ Airport Accommodations			
		MEDFORD-JACKSON COUNTY	Diamond Rated	High Season	Page
N/A	AAA	Candlewood Suites Medford Airport, across from terminal	▽▽	$109-$149 SAVE	376
N/A		Courtyard by Marriott-Medford Airport, just n of terminal	▽▽▽	$161-$197	377

———— WHERE TO STAY ————

BEST WESTERN HORIZON INN   *Book great rates at AAA.com*   Phone: (541)779-5085

AAA SAVE
▽▽▽▽
Hotel
$79-$109 All Year

Address: 1154 E Barnett Rd **Location:** I-5, exit 27 (Barnett Rd), just e. **Facility:** 122 units. 118 one-bedroom standard units. 4 one-bedroom suites, some with whirlpools. 2 stories (no elevator), exterior corridors. *Bath:* combo or shower only. **Parking:** on-site. **Terms:** cancellation fee imposed. **Amenities:** high-speed Internet, irons, hair dryers. **Pool(s):** heated outdoor. **Leisure Activities:** sauna, whirlpool, exercise room. **Guest Services:** valet laundry, wireless Internet. **Business Services:** meeting rooms, business center. **Cards:** AX, DS, MC, VI. **Free Special Amenities:** expanded continental breakfast and high-speed Internet. *(See color ad below)*

🛗 ⬆ 🏊 🚫 ⛶ 🛄 🖥 💻 / SOME UNITS 🛏 🚫

CANDLEWOOD SUITES MEDFORD AIRPORT   *Book great rates at AAA.com*   Phone: (541)772-2800

AAA SAVE
▽▽
Hotel
$109-$149 All Year

Address: 3548 Heathrow Way **Location:** I-5, exit 33, 1.5 mi se via E Pine St and Biddle Rd, just w on O'Hare Pkwy, then just n. **Facility:** 72 units. 60 one-bedroom standard units with efficiencies. 12 one-bedroom suites with efficiencies. 4 stories, interior corridors. *Bath:* combo or shower only. **Parking:** on-site. **Terms:** office hours 7 am-11 pm. **Amenities:** video library, DVD players, CD players, high-speed Internet, dual phone lines, voice mail, irons, hair dryers. **Leisure Activities:** exercise room. **Guest Services:** complimentary and valet laundry, airport transportation-Rogue Valley International-Medford Airport, wireless Internet. **Business Services:** meeting rooms, business center. **Cards:** AX, CB, DC, DS, JC, MC, VI. **Free Special Amenities:** room upgrade (subject to availability with advance reservations) and high-speed Internet.

✈ CALL 🔊M ⛶ 🛄 🖥 💻 / SOME UNITS FEE 🛏 🚫

CEDAR LODGE MOTOR INN   *Book great rates at AAA.com*   Phone: (541)773-7361

AAA SAVE
▽
Motel
$52-$75 All Year

Address: 518 N Riverside Ave **Location:** I-5, exit 27 (Barnett Rd), 0.3 mi w on Barnett Rd, then 1.2 mi n. **Facility:** 79 units. 77 one- and 2 two-bedroom standard units, some with kitchens. 2 stories (no elevator), exterior corridors. *Bath:* combo or shower only. **Parking:** on-site. **Pool(s):** outdoor. **Guest Services:** airport transportation-Medford Airport, wireless Internet. **Cards:** AX, DS, MC, VI. **Free Special Amenities:** continental breakfast and high-speed Internet.

✈ 🛗 ⬆ ⛶ / SOME UNITS FEE 🛏 🚫 🛄 🖥

COMFORT INN NORTH MEDFORD   *Book great rates at AAA.com*   Phone: (541)772-9500

AAA SAVE
▽▽
Hotel
$90-$125 All Year

Address: 2280 Biddle Rd **Location:** I-5, exit 30 southbound, just ne on Crater Lake Hwy, follow signs to Biddle Rd/Airport, then just n; northbound, follow signs to Biddle Rd/Airport, then just ne. **Facility:** Smoke free premises. 52 one-bedroom standard units. 3 stories, interior corridors. *Bath:* combo or shower only. **Parking:** on-site. **Terms:** cancellation fee imposed. **Amenities:** high-speed Internet, safes (fee), irons, hair dryers. *Some:* DVD players. **Pool(s):** heated indoor. **Leisure Activities:** whirlpool. **Guest Services:** valet laundry, airport transportation-Medford Airport, wireless Internet. **Business Services:** PC. **Cards:** AX, DC, DS, JC, MC, VI. **Free Special Amenities:** expanded continental breakfast and high-speed Internet.

✈ 🛗 ⬆ 📶 🚫 ⛶ 🛄 🖥 💻 / SOME UNITS VCR

COMFORT INN SOUTH
Book great rates at AAA.com
Phone: (541)772-8000

AAA SAVE ▼▼▼▼▼
Hotel
$89-$124 All Year

Address: 60 E Stewart Ave **Location:** I-5, exit 27 (Barnett Rd), 0.3 mi w on Barnett Rd, then s. **Facility:** 61 one-bedroom standard units. 3 stories, interior corridors. *Bath:* combo or shower only. **Parking:** on-site. **Terms:** cancellation fee imposed. **Amenities:** high-speed Internet, safes (fee), irons, hair dryers. *Some:* DVD players. **Pool(s):** heated indoor. **Leisure Activities:** whirlpool, exercise room. **Guest Services:** valet and coin laundry, airport transportation-Medford Airport, wireless Internet. **Business Services:** PC. **Cards:** AX, DC, DS, MC, VI. **Free Special Amenities: expanded continental breakfast and high-speed Internet.**

COURTYARD BY MARRIOTT-MEDFORD AIRPORT
Book great rates at AAA.com
Phone: (541)772-5656

▼▼▼▼▼
Hotel
$161-$197 All Year

Address: 600 Airport Rd **Location:** I-5, exit 33, 1.5 mi se via E Pine St and Biddle Rd, then just e. Located just n of airport. **Facility:** Smoke free premises. 100 units. 98 one-bedroom standard units, some with whirlpools. 2 one-bedroom suites. 3 stories, interior corridors. *Bath:* combo or shower only. **Parking:** on-site. **Terms:** cancellation fee imposed. **Amenities:** high-speed Internet, dual phone lines, voice mail, irons, hair dryers. **Pool(s):** heated indoor. **Leisure Activities:** whirlpool, exercise room. **Guest Services:** valet and coin laundry, area transportation, wireless Internet. **Business Services:** meeting rooms, business center. **Cards:** AX, CB, DC, DS, MC, VI.

AAA Benefit:
Members save a minimum 5% off the best available rate.

HAMPTON INN
Book great rates at AAA.com
Phone: (541)779-0660

▼▼▼
Hotel
$149 All Year

Address: 1122 Morrow Rd **Location:** I-5, exit 30 southbound, just e to Poplar Dr, just s, then just e; northbound, just s on Biddle Rd, then just w. Located in a quiet residential area. **Facility:** 75 one-bedroom standard units, some with whirlpools. 3 stories, interior corridors. *Bath:* combo or shower only. **Parking:** on-site. **Terms:** 1-30 night minimum stay, cancellation fee imposed. **Amenities:** video games (fee), dual phone lines, voice mail, irons, hair dryers. *Some:* high-speed Internet. **Pool(s):** heated indoor. **Leisure Activities:** whirlpool, exercise room. **Guest Services:** valet and coin laundry, wireless Internet. **Business Services:** meeting rooms, business center. **Cards:** AX, OD, DC, DS, MC, VI.

AAA Benefit:
Members save up to 10% everyday!

HOLIDAY INN EXPRESS MEDFORD
Book great rates at AAA.com
Phone: (541)732-1400

AAA SAVE ▼▼▼▼▼
Hotel
$99-$139 All Year

Address: 1501 S Pacific Hwy **Location:** I-5, exit 27 (Barnett Rd), 0.4 mi w on Barnett Rd, then 0.3 mi s on SR 99 (Riverside Ave). **Facility:** 63 one-bedroom standard units. 4 stories, interior corridors. *Bath:* combo or shower only. **Parking:** on-site. **Amenities:** video library, DVD players, high-speed Internet, dual phone lines, voice mail, irons, hair dryers. **Pool(s):** heated indoor. **Leisure Activities:** whirlpool, exercise room. **Guest Services:** valet and coin laundry, airport transportation-Medford Airport, wireless Internet. **Business Services:** meeting rooms, business center. **Cards:** AX, CB, DC, DS, JC, MC, VI. **Free Special Amenities: expanded continental breakfast and high-speed Internet.**

MOTEL 6-MEDFORD NORTH - 739
Book at AAA.com
Phone: (541)779-0550

▼
Motel
$55-$65 All Year

Address: 2400 Biddle Rd **Location:** I-5, exit 30 southbound, just ne on Crater Lake Hwy, follow signs to Biddle Rd/Airport, then just n; northbound, follow signs to Biddle Rd/Airport, then just n. Located in a commercial area. **Facility:** 116 one-bedroom standard units. 2 stories (no elevator), exterior corridors. *Bath:* combo or shower only. **Parking:** on-site. **Amenities:** high-speed Internet (fee). **Pool(s):** outdoor. **Guest Services:** coin laundry, wireless Internet. **Cards:** AX, CB, DC, DS, MC, VI.

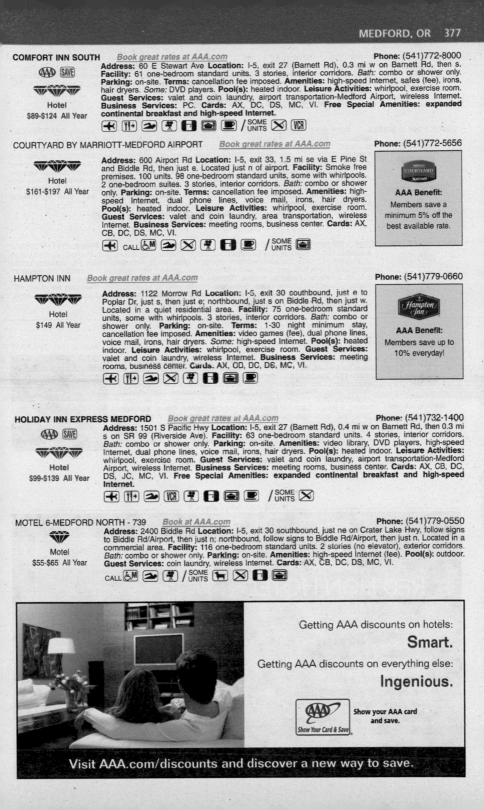

MOTEL 6-MEDFORD SOUTH - #89   *Book at AAA.com*   **Phone:** (541)773-4290

▼
Motel
$49-$59 All Year

Address: 950 Alba Dr **Location:** I-5, exit 27 (Barnett Rd), just e on Barnett Rd, then just n. **Facility:** 101 one-bedroom standard units. 2 stories (no elevator), exterior corridors. *Bath:* combo or shower only. **Parking:** on-site. **Pool(s):** outdoor. **Guest Services:** coin laundry. **Cards:** AX, CB, DC, DS, MC, VI.

CALL 🆓📶 ♨ 🐕 / SOME UNITS 🐾 ✕ 🍴 🖥

QUALITY INN & SUITES   *Book great rates at AAA.com*   **Phone:** 541/779-0050

AAA SAVE
▼ ▼
Hotel
Rates not provided

Address: 1950 Biddle Rd **Location:** I-5, exit 30 southbound, just ne on Crater Lake Hwy, follow signs to Biddle Rd/Airport, then just s; exit northbound, follow signs to Biddle Rd/Airport, then just s. **Facility:** Smoke free premises. 120 one-bedroom standard units, some with whirlpools. 2 stories (no elevator), interior corridors. *Bath:* combo or shower only. **Parking:** on-site. **Amenities:** high-speed Internet, voice mail, safes, irons, hair dryers. *Some:* DVD players. **Pool(s):** heated outdoor. **Leisure Activities:** sauna, whirlpool, bicycles, limited exercise equipment. **Guest Services:** valet and coin laundry, airport transportation-Medford Airport, area transportation-Rogue Valley Mall & within 5 mi, wireless Internet. **Business Services:** PC. **Free Special Amenities: expanded continental breakfast and high-speed Internet.**

✈ 🛏 CALL 🆓📶 ♨ ✕ 🎥 🍴 🖥 / SOME UNITS 🐾 VCR

RED CARPET INN   *Book great rates at AAA.com*   **Phone:** (541)772-6133

AAA SAVE
▼ ▼
Motel
$60-$80 3/1-9/15
$55-$70 9/16-2/28

Address: 525 S Riverside Ave **Location:** I-5, exit 27 (Barnett Rd), 0.3 mi w on Barnett Rd, then 0.4 mi n. **Facility:** 37 units. 36 one-bedroom standard units, some with efficiencies (no utensils) and/or whirlpools. 1 one-bedroom suite with efficiency (no utensils) and whirlpool. 1-2 stories (no elevator), exterior corridors. **Parking:** on-site. **Terms:** office hours 7 am-midnight. **Amenities:** high-speed Internet, wireless Internet. **Guest Services:** coin laundry, wireless Internet. **Business Services:** PC. **Cards:** AX, DS, MC, VI. **Free Special Amenities: continental breakfast and local telephone calls.**

🛏 🎥 🍴 🖥 / SOME UNITS ✕

RED LION HOTEL MEDFORD   *Book great rates at AAA.com*   **Phone:** (541)779-5811

AAA SAVE
▼ ▼
Hotel
$99-$139 All Year

Address: 200 N Riverside Ave **Location:** I-5, exit 27 (Barnett Rd), 0.3 mi w on Barnett Rd, then 1 mi n. **Facility:** 185 units. 183 one-bedroom standard units. 2 one-bedroom suites with whirlpools. 2 stories (no elevator), exterior corridors. *Bath:* combo or shower only. **Parking:** on-site. **Terms:** cancellation fee imposed. **Amenities:** high-speed Internet, voice mail, irons, hair dryers. **Pool(s):** 2 heated outdoor. **Leisure Activities:** exercise room. **Guest Services:** valet and coin laundry, airport transportation-Medford Airport, area transportation-within 2 mi, wireless Internet. **Business Services:** conference facilities, PC. **Cards:** AX, CB, DC, DS, MC, VI. **Free Special Amenities: expanded continental breakfast and high-speed Internet.** *(See color ad below)*

✈ 🛏 🍷 CALL 🆓📶 ♨ ✕ 🎥 🍴 🖥 🛎 / SOME UNITS 🐾

▼ *See AAA listing above* ▼

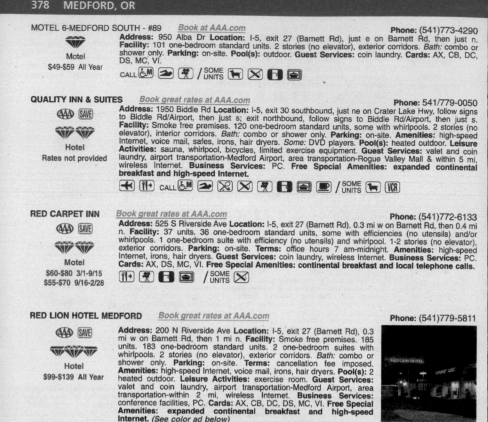

RODEWAY INN   *Book great rates at AAA.com*   Phone: 541/776-9194

AAA [SAVE]

◆◆◆

Motel

Rates not provided

Address: 901 S Riverside Ave **Location:** I-5, exit 27, 0.3 mi w on Barnett Rd, then just n. **Facility:** 40 one-bedroom standard units. 1 story, exterior corridors. *Bath:* combo or shower only. **Parking:** on-site. **Amenities:** high-speed Internet, hair dryers. **Guest Services:** coin laundry, wireless Internet. **Free Special Amenities: continental breakfast and high-speed Internet.**

[icons] / SOME UNITS [X]

ROGUE REGENCY INN & SUITES   *Book great rates at AAA.com*   Phone: (541)770-1234

AAA [SAVE]

◆◆◆

Hotel

$126-$131 All Year

Address: 2300 Biddle Rd **Location:** I-5, exit 30 southbound, just ne on Crater Lake Hwy, follow signs to Biddle Rd/Airport, then just n; northbound, follow signs to Biddle Rd/Airport, then just n. **Facility:** 203 units. 194 one-bedroom standard units. 9 one-bedroom suites with whirlpools, some with kitchens. 4 stories, interior corridors. *Bath:* combo or shower only. **Parking:** on-site. **Amenities:** video games (fee), high-speed Internet, dual phone lines, voice mail, irons, hair dryers. **Dining:** Regency Grill, see separate listing. **Pool(s):** heated indoor. **Leisure Activities:** whirlpool, exercise room. *Fee:* massage. **Guest Services:** valet and coin laundry, airport transportation-Medford Airport, area transportation-Rogue Valley Mall, beauty salon, wireless Internet. **Business Services:** meeting rooms, PC. **Cards:** AX, DC, DS, MC, VI. **Free Special Amenities: continental breakfast and high-speed Internet.** *(See color ad below)*

[icons] CALL [$M] [icons] / SOME UNITS [X] FEE [VCR]

SHILO INN MEDFORD — Book great rates at AAA.com

Phone: (541)770-5151

AAA [SAVE]

▼▼ ▼▼

Hotel
$85-$165 All Year

Address: 2111 Biddle Rd **Location:** I-5, exit 30 southbound, just ne on Crater Lake Hwy, follow signs to Biddle Rd/Airport, then just s; northbound, follow signs to Biddle Rd/Airport, then just s. **Facility:** 48 one-bedroom standard units. 3 stories, interior corridors. **Parking:** on-site. **Amenities:** video games (fee), high-speed Internet, irons, hair dryers. **Leisure Activities:** sauna, whirlpool, steamroom. **Guest Services:** coin laundry, wireless Internet. **Business Services:** PC. **Cards:** AX, CB, DC, DS, JC, MC, VI. **Free Special Amenities: continental breakfast and high-speed Internet.** *(See color ad below)*

SPRINGHILL SUITES BY MARRIOTT — Book great rates at AAA.com

Phone: (541)842-8080

▼▼▼

Hotel
$134-$164 All Year

Address: 1389 Center Dr **Location:** I-5, exit 27 (Barnett Rd) southbound to Stewart Ave, just s; northbound, just w on Barnett Rd, just s on Stewart Ave, then just s. **Facility:** Smoke free premises. 86 one-bedroom standard units. 3 stories, interior corridors. *Bath:* combo or shower only. **Parking:** on-site. **Terms:** cancellation fee imposed. **Amenities:** high-speed Internet, dual phone lines, voice mail, irons, hair dryers. **Pool(s):** heated indoor. **Leisure Activities:** whirlpool, limited exercise equipment. **Guest Services:** valet and coin laundry, wireless Internet. **Business Services:** meeting rooms, business center. **Cards:** AX, DS, MC, VI.

AAA Benefit:
Members save a minimum 5% off the best available rate.

TOWNEPLACE SUITES BY MARRIOTT — Book great rates at AAA.com

Phone: (541)842-5757

▼▼▼

Hotel
$129-$139 All Year

Address: 1395 Center Dr **Location:** I-5, exit 27 (Barnett Rd) southbound to Stewart Ave, just s; northbound, just w on Barnett Rd, just s on Stewart Ave, then just s. **Facility:** Smoke free premises. 76 units. 2 one- and 57 two-bedroom standard units, some with efficiencies or kitchens. 5 one- and 12 two-bedroom suites with kitchens. 3 stories, interior corridors. *Bath:* combo or shower only. **Parking:** on-site. **Terms:** cancellation fee imposed. **Amenities:** high-speed Internet, dual phone lines, voice mail, irons, hair dryers. **Pool(s):** heated outdoor. **Leisure Activities:** limited exercise equipment. **Guest Services:** valet and coin laundry, wireless Internet. **Business Services:** PC. **Cards:** AX, DS, MC, VI.

AAA Benefit:
Members save a minimum 5% off the best available rate.

▼ See AAA listing above ▼

——— **WHERE TO DINE** ———

MAC'S DINER

American
$6-$11

Phone: 541/608-7625

Black-and-white-checkerboard windows adorn the front of the '50s-style diner. The menu lists such burgers as the be-bop-a-lula, sh-boom and yakety yak. Try a phosphate, which is what soda jerks used to concoct. Blue-plate specials are available at dinner. Casual dress. **Bar:** Full bar. **Reservations:** not accepted. **Hours:** 9 am-8 pm, Fri & Sat-9 pm, Sun-3 pm. Closed: 11/26, 12/25. **Address:** 2382 Jacksonville Hwy, Suite F **Location:** I-5, exit 27 (Barnett Rd), 0.3 mi w on Barnett Rd, 0.8 mi n on Riverside Ave, then 1.5 mi w on SR 238 (W Main St/Jacksonville Hwy); in Jackson Creek Shopping Center. **Parking:** on-site. **Cards:** MC, VI.

MCGRATH'S FISH HOUSE

Seafood
$9-$19

Phone: 541/732-1732

The popular chain specializes in fresh Pacific Northwest seafood, including dishes grilled over a wood fire and items from the daily fresh sheet. Also on the menu are steaks, chicken, pasta and gourmet burgers. Casual dress. **Bar:** Full bar. **Reservations:** not accepted. **Hours:** 11 am-10 pm. Closed: 11/26, 12/25. **Address:** 68 E Stewart Ave **Location:** I-5, exit 27 (Barnett Rd), just w to Stewart Ave, then just s; in Harry and David's Country Village. **Parking:** on-site. **Cards:** AX, DC, DS, MC, VI.

PORTERS-DINING AT THE DEPOT

American
$14-$35

Phone: 541/857-1910

A national historic landmark, the 1910 train station has high ceilings and dark wood accents. The atmosphere is warm. Among menu choices are steak, prime rib and seafood preparations, as well as seasonal specials. Try a "martooni" or glass of wine from the good selection. The tree-shaded patio allows for seasonal al fresco dining. Casual dress. **Bar:** Full bar. **Reservations:** accepted. **Hours:** 5 pm-9 pm, Fri & Sat-9:30 pm. Closed: 7/4, 12/25. **Address:** 147 N Front St **Location:** At 5th and Front sts; downtown. **Parking:** on-site and street. **Cards:** AX, CB, DC, DS, MC, VI. **Historic**

REGENCY GRILL   *Menu on AAA.com*

American
$8-$28

Phone: 541/770-1234

The varied menu lists steaks, prime rib, chicken, seafood and pasta dishes, as well as lighter fare and children's and seniors' choices. The setting is pleasant. Casual dress. **Bar:** Full bar. **Reservations:** accepted. **Hours:** 6 am-10 pm. Closed: 11/26, 12/25. **Address:** 2300 Biddle Rd **Location:** I-5, exit 30 southbound, just ne on Crater Lake Hwy, follow signs to Biddle Rd/Airport, then just n; northbound, follow signs to Biddle Rd/Airport, then just n; in Rogue Regency Inn & Suites. **Parking:** on-site. **Cards:** AX, CB, DC, DS, JC, MC, VI. *(See color ad p 379)*

VINNY'S ITALIAN KITCHEN

Italian
$8-$25

Phone: 541/618-8669

Just a short drive from I-5, the restaurant serves traditional Italian family fare, including pasta with varied sauces, fish, veal and chicken dishes and pizza. The two dining rooms are reminiscent of Naples. Counter seats overlook the kitchen. Casual dress. **Bar:** Full bar. **Reservations:** accepted. **Hours:** 11 am-9 pm, Sat & Sun from 3 pm. Closed: 11/26, 12/25; also Mon. **Address:** 970 N Phoenix Rd, Suite 104 **Location:** I-5, exit 27 (Barnett Rd), 2.1 mi e on Barnett Rd, then just s; in Larson Creek Shopping Center. **Parking:** on-site. **Cards:** AX, MC, VI.

MERLIN

——— **WHERE TO STAY** ———

MORRISON'S ROGUE RIVER LODGE

Cabin
$300-$440 9/2-11/15
$175-$320 5/1-9/1

Phone: 541/476-3825

Address: 8500 Galice Rd **Location:** I-5, exit 61, 12 mi w on Merlin-Galice Rd. Located in a quiet area. **Facility:** Smoke free premises. 18 units. 8 one-bedroom standard units. 1 house and 9 cabins. 2 stories (no elevator), interior/exterior corridors. *Bath:* combo or shower only. **Parking:** on-site. **Terms:** open 5/1-11/15, office hours 7 am-11 pm, 45 day cancellation notice-fee imposed. **Amenities:** video library (fee), DVD players, high-speed Internet, irons, hair dryers. **Pool(s):** heated outdoor. **Leisure Activities:** limited beach access, fishing, putting green, 2 tennis courts, hiking trails, limited exercise equipment, basketball, horseshoes, volleyball. **Guest Services:** coin laundry, wireless Internet. **Business Services:** meeting rooms. **Cards:** AX, DS, MC, VI.

[✈] [¶] [⇆] [✕] [✕] [VCR] [▦] / SOME UNITS FEE [🐾] [♿]

MILWAUKIE —*See Portland p. 467.*

MONMOUTH pop. 7,741

——— **WHERE TO DINE** ———

BURGERVILLE

American
$2-$8

Phone: 503/838-6096

First-timers shouldn't let the fast food exterior fool them, as the burgers and chicken here adhere to a higher standard. Northwest ingredients come into play in the sandwiches. Casual dress. **Hours:** 7 am-10 pm. Closed: 11/26, 12/25. **Address:** 615 E Main St **Location:** Jct SR 99 W and E Main St. **Parking:** on-site. **Cards:** DS, MC, VI.

MOSIER pop. 410

——— **WHERE TO STAY** ———

MOSIER HOUSE BED & BREAKFAST

Bed & Breakfast
$85-$135 3/1-11/30

Phone: 541/478-3640

Address: 704 3rd Ave **Location:** I-84, exit 69, 0.3 mi se on US 30, just s on Washington St, then just e. **Facility:** Smoke free premises. 5 one-bedroom standard units. 2 stories (no elevator), interior corridors. *Bath:* some shared or private, combo or shower only. **Parking:** on-site. **Terms:** open 3/1-11/30, office hours 6:30 am-7 pm, check-in 4 pm, 2 night minimum stay - seasonal and/or weekends, 14 day cancellation notice-fee imposed. **Amenities:** high-speed Internet. **Guest Services:** wireless Internet. **Cards:** MC, VI.

[ASK] [✕] [W] [Ⓩ]

──── **WHERE TO DINE** ────

GOOD RIVER RESTAURANT   **Phone:** 541/478-0199

American
$7-$20

Designed after a Western pole barn with a side shed roof and much of the wood from a 100-year-old grain mill, the cafe serves fresh and tasty local food and homemade desserts. In season, guests can relax on the casual front porch and take in views of the Columbia River. Wireless networking is available. Casual dress. **Bar:** Full bar. **Hours:** Open 3/1-11/18 & 2/7-2/28; 11 am-2 & 5-close, Sat & Sun 9 am-close; call for winter hours. Closed: 1/1, 11/26, 12/25, 12/26; also Mon & Tues. **Address:** 904 2nd Ave **Location:** I-84, exit 69, just se on US 30. **Parking:** on-site. **Cards:** AX, DS, MC, VI.

MOUNT ANGEL pop. 3,121

──── **WHERE TO DINE** ────

GLOCKENSPIEL RESTAURANT   **Phone:** 503/845-6222

German
$7-$20

Under the glockenspiel—a clock featuring life-size figures that dance about at 11 am, 1 pm, 4 pm and 7 pm when the bells chime—this restaurant focuses on fresh Northwest foods prepared with a hint of a Bavarian influence. Traditional dishes include fondue, Wiener schnitzel and a sausage platter, along with steaks, pasta and seafood. Apple strudel tops the dessert choices. Casual dress. **Bar:** Full bar. **Reservations:** accepted. **Hours:** 11 am-10 pm, Sat & Sun from 8 am. **Address:** 190 E Charles St **Location:** Downtown. **Parking:** street. **Cards:** AX, MC, VI.

MOUNT HOOD pop. 3,306

──── **WHERE TO STAY** ────

──── *The following lodging was either not evaluated or did not* ────
meet AAA rating requirements but is listed for your information only.

COOPER SPUR MOUNTAIN RESORT   **Phone:** 541/352-6692

[fyi]   Not evaluated. **Address:** 10755 Cooper Spur Rd **Location:** 2.5 mi w of SR 35. Facilities, services, and decor characterize a mid-scale property.

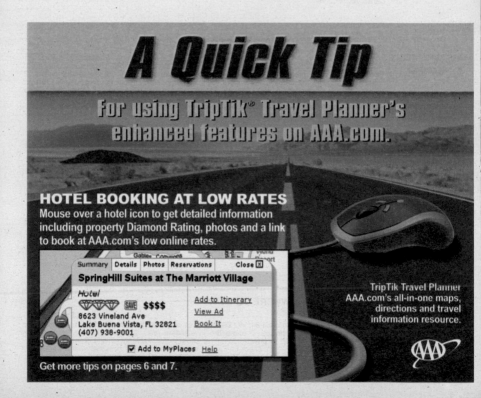

MYRTLE POINT pop. 2,451

―――― WHERE TO STAY ――――

MYRTLE TREES MOTEL

Phone: (541)572-5811

Address: 1010 8th St (Hwy 42) **Location:** On SR 42, 0.5 mi e. Located in a quiet area. **Facility:** 28 one-bedroom standard units. 2 stories (no elevator), exterior corridors. *Bath:* combo or shower only. **Parking:** on-site. **Terms:** 5 day cancellation notice. **Cards:** DS, MC, VI. **Free Special Amenities: local telephone calls and high-speed Internet.**

Motel
$60-$70 All Year

NEWBERG pop. 18,064

―――― WHERE TO STAY ――――

BEST WESTERN NEWBERG INN   *Book great rates at AAA.com*

Phone: (503)537-3000

Hotel
$89-$179 3/1-8/31
$79-$150 9/1-2/28

Address: 2211 Portland Rd **Location:** Northeast of center. **Facility:** 51 one-bedroom standard units, some with whirlpools. 2 stories (no elevator), interior corridors. **Parking:** on-site. **Terms:** cancellation fee imposed. **Amenities:** high-speed Internet, irons, hair dryers. **Pool(s):** heated indoor. **Leisure Activities:** sauna, whirlpool, exercise room. **Guest Services:** valet and coin laundry, wireless Internet. **Business Services:** PC. **Cards:** AX, CB, DC, DS, MC, VI. **Free Special Amenities: expanded continental breakfast and high-speed Internet.**

AAA Benefit:
Members save up to
20%, plus 10%
bonus points with
rewards program.

SHILO INN SUITES - NEWBERG   *Book great rates at AAA.com*

Phone: (503)537-0303

Hotel
$80-$175 All Year

Address: 501 Sitka Ave **Location:** Northeast of center on Portland Rd (SR 99 W). **Facility:** 61 units. 60 one-bedroom standard units. 1 one-bedroom suite with kitchen. 3 stories, interior corridors. **Parking:** on-site. **Amenities:** high-speed Internet, irons, hair dryers. **Pool(s):** heated outdoor. **Leisure Activities:** sauna, whirlpool, steamroom, exercise room. **Guest Services:** coin laundry, wireless Internet. **Business Services:** meeting rooms, PC. **Cards:** AX, CB, DC, DS, JC, MC, VI. **Free Special Amenities: continental breakfast and high-speed Internet.** *(See color ad below)*

——— WHERE TO DINE ———

BURGERVILLE

American
$2-$8

Phone: 503/538-0914
First-timers shouldn't let the fast food exterior fool them, as the burgers and chicken here adhere to a higher standard. Northwest ingredients come into play in the sandwiches. Casual dress. **Hours:** 7 am-10 pm. Closed: 11/26, 12/25. **Address:** 2514 Portland Rd **Location:** East end on SR 99. **Parking:** on-site. **Cards:** DS, MC, VI.

THE PAINTED LADY
American
$45-$60

Phone: 503/538-3850
In a historic home with a comfortable seasonal patio, the restaurant exudes refinement in both its setting and its cuisine. All menus are prix fixe. Dressy casual. **Bar:** Full bar. **Reservations:** suggested. **Hours:** 5 pm-10 pm. Closed: 1/1, 7/4, 12/24, 12/25; also Mon & Tues in winter; Tues in summer. **Address:** 201 S College St **Location:** Jct 2nd and S College sts. **Parking:** street. **Cards:** AX, DC, DS, MC, VI.

YAMHILL GRILL
American
$8-$23

Phone: 503/537-2900
In the heart of wine country, the restaurant presents a menu of burgers, steaks, seafood, pasta, vegetarian fare and such dinner specialties as slow-roasted prime rib. Chicken and ribs are smoked then basted in the eatery's signature barbecue sauce. For dessert, try marionberry cobbler or bumbleberry pie with crisp apples, raspberries, blackberries and rhubarb and wrapped in flaky crust. Beautiful hand-painted murals depicting the wine country adorn the walls. Local wines are featured. Casual dress. **Bar:** Full bar. **Reservations:** accepted. **Hours:** 11 am-9 pm, Fri & Sat-10 pm. Closed: 11/26, 12/25. **Address:** 2818 Portland Rd **Location:** Northeast end on Portland Rd (SR 99 W). **Parking:** on-site. **Cards:** AX, DS, MC, VI.

CALL ⬛🅼

NEWPORT pop. 9,532

——— WHERE TO STAY ———

THE BEST WESTERN AGATE BEACH INN   *Book great rates at AAA.com*   **Phone: (541)265-9411**

ⒶⒶⒶ 〔SAVE〕

Hotel
$133-$225 3/1-9/16
$100-$225 9/17-2/28

Address: 3019 N Coast Hwy **Location:** Jct US 20, 1.5 mi n on US 101. **Facility:** Smoke free premises. 148 units. 147 one-bedroom standard units. 1 one-bedroom suite. 6 stories, interior corridors. **Parking:** on-site. **Terms:** check-in 4 pm. **Amenities:** video library (fee), DVD players, high-speed Internet, voice mail, irons, hair dryers. **Pool(s):** heated indoor. **Leisure Activities:** whirlpool, beach access, exercise room. *Fee:* game room. **Guest Services:** valet laundry, wireless Internet. **Business Services:** conference facilities, PC. **Cards:** AX, DC, DS, MC, VI. **Free Special Amenities: local telephone calls and high-speed Internet.** *(See color ad below)*

AAA Benefit:
Members save up to 20%, plus 10% bonus points with rewards program.

🍽 🍸 🏊 ✂️ ✕ 🚫 🐾 🔌 📺 🖥 / SOME UNITS FEE 🐕

COMFORT INN   *Book great rates at AAA.com*   **Phone: (541)265-6203**

ⒶⒶⒶ 〔SAVE〕
Hotel
$75-$160 All Year

Address: 531 SW Fall St **Location:** Jct US 20, 0.5 mi s on US 101, then just w. **Facility:** Smoke free premises. 70 units. 66 one- and 4 two-bedroom standard units, some with whirlpools. 3 stories, interior corridors. **Parking:** on-site. **Amenities:** high-speed Internet, irons, hair dryers. **Leisure Activities:** exercise room. **Guest Services:** coin laundry, wireless Internet. **Business Services:** meeting rooms, PC. **Cards:** AX, DC, DS, MC, VI. **Free Special Amenities: full breakfast and high-speed Internet.**

✕ 🚫 🐾 🔌 📺 🖥

DAYS INN   *Book great rates at AAA.com*   **Phone: (541)265-5767**

ⒶⒶⒶ 〔SAVE〕
Motel
$75-$90 All Year

Address: 544 SW Coast Hwy **Location:** Jct US 20, 0.5 mi s on US 101. **Facility:** 32 one-bedroom standard units, some with efficiencies, kitchens and/or whirlpools. 2 stories (no elevator), exterior corridors. *Bath:* combo or shower only. **Parking:** on-site. **Terms:** office hours 7 am-11 pm, cancellation fee imposed. **Amenities:** high-speed Internet, irons, hair dryers. **Leisure Activities:** whirlpool. **Guest Services:** wireless Internet. **Cards:** AX, CB, DC, DS, MC, VI.

🏨➔ 🚫 🐾 🔌 📺 🖥 / SOME UNITS ✕

▼ See AAA listing above ▼

ELIZABETH STREET INN

AAA **SAVE**

▼▼▼

Hotel

$169-$319 All Year

Phone: (541)265-9400

Address: 232 SW Elizabeth St **Location:** Oceanfront. Jct US 20, 0.5 mi s on US 101, then w on SW Falls St. Located on the beachfront. **Facility:** Smoke free premises. 68 one-bedroom standard units, some with whirlpools. 6 stories, interior corridors. *Bath:* combo or shower only. **Parking:** on-site. **Terms:** check-in 4 pm, cancellation fee imposed. **Amenities:** video library (fee), DVD players, high-speed Internet, irons, hair dryers. **Pool(s):** heated indoor. **Leisure Activities:** whirlpool, exercise room. **Guest Services:** coin laundry, wireless Internet. **Business Services:** meeting rooms, PC. **Cards:** AX, CB, DC, DS, JC, MC, VI. **Free Special Amenities: expanded continental breakfast and high-speed Internet.**

HALLMARK RESORT OCEANFRONT

fyi

Hotel

$109-$239 All Year

Phone: (541)265-2600

Under major renovation, scheduled to be completed October 2009. **Last rated:** ▼▼▼
Address: 744 SW Elizabeth St **Location:** Oceanfront. Jct US 20, 0.7 mi s on US 101, then just w on SW Bay St. **Facility:** Smoke free premises. 158 one-bedroom standard units, some with whirlpools. 3-5 stories, exterior corridors. *Bath:* combo or shower only. **Parking:** on-site. **Terms:** check-in 4 pm, cancellation fee imposed. **Amenities:** high-speed Internet, voice mail, irons, hair dryers. *Some:* DVD players. **Dining:** Georgie's Beachside Grill, see separate listing. **Pool(s):** heated indoor. **Leisure Activities:** sauna, whirlpool, beach access, playground, exercise room, horseshoes, volleyball. *Fee:* massage. **Guest Services:** coin laundry, area transportation, wireless Internet. **Business Services:** meeting rooms, PC. **Cards:** AX, DC, DS, MC, VI.

HOLIDAY INN EXPRESS

fyi

Hotel

Rates not provided

Too new to rate, opening scheduled for February 2009. **Address:** 135 SE 32nd St **Location:** US 101, just s of Yaquina Bay Bridge. **Amenities:** 85 units, coffeemakers, microwaves, refrigerators, pool. **Terms:** check-in 4 pm.

THE LANDING AT NEWPORT

Book great rates at AAA.com

AAA **SAVE**

▼▼▼

Condominium

$109-$229 All Year

Phone: (541)574-6777

Address: 890 SE Bay Blvd **Location:** Jct US 101, 0.5 mi e on US 20, then 0.3 mi s on John Moore Rd. Located by a marina. **Facility:** Walk along the boardwalk and take in views of the marina and historic bay bridge from this property, where most units boast a fireplace and balcony. Designated smoking area. 57 units. 3 one-bedroom standard units with efficiencies. 39 one- and 15 two-bedroom suites with kitchens. 3 stories, exterior corridors. *Bath:* combo or shower only. **Parking:** on-site. **Terms:** check-in 4 pm, cancellation fee imposed. **Amenities:** video library (fee), high-speed Internet, dual phone lines, voice mail, irons, hair dryers. *Some:* DVD players. **Leisure Activities:** barbecue area, crab cookers, deck, exercise room. **Guest Services:** wireless Internet. **Business Services:** meeting rooms, PC. **Cards:** AX, DS, MC, VI. **Free Special Amenities: local telephone calls and high-speed Internet.**

LA QUINTA INN & SUITES NEWPORT

Book great rates at AAA.com

▼▼ ▼▼

Hotel

$79-$129 All Year

Phone: (541)867-7727

Address: 45 SE 32nd St **Location:** US 101, just s of Yaquina Bay Bridge. **Facility:** 71 units. 59 one-bedroom standard units, some with efficiencies and/or whirlpools. 12 one-bedroom suites with efficiencies. 3 stories, interior corridors. *Bath:* combo or shower only. **Parking:** on-site. **Amenities:** video library, high-speed Internet, dual phone lines, voice mail, irons, hair dryers. *Some:* DVD players. **Pool(s):** heated indoor. **Leisure Activities:** sauna, whirlpool, exercise room. **Guest Services:** coin laundry, wireless Internet. **Business Services:** meeting rooms, PC. **Cards:** AX, DS, JC, MC, VI.

NEWPORT BELLE BED & BREAKFAST

▼▼▼

Bed & Breakfast

Rates not provided

Phone: 541/867-6290

Address: Moored H Dock Newport S Bch Marina **Location:** South end of Yaquina Bay Bridge, follow signs to Marine Science Center, then just w. **Facility:** This newer sternwheeler riverboat offers a unique lodging experience plus views of the marina and Yaquina Bay Bridge. Smoke free premises. 5 one-bedroom standard units. 3 stories (no elevator), exterior corridors. *Bath:* shower only. **Parking:** on-site. **Terms:** open 3/1-10/31, office hours 7:30 am-7 pm, check-in 4 pm, age restrictions may apply. **Amenities:** high-speed Internet, hair dryers. **Guest Services:** TV in common area, wireless Internet. **Business Services:** PC.

OCEAN HOUSE INN-AN OCEANFRONT BED & BREAKFAST

▼▼▼

Bed & Breakfast

$145-$250 All Year

Phone: (541)265-3888

Address: 4920 NW Woody Way **Location:** Jct US 20, 2.6 mi n on US 101, then just w. **Facility:** All guest rooms with fireplaces and ocean views. From the garden area, it is a short walk to the secluded beach below. Smoke free premises. 8 one-bedroom standard units, some with whirlpools. 2 stories, interior corridors. *Bath:* combo or shower only. **Parking:** on-site. **Terms:** office hours 8 am-10 pm, check-in 4 pm, 14 day cancellation notice-fee imposed. **Amenities:** video library, high-speed Internet, hair dryers. *Some:* DVD players. **Leisure Activities:** beach access. *Fee:* massage. **Guest Services:** wireless Internet. **Business Services:** PC. **Cards:** AX, MC, VI.

SHILO INN SUITES OCEANFRONT HOTEL - NEWPORT *Book great rates at AAA.com*

Phone: (541)265-7701

Hotel
$105-$270 All Year

Address: 536 SW Elizabeth St **Location:** Oceanfront. Jct US 20, 0.5 mi s on US 101, then just w on SW Falls St. **Facility:** Smoke free premises. 179 units. 177 one-bedroom standard units. 2 one-bedroom suites with kitchens. 2-4 stories, interior/exterior corridors. **Parking:** on-site. **Terms:** check-in 4 pm. **Amenities:** video games (fee), high-speed Internet, voice mail, irons, hair dryers. **Dining:** 2 restaurants. **Pool(s):** 2 heated indoor. **Leisure Activities:** beach access. **Guest Services:** valet and coin laundry, wireless Internet. **Business Services:** conference facilities, PC. **Cards:** AX, CB, DC, DS, JC, MC, VI. **Free Special Amenities:** newspaper and high-speed Internet. *(See color ad below)*

TYEE LODGE OCEANFRONT BED & BREAKFAST

Phone: (541)265-8953

Bed & Breakfast
$145-$210 All Year

Address: 4925 NW Woody Way **Location:** Jct US 20, 2.6 mi n on US 101, then just w. **Facility:** Located just south of the Yaquina Head Lighthouse on Agate Beach, guest rooms have a gas fireplace. Smoke free premises. 6 one-bedroom standard units. 2 stories (no elevator), interior corridors. *Bath:* combo or shower only. **Parking:** on-site. **Terms:** office hours 8 am-10 pm, check-in 4 pm, age restrictions may apply, cancellation fee imposed. **Amenities:** video library, high-speed Internet, hair dryers. *Some:* DVD players. **Leisure Activities:** beach access. *Fee:* massage. **Guest Services:** wireless Internet. **Business Services:** PC. **Cards:** AX, MC, VI. **Free Special Amenities:** full breakfast and high-speed Internet. *(See color ad below)*

WAVES OF NEWPORT MOTEL AND VACATION RENTALS

Hotel
$68-$129 All Year

Phone: 541/265-4661

Address: 820 NW Coast St **Location:** Jct US 20, 0.5 mi n on US 101, just w on NW 11th St, then just s on Spring St. Located across from the ocean. **Facility:** 64 units. 60 one-bedroom standard units. 1 house, 2 cottages and 1 condominium. 3 stories, exterior corridors. **Parking:** on-site. **Terms:** office hours 8 am-10 pm, 3 day cancellation notice. **Amenities:** video library (fee), DVD players, high-speed Internet, irons, hair dryers. **Pool(s):** heated indoor. **Leisure Activities:** sauna, whirlpool. **Guest Services:** coin laundry, wireless Internet. **Cards:** AX, DS, MC, VI.

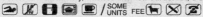

THE WHALER MOTEL

Motel

$115-$175 3/1-10/31
$99-$159 11/1-2/28

Phone: 541/265-9261

Address: 155 SW Elizabeth St **Location:** Jct US 20, just s on US 101, then just w on SW 2nd St. Located across the street from the ocean. **Facility:** Smoke free premises. 73 one-bedroom standard units. 3 stories, exterior corridors. *Bath:* combo or shower only. **Parking:** on-site. **Amenities:** high-speed Internet, irons, hair dryers. **Pool(s):** heated indoor. **Leisure Activities:** whirlpool, beach access, exercise room. **Guest Services:** coin laundry, wireless Internet. **Cards:** AX, DC, DS, MC, VI. **Free Special Amenities: continental breakfast and high-speed Internet.**

------ **WHERE TO DINE** ------

APRIL'S AT NYE BEACH

Regional Italian
$12-$24

Phone: 541/265-6855

An Italian flair is evident in preparations of fresh Northwestern cuisine. Al forno specialties, including four-cheese and grilled portabello mushroom cannelloni, share menu space with such dishes as Tuscan rotini with sun-dried tomatoes, scallions, fresh basil, roasted garlic, grilled chicken and Chardonnay cream sauce. Both Italian and Oregonian wines find their way onto the ample wine list. Ocean view and artwork by the chef's mother lend to the great atmosphere. Casual dress. **Bar:** Beer & wine. **Reservations:** suggested. **Hours:** Open 3/1-12/31 & 2/1-2/28; 5 pm-close. Closed major holidays; also Mon & Tues. **Address:** 749 NW 3rd St **Location:** 0.4 mi w of US 101, jct NW Coast and NW 3rd sts; in Nye Beach. **Parking:** street. **Cards:** DS, MC, VI.

CANYON WAY RESTAURANT & BOOKSTORE

American
$8-$25

Phone: 541/265-8319

Comfortable, informal and catering to its bookstore clientele, this popular restaurant established in 1971 and located in a circa 1910 building serves ample portions of fresh seafood, chicken, steak and pasta. The pasta, bread and desserts are made in house. Diners will find a good selection of beer and wine, along with signature house cocktails, tempting desserts and great coffee. The garden room boasts a view of Yaquina Bay. Casual dress. **Bar:** Full bar. **Reservations:** accepted. **Hours:** 11 am-3 pm, Thurs-Sat to 8:30 pm. Closed major holidays; also Sun. **Address:** 1216 SW Canyon Way **Location:** 4 blks e of jct US 101 and SW Hurbert St; 1 blk from bayfront. **Parking:** on-site. **Cards:** AX, MC, VI.

GEORGIE'S BEACHSIDE GRILL

Regional American
$7-$27

Phone: 541/265-9800

The restaurant specializes in fresh Northwest seafood served in a casual setting. Nearly every table affords wonderful ocean views. Casual dress. **Bar:** Full bar. **Reservations:** not accepted. **Hours:** 7:30 am-9 pm; to 10 pm in summer. **Address:** 744 SW Elizabeth St **Location:** Jct US 20, 0.7 mi s on US 101, then just w on SW Bay St; in Hallmark Resort Oceanfront. **Parking:** on-site. **Cards:** AX, DC, DS, MC, VI.

MAZATLAN MEXICAN RESTAURANT

Mexican
$6-$13

Phone: 541/265-8595

Food prepared the way it's done in Mazatlan is the house specialty. Tasty tacos, burritos and enchiladas can be accompanied by any of a number of imported Mexican beers. The flan is to die for. Casual dress. **Bar:** Full bar. **Hours:** 11 am-9 pm, Fri & Sat-10 pm. Closed: 11/26, 12/25. **Address:** 404 SW Coast Hwy **Location:** Center. **Parking:** street. **Cards:** AX, DS, MC, VI.

MO'S RESTAURANT

Seafood
$7-$14

Phone: 541/265-7512

Overlooking Yaquina Bay and across the street from the Original Mo's, the eatery has satisfied patrons since 1968 with such choices as clam chowder, shrimp and oyster stew, slumgullion (clam chowder with shrimp), seafood dinners and sandwiches. The adjacent clam chowder factory produces 500,000 pounds of clam chowder a year. Casual dress. **Bar:** Beer & wine. **Reservations:** not accepted. **Hours:** 11 am-9 pm; hours vary in winter. Closed: 11/26, 12/25. **Address:** 657 SW Bay Blvd **Location:** Just ne of Bay Bridge; on waterfront. **Parking:** street. **Cards:** AX, DS, MC, VI.

MO'S RESTAURANT

Seafood
$5-$13

Phone: 541/265-2979

The original Mo's location, this modest but busy waterfront cafe is popular with both locals and tourists. Signature dishes are clam chowder and fish and chips. In summer, waits are common, but they're worth it. Casual dress. **Bar:** Beer & wine. **Hours:** 11 am-9 pm. Closed: 11/26, 12/25. **Address:** 622 SW Bay Blvd **Location:** Just ne of Bay Bridge; on waterfront. **Parking:** street. **Cards:** AX, DS, MC, VI.

PANINI BAKERY

Breads/Pastries
$4-$9

Phone: 541/265-5033

The small bakery presents a limited menu of delicious baked items and sandwiches, such as house-roasted pork, eggplant with spinach and feta cheese and portobello mushroom on homemade bread. Waits can be lengthy during busy lunch times. Pizza is prepared only at dinner. Casual dress. **Hours:** 7 am-7 pm. Closed: 12/25. **Address:** 232 NW Coast St **Location:** Jct US 101 and 20, just n on US 101, 0.4 mi w on W 3rd St, then just s. **Parking:** street.

SAFFRON SALMON

Regional American
$10-$34

Phone: 541/265-8921

In a former cannery perched above the water, the restaurant has large windows that overlook the bay. An example of the enjoyable offerings is fresh oven-roasted chinook salmon served with a hazelnut-risotto cake, creamy pesto sauce and orange-saffron vinaigrette. A nice selection of Northwest wines is offered. Casual dress. **Bar:** Beer & wine. **Reservations:** suggested. **Hours:** 11:30 am-2:30 & 5-8:30 pm. Closed: 11/26, 12/25; also Wed & 3 weeks in Nov. **Address:** 859 SW Bay Blvd **Location:** Just ne of Bay Bridge; on Bay Street Pier. **Parking:** street. **Cards:** AX, MC, VI.

TABLES OF CONTENT

Phone: 541/265-5428

Regional American
$24

The oceanside hotel dining room serves multicourse prix fixe dinners only by reservation. Well-prepared meat and seafood entrees are accompanied by soup, salad and dessert, as well as a fine selection of wine and beer. Stimulating tableside conversation is guaranteed. Casual dress. **Bar:** Beer & wine. **Reservations:** required. **Hours:** 8:30-10 am, Mon-Thurs also 7 pm seating, Fri & Sat 6 pm & 8:30 pm seatings. Closed: 1st week in Dec. **Address:** 267 NW Cliff St **Location:** Jct US 20, just n on US 101, then 0.4 mi w on nw 3rd St; in The Sylvia Beach Hotel. **Parking:** on-site and street. **Cards:** AX, MC, VI.

VILLAGE MARKET & DELICATESSEN

Phone: 541/574-9393

Deli
$8-$10

Close to the beach, the delicatessen serves delicious gourmet food items, such as fresh crab bisque and imported meats and cheeses. Casual dress. **Bar:** Beer & wine. **Reservations:** accepted. **Hours:** 11 am-6 pm, Fri & Sat 9 pm. Closed: 12/25; also Mon & Tues. **Address:** 741B NW 3rd St **Location:** Jct US 20, just n on US 101, then 0.4 mi w; in Nye Beach. **Parking:** street. **Cards:** AX, DC, DS, MC, VI.

THE WHALE'S TALE

Phone: 541/265-8660

Seafood
$6-$25

A small, cozy dining room with eclectic decor sets the tone in the colorful establishment, which has served hearty portions of fresh seafood and shellfish for 30 years. This place is well known throughout the community for its well-prepared food. Casual dress. **Bar:** Beer & wine. **Reservations:** accepted. **Hours:** 9 am-9 pm; hours may vary in winter. Closed: 11/26, 12/25. **Address:** 452 SW Bay Blvd **Location:** Just e of jct US 101 and SW Hurbert St; on bayfront. **Parking:** street. **Cards:** AX, CB, DC, DS, MC, VI.

NORTH BEND pop. 9,544

——— WHERE TO STAY ———

COMFORT INN

Book great rates at AAA.com

Phone: (541)756-3191

Motel
$89-$179 All Year

Address: 1503 Virginia Ave **Location:** 0.5 mi w of US 101. Located adjacent to a shopping mall. **Facility:** 96 units. 95 one- and 1 two-bedroom standard units. 2 stories (no elevator), interior/exterior corridors. *Bath:* combo or shower only. **Parking:** on site. **Terms:** check-in 4 pm, cancellation fee imposed. **Amenities:** high-speed Internet, voice mail, safes (fee), irons, hair dryers. **Leisure Activities:** whirlpool, limited exercise equipment. **Guest Services:** valet and coin laundry, area transportation, wireless Internet. **Business Services:** PC, fax (fee). **Cards:** AX, DS, MC, VI.
(See color ad p 323)

THE MILL CASINO & HOTEL

Phone: (541)756-8800

Hotel
$108-$135 All Year

Address: 3201 Tremont Ave **Location:** 0.7 mi n on US 101; downtown. Located on the bayfront. **Facility:** Upscale property with many luxury appointments, attractive public areas and guest units with Northwest forest decor accents. Most rooms with view of bay. 203 units. 180 one-bedroom standard units. 23 one-bedroom suites, some with whirlpools. 7 stories, interior corridors. *Bath:* combo or shower only. **Parking:** on-site. **Terms:** check-in 4 pm, cancellation fee imposed. **Amenities:** voice mail, safes, irons, hair dryers. *Fee:* video games, high-speed Internet. **Pool(s):** heated indoor. **Leisure Activities:** whirlpools, exercise room. **Guest Services:** valet laundry, area transportation, wireless Internet. **Business Services:** meeting rooms. **Cards:** AX, DS, MC, VI.

——— WHERE TO DINE ———

HILLTOP HOUSE RESTAURANT

Menu on AAA.com

Phone: 541/756-4160

Steak & Seafood
$15-$35

A hilltop location affords a nice view of the bay from this restaurant offering seafood, steak, pasta and chicken entrees. A special "daylight" menu is offered from 4-6 pm. Casual dress. **Bar:** Full bar. **Reservations:** accepted. **Hours:** 4 pm-10 pm. Closed: 11/26, 12/25. **Address:** 93405 Wilsey Ln **Location:** 1.8 mi n on US 101; just n of bridge. **Parking:** on-site. **Cards:** AX, DC, DS, MC, VI.

OAKLAND pop. 954

——— WHERE TO STAY ———

BEST WESTERN RICE HILL

Book great rates at AAA.com

Phone: (541)849-3335

Motel
$77 All Year

Address: 621 John Long Rd **Location:** I-5, exit 148, just e. **Facility:** 48 one-bedroom standard units. 2 stories (no elevator), exterior corridors. **Parking:** on-site. **Terms:** check-in 4 pm, 3 day cancellation notice-fee imposed. **Amenities:** irons, hair dryers. *Some:* high-speed Internet. **Pool(s):** heated indoor. **Leisure Activities:** whirlpool, exercise room, basketball. **Guest Services:** wireless Internet. **Business Services:** PC. **Cards:** AX, DS, MC, VI. **Free Special Amenities:** continental breakfast and high-speed Internet.

—— WHERE TO DINE ——

TOLLY'S

American
$6-$30

Phone: 541/459-379

In a former 1903 mercantile, the restaurant boasts an original soda fountain and is decorated in a turn-of-the-20th-century motif. Tempting hors d'oeuvres and entrees feature seasonal ingredients. Romantic candlelight seating is offered in the couples-only room. The patio is open seasonally. Casual dress. **Bar:** Full bar. **Reservations:** suggested. **Hours:** 10:30 am-8 pm, Fri & Sat-9 pm; 9 am-8 pm in winter. Closed: 7/4 11/26, 12/25. **Address:** 115 Locust **Location:** I-5, exit 138 northbound; exit 140 southbound, 1.5 mi e. **Parking:** street. **Cards:** AX, MC, VI. **Historic**

OAKRIDGE pop. 3,148

—— WHERE TO STAY ——

BEST WESTERN OAKRIDGE INN *Book great rates at AAA.com*

Motel
$126-$146 3/1-10/1
$109-$129 10/2-2/28

Phone: (541)782-2212

Address: 47433 Hwy 58 **Location:** West end of SR 58. **Facility:** 40 units. 39 one-bedroom standard units, some with efficiencies (no utensils). 1 one-bedroom suite with efficiency (no utensils). 2 stories (no elevator), exterior corridors. *Bath:* combo or shower only. **Parking:** on-site. **Amenities:** high-speed Internet, voice mail, irons, hair dryers. *Some:* DVD players (fee). **Pool(s):** heated outdoor. **Leisure Activities:** whirlpool. **Guest Services:** coin laundry, wireless Internet. **Business Services:** PC. **Cards:** AX, DC, DS, MC, VI. **Free Special Amenities: continental breakfast and high-speed Internet.**

AAA Benefit:
Members save up to 20%, plus 10% bonus points with rewards program.

CASCADE MOTEL

Motel
$56-$75 All Year

Phone: 541/782-2489

Address: 47487 Hwy 58 **Location:** Center. **Facility:** 10 units. 9 one- and 1 two-bedroom standard units. 1 story, exterior corridors. *Bath:* combo or shower only. **Parking:** on-site. **Terms:** check-in 4 pm cancellation fee imposed. **Amenities:** high-speed Internet. **Leisure Activities:** barbecue facilities picnic area, gazebo. **Guest Services:** wireless Internet. **Business Services:** PC. **Cards:** MC, VI. **Free Special Amenities: continental breakfast and high-speed Internet.**

OCEANSIDE pop. 326

—— WHERE TO DINE ——

ROSEANNA'S CAFE

American
$6-$26

Phone: 503/842-7351

Roses and beachfront touches decorate the small, rustic restaurant from which diners can look out at the relaxing ocean. The varied menu lists seafood, chicken, steak and pasta dishes, as well as tasty soup salad and desserts. Casual dress. **Bar:** Full bar. **Reservations:** not accepted. **Hours:** 10 am-8 pm, Fri & Sat-9 pm; to 9 pm in summer. Closed: 12/25; also 2 weeks in Jan. **Address:** 1490 Pacific Ave **Location:** Center. **Parking:** street. **Cards:** MC, VI.

ONTARIO pop. 10,985

—— WHERE TO STAY ——

BEST WESTERN INN & SUITES *Book great rates at AAA.com*

Hotel
$90-$170 3/1-10/31
$83-$150 11/1-2/28

Phone: (541)889-2600

Address: 251 NE Goodfellow St **Location:** I-84, exit 376B, just nw. **Facility:** 61 units. 49 one-bedroom standard units, some with whirlpools. 12 one-bedroom suites, some with whirlpools. 2 stories (no elevator), interior corridors. **Parking:** on-site. **Amenities:** high-speed Internet, voice mail, irons, hair dryers. **Pool(s):** heated indoor. **Leisure Activities:** whirlpool, exercise room. **Guest Services:** valet and coin laundry, wireless Internet. **Business Services:** PC. **Cards:** AX, CB, DC, DS, MC, VI. **Free Special Amenities: expanded continental breakfast and local telephone calls.**

AAA Benefit:
Members save up to 20%, plus 10% bonus points with rewards program.

CREEK HOUSE BED & BREAKFAST INN

Bed & Breakfast
$99-$139 All Year

Phone: (541)823-0717

Address: 717 SW 2nd St **Location:** I-84, exit 376A, 0.8 mi w on Idaho Ave, then 0.4 mi s. **Facility:** Situated in a quiet residential neighborhood with tree lined streets, this 1908 Queen-Anne-style home was built by a local lumber merchant so only the finest woods and fixtures were used, as is evident by their lasting beauty today. Smoke free premises. 4 units. 3 one-bedroom standard units, some with whirlpools. 1 one-bedroom suite with whirlpool. 4 stories (no elevator), interior corridors. *Bath:* combo, shower or tub only. **Parking:** on-site. **Terms:** office hours 6 am-9 pm, check-in 4 pm, 7 day cancellation notice. **Amenities:** video library, DVD players, high-speed Internet, irons, hair dryers. **Leisure Activities:** horseshoes. **Guest Services:** wireless Internet. **Business Services:** PC. **Cards:** AX, DS, MC, VI.

HOLIDAY INN EXPRESS HOTEL & SUITES

Phone: 541/889-7100

[fyi]

Hotel

$99-$129 All Year

Too new to rate. **Address:** 212 SE 10th St **Location:** I-84, exit 376A, just se. **Amenities:** 96 units, coffeemakers, pool. **Cards:** AX, CB, DC, DS, JC, MC, VI.

HOLIDAY INN-ONTARIO, OR   *Book great rates at AAA.com*

Phone: (541)889-8621

(AAA) [SAVE]

◆◆◆

Hotel

$79-$119 All Year

Address: 1249 Tapadera Ave **Location:** I-84, exit 376B, just nw. **Facility:** 96 one-bedroom standard units. 2 stories (no elevator), interior corridors. *Bath:* combo or shower only. **Parking:** on-site. **Amenities:** high-speed Internet, dual phone lines, voice mail, irons, hair dryers. **Pool(s):** heated outdoor. **Leisure Activities:** whirlpool, exercise room. **Guest Services:** valet laundry, wireless Internet. **Business Services:** meeting rooms, PC. **Cards:** AX, CB, DC, DS, MC, VI. **Free Special Amenities:** local telephone calls and high-speed Internet.

RODEWAY INN   *Book great rates at AAA.com*

Phone: (541)889-9188

(AAA) [SAVE]

◆

Motel

$60-$78 All Year

Address: 615 E Idaho Ave **Location:** I-84, exit 376A, just sw. **Facility:** 71 one-bedroom standard units. 2 stories (no elevator), exterior corridors. **Parking:** on-site. **Amenities:** high-speed Internet. **Pool(s):** heated outdoor. **Guest Services:** wireless Internet. **Business Services:** meeting rooms. **Cards:** AX, CB, DC, DS, MC, VI. **Free Special Amenities:** free continental breakfast and high-speed Internet.

SLEEP INN   *Book great rates at AAA.com*

Phone: (541)881-0007

(AAA) [SAVE]

◆◆

Hotel

$59-$129 All Year

Address: 1221 SE 1st Ave **Location:** I-84, exit 376B, just ne. **Facility:** 65 one-bedroom standard units, some with whirlpools. 3 stories, interior corridors. *Bath:* combo or shower only. **Parking:** on-site. **Amenities:** high-speed Internet, voice mail, irons, hair dryers. **Pool(s):** heated indoor. **Leisure Activities:** whirlpool, exercise room. **Guest Services:** coin laundry, wireless Internet. **Business Services:** PC. **Cards:** AX, CB, DC, DS, JC, MC, VI. **Free Special Amenities:** expanded continental breakfast and newspaper.

SUPER 8   *Book great rates at AAA.com*

Phone: (541)889-8282

(AAA) [SAVE]

◆◆

Hotel

$58-$119 All Year

Address: 266 NE Goodfellow St **Location:** I-84, exit 376B, just nw. **Facility:** 63 units. 62 one-bedroom standard units, some with whirlpools. 1 one-bedroom suite with whirlpool. 2 stories (no elevator), interior corridors. **Parking:** on-site. **Amenities:** high-speed Internet, hair dryers. **Pool(s):** heated indoor. **Leisure Activities:** whirlpool, exercise room. **Guest Services:** coin laundry, wireless Internet. **Business Services:** PC. **Cards:** AX, DC, DS, MC, VI.

OREGON CITY —See Portland p. 467.

PACIFIC CITY pop. 1,027

—— WHERE TO STAY ——

INN AT CAPE KIWANDA

Phone: (503)965-7001

(AAA) [SAVE]

◆◆◆

Hotel

$99-$349 All Year

Address: 33105 Cape Kiwanda Dr **Location:** Just w on Pacific Ave, 1 mi n. Located across the road from the beach. **Facility:** Smoke free premises. 35 units. 34 one-bedroom standard units, some with whirlpools. 1 one-bedroom suite with whirlpool. 3 stories, exterior corridors. **Parking:** on-site. **Terms:** check-in 4 pm, 2 night minimum stay - seasonal and/or weekends. **Amenities:** video library, DVD players, CD players, high-speed Internet, voice mail, hair dryers. **Leisure Activities:** beach access, exercise room. *Fee:* bicycles. **Guest Services:** coin laundry, wireless Internet. **Business Services:** meeting rooms, PC. **Cards:** AX, CB, DC, DS, JC, MC, VI. **Free Special Amenities:** newspaper and high-speed Internet.

PACIFIC CITY INN

Phone: (503)965-6464

(AAA) [SAVE]

◆

Motel

$99 3/1-11/1

$79 11/2-2/28

Address: 35280 Brooten Rd **Location:** Center. **Facility:** Smoke free premises. 17 units. 12 one- and 5 two-bedroom standard units, some with efficiencies or kitchens. 2 stories (no elevator), exterior corridors. *Bath:* shower only. **Parking:** on-site. **Terms:** office hours 8 am-10 pm, 2 night minimum stay - weekends, 3 day cancellation notice-fee imposed. **Amenities:** video library (fee), high-speed Internet, hair dryers. *Some:* DVD players. **Dining:** Delicate Palate Bistro, see separate listing. **Leisure Activities:** picnic tables, garden, bicycle storage. **Guest Services:** wireless Internet. **Cards:** AX, DS, MC, VI. **Free Special Amenities:** local telephone calls and high-speed Internet.

—— WHERE TO DINE ——

DELICATE PALATE BISTRO

Phone: 503/965-6464

(AAA)

◆◆◆

Continental

$25-$29

This charming European bistro serves tasty international cuisine with a Northwest flair. Casual dress. **Bar:** Full bar. **Hours:** Open 3/1-12/24 & 1/15-2/28; 4 pm-9 pm, Sat & Sun from 1 pm; hours may vary in winter. Closed: 11/26, 12/25; also Tues in winter & Mon. **Address:** 35280 Brooten Rd **Location:** Center; in Pacific City Inn. **Parking:** on-site. **Cards:** AX, DS, MC, VI. **Classic**

GRATEFUL BREAD RESTAURANT AND BAKERY

Phone: 503/965-7337

Breads/Pastries
$6-$9

Creative omeletes, wholesome breads, pastries and hearty breakfasts are served at this bright and welcoming village bakery, along with healthful sandwiches, salads, homemade soups and vegetarian dishes. Casual dress. **Bar:** Beer & wine. **Reservations:** not accepted. **Hours:** Open 3/1-12/31 & 2/15-2/28 8 am-4 pm. Closed: 12/25; also Tues & Wed. **Address:** 34805 Brooten Rd **Location:** Center. **Parking:** on-site. **Cards:** MC, VI.

PELICAN PUB & BREWERY

Phone: 503/965-7007

American
$9-$21

Hand-crafted beers brewed on the premises complement pub food, including beer-battered fish and chips, clam chowder, seafood specialties and burgers. The dining area affords views of Haystack Rock and Cape Kiwanda. Deck dining, volleyball and ping pong nights are seasonal offerings. Tables can fill quickly on trivia nights. Casual dress. **Bar:** Full bar. **Hours:** 8 am-10 pm, Fri & Sat-11 pm. **Address:** 33180 Cape Kiwanda Dr **Location:** Just w on Pacific Ave, 1 mi n. **Parking:** on-site. **Cards:** AX, DS, MC, VI.

THE RIVERHOUSE RESTAURANT   *Menu on AAA.com*

Phone: 503/965-6722

American
$9-$25

The intimate riverside eatery presents a dinner menu of fresh seafood and steak dishes, as well as a more casual lunch menu with a wide variety of sandwiches and salads. Casual dress. **Bar:** Full bar. **Reservations:** not accepted. **Hours:** 11 am-9 pm; Sun-Thurs to 8 pm, Fri & Sat-9 pm in winter. Closed 11/26; also 12/10-12/27. **Address:** 34450 Brooten Rd **Location:** North side of street. **Parking:** on-site. **Cards:** MC, VI.

PENDLETON pop. 16,354

——— WHERE TO STAY ———

AMERICAS BEST VALUE INN   *Book great rates at AAA.com*

Phone: (541)276-1400

Motel
$79-$99 3/1-9/30
$69-$89 10/1-2/28

Address: 201 SW Court Ave **Location:** I-84, exit 210 (SR 11), 0.7 mi ne on SE 3rd Dr, then 0.6 mi w. **Facility:** Smoke free premises. 51 units. 49 one-bedroom standard units. 2 one-bedroom suites. 2 stories (no elevator), exterior corridors. **Parking:** on-site. **Amenities:** high-speed Internet, irons, hair dryers. **Pool(s):** heated outdoor. **Guest Services:** wireless Internet. **Business Services:** meeting rooms, PC. **Cards:** AX, CB, DC, DS, MC, VI. **Free Special Amenities:** continental breakfast and early check-in/late check-out.

 / SOME UNITS FEE

BEST WESTERN PENDLETON INN   *Book great rates at AAA.com*

Phone: (541)276-2135

Hotel
$95-$125 All Year

Address: 400 SE Nye Ave **Location:** I-84, exit 210 (SR 11), just se. **Facility:** Smoke free premises. 71 units. 68 one- and 3 two-bedroom standard units. 2 stories (no elevator), interior corridors. *Bath:* combo or shower only. **Parking:** on-site. **Amenities:** high-speed Internet, irons, hair dryers. **Pool(s):** heated outdoor. **Leisure Activities:** whirlpool, exercise room. **Guest Services:** coin laundry, airport transportation-Pendleton Municipal Airport, wireless Internet. **Business Services:** PC. **Cards:** AX, DC, DS, MC, VI. **Free Special Amenities:** expanded continental breakfast and high-speed Internet.

CALL / SOME UNITS FEE

AAA Benefit:
Members save up to 20%, plus 10% bonus points with rewards program.

HAMPTON INN   *Book great rates at AAA.com*

Phone: (541)276-3500

Hotel
$111-$189 All Year

Address: 101 SW Nye Ave **Location:** I-84, exit 210 (SR 11), just sw. **Facility:** Smoke free premises. 74 one-bedroom standard units. 4 stories, interior corridors. *Bath:* combo or shower only. **Parking:** on-site. **Terms:** check-in 4 pm, cancellation fee imposed. **Amenities:** video games (fee), high-speed Internet, voice mail, irons, hair dryers. **Pool(s):** heated indoor. **Leisure Activities:** whirlpool, exercise room. **Guest Services:** coin laundry, wireless Internet. **Business Services:** business center. **Cards:** AX, DS, MC, VI.

CALL / SOME UNITS

AAA Benefit:
Members save up to 10% everyday!

HOLIDAY INN EXPRESS   *Book great rates at AAA.com*

Phone: (541)966-6520

Hotel
$119-$149 3/1-9/5
$109-$139 9/6-2/28

Address: 600 SE Nye Ave **Location:** I-84, exit 210 (SR 11), just se. **Facility:** Smoke free premises. 63 one-bedroom standard units, some with whirlpools. 3 stories, interior corridors. *Bath:* combo or shower only. **Parking:** on-site. **Terms:** cancellation fee imposed. **Amenities:** high-speed Internet, voice mail, irons, hair dryers. **Pool(s):** heated indoor. **Leisure Activities:** whirlpool, exercise room. **Guest Services:** coin laundry, wireless Internet. **Business Services:** meeting rooms, PC. **Cards:** AX, CB, DC, DS, JC, MC, VI. **Free Special Amenities:** expanded continental breakfast and high-speed Internet.

/ SOME UNITS FEE

MOTEL 6 - #349   *Book at AAA.com*

Phone: (541)276-3160

Motel
$51-$61 All Year

Address: 325 SE Nye Ave **Location:** I-84, exit 210 (SR 11), just se. **Facility:** 92 one-bedroom standard units. 2 stories (no elevator), exterior corridors. *Bath:* shower only. **Parking:** on-site. **Amenities:** high-speed Internet (fee). **Pool(s):** heated outdoor. **Guest Services:** coin laundry, wireless Internet. **Cards:** AX, CB, DC, DS, MC, VI.

 / SOME UNITS FEE FEE

OXFORD SUITES

Book at AAA.com

▽▼▽▼▽▼

Hotel

$109-$149 All Year

Phone: (541)276-6000

Address: 2400 SW Court Pl **Location:** I-84, exit 209, just n on SW Emigrant Ave, just nw on SW 20th St, then just sw to SW Court Pl. Located behind a shopping complex. **Facility:** 87 units. 75 one-bedroom standard units. 7 one- and 5 two-bedroom suites. 3 stories, interior corridors. *Bath:* combo or shower only. **Parking:** on-site. **Amenities:** video library (fee), high-speed Internet, voice mail, irons, hair dryers. **Pool(s):** heated indoor. **Leisure Activities:** whirlpool, exercise room. **Guest Services:** coin laundry, wireless Internet. **Business Services:** meeting rooms, PC. **Cards:** AX, DC, DS, MC, VI.

RED LION HOTEL PENDLETON *Book great rates at AAA.com*

[AAA] [SAVE]

▽▼▽▼▽▼

Hotel

$109-$159 All Year

Phone: (541)276-6111

Address: 304 SE Nye Ave **Location:** I-84, exit 210 (SR 11), just sw. **Facility:** Smoke free premises. 170 units. 166 one- and 1 two-bedroom standard units, some with whirlpools. 1 one- and 2 two-bedroom suites. 3 stories, interior/exterior corridors. *Bath:* combo or shower only. **Parking:** on-site. **Terms:** cancellation fee imposed. **Amenities:** video games (fee), high-speed Internet, voice mail, irons, hair dryers. **Pool(s):** heated outdoor. **Leisure Activities:** whirlpool, exercise room. **Guest Services:** valet and coin laundry, airport transportation-Pendleton Municipal Airport, area transportation-within 5 mi, beauty salon, wireless Internet. **Business Services:** conference facilities, PC (fee). **Cards:** AX, DC, DS, MC, VI. **Free Special Amenities: early check-in/late check-out and room upgrade (subject to availability with advance reservations).** *(See color ad below)*

RUGGED COUNTRY LODGE *Book at AAA.com*

▽▼▽▼

Hotel

Rates not provided

Phone: 541/966-6800

Address: 1807 SE Court Ave **Location:** I-84, exit 210 (SR 11), 0.7 mi ne on SE 3rd Dr, then 0.4 mi e. **Facility:** Smoke free premises. 28 one-bedroom standard units. 2 stories (no elevator), interior/exterior corridors. **Parking:** on-site. **Terms:** office hours 6 am-10 pm. **Amenities:** high-speed Internet, voice mail. *Some:* DVD players. **Guest Services:** wireless Internet.

SUPER 8 *Book at AAA.com*

▽▼▽▼

Hotel

Rates not provided

Phone: 541/276-8881

Address: 601 SE Nye Ave **Location:** I-84, exit 210 (SR 11), just se. **Facility:** 50 one-bedroom standard units, some with whirlpools. 2 stories (no elevator), interior corridors. *Bath:* combo or shower only. **Parking:** on-site. **Amenities:** high-speed Internet, hair dryers. **Pool(s):** heated indoor. **Leisure Activities:** whirlpool. **Guest Services:** wireless Internet.

TRAVELODGE *Book great rates at AAA.com*

[AAA] [SAVE]

▽▼▽▼▽▼

Motel

$75-$80 3/1-8/31

$65-$75 9/1-2/28

Phone: (541)276-7531

Address: 411 SW Dorion Ave **Location:** I-84, exit 209, 0.9 mi ne on SW Frazer Ave, then just nw on SW 4th St. Located across from City Hall. **Facility:** 36 one-bedroom standard units. 2 stories (no elevator), exterior corridors. **Parking:** on-site. **Terms:** office hours 6:30 am-11 pm, 2 night minimum stay - seasonal. **Amenities:** high-speed Internet, irons, hair dryers. **Guest Services:** coin laundry, airport transportation-Pendleton Municipal Airport, wireless Internet. **Business Services:** PC. **Cards:** AX, DC, DS, MC, VI. **Free Special Amenities: continental breakfast and high-speed Internet.**

▼ *See AAA listing above* ▼

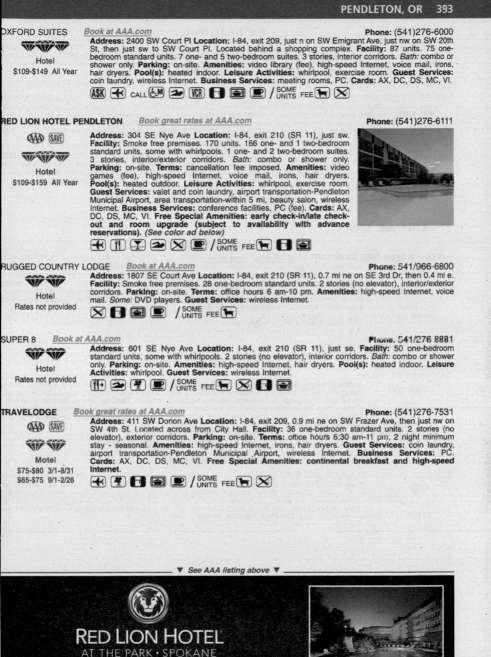

------ **WHERE TO DINE** ------

EL CHARRITO

▼▼▼▼

Mexican

$7-$13

The traditional family-run restaurant features festive mural-painted walls and friendly service. Casual dress. **Bar:** Full bar. **Reservations:** not accepted. **Hours:** 11 am-9 pm. Closed: 11/26, 12/25. **Address:** 212 SV Dorion Ave **Location:** Downtown. **Parking:** on-site. **Cards:** MC, VI.

Phone: 541/276-041

HAMLEY STEAKHOUSE

▼▼▼▼

Steak

$9-$48

This hundred-year-old building has been beautifully restored and is now a popular downtown eatery servin steaks, seafood, burgers, sandwiches and barbecue ribs. Without reservations, there's dining available i the bar area where seating is limited. Casual dress. **Bar:** Full bar. **Reservations:** required. **Hours:** 11:3 am-2 & 5-8 pm, Fri & Sat-9 pm. Closed: 1/1, 12/25. **Address:** 8 SE Court Ave **Location:** Jct S Main S downtown. **Parking:** street. **Cards:** AX, MC, VI.

Phone: 541/278-110

STETSONS HOUSE OF PRIME

▼▼▼▼

Steak

$17-$25

CALL 👍M

The contemporary setting incorporates Western-themed appointments. The restaurant is known for its prime rib and steaks, as well as the signature appetizer of crispy pork shanks with barbecue dipping sauce Casual dress. **Bar:** Full bar. **Hours:** 4:30 pm-close. Closed: 1/1, 12/25. **Address:** 103 SE Court S **Location:** Jct SE 1st St; center. **Parking:** on-site and street. **Cards:** AX, MC, VI.

Phone: 541/966-113

PHOENIX pop. 4,060

------ **WHERE TO STAY** ------

SUPER 8 & PEAR TREE RV RESORT   *Book great rates at AAA.com*

🆎🆎🆎 [SAVE]

▼▼▼▼

Hotel

$60-$85 All Year

🔧 🏊 💻 / SOME UNITS ✖️

Phone: (541)535-444

Address: 300 Pear Tree Ln **Location:** I-5, exit 24, just e on Fern Valley Rd, then just s. Adjacent to truck stop. **Facility:** 46 units. 45 one-bedroom standard units. 1 one-bedroom suite with whirlpool. stories (no elevator), exterior corridors. *Bath:* combo or shower only. **Parking:** on-site **Amenities:** high-speed Internet, irons, hair dryers. **Pool(s):** outdoor. **Leisure Activities:** whirlpool **Guest Services:** coin laundry, wireless Internet. **Cards:** AX, DS, MC, VI. **Free Special Amenities continental breakfast and high-speed Internet.**

PORT ORFORD pop. 1,153

------ **WHERE TO STAY** ------

CASTAWAY BY THE SEA

🆎🆎🆎 [SAVE]

▼▼▼▼

Motel

$65-$160 All Year

✖️ 🐾 / SOME UNITS FEE 🐕 🛏 🖥 💻

Phone: 541/332-450

Address: 545 W 5th St **Location:** Jct US 101, 1 blk w on Harbor Dr, then 1 blk n. **Facility:** Smoke free premises. 13 units. 4 one-bedroom standard units. 8 one- and 1 two-bedroom suites, some wit efficiencies or kitchens. 2 stories (no elevator), exterior corridors. **Parking:** on-site. **Terms:** office hour 8 am-10 pm, 3 day cancellation notice-fee imposed. **Business Services:** fax. **Cards:** AX, DS, MC, V **Free Special Amenities: local telephone calls and room upgrade (subject to availability wit advance reservations).**

------ **WHERE TO DINE** ------

THE SURF SHACK RESTAURANT AND SURF SHOP

▼▼▼▼

American

$3-$13

🐾

Phone: 541/332-045

Diners are treated to ocean views as they nosh on tasty tacos, brick-oven pizzas, panini sandwiches and salads, in addition to weekly dinner specials. Surfing videos play continuously. Casual dress. **Bar:** Beer & wine. **Reservations:** not accepted. **Hours:** Open 3/1-12/15 & 2/1-2/28; 11 am-3 & 5-8 pm; noon-10:30 pm in summer. Closed: 12/25; also Sun & Mon. **Address:** 190 6th St **Location:** On US 101, south end of town across from Battle Rock City Park. **Parking:** on-site. **Cards:** DS, MC, VI.

Destination Portland
pop. 529,121

*E*ntertainment in Portland takes on a carefree, casual feel.

A day can be spent discovering Victorian architecture in Nob Hill, strolling through Gov. Tom McCall Waterfront Park, shopping at a bookstore the size of a city block or skiing at nearby Mount Hood. And options for an evening out range from attending the symphony to cheering on the Trail Blazers.

© Gibson Stock Photography

Nob Hill Shopping District, Portland. Restaurants and trendy boutiques are tucked amid the charming Victorian architecture of Nob Hill, a tree-lined area comprised of N.W. 21st and N.W. 23rd streets. (See mention page 104)

Willamette River, Portland. Enjoy views of downtown while cruising the Willamette River by boat or personal watercraft.

© Gibson Stock Photography

© Richard Cummins SuperStock

Arlene Schnitzer Concert Hall, Portland. This 65-foot-tall "Portland" sign welcomes guests to the concert hall, a restored Italian Rococo Revival structure. (See mention page 105)

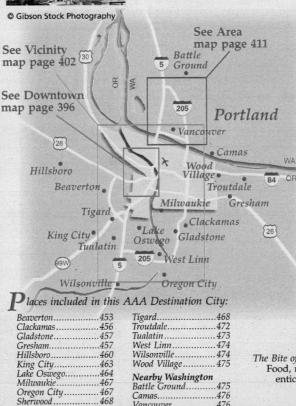

See Vicinity map page 402

See Downtown map page 396

See Area map page 411

Battle Ground

Portland

Vancouver

Camas

Hillsboro

Beaverton

Wood Village

Troutdale

Milwaukie   Gresham

Tigard

Clackamas

King City   Lake Oswego   Gladstone

Tualatin

West Linn

Wilsonville   Oregon City

© Gibson Stock Photography

The Bite of Oregon Festival, Portland. Food, music and regional wines entice locals and visitors alike at this waterfront fest. (See mention page 105)

*P*laces included in this AAA Destination City:

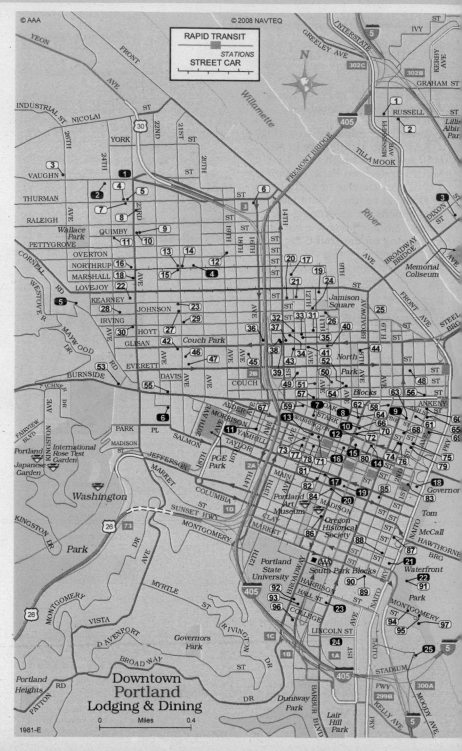

© AAA

© 2008 NAVTEQ

RAPID TRANSIT
STATIONS
STREET CAR

Downtown
Portland
Lodging & Dining

1981-E

0   Miles   0.4

Downtown Portland

This index helps you "spot" where approved lodgings and restaurants are located on the corresponding detailed maps. Lodging daily rate range is for comparison only and show the property's high season. Restaurant rate range is a combination of lunch and/or dinner. Turn to the listing page for more detailed rate information and consult display ads for special promotions.

DOWNTOWN PORTLAND

Map Page	OA	Lodgings	Diamond Rated	High Season	Page
1 / p. 396	AAA	**Holiday Inn Express Hotel & Suites Portland NW Downtown**	▽▽▽	$149-$179 SAVE	414
2 / p. 396		Silver Cloud Inn-Downtown Portland	▽▽▽	$159-$209	420
3 / p. 396	AAA	**Econo Lodge Downtown/Convention Center**	▽	$65-$110 SAVE	413
4 / p. 396		Inn @ Northrup Station	▽▽▽	$139-$219	416
5 / p. 396		Heron Haus Bed & Breakfast	▽▽▽	$145-$350	414
6 / p. 396	AAA	**Park Lane Suites**	▽▽	$129-$249 SAVE	418
7 / p. 396	AAA	**The Mark Spencer Hotel**	▽▽	$99-$249 SAVE	417
8 / p. 396	AAA	**The Benson Hotel, a Coast Hotel**	▽▽▽▽	$129-$359 SAVE	413
9 / p. 396		Embassy Suites Portland Downtown	▽▽▽	$139-$304	413
10 / p. 396	AAA	**Hotel Lucia - see color ad p 416**	▽▽▽	$319 SAVE	416
11 / p. 396	AAA	**Hotel deLuxe - see color ad p 415**	▽▽▽	$169-$369 SAVE	414
12 / p. 396	AAA	**Hotel Vintage Plaza**	▽▽▽▽	Rates not provided SAVE	416
13 / p. 396	AAA	**The Governor Hotel**	▽▽▽▽	$139-$389 SAVE	413
14 / p. 396	AAA	**Hotel Monaco Portland**	▽▽▽▽	Rates not provided SAVE	416
15 / p. 396		Marriott City Center	▽▽▽	$170-$208	417
16 / p. 396	AAA	**The Westin Portland**	▽▽▽▽	$119-$349 SAVE	420
17 / p. 396	AAA	**The Paramount Hotel, a Coast Hotel - see color ad p 418**	▽▽▽	$159-$199 SAVE	418
18 / p. 396	AAA	**Hotel Fifty - see color ad p 415**	▽▽▽	$139-$289 SAVE	415
19 / p. 396	AAA	**Hilton Portland & Executive Tower**	▽▽▽	$139-$239 SAVE	414
20 / p. 396	AAA	**The Heathman Hotel**	▽▽▽	$259-$725 SAVE	414
21 / p. 396		Portland Marriott Downtown Waterfront	▽▽▽	$219-$239	418
22 / p. 396	AAA	**RiverPlace, A Larkspur Collection Hotel - see color ad p 420**	▽▽▽	$249-$525 SAVE	420
23 / p. 396	AAA	**Econo Lodge City Center**	▽▽	$89-$125 SAVE	413
24 / p. 396		University Place	▽▽▽	$108-$159	420
25 / p. 396	AAA	**Residence Inn Portland Downtown at RiverPlace**	▽▽▽	$199-$209 SAVE	419

Map Page	OA	Restaurants	Diamond Rated	Cuisine	Meal Range	Page
1 / p. 396		Widmer Gasthaus	▽▽	German	$7-$22	431
2 / p. 396		Mint & 820	▽▽▽	American	$12-$25	426
3 / p. 396		Meriwether's Restaurant	▽▽▽	American	$8-$34	426
4 / p. 396		Patanegra	▽▽	Spanish	$6-$20	428
5 / p. 396		St. Honore Boulangerie	▽	Breads/Pastries	$7-$9	429
6 / p. 396		Carlyle	▽▽▽	American	$18-$34	422
7 / p. 396		Umenoki Japanese Restaurant	▽▽	Japanese	$6-$21	430
8 / p. 396		Besaw's	▽▽	American	$6-$20	421
9 / p. 396		Sushiville, Sushi Go Round	▽▽	Sushi	$4-$10	430

Map Page	OA	Restaurants (cont'd)	Diamond Rated	Cuisine	Meal Range	Page
⑩ / p. 396		Pastini Pastaria	◆◆	Italian	$5-$10	427
⑪ / p. 396		Stepping Stone Cafe	◆◆	American	$6-$9	429
⑫ / p. 396		Justa Pasta	◆◆	Italian	$5-$14	424
⑬ / p. 396		Wildwood	◆◆◆	American	$9-$33	431
⑭ / p. 396		Paley's Place Bistro & Bar	◆◆◆	Regional American	$16-$32	427
⑮ / p. 396		Marrakesh Moroccan Restaurant	◆◆	Moroccan	$18	426
⑯ / p. 396		BeWon Korean Restaurant	◆◆	Korean	$7-$25	421
⑰ / p. 396		Bridgeport Brewpub & Bakery	◆◆	American	$8-$24	421
⑱ / p. 396		Misohapi	◆◆	Vietnamese	$6-$11	426
⑲ / p. 396		Fenouil	◆◆◆	French	$10-$30	422
⑳ / p. 396	◭◭◭	**On Deck Sports Bar and Grill**	◆◆	American	$6-$18	427
㉑ / p. 396		daily cafe in the Pearl	◆◆	American	$6-$17	422
㉒ / p. 396		Laurelwood Northwest Public House & Brewery	◆◆	American	$9-$15	425
㉓ / p. 396		Serratto	◆◆◆	Regional Mediterranean	$9-$29	429
㉔ / p. 396		Piazza Italia	◆◆	Italian	$10-$14	428
㉕ / p. 396		Wilf's Restaurant	◆◆◆	Steak & Seafood	$10-$46	431
㉖ / p. 396		Sin Ju Japanese Restaurant	◆◆◆	Japanese	$7-$30	429
㉗ / p. 396		Caffe Mingo	◆◆	Italian	$14-$25	422
㉘ / p. 396		Mio Sushi	◆	Sushi	$5-$15	426
㉙ / p. 396		Lucy's Table	◆◆◆	Regional Mediterranean	$15-$28	425
㉚ / p. 396		Papa Haydn West	◆◆◆	Regional American	$9-$27	427
㉛ / p. 396	◭◭◭	**Giorgio's Restaurant**	◆◆◆	Northern Italian	$10-$29	423
㉜ / p. 396	-	Paragon Restaurant & Bar	◆◆	American	$9-$22	427
㉝ / p. 396		Fratelli	◆◆	Italian	$14-$21	423
㉞ / p. 396		OLEA	◆◆	Continental	$14-$25	427
㉟ / p. 396		Oba! Restaurante!	◆◆◆	Latin American	$18-$34	427
㊱ / p. 396	◭◭◭	**Nancy's Kitchen**	◆	American	$6-$9	427
㊲ / p. 396		Holden's Bistro	◆◆	American	$10-$28	423
㊳ / p. 396		Touche' Restaurant & Bar	◆◆◆	Mediterranean	$10-$25	430
㊴ / p. 396		Le Bouchon	◆◆	Regional French	$10-$22	425
㊵ / p. 396		Silk Vietnamese Restaurant	◆◆◆	Vietnamese	$8-$24	429
㊶ / p. 396		Cha! Cha! Cha!	◆	Mexican	$4-$6	422
㊷ / p. 396		Urban Fondue	◆◆◆	Fondue	$15-$23	430
㊸ / p. 396		Andina	◆◆◆	Peruvian	$12-$29	421
㊹ / p. 396		Park Kitchen	◆◆	American	$7-$27	427
㊺ / p. 396		Saint Cupcake	◆	Breads/Pastries	$2-$4	429
㊻ / p. 396		Basta's Italian Restaurant and Bar	◆◆◆	Italian	$15-$22	421
㊼ / p. 396		Ken's Artisan Bakery	◆	Breads/Pastries	$6-$14	424
㊽ / p. 396		House of Louie	◆	Chinese	$5-$12	424

Map Page	OA	Restaurants (cont'd)	Diamond Rated	Cuisine	Meal Range	Page
49 / p. 396		Bluehour	◆◆◆	Continental	$10-$43	421
50 / p. 396		Marinepolis Sushi Land	◆	Sushi	$2-$8	425
51 / p. 396		P.F. Chang's China Bistro	◆◆◆	Chinese	$10-$21	428
52 / p. 396		Fuller's Restaurant	◆	American	$6-$9	423
53 / p. 396		Elephants Delicatessen	◆◆	Deli	$6-$20	422
54 / p. 396		Pearl Bakery	◆	Breads/Pastries	$2-$6	428
55 / p. 396	AAA	**Ringside Steakhouse**	◆◆◆	Steak	$21-$65	428
56 / p. 396		Alexis	◆◆	Greek	$8-$18	421
57 / p. 396		Henry's 12th Street Tavern	◆◆	Regional American	$9-$26	423
58 / p. 396		Portland City Grill	◆◆◆	Pacific Rim	$8-$60	428
59 / p. 396		Jake's Famous Crawfish Restaurant	◆◆◆	Seafood	$7-$28	424
60 / p. 396	AAA	**Dan & Louis Oyster Bar**	◆◆	Traditional Seafood	$7-$30	422
61 / p. 396		Bijou Cafe	◆◆	Natural/Organic	$5-$13	421
62 / p. 396		El Gaucho	◆◆◆	Steak & Seafood	$35-$60	422
63 / p. 396		Kincaid's Fish, Chop & Steak	◆◆◆	American	$10-$46	424
64 / p. 396	AAA	**London Grill**	◆◆◆	Regional American	$9-$56	425
65 / p. 396	AAA	**Kells Irish Restaurant & Pub**	◆◆	Irish	$0-$24	424
66 / p. 396	AAA	**Typhoon!**	◆◆	Thai	$8-$19	430
67 / p. 396		Gracie's	◆◆◆	American	$8-$28	423
68 / p. 396		Ruth's Chris Steak House	◆◆◆	Steak	$20-$40	429
69 / p. 396	AAA	**McCormick & Schmick's**	◆◆◆	Seafood	$15-$25	426
70 / p. 396		Pazzoria Bakery & Cafe	◆	Breads/Pastries	$5-$8	428
71 / p. 396		Jake's Grill	◆◆◆	American	$7-$40	424
72 / p. 396	AAA	**Pazzo Ristorante**	◆◆◆	Italian	$11-$31	428
73 / p. 396		Green Papaya Vietnamese Bistro	◆◆◆	Vietnamese	$7-$24	423
74 / p. 396	AAA	**Huber's**	◆◆	American	$6-$26	424
75 / p. 396		Al-Amir Lebanese Restaurant	◆◆	Lebanese	$6-$17	421
76 / p. 396		Karam Lebanese Cuisine	◆◆	Lebanese	$7-$25	424
77 / p. 396		Three Lions' Bakery and Cafe	◆	Breads/Pastries	$7-$9	430
78 / p. 396		India House	◆◆	Indian	$8-$19	424
79 / p. 396		Mother's Bistro & Bar	◆◆	American	$8-$20	426
80 / p. 396	AAA	**Red Star Tavern**	◆◆◆	Regional American	$12-$35	428
81 / p. 396		Dragonfish Asian Cafe	◆◆◆	Asian	$6-$18	422
82 / p. 396		Southpark Seafood Grill & Wine Bar	◆◆◆	Seafood	$9-$28	429
83 / p. 396		Sungari	◆◆	Chinese	$8-$20	429
84 / p. 396		The Heathman Restaurant	◆◆◆	Regional French	$8-$30	423
85 / p. 396		La Terrazza Italian Grill	◆◆	Italian	$7-$16	425
86 / p. 396		Higgins Restaurant & Bar	◆◆◆	Regional American	$8-$32	423
87 / p. 396		Veritable Quandary	◆◆◆	American	$10-$30	430

Map Page	OA	Restaurants (cont'd)	Diamond Rated	Cuisine	Meal Range	Page
⑧⑧ / p. 396		Mandarin Cove	▽▽	Chinese	$6-$18	425
⑧⑨ / p. 396		Restaurant Murata	▽▽	Japanese	$7-$27	428
⑨⓪ / p. 396		Carafe	▽▽▽	French	$7-$19	422
⑨① / p. 396		Three Degrees - see color ad p 420	▽▽▽	Regional American	$8-$28	430
⑨② / p. 396		Baan-Thai	▽	Thai	$7-$16	421
⑨③ / p. 396		Thanh-Long	▽▽	Vietnamese	$6-$10	430
⑨④ / p. 396		McCormick & Schmick's	▽▽▽	Seafood	$7-$27	426
⑨⑤ / p. 396		Marina Fish House	▽▽	Seafood	$10-$28	425
⑨⑥ / p. 396		Green Onion Restaurant	▽▽	Persian	$7-$17	423
⑨⑦ / p. 396		Stanford's Restaurant & Bar	▽▽▽	American	$10-$38	429

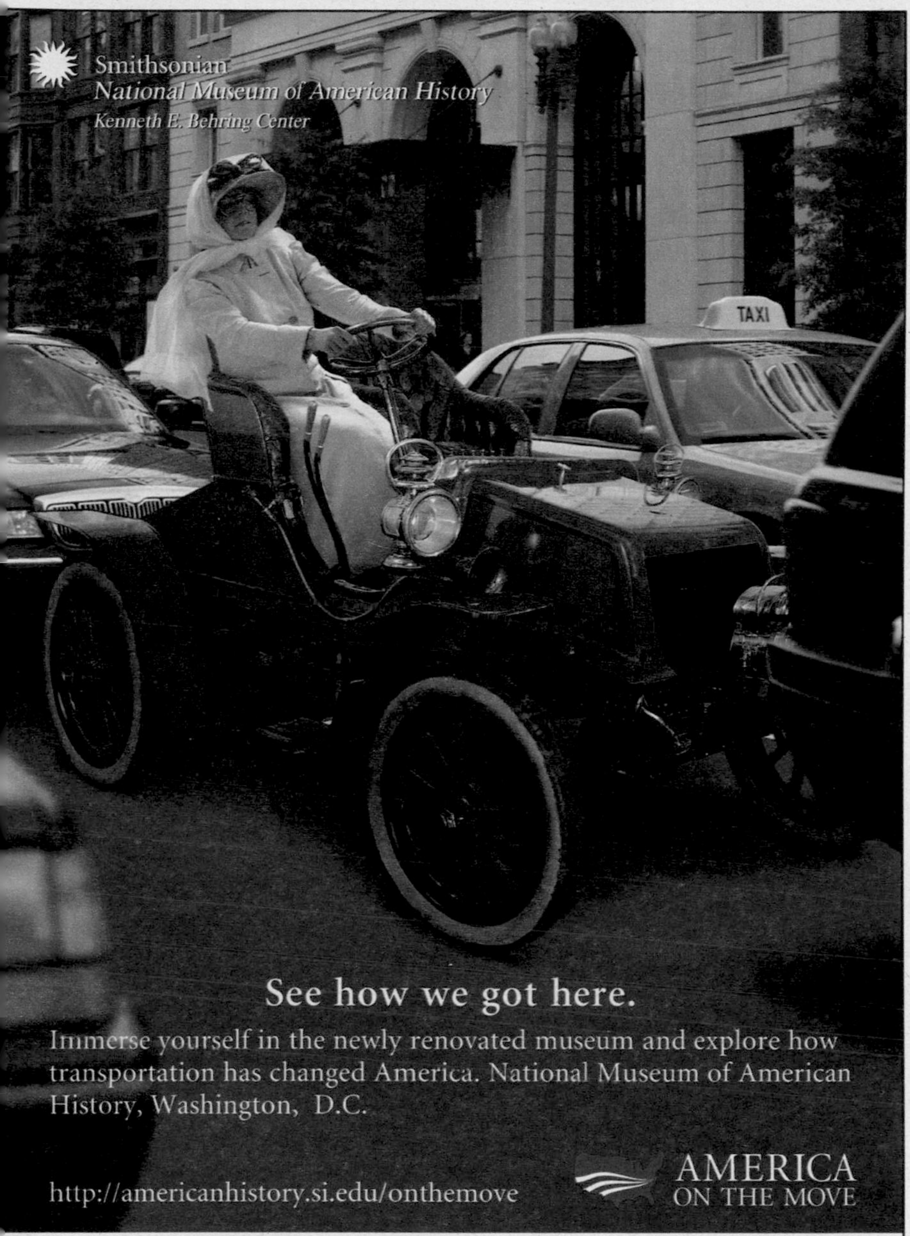

Smithsonian
National Museum of American History
Kenneth E. Behring Center
TAXI
See how we got here.
Immerse yourself in the newly renovated museum and explore how transportation has changed America. National Museum of American History, Washington, D.C.
http://americanhistory.si.edu/onthemove
AMERICA
ON THE MOVE

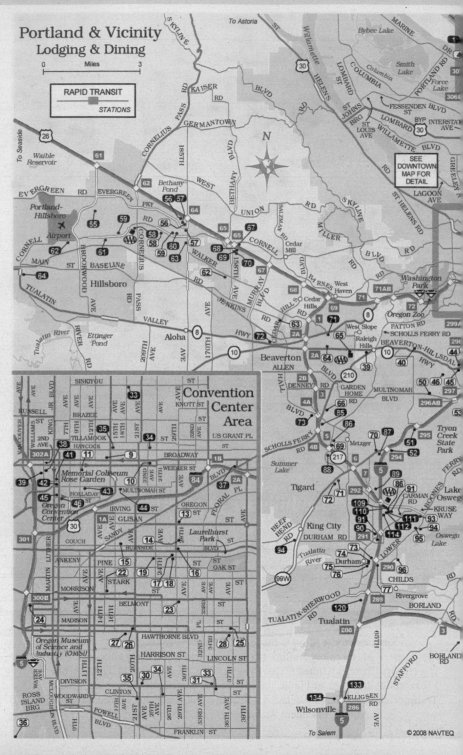

Portland & Vicinity
Lodging & Dining

RAPID TRANSIT
STATIONS

Convention
Center
Area

© 2008 NAVTEQ

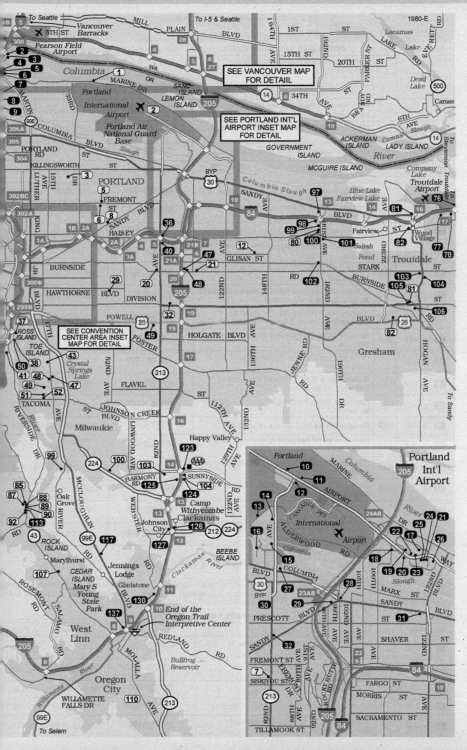

✈ Airport Accommodations

Map Page	OA	PORTLAND INTERNATIONAL	Diamond Rated	High Season	Page
N/A		aloft Portland Airport at Cascade Station, 1.4 mi e of terminal		Rates not provided	431
③⓪ / p. 402		Americas Best Value Inn & Suites-Portland Airport, 2.7 mi s of terminal	◈◈	$54-$79	431
②⑧ / p. 402	AAA	Best Western Pony Soldier Inn-Airport, 3 mi se of terminal	◈◈◈	$109-$209 SAVE	432
①⑨ / p. 402	AAA	Clarion Hotel Portland Airport, 2.3 mi e of terminal	◈◈◈	Rates not provided SAVE	432
②① / p. 402	AAA	Comfort Suites, 2.6 mi e of terminal	◈◈◈	$89-$149 SAVE	435
①③ / p. 402		Country Inn & Suites at Portland Airport, 2.2 mi sw of terminal	◈◈◈	$104-$118	435
②⓪ / p. 402		Courtyard by Marriott, 2.4 mi e of terminal	◈◈◈	$161-$197	435
①② / p. 402	AAA	Embassy Suites at Portland Airport, 0.6 mi s of terminal	◈◈◈	$109-$189 SAVE	437
②③ / p. 402		Fairfield Inn by Marriott, 2.6 mi e of terminal	◈◈◈	$129-$139	437
①① / p. 402		Hampton Inn-Portland Airport, 0.5 mi e of terminal	◈◈◈	$154	438
②⑥ / p. 402	AAA	Hilton Garden Inn-Portland Airport, 2.7 mi e of terminal	◈◈◈	$89-$141 SAVE	438
②④ / p. 402	AAA	Holiday Inn Express Hotel & Suites-Portland Airport, 2.5 mi e of terminal	◈◈◈	$99-$159 SAVE	438
②⑦ / p. 402	AAA	Holiday Inn Portland Airport Hotel & Convention Center, 2.3 mi s of terminal	◈◈◈	$119-$229 SAVE	438
③② / p. 402	AAA	Howard Johnson Portland Airport, 3 mi s of terminal	◈◈	$75-$120 SAVE	439
①⑧ / p. 402		La Quinta Inn & Suites Portland Airport, 2.5 mi e of terminal	◈◈◈	$69-$134	439
②⑨ / p. 402	AAA	Quality Inn & Suites Airport Convention Center, 3 mi se of terminal	◈◈◈	$99-$169 SAVE	441
①⑥ / p. 402	AAA	Radisson Hotel Portland Airport, 1.5 mi s of terminal	◈◈◈	$99-$179 SAVE	441
①⑤ / p. 402	AAA	Ramada Portland, 1.3 mi s of terminal	◈◈	$79-$199 SAVE	441
①④ / p. 402	AAA	Red Lion Hotel Portland Airport, 1.2 mi s of terminal	◈◈◈	Rates not provided SAVE	442
①⓪ / p. 402	AAA	Sheraton Portland Airport Hotel, 0.4 mi e of terminal	◈◈◈	$97-$248 SAVE	443
②② / p. 402	AAA	Shilo Inn Suites Hotel-Portland Airport, 2.4 mi e of terminal	◈◈◈	$120-$220 SAVE	444
②⑤ / p. 402		SpringHill Suites by Marriott Portland Airport, 2.5 mi e of terminal	◈◈◈	$149-$159	444
①⑦ / p. 402		Staybridge Suites Portland-Airport, 2.6 mi e of terminal	◈◈◈	$115-$170	445

Portland and Vicinity

This index helps you "spot" where approved lodgings and restaurants are located on the corresponding detailed maps. Lodging daily rate range is for comparison only and show the property's high season. Restaurant rate range is a combination of lunch and/or dinner. Turn to the listing page for more detailed rate information and consult display ads for special promotions.

PORTLAND

Map Page	OA	Lodgings	Diamond Rated	High Season	Page
① / p. 402	AAA	Holiday Inn Express Hotel & Suites at Jantzen Beach	◈◈◈	$95 SAVE	438
② / p. 402	AAA	Red Lion Hotel on the River Jantzen Beach-Portland	◈◈◈	$169 SAVE	442
③ / p. 402	AAA	Oxford Suites	◈◈◈	$139-$199 SAVE	439
④ / p. 402		Courtyard by Marriott-Portland North Harbour	◈◈◈	$149-$159	435
⑤ / p. 402		Residence Inn by Marriott-Portland North Harbour	◈◈◈	$149-$169	443

PORTLAND (cont'd)

Map Page	OA	Lodgings (cont'd)	Diamond Rated	High Season	Page
6 / p. 402		Fairfield Inn & Suites - Portland North Harbour	◆◆◆	$116-$142	437
7 / p. 402	AAA	**Days Inn-Portland**	◆◆	$72-$81 [SAVE]	436
8 / p. 402	AAA	**Best Western Inn At The Meadows**	◆◆	$121-$141 [SAVE]	432
9 / p. 402		Motel 6 North Portland #4198	◆◆	Rates not provided	439
10 / p. 402	AAA	**Sheraton Portland Airport Hotel**	◆◆◆	$97-$248 [SAVE]	443
11 / p. 402		Hampton Inn-Portland Airport	◆◆◆	$154	438
12 / p. 402	AAA	**Embassy Suites at Portland Airport**	◆◆◆	$109-$189 [SAVE]	437
13 / p. 402		Country Inn & Suites at Portland Airport	◆◆◆	$104-$118	435
14 / p. 402	AAA	**Red Lion Hotel Portland Airport**	◆◆◆	Rates not provided [SAVE]	442
15 / p. 402	AAA	**Ramada Portland**	◆◆	$79-$199 [SAVE]	441
16 / p. 402	AAA	**Radisson Hotel Portland Airport**	◆◆◆	$99-$179 [SAVE]	441
17 / p. 402		Staybridge Suites Portland-Airport	◆◆◆	$115-$170	445
18 / p. 402		La Quinta Inn & Suites Portland Airport	◆◆◆	$69-$134	439
19 / p. 402	AAA	**Clarion Hotel Portland Airport**	◆◆◆	Rates not provided [SAVE]	432
20 / p. 402		Courtyard by Marriott	◆◆◆	$161-$197	435
21 / p. 402	AAA	**Comfort Suites**	◆◆◆	$89-$149 [SAVE]	435
22 / p. 402	AAA	**Shilo Inn Suites Hotel-Portland Airport - see color ad p 444**	◆◆◆	$120-$220	444
23 / p. 402		Fairfield Inn by Marriott	◆◆◆	$129-$139	437
24 / p. 402	AAA	**Holiday Inn Express Hotel & Suites-Portland Airport**	◆◆◆	$99-$159 [SAVE]	438
25 / p. 402		SpringHill Suites by Marriott Portland Airport - see color ad p 445	◆◆◆	$149-$159	444
26 / p. 402	AAA	**Hilton Garden Inn-Portland Airport**	◆◆◆	$89-$141 [SAVE]	438
27 / p. 402	AAA	**Holiday Inn Portland Airport Hotel & Convention Center**	◆◆◆	$119-$229 [SAVE]	438
28 / p. 402	AAA	**Best Western Pony Soldier Inn-Airport**	◆◆◆	$109-$209 [SAVE]	432
29 / p. 402	AAA	**Quality Inn & Suites Airport Convention Center - see color ad p 441**	◆◆◆	$99-$169 [SAVE]	441
30 / p. 402		Americas Best Value Inn & Suites-Portland Airport	◆◆	$54-$79	431
31 / p. 402	AAA	**Nordic Motel**	◆	$72-$95 [SAVE]	439
32 / p. 402	AAA	**Howard Johnson Portland Airport**	◆◆	$75-$120 [SAVE]	439
33 / p. 402		Georgian House Bed & Breakfast	◆◆◆	$90-$135	437
34 / p. 402		Portland's White House	◆◆◆	Rates not provided	439
35 / p. 402	AAA	**Lion and the Rose Victorian Bed & Breakfast Inn**	◆◆◆	$124-$244 [SAVE]	439
36 / p. 402	AAA	**Days Inn Portland Airport**	◆◆	$85-$95 [SAVE]	436
37 / p. 402		Banfield Motel	◆	$65-$115	432
38 / p. 402	AAA	**Shilo Inn-Portland/Rose Garden - see color ad p 443**	◆◆	$92-$200 [SAVE]	444
39 / p. 402		Crowne Plaza Portland Downtown/Convention Center - see color ad p 436	◆◆◆	$129-$199	436
40 / p. 402	AAA	**Comfort Inn**	◆◆◆	$79-$169 [SAVE]	432
41 / p. 402		Courtyard by Marriott-Portland Lloyd Center	◆◆◆	$189-$199	435

PORTLAND (cont'd)

Map Page	OA	Lodgings (cont'd)	Diamond Rated	High Season	Page
42 / p. 402		La Quinta Inn Portland Lloyd Center/Convention Center	◆◆	$69-$120	439
43 / p. 402	AAA	**DoubleTree Hotel Portland**	◆◆◆	$105-$245 SAVE	437
44 / p. 402		Residence Inn by Marriott Portland Downtown/ Lloyd Center - see color ad p 442	◆◆◆	$174-$189	442
45 / p. 402	AAA	**Red Lion Hotel Portland-Convention Center -** see color ad p 418	◆◆◆	$126-$170 SAVE	442
46 / p. 402	AAA	**Shilo Inn Convention Center/Downtown**	◆◆	Rates not provided SAVE	443
47 / p. 402	AAA	**Chestnut Tree Inn**	◆	$55-$85 SAVE	432
48 / p. 402		Holiday Inn Express-I-205 Stark	◆◆	Rates not provided	438
49 / p. 402	AAA	**Briarwood Suites - see color ad p 433**	◆◆	$64-$109 SAVE	432
50 / p. 402	AAA	**Avalon Hotel & Spa**	◆◆◆	$199-$599 SAVE	431
51 / p. 402	AAA	**Hospitality Inn**	◆◆	$79-$129 SAVE	438
52 / p. 402	AAA	**Comfort Suites**	◆◆◆	$109-$159 SAVE	433

Map Page	OA	Restaurants	Diamond Rated	Cuisine	Meal Range	Page
1 / p. 402		Salty's on the Columbia	◆◆◆	Seafood	$10-$45	450
2 / p. 402		Stanford's Restaurant & Bar	◆◆◆	American	$10-$38	451
3 / p. 402	AAA	**Siam Society**	◆◆◆	Thai	$11-$23	451
4 / p. 402		Shenanigans	◆◆◆	American	$10-$58	451
5 / p. 402		Bumblekiss	◆	American	$6-$17	446
6 / p. 402		Fife	◆◆◆	American	$16-$21	447
7 / p. 402		The Original Taco House	◆◆	Mexican	$5-$11	449
8 / p. 402		Rheinlander German Restaurant & Gustav's Bier Stube	◆◆	German	$7-$26	450
9 / p. 402		Pastini Pastaria	◆◆	Italian	$5-$10	449
10 / p. 402		Chez Jose East	◆◆	Mexican	$6-$13	446
11 / p. 402		Stanford's Restaurant & Bar	◆◆◆	American	$10-$38	451
12 / p. 402	AAA	**Ringside Steakhouse**	◆◆◆	Steak	$10-$65	450
13 / p. 402		Pambiche	◆◆	Cuban	$7-$18	449
14 / p. 402		Tabla Mediterranean Bistro	◆◆	Mediterranean	$16-$19	452
15 / p. 402		Lemongrass Thai Restaurant	◆◆	Thai	$9-$24	448
16 / p. 402		Taqueria Nueve	◆◆	Traditional Mexican	$11-$16	452
17 / p. 402		Esparza's Tex Mex Cafe	◆◆	Tex-Mex	$9-$18	447
18 / p. 402		Crema Coffee & Bakery	◆	Breads/Pastries	$6	447
19 / p. 402		Il Piatto	◆◆	Italian	$7-$23	447
20 / p. 402		Ya Hala Lebanese Cuisine	◆◆	Lebanese	$8-$17	452
21 / p. 402	AAA	**Sayler's Old Country Kitchen**	◆◆	Steak	$13-$30	451
22 / p. 402		Nostrana	◆◆◆	Italian	$7-$25	449
23 / p. 402		Genoa	◆◆◆◆	Italian	$65-$130	447
24 / p. 402		Clarklewis	◆◆◆	American	$14-$28	447
25 / p. 402		3 Doors Down Cafe & Lounge	◆◆◆	Regional Mediterranean	$12-$20	446
26 / p. 402		Bombay Cricket Club Restaurant	◆◆	Indian	$13-$20	446

Map Page	OA	Restaurants (cont'd)	Diamond Rated	Cuisine	Meal Range	Page
27 / p. 402		Cafe Castagna	◆◆◆	New American	$11-$21	446
28 / p. 402		Bread & Ink Cafe	◆◆	American	$6-$24	446
29 / p. 402		Sapphire Hotel	◆◆	American	$9-$14	450
30 / p. 402		Nuestra Cocina	◆◆	Mexican	$9-$18	449
31 / p. 402		Lauro Mediterranean Kitchen	◆◆◆	Mediterranean	$15-$19	448
32 / p. 402		Wong's King Seafood Restaurant	◆◆	Chinese	$7-$38	452
33 / p. 402		Pix Patisserie	◆	Breads/Pastries	$5-$7	450
34 / p. 402		NoHo's Hawaiian Cafe	◆	Hawaiian	$6-$19	449
35 / p. 402		Vindalho	◆◆◆	Indian	$14-$19	452
36 / p. 402		Le Hana Japanese Bar & Cafe	◆◆◆	New Japanese	$8-$35	448
37 / p. 402		The Old Spaghetti Factory	◆◆	Italian	$7-$17	449
38 / p. 402		Aquariva Italian Kitchen & Wine Bar	◆◆◆	Regional Italian	$5-$15	446
39 / p. 402		Raccoon Lodge & Brew Pub	◆◆	American	$8-$16	450
40 / p. 402		JoPa	◆◆	Regional American	$7-$24	447
41 / p. 402		Shanghai Noble House	◆◆	Chinese	$6-$14	451
42 / p. 402		Chart House	◆◆◆	Steak & Seafood	$10-$43 [SAVE]	446
43 / p. 402		Papa Haydn	◆◆◆	Regional American	$10 $27	449
44 / p. 402		Salvador Molly's	◆◆	Caribbean	$6-$15	450
45 / p. 402		Three Square Grill	◆◆	American	$7-$25	452
46 / p. 402		Seasons & Regions Seafood Grill	◆◆	Seafood	$6-$20	451
47 / p. 402		Stickers Asian Cafe	◆◆	Asian	$7-$15	451
48 / p. 402		Caprial's Bistro	◆◆	Regional American	$9-$30	446
49 / p. 402		Eleni's Estiatorio	◆◆	Greek	$10-$25	447
50 / p. 402	AAA	**Marco's Cafe & Espresso Bar**	◆◆	American	$8-$16	448
51 / p. 402		Gino's Restaurant & Bar	◆◆	Italian	$14-$39	447
52 / p. 402		Portofino	◆◆	Italian	$11-$19	450
53 / p. 402		Chez Jose West	◆◆	Mexican	$5-$13	447

HILLSBORO

Map Page	OA	Lodgings	Diamond Rated	High Season	Page
55 / p. 402	AAA	**Larkspur Landing Hillsboro/Portland** - see color ad p 460	◆◆◆	$99-$171 [SAVE]	461
56 / p. 402		Courtyard by Marriott	◆◆◆	$179-$219	460
57 / p. 402		Residence Inn by Marriott Portland West	◆◆◆	$179-$219	462
58 / p. 402		SpringHill Suites by Marriott	◆◆◆	$161-$197	462
59 / p. 402		TownePlace Suites by Marriott-Portland Hillsboro	◆◆◆	$170-$208	462
60 / p. 402		Extended Stay Deluxe-Portland-Hillsboro-NW Cornell Rd	◆◆◆	$108-$123	460
61 / p. 402	AAA	**Holiday Inn Express Hillsboro**	◆◆◆	$109-$159 [SAVE]	460
62 / p. 402	AAA	**Red Lion Hotel Hillsboro**	[fyi]	$99-$169 [SAVE]	461
63 / p. 402		Extended StayAmerica-Portland-Beaverton	◆◆	$88-$104	460
64 / p. 402	AAA	**The Dunes Motel**	◆	$55-$95 [SAVE]	460

Map Page	OA	Restaurants	Diamond Rated	Cuisine	Meal Range	Page
56 / p. 402		Stanford's Restaurant & Bar	▽▽▽	American	$10-$38	463
57 / p. 402		Pasta Pronto Cafe	▽	Italian	$8-$13	462
58 / p. 402		Bugatti's Tanasbourne	▽▽	Italian	$8-$19	462
59 / p. 402		P.F. Chang's China Bistro	▽▽▽	Chinese	$10-$21	463

BEAVERTON

Map Page	OA	Lodgings	Diamond Rated	High Season	Page
67 / p. 402	AAA	**Phoenix Inn Suites-Beaverton - see color ad p 440**	▽▽▽	$89-$149 SAVE	454
68 / p. 402		Homewood Suites By Hilton	▽▽▽	$99-$179	454
69 / p. 402	AAA	**Fairfield Inn & Suites by Marriott**	▽▽▽	$139-$149 SAVE	453
70 / p. 402		Hilton Garden Inn Portland/Beaverton	▽▽▽	$99-$199	454
71 / p. 402	AAA	**Shilo Inn Hotel & Suites-Portland/Beaverton - see color ad p 453**	▽▽▽	$107-$187 SAVE	454
72 / p. 402		Comfort Inn & Suites	▽▽	$59-$159	453
73 / p. 402		Courtyard by Marriott	▽▽▽	$159-$169	453

Map Page	OA	Restaurants	Diamond Rated	Cuisine	Meal Range	Page
62 / p. 402	AAA	**Monteaux's Public House**	▽▽	American	$7-$17	455
63 / p. 402		Bugatti's Cedar Hills	▽▽	Italian	$8-$19	455
64 / p. 402		McCormick & Schmick's	▽▽▽	Seafood	$6-$25	455
65 / p. 402		Ernesto's Italian Restaurant	▽▽	Italian	$6-$18	455
66 / p. 402		The Stockpot Broiler	▽▽▽	Regional American	$8-$42	455

TROUTDALE

Map Page	OA	Lodgings	Diamond Rated	High Season	Page
76 / p. 402		Holiday Inn Express-Portland East	▽▽	$89-$159	472
77 / p. 402		Motel 6-Portland Troutdale - 407	▽	$47-$55	472
78 / p. 402	AAA	**Comfort Inn & Suites, Columbia Gorge West**	▽▽	$69-$159 SAVE	472

WOOD VILLAGE

Map Page	OA	Lodgings	Diamond Rated	High Season	Page
81 / p. 402	AAA	**Portland/Troutdale Travelodge**	▽	$44-$89 SAVE	475
82 / p. 402	AAA	**Best Western Cascade Inn & Suites**	▽▽▽	$110-$130 SAVE	475

TIGARD

Map Page	OA	Lodgings	Diamond Rated	High Season	Page
85 / p. 402	AAA	**Embassy Suites Hotel-Portland Washington Square**	▽▽▽	$119-$209 SAVE	468
86 / p. 402	AAA	**Phoenix Inn Suites-Tigard - see color ad p 440**	▽▽▽	$89-$149 SAVE	470
87 / p. 402	AAA	**Quality Inn Tigard**	▽▽	$79-$99 SAVE	470
88 / p. 402	AAA	**Shilo Inn-Tigard/Washington Square**	▽▽	$85-$125 SAVE	470
89 / p. 402		Homestead Studio Suites Hotel Portland-Tigard	▽▽	$85-$100	470
90 / p. 402		Courtyard by Marriott	▽▽▽	$170-$209	468
91 / p. 402		Holiday Inn Express-Portland South	▽▽▽	$89-$149	469

Map Page	OA	Restaurants	Diamond Rated	Cuisine	Meal Range	Page
69 / p. 402		Gustav's Pub & Grill	▽▽▽	German	$9-$20	470
70 / p. 402	AAA	**Banning's Restaurant & Pie House**	▽▽	American	$7-$13	470

Map Page	OA	Restaurants (cont'd)	Diamond Rated	Cuisine	Meal Range	Page
(71) / p. 402		Cafe Allegro	◆◆	Italian	$6-$21	470
(72) / p. 402	AAA	**Max's Fanno Creek Brew Pub**	◆◆	American	$8-$15	471
(73) / p. 402		M & S Grill	◆◆◆	Steak & Seafood	$9-$20	470
(74) / p. 402		Pastini Pastaria	◆◆	Italian	$5-$11	472
(75) / p. 402		Sin Ju Japanese Restaurant	◆◆	Japanese	$9-$32	472
(76) / p. 402		P.F. Chang's China Bistro	◆◆◆	Chinese	$10-$21	472
(77) / p. 402		Miller's Homestead Restaurant	◆◆	American	$8-$16	471

KING CITY

Map Page	OA	Lodging	Diamond Rated	High Season	Page
(94) / p. 402	AAA	**Best Western Northwind Inn & Suites**	◆◆◆	$120-$135 SAVE	463

GRESHAM

Map Page	OA	Lodgings	Diamond Rated	High Season	Page
(97) / p. 402		Hampton Inn Portland East	◆◆◆	$109-$129	458
(98) / p. 402		Extended StayAmerica Portland/Gresham	◆◆	$80-$95	458
(99) / p. 402		Days Inn-Portland East/Gresham	◆◆	$64-$100	458
(100) / p. 402	AAA	**Four Points by Sheraton Portland East**	◆◆◆	$90-$190 SAVE	458
(101) / p. 402	AAA	**Comfort Suites Portland/Gresham**	◆◆◆	$80-$280 SAVE	458
(102) / p. 402	AAA	**Super 8**	◆◆	$64-$79 SAVE	459
(103) / p. 402	AAA	**Days Inn & Suites**	◆◆	$74-$114 SAVE	458
(104) / p. 402		Holiday Inn Portland/Gresham	◆◆◆	$95-$195	458
(105) / p. 402	AAA	**Best Western Pony Soldier Inn**	◆◆◆	$99-$169 SAVE	457
(106) / p. 402	AAA	**Howard Johnson Gresham**	◆◆	$49-$179 SAVE	459

Map Page	OA	Restaurants	Diamond Rated	Cuisine	Meal Range	Page
(80) / p. 402		Francis Xavier's Restaurant and Lounge	◆◆	American	$8-$18	459
(81) / p. 402		Heidi's	◆◆	American	$7-$18	459
(82) / p. 402		Boccelli's Restaurant	◆◆	Italian	$8-$19	459

LAKE OSWEGO

Map Page	OA	Lodgings	Diamond Rated	High Season	Page
(109) / p. 402	AAA	**Phoenix Inn Suites-Lake Oswego** - see color ad p 440	◆◆◆	$84-$164 SAVE	464
(110) / p. 402	AAA	**Crowne Plaza Hotel**	◆◆◆	$79-$249 SAVE	464
(111) / p. 402		Hilton Garden Inn-Lake Oswego	◆◆◆	$109-$149	464
(112) / p. 402		Fairfield Inn & Suites by Marriott	◆◆◆	$139-$149	464
(113) / p. 402		Lakeshore Inn	◆◆	$109-$189	464
(114) / p. 402		Residence Inn by Marriott-Portland South	◆◆◆	$169-$199	464

Map Page	OA	Restaurants	Diamond Rated	Cuisine	Meal Range	Page
(85) / p. 402		Clarke's Restaurant	◆◆◆	American	$18-$30	465
(86) / p. 402		Stanford's Restaurant & Bar	◆◆◆	American	$10-$38	466
(87) / p. 402		Tucci	◆◆◆	Italian	$8-$31	466
(88) / p. 402		Zeppo Italian Ristorante	◆◆	Italian	$7-$22	466
(89) / p. 402		FiveSpice	◆◆◆	Seafood	$9-$26	465
(90) / p. 402		St. Honore Boulangerie	◆	Breads/Pastries	$6-$9	466

Map Page	OA	Restaurants (cont'd)	Diamond Rated	Cuisine	Meal Range	Page
91 / p. 402		Flying Elephants Delicatessen	◆	Deli	$6-$10	465
92 / p. 402		Oswego Lake House	◆◆◆	American	$16-$35	465
93 / p. 402		Amerigo's New Foods Grill	◆◆	American	$8-$17	465
94 / p. 402		La Provence Bakery & Bistro	◆◆	Provincial French	$7-$19	465
95 / p. 402		Riccardo's	◆◆	Northern Italian	$10-$45	466
96 / p. 402		Speedy Linguine	◆◆	Italian	$8-$13	466

MILWAUKIE

Map Page	OA	Lodging	Diamond Rated	High Season	Page
117 / p. 402	AAA	**Econo Lodge Suites Inn**	◆◆	$59-$79 SAVE	467

Map Page	OA	Restaurants	Diamond Rated	Cuisine	Meal Range	Page
99 / p. 402		Amadeus at the Fernwood	◆◆	Continental	$19-$40	467
100 / p. 402	AAA	**Bob's Red Mill Whole Grain Store & Visitor's Center**	◆	American	$6-$9	467

TUALATIN

Map Page	OA	Lodging	Diamond Rated	High Season	Page
120 / p. 402	AAA	**Comfort Inn & Suites - see color ad p 368, p 586, p 499, p 368, p 753, p 473, p 542, p 299, p 344, p 751, p 566, p 500**	◆◆◆	$99-$199 SAVE	473

CLACKAMAS

Map Page	OA	Lodgings	Diamond Rated	High Season	Page
123 / p. 402	AAA	**Days Inn-Portland South**	◆◆	$65-$89 SAVE	456
124 / p. 402	AAA	**Best Western Sunnyside Inn**	◆◆	$76-$106 SAVE	456
125 / p. 402		Courtyard by Marriott Portland-Southeast	◆◆◆	$132-$154	456
126 / p. 402	AAA	**Hampton Inn- see color ad p 456**	◆◆◆	$85-$100 SAVE	457
127 / p. 402		Comfort Suites	◆◆◆	$81-$108	456

Map Page	OA	Restaurants	Diamond Rated	Cuisine	Meal Range	Page
103 / p. 402		Stanford's Restaurant & Bar	◆◆◆	American	$10-$38	457
104 / p. 402		Gustav's German Pub & Grill	◆◆	German	$7-$21	457

GLADSTONE

Map Page	OA	Lodging	Diamond Rated	High Season	Page
130 / p. 402		Oxford Suites	◆◆◆	$95-$125	457

WILSONVILLE

Map Page	OA	Lodgings	Diamond Rated	High Season	Page
133 / p. 402	AAA	**La Quinta Inn Wilsonville**	◆◆◆	$70-$149 SAVE	475
134 / p. 402		Holiday Inn-Wilsonville	◆◆◆	$109-$199	474

OREGON CITY

Map Page	OA	Lodging	Diamond Rated	High Season	Page
137 / p. 402	AAA	**Best Western Rivershore Hotel - see color ad p 467**	◆◆◆	$95-$115 SAVE	467

Map Page	OA	Restaurant	Diamond Rated	Cuisine	Meal Range	Page
110 / p. 402		Bugatti's Hilltop	◆◆	Italian	$10-$19	468

WEST LINN

Map Page	OA	Restaurant	Diamond Rated	Cuisine	Meal Range	Page
107 / p. 402		Bugatti's Ristorante	◆◆◆	Italian	$15-$35	474

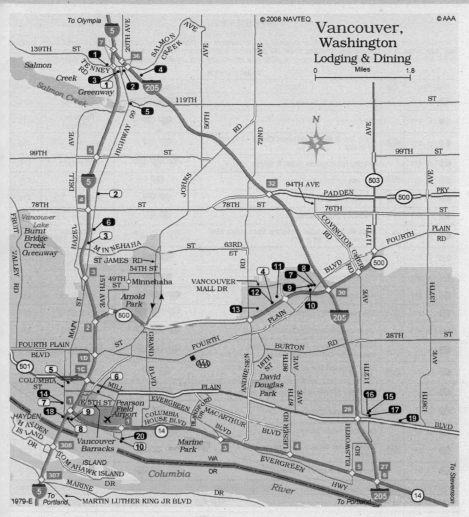

Vancouver,
Washington
Lodging & Dining

© 2008 NAVTEQ   © AAA

Vancouver, Wa

This index helps you "spot" where approved lodgings and restaurants are located on the corresponding detailed maps. Lodging daily rate range is for comparison only and show the property's high season. Restaurant rate range is a combination of lunch and/or dinner. Turn to the listing page for more detailed rate information and consult display ads for special promotions.

VANCOUVER

Map Page	OA	Lodgings	Diamond Rated	High Season	Page
❶ / p. 411		La Quinta Inn & Suites	◆◆◆	$89-$169	479
❷ / p. 411		Comfort Inn	◆◆	Rates not provided	477
❸ / p. 411	ⒶⒶⒶ	Shilo Inn & Suites-Salmon Creek - see color ad p 480	◆◆	$82-$190 [SAVE]	480
❹ / p. 411		Holiday Inn Express Hotel & Suites	◆◆◆	$112-$155	478
❺ / p. 411	ⒶⒶⒶ	**The Inn at Salmon Creek**	◆	$50-$65 [SAVE]	479
❻ / p. 411	ⒶⒶⒶ	**Quality Inn & Suites**	◆◆	$69-$109 [SAVE]	479
❼ / p. 411	ⒶⒶⒶ	**Rodeway Inn & Suites**	◆◆	$79-$96 [SAVE]	480
❽ / p. 411	ⒶⒶⒶ	**Best Western Hotel & Suites Vancouver Mall Dr** - see color ad p 476	◆◆◆	Rates not provided [SAVE]	476
❾ / p. 411		Ramada Inn	◆◆	Rates not provided	479
❿ / p. 411		Comfort Suites	◆◆	$90-$135	477
⓫ / p. 411		Residence Inn Vancouver	◆◆◆	$169-$189	480
⓬ / p. 411	ⒶⒶⒶ	**The Heathman Lodge**	◆◆◆	$139-$169 [SAVE]	477
⓭ / p. 411		Staybridge Suites Vancouver-Portland	◆◆◆	$99-$186	482
⓮ / p. 411	ⒶⒶⒶ	**Hilton Vancouver Washington and Vancouver Convention Center**	◆◆◆	$99-$219 [SAVE]	478
⓯ / p. 411	ⒶⒶⒶ	**Best Western Inn of Vancouver** - see color ad p 477	◆◆	$89-$109 [SAVE]	476
⓰ / p. 411		Extended StayAmerica-Portland-Vancouver	◆◆	$85-$100	477
⓱ / p. 411	ⒶⒶⒶ	**Guest House Motel**	◆	Rates not provided [SAVE]	477
⓲ / p. 411		Red Lion Hotel Vancouver @ the Quay	◆◆◆	$139-$179	479
⓳ / p. 411	ⒶⒶⒶ	**Phoenix Inn Suites-Vancouver** - see color ad p 440	◆◆◆	$79-$149 [SAVE]	479
⓴ / p. 411		Homewood Suites by Hilton	◆◆◆	$109-$179	479

Map Page	OA	Restaurants	Diamond Rated	Cuisine	Meal Range	Page
① / p. 411		Billygan's Roadhouse	◆◆	American	$6-$19	482
② / p. 411		Hazel Dell Brew Pub	◆◆	American	$8-$12	483
③ / p. 411		Peachtree Restaurant & Pie House	◆◆	American	$6-$15	483
④ / p. 411		Hudson's Bar & Grill at The Heathman Lodge	◆◆◆	American	$8-$26	483
⑤ / p. 411		Touch of Athens Greek Cuisina at the Hidden House	◆◆	Greek	$6-$17	484
⑥ / p. 411		The Restaurant at the Historic Reserve	◆◆◆	American	$8-$30	483
⑦ / p. 411		Gray's At The Park	◆◆◆	American	$8-$30	482
⑧ / p. 411		Joe's Crab Shack	◆◆	Seafood	$8-$29 [SAVE]	483
⑨ / p. 411		Who-Song & Larry's	◆◆	Mexican	$6-$15	484
⑩ / p. 411		Beaches Restaurant & Bar	◆◆	American	$5-$24	482

DOWNTOWN PORTLAND   (See map and index starting on p. 396)

──── WHERE TO STAY ────

THE BENSON HOTEL, A COAST HOTEL   *Book great rates at AAA.com*   Phone: (503)228-2000   **8**

(AAA) (SAVE)

▼▼▼ ▼▼▼

Historic
Hotel

$129-$359 All Year

Address: 309 SW Broadway **Location:** At SW Broadway and Oak St. **Facility:** Ornate molded-plaster ceilings, Austrian crystal chandeliers and Italian marble floors are among the standout elements enhancing this 1912 hotel. Smoke free premises. 287 units. 278 one-bedroom standard units. 9 one-bedroom suites, some with whirlpools. 13 stories, interior corridors. *Bath:* combo or shower only. **Parking:** valet. **Terms:** cancellation fee imposed. **Amenities:** dual phone lines, voice mail, honor bars, irons, hair dryers. *Fee:* video games, high-speed Internet. *Some:* CD players. *Fee:* DVD players. **Dining:** El Gaucho, London Grill, see separate listings, entertainment. **Leisure Activities:** exercise room. **Guest Services:** valet laundry, wireless Internet. **Business Services:** conference facilities, business center. **Cards:** AX, DC, DS, JC, MC, VI. **Free Special Amenities: newspaper and early check-in/late check-out.**

🍴 24🕐 📺 CALL 🆓M ✕ 🎥 💻 / SOME UNITS FEE 🐕 FEE VCR FEE 🖨

COURTYARD BY MARRIOTT CITY CENTER

(fyi)

Hotel

Rates not provided

Too new to rate, opening scheduled for February 2009. Address: 550 SW Oak St **Location:** At SW Oak St and SW 6th Ave. **Amenities:** 256 units, restaurant, coffeemakers, microwaves, refrigerators.

COURTYARD *Marriott*

AAA Benefit:

Members save a minimum 5% off the best available rate.

ECONO LODGE CITY CENTER   *Book great rates at AAA.com*   Phone: (503)226-7646   **23**

(AAA) (SAVE)

▼▼▼ ▼▼

Motel

$89-$125 All Year

Address: 1889 SW 4th Ave **Location:** I-5 to I-405, exit 1B (4th Ave). **Facility:** 19 one-bedroom standard units. 2 stories (no elevator), exterior corridors. **Parking:** on-site. **Terms:** office hours 6:30 am-midnight, cancellation fee imposed. **Amenities:** high-speed Internet, irons, hair dryers. **Guest Services:** wireless Internet. **Cards:** AX, DS, MC, VI. **Free Special Amenities: continental breakfast and high-speed Internet.**

🛠 🎥 🖥 💻 / SOME UNITS ✕

ECONO LODGE DOWNTOWN/CONVENTION CENTER   *Book great rates at AAA.com*   Phone: (503)284-5181   **3**

(AAA) (SAVE)

▼▼

Motel

$65-$110 All Year

Address: 305 N Broadway **Location:** I-5, exit 302A northbound, just n on NE Victoria Ave, then just w; exit southbound, just w. Located across from Coliseum and Rose Garden Arena. **Facility:** 19 one-bedroom standard units. 2 stories (no elevator), exterior corridors. **Parking:** on-site. **Terms:** cancellation fee imposed. **Amenities:** high-speed Internet. **Guest Services:** wireless Internet. **Cards:** AX, DC, DS, MC, VI. **Free Special Amenities: continental breakfast and local telephone calls.**

🎥 🖥 💻 / SOME UNITS ✕

EMBASSY SUITES PORTLAND DOWNTOWN   *Book great rates at AAA.com*   Phone: (503)279-9000   **9**

▼▼▼

Classic Historic Hotel

$139-$304 All Year

Address: 319 SW Pine St **Location:** At SW 4th Ave and Pine St. **Facility:** Corinthian columns, gilt ceilings, torchier lighting and spacious suites give this 1912 hotel the opulent look of the Edwardian era. Smoke free premises. 276 units. 19 one-bedroom standard units. 250 one- and 7 two-bedroom suites. 8 stories, interior corridors. *Bath:* combo or shower only. **Parking:** on-site (fee) and valet. **Terms:** check-in 4 pm, 1-30 night minimum stay, cancellation fee imposed. **Amenities:** dual phone lines, voice mail, irons, hair dryers. *Fee:* video games, high-speed Internet. *Some:* DVD players (fee). **Dining:** Kincaid's Fish, Chop & Steak, see separate listing. **Pool(s):** heated indoor. **Leisure Activities:** sauna, whirlpools, exercise room, spa. **Guest Services:** valet and coin laundry, area transportation, wireless Internet. **Business Services:** conference facilities, business center. **Cards:** AX, CB, DC, DS, JC, MC, VI.

🍴 📺 CALL 🆓M 🏊 ✕ ✕ 🎥 🖥 🖨 💻 / SOME UNITS FEE VCR

E

EMBASSY SUITES HOTELS®

AAA Benefit:

Members save 5% or more everyday!

THE GOVERNOR HOTEL   *Book great rates at AAA.com*   Phone: (503)224-3400   **13**

(AAA) (SAVE)

▼▼▼ ▼▼▼

Historic Hotel

$139-$389 All Year

Address: 614 SW 11th Ave **Location:** 11th Ave and Alder St. Light rail line and streetcar nearby. **Facility:** Newly remodeled, the property graciously combines historic charm and modern conveniences; some guest rooms and suites offer a fireplace or terrace. Smoke free premises. 100 units. 76 one-bedroom standard units. 24 one-bedroom suites, some with whirlpools. 6 stories, interior corridors. **Parking:** valet and street. **Terms:** check-in 4 pm. **Amenities:** CD players, high-speed Internet, dual phone lines, voice mail, safes, honor bars, irons, hair dryers. *Some:* DVD players (fee). **Dining:** Jake's Grill, see separate listing. **Leisure Activities:** hot tub & sauna privileges, exercise room. **Guest Services:** valet laundry, area transportation-downtown area, wireless Internet. **Business Services:** conference facilities, PC. **Cards:** AX, DC, DS, MC, VI. **Free Special Amenities: newspaper and high-speed Internet.**

🍴 24🕐 📺 CALL 🆓M ✕ 🎥 💻 / SOME UNITS VCR

(See map and index starting on p. 396)

THE HEATHMAN HOTEL *Book great rates at AAA.com* Phone: (503)241-4100 **20**

AAA SAVE

▼▼▼ ▼▼▼

Historic
Hotel

$259-$725 All Year

Address: 1001 SW Broadway **Location:** At SW Broadway and Salmon St. **Facility:** Situated adjacent to the Portland Performing Arts Center, an extensive library of movies is available to guests at this historic hotel. 150 units. 149 one-bedroom standard units. 1 one-bedroom suite with whirlpool. 10 stories, interior corridors. *Bath:* combo or shower only. **Parking:** valet. **Terms:** check-in 3:30 pm, 2-3 night minimum stay - seasonal and/or weekends, 3 day cancellation notice-fee imposed. **Amenities:** video library, video games (fee), CD players, high-speed Internet, dual phone lines, voice mail, safes, honor bars, irons, hair dryers. *Some:* DVD players. **Dining:** restaurant, see separate listing, entertainment. **Leisure Activities:** lending library, exercise room. **Guest Services:** valet laundry, wireless Internet. **Business Services:** conference facilities, PC. **Cards:** AX, CB, DC, DS, JC, MC, VI. **Free Special Amenities: newspaper and high-speed Internet.**

HERON HAUS BED & BREAKFAST Phone: 503/274-1846 **5**

▼▼▼

Bed & Breakfast

$145-$350 All Year

Address: 2545 NW Westover Rd **Location:** I-405, exit 3 (US 30) northbound; exit Vaughn St southbound, just w on Vaughn St, just s on NW 25th Ave, then just n. Located in a residential neighborhood. **Facility:** Just above Nob Hill shops and restaurants, this beautifully restored 1904 English Tudor home offers casual elegance and a quiet retreat. Smoke free premises. 6 units. 5 one- and 1 two-bedroom standard units, some with whirlpools. 3 stories (no elevator), interior corridors. *Bath:* combo or shower only. **Parking:** on-site. **Terms:** office hours 8:30 am-6 pm, check-in 4 pm, 14 day cancellation notice-fee imposed. **Amenities:** DVD players, CD players, high-speed Internet, hair dryers. **Guest Services:** wireless Internet. **Business Services:** meeting rooms. **Cards:** AX, DS, MC, VI.

HILTON PORTLAND & EXECUTIVE TOWER *Book great rates at AAA.com* Phone: (503)226-1611 **19**

AAA SAVE

▼▼▼

Hotel

$139-$239 All Year

Address: 921 SW 6th Ave **Location:** I-405, exit 1B (6th Ave); at 6th Ave and Taylor St. **Facility:** 782 units. 773 one-bedroom standard units. 1 one- and 8 two-bedroom suites, some with whirlpools. 23 stories, interior corridors. *Bath:* combo or shower only. **Parking:** on-site (fee) and valet. **Terms:** check-in 4 pm, 1-30 night minimum stay, cancellation fee imposed. **Amenities:** dual phone lines, voice mail, irons, hair dryers. *Fee:* video games, high-speed Internet. *Some:* fax. **Dining:** 2 restaurants. **Pool(s):** 2 heated indoor. **Leisure Activities:** sauna, whirlpool, steamroom. *Fee:* massage. **Guest Services:** valet laundry, tanning facilities, wireless Internet. **Business Services:** conference facilities, business center. **Cards:** AX, CB, DC, DS, JC, MC, VI. **Free Special Amenities: newspaper.**

(H) **Hilton**

AAA Benefit:
Members save 5% or more everyday!

**HOLIDAY INN EXPRESS HOTEL & SUITES
PORTLAND NW DOWNTOWN** Phone: (503)484-1100 **1**

AAA SAVE

▼▼▼

Hotel

$149-$179 4/1-2/28
$139-$179 3/1-3/31

Address: 2333 NW Vaughn St **Location:** I-405, exit 3 (US 30), follow Vaughn St, then just w. Located near NW 23rd Ave/NOB Hill. **Facility:** Smoke free premises. 90 one-bedroom standard units. 4 stories, interior corridors. *Bath:* combo or shower only. **Parking:** on-site. **Terms:** cancellation fee imposed. **Amenities:** high-speed Internet, voice mail, irons, hair dryers. **Pool(s):** heated indoor. **Leisure Activities:** whirlpool, exercise room. **Guest Services:** valet and coin laundry, wireless Internet. **Business Services:** meeting rooms, PC. **Cards:** AX, DC, DS, MC, VI. **Free Special Amenities: expanded continental breakfast and high-speed Internet.**

HOTEL DELUXE *Book great rates at AAA.com* Phone: (503)219-2094 **11**

AAA SAVE

▼▼▼

Historic
Hotel

$169-$369 All Year

Address: 729 SW 15th Ave **Location:** I-5 to I-405, exit Salmon St northbound, just n on 14th Ave, w on Morrison. St, then s; exit Couch/Burnside St southbound; at SW 15th Ave and Yamhill St. Located on the light rail line. **Facility:** Located between downtown and the Northwest district, the hotel offers a lobby and dining room with a warm, traditional atmosphere. Smoke free premises. 130 units. 117 one-bedroom standard units. 13 one-bedroom suites. 8 stories, interior corridors. *Bath:* combo or shower only. **Parking:** on-site (fee) and valet. **Terms:** check-in 4 pm, cancellation fee imposed. **Amenities:** dual phone lines, voice mail, safes, honor bars, irons, hair dryers. *Fee:* video games, high-speed Internet. *Some:* DVD players. **Dining:** Gracie's, see separate listing. **Leisure Activities:** exercise room. **Guest Services:** valet laundry, wireless Internet. **Business Services:** meeting rooms, business center. **Cards:** AX, DS, JC, MC, VI. **Free Special Amenities: newspaper.** *(See color ad p 415).*

(See map and index starting on p. 396)

HOTEL FIFTY   *Book great rates at AAA.com*   Phone: (503)221-0711   **18**

AAA SAVE
▼▼▼▼▼
Hotel
$139-$289 All Year

Address: 50 SW Morrison St **Location:** At Morrison St and Naito Pkwy (formerly Front Ave). Located across from Riverfront Park. **Facility:** Smoke free premises. 140 units. 139 one-bedroom standard units. 1 one-bedroom suite. 5 stories, interior corridors. *Bath:* combo or shower only. **Parking:** on-site (fee). **Amenities:** video games (fee), high-speed Internet, dual phone lines, voice mail, irons, hair dryers. **Guest Services:** valet laundry, wireless Internet. **Business Services:** meeting rooms, PC. **Cards:** AX, CB, DC, DS, JC, MC, VI. **Free Special Amenities:** newspaper and high-speed Internet.
(See color ad below)

🍴 🍸 CALL &M 🛗 ✕ 🎥 💻
/ SOME UNITS 🛏 FEE VCR 📶

▼ See AAA listing above ▼

▼ See AAA listing p 414 ▼

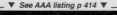

(See map and index starting on p. 396)

HOTEL LUCIA   *Book great rates at AAA.com*   Phone: (503)225-1717   [10]

AAA [SAVE]

▼▼▼▼

Historic Hotel

$319 All Year

Address: 400 SW Broadway **Location:** At SW Broadway and Stark St. **Facility:** This is a trendy, upscale hotel with sleek and contemporary decor throughout; adorning the walls are Pulitzer Prize-winning photographs. Smoke free premises. 127 units. 126 one-bedroom standard units. 1 one-bedroom suite. 9 stories, interior corridors. *Bath:* combo or shower only. **Parking:** valet. **Terms:** check-in 4 pm, cancellation fee imposed. **Amenities:** dual phone lines, voice mail, safes, honor bars, irons, hair dryers. *Fee:* video games, high-speed Internet. *Some:* DVD players. **Dining:** Typhoon!, see separate listing. **Leisure Activities:** exercise room. **Guest Services:** valet laundry, wireless Internet. **Business Services:** meeting rooms, business center. **Cards:** AX, CB, DC, DS, JC, MC, VI. **Free Special Amenities: newspaper.** *(See color ad below)*

[icons] 🍴 24🕐 🍸 CALL 🅜 ⊗ 📶 📺 / SOME UNITS FEE 🛏 VCR 📠

HOTEL MONACO PORTLAND   *Book great rates at AAA.com*   Phone: 503/222-0001   [14]

AAA [SAVE]

▼▼▼▼

Historic Hotel

Rates not provided

Address: 506 SW Washington St **Location:** At SW 5th Ave and SW Washington St. **Facility:** A complimentary nightly wine tasting by the living room fireplace is a tradition at this attractively decorated hotel. 221 units. 86 one-bedroom standard units, some with whirlpools. 135 one-bedroom suites, some with whirlpools. 10 stories, interior corridors. *Bath:* combo or shower only. **Parking:** valet. **Amenities:** DVD players, video games (fee), CD players, high-speed Internet, dual phone lines, voice mail, safes, honor bars, irons, hair dryers. **Dining:** Red Star Tavern, see separate listing. **Leisure Activities:** exercise room, spa. **Guest Services:** valet laundry, wireless Internet. **Business Services:** conference facilities, business center. **Free Special Amenities: newspaper and early check-in/late check-out.**

[icons] 🍴 24🕐 🍸 CALL 🅜 📺 / SOME UNITS 🐕 ⊗ VCR

HOTEL VINTAGE PLAZA   *Book great rates at AAA.com*   Phone: 503/228-1212   [12]

AAA [SAVE]

▼▼▼▼

Historic Boutique Hotel

Rates not provided

Address: 422 SW Broadway **Location:** At Broadway and Washington St. **Facility:** Tuscan-style decor is featured at this boutique hotel, which offers some two-level townhouse suites and specialty starlight guest rooms. Garden spa rooms feature their own outdoor patio with private spa tub. 117 one-bedroom standard units, some with whirlpools. 10 stories, interior corridors. **Parking:** valet. **Amenities:** video games (fee), CD players, high-speed Internet, dual phone lines, voice mail, honor bars, irons, hair dryers. *Some:* DVD players. **Dining:** Pazzoria Bakery & Cafe, Pazzo Ristorante, see separate listings. **Leisure Activities:** exercise room. **Guest Services:** valet laundry, wireless Internet. *Fee:* barber shop. **Business Services:** conference facilities, business center. **Free Special Amenities: newspaper and early check-in/late check-out.**

[icons] 🍴 🍸 📺 / SOME UNITS 🐕 ⊗ VCR

INN @ NORTHRUP STATION   *Book at AAA.com*   Phone: (503)224-0543   [4]

▼▼▼▼

Hotel

$139-$219 All Year

Address: 2025 NW Northrup St **Location:** I-405, exit Everett St northbound, 0.3 mi w on Glisan St, then just n on NW 21st Ave; just e of jct Northrup St and NW 21st Ave. Located on streetcar line. **Facility:** Smoke free premises. 70 one-bedroom standard units, some with kitchens. 3 stories, interior corridors. *Bath:* combo or shower only. **Parking:** on-site. **Terms:** cancellation fee imposed. **Amenities:** video games (fee), CD players, high-speed Internet, dual phone lines, voice mail, irons, hair dryers. **Guest Services:** valet laundry, wireless Internet. **Business Services:** PC (fee). **Cards:** AX, DS, MC, VI.

[icons] 🍴↕ FEE 🛅 ⊗ 📶 🗄 🖥 🖨

———— ▼ *See AAA listing above* ▼ ————

(See map and index starting on p. 396)

THE MARK SPENCER HOTEL   *Book great rates at AAA.com*   Phone: (503)224-3293   **7**

AAA [SAVE]
♦♦♦♦
Hotel
$99-$249 All Year

Address: 409 SW 11th Ave **Location:** At SW Stark St and SW 11th Ave. **Facility:** Smoke free premises. 101 units. 55 one-bedroom standard units with kitchens. 46 one-bedroom suites with kitchens. 6 stories, interior corridors. *Bath:* combo or shower only. **Parking:** on-site (fee). **Terms:** check-in 4 pm, cancellation fee imposed. **Amenities:** voice mail, irons, hair dryers. *Fee:* video games, high-speed Internet. **Leisure Activities:** rooftop garden. **Guest Services:** valet and coin laundry, wireless Internet. **Business Services:** meeting rooms, PC. **Cards:** AX, CB, DC, DS, JC, MC, VI. **Free Special Amenities: continental breakfast and newspaper.**

[icons] / SOME UNITS FEE

MARRIOTT CITY CENTER   *Book great rates at AAA.com*   Phone: (503)226-6300   **15**

♦♦♦♦
Hotel
$170-$208 All Year

Address: 520 SW Broadway **Location:** At Washington St and SW Broadway. Located near light rail line. **Facility:** Smoke free premises. 249 units. 238 one-bedroom standard units. 11 one-bedroom suites. 20 stories, interior corridors. *Bath:* combo or shower only. **Parking:** valet. **Terms:** check-in 4 pm, cancellation fee imposed. **Amenities:** dual phone lines, voice mail, irons, hair dryers. *Fee:* video games, high-speed Internet. *Some:* DVD players (fee), CD players. **Leisure Activities:** whirlpool, exercise room. **Guest Services:** valet and coin laundry, wireless Internet. **Business Services:** meeting rooms, business center. **Cards:** AX, CB, DC, DS, JC, MC, VI.

[icons] / SOME UNITS FEE VCR

Marriott
HOTELS & RESORTS

AAA Benefit:
Members save a minimum 5% off the best available rate.

THE NINES   Phone: 503/222-9996

[fyi]
Hotel
Rates not provided

Too new to rate, opening scheduled for November 2008. **Address:** 525 SW Morrison St **Location:** At SW Morrison St and SW 5th Ave. **Amenities:** 331 units, restaurant, coffeemakers.

THE LUXURY COLLECTION

AAA Benefit:
Inspiring travels with your AAA Preferred rates

(See map and index starting on p. 396)

THE PARAMOUNT HOTEL, A COAST HOTEL   *Book great rates at AAA.com*   Phone: (503)223-9900   **17**

Hotel
$159-$199 All Year

Address: 808 SW Taylor St **Location:** At SW 8th Ave and SW Taylor St. **Facility:** 154 units. 152 one-bedroom standard units, some with whirlpools. 2 one-bedroom suites with whirlpools. 15 stories, interior corridors. *Bath:* combo or shower only. **Parking:** valet. **Terms:** check-in 4 pm, cancellation fee imposed. **Amenities:** dual phone lines, voice mail, honor bars, irons, hair dryers. *Fee:* video games, high-speed Internet. *Some:* CD players. **Dining:** Dragonfish Asian Cafe, see separate listing. **Leisure Activities:** exercise room. **Guest Services:** valet laundry, wireless Internet. **Business Services:** meeting rooms, business center. **Cards:** AX, DC, DS, JC, MC, VI. **Free Special Amenities:** newspaper. (See color ad below)

PARK LANE SUITES   *Book great rates at AAA.com*   Phone: (503)226-6288   **6**

Motel
$129-$249 All Year

Address: 809 SW King Ave **Location:** I-405, exit Couch/Burnside St southbound, 0.5 mi w on Burnside St, then just s; exit Everett St northbound, 0.3 mi w on Glisan St, just s on NW 21st Ave, just w on Burnside St, then just s. **Facility:** Smoke free premises. 44 units. 1 one-bedroom standard unit with efficiency. 38 one- and 5 two-bedroom suites with efficiencies. 5 stories, exterior corridors. *Bath:* combo or shower only. **Parking:** on-site. **Amenities:** DVD players, high-speed Internet, voice mail, irons, hair dryers. **Guest Services:** coin laundry. **Cards:** AX, CB, DC, DS, JC, MC, VI.

PORTLAND MARRIOTT DOWNTOWN WATERFRONT   *Book great rates at AAA.com*   Phone: (503)226-7600   **21**

Hotel
$219-$239 All Year

Address: 1401 SW Naito Pkwy **Location:** Between Columbia and Clay sts. Located across from Waterfront Park. **Facility:** Smoke free premises. 503 units. 501 one-bedroom standard units. 2 one-bedroom suites. 15 stories, interior corridors. *Bath:* combo or shower only. **Parking:** valet. **Terms:** check-in 4 pm, cancellation fee imposed. **Amenities:** high-speed Internet (fee), dual phone lines, voice mail, irons, hair dryers. **Pool(s):** heated indoor. **Leisure Activities:** whirlpool. **Guest Services:** valet and coin laundry, wireless Internet. **Business Services:** conference facilities, business center. **Cards:** AX, CB, DC, DS, JC, MC, VI.

Marriott
HOTELS & RESORTS

AAA Benefit:
Members save a minimum 5% off the best available rate.

─────────── ▼ See AAA listing above ▼ ───────────

(See map and index starting on p. 396)

RESIDENCE INN PORTLAND DOWNTOWN AT RIVERPLACE *Book great rates at AAA.com*

Phone: (503)552-9500   25

AAA SAVE
▼▼▼▼
Hotel
$199-$209 All Year

Address: 2115 SW River Pkwy **Location:** At SW Moody Ave and SW River Pkwy; on the Willamette River Waterfront. Located by Portland Street Car Line. **Facility:** Smoke free premises. 258 units. 106 one-bedroom standard units with efficiencies. 119 one- and 33 two-bedroom suites, some with efficiencies or kitchens. 9 stories, interior corridors. *Bath:* combo or shower only. **Parking:** on-site (fee). **Terms:** check-in 4 pm, cancellation fee imposed. **Amenities:** video games (fee), high-speed Internet, dual phone lines, voice mail, irons, hair dryers. **Pool(s):** heated indoor. **Leisure Activities:** whirlpool, exercise room. **Guest Services:** valet and coin laundry, area transportation-within 5 mi, wireless Internet. **Business Services:** meeting rooms, business center. **Cards:** AX, CB, DC, DS, JC, MC, VI. **Free Special Amenities:** expanded continental breakfast and high-speed Internet.

Residence Inn Marriott
AAA Benefit:
Members save a minimum 5% off the best available rate.

🌊 ❌ 🍴 🔋 📷 💻 / SOME UNITS FEE 🐂

(See map and index starting on p. 396)

RIVERPLACE, A LARKSPUR COLLECTION HOTEL
Book great rates at AAA.com   Phone: (503)228-3233   22

(AAA) (SAVE)

▼▼▼▼ ▼▼▼▼

Hotel
$249-$525 3/1-10/30
$239-$525 10/31-2/28

Address: 1510 SW Harbor Way **Location:** At Naito Pkwy (formerly Front Ave) and SW Harbor Way. Located on the Riverfront Esplanade. **Facility:** Many of the rooms in this hotel, which is newly renovated in the Northwest Craftsman style, offer a view of the Willamette River and the marina. Smoke free premises. 84 units. 50 one-bedroom standard units. 32 one- and 2 two-bedroom suites, some with kitchens. 4 stories, interior corridors. *Bath:* combo or shower only. **Parking:** on-site (fee) and valet. **Terms:** check-in 4 pm, cancellation fee imposed. **Amenities:** video library, DVD players, video games (fee), CD players, high-speed Internet, dual phone lines, voice mail, irons, hair dryers. **Dining:** Three Degrees, see separate listing. **Leisure Activities:** sauna, whirlpool. **Guest Services:** valet laundry, wireless Internet. **Business Services:** conference facilities, business center. **Cards:** AX, CB, DC, DS, JC, MC, VI. **Free Special Amenities: newspaper and high-speed Internet.** *(See color ad below)*

SILVER CLOUD INN-DOWNTOWN PORTLAND
Book at AAA.com   Phone: (503)242-2400   2

▼▼▼

Hotel
$159-$209 All Year

Address: 2426 NW Vaughn St **Location:** I-405, exit 3 (US 30), follow Vaughn St, then just w. Located near NW 23rd Ave/Nob Hill. **Facility:** Smoke free premises. 82 one-bedroom standard units, some with whirlpools. 4 stories, interior corridors. *Bath:* combo or shower only. **Parking:** on-site. **Amenities:** high-speed Internet, voice mail, irons, hair dryers. **Leisure Activities:** exercise room. **Guest Services:** complimentary and valet laundry, area transportation, wireless Internet. **Business Services:** PC. **Cards:** AX, DC, DS, JC, MC, VI.

UNIVERSITY PLACE
Book at AAA.com   Phone: (503)221-0140   24

▼▼▼

Hotel
$108-$159 All Year

Address: 310 SW Lincoln St **Location:** I-5 to I-405, exit 4th Ave, just n, then just e. **Facility:** Smoke free premises. 235 units. 232 one-bedroom standard units. 3 one-bedroom suites, some with whirlpools. 3 stories, interior/exterior corridors. *Bath:* combo or shower only. **Parking:** on-site (fee). **Terms:** cancellation fee imposed. **Amenities:** high-speed Internet, voice mail, irons, hair dryers. *Some:* DVD players, CD players. **Pool(s):** heated outdoor. **Leisure Activities:** exercise room. **Guest Services:** valet and coin laundry, wireless Internet. **Business Services:** conference facilities, PC (fee). **Cards:** AX, MC, VI.

THE WESTIN PORTLAND
Book great rates at AAA.com   Phone: (503)294-9000   16

(AAA) (SAVE)

▼▼▼▼ ▼▼▼▼

Hotel
$119-$349 All Year

Address: 750 SW Alder St **Location:** At Park Ave and SW Alder St. **Facility:** Original artwork, spacious rooms, and public areas with an upscale contemporary look characterize this full-service hotel. Smoke free premises. 205 units. 204 one-bedroom standard units. 1 two-bedroom suite with whirlpool. 19 stories, interior corridors. *Bath:* combo or shower only. **Parking:** valet. **Amenities:** dual phone lines, voice mail, safes, honor bars, irons, hair dryers. *Fee:* video games, high-speed Internet. **Dining:** Daily Grill, see separate listing. **Leisure Activities:** exercise room. **Guest Services:** valet laundry, wireless Internet. **Business Services:** conference facilities, business center. **Cards:** AX, CB, DC, DS, JC, MC, VI. **Free Special Amenities: newspaper.**

WESTIN
HOTELS & RESORTS

AAA Benefit:
Enjoy up to 15% off your next stay, plus Starwood Preferred Guest® bonuses.

(See map and index starting on p. 396)

──────── **WHERE TO DINE** ────────

AL-AMIR LEBANESE RESTAURANT
Phone: 503/274-0010 ⑦⑤

Lebanese
$6-$17

Family owned since 1988, the restaurant invites guests to experience Lebanese dishes from inside a former archbishop's residence. Recommended for sampling is the tour of five appetizers. The house specialty, seasoned lamb, is roasted slowly over a low flame and served with yogurt-cucumber sauce. Charcoal broiling adds flavor to the beef, chicken and shrimp kebabs. Vegetarians have many options here. Live music and belly dancing enhance the atmosphere on Friday and Saturday nights. Casual dress. **Bar:** Full bar. **Reservations:** suggested. **Hours:** 11 am-2:30 & 4:30-9:30 pm, Fri-midnight, Sat 4:30 pm-midnight, Sun 4:30 pm-9 pm. Closed major holidays. **Address:** 223 SW Stark St **Location:** At SW 2nd Ave and SW Stark St. **Parking:** street. **Cards:** AX, CB, DC, DS, MC, VI.

ALEXIS
Phone: 503/224-8577 ⑤⑥

Greek
$8-$18

Traditional Greek recipes handed down by the owner's mother include homemade bread, Greek salad, souvlaki, melitzano, tzatziki, dolmathakia and saganaki. The menu lines up a good selection of appetizers and other specialties that pair with regional beers and local and Greek wines. Casual dress. **Bar:** Full bar. **Reservations:** not accepted. **Hours:** 11:30 am-2 & 5-10 pm, Fri-11 pm, Sat 5 pm-11 pm. Closed major holidays; also Sun. **Address:** 215 W Burnside St **Location:** Northwest corner of Burnside St and 2nd Ave. **Parking:** street. **Cards:** AX, DC, DS, MC, VI.

ANDINA
Phone: 503/228-9535 ④③

Peruvian
$12-$29

In the Pearl District, this taste of Peru has warm decor, including Peruvian art. Peruvian chefs prepare gourmet versions of traditional dishes and Novoandina cuisine. Among interesting appetizers are seviche, the country's flagship dish and chicharrones, prawns deep-fried in quinoa. A good South American wine list is presented. Specialty drinks include pisco, made from Peruvian white grape brandy. Patrons seated at the kitchen bar can watch the chefs work. A late-night tapas menu is available in the bar. Casual dress. Entertainment. **Bar:** Full bar. **Reservations:** suggested. **Hours:** 11:30 am-2:30 & 5-9:30 pm, Fri & Sat 5 pm-10:30 pm. Closed: 11/26, 12/25. **Address:** 1314 NW Glisan St **Location:** I-405, exit Everett St northbound, just n on NW 14th Ave, just e to 13th Ave, then just n; exit Couch/Burnside St southbound, just e; at 13th Ave and NW Glisan St. **Parking:** street. **Cards:** AX, DS, MC, VI.

BAAN-THAI
Phone: 503/224-8424 ⑨②

Thai
$7-$16

In a converted house in the University District, this popular, family-run restaurant features colorful decor and prepares a variety of dishes, including curries, soups, stir-fried noodles and house specials. The spiciness can be adjusted to diners' tastes. A few outdoor tables overlook the street scene. Long waits at lunchtime are common. Casual dress. **Bar:** Beer & wine. **Hours:** 11 am-10 pm. Closed: 11/26, 12/25; also Sun. **Address:** 1924 SW Broadway, 2nd Floor **Location:** Jct College St. **Parking:** street. **Cards:** MC, VI.

BASTA'S ITALIAN RESTAURANT AND BAR
Phone: 503/274-1572 ④⑥

Italian
$15-$22

This popular neighborhood favorite offers creative presentations and a good wine list in a warm, unpretentious setting. Dressy casual. **Bar:** Full bar. **Reservations:** suggested. **Hours:** 5 pm-10 pm, Fri & Sat-11 pm. Closed major holidays. **Address:** 410 NW 21st Ave **Location:** Jct Flanders St; in Pearl District. **Parking:** on-site. **Cards:** AX, MC, VI.

BESAW'S
Phone: 503/228-2619 ⑧

American
$6-$20

Serving the Portland community since 1903, this Northwest neighborhood cafe caters to those in a hurry yet choose to have fresh, well-prepared cuisine. The breakfasts are known throughout the area, plus daily specials and delicious desserts. An outdoor patio is heated. Casual dress. **Bar:** Full bar. **Reservations:** accepted, for dinner. **Hours:** 7 am-10 pm, Sat from 8 am, Sun 8 am-3 pm, Mon 7 am-3 pm; Sunday brunch. Closed: 11/26, 12/25. **Address:** 2301 NW Savier St **Location:** Corner of NW 23rd Ave and NW Savier St. **Parking:** on-site. **Cards:** AX, MC, VI.

BEWON KOREAN RESTAURANT
Phone: 503/464-9222 ⑯

Korean
$7-$25

The distinctive culinary experience centers on the presentation of rich-with-tradition Korean recipes. Dishes are served with seven seasonal side dishes. A seven-course meal is another option. Korean rice wine goes well with the cuisine. Casual dress. **Bar:** Beer & wine. **Reservations:** suggested. **Hours:** 11:30 am-2:30 & 5-9 pm, Fri-10 pm, Sat 5 pm-10 pm, Sun 5 pm-9 pm. Closed: 1/1, 11/26, 12/25. **Address:** 1203 NW 23rd Ave **Location:** I-405, exit Everett St northbound, 1 mi w on Glisan St, then just n; jct Northrup St. **Parking:** on-site. **Cards:** AX, DS, MC, VI.

BIJOU CAFE
Phone: 503/222-3187 ⑥①

Natural/Organic
$5-$13

In a renovated warehouse, the classic cafe lets in lots of natural light, which gives it a spacious, airy feel. Organic and regionally grown ingredients factor into breakfast specialties and lunch dishes that change daily. Casual dress. **Bar:** Beer & wine. **Hours:** 7 am-2 pm, Sat & Sun from 8 am. Closed: 11/26, 12/25. **Address:** 132 SW 3rd Ave **Location:** At Pine St and 3rd Ave. **Parking:** street. **Cards:** MC, VI.

BLUEHOUR
Phone: 503/226-3394 ④⑨

Continental
$10-$43

The restaurant occupies a converted warehouse in the fashionable Pearl District. The interior can best be described as industrial meets modern in a soft, chic way. Northwest cuisine reflects Italian and French influences. Outdoor seating is a seasonal option. Dressy casual. **Bar:** Full bar. **Reservations:** suggested. **Hours:** 11:30 am-2 & 5:30-10 pm, Fri-10:30 pm, Sat 5 pm-10:30 pm, Sun 5 pm-10 pm; Sunday brunch 10 am-2 pm. Closed: 1/1, 9/7, 12/25. **Address:** 250 NW 13th Ave **Location:** At 13th Ave and Everett St. **Parking:** valet and street. **Cards:** AX, DC, MC, VI.

BRIDGEPORT BREWPUB & BAKERY
Phone: 503/241-3612 ⑰

American
$8-$24

In a century-old historic building that was once a rope factory, this brewpub is Oregon's oldest craft brewery. Pub fare washes down easily with freshly brewed handcrafted Bridgeport ales. From Sunday through Wednesday, a three-course special is an option. Patrons can tour the brewery Saturdays at 1, 3 and 5 pm and weekdays by appointment. Casual dress. **Bar:** Full bar. **Reservations:** accepted. **Hours:** 7 am-11 pm, Fri & Sat-midnight, Sun & Mon-10 pm. Closed major holidays. **Address:** 1313 NW Marshall St **Location:** Jct 13th Ave; in Pearl District. **Parking:** street. **Cards:** AX, DS, MC, VI.

(See map and index starting on p. 396)

CAFFE MINGO
Phone: 503/226-4646 (27)

Italian
$14-$25

Simply prepared food is the draw at the popular bistro-style establishment. Among the interesting pasta dishes are penne pasta tossed with beef braised in Chianti and espresso. Be prepared to wait for a table. Casual dress. **Bar:** Beer & wine. **Reservations:** not accepted. **Hours:** 5 pm-10 pm, Fri & Sat-10:30 pm. Closed major holidays. **Address:** 807 NW 21st Ave **Location:** I-405, exit Everett St, just n, 1 mi on Glisan St, then just n; at NW Kearny St and 21st Ave. **Parking:** valet and street. **Cards:** AX, DC, DS, MC, VI.

CARAFE
Phone: 503/248-0004 (90)

French
$7-$19

Hearty, traditional country French food is always on the menu at Carafe. Try the roasted beet salad and the duck leg confit served on a bean cassoulet with duck sausage. Diners may validate parking in the 200 Market building. Casual dress. **Bar:** Full bar. **Reservations:** accepted. **Hours:** 11 am-9 pm, Fri & Sat-10 pm. Closed major holidays; also Sun. **Address:** 200 SW Market St **Location:** Jct SW 2nd Ave. **Parking:** on-site and valet. **Cards:** AX, DS, MC, VI.

CARLYLE
Phone: 503/595-1782 (6)

American
$18-$34

Located in the Alphabet District and named after the Carlyle Hotel in New York, the restaurant offers creative presentations of fresh, regionally available foods and an excellent wine list in an upscale setting. Dressy casual. **Bar:** Full bar. **Reservations:** suggested. **Hours:** 3 pm-9:30 pm, Sat 5:30 pm-10:30 pm, Sun 5:30 pm-9:30 pm. Closed: 11/26, 12/25. **Address:** 1632 NW Thurman St **Location:** Jct 17th Ave; beneath Fremont Bridge. **Parking:** street. **Cards:** AX, DC, DS, MC, VI.

CHA! CHA! CHA!
Phone: 503/221-2111 (41)

Mexican
$4-$6

Those in a hurry appreciate the quick counter service. Burritos and tacos are among items served in large portions. Casual dress. **Bar:** Full bar. **Hours:** 10 am-10 pm. **Address:** 1208 NW Glisan St **Location:** Between 12th and 13th aves NW. **Parking:** street. **Cards:** AX, MC, VI.

DAILY CAFE IN THE PEARL
Phone: 503/242-1916 (21)

American
$6-$17

Creative menu selections center on organic and seasonal ingredients. The neighborhood establishment bases its daily specials on market availability. Casual dress. **Bar:** Beer & wine. **Reservations:** accepted, for dinner. **Hours:** 7 am-5 pm, Wed-Fri to 9 pm, Sat 9 am-9 pm, Sun 9 am-2 pm. Closed major holidays. **Address:** 902 NW 13th Ave **Location:** Jct NW Kearny St; in Pearl District. **Parking:** street. **Cards:** AX, MC, VI.

DAILY GRILL
Phone: 503/294-7001

American
$8-$28

Downtown in the cultural district, this regional chain offers well-prepared selections of contemporary American classics that include meatloaf, fish and chips, 28-day aged Angus beef steaks, pan-fried trout, pot pies and pasta selections. The signature dessert, fresh fruit cobbler, is tasty and enough for two. Seasonal patio dining is available. Casual dress. **Bar:** Full bar. **Reservations:** accepted. **Hours:** 6:30 am-10 pm, Fri & Sat-11 pm. **Address:** 614 SW Park Ave **Location:** At Park Ave and SW Alder St; in The Westin Portland. **Parking:** valet and street. **Cards:** AX, CB, DC, DS, MC, VI.

CALL ⑤ℳ

DAN & LOUIS OYSTER BAR
Phone: 503/227-5906 (60)

AAA

Traditional
Seafood
$7-$30

Four generations of Wachsmuths have owned this establishment since its humble 1907 beginning, when Louis Wachsmuth carted boxes of live crab to a big crab pot inside. The dining room has a sailing ship interior with many nautical curios. Recommended is the captain's assorted seafood fry, a delicious sampling of shrimp, scallops, oysters, cod, calamari and halibut. Several types of seafood stew as well as a late-night menu also are offered. Casual dress. **Bar:** Full bar. **Reservations:** suggested. **Hours:** 11 am-9 pm, Fri & Sat-10 pm. Closed major holidays. **Address:** 208 SW Ankeny St **Location:** At Ankeny St and 2nd Ave. **Parking:** street. **Cards:** AX, CB, DC, DS, JC, MC, VI. **Historic**

DRAGONFISH ASIAN CAFE
Phone: 503/243-5991 (81)

Asian
$6-$18

The upscale restaurant serves fresh, assorted Asian cuisines in a sleek Asian decor. Dressy casual. **Bar:** Full bar. **Reservations:** accepted. **Hours:** 6:30 am-10 pm, Fri & Sat-11 pm. Closed: 1/1, 11/26, 12/25. **Address:** 909 SW Park Ave **Location:** At SW 8th Ave and SW Taylor St; in The Paramount Hotel, a Coast Hotel. **Parking:** street. **Cards:** AX, DC, DS, MC, VI.

CALL ⑤ℳ

ELEPHANTS DELICATESSEN
Phone: 503/299-6304 (53)

Deli
$6-$20

The upscale delicatessen serves interesting food, including salads of all kinds, olive and antipasto bars, hand-made pizzas, grill items, sandwiches, soups and fresh, delectable bakery goods. Sidewalk tables are available in season. Casual dress. **Bar:** Full bar. **Reservations:** not accepted. **Hours:** 7 am-8:30 pm, Sun 9:30 am-6:30 pm. Closed major holidays. **Address:** 115 NW 22nd Ave **Location:** Just n of Burnside St; jct NW Davis St; nw of downtown; in Nob Hill District. **Parking:** on-site. **Cards:** AX, MC, VI.

EL GAUCHO
Phone: 503/227-8794 (62)

Steak & Seafood
$35-$60

Sumptuous, aged steaks are served in a casually elegant atmosphere. One of the specialties is flaming brochette. Included in the good selection of wines is an impressive reserve wine list. Dressy casual. Entertainment. **Bar:** Full bar. **Reservations:** suggested. **Hours:** 4:30 pm-1 am, Sun-11 pm. Closed major holidays. **Address:** 319 SW Broadway **Location:** At SW Broadway and Oak St; in The Benson Hotel, a Coast Hotel. **Parking:** valet and street. **Cards:** AX, DC, DS, MC, VI.

FENOUIL
Phone: 503/525-2225 (19)

French
$10-$30

Fenouil, pronounced "fen-wee," means fennel in French, and modern French cuisine is the refined restaurant's specialty. Soaring windows overlook Jameson Square, and two dual-sided fireplaces contribute to the cheery decor. Retractable glass garage doors open in season. Valet parking is offered in the evenings, Friday & Saturday. Dressy casual. **Bar:** Full bar. **Reservations:** suggested. **Hours:** 11 am-2 & 5-10 pm, Fri-11 pm, Sat 5 pm-11 pm, Sun 9 am-2 & 5-10 pm; Sunday brunch. Closed: 1/1, 11/26, 12/25. **Address:** 900 NW 11th Ave **Location:** At NW Lovejoy St; in Pearl District. **Parking:** street. **Cards:** AX, DS, MC, VI.

(See map and index starting on p. 396)

FRATELLI
Phone: 503/241-8800   ③③
Italian
$14-$21
Organic produce and fresh products are prominent in this seasonally changing menu in which inventive, complex Italian cooking is prepared. An interesting selection of antipasti and house-made ravioli, gnocchi or the house favorite, polenta with fresh wild mushrooms, are recommended for the first course. Some unique second course offerings may include Sardinian flatbread filled with veal sausage, hazelnuts and goat cheese or roast crepe with wild mushroom and sheep ricotta with black pepper sauce. Casual dress. **Bar:** Full bar. **Reservations:** suggested. **Hours:** 5 pm-9 pm, Fri & Sat-10 pm. Closed major holidays; also Super Bowl Sun. **Address:** 1230 NW Hoyt St **Location:** Jct NW 12th Ave; in Pearl District. **Parking:** street. **Cards:** AX, MC, VI.

FULLER'S RESTAURANT
Phone: 503/222-5608   ⑤②
American
$6-$9
A fixture in the Pearl District since 1947, the modest eatery invites patrons to grab a seat at the counter (the only seating offered) for a meal in friendly, unpretentious environs. Freshly made breads, comfort foods and all-day breakfast items are among offerings. Portions are generous. Casual dress. **Hours:** 6 am-3 pm, Sat 7 am-2 pm, Sun 8 am-2 pm. Closed major holidays. **Address:** 136 NW 9th Ave **Location:** Corner of NW Davis St and NW 9th Ave. **Parking:** street.

GIORGIO'S RESTAURANT
Phone: 503/221-1888   ③①

Northern Italian
$10-$29
It's all about the food at Giorgio's. While the intimately sized dining room presents a casual, bistro-like ambience, the food preparation is remarkably sophisticated. Each dish is beautifully arranged and colorfully presented, adding to the meal's festivity. Black bass, pan-roasted and served with an artichoke puree, English thyme and crispy potato squares, is exceptional. The daily changing menu includes several made-in-house pasta dishes. The wait staff appears enthusiastic and well-informed. Dressy casual. **Bar:** Full bar. **Reservations:** suggested. **Hours:** 11:30 am-2 & 5-10 pm, Fri & Sat-11 pm. Closed: 1/1, 11/26, 12/25; also Sun & Mon. **Address:** 1131 NW Hoyt St **Location:** Jct NW 12th Ave; in Pearl District. **Parking:** street. **Cards:** AX, DC, DS, MC, VI.

GRACIE'S
Phone: 503/222-2171   ⑥⑦
American
$8-$28
Lending to the historic hotel dining room's updated style are fluted columns, gilded moldings and crystal chandeliers. The menu features Hollywood-inspired cuisine infused with Northwest sensibilities. Casual dress. **Bar:** Full bar. **Reservations:** accepted. **Hours:** 6:30-10:30 am, 11-2 & 5-10 pm, Fri & Sat-midnight; Saturday & Sunday brunch. **Address:** 729 SW 15th Ave **Location:** I-5 to I-405, exit Salmon St northbound, just n on 14th Ave, w on Morrison St, then s; exit Couch/Burnside St southbound; at SW 15th Ave and Yamhill St; in Hotel deLuxe. **Parking:** on-site and valet. **Cards:** AX, CB, DC, DS, JC, MC, VI.

GREEN ONION RESTAURANT
Phone: 503/274-4294   ⑨⑤
Persian
$7-$17
Smells of Persian cooking waft in the air from this restaurant perched in the living room of a converted Victorian home. Don't let the exterior deceive you—the dining room is intimate in size and features two sections for dining. The welcoming chef/owner both prepares and serves tasty, authentic food. Selections include kebabs, chicken and vegetarian dishes, aromatic basmati saffron rice and desserts such as the made-in-house Persian ice cream with pistachios, rosewater and saffron. Casual dress. **Bar:** Beer & wine. **Reservations:** accepted. **Hours:** 11 am-11 pm; seasonal hours vary. Closed major holidays; also Sun. **Address:** 636 SW Jackson St **Location:** Jct SW Broadway; close to Portland State University (PSU). **Parking:** street. **Cards:** DS, MC, VI.

GREEN PAPAYA VIETNAMESE BISTRO
Phone: 503/248-2112   ⑦③
Vietnamese
$7-$24
Soft lighting and background music lend to the upscale feel. A good choice of wines and creative cocktails pairs with the excellent seafood dishes for which this place is known. Casual dress. **Bar:** Full bar. **Reservations:** accepted. **Hours:** 11 am-2:30 & 4-10 pm. Closed major holidays. **Address:** 1135 SW Morrison St **Location:** Corner of SW 11th Ave and SW Morrison St. **Parking:** street. **Cards:** AX, DC, DS, MC, VI.

THE HEATHMAN RESTAURANT
Phone: 503/790-7752   ⑧④
Regional French
$8-$30
A distinctive French influence, courtesy of the only known French master chef in the Pacific Northwest, enhances the creative Northwest cuisine of this upscale restaurant. The menu lists innovative dishes, as well as delightfully sinful desserts such as white chocolate coconut flan. Casual dress. Entertainment. **Bar:** Full bar. **Reservations:** suggested. **Hours:** 6:30 am-10 pm, Fri & Sat-11 pm. **Address:** 1001 SW Broadway **Location:** At SW Broadway and Salmon St; in The Heathman Hotel. **Parking:** valet and street. **Cards:** AX, CB, DC, DS, JC, MC, VI.

CALL

HENRY'S 12TH STREET TAVERN
Phone: 503/227-5320   ⑤⑦
Regional American
$9-$26
In a former brewery in the historic brewery blocks, the four-level tavern with rustic exposed walls prepares contemporary Northwest fare (not your typical pub food). Choices include fresh seafood, USDA Choice steaks, pasta and Asian preparations. In addition to 100 draft beers, beverage choices include listings on the interesting martini menu. Outside seating can be requested in season. A billiards room is on site. Casual dress. **Bar:** Full bar. **Reservations:** accepted. **Hours:** 11 am-11 pm, Fri & Sat-midnight. Closed: 12/25. **Address:** 10 NW 12th Ave **Location:** At NW Burnside St and NW 12th Ave; in Pearl District. **Parking:** street. **Cards:** AX, DC, DS, MC, VI.

HIGGINS RESTAURANT & BAR
Phone: 503/222-9070   ⑧⑥
Regional American
$8-$32
The restaurant's cuisine emphasizes local, organic and seasonal foods from the Northwest. Large windows on three levels of cozy dining rooms overlook Broadway. Casual dress. **Bar:** Full bar. **Reservations:** suggested. **Hours:** 11:30 am-2 & 5-10:30 pm, Sat & Sun from 5 pm. Closed major holidays; also 12/24. **Address:** 1239 SW Broadway **Location:** At SW Broadway and Jefferson St. **Parking:** street. **Cards:** AX, DC, DS, JC, MC, VI.

HOLDEN'S BISTRO
Phone: 503/916-0099   ③⑦
American
$10-$28
The candlelit storefront restaurant has a cozy, minimalist feel both inside and at sidewalk tables. American food is prepared with a twist, and varied small plates are offered. Key lime pie compares well with its Florida counterpart. Casual dress. **Bar:** Full bar. **Reservations:** accepted. **Hours:** 5 pm-10 pm. Closed major holidays; also Sun & Mon. **Address:** 524 NW 14th Ave **Location:** Between Hoyt and Glisan sts; in Pearl District. **Parking:** street. **Cards:** AX, DS, MC, VI.

(See map and index starting on p. 396)

HOUSE OF LOUIE　　　　　　　　　　　　　　　　　　　**Phone: 503/228-9898**　④⑧

Chinese
$5-$12

Dragon pillars mark the entry of this long-established city fixture, which offers reasonably priced dim sum each day from carts that circulate the dining area. In the evening, diners order from the menu. Casual dress. **Reservations:** not accepted. **Hours:** 10 am-10 pm. Closed major holidays. **Address:** 331 NW Davis St **Location:** Jct NW 4th Ave; in Chinatown. **Parking:** street. **Cards:** MC, VI.

HUBER'S　　*Menu on AAA.com*　　　　　　　　　　　　**Phone: 503/228-5686**　⑦④

American
$6-$26

Established in 1879, the busy local landmark is renowned for great turkey dinners, delicious clam chowder and Spanish coffee. Also on the menu are steaks and other seafood selections. The original decor from 1911 includes an arched stained-glass skylight, rich mahogany paneling and a terrazzo floor. This place is open on Thanksgiving. Casual dress. **Bar:** Full bar. **Reservations:** suggested. **Hours:** 11:30 am-10 pm, Fri-11 pm, Sat 11 am-11 pm, Sun 4 pm-10 pm. Closed major holidays. **Address:** 411 SW 3rd Ave **Location:** At Stark St and SW 3rd Ave; in Oregon Pioneer Building. **Parking:** street. **Cards:** AX, CB, DC, DS, MC, VI. **Historic**

INDIA HOUSE　　　　　　　　　　　　　　　　　　　　**Phone: 503/274-1017**　⑦⑧

Indian
$8-$19

Conveniently located on the light rail line, this popular restaurant serves chicken, lamb and seafood curries that are spiced according to your taste. Several varieties of tandoori breads and specialties are cooked in a tandoori (clay) oven. Casual dress. **Bar:** Beer & wine. **Reservations:** suggested. **Hours:** 11:30 am-2 & 5:30-10 pm, Fri-10:30 pm, Sat noon-2:30 & 5:30-10:30 pm, Sun 5:30 pm-10:30 pm. Closed major holidays. **Address:** 1038 SW Morrison St **Location:** Jct SW 11th Ave. **Parking:** street. **Cards:** AX, DC, DS, MC, VI.

JAKE'S FAMOUS CRAWFISH RESTAURANT　　　　　　　**Phone: 503/226-1419**　⑤⑨

Seafood
$7-$28

For more than 115 years, the casual downtown restaurant has served as a veritable temple for the worship of seafood. The menu changes daily to reflect market availability but is consistently an encyclopedia of piscatorial delights. Signature dishes include Jake's New England-style clam chowder, king salmon oven-roasted on a cedar plank and Dungeness crab and bay shrimp cakes. For dessert, splurge on the decadent chocolate truffle cake. Casual dress. **Bar:** Full bar. **Reservations:** suggested. **Hours:** 11 am-midnight, Fri-1 am, Sat noon-1 am, Sun 3 pm-midnight. Closed: 12/25. **Address:** 401 SW 12th Ave **Location:** At 12th Ave and Stark St. **Parking:** valet and street. **Cards:** AX, CB, DC, DS, JC, MC, VI. **Historic**

JAKE'S GRILL　　　　　　　　　　　　　　　　　　　　**Phone: 503/220-1850**　⑦①

American
$7-$40

The lively, classic American bistro prepares more than 30 varieties of fresh fish and shellfish, as well as chops, poultry and USDA Prime steaks. The menu changes daily to reflect the fresh seafood selection. Casual dress. **Bar:** Full bar. **Reservations:** suggested. **Hours:** 6:30 am-11 pm, Fri & Sat-midnight; Saturday & Sunday brunch 7:30 am-2 pm. **Address:** 611 SW 10th Ave **Location:** 11th Ave and Alder St; in The Governor Hotel. **Parking:** valet and street. **Cards:** AX, DC, DS, MC, VI. **Historic**

JUSTA PASTA　　　　　　　　　　　　　　　　　　　　**Phone: 503/243-2249**　①②

Italian
$5-$14

Tucked away in the trendy Pearl District, this restaurant is known for its house-made pastas; enjoy them in the casual and bustling dining room or at the patio tables overlooking a primarily residential area. You may also purchase pasta by the pound and take it home to serve with your own sauces. Casual dress. **Bar:** Beer & wine. **Reservations:** not accepted. **Hours:** 11:30 am-3 & 4:30-9 pm, Fri-9:30 pm, Sat 4 pm-9:30 pm, Sun 4 pm-8:30 pm; hours extended 1/2 hour in summer. Closed major holidays. **Address:** 1336 NW 19th Ave **Location:** Between Overton and Pettygrove sts; in Pearl District. **Parking:** on-site. **Cards:** AX, DS, MC, VI.

KARAM LEBANESE CUISINE　　　　　　　　　　　　　　**Phone: 503/223-0830**　⑦⑥

Lebanese
$7-$25

This friendly, family-run restaurant offers a varied menu of delicious and authentic cuisine; try the mezza platter if you can't decide on a selection. Casual dress. **Bar:** Full bar. **Reservations:** accepted. **Hours:** 10 am-9 pm, Sat from 11 am. Closed: 11/26, 12/25; also Sun. **Address:** 316 SW Stark St **Location:** Jct 3rd Ave. **Parking:** street. **Cards:** AX, DS, MC, VI.

KELLS IRISH RESTAURANT & PUB　　　　　　　　　　　**Phone: 503/227-4057**　⑥⑤

Irish
$6-$24

Famous for its shepherd's pie, this warm, inviting neighborhood establishment is housed in a building dating from 1889. Traditional and new world Irish cuisine is served while live Irish music plays each night. A late-night pub menu is available, and breakfast is offered on the weekends. Casual dress. **Entertainment. Bar:** Full bar. **Reservations:** accepted. **Hours:** 11:30 am-1 am, Sat & Sun from 9 am. Closed: 11/26, 12/25. **Address:** 112 SW 2nd Ave **Location:** Just n of SW Pine St. **Parking:** street. **Cards:** AX, CB, DC, JC, MC, VI. **Historic**

KEN'S ARTISAN BAKERY　　　　　　　　　　　　　　　**Phone: 503/248-2202**　④⑦

Breads/Pastries
$6-$14

A simple, no-nonsense escape from the damp Oregon weather, the bakery is permeated with the aromas of freshly baked breads and desserts. Every case and rack is filled with mouthwatering delights from pain au chocolat to soft caneles to croissants with Gruyere and spinach. From the airy ciabatta to dense country bread and classic baguettes, the sandwich selection is a sheer delight simply because of the breads. As much as possible, everything is made from fresh, local and organic ingredients. Pizza is served on Monday nights. Parking is available until 5 pm at nearby Basta's Restaurant. Casual dress. **Bar:** Beer & wine. **Hours:** 7 am-6 pm, Sun 8 am-5 pm. Closed: 11/26, 12/25. **Address:** 338 NW 21st Ave **Location:** I-405, exit Everett St northbound, 1 mi w on Glisan St, then just n; jct NW Flanders St; in Northwest District. **Parking:** street. **Cards:** MC, VI.

KINCAID'S FISH, CHOP & STEAK　　　　　　　　　　　**Phone: 503/223-6200**　⑥③

American
$10-$46

This popular restaurant has a bustling, warm ambience. The varied menu includes seafood, steak and excellent prime rib. Ample wine and dessert choices round out the meal. Dressy casual. **Bar:** Full bar. **Reservations:** accepted. **Hours:** 11 am-11 pm, Fri & Sat-midnight. **Address:** 121 SW 3rd Ave **Location:** At SW 4th Ave and Pine St; in Embassy Suites Portland Downtown. **Parking:** valet and street. **Cards:** AX, DC, DS, MC, VI.

(See map and index starting on p. 396)

LA TERRAZZA ITALIAN GRILL
Phone: 503/223-8200   85

Italian
$7-$16

The eatery offers a good selection of traditional Italian dishes, homemade pastas and efficient, polite service. Seating options include counter seats, which overlook the grill, or patio seating, open in season. Casual dress. **Bar:** Full bar. **Reservations:** accepted. **Hours:** 11 am-9 pm, Fri & Sat-10 pm. Closed major holidays; also Sun. **Address:** 933 SW 3rd Ave **Location:** Jct Salmon St. **Parking:** street. **Cards:** AX, CB, DS, MC, VI.

LAURELWOOD NORTHWEST PUBLIC HOUSE & BREWERY
Phone: 503/228-5553   22

American
$9-$15

Set in a classic 1902 home just off popular 23rd Avenue, the neighborhood eatery is a popular dinner spot thanks to its children's play area. Hand-crafted beers are brewed on site, and outside porch seating is an option in season. Casual dress. **Bar:** Full bar. **Reservations:** not accepted. **Hours:** 11 am-10 pm, Fri & Sat-11 pm. Closed major holidays. **Address:** 2327 NW Kearney St **Location:** I-405; exit Everett St, 1 mi w on Glisan St, 0.4 mi n on 23rd Ave, then just w. **Parking:** street. **Cards:** AX, DS, MC, VI.

LE BOUCHON
Phone: 503/248-2193   39

Regional French
$10-$22

Le Bouchon translates to "the cork," but the French use the term to refer to a casual bistro, which in this case is also a lively one. A light menu of Bordeaux-style classic French cuisine prepared with country touches pairs with wines from all over France. Mussel soup prepared with saffron is recommended, as is lobster bisque. Casual dress. **Bar:** Full bar. **Reservations:** suggested. **Hours:** 11:30 am-2 & 5:30-10 pm, Fri-11 pm, Sat 5:30 pm-11 pm. Closed major holidays; also Sun & Mon. **Address:** 517 NW 14th Ave **Location:** I-405, exit Everett St northbound, just n; in Pearl District. **Parking:** street. **Cards:** AX, DS, MC, VI.

LONDON GRILL   *Menu on AAA.com*
Phone: 503/295-4110   64

Regional American
$9-$56

Live piano music or acoustical guitar lends to the dignified aura that personifies the warm and spacious dining room. For more than 50 years, this restaurant has served such classics as Caesar salad and steak Diane prepared tableside, and cedar-smoked salmon with juniper berry sage Pinot Gris sauce. Dessert choices include bananas Foster. A broad selection of wines is housed in the wine cellar, which can be reserved for secluded dining and is accessed via a secret door. Dressy casual. **Entertainment. Bar:** Full bar. **Reservations:** suggested. **Hours:** 6:30-11 am, 11:30-2 & 5-9 pm, Fri & Sat-10 pm; Sunday brunch 9:30 am-2 pm. **Address:** 309 SW Broadway **Location:** At SW Broadway and Oak St; in The Benson Hotel, a Coast Hotel. **Parking:** on-site and valet. **Cards:** AX, CB, DC, DS, JC, MC, VI.

LUCY'S TABLE
Phone: 503/226-6126   29

Regional Mediterranean
$15-$28

The seasonally changing menu lists creative Northwest cuisine infused with French and Mediterranean influences. Courteous staff members lend to the welcoming feel of the warm, inviting space. Sidewalk seating is a seasonal option. From Wednesday through Saturday, valet parking service is offered one block north at Johnson Street. Casual dress. **Bar:** Full bar. **Reservations:** suggested. **Hours:** 5 pm-9:30 pm, Fri & Sat-10:30 pm. Closed major holidays; also Sun. **Address:** 704 NW 21st Ave **Location:** I-405, exit Everett St northbound, 1 mi w on Glisan St, then just n; jct Irving St. **Parking:** valet and street. **Cards:** AX, DC, DS, MC, VI.

MANDARIN COVE
Phone: 503/222-0006   88

Chinese
$6-$18

The restaurant's menu lists both Hunan and Szechuan specialties, as well as classic Chinese entrees. Try the assorted platter appetizer and the sizzling rice shrimp as a main course. Service is prompt, and you'll find complimentary parking after 4:30 pm on weekdays and all day Saturday and Sunday in the Columbia Square parking garage off of Jefferson Street between First and Second avenues. Casual dress. **Bar:** Full bar. **Reservations:** accepted. **Hours:** 11 am-2 & 4:30-9 pm, Fri 4:30 pm-10 pm, Sat noon-10 pm, Sun 4 pm-9 pm. Closed major holidays. **Address:** 111 SW Columbia St **Location:** At Columbia St and 1st Ave. **Parking:** on-site (fee). **Cards:** AX, MC, VI.

MARINA FISH HOUSE
Phone: 503/227-3474   95

Seafood
$10-$28

At Riverplace Marina on the Willamette River, the floating restaurant affords views of downtown and water activity. Although the menu centers on diverse offerings of seafood, it also lists pasta, beef and chicken dishes. Outside dining on the floating dock is available in season. Guests can park for half-price validation in the lot adjacent to Stanford's Restaurant. Casual dress. **Bar:** Full bar. **Reservations:** suggested. **Hours:** 11 am-11 pm, Fri & Sat-midnight, Sun 9 am-11 pm; to 10 pm, Fri & Sat-11 pm, Sun 10 am-10 pm in winter; Sunday brunch. Closed: 11/26, 12/25. **Address:** 0425 SW Montgomery St **Location:** Just e of Naito Pkwy (formerly Front Ave) and Market St; at Riverplace Marina. **Parking:** on-site (fee) and street. **Cards:** AX, CB, DC, DS, MC, VI.

MARINEPOLIS SUSHI LAND
Phone: 503/546-9933   50

Sushi
$2-$8

Guests sit and watch the various freshly prepared sushi choices circulate on the conveyor belt as they dine at this light and bright eatery. Fast and affordable, this place displays color-coded plates marked with the price per plate on its wall. Casual dress. **Bar:** Beer only. **Reservations:** not accepted. **Hours:** 11 am-9 pm. Closed: 12/25. **Address:** 138 NW 10th Ave **Location:** Jct NW Davis St; in Pearl District. **Parking:** street. **Cards:** MC, VI.

CALL

(See map and index starting on p. 396)

MARRAKESH MOROCCAN RESTAURANT
Moroccan
$18

Phone: 503/248-9442 ⑮

A lively Moroccan feast awaits inside the doors of this welcoming oasis. The prix fixe menu includes salad Marrakesh; bastela royale, phyllo dough filled with ground chicken and spices; and a choice of entree, dessert and mint tea. A good entree is lamb m'rouzia served with onions, raisins and honey sauce. A la carte items also are available. Moroccan wines and beers are served. Belly dancing lends to the atmosphere Wednesday through Sunday. Casual dress. Entertainment. **Bar:** Beer & wine. **Reservations:** suggested. **Hours:** 5 pm-10 pm. **Address:** 1201 NW 21st Ave **Location:** Jct NW Northrup St. **Parking:** street. **Cards:** AX, CB, DC, DS, MC, VI.

MCCORMICK & SCHMICK'S
Seafood
$7-$27

Phone: 503/220-1865 ⑭

This place is all about seafood, which is imported from all over the world. Among good choices are Washington state oysters, Maine clams, delicate Hawaiian escolar and tuna from Ecuador. The clublike decor is cozy, and expert staff provide able assistance. Casual dress. **Bar:** Full bar. **Reservations:** suggested. **Hours:** 11 am-10 pm, Fri & Sat-11 pm. **Address:** 0309 SW Montgomery St **Location:** Just n of jct SW River Dr and SW Montgomery St; on the riverfront esplanade. **Parking:** street. **Cards:** AX, DC, DS, MC, VI.

MCCORMICK & SCHMICK'S
AAA

Seafood
$15-$25

Phone: 503/224-7522 ⑯

This place is all about seafood, which is imported from all over the world. Among good choices are Washington state oysters, Maine clams, delicate Hawaiian escolar and tuna from Ecuador. The clublike decor is cozy, and expert staff provide able assistance. Casual dress. **Bar:** Full bar. **Reservations:** suggested. **Hours:** 4 pm-10 pm, Fri & Sat-11 pm. Closed: 12/25. **Address:** 235 SW 1st Ave **Location:** At SW 1st Ave and Oak St. **Parking:** on-site. **Cards:** AX, DC, DS, JC, MC, VI. **Historic**

MCMENAMINS
American
$5-$20

Phone: 503/282-6810

The casual neighborhood eatery is where friends gather for classic pub and comfort fare, all washed down by pints of locally made beer. Large wooden booths or tables easily accommodate larger groups, and the eclectic, custom-painted walls and varied period light fixtures keep diners' eyes busy should the conversation lag. Casual dress. Entertainment. **Bar:** Full bar. **Hours:** 11 am-11 pm, Fri & Sat-midnight, Sun 4 pm-11 pm. **Address:** 836 N Russell St **Location:** Just n of N Interstate Ave. **Parking:** on-site. **Cards:** MC, VI.

MCMENAMINS MARKET STREET PUB
American
$5-$20

Phone: 503/497-0160

The casual neighborhood eatery is where friends gather for classic pub and comfort fare, all washed down by pints of locally made beer. Large wooden booths or tables easily accommodate larger groups, and the eclectic, custom-painted walls and varied period light fixtures keep diners' eyes busy should the conversation lag. Casual dress. **Bar:** Full bar. **Hours:** 11 am-1 am, Sun noon-midnight. Closed: 11/26, 12/25. **Address:** 1526 SW 10th Ave **Location:** Corner of Clay St and SW 10th Ave. **Parking:** street. **Cards:** MC, VI.

MERIWETHER'S RESTAURANT
American
$8-$34

Phone: 503/228-1250 ③

A little off the beaten path, the restaurant is a great place to gather around the fireplace on a cold night or escape the summer sun in the year-round covered garden. Most menu items originate in the Northwest and are created fresh daily with such items as salmon gravlax, rainbow trout and grilled venison. Dishes may be as simple as a smoked ham and Tillamook cheddar cheese sandwich. Casual dress. **Bar:** Full bar. **Reservations:** accepted. **Hours:** 11:30 am-9 pm, Sat & Sun from 8 am. Closed: 1/1, 7/4, 12/25. **Address:** 2601 NW Vaughn St **Location:** Jct NW 26 Ave. **Parking:** on-site. **Cards:** AX, DC, DS, MC, VI.

MINT & 820
American
$12-$25

Phone: 503/284-5518 ②

Sleek styling, specialty cocktails and Latino cuisine are found at the trendy establishment. Guests might start off with roasted poblano chile soup and then enjoy braised Muscovite duck legs in dried fig-ancho mole served over grilled leeks. Upbeat dinner music lends to the atmosphere. Cocktail classes are scheduled regularly. Casual dress. **Bar:** Full bar. **Reservations:** suggested. **Hours:** 5 pm-10 pm, Fri & Sat-11 pm. Closed: 11/26, 12/24, 12/25; also Sun. **Address:** 816 N Russell St **Location:** I-5, exit 302A northbound, e on NE Weidler St, n on NE Victoria Ave, w on NE Broadway, 0.4 mi nw on Interstate Ave, then just e; exit Broadway southbound, just w, 0.4 mi nw on Interstate Ave, then just e. **Parking:** street. **Cards:** AX, MC, VI.

MIO SUSHI
Sushi
$5-$15

Phone: 503/221-1469 ㉘

In an old house in the historic King's Hill area, the no-nonsense sushi bar has limited space, which means a reservation is a good idea. Guests can fill up on their favorite raw fish or opt for one of the many cooked dishes, such as tempura, teriyaki and noodles. Take-out service is another option. Casual dress. **Bar:** Beer & wine. **Reservations:** suggested. **Hours:** 11:30 am-9:30 pm, Fri-10 pm, Sat noon-10 pm. Closed: major holidays; also 12/24, Sun. **Address:** 2271 NW Johnson St **Location:** I-405, exit Everett St northbound, 1 mi w on Glisan St, then just n on NW 23rd Ave; in Northwest District. **Parking:** street. **Cards:** AX, MC, VI.

MISOHAPI
Vietnamese
$6-$11

Phone: 503/796-2012 ⑱

Specializing in Vietnamese and Thai cuisine, the restaurant offers a variety of chicken, pork, beef, vegetarian and seafood dishes, along with interesting soups and noodle bowls. Billowing contemporary sails hang from the ceiling to create a light, airy feel. Large windows look out onto busy NW 23rd Avenue. Casual dress. **Bar:** Beer & wine. **Reservations:** not accepted. **Hours:** 11 am-10 pm. Closed major holidays, also 12/24 & Sun. **Address:** 1123 NW 23rd Ave **Location:** I-405, exit Everett St northbound, 1 mi w on Glisan St, then just n. **Parking:** street. **Cards:** AX, DS, MC, VI.

MOTHER'S BISTRO & BAR
American
$8-$20

Phone: 503/464-1122 ⑲

The bistro offers the notion that home-cooked food can be creative and wonderful for breakfast, lunch and dinner. The dining room appears both eclectic and intimate. There are some international offerings, but features focus on Mother's special recipes, changing monthly specials, M.O.M. (Mother of the Month) special dishes and interesting desserts. Casual dress. **Bar:** Full bar. **Reservations:** accepted. **Hours:** 7 am-9 pm, Fri & Sat-10 pm, Sun 9 am-2:30 pm. Closed: 12/25; also Mon. **Address:** 212 SW Stark St **Location:** Corner of SW 2nd Ave and SW Stark St. **Parking:** street. **Cards:** AX, CB, DC, DS, MC, VI.

(See map and index starting on p. 396)

NANCY'S KITCHEN *Menu on AAA.com*   Phone: 503/241-1137   36

Tucked away in a commercial strip near the resurgent Pearl District, the restaurant is open only for breakfast and lunch. Offerings include house specialty sandwiches, wraps, salads, desserts baked in house, and take-and-bake casseroles. Casual dress. **Reservations:** not accepted. **Hours:** 8 am-4 pm, Sat-3 pm, Sun-2 pm. Closed: 1/1, 12/25; also Mon. **Address:** 1611 NW Glisan St **Location:** I-405, exit Everett St northbound, just w; in Pearl District. **Parking:** on-site. **Cards:** MC, VI.

American
$6-$9

OBA! RESTAURANTE!   Phone: 503/228-6161   35

The upscale Nuevo Latino restaurant is part comfortable Mexican hacienda and part Havana nightlife. The atmosphere sizzles with the accompaniment of lively salsa music. An extensive wine list complements spicy food delivered by energetic servers who aim to please. Valet parking is available Thursday through Saturday. Dressy casual. **Bar:** Full bar. **Reservations:** suggested. **Hours:** 5:30 pm-9:30 pm, Fri & Sat-10:30 pm, Sun & Mon-9 pm. Closed: 7/4, 11/26, 12/25. **Address:** 555 NW 12th Ave **Location:** At Hoyt St; in Pearl District. **Parking:** valet and street. **Cards:** AX, DS, MC, VI.

Latin American
$18-$34

OLEA   Phone: 503/274-0800   34

In a former warehouse, the inviting restaurant has a cozy dining loft in which diffused lighting permeates through oversize lampshades. Creative preparations of delightful contemporary Mediterranean-inspired cuisine represent an assortment of countries, including France, Italy, Spain and Morocco. Among popular features are happy hour from 5 to 7 pm and live jazz on Thursday evenings. Casual dress. **Bar:** Full bar. **Reservations:** suggested. **Hours:** 5 pm-11 pm. Closed major holidays. **Address:** 1338 NW Hoyt St **Location:** At 13th Ave and Hoyt St; in Pearl District. **Parking:** street. **Cards:** AX, CB, DC, DS, MC, VI.

Continental
$14-$25

CALL ⓁⓂ

ON DECK SPORTS BAR AND GRILL   Phone: 503/227-7020   20

Patrons ascend the stairs to the popular and lively sports bar. In summer, the expansive deck offers good views of the surrounding Pearl District. Casual dress. **Bar:** Full bar. **Reservations:** not accepted. **Hours:** 11 am-midnight, Fri-1:30 am, Sat 9 am-1:30 am, Sun 9 am-11 pm. Closed: 12/25. **Address:** 910 NW 14th Ave **Location:** At Kearney St; in Pearl District. **Parking:** street. **Cards:** AX, MC, VI.

American
$6-$18

PALEY'S PLACE BISTRO & BAR   Phone: 503/243-2403   14

In a casually elegant setting, this establishment serves artfully prepared cuisine. Enjoy the flavors of roasted summer vegetables served with polenta or halibut poached in olive oil. For dessert, the plate of gourmet cookies and truffles may be shared, but why would you? Casual dress. **Bar:** Full bar. **Reservations:** suggested. **Hours:** 5:30 pm-10 pm, Fri & Sat-11 pm, Sun 5 pm-10 pm. Closed major holidays. **Address:** 1204 NW 21st Ave **Location:** Jct NW Northrup St; in Northwest District. **Parking:** street. **Cards:** AX, MC, VI.

Regional American
$16-$32

PALOMINO RESTAURANT   Phone: 503/248-1690

This national chain restaurant offers patrons an impressive assortment of dishes including seafood, pasta and steak. Rounding out the menu are pizzas, salads and Tuscan-style rotisserie roasted chicken all served up in a trendy, casual upscale atmosphere. Casual dress. **Bar:** Full bar. **Reservations:** accepted. **Hours:** 11 am-11 pm, Fri-midnight, Sat 8:30 am-midnight, Sun 8:30 am-10 pm. Closed: 12/25. **Address:** 1203 NW Glisan St **Location:** I-405, Everett St northbound, just e, then just n on 12th Ave; jct NW 12th Ave and Glisan St; in Pearl District. **Parking:** street. **Cards:** AX, DC, DS, MC, VI.

American
$8-$30

PAPA HAYDN WEST   Phone: 503/228-7317   30

A hot spot for people-watching, the trendy restaurant features a partially open kitchen, quality art and popular sidewalk seating. Although the menu's Northwest specialties are tasty, the desserts, more than 30 temptations made in-house, take top billing. Patrons can park behind the brick building on Irving Street near 23rd Avenue. Casual dress. **Bar:** Full bar. **Reservations:** accepted, Sun-Thurs. **Hours:** 11:30 am-10 pm, Fri & Sat-midnight, Sun 10 am-10 pm; Mon-Thurs to 11 pm in summer; Sunday brunch. Closed: 1/1, 11/26, 12/25. **Address:** 701 NW 23rd Ave **Location:** I-405, exit Everett St northbound, 1 mi w on Glisan St, then just n; jct NW Irving St. **Parking:** on-site. **Cards:** AX, MC, VI.

Regional American
$9-$27

PARAGON RESTAURANT & BAR   Phone: 503/833-5060   32

Some sidewalk tables are available at the comfortable, casual bar and restaurant, where offerings include wild mushroom-stuffed chicken and rock shrimp cakes. Casual dress. Entertainment. **Bar:** Full bar. **Reservations:** accepted. **Hours:** 11:30 am-4 & 5:30-10 pm, Fri & Sat-10:30 pm. Closed major holidays. **Address:** 1309 NW Hoyt St **Location:** Jct NW 13th Ave; in Pearl District. **Parking:** street. **Cards:** AX, DC, DS, MC, VI.

American
$9-$22

PARK KITCHEN   Phone: 503/223-7275   44

A popular spot for both lunch and dinner, this spot is located in the North Park Blocks area, on the edge of the Pearl District. Seating is limited (find sidewalk tables in season), but the food is prepared inventively, utilizing farm-fresh ingredients. Small hot and cold plates, along with large plates, are available. Casual dress. **Bar:** Full bar. **Reservations:** suggested. **Hours:** 11:30 am-2 & 5-9 pm, Fri-9:30 pm, Sat 5 pm-9:30 pm. Closed major holidays; also Sun. **Address:** 422 NW 8th Ave **Location:** Just s of jct NW Glisan St. **Parking:** street. **Cards:** AX, MC, VI.

American
$7-$27

PASTINI PASTARIA   Phone: 503/595-1205   10

Fresh, affordable pasta dishes, along with grilled panini sandwiches, are served at the contemporary, Italian-style bistro. Casual dress. **Bar:** Full bar. **Reservations:** not accepted. **Hours:** 11:30 am-9 pm, Fri & Sat-10 pm, Sun 4 pm-9 pm. Closed major holidays; also 12/24. **Address:** 1506 NW 23rd Ave **Location:** At Quimby St and NW 23rd Ave. **Parking:** street. **Cards:** AX, MC, VI.

Italian
$5-$10

(See map and index starting on p. 396)

PATANEGRA   Phase: 503/227-7282   ④

Spanish
$6-$20

In a former warehouse, this neighborhood restaurant serves small and large portions of cold and hot tapas, along with hearty paellas. Recommended is warm grilled squid. The wine list includes an excellent selection from Spain. Rustic wooden beams, warm decor and large wooden tables for community dining add to the welcoming feel. Casual dress. **Bar:** Full bar. **Hours:** 5 pm-10 pm, Mon-9 pm. Closed: Sun. **Address:** 1818 NW 23rd Pl **Location:** I-405, exit 3 (US 30) northbound; exit Vaughn St southbound, just s on NW 23rd Ave, w on NW Thurman St, then just n. **Parking:** street. **Cards:** AX, DS, MC, VI.

PAZZORIA BAKERY & CAFE   Phone: 503/228-1515   ⑦⓪

Breads/Pastries
$5-$8

A casual complement to the upscale Pazzo Ristorante next door, the cafe makes Italian artisan-style breads and pastries on site daily. The lunch menu lists pasta, trattoria-style pizza by the slice and panini sandwiches. Casual dress. **Hours:** 7 am-4 pm, Sat & Sun 9 am-3 pm. Closed major holidays. **Address:** 621 SW Washington St **Location:** At Broadway and Washington St; in Hotel Vintage Plaza. **Parking:** street. **Cards:** AX, DC, DS, MC, VI.

PAZZO RISTORANTE   Phone: 503/228-1515   ⑦②

Italian
$11-$31

The casually upscale restaurant is known for exceptional Italian dishes. The calorie-conscious should tune out their inner voice's warning to bypass dessert, as the decadent creations shouldn't be missed. A good selection of wines is available. Casual dress. **Bar:** Full bar. **Reservations:** suggested. **Hours:** 7-10:30 am, 11:30-2:30 & 5-10 pm, Fri-11 pm, Sat 8 am-2 & 4:30-11 pm, Sun 8 am-2 & 4-9:30 pm; Saturday & Sunday brunch. Closed major holidays. **Address:** 627 SW Washington St **Location:** At Broadway and Washington St; in Hotel Vintage Plaza. **Parking:** valet and street. **Cards:** AX, DC, DS, MC, VI.

PEARL BAKERY   Phone: 503/827-0910   ⑤④

Breads/Pastries
$2-$6

The bakery crafts high-quality artisan breads and European pastries from carefully chosen ingredients. Sandwiches are tasty. Casual dress. **Hours:** 6:30 am-5:30 pm, Sat 7 am-5 pm, Sun 8 am-2 pm. Closed major holidays. **Address:** 102 NW 9th Ave **Location:** I-405, exit Everett St northbound, just n on NW 14th Ave to Everett St, then just s; exit southbound, just s; at NW 9th Ave and Couch St. **Parking:** on-site. **Cards:** MC, VI.

P.F. CHANG'S CHINA BISTRO   Phone: 503/432-4000   ⑤①

Chinese
$10-$21

Trendy, upscale decor provides a pleasant backdrop for New Age Chinese dining. Appetizers, soups and salads are a meal by themselves. Vegetarian plates and sides, noodles, meins, chicken and meat dishes are created from exotic, fresh ingredients. Casual dress. **Bar:** Full bar. **Reservations:** suggested. **Hours:** 11 am-11 pm, Fri & Sat-midnight. Closed: 11/26, 12/25. **Address:** 1139 NW Couch St **Location:** Near jct NW 11th Ave; in Pearl District. **Cards:** AX, DC, DS, MC, VI.

PIAZZA ITALIA   Phone: 503/478-0619   ②④

Italian
$10-$14

The popular bistro builds its menu on such classics as pasta bolognese. Some sidewalk seating is available. Any of several flavors of gelato can be enjoyed for dessert. Casual dress. **Bar:** Beer & wine. **Reservations:** suggested. **Hours:** 11:30 am-11 pm, Sun-9 pm. Closed major holidays. **Address:** 1129 NW Johnson St **Location:** Between NW 11th and 12th aves; in Pearl District. **Parking:** street. **Cards:** AX, DS, MC, VI.

PORTLAND CITY GRILL   Phone: 503/450-0030   ⑤⑧

Pacific Rim
$8-$60

Patrons enjoy spectacular views of downtown, the Willamette River and beyond from the 30th-floor setting. Northwestern, island and Asian influences spring forth from USDA Prime steaks, sushi preparations and fresh Hawaiian, Pacific Coast and Alaskan seafood. The sounds of piano music float from the lounge nightly. Parking in the underground facility is validated for 2 hours. Those who wish to avoid disappointment should reserve a window table in advance. Casual dress. Entertainment. **Bar:** Full bar. **Reservations:** suggested. **Hours:** 11 am-midnight, Fri-1 am, Sat 4 pm-1 am, Sun 4 pm-11 pm. **Address:** 111 SW 5th Ave **Location:** At SW 5th Ave and Pine St; in Unico/US Bancorp Tower, on the 30th floor. **Parking:** on-site. **Cards:** AX, MC, VI.

CALL 🅶M

RED STAR TAVERN   Phone: 503/222-0005   ⑧⓪

Regional American
$12-$35

The warm, inviting establishment features an open exhibition kitchen where many food items are roasted, such as mussels with tequila cascabel cream, and the rosemary-mustard marinated pork chop. Rotisserie game is available only during the week. Two-hour validated parking can be found at two nearby lots. Casual dress. **Bar:** Full bar. **Reservations:** suggested. **Hours:** 6:30-10:30 am, 11:30-2:30 & 5-10 pm, Fri-11 pm, Sat 8 am-3 & 5-11 pm, Sun 8 am-3 & 5-10 pm. Closed major holidays; also for dinner 1/1. **Address:** 506 SW Washington St **Location:** At SW 5th Ave and SW Washington St; in Hotel Monaco Portland. **Parking:** on-site. **Cards:** AX, CB, DC, DS, JC, MC, VI.

RESTAURANT MURATA   Phone: 503/227-0080   ⑧⑨

Japanese
$7-$27

Patrons can take advantage of validated parking in the 200 Market Building then head inside the restaurant's cozy dining room, one of a few semi-private tatami rooms or the small sushi bar for a nice choice of sushi, hot pot dishes, rice bowls, traditional Japanese cuisine and some unique items not often seen. Casual dress. **Bar:** Beer & wine. **Reservations:** suggested. **Hours:** 11:30 am-2 & 5:30-9:30 pm, Sat from 5:30 pm. Closed major holidays; also Sun. **Address:** 200 SW Market St **Location:** Corner of SW 2nd Ave and SW Market St. **Parking:** street. **Cards:** AX, DC, MC, VI.

RINGSIDE STEAKHOUSE   Phone: 503/223-1513   ⑤⑤

Steak
$21-$65

For more than 60 years, the established dinner house has been serving steaks, seafood and specialty onion rings. House specialties include bone-in steaks and slow-roasted prime rib. An extensive selection of wines and microbrews complements the menu choices. Low lighting and cherry paneling lend to the interior's rustic, cozy feel. Early supper specials must be ordered before 5:45 pm. Dressy casual. **Bar:** Full bar. **Reservations:** suggested. **Hours:** 5 pm-midnight, Sun 4 pm-11:30 pm. Closed major holidays. **Address:** 2165 W Burnside St **Location:** At 22nd Ave and W Burnside St. **Parking:** valet and street. **Cards:** AX, DC, DS, JC, MC, VI.

(See map and index starting on p. 396)

RUTH'S CHRIS STEAK HOUSE
Phone: 503/221-4518   68

Steak
$20-$40

The main fare is steak, which is prepared from several cuts of prime beef and cooked to perfection, but the menu also lists lamb, chicken and seafood dishes. Guests should come hungry because the side dishes, which are among the a la carte offerings, could make a meal in themselves. Casual dress. **Bar:** Full bar. **Reservations:** suggested. **Hours:** 5 pm-10 pm, Sun from 4 pm. Closed major holidays. **Address:** 309 SW 3rd Ave **Location:** Just s of jct SW Oak St. **Parking:** valet and street. **Cards:** AX, CB, DC, DS, JC, MC, VI.

SAINT CUPCAKE
Phone: 503/473-8760   45

Breads/Pastries
$2-$4

Named after the patron saint of sweet, this bakery features cupcakes with cute toppings in two sizes: the two- to three-bite dot-size and the larger regular. Each day means a different spread of temptations, and those who have favorites can check the Web site to know the right day to visit. The toasted twisted coconut and Fat Elvis are favorites. Vegan cupcakes also are available. Casual dress. **Reservations:** not accepted. **Hours:** 9 am-8 pm, Fri-10 pm, Sat 10 am-10 pm, Sun 10 am-6 pm. Closed: 1/1, 11/26, 12/25; also Mon. **Address:** 407 NW 17th Ave, #4 **Location:** Jct NW Flanders St. **Parking:** street. **Cards:** MC, VI.

ST. HONORE BOULANGERIE
Phone: 503/445-4342   5

Breads/Pastries
$7-$9

Honored as a leading baker in France, Dominique Geulin now creates an array of tempting pastries and breads for this bakery. Enhancing the dining area's cozy, informal decor are a baker's cart and massive wooden table similar to that in a French farmhouse. Large windows overlook the street scene, and sidewalk seating is offered in season. Casual dress. **Bar:** Beer & wine. **Reservations:** not accepted. **Hours:** 7 am-8 pm. Closed: 12/25. **Address:** 2335 NW Thurman St **Location:** Jct NW 23rd Ave, just w. **Parking:** street. **Cards:** MC, VI.

SERRATTO
Phone: 503/221-1195   23

Regional
Mediterranean
$9-$29

This restaurant features innovative dishes from Italy, France and the Mediterranean. Serratto appears intimate, yet casual, and it boasts a fine reputation for serving excellent food. The menu changes seasonally and features chicken dishes, pork and beef selections, seafood and creative desserts. A congenial staff provides near-seamless service. Sidewalk seating is available in season, and you can find parking for lunch and dinner at a nearby lot at N.W. Johnson, just west of N.W. 21st Avenue (there is a $4 parking charge at dinner). Dressy casual. **Bar:** Full bar. **Reservations:** accepted. **Hours:** 11 am-10 pm, Fri & Sat-11 pm. Closed major holidays. **Address:** 2112 NW Kearney St **Location:** Jct NW 21st Ave. **Parking:** on-site (fee) and valet. **Cards:** AX, CB, DS, MC, VI.

SILK VIETNAMESE RESTAURANT
Phone: 503/248-2172   40

Vietnamese
$8-$24

The quiet restaurant with gracious and understated decor tempts diners with Vietnamese culinary classics, including noodle soups, ginger chicken and shaken beef. Among grilled dishes are kaffir lime leaf beef. A few vegetarian choices also grace the menu. Casual dress. **Bar:** Full bar. **Reservations:** accepted, for dinner. **Hours:** 11 am-3 & 5-10 pm. Closed: 11/26, 12/25; also Sun. **Address:** 1012 NW Glisan St **Location:** Jct 10th Ave. **Parking:** street. **Cards:** AX, DS, MC, VI.

SIN JU JAPANESE RESTAURANT
Phone: 503/223-6535   26

Japanese
$7-$30

In the Pearl district, the trendy Japanese restaurant incorporates a sushi bar and tatami rooms. Extensive menu options range from fresh, hand-rolled, creative sushi to sukiyaki. Casual dress. **Bar:** Full bar. **Reservations:** suggested. **Hours:** 11:30 am-2:30 & 5-9:30 pm, Fri & Sat-10:30 pm, Sun 5 pm-9:30 pm. Closed major holidays. **Address:** 1022 NW Johnson St **Location:** At 10th Ave and Johnson St. **Parking:** street. **Cards:** AX, DS, MC, VI.

SOUTHPARK SEAFOOD GRILL & WINE BAR
Phone: 503/326-1300   82

Seafood
$9-$28

The menu merges fresh, local seafood and Mediterranean dishes. Lending character to the quiet, upscale dining room are an open kitchen with a wood-burning oven and a view of the Portland streetscape. Table spacing is a bit tight. There is a generous selection of wines by the glass and microbrewed beers. Casual dress. **Bar:** Full bar. **Reservations:** suggested. **Hours:** 11:30 am-3 & 5-midnight, Fri-1 am, Sat 11 am-1 am, Sun 11:30 am-11 pm. Closed major holidays. **Address:** 901 SW Salmon St **Location:** Jct SW 9th Ave. **Parking:** on-site. **Cards:** AX, DS, MC, VI.

STANFORD'S RESTAURANT & BAR
Phone: 503/241-5051   97

American
$10-$38

Near the Willamette riverfront, the restaurant offers a casual dining experience. Nightly dinner features and other menu items include hand-picked fresh seafood, quality steak, rock-salt-roasted prime rib and pasta selections. The patio opens seasonally. There is off-site parking in a nearby parking garage with 50 percent validation. Casual dress. **Bar:** Full bar. **Reservations:** accepted. **Hours:** 11 am-11 pm, Fri & Sat-midnight. Closed: 11/26, 12/25. **Address:** 1831 SW River Dr **Location:** I-5, exit 299B, just e on SW Montgomery St, then just s; at Riverplace Marina. **Parking:** street. **Cards:** AX, DC, DS, VI.

CALL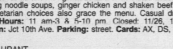

STEPPING STONE CAFE
Phone: 503/222-1132   11

American
$6-$9

The true neighborhood morning cafe serves from-scratch buttermilk pancakes with real maple syrup. The menu mixes such breakfast classics as three-egg omelets and lunch staples of burgers, sandwiches and salads. Casual dress. **Bar:** Full bar. **Reservations:** not accepted. **Hours:** 6 am-10 pm, Fri-3 am, Sat 7:30 am-3 am, Sun 7:30 am-10 pm. Closed: 12/25. **Address:** 2390 NW Quimby St **Location:** Corner of Quimby St and NW 24th Ave. **Parking:** street. **Cards:** DS, MC, VI.

SUNGARI
Phone: 503/224-0800   83

Chinese
$8-$20

Located right downtown on a busy street corner, the dining room's decor is a bit more upscale than a typical ethnic eatery, and window seats afford great people-watching opportunities. An extensive Chinese menu is full of family favorites prepared without MSG. For those undecided, the house specialties are always a solid bet. Casual dress. **Bar:** Full bar. **Reservations:** accepted. **Hours:** 11:30 am-2:30 & 5:30-9 pm, Fri & Sat-10 pm, Sun 4:30 pm-9:30 pm. Closed major holidays. **Address:** 735 SW 1st Ave **Location:** Corner of SW First Ave and Yamhill St. **Parking:** street. **Cards:** AX, MC, VI.

(See map and index starting on p. 396)

SUSHIVILLE, SUSHI GO ROUND Phone: 503/226-4710 ⑨

Sushi
$4-$10

A great place for a quick lunch, the restaurant has a meandering, vaguely horseshoe-shaped sushi bar with two inset conveyor belts used to keep a steady parade of dishes passing by the eyes of the diner. Plates are color coded for pricing at the end of the meal. The interesting concept, which is typically less expensive than traditional sushi bars, should appeal to sushi lovers who don't have a lot of time. Casual dress. **Bar:** Full bar. **Reservations:** accepted, weekdays. **Hours:** 11 am-9 pm, Fri & Sat-10 pm. Closed major holidays. **Address:** 1514 NW 23rd Ave **Location:** Jct NW Quimby St; in Northwest District. **Parking:** street. **Cards:** AX, DS, MC, VI.

THAI ORCHID RESTAURANT Phone: 503/226-4542

Thai
$7-$15

Patrons can enjoy fresh, flavorful Thai food with no added monosodium glutamate at this restaurant. The varied menu includes salads, soups, stir-fried dishes, distinctive curries, seafood and noodles. Casual dress. **Bar:** Beer & wine. **Hours:** 11:30 am-9 pm. Closed: 7/4, 12/25. **Address:** 2231 W Burnside St **Location:** Jct NW 22nd Ave. **Parking:** street. **Cards:** AX, DS, MC, VI.

THANH-LONG Phone: 503/223-1660 ⑨③

Vietnamese
$6-$10

Patrons find freshly prepared Vietnamese cuisine—such as glass noodle dishes, traditional cold rice vermicelli topped with grilled pork, chicken or shrimp, pho (beef noodle soup) and a variety of vegetarian dishes and curries—as well as tempting desserts and bakery items. Lunch specials are another offering. Casual dress. **Bar:** Beer & wine. **Reservations:** accepted. **Hours:** 10 am-9 pm. Closed major holidays; also Sun. **Address:** 635 SW College St **Location:** Jct SW Broadway. **Parking:** on-site. **Cards:** MC, VI.

THREE DEGREES Phone: 503/295-6166 ⑨①

Regional American
$8-$28

Northwestern cuisine emphasizes fresh, locally grown ingredients. Tiered seating in the dining room allows for beautiful views of the Willamette River and marina, while the outdoor patio seating overlooks RiverPlace Esplanade. Parking is validated for 2 hours. Casual dress. **Bar:** Full bar. **Reservations:** suggested. **Hours:** 6:30 am-2 & 5-10 pm. **Address:** 1510 SW Harbor Way **Location:** At Naito Pkwy (formerly Front Ave) and SW Harbor Way; in RiverPlace, A Larkspur Collection Hotel. **Parking:** valet and street. **Cards:** AX, CB, DC, DS, JC, MC, VI. *(See color ad p 420)*

THREE LIONS' BAKERY AND CAFE Phone: 503/224-3429 ⑦⑦

Breads/Pastries
$7-$9

Soups and sandwiches feature prominently on the lunch menu of the bakery/eatery, which prepares fresh, made-from-scratch daily bakery specials and nearly-famous desserts, especially the cakes. Casual dress. **Hours:** 7:30 am-4:30 pm. Closed major holidays; also Sat & Sun. **Address:** 1138 SW Morrison St **Location:** At 12th Ave and Morrison St. **Parking:** street. **Cards:** AX, MC, VI.

TOUCHE' RESTAURANT & BAR Phone: 503/221-1150 ㉜

Mediterranean
$10-$25

The warm, comfortable restaurant is capable of handling parties of up to 100 people. With good food downstairs and pool tables upstairs, this place is great for hanging out and enjoying Italian/Mediterranean food with myriad libations. The delicious rack of lamb comes in a portion nearly large enough for two. Pasta or pizza are other options. Casual dress. **Bar:** Full bar. **Hours:** 4 pm-2:30 am. Closed: 7/4, 11/26, 12/24, 12/25. **Address:** 1425 NW Glisan St **Location:** Between 14th and 15th aves; in Pearl District. **Parking:** on-site. **Cards:** MC, VI.

TYPHOON! Phone: 503/224-8285 ㉖

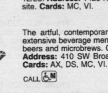

Thai
$8-$19

The artful, contemporary Thai restaurant features classic entrees and new twists on old favorites. The extensive beverage menu lists an impressive tea selection from China, Japan and Thailand, as well as Thai beers and microbrews. Casual dress. **Bar:** Full bar. **Reservations:** suggested. **Hours:** 11 am-2 & 5-10 pm. **Address:** 410 SW Broadway **Location:** At SW Broadway and Stark St; in Hotel Lucia. **Parking:** street. **Cards:** AX, DS, MC, VI.

CALL

TYPHOON! Phone: 503/243-7557

Thai
$8-$19

The artful, contemporary Thai restaurant features classic entrees and new twists on old favorites. The extensive beverage menu lists an impressive tea selection from China, Japan and Thailand, as well as Thai beers and microbrews. Casual dress. **Bar:** Full bar. **Reservations:** suggested. **Hours:** 11 am-2 & 5-10 pm. Closed: 11/26, 12/25. **Address:** 2310 NW Everett St **Location:** Corner of NW 23rd Ave and NW Everett St. **Parking:** on-site. **Cards:** AX, DS, MC, VI.

UMENOKI JAPANESE RESTAURANT Phone: 503/242-6404 ⑦

Japanese
$6-$21

Featuring primarily a large variety of sushi and sashimi menu choices, the menu at this casual restaurant also has a good selection of other traditional Japanese food, including tempura items and combination meals served in a black box with multiple compartments. The dining room sports olive-colored walls with booth seating and light wood partitions dividing the room. Another option is to sit at the sushi bar and watch the chef at work. Casual dress. **Bar:** Beer & wine. **Reservations:** accepted. **Hours:** 11:30 am-2 & 5-9:30 pm, Fri & Sat-10 pm. Closed: 11/26, 12/25; also Sun. **Address:** 2330 NW Thurman St **Location:** Jct NW 23rd Ave, just w. **Parking:** on-site. **Cards:** MC, VI.

URBAN FONDUE Phone: 503/242-1400 ㊷

Fondue
$15-$23

This distinctive restaurant features interesting fondues to share, including smoked farmhouse cheddar for an appetizer, a variety of entree cooking broths and dipping sauces. There are also non-fondue items available. Dessert dips include white chocolate with lavender and bittersweet chocolate with hazelnuts. Plush seating, marble tables and contemporary decor enhance the delightful dining experience. Casual dress. **Bar:** Full bar. **Reservations:** suggested. **Hours:** 5 pm-10 pm, Fri & Sat-11 pm, Sun 5 pm-9 pm. Closed major holidays. **Address:** 2114 NW Glisan St **Location:** I-405, exit Everett St, 1 mi w on Glisan St; in Northwest District. **Parking:** street. **Cards:** AX, MC, VI.

VERITABLE QUANDARY Phone: 503/227-7342 ㊇⑦

American
$10-$30

Osso buco is a favorite among the changing menu selections. This is a popular after-hours spot, with an intimate, though sometimes lively, atmosphere. Dressy casual. **Bar:** Full bar. **Reservations:** accepted. **Hours:** 11 am-3 & 5-10 pm, Sat & Sun from 9:30 am; Saturday and Sunday brunch. Closed: 1/1, 11/26, 12/25. **Address:** 1220 SW 1st Ave **Location:** At SW Madison St. **Parking:** street. **Cards:** AX, CB, DC, DS, JC, MC, VI.

(See map and index starting on p. 396)

WIDMER GASTHAUS

German
$7-$22

Phone: 503/281-3333 ①

In a circa 1890 building not far from the convention center, the establishment serves German fare, along with sandwiches and burgers. Diners might want to start with cheese fondue before moving on to pork schnitzel and any of three types of slow-roasted sausage finished in Widmer Brothers Pale Ale. Beverage choices include fresh beers from the brewery and hand-crafted root beer. Brewery tours are given Friday at 3 and Saturday at 11 and noon; call 503-281-2437 for reservations. Casual dress. **Bar:** Beer & wine. **Hours:** 11 am-11 pm, Fri & Sat-1 am. Closed major holidays. **Address:** 955 N Russell St **Location:** Jct N Interstate Ave. **Parking:** on-site. **Cards:** AX, DS, MC, VI.

WILDWOOD
American
$9-$33

CALL ⑤ᴹ

Phone: 503/248-9663 ⑬

Art deco touches lend to the restaurant's trendy, upbeat atmosphere. An extensive selection of West Coast wines complements the seasonal market-driven menu, which emphasizes local Northwest food items. Casual dress. **Bar:** Full bar. **Reservations:** suggested. **Hours:** 11:30 am-9 pm, Fri & Sat-10 pm, Sun 5 pm-8:30 pm; to 10 pm, Fri & Sat-11 pm, Sun 5 pm-9 pm in summer. Closed major holidays. **Address:** 1221 NW 21st Ave **Location:** Jct NW Overton St. **Parking:** on-site. **Cards:** AX, MC, VI.

WILF'S RESTAURANT
Steak & Seafood
$10-$46

Phone: 503/223-0070 ㉕

In Union Station, which is on the National Historic Registry, the restaurant offers tableside preparation of selected dishes, including Caesar salad for two, steak Diane and mixed berry flambe. Wilf's prides itself on being a sustainable restaurant, and all meats and seafood are organic and hormone-free. Large windows afford a trackside view. Jazz entertainment adds to the enjoyable atmosphere. A casual bar menu is available. Casual dress. Entertainment. **Bar:** Full bar. **Reservations:** suggested. **Hours:** 11:30 am-11 pm, Fri-midnight, Sat 5 pm-midnight. Closed major holidays; also Sun. **Address:** 800 NW 6th Ave **Location:** Jct NW Irving St; in Union Station. **Parking:** on-site. **Cards:** AX, MC, VI. **Historic**

The following restaurants have not been evaluated by AAA but are listed for your information only.

DESCHUTES BREWERY & PUBLIC HOUSE
[fyi]

Phone: 503/296-4906

Not evaluated. A relative newcomer to the local dining scene, the brewery serves casual pub food with a variety of freshly made beers. **Address:** 210 NW 11th Ave **Location:** Corner NW 11th Ave and NW Davis St.

VIA DELIZIA
[fyi]

Phone: 503/225-9300

Not evaluated. A dessert cafe known for its 24 interesting flavors of delicious hand-crafted gelatos, the "street of delights" lives up to its name. The decor replicates an Italian courtyard beneath an olive tree. Those who want more than dessert can try panini sandwiches and a few entrees. **Address:** 1105 NW Marshall St **Location:** Jct NW 11th Ave; in Pearl District.

PORTLAND pop. 529,121 (See map and index starting on p. 402)

——— WHERE TO STAY ———

ALOFT PORTLAND AIRPORT AT CASCADE STATION
[fyi]
Hotel
Rates not provided

Phone: 503/200-5678

Too new to rate, opening scheduled for September 2008. **Address:** 9920 NE Cascade Pkwy **Location:** I-205, exit 24A northbound; exit 24 southbound, 0.5 mi w on Airport Way, then just se. **Amenities:** 136 units, pets, coffeemakers, refrigerators, pool.

AAA Benefit:
Enjoy the new twist, get up to 15% off Starwood Preferred Guest® bonuses.

AMERICAS BEST VALUE INN & SUITES-PORTLAND AIRPORT
Book at AAA.com
Hotel
$54-$79 All Year

Phone: (503)255-9771 ㉚

Address: 4911 NE 82nd Ave **Location:** I-84, exit 5 eastbound, 2 mi n; westbound, exit I-205 N to exit 23B (Killingsworth St), 0.5 mi w, then 0.6 mi s. **Facility:** 51 units. 29 two-bedroom standard units with kitchens (utensils extra charge). 22 one-bedroom suites with kitchens (utensils extra charge). 2 stories (no elevator), interior corridors. **Parking:** on-site. **Amenities:** high-speed Internet, voice mail, safes (fee), irons, hair dryers. **Pool(s):** heated outdoor. **Guest Services:** coin laundry, wireless Internet. **Cards:** AX, DS, MC, VI.

AVALON HOTEL & SPA
(AAA) [SAVE]
Hotel
$199-$599 All Year

Book great rates at AAA.com

Phone: (503)802-5800 ㊿

Address: 0455 SW Hamilton Ct **Location:** I-5, exit 298 northbound, just s on SW Corbett Ave, e on SW Richardson Ct, 0.3 mi n on Macadam Ave (SR 43), then just e; exit 299A southbound, follow signs for Johns Landing/Lake Oswego 0.8 mi s, then just e. Located adjacent to the Willamette River. **Facility:** Smoke free premises. 99 units. 81 one-bedroom standard units. 18 one-bedroom suites, some with whirlpools. 6 stories, interior corridors. *Bath:* combo or shower only. **Terms:** cancellation fee imposed. **Amenities:** CD players, high-speed Internet, dual phone lines, voice mail, safes, irons, hair dryers. *Some:* DVD players (fee). **Dining:** Aquariva Italian Kitchen & Wine Bar, see separate listing. **Leisure Activities:** saunas, whirlpools, steamrooms, jogging, spa. *Fee:* fitness instruction; riverfront trail. **Guest Services:** valet laundry, area transportation-downtown & train station, beauty salon, wireless Internet. **Business Services:** meeting rooms, business center. **Cards:** AX, CB, DC, DS, JC, MC, VI. **Free Special Amenities:** newspaper and high-speed Internet.

(See map and index starting on p. 402)

BANFIELD MOTEL

Book at AAA.com   Phone: (503)280-1400   37

Hotel
$65-$115 All Year

Address: 1525 NE 37th Ave **Location:** I-84, exit 2 eastbound, just n on NE 39th Ave, just w on NE Broadway St, then just s; exit southbound, just w on NE Halsey, just n on NE 39th Ave, just w on NE Broadway St, then just s. **Facility:** 50 one-bedroom standard units. 2 stories (no elevator), exterior corridors. **Parking:** on-site. **Amenities:** high-speed Internet, voice mail. **Pool(s):** heated outdoor. **Guest Services:** coin laundry, wireless Internet. **Cards:** AX, DS, MC, VI.

BEST WESTERN INN AT THE MEADOWS   *Book great rates at AAA.com*   Phone: (503)286-9600   8

Hotel
$121-$141 3/1-10/31
$105-$125 11/1-2/28

Address: 1215 N Hayden Meadows Dr **Location:** I-5, exit 306B, just e. **Facility:** 146 units. 144 one-bedroom standard units. 2 one-bedroom suites. 3 stories, interior corridors. **Parking:** on-site. **Amenities:** video games (fee), high-speed Internet, irons, hair dryers. **Leisure Activities:** whirlpool. **Guest Services:** valet and coin laundry, airport transportation-Portland International Airport, area transportation-within 5 mi, wireless Internet. **Business Services:** meeting rooms, PC. **Cards:** AX, DC, DS, MC, VI. **Free Special Amenities: expanded continental breakfast and high-speed Internet.**

AAA Benefit:
Members save up to 20%, plus 10% bonus points with rewards program.

BEST WESTERN PONY SOLDIER INN-AIRPORT   *Book great rates at AAA.com*   Phone: (503)256-1504   28

Hotel
$109-$209 All Year

Address: 9901 NE Sandy Blvd **Location:** I-205, exit 23A, just e. **Facility:** 102 one-bedroom standard units, some with efficiencies and/or whirlpools. 2 stories, interior corridors. **Parking:** on-site. **Amenities:** video games (fee), high-speed Internet, voice mail, irons, hair dryers. *Some:* DVD players, dual phone lines. **Pool(s):** outdoor. **Leisure Activities:** sauna, whirlpool, exercise room. **Guest Services:** complimentary and valet laundry, airport transportation-Portland International Airport, area transportation-within 5 mi, wireless Internet. **Business Services:** meeting rooms, PC. **Cards:** AX, CB, DC, DS, JC, MC, VI. **Free Special Amenities: expanded continental breakfast and high-speed Internet.**

AAA Benefit:
Members save up to 20%, plus 10% bonus points with rewards program.

BRIARWOOD SUITES   *Book great rates at AAA.com*   Phone: (503)788-9394   49

Motel
$64-$109 All Year

Address: 7740 SE Powell Blvd **Location:** I-205, exit 19, 1 mi w. **Facility:** 40 one-bedroom standard units. 2 stories, exterior corridors. **Parking:** on-site. **Terms:** cancellation fee imposed. **Amenities:** high-speed Internet, voice mail, hair dryers. **Guest Services:** coin laundry, wireless Internet. **Cards:** AX, DS, MC, VI. **Free Special Amenities: newspaper and high-speed Internet.** *(See color ad p 433)*

CHESTNUT TREE INN   Phone: (503)255-4444   47

Motel
$55-$85 All Year

Address: 9699 SE Stark St **Location:** I-205, exit 21A southbound; exit 20 northbound, just e on Washington St, just n on SE 99th St, then just w. **Facility:** 58 one-bedroom standard units, some with kitchens (no utensils). 2 stories (no elevator), exterior corridors. **Parking:** on-site. **Cards:** AX, CB, DC, MC, VI. **Free Special Amenities: expanded continental breakfast and local telephone calls.**

CLARION HOTEL PORTLAND AIRPORT   *Book great rates at AAA.com*   Phone: 503/252-2222   19

Hotel
Rates not provided

Address: 11518 NE Glenn Widing Dr **Location:** I-205, exit 24B northbound; exit 24 southbound, 0.4 mi e, then just n. **Facility:** 101 units. 94 one-bedroom standard units, some with whirlpools. 7 one-bedroom suites. 4 stories, interior corridors. *Bath:* combo or shower only. **Parking:** on-site. **Amenities:** high-speed Internet, voice mail, irons, hair dryers. **Pool(s):** heated indoor. **Leisure Activities:** whirlpool, exercise room. **Guest Services:** valet and coin laundry, airport transportation-Portland International Airport, wireless Internet. **Business Services:** meeting rooms, PC. **Free Special Amenities: local telephone calls and high-speed Internet.**

COMFORT INN   *Book great rates at AAA.com*   Phone: (503)408-8000   40

Hotel
$79-$169 All Year

Address: 8225 NE Wasco St **Location:** I-84, exit 5 eastbound, just n on NE 82nd Ave, then just e; I-205, exit 21A northbound, 0.7 mi w on Glisan St, then 0.4 mi n on 82nd Ave; I-84 westbound and I-205 southbound follow signs to I-205 southbound, exit 21A, 0.7 mi w on Glisan St, then 0.4 mi n on 82nd Ave. Located near the lightrail line. **Facility:** 66 one-bedroom standard units, some with whirlpools. 3 stories, interior corridors. *Bath:* combo or shower only. **Parking:** on-site. **Terms:** cancellation fee imposed. **Amenities:** high-speed Internet, voice mail, irons, hair dryers. **Pool(s):** heated indoor. **Leisure Activities:** whirlpool, exercise room. **Guest Services:** coin laundry, wireless Internet. **Business Services:** meeting rooms, PC. **Cards:** AX, DC, DS, MC, VI.

(See map and index starting on p. 402)

COMFORT SUITES

Book great rates at AAA.com

Hotel

$109-$159 3/1-9/30
$99-$149 10/1-2/28

Phone: (503)768-4400 **52**
Address: 11340 SW 60th Ave **Location:** I-5, exit 296A (Barbur Blvd) southbound, 2 mi s, then just e; exit 294 northbound, just e. Located in a quiet area. **Facility:** Smoke free premises. 52 one-bedroom standard units, some with whirlpools. 3 stories, interior corridors. *Bath:* combo or shower only. **Parking:** on-site. **Amenities:** high-speed Internet, dual phone lines, voice mail, irons, hair dryers. **Pool(s):** heated indoor. **Leisure Activities:** whirlpool, small library, exercise room. **Guest Services:** valet and coin laundry, wireless Internet. **Business Services:** meeting rooms, business center. **Cards:** AX, CB, DC, DS, JC, MC, VI. **Free Special Amenities:** expanded continental breakfast and high-speed Internet.

▼ See AAA listing p 432 ▼

At 60 mph, if you reach down
to change the radio station
you can travel the length
of a football field.

Stay Focused

Keep your mind on the road.

(See map and index starting on p. 402)

COMFORT SUITES

Hotel
$89-$149 All Year

Book great rates at AAA.com **Phone:** (503)261-9000 **21**

Address: 12010 NE Airport Way **Location:** I-205, exit 24B northbound; exit 24 southbound, 0.7 mi e. **Facility:** Smoke free premises. 81 one-bedroom standard units, some with whirlpools. 3 stories, interior corridors. *Bath:* combo or shower only. **Parking:** on-site. **Amenities:** high-speed Internet, dual phone lines, voice mail, irons, hair dryers. **Pool(s):** heated indoor. **Leisure Activities:** sauna, whirlpool, exercise room. **Guest Services:** valet and coin laundry, airport transportation-Portland International Airport, area transportation-light rail, wireless Internet. **Business Services:** meeting rooms, PC. **Cards:** AX, DS, MC, VI. **Free Special Amenities:** full breakfast and high-speed Internet.

COUNTRY INN & SUITES AT PORTLAND AIRPORT *Book at AAA.com* **Phone:** (503)255-2700 **13**

Hotel
$104-$118 All Year

Address: 7025 NE Alderwood Rd **Location:** I-205, exit 24A (Airport Way) northbound; exit 24 southbound, 1.3 mi w on Airport Way, 0.4 mi sw on NE 82nd Ave, then just w. **Facility:** 153 one-bedroom standard units, some with kitchens and/or whirlpools. 4 stories, interior corridors. *Bath:* combo or shower only. **Parking:** on-site. **Terms:** cancellation fee imposed. **Amenities:** video games (fee), high-speed Internet, dual phone lines, voice mail, irons, hair dryers. **Pool(s):** heated indoor. **Leisure Activities:** whirlpool, exercise room. **Guest Services:** valet and coin laundry, area transportation, wireless Internet. **Business Services:** meeting rooms, business center. **Cards:** AX, CB, DC, DS, MC, VI.

COURTYARD BY MARRIOTT *Book great rates at AAA.com* **Phone:** (503)252-3200 **20**

Hotel
$161-$197 All Year

Address: 11550 NE Airport Way **Location:** I-205, exit 24B northbound; exit 24 southbound, 0.5 mi e. **Facility:** Smoke free premises. 150 units. 140 one-bedroom standard units. 10 one-bedroom suites. 6 stories, interior corridors. *Bath:* combo or shower only. **Parking:** on-site. **Terms:** cancellation fee imposed. **Amenities:** video games (fee), high-speed Internet, dual phone lines, voice mail, irons, hair dryers. **Pool(s):** heated outdoor. **Leisure Activities:** whirlpool, exercise room. **Guest Services:** valet and coin laundry, area transportation, wireless Internet. **Business Services:** meeting rooms, business center. **Cards:** AX, CB, DC, DS, JC, MC, VI.

AAA Benefit:
Members save a
minimum 5% off the
best available rate.

COURTYARD BY MARRIOTT-PORTLAND LLOYD CENTER *Book great rates at AAA.com* **Phone:** (503)234-3200 **41**

Hotel
$189-$199 All Year

Address: 435 NE Wasco St **Location:** I-5, exit 302A, just e on NE Weidler St, just s on NE Martin Luther King Jr Blvd, then just e. **Facility:** Smoke free premises. 202 units. 193 one-bedroom standard units, some with whirlpools. 9 one-bedroom suites. 6 stories, interior corridors. *Bath:* combo or shower only. **Parking:** on-site (fee). **Terms:** cancellation fee imposed. **Amenities:** video games (fee), high-speed Internet, dual phone lines, voice mail, irons, hair dryers. **Pool(s):** heated indoor. **Leisure Activities:** whirlpool, exercise room. **Guest Services:** valet and coin laundry, area transportation, wireless Internet. **Business Services:** meeting rooms, business center. **Cards:** AX, CB, DC, DS, JC, MC, VI.

AAA Benefit:
Members save a
minimum 5% off the
best available rate.

COURTYARD BY MARRIOTT-PORTLAND NORTH HARBOUR *Book great rates at AAA.com* **Phone:** (503)735-1818 **4**

Hotel
$149-$159 All Year

Address: 1231 N Anchor Way **Location:** I-5, exit 307, follow signs to Marine Dr E, then just n. Located by a river. **Facility:** Smoke free premises. 133 units. 128 one-bedroom standard units, some with whirlpools. 5 one-bedroom suites. 4 stories, interior corridors. *Bath:* combo or shower only. **Parking:** on-site. **Terms:** cancellation fee imposed. **Amenities:** video games (fee), high-speed Internet, dual phone lines, voice mail, irons, hair dryers. **Pool(s):** heated indoor. **Leisure Activities:** whirlpool, exercise room. **Guest Services:** valet and coin laundry, area transportation, wireless Internet. **Business Services:** conference facilities, business center. **Cards:** AX, CB, DC, DS, JC, MC, VI.

AAA Benefit:
Members save a
minimum 5% off the
best available rate.

(See map and index starting on p. 402)

CROWNE PLAZA PORTLAND DOWNTOWN/CONVENTION CENTER   *Book great rates at AAA.com*   Phone: (503)233-2401   **39**

Hotel
$129-$199 All Year

Address: 1441 NE 2nd Ave **Location:** I-5, exit 302A, just e on NE Weidler St, then just s. **Facility:** Smoke free premises. 241 units. 239 one-bedroom standard units. 2 one-bedroom suites. 10 stories, interior corridors. *Bath:* combo or shower only. **Parking:** on-site (fee). **Terms:** 5 day cancellation notice. **Amenities:** CD players, high-speed Internet, voice mail, irons, hair dryers. *Some:* safes. **Pool(s):** heated indoor. **Leisure Activities:** whirlpool, exercise room. **Guest Services:** valet and coin laundry, area transportation, wireless Internet. **Business Services:** conference facilities, business center. **Cards:** AX, CB, DC, DS, JC, MC, VI. *(See color ad below)*

DAYS INN-PORTLAND   *Book great rates at AAA.com*   Phone: (503)289-1800   **7**

Hotel
$72-$81 All Year

Address: 9930 N Whitaker Rd **Location:** I-5, exit 306B, just e. **Facility:** 210 one-bedroom standard units, some with efficiencies. 4 stories, interior corridors. *Bath:* combo or shower only. **Parking:** on-site. **Amenities:** video games (fee), high-speed Internet, voice mail, hair dryers. **Leisure Activities:** exercise room. **Guest Services:** valet and coin laundry, airport transportation-Portland International Airport, area transportation-within 9 mi & Expo Center, wireless Internet. **Business Services:** meeting rooms, PC (fee). **Cards:** AX, DC, DS, MC, VI. **Free Special Amenities: expanded continental breakfast and high-speed Internet.**

DAYS INN PORTLAND AIRPORT   *Book great rates at AAA.com*   Phone: (503)253-1151   **36**

Hotel
$85-$95 7/1-2/28
$75-$85 3/1-6/30

Address: 1530 NE 82nd Ave **Location:** I-84, exit 5 eastbound, just n on NE 82nd Ave, then just e on Jonesmore St; exit westbound, follow signs to I-205 northbound, exit 21A, 0.7 mi w on Glisan St, 0.5 mi n on 82nd Ave, then just e on Jonesmore St. **Facility:** 40 one-bedroom standard units. 2 stories (no elevator), exterior corridors. **Parking:** on-site. **Terms:** cancellation fee imposed. **Amenities:** high-speed Internet, irons, hair dryers. **Guest Services:** wireless Internet. **Cards:** AX, DS, MC, VI. **Free Special Amenities: continental breakfast and high-speed Internet.**

▼ *See AAA listing above* ▼

(See map and index starting on p. 402)

DOUBLETREE HOTEL PORTLAND   *Book great rates at AAA.com*   Phone: (503)281-6111   **43**

Hotel
$105-$245 All Year

Address: 1000 NE Multnomah St **Location:** I-5, exit 302A, just e, just s on 9th Ave, then just e; I-84 westbound, exit Lloyd Center. Located opposite Lloyd Center Mall, park and light rail. **Facility:** Smoke free premises. 476 units. 459 one-bedroom standard units. 17 one-bedroom suites, some with whirlpools. 9-15 stories, interior corridors. *Bath:* combo or shower only. **Parking:** on-site (fee) and valet. **Terms:** 1-30 night minimum stay, cancellation fee imposed. **Amenities:** voice mail, irons, hair dryers. *Fee:* video games, high-speed Internet. *Some:* DVD players. **Dining:** 2 restaurants. **Pool(s):** heated outdoor. **Leisure Activities:** exercise room. **Guest Services:** valet laundry, area transportation-hospitals within 5 mi & train station, wireless Internet. **Business Services:** conference facilities, business center. **Cards:** AX, CB, DC, DS, JC, MC, VI.

DoubleTree
HOTELS·SUITES·RESORTS·CLUBS

AAA Benefit:
Members save 5% or more everyday!

EMBASSY SUITES AT PORTLAND AIRPORT   *Book great rates at AAA.com*   Phone: (503)460-3000   **12**

Hotel
$109-$189 All Year

Address: 7900 NE 82nd Ave **Location:** I-205, exit 24A northbound; exit 24 southbound, 1.3 mi w. **Facility:** 251 one-bedroom suites, some with whirlpools. 8 stories, interior corridors. *Bath:* combo or shower only. **Parking:** on-site. **Terms:** 1-30 night minimum stay, cancellation fee imposed. **Amenities:** dual phone lines, voice mail, irons, hair dryers. *Fee:* video games, high-speed Internet. **Pool(s):** heated indoor. **Leisure Activities:** sauna, whirlpool, sun deck, exercise room. **Guest Services:** valet and coin laundry, airport transportation-Portland International Airport, wireless Internet. **Business Services:** conference facilities, business center. **Cards:** AX, CB, DC, DS, JC, MC, VI. **Free Special Amenities:** full breakfast and newspaper.

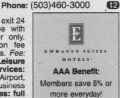

E
EMBASSY SUITES
HOTELS·

AAA Benefit:
Members save 5% or more everyday!

FAIRFIELD INN & SUITES - PORTLAND NORTH
HARBOUR   *Book great rates at AAA.com*   Phone: (503)286-6336   **6**

Hotel
$116-$142 All Year

Address: 1200 N Anchor Way **Location:** I-5, exit 307, follow signs to Marine Dr E, then just n. **Facility:** Smoke free premises. 93 one-bedroom standard units. 3 stories, interior corridors. *Bath:* combo or shower only. **Parking:** on-site. **Terms:** cancellation fee imposed. **Amenities:** high-speed Internet, voice mail, irons, hair dryers. **Pool(s):** heated indoor. **Leisure Activities:** whirlpool, exercise room. **Guest Services:** valet and coin laundry, area transportation, wireless Internet. **Business Services:** PC. **Cards:** AX, DS, MC, VI.

FAIRFIELD
INN & SUITES
Marriott

AAA Benefit:
Members save a minimum 5% off the best available rate.

FAIRFIELD INN BY MARRIOTT   *Book great rates at AAA.com*   Phone: (503)253-1400   **23**

Hotel
$129-$139 All Year

Address: 11929 NE Airport Way **Location:** I-205, exit 24B northbound; exit 24 southbound, 0.7 mi e. **Facility:** Smoke free premises. 106 one-bedroom standard units. 3 stories, interior corridors. *Bath:* combo or shower only. **Parking:** on-site. **Terms:** cancellation fee imposed. **Amenities:** high-speed Internet, voice mail, irons, hair dryers. **Pool(s):** heated outdoor. **Leisure Activities:** whirlpool, exercise room. **Guest Services:** valet laundry, area transportation, wireless Internet. **Business Services:** PC. **Cards:** AX, CB, DC, DS, JC, MC, VI.

FAIRFIELD
INN
Marriott

AAA Benefit:
Members save a minimum 5% off the best available rate.

GEORGIAN HOUSE BED & BREAKFAST   Phone: 503/281-2250   **33**

Bed & Breakfast
$90-$135 All Year

Address: 1828 NE Siskiyou St **Location:** I-5, exit 302A, 0.7 mi e on Weidler St, then 0.7 mi n on NE 15th Ave, then just e; jct NE 19th Ave. Located in Historic Irvington District. **Facility:** In a quiet residential neighborhood, this Georgian colonial B&B offers a gazebo, a deck and a lovely English garden; guest rooms have antiques. Smoke free premises. 4 one-bedroom standard units. 3 stories (no elevator), interior corridors. *Bath:* some shared or private. **Parking:** on-site and street. **Terms:** office hours 6 am-10 pm, 14 day cancellation notice-fee imposed. **Amenities:** video library, hair dryers. *Some:* DVD players, CD players. **Cards:** MC, VI.

(See map and index starting on p. 402)

HAMPTON INN-PORTLAND AIRPORT Book great rates at AAA.com   Phone: (503)288-2423   ⑪

Hotel
$154 All Year

Address: 8633 NE Airport Way **Location:** I-205, exit 24A northbound; exit 24 southbound, 1.4 mi w. **Facility:** 129 one-bedroom standard units. 4 stories, interior corridors. *Bath:* combo or shower only. **Parking:** on-site. **Terms:** 1-30 night minimum stay, cancellation fee imposed. **Amenities:** video games (fee), high-speed Internet, voice mail, irons, hair dryers. **Pool(s):** outdoor. **Leisure Activities:** whirlpool. **Guest Services:** valet laundry, wireless Internet. **Business Services:** meeting rooms, PC. **Cards:** AX, CB, DC, DS, MC, VI.

AAA Benefit:
Members save up to 10% everyday!

HILTON GARDEN INN-PORTLAND AIRPORT   Book great rates at AAA.com   Phone: (503)255-8600   ㉖

Hotel
$89-$141 All Year

Address: 12048 NE Airport Way **Location:** I-205, exit 24B northbound; exit 24 southbound, 0.8 mi e. **Facility:** Smoke free premises. 121 units. 113 one-bedroom standard units. 8 one-bedroom suites. 4 stories, interior corridors. *Bath:* combo or shower only. **Parking:** on-site. **Terms:** 1-30 night minimum stay, cancellation fee imposed. **Amenities:** high-speed Internet, dual phone lines, voice mail, irons, hair dryers. **Pool(s):** heated indoor. **Leisure Activities:** whirlpool, exercise room. **Guest Services:** valet and coin laundry, airport transportation-Portland International Airport, wireless Internet. **Business Services:** meeting rooms, business center. **Cards:** AX, CB, DC, DS, JC, MC, VI. **Free Special Amenities:** newspaper and early check-in/late check-out.

Hilton Garden Inn

AAA Benefit:
Members save 5% or more everyday!

HOLIDAY INN EXPRESS HOTEL & SUITES AT JANTZEN BEACH   Book great rates at AAA.com   Phone: (503)283-8000   ❶

Hotel
$95 All Year

Address: 2300 N Hayden Island Dr **Location:** I-5, exit 308, 0.6 mi w. **Facility:** 74 units. 68 one- and 6 two-bedroom standard units, some with whirlpools. 4 stories, interior corridors. *Bath:* combo or shower only. **Parking:** on-site. **Amenities:** high-speed Internet, dual phone lines, voice mail, irons, hair dryers. **Pool(s):** heated indoor. **Leisure Activities:** sauna, whirlpool, exercise room. **Guest Services:** valet and coin laundry, wireless Internet. **Business Services:** meeting rooms, PC. **Cards:** AX, DC, DS, MC, VI. **Free Special Amenities:** expanded continental breakfast and high-speed Internet.

HOLIDAY INN EXPRESS HOTEL & SUITES-PORTLAND AIRPORT   Book great rates at AAA.com   Phone: (503)251-9991   ㉔

Hotel
$99-$159 3/1-11/30
$79-$139 12/1-2/28

Address: 11938 NE Airport Way **Location:** I-205, exit 24B northbound; exit 24 southbound, 0.6 mi e. **Facility:** Smoke free premises. 79 units. 76 one-bedroom standard units, some with whirlpools. 3 one-bedroom suites. 3 stories, interior corridors. *Bath:* combo or shower only. **Parking:** on-site. **Terms:** check-in 4 pm, cancellation fee imposed. **Amenities:** high-speed Internet, dual phone lines, voice mail, irons, hair dryers. **Leisure Activities:** sauna, whirlpool, exercise room. **Guest Services:** valet and coin laundry, airport transportation-Portland International Airport, area transportation-light rail station, wireless Internet. **Business Services:** PC. **Cards:** AX, DS, MC, VI.

HOLIDAY INN EXPRESS-I-205 STARK   Book great rates at AAA.com   Phone: 503/252-7400   ㊽

Hotel
Rates not provided

Address: 9707 SE Stark St **Location:** I-205, exit 21A southbound; exit 20 northbound, just e on Washington St, just n on SE 99th Ave, then just w. **Facility:** Smoke free premises. 84 one-bedroom standard units. 3 stories, interior corridors. *Bath:* combo or shower only. **Parking:** on-site. **Amenities:** video games (fee), high-speed Internet, dual phone lines, voice mail, irons, hair dryers. **Leisure Activities:** whirlpool, exercise room. **Guest Services:** valet laundry, wireless Internet. **Business Services:** meeting rooms, PC.

HOLIDAY INN PORTLAND AIRPORT HOTEL & CONVENTION CENTER   Book great rates at AAA.com   Phone: (503)256-5000   ㉗

Hotel
$119-$229 All Year

Address: 8439 NE Columbia Blvd **Location:** I-205, exit 23B, 0.5 mi w. **Facility:** 284 units. 268 one-bedroom standard units. 16 one-bedroom suites. 8 stories, interior corridors. *Bath:* some combo or shower only. **Parking:** on-site. **Amenities:** video games (fee), high-speed Internet, dual phone lines, voice mail, irons, hair dryers. **Dining:** nightclub. **Pool(s):** heated indoor. **Leisure Activities:** whirlpool, exercise room. **Guest Services:** valet and coin laundry, airport transportation-Portland International Airport, area transportation-light rail station, wireless Internet. **Business Services:** conference facilities, PC. **Cards:** AX, CB, DC, DS, JC, MC, VI. **Free Special Amenities:** newspaper.

HOSPITALITY INN   Book great rates at AAA.com   Phone: (503)244-6684   ㊿①

Hotel
$79-$129 All Year

Address: 10155 SW Capitol Hwy **Location:** I-5, exit 295 southbound; exit 294 northbound, just e. **Facility:** 53 one-bedroom standard units, some with whirlpools. 3 stories, interior corridors. *Bath:* combo or shower only. **Parking:** on-site. **Terms:** cancellation fee imposed. **Amenities:** video library (fee), DVD players, high-speed Internet, irons, hair dryers. **Leisure Activities:** whirlpool, limited exercise equipment. **Guest Services:** coin laundry, wireless Internet. **Business Services:** meeting rooms. **Cards:** AX, DS, MC, VI. **Free Special Amenities:** expanded continental breakfast and high-speed Internet.

(See map and index starting on p. 402)

HOWARD JOHNSON PORTLAND AIRPORT *Book great rates at AAA.com* **Phone: (503)256-4111** **32**

Address: 8247 NE Sandy Blvd **Location:** I-84, exit 5 eastbound, 1.5 mi n on 82nd Ave; exit I-205 N westbound; I-205, exit 23A southbound; exit 23B northbound (US 30 business route/Sandy Blvd W), 1 mi w. **Facility:** 110 units. 108 one-bedroom standard units, some with whirlpools. 2 one-bedroom suites. 3 stories (no elevator), interior/exterior corridors. **Parking:** on-site. **Amenities:** high-speed Internet, irons, hair dryers. **Pool(s):** heated outdoor. **Guest Services:** valet and coin laundry, airport transportation-Portland International Airport, area transportation-light rail station, wireless Internet. **Business Services:** meeting rooms, PC. **Cards:** AX, CB, DC, DS, JC, MC, VI. **Free Special Amenities: expanded continental breakfast and high-speed Internet.**

Hotel
$75-$120 6/1-2/28
$65-$105 3/1-5/31

LA QUINTA INN & SUITES PORTLAND AIRPORT *Book great rates at AAA.com* **Phone: (503)382-3820** **18**

Address: 11207 NE Holman St **Location:** I-205, exit 24B northbound; exit 24 southbound, 0.4 mi e on Airport Way, then just sw. **Facility:** Smoke free premises. 98 one-bedroom standard units. 4 stories, interior corridors. *Bath:* combo or shower only. **Parking:** on-site. **Amenities:** high-speed Internet, dual phone lines, voice mail, irons, hair dryers. **Pool(s):** heated indoor. **Leisure Activities:** whirlpool, exercise room. **Guest Services:** valet and coin laundry, area transportation, wireless Internet. **Business Services:** meeting rooms, PC. **Cards:** AX, CB, DS, MC, VI.

Hotel
$69-$134 All Year

LA QUINTA INN PORTLAND LLOYD CENTER/ CONVENTION CENTER *Book great rates at AAA.com* **Phone: (503)233-7933** **42**

Address: 431 NE Multnomah St **Location:** I-5, exit 302A, just e on NE Weidler St, just s on NE Martin Luther King Jr Blvd, then just e. **Facility:** 79 one-bedroom standard units, some with whirlpools. 2 stories, interior corridors. *Bath:* combo or shower only. **Parking:** on-site. **Amenities:** high-speed Internet, voice mail, irons, hair dryers. **Pool(s):** heated indoor. **Leisure Activities:** exercise room. **Guest Services:** valet laundry, wireless Internet. **Business Services:** meeting rooms, PC. **Cards:** AX, CB, DS, JC, MC, VI.

Hotel
$69-$120 All Year

LION AND THE ROSE VICTORIAN BED & BREAKFAST INN **Phone: 503/287-9245** **35**

Address: 1810 NE 15th Ave **Location:** I-5, exit 302A, 0.7 mi e on Weidler St, then just n. Located in Historic Irvington District. **Facility:** This landmark 1906 Queen Anne home is within walking distance of shops, theaters and restaurants and is near the light rail and convention center. Smoke free premises. 7 one-bedroom standard units, some with whirlpools. 2 stories (no elevator), interior corridors. *Bath:* combo or shower only. **Parking:** street. **Terms:** office hours 7 am-10 pm, 7 day cancellation notice-fee imposed. **Amenities:** high-speed Internet, irons, hair dryers. **Guest Services:** wireless Internet. **Business Services:** PC. **Cards:** AX, DS, MC, VI. **Free Special Amenities: local telephone calls and high-speed Internet.**

Historic Bed & Breakfast
$124-$244 All Year

MOTEL 6 NORTH PORTLAND #4198 *Book at AAA.com* **Phone: 503/247-3700** **9**

Address: 1125 N Schmeer Rd **Location:** I-5, exit 306B, 0.4 mi s on N Whitaker Rd, then just e. **Facility:** 65 one-bedroom standard units. 3 stories, interior corridors. *Bath:* combo or shower only. **Parking:** on-site. **Amenities:** high-speed Internet, voice mail. **Leisure Activities:** whirlpool. **Guest Services:** coin laundry, wireless Internet.

Hotel
Rates not provided

NORDIC MOTEL *Book great rates at AAA.com* **Phone: (503)253-6427** **31**

Address: 11942 NE Sandy Blvd **Location:** I-205, exit 23A (Sandy Blvd), 1 mi e. **Facility:** 24 units. 21 one- and 3 two-bedroom standard units, some with kitchens (no utensils). 1 story, exterior corridors. *Bath:* combo or shower only. **Parking:** on-site. **Terms:** cancellation fee imposed. **Amenities:** dual phone lines. **Guest Services:** wireless Internet. **Cards:** AX, DS, MC, VI. **Free Special Amenities: early check-in/late check-out and high-speed Internet.**

Motel
$72-$95 3/1-9/15
$72-$90 9/16-2/28

OXFORD SUITES *Book great rates at AAA.com* **Phone: (503)283-3030** **3**

Address: 12226 N Jantzen Dr **Location:** I-5, exit 308, just e on Hayden Island Dr. Located at Jantzen Beach. **Facility:** 200 units. 190 one- and 4 two-bedroom standard units, some with whirlpools. 2 one- and 4 two-bedroom suites. 4 stories, interior corridors. *Bath:* combo or shower only. **Parking:** on-site. **Terms:** cancellation fee imposed. **Amenities:** video library (fee), high-speed Internet, voice mail, irons, hair dryers. *Some:* DVD players. **Pool(s):** heated indoor. **Leisure Activities:** sauna, whirlpool, steamroom. **Guest Services:** valet and coin laundry, airport transportation-Portland International Airport, area transportation-Expo Center & Portland International Raceway, wireless Internet. **Business Services:** meeting rooms, business center. **Cards:** AX, DC, DS, MC, VI. **Free Special Amenities: full breakfast and high-speed Internet.**

Hotel
$139-$199 All Year

PORTLAND'S WHITE HOUSE **Phone: 503/287-7131** **34**

Address: 1914 NE 22nd Ave **Location:** I-5, exit 302A, 1.1 mi e on NE Weidler St, just n on NE 22nd Ave, then n. Located in a historical residential area. **Facility:** This beautiful historic property built in 1911 offers upscale appointments and is convenient to restaurants and shopping. 8 one-bedroom standard units, some with whirlpools. 3 stories (no elevator), interior corridors. *Bath:* combo or shower only. **Parking:** street. **Amenities:** CD players, high-speed Internet, hair dryers. *Some:* DVD players. **Guest Services:** wireless Internet. **Business Services:** meeting rooms.

Classic Historic Bed & Breakfast
Rates not provided

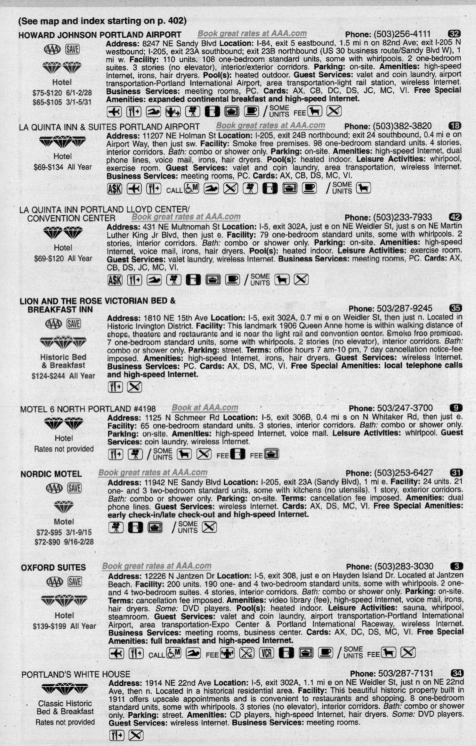

(See map and index starting on p. 402)

QUALITY INN & SUITES AIRPORT CONVENTION CENTER *Book great rates at AAA.com*   Phone: (503)255-1404 **29**

AAA [SAVE]
▼▼▼▼
Hotel
$99-$169 All Year

Address: 9727 NE Sandy Blvd **Location:** I-205, exit 23A, just e. Located near light rail. **Facility:** Smoke free premises. 65 units. 61 one-bedroom standard units. 4 one-bedroom suites with efficiencies. 2 stories (no elevator), exterior corridors. *Bath:* combo or shower only. **Parking:** on-site. **Amenities:** high-speed Internet, voice mail, irons, hair dryers. **Pool(s):** heated outdoor. **Leisure Activities:** exercise room. **Guest Services:** valet and coin laundry, airport transportation-Portland International Airport, area transportation-within 5 mi, wireless Internet. **Business Services:** conference facilities. **Cards:** AX, DC, DS, JC, MC, VI. **Free Special Amenities: expanded continental breakfast and high-speed Internet.** *(See color ad below)*

RADISSON HOTEL PORTLAND AIRPORT *Book great rates at AAA.com*   Phone: (503)251-2000 **16**

AAA [SAVE]
▼▼▼
Hotel
$99-$179 All Year

Address: 6233 NE 78th Ct **Location:** I-205, exit 23B (Killingsworth St), 0.9 mi w on NE Columbia Blvd, just n on NE 80th Ave, then just w on NE Holman St. Adjacent to a golf course. **Facility:** 192 units. 186 one-bedroom standard units, some with whirlpools. 6 one-bedroom suites. 4 stories, interior corridors. *Bath:* combo or shower only. **Parking:** on-site. **Amenities:** video games (fee), high-speed Internet, dual phone lines, voice mail, irons, hair dryers. *Some:* CD players. **Pool(s):** heated indoor. **Leisure Activities:** sauna, whirlpool, sun deck, walking path, exercise room. **Guest Services:** complimentary and valet laundry, airport transportation-Portland International Airport, area transportation-light rail station, wireless Internet. **Business Services:** meeting rooms, business center. **Cards:** AX, CB, DC, DS, JC, MC, VI. **Free Special Amenities: newspaper and high-speed Internet.**

RAMADA PORTLAND *Book great rates at AAA.com*   Phone: (503)255-6511 **15**

AAA [SAVE]
▼▼ ▼
Hotel
$79-$199 3/1-10/31
$69-$159 11/1-2/28

Address: 6221 NE 82nd Ave **Location:** I-205, exit 23B (Killingsworth St), just w on Columbia Blvd, then just n on 80th Ave. **Facility:** 198 units. 196 one-bedroom standard units. 2 one-bedroom suites with whirlpools. 2 stories, interior corridors. *Bath:* combo or shower only. **Parking:** on-site. **Amenities:** voice mail, irons, hair dryers. *Some:* safes. **Pool(s):** heated outdoor. **Leisure Activities:** sauna, whirlpool, exercise room. **Guest Services:** valet and coin laundry, airport transportation-Portland International Airport, wireless Internet. **Business Services:** PC. **Cards:** AX, DS, MC, VI. **Free Special Amenities: local telephone calls and high-speed Internet.**

(See map and index starting on p. 402)

RED LION HOTEL ON THE RIVER JANTZEN BEACH-PORTLAND
Book great rates at AAA.com   Phone: (503)283-4466   **2**

Hotel
$169 All Year

Address: 909 N Hayden Island Dr **Location:** I-5, exit 308, just ne. **Facility:** Smoke free premises. 318 units. 307 one- and 4 two-bedroom standard units. 7 one-bedroom suites. 4 stories, interior corridors. *Bath:* combo or shower only. **Parking:** on-site. **Terms:** cancellation fee imposed. **Amenities:** high-speed Internet, voice mail, safes, irons, hair dryers. **Dining:** 2 restaurants, also, Shenanigans, see separate listing. **Pool(s):** heated outdoor. **Leisure Activities:** whirlpool, boat dock, 2 lighted tennis courts, exercise room. **Guest Services:** valet and coin laundry, airport transportation-Portland International Airport, area transportation-shopping mall & light rail station, wireless Internet. **Business Services:** conference facilities, business center. **Cards:** AX, CB, DC, DS, JC, MC, VI. **Free Special Amenities: local telephone calls and high-speed Internet.**

RED LION HOTEL PORTLAND AIRPORT
Book great rates at AAA.com   Phone: 503/255-6722   **14**

Hotel
Rates not provided

Address: 7101 NE 82nd Ave **Location:** I-205, exit 24A northbound; exit 24 southbound, 1.3 mi w on NE Airport Way, then 0.5 mi s. **Facility:** Smoke free premises. 136 units. 134 one-bedroom standard units. 2 one-bedroom suites. 2 stories (no elevator), interior/exterior corridors. *Bath:* combo or shower only. **Parking:** on-site. **Amenities:** high-speed Internet, voice mail, irons, hair dryers. **Pool(s):** heated outdoor. **Leisure Activities:** sauna, whirlpool, exercise room. **Guest Services:** valet and coin laundry, airport transportation-Portland International Airport, area transportation-light rail station, wireless Internet. **Business Services:** meeting rooms, PC (fee). **Free Special Amenities: local telephone calls and high-speed Internet.**

RED LION HOTEL PORTLAND-CONVENTION CENTER
Book great rates at AAA.com   Phone: (503)235-2100   **45**

Hotel
$126-$170 All Year

Address: 1021 NE Grand Ave **Location:** I-5, exit 302A, just e on NE Weidler St, just s on NE Martin Luther King Jr Blvd, then just e. Located adjacent to the convention center. **Facility:** Smoke free premises. 174 units. 172 one-bedroom standard units. 2 one-bedroom suites with whirlpools. 6 stories, interior corridors. **Parking:** on-site (fee). **Terms:** cancellation fee imposed. **Amenities:** video games (fee), high-speed Internet, voice mail, irons, hair dryers. *Some:* DVD players, CD players. **Leisure Activities:** exercise room. **Guest Services:** valet and coin laundry, wireless Internet. **Business Services:** conference facilities, PC. **Cards:** AX, DS, MC, VI. **Free Special Amenities: local telephone calls and high-speed Internet.** *(See color ad p 418)*

RESIDENCE INN BY MARRIOTT PORTLAND DOWNTOWN/LLOYD CENTER
Book great rates at AAA.com   Phone: (503)288-1400   **44**

Hotel
$174-$189 All Year

Address: 1710 NE Multnomah St **Location:** I-5, exit 302A, 0.8 mi e on Weidler St, then just s on 15th Ave; I-84, exit 1 (Lloyd Center) westbound, just n on 13th St, then just e. **Facility:** Smoke free premises. 168 units. 128 one-bedroom standard units, some with kitchens. 16 one- and 24 two-bedroom suites with kitchens. 3 stories (no elevator), exterior corridors. *Bath:* combo or shower only. **Parking:** on-site. **Terms:** check-in 4 pm, cancellation fee imposed. **Amenities:** high-speed Internet, dual phone lines, voice mail, irons, hair dryers. **Pool(s):** heated outdoor. **Leisure Activities:** whirlpool, lighted tennis court, exercise room, sports court. **Guest Services:** valet and coin laundry, wireless Internet. **Business Services:** meeting rooms, business center. **Cards:** AX, CB, DC, DS, JC, MC, VI. *(See color ad below)*

AAA Benefit:
Members save a minimum 5% off the best available rate.

▼ See AAA listing above ▼

(See map and index starting on p. 402)

RESIDENCE INN BY MARRIOTT-PORTLAND NORTH HARBOUR *Book great rates at AAA.com*

Phone: (503)285-9888 **5**

Hotel
$149-$169 All Year

Address: 1250 N Anchor Way **Location:** I-5, exit 307, follow signs to Marine Dr E, then just n. **Facility:** Smoke free premises. 102 units. 24 one-bedroom standard units, some with efficiencies or kitchens. 50 one- and 28 two-bedroom suites, some with efficiencies or kitchens. 4 stories, interior corridors. *Bath:* combo or shower only. **Parking:** on-site. **Terms:** cancellation fee imposed. **Amenities:** high-speed Internet, dual phone lines, voice mail, irons, hair dryers. **Pool(s):** heated outdoor. **Leisure Activities:** whirlpool, exercise room, sports court. **Guest Services:** valet and coin laundry, area transportation, wireless Internet. **Business Services:** meeting rooms, PC. **Cards:** AX, CB, DC, DS, JC, MC, VI.

AAA Benefit:
Members save a minimum 5% off the best available rate.

SHERATON PORTLAND AIRPORT HOTEL *Book great rates at AAA.com*

Phone: (503)281-2500 **10**

Hotel
$97-$248 All Year

Address: 8235 NE Airport Way **Location:** I-205, exit 24A northbound; exit 24 southbound, 1.5 mi w. **Facility:** Smoke free premises. 213 units. 204 one-bedroom standard units. 9 one-bedroom suites, some with whirlpools. 5 stories, interior corridors. **Parking:** on-site. **Terms:** cancellation fee imposed. **Amenities:** video games (fee), high-speed Internet, dual phone lines, voice mail, honor bars, irons, hair dryers. *Some:* DVD players, CD players, safes. **Pool(s):** heated indoor. **Leisure Activities:** saunas, exercise room. **Guest Services:** valet laundry, airport transportation-Portland International Airport, area transportation-within 3 mi & light rail station, wireless Internet. **Business Services:** conference facilities, PC (fee). **Cards:** AX, CB, DC, DS, JC, MC, VI. **Free Special Amenities:** local telephone calls and high-speed Internet.

S Sheraton
HOTELS & RESORTS

AAA Benefit:
Members get up to 15% off, plus Starwood Preferred Guest® bonuses.

SHILO INN CONVENTION CENTER/DOWNTOWN *Book great rates at AAA.com*

Phone: 503/234-4391 **46**

Motel
Rates not provided

Address: 518 NE Holladay St **Location:** I-5, exit 302A, just e on NE Weidler St, just s on NE Martin Luther King Jr Blvd, then just e. **Facility:** 36 one-bedroom standard units. 2 stories (no elevator), exterior corridors. **Parking:** on-site. **Amenities:** high-speed Internet, irons, hair dryers. **Guest Services:** wireless Internet. **Free Special Amenities:** continental breakfast and high-speed Internet.

▼ See AAA listing p 444 ▼

(See map and index starting on p. 402)

SHILO INN-PORTLAND/ROSE GARDEN   *Book great rates at AAA.com*   Phone: (503)736-6300   38

Ⓐ SAVE
▼▼▼
Hotel
$92-$200 All Year

Address: 1506 NE 2nd Ave **Location:** I-5, exit 302A, just e on NE Weidler St, then just s. **Facility:** 44 units. 43 one-bedroom standard units. 1 one-bedroom suite with kitchen. 2 stories (no elevator), interior corridors. **Parking:** on-site. **Amenities:** video games (fee), high-speed Internet, voice mail, irons, hair dryers. **Leisure Activities:** sauna. **Guest Services:** coin laundry, wireless Internet. **Cards:** AX, CB, DC, DS, JC, MC, VI. **Free Special Amenities: continental breakfast and high-speed Internet.** *(See color ad p 443)*

SHILO INN SUITES HOTEL-PORTLAND AIRPORT   *Book great rates at AAA.com*   Phone: (503)252-7500   22

Ⓐ SAVE
▼▼▼
Hotel
$120-$220 All Year

Address: 11707 NE Airport Way **Location:** I-205, exit 24B northbound; exit 24 southbound, 0.5 mi e. **Facility:** 200 units. 199 one-bedroom standard units. 1 one-bedroom suite with kitchen. 4 stories, interior corridors. **Parking:** on-site. **Amenities:** video games (fee), high-speed Internet, dual phone lines, voice mail, irons, hair dryers. **Dining:** entertainment. **Pool(s):** heated indoor. **Leisure Activities:** sauna, whirlpool, steamroom, exercise room. **Guest Services:** valet and coin laundry, airport transportation-Portland International Airport, area transportation-light rail station, wireless Internet. **Business Services:** conference facilities, business center. **Cards:** AX, CB, DC, DS, JC, MC, VI. **Free Special Amenities: expanded continental breakfast and high-speed Internet.** *(See color ad below)*

SPRINGHILL SUITES BY MARRIOTT PORTLAND AIRPORT   *Book great rates at AAA.com*   Phone: (503)253-4095   25

▼▼▼
Hotel
$149-$159 All Year

Address: 11922 NE Airport Way **Location:** I-205, exit 24B northbound; exit 24 southbound, 0.6 mi e. **Facility:** Smoke free premises. 81 one-bedroom standard units, some with whirlpools. 5 stories, interior corridors. *Bath:* combo or shower only. **Parking:** on-site. **Terms:** cancellation fee imposed. **Amenities:** high-speed Internet, dual phone lines, voice mail, irons, hair dryers. **Pool(s):** heated indoor. **Leisure Activities:** whirlpool, exercise room. **Guest Services:** valet and coin laundry, wireless Internet. **Business Services:** meeting rooms, business center. **Cards:** AX, CB, DC, DS, JC, MC, VI. *(See color ad p 445)*

SPRINGHILL SUITES Marriott

AAA Benefit:
Members save a minimum 5% off the best available rate.

▼ See AAA listing above ▼

(See map and index starting on p. 402)

STAYBRIDGE SUITES PORTLAND-AIRPORT   *Book at AAA.com*   **Phone:** (503)262-8888   **17**

Hotel
$115-$170 All Year

Address: 11936 NE Glenn Widing Dr **Location:** I-205, exit 24B northbound; exit 24 southbound, 0.7 mi e, then just nw. **Facility:** Smoke free premises. 106 units. 47 one-bedroom standard units with efficiencies. 50 one- and 9 two-bedroom suites with efficiencies. 3 stories, interior corridors. *Bath:* combo or shower only. **Parking:** on-site. **Terms:** cancellation fee imposed. **Amenities:** video library (fee), DVD players, high-speed Internet, dual phone lines, voice mail, irons, hair dryers. **Pool(s):** heated indoor. **Leisure Activities:** sauna, whirlpool, exercise room. **Guest Services:** complimentary and valet laundry, area transportation, wireless Internet. **Business Services:** business center. **Cards:** AX, CB, DC, DS, JC, MC, VI.

(ASK) (✦) (¶✦) CALL (&M) (🍴) (✕) (⊠) (🎦) (📠) (🖨) (💻) / SOME UNITS FEE (🐾)

──── ▼ See AAA listing p 444 ▼ ────

Always at Your Service...

Your AAA membership card is the key to obtaining Emergency Road Service. AAA can help when your car stalls, you get a flat tire, you run out of gas and even when you're locked out. Anytime, anywhere, call **800-AAA-HELP** to get going again.

(See map and index starting on p. 402)

──────── *The following lodging was either not evaluated or did not* ────────
meet AAA rating requirements but is listed for your information only.

MCMENAMINS KENNEDY SCHOOL   **Phone: 503/249-3983**
[fyi]   Not evaluated. **Address:** 5736 NE 33rd Ave **Location:** I-5, exit 303 (N Killingsworth St), 2.3 mi e, then
               just n. Facilities, services, and decor characterize a mid-scale property.

──────── **WHERE TO DINE** ────────

3 DOORS DOWN CAFE & LOUNGE   **Phone: 503/236-6886** (25)
▼▼▼▼   The trendy, lively neighborhood restaurant serves Mediterranean/Italian cuisine with Northwest influences.
               To ensure a spot, diners should call ahead to be put on a wait list. Recommended is the signature seafood
Regional   fra diavolo, with ample clams, mussels, shrimp and halibut tossed with fettuccine in a robust red sauce.
Mediterranean Banana creme pie goes way beyond the standard. Casual dress. **Bar:** Full bar. **Hours:** 5 pm-10 pm, Sun 4
$12-$20   pm-9 pm. Closed: 4/12, 11/26, 12/25; also Mon. **Address:** 1429 SE 37th Ave **Location:** I-84, exit 2, 1.4 mi s
               on 39th Ave, then just w; at SE 37th Ave and Hawthorne Blvd. **Parking:** street. **Cards:** AX, DC, DS, JC,
               MC, VI.

AQUARIVA ITALIAN KITCHEN & WINE BAR   **Phone: 503/802-5850** (38)
▼▼▼   Lighter portions and tapas-style menu items can pair with either red or white wines, more than 40 of which
               are available by the glass, at this restaurant on the banks of the Willamette River. A romantic feel
Regional Italian punctuates the newly renovated dining room and seasonal riverfront patio, which afford serene river views.
$5-$15   Dressy casual. **Bar:** Full bar. **Reservations:** suggested. **Hours:** 11 am-midnight. Closed: 7/4, 11/26, 12/25.
               Address: 0470 SW Hamilton Ct **Location:** I-5, exit 298 northbound, just s on SW Corbett Ave, e on SW
               Richardson Ct, 0.3 mi n on Macadam Ave (SR 43), then just e; exit 299A southbound, follow signs for Johns
               Landing/Lake Oswego 0.8 mi s, then just e; in Avalon Hotel & Spa. **Parking:** valet. **Cards:** AX, DS,
               MC, VI.

BOMBAY CRICKET CLUB RESTAURANT   **Phone: 503/231-0740** (26)
▼▼▼   Patrons can watch cricket matches on a large-screen TV as they dine on Indian and Middle Eastern
               specialties. Among varied curries are preparations of chicken, lamb, seafood and vegetarian ingredients.
Indian   Tandoori specialties are marinated overnight then grilled in a clay oven. Casual dress. **Bar:** Full bar.
$13-$20   **Reservations:** suggested. **Hours:** 5 pm-9 pm, Fri & Sat-10 pm. Closed: 1/1, 11/26, 12/25. **Address:** 1925
               SE Hawthorne Blvd **Location:** Jct SE 19th Ave. **Parking:** on-site. **Cards:** AX, DS, MC, VI.

BREAD & INK CAFE   **Phone: 503/239-4756** (28)
▼▼▼   A savory mix of sure-to-please cuisines is what is found at the comfortable establishment. Large windows
               overlook Hawthorne Boulevard. Among interesting salads and entrees are risotto with roasted butternut
American   squash and rack of lamb with Italian salsa verde. Desserts are wonderful. If it's available, be sure to try
$6-$24   cassatta Siciliana, which comprises seven layers of lemon pound cake filled with lightly sweetened and
               flavored ricotta. Casual dress. **Bar:** Full bar. **Reservations:** accepted. **Hours:** 8 am-9 pm, Fri & Sat-10 pm;
               Sunday brunch. Closed: 12/25. **Address:** 3610 SE Hawthorne Blvd **Location:** Jct SE 36th Ave. **Parking:**
               on-site. **Cards:** AX, DS, MC, VI.

BUMBLEKISS   **Phone: 503/282-6313** (5)
▼   The popular neighborhood favorite is known for its location in a brightly colored house and for its interesting
               scrambles. No hydrogenated oils are used in preparations that incorporate organic and local ingredients
American   whenever possible. Breakfast served until 3 pm offers an alternative lunch choice to gourmet sandwiches
$6-$17   and free-range hand-patted burgers. The patio on the side of the house opens in season. Casual dress.
               Bar: Beer & wine. **Hours:** 8 am-3 pm, Wed-Sat to 9 pm. **Address:** 3517 NE 46th Ave **Location:** Corner of
               NE 46th Ave and NE Fremont St; in Beaumont Village. **Parking:** street. **Cards:** MC, VI.

               CALL

CAFE CASTAGNA   **Phone: 503/231-9959** (27)
▼▼▼   A casual complement to the upscale Castagna Restaurant next door, the cafe focuses on comfort food done
               with expert, skilled attention to detail. An outdoor patio area is available in season. Casual dress. **Bar:** Full
New American   bar. **Hours:** 11:30 am-2 & 5-close, Mon from 5 pm. Closed major holidays. **Address:** 1758 SE Hawthorne
$11-$21   Blvd **Location:** I-5, exit 300, follow signs to SW Water Ave, just s to Hawthorne Blvd, then 0.7 mi e.
               Parking: street. **Cards:** AX, DC, DS, MC, VI.

CAPRIAL'S BISTRO   **Phone: 503/236-6457** (48)
▼▼▼ ▼▼▼   The renowned chef, who has her own television show on PBS, expertly crafts ethnically-influenced
               Northwest cuisine into innovative dishes. The menu changes monthly to reflect the season. The bright
Regional American dining room features an impressively stocked "wine wall" and an open kitchen amid its contemporary decor.
$9-$30   Casual dress. **Bar:** Full bar. **Reservations:** suggested, for dinner. **Hours:** 11:30 am-2:30 & 5-9 pm, Fri &
               Sat-10 pm. Closed major holidays; also Sun & Mon. **Address:** 7015 SE Milwaukie Ave **Location:** Jct SE
               Bybee Blvd; in Westmoreland neighborhood of southeast Portland. **Parking:** street. **Cards:** AX, MC, VI.

CHART HOUSE   **Phone: 503/246-6963** (42)
[SAVE]   The restaurant's two-level dining area, particularly its top level, affords some of the city's best views, which
               incorporate panoramic vistas of the city and mountains. Recent renovations enhance this established spot,
▼▼▼   which presents a menu of fresh fish, selections and specials, along with prime rib and steaks. Dressy
               casual. **Bar:** Full bar. **Reservations:** suggested. **Hours:** 11:30 am-2 & 5-9:30 pm, Fri-10 pm, Sat 5 pm-10
Steak & Seafood pm, Sun 5 pm-9 pm. **Address:** 5700 SW Terwilliger Blvd **Location:** I-5, exit 297 (SW Terwilliger Blvd), 1.2
$10-$43   mi n. **Parking:** valet. **Cards:** AX, DS, MC, VI.

CHEZ JOSE EAST   **Phone: 503/280-9888** (10)
▼▼▼   This popular neighborhood eatery serves tasty Mexican cuisine in a family-friendly atmosphere. The patio
               opens seasonally. Casual dress. **Bar:** Full bar. **Reservations:** not accepted. **Hours:** 4 pm-11 pm, Fri & Sat-
Mexican   midnight, Sun 5 pm-10 pm. Closed: 4/12, 11/26, 12/24, 12/25. **Address:** 2200 NE Broadway **Location:** Jct
$6-$13   NE 22nd Ave. **Parking:** on-site. **Cards:** AX, MC, VI.

(See map and index starting on p. 402)

CHEZ JOSE WEST

Phone: 503/244-0007   53

Mexican
$5-$13

The busy neighborhood eatery features counter seating, contemporary industrial decor and tasty Mexican food. A few interesting food choices include squash enchiladas with spicy peanut sauce and chipotle-honey camarones (prawns). Patrons can choose from a large selection of premium tequilas. Casual dress. **Bar:** Full bar. **Hours:** 11 am-10 pm, Sun 5 pm-9 pm. Closed: 11/26, 12/25. **Address:** 8502 SW Terwilliger Blvd **Location:** I-5, exit 297 (SW Terwilliger Blvd), 0.5 mi s. **Parking:** on-site. **Cards:** AX, DS, MC, VI.

CLARKLEWIS

Phone: 503/235-2294   24

American
$14-$28

In what was once a loading dock built in 1910 on the "other" side of the river, the restaurant has a contemporary industrial feel, with a large garage door that's open in warm weather. On each table are hand-blown, clear-glass water carafes. Dishes might include peasant salad, a hearth-roasted pork or one of several delicious pasta selections. Ingredients are fresh and interesting, and the menu is ever-changing. Dressy casual. **Bar:** Full bar. **Reservations:** suggested. **Hours:** 5:30 pm-close. Closed major holidays; also Sun & Mon. **Address:** 1001 SE Water Ave **Location:** Jct Taylor Ave; east side of Morrison Bridge. **Parking:** on-site. **Cards:** AX, MC, VI.

CREMA COFFEE & BAKERY

Phone: 503/234-0206   18

Breads/Pastries
$6

In a former garage, the sleek contemporary bakery tempts patrons with delectable pastries and desserts. Casual dress. **Hours:** 7 am-6 pm, Sun-5 pm. Closed major holidays. **Address:** 2728 SE Ankeny St **Location:** I-5, exit 300B, 2.3 mi e. **Parking:** street. **Cards:** MC, VI.

ELENI'S ESTIATORIO

Phone: 503/230-2165   49

Greek
$10-$25

Greek specialties range from familiar favorites to unusual fare, with some dishes from the island of Crete. The appetizer sampler is recommended from the extensive selection of interesting starters. Pasta and lamb dishes match well with the Greek wines. Casual dress. **Bar:** Full bar. **Reservations:** suggested. **Hours:** 5 pm-10 pm, Fri & Sat-11 pm. Closed: 11/26, 12/25; also Sun & Mon. **Address:** 7712 SE 13th Ave **Location:** I-5, exit 300B, 1.2 mi s on US 99E, exit Milwaukie Ave/Westmoreland, 1 mi s to SE Bybee Blvd, w to 13th Ave, then just s; in Sellwood District. **Parking:** street. **Cards:** AX, DS, MC, VI.

ESPARZA'S TEX MEX CAFE

Phone: 503/234-7909   17

Tex-Mex
$9-$18

Esparza's has its own brand of Tex-Mex cooking that includes smoking its own meats. Spicy ground buffalo enchilada, jalapeno-marinated lamb chops, smoked beef brisket and fried catfish with green tomatillo sauce are just some of the entree choices to enjoy while dining in very retro/eclectic surroundings. This spot has possibly the best Tex-Mex this side of the Rio Grande as well as 20 kinds of tequila. Casual dress. **Bar:** Full bar. **Reservations:** not accepted. **Hours:** 11:30 am-10 pm; Fri & Sat-10:30 pm in summer. Closed: 11/26, 12/25; also Sun. **Address:** 2725 SE Ankeny St **Location:** At SE 28th Ave and Ankeny St; 1 blk s of E Burnside St. **Parking:** on-site. **Cards:** AX, CB, DC, DS, MC, VI.

FIFE

Phone: 971/222-3433   6

American
$16-$21

The new restaurant is decorated with oversized lampshades, and an open kitchen has kitchen-view seating. Exciting American cuisine is prepared from local and organic ingredients. Most menu items change daily, but if it's available, try the pan-roasted quail with mushrooms, wild rice and shoot garlic confit. Casual dress. **Bar:** Full bar. **Reservations:** suggested. **Hours:** 5 pm-9 pm, Fri & Sat-10 pm. Closed major holidays; also 12/24, Sun & Mon. **Address:** 4440 NE Fremont St **Location:** Corner of NE 45th Ave and NE Fremont St; in Beaumont Village. **Parking:** on-site. **Cards:** DS, MC, VI.

CALL   📞♿

GENOA

Phone: 503/238-1464   23

Italian
$65-$130

An intimate air envelops the sophisticated restaurant, which welcomes guests into a beautiful sitting room for pre- or post-dining relaxation. Seven- and 12-course meals are leisurely paced, allowing for plenty of conversation in between bites of delectable cuisine. Dishes draw on regional and classic influences. Dressy casual. **Bar:** Full bar. **Reservations:** required. **Hours:** 5:30 pm-9:30 pm. Closed major holidays; also 12/24 & Mon. **Address:** 2832 SE Belmont St **Location:** I-5, exit 300B, 2 mi e; jct SE 28th Ave. **Parking:** street. **Cards:** AX, CB, DC, DS, MC, VI.

GINO'S RESTAURANT & BAR

Phone: 503/233-4613   51

Italian
$14-$39

A great place to gather with friends after antiquing in the Sellwood District, this neighborhood Italian eatery serves large portions in a homelike setting that feels more East Coast. In addition to such great specialties as wild mushroom risotto, hand-stuffed ravioli and Grandma Jean's pasta, the menu lists steaks, chops and chicken. The wine list shows some depth and creativity, and desserts are large enough to share. Casual dress. **Bar:** Full bar. **Reservations:** not accepted. **Hours:** 4 pm-10 pm, Fri & Sat-11 pm. Closed: 7/4, 11/26, 12/24, 12/25. **Address:** 8051 SE 13th Ave **Location:** I-5, exit 300B, 1.2 mi s on SR 99E, exit Milwaukie Ave/Westmoreland, 1 mi s to SE Bybee Blvd, just w to 13th Ave, then just s; in Sellwood District. **Parking:** on-site and street. **Cards:** MC, VI.

📷

IL PIATTO

Phone: 503/236-4997   19

Italian
$7-$23

In a former corner grocery store, the neighborhood eatery serves a variety of pastas in an eclectic, yet warm and casual, Italian-style dining room. The extensive wine list features regional wines of Italy. Outside seating is available in season. Casual dress. **Bar:** Full bar. **Reservations:** suggested. **Hours:** 11:30 am-2 & 5:30-9:30 pm, Fri-10:30 pm, Sat 5:30 pm-10 pm, Sun & Mon 5:30 pm-9:30 pm. Closed: 1/1, 11/26, 12/25. **Address:** 2348 SE Ankeny St **Location:** Corner of SE Ankeny St and SE 23rd Ave. **Parking:** street. **Cards:** AX, DS, MC, VI.

JOPA

Phone: 503/892-6686   40

Regional American
$7-$24

The comfortable restaurant serves Northwest fare, with some pastas, pizzas and calzones. Daily specials can include unusual fish entrees. A whimsical mural adorns one wall. The patio opens seasonally. Casual dress. **Bar:** Full bar. **Reservations:** not accepted. **Hours:** 11:30 am-9:30 pm, Fri & Sat-10 pm, Sun 5 pm-9 pm. Closed: 1/1, 11/26, 12/24-12/26; also Mon. **Address:** 4439 SW Beaverton-Hillsdale Hwy (SR 10) **Location:** I-5, exit 297 northbound, just n to SW Barbur Blvd, just w, 0.8 mi nw on Bertha Blvd, then 0.9 mi nw; exit southbound, follow signs to Bertha Blvd, 0.8 mi nw, then 0.9 mi nw. **Parking:** on-site. **Cards:** AX, MC, VI.

CALL

(See map and index starting on p. 402)

LAURO MEDITERRANEAN KITCHEN
Phone: 503/239-7000

Mediterranean
$15-$19

Attention to detail is evidenced in creative fare inspired by Spain, Portugal, Morocco, Italy and Greece. An oversize chalkboard lists nightly specials. The blue-tiled gas-fired pizza oven adds a nice touch, as do the knowledgeable servers. Diners who sit at the neighborhood restaurant's counter can observe food preparation. Casual dress. **Bar:** Full bar. **Reservations:** not accepted. **Hours:** 5 pm-9 pm, Fri & Sat-10 pm. Closed major holidays. **Address:** 3377 SE Division St **Location:** Jct SE 34th Ave; in Richmond District. **Parking:** on-site. **Cards:** AX, DS, MC, VI.

CALL

LE HANA JAPANESE BAR & CAFE
Phone: 503/467-7533   36

New Japanese
$8-$35

An extensive choice of sakes and sake cocktails complements the cafe's creative sushi fusions, seafood and meat entrees, some of which incorporate French fusion elements. Contemporary flair marks the casually upscale setting, where courteous staff help guests feel comfortable. Casual dress. **Bar:** Full bar. **Reservations:** accepted. **Hours:** 11 am-10 pm, Fri-10:30 pm, Sat 4:30 pm-10 pm, Sun 4 pm-10 pm. Closed major holidays. **Address:** 3500 SW River Pkwy **Location:** Just e of SW Macadam Ave (SR 43) and the OHSU tram; ground level of the Meriwether Condominium; in South Waterfront District. **Parking:** street. **Cards:** AX, DS, MC, VI.

LEMONGRASS THAI RESTAURANT
Phone: 503/231-5780   15

Thai
$9-$24

On the main floor of an old home, the casual restaurant can be difficult to find. Those who make the extra effort are rewarded. Because the owner does much of the cooking and serving, arriving guests sometimes must wait in the small entry. The kitchen doesn't shy away from spices, so guests should make their preferences known. Casual dress. **Bar:** Beer & wine. **Reservations:** not accepted. **Hours:** Open 3/1-6/30 & 8/1-2/28; 11:45 am-2 & 6-9:30 pm, Fri-10 pm, Sat 5:30 pm-10 pm. Closed major holidays; also Sun & Mon. **Address:** 1705 NE Couch St **Location:** Northeast corner of 17th and Couch sts; just n of E Burnside St. **Parking:** street.

MARCO'S CAFE & ESPRESSO BAR
Phone: 503/245-0199   50

American
$8-$16

Efficient servers circulate through the popular neighborhood eatery, which is housed in a building dating from 1913 that was once a grocery store. The menu lists a good selection of salads, sandwiches and burgers as well as lunch and dinner specials. Entrees include jumbo sea scallops broiled with port wine, and chocolate velvet cake is among dessert options. Breakfast is served all day. Casual dress. **Bar:** Beer & wine. **Reservations:** not accepted. **Hours:** 7 am-9 pm, Sat from 8 am, Sun 8 am-2 pm. Closed major holidays. **Address:** 7910 SW 35th Ave **Location:** I-5, exit 295, 1.2 mi n on SW Capitol Hwy, then just s; at SW 35th Ave and Multnomah St. **Parking:** on-site. **Cards:** AX, DS, MC, VI.

MCMENAMINS
Phone: 503/286-0372

American
$5-$20

The casual neighborhood eatery is where friends gather for classic pub and comfort fare, all washed down by pints of locally made beer. Large wooden booths or tables easily accommodate larger groups, and the eclectic, custom-painted walls and varied period light fixtures keep diners' eyes busy should the conversation lag. Casual dress. **Bar:** Full bar. **Hours:** 11 am-11 pm, Thurs-midnight, Fri & Sat-1 am, Sun noon-11 pm. **Address:** 430 NW Killingsworth St **Location:** I-5, exit 303 (N Killingsworth St), then e; jct N Haight St. **Parking:** on-site. **Cards:** MC, VI.

MCMENAMINS
Phone: 503/288-9498

American
$5-$20

The casual neighborhood eatery is where friends gather for classic pub and comfort fare, all washed down by pints of locally made beer. Large wooden booths or tables easily accommodate larger groups, and the eclectic, custom-painted walls and varied period light fixtures keep diners' eyes busy should the conversation lag. Casual dress. **Bar:** Full bar. **Hours:** 11 am-1 am, Sun noon-midnight. Closed: 11/26, 12/25. **Address:** 1504 NE Broadway **Location:** I-5, exit 302A, 0.8 mi e on NE Weidler St, then just n on NE 15th Ave. **Parking:** street. **Cards:** MC, VI.

MCMENAMINS
Phone: 503/288-2192

American
$5-$20

The casual neighborhood eatery is where friends gather for classic pub and comfort fare, all washed down by pints of locally made beer. Large wooden booths or tables easily accommodate larger groups, and the eclectic, custom-painted walls and varied period light fixtures keep diners' eyes busy should the conversation lag. Casual dress. **Bar:** Full bar. **Reservations:** not accepted. **Hours:** 7 am-1 am, Sun-midnight. **Address:** 5736 NE 33rd Ave **Location:** I-84, exit 33rd Ave eastbound, 2 mi n; exit 43rd Ave westbound, follow signs to Broadway, 1 mi w on Broadway, then 2 mi n. **Parking:** on-site. **Cards:** MC, VI.

MCMENAMINS
Phone: 503/254-5411

American
$5-$20

The casual neighborhood eatery is where friends gather for classic pub and comfort fare, all washed down by pints of locally made beer. Large wooden booths or tables easily accommodate larger groups, and the eclectic, custom-painted walls and varied period light fixtures keep diners' eyes busy should the conversation lag. Casual dress. **Bar:** Full bar. **Hours:** 11 am-1 am, Sun noon-midnight. Closed: 12/25. **Address:** 9710 SE Washington St **Location:** I-205, exit 20 northbound, 0.5 mi e on Washington St, then just s; exit 21A southbund, just e on Glisan St, then s. **Parking:** on-site. **Cards:** MC, VI.

NEWPORT BAY RESTAURANT
Phone: 503/493-0100

Seafood
$8-$25

This restaurant is for those seeking a casual, relaxing time. A menu favorite is New England clam chowder, which is available nightly. Fresh Northwest salmon and Alaskan halibut prepared several ways share menu space with pasta, chicken and salads. Casual dress. **Bar:** Full bar. **Reservations:** accepted. **Hours:** 11 am-10 pm, Fri & Sat-11 pm, Sun 9 am-10 pm. Closed: 11/26, 12/25. **Address:** 1200 NE Broadway **Location:** I-5, exit 302A, 0.7 mi e on NE Weidler St, just n on 14th Ave, then just w. **Parking:** on-site. **Cards:** AX, DS, MC, VI.

NEWPORT BAY RESTAURANT
Phone: 503/255-2722

American
$8-$25

This restaurant is for those seeking a casual, relaxing time. A menu favorite is New England clam chowder, which is available nightly. Fresh Northwest salmon and Alaskan halibut prepared several ways share menu space with pasta, chicken and salads. Casual dress. **Bar:** Full bar. **Reservations:** accepted. **Hours:** 11 am-10 pm, Fri & Sat-11 pm, Sun 9 am-10 pm. Closed: 11/26, 12/25. **Address:** 9722 SE Washington St **Location:** I-205, exit 20 northbound, 0.5 mi e on Washington St, then just s; exit 21A southbound, just e on Glisan St, then s. **Parking:** on-site. **Cards:** AX, DS, MC, VI.

CALL

(See map and index starting on p. 402)

NEWPORT BAY RESTAURANT
Phone: 503/283-3474

American
$8-$25

This restaurant is for those seeking a casual, relaxing time. A menu favorite is New England clam chowder, which is available nightly. Fresh Northwest salmon and Alaskan halibut prepared several ways share menu space with pasta, chicken and salads. Casual dress. **Bar:** Full bar. **Reservations:** accepted. **Hours:** 11 am-10 pm, Fri & Sat-11 pm, Sun 9 am-10 pm. Closed: 11/26, 12/25. **Address:** 11950 N Center Ave **Location:** I-5, exit 308, just w on Hayden Island Dr, then just s. **Parking:** on-site. **Cards:** AX, DS, MC, VI.

CALL 🔊M

NOHO'S HAWAIIAN CAFE
Phone: 503/233-5301 ㉞

Hawaiian
$6-$19

A treat from the islands, this eatery has been preparing authentic Hawaiian plate lunch-style food served with traditional sauces since 1992. The menu lists heaping portions of an assortment of pupus (appetizers) as well as teriyaki, rib, seafood and noodle dishes. Daily specials are another option. Casual dress. **Bar:** Beer & wine. **Reservations:** accepted, until 6:30 pm. **Hours:** 10:30 am-9 pm, Fri-10 pm, Sat noon-10 pm, Sun noon-9 pm. Closed: 1/1, 11/26, 12/25. **Address:** 2525 SE Clinton St **Location:** E on US 26; from Ross Island Bridge, 1.1 mi e, then 0.4 mi n on SE 26th Ave. **Parking:** street. **Cards:** AX, DS, MC, VI.

NOSTRANA
Phone: 503/234-2427 ㉒

Italian
$7-$25

Inventive and mostly contemporary Italian cuisine is well-prepared at this neighborhood restaurant, which turns out wood-oven-baked pizzas and fresh pasta dishes made from primarily locally supplied ingredients. Counter seats give diners close-up views inside the exhibition kitchen. Service is relaxed. Those who don't arrive early should be prepared for a long wait most nights, as reservations are not accepted. Casual dress. **Bar:** Full bar. **Reservations:** not accepted. **Hours:** 11:30 am-2 & 5-10 pm, Fri-11 pm, Sat 5 pm-11 pm, Sun 5 pm-10 pm. Closed major holidays; also 12/24. **Address:** 1401 SE Morrison St **Location:** Jct SE 14th Ave and SE Morrison St; east side of Morrison Bridge. **Parking:** on-site. **Cards:** AX, MC, VI.

CALL 🔊M

NUESTRA COCINA
Phone: 503/232-2135 ㉚

Mexican
$9-$18

Homemade tortillas begin each meal at the popular restaurant. Minced ceviche is among the interesting appetizers, which lead in to the not-to-be-missed main courses. Patrons can choose from a good selection of tequilas. The mosaic counter allows for viewing of meal preparations; patio seating is another option. It's best to arrive early to avoid long waits. Casual dress. **Bar:** Full bar. **Reservations:** not accepted. **Hours:** 5 pm-10 pm. Closed: 1/1, 11/26; also Sun, Mon & Christmas week. **Address:** 2135 SE Division **Location:** Jct SE 22nd Ave, just s of Ladd's Addition. **Parking:** street. **Cards:** AX, DS, MC, VI.

THE OLD SPAGHETTI FACTORY
Phone: 503/222-5375 ㊲

Italian
$7-$17

As the original Old Spaghetti Factory, this spacious restaurant with its beautiful blue-tiled roof features a trolley car with seats made from antique bed frames. Spaghetti, of course, is the featured item and is served with sauces made fresh daily. Other favorite Italian classics share space on the menu. A few tables overlook the Willamette River. Casual dress. **Bar:** Full bar. **Hours:** 11:30 am-2:30 & 4:30-9:30 pm, Fri-10:30 pm, Sat noon-10:30 pm, Sun noon-9:30 pm. Closed: 12/25. **Address:** 0715 SW Bancroft **Location:** I-5, exit 298 northbound, just s on SW Corbett, e on SW Richardson Ct, 0.4 mi n on Macadem Ave (SR 43), then just e; exit 299A southbound, just n on Macadem Ave (SR 43), then just e. **Parking:** on-site. **Cards:** AX, DS, MC, VI.

CALL 🔊M

THE ORIGINAL TACO HOUSE
Phone: 503/252-1695 ⑦

Mexican
$5-$11

Since 1960, the establishment has served little and big burritos, halibut tacos and other Mexican and gringo favorites. Lunch specials are prepared daily. Casual dress. **Bar:** Full bar. **Reservations:** not accepted. **Hours:** 11 am-10 pm. Closed major holidays. **Address:** 3255 NE 82nd Ave **Location:** I-84, exit 5 eastbound, 1 mi n; exit I-205 westbound to exit 23A southbound; exit 23B northbound (Sandy Blvd), 1 mi w on NE Sandy Blvd, then 0.5 mi s. **Parking:** on-site. **Cards:** AX, DS, MC, VI.

🔖

PAMBICHE
Phone: 503/233-0511 ⑬

Cuban
$7-$18

Colorful walls and Caribbean artwork add spice inside the small neighborhood restaurant, which often has long lines in part because of limited seating in its dining room and on the lamp-heated patio. European influences come into play in African and indigenous Caribbean dishes collectively referred to as Cuban Creole cuisine. Recommended is the empanada puerro prepared with fresh leeks in savory Spanish custard cream. Interesting desserts merit a splurge. Casual dress. **Bar:** Full bar. **Hours:** 11 am-10 pm, Fri & Sat-midnight. Closed: 12/25. **Address:** 2811 NE Glisan St **Location:** Corner of NE 28th Ave and NE Glisan St. **Parking:** street. **Cards:** MC, VI.

PAPA HAYDN
Phone: 503/232-9440 ㊸

Regional American
$10-$27

For 26 years, the landmark neighborhood bistro has featured delicious Northwest cuisine and fabulous desserts that shouldn't be missed. Sidewalk seating is a seasonal option. Casual dress. **Bar:** Full bar. **Reservations:** not accepted. **Hours:** 11:30 am-10 pm, Fri & Sat-midnight, Sun 10 am-9 pm; Sunday brunch. Closed: 1/1, 11/26, 12/25. **Address:** 5829 SE Milwaukie Ave **Location:** Jct SE Ramone St; in Westmoreland neighborhood of southeast Portland. **Parking:** street. **Cards:** AX, MC, VI.

PASTINI PASTARIA
Phone: 503/288-4300 ⑨

Italian
$5-$10

The lively, Italian-style bistro prepares a variety of fresh, affordable pasta dishes, including several low in fat and oil. Wood accents throughout add to the warmth. Casual dress. **Bar:** Full bar. **Reservations:** not accepted. **Hours:** 11:30 am-9 pm, Fri & Sat-10 pm, Sun 4 pm-9 pm. Closed: 9/7, 11/26, 12/24, 12/25. **Address:** 1426 NE Broadway **Location:** Corner of NE Broadway and NE 15th Ave. **Parking:** street. **Cards:** AX, MC, VI.

(See map and index starting on p. 402)

PIX PATISSERIE
Phone: 503/232-4407 (33)

Breads/Pastries
$5-$7

Fanciful flair characterizes the pastries and other treats lined up in the dessert case at this busy spot. Standouts among the inventive creations include French-style macaroons, homemade ice creams and beer floats. Whimsy reigns in the dining room, while the seasonal streetside seating has an entirely different appeal. As for more substantial offerings, grilled panini sandwiches pair well with interesting selections of beer and wine. Casual dress. **Bar:** Beer & wine. **Reservations:** not accepted. **Hours:** 10 am-midnight, Fri & Sat-2 am. **Address:** 3402 SE Division St **Location:** Jct SE 34th Ave; in Richmond District. **Parking:** street. **Cards:** MC, VI.

PORTOFINO
Phone: 503/234-8259 (52)

Italian
$11-$19

At the cozy, romantic restaurant, Northern Italian and French cuisine share menu space. Among preparations are tortellini with vodka tomato cream sauce, homemade cannelloni and several tempting veal and vegetarian dishes. Particularly popular are the entrees made with sambuca sauce. Tiramisu comes highly recommended. Patrons can park in the rear of the building. Casual dress. **Bar:** Full bar. **Reservations:** suggested. **Hours:** 4:30 pm-9:30 pm, Fri & Sat-10 pm. Closed major holidays; also Mon & Tues. **Address:** 8075 SE 13th Ave **Location:** In Sellwood District. **Parking:** on-site. **Cards:** DS, MC, VI.

CALL

RACCOON LODGE & BREW PUB
Phone: 503/296-0110 (39)

American
$8-$16

Trophy heads of deer and elk adorn the walls of the Northwest lodge-style restaurant. Varied sandwiches, burgers and salads are served. Fry types include shoestring, sweet potato and ale-battered with eight dipping sauces. Among entrees are meatloaf in stout gravy. The eatery brews its own ales and a cream-style root beer. Outside seating is available in season. Casual dress. **Bar:** Full bar. **Reservations:** accepted. **Hours:** 11:30 am-10 pm, Sun-9 pm. Closed: 11/26, 12/25. **Address:** 7424 SW Beaverton-Hillsdale Hwy **Location:** SR 217, exit 2 (SR 10/Beaverton-Hillsdale Hwy), 1.9 mi e. **Parking:** on-site. **Cards:** AX, DS, MC, VI.

CALL

RHEINLANDER GERMAN RESTAURANT & GUSTAV'S BIER STUBE
Phone: 503/288-5503 (8)

German
$7-$26

The festive Bavarian restaurant bustles with activity as strolling musicians and singers set a lively tempo. The complimentary pre-meal fondue prepares guests for traditional and creative entrees, such as schnitzel cordon bleu, sauerbraten and the family feast. Casual dress. Entertainment. **Bar:** Full bar. **Reservations:** suggested. **Hours:** 5 pm-9 pm, Fri-10 pm, Sat 4 pm-10 pm, Sun 4 pm-9 pm. Closed: 12/25. **Address:** 5035 NE Sandy Blvd **Location:** I-84, exit 2 eastbound, just n, then 0.8 mi ne; exit westbound, just e on Halsey St, just n on 47th Ave, then just ne. **Parking:** on-site. **Cards:** AX, MC, VI.

RINGSIDE STEAKHOUSE
Phone: 503/255-0759 (12)

Steak
$10-$65

For more than 29 years, this dinner house at the Glendoveer Golf Course has been known for its hand-cut, aged USDA prime and bone-in steaks as well as its attentive service. More than 600 wines are available. A fireplace enhances an already warm, inviting atmosphere. Early or late supper is available for $25 for select entrees before 5:45 pm or after 9 pm and all evening on Sunday and Monday. Casual dress. **Bar:** Full bar. **Reservations:** suggested. **Hours:** 11:30 am-2:30 & 4:30-10:30 pm, Fri-11:30 pm, Sat 4:30 pm-11:30 pm, Sun 4 pm-10 pm. Closed major holidays. **Address:** 14021 NE Glisan St **Location:** I-205, exit 21A (Glisan St/Stark St) southbound, 2.2 mi e. **Parking:** on-site. **Cards:** AX, DC, DS, JC, MC, VI.

CALL

SALTY'S ON THE COLUMBIA
Phone: 503/288-4444 (1)

Seafood
$10-$45

Patrons take in wonderful views of the Columbia River while savoring tasty, attractively presented preparations of Northwest seafood, such as oysters on the half-shell, live Dungeness crab and salmon prepared several ways. The daily sheet menu is a showcase for the freshest market ingredients. The dining deck opens seasonally. Casual dress. **Bar:** Full bar. **Reservations:** suggested. **Hours:** 11:15 am-10:30 pm, Fri & Sat-11 pm, Sun 9:30 am-2 & 4:30-9 pm; 11:15 am-9:30 pm, Fri & Sat-10 pm in winter; Sunday brunch. Closed: 12/25. **Address:** 3839 NE Marine Dr **Location:** I-5, exit 307, 3 mi e. **Parking:** on-site and valet. **Cards:** AX, DC, DS, MC, VI.

CALL

SALVADOR MOLLY'S
Phone: 503/293-1790 (44)

Caribbean
$6-$15

Diners can grab peanuts at the counter and throw the shells on the floor at the funky eatery, which displays eclectic decor. The many Caribbean libations pair with "pirate cooking," the tropical cuisine of the Caribbean, Mexico and South America. The "wall of flames" proudly lists the names of those who dare to polish off the habanero fritters (a.k.a., "great balls of fire"). Casual dress. **Bar:** Full bar. **Reservations:** not accepted. **Hours:** 11 am-10 pm, Fri & Sat-11 pm, Sun & Mon-9 pm. Closed: 1/1, 11/26, 12/25. **Address:** 1523 SW Sunset Blvd **Location:** Jct SW Capitol Way. **Parking:** on-site. **Cards:** AX, DS, MC, VI.

SAPPHIRE HOTEL
Phone: 503/232-6333 (29)

American
$9-$14

Part bar, part restaurant, part live jazz club (on Sundays), this restaurant is located in a turn-of-the-20th-century hotel lobby near Mt Tabor. The eclectic, funky spot continues to be a place to eat and drink. Known for specialty drinks and music, the somewhat limited menu is interesting with creative desserts. Casual dress. **Bar:** Full bar. **Hours:** 4 pm-2 am, Sun-1 am. Closed: 1/1, 12/25. **Address:** 5008 SE Hawthorne Blvd **Location:** Jct SE 50th Ave. **Parking:** street. **Cards:** AX, MC, VI.

(See map and index starting on p. 402)

SAYLER'S OLD COUNTRY KITCHEN
Phone: 503/252-4171   (21)

Steak
$13-$30

Since 1946, friendly staffers at the casual, family-owned steakhouse have served a broad selection of USDA Choice steak dinners, as well as chicken and seafood. A whopping 72-ounce top sirloin dinner is free to anyone who can eat the entire steak and trimmings within an hour. Those with lesser appetites should stray toward the lighter menu. A rustic, open fireplace is the room's focal point. A wait for seating is common on the weekends. Casual dress. **Bar:** Full bar. **Reservations:** not accepted. **Hours:** 4 pm-10 pm, Fri-11 pm, Sat 3 pm-11 pm, Sun noon-10 pm. Closed: 7/4, 11/26, 12/24, 12/25. **Address:** 10519 SE Stark St **Location:** I-205, exit 20 northbound, 0.5 mi e on Washington St, then just n; exit 21A southbound. **Parking:** on-site. **Cards:** AX, DS, MC, VI.

SEASONS & REGIONS SEAFOOD GRILL
Phone: 503/244-6400   (46)

Seafood
$6-$20

A Northwestern flair punctuates the popular neighborhood grill's offerings of fresh seafood, meat, chicken and pasta, as well as sandwiches. The patio is heated, making for cozier seating on cooler days. The "curlers and fuzzy slippers pick-up window" comes in handy. Casual dress. **Bar:** Full bar. **Reservations:** not accepted. **Hours:** 11:15 am-9:30 pm, Fri-10 pm, Sat 9 am-10 pm, Sun 9 am-9 pm; Saturday & Sunday brunch. Closed major holidays. **Address:** 6660 SW Capitol Hwy **Location:** I-5, exit 297 (SW Terwilliger Blvd), 0.9 mi n on SW Bertha Blvd, then 0.4 mi w. **Parking:** on-site. **Cards:** AX, DS, MC, VI.

SHANGHAI NOBLE HOUSE
Phone: 503/227-3136   (41)

Chinese
$6-$14

Live seafood and Northern Szechuan specialties are at the heart of the restaurant's menu. Casual dress. **Bar:** Full bar. **Reservations:** accepted. **Hours:** 11 am-10:30 pm. Closed: 11/26. **Address:** 5331 SW Macadam Ave **Location:** Jct SW Sweeney St; in John's Landing Water Tower Building. **Parking:** on-site. **Cards:** AX, MC, VI.

SHENANIGANS
Phone: 503/289-0966   (4)

American
$10-$58

Guests savor flavorful steaks and fresh seafood as they take in beautiful views of the river. The Sunday buffet is a must. A loyal clientele of locals makes this place popular. Casual dress. **Bar:** Full bar. **Reservations:** accepted. **Hours:** 11 am-10 pm, Fri & Sat-11 pm, Sun 9 am-2:30 & 4-10 pm; Sunday brunch. **Address:** 909 N Hayden Island Dr **Location:** I-5, exit 308, just ne; in Red Lion Hotel on the River Jantzen Beach-Portland. **Parking:** on-site. **Cards:** AX, DC, DS, MC, VI.

SIAM SOCIETY
Phone: 503/922-3675   (3)

Thai
$11-$23

In the 1920 Alberta electric substation, this dining venue exudes character. With its discounted prices on select entrees and appetizers, happy hour is popular. Menu items include many traditional Thai dishes, including sexy beef and a banana roasted pork that takes five days to create. Many kitchen and bar ingredients are gathered fresh daily at local markets, and a full-time mixologist busily conjures the "Thai me up" and "hibiscus Mojito," fun and tasty drinks. Casual dress. **Bar:** Full bar. **Reservations:** accepted. **Hours:** 4 pm-10 pm, Fri & Sat-11 pm. Closed major holidays; also Sun. **Address:** 2703 NE Alberta St **Location:** I-5, exit 303 (Alberta St), 2 mi e. **Parking:** street. **Cards:** MC, VI.

STANFORD'S RESTAURANT & BAR
Phone: 503/493-4056   (2)

American
$10-$38

While waiting for a flight, patrons can grab a bite at this spot, which offers a casual, tasteful dining experience. Fresh seafood and quality steaks are emphasized on a menu that also lists several dishes grilled over a wood fire, as well as rock-salt-roasted prime rib, pizza, sandwiches and vegetarian selections. A "grab & go counter" allows for on-the-run repasts. Casual dress. **Bar:** Full bar. **Reservations:** accepted. **Hours:** 11 am-11 pm. **Address:** 7000 NE Airport Way, #2600 **Location:** I-205, exit 24A northbound; exit 24 southbound, 1.7 mi w; in Portland International Airport; adjacent to entrance for gates A, B & C. **Parking:** on-site (fee). **Cards:** AX, DC, DS, MC, VI.

CALL

STANFORD'S RESTAURANT & BAR
Phone: 503/285-2005

American
$10-$36

Near Jantzen Beach Shopping Center, the restaurant offers an upscale yet casual dining experience. Menu items include fresh seafood, quality steaks and pasta, and several menu items are prepared on a wood-fire grill. Patio seating is available in season. Casual dress. **Bar:** Full bar. **Reservations:** accepted. **Hours:** 11 am-11 pm, Fri & Sat-midnight. Closed: 11/26, 12/25. **Address:** 1440 N Jantzen Beach Center **Location:** I-5, exit 308, just w on Hayden Island Dr, then just s; across from Jantzen Beach Super Center. **Parking:** on-site. **Cards:** AX, DC, DS, MC, VI.

STANFORD'S RESTAURANT & BAR
Phone: 503/335-0811   (11)

American
$10-$38

This full-service restaurant offers upscale casual service, a warm interior and a wide variety of menu items including seafood, pasta and vegetarian dishes. The menu also has pizza, chicken, ribs, steak and rock-salt-roasted prime rib. Specialties of fresh Pacific Northwest salmon can be pan-seared or grilled over a wood fire. Outside seating is a seasonal option. Casual dress. **Bar:** Full bar. **Reservations:** accepted. **Hours:** 11 am-11 pm, Fri & Sat-midnight. Closed: 11/26, 12/25. **Address:** 913 Lloyd Center **Location:** Jct NE 9th Ave and NE Multnomah St; in west end of Lloyd Center Mall; near Nordstrom's. **Parking:** on-site. **Cards:** AX, DC, DS, MC, VI.

STICKERS ASIAN CAFE
Phone: 503/239-8739   (47)

Asian
$7-$15

An intriguing blend of East Indian and Asian cuisines graces the menu, which features items typical of popular Asian street food, made without MSG. You'll find an assortment of pot stickers and dumplings, satays, curries and noodles. Casual dress. **Bar:** Full bar. **Reservations:** not accepted. **Hours:** 11:30 am-9 pm, Fri & Sat-10 pm. Closed: 11/26, 12/25. **Address:** 6808 SE Milwaukie Ave **Location:** Jct SE Bybee Blvd; in Westmoreland neighborhood of southeast Portland. **Parking:** on-site. **Cards:** AX, DS, MC, VI.

(See map and index starting on p. 402)

TABLA MEDITERRANEAN BISTRO

Mediterranean
$16-$19

Phone: 503/238-3777 (14)

The lively neighborhood bistro offers interesting fare, including French, Italian and Spanish cuisines with a Mediterranean flair. Everything on the menu is locally produced and organic, including the delicious house-made pasta selections. Half portions provide an opportunity to try various dishes, and a three-course dinner is available for $24. Counter seating oversees the busy kitchen. The wine list offers moderately priced options. Casual dress. **Bar:** Full bar. **Reservations:** suggested. **Hours:** 5:30 pm-9:30 pm, Fri & Sat-10 pm. Closed: 1/1, 11/26, 12/25; also Mon. **Address:** 200 NE 28th Ave **Location:** Corner of NE 28th Ave and Davis St. **Parking:** street. **Cards:** AX, DC, DS, MC, VI.

TAQUERIA NUEVE

Traditional
Mexican
$11-$16

Phone: 503/236-6195 (16)

The lively restaurant combines tasty, traditional Oaxacan-style Mexican cuisine with local foods and some spicy flavors. Warm-colored walls add to the tropical ambience. Parking is available behind the building. Casual dress. **Bar:** Full bar. **Reservations:** not accepted. **Hours:** 5 pm-10 pm. Closed major holidays; also 12/24. **Address:** 28 NE 28th Ave **Location:** Just n of E Burnside St. **Parking:** on-site. **Cards:** AX, MC, VI.

THREE SQUARE GRILL

American
$7-$25

Phone: 503/244-4467 (45)

In a small shopping center, the neighborhood establishment shines with such seasonal offerings as the sauteed Pacific crab cake with sauce remoulade appetizer and the bluefin tuna with olive tapenade entree. Ginger cake with caramel is a can't-miss dessert. Casual dress. **Bar:** Beer & wine. **Reservations:** accepted. **Hours:** 5 pm-9 pm. Closed major holidays; also 12/24. **Address:** 6320 SW Capitol Hwy **Location:** I-5, exit 297 (SW Terwilliger Blvd), 0.9 mi n on SW Bertha Blvd, then 0.4 mi e; in Hillsdale Shopping Center. **Parking:** on-site. **Cards:** MC, VI.

CALL ♿Ⓜ

VINDALHO

Indian
$14-$19

Phone: 503/467-4550 (35)

Contemporary India-inspired cuisine is prepared from fresh ingredients and with a Northwest flair. The neighborhood spot also turns out several tandoori items. The back patio opens seasonally. Casual dress. **Bar:** Full bar. **Reservations:** suggested. **Hours:** 5 pm-10 pm. Closed major holidays; also Sun & Mon. **Address:** 2038 Clinton St **Location:** E on US 26; from Ross Island Bridge, just n on SE 21st Ave, then just w. **Parking:** street. **Cards:** AX, MC, VI.

WONG'S KING SEAFOOD RESTAURANT

Chinese
$7-$38

Phone: 503/788-8883 (32)

Popular with Portlanders, this restaurant serves daily dim sum lunches. It's wise to arrive early or late to find parking and avoid long waits. The hostess provides numbers to incoming guests. In the evening, a variety of seafood dishes and interesting food items are prepared. No monosodium glutamate is added to the food. Casual dress. **Bar:** Full bar. **Reservations:** accepted, for dinner. **Hours:** 10 am-11 pm, Fri & Sat-midnight. **Address:** 8733 SE Division St **Location:** Jct SE 87th Ave. **Parking:** on-site. **Cards:** AX, DS, MC, VI.

CALL ♿Ⓜ

YA HALA LEBANESE CUISINE

Lebanese
$8-$17

Phone: 503/256-4484 (20)

Ya Hala means "welcome" in Lebanon, and guests surely are welcomed here. The menu lists a variety of interesting and more traditional hot and cold mezzas (appetizers), as well as kebabs and such entrees as lamb, eggplant casserole and kafta. Desserts are tasty. Beverages include Lebanese wine and distinctive nonalcoholic drinks. Those who don't come early on weekends can expect a wait. Casual dress. **Bar:** Full bar. **Reservations:** not accepted. **Hours:** 11 am-9 pm. Closed: 5/25, 11/26, 12/25; also Sun. **Address:** 8005 SE Stark St **Location:** I-84, exit 5, 1 mi s on SE 82nd Ave, then just w; I-205, exit 21A southbound; exit 20 northbound, 0.8 mi w. **Parking:** street. **Cards:** AX, DS, MC, VI.

The Portland Vicinity

BEAVERTON pop. 76,129   (See map and index starting on p. 402)

———— WHERE TO STAY ————

COMFORT INN & SUITES   *Book at AAA.com*   **Phone:** (503)643-9100   **72**

Hotel
$59-$159 All Year

Address: 13455 SW Tualatin Valley Hwy **Location:** SR 217, exit 2A (Canyon Rd/SR 8), 1 mi w. Located near light rail line. **Facility:** 105 units. 70 one-bedroom standard units. 35 one-bedroom suites, some with whirlpools. 4 stories, interior corridors. **Parking:** on-site. **Amenities:** high-speed Internet, voice mail, safes (fee), irons, hair dryers. *Some:* DVD players. **Pool(s):** heated outdoor. **Leisure Activities:** exercise room. **Guest Services:** valet and coin laundry, wireless Internet. **Business Services:** meeting rooms, PC. **Cards:** AX, DS, MC, VI.

COURTYARD BY MARRIOTT   *Book great rates at AAA.com*   **Phone:** (503)641-3200   **73**

Hotel
$159-$169 All Year

Address: 8500 SW Nimbus Ave **Location:** SR 217, exit 4 (Scholls Ferry Rd) northbound, just ne on Scholls Ferry Rd, just 0.3 mi w on Hall Blvd, then just s; exit 4A (Hall Blvd) southbound, just w on Hall Blvd, then just s. Located in a corporate business park. **Facility:** Smoke free premises. 149 units. 137 one-bedroom standard units. 12 one-bedroom suites. 3 stories, interior corridors. *Bath:* combo or shower only. **Parking:** on-site. **Terms:** cancellation fee imposed. **Amenities:** high-speed Internet, voice mail, irons, hair dryers. **Pool(s):** heated indoor. **Leisure Activities:** whirlpool, exercise room. **Guest Services:** valet and coin laundry, wireless Internet. **Business Services:** meeting rooms, PC. **Cards:** AX, CB, DC, DS, MC, VI.

AAA Benefit:
Members save a minimum 5% off the best available rate.

FAIRFIELD INN & SUITES BY MARRIOTT   *Book great rates at AAA.com*   **Phone:** (503)972-0048   **69**

Hotel
$139-$149 All Year

Address: 15583 NW Gateway Ct **Location:** US 26, exit 65, just sw on nw Cornell Rd, just s on NW 158th Ave, just se on nw Waterhouse Ave, then just e. **Facility:** Smoke free premises. 106 one-bedroom standard units. 4 stories, interior corridors. *Bath:* combo or shower only. **Parking:** on-site. **Terms:** cancellation fee imposed. **Amenities:** video games (fee), high-speed Internet, voice mail, irons, hair dryers. *Some:* CD players. **Pool(s):** heated indoor. **Leisure Activities:** whirlpool, exercise room. **Guest Services:** valet and coin laundry, wireless Internet. **Business Services:** meeting rooms, PC. **Cards:** AX, CB, DC, DS, MC, VI. **Free Special Amenities:** continental breakfast and high-speed Internet.

AAA Benefit:
Members save a minimum 5% off the best available rate.

▼ See AAA listing p 454 ▼

(See map and index starting on p. 402)

HILTON GARDEN INN PORTLAND/BEAVERTON   *Book great rates at AAA.com*   Phone: (503)439-1717   70

Hotel
$99-$199 All Year

Address: 15520 NW Gateway Ct **Location:** US 26, exit 65, just sw on NW Cornell Rd, just s on NW 158th Ave, just se on NW Waterhouse Ave, then just e. **Facility:** 150 one-bedroom standard units, some with whirlpools. 4 stories, interior corridors. *Bath:* combo or shower only. **Parking:** on-site. **Terms:** 1-30 night minimum stay, cancellation fee imposed. **Amenities:** video games (fee), high-speed Internet, voice mail, irons, hair dryers. **Pool(s):** heated indoor. **Leisure Activities:** whirlpool, exercise room. **Guest Services:** valet and coin laundry, area transportation, wireless Internet. **Business Services:** meeting rooms, business center. **Cards:** AX, CB, DC, DS, MC, VI.

AAA Benefit:
Members save 5% or more everyday!

HOMEWOOD SUITES BY HILTON   *Book great rates at AAA.com*   Phone: (503)614-0900   68

Hotel
$99-$179 All Year

Address: 15525 NW Gateway Ct **Location:** US 26, exit 65, just sw on NW Cornell Rd, just s on NW 158th Ave, just se on NW Waterhouse Ave, then just e. **Facility:** 123 units. 116 one- and 7 two-bedroom suites with efficiencies. 4 stories, interior corridors. *Bath:* combo or shower only. **Parking:** on-site. **Terms:** 1-30 night minimum stay, cancellation fee imposed. **Amenities:** video games (fee), high-speed Internet, dual phone lines, voice mail, irons, hair dryers. **Pool(s):** outdoor. **Leisure Activities:** exercise room, barbecue grills. **Guest Services:** valet and coin laundry, area transportation, wireless Internet. **Business Services:** meeting rooms, business center. **Cards:** AX, CB, DC, DS, MC, VI.

HOMEWOOD SUITES Hilton

AAA Benefit:
Members save 5% or more everyday!

PHOENIX INN SUITES-BEAVERTON   *Book great rates at AAA.com*   Phone: (503)614-8100   67

Hotel
$89-$149 All Year

Address: 15402 NW Cornell Rd **Location:** US 26, exit 65, just ne. **Facility:** Smoke free premises. 98 units. 96 one- and 2 two-bedroom standard units, some with whirlpools. 4 stories, interior corridors. *Bath:* combo or shower only. **Parking:** on-site. **Terms:** check-in 4 pm, cancellation fee imposed. **Amenities:** high-speed Internet, dual phone lines, voice mail, irons, hair dryers. *Some:* DVD players. **Pool(s):** heated indoor. **Leisure Activities:** whirlpool, exercise room. **Guest Services:** valet and coin laundry, area transportation-within 5 mi, wireless Internet. **Business Services:** meeting rooms, business center. **Cards:** AX, CB, DC, DS, MC, VI. **Free Special Amenities:** expanded continental breakfast and high-speed Internet. *(See color ad p 440)*

SHILO INN HOTEL & SUITES-PORTLAND/BEAVERTON   *Book great rates at AAA.com*   Phone: (503)297-2551   71

Hotel
$107-$187 All Year

Address: 9900 SW Canyon Rd **Location:** SR 217, exit 2A (Canyon Rd/Beaverton Hillsdale Hwy), 0.3 mi e on feeder road to SR 8 (Canyon Rd), then 0.6 mi e. **Facility:** 142 units. 139 one-bedroom standard units. 3 one-bedroom suites with kitchens. 2 stories (no elevator), interior corridors. *Bath:* combo or shower only. **Parking:** on-site. **Amenities:** video games (fee), high-speed Internet, voice mail, irons, hair dryers. **Pool(s):** heated outdoor. **Leisure Activities:** whirlpool, exercise room. **Guest Services:** valet and coin laundry, area transportation-St Vincent & local hospitals, wireless Internet. **Business Services:** PC. **Cards:** AX, CB, DC, DS, JC, MC, VI. **Free Special Amenities:** full breakfast and high-speed Internet. *(See color ad p 453)*

(See map and index starting on p. 402)

──────── **WHERE TO DINE** ────────

BUGATTI'S CEDAR HILLS
Phone: 503/626-1400   63
Italian
$8-$19
Delicious pizza, steak, pasta and seafood, along with burgers and panini sandwiches, make up the menu at this spot in a busy shopping area. Casual dress. **Bar:** Full bar. **Hours:** 11 am-10 pm, Fri-11 pm, Sat noon-11 pm, Sun noon-10 pm. Closed major holidays. **Address:** 2905 SW Cedar Hills Blvd **Location:** US 26, exit 68, 1.3 mi s; at SW Jenkins Rd and SW Cedar Hills Blvd. **Parking:** on-site. **Cards:** AX, DS, MC, VI.

ERNESTO'S ITALIAN RESTAURANT
Phone: 503/292-0119   65
Italian
$6-$18
Examples of traditional Italian fare include spaghetti with meatballs, tortellini with Alfredo or pesto sauce, cannelloni, manicotti, pizzas and calzones. Complete family-style dinners and early-bird specials are among offerings. Casual dress. **Bar:** Full bar. **Reservations:** suggested. **Hours:** 11 am-10 pm, Fri-11 pm, Sat 4:30 pm-11 pm, Sun 4 pm-9 pm. Closed major holidays. **Address:** 8544 SW Apple Way **Location:** SR 217, exit 2 (SR 10/Beaverton-Hillsdale Hwy), 1.4 mi e. **Parking:** on-site. **Cards:** AX, DS, MC, VI.

MCCORMICK & SCHMICK'S
Phone: 503/643-1322   64
Seafood
$6-$25
This place is all about seafood, which is imported from all over the world. Among good choices are Washington state oysters, Maine clams, delicate Hawaiian escolar and tuna from Ecuador. The clublike decor is cozy, and expert staff provide able assistance. Casual dress. **Bar:** Full bar. **Reservations:** suggested. **Hours:** 11:15 am-11 pm, Fri & Sat-midnight, Sun 4 pm-10 pm. Closed: 1/1, 12/25. **Address:** 9945 SW Beaverton-Hillsdale Hwy **Location:** SR 217, exit Beaverton-Hillsdale Hwy (SR 10), 0.6 mi e. **Parking:** on-site. **Cards:** AX, CB, DC, DS, MC, VI.

MCGRATH'S FISH HOUSE
Phone: 503/646-1881
Seafood
$9-$19
The popular chain specializes in fresh Pacific Northwest seafood, including dishes grilled over a wood fire and items from the daily fresh sheet. Also on the menu are steaks, chicken, pasta and gourmet burgers. Casual dress. **Bar:** Full bar. **Reservations:** not accepted. **Hours:** 11 am-10 pm. Closed: 11/26, 12/25. **Address:** 3211 SW Cedar Hills Blvd **Location:** US 26, exit 68, 1.5 mi s; at Cedar Hills Crossing Mall. **Parking:** on-site. **Cards:** AX, DC, DS, MC, VI.
CALL 🅼

MONTEAUX'S PUBLIC HOUSE
Phone: 503/439-9942   62
American
$7-$17
Each month, the restaurant features the cuisine of a different country, as well as house favorites, salads and pub fare. Casual dress. **Bar:** Full bar. **Reservations:** not accepted. **Hours:** 11 am-10 pm. Closed major holidays; also Sun. **Address:** 16165 SW Regatta Ln, Suite 1000 **Location:** US 26, exit 65, just s on Cornell Rd, 0.9 mi se on 158th Ave, just w on NW Walker Rd, then s on NW Schendel Ave. **Parking:** on-site. **Cards:** AX, DC, DS, MC, VI.
CALL 🅼

NEWPORT BAY RESTAURANT
Phone: 503/645-2526
Seafood
$8-$25
This restaurant is for those seeking a casual, relaxing time. A menu favorite is New England clam chowder, which is available nightly. Fresh Northwest salmon and Alaskan halibut prepared several ways share menu space with pasta, chicken and salads. Casual dress. **Bar:** Full bar. **Reservations:** accepted. **Hours:** 11 am-10 pm, Fri & Sat-11 pm, Sun 9 am-10 pm. Closed: 11/26, 12/25. **Address:** 2865 NW Town Center Loop **Location:** US 26, exit 64 (185th Ave). **Parking:** on-site. **Cards:** AX, DS, MC, VI.

THE STOCKPOT BROILER
Phone: 503/643-5451   66
Regional American
$8-$42
Views of the golf course enhance the dining experience at this restaurant. Northwest and international ingredients mingle in the dishes, which range from hand-cut steaks to such fresh seafood offerings as seared Pacific ahi and Alaskan halibut. Casual dress. **Bar:** Full bar. **Reservations:** suggested. **Hours:** 11:30 am-10:30 pm, Sun from 10 am; Sunday brunch. Closed: 1/1. **Address:** 8200 SW Scholls Ferry Rd **Location:** Just ne from jct SW Hall Blvd and SW Scholls Ferry Rd (SR 210); at Red Tail Golf Course. **Parking:** on-site. **Cards:** AX, DS, MC, VI.

THAI ORCHID RESTAURANT
Phone: 503/439-6683
Thai
$7-$15
Patrons can enjoy fresh, flavorful Thai food with no added monosodium glutamate at this restaurant. The varied menu includes salads, soups, stir-fried dishes, distinctive curries, seafood and noodles. Casual dress. **Bar:** Beer & wine. **Reservations:** accepted. **Hours:** 11:30 am-9 pm. Closed: 7/4, 12/25. **Address:** 18070 Evergreen Pkwy, Suite C **Location:** US 26, exit 64 (185th Ave), just s, then just e. **Parking:** on-site. **Cards:** AX, DS, MC, VI.

THAI ORCHID RESTAURANT
Phone: 503/617-4602
Thai
$7-$15
Patrons can enjoy fresh, flavorful Thai food with no added monosodium glutamate at this restaurant. The varied menu includes salads, soups, stir-fried dishes, distinctive curries, seafood and noodles. Casual dress. **Bar:** Beer & wine. **Reservations:** accepted. **Hours:** 11:30 am-9 pm. Closed: 7/4, 12/25. **Address:** 16165 SW Regatta Dr, Suite 300 **Location:** US 26, exit 65 westbound, just s on Cornell Rd, 0.9 mi s on 158th Ave, just nw on Walker Rd, then just s; exit eastbound, just straight on feeder road, then same directions as westbound. **Parking:** on-site. **Cards:** AX, DS, MC, VI.

TYPHOON!
Phone: 503/644-8010
Thai
$8-$19
The artful, contemporary Thai restaurant features classic entrees and new twists on old favorites. The extensive beverage menu lists an impressive tea selection from China, Japan and Thailand, as well as Thai beers and microbrews. Casual dress. **Bar:** Full bar. **Reservations:** suggested. **Hours:** 11 am-2 & 5-10 pm. Closed: 11/26, 12/25. **Address:** 12600 SW Crescent St **Location:** SR 217, exit 2A (Canyon Rd/SR 8), 0.5 mi w on SW Canyon Rd, then just n on Hall Blvd; at The Round and adjacent to Beaverton Central MAX rail station. **Parking:** on-site. **Cards:** AX, DS, MC, VI.
CALL 🅼

CLACKAMAS pop. 5,177   (See map and index starting on p. 402)

———— WHERE TO STAY ————

BEST WESTERN SUNNYSIDE INN   *Book great rates at AAA.com*

Hotel
$76-$106 All Year

Phone: (503)652-1500   124

Address: 12855 SE 97th Ave **Location:** I-205, exit 14, follow signs for Sunnyside Rd E, just e on Sunnyside Rd, then just s. **Facility:** 141 one-bedroom standard units, some with whirlpools. 3 stories, exterior corridors. **Parking:** on-site. **Terms:** check-in 4 pm, 7 day cancellation notice-fee imposed. **Amenities:** video games (fee), high-speed Internet, irons, hair dryers. **Pool(s):** heated outdoor. **Guest Services:** valet and coin laundry, airport transportation-Portland International Airport, area transportation-within 3 mi, wireless Internet. **Business Services:** meeting rooms, PC. **Cards:** AX, DC, DS, JC, MC, VI.

AAA Benefit:
Members save up to 20%, plus 10% bonus points with rewards program.

COMFORT SUITES   *Book at AAA.com*

Hotel
$81-$108 All Year

Phone: (503)723-3450   127

Address: 15929 SE McKinley Ave **Location:** I-205, exit 12 northbound, exit 12B southbound, just w. **Facility:** Smoke free premises. 50 units. 47 one-bedroom standard units. 3 one-bedroom suites with whirlpools. 3 stories, interior corridors. *Bath:* combo or shower only. **Parking:** on-site. **Terms:** cancellation fee imposed. **Amenities:** high-speed Internet, dual phone lines, voice mail, safes, irons, hair dryers. **Pool(s):** heated indoor. **Leisure Activities:** sauna, whirlpool, exercise room. **Guest Services:** coin laundry, wireless Internet. **Business Services:** meeting rooms, PC. **Cards:** AX, DS, MC, VI.

COURTYARD BY MARRIOTT PORTLAND-SOUTHEAST   *Book great rates at AAA.com*
Hotel
$132-$154 All Year

Phone: (503)652-2900   125

Address: 9300 SE Sunnybrook Blvd **Location:** I-205, exit 14, follow signs for SE Sunnybrook Blvd W, then just w. Located near Clackamas Promenade. **Facility:** Smoke free premises. 136 units. 129 one-bedroom standard units, some with whirlpools. 7 one-bedroom suites. 4 stories, interior corridors. *Bath:* combo or shower only. **Parking:** on-site. **Terms:** cancellation fee imposed. **Amenities:** video games (fee), high-speed Internet, dual phone lines, voice mail, irons, hair dryers. **Pool(s):** heated indoor. **Leisure Activities:** whirlpool, exercise room. **Guest Services:** valet and coin laundry, area transportation, wireless Internet. **Business Services:** meeting rooms, business center. **Cards:** AX, CB, DC, DS, JC, MC, VI.

AAA Benefit:
Members save a minimum 5% off the best available rate.

DAYS INN-PORTLAND SOUTH   *Book great rates at AAA.com*
Hotel
$65-$89 All Year

Phone: (503)654-1699   123

Address: 9717 SE Sunnyside Rd **Location:** I-205, exit 14, follow signs for SE Sunnyside Rd, just e on SE Sunnyside Rd, then just n on SE Stevens Rd. **Facility:** 96 units. 95 one-bedroom standard units. 1 one-bedroom suite with kitchen. 3 stories, interior corridors. *Bath:* combo or shower only. **Parking:** on-site. **Terms:** check-in 4 pm. **Amenities:** video games (fee), high-speed Internet. *Some:* DVD players, irons. **Pool(s):** heated outdoor. **Leisure Activities:** sauna, whirlpool, limited exercise equipment. **Guest Services:** valet laundry, airport transportation-Portland International Airport, area transportation-within 2 mi, wireless Internet. **Business Services:** meeting rooms, PC. **Cards:** AX, DS, MC, VI. **Free Special Amenities:** expanded continental breakfast and high-speed Internet.

▼ See AAA listing p 457 ▼

(See map and index starting on p. 402)

HAMPTON INN — *Book great rates at AAA.com* — Phone: (503)655-7900 — **126**

AAA SAVE

Hotel
$85-$100 All Year

Address: 9040 SE Adams **Location:** I-205, exit 12A southbound; exit 12 northbound, just e on SR 212, then just n on SE 82nd Dr. **Facility:** 114 one-bedroom standard units. 4 stories, interior corridors. *Bath:* combo or shower only. **Parking:** on-site. **Terms:** 1-30 night minimum stay, cancellation fee imposed. **Amenities:** video games (fee), high-speed Internet, voice mail, irons, hair dryers. **Leisure Activities:** whirlpool, exercise room. **Guest Services:** valet and coin laundry, wireless Internet. **Business Services:** meeting rooms, PC. **Cards:** AX, CB, DC, DS, JC, MC, VI. **Free Special Amenities:** expanded continental breakfast and high-speed Internet. *(See color ad p 456)*

AAA Benefit:
Members save up to 10% everyday!

——— WHERE TO DINE ———

GUSTAV'S GERMAN PUB & GRILL — Phone: 503/653-1391 — **104**

German
$7-$21

The restaurant serves traditional German fare, including wood-smoked bier sausage, schnitzel, red cabbage and sauerkraut and rotisserie pork, turkey and lamb. Those who want to try it all should try Gustav's party feast and the memorable Swiss cheese fondue. Many local and imported beers are available, as is a choice of desserts that includes English bread pudding made with oven-baked croissants. Casual dress. **Bar:** Full bar. **Reservations:** not accepted. **Hours:** 11 am-11 pm, Fri & Sat-midnight. Closed: 12/25. **Address:** 12605 SE 97th **Location:** I-205, exit 14, follow signs for Sunnyside Rd E, just e on SE Sunnyside Rd, then just s. **Parking:** on-site. **Cards:** AX, MC, VI.

CALL

STANFORD'S RESTAURANT & BAR — Phone: 503/653-9400 — **103**

American
$10-$08

Fresh seafood and quality steaks are the norm at the restaurant, where several dishes are prepared using wood-fire grilling. This place is near a mall. Casual dress. **Bar:** Full bar. **Reservations:** accepted. **Hours:** 11 am-11 pm, Fri & Sat-midnight. Closed: 11/26, 12/25. **Address:** 8416 SE Sunnyside Rd **Location:** I-205, exit 14, follow signs for Sunnyside Rd, then just w; at Clackamas Promenade. **Parking:** on-site. **Cards:** AX, DS, MC, VI.

CALL

GLADSTONE pop. 11,438 (See map and index starting on p. 402)

——— WHERE TO STAY ———

OXFORD SUITES — *Book at AAA.com* — Phone: (503)722-7777 — **130**

Hotel
$95-$125 All Year

Address: 75 82nd Dr **Location:** I-205, exit 11, 0.3 mi sw. **Facility:** Smoke free premises. 98 units. 90 one- and 8 two-bedroom standard units. 5 stories, interior corridors. *Bath:* combo or shower only. **Parking:** on-site. **Amenities:** video library (fee), voice mail, irons, hair dryers. **Pool(s):** heated indoor. **Leisure Activities:** whirlpool, steamroom, exercise room. **Guest Services:** valet and coin laundry, area transportation, wireless Internet. **Business Services:** meeting rooms, PC. **Cards:** AX, DS, MC, VI.

——— WHERE TO DINE ———

BURGERVILLE — Phone: 503/655-3932

American
$2-$8

First-timers shouldn't let the fast food exterior fool them, as the burgers and chicken here adhere to a higher standard. Northwest ingredients come into play in the sandwiches. Casual dress. **Hours:** 7 am-10 pm. Closed: 11/26, 12/25. **Address:** 19119 SE McLoughlin Blvd **Location:** I-205, exit 9, 1.4 mi n on SR 99 E (McLoughlin Blvd). **Parking:** on-site. **Cards:** DS, MC, VI.

GRESHAM pop. 90,205 (See map and index starting on p. 402)

——— WHERE TO STAY ———

BEST WESTERN PONY SOLDIER INN — *Book great rates at AAA.com* — Phone: (503)665-1591 — **105**

AAA SAVE

Hotel
$99-$169 All Year

Address: 1060 NE Cleveland Ave **Location:** I-84, exit 14 (Fairview Pkwy), 0.9 mi s, 0.4 mi e on NE Glisan St, 1.2 mi s on NE 223rd Ave, 0.7 mi e on Burnside Rd, then just s. **Facility:** 74 one-bedroom standard units. 2 stories (no elevator), interior corridors. **Parking:** on-site. **Terms:** 7 day cancellation notice. **Amenities:** video games (fee), high-speed Internet, irons, hair dryers. *Some:* dual phone lines. **Pool(s):** heated outdoor. **Leisure Activities:** sauna, whirlpool, exercise room. **Guest Services:** complimentary and valet laundry, wireless Internet. **Business Services:** meeting rooms, PC. **Cards:** AX, DC, DS, MC, VI. **Free Special Amenities:** expanded continental breakfast and high-speed Internet.

AAA Benefit:
Members save up to 20%, plus 10% bonus points with rewards program.

(See map and index starting on p. 402)

COMFORT SUITES PORTLAND/GRESHAM

Book great rates at AAA.com   Phone: (503)661-2200   101

AAA SAVE
▼▼▼
Hotel
$80-$280 All Year

Address: 1477 NE 183rd St **Location:** I-84, exit 13, 0.5 mi s on NE 181st Ave, just e on NE Halsey St, then just s. **Facility:** Smoke free premises. 83 units. 79 one- and 3 two-bedroom standard units, some with whirlpools. 1 one-bedroom suite. 4 stories, interior corridors. **Parking:** on-site. **Amenities:** high-speed Internet, dual phone lines, voice mail, irons, hair dryers. **Pool(s):** heated indoor. **Leisure Activities:** sauna, whirlpool, exercise room. **Guest Services:** valet and coin laundry, wireless Internet. **Business Services:** meeting rooms, PC. **Cards:** AX, DC, DS, MC, VI. **Free Special Amenities:** expanded continental breakfast and high-speed Internet.

DAYS INN & SUITES

Book great rates at AAA.com   Phone: (503)465-1515   103

AAA SAVE
▼▼▼
Hotel
$74-$114 All Year

Address: 24124 SE Stark St **Location:** I-84, exit 16, 1.5 mi s on NE 238th Dr/NE 242nd Dr, then just w. **Facility:** 53 one-bedroom standard units, some with whirlpools. 2 stories (no elevator), interior corridors. *Bath:* combo or shower only. **Parking:** on-site. **Terms:** cancellation fee imposed. **Amenities:** high-speed Internet, hair dryers. *Some:* DVD players (fee), irons. **Pool(s):** heated indoor. **Leisure Activities:** whirlpool, exercise room. **Guest Services:** coin laundry, wireless Internet. **Business Services:** PC. **Cards:** AX, DC, DS, MC, VI. **Free Special Amenities:** continental breakfast and high-speed Internet.

DAYS INN-PORTLAND EAST/GRESHAM

Book at AAA.com   Phone: (503)618-8400   99

▼▼▼
Hotel
$64-$100 All Year

Address: 2261 NE 181st Ave **Location:** I-84, exit 13, just sw. **Facility:** 75 one-bedroom standard units, some with whirlpools. 4 stories, interior corridors. *Bath:* combo or shower only. **Parking:** on-site. **Amenities:** high-speed Internet, dual phone lines, voice mail, irons, hair dryers. **Pool(s):** heated indoor. **Leisure Activities:** exercise room. **Guest Services:** valet and coin laundry, wireless Internet. **Business Services:** meeting rooms, PC. **Cards:** AX, DS, MC, VI.

EXTENDED STAYAMERICA PORTLAND/GRESHAM

Book at AAA.com   Phone: (503)661-0226   98

▼▼
Hotel
$80-$95 All Year

Address: 17777 NE Sacramento St **Location:** I-84, exit 13, 0.3 mi s on NE 181st Ave, just s on NE San Rafael St, then just n on NE 178th Ave. **Facility:** 104 one-bedroom standard units with efficiencies. 3 stories, interior corridors. *Bath:* combo or shower only. **Parking:** on-site. **Terms:** office hours 7 am-11 pm, cancellation fee imposed. **Amenities:** high-speed Internet (fee), voice mail, irons. **Guest Services:** coin laundry, wireless Internet. **Cards:** AX, CB, DC, DS, JC, MC, VI.

FOUR POINTS BY SHERATON PORTLAND EAST

Book great rates at AAA.com   Phone: (503)491-1818   100

AAA SAVE
▼▼▼
Hotel
$90-$190 All Year

Address: 1919 NE 181st Ave **Location:** I-84, exit 13, 0.3 mi s on NE 181st Ave, then just w on NE San Rafael St. **Facility:** Smoke free premises. 74 units. 71 one-bedroom standard units, some with whirlpools. 3 one-bedroom suites. 3 stories, interior corridors. *Bath:* combo or shower only. **Parking:** on-site. **Amenities:** video games (fee), high-speed Internet, dual phone lines, voice mail, irons, hair dryers. **Dining:** Francis Xavier's Restaurant and Lounge, see separate listing. **Pool(s):** heated indoor. **Leisure Activities:** whirlpool, library, exercise room. **Guest Services:** valet and coin laundry, wireless Internet. **Business Services:** meeting rooms, business center. **Cards:** AX, CB, DC, DS, JC, MC, VI. **Free Special Amenities:** continental breakfast and high-speed Internet.

FOUR ✦ POINTS
BY SHERATON

AAA Benefit:
Members get up to 15% off, plus Starwood Preferred Guest® bonuses.

HAMPTON INN PORTLAND EAST

Book great rates at AAA.com   Phone: (503)669-7000   97

▼▼▼
Hotel
$109-$129 All Year

Address: 3039 NE 181st Ave **Location:** I-84, exit 13, just nw. **Facility:** 60 one-bedroom standard units, some with whirlpools. 3 stories, interior corridors. *Bath:* combo or shower only. **Parking:** on-site. **Terms:** 1-30 night minimum stay, cancellation fee imposed. **Amenities:** high-speed Internet, voice mail, irons, hair dryers. **Pool(s):** heated indoor. **Leisure Activities:** whirlpool, exercise room. **Guest Services:** valet and coin laundry, wireless Internet. **Business Services:** meeting rooms, business center. **Cards:** AX, CB, DC, DS, MC, VI.

Hampton Inn

AAA Benefit:
Members save up to 10% everyday!

HOLIDAY INN PORTLAND/GRESHAM

Book great rates at AAA.com   Phone: (503)907-1777   104

▼▼▼
Hotel
$95-$195 All Year

Address: 2752 NE Hogan Dr **Location:** I-84, exit 16, 1.8 mi s on 238th/Hogan drs. **Facility:** 168 one-bedroom standard units, some with whirlpools. 4 stories, interior corridors. *Bath:* combo or shower only. **Parking:** on-site. **Terms:** check-in 4 pm, cancellation fee imposed. **Amenities:** high-speed Internet, voice mail, irons, hair dryers. **Pool(s):** heated indoor. **Leisure Activities:** whirlpool, exercise room. **Guest Services:** valet and coin laundry, wireless Internet. **Business Services:** conference facilities, PC. **Cards:** AX, DS, MC, VI.

(See map and index starting on p. 402)

HOWARD JOHNSON GRESHAM   *Book great rates at AAA.com*   Phone: (503)666-9545   106

(AAA) [SAVE]

▼▼ ▼▼

Hotel
$49-$179 All Year

Address: 1572 NE Burnside Rd **Location:** I-84, exit 16, 2.7 mi s on NE 238th Dr, just w on Division St, then just se; I-205, exit 19, 5.5 mi e on Division St, then just se. **Facility:** 72 units. 68 one- and 4 two-bedroom standard units, some with whirlpools. 2 stories, interior corridors. *Bath:* combo or shower only. **Parking:** on-site. **Terms:** cancellation fee imposed. **Pool(s):** outdoor. **Leisure Activities:** limited exercise equipment. **Guest Services:** coin laundry, wireless Internet. **Business Services:** meeting rooms, PC. **Cards:** AX, DS, MC, VI. **Free Special Amenities: continental breakfast and high-speed Internet.**

[icons]

SUPER 8   *Book great rates at AAA.com*   Phone: (503)661-5100   102

(AAA) [SAVE]

▼▼ ▼▼

Hotel
$64-$79 All Year

Address: 121 NE 181st Ave **Location:** I-84, exit 13, 1 mi s. Located on light rail. **Facility:** 44 one-bedroom standard units. 2 stories (no elevator), interior corridors. **Parking:** on-site. **Terms:** cancellation fee imposed. **Amenities:** high-speed Internet, hair dryers. **Guest Services:** coin laundry, wireless Internet. **Business Services:** meeting rooms, PC. **Cards:** AX, CB, DC, DS, JC, MC, VI. **Free Special Amenities: expanded continental breakfast and high-speed Internet.**

[icons]

——— WHERE TO DINE ———

BOCCELLI'S RESTAURANT   Phone: 503/492-9534   82

▼▼ ◆◆

Italian
$8-$19

Splashed in contemporary decor, this restaurant serves classic pasta dishes, including ravioli, with made-from-scratch sauces that combine the freshest ingredients. Salads, steaks and sandwiches round out the menu. Al fresco meals can be enjoyed on the sidewalk patio in front or on the small cozy patio in the back. Casual dress. **Bar:** Beer & wine. **Reservations:** accepted. **Hours:** 11 am-9 pm, Fri & Sat-10 pm, Sun noon-9 pm. Closed major holidays. **Address:** 246 N Main St **Location:** I-84, exit 13, 1.3 mi s on NE 181st Ave, 2.4 mi e on SE Burnside Rd, then 0.6 mi s; jct NE 3rd St; in historic downtown. **Parking:** on-site. **Cards:** AX, DS, MC, VI.

BURGERVILLE   Phone: 503/665-0931

◆

American
$2-$8

First-timers shouldn't let the fast food exterior fool them, as the burgers and chicken here adhere to a higher standard. Northwest ingredients come into play in the sandwiches. Casual dress. **Hours:** 7 am-10 pm. Closed: 11/26, 12/25. **Address:** 2975 NE Hogan Dr **Location:** I-84, exit 16, 1.7 mi s on 238th/Hogan Dr. **Parking:** on-site. **Cards:** DS, MC, VI.

FRANCIS XAVIER'S RESTAURANT AND LOUNGE   Phone: 503/666-1957   80

▼▼ ◆◆

American
$8-$18

All-day breakfast items and cooked-from-scratch family-style specials are among restaurant offerings. Steaks, seafood, burgers and sandwiches round out the menu. Casual dress. **Bar:** Full bar. **Reservations:** accepted. **Hours:** 6 am-10 pm. Closed: 11/26, 12/25. **Address:** 1933 NE 181st Ave **Location:** I-84, exit 13, 0.3 mi s on NE 181st Ave, then just w on NE San Rafael St; in Four Points by Sheraton Portland East. **Parking:** on-site. **Cards:** AX, DC, DS, MC, VI.

HEIDI'S   Phone: 503/667-4200   81

▼▼ ◆◆

American
$7-$18

Since 1968, this family-owned-and-operated establishment has served Swiss-German entrees, including Swiss cabbage rolls as well as homemade soups, creative burgers, tasty sandwiches and seafood, beef and poultry selections. Fresh bakery items also tempt. Casual dress. **Bar:** Full bar. **Reservations:** accepted. **Hours:** 6:30 am-9:30 pm. Closed: 12/25. **Address:** 1230 NE Cleveland Ave **Location:** I-84, exit 16, 2.5 mi s on NE 238th Dr, just w on Division St, then just n on Burnside; I-205, exit 19, 5.5 mi e on Division St, then just n on Burnside Rd. **Parking:** on-site. **Cards:** AX, DC, DS, MC, VI.

NEWPORT BAY RESTAURANT   Phone: 503/661-2722

▼▼ ▼▼

Seafood
$8-$25

This restaurant is for those seeking a casual, relaxing time. A menu favorite is New England clam chowder, which is available nightly. Fresh Northwest salmon and Alaskan halibut prepared several ways share menu space with pasta, chicken and salads. Casual dress. **Bar:** Full bar. **Reservations:** accepted. **Hours:** 11 am-10 pm, Fri & Sat-11 pm, Sun 9 am-10 pm. Closed: 11/26, 12/25. **Address:** 2757 SE Burnside Rd **Location:** I-84, exit 16, just s on 238th Dr, 2.8 mi s, then 0.9 mi e; near jct Powell Blvd and Burnside Rd. **Parking:** on-site. **Cards:** AX, DS, MC, VI.

CALL [icons]

TYPHOON!   Phone: 503/669-9995

▼▼ ◆◆

Thai
$9-$24

The artful, contemporary Thai restaurant features classic entrees and new twists on old favorites. The extensive beverage menu lists an impressive tea selection from China, Japan and Thailand, as well as Thai beers and microbrews. Casual dress. **Bar:** Full bar. **Reservations:** suggested. **Hours:** 11 am-2 & 5-10 pm. Closed: 11/26, 12/25. **Address:** 543 NW 12th St **Location:** Near jct Division St and Eastman Pkwy; in Gresham Station Shopping Center. **Parking:** on-site. **Cards:** AX, DS, MC, VI.

HILLSBORO   pop. 70,186   (See map and index starting on p. 402)

——— **WHERE TO STAY** ———

COURTYARD BY MARRIOTT   *Book great rates at AAA.com*   Phone: (503)690-1800   56

Hotel
$179-$219 All Year

Address: 3050 NW Stucki Pl **Location:** US 26, exit 64, just s on NW 185th Ave, 0.3 mi w on NW Evergreen Pkwy, then just n. Located in a corporate business park. **Facility:** Smoke free premises. 155 units. 149 one-bedroom standard units. 6 one-bedroom suites. 3 stories, interior corridors. *Bath:* combo or shower only. **Parking:** on-site. **Terms:** cancellation fee imposed. **Amenities:** high-speed Internet, dual phone lines, voice mail, irons, hair dryers. **Pool(s):** heated indoor. **Leisure Activities:** whirlpool, exercise room. **Guest Services:** valet and coin laundry, area transportation, wireless Internet. **Business Services:** meeting rooms, PC. **Cards:** AX, CB, DC, DS, JC, MC, VI.

AAA Benefit:
Members save a minimum 5% off the best available rate.

THE DUNES MOTEL   Phone: (503)648-8991   64

Motel
$55-$95 All Year

Address: 452 SE 10th Ave (SR 8) **Location:** US 26, exit 62A westbound; exit 62 eastbound, 1.1 mi s on NW Cornelius Pass Rd, then 4.4 mi w on NE Cornell Rd. **Facility:** 40 one-bedroom standard units. 2 stories (no elevator), interior corridors. **Parking:** on-site. **Terms:** cancellation fee imposed. **Amenities:** *Some:* DVD players, high-speed Internet. **Guest Services:** wireless Internet. **Cards:** AX, DS, MC, VI. **Free Special Amenities:** early check-in/late check-out and high-speed Internet.

EXTENDED STAYAMERICA-PORTLAND-BEAVERTON   *Book at AAA.com*   Phone: (503)439-1515   63

Hotel
$88-$104 All Year

Address: 18665 NW Eider Ct **Location:** US 26, exit 64, 0.7 mi s on NW 185th Ave, then just w. **Facility:** 122 one-bedroom standard units with efficiencies. 3 stories, interior corridors. *Bath:* combo or shower only. **Parking:** on-site. **Terms:** office hours 7 am-11 pm, cancellation fee imposed. **Amenities:** high-speed Internet (fee), voice mail, irons. **Guest Services:** coin laundry, wireless Internet. **Cards:** AX, CB, DC, DS, JC, MC, VI.

EXTENDED STAY DELUXE-PORTLAND-HILLSBORO-NW CORNELL RD   *Book at AAA.com*   Phone: (503)439-0706   60

Hotel
$108-$123 All Year

Address: 19311 NW Cornell Rd **Location:** US 26, exit 64, 0.5 mi s on NW 185th Ave, then 0.4 mi w. **Facility:** 136 units. 113 one-bedroom standard units with efficiencies. 23 one-bedroom suites with efficiencies. 3 stories, interior corridors. *Bath:* combo or shower only. **Parking:** on-site. **Terms:** office hours 7 am-11 pm, cancellation fee imposed. **Amenities:** DVD players, high-speed Internet (fee), dual phone lines, voice mail, irons, hair dryers. **Pool(s):** heated outdoor. **Leisure Activities:** exercise room. **Guest Services:** coin laundry, wireless Internet. **Cards:** AX, CB, DC, DS, JC, MC, VI.

HOLIDAY INN EXPRESS HILLSBORO   *Book great rates at AAA.com*   Phone: (503)844-9696   61

Hotel
$109-$159 All Year

Address: 5900 NE Ray Cir **Location:** US 26, exit 62A westbound; exit 62 eastbound, 1 mi s on Cornelius Pass Rd, 1.1 mi w on NW Cornell Rd, then just s. **Facility:** 86 one-bedroom standard units. 4 stories, interior corridors. *Bath:* combo or shower only. **Parking:** on-site. **Amenities:** video games (fee), high-speed Internet, dual phone lines, voice mail, safes, irons, hair dryers. **Leisure Activities:** whirlpool, exercise room. **Guest Services:** valet and coin laundry, wireless Internet. **Business Services:** meeting rooms, business center. **Cards:** AX, CB, DC, DS, MC, VI. **Free Special Amenities:** full breakfast and high-speed Internet.

▼ See AAA listing p 461 ▼

(See map and index starting on p. 402)

LARKSPUR LANDING HILLSBORO/PORTLAND   *Book great rates at AAA.com*   Phone: (503)681-2121   55

AAA (SAVE)
▼▼◇▼▼
Hotel
$99-$171 All Year

Address: 3133 NE Shute Rd **Location:** US 26, exit 61, 1.1 mi s. Located in Dawson Creek Park area. **Facility:** 125 units. 77 one-bedroom standard units with efficiencies. 48 one-bedroom suites, some with efficiencies or kitchens. 4 stories, interior corridors. *Bath:* combo or shower only. **Parking:** on-site. **Terms:** cancellation fee imposed. **Amenities:** video library, DVD players, CD players, high-speed Internet, dual phone lines, voice mail, irons, hair dryers. **Leisure Activities:** whirlpool, barbecue area, gazebo, exercise room. **Guest Services:** complimentary and valet laundry, airport transportation-Hillsboro Airport, area transportation-within 5 mi, wireless Internet. **Business Services:** business center. **Cards:** AX, DS, MC, VI. **Free Special Amenities:** expanded continental breakfast and high-speed Internet.
(See color ad p 460)

✈ ⊠ 🐾 🛗 📷 💻 / SOME UNITS FEE 🐕 ⊠

RED LION HOTEL HILLSBORO   Phone: (503)648-3500   62

AAA (SAVE)
(fyi)
Hotel
$99-$169 All Year

Under major renovation, scheduled to be completed January 2009. Last rated: ▼▼▼ **Address:** 3500 NE Cornell Rd **Location:** US 26, exit 62A, 1 mi s on Cornelius Pass Rd, then 2.5 mi w. Located opposite Hillsboro Airport. **Facility:** Smoke free premises. 122 one-bedroom standard units, some with whirlpools. 2 stories (no elevator), interior corridors. *Bath:* combo or shower only. **Parking:** on-site. **Terms:** cancellation fee imposed. **Amenities:** video games (fee), high-speed Internet, voice mail, irons, hair dryers. **Pool(s):** heated outdoor. **Leisure Activities:** whirlpool, exercise room. **Guest Services:** valet and coin laundry, airport transportation-Hillsboro Airport, area transportation-within 10 mi, wireless Internet. **Business Services:** conference facilities. **Cards:** AX, CB, DC, DS, JC, MC, VI. **Free Special Amenities:** newspaper and high-speed Internet.

✈ 🍴 🍸 🐾 ⊠ 🐾 🛗 📷 💻 / SOME UNITS FEE 🐕

(See map and index starting on p. 402)

RESIDENCE INN BY MARRIOTT PORTLAND WEST   *Book great rates at AAA.com*   Phone: (503)531-3200   57

Hotel
$179-$219 All Year

Address: 18855 NW Tanasbourne Dr **Location:** US 26, exit 64, just s on NW 185th Ave, then just w. Located in a corporate business park. **Facility:** Smoke free premises. 122 units. 73 one-bedroom standard units with kitchens. 17 one- and 32 two-bedroom suites with kitchens. 2 stories, interior/exterior corridors. *Bath:* combo or shower only. **Parking:** on-site. **Terms:** cancellation fee imposed. **Amenities:** high-speed Internet, voice mail, irons, hair dryers. **Pool(s):** outdoor. **Leisure Activities:** whirlpools, exercise room, sports court. **Guest Services:** valet and coin laundry, area transportation, wireless Internet. **Business Services:** meeting rooms, business center. **Cards:** AX, CB, DC, DS, JC, MC, VI.

AAA Benefit:
Members save a minimum 5% off the best available rate.

SPRINGHILL SUITES BY MARRIOTT   *Book great rates at AAA.com*   Phone: (503)547-0202   58

Hotel
$161-$197 All Year

Address: 7351 NE Butler St **Location:** US 26, exit 62A westbound; exit 62 eastbound, 1 mi s on Cornelius Pass Rd, then just w. **Facility:** Smoke free premises. 106 one-bedroom standard units, some with whirlpools. 4 stories, interior corridors. *Bath:* combo or shower only. **Parking:** on-site. **Terms:** cancellation fee imposed. **Amenities:** video games (fee), high-speed Internet, dual phone lines, voice mail, irons, hair dryers. *Some:* DVD players. **Pool(s):** heated indoor. **Leisure Activities:** whirlpool, exercise room. **Guest Services:** valet and coin laundry, area transportation, wireless Internet. **Business Services:** meeting rooms, PC. **Cards:** AX, CB, DC, DS, JC, MC, VI.

AAA Benefit:
Members save a minimum 5% off the best available rate.

TOWNEPLACE SUITES BY MARRIOTT-PORTLAND HILLSBORO   *Book great rates at AAA.com*   Phone: (503)268-6000   59

Hotel
$170-$208 All Year

Address: 6550 NE Brighton St **Location:** US 26, exit 62A westbound; exit 62 eastbound, just s, 1 mi s on Cornelius Pass Rd, 0.7 mi w on Cornell Rd, just n on NW 229th Ave, then just w. **Facility:** Smoke free premises. 136 one-bedroom standard units, some with efficiencies. 2 stories (no elevator), interior/exterior corridors. *Bath:* combo or shower only. **Parking:** on-site. **Terms:** cancellation fee imposed. **Amenities:** high-speed Internet, voice mail, irons, hair dryers. *Some:* dual phone lines. **Pool(s):** heated outdoor. **Leisure Activities:** whirlpool, exercise room, sports court. **Guest Services:** valet and coin laundry, area transportation, wireless Internet. **Business Services:** meeting rooms, business center. **Cards:** AX, CB, DC, DS, JC, MC, VI.

AAA Benefit:
Members save a minimum 5% off the best available rate.

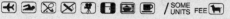

——— WHERE TO DINE ———

BUGATTI'S TANASBOURNE   Phone: 503/352-5252   58

Italian
$8-$19

Delicious pizza, steak, pasta and seafood, along with burgers and panini sandwiches, make up the menu at the attractive restaurant, which isn't far from the busy Tanasbourne shopping center. Casual dress. **Bar:** Full bar. **Reservations:** not accepted. **Hours:** 11 am-10 pm, Fri-11 pm, Sat noon-11 pm, Sun noon-10 pm. Closed major holidays. **Address:** 2364 NW Amberbrook Dr **Location:** US 26, exit 64 (185th Ave), 0.5 mi s on NW 185th Ave, 0.8 mi w on NW Cornell Rd, then just s. **Parking:** on-site. **Cards:** AX, DS, MC, VI.

BURGERVILLE   Phone: 503/690-0299

American
$2-$8

First-timers shouldn't let the fast food exterior fool them, as the burgers and chicken here adhere to a higher standard. Northwest ingredients come into play in the sandwiches. Casual dress. **Hours:** 7 am-10 pm. Closed: 11/26, 12/25. **Address:** 1245 NW 185th Ave **Location:** US 26, exit 64, 0.8 mi s. **Parking:** on-site. **Cards:** DS, MC, VI.

MCMENAMINS   Phone: 503/640-6174

American
$5-$20

The casual neighborhood eatery is where friends gather for classic pub and comfort fare, all washed down by pints of locally made beer. Large wooden booths or tables easily accommodate larger groups, and the eclectic, custom-painted walls and varied period light fixtures keep diners' eyes busy should the conversation lag. Casual dress. **Bar:** Full bar. **Hours:** 11 am-11 pm, Fri & Sat-midnight, Sun & Mon-10 pm. Closed: 12/25. **Address:** 4045 NW Cornelius Pass Rd **Location:** US 26 westbound, exit 62A south, 0.3 mi s; exit 62 eastbound, 0.3 mi s. **Parking:** on-site. **Cards:** MC, VI.

PASTA PRONTO CAFE   Phone: 503/690-8888   57

Italian
$8-$13

Tucked away in a shopping center, this popular cafe's menu offerings include crostinis, Italian sandwiches, pasta prepared with any of nine sauces, pizzas and such house specialties as salmon with bowtie pasta and four-cheese ravioli. Several "grab 'n' go, heat 'n' eat specials" appeal to diners in a hurry. Casual dress. **Bar:** Beer & wine. **Hours:** 11 am-9 pm, Sun 11:30 am-8 pm. Closed major holidays. **Address:** 2467 NW 185th Ave **Location:** US 26, exit 64, just s; in Tanasbourne Village Shopping Center, northwest corner. **Parking:** on-site. **Cards:** AX, DS, MC, VI.

(See map and index starting on p. 402)

P.F. CHANG'S CHINA BISTRO   **Phone:** 503/533-4580   59

Chinese
$10-$21

Trendy, upscale decor provides a pleasant backdrop for New Age Chinese dining. Appetizers, soups and salads are a meal by themselves. Vegetarian plates and sides, noodles, meins, chicken and meat dishes are created from exotic, fresh ingredients. Casual dress. **Bar:** Full bar. **Reservations:** accepted. **Hours:** 11 am-11 pm, Fri & Sat-midnight. Closed: 11/26, 12/25. **Address:** 19320 NW Emma Way **Location:** US 26, exit 64, 1 mi s, then 0.5 mi w on NW Cornell Rd; jct NW Cornell Rd and NW Stucki Pl; in the Streets of Tanasbourne. **Parking:** on-site. **Cards:** AX, DC, DS, MC, VI.

CALL ⓦⓜ

STANFORD'S RESTAURANT & BAR   **Phone:** 503/645-8000   56

American
$10-$38

A casual spot convenient to the Sunset Highway (US 26), Stanford's presents a menu of daily fresh fish choices, in addition to quality steaks, rock-salt-roasted prime rib, vegetarian selections and pasta. Lighter fare, such as burgers and sandwiches, also is available, and several items are prepared over a wood-fire grill. The seasonal patio overlooks a water feature. Casual dress. **Bar:** Full bar. **Reservations:** accepted. **Hours:** 11 am-11 pm, Fri & Sat-midnight. Closed: 11/26, 12/25. **Address:** 2770 NW 188th Ave **Location:** US 26, exit 64, just s. **Parking:** on-site. **Cards:** AX, DC, DS, MC, VI.

THAI ORCHID RESTAURANT   **Phone:** 503/681-2611

Thai
$7-$15

Patrons can enjoy fresh, flavorful Thai food with no added monosodium glutamate at this restaurant. The varied menu includes salads, soups, stir-fried dishes, distinctive curries, seafood and noodles. Casual dress. **Bar:** Beer & wine. **Reservations:** accepted. **Hours:** 11:30 am-9 pm. Closed: 7/4, 12/25. **Address:** 4550 NE Cornell Rd **Location:** US 26 W, exit 62A southbound, 1.1 mi s on Cornelius Pass Rd, then 1.8 mi w; exit 62 eastbound, 1.1 mi s on Cornelius Pass Rd, then 1.8 mi w. **Parking:** on-site. **Cards:** AX, DS, MC, VI.

KING CITY pop. 1,949 (See map and index starting on p. 402)

———— **WHERE TO STAY** ————

BEST WESTERN NORTHWIND INN & SUITES   *Book great rates at AAA.com*   **Phone:** (503)431-2100   94

Hotel
$120-$135 All Year

Address: 16105 SW Pacific Hwy **Location:** I-5, exit 292, just nw on SR 217, exit 6 (SR 99W), then 2.5 mi s. **Facility:** 71 units. 69 one- and 2 two-bedroom standard units, some with whirlpools. 3 stories, interior corridors. *Bath:* combo or shower only. **Parking:** on-site. **Terms:** cancellation fee imposed. **Amenities:** high-speed Internet, dual phone lines, voice mail, irons, hair dryers. **Pool(s):** heated indoor. **Leisure Activities:** whirlpool, exercise room. **Guest Services:** valet and coin laundry, wireless Internet. **Business Services:** meeting rooms, PC. **Cards:** AX, DC, DS, JC, MC, VI. **Free Special Amenities:** expanded continental breakfast and high-speed Internet.

AAA Benefit:
Members save up to 20%, plus 10% bonus points with rewards program.

⊺▷ CALL ⓦⓜ ⌿ ⧖ 🛏 📺 🖵 / SOME UNITS FEE 🐾 ⊠

LAKE OSWEGO pop. 35,278 (See map and index starting on p. 402)

──── WHERE TO STAY ────

CROWNE PLAZA HOTEL · *Book great rates at AAA.com* · Phone: (503)624-8400 · 110

Hotel
$79-$249 All Year

Address: 14811 Kruse Oaks Dr **Location:** I-5, exit 292B northbound; exit 292 southbound, just e on Kruse Way, then just s. **Facility:** 161 units. 150 one-bedroom standard units. 11 one-bedroom suites, some with whirlpools. 6 stories, interior corridors. *Bath:* combo or shower only. **Parking:** on-site. **Amenities:** CD players, dual phone lines, voice mail, irons, hair dryers. *Fee:* video games, high-speed Internet. **Pool(s):** heated indoor/outdoor. **Leisure Activities:** sauna, whirlpool, exercise room. **Guest Services:** valet laundry, area transportation-within 5 mi, wireless Internet. **Business Services:** conference facilities, business center. **Cards:** AX, DC, DS, JC, MC, VI. **Free Special Amenities:** newspaper and early check-in/late check-out.

FAIRFIELD INN & SUITES BY MARRIOTT · *Book great rates at AAA.com* · Phone: (503)670-7557 · 112

Hotel
$139-$149 All Year

Address: 6100 SW Meadows Rd **Location:** I-5, exit 292B northbound; 292 southbound, just s on SW Bangy Rd, then just e. Located in a quiet area. **Facility:** Smoke free premises. 124 one-bedroom standard units. 5 stories, interior corridors. *Bath:* combo or shower only. **Parking:** on-site. **Terms:** cancellation fee imposed. **Amenities:** video games (fee), high-speed Internet, voice mail, irons, hair dryers. **Pool(s):** heated indoor. **Leisure Activities:** whirlpool, exercise room. **Guest Services:** valet and coin laundry, wireless Internet. **Business Services:** meeting rooms, PC. **Cards:** AX, CB, DC, DS, JC, MC, VI.

AAA Benefit:
Members save a minimum 5% off the best available rate.

HILTON GARDEN INN-LAKE OSWEGO · *Book great rates at AAA.com* · Phone: (503)684-8900 · 111

Hotel
$109-$149 All Year

Address: 14850 Kruse Oaks Dr **Location:** I-5, exit 292B northbound; exit 292 southbound, just e on Kruse Way, then just s. **Facility:** 179 one-bedroom standard units, some with whirlpools. 6 stories, interior corridors. *Bath:* combo or shower only. **Parking:** on-site. **Terms:** 1-30 night minimum stay, cancellation fee imposed. **Amenities:** high-speed Internet, dual phone lines, voice mail, irons, hair dryers. **Pool(s):** heated indoor. **Leisure Activities:** whirlpool, exercise room. **Guest Services:** valet and coin laundry, wireless Internet. **Business Services:** meeting rooms, business center. **Cards:** AX, CB, DC, DS, JC, MC, VI.

Hilton Garden Inn

AAA Benefit:
Members save 5% or more everyday!

LAKESHORE INN · *Book at AAA.com* · Phone: (503)636-9679 · 113

Motel
$109-$189 3/1-9/30
$94-$159 10/1-2/28

Address: 210 N State St **Location:** I-205, exit 8, just nw, then 4.8 mi on SR 43 (State St/Willamette Dr); exit 3, ne on Stafford Rd, then just n; center. Located adjacent to Millennium Park. **Facility:** 33 units. 17 one-bedroom standard units. 13 one- and 3 two-bedroom suites, some with efficiencies or kitchens. 4 stories, exterior corridors. **Parking:** on-site. **Terms:** 3 day cancellation notice-fee imposed. **Amenities:** DVD players, voice mail, irons, hair dryers. **Pool(s):** heated outdoor. **Guest Services:** coin laundry, wireless Internet. **Business Services:** meeting rooms, fax. **Cards:** AX, DC, DS, MC, VI.

PHOENIX INN SUITES-LAKE OSWEGO · *Book great rates at AAA.com* · Phone: (503)624-7400 · 109

Hotel
$84-$164 All Year

Address: 14905 SW Bangy Rd **Location:** I-5, exit 292 southbound, just e, then just s; exit 292B northbound, just s. **Facility:** 62 one-bedroom standard units, some with whirlpools. 4 stories, interior corridors. *Bath:* combo or shower only. **Parking:** on-site. **Terms:** check-in 4 pm, cancellation fee imposed. **Amenities:** dual phone lines, voice mail, irons, hair dryers. *Some:* DVD players. **Pool(s):** heated indoor. **Leisure Activities:** whirlpool, exercise room. **Guest Services:** valet and coin laundry, area transportation-within 5 mi, wireless Internet. **Business Services:** meeting rooms, PC. **Cards:** AX, DC, DS, MC, VI. **Free Special Amenities:** expanded continental breakfast and high-speed Internet. (See color ad p 440)

RESIDENCE INN BY MARRIOTT-PORTLAND SOUTH · *Book great rates at AAA.com* · Phone: (503)684-2603 · 114

Hotel
$169-$199 All Year

Address: 15200 SW Bangy Rd **Location:** I-5, exit 292B northbound; 292 southbound, just e, then 0.3 mi s. Located in a quiet area. **Facility:** Smoke free premises. 112 units. 84 one-bedroom standard units with kitchens. 28 two-bedroom suites with kitchens. 2 stories (no elevator), exterior corridors. *Bath:* combo or shower only. **Parking:** on-site. **Terms:** check-in 4 pm, cancellation fee imposed. **Amenities:** video games (fee), high-speed Internet, dual phone lines, voice mail, irons, hair dryers. *Some:* DVD players. **Pool(s):** heated outdoor. **Leisure Activities:** whirlpools, exercise room, sports court. **Guest Services:** valet and coin laundry, area transportation, wireless Internet. **Business Services:** meeting rooms, business center. **Cards:** AX, CB, DC, DS, JC, MC, VI.

Residence Inn

AAA Benefit:
Members save a minimum 5% off the best available rate.

(See map and index starting on p. 402)

──────── WHERE TO DINE ────────

AMERIGO'S NEW FOODS GRILL Phone: 503/699-1688 93
American
$8-$17
American cuisine draws on Italian and international influences, and house specialty pizzas and pasta dishes are prepared with several choices of sauce. Everything here is made from scratch, including desserts, which come in an array of delicious options. The covered patio opens in season. Casual dress. **Bar:** Beer & wine. **Reservations:** accepted. **Hours:** 11 am-9 pm, Fri-9:30 pm, Sat 8:30 am-9:30 pm, Sun 8:30 am-8:30 pm; Saturday & Sunday brunch, 8:30 am-2 pm. Closed major holidays. **Address:** 4200 SW Mercantile Dr **Location:** I-5, exit 292B northbound; exit 292 southbound, 0.8 mi e on Kruse Way. **Parking:** on-site. **Cards:** AX, DS, MC, VI.

BURGERVILLE Phone: 503/684-8142
American
$2-$8
First-timers shouldn't let the fast food exterior fool them, as the burgers and chicken here adhere to a higher standard. Northwest ingredients come into play in the sandwiches. Casual dress. **Hours:** 7 am-10 pm. Closed: 11/26, 12/25. **Address:** 15650 SW Upper Boones Ferry Rd **Location:** I-5, exit 291, just w. **Parking:** on-site. **Cards:** DS, MC, VI.

CLARKE'S RESTAURANT Phone: 503/636-2667 85
American
$18-$30
The trendy downtown establishment shouldn't be missed. Fresh, delectable items from the seasonally changing menu include grilled beef tenderloin topped with morels and crawfish and panache of petrale sole and king salmon over tagliolini. Lobster and shrimp risotto is the signature dish. Patio seating is a seasonal option. Dressy casual. **Bar:** Full bar. **Reservations:** suggested. **Hours:** 5 pm-9 pm. Closed major holidays; also Super Bowl Sun & week of 7/4. **Address:** 455 2nd St **Location:** Just w of SR 43 (State St); between A and B aves. **Parking:** on-site. **Cards:** AX, DS, MC, VI.

FIVESPICE Phone: 503/697-8889 89
Seafood
$9-$26
Interesting Pan-Asian cuisine is featured at this restaurant which combines Asian flavors with fresh Pacific Northwest ingredients. Views of the lake and a heated terrace are also featured. Casual dress. **Bar:** Full bar. **Reservations:** accepted. **Hours:** 11:30 am-10 pm, Sun-9 pm. Closed: 11/26, 12/25. **Address:** 315 First St, Suite 201 **Location:** Just s of A Ave; downtown; adjacent to Millennium Park; at Lake View Village Shopping Center. **Parking:** on-site. **Cards:** AX, DS, MC, VI.
CALL ♿

FLYING ELEPHANTS DELICATESSEN Phone: 503/620-2444 91
Deli
$6-$10
Set back in an office building (look for the green awning), this upscale deli features tasty sandwiches on freshly baked bread as well as soups and delicious bakery items. Outdoor patio seating is available in season. Casual dress. **Bar:** Beer & wine. **Hours:** 6:30 am-6 pm. Closed major holidays; also Sat & Sun. **Address:** 5885 SW Meadows Rd **Location:** I-5, exit 292B northbound, just s on SW Bangy Rd, then just e; exit 292 southbound, just e, just s on SW Bangy Rd, then just e; in Kruse Woods Business Park. **Parking:** on-site. **Cards:** AX, MC, VI.

LA PROVENCE BAKERY & BISTRO Phone: 503/635-4533 94
Provincial French
$7-$19
Enjoy provincial French food in a country-style home. Guests dine on such selections as roasted duck breast with pomegranate, toasted hazelnut lamb chops and daily quiche, as well as fresh pastas, risottos and seafood selections. The French pastries and desserts are exquisite. Casual dress. **Bar:** Beer & wine. **Reservations:** suggested. **Hours:** 7 am-9 pm, Sun-Tues to 8 pm. Closed: 12/25. **Address:** 15964 SW Boones Ferry Rd **Location:** I-5, exit 292, 1 mi e, then 0.5 mi s. **Parking:** on-site. **Cards:** AX, DS, MC, VI.

MANZANA ROTISSERIE GRILL Phone: 503/675-3322
American
$10-$30
Specialties here include fish grilled over an apple-wood fire and chicken cooked on the rotisserie. Recommended for an appetizer is the jumbo wood-grilled artichoke. The seasonal patio affords a partial view of a lake and park, but reservations are not accepted for the patio, so arrive early. Casual dress. **Bar:** Full bar. **Reservations:** accepted. **Hours:** 11 am-11 pm, Fri-midnight, Sat 8:30 am-midnight, Sun 8:30 am-10 pm. Closed: 11/26, 12/25. **Address:** 305 SW First St **Location:** I-205, exit 8 westbound, just nw, 5.1 mi on SR 43 (State St/Willamette Dr); exit 3 eastbound 2.9 mi ne on Stafford Rd/McVey Ave, then just n; center; adjacent to Millennium Park; at Lake View Village Shopping Center. **Parking:** on-site. **Cards:** AX, DC, DS, MC, VI.
CALL ♿

OSWEGO LAKE HOUSE Phone: 503/636-4561 92
American
$16-$35
The downtown restaurant offers relaxed yet sophisticated lakeside dining. Reservations for deck tables book quickly in season. Recommended is the decadent ultimate burger, a Kobe beef patty and half Australian lobster tail served on an oversize bun. Also worth considering are fresh salads, steaks and pasta dishes. A heated patio, outdoor fireplace and boat dock are also featured, and parking is available in a nearby lot. Casual dress. **Bar:** Full bar. **Reservations:** suggested. **Hours:** 4:30 pm-10 pm, Sun 10 am-9 pm. Closed: 1/1, 11/26, 12/25. **Address:** 40 N State St **Location:** I-205, exit 8, 5.1 mi nw on SR 43 (State St/Willamette Dr); exit 3, 2.9 mi ne on Stafford Rd/McVey Ave, then just n; center. **Parking:** street. **Cards:** AX, DS, MC, VI.

RAM RESTAURANT AND BREWERY Phone: 503/697-8818
American
$8-$22
The enormous restaurant features high ceilings, huge television screens, large sports-themed banners and a brew pub area. The menu is equally enormous, with steaks, poultry, pasta, seafood, salads, sandwiches and pizza. The on-site brewery turns out a large selection of microbrews. Casual dress. **Bar:** Full bar. **Reservations:** suggested. **Hours:** 11 am-close. Closed: 12/25. **Address:** 320 Oswego Pointe Dr **Location:** SR 43 (State St), just se on Foothills Rd. **Parking:** on-site. **Cards:** AX, MC, VI.

(See map and index starting on p. 402)

RICCARDO'S

Northern Italian
$10-$45

Phone: 503/636-4104 (95)

This cozy and colorful restaurant serves creative pasta, veal, lamb, seafood and chicken dishes, including such excellent selections as Adriatic-style lasagna, with selections from an extensive Italian wine list. Moist tiramisu is a tempting meal-ender. The attractive outdoor patio is relaxing. Casual dress. **Bar:** Full bar. **Reservations:** suggested. **Hours:** 11 am-4 & 5-10 pm, Fri & Sat-10:30 pm; to 9:30 pm, Fri & Sat-10 pm in winter. Closed major holidays; also Sun. **Address:** 16035 SW Boones Ferry Rd **Location:** I-5, exit 292, 1 mi e on Kruse Way, then 0.5 mi s. **Parking:** on-site. **Cards:** AX, DC, MC, VI.

ST. HONORE BOULANGERIE

Breads/Pastries
$6-$9

Phone: 503/496-5596 (90)

St. Honore, the patron saint of bakers, watches over the handcrafted French breads and pastries being made in the clay firebrick oven at this upscale bakery. Crisp baguettes, croissants, sweets, salads and sandwiches pair with French wines and beer. In season, patio seating is available. Casual dress. **Bar:** Beer & wine. **Reservations:** not accepted. **Hours:** 7 am-8 pm. Closed: 12/24, 12/25. **Address:** 315 First St, Suite 103 **Location:** I-205, exit 8 westbound, 5.1 mi nw of SR 43 (State St/Willamette Dr); exit 3 eastbound, 2.9 mi ne on Stafford Rd/McVey Ave, then just n; adjacent to Millenium Park; at Lake View Village Shopping Center; center. **Parking:** on-site. **Cards:** MC, VI.

CALL

SPEEDY LINGUINE

Italian
$8-$13

Phone: 503/636-3610 (96)

Hearth-baked pizzas, fresh egg linguines and sautes, such as chicken Cabernet (chicken, mushrooms, red onions and tomatoes sauteed in olive oil and garlic, then splashed with dry Cabernet wine and tossed with smoked mozzarella cheese and egg linguine) are some of the items diners find at the neighborhood restaurant. An outside seating area opens seasonally. Casual dress. **Bar:** Full bar. **Reservations:** accepted. **Hours:** 11 am-2 & 4-8 pm, Fri-9 pm, Sat & Sun 4 pm-9 pm. Closed major holidays. **Address:** 5405 SW Jean Rd **Location:** I-5, exit 290, 0.4 mi w to Jean Rd, then 0.4 mi se. **Parking:** on-site. **Cards:** AX, DS, MC, VI.

STANFORD'S RESTAURANT & BAR

American
$10-$38

Phone: 503/620-3541 (86)

Guests can look forward to a tasteful dining experience at the casual restaurant, where fresh seafood, quality steaks and pasta dominate the menu. Several dishes are prepared using wood-fire grilling. Recommended are the Tex-Mex egg roll appetizer and the fresh Hawaiian ahi tuna entree, which is seared rare with a mild wasabi/ginger sauce. It's hard to beat the decadent white chocolate macadamia nut brownie topped with toasted macadamias on a warm cream anglaise sauce drizzled with caramel. Casual dress. **Bar:** Full bar. **Reservations:** accepted. **Hours:** 11 am-11 pm, Fri & Sat-midnight. Closed: 11/26, 12/25. **Address:** 14801 Kruse Oaks Dr **Location:** I-5, exit 292, just e. **Parking:** on-site. **Cards:** AX, DC, DS, MC, VI.

CALL

TUCCI

Italian
$8-$31

Phone: 503/697-3383 (87)

Guests park in the lot behind the building and head inside the warm, cozy dinner house for modern Italian cuisine. Selections such as pan-roasted filet mignon in a grappa reduction or pasta of capellini and Dungeness crab pair with choices from the all-Italian wine list. Servers display solid knowledge of the menu, which changes frequently. Warm chocolate polenta cake is just one of the delicious desserts. Patio or sidewalk seating is available in season. Dressy casual. **Bar:** Full bar. **Reservations:** suggested. **Hours:** 11 am-10 pm, Fri-11 pm, Sat 4 pm-11 pm, Sun 9 am-2 & 4-9 pm, Mon 11 am-9 pm; Sunday brunch. Closed: 1/1, 12/25. **Address:** 220 A Ave **Location:** Just w of SR 43 (State St); near 2nd St and A Ave. **Parking:** on-site. **Cards:** AX, DS, MC, VI.

ZEPPO ITALIAN RISTORANTE

Italian
$7-$22

Phone: 503/675-2726 (88)

Light fixtures fashioned from colanders and graters lend to the eatery's warm, contemporary atmosphere. The menu lists fresh pasta and meat dishes, as well as flavorful desserts. Casual dress. **Bar:** Full bar. **Reservations:** accepted. **Hours:** 11 am-10 pm, Fri-11 pm, Sat 8 am-11 pm, Sun 8 am-9 pm. Closed major holidays. **Address:** 345 1st Ave, Suite 105 **Location:** I-205, exit 8 westbound, 5.1 mi nw on SR 43 (State St/Willamette Dr); exit 3 eastbound, 2.9 mi ne on Stafford Rd/McVey Ave, then just n; center; adjacent to Millennium Park; at Lake View Village Shopping Center. **Parking:** on-site. **Cards:** AX, DC, DS, MC, VI.

CALL

MILWAUKIE pop. 20,490   (See map and index starting on p. 402)

──── WHERE TO STAY ────

ECONO LODGE SUITES INN   *Book great rates at AAA.com*   Phone: (503)654-2222   117

AAA SAVE
◆◆ ◆◆
Motel
$59-$79 All Year

Address: 17330 SE McLoughlin Blvd **Location:** I-205, exit 9, 2.3 mi n on SR 99 E (McLoughlin Blvd). **Facility:** 25 one-bedroom standard units, some with whirlpools. 2 stories (no elevator), exterior corridors. **Parking:** on-site. **Terms:** cancellation fee imposed. **Amenities:** high-speed Internet. *Some:* DVD players (fee). **Pool(s):** heated outdoor. **Leisure Activities:** whirlpool. **Guest Services:** coin laundry, wireless Internet. **Cards:** AX, CB, DC, DS, MC, VI. **Free Special Amenities: continental breakfast and newspaper.**

[amenity icons] / SOME UNITS FEE / FEE VCR

──── WHERE TO DINE ────

AMADEUS AT THE FERNWOOD   Phone: 503/659-1735   99

◆◆ ◆◆
Continental
$19-$40

Enter a chateau-style home tucked away in a forested hillside with a view of the Willamette River. Relish delicious seafood, poultry and steak selections while the gentle strains of piano music soothe away the day's cares. Enjoy patio dining in season. Dressy casual. **Bar:** Full bar. **Reservations:** suggested. **Hours:** 5 pm-10 pm, Sun 10 am-2:30 & 5-close; Sunday brunch. Closed: 1/1, 12/25; also Mon. **Address:** 2122 SE Sparrow Rd **Location:** Off SR 99 E (McLoughlin Blvd), take N River Rd. **Parking:** on-site. **Cards:** AX, MC, VI.

BOB'S RED MILL WHOLE GRAIN STORE & VISITOR'S CENTER   *Menu on AAA.com*   Phone: 503/607-6455   100

AAA
◆◆◆
American
$6-$9

With a water wheel out front, this distinctive, contemporary-style mill offers sandwiches made with whole grain flours. Vegan menus are available for both lunch and breakfast. Guests can sit in the second-floor dining room or on the seasonal patio. Open until 6 pm, an on-site whole grain store features Bob's products and some historical displays. Casual dress. **Reservations:** not accepted. **Hours:** 8 am-3 pm, Sat from 7 am. Closed major holidays; also Sun. **Address:** 5000 SE International Way **Location:** I-205, exit 13 (SR 224), 2.1 mi w, just ne on SE Freeman Way, then just s. **Parking:** on-site. **Cards:** DS, MC, VI.

CALL ⬛M

MCGRATH'S FISH HOUSE   Phone: 503/653-8070

◆◆ ◆◆
Steak & Seafood
$9-$19

The popular chain specializes in fresh Pacific Northwest seafood, including dishes grilled over a wood fire and items from the daily fresh sheet. Also on the menu are steaks, chicken, pasta and gourmet burgers. Casual dress. **Bar:** Full bar. **Hours:** 11 am-10 pm. Closed: 11/26, 12/25. **Address:** 11050 SE Oak St **Location:** I-205, exit 13 (SR 224/SE 82nd Dr), 3.2 mi w, then just ne. **Parking:** on-site. **Cards:** AX, DC, DS, MC, VI.

OREGON CITY pop. 25,754   (See map and index starting on p. 402)

──── WHERE TO STAY ────

BEST WESTERN RIVERSHORE HOTEL   *Book great rates at AAA.com*   Phone: (503)655-7141   137

AAA SAVE
◆◆◆
Hotel
$95-$115 All Year

Address: 1900 Clackamette Dr **Location:** I-205, exit 9, just n. **Facility:** Smoke free premises. 114 units. 113 one-bedroom standard units. 1 one-bedroom suite. 3 stories, interior corridors. *Bath:* combo or shower only. **Parking:** on-site. **Amenities:** video library (fee), high-speed Internet, voice mail, irons, hair dryers. *Some:* DVD players (fee). **Pool(s):** heated outdoor. **Leisure Activities:** whirlpool, fishing, exercise room. **Guest Services:** coin laundry, area transportation-within 10 mi, wireless Internet. **Business Services:** meeting rooms, PC. **Cards:** AX, DC, DS, MC, VI. **Free Special Amenities: local telephone calls and high-speed Internet.** (See color ad below)

[Best Western logo]

AAA Benefit:
Members save up to 20%, plus 10% bonus points with rewards program.

[amenity icons] CALL ⬛M / SOME UNITS FEE

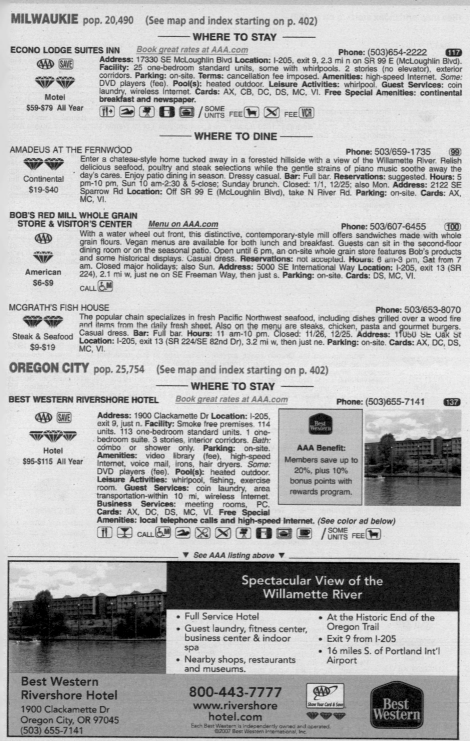

(See map and index starting on p. 402)

———— **WHERE TO DINE** ————

BUGATTI'S HILLTOP

Italian
$10-$19

Phone: 503/722-8222   (110)

Delicious pizza, steak, pasta and seafood, along with burgers and panini sandwiches, make up the menu at the attractive restaurant not far from downtown. The patio area opens seasonally. Casual dress. **Bar:** Full bar. **Reservations:** not accepted. **Hours:** 11 am-9 pm, Fri-10 pm, Sat noon-10 pm, Sun noon-9 pm. Closed major holidays. **Address:** 334 Warner Milne Rd **Location:** Just w of jct Molalla Ave; in Danielson's Hilltop Shopping Center. **Parking:** on-site. **Cards:** AX, DS, MC, VI.

BURGERVILLE

American
$2-$8

Phone: 503/655-0013

First-timers shouldn't let the fast food exterior fool them, as the burgers and chicken here adhere to a higher standard. Northwest ingredients come into play in the sandwiches. Casual dress. **Hours:** 7 am-10 pm. Closed: 11/26, 12/25. **Address:** 1900 Molalla Ave **Location:** Just s of jct Warner Milne Rd and Molalla Ave. **Parking:** on-site. **Cards:** DS, MC, VI.

MCMENAMINS

American
$5-$20

Phone: 503/655-8032

The casual neighborhood eatery is where friends gather for classic pub and comfort fare, all washed down by pints of locally made beer. Large wooden booths or tables easily accommodate larger groups, and the eclectic, custom-painted walls and varied period light fixtures keep diners' eyes busy should the conversation lag. Casual dress. **Bar:** Full bar. **Hours:** 11 am-midnight, Fri & Sat-1 am, Sun noon-11 pm. Closed: 12/25. **Address:** 102 Ninth St **Location:** I-205, exit 9, 0.5 mi s on SR 99 (McLoughlin Blvd). **Parking:** on-site. **Cards:** MC, VI.

STONE CLIFF INN

Regional American
$9-$30

Phone: 503/631-7900

This warm and inviting lodge-style restaurant has a delightful deck overlooking the river. When venison rib rack braised with shallot and brandy sauce is on the menu, it should be given serious consideration. Casual dress. **Bar:** Full bar. **Reservations:** suggested. **Hours:** 11:30 am-9 pm, Fri & Sat-10 pm, Sun 10 am-9 pm; Sunday brunch. Closed: 7/4, 12/25. **Address:** 17900 Clackamas River Dr **Location:** I-205, exit 12, 3.5 mi e on SR 212, 1 mi s on SR 224, at Y, cross Carver Bridge, then just s. **Parking:** on-site. **Cards:** AX, DC, DS, MC, VI.

CALL

SHERWOOD pop. 11,791

———— **WHERE TO DINE** ————

HUNTER'S RIDGE GRILL

American
$8-$28

Phone: 503/625-1912

When returning from the Oregon coast, explorers often stop at this restaurant for a casual fine-dining experience. Dishes on the ever-changing menu feature local and seasonal ingredients. When it's open, the seasonal terrace allows for dining amid a grove of tall trees. Casual dress. **Bar:** Full bar. **Reservations:** suggested. **Hours:** 11:30 am-9 pm, Fri-10 pm, Sat 4 pm-10 pm, Sun 4:30 pm-9 pm; Sunday brunch 10 am-2 pm. Closed: 12/25; also Mon. **Address:** 20510 Roy Rogers Rd, Suite 160 **Location:** SR 99, just w on Roy Rogers Rd, then just e on SW Borchers Dr; across from Safeway. **Parking:** on-site. **Cards:** AX, DS, MC, VI.

TIGARD pop. 41,223   (See map and index starting on p. 402)

———— **WHERE TO STAY** ————

COURTYARD BY MARRIOTT
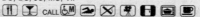 *Book great rates at AAA.com*

Hotel
$170-$208 All Year

Phone: (503)684-7900   (90)

Address: 15686 SW Sequoia Pkwy **Location:** I-5, exit 291, just w on Upper Boones Ferry Rd, then just n. Located in a business park. **Facility:** Smoke free premises. 110 units. 106 one-bedroom standard units. 4 one-bedroom suites. 4 stories, interior corridors. *Bath:* combo or shower only. **Parking:** on-site. **Terms:** cancellation fee imposed. **Amenities:** CD players, high-speed Internet, dual phone lines, voice mail, irons, hair dryers. **Pool(s):** heated indoor. **Leisure Activities:** whirlpool, exercise room. **Guest Services:** valet and coin laundry, area transportation, wireless Internet. **Business Services:** meeting rooms, PC. **Cards:** AX, CB, DC, DS, JC, MC, VI.

AAA Benefit:
Members save a minimum 5% off the best available rate.

EMBASSY SUITES HOTEL-PORTLAND
WASHINGTON SQUARE   *Book great rates at AAA.com*

(AAA) (SAVE)

Hotel
$119-$209 All Year

Phone: (503)644-4000   (85)

Address: 9000 SW Washington Square Rd **Location:** SR 217, exit 4B (Progress/Scholls Ferry Rd), just ne on SW Scholls Ferry Rd, just e on SW Hall Blvd, then just s. Located adjacent to Washington Square Mall. **Facility:** 354 units. 352 one- and 2 two-bedroom suites, some with whirlpools. 9 stories, interior corridors. *Bath:* combo or shower only. **Parking:** on-site. **Terms:** 1-30 night minimum stay, cancellation fee imposed. **Amenities:** voice mail, irons, hair dryers. *Fee:* video games, high-speed Internet. **Pool(s):** heated indoor. **Leisure Activities:** whirlpool, exercise room. **Guest Services:** valet and coin laundry, area transportation-within 1 mi, mall & light rail station, wireless Internet. **Business Services:** conference facilities, business center. **Cards:** AX, CB, DC, DS, JC, MC, VI. **Free Special Amenities:** full breakfast and newspaper.

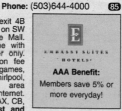

AAA Benefit:
Members save 5% or more everyday!

(See map and index starting on p. 402)

HOLIDAY INN EXPRESS-PORTLAND SOUTH   *Book great rates at AAA.com*   **Phone:** (503)620-2980   **91**

◆◆◆◆◆

Hotel

$89-$149 All Year

Address: 15700 SW Upper Boones Ferry Rd **Location:** I-5, exit 291, just sw. **Facility:** 94 units. 86 one- and 5 two-bedroom standard units, some with whirlpools. 3 one-bedroom suites. 3-4 stories, interior corridors. *Bath:* combo or shower only. **Parking:** on-site. **Terms:** check-in 4 pm. **Amenities:** high-speed Internet, voice mail, irons, hair dryers. **Pool(s):** heated indoor. **Leisure Activities:** exercise room. **Guest Services:** valet and coin laundry, wireless Internet. **Business Services:** meeting rooms, PC. **Cards:** AX, CB, DC, DS, JC, MC, VI.

(ASK) (☂) (➙) (🏊) (🔒) (🛏) (💻) / SOME UNITS (✖)

▼ *See AAA listing p 470* ▼

Phoenix Grand Hotel at Bridgeport
Tualatin, Oregon

- 124 beautifully appointed guest rooms
- Luxury Business Class Hotel
- Located within the Bridgeport District of Tualatin
- Amenities include· complimentary hot breakfast buffet, high speed wireless internet, garage parking, pool, Jacuzzi & fitness room
- Visit our website at www.phoenixgrandhotel.com

PHOENIX GRAND HOTEL

1-866-968-5757 · 503-968-5757
7265 SW Hazel Fern Rd · Tigard, OR 97224
Opening August 2009

(See map and index starting on p. 402)

HOMESTEAD STUDIO SUITES HOTEL
PORTLAND-TIGARD   *Book at AAA.com*

▼▼▼ Hotel
$85-$100 All Year

Phone: (503)670-0555 89

Address: 13009 SW 68th Pkwy **Location:** I-5, exit 293 (Haines St) southbound, 0.5 mi s on SW 68th Ave; exit 293 northbound, just w on Atlanta Ave, then 0.7 mi s; SR 217, exit 7 (72nd Ave), just ne, just e on Hampton St, then just s. Wetlands area on property. **Facility:** 137 units. 127 one-bedroom standard units with efficiencies. 10 one-bedroom suites with efficiencies. 2 stories (no elevator), exterior corridors. *Bath:* combo or shower only. **Parking:** on-site. **Terms:** office hours 7 am-11 pm, cancellation fee imposed. **Amenities:** high-speed Internet (fee), voice mail, irons, hair dryers. **Guest Services:** coin laundry, wireless Internet. **Cards:** AX, CB, DC, DS, JC, MC, VI.

PHOENIX GRAND HOTEL

[fyi] Hotel

Phone: 503/968-5757

Under construction, scheduled to open August 2009. **Address:** 7265 SW Hazel Fern Rd **Location:** I-5, exit 290, just w via Lower Boones Ferry and SW Bridgeport rds, then just s. **Amenities:** 123 units, coffeemakers, microwaves, refrigerators, pool. *(See color ad p 469)*

PHOENIX INN SUITES-TIGARD   *Book great rates at AAA.com*

AAA SAVE
▼▼▼ Hotel
$89-$149 All Year

Phone: (503)624-9000 86

Address: 9575 SW Locust St **Location:** SR 217, exit 5 (Greenburg Rd), just ne on SW Greenburg Rd, then just e. **Facility:** 101 units. 98 one-bedroom standard units, some with whirlpools. 3 one-bedroom suites with whirlpools. 3 stories, interior corridors. *Bath:* combo or shower only. **Parking:** on-site. **Terms:** cancellation fee imposed. **Amenities:** high-speed Internet, dual phone lines, voice mail, irons, hair dryers. *Some:* DVD players. **Pool(s):** heated indoor. **Leisure Activities:** whirlpool, exercise room. **Guest Services:** valet and coin laundry, area transportation-within 5 mi, wireless Internet. **Business Services:** meeting rooms, PC. **Cards:** AX, CB, DC, DS, JC, MC, VI. **Free Special Amenities:** expanded continental breakfast and high-speed Internet. *(See color ad p 440)*

QUALITY INN TIGARD   *Book great rates at AAA.com*

AAA SAVE
▼▼▼ Hotel
$79-$99 All Year

Phone: (503)245-6421 87

Address: 11460 SW Pacific Hwy **Location:** I-5, exit 294, just w. **Facility:** 115 one-bedroom standard units. 4 stories, interior corridors. **Parking:** on-site. **Amenities:** high-speed Internet, voice mail, irons, hair dryers. **Pool(s):** heated outdoor. **Leisure Activities:** sauna, steamroom, exercise room. **Guest Services:** valet laundry, wireless Internet. **Business Services:** meeting rooms, PC. **Cards:** AX, DS, MC, VI. **Free Special Amenities:** continental breakfast and high-speed Internet.

SHILO INN-TIGARD/WASHINGTON SQUARE   *Book great rates at AAA.com*

AAA SAVE
▼▼▼ Hotel
$85-$125 All Year

Phone: (503)620-4320 88

Address: 10830 SW Greenburg Rd **Location:** SR 217, exit 5 (Greenburg Rd), just sw. **Facility:** 77 one-bedroom standard units, some with efficiencies. 4 stories, interior corridors. *Bath:* combo or shower only. **Parking:** on-site. **Terms:** cancellation fee imposed. **Amenities:** video games (fee), high-speed Internet, irons, hair dryers. **Leisure Activities:** sauna, whirlpool, steamroom, exercise room. **Guest Services:** coin laundry, wireless Internet. **Business Services:** PC. **Cards:** AX, DS, MC, VI. **Free Special Amenities:** continental breakfast and high-speed Internet.

--- **WHERE TO DINE** ---

BANNING'S RESTAURANT & PIE HOUSE

AAA
▼▼▼ American
$7-$13

Phone: 503/244-2558 70

For 25 years, the establishment has been serving home-cooked meals, sandwiches, burgers and unbeatable breakfasts, along with delicious pies and cakes that are made fresh daily. Casual dress. **Bar:** Beer & wine. **Reservations:** not accepted. **Hours:** 24 hours. Closed: 12/25. **Address:** 11477 SW Pacific Hwy **Location:** I-5, exit 294, just w. **Parking:** on-site. **Cards:** AX, DS, MC, VI.

CAFE ALLEGRO

▼▼▼ Italian
$6-$21

Phone: 503/684-0130 71

Hearth-baked lasagna al forno, calzones and pizzas, as well as fresh linguine, ravioli and seafood sautes served over pasta are some of the menu offerings at the small neighborhood eatery. Casual dress. **Bar:** Beer & wine. **Reservations:** not accepted. **Hours:** 11 am-9 pm, Fri-10 pm, Sat noon-10 pm, Sun 4 pm-9 pm. Closed major holidays; also 12/24. **Address:** 12386 SW Main St **Location:** Just sw of Greenburg Rd and SW Pacific Hwy (SR 99). **Parking:** on-site. **Cards:** AX, DS, MC, VI.

GUSTAV'S PUB & GRILL

▼▼▼ German
$9-$20

Phone: 503/639-4544 69

Guests can dine amid contemporary German decor. Among specialties are various schnitzels, grilled sausages and sauerbraten. Rotisserie chicken and turkey, along with a few fish selections, round out the menu nicely. Those who can't make up their mind might try the Bavarian sampler or Gustav's family feast. An outdoor patio is open in summer. Casual dress. **Bar:** Full bar. **Reservations:** not accepted. **Hours:** 11 am-11 pm, Fri & Sat-midnight. Closed: 12/25. **Address:** 10350 SW Greenburg Rd **Location:** SR 217, exit 5 (Greenburg Rd), just e. **Parking:** on-site. **Cards:** AX, DS, MC, VI.

M & S GRILL

▼▼▼ Steak & Seafood
$9-$20

Phone: 503/684-5490 73

Aged steaks, fresh seafood and pasta are served at this newest addition to the ever-popular McCormick & Schmick's chain of restaurants. Private, curtained booths are available by reservation. Dressy casual. **Bar:** Full bar. **Reservations:** suggested. **Hours:** 11 am-11 pm, Sun-10 pm. **Address:** 17015 SW 72nd Ave **Location:** I-5, exit 290, just nw; in Bridgeport Village Shopping Center. **Parking:** on-site. **Cards:** AX, DS, MC, VI.

(See map and index starting on p. 402)

MAX'S FANNO CREEK BREW PUB
Phone: 503/624-9400 (72)

American
$8-$15

A relaxed and casual gathering place for family and friends, the brew pub affords seating in semiprivate booths, at open group tables, at the bar or in an area near the small children's play zone. Guests sip hand-crafted beers with their choice of pub grub such as burgers, pasta, paninis, pizza, sandwiches or even Scotch eggs. Casual dress. **Bar:** Full bar. **Reservations:** not accepted. **Hours:** 11:30 am-9 pm, Fri & Sat-10 pm. Closed: 11/26, 12/25. **Address:** 12562 SW Main St **Location:** SR 217, exit 6, just sw on SW Pacific Hwy, then 0.4 mi sw. **Parking:** street. **Cards:** MC, VI.

MCMENAMINS
Phone: 503/684-2688

American
$5-$20

The casual neighborhood eatery is where friends gather for classic pub and comfort fare, all washed down by pints of locally made beer. Large wooden booths or tables easily accommodate larger groups, and the eclectic, custom-painted walls and varied period light fixtures keep diners' eyes busy should the conversation lag. Casual dress. **Bar:** Full bar. **Hours:** 11 am-1 am, Fri-2:30 am, Sun noon-midnight, Mon 11 am-midnight. Closed: 11/26, 12/25. **Address:** 14610 SW Sequoia Pkwy **Location:** I-5, exit 291, just sw on SW Upper Boones Ferry Rd, then 0.3 mi n. **Parking:** on-site. **Cards:** MC, VI.

MILLER'S HOMESTEAD RESTAURANT
Phone: 503/684-2831 (77)

American
$8-$16

For more than 20 years, the warm, comfortable and casual restaurant has served tasty homemade food, such as burgers, sandwiches and an extensive selection of all-day breakfast items, including pancakes and omelets. Seniors also have an array of choices. Delicious Oregon gooseberry pie is sometimes among the daily baked pies. A covered wagon and windmill are out front. Casual dress. **Hours:** 5:30 am-8 pm, Sun from 6:30 am. **Address:** 17933 SW McEwan Rd **Location:** I-5, exit 290, just e to McEwan Rd, then just s. **Parking:** on-site. **Cards:** DS, MC, VI.

NEWPORT BAY RESTAURANT
Phone: 503/620-3474

American
$8-$25

This restaurant is for those seeking a casual, relaxing time. A menu favorite is New England clam chowder, which is available nightly. Fresh Northwest salmon and Alaskan halibut prepared several ways share menu space with pasta, chicken and salads. Casual dress. **Bar:** Full bar. **Reservations:** accepted. **Hours:** 11 am-9 pm, Sun-7 pm. Closed: 11/26, 12/25. **Address:** 9699 SW Washington Square Rd **Location:** SR 217, exit 5 (Greenburg Rd), just e; in Washington Square Mall, on east side. **Parking:** on-site. **Cards:** AX, DS, MC, VI.

CALL

NEWPORT BAY RESTAURANT
Phone: 503/245-3474

American
$8-$25

This restaurant is for those seeking a casual, relaxing time. A menu favorite is New England clam chowder, which is available nightly. Fresh Northwest salmon and Alaskan halibut prepared several ways share menu space with pasta, chicken and salads. Casual dress. **Bar:** Full bar. **Reservations:** accepted. **Hours:** 11 am-10 pm, Fri & Sat-11 pm, Sun 9 am-10 pm. Closed: 11/26, 12/25. **Address:** 10935 SW 68th Pkwy **Location:** I-5, exit 294, 0.3 mi w on Pacific Hwy (SR 99 W). **Parking:** on-site. **Cards:** AX, DS, MC, VI.

CALL

(See map and index starting on p. 402)

PASTINI PASTARIA

Phone: 503/718-2300　74

Italian
$5-$11

The lively pastaria prepares more than two dozen pasta dishes with homemade sauces and pestos. In addition to steaming pasta bowls, the menu lists antipasti, salads and grilled panini. Patio seating is a warm-weather option. Casual dress. **Bar:** Full bar. **Reservations:** not accepted. **Hours:** 11 am-9 pm, Fri & Sat-10 pm. Closed: 11/26, 12/25. **Address:** 7307 SW Bridgeport, Suite B-105 **Location:** I-5, exit 290, just w; in Bridgeport Village Shopping Center. **Parking:** on-site. **Cards:** AX, MC, VI.

P.F. CHANG'S CHINA BISTRO

Phone: 503/430-3020　76

Chinese
$10-$21

Trendy, upscale decor provides a pleasant backdrop for New Age Chinese dining. Appetizers, soups and salads are a meal by themselves. Vegetarian plates and sides, noodles, meins, chicken and meat dishes are created from exotic, fresh ingredients. Casual dress. **Bar:** Full bar. **Reservations:** accepted. **Hours:** 11 am-11 pm, Fri & Sat-midnight. Closed: 11/26, 12/25. **Address:** 7463 SW Bridgeport Rd **Location:** I-5, exit 290, just w; in Bridgeport Village Shopping Center. **Parking:** on-site. **Cards:** AX, DC, DS, MC, VI.

SIN JU JAPANESE RESTAURANT

Phone: 503/352-3815　75

Japanese
$9-$32

Contemporary Japanese cuisine is prepared at the sleek restaurant, where hot and cold appetizers and sushi are served all day. The cozy fireplace lounge area invites relaxation. This place is in the northwest corner of a shopping center. Casual dress. **Bar:** Full bar. **Reservations:** suggested. **Hours:** 11 am-10 pm, Fri & Sat 10 am-10:30 pm. **Address:** 7339 SW Bridgeport Rd **Location:** I-5, exit 290, just w; in Bridgeport Village Shopping Center. **Parking:** on-site. **Cards:** AX, DS, MC, VI.

TROUTDALE pop. 13,777 (See map and index starting on p. 402)

———— WHERE TO STAY ————

COMFORT INN & SUITES, COLUMBIA GORGE WEST
Book great rates at AAA.com

Phone: (503)669-6500　78

Hotel
$69-$159 All Year

Address: 477 NW Phoenix Dr **Location:** I-84, exit 17, south side of interstate, just s off Frontage Rd. **Facility:** 73 one-bedroom standard units, some with whirlpools. 3 stories, interior corridors. **Parking:** on-site. **Terms:** cancellation fee imposed. **Amenities:** high-speed Internet, irons, hair dryers. **Pool(s):** heated indoor. **Leisure Activities:** whirlpool, exercise room. **Guest Services:** valet and coin laundry, wireless Internet. **Business Services:** meeting rooms. **Cards:** AX, CB, DC, DS, JC, MC, VI. **Free Special Amenities:** expanded continental breakfast and high-speed Internet.

HOLIDAY INN EXPRESS-PORTLAND EAST
Book at AAA.com

Phone: (503)492-2900　76

Hotel
$89-$159 All Year

Address: 1000 NW Graham Rd **Location:** I-84, exit 17 eastbound, e on Frontage Rd, then just n; westbound, just n. **Facility:** 77 one-bedroom standard units, some with whirlpools. 3 stories, interior corridors. *Bath:* combo or shower only. **Parking:** on-site. **Terms:** cancellation fee imposed. **Amenities:** high-speed Internet, dual phone lines, voice mail, irons, hair dryers. **Leisure Activities:** whirlpool, exercise room. **Guest Services:** valet and coin laundry, wireless Internet. **Business Services:** PC. **Cards:** AX, CB, DC, DS, JC, MC, VI.

MOTEL 6-PORTLAND TROUTDALE - 407
Book at AAA.com

Phone: (503)665-2254　77

Motel
$47-$55 All Year

Address: 1610 NW Frontage Rd **Location:** I-84, exit 17 eastbound, just sw; westbound, just w on Frontage Rd, then just sw. **Facility:** 123 one-bedroom standard units. 2 stories (no elevator), exterior corridors. *Bath:* shower only. **Parking:** on-site. **Pool(s):** heated outdoor. **Guest Services:** coin laundry. **Cards:** AX, CB, DC, DS, MC, VI.

———— *The following lodging was either not evaluated or did not* ————
meet AAA rating requirements but is listed for your information only.

MCMENAMINS EDGEFIELD

Phone: 503/669-8610

(fyi)

Not evaluated. **Address:** 2126 SW Halsey St **Location:** I-84, exit 16, just s on 238th Dr, then just e. Facilities, services, and decor characterize a mid-scale property.

———— WHERE TO DINE ————

TAD'S CHICKEN 'N DUMPLINS

Phone: 503/666-5337

American
$12-$28

This roadhouse restaurant has been serving motorists since the late 1920s. What began as a hot dog stand now serves chicken and dumplings, seafood, beef, pasta and salads. The enclosed deck overlooks the Sandy River, in a wooded setting. Call ahead seating available. Casual dress. **Bar:** Full bar. **Reservations:** not accepted. **Hours:** 5 pm-10 pm, Sat from 4 pm, Sun from 2 pm. Closed: 11/26, 12/25. **Address:** 1325 E Historic Columbia River Hwy **Location:** I-84, exit 18, 1 mi s. **Parking:** on-site. **Cards:** AX, DS, MC, VI. **Classic**

(See map and index starting on p. 402)

TROUTDALE GENERAL STORE   Phone: 503/492-7912

American
$4-$8

This charming store not only serves a variety of fresh sandwiches, but doubles as an ice cream parlor and confectionery as well, making for a nice stop when traveling to or from the Columbia Gorge. Dine on the main floor or upstairs, where there are a few tables on the deck. Casual dress. **Bar:** Beer & wine. **Hours:** 7:30 am-5 pm, Sat & Sun from 9 am. Closed major holidays. **Address:** 289 E Historic Columbia River Hwy **Location:** I-84, exit 17, just e on south frontage road, just s on Graham Rd, then just e. **Parking:** on-site. **Cards:** DS, MC, VI.

TUALATIN pop. 22,791   (See map and index starting on p. 402)

——— WHERE TO STAY ———

COMFORT INN & SUITES   *Book great rates at AAA.com*   Phone: (503)612-9952   [120]

Hotel
$99-$199 All Year

Address: 7640 SW Warm Springs St **Location:** I-5, exit 289, just w on Nyberg Rd, just s on Martinazzi Ave, then just e; just behind Fred Meyer. **Facility:** Smoke free premises. 59 units. 58 one-bedroom standard units, some with efficiencies and/or whirlpools. 1 one-bedroom suite. 3 stories, interior corridors. *Bath:* combo or shower only. **Parking:** on-site. **Terms:** check-in 4 pm, cancellation fee imposed. **Amenities:** high-speed Internet, dual phone lines, voice mail, irons, hair dryers. **Pool(s):** heated indoor. **Leisure Activities:** whirlpool, exercise room. **Guest Services:** valet and coin laundry, wireless Internet. **Business Services:** meeting rooms, PC. **Cards:** AX, CB, DC, DS, JC, MC, VI. **Free Special Amenities:** full breakfast and high-speed Internet.

(See color ad p 368, p 586, p 499, p 368, p 752, below, p 542, p 299, p 344, p 751, p 566 & p 500)

WEST LINN pop. 22,261   (See map and index starting on p. 402)

——— WHERE TO DINE ———

BUGATTI'S RISTORANTE
Phone: 503/636-9555   (107)

Italian
$15-$35

The popular neighborhood restaurant presents a creative seasonal menu with many flavorful pasta dishes, as well as fresh salmon and steaks. The wine selection is good. Tiramisu translates to "carry me up," and diners might feel as though they're in heaven after indulging. Guests can sit on the deck in season. Casual dress. **Bar:** Full bar. **Reservations:** suggested. **Hours:** 5 pm-9 pm, Fri & Sat-10 pm. Closed major holidays. **Address:** 18740 Willamette Dr **Location:** I-205, exit 8, 2.5 mi n on SR 43 (Willamette Dr). **Parking:** on-site. **Cards:** AX, DS, MC, VI.

BURGERVILLE
Phone: 503/635-7339

American
$2-$8

First-timers shouldn't let the fast food exterior fool them, as the burgers and chicken here adhere to a higher standard. Northwest ingredients come into play in the sandwiches. Casual dress. **Hours:** 7 am-10 pm. Closed: 11/26, 12/25. **Address:** 18350 Willamette Dr **Location:** I-205, exit 8, 3 mi nw on SR 43 (Willamette Dr). **Parking:** on-site. **Cards:** DS, MC, VI.

THAI ORCHID RESTAURANT
Phone: 503/699-4195

Thai
$7-$15

Patrons can enjoy fresh, flavorful Thai food with no added monosodium glutamate at this restaurant. The varied menu includes salads, soups, stir-fried dishes, distinctive curries, seafood and noodles. Casual dress. **Bar:** Beer & wine. **Reservations:** accepted. **Hours:** 11:30 am-9 pm. Closed: 7/4, 12/25. **Address:** 18740 Willamette Dr **Location:** I-205, exit 8, 2.9 mi nw on SR 43 (Willamette Dr). **Parking:** on-site. **Cards:** AX, DS, MC, VI.

WILSONVILLE pop. 13,991   (See map and index starting on p. 402)

——— WHERE TO STAY ———

BEST WESTERN WILLAMETTE INN   *Book great rates at AAA.com*

Phone: (503)682-2288

(AAA) (SAVE)

Hotel
$96-$106 All Year

Address: 30800 SW Parkway Ave **Location:** I-5, exit 283, just e on Wilsonville Rd, then 0.3 mi s. **Facility:** 63 one-bedroom standard units. 2 stories (no elevator), interior corridors. **Parking:** on-site. **Terms:** 7 day cancellation notice. **Amenities:** high-speed Internet, voice mail, irons, hair dryers. **Pool(s):** heated outdoor. **Leisure Activities:** whirlpool, exercise room. **Guest Services:** coin laundry, wireless Internet. **Business Services:** conference facilities, business center. **Cards:** AX, DC, DS, MC, VI. **Free Special Amenities:** expanded continental breakfast and high-speed Internet.

AAA Benefit:
Members save up to 20%, plus 10% bonus points with rewards program.

HOLIDAY INN-WILSONVILLE   *Book at AAA.com*
Phone: (503)682-2211   (134)

Hotel
$109-$199 All Year

Address: 25425 SW 95th Ave **Location:** I-5, exit 286, just w on Boones Ferry Rd, then just se. **Facility:** Smoke free premises. 170 units. 166 one-bedroom standard units. 4 one-bedroom suites. 5 stories, interior corridors. **Bath:** combo or shower only. **Parking:** on-site. **Amenities:** high-speed Internet, voice mail, irons, hair dryers. **Pool(s):** heated indoor. **Leisure Activities:** whirlpool, exercise room. **Guest Services:** valet and coin laundry, area transportation, wireless Internet. **Business Services:** conference facilities, business center. **Cards:** AX, CB, DC, DS, JC, MC, VI.

(See map and index starting on p. 402)

LA QUINTA INN WILSONVILLE   *Book great rates at AAA.com*   Phone: (503)682-3184   [133]

AAA [SAVE]
▼▼▼▼
Hotel
$70-$149 All Year

Address: 8815 SW Sun Pl **Location:** I-5, exit 286, just e on Elligsen Rd, just n on Parkway Ave, then just w. **Facility:** Smoke free premises. 75 one-bedroom standard units, some with whirlpools. 3 stories, interior corridors. *Bath:* combo or shower only. **Parking:** on-site. **Amenities:** high-speed Internet, voice mail, irons, hair dryers. **Pool(s):** heated outdoor. **Leisure Activities:** exercise room. **Guest Services:** valet and coin laundry, wireless Internet. **Business Services:** meeting rooms, PC. **Cards:** AX, DS, MC, VI. **Free Special Amenities: expanded continental breakfast and high-speed Internet.**

CALL [&M] [≈] [✕] [✦] [🗎] [🖼] [🖳] / SOME UNITS [🐾]

WILSONVILLE INN & SUITES   *Book great rates at AAA.com*   Phone: (503)570-9700

AAA [SAVE]
▼▼▼▼
Hotel
$69-$159 All Year

Address: 29769 SW Boones Ferry Rd **Location:** I-5, exit 283, just w on Wilsonville Rd, then just n. **Facility:** 56 units. 53 one-bedroom standard units. 3 one-bedroom suites with whirlpools. 4 stories, interior corridors. *Bath:* combo or shower only. **Parking:** on-site. **Amenities:** high-speed Internet, dual phone lines, voice mail, irons, hair dryers. **Pool(s):** heated indoor. **Leisure Activities:** whirlpool, exercise room. **Guest Services:** valet and coin laundry, area transportation-within 10 mi, wireless Internet. **Business Services:** meeting rooms, business center. **Cards:** AX, DC, DS, MC, VI. **Free Special Amenities: expanded continental breakfast and high-speed Internet.**

[¶†] CALL [&M] [≈] [✦] [🗎] [🖼] [🖳] / SOME UNITS FEE[🐾] [✕]

WOOD VILLAGE   (See map and index starting on p. 402)

—— WHERE TO STAY ——

BEST WESTERN CASCADE INN & SUITES   *Book great rates at AAA.com*   Phone: (503)491-9700   [82]

AAA [SAVE]
▼▼▼▼
Hotel
$110-$130 3/1-9/30
$89-$119 10/1-2/28

Address: 23525 NE Halsey St **Location:** I-84, exit 16, just s on NE 238th Dr, then just w. **Facility:** 60 one-bedroom standard units, some with whirlpools. 3 stories, interior corridors. *Bath:* combo or shower only. **Parking:** on-site. **Amenities:** high-speed Internet, voice mail, irons, hair dryers. **Pool(s):** heated indoor. **Leisure Activities:** sauna, whirlpool, exercise room. **Guest Services:** valet and coin laundry, airport transportation-Portland International Airport, wireless Internet. **Business Services:** meeting rooms, PC. **Cards:** AX, DC, DS, JC, MC, VI.

[✈] CALL [&M] [≈] [✕] [✦] [▯] [🗎] [🖳] / SOME UNITS [✕]

┌─────────────────┐
│ **Best Western** │
│   │
│ **AAA Benefit:** │
│ Members save up to │
│ 20%, plus 10%   │
│ bonus points with │
│ rewards program. │
└─────────────────┘

PORTLAND/TROUTDALE TRAVELODGE   *Book great rates at AAA.com*   Phone: (503)666-6623   [81]

AAA [SAVE]
▼
Hotel
$44-$89 All Year

Address: 23705 NE Sandy Blvd **Location:** I-84, exit 16, just n on NE 238th Dr. **Facility:** 44 one-bedroom standard units, some with efficiencies or kitchens. 2 stories (no elevator), interior corridors. *Bath:* combo or shower only. **Parking:** on-site. **Amenities:** high-speed Internet, hair dryers. **Guest Services:** coin laundry, wireless Internet. **Cards:** AX, DC, DS, MC, VI. **Free Special Amenities: expanded continental breakfast and high-speed Internet.**

[¶] [✦] [🖳] / SOME UNITS [✕] [🗎] [🖼]

Nearby Washington

BATTLE GROUND   pop. 9,296

—— WHERE TO STAY ——

BEST WESTERN BATTLE GROUND INN & SUITES   *Book great rates at AAA.com*   Phone: (360)687-8881

AAA [SAVE]
▼▼▼▼
Motel
$100-$160 3/1-8/31
$70-$130 9/1-2/28

Address: 1419 W Main St **Location:** 0.5 mi nw, 0.9 mi w, just s, then 5.2 mi w. **Facility:** Smoke free premises. 46 units. 45 one-bedroom standard units, some with whirlpools. 1 one-bedroom suite with efficiency (no utensils). 3 stories, interior corridors. **Parking:** on-site. **Amenities:** high-speed Internet, dual phone lines, irons, hair dryers. **Pool(s):** heated indoor. **Leisure Activities:** whirlpool, exercise room. **Guest Services:** coin laundry, wireless Internet. **Business Services:** meeting rooms, PC. **Cards:** AX, DC, DS, MC, VI. **Free Special Amenities: expanded continental breakfast and high-speed Internet.**

CALL [&M] [≈] [✕] [🗎] [🖼] [🖳]

┌─────────────────┐
│ **Best Western** │
│   │
│ **AAA Benefit:** │
│ Members save up to │
│ 20%, plus 10%   │
│ bonus points with │
│ rewards program. │
└─────────────────┘

—— WHERE TO DINE ——

BURGERVILLE   Phone: 360/687-7308

▼
American
$2-$8

First-timers shouldn't let the fast food exterior fool them, as the burgers and chicken here adhere to a higher standard. Northwest ingredients come into play in the sandwiches. Casual dress. **Hours:** 7 am-10 pm. Closed: 11/26, 12/25. **Address:** 217 Main St **Location:** At Main St and SW 3rd Ave; downtown. **Parking:** on-site. **Cards:** DS, MC, VI.

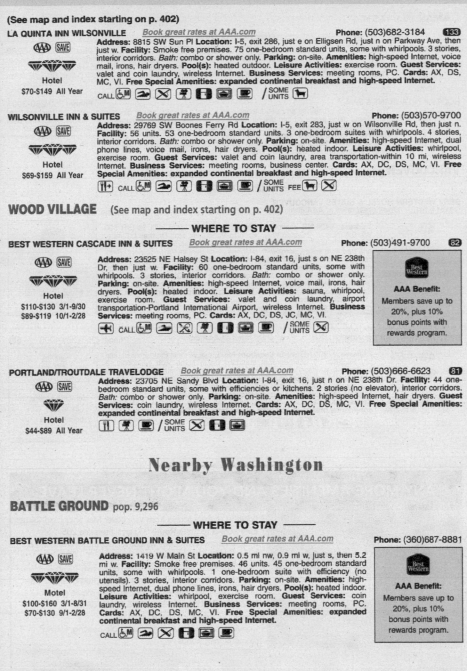

CAMAS pop. 12,534

---------- WHERE TO DINE ----------

BURGERVILLE

American
$2-$8

Phone: 360/834-3289
First-timers shouldn't let the fast food exterior fool them, as the burgers and chicken here adhere to a higher standard. Northwest ingredients come into play in the sandwiches. Casual dress. **Hours:** 7 am-10 pm. Closed: 11/26, 12/25. **Address:** 518 NE 3rd Ave **Location:** At NE 3rd Ave and NE Dallas St; downtown. **Parking:** on-site. **Cards:** DS, MC, VI.

ROOTS RESTAURANT & BAR

Regional American
$7-$22

Phone: 360/260-3001
The hip, trendy place has an open kitchen and a chef's counter where diners can watch the freshest local ingredients being prepared into dishes for the ever-changing menu. Choices range from spinach and beet salads to pan-seared wild salmon, roasted chicken and top sirloin steak. Semi-formal attire. **Bar:** Full bar. **Reservations:** suggested. **Hours:** 11:30 am-2:30 & 5-10 pm, Sun 11 am-2 & 5-9 pm; Sunday brunch. Closed: 7/4, 9/7, 12/25. **Address:** 19215 SE 34th St **Location:** SR 14, exit 8, just n on 164th Ave, then 1.3 mi e. **Parking:** on-site. **Cards:** AX, DS, MC, VI.

VANCOUVER pop. 143,560   (See map and index starting on p. 411)

---------- WHERE TO STAY ----------

BEST WESTERN HOTEL & SUITES VANCOUVER MALL DR   *Book great rates at AAA.com*

Hotel
Rates not provided

Phone: 360/256-0707   [8]
Address: 9420 NE Vancouver Mall Dr **Location:** I-205, exit 30 (SR 500 W), 0.6 mi w to Thurston Way, just n to Vancouver Mall Dr, then 0.7 mi e. **Facility:** 75 units. 71 one-bedroom standard units, some with whirlpools. 4 one-bedroom suites, some with kitchens. 4 stories, interior corridors. *Bath:* combo or shower only. **Parking:** on-site. **Amenities:** high-speed Internet, dual phone lines, voice mail, irons, hair dryers. **Pool(s):** heated indoor. **Leisure Activities:** sauna, whirlpool, exercise room. **Guest Services:** coin laundry, wireless Internet. **Business Services:** meeting rooms, PC. **Free Special Amenities:** continental breakfast and high-speed Internet. *(See color ad below)*

BEST WESTERN INN OF VANCOUVER   *Book great rates at AAA.com*

Hotel
$89-$109 3/1-9/15
$85-$105 9/16-2/28

Phone: (360)254-4000   [15]
Address: 11506 NE 3rd St **Location:** I-205, exit 28 (Mill Plain Blvd E), just ne. **Facility:** 59 one-bedroom standard units, some with whirlpools. 2 stories (no elevator), exterior corridors. **Parking:** on-site. **Terms:** 3 day cancellation notice-fee imposed. **Amenities:** high-speed Internet, irons, hair dryers. **Pool(s):** heated indoor. **Leisure Activities:** whirlpool, limited exercise equipment. **Guest Services:** coin laundry, wireless Internet. **Cards:** AX, CB, DC, DS, JC, MC, VI. **Free Special Amenities:** continental breakfast and high-speed Internet. *(See color ad p 477)*

▼ *See AAA listing above* ▼

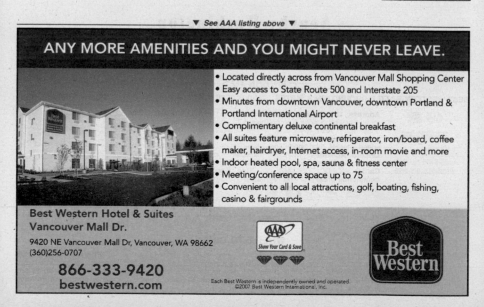

(See map and index starting on p. 411)

COMFORT INN   *Book at AAA.com*   Phone: 360/574-6000   **2**

Hotel
Rates not provided

Address: 13207 NE 20th Ave **Location:** I-5, exit 7, just e; I-205, exit 36, just w. **Facility:** 58 units. 56 one-bedroom standard units, some with whirlpools. 2 one-bedroom suites with whirlpools. 2 stories (no elevator), interior corridors. **Parking:** on-site. **Amenities:** high-speed Internet, irons, hair dryers. **Pool(s):** heated indoor. **Leisure Activities:** whirlpool, exercise room. **Guest Services:** coin laundry, wireless Internet. **Business Services:** meeting rooms, PC.

COMFORT SUITES   *Book at AAA.com*   Phone: (360)253-3100   **10**

Hotel
$90-$135 All Year

Address: 4714 NE 94th Ave **Location:** I-205, exit 30 (SR 500 W), 0.6 mi w to Thurston Way, just n to Vancouver Mall Dr, then 0.5 mi e; southeast edge of Westfield Shopping Center. **Facility:** Smoke free premises. 67 one-bedroom standard units, some with whirlpools. 2 stories (no elevator), interior corridors. **Parking:** on-site. **Amenities:** high-speed Internet, irons, hair dryers. *Some:* DVD players (fee). **Pool(s):** heated indoor. **Leisure Activities:** whirlpool, exercise room. **Guest Services:** coin laundry, tanning facilities, wireless Internet. **Business Services:** meeting rooms, PC. **Cards:** AX, CB, DC, DS, JC, MC, VI.

EXTENDED STAYAMERICA-PORTLAND-VANCOUVER   *Book at AAA.com*   Phone: (360)604-8530   **16**

Hotel
$85-$100 All Year

Address: 300 NE 115th Ave **Location:** I-205, exit 28 (Mill Plain Blvd E), just ne. **Facility:** 116 one-bedroom standard units with efficiencies. 3 stories, interior corridors. *Bath:* combo or shower only. **Parking:** on-site. **Terms:** cancellation fee imposed. **Amenities:** high-speed Internet (fee), voice mail, irons. **Guest Services:** coin laundry, wireless Internet. **Cards:** AX, CB, DC, DS, JC, MC, VI.

GUEST HOUSE MOTEL   Phone: 360/254-4511   **17**

Motel
Rates not provided

Address: 11504 NE 2nd St **Location:** I-205, exit 28 (Mill Plain Blvd E), just ne. **Facility:** 46 one-bedroom standard units. 2 stories (no elevator), exterior corridors. **Parking:** on-site. **Terms:** office hours 7 am-10:30 pm. **Amenities:** high-speed Internet. **Guest Services:** coin laundry, wireless Internet. **Free Special Amenities: continental breakfast and high-speed Internet.**

THE HEATHMAN LODGE   *Book great rates at AAA.com*   Phone: (360)254-3100   **12**

Hotel
$139-$169 All Year

Address: 7801 NE Greenwood Dr **Location:** I-205, exit 30 (SR 500 W), 0.5 mi w to Thurston Way, just n to NE Parkway Dr, then just w. **Facility:** 142 units. 121 one-bedroom standard units. 21 one-bedroom suites, some with whirlpools. 4 stories, interior corridors. *Bath:* combo or shower only. **Parking:** on-site. **Terms:** check-in 4 pm, cancellation fee imposed. **Amenities:** video games (fee), high-speed Internet, dual phone lines, voice mail, irons, hair dryers. *Some:* DVD players, CD players. **Dining:** Hudson's Bar & Grill at The Heathman Lodge, see separate listing. **Pool(s):** heated indoor. **Leisure Activities:** sauna, whirlpool, exercise room. **Guest Services:** complimentary and valet laundry, wireless Internet. **Business Services:** meeting rooms, business center. **Cards:** AX, CB, DC, DS, MC, VI. **Free Special Amenities: continental breakfast and high-speed Internet.**

▼ *See AAA listing p 476* ▼

(See map and index starting on p. 411)

HILTON VANCOUVER WASHINGTON AND VANCOUVER CONVENTION CENTER

Book great rates at AAA.com

Phone: (360)993-4500 **14**

(AAA) (SAVE)

▼▼▼

Hotel

$99-$219 All Year

Address: 301 W 6th St **Location:** I-5, exit 1C (Mill Plain Blvd) southbound, 0.3 mi w, then 0.3 mi s on W Columbia St; exit 1B northbound, 0.5 mi, follow signs to City Center/6th St. **Facility:** 226 units. 224 one-bedroom standard units. 2 one-bedroom suites. 7 stories, interior corridors. *Bath:* combo or shower only. **Parking:** on-site (fee) and valet. **Terms:** check-in 4 pm, 1-30 night minimum stay, cancellation fee imposed. **Amenities:** dual phone lines, voice mail, irons, hair dryers. *Fee:* video games, high-speed Internet. **Dining:** Gray's At The Park, see separate listing. **Pool(s):** heated indoor. **Leisure Activities:** whirlpool, exercise room. **Guest Services:** valet laundry, wireless Internet. **Business Services:** conference facilities, business center. **Cards:** AX, CB, DC, DS, JC, MC, VI.

Hilton

AAA Benefit:
Members save 5% or more everyday!

🍽 CALL 👍M 🏊 ✕ 🎦 🖥 / SOME UNITS FEE 🛏 FEE 🖨 FEE 🖼

HOLIDAY INN EXPRESS HOTEL & SUITES

Book at AAA.com

Phone: (360)576-1040 **4**

▼▼▼

Hotel

$112-$155 6/1-2/28
$112-$143 3/1-5/31

Address: 13101 NE 27th Ave **Location:** I-205, exit 36, just e on NE 134th St-WSU; I-5, exit 7 (I-205) southbound, exit 36, just e; exit 7 northbound, 0.5 mi e on NE 134th St-WSU. **Facility:** 78 units. 76 one-bedroom standard units. 2 one-bedroom suites with whirlpools. 3 stories, interior corridors. *Bath:* combo or shower only. **Parking:** on-site. **Amenities:** high-speed Internet, dual phone lines, voice mail, irons, hair dryers. **Pool(s):** heated indoor. **Leisure Activities:** whirlpool, exercise room. **Guest Services:** valet and coin laundry, wireless Internet. **Business Services:** meeting rooms, business center. **Cards:** AX, CB, DC, DS, JC, MC, VI.

(ASK) CALL 👍M 🏊 🖥 / SOME UNITS ✕ 🖨 🖼

Hertz rents Fords and other fine cars.
® REG. U.S. PAT. OFF. © HERTZ SYSTEM INC., 1999/2006-99.

Savings for all Seasons

No matter the season, Hertz offers AAA members exclusive discounts and benefits.

Operating in 145 countries at over 8,000 locations, Hertz makes traveling more convenient and efficient wherever and whenever you go. Hertz offers AAA members discounts up to 20% on car rentals worldwide.

To receive your exclusive AAA member discounts and benefits, mention your AAA membership card at time of reservation and present it at time of rental. **In addition**, to receive a free one car class upgrade on daily, weekly or weekend rental in the United States, Puerto Rico and Canada, mention PC# 969194 at the time of reservation. Offer is valid for vehicle pick-up on or before 12/15/09.

For reservations and program details, visit AAA.com/hertz, call your AAA Travel office or the Hertz/AAA Desk at **1-800-654-3080.**

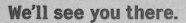

AAA **AAA TourBookMark**

Lodging Listing Symbols

Member Values *(see pgs. 12-13)*

- **AAA** Official Appointment
- **[SAVE]** Offers lowest public rate or minimum 10% discount
- **[A$K]** May offer discount
- **[fyi]** Informational listing only

Member Services

- Airport transportation
- Pets allowed (call property for restrictions and fees)
- Restaurant on premises
- Restaurant off premises (walking distance)
- 24-hour room service
- Full bar
- Child care
- Accessible features (call property for available services and amenities)

Leisure Activities

- Full-service casino
- Pool
- Health club on premises
- Health club off premises (walking distance)
- Recreational activities

In-Room Amenities

- Designated non-smoking rooms
- VCR
- Movies
- Refrigerator
- Microwave
- Coffee maker
- No air conditioning
- No TV
- No cable TV
- No telephones

Safety Features *(see page 24)*
(Mexico and Caribbean only)

- **[S]** Sprinklers
- **[D]** Smoke detectors

Call property for detailed information about fees and restrictions relating to the lodging listing symbols.

CHOICE HOTELS
INTERNATIONAL

Book today
at choicehotels.com
or 800.228.1222

We'll see you there.

CHOICE HOTELS INTERNATIONAL®

(See map and index starting on p. 411)

HOMEWOOD SUITES BY HILTON   *Book great rates at AAA.com*   Phone: (360)750-1100   **20**

Hotel
$109-$179 All Year

Address: 701 SE Columbia Shores Blvd **Location:** SR 14, exit 1, just s. Located in a residential commercial area. **Facility:** 104 units. 96 one- and 8 two-bedroom suites with efficiencies. 2-3 stories, interior/exterior corridors. *Bath:* combo or shower only. **Parking:** on-site. **Terms:** 1-30 night minimum stay, cancellation fee imposed. **Amenities:** video games (fee), high-speed Internet, dual phone lines, voice mail, irons, hair dryers. **Pool(s):** heated outdoor. **Leisure Activities:** whirlpool, exercise room, sports court. **Guest Services:** valet and coin laundry, area transportation, wireless Internet. **Business Services:** meeting rooms, business center. **Cards:** AX, CB, DC, DS, JC, MC, VI.

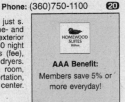

AAA Benefit:
Members save 5% or more everyday!

THE INN AT SALMON CREEK   *Book great rates at AAA.com*   Phone: (360)573-0751   **5**

Motel
$50-$65 All Year

Address: 11901 NE Hwy 99 **Location:** I-5, exit 7, 1 mi se; I-205, exit 36, 1 mi sw. **Facility:** 19 units. 15 one-bedroom standard units, some with kitchens (no utensils). 4 one-bedroom suites with kitchens (no utensils). 1 story, exterior corridors. **Parking:** on-site. **Terms:** cancellation fee imposed. **Amenities:** high-speed Internet. **Guest Services:** wireless Internet. **Cards:** AX, CB, DC, DS, JC, MC, VI. **Free Special Amenities: local telephone calls and preferred room (subject to availability with advance reservations).**

LA QUINTA INN & SUITES   *Book at AAA.com*   Phone: (360)566-1100   **1**

Hotel
$89-$169 All Year

Address: 1500 NE 134th St **Location:** I-5, exit 7, just w; I-205, exit 36, 0.5 mi w. **Facility:** Smoke free premises. 89 units. 82 one-bedroom standard units. 7 one-bedroom suites. 4 stories, interior corridors. *Bath:* combo or shower only. **Parking:** on-site. **Amenities:** high-speed Internet, voice mail, irons, hair dryers. **Pool(s):** heated indoor. **Guest Services:** valet and coin laundry, wireless Internet. **Business Services:** meeting rooms, business center. **Cards:** AX, CB, DC, DS, MC, VI.

PHOENIX INN SUITES-VANCOUVER   *Book great rates at AAA.com*   Phone: (360)891-9777   **19**

Hotel
$79-$149 All Year

Address: 12712 SE 2nd Cir **Location:** I-205, exit 28 (Mill Plain Blvd E), 0.8 mi e, then just n on SE 126th Ave. **Facility:** Smoke free premises. 98 units. 95 one- and 3 two-bedroom standard units, some with whirlpools. 3 stories, interior corridors. *Bath:* combo or shower only. **Parking:** on-site. **Terms:** cancellation fee imposed. **Amenities:** high-speed Internet, dual phone lines, voice mail, irons, hair dryers. **Pool(s):** heated indoor. **Leisure Activities:** whirlpool, exercise room. **Guest Services:** valet and coin laundry, airport transportation-Portland International Airport, wireless Internet. **Business Services:** meeting rooms, business center. **Cards:** AX, CB, DC, DS, JC, MC, VI. **Free Special Amenities: expanded continental breakfast and high-speed Internet. (See color ad p 440)**

QUALITY INN & SUITES   *Book great rates at AAA.com*   Phone: (360)696-0516   **6**

Hotel
$69-$109 All Year

Address: 7001 NE Hwy 99 **Location:** I-5, exit 4, 0.5 mi se. **Facility:** Smoke free premises. 72 one-bedroom standard units, some with kitchens (no utensils). 2 stories (no elevator), interior corridors. **Parking:** on-site. **Terms:** check-in 4 pm, cancellation fee imposed. **Amenities:** high-speed Internet, voice mail, irons, hair dryers. **Pool(s):** heated outdoor. **Leisure Activities:** whirlpool, limited exercise equipment. **Guest Services:** valet and coin laundry, wireless Internet. **Business Services:** meeting rooms, PC. **Cards:** AX, CB, DC, DS, JC, MC, VI. **Free Special Amenities: expanded continental breakfast and high-speed Internet.**

RAMADA INN   *Book at AAA.com*   Phone: 360/253-5000   **9**

Hotel
Rates not provided

Address: 9107 NE Vancouver Mall Dr **Location:** I-205, exit 30 (SR 500 W), 0.6 mi w to Thurston Way, just n to Vancouver Mall Dr, then 0.5 mi e; southeast edge of Westfield Shopping Center. **Facility:** 55 one-bedroom standard units. 2 stories (no elevator), interior corridors. **Parking:** on-site. **Amenities:** high-speed Internet, dual phone lines, voice mail, irons, hair dryers. **Pool(s):** heated indoor. **Leisure Activities:** whirlpool. **Guest Services:** wireless Internet. **Business Services:** PC.

RED LION HOTEL VANCOUVER @ THE QUAY   *Book great rates at AAA.com*   Phone: (360)694-8341   **18**

Hotel
$139-$179 3/1-10/31
$129-$169 11/1-2/28

Address: 100 Columbia St **Location:** 0.5 mi s on dock at foot of Columbia St. **Facility:** Smoke free premises. 160 units. 157 one-bedroom standard units. 3 one-bedroom suites, some with kitchens and/or whirlpools. 3 stories, interior corridors. *Bath:* combo or shower only. **Parking:** on-site. **Terms:** check-in 4 pm. **Amenities:** high-speed Internet, voice mail, irons, hair dryers. **Pool(s):** heated outdoor. **Leisure Activities:** jogging, exercise room. **Guest Services:** valet and coin laundry, wireless Internet. **Business Services:** conference facilities, business center. **Cards:** AX, DS, MC, VI.

(See map and index starting on p. 411)

RESIDENCE INN VANCOUVER *Book great rates at AAA.com* Phone: (360)253-4800 11

Hotel
$169-$189 All Year

Address: 8005 NE Parkway Dr **Location:** I-205, exit 30 (SR 500 W), 0.5 mi w to Thurston Way, just n to NE Parkway Dr, then just w. **Facility:** Smoke free premises. 120 units. 84 one-bedroom standard units with kitchens. 6 one- and 30 two-bedroom suites with kitchens. 2 stories (no elevator), exterior corridors. *Bath:* combo or shower only. **Parking:** on-site. **Terms:** cancellation fee imposed. **Amenities:** video games (fee), high-speed Internet, dual phone lines, voice mail, irons, hair dryers. **Pool(s):** heated outdoor. **Leisure Activities:** whirlpools, exercise room, sports court. **Guest Services:** valet and coin laundry, wireless Internet. **Business Services:** meeting rooms, PC. **Cards:** AX, CB, DC, DS, JC, MC, VI.

AAA Benefit:
Members save a minimum 5% off the best available rate.

RODEWAY INN & SUITES *Book great rates at AAA.com* Phone: (360)254-0900 7

Hotel
$79-$96 All Year

Address: 9201 NE Vancouver Mall Dr **Location:** I-205, exit 30 (SR 500 W), just n to Vancouver Mall Dr, then 0.5 mi e; southeast edge of Westfield Shopping Center. **Facility:** 63 one-bedroom standard units. 3 stories, interior corridors. *Bath:* combo or shower only. **Parking:** on-site. **Amenities:** high-speed Internet, safes, irons, hair dryers. **Pool(s):** heated indoor. **Leisure Activities:** whirlpool. **Guest Services:** coin laundry, wireless Internet. **Business Services:** PC. **Cards:** AX, DC, DS, JC, MC, VI. **Free Special Amenities:** expanded continental breakfast and high-speed Internet.

SHILO INN & SUITES-SALMON CREEK *Book great rates at AAA.com* Phone: (360)573-0511 3

Hotel
$82-$190 All Year

Address: 13206 Hwy 99 **Location:** I-5, exit 7, just e; I-205, exit 36, just w. **Facility:** Smoke free premises. 66 one-bedroom standard units, some with efficiencies. 2 stories (no elevator), interior corridors. *Bath:* combo or shower only. **Parking:** on-site. **Amenities:** video games (fee), high-speed Internet, irons, hair dryers. **Pool(s):** heated indoor. **Leisure Activities:** sauna, whirlpool, steamroom. **Guest Services:** coin laundry, wireless Internet. **Business Services:** meeting rooms, PC. **Cards:** AX, CB, DC, DS, JC, MC, VI. **Free Special Amenities:** continental breakfast and high-speed Internet. *(See color ad below)*

See map and index starting on p. 411)

SPRINGHILL SUITES BY MARRIOTT VANCOUVER
COLUMBIA TECH CENTER   *Book great rates at AAA.com*   Phone: (360)260-1000

Hotel
$134-$164 All Year

Address: 1421 SE Tech Center Dr **Location:** SR 14, exit 8, 1.3 mi n on SE 164th Ave, then just e. **Facility:** Smoke free premises. 119 one-bedroom standard units. 4 stories, interior corridors. *Bath:* combo or shower only. **Parking:** on-site. **Terms:** cancellation fee imposed. **Amenities:** high-speed Internet, voice mail, irons, hair dryers. **Pool(s):** heated indoor. **Leisure Activities:** whirlpool, exercise room. **Guest Services:** valet and coin laundry, area transportation, wireless Internet. **Business Services:** meeting rooms, PC. **Cards:** AX, CB, DC, DS, JC, MC, VI.

AAA Benefit:
Members save a
minimum 5% off the
best available rate.

Know the Local Driving Laws When Traveling

Across the U.S. and Canada, check the *Digest of Motor Laws* for local information on automated enforcement laws, occupant protection, alcohol laws, and traffic safety. Topics also include driver licensing laws and motor vehicle fees and taxes.

Contact your local AAA club for purchasing information.

Retail price: $13.95

DIGEST OF MOTOR LAWS

75TH EDITION

(See map and index starting on p. 411)

STAYBRIDGE SUITES VANCOUVER-PORTLAND   *Book at AAA.com*   Phone: (360)891-8282   ❶

▼▼▼

Hotel
$99-$186 All Year

Address: 7301 NE 41st St **Location:** I-205, exit 30 (SR 500 W), 1.5 mi w to NE Andresen Rd, just to NE 40th St, just e to NE 72nd St, just n to NE 41st St, then just e. **Facility:** 117 units. 63 one-bedroom standard units with efficiencies. 31 one- and 23 two-bedroom suites with efficiencies. stories, interior corridors. *Bath:* combo or shower only. **Parking:** on-site. **Amenities:** DVD player, high-speed Internet, dual phone lines, voice mail, irons, hair dryers. **Pool(s):** heated outdoor. **Leisure Activities:** whirlpool, exercise room, sports court. **Guest Services:** complimentary and valet laundry, area transportation, wireless Internet. **Business Services:** meeting rooms, business cente. **Cards:** AX, CB, DC, DS, JC, MC, VI.

✈ CALL 🛗 ➤ ✕ VCR 🎦 🖥 🍴 🖥 / SOME UNITS FEE 🐾 ✕

──────── **WHERE TO DINE** ────────

ARAWAN THAI CUISINE   Phone: 360/882-811

▼▼▼

Thai
$6-$10

In a small shopping complex, the basic storefront opens to a bright restaurant where the menu lines up wide selection of both Thai and sushi dishes. Casual dress. **Bar:** Full bar. **Hours:** 11 am-9:30 pm. Closed 7/4, 11/26, 12/25. **Address:** 700 SE 160th Ave **Location:** SR 14, exit 8, 1.5 mi n, then just nw; in Mill Plai Town Center. **Parking:** on-site. **Cards:** AX, CB, DC, DS, MC, VI.

CALL 🛗

BEACHES RESTAURANT & BAR   Phone: 360/699-1592   ❶

▼▼

American
$5-$24

Northwest foods include wood-oven specialties and large salads. Tables overlook the Columbia River and sand volleyball court. Casual dress. **Bar:** Full bar. **Reservations:** accepted. **Hours:** 11 am-10 pm, Sun Mon-9 pm. Closed: 1/1, 11/26, 12/25. **Address:** 1919 SE Columbia River Dr **Location:** SR 14, exit 1, just s **Parking:** on-site. **Cards:** AX, DC, DS, MC, VI.

BILLYGAN'S ROADHOUSE   Phone: 360/573-2711   ❶

▼▼

American
$6-$19

Snack on peanuts as you peruse the menu, where you'll find prime rib, steak and fish cooked over mesquit wood. The tangy Key lime cheesecake is the perfect way to end your meal. Servers are casual, upbeat an friendly. Casual dress. **Bar:** Full bar. **Hours:** 7 am-10 pm, Fri & Sat-11 pm. Closed major holidays **Address:** 13200 NE Hwy 99 **Location:** I-5, exit 7, just e; I-205, exit 36, just w. **Parking:** on-site. **Cards:** AX DS, MC, VI.

BURGERVILLE   Phone: 360/944-623

▼▼

American
$2-$8

First-timers shouldn't let the fast food exterior fool them, as the burgers and chicken here adhere to a highe standard. Northwest ingredients come into play in the sandwiches. Casual dress. **Hours:** 7 am-10 pm Closed: 11/26, 12/25. **Address:** 8320 NE Vancouver Plaza Dr **Location:** I-205, exit 30 (SR 500 W), 0.5 n w on Thurston Way, then just s. **Parking:** on-site. **Cards:** DS, MC, VI.

BURGERVILLE   Phone: 360/253-943

▼▼

American
$2-$8

First-timers shouldn't let the fast food exterior fool them, as the burgers and chicken here adhere to a highe standard. Northwest ingredients come into play in the sandwiches. Casual dress. **Hours:** 7 am-10 pm Closed: 11/26, 12/25. **Address:** 16416 SE McGillivray Blvd **Location:** SR 14, exit 8, 1.3 mi n, then just w **Parking:** on-site. **Cards:** DS, MC, VI.

BURGERVILLE   Phone: 360/573-822

▼▼

American
$2-$8

First-timers shouldn't let the fast food exterior fool them, as the burgers and chicken here adhere to a highe standard. Northwest ingredients come into play in the sandwiches. Casual dress. **Hours:** 7 am-10 pm Closed: 11/26, 12/25. **Address:** 13301 NE Hwy 99 **Location:** I-5, exit 7, just e; I-205, exit 36, just w **Parking:** on-site. **Cards:** DS, MC, VI.

BURGERVILLE   Phone: 360/693-880

▼▼

American
$2-$8

First-timers shouldn't let the fast food exterior fool them, as the burgers and chicken here adhere to a highe standard. Northwest ingredients come into play in the sandwiches. Casual dress. **Hours:** 7 am-10 pm Closed: 11/26, 12/25. **Address:** 307 E Mill Plain Blvd **Location:** I-5, exit 1C (Mill Plain Blvd), just w **Parking:** on-site. **Cards:** DS, MC, VI.

🅜

BURGERVILLE   Phone: 360/254-930

▼▼

American
$2-$8

First-timers shouldn't let the fast food exterior fool them, as the burgers and chicken here adhere to a highe standard. Northwest ingredients come into play in the sandwiches. Casual dress. **Hours:** 7 am-10 pm Closed: 11/26, 12/25. **Address:** 11704 E Mill Plain Blvd **Location:** I-205, exit 28 (E Mill Plain Blvd), just e **Parking:** on-site. **Cards:** DS, MC, VI.

CATHEDRAL TAPATIA MEXICAN RESTAURANT   Phone: 360/891-0055

▼▼▼

Mexican
$8-$15

Jalisco cuisine is served in a large vaulted room that is festively painted with Mexican murals. Casual dress **Bar:** Full bar. **Hours:** 11 am-10 pm, Fri & Sat-11 pm. Closed: 7/4, 11/26, 12/25. **Address:** 707 SE 164th Ave **Location:** SR 14, exit 8, 1.5 mi n. **Parking:** on-site. **Cards:** AX, DS, MC, VI.

GRAY'S AT THE PARK   Phone: 360/828-4343   ❼

▼▼▼

American
$8-$30

Diners sit down to America-inspired dishes prepared with regional products and a Northwest flair. The dining room incorporates a crisp, clean and contemporary dining room and a sharp, trendy lounge in which classic cocktails are served. Casual dress. **Bar:** Full bar. **Reservations:** accepted. **Hours:** 6 am-10 pm, Fri & Sat 11 pm. **Address:** 301 W 6th St **Location:** I-5, exit 1C (Mill Plain Blvd) southbound, 0.3 mi w, then 0.3 mi s on W Columbia St; exit 1B northbound, 0.5 mi, follow signs to City Center/6th St; in Hilton Vancouver Washington and Vancouver Convention Center. **Parking:** on-site and valet. **Cards:** AX, CB, DC, DS, JC MC, VI.

CALL 🛗

(See map and index starting on p. 411)

GUSTAV'S PUB & GRILL
Phone: 360/883-0222

German
$8-$23

Select from such favorites as wood-smoked bier sausage, schnitzel, red cabbage and sauerkraut or pork, turkey and lamb rotisserie entrees. Gustav's party feast or the memorable Swiss cheese fondue are ideal for larger appetites. Local and imported beers are available as is a choice of desserts that includes English bread pudding made with oven-baked croissants. Casual dress. **Bar:** Full bar. **Reservations:** accepted. **Hours:** 11 am-11 pm, Fri & Sat-midnight. Closed: 12/25. **Address:** 1705 SE 164th **Location:** SR 14, exit 8, 1.1 mi n. **Parking:** on-site. **Cards:** AX, DS, MC, VI.

CALL M

HAZEL DELL BREW PUB
Phone: 360/576-0996   2

American
$8-$12

The pub serves a large assortment of freshly brewed ales and delicious fish-and-chips. Also on the menu are burgers, chicken and sausage as well as traditional, Cajun and West Indies sandwiches. Casual dress. **Bar:** Beer & wine. **Hours:** 11:30 am-11 pm, Fri & Sat 11 am-1 am, Sun 11 am-midnight. Closed: 12/25. **Address:** 8513 NE Hwy 99 **Location:** I-5, exit 4, 0.6 mi ne. **Parking:** on-site. **Cards:** MC, VI.

CALL M

HUDSON'S BAR & GRILL AT THE HEATHMAN LODGE
Phone: 360/816-6100   4

American
$8-$26

Sit back and enjoy the show of spinach Gorgonzola raviolis, grilled portobello mushroom caps, oven-roasted venison and herb-crusted pork tenderloin being prepared before your eyes in the open kitchen. Casual dress. **Bar:** Full bar. **Reservations:** accepted. **Hours:** 6 am-10 pm, Sat from 8 am, Sun 8 am-9 pm. **Address:** 7801 NE Greenwood Dr **Location:** I-205, exit 30 (SR 500 W), 0.5 mi w to Thurston Way, just n to NE Parkway Dr, then just w; in The Heathman Lodge. **Parking:** on-site. **Cards:** AX, CB, DC, DS, JC, MC, VI.

CALL M

JOE'S CRAB SHACK
Phone: 360/693-9211   8

SAVE

Seafood
$8-$29

The popular seafood restaurant specializes in a year-round variety of crab: Alaskan king, Dungeness, snow and blue. Among other offerings are fresh shrimp, hearty gumbo, clam chowder and classic steaks and chicken. Casual dress. **Bar:** Full bar. **Reservations:** accepted. **Hours:** 11 am-10 pm, Fri & Sat-11 pm. Closed: 11/26, 12/25. **Address:** 101 SE Columbia Way **Location:** I-5, exit 1A (SR 14), SR 14, exit 1, just s, then 0.5 mi w. **Parking:** on-site. **Cards:** AX, DC, DS, MC, VI.

MCGRATH'S FISH HOUSE
Phone: 360/514-9555

Seafood
$9-$19

The popular chain specializes in fresh Pacific Northwest seafood, including dishes grilled over a wood fire and items from the daily fresh sheet. Also on the menu are steaks, chicken, pasta and gourmet burgers. Casual dress. **Bar:** Full bar. **Reservations:** not accepted. **Hours:** 11 am-10 pm. Closed: 11/26, 12/25. **Address:** 12501 SE 2nd Cir **Location:** I-205, exit 28 (E Mill Plain Blvd), 0.8 mi e, then just n. **Parking:** on-site. **Cards:** AX, DC, DS, MC, VI.

MCMENAMINS
Phone: 360/699-1521

American
$5-$20

The casual neighborhood eatery is where friends gather for classic pub and comfort fare, all washed down by pints of locally made beer. Large wooden booths or tables easily accommodate larger groups, and the eclectic, custom-painted walls and varied period light fixtures keep diners' eyes busy should the conversation lag. Casual dress. **Bar:** Full bar. **Reservations:** not accepted. **Hours:** 11 am-midnight, Fri & Sat-1 am. **Address:** 1801 SE Columbia River Dr **Location:** SR 14, exit 1, just s. **Parking:** on-site. **Cards:** MC, VI.

MCMENAMINS
Phone: 360/254-3950

American
$5-$20

The casual neighborhood eatery is where friends gather for classic pub and comfort fare, all washed down by pints of locally made beer. Large wooden booths or tables easily accommodate larger groups, and the eclectic, custom-painted walls and varied period light fixtures keep diners' eyes busy should the conversation lag. Casual dress. **Bar:** Full bar. **Reservations:** not accepted. **Hours:** 11 am-11 pm, Fri & Sat-1 am, Sun noon-11 pm. **Address:** 1900 NE 162nd Ave, Suite B-107 **Location:** SR 14, exit 8, 2.5 mi n via 164th and 162nd aves. **Parking:** on-site. **Cards:** MC, VI.

CALL M

NEWPORT BAY RESTAURANT
Phone: 360/896-9795

Seafood
$8-$25

This restaurant is for those seeking a casual, relaxing time. A menu favorite is New England clam chowder, which is available nightly. Fresh Northwest salmon and Alaskan halibut prepared several ways share menu space with pasta, chicken and salads. Casual dress. **Bar:** Full bar. **Hours:** 11 am-10 pm, Fri & Sat-11 pm, Sun 9 am-10 pm. Closed: 11/26, 12/25. **Address:** 7717 NE Vancouver Plaza Dr **Location:** I-205, exit 30 (SR 500 W), just s on Thurston Way, then just w. **Parking:** on-site. **Cards:** AX, DS, MC, VI.

PEACHTREE RESTAURANT & PIE HOUSE
Phone: 360/693-6736   3

American
$6-$15

Locals gather for breakfast served all day, a selection of at least 10 to 15 freshly baked pies and hardy comfort food along the lines of chicken-fried steak and Yankee pot roast, which are served for dinner. Casual dress. **Reservations:** not accepted. **Hours:** 6 am-10 pm, Fri & Sat-11 pm. **Address:** 6600 NE Hwy 99 **Location:** I-5, exit 4, 0.9 mi se. **Parking:** on-site. **Cards:** AX, DS, MC, VI.

THE RESTAURANT AT THE HISTORIC RESERVE
Phone: 360/906-1101   6

American
$8-$30

Travel back in time to Fort Vancouver and Officer's Row, where a residence has been converted into an eatery. The home and area carry a lot of history that the staff is happy to relate while providing pleasant service. A glass enclosed back porch is always an enjoyable dining venue on sunny summer days. Entrees to choose from include chutney stuffed pork tenderloin, pan seared sturgeon with a pine nut crust or maybe a sauteed veal scalloppini. Casual dress. **Bar:** Full bar. **Reservations:** suggested. **Hours:** 11 am-2 & 5-8 pm, Sat from 5 pm, Sun 10 am-2 & 5-8 pm. Closed major holidays. **Address:** 1101 Officers Row **Location:** I-5, exit 1C (Mill Plain Blvd), just e, just s on Fort Vancouver Way, then just e. **Parking:** on-site. **Cards:** AX, DS, MC, VI.

(See map and index starting on p. 411)

ROUND TABLE PIZZA

◆◆ Pizza

$11-$26

Phone: 360/892-0450

This casual, family-oriented pizza place features high-quality ingredients and dough rolled fresh daily. Distinctive specialty pizzas are piled high with toppings. Casual dress. **Bar:** Beer & wine. **Reservations:** not accepted. **Hours:** 11 am-10 pm, Fri & Sat-11 pm. Closed: 11/26, 12/25. **Address:** 5016 NE Thurston Way. **Location:** Jct NE Thurston Way and NE 50th St. **Parking:** on-site. **Cards:** AX, DS, MC, VI.

ROUND TABLE PIZZA

◆◆ Pizza

$10-$17

Phone: 360/574-5755

This casual, family-oriented pizza place features high-quality ingredients and dough rolled fresh daily. Distinctive specialty pizzas are piled high with toppings. Casual dress. **Bar:** Beer & wine. **Reservations:** not accepted. **Hours:** 11 am-10 pm, Fri & Sat-11 pm. Closed: 11/26, 12/25. **Address:** 13009 NE Hwy 99. **Location:** I-5, exit 7, just e. **Parking:** on-site. **Cards:** AX, MC, VI.

THAI ORCHID RESTAURANT

◆◆ ◆◆ Thai

$7-$15

Phone: 360/695-7786

Patrons can enjoy fresh, flavorful Thai food with no added monosodium glutamate at this restaurant. The varied menu includes salads, soups, stir-fried dishes, distinctive curries, seafood and noodles. Casual dress. **Bar:** Beer & wine. **Reservations:** accepted. **Hours:** 11:30 am-9 pm. Closed: 7/4, 12/25. **Address:** 1004 Washington St **Location:** Southwest corner of W Evergreen St. **Parking:** on-site. **Cards:** AX, DS, MC, VI.

TOUCH OF ATHENS GREEK CUISINA AT THE HIDDEN HOUSE

◆◆ ◆◆ Greek

$6-$17

Phone: 360/695-6198   ⑤

It's a good idea to arrive early and linger on the front porch in preparation for a Greek experience that will include belly-dancing and attentive service from a Greek staff. Diners might start the evening with saganaki (a flaming cheese dish) and then move onto kebabs or maybe leg of lamb. Casual dress. **Bar:** Full bar. **Reservations:** accepted. **Hours:** 11 am-2 & 5-9 pm, Fri & Sat-10 pm. Closed: 11/26, 12/25; also Sun. **Address:** 100 W 13th St **Location:** Corner of Main and W 13th sts; downtown. **Parking:** on-site. **Cards:** AX, DS, MC, VI.

WHO-SONG & LARRY'S

◆◆ ◆◆ Mexican

$6-$15

Phone: 360/695-1198   ⑨

A south-of-the-border flair gives the casual restaurant, set on the Columbia River, its personality. Dishes such as chicken soft tacos are attractively garnished with lettuce leaves and chunky guacamole. The outdoor seating is popular in season. Casual dress. **Bar:** Full bar. **Hours:** 11 am-10 pm, Fri & Sat-11 pm. Closed: 11/26. **Address:** 111 E Columbia River Way **Location:** I-5, exit 1A (SR 14), SR 14, exit 1, just s, then 0.5 mi w. **Parking:** on-site. **Cards:** AX, CB, DC, DS, JC, MC, VI.

Portland Rose Festival / © Janis Miglavs / Danita Delimont Stock Photography

This ends listings for the Portland Vicinity.
The following page resumes the alphabetical listings of cities in Oregon.

PRINEVILLE pop. 7,356

—— WHERE TO STAY ——

BEST WESTERN PRINEVILLE INN *Book great rates at AAA.com*

Phone: (541)447-8080

AAA SAVE
Hotel
$76-$135 All Year

Address: 1475 NE 3rd St **Location:** 0.8 mi e on US 26. **Facility:** Smoke free premises. 67 one-bedroom standard units, some with whirlpools. 2 stories (no elevator), interior corridors. **Parking:** on-site. **Terms:** 3 day cancellation notice. **Amenities:** high-speed Internet, voice mail, irons, hair dryers. **Pool(s):** heated indoor. **Leisure Activities:** whirlpool. **Guest Services:** coin laundry, wireless Internet. **Business Services:** meeting rooms, PC. **Cards:** AX, DC, DS, MC, VI.

AAA Benefit:
Members save up to 20%, plus 10% bonus points with rewards program.

ECONO LODGE *Book at AAA.com*

Phone: 541/447-6231

Hotel
Rates not provided

Address: 123 NE 3rd St **Location:** Center; downtown. **Facility:** 33 one-bedroom standard units. 2 stories (no elevator), interior corridors. **Parking:** on-site. **Terms:** office hours 7 am-11 pm. **Amenities:** high-speed Internet. *Some:* irons, hair dryers. **Guest Services:** wireless Internet. **Business Services:** PC.

STAFFORD INN

Phone: (541)447-7100

Hotel
$87-$117 3/1-9/30
$82-$112 10/1-2/28

Address: 1773 NE 3rd St **Location:** 1 mi e on US 26. **Facility:** 63 units. 57 one-bedroom standard units. 6 one-bedroom suites with whirlpools. 3 stories, interior corridors. *Bath:* combo or shower only. **Parking:** on-site. **Amenities:** video games (fee), high-speed Internet, voice mail, irons, hair dryers. **Pool(s):** heated indoor. **Leisure Activities:** whirlpool, exercise room. **Guest Services:** valet and coin laundry, wireless Internet. **Business Services:** meeting rooms, PC. **Cards:** AX, CB, DC, DS, JC, MC, VI.

PROSPECT

—— WHERE TO STAY ——

PROSPECT HISTORIC HOTEL-MOTEL & DINNER HOUSE

Phone: (541)560-3664

Historic Motel
$70-$190 All Year

Address: 391 Mill Creek Dr **Location:** Jct SR 62, 0.3 mi s on 1st St (0.7 mi e of MM 43), just w. **Facility:** Handmade quilts drape all of the beds in this historic motel; family units for up to six people are offered. Smoke free premises. 24 units. 18 one- and 6 two-bedroom standard units, some with efficiencies. 1-3 stories (no elevator), interior/exterior corridors. *Bath:* combo or shower only. **Parking:** on-site. **Terms:** office hours 8 am-10 pm, cancellation fee imposed. **Amenities:** high-speed Internet. **Leisure Activities:** fishing, hiking trails, horseshoes. **Guest Services:** wireless Internet. **Business Services:** meeting rooms. **Cards:** DC, DS, MC, VI.

REDMOND pop. 13,481

—— WHERE TO STAY ——

BEST WESTERN RAMA INN *Book great rates at AAA.com*

Phone: (541)548-8080

AAA SAVE
Hotel
$99-$130 All Year

Address: 2630 SW 17th Pl **Location:** 1.3 mi s on US 97 from jct SR 126, then just sw. **Facility:** Smoke free premises. 74 units. 71 one-bedroom standard units. 3 one-bedroom suites. 2 stories (no elevator), interior corridors. *Bath:* combo or shower only. **Parking:** on-site. **Terms:** cancellation fee imposed. **Amenities:** high-speed Internet, voice mail, irons, hair dryers. **Pool(s):** heated indoor. **Leisure Activities:** whirlpool, sun deck, exercise room. **Guest Services:** coin laundry, airport transportation-Redmond Airport, wireless Internet. **Business Services:** meeting rooms, business center. **Cards:** AX, DC, DS, MC, VI. **Free Special Amenities: expanded continental breakfast and high-speed Internet.**

AAA Benefit:
Members save up to 20%, plus 10% bonus points with rewards program.

COMFORT SUITES-REDMOND AIRPORT *Book at AAA.com*

Phone: 541/504-8900

Hotel
Rates not provided

Address: 2243 SW Yew Ave **Location:** US 97, exit 124 (Yew Ave/Airport Way/Redmond Airport), just nw; 2 mi s of jct SR 126. **Facility:** Smoke free premises. 92 units. 84 one-bedroom standard units, some with whirlpools. 8 one-bedroom suites with efficiencies. 3 stories, interior corridors. *Bath:* combo or shower only. **Parking:** on-site. **Amenities:** high-speed Internet, dual phone lines, voice mail, irons, hair dryers. **Pool(s):** heated indoor. **Leisure Activities:** whirlpool, exercise room. **Guest Services:** coin laundry, wireless Internet. **Business Services:** meeting rooms, PC.

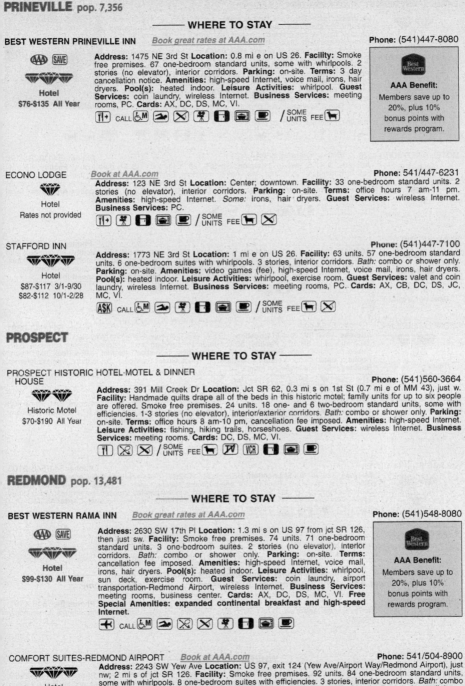

EAGLE CREST RESORT   *Book great rates at AAA.com*   Phone: 541/923-2453

Resort
Hotel
Rates not provided

Address: 1522 Cline Falls Rd **Location:** 4.5 mi w on SR 126, 1 mi s. **Facility:** Rooms in this resort come in varying sizes, some with a view, balcony, patio or gas fireplace. Smoke free premises. 100 units. 54 one-bedroom standard units. 46 one-bedroom suites. 2 stories, interior corridors. *Bath:* combo or shower only. **Parking:** on-site. **Terms:** check-in 4 pm. **Amenities:** video library (fee), DVD players, voice mail, irons, hair dryers. **Dining:** Niblick and Greene's, see separate listing. **Pool(s):** 3 heated outdoor, heated indoor. **Leisure Activities:** whirlpools, fishing, recreation programs, rental bicycles, hiking trails, playground, exercise room, spa, sports court, horseshoes, volleyball. *Fee:* golf-54 holes, 4 tennis courts (2 indoor, 2 lighted), racquetball courts, sports center. **Guest Services:** valet and coin laundry, area transportation (fee), beauty salon, wireless Internet. **Business Services:** conference facilities, PC. *(See color ad p 53)*

MOTEL 6 REDMOND-4076   *Book great rates at AAA.com*   Phone: (541)923-2100

AAA SAVE

Hotel
$60-$100 All Year

Address: 2247 S Hwy 97 **Location:** Jct SR 126, 1 mi s on US 97, then just w. **Facility:** 83 one-bedroom standard units. 3 stories, interior corridors. *Bath:* combo or shower only. **Parking:** on-site. **Amenities:** *Some:* high-speed Internet. **Leisure Activities:** whirlpool. **Guest Services:** coin laundry, wireless Internet. **Business Services:** PC. **Cards:** AX, DS, MC, VI. **Free Special Amenities:** local telephone calls and high-speed Internet.

REDMOND INN   Phone: 541/548-1091

AAA SAVE

Motel
Rates not provided

Address: 1545 S US 97 **Location:** 0.5 mi s on US 97 from jct SR 126. **Facility:** 46 one-bedroom standard units, some with efficiencies and/or whirlpools. 2 stories (no elevator), exterior corridors. **Parking:** on-site. **Pool(s):** heated outdoor. **Guest Services:** airport transportation-Redmond Airport, wireless Internet. **Free Special Amenities: continental breakfast and high-speed Internet.**

REDMOND SUPER 8   *Book at AAA.com*   Phone: 541/548-8881

Hotel
Rates not provided

Address: 3629 SW 21st Pl **Location:** US 97, exit 124 (Yew Ave/Airport Way/Redmond Airport), just ne; 2 mi s of jct SR 126. **Facility:** 85 one-bedroom standard units. 3 stories, interior corridors. *Bath:* combo or shower only. **Parking:** on-site. **Amenities:** high-speed Internet, safes (fee), hair dryers. **Pool(s):** heated indoor. **Leisure Activities:** whirlpool. **Guest Services:** coin laundry, wireless Internet. **Business Services:** meeting rooms.

SLEEP INN & SUITES-REDMOND   Phone: 541/504-1500

fyi

Hotel
Rates not provided

Too new to rate, opening scheduled for October 2008. **Address:** 1847 N US 97 **Location:** 1 mi n of downtown. **Amenities:** 72 units, coffeemakers, microwaves, refrigerators, pool.

VILLAGE SQUIRE MOTEL   Phone: 541/548-2105

AAA SAVE

Motel
$69-$79 3/1-9/30
$59-$69 10/1-2/28

Address: 629 SW 5th St **Location:** US 97, exit SR 126W (Sisters Eugene City Center), just nw; jct sw Glacier Ave; downtown. **Facility:** 24 one-bedroom standard units. 2 stories (no elevator), exterior corridors. **Parking:** on-site. **Terms:** check-in 4 pm, cancellation fee imposed. **Amenities:** video library (fee). **Guest Services:** airport transportation-Redmond Airport, wireless Internet. **Cards:** AX, MC, VI.

The following lodging was either not evaluated or did not meet AAA rating requirements but is listed for your information only.

GREENWAY MOTEL   Phone: 541/548-4591

fyi

Not evaluated. **Address:** 517 W Birch Ave. Facilities, services, and decor characterize an economy property.

--- **WHERE TO DINE** ---

MUSTARD SEED CAFE   Phone: 541/923-2599

American
$8-$25

The small restaurant is in the Dawson Station area of the city, where several shops occupy some historic homes. Specialties are salads, sandwiches and burgers, but a few full-course entrees round out the menu. Although the menu centers on American cuisine, hints of Continental cuisine are evident. Casual dress. **Bar:** Beer & wine. **Reservations:** suggested. **Hours:** 8 am-2 & 5-8 pm, Sun from 9 am, Tues & Wed 8 am-2 pm. Closed: 4/12, 7/4, 12/25; also Mon. **Address:** 614 NW Cedar Ave **Location:** Just n of jct US 97 S and SR 126; between NW 6th and NW 7th sts. **Parking:** on-site and street. **Cards:** MC, VI.

NIBLICK AND GREENE'S

American
$9-$36

Phone: 541/548-4220

The golf-themed restaurant overlooks Eagle Lake. On the menu are pasta, seafood, birdies (chicken), prime rib and steak dishes. Outside seating on the patio can be requested in season. Casual dress. **Bar:** Full bar. **Reservations:** accepted. **Hours:** 5 pm-9 pm, Fri & Sat-9:30 pm. Closed: 1/1, 11/26, 12/25. **Address:** 7535 Falcon Crest Dr, #100 **Location:** 4.5 mi w on SR 126, 1 mi s; in Eagle Crest Resort. **Parking:** on-site. **Cards:** MC, VI.

RED DOG DEPOT

American
$8-$16

Phone: 541/923-6400

Serving simpler fare like burgers and sandwiches with a few heartier dishes, salads and appetizers, the restaurant is true to its name. Set in an old train depot with covered patio seating in summer, the interior walls are lined with pictures of local canines. Casual dress. **Bar:** Full bar. **Reservations:** not accepted. **Hours:** 11 am-11 pm. **Address:** 3716 SW 21st Pl **Location:** US 97, exit 124 (Yew Ave/Airport Way/Redmond Airport), just ne; 2 mi s of jct SR 126. **Parking:** on-site. **Cards:** MC, VI.

SULLY'S ITALIAN RESTAURANT

Italian
$9-$16

Phone: 541/548-5483

The nice, casual restaurant offers a good selection of pasta, chicken, seafood and steak preparations, as well as fun foods such as pizza, calzones and sandwiches. Recommended is the made-from-scratch lasagna, smothered in a tasty meat sauce and topped with Parmesan cheese. Daily specials are also worth trying. Casual dress. **Bar:** Full bar. **Reservations:** not accepted. **Hours:** 4 pm-10 pm; to 9 pm in winter. Closed: 7/4, 11/26, 12/25. **Address:** 314 SW 5th St **Location:** On US 97 N, just n of jct SR 126; downtown. **Parking:** on-site. **Cards:** DS, MC, VI.

REEDSPORT pop. 4,378

———— WHERE TO STAY ————

ANCHOR BAY INN

Motel
$50-$80 All Year

Phone: (541)271-2149

Address: 1821 Winchester Ave (US 101) **Location:** Jct SR 38, 0.8 mi s. **Facility:** 21 units. 20 one- and 1 two-bedroom standard units. 2 stories (no elevator), exterior corridors. *Bath:* combo or shower only. **Parking:** on-site. **Terms:** office hours 7:30 am-11 pm. **Amenities:** high-speed Internet. **Pool(s):** outdoor. **Guest Services:** coin laundry, wireless Internet. **Cards:** AX, CB, DC, DS, MC, VI. **Free Special Amenities:** expanded continental breakfast and high-speed Internet.

BEST WESTERN SALBASGEON INN

Book great rates at AAA.com

Motel
Rates not provided

Phone: 541/271-4831

Address: 1400 US 101 S **Location:** Jct SR 38, 0.4 mi s. **Facility:** 57 units. 56 one-bedroom standard units, some with whirlpools. 1 two-bedroom suite with kitchen and whirlpool. 2 stories (no elevator), exterior corridors. **Parking:** on-site. **Amenities:** high-speed Internet, voice mail, irons, hair dryers. **Pool(s):** heated indoor. **Leisure Activities:** whirlpool, exercise room. **Guest Services:** coin laundry, wireless Internet. **Business Services:** PC. **Free Special Amenities:** expanded continental breakfast and high-speed Internet.

AAA Benefit:
Members save up to 20%, plus 10% bonus points with rewards program.

ECONOMY INN

Book great rates at AAA.com

Motel
Rates not provided

Phone: 541/271-3671

Address: 1593 US 101 S **Location:** Jct SR 38, 0.5 mi s. **Facility:** 39 one-bedroom standard units. 2 stories (no elevator), exterior corridors. **Parking:** on-site. **Terms:** office hours 7 am-10 pm, check-in 4 pm. **Amenities:** high-speed Internet. **Pool(s):** heated outdoor. **Guest Services:** wireless Internet. **Free Special Amenities:** continental breakfast and high-speed Internet.

SALBASGEON INN OF THE UMPQUA

Motel
Rates not provided

Phone: 541/271-2025

Address: 45209 SR 38 **Location:** Jct US 101, 7.5 mi e. **Facility:** Smoke free premises. 14 units. 13 one-bedroom standard units, some with kitchens and/or whirlpools. 1 house. 2 stories (no elevator), exterior corridors. *Bath:* combo or shower only. **Parking:** on-site. **Terms:** office hours 6 am-10 pm, check-in 4 pm. **Amenities:** hair dryers. **Leisure Activities:** fishing, putting green, horseshoes. *Fee:* golf instruction. **Free Special Amenities:** continental breakfast and high-speed Internet.

ROCKAWAY BEACH pop. 1,267

———— WHERE TO STAY ————

SILVER SANDS MOTEL

Motel
Rates not provided

Phone: 503/355-2206

Address: 215 S Pacific St **Location:** Just w off US 101, on S 2nd Ave, then just w. **Facility:** 40 units. 24 one-bedroom standard units. 16 one-bedroom suites with efficiencies. 2 stories (no elevator), exterior corridors. **Parking:** on-site. **Terms:** office hours 7 am-11 pm, check-in 4 pm. **Amenities:** high-speed Internet, hair dryers. **Pool(s):** heated indoor. **Leisure Activities:** sauna, whirlpool, playground. **Guest Services:** wireless Internet.

TRADEWINDS MOTEL

Phone: 503/355-2112

🔺🔺 SAVE
▼▼ ▼▼
Motel
$85-$169 3/1-9/25
$58-$97 9/26-2/28

Address: 523 N Pacific St **Location:** Oceanfront. Just w off US 101, on NW 6th Ave, then just s. **Facility:** 19 one-bedroom standard units, some with efficiencies and/or whirlpools. 2 stories (no elevator), exterior corridors. **Parking:** on-site. **Terms:** office hours 8 am-11 pm, 2 night minimum stay - seasonal and/or weekends, 7 day cancellation notice-fee imposed. **Amenities:** high-speed Internet, hair dryers. **Leisure Activities:** beachfront picnic tables & barbecue grills. **Guest Services:** wireless Internet. **Cards:** AX, CB, DC, DS, MC, VI.

🅰️ VCR 📷 🛜 🖥️ 💻 / SOME UNITS FEE 🐾 ✖️

ROSEBURG pop. 20,017

———— WHERE TO STAY ————

BEST WESTERN GARDEN VILLA INN
Book great rates at AAA.com

Phone: (541)672-1601

🔺🔺 SAVE
▼▼ ▼▼
Motel
$89-$139 All Year

Address: 760 NW Garden Valley Blvd **Location:** I-5, exit 125, just nw. Located in the Garden Valley Shopping Center. **Facility:** Smoke free premises. 66 one-bedroom standard units. 2 stories (no elevator), exterior corridors. **Parking:** on-site. **Amenities:** high-speed Internet, irons, hair dryers. **Pool(s):** heated outdoor. **Leisure Activities:** whirlpool. **Guest Services:** valet and coin laundry, wireless Internet. **Business Services:** PC. **Cards:** AX, CB, DC, DS, JC, MC, VI. **Free Special Amenities: full breakfast and high-speed Internet.**

Best Western

AAA Benefit:

Members save up to 20%, plus 10% bonus points with rewards program.

🏊 ✖️ 📷 🛜 🖥️ 💻 / SOME UNITS FEE 🐾

COMFORT INN
Book great rates at AAA.com

Phone: (541)957-1100

🔺🔺 SAVE
▼▼ ▼▼
Hotel
$69-$169 All Year

Address: 1539 Mulholland Dr **Location:** I-5, exit 125, just ne. **Facility:** Smoke free premises. 50 units. 47 one- and 1 two-bedroom standard units. 2 one-bedroom suites, some with whirlpools. 2 stories (no elevator), interior corridors. *Bath:* combo or shower only. **Parking:** on-site. **Terms:** check-in 4 pm, cancellation fee imposed. **Amenities:** high-speed Internet, irons, hair dryers. *Some:* DVD players (fee). **Pool(s):** heated indoor. **Leisure Activities:** whirlpool, exercise room. **Guest Services:** coin laundry, airport transportation-Roseburg Airport, wireless Internet. **Business Services:** meeting rooms, PC. **Cards:** AX, DC, DS, MC, VI. **Free Special Amenities: expanded continental breakfast and high-speed Internet.**

🛬 🍴 CALL 📶M 🏊 ✖️ 📷 💻 / SOME UNITS FEE VCR 🛜 🖥️

HOLIDAY INN EXPRESS
Book great rates at AAA.com

Phone: 541/673-7517

🔺🔺 SAVE
▼▼▼▼▼▼
Hotel
Rates not provided

Address: 375 W Harvard Ave **Location:** I-5, exit 124, just se. **Facility:** 100 one-bedroom standard units, some with whirlpools. 4 stories, interior/exterior corridors. *Bath:* combo or shower only. **Parking:** on-site. **Amenities:** high-speed Internet, voice mail, irons, hair dryers. **Pool(s):** heated indoor. **Leisure Activities:** whirlpool, barbecue grill, exercise room. **Guest Services:** valet and coin laundry, wireless Internet. **Business Services:** meeting rooms, business center. **Free Special Amenities: expanded continental breakfast and high-speed Internet.**

CALL 📶M 🏊 ✖️ 📷 🛜 🖥️ 💻 / SOME UNITS FEE 🐾 ✖️

HOWARD JOHNSON EXPRESS INN
Book great rates at AAA.com

Phone: (541)673-5082

🔺🔺 SAVE
▼▼
Motel
$68-$95 3/1-9/30
$63-$89 10/1-2/28

Address: 978 NE Stephens St **Location:** I-5, exit 125, 0.6 mi e on Garden Valley Blvd, then 0.4 mi s. **Facility:** 31 one-bedroom standard units, some with efficiencies and/or whirlpools. 2 stories (no elevator), exterior corridors. **Parking:** on-site. **Amenities:** high-speed Internet, voice mail, safes (fee), irons, hair dryers. **Guest Services:** coin laundry, airport transportation-Roseburg Airport, wireless Internet. **Cards:** AX, CB, DC, DS, MC, VI. **Free Special Amenities: continental breakfast and high-speed Internet.**

🛬 🍴 📶 📷 💻 / SOME UNITS ✖️ 🛜 🖥️

MOTEL 6 #4108
Book great rates at AAA.com

Phone: (541)464-8000

🔺🔺 SAVE
▼▼ ▼▼
Hotel
$40-$72 All Year

Address: 3100 NW Aviation Dr **Location:** I-5, exit 127, just se. **Facility:** 81 one-bedroom standard units. 3 stories, interior corridors. *Bath:* combo or shower only. **Parking:** on-site. **Amenities:** high-speed Internet. *Some:* irons, hair dryers. **Guest Services:** coin laundry, wireless Internet. **Business Services:** PC. **Cards:** AX, DS, MC, VI. **Free Special Amenities: newspaper and high-speed Internet.**

🍴 CALL 📶M 📷 / SOME UNITS 🐾 ✖️ 🛜 🖥️

QUALITY INN *Book great rates at AAA.com* Phone: (541)673-5561

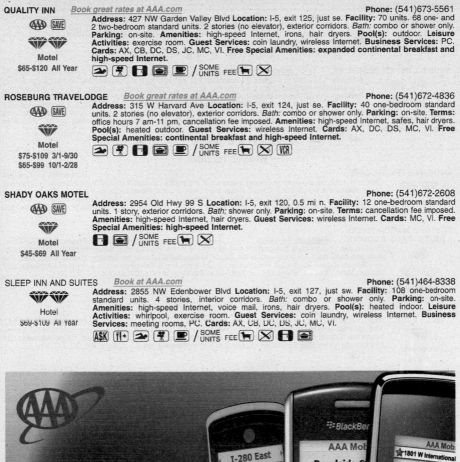

AAA SAVE

◆◆◆ ◆◆◆

Motel

$65-$120 All Year

Address: 427 NW Garden Valley Blvd **Location:** I-5, exit 125, just se. **Facility:** 70 units. 68 one- and 2 two-bedroom standard units. 2 stories (no elevator), exterior corridors. *Bath:* combo or shower only. **Parking:** on-site. **Amenities:** high-speed Internet, irons, hair dryers. **Pool(s):** outdoor. **Leisure Activities:** exercise room. **Guest Services:** coin laundry, wireless Internet. **Business Services:** PC. **Cards:** AX, CB, DC, DS, JC, MC, VI. **Free Special Amenities: expanded continental breakfast and high-speed Internet.**

ROSEBURG TRAVELODGE *Book great rates at AAA.com* Phone: (541)672-4836

AAA SAVE

◆◆◆

Motel

$75-$109 3/1-9/30
$65-$99 10/1-2/28

Address: 315 W Harvard Ave **Location:** I-5, exit 124, just se. **Facility:** 40 one-bedroom standard units. 2 stories (no elevator), exterior corridors. *Bath:* combo or shower only. **Parking:** on-site. **Terms:** office hours 7 am-11 pm, cancellation fee imposed. **Amenities:** high-speed Internet, safes, hair dryers. **Pool(s):** heated outdoor. **Guest Services:** wireless Internet. **Cards:** AX, DC, DS, MC, VI. **Free Special Amenities: continental breakfast and high-speed Internet.**

SHADY OAKS MOTEL Phone: (541)672-2608

AAA SAVE

◆◆◆

Motel

$45-$69 All Year

Address: 2954 Old Hwy 99 S **Location:** I-5, exit 120, 0.5 mi n. **Facility:** 12 one-bedroom standard units. 1 story, exterior corridors. *Bath:* shower only. **Parking:** on-site. **Terms:** cancellation fee imposed. **Amenities:** high-speed Internet, hair dryers. **Guest Services:** wireless Internet. **Cards:** MC, VI. **Free Special Amenities: high-speed Internet.**

SLEEP INN AND SUITES *Book at AAA.com* Phone: (541)464-8338

◆◆◆ ◆◆◆

Hotel

$69-$109 All Year

Address: 2855 NW Edenbower Blvd **Location:** I-5, exit 127, just sw. **Facility:** 108 one-bedroom standard units. 4 stories, interior corridors. *Bath:* combo or shower only. **Parking:** on-site. **Amenities:** high-speed Internet, voice mail, irons, hair dryers. **Pool(s):** heated indoor. **Leisure Activities:** whirlpool, exercise room. **Guest Services:** coin laundry, wireless Internet. **Business Services:** meeting rooms, PC. **Cards:** AX, CB, DC, DS, JC, MC, VI.

SUPER 8   *Book at AAA.com*   Phone: 541-672-8880

Hotel
Rates not provided

Address: 3200 NW Aviation Dr **Location:** I-5, exit 127, just ne. **Facility:** 88 one-bedroom standard units. 3 stories, interior corridors. *Bath:* combo or shower only. **Parking:** on-site. **Amenities:** high-speed Internet, safes (fee), hair dryers. **Pool(s):** heated indoor. **Leisure Activities:** whirlpool. **Guest Services:** coin laundry, wireless Internet. **Business Services:** meeting rooms.

CALL 🚭🖩 🏊 🎥 / SOME UNITS FEE 🐾 ✕ 🖥

WINDMILL INN OF ROSEBURG   *Book great rates at AAA.com*   Phone: 541-673-0901

🔺🔺🔺 SAVE

Hotel
Rates not provided

Address: 1450 NW Mulholland Dr **Location:** I-5, exit 125, just ne. **Facility:** Smoke free premises. 128 one-bedroom standard units. 2 stories (no elevator), interior corridors. *Bath:* combo or shower only. **Parking:** on-site. **Terms:** check-in 4 pm. **Amenities:** high-speed Internet, voice mail, irons, hair dryers. *Some:* DVD players. **Pool(s):** heated outdoor. **Leisure Activities:** sauna, whirlpool, bicycles, exercise room. **Guest Services:** valet and coin laundry, airport transportation-Roseburg Airport, area transportation-shopping, wireless Internet. **Business Services:** meeting rooms, PC. **Free Special Amenities:** newspaper and high-speed Internet.

🛬 🍴 🏊 ✕ ✕ 🎥 🖥 🖥 🖥 / SOME UNITS 🐾

——— **WHERE TO DINE** ———

ANTHONY'S ITALIAN CAFE   Phone: 541-229-2233

Italian
$6-$17

This cafe whips up a variety of entrees prepared in the traditional Italian style, in addition to good pizza and Italian submarine sandwiches. Casual dress. **Bar:** Beer & wine. **Reservations:** accepted. **Hours:** 11 am-9 pm, Sat from 12:30 pm. Closed: Sun & Mon. **Address:** 500 SE Cass Ave, Suite 120 **Location:** I-5, exit 124, 0.5 mi e on SE Oak Ave, just s on SE Pine St, then just w; in Village Station. **Parking:** on-site. **Cards:** AX, DS, MC, VI.

**BRUTKE'S WAGON WHEEL
RESTAURANT & LOUNGE**   *Menu on AAA.com*   Phone: 541-672-7555

🔺🔺🔺

🔺🔺🔺
American
$5-$35

Dependable country-style preparations—most notably prime rib and ribs, which come in barbecue beef, pork and baby back varieties—make the casual restaurant a favorite for families. Casual dress. **Bar:** Full bar. **Reservations:** suggested. **Hours:** 9 am-2 & 4-9 pm, Fri & Sat-10 pm, Sun 7 am-8 pm. **Address:** 227 Garden Valley Blvd **Location:** I-5, exit 125, just e. **Parking:** on-site. **Cards:** AX, DS, MC, VI.

🚫

CASEY'S FAMILY RESTAURANT   Phone: 541-672-1512

🔺🔺🔺
American
$6-$16

This recently remodeled long-loved local favorite serves homemade fare, including hard-to-resist freshly baked pie. Casual dress. **Reservations:** not accepted. **Hours:** 6 am-10 pm. Closed: 12/25. **Address:** 326 NW Garden Valley Blvd **Location:** I-5, exit 125, just e. **Parking:** on-site. **Cards:** AX, DS, MC, VI.

CALL 🚭🖩

D'S MAGNOLIA RESTAURANT & LOUNGE   Phone: 541-672-1235

🔺🔺🔺
Continental
$7-$21

Menu items include pasta, beef, chicken and vegetarian entrees, which pair with the good selection of wines. Heavenly homemade desserts feature chocolate, fresh berries and other favorite ingredients. Casual dress. **Bar:** Full bar. **Reservations:** suggested. **Hours:** 11 am-2 & 5-8 pm, Fri-9 pm, Sat 5 pm-9 pm. Closed: 1/1, 12/25; also Sun. **Address:** 647 SE Jackson St **Location:** Downtown. **Parking:** street. **Cards:** AX, MC, VI.

MCMENAMINS   Phone: 541-672-1934

🔺🔺🔺
American
$5-$20

The casual neighborhood eatery is where friends gather for classic pub and comfort fare, all washed down by pints of locally made beer. Large wooden booths or tables easily accommodate larger groups, and the eclectic, custom-painted walls and varied period light fixtures keep diners' eyes busy should the conversation lag. Casual dress. **Bar:** Full bar. **Hours:** 11 am-11 pm, Fri & Sat-midnight, Sun-10 pm. Closed: 11/26, 12/25. **Address:** 700 SE Sheridan St **Location:** I-5, exit 124, 0.5 mi e, then just s; in Village Station. **Parking:** on-site. **Cards:** MC, VI.

ST. HELENS pop. 10,019

——— **WHERE TO STAY** ———

BEST WESTERN OAK MEADOWS INN   *Book great rates at AAA.com*   Phone: (503)397-3000

🔺🔺🔺 SAVE

🔺🔺🔺
Hotel
$99-$169 3/1-9/30
$89-$149 10/1-2/28

Address: 585 S Columbia River Hwy **Location:** South end of town on US 30. **Facility:** Smoke free premises. 81 one-bedroom standard units. 2 stories (no elevator), interior corridors. *Bath:* combo or shower only. **Parking:** on-site. **Terms:** 3 day cancellation notice. **Amenities:** high-speed Internet, voice mail, irons, hair dryers. **Pool(s):** heated indoor. **Leisure Activities:** whirlpool. **Guest Services:** valet and coin laundry, wireless Internet. **Business Services:** meeting rooms. **Cards:** AX, CB, DC, DS, JC, MC, VI.

🏊 ✕ 🎥 🖥 🖥 🖥 / SOME UNITS FEE 🐾

Best Western

AAA Benefit:
Members save up to 20%, plus 10% bonus points with rewards program.

——— **WHERE TO DINE** ———

BURGERVILLE   Phone: 503/397-5885

🔺
American
$2-$8

First-timers shouldn't let the fast food exterior fool them, as the burgers and chicken here adhere to a higher standard. Northwest ingredients come into play in the sandwiches. Casual dress. **Hours:** 7 am-10 pm. Closed: 11/26, 12/25. **Address:** 715 S Columbia River Hwy **Location:** Jct US 30 and Sykes Rd. **Parking:** on-site. **Cards:** DS, MC, VI.

DOCKSIDE STEAK & PASTA   Phone: 503/366-0877

Italian
$10-$25

Booth seating offers a glimpse over the log yard to the gently flowing Columbia River. During the summer, sidewalk tables line the peaceful street and the rooftop deck affords panoramic views. Guests who have trouble narrowing their choices should consider the Tour of Italy combination, which includes three small entrees. Also on the menu are several steak selections with a choice of specialty sauces, fresh seafood, classic sandwiches, chicken and gourmet burgers. Casual dress. **Bar:** Full bar. **Reservations:** accepted. **Hours:** 11 am-9 pm, Fri & Sat-10 pm, Sun 4 pm-9 pm. Closed major holidays. **Address:** 343 S 1st St **Location:** South end of 1st St; downtown. **Parking:** on-site. **Cards:** MC, VI.

SALEM pop. 136,924

——— WHERE TO STAY ———

BEST WESTERN BLACK BEAR INN   *Book great rates at AAA.com*   Phone: (503)581-1559

Motel
$110-$130 3/1-9/15
$90-$100 9/16-2/28

Address: 1600 Motor Ct NE **Location:** I-5, exit 256, just e, then just s. **Facility:** 101 one-bedroom standard units, some with whirlpools. 2 stories (no elevator), exterior corridors. *Bath:* combo or shower only. **Parking:** on-site. **Terms:** 7 day cancellation notice-fee imposed. **Amenities:** high-speed Internet, voice mail, irons, hair dryers. **Pool(s):** heated indoor. **Leisure Activities:** saunas, whirlpool, 2 tennis courts, mobile basketball, playground, exercise room. **Guest Services:** valet and coin laundry, airport transportation-Salem Airport, area transportation-train & bus stations, wireless Internet. **Business Services:** meeting rooms, PC. **Cards:** AX, DS, MC, VI. **Free Special Amenities: full breakfast.**

AAA Benefit:
Members save up to 20%, plus 10% bonus points with rewards program.

BEST WESTERN MILL CREEK INN   *Book great rates at AAA.com*   Phone: (503)585-3332

Hotel
$112-$168 All Year

Address: 3125 Ryan Dr SE **Location:** I-5, exit 253, just w on Mission St (SR 22), just n on Hawthorn Ave, then just w. **Facility:** Smoke free premises. 109 units. 104 one-bedroom standard units. 5 one-bedroom suites, some with kitchens. 0 stories, interior corridors. *Bath:* combo or shower only. **Parking:** on-site. **Amenities:** high-speed Internet, voice mail, irons, hair dryers. *Some:* DVD players (fee). **Pool(s):** heated indoor. **Leisure Activities:** saunas, whirlpool, exercise room. **Guest Services:** valet and coin laundry, airport transportation-Salem Airport, area transportation-bus & train stations, wireless Internet. **Business Services:** meeting rooms, business center. **Cards:** AX, DC, DS, MC, VI. **Free Special Amenities: full breakfast and high-speed Internet.**

AAA Benefit:
Members save up to 20%, plus 10% bonus points with rewards program.

BEST WESTERN PACIFIC HWY INN   *Book great rates at AAA.com*   Phone: 503/390-3200

Motel
Rates not provided

Address: 4646 Portland Rd NE **Location:** I-5, exit 258, 0.3 mi e. **Facility:** 52 one-bedroom standard units. 2 stories (no elevator), exterior corridors. *Bath:* combo or shower only. **Parking:** on-site. **Amenities:** high-speed Internet, irons, hair dryers. **Pool(s):** heated indoor. **Leisure Activities:** whirlpool, exercise room. **Guest Services:** valet and coin laundry, airport transportation-Salem Airport, area transportation-bus & train stations, wireless Internet. **Business Services:** meeting rooms. **Free Special Amenities: expanded continental breakfast and high-speed Internet.**

AAA Benefit:
Members save up to 20%, plus 10% bonus points with rewards program.

COMFORT INN & SUITES   *Book great rates at AAA.com*   Phone: (503)588-0515

Hotel
$77-$235 All Year

Address: 1775 Freeway Ct NE **Location:** I-5, exit 256, just nw. **Facility:** Smoke free premises. 64 units. 60 one- and 3 two-bedroom standard units, some with whirlpools. 1 one-bedroom suite with kitchen. 4 stories, interior corridors. *Bath:* combo or shower only. **Parking:** on-site. **Terms:** cancellation fee imposed. **Amenities:** high-speed Internet, safes (fee), irons, hair dryers. **Pool(s):** heated indoor. **Leisure Activities:** whirlpool. **Guest Services:** valet and coin laundry, wireless Internet. **Business Services:** meeting rooms, PC. **Cards:** AX, DC, DS, JC, MC, VI. **Free Special Amenities: expanded continental breakfast and high-speed Internet.**

CROSSLAND STUDIOS SALEM NORTH   *Book at AAA.com*   Phone: (503)363-7557

Motel
$69-$84 All Year

Address: 3535 Fisher Rd NE **Location:** I-5, exit 258, just e on Portland Rd NE, 0.4 mi s on Ward Dr, then 0.8 mi s. **Facility:** 129 one-bedroom standard units with efficiencies. 3 stories, exterior corridors. *Bath:* combo or shower only. **Parking:** on-site. **Terms:** office hours 7 am-11 pm, cancellation fee imposed. **Amenities:** high-speed Internet (fee), voice mail. **Guest Services:** coin laundry, wireless Internet. **Cards:** AX, CB, DC, DS, JC, MC, VI.

HOLIDAY INN EXPRESS *Book great rates at AAA.com* Phone: (503)391-7000

Hotel
$109-$149 3/1-9/30
$89-$129 10/1-2/28

Address: 890 Hawthorne Ave SE **Location:** I-5, exit 253, just w on Mission St (SR 22), then just n. **Facility:** Smoke free premises. 113 one-bedroom standard units, some with whirlpools. 4 stories, interior corridors. *Bath:* combo or shower only. **Parking:** on-site. **Amenities:** high-speed Internet, dual phone lines, voice mail, irons, hair dryers. **Pool(s):** heated indoor. **Leisure Activities:** exercise room. **Guest Services:** valet and coin laundry, wireless Internet. **Business Services:** meeting rooms, PC. **Cards:** AX, CB, DC, DS, MC, VI. **Free Special Amenities:** expanded continental breakfast and high-speed Internet. *(See color ad below)*

HOWARD JOHNSON INN *Book great rates at AAA.com* Phone: (503)375-7710

Hotel
$70-$110 All Year

Address: 2250 Mission St SE **Location:** I-5, exit 253, 1.4 mi w. **Facility:** Smoke free premises. 68 one-bedroom standard units. 2 stories (no elevator), interior corridors. *Bath:* combo or shower only. **Parking:** on-site. **Terms:** cancellation fee imposed. **Amenities:** high-speed Internet, voice mail, safes (fee), irons, hair dryers. *Some: Fee:* DVD players. **Pool(s):** heated outdoor. **Leisure Activities:** exercise room. **Guest Services:** coin laundry, wireless Internet. **Cards:** AX, DC, DS, MC, VI. **Free Special Amenities:** continental breakfast and high-speed Internet.

PHOENIX GRAND HOTEL   *Book great rates at AAA.com*   **Phone:** (503)540-7800

Hotel
$159-$449 All Year

Address: 201 Liberty St SE **Location:** I-5, exit 253, 3.1 mi w on Mission St (SR 22), follow signs to City Center, then 0.4 mi n; at Ferry and Liberty sts; downtown. **Facility:** 193 units. 146 one-bedroom standard units, some with whirlpools. 47 one-bedroom suites, some with whirlpools. 5 stories, interior corridors. *Bath:* combo or shower only. **Parking:** on-site. **Terms:** cancellation fee imposed. **Amenities:** video games (fee), high-speed Internet, voice mail, irons, hair dryers. *Some:* DVD players. **Dining:** Bentley's Grill, see separate listing. **Pool(s):** heated indoor. **Leisure Activities:** whirlpool, exercise room. **Guest Services:** valet and coin laundry, airport transportation-Salem Airport, wireless Internet. **Business Services:** conference facilities, business center. **Cards:** AX, DC, DS, MC, VI. **Free Special Amenities:** expanded continental breakfast and high-speed Internet.
(See color ad below)

PHOENIX INN SUITES-NORTH SALEM   *Book great rates at AAA.com*   **Phone:** (503)581-7004

Hotel
$79-$139 All Year

Address: 1590 Weston Ct NE **Location:** I-5, exit 256, just w, then just s. **Facility:** 80 units. 76 one- and 4 two-bedroom standard units, some with whirlpools. 4 stories, interior corridors. *Bath:* combo or shower only. **Parking:** on-site. **Terms:** check-in 4 pm, cancellation fee imposed. **Amenities:** high-speed Internet, dual phone lines, voice mail, irons, hair dryers. *Some:* DVD players (fee). **Pool(s):** heated indoor. **Leisure Activities:** whirlpool, exercise room. **Guest Services:** valet and coin laundry, wireless Internet. **Business Services:** meeting rooms, PC. **Cards:** AX, DS, MC, VI. **Free Special Amenities:** expanded continental breakfast and high-speed Internet.
(See color ad p 440 & below)

PHOENIX INN SUITES-SOUTH SALEM *Book great rates at AAA.com* **Phone:** (503)588-9220

Hotel
$79-$139 All Year

Address: 4370 Commercial SE **Location:** I-5, exit 252, 1.5 mi w on Kuebler Rd, then 0.7 mi n. **Facility:** 89 units. 86 one- and 3 two-bedroom standard units, some with whirlpools. 4 stories, interior corridors. **Parking:** on-site. **Terms:** check-in 4 pm, cancellation fee imposed. **Amenities:** high-speed Internet, dual phone lines, voice mail, irons, hair dryers. *Some:* DVD players. **Pool(s):** heated indoor. **Leisure Activities:** whirlpool, exercise room. **Guest Services:** valet and coin laundry, wireless Internet. **Business Services:** meeting rooms, PC. **Cards:** AX, DC, DS, MC, VI. **Free Special Amenities: expanded continental breakfast and high-speed Internet.** *(See color ad p 440 & p 493)*

CALL / SOME UNITS FEE

RED LION HOTEL SALEM *Book great rates at AAA.com* **Phone:** (503)370-7888

Hotel
$124-$169 All Year

Address: 3301 Market St NE **Location:** I-5, exit 256, just w. **Facility:** Smoke free premises. 148 units. 146 one-bedroom standard units. 2 one-bedroom suites with whirlpools. 4 stories, interior corridors. *Bath:* combo or shower only. **Parking:** on-site. **Amenities:** high-speed Internet, voice mail, irons, hair dryers. *Some:* DVD players (fee). **Pool(s):** heated indoor. **Leisure Activities:** sauna, exercise room. **Guest Services:** valet and coin laundry, airport transportation (fee)-Portland International Airport, area transportation-within 6 mi, wireless Internet. **Business Services:** conference facilities, PC. **Cards:** AX, CB, DC, DS, JC, MC, VI. **Free Special Amenities: newspaper and high-speed Internet.** *(See color ad below)*

FEE CALL / SOME UNITS FEE

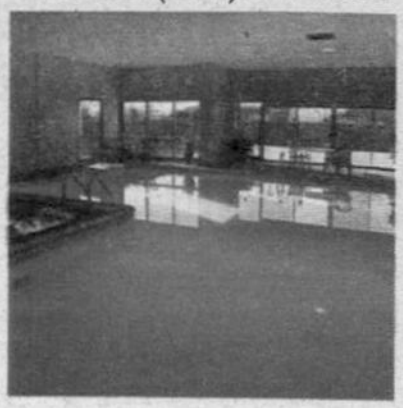

RESIDENCE INN BY MARRIOTT *Book great rates at AAA.com* **Phone:** (503)585-6500

Hotel
$170-$180 All Year

Address: 640 Hawthorne Ave SE **Location:** I-5, exit 253, just w, then n. **Facility:** Smoke free premises. 90 units. 49 one-bedroom standard units with kitchens. 24 one- and 17 two-bedroom suites with kitchens. 3 stories, interior corridors. *Bath:* combo or shower only. **Parking:** on-site. **Terms:** cancellation fee imposed. **Amenities:** dual phone lines, voice mail, irons, hair dryers. *Some:* DVD players, high-speed Internet. **Pool(s):** heated indoor. **Leisure Activities:** whirlpool, exercise room, sports court. **Guest Services:** valet and coin laundry, wireless Internet. **Business Services:** meeting rooms, PC. **Cards:** AX, DS, MC, VI.

CALL / SOME UNITS FEE

AAA Benefit:
Members save a minimum 5% off the best available rate.

SALEM COMFORT SUITES *Book at AAA.com* **Phone:** (503)585-9705

Hotel
$129-$220 All Year

Address: 630 Hawthorne Ave SE **Location:** I-5, exit 253, just w, then 0.4 mi n. **Facility:** Smoke free premises. 85 units. 80 one-bedroom standard units. 5 one-bedroom suites with whirlpools. 3 stories, interior corridors. *Bath:* combo or shower only. **Parking:** on-site. **Terms:** cancellation fee imposed. **Amenities:** high-speed Internet, dual phone lines, voice mail, irons, hair dryers. *Fee:* video library, safes. **Pool(s):** heated indoor. **Leisure Activities:** sauna, whirlpool, exercise room. **Guest Services:** valet and coin laundry, area transportation, wireless Internet. **Business Services:** meeting rooms, PC. **Cards:** AX, DC, DS, MC, VI.

CALL / SOME UNITS

▼ *See AAA listing above* ▼

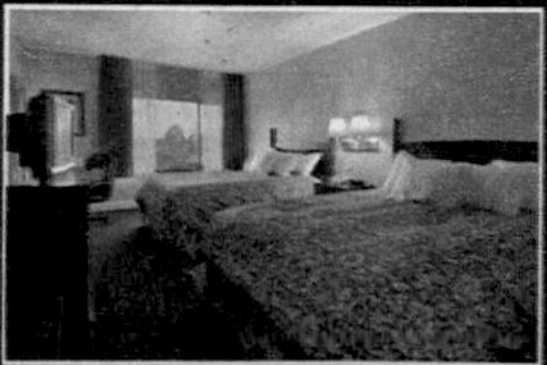

SHILO INN SUITES-SALEM   *Book great rates at AAA.com*   **Phone:** (503)581-4001

AAA SAVE
▼▼◆▼▼
Hotel
$90-$180 All Year

Address: 3304 Market St NE **Location:** I-5, exit 256, just w. **Facility:** 89 one-bedroom standard units. 4 stories, interior corridors. **Parking:** on-site. **Amenities:** video games (fee), high-speed Internet, voice mail, irons, hair dryers. **Pool(s):** heated indoor. **Leisure Activities:** sauna, whirlpool, steamroom, exercise room. **Guest Services:** valet and coin laundry, airport transportation-Salem Airport, area transportation-bus & train stations, wireless Internet. **Business Services:** meeting rooms, PC. **Cards:** AX, DC, DS, JC, MC, VI. **Free Special Amenities: continental breakfast and high-speed Internet.** *(See color ad below)*

SUPER 8 SALEM   *Book at AAA.com*   **Phone:** (503)370-8888

▼▼◆ ▼▼◆
Hotel
$70-$90 All Year

Address: 1288 Hawthorne Ave NE **Location:** I-5, exit 256, just w, then just s. **Facility:** 80 units. 79 one-bedroom standard units. 1 one-bedroom suite with kitchen. 3 stories, interior corridors. **Parking:** on-site. **Amenities:** high-speed Internet, safes (fee), hair dryers. **Pool(s):** heated indoor. **Leisure Activities:** whirlpool. **Guest Services:** coin laundry, wireless Internet. **Business Services:** meeting rooms. **Cards:** AX, DS, MC, VI.

TRAVELODGE SALEM CAPITAL   *Book great rates at AAA.com*   **Phone:** (503)581-2466

AAA SAVE
▼◆▼
Motel
$57-$73 All Year

Address: 1555 State St **Location:** I-5, exit 256, just w on SR 22/99 (Mission St), 0.6 mi n on Airport Rd SE, then 1 mi w. **Facility:** 42 one-bedroom standard units. 2 stories (no elevator), exterior corridors. *Bath:* combo or shower only. **Parking:** on-site. **Terms:** office hours 7 am-11 pm. **Amenities:** high-speed Internet, hair dryers. **Pool(s):** heated outdoor. **Guest Services:** wireless Internet. **Cards:** AX, DS, MC, VI. **Free Special Amenities: continental breakfast and high-speed Internet.**

▼ *See AAA listing above* ▼

——— WHERE TO DINE ———

ALESSANDRO'S RISTORANTE & GALLERIA   *Menu on AAA.com*
             Phone: 503/370-9951

In an 1870s building that originally was a livery stable, this downtown restaurant prepares fresh pasta entrees, as well as seafood, poultry and veal dishes. The chef's table multi-course dinner is $42.50 without wine pairings and $53.50 with them. Casual dress. **Bar:** Full bar. **Reservations:** suggested. **Hours:** 11 am-2 & 5-9 pm, Fri & Sat 5:30 pm-10 pm. Closed major holidays; also Sun. **Address:** 120 Commercial St NE **Location:** Corner of State St; center. **Parking:** on-site. **Cards:** AX, DS, MC, VI.

Italian
$8-$32

BENTLEY'S GRILL
             Phone: 503/779-1660

In historic downtown, this spacious restaurant, which has a large copper vented fire bowl, offers well-prepared steaks, seafood, a few rotisserie items, pizzas and sandwiches. The signature prime rib is slow-roasted in a hardwood smoker. Delicious cakes come from the local Konditorei Bakery. Casual dress. **Bar:** Full bar. **Reservations:** suggested. **Hours:** 11 am-10 pm, Fri & Sat-midnight, Sun 4 pm-10 pm. Closed: 7/4, 12/25. **Address:** 291 Liberty St SE **Location:** I-5, exit 253, 3.1 mi w on Mission St (SR 22), follow signs to City Center, then 0.4 mi n; at Ferry and Liberty sts; downtown; in Phoenix Grand Hotel. **Parking:** on-site. **Cards:** AX, DC, DS, MC, VI. *(See color ad p 493)*

American
$8-$30

CALL

DAVINCI ITALIAN RISTORANTE WINE BAR
             Phone: 503/399-1413

The popular eatery envelops diners in a romantic setting accented by faux marble walls, exposed brick, Tiffany-style lamps and lush tropical plants. Northern Italian dishes are cooked to order, and pasta specials are made fresh daily. Specialties include fettuccine al Guglielmo—a delicious combination of scallops, prawns and tomatoes served with fresh pasta and a cream sauce—and ravioli con salmon affumicato, a heavenly blend of smoked salmon and cheese. The wine selection is good. Dressy casual. **Bar:** Full bar. **Reservations:** not accepted. **Hours:** 4:30 pm-9 pm, Fri & Sat-10 pm, Sun 5 pm-8 pm. Closed: 5/25, 11/26, 12/25. **Address:** 180 High St SE **Location:** Jct Ferry St SW; downtown. **Parking:** on-site. **Cards:** AX, DS, MC, VI.

Traditional Italian
$16-$28

GERRY FRANK'S KONDITOREI
             Phone: 503/585-7070

For more than 25 years, this cheery Viennese-style bakery and cafe has served delightful sandwiches, salads and a daily quiche. Recommended is the Konditorei special, which includes a half-sandwich, cup of soup and dessert. The extravagant cakes on display are the real draw here and shouldn't be missed. Lines can form early. Casual dress. **Bar:** Wine only. **Reservations:** not accepted. **Hours:** 7:30 am-10 pm, Fri & Sat-11 pm, Sun 11 am-9 pm. Closed major holidays. **Address:** 310 Kearny St SE **Location:** I-5, exit 253, 2.8 mi w on Mission St (SR 22), then just s on Commercial St SE. **Parking:** on-site. **Cards:** DS, MC, VI.

Breads/Pastries
$3-$13

JONATHAN'S OYSTER BAR & LONG BAR CAFE
             Phone: 503/362-7219

The friendly, casual restaurant dabbles in a variety of food styles, including Cajun and Mexican. However, fresh seafood and steaks are the main focus. Parking in the adjacent lot is complimentary after 5 pm. Casual dress. **Bar:** Full bar. **Reservations:** suggested, for dinner Fri & Sat. **Hours:** 11:30 am-9 pm, Fri-9:30 pm, Sat 5 pm-9:30 pm. Closed major holidays; also Sun. **Address:** 445 State St **Location:** On north side of State St; between Liberty and High sts; center. **Parking:** on-site. **Cards:** AX, CB, DC, DS, MC, VI.

American
$9-$29

CALL

MCGRATH'S FISH HOUSE
             Phone: 503/485-3086

The popular chain specializes in fresh Pacific Northwest seafood, including dishes grilled over a wood fire and items from the daily fresh sheet. Also on the menu are steaks, chicken, pasta and gourmet burgers. Casual dress. **Bar:** Full bar. **Hours:** 11 am-10 pm. Closed: 11/26, 12/25. **Address:** 3805 Center St NE **Location:** I-5, exit 256, just e on Market St, then just s on Lancaster Dr NE; near Lancaster Mall. **Parking:** on-site. **Cards:** AX, DC, DS, MC, VI.

Steak & Seafood
$9-$19

MCGRATH'S FISH HOUSE   *Menu on AAA.com*
             Phone: 503/362-0736

The popular chain specializes in fresh Pacific Northwest seafood, including dishes grilled over a wood fire and items from the daily fresh sheet. Also on the menu are steaks, chicken, pasta and gourmet burgers. Casual dress. **Bar:** Full bar. **Hours:** 11 am-10 pm. Closed: 11/26, 12/25. **Address:** 350 Chemeketa St NE **Location:** Between Commercial and Liberty sts; center. **Parking:** street. **Cards:** AX, DC, DS, MC, VI.

Steak & Seafood
$9-$19

MCMENAMINS
             Phone: 503/399-9062

The casual neighborhood eatery is where friends gather for classic pub and comfort fare, all washed down by pints of locally made beer. Large wooden booths or tables easily accommodate larger groups, and the eclectic, custom-painted walls and varied period light fixtures keep diners' eyes busy should the conversation lag. Casual dress. **Hours:** 11 am-midnight, Fri & Sat-1 am, Sun noon-11 pm. Closed: 12/25. **Address:** 888 Liberty St NE **Location:** 0.6 mi ne. **Parking:** on-site. **Cards:** MC, VI.

American
$5-$20

MCMENAMINS
             Phone: 503/363-7286

The casual neighborhood eatery is where friends gather for classic pub and comfort fare, all washed down by pints of locally made beer. Large wooden booths or tables easily accommodate larger groups, and the eclectic, custom-painted walls and varied period light fixtures keep diners' eyes busy should the conversation lag. Casual dress. **Bar:** Full bar. **Reservations:** not accepted. **Hours:** 11 am-10 pm, Tues-Thurs to midnight, Fri & Sat-1 am, Sun noon-10 pm. Closed: 11/26, 12/24, 12/25. **Address:** 3575 Liberty Rd S **Location:** I-5, exit 252, 1.5 mi w on Kuebler Blvd SE, 1.7 mi n on Commercial St SE, 0.4 mi w on Madrona Ave SE, then just s. **Parking:** on-site. **Cards:** MC, VI.

American
$5-$20

NEWPORT BAY RESTAURANT

Phone: 503/315-7100

Steak & Seafood
$8-$25

This restaurant is for those seeking a casual, relaxing time. A menu favorite is New England clam chowder, which is available nightly. Fresh Northwest salmon and Alaskan halibut prepared several ways share menu space with pasta, chicken and salads. Casual dress. **Bar:** Full bar. **Reservations:** accepted. **Hours:** 11 am-10 pm, Fri & Sat-11 pm, Sun 9 am-10 pm. Closed: 11/26, 12/25. **Address:** 1717 Freeway Ct NE **Location:** I-5, exit 256; northwest corner. **Parking:** on-site. **Cards:** AX, DS, MC, VI.

CALL

RAM RESTAURANT AND BREWERY

Phone: 503/363-1904

American
$8-$22

The enormous restaurant features high ceilings, huge television screens, large sports-themed banners and a brew pub area. The menu is equally enormous, with steaks, poultry, pasta, seafood, salads, sandwiches and pizza. The on-site brewery turns out a large selection of microbrews. Casual dress. **Bar:** Full bar. **Hours:** 11 am-close. Closed: 12/25. **Address:** 515 12th St SE **Location:** At 12th and Trade (Bellevue) sts; across from train station. **Parking:** on-site. **Cards:** AX, MC, VI.

SANDY pop. 5,385

——— **WHERE TO STAY** ———

BEST WESTERN SANDY INN

Book great rates at AAA.com

Phone: (503)668-7100

Hotel
$75-$110 All Year

Address: 37465 US 26 **Location:** West side of town. **Facility:** 45 one-bedroom standard units, some with whirlpools. 2 stories (no elevator), interior corridors. **Parking:** on-site. **Terms:** check-in 4 pm, 3 day cancellation notice-fee imposed. **Amenities:** high-speed Internet, irons, hair dryers. **Pool(s):** heated indoor. **Leisure Activities:** whirlpool, exercise room. **Guest Services:** coin laundry, wireless Internet. **Business Services:** PC. **Cards:** AX, CB, DC, DS, JC, MC, VI. **Free Special Amenities:** early check-in/late check-out and high-speed Internet.

AAA Benefit:
Members save up to 20%, plus 10% bonus points with rewards program.

——— **WHERE TO DINE** ———

TOLLGATE INN RESTAURANT, BAKERY & SALOON

Phone: 503/668-8456

American
$6-$20

For more than 25 years, this eatery has been serving hearty offerings. Varied sandwiches and such entrees as slow-cooked Yankee pot roast are good options, and a full-service bakery and espresso bar are on the premises. Senior and light-eaters menus are available. Casual dress. **Bar:** Full bar. **Hours:** 6 am-9:30 pm; Fri & Sat-10 pm in summer. Closed: 11/26, 12/25. **Address:** 38100 US 26 **Location:** South end of town. **Parking:** on-site. **Cards:** AX, DS, MC, VI.

SCAPPOOSE pop. 4,976

——— **WHERE TO DINE** ———

MARK'S ON THE CHANNEL

Phone: 503/543-8765

Regional
International
$7-$20

This casual floating restaurant entices with regional and a few distinctive globally influenced dishes. Guests can sit outside along the channel and enjoy a relaxing meal with views of the marina. Musicians kick up the atmosphere on Tuesday, Friday and Saturday. Casual dress. **Bar:** Full bar. **Hours:** 11 am-9 pm, Fri & Sat 10 am-10 pm, Sun 10 am-8 pm; Friday & Sunday brunch; hours may vary in winter. Closed: 7/4, 11/26, 12/25; also Mon. **Address:** 34326 Johnsons Landing Rd, #17 **Location:** US 30, 0.8 mi e; in McCuddy's Landing Marina. **Parking:** on-site. **Cards:** AX, DS, MC, VI.

CALL

SEASIDE pop. 5,900

——— **WHERE TO STAY** ———

10TH AVENUE INN B&B AND VACATION RENTAL

Phone: 503/738-0643

Bed & Breakfast
$119-$170 All Year

Address: 125 10th Ave **Location:** US 101, exit 12th Ave, 0.3 mi w, just s on Necanicum Dr, then just w. Located in a residential neighborhood. **Facility:** Convenient to the beach, the B&B's guest rooms offer ocean views; an adjacent cottage is geared to families. Smoke free premises. 4 units. 2 one-bedroom standard units. 1 one-bedroom suite. 1 cottage. 2 stories (no elevator), interior/exterior corridors. *Bath:* combo or shower only. **Parking:** on-site. **Terms:** check-in 4 pm, age restrictions may apply, 30 day cancellation notice-fee imposed. **Amenities:** video library, high-speed Internet, hair dryers. *Some:* irons. **Leisure Activities:** beach access. **Guest Services:** wireless Internet. **Cards:** AX, DS, MC, VI.

BEST WESTERN OCEAN VIEW RESORT   *Book great rates at AAA.com*

Phone: (503)738-3334

AAA SAVE

Hotel
$79-$489 3/1-9/30
$59-$289 10/1-2/28

Address: 414 N Prom **Location:** Oceanfront. US 101, exit 1st Ave, just w, just n on Necanicum Dr, then just w on 4th Ave. Located on the Promenade. **Facility:** Smoke free premises. 107 one-bedroom standard units, some with efficiencies and/or whirlpools. 5 stories, interior/exterior corridors. *Bath:* combo or shower only. **Parking:** on-site. **Terms:** check-in 4 pm, 3 day cancellation notice. **Amenities:** video library (fee), DVD players, high-speed Internet, voice mail, irons, hair dryers. **Dining:** Salvatore's Cafe & Sal's Pub, see separate listing. **Pool(s):** heated indoor. **Leisure Activities:** whirlpool, beach access. **Guest Services:** coin laundry, wireless Internet. **Business Services:** conference facilities. **Cards:** AX, DC, DS, MC, VI. **Free Special Amenities: local telephone calls and high-speed Internet.**

AAA Benefit:
Members save up to 20%, plus 10% bonus points with rewards program.

COMFORT INN & SUITES BY CONVENTION CENTER/BOARDWALK   *Book great rates at AAA.com*

Phone: (503)738-3011

AAA SAVE

Hotel
$99-$399 3/1-9/30
$89-$199 10/1-2/28

Address: 545 Broadway **Location:** US 101, just w on Ave A; downtown. **Facility:** Smoke free premises. 65 one-bedroom standard units, some with whirlpools. 3 stories, interior corridors. *Bath:* combo or shower only. **Parking:** on-site. **Terms:** check-in 4 pm, cancellation fee imposed. **Amenities:** high-speed Internet, irons, hair dryers. **Pool(s):** heated indoor. **Leisure Activities:** sauna, whirlpool. **Guest Services:** coin laundry, wireless Internet. **Business Services:** PC. **Cards:** AX, CB, DC, DS, MC, VI. **Free Special Amenities: expanded continental breakfast and high-speed Internet.**
(See color ad p 368, p 586, p 499, p 368, p 752, p 473, p 542, p 299, p 344, p 751, p 566 & p 500)

EBB-TIDE RESORT

Phone: (503)738-8371

AAA SAVE

Hotel
$60-$200 All Year

Address: 300 N Prom **Location:** Oceanfront. US 101, exit 1st Ave, 0.4 mi w, just n on Columbia St, then just w on 2nd Ave. Located on the Promenade. **Facility:** 99 units. 61 one- and 38 two-bedroom standard units, some with efficiencies and/or whirlpools. 4 stories, interior/exterior corridors. *Bath:* combo or shower only. **Parking:** on-site. **Terms:** check-in 5 pm, 3 day cancellation notice-fee imposed. **Amenities:** video library (fee), DVD players, voice mail, hair dryers. **Pool(s):** heated indoor. **Leisure Activities:** sauna, whirlpool, beach access, limited exercise equipment. **Guest Services:** coin laundry. **Cards:** AX, DS, MC, VI. **Free Special Amenities: local telephone calls and high-speed Internet.**

GILBERT INN BED AND BREAKFAST

Phone: 503/738-9770

AAA SAVE

Historic Bed & Breakfast
$89-$160 All Year

Address: 341 Beach Dr **Location:** US 101, exit Ave B, 0.6 mi w. **Facility:** Near the beach, promenade, shopping and restaurants, this 1892 Queen Anne home boasts a parlor fireplace, period furnishings and family heirlooms. Smoke free premises. 10 one-bedroom standard units. 3 stories (no elevator), interior corridors. **Parking:** on-site. **Terms:** office hours 7:30 am-8 pm, check-in 4 pm, 2 night minimum stay - weekends, age restrictions may apply, 7 day cancellation notice-fee imposed. **Amenities:** DVD players, high-speed Internet, hair dryers. *Some:* irons. **Guest Services:** wireless Internet. **Cards:** AX, DS, MC, VI.

HILLCREST INN

Motel

$55-$325 All Year

Phone: 503/738-6273

Address: 118 N Columbia St **Location:** US 101, exit Broadway St, 0.4 mi w, then just n. **Facility:** 27 units. 18 one-bedroom standard units, some with kitchens and/or whirlpools. 4 one-bedroom suites with efficiencies. 2 houses and 3 cottages. 2 stories (no elevator), interior/exterior corridors. *Bath:* combo or shower only. **Parking:** on-site. **Terms:** office hours 8 am-10 pm, check-in 4 pm. **Amenities:** high-speed Internet, irons. *Some:* DVD players, hair dryers. **Leisure Activities:** sauna, limited beach access, barbecue. **Guest Services:** coin laundry, wireless Internet. **Cards:** AX, DS, MC, VI. **Free Special Amenities:** local telephone calls and high-speed Internet.
(See color ad below)

▼ See AAA listing above ▼

HI-TIDE RESORT

Phone: (503)738-8414

AAA (SAVE)

Motel
$100-$160 All Year

Address: 30 Ave G **Location:** Oceanfront. US 101, exit Ave G, 0.6 mi w. **Facility:** Smoke free premises. 64 one-bedroom standard units, some with efficiencies. 3 stories, exterior corridors. **Parking:** on-site. **Terms:** office hours 7 am-11 pm, check-in 5 pm, 3 day cancellation notice. **Amenities:** video library (fee), DVD players, high-speed Internet, hair dryers. **Pool(s):** heated indoor. **Leisure Activities:** whirlpool, beach access. **Guest Services:** wireless Internet. **Cards:** AX, DC, DS, MC, VI. **Free Special Amenities: local telephone calls and high-speed Internet.**

HOLIDAY INN EXPRESS HOTEL & SUITES   *Book great rates at AAA.com*

Phone: (503)717-8000

AAA (SAVE)

Hotel
$99-$399 3/1-9/30
$89-$199 10/1-2/28

Address: 34 Holladay Dr **Location:** US 101, exit Broadway St, just w, then just n. **Facility:** Smoke free premises. 79 units. 71 one- and 5 two-bedroom standard units. 3 one-bedroom suites with whirlpools. 4 stories, interior corridors. *Bath:* combo or shower only. **Parking:** on-site. **Terms:** check-in 4 pm, cancellation fee imposed. **Amenities:** DVD players, high-speed Internet, voice mail, irons, hair dryers. **Pool(s):** heated indoor. **Leisure Activities:** sauna, whirlpool, exercise room. **Guest Services:** coin laundry, wireless Internet. **Business Services:** meeting rooms, PC. **Cards:** AX, CB, DC, DS, MC, VI.

(See color ad p 368, p 586, p 499, p 368, p 752, p 473, p 542, p 299, p 344, p 751, p 566 & below)

INN AT SEASIDE   *Book at AAA.com*

Phone: (503)738-9581

Motel
$65-$209 All Year

Address: 441 2nd Ave **Location:** US 101, exit 1st Ave, then just w. Located adjacent to the convention center. **Facility:** Smoke free premises. 47 units. 43 one- and 1 two-bedroom standard units, some with efficiencies or kitchens. 3 two-bedroom suites. 3 stories, interior/exterior corridors. *Bath:* combo or shower only. **Parking:** on-site. **Terms:** office hours 8 am-10 pm, 3 day cancellation notice. **Amenities:** video library (fee), DVD players, high-speed Internet, irons, hair dryers. **Pool(s):** heated indoor. **Leisure Activities:** whirlpool. **Guest Services:** coin laundry, wireless Internet. **Business Services:** meeting rooms. **Cards:** AX, DS, MC, VI.

INN AT THE SHORE

Phone: 503/738-3113

Motel
Rates not provided

Address: 2275 S Prom **Location:** Oceanfront. US 101, exit Ave U, just w. **Facility:** Smoke free premises. 18 units. 12 one-bedroom standard units, some with whirlpools. 6 two-bedroom suites with efficiencies. 3 stories (no elevator), exterior corridors. **Parking:** on-site. **Terms:** office hours 8 am-9 pm, check-in 4 pm. **Amenities:** video library, DVD players, high-speed Internet, hair dryers. **Leisure Activities:** beach access, bicycles. **Guest Services:** wireless Internet.

INN OF THE FOUR WINDS

AAA SAVE

▼▼ ▼▼

Motel

$169-$249 3/1-10/15
$159-$209 10/16-2/28

Phone: (503)738-9524

Address: 820 N Prom **Location:** Oceanfront. US 101, exit 12th Ave, 0.3 mi w, just s on Necanicum Dr, then just w on 9th Ave. Located on the Promenade. **Facility:** Smoke free premises. 19 units. 6 one- and 6 two-bedroom standard units. 2 one-bedroom suites. 4 houses and 1 cottage. 2 stories (no elevator), exterior corridors. *Bath:* combo or shower only. **Parking:** on-site. **Terms:** office hours 9 am-10 pm, 2-3 night minimum stay - seasonal and/or weekends, 3 day cancellation notice. **Amenities:** video library (fee), DVD players, CD players, high-speed Internet, voice mail, irons, hair dryers. **Guest Services:** wireless Internet. **Cards:** AX, CB, DC, DS, MC, VI. **Free Special Amenities: local telephone calls and high-speed Internet.**

MICROTEL INN & SUITES *Book great rates at AAA.com*

AAA SAVE

▼▼ ▼▼

Hotel

$89-$199 All Year

Phone: (503)738-8971

Address: 2455 S Roosevelt Dr (US 101) **Location:** Just s of downtown on US 101. **Facility:** 60 one-bedroom standard units, some with whirlpools. 3 stories, interior corridors. *Bath:* combo or shower only. **Parking:** on-site. **Terms:** 2 night minimum stay - seasonal and/or weekends, 3 day cancellation notice-fee imposed. **Amenities:** high-speed Internet. *Some:* DVD players (fee). **Guest Services:** wireless Internet. **Business Services:** meeting rooms, PC. **Cards:** AX, DS, MC, VI. **Free Special Amenities: continental breakfast and high-speed Internet.**

RIVERTIDE SUITES

AAA SAVE

▼▼▼ ▼

Hotel

$95-$525 All Year

Phone: (503)717-1100

Address: 102 N Holladay **Location:** US 101, just w on Broadway St, then just n. **Facility:** Smoke free premises. 70 units. 22 one-bedroom standard units, some with whirlpools. 18 one- and 30 two-bedroom suites, some with whirlpools. 4 stories, interior corridors. *Bath:* combo or shower only. **Parking:** on-site. **Terms:** check-in 4 pm, 3 day cancellation notice-fee imposed. **Amenities:** video library, DVD players, high-speed Internet, dual phone lines, voice mail, irons, hair dryers. **Pool(s):** heated indoor. **Leisure Activities:** whirlpool, exercise room. **Guest Services:** complimentary laundry, wireless Internet. **Business Services:** meeting rooms, PC. **Cards:** AX, DS, MC, VI. **Free Special Amenities: expanded continental breakfast and early check-in/late check-out.** *(See color ad below)*

SEASHORE INN..ON THE BEACH *Book great rates at AAA.com*

AAA SAVE

▼▼ ▼▼

Motel

$75-$249 All Year

Phone: (503)738-6368

Address: 60 N Prom **Location:** Oceanfront. US 101, exit 1st Ave, 0.4 mi w. Located on the Promenade. **Facility:** 54 one-bedroom standard units, some with efficiencies or kitchens. 3 stories, interior/exterior corridors. *Bath:* combo or shower only. **Parking:** on-site. **Terms:** office hours 8 am-11 pm. **Amenities:** video library (fee), high-speed Internet, hair dryers. *Some:* DVD players, CD players. **Pool(s):** heated indoor. **Leisure Activities:** sauna, whirlpool, beach access. **Guest Services:** coin laundry, wireless Internet. **Cards:** AX, DS, MC, VI. **Free Special Amenities: continental breakfast and newspaper.** *(See color ad p 502)*

THE SEASIDE INN

▼▼ ▼▼

Hotel

Rates not provided

Phone: 503/738-6403

Address: 581 S Prom **Location:** US 101, exit Ave G, 0.6 mi w, then just n. Located on the Promenade. **Facility:** Smoke free premises. 14 units. 13 one- and 1 two-bedroom standard units, some with whirlpools. 5 stories, interior corridors. *Bath:* combo or shower only. **Parking:** on-site. **Terms:** office hours 7:30 am-10 pm, check-in 4 pm. **Amenities:** video library, DVD players, high-speed Internet, hair dryers. **Leisure Activities:** beach access. *Fee:* massage. **Guest Services:** wireless Internet. **Business Services:** meeting rooms.

SHILO INN SUITES OCEANFRONT HOTEL-SEASIDE

Book great rates at AAA.com

Phone: (503)738-9571

AAA SAVE
▼▼▼▼
Hotel
$100-$550 All Year

Address: 30 N Prom **Location:** Oceanfront. US 101, exit Broadway St, 0.4 mi w. **Facility:** 113 units. 112 one-bedroom standard units, some with efficiencies. 1 one-bedroom suite with kitchen. 5 stories, exterior corridors. *Bath:* combo or shower only. **Parking:** on-site. **Terms:** check-in 4 pm. **Amenities:** high-speed Internet, voice mail, irons, hair dryers. **Pool(s):** heated indoor. **Leisure Activities:** sauna, whirlpool, steamroom, limited beach access, exercise room. *Fee:* game room. **Guest Services:** coin laundry, area transportation-within 5 mi, wireless Internet. **Business Services:** conference facilities, PC. **Cards:** AX, CB, DC, DS, JC, MC, VI. **Free Special Amenities:** newspaper and high-speed Internet. *(See color ad below)*

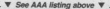

SUNDOWNER MOTOR INN

Phone: 503/738-8301

AAA SAVE
▼▼▼
Motel
$70-$145 All Year

Address: 125 Ocean Way **Location:** US 101, exit Broadway St, just w, just n on Columbia, then just w. **Facility:** 22 units. 20 one-bedroom standard units. 2 one-bedroom suites with kitchens. 2 stories (no elevator), exterior corridors. **Parking:** on-site. **Terms:** office hours 8 am-10 pm, 2 night minimum stay - seasonal and/or weekends, cancellation fee imposed. **Amenities:** DVD players, high-speed Internet, irons, hair dryers. **Pool(s):** heated indoor. **Guest Services:** coin laundry, wireless Internet. **Cards:** DS, MC, VI. **Free Special Amenities:** local telephone calls and high-speed Internet.

WEISS' PARADISE SUITES & HOMES

Motel
$125-$195 All Year

Phone: (503)738-6691

Address: 741 S Downing St **Location:** US 101, exit Ave G, just w. Located in a residential area. **Facility:** 4 one-bedroom suites with kitchens, some with whirlpools. 1 story, exterior corridors. *Bath:* combo or shower only. **Parking:** on-site. **Terms:** office hours 8 am-9 pm, check-in 4 pm, 2 night minimum stay, 7 day cancellation notice. **Amenities:** video library, DVD players, high-speed Internet, irons, hair dryers. **Guest Services:** wireless Internet. **Cards:** AX, MC, VI. **Free Special Amenities:** local telephone calls and early check-in/late check-out.

—————— WHERE TO DINE ——————

BAGELS BY THE SEA

American
$5-$8

Phone: 503/717-9145

The on-premises bakery makes 20 savory varieties of soft bagels, including designer bagels, for its full-service delicatessen sandwiches, which are stacked high with in-house roasted meats. Several varieties of cream cheese spreads also make good toppers. Gourmet coffees, along with such baked treats as giant cookies and bars, are other temptations. A covered patio and drive-through service are available. Casual dress. **Hours:** 6:30 am-3 pm. Closed: 4/12, 11/26, 12/25. **Address:** 210 S Holladay Dr **Location:** US 101, just w on Ave A, then just s. **Parking:** on-site. **Cards:** AX, DS, MC, VI.

THE BUOY'S BEST FISH HOUSE
Phone: 503/738-6348

The basic eatery prepares fresh seafood cocktail, melts and baskets. Seasonal outside seats are near the river's edge. Casual dress. **Reservations:** not accepted. **Hours:** 11:30 am-7 pm. Closed: 11/26, 12/25; also Tues & Wed in winter. **Address:** 1800 S Roosevelt Dr **Location:** On US 101; south end of town, near Ave S. **Parking:** on-site. **Cards:** MC, VI.

Seafood
$8-$12

DOOGERS SEAFOOD & GRILL
Phone: 503/738-3773

Popular with families, the comfortable restaurant is rustic in decor with quaint touches. On the menu are traditional preparations of primarily seafood dishes, with a handful of pasta, chicken and beef entrees. Casual dress. **Bar:** Beer & wine. **Hours:** 11 am-10 pm, Fri & Sat-10:30 pm; to 9 pm in winter. Closed: 11/26, 12/25. **Address:** 505 Broadway St **Location:** US 101, just w on Broadway St. **Parking:** on-site. **Cards:** AX, DS, MC, VI.

Seafood
$7-$39   CALL 👍M

GUIDO & VITO'S ITALIAN EATERY
Phone: 503/717-1229

The casual restaurant serves traditional and specialty pasta, meat and seafood dishes, which are made to order along with the sauces. Casual dress. **Bar:** Full bar. **Reservations:** not accepted. **Hours:** 4:30 pm-9 pm, Sat-9:30 pm. Closed: 12/25. **Address:** 604 Broadway St **Location:** US 101, exit Broadway St, just w. **Parking:** street. **Cards:** DS, MC, VI.

Italian
$4-$22

LIL' BAYOU RESTAURANT & MAGNOLIA LOUNGE
Phone: 503/717-0624

Southern flavors come together in traditional Cajun and Creole preparations of local seafood, meats and produce. Casual dress. **Bar:** Full bar. **Reservations:** not accepted. **Hours:** 5 pm-10 pm; call for winter hours. Closed major holidays; also Tues in winter. **Address:** 20 N Holladay Dr **Location:** US 101, exit Broadway St, just w, then just n. **Parking:** street. **Cards:** AX, MC, VI.

Cajun
$15-$20

MCKEOWN'S COURTYARD CAFE AND BAR
Phone: 503/738-5232

Breakfast at the beach includes omelets, Benedicts and lightweight breakfasts. For lunch and dinner, the menu lists several seafood selections, tender prime rib and steaks, pasta dishes, salads and quesadillas. To look out over the dining room, guests can reserve the loft. Casual dress. **Bar:** Full bar. **Reservations:** accepted. **Hours:** 8 am-10 pm; Sunday brunch 9:30 am-1:30 pm. **Address:** 714 Broadway St **Location:** US 101, exit Broadway St, just w. **Parking:** street. **Cards:** AX, DS, MC, VI.

American
$7-$24

NORMA'S OCEAN DINER   *Menu on AAA.com*
Phone: 503/738-4331

Located just off the Prom, this restaurant serves fresh and tasty seafood. Photos of lighthouses adorn the walls. Casual dress. **Bar:** Beer & wine. **Reservations:** not accepted. **Hours:** 11 am-10 pm; hours may vary in winter. Closed: 11/26; also 12/15-12/31. **Address:** 20 N Columbia St **Location:** US 101, exit Broadway St, 0.4 mi w, then just n. **Parking:** street. **Cards:** AX, DS, MC, VI.

Regional
Seafood
$7-$25

SALVATORE'S CAFE & SAL'S PUB
Phone: 503/738-3334

The casual restaurant with a fireplace has a cozy feel. Several seafood, pasta and chicken dishes are prepared from fresh ingredients. Pizza and lighter cafe items round out the offerings. Casual dress. **Bar:** Full bar. **Reservations:** accepted. **Hours:** 7 am-11 & 5-9 pm, Fri & Sat-10 pm, Sun 8 am-1 & 5-9 pm; Sunday brunch. **Address:** 414 N Prom **Location:** US 101, exit 1st Ave, just w, just n on Necanicum Dr, then just w on 4th Ave; in Best Western Ocean View Resort. **Parking:** on-site. **Cards:** AX, CB, DC, DS, MC, VI.

Italian
$10-$20   CALL 👍M

SHADY COVE pop. 2,307

—————— WHERE TO DINE ——————

TWO PINES SMOKEHOUSE
Phone: 541/878-7463

Tex-Mex and smoked barbecue are prepared in a Western lodge atmosphere. Steaks and prime rib also find their way onto the menu. Casual dress. **Bar:** Full bar. **Reservations:** accepted. **Hours:** 7 am-9 pm. Closed: 12/25. **Address:** 21331 Hwy 62 **Location:** Center of town. **Parking:** on-site. **Cards:** AX, CB, DC, DS, MC, VI.

Barbecue
$8-$25

SHERWOOD —*See Portland p. 468.*

SILVERTON pop. 7,414

—————— WHERE TO STAY ——————

WATER STREET INN
Phone: 503/873-3344

Address: 421 N Water St **Location:** Downtown. **Facility:** Built in 1890, this renovated inn features a backyard garden and is convenient to the Oregon Garden, Silver Falls State Park and restaurants. Smoke free premises. 5 one-bedroom standard units, some with whirlpools. 2 stories (no elevator), interior corridors. *Bath:* combo or shower only. **Parking:** on-site. **Terms:** office hours 8 am-9 pm, check-in 4 pm, age restrictions may apply, 8 day cancellation notice. **Amenities:** video library, high-speed Internet. **Guest Services:** wireless Internet. **Cards:** AX, MC, VI.

Bed & Breakfast
$95-$165 All Year

The following lodging was either not evaluated or did not
meet AAA rating requirements but is listed for your information only.

SILVERTON INN
[fyi]

Phone: 503/873-1000

Not evaluated. **Address:** 310 N Water St **Location:** Center. Facilities, services, and decor characterize an economy property.

--- **WHERE TO DINE** ---

SILVER GRILLE
▼▼▼ ▼▼▼

Regional American
$16-$21

Phone: 503/873-4035

In historic downtown, the casually upscale bistro prepares seasonally changing examples of Willamette Valley cuisine. Featured is the chef's choice, a nightly four-course prix fixe menu. Casual dress. **Bar:** Full bar. **Reservations:** suggested. **Hours:** 5 pm-9 pm. Closed: 11/26, 12/25; also Mon & Tues. **Address:** 206 E Main St **Location:** Just e of jct S Water St; downtown. **Parking:** street. **Cards:** AX, DS, MC, VI.

The following restaurants have not been evaluated by AAA
but are listed for your information only.

O'BRIEN'S CAFE
[fyi]

Phone: 503/873-7554

Not evaluated. Guests of the homey eatery will find hot and cold sandwiches, burgers and breakfast served all day. The seasonal outdoor deck overlooks Silver Creek. **Address:** 105 N Water St **Location:** Just n of Main St; center.

RED THAI ROOM
[fyi]

Phone: 503/873-1122

Not evaluated. The warm, eclectic dining room serves as a prelude to the delicious Thai-Asian country fare, which includes curries, vegetarian selections and dishes prepared with homemade sauces. **Address:** 211 Oak St **Location:** Just e of jct S Water St; downtown.

SISTERS pop. 959

--- **WHERE TO STAY** ---

BEST WESTERN PONDEROSA LODGE   *Book great rates at AAA.com*

(AAA) [SAVE]
▼▼▼ ▼▼▼

Motel
$130-$270 3/1-10/31
$100-$250 11/1-2/28

Phone: (541)549-1234

Address: 500 Hwy 20 W **Location:** Just w on US 20 from jct SR 242; at Barclay Dr; west end of town. Located in a quiet location. **Facility:** Designated smoking area. 75 units. 68 one-bedroom standard units, some with whirlpools. 7 one-bedroom suites with whirlpools. 2 stories (no elevator), exterior corridors. **Parking:** on-site. **Amenities:** video library, irons, hair dryers. *Some:* DVD players, high-speed Internet. **Pool(s):** heated outdoor. **Leisure Activities:** whirlpool, walking trails. **Guest Services:** coin laundry, wireless Internet. **Business Services:** meeting rooms, PC. **Cards:** AX, CB, DC, DS, JC, MC, VI. **Free Special Amenities:** expanded continental breakfast and high-speed Internet.

AAA Benefit:
Members save up to 20%, plus 10% bonus points with rewards program.

[❗] [🛏] [✕] [VCR] [▯] [▱] [▱] / SOME UNITS FEE [🐾]

BLUE SPRUCE BED & BREAKFAST
▼▼▼ ▼▼▼

Bed & Breakfast
Rates not provided

Phone: 541/549-9644

Address: 444 S Spruce St **Location:** Just se of US 20/SR 126; downtown. **Facility:** Located in a residential neighborhood, the inn features a wrap-around porch and guest rooms with a contemporary Northwest decor. Designated smoking area. 5 one-bedroom standard units with whirlpools. 2 stories (no elevator), interior corridors. **Parking:** on-site. **Terms:** office hours 8 am-9 pm, check-in 4 pm, age restrictions may apply. **Amenities:** video library, irons, hair dryers. **Leisure Activities:** bicycles, horseshoes. **Guest Services:** complimentary laundry, wireless Internet. **Business Services:** PC.

[🖐] [✕] [VCR] [✆] [▯]

FIVEPINE LODGE & SPA RESORT   *Book at AAA.com*
▼▼▼ ▼▼▼

Cottage
$159-$219 All Year

Phone: (541)549-5900

Address: 1021 Desperado Tr **Location:** Jct SR 126 and US 20, just e on US 20; east end of town. **Facility:** A huge dual-sided fireplace welcomes guests to the cozy lobby area; select from individual cottages or standard rooms in the main lodge. 32 units. 6 one-bedroom suites. 26 cottages. 2 stories (no elevator), interior corridors. **Parking:** on-site. **Terms:** office hours 7 am-10 pm, check-in 4 pm, 2 night minimum stay - seasonal and/or weekends, 7 day cancellation notice-fee imposed. **Amenities:** video library, DVD players, high-speed Internet, voice mail, irons, hair dryers. **Pool(s):** heated outdoor. **Leisure Activities:** bicycles, hiking trails, jogging, spa, croquet. *Fee:* movie theatre. **Guest Services:** wireless Internet. **Business Services:** conference facilities, PC. **Cards:** AX, DS, MC, VI.

[🍴] [🍸] [🛏] [🖐] [✕] [✕] [▯] [▱] / SOME UNITS FEE [🐾]

--- **WHERE TO DINE** ---

BRONCO BILLY'S RANCH GRILL & SALOON
▼▼ ▼▼

American
$8-$27

Phone: 541/549-7427

A quaint Western setting in a historic hotel, settle in and enjoy a hearty meal of steak, seafood or chicken, or perhaps barbecue dishes like ribs and burgers served with Western flair. Let fresh air whet your appetite on the covered outdoor deck. Casual dress. **Bar:** Full bar. **Reservations:** accepted. **Hours:** 11:30 am-10 pm; to 8 pm in winter. Closed: 11/26, 12/25. **Address:** 190 E Cascade St **Location:** On SR 126; center. **Parking:** street. **Cards:** MC, VI. **Historic**

SPRINGFIELD pop. 52,864—*See also EUGENE.*

—————— **WHERE TO STAY** ——————

BEST WESTERN GRAND MANOR INN *Book great rates at AAA.com*

Phone: (541)726-4769

Hotel
$93-$156 All Year

Address: 971 Kruse Way **Location:** I-5, exit 195A, just se. **Facility:** 65 units. 62 one-bedroom standard units. 3 one-bedroom suites. 3 stories, interior corridors. *Bath:* combo or shower only. **Parking:** on-site. **Amenities:** high-speed Internet, voice mail, irons, hair dryers. **Pool(s):** heated outdoor. **Leisure Activities:** sauna, exercise room. **Guest Services:** valet and coin laundry, wireless Internet. **Business Services:** meeting rooms, PC. **Cards:** AX, CB, DC, DS, JC, MC, VI. **Free Special Amenities: expanded continental breakfast and high-speed Internet.**

AAA Benefit:
Members save up to 20%, plus 10% bonus points with rewards program.

COMFORT SUITES EUGENE/SPRINGFIELD *Book great rates at AAA.com*

Phone: (541)746-5359

Hotel
$99-$179 All Year

Address: 969 Kruse Way **Location:** I-5, exit 195A, just se. **Facility:** Smoke free premises. 77 units. 75 one-bedroom standard units, some with whirlpools. 2 one-bedroom suites with whirlpools. 3 stories, interior corridors. *Bath:* combo or shower only. **Parking:** on-site. **Terms:** cancellation fee imposed. **Amenities:** video games (fee), high-speed Internet, voice mail, irons, hair dryers. **Pool(s):** heated indoor. **Leisure Activities:** whirlpool, exercise room. **Guest Services:** valet and coin laundry, wireless Internet. **Business Services:** meeting rooms, PC. **Cards:** AX, CB, DC, DS, JC, MC, VI.

COURTYARD BY MARRIOTT *Book great rates at AAA.com*

Phone: (541)726-2121

Hotel
$143-$175 All Year

Address: 3443 Hutton St **Location:** I-5, exit 195A, just se. **Facility:** Smoke free premises. 116 units. 112 one-bedroom standard units, some with whirlpools. 4 one-bedroom suites. 2 stories, interior corridors. *Bath:* combo or shower only. **Parking:** on-site. **Terms:** cancellation fee imposed. **Amenities:** video games (fee), high-speed Internet, voice mail, irons, hair dryers. **Pool(s):** heated indoor. **Leisure Activities:** whirlpool, exercise room. **Guest Services:** valet and coin laundry, area transportation, wireless Internet. **Business Services:** meeting rooms, PC. **Cards:** AX, CB, DC, DS, JC, MC, VI.

AAA Benefit:
Members save a minimum 5% off the best available rate.

HOLIDAY INN EUGENE - SPRINGFIELD *Book great rates at AAA.com*

Phone: (541)284-0707

Hotel
$129-$209 All Year

Address: 919 Kruse Way **Location:** I-5, exit 195A, just se. **Facility:** Smoke free premises. 153 units. 148 one-bedroom standard units, some with whirlpools. 5 one-bedroom suites. 6 stories, interior corridors. *Bath:* combo or shower only. **Parking:** on-site. **Terms:** check-in 4 pm. **Amenities:** high-speed Internet, voice mail, irons, hair dryers. **Pool(s):** heated indoor. **Leisure Activities:** whirlpool, exercise room. **Guest Services:** valet and coin laundry, airport transportation-Eugene Airport, wireless Internet. **Business Services:** meeting rooms, business center. **Cards:** AX, CB, DC, DS, JC, MC, VI. **Free Special Amenities: local telephone calls and high-speed Internet.**

HOLIDAY INN EXPRESS HOTEL & SUITES *Book great rates at AAA.com*

Phone: (541)746-8471

Hotel
$109-$179 All Year

Address: 3480 Hutton St **Location:** I-5, exit 195A, just se. Located in a commercial area. **Facility:** 85 one-bedroom standard units, some with whirlpools. 3 stories, interior corridors. *Bath:* combo or shower only. **Parking:** on-site. **Amenities:** video games (fee), high-speed Internet, voice mail, irons, hair dryers. **Pool(s):** heated indoor. **Leisure Activities:** exercise room. **Guest Services:** valet and coin laundry, wireless Internet. **Business Services:** PC. **Cards:** AX, CB, DC, DS, JC, MC, VI.

MOTEL 6 #418 *Book at AAA.com*

Phone: (541)741-1105

Motel
$51-$61 All Year

Address: 3752 International Ct **Location:** I-5, exit 195A, just e on Beltline Rd, just nw on Gateway St, then just n. **Facility:** 131 one-bedroom standard units. 2 stories (no elevator), exterior corridors. *Bath:* shower only. **Parking:** on-site. **Amenities:** high-speed Internet (fee). **Pool(s):** heated outdoor. **Guest Services:** coin laundry, wireless Internet. **Cards:** AX, CB, DC, DS, MC, VI.

SUPER 8 *Book great rates at AAA.com*

Phone: 541/746-1314

Hotel
Rates not provided

Address: 3315 Gateway St **Location:** I-5, exit 195A, just e on Beltline Rd, then just s. **Facility:** 71 one-bedroom standard units. 3 stories (no elevator), interior corridors. *Bath:* combo or shower only. **Parking:** on-site. **Amenities:** high-speed Internet, irons, hair dryers. **Leisure Activities:** whirlpool. **Guest Services:** coin laundry, wireless Internet. **Free Special Amenities: continental breakfast and high-speed Internet.**

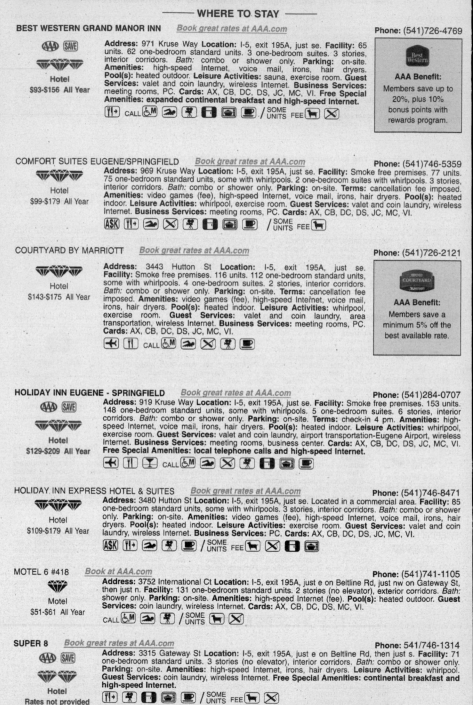

VILLAGE INN

AAA SAVE

▼▼ ▼▼

Motel

$79 All Year

Phone: (541)747-4546

Address: 1875 Mohawk Blvd **Location:** I-5, exit 194A, 2.5 mi e on SR 126, exit Mohawk Blvd, then just n. **Facility:** 66 one-bedroom standard units, some with efficiencies. 2 stories (no elevator), exterior corridors. **Parking:** on-site. **Amenities:** high-speed Internet, hair dryers. *Some:* irons. **Pool(s):** heated outdoor. **Leisure Activities:** whirlpool, exercise room. **Guest Services:** coin laundry, wireless Internet. **Business Services:** meeting rooms. **Cards:** AX, DS, MC, VI. **Free Special Amenities: local telephone calls and high-speed Internet.**

⊞ ⊻ ⊇ ⊛ ⊡ / SOME UNITS ⊢ ⊠ ⊟ ⊟

——— **WHERE TO DINE** ———

SOFIA'S RESTAURANT & BAVARIAN BREWERY   Phone: 541-744-3330

▼▼ ▼▼

German

$8-$22

A variety of schnitzels and other German favorites, along with a few American specialties and the highly recommended smoked pork chop, make up the menu at this restaurant. Complementing them is a good selection of imported German draft beers and house brews. The patio opens seasonally. Casual dress. **Bar:** Full bar. **Reservations:** accepted. **Hours:** 11:30 am-9:30 pm, Fri & Sat-10:30 pm, Sun 4:30 pm-9:30 pm. Closed: 11/26, 12/25. **Address:** 980 Kruse Way **Location:** I-5, exit 195A, just e, then s on Gateway St. **Parking:** on-site. **Cards:** AX, DS, MC, VI.

CALL ⊡M

SUNRIVER

——— **WHERE TO STAY** ———

DISCOVER SUNRIVER VACATION RENTALS   Phone: (541)593-2482

AAA SAVE

▼▼ ▼▼

Vacation Rental House

$90-$140 All Year

Location: US 97, exit 153 (S Century Dr), 2 mi w to Abbott Dr, then just n on Beaver Dr. Located in Sunriver Village Mall; adjacent to Coldwell Banker. **Facility:** Many units feature a fireplace, ceiling fan and whirlpool or hot tub, some have a loft; the property's recreational opportunities are expansive. 145 units. 98 houses, 12 cabins and 35 condominiums. 1-2 stories (no elevator), interior corridors. **Parking:** on-site. **Terms:** office hours 8 am-6 pm, check-in 4 pm, 2 night minimum stay - seasonal, 60 day cancellation notice-fee imposed. **Amenities:** DVD players, CD players, high-speed Internet, irons, hair dryers. **Pool(s):** 2 heated outdoor, heated indoor. **Leisure Activities:** saunas, whirlpool, waterslide, wave machine, 28 tennis courts, rock climbing, access to Mavericks Recreation Facility, bicycles, playground, exercise room, fitness classes, sports court, basketball, horseshoes, volleyball. *Fee:* massage, game room. **Guest Services:** coin laundry, wireless Internet. **Business Services:** meeting rooms, PC. **Cards:** DS, MC, VI. **Free Special Amenities: local telephone calls and high-speed Internet.**

⊇ ⊠ ⊠ (VCR) ⊛ ⊟ ⊟ ⊡ / SOME UNITS FEE ⊢ ⊞

SUNRAY VACATION RENTALS   Phone: (541)593-3225

AAA SAVE

▼▼ ▼▼

Vacation Rental House

$100-$800 All Year

Location: US 97, exit 153 (Century Dr), 2 mi w, follow signs to Mt Bachelor, just s on Century Dr, then just e. Located in Sunriver Business Park. **Facility:** Luxury homes and condos, each with a fireplace and hot tub, are conveniently located in this eco-friendly town; bike paths are available. 180 units. 168 houses and 12 condominiums. 1-3 stories (no elevator), exterior corridors. **Parking:** on-site. **Terms:** office hours 8 am-7 pm, check-in 4 pm, 2 night minimum stay - seasonal, 60 day cancellation notice-fee imposed. **Amenities:** CD players. *Some:* DVD players, high-speed Internet, voice mail, irons, hair dryers. **Pool(s):** 2 heated outdoor. **Leisure Activities:** saunas, whirlpool, wave machine, 20 tennis courts, cross country skiing, ice skating, access to Maverick's Recreation Facility, bicycles, hiking trails, jogging, playground, basketball, volleyball. *Fee:* golf-18 holes, miniature golf, massage, game room. **Guest Services:** complimentary laundry, wireless Internet. **Business Services:** meeting rooms. **Cards:** AX, DC, DS, MC, VI. **Free Special Amenities: local telephone calls and preferred room (subject to availability with advance reservations).**

⊞ ⊇ ⊕ ⊠ ⊠ (VCR) ⊟ ⊟ ⊡ / SOME UNITS FEE ⊢ ⊞

SUNRIVER RESORT   Phone: (541)593-1000

AAA SAVE

▼▼ ▼▼

Resort Hotel

$149-$274 All Year

Address: 17600 Center Dr **Location:** US 97, exit 153 (S Century Dr), 2 mi w to Abbott Dr, then just w. **Facility:** Some rooms have views of the mountains, the golf course or a stream; all have a fireplace and upscale Northwest decor. 655 units. 163 one-bedroom standard units. 75 one-, 111 two- and 35 three-bedroom suites, some with efficiencies or kitchens. 266 houses and 5 cabins. 2 stories, exterior corridors. **Bath:** combo or shower only. **Parking:** on-site. **Terms:** check-in 4 pm, 21 day cancellation notice-fee imposed. **Amenities:** voice mail, irons, hair dryers. *Some:* DVD players, video games (fee), CD players, dual phone lines, safes, honor bars. **Dining:** 3 restaurants, also, Meadows at the Lodge, see separate listing. **Pool(s):** 3 heated outdoor. **Leisure Activities:** saunas, whirlpools, steamrooms, waterslide, rental boats, marina, fishing, cross country skiing, recreation programs, bike trails, children's program, hiking trails, jogging, playground, spa, sports court, basketball, volleyball. *Fee:* canoes, kayaks, family canoe , raft float trips, white water rafting, golf-54 holes, golf instruction, 4 tennis courts (3 indoor, 4 lighted), snowmobiling, ice skating, tobogganing, sleigh rides, carriage ride, aerobics, bike tours, gliders & bi-plane rides in summer, bicycles, horseback riding, horseshoes. **Guest Services:** complimentary and valet laundry, airport transportation-Sunriver & Redmond-Roberts Field airports, area transportation (fee)-Mt Bachelor, wireless Internet. **Business Services:** conference facilities, business center. **Cards:** AX, DC, DS, MC, VI. *(See color ad p 53)*

⊞ ⊞ ⊻ ⊕ ⊇ ⊕ ⊠ ⊠ ⊡ / SOME UNITS FEE ⊢ (VCR) ⊟ ⊟

——— *The following lodging was either not evaluated or did not* ———
meet AAA rating requirements but is listed for your information only.

MOUNTAIN RESORT PROPERTIES   Phone: 541/593-8685

fyi   Not evaluated. **Location:** US 97, exit S Century Dr, 1 mi w; behind Bank of the Cascades. Facilities, services, and decor characterize a mid-scale property.

------ **WHERE TO DINE** ------

MEADOWS AT THE LODGE
Phone: 541/593-3740

▼▼▼▼
Regional American
$9-$36

Patrons can enjoy a beautiful view of the Cascade Mountains and the golf course. Examples of Northwest cuisine that may appear on the menu include pan-roasted elk loin and grilled salmon with marionberry compote. Outdoor seating is an option, and brunch is served on Sunday. Dressy casual. **Bar:** Full bar. **Reservations:** suggested. **Hours:** 6:30 am-9:30 pm, Fri & Sat-10 pm; 7 am-9 pm in winter; Sunday brunch. **Address:** 17600 Center Dr **Location:** US 97, exit 153 (S Century Dr), 2 mi w to Abbott Dr, then just w; in Sunriver Resort. **Parking:** on-site. **Cards:** AX, DC, DS, MC, VI.

SUTHERLIN pop. 6,669

------ **WHERE TO STAY** ------

BEST WESTERN HARTFORD LODGE
Phone: (541)459-1424

(AAA) (SAVE)
(fyi)
Hotel
$89-$139 All Year

Under major renovation, scheduled to be completed February 2009. **Last rated:** ▼▼ **Address:** 150 Myrtle St **Location:** I-5, exit 136, just ne. **Facility:** Smoke free premises. 61 one-bedroom standard units. 2 stories, exterior corridors. **Parking:** on-site. **Terms:** cancellation fee imposed. **Amenities:** video library (fee), DVD players, high-speed Internet, voice mail, irons, hair dryers. **Pool(s):** heated indoor. **Leisure Activities:** whirlpool, exercise room. **Guest Services:** valet and coin laundry, wireless Internet. **Business Services:** meeting rooms, PC. **Cards:** AX, DS, MC, VI. **Free Special Amenities:** full breakfast and high-speed Internet.

🐾 ✕ 🎦 🛢 📷 💻 / SOME UNITS FEE 🐕

AAA Benefit:
Members save up to 20%, plus 10% bonus points with rewards program.

MICROTEL INN *Book at AAA.com*
Phone: 541/459-6800

▼▼ ▼▼
Hotel
Rates not provided

Address: 1400 Hospitality Pl **Location:** I-5, exit 136, just se. **Facility:** 80 one-bedroom standard units. 3 stories, interior corridors. *Bath:* combo or shower only. **Parking:** on-site. **Amenities:** high-speed Internet. *Some:* hair dryers. **Guest Services:** coin laundry, wireless Internet. **Business Services:** PC.

🍴 🎦 / SOME UNITS FEE 🐕 ✕ 🛢 📷 💻

------ **WHERE TO DINE** ------

PEDOTTI'S ITALIAN RESTUARANT
Phone: 541/459-3773

▼▼ ▼▼
Italian
$6-$17

Among homemade specialties are baked lasagna, manicotti, ravioli, calzones, oven-baked submarine sandwiches and pizza. Early-bird specials are offered from 4 to 6 pm Monday through Thursday. Nightly dinner specials are tempting. Casual dress. **Bar:** Full bar. **Reservations:** suggested. **Hours:** 11 am-9 pm, Sat from 4 pm, Sun from noon. Closed major holidays. **Address:** 1332 W Central Ave **Location:** I-5, exit 136, just e. **Parking:** on-site. **Cards:** MC, VI.

SWEET HOME pop. 8,016

------ **WHERE TO STAY** ------

SWEET HOME INN
Phone: (541)367-5137

(AAA) (SAVE)
▼▼ ▼▼
Motel
$79-$99 3/1-9/14
$69-$89 9/15-2/28

Address: 805 Long St **Location:** Just e of jct US 20 and SR 228; just s on 10th Ave, then just w. **Facility:** 28 units. 27 one- and 1 two-bedroom standard units, some with whirlpools. 1-2 stories (no elevator), exterior corridors. *Bath:* combo or shower only. **Parking:** on-site. **Terms:** office hours 7 am-midnight. **Amenities:** high-speed Internet, irons, hair dryers. **Leisure Activities:** sauna, whirlpool. **Guest Services:** coin laundry, wireless Internet. **Cards:** AX, CB, DC, DS, JC, MC, VI. **Free Special Amenities:** local telephone calls and high-speed Internet.

🎦 🛢 📷 💻 / SOME UNITS FEE 🐕 ✕

------ **WHERE TO DINE** ------

THE POINT RESTAURANT & LOUNGE
Phone: 541/367-1560

(AAA)
▼▼ ▼▼
Steak & Seafood
$5-$24

Across the highway from Foster Lake, the establishment offers Angus steaks, pasta dishes, sandwiches and such seafood preparations as pecan-encrusted halibut and hickory-smoked salmon. Save room for the signature raisin cream pie. The patio opens seasonally. Breakfast is available. Casual dress. **Bar:** Full bar. **Reservations:** accepted. **Hours:** 7 am-9 pm. Closed: 11/26, 12/25. **Address:** 6305 US 20 **Location:** 3.5 mi e. **Parking:** on-site. **Cards:** MC, VI.

CALL 👤M

THE DALLES pop. 12,156

------ **WHERE TO STAY** ------

COMFORT INN COLUMBIA GORGE *Book great rates at AAA.com*
Phone: (541)298-2800

(AAA) (SAVE)
▼▼ ▼▼
Hotel
$85-$174 All Year

Address: 351 Lone Pine Dr **Location:** I-84, exit 87, just nw. **Facility:** Smoke free premises. 56 one-bedroom standard units, some with whirlpools. 2 stories (no elevator), interior corridors. **Parking:** on-site. **Terms:** cancellation fee imposed. **Amenities:** high-speed Internet, irons, hair dryers. **Pool(s):** heated indoor. **Leisure Activities:** whirlpool, playground, exercise room. **Guest Services:** coin laundry, wireless Internet. **Business Services:** meeting rooms. **Cards:** AX, CB, DC, DS, JC, MC, VI. **Free Special Amenities:** expanded continental breakfast and high-speed Internet.

🐾 ✕ ✕ 🎦 🛢 📷 💻 / SOME UNITS FEE 🐕

COUSINS COUNTRY INN   *Book great rates at AAA.com*   Phone: 541/298-5161

AAA [SAVE]
▼▼ ▼▼
Hotel
Rates not provided

Address: 2114 W 6th St **Location:** I-84, exit 83 eastbound, just nw; exit 84 westbound, just nw on W 2nd St, just sw on Webber St, then just n. **Facility:** 93 one-bedroom standard units, some with efficiencies or kitchens. 2 stories (no elevator), exterior corridors. *Bath:* combo or shower only. **Parking:** on-site. **Terms:** check-in 4 pm. **Amenities:** video library (fee), DVD players, high-speed Internet, irons, hair dryers. **Dining:** Cousins' Restaurant and Saloon, see separate listing. **Pool(s):** heated outdoor. **Leisure Activities:** whirlpool. **Guest Services:** coin laundry, airport transportation-The Dalles Municipal Airport, wireless Internet. **Business Services:** meeting rooms, PC. **Free Special Amenities:** newspaper and high-speed Internet.

🛬 🍽 🍸 CALL 🏋M 🏊 🛁 🎮 🖥 🖨 🖳 / SOME UNITS FEE 🐕 ✕

THE DALLES INN   *Book at AAA.com*   Phone: (541)296-9107

▼▼ ▼▼
Hotel
$79-$139 All Year

Address: 112 W 2nd St **Location:** I-84, exit 84 eastbound, just se; exit 85 westbound, 0.8 mi nw; at Liberty and W 2nd sts; downtown. Located near train tracks. **Facility:** 63 one-bedroom standard units, some with whirlpools. 1 one-bedroom suite with kitchen. 2-4 stories, interior/exterior corridors. **Parking:** on-site. **Amenities:** video library (fee), DVD players, high-speed Internet, voice mail, irons, hair dryers. **Pool(s):** heated outdoor. **Guest Services:** coin laundry, wireless Internet. **Business Services:** meeting rooms, PC. **Cards:** AX, DC, DS, MC, VI.

(ASK) 🍽 🏊 🎮 🖥 🖨 🖳 / SOME UNITS FEE 🐕 ✕

MOTEL 6 #4268   *Book at AAA.com*   Phone: 541/296-1191

▼▼
Hotel
Rates not provided

Address: 2500 W 6th St **Location:** I-84, exit 83 eastbound, just nw exit 84 westbound, just nw on w 2nd St, just sw on Webber St, then just n. **Facility:** 70 one-bedroom standard units. 2 stories (no elevator), interior corridors. **Parking:** on-site. **Amenities:** high-speed Internet. **Pool(s):** heated outdoor. **Guest Services:** coin laundry, wireless Internet.

🏊 🎮 🖥 / SOME UNITS FEE 🐕 ✕

SHILO INN SUITES HOTEL-THE DALLES   *Book great rates at AAA.com*   Phone: 541/298-5502

AAA [SAVE]
▼▼ ▼▼
Hotel
Rates not provided

Address: 3223 Bret Clodfelter Way **Location:** I-84, exit 87, just ne. Located overlooking The Dalles Dam. **Facility:** Smoke free premises. 112 units. 110 one-bedroom standard units. 2 two-bedroom suites, some with whirlpools. 2 stories (no elevator), interior corridors. **Parking:** on-site. **Amenities:** video games (fee), high-speed Internet, voice mail, irons, hair dryers. **Pool(s):** heated outdoor. **Leisure Activities:** sauna, whirlpool, limited exercise equipment. **Guest Services:** coin laundry, airport transportation (fee)-The Dalles Municipal Airport, area transportation-bus & train depot, wireless Internet. **Business Services:** meeting rooms, PC. **Free Special Amenities:** continental breakfast and high-speed Internet. *(See color ad below)*

FEE 🛬 🍽 🏊 🏋 ✕ 🎮 🖥 🖨 🖳 / SOME UNITS FEE 🐕

SUPER 8 MOTEL   *Book at AAA.com*   Phone: 541/296-6888

▼▼ ▼▼
Hotel
Rates not provided

Address: 609 Cherry Heights Rd **Location:** I-84, exit 84 eastbound, just se on W 2nd St, then just sw; exit 84 westbound, just nw on W 2nd St, just sw on Webber St, then just se on W 8th St. **Facility:** 73 one-bedroom standard units, some with whirlpools. 3 stories, interior corridors. *Bath:* combo or shower only. **Parking:** on-site. **Amenities:** high-speed Internet, irons, hair dryers. **Pool(s):** heated outdoor. **Guest Services:** coin laundry, wireless Internet.

🏊 🎮 🖥 🖨 🖳 / SOME UNITS FEE 🐕 ✕

▼ See AAA listing above ▼

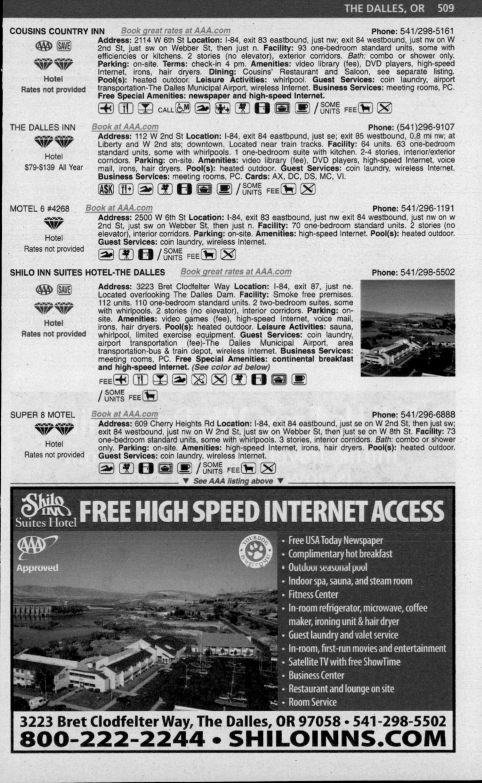

─────── **WHERE TO DINE** ───────

BALDWIN SALOON *Menu on AAA.com* Phone: 541/296-5666

Steak & Seafood
$7-$24

The restored 1876 restaurant and bar is one of the town's oldest commercial buildings—it was a saloon and later a steamboat office and grain warehouse. The original bar, brick walls and an antique painting collection contribute to the decor. Fresh seafood, oysters and meat entrees are available with homemade soup, salad and dessert. The patio is open seasonally. Casual dress. **Bar:** Full bar. **Reservations:** not accepted. **Hours:** 11 am-9 pm, Fri & Sat-10 pm; to 10 pm in summer. Closed major holidays; also Sun. **Address:** 205 Court St **Location:** Jct E 1st and Court sts; downtown. **Parking:** street. **Cards:** DS, MC, VI.

BURGERVILLE Phone: 541/298-5753

American
$2-$8

First-timers shouldn't let the fast food exterior fool them, as the burgers and chicken here adhere to a higher standard. Northwest ingredients come into play in the sandwiches. Casual dress. **Hours:** 7 am-10 pm. Closed: 11/26, 12/25. **Address:** 118 W 3rd St **Location:** I-84, exit 84 eastbound, just se; exit 85 westbound, 0.8 mi nw; downtown. **Parking:** on-site. **Cards:** DS, MC, VI.

CASA EL MIRADOR Phone: 541/298-7388

Mexican
$6-$15

Large windows make the restaurant a bright, cheerful place. Southwestern-style artwork adorns the walls, and lively colors add to the festive atmosphere. Traditional Mexican selections reflect straightforward presentation and are offered in two portion sizes. Varied choices—including seafood, chicken, egg dishes and Mexican favorites—and good prices keep this place popular. A good selection of margaritas is available. Casual dress. **Bar:** Full bar. **Reservations:** accepted. **Hours:** 11 am-9 pm, Fri & Sat-10 pm; to 10 pm in summer. Closed major holidays. **Address:** 1424 W 2nd St **Location:** I-84, exit 83 eastbound, just se on W 6th St, just n on Webber St, then just se; exit 85 westbound, just nw. **Parking:** on-site. **Cards:** AX, DS, MC, VI.

COUSINS' RESTAURANT AND SALOON Phone: 541/298-2771

American
$7-$20

This fun place has home-style cooking along the lines of pot roast, roast turkey and homemade biscuits, breads and pies in a country-cousin atmosphere. The establishment is renowned for its giant cinnamon rolls. Breakfast is served all day, and daily blue plate specials are good choices. The dining room's "milk house" section is complete with cowhide booths and milk can seats at the counter. Casual dress. **Bar:** Full bar. **Reservations:** not accepted. **Hours:** 6 am-10 pm; to 9 pm in winter. Closed: 12/25. **Address:** 2114 W 6th St **Location:** I-84, exit 83 eastbound, just nw; exit 84 westbound, just nw on W 2nd St, just sw on Webber St, then just n; in Cousins Country Inn. **Parking:** on-site. **Cards:** AX, DC, DS, MC, VI.

WINDSEEKER RESTAURANT & PORTSIDE PUB

Phone: 541/298-7171

American
$6-$22

On the banks of the Columbia River, the restaurant prepares steaks, seafood, pasta, burgers and fresh salads. Good choices include salmon Oscar (rock shrimp in Alfredo sauce served over a salmon fillet, fried razor clams or stuffed halibut) and an 8-ounce fillet of Alaskan halibut stuffed with bay shrimp and blue cheese, oven baked and finished with raspberry beurre blanc sauce. During nice weather, diners can opt for outside seating. Casual dress. **Bar:** Full bar. **Reservations:** suggested, weekends & holidays. **Hours:** 11 am-9 pm, Sat & Sun from 9 am; Sunday brunch. **Address:** 1535 Barge Way Rd **Location:** I-84, exit 83 eastbound; exit 84 westbound, follow signs to Port area, cross railroad tracks, then just e. **Parking:** on-site. **Cards:** AX, DS, MC, VI.

TIGARD —See Portland p. 468.

TILLAMOOK pop. 4,352

——— WHERE TO STAY ———

BEST WESTERN INN & SUITES   *Book great rates at AAA.com*

Phone: (503)842-7599

Hotel
$130-$200 3/1-9/30
$98-$150 10/1-2/28

Address: 1722 N Makinster Rd **Location:** 1 mi n on US 101. **Facility:** Smoke free premises. 51 one-bedroom standard units. 3 stories, interior corridors. *Bath:* combo or shower only. **Parking:** on-site. **Terms:** check-in 4 pm, 7 day cancellation notice-fee imposed. **Amenities:** video library (fee), DVD players, high-speed Internet, safes, irons, hair dryers. **Pool(s):** heated indoor/outdoor. **Leisure Activities:** sauna, whirlpool, limited exercise equipment. **Guest Services:** coin laundry, wireless Internet. **Business Services:** business center. **Cards:** AX, DS, MC, VI. **Free Special Amenities:** expanded continental breakfast and high-speed Internet.

AAA Benefit:
Members save up to 20%, plus 10% bonus points with rewards program.

MAR-CLAIR INN

Phone: (503)842-7571

Motel
$86-$106 All Year

Address: 11 Main Ave **Location:** US 101, just n of jct SR 6. **Facility:** 47 units. 41 one-bedroom standard units. 6 one-bedroom suites with kitchens. 1-2 stories (no elevator), interior/exterior corridors. *Bath:* combo or shower only. **Parking:** on-site. **Pool(s):** outdoor. **Leisure Activities:** sauna, whirlpool. **Guest Services:** beauty salon, tanning facilities. **Cards:** AX, DS, MC, VI.

▼ See AAA listing p 512 ▼

SHILO INN SUITES HOTEL-TILLAMOOK *Book great rates at AAA.com*

Phone: (503)842-7971

AAA SAVE

Hotel
$95-$200 All Year

Address: 2515 Main Ave **Location:** 1 mi n on US 101. **Facility:** 101 units. 100 one-bedroom standard units, some with efficiencies. 1 one-bedroom suite with kitchen. 2 stories (no elevator), interior corridors. **Parking:** on-site. **Terms:** check-in 4 pm. **Amenities:** high-speed Internet, voice mail, irons, hair dryers. **Pool(s):** heated indoor. **Leisure Activities:** sauna, whirlpool, steamroom, fish cleaning facilities, exercise room. **Guest Services:** coin laundry, airport transportation-Tillamook Airport, wireless Internet. **Business Services:** meeting rooms, PC. **Cards:** AX, CB, DC, DS, JC, MC, VI. **Free Special Amenities:** newspaper and high-speed Internet. *(See color ad p 511)*

--------- WHERE TO DINE ---------

BLUE HERON FRENCH CHEESE COMPANY

Phone: 503/842-8281

AAA

American
$5-$7

Resembling an old barn, the simple, no-frills restaurant carries that theme into its country decor and its menu of delicatessen-style fare. An espresso bar sits in the middle of the dining area, and a wine-tasting and cheese-sampling area is in the back. Picnic tables let diners enjoy the view of the coastal range on a clear day. Casual dress. **Bar:** Beer & wine. **Reservations:** not accepted. **Hours:** 8 am-8 pm; 9 am-6 pm 10/1-5/31. Closed: 11/26, 12/25. **Address:** 2001 Blue Heron Dr **Location:** 0.9 mi n on US 101. **Parking:** on-site. **Cards:** AX, DS, MC, VI.

TIMBERLINE LODGE

--------- WHERE TO STAY ---------

TIMBERLINE LODGE

Phone: (503)622-7979

Classic Historic
Hotel
$130-$325 All Year

Address: 27500 Timberline Rd **Location:** Off US 26; 6 mi n of Government Camp jct at 6000 ft level. Located on south slope of Mount Hood. **Facility:** Built by artisans in 1937, this mountain resort lodge features well-maintained guest rooms (some with fireplaces) and an on-site museum. Smoke free premises. 71 one-bedroom standard units. 3 stories, interior corridors. *Bath:* some shared or private, shower only. **Parking:** on-site. **Terms:** check-in 4 pm, 7 day cancellation notice. **Amenities:** video library, voice mail. *Some:* DVD players, irons, hair dryers. **Dining:** Cascade Dining Room At Timberline Lodge, see separate listing. **Pool(s):** heated outdoor. **Leisure Activities:** sauna, whirlpool, downhill skiing, hiking trails, exercise room. **Guest Services:** complimentary laundry, wireless Internet. **Business Services:** meeting rooms, PC. **Cards:** AX, DS, MC, VI.

--------- WHERE TO DINE ---------

CASCADE DINING ROOM AT TIMBERLINE LODGE

Phone: 503/272-3700

Regional
Continental
$14-$39

Guests can experience fine dining in the impressive, hand-crafted lodge, which was built on a mountainside during the Depression. Still sporting the original 1937 Cascadian architecture and artwork, the location is an excellent spot for Pacific Northwest cuisine. Casual dress. **Bar:** Full bar. **Reservations:** suggested. **Hours:** 7:30 am-10, noon-2 & 6-8 pm. **Address:** 27500 Timberline Rd **Location:** Off US 26; 6 mi n of Government Camp jct at 6000 ft level; in Timberline Lodge. **Parking:** on-site. **Cards:** AX, DC, DS, MC, VI. **Classic Historic**

CALL

TROUTDALE *—See Portland p. 472.*

TUALATIN *—See Portland p. 473.*

WALDPORT pop. 2,050

--------- WHERE TO STAY ---------

CLIFF HOUSE BED & BREAKFAST

Phone: (541)563-2506

Historic Bed
& Breakfast
$110-$225 All Year

Address: 1450 Adahi Rd **Location:** Jct SR 34, 0.8 mi s on US 101, then just w. **Facility:** This rustic-looking restored home with balconies and antique wood-burning stoves is nestled on a coastal bluff on Yaquina John Point. Smoke free premises. 4 one-bedroom standard units, some with whirlpools. 2 stories (no elevator), interior/exterior corridors. *Bath:* combo or shower only. **Parking:** on-site. **Terms:** office hours 7:30 am-10 pm, 2 night minimum stay - seasonal and/or weekends, age restrictions may apply, 14 day cancellation notice-fee imposed. **Amenities:** video library, CD players, high-speed Internet, hair dryers. **Leisure Activities:** whirlpool, beach access, putting green. *Fee:* massage. **Guest Services:** wireless Internet. **Cards:** MC, VI.

WARRENTON pop. 4,096

------ WHERE TO STAY ------

SHILO INN SUITES HOTEL - WARRENTON/ASTORIA   *Book great rates at AAA.com*   Phone: (503)861-2181

AAA (SAVE)

◇◇◇◇

Hotel

$125-$250 All Year

Address: 1609 E Harbor Dr **Location:** On US 26/101; near west end of Young's Bay Bridge. **Facility:** 63 units. 62 one-bedroom standard units, some with efficiencies. 1 one-bedroom suite with kitchen. 4 stories, interior corridors. **Parking:** on-site. **Terms:** check-in 4 pm. **Amenities:** video games (fee), high-speed Internet, voice mail, irons, hair dryers. **Pool(s):** heated indoor. **Leisure Activities:** sauna, whirlpool, steamroom, exercise room. **Guest Services:** valet and coin laundry, airport transportation-Astoria Airport, wireless Internet. **Business Services:** meeting rooms, PC. **Cards:** AX, CB, DC, DS, JC, MC, VI. **Free Special Amenities: continental breakfast and high-speed Internet.** *(See color ad below)*

（icons） / SOME UNITS FEE ⊡ ⊠

------ WHERE TO DINE ------

DOOGERS SEAFOOD & GRILL   Phone: 503/861-2839

◇◇ ◇◇

Seafood

$9-$38

Popular with families, the comfortable restaurant is rustic in decor with quaint touches. On the menu are traditional preparations of primarily seafood dishes, with a handful of pasta, chicken and beef entrees. Casual dress. **Bar:** Full bar. **Reservations:** not accepted. **Hours:** 8 am-9 pm, Fri & Sat-10 pm; to 10 pm in summer. Closed: 11/26, 12/25. **Address:** 103 S US 101 **Location:** US 26/101; near west end of Young's Bay Bridge. **Parking:** on-site. **Cards:** AX, DS, MC, VI.

WELCHES

------ WHERE TO STAY ------

THE CABINS CREEKSIDE AT WELCHES   Phone: (503)622-4275

AAA (SAVE)

◇◇ ◇◇

Motel

$119-$139 All Year

Address: 25080 E Welches Rd **Location:** 0.0 mi s of US 20. **Facility:** Smoke free premises. 9 one-bedroom standard units with kitchens. 1 story, exterior corridors. **Parking:** on-site. **Terms:** office hours 11 am-6:30 pm, 7 day cancellation notice-fee imposed. **Amenities:** video library, DVD players, high-speed Internet, irons, hair dryers. **Leisure Activities:** whirlpool. **Guest Services:** coin laundry, wireless Internet. **Cards:** AX, DS, MC, VI.

（icons）

▼ *See AAA listing above* ▼

THE RESORT AT THE MOUNTAIN   *Book great rates at AAA.com*   **Phone:** (503)622-3101

AAA [SAVE]

▼▼▼▼
Resort
Hotel
$139-$475 5/1-2/28
$450 3/1-4/30

Address: 68010 E Fairway Ave **Location:** 0.8 mi s of US 26 on E Welches Rd. Located in a forest setting. **Facility:** A Scottish ambiance pervades this resort, which is in a scenic mountain setting with landscaped grounds near the ski area; guest suites have balconies. Smoke free premises. 160 units. 144 one-bedroom standard units. 8 one- and 4 two-bedroom suites, some with efficiencies. 4 houses. 2 stories, exterior corridors. *Bath:* combo or shower only. **Parking:** on-site. **Terms:** check-in 4 pm, 3 day cancellation notice-fee imposed. **Amenities:** video library (fee), DVD players, voice mail, irons, hair dryers. *Some:* high-speed Internet. **Dining:** 2 restaurants. **Pool(s):** heated outdoor. **Leisure Activities:** whirlpool, fishing, 4 tennis courts, recreation programs in summer, badminton, bicycles, hiking trails, jogging, playground, exercise room, volleyball. *Fee:* golf-27 holes, croquet, lawn bowling, massage. **Guest Services:** coin laundry, area transportation, wireless Internet. **Business Services:** conference facilities, PC. **Cards:** AX, DC, DS, MC, VI. **(See color ad below)**

[icons] / SOME UNITS FEE [icons]

WHISPERING WOODS RESORT   *Book great rates at AAA.com*   **Phone:** (503)622-3171

AAA [SAVE]

▼▼▼
Condominium
$139-$209 All Year

Address: 67800 E Nicklaus Way **Location:** 0.8 mi s of US 26 on Welches Rd, just w on Woodruff Way. **Facility:** Offering very well-equipped and nicely maintained units, many with views of an adjacent golf course or forest; convenient to Mount Hood. Smoke free premises. 65 units. 16 one- and 49 two-bedroom suites with kitchens. 1-3 stories (no elevator), exterior corridors. **Parking:** on-site. **Terms:** office hours 8 am-8 pm, check-in 5 pm, 3 day cancellation notice-fee imposed. **Amenities:** video library (fee), DVD players, CD players, irons, hair dryers. **Pool(s):** heated outdoor. **Leisure Activities:** sauna, whirlpool, recreation programs, barbecue grills, playground, exercise room, basketball. *Fee:* tennis racquets, bicycles. **Guest Services:** complimentary laundry, wireless Internet. **Cards:** AX, DC, DS, MC, VI.

[icons]

▼ *See AAA listing above* ▼

——— **WHERE TO DINE** ———

BACKYARD BISTRO　　　　　　　　　　　　　　　　　　　Phone: 503/622-6302

▼▼ ▼▼
American
$6-$14

Nicely prepared food items, including the highly recommended zucchini patty appetizers, are served in an attractive setting, which includes a delightful seasonal patio. Casual dress. **Bar:** Wine only. **Reservations:** accepted. **Hours:** 11 am-8 pm, Sun 10 am-4 pm. Closed: 11/26, 12/25; also Mon. **Address:** 67898 E US 26 **Location:** On US 26. **Parking:** on-site. **Cards:** AX, DS, MC, VI.

AC

THE RENDEZVOUS GRILL　　　　　　　　　　　　　　　　Phone: 503/622-6837

▼▼ ▼▼
American
$8-$24

The restaurant is known for its innovative cuisine. Blending elements of traditional Pacific Northwest and pasta dishes is the signature creation of alder-smoked chicken and fresh rigatoni with dried cranberries and toasted hazelnuts in champagne cream sauce. Another good choice is Dungeness crab and bay shrimp cakes with chipotle aioli. The master baker creates sinful desserts on the premises. The open, airy patio is a great place to relax. Dressy casual. **Bar:** Full bar. **Reservations:** suggested. **Hours:** 11:30 am-9 pm. Closed: 11/26, 12/24, 12/25. **Address:** 67149 E US 26 **Location:** 15 mi e of Sandy; 0.5 mi w of Welches Rd; at Milepost 40. **Parking:** on-site. **Cards:** AX, DS, MC, VI.

WEST LINN —See Portland p. 474.

WHEELER pop. 391

——— **WHERE TO STAY** ———

OLD WHEELER HOTEL　　　　　　　　　　　　　　　　　Phone: (503)368-6000

▼▼ ▼▼
Bed & Breakfast
$65-$150 All Year

Address: 495 US 101 **Location:** On US 101; center. **Facility:** Smoke free premises. 7 one-bedroom standard units, some with whirlpools. 2 stories, interior corridors. *Bath:* combo or shower only. **Parking:** street. **Terms:** 7 day cancellation notice-fee imposed. **Amenities:** video library, DVD players, high-speed Internet. **Guest Services:** wireless Internet. **Business Services:** PC. **Cards:** AX, DS, MC, VI.

ASK ▥✚ ✕ ☎

WHEELER ON THE BAY LODGE AND MARINA　　　　　Phone: 503/368-5858

▼▼
Motel
$80-$155 All Year

Address: 580 Marine Dr **Location:** On US 101; center. Located on Nehalem Bay. **Facility:** Smoke free premises. 10 one-bedroom standard units, some with whirlpools. 1 story, exterior corridors. *Bath:* combo or shower only. **Parking:** on site. **Terms:** office hours 9 am-10 pm, 3 day cancellation notice-fee imposed. **Amenities:** video library (fee), DVD players. **Leisure Activities:** fishing. *Fee:* boat dock, charter fishing, massage. **Cards:** AX, MC, VI.

▥✚ ✕ ✕ AC VCR ▥ ▤ ▤ ▥ / SOME UNITS FEE ▥

WILSONVILLE —See Portland p. 474.

WINSTON pop. 4,613

──────── WHERE TO STAY ────────

SWEET BREEZE INN II
Phone: (541)679-2420

(AAA) (SAVE)
▼▼▼
Motel
$49-$89 All Year

Address: 251 NE Main St **Location:** I-5, exit 119, 3 mi w. **Facility:** Smoke free premises. 32 one-bedroom standard units. 2 stories (no elevator), exterior corridors. *Bath:* combo or shower only. **Parking:** on-site. **Terms:** 3 day cancellation notice-fee imposed. **Cards:** AX, CB, DC, DS, MC, VI.

📶 ✕ 🔲 🖼 / SOME UNITS FEE 🐕

WOLF CREEK

──────── WHERE TO STAY ────────

──────── *The following lodging was either not evaluated or did not* ────────
meet AAA rating requirements but is listed for your information only.

WOLF CREEK INN
Phone: 541/866-2474

[fyi]

Not evaluated. **Address:** 100 Front St **Location:** I-5, exit 76, just w. Facilities, services, and decor characterize a mid-scale property.

──────── WHERE TO DINE ────────

──────── *The following restaurant has not been evaluated by AAA* ────────
but is listed for your information only.

WOLF CREEK INN
Phone: 541/866-2474

[fyi]

Not evaluated. Serving lunch and dinner, the 1883 hostelry offers traditional dishes reminiscent of those served in a bygone country inn, along with creative fare. Specialty theme dinners are prepared throughout the year. **Address:** 100 Front St **Location:** I-5, exit 76, just w; in Wolf Creek Inn.

WOODBURN pop. 20,100

──────── WHERE TO STAY ────────

BEST WESTERN WOODBURN INN   *Book great rates at AAA.com*
Phone: (503)982-6515

(AAA) (SAVE)
▼▼▼
Hotel
$99-$229 All Year

Address: 2887 Newburg Hwy **Location:** I-5, exit 271, just ne. Located near an outlet mall. **Facility:** 81 units. 79 one-bedroom standard units, some with whirlpools. 3 one-bedroom suites. 3 stories, interior corridors. *Bath:* combo or shower only. **Parking:** on-site. **Terms:** 3 day cancellation notice. **Amenities:** high-speed Internet, voice mail, irons, hair dryers. **Pool(s):** heated outdoor. **Leisure Activities:** whirlpool, exercise room. **Guest Services:** coin laundry, wireless Internet. **Business Services:** meeting rooms, business center. **Cards:** AX, CB, DC, DS, JC, MC, VI. **Free Special Amenities: continental breakfast.**

📶 CALL 🖥 🏊 🎥 🔲 🖼 🖳 / SOME UNITS FEE 🐕 ✕

> Best Western
>
> **AAA Benefit:**
> Members save up to
> 20%, plus 10%
> bonus points with
> rewards program.

LA QUINTA INN & SUITES WOODBURN   *Book great rates at AAA.com*
Phone: (503)982-1727

▼▼▼
Hotel
$59-$104 All Year

Address: 120 Arney Rd NE **Location:** I-5, exit 271, just nw. Located near an outlet mall. **Facility:** 60 units. 46 one- and 1 two-bedroom standard units, some with kitchens and/or whirlpools. 13 one-bedroom suites with efficiencies. 3 stories, interior corridors. **Parking:** on-site. **Amenities:** high-speed Internet, irons, hair dryers. *Some:* DVD players. **Pool(s):** heated outdoor. **Leisure Activities:** whirlpool, exercise room. **Guest Services:** coin laundry, wireless Internet. **Business Services:** business center. **Cards:** AX, DC, DS, MC, VI.

(ASK) 📶 🏊 🎥 🖳 / SOME UNITS 🐕 ✕ (VCR) 🔲 🖼

WOOD VILLAGE —See Portland p. 475.

YACHATS pop. 617

──────── WHERE TO STAY ────────

THE ADOBE RESORT
Phone: (541)547-3141

(AAA) (SAVE)
▼▼▼
Hotel
$75-$405 All Year

Address: 1555 US 101 **Location:** Oceanfront. 0.5 mi n; just w of US 101. **Facility:** Smoke free premises. 110 units. 103 one-bedroom standard units, some with whirlpools. 2 one- and 5 two-bedroom suites, some with kitchens. 2-3 stories, interior corridors. *Bath:* combo or shower only. **Parking:** on-site. **Terms:** check-in 4 pm, cancellation fee imposed. **Amenities:** video library (fee), DVD players, high-speed Internet, voice mail, irons, hair dryers. *Some:* CD players. **Pool(s):** heated indoor. **Leisure Activities:** sauna, whirlpool, beach access, exercise room, game room. *Fee:* massage. **Guest Services:** coin laundry, wireless Internet. **Business Services:** conference facilities, PC. **Cards:** AX, CB, DC, DS, JC, MC, VI. **Free Special Amenities: high-speed Internet.** *(See color ad p 517)*

📶 🍽 🏊 🎿 ✕ 🎿 🎥 🔲 🖼 🖳 / SOME UNITS FEE 🐕

THE DUBLIN HOUSE

Motel
$49-$135 All Year

Phone: 541/547-3703
Address: 251 W 7th St **Location:** US 101 at 7th St; downtown. **Facility:** 27 one-bedroom standard units, some with kitchens. 2 stories (no elevator), exterior corridors. *Bath:* combo or shower only. **Parking:** on-site. **Terms:** office hours 9 am-10 pm. **Pool(s):** heated indoor. **Cards:** DS, MC, VI.

FIRESIDE MOTEL

AAA SAVE

Motel
$60-$155 All Year

Phone: (541)547-3636
Address: 1881 US 101 N **Location:** Oceanfront. 0.6 mi n; just w of US 101. **Facility:** Smoke free premises. 43 units. 42 one-bedroom standard units, some with whirlpools. 1 one-bedroom suite with kitchen. 2 stories (no elevator), exterior corridors. **Parking:** on-site. **Terms:** office hours 8 am-10 pm, cancellation fee imposed. **Amenities:** video library (fee), DVD players, high-speed Internet, hair dryers. **Leisure Activities:** walking trail along ocean, barbecue grills, picnic area, hiking trails, jogging. *Fee:* massage. **Guest Services:** wireless Internet. **Cards:** AX, DS, MC, VI. **Free Special Amenities:** local telephone calls and high-speed Internet. *(See color ad below)*

OVERLEAF LODGE

AAA SAVE

Hotel
$135-$450 All Year

Phone: (541)547-4880
Address: 280 Overleaf Lodge Ln **Location:** Oceanfront. 0.6 mi n; just w of US 101. **Facility:** Smoke free premises. 60 units. 50 one-bedroom standard units, some with efficiencies and/or whirlpools. 3 one- and 1 two-bedroom suites, some with efficiencies, kitchens and/or whirlpools. 6 houses. 3 stories, interior/exterior corridors. *Bath:* combo or shower only. **Parking:** on-site. **Terms:** office hours 8 am-10 pm, cancellation fee imposed. **Amenities:** video library (fee), DVD players, CD players, high-speed Internet, irons, hair dryers. **Leisure Activities:** sauna, picnic tables, walking trail along ocean, hiking trails, jogging, exercise room, spa. **Guest Services:** complimentary laundry, wireless Internet. **Business Services:** meeting rooms, business center. **Cards:** AX, DS, MC, VI. **Free Special Amenities:** expanded continental breakfast and high-speed Internet. *(See color ad below)*

SEA QUEST INN BED & BREAKFAST

Phone: 541/547-3782

Bed & Breakfast
$145-$350 All Year

Address: 95354 US 101 **Location:** Oceanfront. Between MM 171 and 172, 6 mi s, then just w. Located in a secluded rural area along the coast. **Facility:** A rambling, seaside B&B with splendid ocean views, the Sea Quest features distinctive decor and accommodating, gregarious staff. Smoke free premises. 7 one-bedroom standard units, some with whirlpools. 2 stories (no elevator), interior corridors. *Bath:* combo or shower only. **Parking:** on-site. **Terms:** 10 day cancellation notice-fee imposed. **Amenities:** video library, CD players, high-speed Internet, hair dryers. *Some:* DVD players. **Leisure Activities:** beach access. **Guest Services:** wireless Internet. **Business Services:** PC. **Cards:** AX, DS, MC, VI.

SHAMROCK LODGETTES   *Book at AAA.com*

Phone: 541/547-3312

Cabin
Rates not provided

Address: 105 US 101 S **Location:** On US 101, just s. **Facility:** Designated smoking area. 21 units. 12 one-bedroom standard units, some with efficiencies. 9 cabins. 1 story, exterior corridors. *Bath:* combo or shower only. **Parking:** on-site. **Terms:** office hours 9 am-9 pm. **Amenities:** *Some:* DVD players. **Leisure Activities:** sauna, whirlpool, beach access, exercise room.

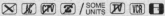

──────── **WHERE TO DINE** ────────

THE DRIFT INN

Phone: 541/547-4477

American
$10-$22

Patrons can sample seafood entrees and Northwestern crafted beers while enjoying a partial ocean view. Entertainment is provided on weekends. Casual dress. **Bar:** Full bar. **Reservations:** not accepted. **Hours:** 8 am-10 pm. Closed: 12/25. **Address:** 124 US 101 N **Location:** Downtown. **Parking:** street. **Cards:** MC, VI.

Washington

Mount Vernon
© William Neill
Larry Ulrich Stock

ABERDEEN pop. 16,461—*See also HOQUIAM.*

——— WHERE TO STAY ———

A HARBOR VIEW BED AND BREAKFAST   Phone: 360/533-7996

Bed & Breakfast
$139-$250 All Year

Address: 111 W 11th St **Location:** US 101, 1 mi n on Broadway, then just w. Located in the Historic Broadway Hill District. **Facility:** Built in 1905, this B&B is decorated mainly with Victorian pieces, heirloom quilts and some modern American pieces. Smoke free premises. 5 units. 4 one-bedroom standard units. 1 two-bedroom suite with kitchen. 2 stories (no elevator), interior corridors. *Bath:* combo or shower only. **Parking:** on-site. **Terms:** check-in 4 pm, 2 night minimum stay - seasonal and/or weekends, age restrictions may apply, 7 day cancellation notice-fee imposed. **Amenities:** video library, DVD players, high-speed Internet, irons, hair dryers. **Guest Services:** wireless Internet. **Business Services:** PC. **Cards:** AX, MC, VI.

GUESTHOUSE INTERNATIONAL INN & SUITES   *Book at AAA.com*   Phone: 360/537-7460

Hotel
Rates not provided

Address: 701 E Heron St **Location:** Just e on US 12, cross street to Kansas St; downtown. **Facility:** 87 units. 76 one- and 2 two-bedroom standard units, some with whirlpools. 9 one-bedroom suites with efficiencies. 3 stories, interior corridors. *Bath:* combo or shower only. **Parking:** on-site. **Amenities:** video library (fee), high-speed Internet, voice mail, irons, hair dryers. *Some:* video games (fee). **Pool(s):** heated indoor. **Leisure Activities:** whirlpool, exercise room. **Guest Services:** coin laundry, wireless Internet. **Business Services:** meeting rooms, business center.

——— WHERE TO DINE ———

BRIDGES RESTAURANT   Phone: 360/532-6563

American
$9-$27

Contributing to a relaxed, fine-dining atmosphere are brass, glass and dark wood paneling. The menu centers on the classics: steak, lobster, chicken and prime rib. **Bar:** Full bar. **Reservations:** suggested. **Hours:** 11 am-9 pm, Fri & Sat-10 pm, Sun 4 pm-9 pm. Closed: 1/1, 7/4, 12/25. **Address:** 112 N G St **Location:** 1st and G sts. **Parking:** on-site. **Cards:** AX, CB, DC, DS, MC, VI.

AIRWAY HEIGHTS pop. 4,500

——— WHERE TO STAY ———

DAYS INN & SUITES   *Book great rates at AAA.com*   Phone: 509/244-0222

Hotel
Rates not provided

Address: 1215 S Garfield Rd **Location:** I-90, exit 277 to SR 2, 4 mi w. **Facility:** 61 one-bedroom standard units, some with whirlpools. 2 stories (no elevator), interior corridors. *Bath:* combo or shower only. **Parking:** on-site, winter plug-ins. **Amenities:** voice mail, irons, hair dryers. **Guest Services:** wireless Internet. **Business Services:** meeting rooms, business center. **Free Special Amenities:** continental breakfast and high-speed Internet.

STRATFORD SUITES   *Book at AAA.com*   Phone: (509)321-1600

Hotel
$129-$225 All Year

Address: 11808 W Center Ln **Location:** I-90, exit 277, 4 mi w on SR 2. **Facility:** Smoke free premises. 60 two-bedroom suites with kitchens. 1 story, exterior corridors. *Bath:* combo or shower only. **Parking:** on-site. **Terms:** office hours 8 am-6 pm, cancellation fee imposed. **Amenities:** DVD players, high-speed Internet, voice mail, irons. **Guest Services:** complimentary laundry, wireless Internet. **Business Services:** business center. **Cards:** AX, DS, MC, VI.

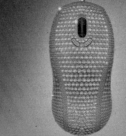

ANACORTES pop. 14,557

───── WHERE TO STAY ─────

ANACO BAY INN

(AAA) (SAVE)

▼▼▼▼

Hotel
$64-$139 All Year

Phone: 360/299-3320

Address: 916 33rd St **Location:** Just s of downtown. Located in a commerical area. **Facility:** Smoke free premises. 22 units. 17 one-bedroom standard units, some with efficiencies and/or whirlpools. 1 one- and 4 two-bedroom suites, some with efficiencies or kitchens. 2 stories (no elevator), interior corridors. **Parking:** on-site. **Terms:** office hours 7 am-10 pm, 2 night minimum stay - seasonal and/or weekends, 3 day cancellation notice. **Amenities:** video library (fee), high-speed Internet, dual phone lines, hair dryers. *Some:* irons. **Leisure Activities:** whirlpool. **Guest Services:** coin laundry, wireless Internet. **Business Services:** PC. **Cards:** AX, DS, MC, VI. **Free Special Amenities: expanded continental breakfast and local telephone calls.** *(See color ad below)*

FEE (icons)

▼ See AAA listing p 522 ▼

Anaco Inn

anacoinn@verizon.net
www.anacoinn.com

"Your Home Away From Home"

Jetted Tubs • Fire Places • Cont. Breakfast

Kitchen • Non-smoking • Rooms with view

Spa Services • Security Cameras

Gateway to the San Juans • 7 min from Ferry

905 20th Street Anacortes, WA 98221

Reservations: **(888) 293-8833**
(360) 293-8833

▼ See AAA listing above ▼

ANACO Bay Inn

An Elegant Affordable European Style Inn

Fireplaces • Jetted Tubs • Cont. Breakfast • Kitchens
Non-Smoking • Hot Tub with View • Security
Conference Room • WiFi • Business Center Amenities

916 33rd Street • Anacortes WA 98221 • 360-299-3320

RESERVATIONS **877-299-3320** • anacobayinn.com

ANACO INN

Hotel
$79-$149 3/1-9/15
$59-$109 9/16-2/28

Phone: 360/293-8833

Address: 905 20th St **Location:** Just s of downtown. Located in a commercial area. **Facility:** Smoke free premises. 14 units. 9 one-bedroom standard units, some with efficiencies and/or whirlpools. 3 one- and 2 two-bedroom suites, some with efficiencies or kitchens. 2 stories (no elevator), interior/exterior corridors. **Parking:** on-site. **Terms:** office hours 7 am-10 pm, 3 day cancellation notice-fee imposed. **Amenities:** video library (fee), high-speed Internet, hair dryers. **Guest Services:** coin laundry, wireless Internet. **Cards:** AX, DS, MC, VI. **Free Special Amenities:** continental breakfast and high-speed Internet.
(See color ad p 521)

ANACORTES INN

Motel
Rates not provided

Phone: 360/293-3153

Address: 3006 Commercial Ave **Location:** Just s of downtown. Located in a commercial area. **Facility:** 44 one-bedroom standard units, some with efficiencies and/or whirlpools. 2 stories (no elevator), exterior corridors. **Parking:** on-site. **Terms:** office hours 7 am-11 pm. **Amenities:** high-speed Internet. **Pool(s):** heated outdoor. **Guest Services:** wireless Internet. **Free Special Amenities:** continental breakfast and high-speed Internet.

ANACORTES SHIP HARBOR INN

Motel
Rates not provided

Phone: 360/293-5177

Address: 5316 Ferry Terminal Rd **Location:** 0.3 mi s of ferry landing. **Facility:** Smoke free premises. 28 units. 19 one-bedroom standard units, some with efficiencies and/or whirlpools. 2 one-bedroom suites with whirlpools. 1 house and 6 cottages. 2 stories (no elevator), exterior corridors. **Parking:** on-site. **Amenities:** hair dryers. *Some:* irons. **Guest Services:** coin laundry, wireless Internet. **Free Special Amenities:** expanded continental breakfast and high-speed Internet.

▼ See AAA listing p 523 ▼

CAP SANTE INN

(AAA) (SAVE)

◆◆◆ ◆◆◆

Motel
$78-$135 3/1-9/30
$68-$105 10/1-2/28

Phone: 360/293-0602
Address: 906 9th St **Location:** On 9th St, just e. **Facility:** Smoke free premises. 34 units. 33 one- and 1 two-bedroom standard units. 2 stories (no elevator), exterior corridors. *Bath:* combo or shower only. **Parking:** on-site. **Terms:** office hours 7 am-11 pm. **Amenities:** high-speed Internet, hair dryers. **Guest Services:** coin laundry, wireless Internet. **Cards:** AX, DS, MC, VI. **Free Special Amenities:** continental breakfast and high-speed Internet. *(See color ad p 522)*

[⊞+] [⊠] [⊠] [⊟] [⊡] / SOME UNITS FEE [⊞]

FIDALGO COUNTRY INN & SUITES *Book great rates at AAA.com*

◆◆◆ ◆◆◆

Hotel
$100-$400 3/1-9/30
$90-$400 10/1-2/28

Phone: (360)293-3494
Address: 7645 SR 20 **Location:** Jct Fidalgo Bay Rd. **Facility:** 50 units. 48 one-bedroom standard units. 2 one-bedroom suites with whirlpools. 2 stories (no elevator), interior/exterior corridors. **Parking:** on-site. **Terms:** cancellation fee imposed. **Amenities:** high-speed Internet, irons, hair dryers. *Some:* DVD players. **Pool(s):** heated outdoor. **Leisure Activities:** whirlpool. **Guest Services:** coin laundry, wireless Internet. **Business Services:** meeting rooms, PC. **Cards:** AX, DC, DS, MC, VI. *(See color ad below)*

[ASK] [⊞+] CALL [⊆M] [⊇] [▣] [⊟] [⊡] [⊡] / SOME UNITS FEE [⊞] [⊠] [VCR]

HERON HOUSE GUEST SUITES

◆◆◆ ◆◆◆

Bed & Breakfast
$180-$235 All Year

Phone: 360/293-4477
Address: 11110 Marine Dr **Location:** From ferry terminal, just w on Sunset Ave, then 2 mi s on Anaco Beach Dr/Marine Dr. **Facility:** From the wrap-around porch the B&B offers views of the setting sun over Burrow's Bay, the San Juan Islands and the Olympic mountain range. Smoke free premises. 4 units. 2 one-bedroom standard units with whirlpools. 2 one-bedroom suites. 2 stories (no elevator), interior/exterior corridors. *Bath:* combo or shower only. **Parking:** on-site. **Terms:** check-in 4 pm, 7 day cancellation notice-fee imposed. **Amenities:** video library, DVD players, CD players, voice mail, hair dryers. **Guest Services:** area transportation, wireless Internet. **Cards:** MC, VI.

[ASK] [⊬] [⊠]

▼ See AAA listing p 524 ▼

The Marina Inn

AAA
◆◆◆ ◆◆◆

- 24 hour service with warm and friendly staff
- Fresh hot baked cookies every night
- Expanded Continental Breakfast
- Children Under 12 Stay Free
- Free Wireless Internet
- Jacuzzi Tub Rooms
- Queen / King Beds

3300 Commercial Ave • Anacortes, Washington 98221
Phone / Fax: 360-293-1100
themarinainn@comcast.net • www.marinainnwa.com

▼ See AAA listing above ▼

Fidalgo Country Inn
WELCOME TO FIDALGO ISLAND.

50 deluxe air conditioned rooms and suites
• Non-smoking rooms • Full breakfast • Free Wireless
• Hospitality room for groups up to 40 • Outdoor pool
& Hot Tub • 10-minute drive to State Parks and ferry
service to San Juan Islands and Sidney, B.C.

7645 SR 20, Anacortes, WA 98221
360-293-3494 • fidalgocountryinn.com

FOR RESERVATIONS CALL: 1-800-244-4179

ISLANDS INN

Motel
$94-$150 3/1-9/30
$79-$110 10/1-2/28

Phone: 360/293-4644

Address: 3401 Commercial Ave **Location:** Just s of downtown. **Facility:** 36 units. 30 one-bedroom standard units. 6 one-bedroom suites. 2 stories (no elevator), exterior corridors. **Parking:** on-site. **Terms:** office hours 6:30 am-11 pm, cancellation fee imposed. **Amenities:** voice mail, hair dryers. *Some:* DVD players, high-speed Internet. **Pool(s):** heated outdoor. **Leisure Activities:** whirlpool. **Guest Services:** wireless Internet. **Business Services:** PC. **Cards:** AX, DS, MC, VI.

ASK ⏸ 🏊 📶 🖥 / SOME UNITS FEE 🐕 ✕ 🍴

MAJESTIC INN & SPA

Hotel
$189-$219 All Year

Phone: (360)299-1400

Address: 419 Commercial Ave **Location:** Downtown. **Facility:** Smoke free premises. 21 units. 20 one-bedroom standard units. 1 one-bedroom suite with whirlpool. 5 stories, interior corridors. **Parking:** on-site. **Amenities:** video library (fee), DVD players, CD players, high-speed Internet, voice mail, irons, hair dryers. **Leisure Activities:** spa. **Guest Services:** area transportation-within 5 mi, wireless Internet. **Business Services:** meeting rooms. **Cards:** AX, MC, VI. **Free Special Amenities:** newspaper and high-speed Internet.

⏸ 🍽 ♿ ✕ 🍴 📷 / SOME UNITS FEE 🐕 📶 🖥

MARINA INN

Hotel
$74-$119 All Year

Phone: (360)293-1100

Address: 3300 Commercial Ave **Location:** Just s of downtown. Located in a commercial area. **Facility:** 52 one-bedroom standard units, some with whirlpools. 2 stories (no elevator), interior corridors. **Parking:** on-site. **Terms:** cancellation fee imposed. **Amenities:** high-speed Internet, hair dryers. **Guest Services:** coin laundry, wireless Internet. **Cards:** AX, DC, DS, MC, VI. **Free Special Amenities:** expanded continental breakfast and high-speed Internet. *(See color ad p 523)*

✕ 📷 📶 🖥 🖥 / SOME UNITS 🍴

——— WHERE TO DINE ———

CALICO CUPBOARD CAFE & BAKERY

American
$7-$9

Phone: 360/293-7315

Mouthwatering aromas waft from the old-fashioned organic bakery, where sinful cinnamon rolls, soft bread and warm cookies come straight from the oven. The menu's focus is light fare, such as soups, salads, sandwiches, omelets and vegetarian entrees. Casual dress. **Bar:** Beer & wine. **Reservations:** not accepted. **Hours:** 7 am-3 pm. Closed: 11/26, 12/25. **Address:** 901 Commercial Ave **Location:** Jct 9th St. **Parking:** on-site. **Cards:** MC, VI.

CHARLIE'S

Traditional
American
$9-$25

Phone: 360/293-7377

Overlooking the ferry terminal and bay, the restaurant offers two levels of seating to take advantage of the view. Quaint nautical decor characterizes the dining area, while a rooftop patio maximizes the setting's appeal. Clam chowder and oyster stew stand out on the tempting menu. Casual dress. **Bar:** Full bar. **Reservations:** suggested. **Hours:** 11:30 am-9 pm. Closed: 12/24, 12/25. **Address:** 5407 Ferry Terminal Rd **Location:** 3 mi nw of town; 0.5 mi n of BC-San Juan Ferry Terminal. **Parking:** on-site. **Cards:** AX, DS, MC, VI.

🍴

RANDY'S PIER 61

Seafood
$7-$25

Phone: 360/293-5108

The casual dining room overlooks Guemes Channel and Island for gorgeous water and sunset views. In addition to smoked prime rib and baby back ribs, try the house specialty gumbo, a rich, Cajun-style seafood dish thick with oysters, shrimp, salmon and clams. Casual dress. **Bar:** Full bar. **Reservations:** suggested, for dinner. **Hours:** 11:30 am-9 pm, Sun from 10 am. Closed: 12/25. **Address:** 209 T Ave **Location:** 0.4 mi e of Commercial Ave, just n of 4th St. **Parking:** on-site. **Cards:** AX, DS, MC, VI.

ROCKFISH GRILL/ANACORTES BREWING

American
$7-$21

Phone: 360/588-1720

At the casual downtown eatery, locals gather for a variety of food, from pizza and sandwiches to beef and fish dishes. Patrons often enjoy downing a pint of beer that's made in-house. Casual dress. **Bar:** Beer & wine. **Hours:** 11:30 am-10 pm, Fri & Sat-midnight. Closed major holidays. **Address:** 320 Commercial Ave **Location:** Downtown. **Parking:** street. **Cards:** AX, MC, VI.

STAR BAR

International
$21-$30

Phone: 360/299-2120

The trendy new downtown restaurant has more of a metropolitan feel. A large bar features private curtained seating with ottomans, pillows and Bombay style, while the dining room applies a Northwest arts and crafts spin to the same Far East decor. Chef/owner Robert Zutter infuses Northwest fare with international influences. Daily risotto and fish specials merit a look, as do features such as pork tenderloin, roasted chicken, Cuban marinated flank steak and spicy garlic shrimp. Casual dress. **Bar:** Full bar. **Reservations:** suggested. **Hours:** 5 pm-9:30 pm. Closed major holidays; also Mon. **Address:** 416 1/2 Commercial Ave **Location:** Downtown. **Parking:** street. **Cards:** AX, MC, VI.

ARLINGTON —See Seattle p. 665.

ASHFORD pop. 267

——— WHERE TO STAY ———

ALEXANDER'S COUNTRY INN

Phone: (360)569-2300

Historic Country Inn
$99-$235 All Year

Address: 37515 SR 706 E **Location:** 1 mi w of Nisqually entrance to Mount Rainier National Park. **Facility:** Each guest room is unique in size and layout and furnished in a collection of period pieces befitting the age of the inn. Smoke free premises. 14 units. 7 one-bedroom standard units. 5 one-bedroom suites. 2 houses. 1-3 stories (no elevator), interior/exterior corridors. *Bath:* combo or shower only. **Parking:** on-site. **Terms:** office hours 8 am-9 pm, 14 day cancellation notice-fee imposed. **Amenities:** video library. *Some:* CD players. **Dining:** Alexander's Restaurant, see separate listing. **Leisure Activities:** whirlpool. *Fee:* massage. **Business Services:** meeting rooms. **Cards:** MC, VI.

MOUNTAIN MEADOWS INN BED & BREAKFAST

Phone: 360/569-2788

Historic Bed & Breakfast
$99-$165 All Year

Address: 28912 SR 706 E **Location:** West end of town. **Facility:** The restored 1910 home is set on 11 wooded acres six miles from Mount Rainier National Park; several nature trails are on the property. Smoke free premises. 6 units. 5 one- and 1 two-bedroom standard units, some with efficiencies or kitchens. 2 stories (no elevator), interior/exterior corridors. *Bath:* combo or shower only. **Parking:** on-site. **Terms:** check-in 4 pm, 2-3 night minimum stay - seasonal and/or weekends, age restrictions may apply, 14 day cancellation notice-fee imposed. **Leisure Activities:** whirlpool. **Cards:** MC, VI.

THE NISQUALLY LODGE & CONFERENCE CENTER

Phone: 360/569-8804

Hotel
Rates not provided

Address: 31609 SR 706 **Location:** 5.1 mi w of Nisqually entrance to Mount Rainier National Park. **Facility:** Smoke free premises. 24 one-bedroom standard units. 2 stories (no elevator), interior corridors. **Parking:** on-site. **Terms:** office hours 7:30 am-9 pm. **Amenities:** hair dryers. **Leisure Activities:** whirlpool. **Guest Services:** coin laundry, wireless Internet. **Business Services:** meeting rooms.

——— WHERE TO DINE ———

ALEXANDER'S RESTAURANT

Phone: 360/569-2300

American
$8-$23

Just outside Mount Rainier National Park, the restaurant nurtures a relaxed country atmosphere. Homemade bread and desserts tempt the taste buds. Casual dress. **Bar:** Beer & wine. **Reservations:** accepted. **Hours:** 8 am-8:30 pm. Closed: 11/26, 12/25. **Address:** 37515 SR 706 E **Location:** 1 mi w of Nisqually entrance to Mount Rainier National Park; in Alexander's Country Inn. **Parking:** on-site. **Cards:** MC, VI. **Historic**

CALL

AUBURN —See Seattle p. 665.

BAINBRIDGE ISLAND —See Seattle p. 666.

BATTLE GROUND —See Nearby Portland, OR p. 475.

BELFAIR

——— WHERE TO STAY ———

SELAH INN

Phone: (360)275-0916

Bed & Breakfast
$100-$205 All Year

Address: 130 NE Dulalip Landing **Location:** Jct SR 3, 3.6 mi w on SR 300, 0.4 mi s. **Facility:** This contemporary B&B, located on the shores of the Hood Canal in a small rural community, offers a suite with a large whirlpool tub and gas fireplace. Smoke free premises. 4 one-bedroom standard units, some with whirlpools. 2 stories (no elevator), interior corridors. *Bath:* combo or shower only. **Parking:** on-site. **Terms:** age restrictions may apply, 7 day cancellation notice-fee imposed. **Amenities:** video library, DVD players, CD players, high-speed Internet, hair dryers. **Leisure Activities:** whirlpool. **Business Services:** meeting rooms. **Cards:** MC, VI.

BELLEVUE —See Seattle p. 667.

BELLINGHAM pop. 67,171

✈ **Airport Accommodations**

Map Page	OA	BELLINGHAM INTERNATIONAL	Diamond Rated	High Season	Page
N/A	AAA	Hampton Inn Bellingham Airport, just n	▽▽▽	$89-$164 SAVE	527

——— WHERE TO STAY ———

BEST WESTERN HERITAGE INN   *Book great rates at AAA.com*

Phone: (360)647-1912

AAA SAVE
▽▽▽▽

Hotel
$129-$149 3/1-9/1
$109-$129 9/2-2/28

Address: 151 E McLeod Rd **Location:** I-5, exit 256A, just e. **Facility:** Smoke free premises. 90 one-bedroom standard units, some with kitchens. 3-4 stories (no elevator), interior corridors. *Bath:* combo or shower only. **Parking:** on-site. **Terms:** 3 night minimum stay - seasonal and/or weekends. **Amenities:** DVD players, high-speed Internet, voice mail, irons, hair dryers. **Pool(s):** heated outdoor. **Leisure Activities:** whirlpool. **Guest Services:** valet and coin laundry, airport transportation-Bellingham International Airport, wireless Internet. **Business Services:** meeting rooms, PC. **Cards:** AX, DC, DS, MC, VI. **Free Special Amenities: expanded continental breakfast and high-speed Internet.**

AAA Benefit:
Members save up to 20%, plus 10% bonus points with rewards program.

✈ 🍴 🛳 🏋 ✕ 📷 🔒 📺 💻 / SOME UNITS FEE 🐾

BEST WESTERN LAKEWAY INN & CONFERENCE CENTER   *Book great rates at AAA.com*

Phone: (360)671-1011

AAA SAVE
▽▽▽▽

Hotel
$99-$209 All Year

Address: 714 Lakeway Dr **Location:** I-5, exit 253 (Lakeway Dr), just se. **Facility:** Smoke free premises. 132 units. 124 one-bedroom standard units. 8 one-bedroom suites. 4 stories, interior corridors. **Parking:** on-site. **Amenities:** high-speed Internet, dual phone lines, voice mail, irons, hair dryers. **Dining:** 2 restaurants. **Pool(s):** heated indoor. **Leisure Activities:** saunas, whirlpool, exercise room. **Guest Services:** valet and coin laundry, airport transportation-Bellingham International Airport, area transportation, wireless Internet. **Business Services:** conference facilities, business center. **Cards:** AX, CB, DC, DS, JC, MC, VI. **Free Special Amenities: local telephone calls and high-speed Internet.** *(See color ad below)*

AAA Benefit:
Members save up to 20%, plus 10% bonus points with rewards program.

✈ 🍴 🍸 🛳 ✕ ✕ 📷 🔒 💻
/ SOME UNITS FEE 🐾 FEE 🍽

THE CHRYSALIS INN & SPA

Phone: (360)756-1005

AAA SAVE
▽▽▽▽

Hotel
$209-$355 All Year

Address: 804 10th St **Location:** I-5, exit 250, 1.3 mi nw on Old Fairhaven Pkwy, 0.6 mi n via 12th and 11th sts, just w on Taylor Ave, then just n. **Facility:** Smoke free premises. 43 units. 34 one-bedroom standard units. 9 one-bedroom suites with whirlpools. 3 stories, interior corridors. **Parking:** on-site. **Terms:** check-in 4 pm, cancellation fee imposed. **Amenities:** video library, DVD players, CD players, high-speed Internet, dual phone lines, voice mail, honor bars, irons, hair dryers. **Dining:** Fino, see separate listing. **Leisure Activities:** jogging, spa. **Guest Services:** valet laundry, wireless Internet. **Business Services:** meeting rooms, PC. **Cards:** AX, DC, DS, MC, VI. **Free Special Amenities: full breakfast and high-speed Internet.**

🍴 ✕ 📷 🔒 💻 / SOME UNITS FEE 🐾

▼ See AAA listing above ▼

COMFORT INN *Book great rates at AAA.com* Phone: 360/738-1100

AAA [SAVE]
◆◆◆◆
Hotel
Rates not provided

Address: 4282 Meridian St **Location:** I-5, exit 256A, 1 mi e. **Facility:** Smoke free premises. 85 units. 83 one-bedroom standard units, some with kitchens and/or whirlpools. 2 one-bedroom suites with kitchens, some with whirlpools. 3 stories, interior corridors. **Parking:** on-site. **Amenities:** high-speed Internet, voice mail, irons, hair dryers. *Some:* DVD players (fee). **Pool(s):** heated indoor. **Leisure Activities:** whirlpool, exercise room. **Guest Services:** valet and coin laundry, wireless Internet. **Business Services:** meeting rooms, PC. **Free Special Amenities: expanded continental breakfast and high-speed Internet.**

⟨†↑⟩ CALL ⟨&M⟩ ⟨⊇⟩ ⟨✕⟩ ⟨⚏⟩ ⟨🍴⟩ ⟨🖥⟩ ⟨📺⟩ / SOME UNITS FEE ⟨VCR⟩

ECONO LODGE INN & SUITES *Book great rates at AAA.com* Phone: 360/671-4600

AAA [SAVE]
◆◆◆◆
Hotel
Rates not provided

Address: 3750 Meridian St **Location:** I-5, exit 256A, just w. **Facility:** 126 units. 123 one-bedroom standard units. 3 one-bedroom suites. 3 stories, exterior corridors. **Parking:** on-site. **Amenities:** high-speed Internet. *Some:* hair dryers. *Fee:* DVD players. **Pool(s):** heated outdoor. **Leisure Activities:** whirlpool. **Guest Services:** coin laundry, wireless Internet. **Free Special Amenities: continental breakfast and high-speed Internet.**

⟨†↑⟩ ⟨⊇⟩ ⟨⚏⟩ / SOME UNITS FEE ⟨🛏⟩ ⟨✕⟩ FEE ⟨VCR⟩ FEE ⟨🍴⟩ FEE ⟨🖥⟩

FAIRHAVEN VILLAGE INN Phone: (360)733-1311

AAA [SAVE]
◆◆◆◆
Hotel
$189-$329 All Year

Address: 1200 10th St **Location:** I-5, exit 250, 1.5 mi w. Located in Old Fairhaven Historic District. **Facility:** Smoke free premises. 22 units. 21 one-bedroom standard units. 1 one-bedroom suite with whirlpool. 3 stories, interior corridors. *Bath:* combo or shower only. **Parking:** on-site. **Terms:** office hours 7 am-10 pm, 2 night minimum stay - seasonal and/or weekends, cancellation fee imposed. **Amenities:** CD players, high-speed Internet, voice mail, irons, hair dryers. **Guest Services:** valet laundry, wireless Internet. **Business Services:** meeting rooms. **Cards:** AX, MC, VI. **Free Special Amenities: expanded continental breakfast and high-speed Internet.**

⟨†↑⟩ CALL ⟨&M⟩ ⟨✕⟩ ⟨⚏⟩ ⟨📺⟩ / SOME UNITS FEE ⟨🛏⟩ ⟨🍴⟩ ⟨🖥⟩

GUESTHOUSE INN *Book at AAA.com* Phone: (360)671-9600

◆◆ ◆◆
Hotel
$79-$120 All Year

Address: 805 Lakeway Dr **Location:** I-5, exit 253 (Lakeway Dr), just ne. **Facility:** 81 units. 80 one-bedroom standard units. 1 one-bedroom suite with kitchen. 3 stories, interior corridors. **Parking:** on-site. **Amenities:** high-speed Internet, voice mail, irons, hair dryers. **Leisure Activities:** whirlpool. **Guest Services:** valet and coin laundry, wireless Internet. **Business Services:** PC. **Cards:** AX, CB, DC, DS, MC, VI.

[ASK] ⟨+⟩ ⟨†↑⟩ ⟨⚏⟩ ⟨🍴⟩ ⟨🖥⟩ ⟨📺⟩ / SOME UNITS FEE ⟨🛏⟩ ⟨✕⟩

HAMPTON INN BELLINGHAM AIRPORT *Book great rates at AAA.com* Phone: (360)676-7700

AAA [SAVE]
◆◆◆◆
Hotel
$89-$164 All Year

Address: 3985 Bennett Dr **Location:** I-5, exit 258, just nw. **Facility:** 132 one-bedroom standard units, some with whirlpools. 4 stories, interior corridors. *Bath:* some combo or shower only. **Parking:** on-site. **Terms:** 1-30 night minimum stay, cancellation fee imposed. **Amenities:** video games (fee), high-speed Internet, voice mail, irons, hair dryers. **Pool(s):** heated outdoor. **Leisure Activities:** exercise room. **Guest Services:** valet and coin laundry, airport transportation-Bellingham International Airport, wireless Internet. **Business Services:** meeting rooms, PC. **Cards:** AX, CB, DC, DS, JC, MC, VI. **Free Special Amenities: expanded continental breakfast and high-speed Internet.**

<table>
<tr><td colspan="2">Hampton Inn</td></tr>
<tr><td colspan="2">**AAA Benefit:**
Members save up to 10% everyday!</td></tr>
</table>

⟨+⟩ ⟨†↑⟩ CALL ⟨&M⟩ ⟨⊇⟩ ⟨⚏⟩ ⟨🍴⟩ ⟨🖥⟩ ⟨📺⟩ / SOME UNITS ⟨✕⟩ ⟨🍴⟩ ⟨🖥⟩

HOLIDAY INN EXPRESS-BELLINGHAM *Book great rates at AAA.com* Phone: (360)671-4800

AAA [SAVE]
◆◆◆◆
Hotel
$107-$145 All Year

Address: 4160 Meridian St **Location:** I-5, exit 256A, 0.7 mi e. **Facility:** 101 one-bedroom standard units. 3 stories, interior corridors. *Bath:* combo or shower only. **Parking:** on-site. **Terms:** cancellation fee imposed. **Amenities:** video games (fee), high-speed Internet, dual phone lines, voice mail, irons, hair dryers. **Pool(s):** heated indoor. **Leisure Activities:** whirlpool. **Guest Services:** valet laundry, airport transportation-Bellingham International Airport, area transportation-ferry terminal, wireless Internet. **Cards:** AX, DC, DS, MC, VI. **Free Special Amenities: expanded continental breakfast and high-speed Internet.**

⟨+⟩ ⟨†↑⟩ CALL ⟨&M⟩ ⟨⊇⟩ ⟨👥⟩ ⟨⚏⟩ ⟨🍴⟩ ⟨🖥⟩ ⟨📺⟩ / SOME UNITS FEE ⟨🛏⟩ ⟨✕⟩

▼ See AAA listing p 546 ▼

HOTEL BELLWETHER   *Book great rates at AAA.com*   Phone: (360)392-3100

AAA [SAVE]

▼▼▼

Hotel

$188-$710 3/1-9/30
$156-$566 10/1-2/28

Address: One Bellwether Way **Location:** I-5, exit 253 (Lakeway Dr), 0.9 mi nw via Lakeway Dr and E Holly St, just w on Bay St, 0.6 mi n via W Chestnut St and Roeder Ave, then just w. **Facility:** Smoke free premises. 66 units. 58 one-bedroom standard units with whirlpools. 8 one-bedroom suites with whirlpools. 3 stories, interior corridors. **Parking:** on-site. **Terms:** check-in 4 pm, 3 day cancellation notice-fee imposed. **Amenities:** video library (fee), DVD players, CD players, high-speed Internet, dual phone lines, voice mail, safes, honor bars, irons, hair dryers. **Leisure Activities:** putting green, exercise room, spa. *Fee:* boat dock. **Guest Services:** valet laundry, wireless Internet. **Business Services:** conference facilities, business center. **Cards:** AX, CB, DC, DS, JC, MC, VI. Affiliated with A Preferred Hotel.

[icons] / SOME UNITS FEE [icon] FEE [VCR] [icons]

LA QUINTA INN BELLINGHAM   *Book great rates at AAA.com*   Phone: (360)671-6200

AAA [SAVE]

▼▼▼

Hotel

$59-$169 All Year

Address: 125 E Kellogg Rd **Location:** I-5, exit 256A, 1 mi ne via Meridian St. **Facility:** 70 one-bedroom standard units, some with efficiencies and/or whirlpools. 3 stories, interior corridors. **Parking:** on-site. **Amenities:** high-speed Internet, voice mail, irons, hair dryers. **Pool(s):** heated outdoor. **Leisure Activities:** whirlpool. **Guest Services:** valet and coin laundry, wireless Internet. **Business Services:** PC. **Cards:** AX, CB, DS, MC, VI. **Free Special Amenities: continental breakfast and local telephone calls.**

[icons] / SOME UNITS FEE [icons] FEE [icon] FEE [icon]

MOTEL 6 - 44   *Book at AAA.com*   Phone: (360)671-4494

▼

Motel

$55-$75 All Year

Address: 3701 Byron Ave **Location:** I-5, exit 252, just nw. **Facility:** 60 one-bedroom standard units. 2 stories, exterior corridors. *Bath:* shower only. **Parking:** on-site. **Pool(s):** heated outdoor. **Guest Services:** coin laundry. **Cards:** AX, CB, DC, DS, MC, VI.

[icons] CALL [icons] / SOME UNITS [icons] FEE [icon] FEE [icon]

QUALITY INN BARON SUITES   *Book great rates at AAA.com*   Phone: (360)647-8000

AAA [SAVE]

▼▼▼

Hotel

$109-$219 5/23-2/28
$85-$189 3/1-5/22

Address: 100 E Kellogg Rd **Location:** I-5, exit 256A, 1 mi ne via Meridian St. **Facility:** 86 units. 85 one-bedroom standard units, some with efficiencies and/or whirlpools. 1 one-bedroom suite with kitchen and whirlpool. 3 stories, interior/exterior corridors. **Parking:** on-site. **Terms:** cancellation fee imposed. **Amenities:** high-speed Internet, voice mail, irons, hair dryers. *Some:* DVD players, dual phone lines. **Pool(s):** heated outdoor. **Leisure Activities:** whirlpool, exercise room. **Guest Services:** valet and coin laundry, area transportation-within 5 mi, wireless Internet. **Business Services:** meeting rooms, PC. **Cards:** AX, CB, DC, DS, JC, MC, VI. **Free Special Amenities: expanded continental breakfast and high-speed Internet.**

[icons] / SOME UNITS FEE [icons]

——— WHERE TO DINE ———

ARCHER ALE HOUSE   Phone: 360/647-7002

▼▼

American

$8-$14

In the renovated cellar of the historic 1903 Shering Block, this English pub comes complete with an antique oak bar, stained-glass windows and an embossed tin ceiling. Offerings of traditional pub fare include pizza, sandwiches and snacks, which patrons can wash down with a great pint of beer. **Bar:** Beer & wine. **Reservations:** not accepted. **Hours:** 3 pm-11 pm, Thurs & Fri-midnight, Sat 1 pm-midnight, Sun 1 pm-9 pm. Closed major holidays. **Address:** 1212 10th St **Location:** I-5, exit 250, 1.3 mi w on Fairhaven Pkwy; in Fairhaven Historic District. **Parking:** on-site. **Cards:** MC, VI.

BILLY MCHALE'S   Phone: 360/647-7763

▼▼

American

$8-$19

The family-oriented restaurant, which serves chicken, steak and fresh seafood, is known for its succulent ribs and tasty onion loaf. Drinks include 31 varieties of margaritas. The bustling dining room teems with upbeat colors, signs and memorabilia. Casual dress. **Bar:** Full bar. **Reservations:** not accepted. **Hours:** 11 am-10 pm, Fri & Sat-11 pm, Sun & Mon-9 pm. Closed: 11/26, 12/25. **Address:** 4301 Meridian St **Location:** I-5, exit 256A, 1 mi n. **Parking:** on-site. **Cards:** AX, CB, DC, DS, MC, VI.

BOUNDARY BAY BREWERY & BISTRO   Phone: 360/647-5593

▼▼

American

$7-$19

Close to the bay, the restaurant is in an artsy historic downtown area rich with folklore. One of this place's claims to fame is its award-winning brewery from The Great American Beer Festival. Distinctive menu items include hand-made ravioli with a choice of sauce, and yummy desserts such as creme brulee and the delicious brownie with a heaping pile of whipped cream. Casual dress. **Bar:** Beer & wine. **Reservations:** accepted. **Hours:** 11 am-11 pm. Closed major holidays. **Address:** 1107 Railroad Ave **Location:** I-5, exit 253 (Lakeway Dr), 3 mi nw, then just sw. **Parking:** on-site. **Cards:** MC, VI.

[icon]

THE CLIFF HOUSE   Phone: 360/734-8660

▼▼

Steak & Seafood

$20-$40

The attractive rooftop dining room affords breathtaking panoramas of Bellingham Bay. Steak and seafood are at the heart of the well-established restaurant's menu. Casual dress. **Bar:** Full bar. **Reservations:** suggested. **Hours:** 5 pm-9:30 pm. Closed: 11/26, 12/25. **Address:** 331 N State St **Location:** I-5, exit 254, 2 mi w via Iowa and State sts. **Parking:** on-site. **Cards:** AX, DC, DS, MC, VI.

COLOPHON CAFE   Phone: 360/647-0092

AAA

▼▼

American

$6-$12

Upstairs is a delicatessen with a more casual feel, while downstairs houses a larger dining room with an adjacent bookstore. The diverse menu includes exotic soup and salad, sandwiches, quiche and pot pies, as well as espresso and homemade desserts. **Hours:** 9 am-8 pm, Fri & Sat-10 pm, Sun 10 am-8 pm; 9 am-10 pm, Sun-8 pm 5/26-9/30. Closed: 11/26, 12/25. **Address:** 1208 11th St **Location:** I-5, exit 250, 1.5 mi nw; in Fairhaven Historic District. **Parking:** street. **Cards:** AX, DS, MC, VI.

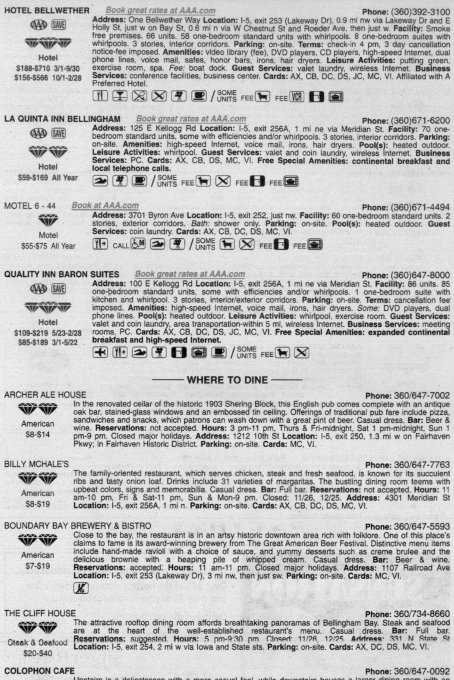

DIRTY DAN HARRIS   Phone: 360/676-1011

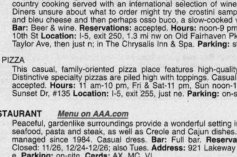

American
$17-$25

The upscale historic restaurant specializes in local seafood, aged steaks, slow-roasted prime rib, premium spirits and fine wines. The extensive wine cellar concentrates heavily on selections from Washington, California and Oregon vineyards. Casual dress. **Bar:** Full bar. **Reservations:** suggested. **Hours:** 5 pm-9:30 pm, Fri & Sat-10 pm. Closed: 1/1, 11/26, 12/25. **Address:** 1211 11th St **Location:** I-5, exit 250, 1.5 mi nw; in Fairhaven Historic District. **Parking:** on-site. **Cards:** AX, DC, DS, MC, VI. **Historic**

FINO   Phone: 360/676-9463

International
$13-$32

A quiet place to gather after a day of shopping in Old Fairhaven, the restaurant specializes in European country cooking served with an international selection of wines and a panoramic view of Bellingham Bay. Diners unsure about what to order might try the crostini sampler, a watercress salad with apples, walnuts and bleu cheese and then perhaps osso buco, a slow-cooked veal shank with tomato risotto. Casual dress. **Bar:** Beer & wine. **Reservations:** accepted. **Hours:** noon-9 pm. Closed: 11/26, 12/24, 12/25. **Address:** 804 10th St **Location:** I-5, exit 250, 1.3 mi nw on Old Fairhaven Pkwy, 0.6 mi n via 12th and 11th sts, just w on Taylor Ave, then just n; in The Chrysalis Inn & Spa. **Parking:** street. **Cards:** AX, MC, VI.

ROUND TABLE PIZZA   Phone: 360/671-6305

Pizza
$10-$17

This casual, family-oriented pizza place features high-quality ingredients and dough rolled fresh daily. Distinctive specialty pizzas are piled high with toppings. Casual dress. **Bar:** Beer & wine. **Reservations:** not accepted. **Hours:** 11 am-10 pm, Fri & Sat-11 pm, Sun noon-10 pm. Closed: 1/1, 12/25. **Address:** 1145 E Sunset Dr, #135 **Location:** I-5, exit 255, just ne. **Parking:** on-site. **Cards:** AX, DS, MC, VI.

SADIGHI'S RESTAURANT   *Menu on AAA.com*   Phone: 360/647-1109

Continental
$7-$24

Peaceful, gardenlike surroundings provide a wonderful setting in which diners can sample fresh, wholesome seafood, pasta and steak, as well as Creole and Cajun dishes. The restaurant has been family-owned-and-managed since 1984. Casual dress. **Bar:** Full bar. **Reservations:** suggested. **Hours:** 4:30 pm-10 pm. Closed: 11/26, 12/24-12/26; also Tues. **Address:** 921 Lakeway Dr **Location:** I-5, exit 253 (Lakeway Dr), just e. **Parking:** on-site. **Cards:** AX, MC, VI.

THAI HOUSE RESTAURANT   Phone: 360/734-5111

Thai
$8-$13

A traditional family-operated restaurant for 8 years, this storefront restaurant features authentic classics such as pad thai and tom yam. Casual dress. **Bar:** Beer & wine. **Hours:** 11 am-10 pm, Sun noon-9 pm. Closed major holidays. **Address:** 187 Telegraph Rd **Location:** I-5, exit 256A, just e. **Parking:** on-site. **Cards:** AX, DS, MC, VI.

BLAINE pop. 3,770

------ **WHERE TO STAY** ------

SEMIAHMOO RESORT   *Book great rates at AAA.com*   Phone: (360)318-2000

Resort
Hotel
$119-$399 All Year

Address: 9565 Semiahmoo Pkwy **Location:** I-5, exit 270, 9.5 mi nw on Semiahmoo Spit. Located in a quiet area. **Facility:** This waterfront resort in a 1,100-acre wildlife area features rustic decor, two waterfront restaurants, a spa, two golf courses and a health facility. 194 one-bedroom standard units. 4 stories, interior corridors. **Parking:** on-site and valet. **Terms:** check-in 4 pm, 2 night minimum stay - seasonal and/or weekends, 3 day cancellation notice. **Amenities:** high-speed Internet, dual phone lines, voice mail, honor bars, irons, hair dryers. **Dining:** Stars, see separate listing. **Pool(s):** heated indoor/outdoor. **Leisure Activities:** saunas, whirlpool, marina, croquet, jogging, spa, horseshoes, volleyball. **Fee:** charter fishing, golf-36 holes, 6 tennis courts (1 indoor, 1 lighted), racquetball court, basketball. **Guest Services:** valet laundry, area transportation-golf courses & club house, wireless Internet. **Business Services:** conference facilities, business center. **Cards:** AX, DC, DS, MC, VI. **Free Special Amenities:** newspaper and high-speed Internet.

------ **WHERE TO DINE** ------

STARS   Phone: 360/371-2000

Regional
Continental
$22-$38

A nautical theme is carried out in the upscale bayfront restaurant's dining room, where a pianist tickles the ivories of a handsome baby grand in the background on weekend evenings. Specialties are Northwest cuisine are pleasing both in taste and presentation. Dressy casual. **Bar:** Full bar. **Reservations:** suggested. **Hours:** 6:30 am-11:30 & 5-9 pm, Sat & Sun 6:30 am-noon & 5-10 pm. Closed: Mon, for dinner Sun in winter. **Address:** 9565 Semiahmoo Pkwy **Location:** I-5, exit 270, 9.5 mi nw on Semiahmoo Spit; in Semiahmoo Resort. **Parking:** on-site and valet. **Cards:** AX, DS, MC, VI.

BOTHELL —See Seattle p. 672.

BOW

------ **WHERE TO STAY** ------

THE SKAGIT RIDGE HOTEL   Phone: 360/724-0640

Hotel
$69-$169 All Year

Address: 18444 Bow Ridge Dr **Location:** I-5, exit 236, just se. **Facility:** 41 units. 40 one-bedroom standard units. 1 one-bedroom suite with whirlpool. 3 stories, interior corridors. **Bath:** combo or shower only. **Parking:** on-site. **Terms:** check-in 4 pm, 3 day cancellation notice-fee imposed. **Amenities:** high-speed Internet, voice mail, irons, hair dryers. **Leisure Activities:** Fee: pool, whirlpool & exercise privileges. **Guest Services:** area transportation-casino shuttle, wireless Internet. **Business Services:** meeting rooms. **Cards:** AX, DC, DS, MC, VI. **Free Special Amenities:** expanded continental breakfast and high-speed Internet.

SKAGIT VALLEY CASINO RESORT

Hotel
$89-$139 All Year

Phone: 360/724-7777

Address: 5984 N Darrk Ln **Location:** I-5, exit 236, just ne. **Facility:** This casino resort features a full-service, Las Vegas-style casino, live music and headline entertainment, three restaurants and a luxury hotel. 103 units. 75 one-bedroom standard units. 28 one-bedroom suites with whirlpools. 4 stories, interior corridors. *Bath:* combo or shower only. **Parking:** on-site. **Terms:** check-in 4 pm, 3 day cancellation notice-fee imposed. **Amenities:** high-speed Internet, dual phone lines, voice mail, irons, hair dryers. *Some:* safes. **Dining:** 3 restaurants. **Pool(s):** heated indoor. **Leisure Activities:** sauna, whirlpool, exercise room. **Guest Services:** valet and coin laundry, wireless Internet. **Business Services:** meeting rooms. **Cards:** AX, DS, MC, VI. **Free Special Amenities:** continental breakfast and high-speed Internet.

——— WHERE TO DINE ———

CHUCKANUT MANOR SEAFOOD & GRILL

Seafood
$8-$35

Phone: 360/766-6191

Panoramic views of Samish Bay awe guests from the dining room of the 1920s building. Entrees such as Cajun prawns with orange marmalade-horseradish sauce intrigue. Sunday brunch is exceptionally popular, as is the luscious cheesecake. Deck seating is a nice summer option. Casual dress. **Bar:** Full bar. **Reservations:** suggested. **Hours:** 11:30 am-10 pm, Sun 10:30 am-2:30 & 3-10 pm. Closed: 1/1, 7/4, 12/24, 12/25; also Mon. **Address:** 3056 Chuckanut Dr (SR 11) **Location:** I-5, exit 231, 9.5 mi nw; exit 250, 12 mi sw on SR 11; between MM 9 and 10. **Parking:** on-site. **Cards:** AX, CB, DC, DS, MC, VI. **Historic**

THE OYSTER BAR

American
$9-$55

Phone: 360/766-6185

Perched on the side of a hill, the restaurant has provided an elegant atmosphere to travelers of Chuckanut Drive since 1930. The dining room is softly lit by candles, and service is attentive yet unobtrusive so diners can enjoy the romantic water views and delectable foods such as salmon wrapped in parchment. The experience is adult-oriented, so smaller children typically are not encouraged to visit. Dressy casual. **Bar:** Beer & wine. **Reservations:** suggested. **Hours:** 11:30 am-10 pm. Closed: 12/25. **Address:** 2578 Chuckanut Dr (SR 11) **Location:** I-5, exit 236, 3.8 mi w on Bow Hill Rd, then 3.5 mi n; halfway between Bellingham and Burlington. **Parking:** on-site. **Cards:** AX, MC, VI. **Classic**

RHODODENDRON CAFE

Ethnic
$7-$20

Phone: 360/766-6667

Each month ushers in a different ethnic theme, with all menu items made from scratch. Clam chowder, freshly baked bread, apple-raisin pork chops and homemade pies are only a few of the deliciously prepared and well-presented dishes offered. Casual dress. **Bar:** Beer & wine. **Hours:** Open 3/1-11/22 & 1/1-2/28; 11:30 am-9 pm, Sat & Sun from 9 am; Saturday & Sunday brunch. Closed: 7/4; also Mon & Tues. **Address:** 5521 Chuckanut Dr (SR 11) **Location:** I-5, exit 236, 3.8 mi w on Bow Hill Rd, then just n. **Parking:** on-site. **Cards:** AX, DS, MC, VI.

BREMERTON —See Seattle p. 674.

BURIEN —See Seattle p. 675.

BURLINGTON pop. 6,757

——— WHERE TO STAY ———

COCUSA MOTEL

Hotel
$75-$135 3/1-9/30
$63-$135 10/1-2/28

Phone: (360)757-6044

Address: 370 W Rio Vista **Location:** I-5, exit 230, just e. **Facility:** 63 one-bedroom standard units, some with efficiencies and/or whirlpools. 2 stories (no elevator), exterior corridors. *Bath:* combo or shower only. **Parking:** on-site. **Amenities:** high-speed Internet. **Pool(s):** heated outdoor. **Guest Services:** coin laundry, wireless Internet. **Business Services:** meeting rooms. **Cards:** AX, DC, DS, MC, VI. **Free Special Amenities: continental breakfast and high-speed Internet.**

FAIRFIELD INN & SUITES BY MARRIOTT
BURLINGTON   *Book great rates at AAA.com*

Hotel
$139-$149 All Year

Phone: (360)757-2717

Address: 9384 Old Hwy 99 N **Location:** I-5, exit 232, just ne. **Facility:** Smoke free premises. 78 one-bedroom standard units, some with whirlpools. 3 stories, interior corridors. *Bath:* combo or shower only. **Parking:** on-site. **Terms:** cancellation fee imposed. **Amenities:** high-speed Internet, dual phone lines, voice mail, irons, hair dryers. **Pool(s):** heated indoor. **Leisure Activities:** whirlpool, exercise room. **Guest Services:** valet and coin laundry, wireless Internet. **Business Services:** PC. **Cards:** AX, CB, DC, DS, JC, MC, VI. **Free Special Amenities: expanded continental breakfast and high-speed Internet.** *(See color ad below)*

AAA Benefit:
Members save a minimum 5% off the best available rate.

HAMPTON INN & SUITES   *Book great rates at AAA.com*

Hotel
$99-$149 All Year

Phone: (360)767-7100

Address: 1860 S Burlington Blvd **Location:** I-5, exit 229, just e on George Hopper Dr, then just s. **Facility:** 102 one-bedroom standard units, some with whirlpools. 4 stories, interior corridors. *Bath:* combo or shower only. **Parking:** on-site. **Terms:** check-in 4 pm, 1-30 night minimum stay, cancellation fee imposed. **Amenities:** high-speed Internet, voice mail, irons, hair dryers. **Pool(s):** heated indoor. **Leisure Activities:** whirlpool, exercise room. **Guest Services:** valet and coin laundry, wireless Internet. **Business Services:** meeting rooms, business center. **Cards:** AX, CB, DC, DS, MC, VI.

AAA Benefit:
Members save up to 10% everyday!

▼ *See AAA listing above* ▼

HOLIDAY INN EXPRESS HOTEL & SUITES

Book great rates at AAA.com

Phone: (360)755-7338

▼▼▼

Hotel
$119-$179 All Year

Address: 1003 Goldenrod Rd **Location:** I-5, exit 230, just sw. **Facility:** Smoke free premises. 75 units. 63 one-bedroom standard units, some with whirlpools. 12 one-bedroom suites, some with whirlpools. 3 stories, interior corridors. *Bath:* combo or shower only. **Parking:** on-site. **Terms:** check-in 4 pm. **Amenities:** high-speed Internet, dual phone lines, voice mail, irons, hair dryers. **Pool(s):** heated indoor. **Leisure Activities:** whirlpool, exercise room. **Guest Services:** valet and coin laundry, wireless Internet. **Business Services:** business center. **Cards:** AX, DC, DS, JC, MC, VI.

[ASK] 🏊 ✕ 🎣 🍴 📷 ☕

——— WHERE TO DINE ———

BOB'S BURGERS & BREW

Phone: 360/757-9097

▼▼ ▼▼

American
$7-$19

More than 20 beef and chicken combinations are on a menu that also lists other sandwiches and entrees. Padded booths are a comfortable spot for kicking back while watching sports on a nearby TV. Casual dress. **Bar:** Full bar. **Reservations:** accepted, weekdays only. **Hours:** 6:30 am-10 pm, Fri & Sat-11 pm, Sun 9 am-10 pm. Closed: 11/26, 12/25. **Address:** 9394 Old Hwy 99 N Rd **Location:** I-5, exit 232, just ne. **Parking:** on-site. **Cards:** AX, CB, DC, MC, VI.

CAMAS —*See Nearby Portland, OR p. 476.*

CASHMERE pop. 2,965

——— WHERE TO STAY ———

VILLAGE INN MOTEL

Phone: (509)782-3522

(AAA) [SAVE]

▼▼ ▼▼

Motel
$59-$94 All Year

Address: 229 Cottage Ave **Location:** On Business Rt US 2 and 97; downtown. **Facility:** 21 one-bedroom standard units. 2 stories (no elevator), exterior corridors. *Bath:* combo or shower only. **Parking:** on-site. **Terms:** office hours 7 am-10:30 pm, 2-3 night minimum stay - seasonal, 7 day cancellation notice-fee imposed. **Guest Services:** wireless Internet. **Cards:** AX, DS, MC, VI. **Free Special Amenities:** local telephone calls and high-speed Internet.

/ SOME UNITS FEE 🐾 ✕ 🍴 📷

CASTLE ROCK pop. 2,130

——— WHERE TO STAY ———

BLUE HERON INN B&B

Phone: 360/274-9595

▼▼▼

Bed & Breakfast
Rates not provided

Address: 2846 Spirit Lake Hwy **Location:** I-5, exit 49, 5 mi e on US 504. **Facility:** Just across from the Mount St. Helens Volcanic Monument Visitor Center, this B&B offers both mountain and lake views. Smoke free premises. 7 one-bedroom standard units. 3 stories (no elevator), interior corridors. *Bath:* combo or shower only. **Parking:** on-site. **Terms:** office hours 7:30 am-9 pm, age restrictions may apply. **Amenities:** hair dryers. *Some:* DVD players. **Pool(s):** heated outdoor. **Guest Services:** wireless Internet.

CALL 📞M 🏊 ✕ / SOME UNITS [VCR]

TIMBERLAND INN & SUITES

Phone: (360)274-6002

(AAA) [SAVE]

▼▼▼

Motel
$80-$200 3/1-10/31
$60-$125 11/1-2/28

Address: 1271 Mount St. Helens Way **Location:** I-5, exit 49, just ne. Located next to Mount St. Helens Cinedome Theater. **Facility:** 40 one-bedroom standard units, some with whirlpools. 2 stories (no elevator), exterior corridors. **Parking:** on-site. **Terms:** office hours 7 am-11 pm, cancellation fee imposed. **Amenities:** high-speed Internet, hair dryers. *Some:* irons. **Guest Services:** coin laundry. **Cards:** AX, DS, MC, VI. *(See color ad p 186)*

 🎣 🍴 / SOME UNITS FEE 🐾 ✕ 🍴 ☕

——— WHERE TO DINE ———

HATTIE'S

Phone: 360/274-7019

▼▼ ▼▼

American
$6-$20

In the city center, the restaurant presents a menu that includes prime rib and a few pasta dishes as choices. Guests are treated to uptown class and down-home cooking. This is the kind of place where people meet new friends and always feel at home. Casual dress. **Bar:** Beer & wine. **Reservations:** accepted. **Hours:** 8 am-8 pm, Sun from 9 am. Closed: 1/1, 7/4, 12/25. **Address:** 51 Cowlitz St W **Location:** I-5, exit 49, 0.7 mi sw, then just w. **Parking:** street. **Cards:** AX, DS, MC, VI.

CENTRALIA pop. 14,742

———— WHERE TO STAY ————

GREAT WOLF LODGE-GRAND MOUND   *Book great rates at AAA.com*   Phone: (360)273-7718

AAA **SAVE**

Hotel
$329-$589 All Year

Address: 20500 Old Hwy 99 SW **Location:** I-5, exit 88 southbound, just w, then 0.8 mi s; exit 88B northbound to Aberdeen, just w, then 0.8 mi s. **Facility:** Smoke free premises. 398 one-bedroom standard units, some with whirlpools. 8 stories, interior corridors. **Parking:** on-site. **Terms:** check-in 4 pm, 3 day cancellation notice-fee imposed. **Amenities:** video games (fee), high-speed Internet, voice mail, safes, irons, hair dryers. *Some:* CD players. **Dining:** 2 restaurants. **Leisure Activities:** whirlpool, exercise room, spa. *Fee:* indoor waterpark. **Guest Services:** coin laundry, wireless Internet. **Business Services:** conference facilities, PC. **Cards:** AX, DC, DS, MC, VI. *(See color ad p 577)*

MOTEL 6 - 394   *Book at AAA.com*   Phone: (360)330-2057

Motel
$45-$55 All Year

Address: 1310 Belmont Ave **Location:** I-5, exit 82, just w on Harrison Ave, then just n. **Facility:** 122 one-bedroom standard units. 2 stories (no elevator), exterior corridors. *Bath:* shower only. **Parking:** on-site. **Pool(s):** heated outdoor. **Guest Services:** coin laundry. **Cards:** AX, CB, DC, DS, MC, VI.

PEPPERMILL EMPRESS INN   *Book great rates at AAA.com*   Phone: 360/330-9441

AAA **SAVE**

Hotel
$105-$135 All Year

Address: 1233 Alder St **Location:** I-5, exit 81, just se. **Facility:** 71 one-bedroom standard units. 3 stories, interior corridors. *Bath:* combo or shower only. **Parking:** on-site. **Amenities:** high-speed Internet, dual phone lines, irons, hair dryers. **Pool(s):** heated indoor. **Leisure Activities:** whirlpool. **Guest Services:** valet and coin laundry, wireless Internet. **Cards:** AX, CB, DC, DS, JC, MC, VI. **Free Special Amenities:** continental breakfast and high-speed Internet.

———— *The following lodging was either not evaluated or did not* ————
meet AAA rating requirements but is listed for your information only.

MCMENAMINS OLYMPIC CLUB HOTEL   **Phone:** 360/736-5164
[fyi]   Not evaluated. **Address:** 112 N Tower Ave **Location:** Downtown. Facilities, services, and decor
                characterize a mid-scale property.

———— **WHERE TO DINE** ————

BERRY FIELDS CAFE   **Phone:** 360/736-1183

Adjoining an antiques mall, the restaurant enables guests to rest their feet after a morning of browsing
selections of Depression glass. Portions of fresh food are on the generous side; a salad is a meal, and
sandwiches can easily serve two or work as leftovers. A slice of freshly made pie provides a sweet finish.
Casual dress. **Reservations:** accepted. **Hours:** 8 am-5 pm. Closed major holidays. **Address:** 201 S Pearl
American   St **Location:** At Pearl and Locust sts; downtown. **Parking:** on-site. **Cards:** MC, VI.
$5-$9

BURGERVILLE   **Phone:** 360/736-5212

First-timers shouldn't let the fast food exterior fool them, as the burgers and chicken here adhere to a higher
standard. Northwest ingredients come into play in the sandwiches. Casual dress. **Hours:** 7 am-10 pm.
American   Closed: 11/26, 12/25. **Address:** 818 Harrison Ave **Location:** I-5, exit 82, just e. **Parking:** on-site.
$2-$8   **Cards:** DS, MC, VI.

COUNTRY COUSIN   **Phone:** 360/736-2200

Pot roast and all-day breakfast items are representative of the restaurant's comfort food, which is served by
laid-back staffers. The sounds of farm animals can be heard in the background, and patrons are greeted like
American   family. Casual dress. **Bar:** Full bar. **Reservations:** accepted. **Hours:** 5:30 am-10 pm, Fri & Sat-11 pm.
$7-$25   Closed: 12/24, 12/25. **Address:** 1054 Harrison Ave **Location:** I-5, exit 82, just nw. **Parking:** on-site.
               Cards: AX, DS, MC, VI.
               CALL ⟨M⟩

MCMENAMINS   **Phone:** 360/736-5164

The casual neighborhood eatery is where friends gather for classic pub and comfort fare, all washed down
by pints of locally made beer. Large wooden booths or tables easily accommodate larger groups, and the
American   eclectic, custom-painted walls and varied period light fixtures keep diners' eyes busy should the
$5-$20   conversation lag. Casual dress. **Bar:** Full bar. **Hours:** 7 am-midnight, Fri & Sat-1 am. **Address:** 112 N
               Tower Ave **Location:** Downtown. **Parking:** street. **Cards:** MC, VI.

CHEHALIS pop. 7,057

———— **WHERE TO STAY** ————

BEST WESTERN PARK PLACE INN & SUITES   *Book great rates at AAA.com*   **Phone:** (360)748-4040

Hotel   **Address:** 201 SW Interstate Ave **Location:** I-5, exit 76, just se.
$97-$124 3/1-9/30   **Facility:** Smoke free premises. 61 one-bedroom standard units, some with
$91-$106 10/1-2/28 whirlpools. 3 stories, interior corridors. *Bath:* combo or shower only.
                Parking: on-site. **Terms:** 2 night minimum stay - weekends, 3 day
                cancellation notice-fee imposed. **Amenities:** high-speed Internet, irons,
                hair dryers. *Some:* dual phone lines. **Pool(s):** heated indoor. **Leisure
                Activities:** whirlpool, exercise room. **Guest Services:** coin laundry,
                wireless Internet. **Business Services:** meeting rooms, PC. **Cards:** AX, CB,
                DC, DS, JC, MC, VI. **Free Special Amenities: expanded continental
                breakfast and high-speed Internet.**

AAA Benefit:
Members save up to
20%, plus 10%
bonus points with
rewards program.

———— **WHERE TO DINE** ————

**HISTORIC MARY MCCRANKS
RESTAURANT**   **Phone:** 360/748-3662

This roadside country inn restaurant, in operation since 1935, is known for its fresh, from-scratch cooking.
The menu features country pork chops, fried chicken, seafood, prime rib and homemade desserts. Casual
dress. **Bar:** Full bar. **Reservations:** suggested. **Hours:** 11:30 am-8:30 pm, Sun noon-8 pm. Closed: 7/4,
12/24-12/26; also Mon. **Address:** 2923 Jackson Hwy **Location:** I-5, exit 72 northbound, 0.8 mi ne on Rush
American   Rd, 0.8 mi e on Bishop, then just n; exit 76 southbound, 0.7 mi e on 13th, then 3.6 mi s via Market St and
$6-$19   Jackson Hwy. **Parking:** on-site. **Cards:** AX, DS, MC, VI.

SPIFFY'S RESTAURANT & BAKERY   **Phone:** 360/262-3561

A great pit stop after a long haul down the interstate, the eatery opens 24 hours a day and always serves
breakfast. Families appreciate the comfortable setting, early-bird specials from Monday through Thursday
and mouthwatering homemade pies and fresh cinnamon rolls. Casual dress. **Reservations:** not accepted.
American   **Hours:** 24 hours. Closed: 12/24, 12/25. **Address:** 110 US 12 **Location:** I-5, exit 68, just se. **Parking:** on-
$7-$17   site. **Cards:** AX, DS, MC, VI.

CHELAN pop. 3,522

APPLE INN MOTEL

Motel
Rates not provided

Phone: 509/682-4044

Address: 1002 E Woodin Ave **Location:** Jct Alternate Rt US 97 N and SR 150, 0.6 mi e on Alternate Rt US 97 N. **Facility:** 41 units. 37 one-bedroom standard units. 4 one-bedroom suites with kitchens. 1-2 stories (no elevator), interior/exterior corridors. *Bath:* combo or shower only. **Parking:** on-site, winter plug-ins. **Terms:** office hours 7 am-11 pm. **Amenities:** video library. *Some:* high-speed Internet. **Pool(s):** heated outdoor. **Leisure Activities:** whirlpool. **Guest Services:** area transportation, wireless Internet. **Business Services:** meeting rooms.

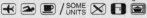

BEST WESTERN LAKESIDE LODGE & SUITES   *Book great rates at AAA.com*

AAA **SAVE**

Hotel
$100-$400 3/1-10/15
$100-$150 10/16-2/28

Phone: (509)682-4396

Address: 2312 W Woodin Ave **Location:** West end of town. **Facility:** Smoke free premises. 93 units. 35 one-bedroom standard units, some with efficiencies and/or whirlpools. 58 one-bedroom suites, some with efficiencies, kitchens and/or whirlpools. 2-4 stories, exterior corridors. *Bath:* combo or shower only. **Parking:** on-site. **Terms:** 2-3 night minimum stay - seasonal and/or weekends, 7 day cancellation notice-fee imposed. **Amenities:** video library (fee), DVD players, irons, hair dryers. *Some:* high-speed Internet. **Pool(s):** heated outdoor, heated indoor. **Leisure Activities:** whirlpools, limited exercise equipment. **Guest Services:** coin laundry, wireless Internet. **Business Services:** meeting rooms. **Cards:** AX, DC, DS, MC, VI.

AAA Benefit:
Members save up to 20%, plus 10% bonus points with rewards program.

CAMPBELL HOUSE CAFE VERANDA GRILL

AAA

American
$7-$27

Phone: 509/682-4250

Located on the shores of Lake Chelan. The upstairs is a casual cafe and pub while the lower level is a more full service experience. Come enjoy a dark porter beer and slow roasted prime rib. Casual dress. **Bar:** Full bar. **Reservations:** suggested. **Hours:** 6:45 am-1 & 5-9 pm; hours may vary. Closed: 12/25; also 1/2-1/15. **Address:** 104 W Woodin Ave **Location:** On Lake Chelan; in Campbell's Resort and Conference Center. **Parking:** on-site. **Cards:** AX, MC, VI. **Historic**

CHENEY pop. 8,832

HOLIDAY INN EXPRESS HOTEL & SUITES-CHENEY UNIVERSITY AREA   *Book great rates at AAA.com*

Hotel
$99-$169 3/1-10/31
$79-$99 11/1-2/28

Phone: (509)235-1100

Address: 111 Betz Rd **Location:** I-90, exit 270, 5 mi s, then just w. **Facility:** Smoke free premises. 76 one-bedroom standard units. 3 stories, interior corridors. *Bath:* combo or shower only. **Parking:** on-site. **Terms:** check-in 4 pm, cancellation fee imposed. **Amenities:** high-speed Internet, voice mail, irons, hair dryers. **Pool(s):** heated indoor. **Leisure Activities:** whirlpool, exercise room. **Guest Services:** coin laundry, wireless Internet. **Business Services:** meeting rooms, business center. **Cards:** AX, CB, DC, DS, MC, VI.

CHEWELAH pop. 2,186

——— WHERE TO STAY ———

NORDLIG MOTEL

AAA SAVE
♦♦ ♦♦
Motel
$58-$63 All Year

Phone: (509)935-6704

Address: W 101 Grant Ave **Location:** North edge of town on US 395. Located across from a city park. **Facility:** 14 one-bedroom standard units. 2 stories (no elevator), exterior corridors. *Bath:* shower only. **Parking:** on-site, winter plug-ins. **Terms:** office hours 7 am-10 pm. **Guest Services:** wireless Internet. **Cards:** AX, DS, MC, VI. **Free Special Amenities: continental breakfast and high-speed Internet.**

📷 🛏 / SOME UNITS FEE 🐕 ⊗ VCR 📷

CLARKSTON pop. 7,337

——— WHERE TO STAY ———

BEST WESTERN RIVERTREE INN *Book great rates at AAA.com*

AAA SAVE
♦♦ ♦♦
Hotel
$99-$169 All Year

Phone: (509)758-9551

Address: 1257 Bridge St **Location:** 0.9 mi w of Snake River Bridge on US 12. **Facility:** Smoke free premises. 62 units. 60 one-bedroom standard units, some with efficiencies (no utensils) and/or whirlpools. 2 one-bedroom suites. 2 stories (no elevator), exterior corridors. *Bath:* combo or shower only. **Parking:** on-site, winter plug-ins. **Terms:** 2 night minimum stay - weekends. **Amenities:** high-speed Internet, irons, hair dryers. *Some:* DVD players. **Pool(s):** heated outdoor. **Leisure Activities:** sauna, whirlpool, exercise room. **Guest Services:** coin laundry, wireless Internet. **Business Services:** business center. **Cards:** AX, DC, DS, MC, VI. **Free Special Amenities: expanded continental breakfast and high-speed Internet.**

AAA Benefit:
Members save up to 20%, plus 10% bonus points with rewards program.

🍴 CALL 🅖M 🏊 ⊗ 📷 🛏 📶 📷 / SOME UNITS 🐕

MOTEL 6   *Book at AAA.com*

♦♦
Motel
Rates not provided

Phone: 509/758-1631

Address: 222 Bridge St **Location:** Just w of Snake River Bridge. **Facility:** 87 units. 86 one-bedroom standard units. 1 two-bedroom suite with kitchen. 2 stories (no elevator), exterior corridors. *Bath:* combo or shower only. **Parking:** on-site. **Amenities:** *Some:* DVD players. **Pool(s):** heated indoor. **Leisure Activities:** whirlpool. **Guest Services:** coin laundry, wireless Internet.

🍴 CALL 🅖M 🏊 📷 / SOME UNITS 🐕 ⊗ VCR 📶 📷

QUALITY INN & SUITES CONFERENCE CENTER *Book great rates at AAA.com*

AAA SAVE
♦♦♦
Hotel
$110-$170 3/1-10/31
$100-$160 11/1-2/28

Phone: (509)758-9500

Address: 700 Port Dr **Location:** Just w of Snake River Bridge on US 12, just n on 5th St. Located in a quiet area. **Facility:** Smoke free premises. 97 units. 76 one-bedroom standard units, some with whirlpools. 21 one-bedroom suites, some with whirlpools. 3 stories, interior corridors. *Bath:* combo or shower only. **Terms:** 14 day cancellation notice. **Amenities:** high-speed Internet, irons, hair dryers. *Some:* dual phone lines. **Dining:** Bogey's Restaurant, see separate listing. **Pool(s):** heated outdoor. **Leisure Activities:** whirlpool, driving range, putting course, exercise room. **Guest Services:** valet and coin laundry, airport transportation-Lewiston Airport, wireless Internet. **Business Services:** conference facilities, business center. **Cards:** AX, DC, DS, MC, VI. **Free Special Amenities: full breakfast and high-speed Internet.**

✈ 🍴 CALL 🅖M 🏊 ⊗ 📷 📶 📷 📷

——— WHERE TO DINE ———

BOGEY'S RESTAURANT

♦♦ ♦♦
American
$6-$23

Phone: 509/758-9500

Enjoy your steak or seafood in a comfortable, contemporary dining room with views of the river and the manicured grounds of the hotel. Casual dress. **Bar:** Full bar. **Reservations:** accepted. **Hours:** 6 am-2 & 5-9 pm. Closed: 12/25; also Sun. **Address:** 700 Port Dr **Location:** Just w of Snake River Bridge on US 12, just n on 5th St; in Quality Inn & Suites Conference Center. **Parking:** on-site. **Cards:** AX, CB, DC, DS, MC, VI.

CALL 🅖M

ROOSTER'S WATERFRONT RESTAURANT

♦♦ ♦♦
American
$5-$20

Phone: 509/751-0155

The casual, nautical-themed restaurant sits on the banks of the Snake River. Casual dress. **Bar:** Full bar. **Hours:** 11 am-9 pm, Fri & Sat-10 pm. Closed: 1/1, 11/26, 12/25. **Address:** 1550 Port Dr **Location:** 1.4 mi w of Snake River Bridge on US 12, just n. **Parking:** on-site. **Cards:** AX, DS, MC, VI.

CLE ELUM pop. 1,755

------ WHERE TO STAY ------

BEST WESTERN SNOWCAP LODGE   *Book great rates at AAA.com*   Phone: (509)674-0200

(AAA) (SAVE)
▼▼◆▼▼
Hotel
$120-$130 All Year

Address: 809 W Davis St **Location:** I-90, exit 84 eastbound, just n; exit westbound, 0.6 mi w, then just s. **Facility:** Smoke free premises. 50 one-bedroom standard units. 2 stories (no elevator), interior corridors. *Bath:* combo or shower only. **Parking:** on-site. **Terms:** check-in 4 pm. **Amenities:** high-speed Internet, dual phone lines, voice mail, irons, hair dryers. **Pool(s):** heated indoor. **Leisure Activities:** whirlpool, exercise room. **Guest Services:** complimentary laundry, wireless Internet. **Business Services:** meeting rooms. **Cards:** AX, DS, MC, VI. **Free Special Amenities: expanded continental breakfast and high-speed Internet.**

AAA Benefit:
Members save up to 20%, plus 10% bonus points with rewards program.

⟳ ✕ 🎥 🛏 🖥 🖨

CASCADE MOUNTAIN INN   Phone: (509)674-2380

(AAA) (SAVE)
▼◆▼
Motel
$49-$99 All Year

Address: 906 E 1st St **Location:** I-90, exit 85, 1 mi nw. **Facility:** 43 one-bedroom standard units, some with whirlpools. 2 stories, interior corridors. *Bath:* combo or shower only. **Parking:** on-site. **Amenities:** hair dryers. **Business Services:** meeting rooms, PC. **Cards:** AX, CB, DC, DS, MC, VI. **Free Special Amenities: continental breakfast and high-speed Internet.**

CALL 🔊M 🎥 🛏 🖥 🖨 / SOME UNITS 🐾 ✕

CLE ELUM TRAVELERS INN   *Book great rates at AAA.com*   Phone: (509)674-5535

(AAA) (SAVE)
▼◆▼
Motel
$60-$85 All Year

Address: 1001 E 1st St **Location:** I-90, exit 85, 1 mi w on SR 903. **Facility:** 33 units. 32 one- and 1 two-bedroom standard units. 1-2 stories (no elevator), interior/exterior corridors. *Bath:* combo or shower only. **Parking:** on-site. **Terms:** office hours 7 am-11 pm. **Amenities:** hair dryers. **Guest Services:** wireless Internet. **Business Services:** PC. **Cards:** AX, DS, MC, VI. **Free Special Amenities: full breakfast and high-speed Internet.**

📶 🎥 / SOME UNITS FEE 🐾 ✕ ☎ 🛏 🖨

A Quick Tip

For using TripTik® Travel Planner's enhanced features on AAA.com.

NO MAP CLUTTER
Click your right mouse button to access more navigation tools that pan, zoom and identify roads.

TripTik Travel Planner
AAA.com's all-in-one maps, directions and travel information resource.

Get more tips on pages 6 and 7.

THE INN AT SUNCADIA
Book at AAA.com
Phone: (509)649-6405

▼▼▼▼
Hotel
$179-$339 All Year

Address: 3320 Suncadia Tr **Location:** I-90, exit 80, 2 mi n, then 0.3 mi w. **Facility:** Smoke free premises. 18 one-bedroom standard units. 2 stories, interior corridors. **Parking:** on-site and valet. **Terms:** check-in 4 pm, 7 day cancellation notice-fee imposed. **Amenities:** video games (fee), CD players, high-speed Internet, dual phone lines, voice mail, safes, irons, hair dryers. *Some:* DVD players. **Dining:** Inn at Suncadia - Gas Lamp Grille - see separate listing. **Pool(s):** heated outdoor, heated indoor. **Leisure Activities:** saunas, whirlpools, steamrooms, waterslide, 4 lighted tennis courts, cross country skiing, ice skating, recreation programs, rental bicycles, hiking trails, jogging, basketball, game room. *Fee:* golf-18 holes, horseback riding, massage. **Guest Services:** area transportation, wireless Internet. **Business Services:** meeting rooms, business center. **Cards:** AX, CB, DC, DS, JC, MC, VI.

ASK ▮▮ CALL &M 🏊 🛁 ✕ ✕ 📷 🖥 💻 / SOME UNITS VCR

LODGE AT SUNCADIA
Phone: 509/649-6460

▼▼▼▼
Resort
Hotel
Rates not provided

Address: 3600 Suncadia Tr **Location:** I-90, exit 80, 2 mi n, then 0.3 mi w. **Facility:** One of two lodges in the newly created Suncadia Resort, this lodge boasts a panoramic view of the Cascade Mountains. The lodge features artwork and furniture from local artisans. Smoke free premises. 254 units. 127 one-bedroom standard units with kitchens. 92 one- and 35 two-bedroom suites, some with efficiencies and/or whirlpools. 6 stories, interior/exterior corridors. *Bath:* combo or shower only. **Parking:** on-site. **Terms:** check-in 4 pm. **Amenities:** video games (fee), high-speed Internet, dual phone lines, voice mail, irons, hair dryers. *Some:* DVD players. **Dining:** Portals, see separate listing. **Pool(s):** heated outdoor. **Leisure Activities:** whirlpool, waterslide, lifeguard on duty, 2 tennis courts, cross country skiing, recreation programs, hiking trails, jogging, spa. *Fee:* boats, canoes, paddleboats, fishing, golf-18 holes, ice skating, bicycles, horseback riding. **Guest Services:** valet and coin laundry, area transportation, wireless Internet. **Business Services:** meeting rooms, business center.

▮▮ Y CALL &M 🏊 🛁 ✕ ✕ 📷 🖥 💻 / SOME UNITS 🖥 📷

STEWART LODGE
Book great rates at AAA.com
Phone: (509)674-4548

AAA SAVE
▼▼ ▼▼
Motel
$90-$99 5/1-2/28
$86-$94 3/1-4/30

Address: 805 W 1st St **Location:** I-90, exit 84 eastbound, just n; exit westbound, 0.6 mi w. **Facility:** 37 units. 36 one-bedroom standard units. 1 cottage. 1-2 stories (no elevator), exterior corridors. *Bath:* combo or shower only. **Parking:** on-site. **Terms:** office hours 7 am-11 pm, cancellation fee imposed. **Amenities:** voice mail, hair dryers. *Some:* irons. **Pool(s):** heated outdoor. **Leisure Activities:** whirlpool, playground. **Cards:** AX, DS, MC, VI. **Free Special Amenities:** continental breakfast and local telephone calls.

▮▮→ 🏊 📷 🖥 📷 💻 / SOME UNITS FEE 🐾 ✕

TIMBER LODGE INN
Phone: 509/674-5966

▼▼▼
Motel
$70-$90 All Year

Address: 301 W 1st St **Location:** I-90, exit 84 eastbound, 1 mi ne; exit westbound, just w; downtown. **Facility:** 33 one-bedroom standard units. 2 stories (no elevator), interior/exterior corridors. **Parking:** on-site, winter plug-ins. **Terms:** cancellation fee imposed. **Leisure Activities:** whirlpool. **Guest Services:** coin laundry, wireless Internet. **Business Services:** meeting rooms, PC. **Cards:** AX, DS, MC, VI.

ASK ▮▮→ CALL &M 🖥 📷 / SOME UNITS FEE 🐾 ✕

─────── **WHERE TO DINE** ───────

THE COTTAGE CAFE
Phone: 509/674-2922

AAA
▼▼
American
$6-$12

A local favorite since 1935, the unpretentious restaurant specializes in family-style home cooking. It's hard to find a time when the place isn't busy. The on-premises bakery churns out temptations such as pies, sweet rolls and other desserts. Casual dress. **Bar:** Full bar. **Hours:** 24 hours. Closed: 12/25. **Address:** 911 E 1st St **Location:** I-90, exit 85, 1.1 mi w on SR 903. **Parking:** on-site. **Cards:** AX, CB, DC, DS, MC, VI.

CALL &M

INN AT SUNCADIA - GAS LAMP GRILLE
Phone: 509/649-6402

▼▼▼
American
$10-$41

The restaurant affords beautiful views of pristine forests, impressive mountains and its own well-manicured grounds, including the golf course. In the casually elegant dining room, diners partake of American food prepared with a Continental flair. Diverse offerings include locally raised Washington lamb for dinner and a distinctive take on the BLT, which substitutes grilled wild salmon for bacon, for lunch. Casual dress. **Bar:** Full bar. **Reservations:** suggested. **Hours:** 6:30 am-9 pm, seasonal hours may vary. **Address:** 3320 Suncadia Tr **Location:** I-90, exit 80, 2 mi n, then 0.3 mi w; in The Inn at Suncadia. **Parking:** on-site. **Cards:** AX, CB, DC, DS, JC, MC, VI.

MA MA VALLONE'S STEAK HOUSE & INN
Phone: 509/674-5174

▼▼▼
Steak
$9-$24

In a turn-of-the-20th-century boarding house with its original warm woodwork and many original fixtures, the homey restaurant serves up dishes such as garlic chicken, codfish Siciliano and excellent prime rib. The uncrowded dining room features a few quiet nooks, perfect places for cozy, romantic chats. Service is casual but attentive. Casual dress. **Bar:** Full bar. **Reservations:** suggested. **Hours:** 4:30 pm-9:30 pm. Closed: 12/24, 12/25. **Address:** 302 W 1st St **Location:** I-90, exit 84 eastbound, 1 mi ne; exit westbound, 2.5 mi ne. **Parking:** on-site. **Cards:** AX, DS, MC, VI.

PORTALS
Phone: 509/649-6473

▼▼▼
Western American
$12-$36

The elegant restaurant offers a spectacular view of the Cascade Mountains. The menu showcases fresh and local artisanal produce, not to mention great steaks. Casual resort wear is appropriate here. Dressy casual. **Bar:** Full bar. **Hours:** 6:30 am-4 & 5-9 pm. **Address:** 3600 Suncadia Tr **Location:** I-90, exit 80, 2 mi n, then 0.3 mi w; in Lodge at Suncadia. **Parking:** on-site. **Cards:** DC, DS, MC, VI.

CALL &M

SPACONE'S

▼▼▼
Italian
$13-$34

Phone: 509/674-9609

This cozy, homey and comfortable eatery serves a delicious array of traditional cuisine including ravioli, spaghetti carbonara and veal piccata. Being a relatively small establishment allows the chef considerable flexibility and creativity and makes for very personal service. At times, the small staff seems stretched, but management makes efforts to bring in reinforcements for times expected to be busy. Casual dress. **Bar:** Full bar. **Reservations:** suggested. **Hours:** 5 pm-9 pm, Fri & Sat-10 pm. Closed major holidays; also Mon. **Address:** 212 W Railroad Ave **Location:** I-90, exit 84 eastbound, 1 mi ne, then just s; exit westbound, just w. **Parking:** on-site. **Cards:** AX, MC, VI.

COLFAX pop. 2,844

———— WHERE TO STAY ————

WHEATLAND INN

▼▼▼
Hotel
$99-$139 All Year

Book at AAA.com   Phone: 509/397-0397

Address: 701 N Main **Location:** Downtown. **Facility:** Smoke free premises. 50 one-bedroom standard units, some with whirlpools. 2 stories (no elevator), interior corridors. *Bath:* combo or shower only. **Parking:** on-site. **Amenities:** high-speed Internet, voice mail, irons, hair dryers. **Pool(s):** heated indoor. **Leisure Activities:** whirlpool, exercise room. **Guest Services:** coin laundry, wireless Internet. **Business Services:** meeting rooms, PC. **Cards:** AX, CB, DC, DS, JC, MC, VI.

[ASK] CALL [⅚M] [🏊] [✕] [🐾] [📠] / SOME UNITS FEE [🐕] [🛗] [🍽️]

COLVILLE pop. 4,988

———— WHERE TO DINE ————

CAFE ITALIANO

▼▼▼
Italian
$5-$13

Phone: 509/684-5957

Italian and Greek dishes line the menu of the casual, comfortable and exceedingly friendly restaurant. A serene and shaded fountain courtyard allows for seasonal dining. Casual dress. **Bar:** Beer & wine. **Reservations:** accepted. **Hours:** 11 am-2 & 4-9 pm. Closed: 1/1, 11/26, 12/25. **Address:** 153 W 2nd Ave **Location:** Downtown. **Parking:** street. **Cards:** MC, VI.

———— *The following restaurant has not been evaluated by AAA but is listed for your information only.* ————

LOVITT RESTAURANT

[fyi]

Phone: 509/684-5444

Not evaluated. In a tree-shaded gingerbread Victorian house, the restaurant makes everything on the menu in house using local and organic ingredients whenever possible. The menu changes seasonally to ensure that no palates become bored. Even the pasta is freshly made, enhancing the delightful flavor of morel tagliatelle (with morel mushrooms, asparagus tips and Parmesan) and other dishes sure to please pasta lovers. Diners appreciate the variety and artistry. **Address:** 149 Hwy 395 S **Location:** US 395, Mile Post 228.

CONCRETE pop. 790

———— WHERE TO STAY ————

OVENELL'S HERITAGE INN B&B AND LOG CABINS

[AAA] [SAVE]

▼▼▼
Cabin
$110-$160 3/1-9/30
$105-$150 10/1-2/28

Phone: 360/853-8494

Address: 46276 Concrete Sauk Valley Rd **Location:** 0.5 mi w of downtown on SR 20, 3 mi se. **Facility:** Situated on 500 acres, modern cabins with a rustic feel are nestled in a meadow close to the river. Smoke free premises. 6 cabins. 2 stories (no elevator), interior/exterior corridors. *Bath:* combo or shower only. **Parking:** on-site. **Terms:** age restrictions may apply, 3 day cancellation notice-fee imposed. **Amenities:** video library, hair dryers. **Leisure Activities:** fishing, croquet, hiking trails, playground, horseshoes, volleyball. **Cards:** DS, MC, VI. **Free Special Amenities: local telephone calls.**

[✕] [✕] [VCR] [🛗] [🍽️] [📠] / SOME UNITS FEE [🐕] [☎]

COULEE DAM pop. 1,044

———— WHERE TO STAY ————

COLUMBIA RIVER INN

[AAA] [SAVE]

▼▼▼
Motel
$95-$115 3/1-9/30
$69-$95 10/1-2/28

Phone: (509)633-2100

Address: 10 Lincoln Ave **Location:** On SR 155 at Visitor Center. **Facility:** Smoke free premises. 35 units. 34 one-bedroom standard units, some with whirlpools. 1 two-bedroom suite with kitchen. 2 stories (no elevator), exterior corridors. *Bath:* combo or shower only. **Parking:** on-site, winter plug-ins. **Terms:** office hours 7 am-10 pm, check-in 4 pm. **Amenities:** high-speed Internet, voice mail, irons, hair dryers. **Pool(s):** heated outdoor. **Leisure Activities:** sauna, whirlpool, exercise room. **Guest Services:** coin laundry. **Business Services:** meeting rooms, PC, fax (fee). **Cards:** AX, DS, MC, VI. **Free Special Amenities: local telephone calls and high-speed Internet.**

[🏊] [✕] [✕] [🐾] [🛗] [🍽️] [📠]

COULEE HOUSE INN & SUITES

▼▼▼
Motel
$99-$199 All Year

Phone: (509)633-1101

Address: 110 Roosevelt Way **Location:** Just e of river bridge. **Facility:** 61 units. 57 one- and 2 two-bedroom standard units, some with efficiencies. 2 one-bedroom suites with kitchens. 2 stories (no elevator), exterior corridors. *Bath:* combo or shower only. **Parking:** on-site. **Terms:** office hours 7 am-10 pm, 7 day cancellation notice. **Amenities:** high-speed Internet, voice mail, hair dryers. *Some:* safes, irons. **Pool(s):** heated outdoor. **Leisure Activities:** sauna, whirlpools, limited exercise equipment. **Guest Services:** coin laundry, wireless Internet. **Business Services:** PC. **Cards:** AX, CB, DC, DS, JC, MC, VI.

[ASK] [🍴] [🏊] [✕] [🐾] [🛗] [🍽️] [📠] / SOME UNITS FEE [🐕] [✕]

COUPEVILLE pop. 1,723

──────── WHERE TO STAY ────────

ANCHORAGE INN BED & BREAKFAST
Phone: 360/678-5581

(AAA) (SAVE)

◆◆◆

Bed & Breakfast
$99-$159 All Year

Address: 807 N Main St **Location:** Just s of Front St; 0.5 mi n of jct SR 20; downtown. **Facility:** Billed as the "Hotel Del of Whidbey Island," the inn offers sweeping views of Penn Cove and Mt. Baker from its wrap-around front porch and most rooms. Smoke free premises. 7 one-bedroom standard units. 3 stories (no elevator), interior corridors. *Bath:* combo or shower only. **Parking:** on-site. **Terms:** age restrictions may apply, 3 day cancellation notice-fee imposed. **Amenities:** video library, hair dryers. *Some:* DVD players. **Guest Services:** wireless Internet. **Business Services:** PC. **Cards:** DS, MC, VI.

(icons)

THE BLUE GOOSE INN   *Book at AAA.com*
Phone: (360)678-4284

◆◆◆

Historic Bed & Breakfast
$109-$149 All Year

Address: 702 N Main St **Location:** 0.3 mi n of jct SR 20; downtown. **Facility:** Furnished with period antiques, the property consists of two neighboring homes built in 1887 and 1891; located within walking distance of downtown. Smoke free premises. 6 units. 5 one-bedroom standard units, some with whirlpools. 1 one-bedroom suite. 2 stories (no elevator), interior corridors. *Bath:* combo or shower only. **Parking:** on-site. **Terms:** check-in 4 pm, age restrictions may apply, 7 day cancellation notice-fee imposed. **Amenities:** DVD players, irons, hair dryers. **Guest Services:** wireless Internet. **Cards:** AX, DS, MC, VI.

(icons)

CAPTAIN WHIDBEY INN
Phone: 360/678-4097

◆◆

Historic Country Inn
Rates not provided

Address: 2072 Captain Whidbey Inn Rd **Location:** 3.5 mi e on SR 20, 0.8 mi s on Madrona Way, then just w. Located in a quiet area. **Facility:** Located on the wooded shore of Penn Cove, this 1907 inn offers rustic cabins and spacious rooms in a two-story building overlooking a lagoon. Smoke free premises. 29 units. 25 one-bedroom standard units. 4 cabins. 2 stories (no elevator), interior/exterior corridors. *Bath:* some shared or private, combo or shower only. **Parking:** on-site. **Terms:** check-in 4 pm, age restrictions may apply. **Amenities:** *Some:* high-speed Internet. **Leisure Activities:** boat dock, fishing, hiking trails. *Fee:* bicycles. **Guest Services:** TV in common area, wireless Internet. **Business Services:** meeting rooms.

(icons)

COMPASS ROSE
Phone: (360)678-5318

◆◆◆

Historic Bed & Breakfast
$115 All Year

Address: 508 S Main St **Location:** 0.5 mi s of jct SR 20. Located in the historic district. **Facility:** Breakfast served on fine china complemented by crystal, silver, linen and lace distinguishes this 1890 Queen Anne home. Smoke free premises. 2 one-bedroom standard units. 2 stories (no elevator), interior corridors. *Bath:* combo or shower only. **Parking:** on-site. **Terms:** check-in 4 pm. **Guest Services:** TV in common area, wireless Internet.

(icons)

THE COUPEVILLE INN
Phone: 360/678-6668

(AAA) (SAVE)

◆◆◆

Hotel
$105-$225 All Year

Address: 200 Coveland St **Location:** Just s of Front St; w of Main St; downtown. **Facility:** 26 units. 24 one-bedroom standard units. 1 one- and 1 two-bedroom suites with kitchens. 2 stories (no elevator), interior corridors. *Bath:* combo or shower only. **Parking:** on-site. **Terms:** office hours 6 am-9 pm, 2 night minimum stay - weekends. **Amenities:** video library (fee), voice mail, hair dryers. *Some:* DVD players. **Guest Services:** wireless Internet. **Business Services:** meeting rooms, PC. **Cards:** AX, DS, MC, VI. **Free Special Amenities:** expanded continental breakfast and high-speed Internet. *(See color ad below)*

(icons)

──────── ▼ *See AAA listing above* ▼ ────────

GARDEN ISLE GUEST COTTAGES/VACATION
  HOME   Phone: 360-678-5641

▼▼▼
Cottage
$130-$275 All Year

Address: 207 NW Coveland St **Location:** 0.3 mi w of Main St; downtown. **Facility:** Two quaint guest cottages are situated in a small fruit orchard with views of Penn Cove; one cottage features a gas stove. Smoke free premises. 3 units. 1 house and 2 cottages. 1 story, exterior corridors. *Bath:* combo or shower only. **Parking:** on-site. **Terms:** 2 night minimum stay - seasonal and/or weekends, 7 day cancellation notice-fee imposed. **Amenities:** DVD players, CD players, irons, hair dryers. *Some:* high-speed Internet. **Leisure Activities:** whirlpool. **Guest Services:** wireless Internet. **Cards:** MC, VI.

[icons]

——— WHERE TO DINE ———

CHRISTOPHER'S ON WHIDBEY   Phone: 360/678-5480

▼▼▼
American
$8-$21

Packed with local flavor, any dish at this cafe is sure to please, but those with fresh seafood and the famous Penn Cove mussels are the first choice of most regulars. Casual dress. **Bar:** Beer & wine. **Reservations:** accepted. **Hours:** 11:30 am-2 & 5-close, Sat noon-2:30 & 5-close. Closed major holidays; also Sun. **Address:** 103 NW Coveland St **Location:** Downtown. **Parking:** on-site. **Cards:** AX, MC, VI.

KNEAD & FEED   Phone: 360/678-5431

▼▼▼
Deli
$7-$13

Down a narrow set of stairs from street level, this small facility has great freshly made breads, salads, sandwiches and soup, not to mention killer cinnamon rolls. Patrons are treated to great water views from every table. Casual dress. **Reservations:** accepted. **Hours:** 11 am-3 pm, Sat & Sun 9 am-4 pm. Closed major holidays. **Address:** 4 Front St **Location:** Downtown. **Parking:** street. **Cards:** AX, MC, VI.

[icon]

DAYTON pop. 2,655

——— WHERE TO STAY ———

THE WEINHARD HOTEL   Phone: 509/382-4032

▼▼▼
Historic
Hotel
$125-$180 All Year

Address: 235 E Main St **Location:** Downtown. **Facility:** Turn-of-the-20th-century Victorian ambience at base of Blue Mountains. Originally built by a member of the Weinhard brewing family as a saloon and fraternal lodge meeting place. Smoke free premises. 15 one-bedroom standard units, some with whirlpools. 2 stories (no elevator), interior corridors. **Parking:** on-site. **Terms:** office hours 7 am-9 pm, check-in 4 pm, 7 day cancellation notice-fee imposed. **Amenities:** high-speed Internet, hair dryers. *Some:* irons. **Guest Services:** PC (fee). **Cards:** AX, DS.

[icons]

——— WHERE TO DINE ———

PATIT CREEK RESTAURANT   Phone: 509/382-2625

▼▼▼
Continental
$8-$34

The menu changes weekly at the restaurant, which boasts an intimate dining room appointed with art deco touches and framed photos of '30s and '40s movie stars. The owner-chef personally selects all ingredients and prepares entrees, while his wife concocts tasty desserts such as espresso fudge torte, fresh strawberry shortcake and the rich signature floating island, meringue served on creme anglaise. Daily lunch and dinner specials might include veal parmigiana or sea bass prepared fisherman style. Casual dress. **Bar:** Beer & wine. **Reservations:** required. **Hours:** 11:30 am-1:30 & 4:30-8 pm, Sat from 4:30 pm; hours may vary. Closed major holidays; also Sun-Tues. **Address:** 725 E Dayton Ave **Location:** On US 12; north edge of town. **Parking:** on-site. **Cards:** MC, VI.

DEMING pop. 210

——— WHERE TO DINE ———

THE NORTH FORK BREWERY   Phone: 360/599-2337

▼▼
Pizza
$8-$20

The eatery is out of the way to those who aren't heading to Mount Baker, but it's worth the scenic drive. Craft beers taste good with hearty Italian food. Casual dress. **Bar:** Beer & wine. **Hours:** 2 pm-10 pm, Sat & Sun noon-11 pm. Closed: major holidays; also 12/24. **Address:** 6186 Mt Baker Hwy (SR 542) **Location:** 6 mi e on SR 542 (Mt Baker Hwy) at MM 21. **Parking:** on-site. **Cards:** AX, DS, MC, VI.

[icon]

DES MOINES —See Seattle p. 675.

DUPONT —See Seattle p. 675.

EAST WENATCHEE pop. 5,757—See also WENATCHEE.

——— WHERE TO STAY ———

CEDARS INN, EAST WENATCHEE   *Book at AAA.com*   Phone: (509)886-8000

▼▼▼
Hotel
$61-$190 All Year

Address: 80 Ninth St NE **Location:** Just e of SR 28. **Facility:** 94 one-bedroom standard units, some with whirlpools. 3 stories, interior corridors. **Parking:** on-site. **Terms:** check-in 4 pm, cancellation fee imposed. **Amenities:** hair dryers. **Pool(s):** heated indoor. **Leisure Activities:** whirlpool, exercise room. **Guest Services:** valet and coin laundry, wireless Internet. **Business Services:** meeting rooms, PC. **Cards:** AX, DC, DS, MC, VI.

[icons]

EATONVILLE pop. 2,012

------ WHERE TO STAY ------

MILL VILLAGE MOTEL

AAA SAVE
Motel
$80-$100 All Year

Phone: 360/832-3200
Address: 210 Center St E **Location:** Just e of jct SR 161; center. **Facility:** 32 one-bedroom standard units. 2 stories (no elevator), exterior corridors. *Bath:* combo or shower only. **Parking:** on-site. **Terms:** office hours 7 am-10 pm. **Amenities:** high-speed Internet, voice mail, hair dryers. **Guest Services:** wireless Internet. **Business Services:** meeting rooms, PC. **Cards:** AX, DC, DS, MC, VI. **Free Special Amenities:** expanded continental breakfast and high-speed Internet.

EDMONDS —See Seattle p. 676.

ELLENSBURG pop. 15,414

------ WHERE TO STAY ------

BEST WESTERN LINCOLN INN & SUITES   *Book great rates at AAA.com*

AAA SAVE
Hotel
$99-$299 All Year

Phone: (509)925-4244

AAA Benefit:
Members save up to 20%, plus 10% bonus points with rewards program.

Address: 211 W Umptanum Rd **Location:** I-90, exit 109, just n, then just w. **Facility:** Smoke free premises. 55 units. 52 one-bedroom standard units, some with whirlpools. 3 one-bedroom suites with efficiencies. 3 stories, interior corridors. *Bath:* combo or shower only. **Parking:** on-site. **Terms:** cancellation fee imposed. **Amenities:** high-speed Internet, dual phone lines, voice mail, irons, hair dryers. **Pool(s):** heated indoor. **Leisure Activities:** whirlpool, barbecue area with picnic tables, fish cleaning facilities, exercise room. *Fee:* massage. **Guest Services:** coin laundry, wireless Internet. **Business Services:** meeting rooms, business center. **Cards:** AX, CB, DC, DS, JC, MC, VI. **Free Special Amenities:** full breakfast and high-speed Internet. *(See color ad p 368, p 586, p 499, p 368, p 752, p 473, below, p 299, p 344, p 751, p 566 & p 500)*

DAYS INN   *Book at AAA.com*

Hotel
$75-$120 All Year

Phone: (509)933-1500
Address: 901 Berry Rd **Location:** I-90, exit 109, just s. **Facility:** Smoke free premises. 50 one-bedroom standard units, some with kitchens (no utensils) and/or whirlpools. 2 stories (no elevator), interior corridors. *Bath:* combo or shower only. **Parking:** on-site. **Terms:** cancellation fee imposed. **Amenities:** hair dryers. **Pool(s):** heated indoor. **Leisure Activities:** whirlpool, lighted tennis court, limited exercise equipment, basketball, game room. **Guest Services:** coin laundry, wireless Internet. **Business Services:** meeting rooms, PC. **Cards:** AX, DS, MC, VI.

ELLENSBURG COMFORT INN   *Book at AAA.com*   **Phone:** (509)925-7037

Hotel
$109-$139 5/1-2/28
$89-$119 3/1-4/30

Address: 1722 Canyon Rd **Location:** I-90, exit 109. **Facility:** 52 one-bedroom standard units, some with whirlpools. 2 stories (no elevator), interior corridors. *Bath:* combo or shower only. **Parking:** on-site. **Amenities:** voice mail, safes (fee), irons, hair dryers. **Pool(s):** heated indoor. **Leisure Activities:** whirlpool. **Guest Services:** coin laundry, wireless Internet. **Business Services:** meeting rooms, PC. **Cards:** AX, DC, DS, MC, VI.

HOLIDAY INN EXPRESS   *Book at AAA.com*   **Phone:** (509)962-9400

Hotel
$145-$175 All Year

Address: 1620 Canyon Rd **Location:** I-90, exit 109, just n. **Facility:** Smoke free premises. 66 units. 63 one-bedroom standard units, some with whirlpools. 3 one-bedroom suites with whirlpools. 3 stories, interior corridors. *Bath:* combo or shower only. **Amenities:** voice mail, irons, hair dryers. *Some:* high-speed Internet. **Pool(s):** heated indoor. **Leisure Activities:** whirlpool, exercise room. **Guest Services:** coin laundry, wireless Internet. **Business Services:** meeting rooms, business center. **Cards:** AX, CB, DC, DS, JC, MC, VI.

I-90 INN MOTEL   **Phone:** (509)925-9844

Motel
$64-$84 All Year

Address: 1390 Dollar Way N **Location:** I-90, exit 106, just n. **Facility:** 72 one-bedroom standard units. 2 stories (no elevator), exterior corridors. **Parking:** on-site, winter plug-ins. **Amenities:** video library. *Some:* hair dryers. **Leisure Activities:** fishing. **Guest Services:** coin laundry, wireless Internet. **Cards:** AX, DS, MC, VI. **Free Special Amenities:** continental breakfast and high-speed Internet.

NITES INN   **Phone:** 509/962-9600

Motel
$58-$69 All Year

Address: 1200 S Ruby **Location:** I-90, exit 109, 0.5 mi n. **Facility:** 32 one-bedroom standard units. 2 stories (no elevator), exterior corridors. **Parking:** on-site, winter plug-ins. **Guest Services:** coin laundry. **Cards:** AX, CB, DC, MC, VI.

QUALITY INN & CONFERENCE CENTER   *Book at AAA.com*   Phone: 509/925-9800

Hotel
Rates not provided

Address: 1700 Canyon Rd **Location:** I-90, exit 109, just n. **Facility:** 106 one-bedroom standard units. 2 stories (no elevator), interior corridors. **Parking:** on-site, winter plug-ins. **Amenities:** high-speed Internet, voice mail, hair dryers. **Pool(s):** heated indoor. **Leisure Activities:** whirlpool. **Guest Services:** coin laundry, wireless Internet. **Business Services:** meeting rooms.

──────── WHERE TO DINE ────────

PEARL'S ON PEARL WINE BAR & BISTRO

AAA

American
$8-$22

Phone: 509/962-8899

The exceedingly friendly, family-owned restaurant specializes in New American cuisine paired with an excellent wine selection. The menu, which changes every other month, is inventive and interesting. Casual dress. **Bar:** Full bar. **Reservations:** suggested. **Hours:** 4 pm-10 pm; hours may vary in winter. Closed major holidays; also Sun. **Address:** 311 N Pearl St **Location:** Downtown. **Parking:** street. **Cards:** AX, MC, VI.

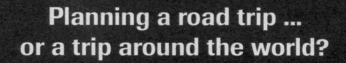

VALLEY CAFE, DELI & WINE SHOP

Phone: 509/925-3050

◈◈ ◈◈
American
$4-$20

The 1930 art deco building carries over that design into its small, cozy dining room. Eclectic dishes mix Asian, Mediterranean and Pacific Northwest influences. The use of spices is restrained but inventive. Casual dress. **Bar:** Beer & wine. **Reservations:** accepted. **Hours:** 11 am-9 pm. Closed: 1/1, 11/26, 12/24, 12/25. **Address:** 105 W 3rd Ave **Location:** Downtown. **Parking:** street. **Cards:** AX, DC, DS, MC, VI.

YELLOW CHURCH CAFE

Phone: 509/933-2233

◈◈ ◈◈
American
$6-$19

The eclectic favorite occupies an old church with a choir loft where diners are seated and an altar area housing an open kitchen lighted through stained-glass windows. On the menu are soup, sandwiches and daily specials for lunch and a wide selection of steaks and pasta for dinner. Casual dress. **Bar:** Beer & wine. **Reservations:** accepted. **Hours:** 11 am-close, Sat & Sun from 8 am. Closed: 7/4, 11/26, 12/25. **Address:** 111 S Pearl St **Location:** Just s of downtown; at Capitol. **Parking:** street. **Cards:** AX, CB, DC, JC, MC, VI.

ELMA pop. 3,049

------ WHERE TO STAY ------

MICROTEL INN & SUITES-ELMA   *Book at AAA.com*

Phone: 360/482-6868

◈◈ ◈◈
Hotel
Rates not provided

Address: 800 E Main St **Location:** Just ne of jct US 12 and SR 8. **Facility:** 71 one-bedroom standard units, some with whirlpools. 3 stories, interior corridors. *Bath:* combo or shower only. **Parking:** on-site. **Amenities:** high-speed Internet, voice mail, irons, hair dryers. **Guest Services:** coin laundry, wireless Internet. **Business Services:** meeting rooms, PC.

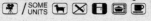

ENUMCLAW pop. 11,116

------ WHERE TO DINE ------

LEE'S RESTAURANT & LOUNGE

Phone: 360/825-3761

◈◈ ◈◈
American
$4-$12

More of a diner in feel, the casual downtown eatery is one where the staff recognizes locals by name. Comfort food is the special of the day, and the chicken-fried steak is hot and smothered in thick brown gravy. Dessert is probably something simple, like ice cream, homemade apple pie or tapioca. Casual dress. **Bar:** Full bar. **Reservations:** accepted. **Hours:** 6 am-10 pm, Sat & Sun 7 am-9 pm. Closed: 11/26, 12/25. **Address:** 1110 Griffin Ave **Location:** Downtown. **Parking:** on-site. **Cards:** AX, MC, VI.

EPHRATA pop. 6,808

------ WHERE TO STAY ------

BEST WESTERN RAMA INN   *Book great rates at AAA.com*

Phone: (509)754-7111

AAA SAVE
◈◈ ◈◈
Hotel
$90-$150 3/1-8/31
$80-$120 9/1-2/28

Address: 1818 Basin St SW **Location:** West end of town on SR 28. **Facility:** 46 units. 45 one-bedroom standard units, some with whirlpools. 1 one-bedroom suite with kitchen. 2 stories (no elevator), interior corridors. *Bath:* combo or shower only. **Parking:** on-site. **Terms:** 3 day cancellation notice. **Amenities:** high-speed Internet, voice mail, irons, hair dryers. **Pool(s):** heated indoor. **Leisure Activities:** sauna, whirlpool. **Guest Services:** coin laundry, wireless Internet. **Business Services:** meeting rooms, PC. **Cards:** AX, DC, DS, MC, VI. **Free Special Amenities:** expanded continental breakfast and high-speed Internet. *(See color ad below)*

AAA Benefit:
Members save up to 20%, plus 10% bonus points with rewards program.

CALL ✆M 🏊 🏋 🍴 🖥 💻 / SOME UNITS FEE 🐾 ✕

▼ See AAA listing above ▼

EVERETT —See Seattle p. 677.

EVERSON pop. 2,035

———— WHERE TO DINE ————

BLACK FOREST STEAK & SCHNITZEL HOUSE   **Phone:** 360/966-2855

▼▼▼ ▼▼▼
Steak
$14-$24

Although the steakhouse is not easy to find, its steaks make the effort worthwhile. A mesquite grilling technique is employed in flavorful food preparations. Casual dress. **Bar:** Full bar. **Hours:** 5 pm-10 pm. Closed major holidays. **Address:** 203 W Main St **Location:** Center. **Parking:** street. **Cards:** AX, MC, VI.

FEDERAL WAY —See Seattle p. 680.

FERNDALE pop. 8,758

———— WHERE TO STAY ————

FERNDALE SUPER 8   *Book at AAA.com*   **Phone:** (360)384-8881

▼▼ ▼▼
Hotel
$70-$185 All Year

Address: 5788 Barrett Ave **Location:** I-5, exit 262, just ne. **Facility:** 78 units. 77 one-bedroom standard units. 1 one-bedroom suite. 3 stories, interior corridors. *Bath:* combo or shower only. **Parking:** on-site. **Amenities:** high-speed Internet, hair dryers. **Pool(s):** heated indoor. **Leisure Activities:** whirlpool. **Guest Services:** coin laundry, wireless Internet. **Business Services:** meeting rooms. **Cards:** AX, CB, DC, DS, MC, VI.

(ASK) (TI+) CALL (ÊM) 🛄 🎦 🗂 🖳 / SOME UNITS FEE 🐾 ☒ 🖼

SILVER REEF HOTEL CASINO & SPA   *Book great rates at AAA.com*   **Phone:** (360)383-0777

(AAA) (SAVE)
▼▼▼
Hotel
$116-$269 All Year

Address: 4876 Haxton Way **Location:** I-5, exit 260, 3.6 mi w. **Facility:** Modern, spacious guest rooms are conveniently located above a spa, restaurants and a full-service casino; property charges no room tax. 105 units. 101 one-bedroom standard units. 4 one-bedroom suites with whirlpools. 6 stories, interior corridors. *Bath:* combo or shower only. **Parking:** on-site. **Terms:** check-in 4 pm. **Amenities:** high-speed Internet, voice mail, irons, hair dryers. *Some:* safes. **Dining:** 4 restaurants, also, The Steak House at Silver Reef, see separate listing, entertainment. **Pool(s):** heated indoor. **Leisure Activities:** sauna, whirlpool, steamroom, exercise room, spa. **Guest Services:** valet laundry, wireless Internet. **Business Services:** meeting rooms, PC. **Cards:** AX, CB, DC, DS, JC, MC, VI. **Free Special Amenities:** expanded continental breakfast and high-speed Internet. *(See color ad p 527)*

🎰 🍴 🍸 🛄 ☒ 🎦 🖳 / SOME UNITS FEE 🐾 ☒ 🗂 🖼

———— WHERE TO DINE ————

THE STEAK HOUSE AT SILVER REEF   **Phone:** 360/543-7178

▼▼▼
Steak
$24-$40

Just off the casino floor, this steakhouse feels like an intimate formal retreat from the bells and whistles of whirling slots. Steak butter bastes broiled aged Prime steaks, and tableside preparations include steak Diane and cherries jubilee. On Friday and Saturday, patrons can request the featured slow-roasted prime rib. Casual dress. **Bar:** Full bar. **Reservations:** suggested. **Hours:** 5 pm-9 pm, Fri & Sat-10 pm. **Address:** 4876 Haxton Way **Location:** I-5, exit 260, 3.6 mi w; in Silver Reef Hotel Casino & Spa. **Parking:** on-site. **Cards:** AX, CB, DC, DS, JC, MC, VI. *(See color ad p 527)*

FIFE —See Seattle p. 682.

FORKS pop. 3,120—See also OLYMPIC NATIONAL PARK.

———— WHERE TO STAY ————

FORKS MOTEL   **Phone:** (360)374-6243

(AAA) (SAVE)
▼▼▼
Motel
$57-$150 All Year

Address: 351 US 101 (S Forks Ave) **Location:** Just s. **Facility:** 73 units. 64 one- and 8 two-bedroom standard units, some with kitchens. 1 two-bedroom suite with whirlpool. 1-2 stories (no elevator), exterior corridors. *Bath:* combo or shower only. **Parking:** on-site. **Terms:** office hours 7 am-11 pm. **Amenities:** *Some:* DVD players, hair dryers. **Pool(s):** heated outdoor. **Guest Services:** coin laundry, wireless Internet. **Cards:** AX, CB, DC, DS, JC, MC, VI. **Free Special Amenities:** local telephone calls and high-speed Internet.

(TI+) 🛄 🎦 🖳 / 00ME UNITS FEE 🐾 ☒ 🕎 🗂 🖼

MANITOU LODGE   **Phone:** 360/374-6295

▼▼▼
Bed & Breakfast
$99-$179 All Year

Address: 813 Kilmer Rd **Location:** 7.7 mi sw on SR 110 (LaPush Rd), 0.7 mi w on Mora Rd, then 0.8 mi n. **Facility:** Designated smoking area. 7 units. 5 one-bedroom standard units. 2 cabins. 1-2 stories (no elevator), interior/exterior corridors. *Bath:* combo or shower only. **Parking:** on-site. **Terms:** check-in 4 pm, age restrictions may apply, 14 day cancellation notice-fee imposed. **Amenities:** hair dryers. **Leisure Activities:** hiking trails. **Guest Services:** wireless Internet. **Cards:** AX, DC, MC, VI.

☒ 🕎 🔲 🖾 🗂 🖼 🖳 / SOME UNITS FEE 🐾

MILLER TREE INN BED & BREAKFAST

Phone: (360)374-6806

Historic Bed & Breakfast

$115-$205 3/1-9/20
$95-$175 9/21-2/28

Address: 654 E Division St **Location:** 0.3 mi e of US 101 (S Forks Ave). **Facility:** On the edge of town, this restored farm home is a short drive from the mountains and ocean; rooms have views of the surrounding pasture and trees. Smoke free premises. 8 units. 7 one-bedroom standard units, some with whirlpools. 1 one-bedroom suite with efficiency and whirlpool. 3 stories (no elevator), interior/exterior corridors. *Bath:* combo or shower only. **Parking:** on-site. **Terms:** check-in 4:30 pm, 7 day cancellation notice-fee imposed. **Amenities:** video library, hair dryers. *Some:* DVD players, CD players. **Leisure Activities:** whirlpool. **Guest Services:** wireless Internet. **Business Services:** PC. **Cards:** AX, DS, MC, VI.

MISTY VALLEY INN BED AND BREAKFAST

Phone: 360/374-9389

Bed & Breakfast

$110-$130 3/1-9/23
$95-$115 9/24-2/28

Address: 194894 US 101 N **Location:** 3 mi n of downtown on US 101 (S Forks Ave) at MM 195. **Facility:** Smoke free premises. 4 one-bedroom standard units. 2 stories (no elevator), interior corridors. *Bath:* combo or shower only. **Parking:** on-site. **Terms:** check-in 4 pm, age restrictions may apply. **Amenities:** hair dryers. **Leisure Activities:** whirlpool. **Guest Services:** TV in common area, wireless Internet. **Business Services:** PC. **Cards:** AX, DS, MC, VI.

OLYMPIC SUITES INN

Phone: (360)374-5400

AAA SAVE

Motel

$49-$129 All Year

Address: 800 Olympic Dr **Location:** North end of town; just ne off US 101 (S Forks Ave). Located in a quiet area. **Facility:** 33 units. 3 one- and 2 two-bedroom standard units. 16 one- and 12 two-bedroom suites with kitchens (utensils extra charge). 2 stories (no elevator), exterior corridors. *Bath:* combo or shower only. **Parking:** on-site. **Terms:** office hours 8 am-11 pm. **Amenities:** CD players, hair dryers. *Some:* DVD players (fee). **Guest Services:** coin laundry, wireless Internet. **Cards:** DS, MC, VI. **Free Special Amenities:** local telephone calls and high-speed Internet.

PACIFIC INN MOTEL

Phone: (360)374-9400

Motel

$59-$200 All Year

Address: 352 US 101 (S Forks Ave) **Location:** Just s. **Facility:** 35 units. 34 one-bedroom standard units. 1 one-bedroom suite with kitchen. 2 stories (no elevator), exterior corridors. *Bath:* combo or shower only. **Parking:** on-site. **Terms:** office hours 7 am-11 pm. **Amenities:** *Some:* DVD players (fee). **Guest Services:** coin laundry, wireless Internet. **Business Services:** PC. **Cards:** AX, DS, MC, VI.

—— WHERE TO DINE ——

SMOKEHOUSE RESTAURANT

Phone: 360/374-6258

Steak & Seafood

$7-$27

Located at the edge of town just past a stream, the eatery offers such fresh selections of salmon that patrons may question if the fish were caught the same day. Aromas of smoked salmon linger in the dining room adorned with photos of locally spotted American bald eagles. The menu lists other selections of seafood as well as poultry and other meats, and diners can buy smoked salmon to take home. Parking is ample. Casual dress. **Bar:** Full bar. **Reservations:** suggested, weekends. **Hours:** 11 am-10 pm; to 9 pm off season. Closed: 11/26, 12/24, 12/25. **Address:** 193161 US 101 **Location:** 1 mi n on US 101 (S Forks Ave) at SR 110 (LaPush Rd). **Parking:** on-site. **Cards:** DS, MC, VI.

GIG HARBOR —*See Seattle p. 682.*

GOLDENDALE pop. 3,760

—— WHERE TO STAY ——

QUALITY INN & SUITES

Book great rates at AAA.com   **Phone:** (509)773-5881

AAA SAVE

Hotel

$89-$149 All Year

Address: 808 E Simcoe Dr **Location:** US 97, exit Simcoe Dr, just sw. **Facility:** 48 units. 46 one-bedroom standard units, some with whirlpools. 2 one-bedroom suites with kitchens. 2 stories (no elevator), exterior corridors. **Parking:** on-site. **Terms:** cancellation fee imposed. **Amenities:** high-speed Internet, voice mail, irons, hair dryers. **Pool(s):** heated outdoor. **Guest Services:** wireless Internet. **Business Services:** meeting rooms, PC. **Cards:** AX, DC, DS, MC, VI. **Free Special Amenities:** local telephone calls and high-speed Internet.

HOODSPORT

—— WHERE TO STAY ——

GLEN-AYR HOOD CANAL WATERFRONT RESORT

Phone: (360)877-9522

Hotel

$79-$199 All Year

Address: 25381 N US 101 **Location:** 1.5 mi n. **Facility:** Smoke free premises. 17 units. 14 one-bedroom standard units. 2 one-bedroom suites with efficiencies. 1 condominium. 2 stories (no elevator), exterior corridors. **Parking:** on-site. **Terms:** office hours 10 am-8 pm, 2 night minimum stay - seasonal and/or weekends, 14 day cancellation notice, 3 day in winter-fee imposed. **Amenities:** hair dryers. *Some:* DVD players, CD players. **Leisure Activities:** whirlpool, scuba diving, fishing. *Fee:* boat dock. **Guest Services:** coin laundry, wireless Internet. **Business Services:** meeting rooms. **Cards:** AX, DS, MC, VI.

HOQUIAM pop. 9,097—*See also ABERDEEN.*

———— WHERE TO STAY ————

HOQUIAM'S CASTLE BED & BREAKFAST
▼▼▼▼

Historic Bed
& Breakfast

$145-$195 3/1-9/30
$125-$175 10/1-2/28

Phone: (360)533-2005

Address: 515 Chenault Ave **Location:** Just w of jct US 101 and SR 109, just n on Grant St, then just e. **Facility:** This 1897 home overlooking the harbor is decorated with Victorian and museum pieces, including a Reginaphone and Brunswick Victrola. Smoke free premises. 4 one-bedroom standard units. 3 stories (no elevator), interior corridors. *Bath:* combo or shower only. **Parking:** on-site. **Terms:** check-in 4 pm, age restrictions may apply, 3 day cancellation notice. **Guest Services:** TV in common area, wireless Internet. **Business Services:** meeting rooms. **Cards:** MC, VI.

(ASK) ⊠ (AC) (W) (Z)

ILWACO pop. 950

———— WHERE TO STAY ————

HEIDI'S INN
(AAA) (SAVE)

▼

Motel
Rates not provided

Phone: 360-642-2387

Address: 126 Spruce St **Location:** Downtown. **Facility:** 26 one-bedroom standard units, some with kitchens. 2 stories (no elevator), exterior corridors. *Bath:* combo or shower only. **Parking:** on-site. **Terms:** office hours 8 am-midnight. **Amenities:** high-speed Internet. **Guest Services:** coin laundry, wireless Internet. **Free Special Amenities:** local telephone calls and high-speed Internet.

(AC) (🎥) (📶) / SOME UNITS FEE (🐾) ⊠ (📷) (📺)

INN AT HARBOUR VILLAGE
(AAA) (SAVE)

▼▼▼

Bed & Breakfast
$85-$185 All Year

Phone: (360)642-0087

Address: 120 Williams Ave NE **Location:** Just e of US 101. **Facility:** Nestled on a knoll, a short stroll from the activities at Port of Ilwaco, the inn is situated in a converted circa 1928 New England-style church. Smoke free premises. 10 one-bedroom standard units. 3 stories (no elevator), interior corridors. *Bath:* combo or shower only. **Parking:** on-site. **Terms:** office hours 7 am-10 pm, check-in 4 pm, age restrictions may apply, cancellation fee imposed. **Amenities:** video library, high-speed Internet, hair dryers. *Some:* DVD players, CD players, irons. **Guest Services:** wireless Internet. **Business Services:** meeting rooms. **Cards:** AX, DS, MC, VI. **Free Special Amenities:** continental breakfast and high-speed Internet.

⊠ (AC) (Z) (📺) / SOME UNITS (VCR)

———— WHERE TO DINE ————

THE PORT BISTRO
▼▼▼

American
$16-$30

Phone: 360-642-8447

By the Port of Ilwaco, the casual bistro presents a menu of creative fresh local seafood and steaks. Soft candles glow during stormy winter nights. Casual dress. **Bar:** Beer & wine. **Reservations:** accepted. **Hours:** 4 pm-9 pm. Closed: 11/26, 12/25; also Tues & Wed in winter. **Address:** 235 Howerton Way SE **Location:** South end of Port of Ilwaco. **Parking:** on-site. **Cards:** AX, MC, VI.

(AC)

ISSAQUAH —*See Seattle p. 683.*
KALAMA pop. 1,783

———— WHERE TO STAY ————

KALAMA RIVER INN
(AAA) (SAVE)

▼

Motel
$56-$70 3/1-9/6
$53-$65 9/7-2/28

Book great rates at AAA.com

Phone: (360)673-2855

Address: 602 NE Frontage Rd **Location:** I-5, exit 30 northbound, 0.4 mi n; exit southbound, 0.4 mi s. **Facility:** 44 one-bedroom standard units. 2 stories (no elevator), exterior corridors. **Parking:** on-site. **Terms:** office hours 7 am-11 pm, cancellation fee imposed. **Amenities:** high-speed Internet. *Some:* irons, hair dryers. **Guest Services:** wireless Internet. **Cards:** AX, DS, MC, VI. **Free Special Amenities:** continental breakfast and high-speed Internet.

(🍴) (🎥) (📶) (📷) / SOME UNITS FEE (🐾) ⊠

——— **WHERE TO DINE** ———

KALAMA BURGER BAR

American
$2-$4

Phone: 360/673-2091

This place is reminiscent of those simple little burger joints folks might remember from their childhood. The restaurant started as a small shack with a walk-up window and has matured into what it is today. Staples here are fast burgers, thick milk shakes and wavy fries. Those who don't do burgers might opt for a chili dog, chicken dinner, or captain's plate. If it's grilled or fried and fast, it's probably here. Casual dress. **Reservations:** not accepted. **Hours:** 9 am-9 pm. Closed major holidays. **Address:** 49 Ivy St **Location:** I-5, exit 30, 0.4 mi n; exit southbound, 0.4 mi s. **Parking:** on-site and street. **Cards:** AX, DS, MC, VI.

CALL 🚹

KELSO pop. 11,895

——— **WHERE TO STAY** ———

BEST WESTERN ALADDIN   *Book great rates at AAA.com*

Hotel
$99-$120 3/1-9/15
$90-$120 9/16-2/28

Phone: (360)425-9660

Address: 310 Long Ave **Location:** I-5, exit 39, 1.1 mi w via Allen and W Main sts, then just n on 5th Ave NW. **Facility:** 78 one-bedroom standard units, some with kitchens. 2 stories (no elevator), interior corridors. **Parking:** on-site. **Amenities:** high-speed Internet, irons, hair dryers. *Some:* DVD players (fee). **Pool(s):** heated indoor. **Leisure Activities:** whirlpool. **Guest Services:** coin laundry. **Cards:** AX, CB, DC, DS, JC, MC, VI. **Free Special Amenities:** expanded continental breakfast and high-speed Internet.

COMFORT INN   *Book great rates at AAA.com*

Hotel
$85-$99 3/1-9/30
$80-$90 10/1-2/28

Phone: (360)425-4600

Address: 440 Three Rivers Dr **Location:** I-5, exit 39, just sw. Adjacent to Three Rivers Mall. **Facility:** 57 one-bedroom standard units, some with whirlpools. 2 stories (no elevator), interior corridors. **Parking:** on-site. **Amenities:** high-speed Internet, irons, hair dryers. **Pool(s):** heated indoor. **Leisure Activities:** whirlpool, limited exercise equipment. **Guest Services:** valet laundry, wireless Internet. **Business Services:** PC. **Cards:** AX, DC, DS, MC, VI. **Free Special Amenities:** continental breakfast and high-speed Internet.

GUESTHOUSE INN & SUITES   *Book at AAA.com*

Hotel
Rates not provided

Phone: 360/414-5953

Address: 501 Three Rivers Dr **Location:** I-5, exit 39, 0.3 mi w on Allen St, then 0.3 mi s. Located adjacent to Three Rivers Mall. **Facility:** 60 units. 56 one- and 2 two-bedroom standard units, some with whirlpools. 2 one-bedroom suites with efficiencies. 3 stories, interior corridors. *Bath:* combo or shower only. **Parking:** on-site. **Amenities:** video library (fee), high-speed Internet, voice mail, irons, hair dryers. **Pool(s):** heated indoor. **Leisure Activities:** whirlpool, exercise room. **Guest Services:** valet and coin laundry, wireless Internet. **Business Services:** meeting rooms, PC.

MOTEL 6 - 43   *Book at AAA.com*   Phone: (360)425-3229
Motel
Address: 106 Minor Rd **Location:** I-5, exit 39, 0.3 mi ne. **Facility:** 63 one-bedroom standard units. 2 stories (no elevator), exterior corridors. *Bath:* shower only. **Parking:** on-site. **Pool(s):** heated outdoor. **Guest Services:** coin laundry. **Cards:** AX, CB, DC, DS, MC, VI.
$55-$65 All Year

RED LION HOTEL & CONFERENCE CENTER
KELSO/LONGVIEW   *Book great rates at AAA.com*   Phone: 360/636-4400
Hotel
Rates not provided
Address: 510 Kelso Dr **Location:** I-5, exit 39, 0.3 mi se. **Facility:** 161 units. 159 one-bedroom standard units. 2 one-bedroom suites. 2 stories (no elevator), interior corridors. *Bath:* combo or shower only. **Parking:** on-site. **Amenities:** high-speed Internet, voice mail, irons, hair dryers. **Pool(s):** heated outdoor. **Leisure Activities:** whirlpool, exercise room. **Guest Services:** valet and coin laundry, wireless Internet. **Business Services:** conference facilities. **Free Special Amenities: local telephone calls and high-speed Internet.**

SUPER 8 MOTEL   *Book at AAA.com*   Phone: 360/423-8880
Hotel
Rates not provided
Address: 250 Kelso Dr **Location:** I-5, exit 39, just se. **Facility:** 84 units. 82 one-bedroom standard units. 2 one-bedroom suites. 3 stories, interior corridors. *Bath:* combo or shower only. **Parking:** on-site. **Amenities:** high-speed Internet, hair dryers. **Pool(s):** heated indoor. **Leisure Activities:** whirlpool. **Guest Services:** coin laundry, wireless Internet.

------- **WHERE TO DINE** -------

BURGERVILLE   Phone: 360/501-4354
American
$2-$8
First-timers shouldn't let the fast food exterior fool them, as the burgers and chicken here adhere to a higher standard. Northwest ingredients come into play in the sandwiches. Casual dress. **Hours:** 7 am-10 pm. Closed: 11/26, 12/25. **Address:** 600 W Main St **Location:** I-5, exit 39, 1.1 mi w via Allen and W Main sts. **Parking:** on-site. **Cards:** DS, MC, VI.

KENNEWICK pop. 54,693

------- **WHERE TO STAY** -------

BEST WESTERN KENNEWICK INN   *Book great rates at AAA.com*   Phone: (509)586-1332
Hotel
$100-$140 All Year
Address: 4001 W 27th Ave **Location:** I-82, exit 113 (US 395), 0.8 mi n. **Facility:** Smoke free premises. 88 units. 87 one-bedroom standard units, some with whirlpools. 1 one-bedroom suite with kitchen. 3 stories, interior corridors. *Bath:* combo or shower only. **Parking:** on-site, winter plug-ins. **Amenities:** voice mail, safes, irons, hair dryers. *Some:* high-speed Internet. **Pool(s):** heated indoor. **Leisure Activities:** sauna, whirlpool, exercise room. **Guest Services:** valet and coin laundry, wireless Internet. **Business Services:** meeting rooms, business center. **Cards:** AX, DC, DS, MC, VI. **Free Special Amenities: full breakfast and high-speed Internet.**

AAA Benefit:
Members save up to 20%, plus 10% bonus points with rewards program.

CLOVER ISLAND INN   *Book at AAA.com*   Phone: (509)586-0541
Hotel
$89-$349 All Year
Address: 435 Clover Island Dr **Location:** US 395, exit Port of Kennewick, 1 mi e on Columbia Dr, then just n. **Facility:** 151 units. 147 one-bedroom standard units. 4 one-bedroom suites, some with whirlpools. 4 stories, interior corridors. **Parking:** on-site. **Amenities:** voice mail, irons, hair dryers. **Pool(s):** heated outdoor. **Leisure Activities:** sauna, whirlpool, boat dock, fishing, exercise room. **Guest Services:** wireless Internet. **Business Services:** conference facilities. **Cards:** AX, DS, MC, VI.

COMFORT INN   *Book at AAA.com*   Phone: (509)783-8396
Motel
$85-$130 All Year
Address: 7801 W Quinault Ave **Location:** 0.5 mi s on Columbia Center Blvd from SR 240. Located in a quiet area. **Facility:** 56 one-bedroom standard units, some with whirlpools. 2 stories (no elevator), interior corridors. *Bath:* combo or shower only. **Parking:** on-site. **Amenities:** safes (fee), irons, hair dryers. **Pool(s):** heated indoor. **Leisure Activities:** whirlpool. **Guest Services:** valet and coin laundry, wireless Internet. **Business Services:** PC. **Cards:** AX, DS, MC, VI.

DAYS INN KENNEWICK   *Book great rates at AAA.com*   Phone: (509)735-9511
Hotel
$72-$130 3/1-9/30
$63-$100 10/1-2/28
Address: 2811 W 2nd Ave **Location:** Jct US 395 and Clearwater Ave, just s, just w. **Facility:** 104 units. 103 one-bedroom standard units, some with efficiencies. 1 one-bedroom suite with efficiency and whirlpool. 3 stories (no elevator), interior/exterior corridors. **Parking:** on-site. **Amenities:** irons, hair dryers. **Pool(s):** heated outdoor. **Leisure Activities:** limited exercise equipment. **Guest Services:** coin laundry, wireless Internet. **Business Services:** meeting rooms, PC. **Cards:** AX, CB, DC, DS, MC, VI.

ECONO LODGE   *Book at AAA.com*   Phone: 509/783-6191
▼▼▼▼
Motel
Rates not provided

Address: 300 N Ely St, #A **Location:** On US 395, jct Clearwater Ave. **Facility:** 60 one-bedroom standard units. 2 , stories (no elevator), exterior corridors. **Parking:** on-site, winter plug-ins. **Amenities:** high-speed Internet, voice mail. **Guest Services:** coin laundry, wireless Internet.

FAIRFIELD INN BY MARRIOTT   *Book great rates at AAA.com*   Phone: (509)783-2164
▼▼▼▼
Hotel
$134-$164 All Year

Address: 7809 W Quinault Ave **Location:** 0.5 mi s on Columbia Center Blvd from SR 240. Located in a quiet area. **Facility:** Smoke free premises. 63 one-bedroom standard units. 3 stories, interior corridors. **Bath:** combo or shower only. **Parking:** on-site. **Terms:** cancellation fee imposed. **Amenities:** voice mail, irons, hair dryers. **Pool(s):** heated indoor. **Leisure Activities:** whirlpool, exercise room. **Guest Services:** valet laundry, wireless Internet. **Business Services:** business center. **Cards:** AX, CB, DC, DS, JC, MC, VI.

AAA Benefit:
Members save a minimum.5% off the best available rate.

GUESTHOUSE INTERNATIONAL SUITES   *Book great rates at AAA.com*   Phone: (509)735-2242
(AAA) [SAVE]
▼▼ ▼▼
Hotel
$72-$82 All Year

Address: 5616 W Clearwater Ave **Location:** US 395, 1.9 mi w. **Facility:** 56 one-bedroom standard units. 2 stories (no elevator), interior corridors. **Bath:** combo or shower only. **Parking:** on-site. **Terms:** cancellation fee imposed. **Amenities:** high-speed Internet, voice mail, irons, hair dryers. **Leisure Activities:** exercise room. **Guest Services:** coin laundry, wireless Internet. **Business Services:** business center. **Cards:** AX, DS, MC, VI. **Free Special Amenities: expanded continental breakfast and high-speed Internet.**

HILTON GARDEN INN   *Book great rates at AAA.com*   Phone: (509)735-4600
▼▼▼
Hotel
$89-$169 All Year

Address: 701 N Young St **Location:** 1 mi s of SR 240, just e. **Facility:** 120 units. 118 one-bedroom standard units. 2 one-bedroom suites. 3 stories, interior corridors. **Bath:** combo or shower only. **Parking:** on-site. **Terms:** 1-30 night minimum stay, cancellation fee imposed. **Amenities:** video games (fee), high-speed Internet, dual phone lines, voice mail, irons, hair dryers. **Pool(s):** heated indoor. **Leisure Activities:** whirlpool, exercise room. **Guest Services:** valet and coin laundry, wireless Internet. **Business Services:** meeting rooms, business center. **Cards:** AX, CB, DC, DS, JC, MC, VI.

AAA Benefit:
Members save 5% or more everyday!

KENNEWICK SUPER 8   *Book great rates at AAA.com*   Phone: (509)736-6888
(AAA) [SAVE]
▼▼▼
Hotel
$76-$91 3/1-10/1
$71-$86 10/2-2/28

Address: 626 N Columbia Center Blvd **Location:** 1.1 mi s of SR 240. **Facility:** 95 one-bedroom standard units. 3 stories, interior corridors. **Bath:** combo or shower only. **Parking:** on-site, winter plug-ins. **Terms:** 10 day cancellation notice. **Amenities:** hair dryers. **Pool(s):** heated indoor. **Leisure Activities:** whirlpool. **Guest Services:** coin laundry, wireless Internet. **Business Services:** PC. **Cards:** AX, CB, DC, DS, MC, VI. **Free Special Amenities: continental breakfast and high-speed Internet.**

LA QUINTA INN & SUITES KENNEWICK   *Book great rates at AAA.com*   Phone: (509)736-3326
▼▼▼
Hotel
$69-$119 All Year

Address: 4220 W 27th Pl **Location:** I-82, exit 113 (US 395), 0.8 mi n. Located in a quiet area. **Facility:** 53 one-bedroom standard units, some with efficiencies and/or whirlpools. 2 stories (no elevator), interior corridors. **Bath:** combo or shower only. **Parking:** on-site. **Amenities:** voice mail, irons, hair dryers. *Some:* dual phone lines. **Pool(s):** heated indoor. **Leisure Activities:** sauna, whirlpool, exercise room. **Guest Services:** valet and coin laundry, wireless Internet. **Business Services:** meeting rooms, business center. **Cards:** AX, CB, DS, JC, MC, VI.

QUALITY INN KENNEWICK   *Book at AAA.com*   Phone: (509)735-6100
▼▼▼
Hotel
$70-$90 All Year

Address: 7901 W Quinault Ave **Location:** 0.5 mi s on Columbia Center Blvd from SR 240. **Facility:** Smoke free premises. 125 units. 122 one-bedroom standard units, some with whirlpools. 3 one-bedroom suites. 4 stories, interior corridors. **Bath:** combo or shower only. **Parking:** on-site. **Amenities:** high-speed Internet, voice mail, irons, hair dryers. **Pool(s):** heated outdoor, heated indoor. **Leisure Activities:** whirlpool, exercise room. **Guest Services:** complimentary and valet laundry, wireless Internet. **Business Services:** meeting rooms, business center. **Cards:** AX, DS, MC, VI.

RED LION HOTEL COLUMBIA CENTER-KENNEWICK   *Book great rates at AAA.com*   Phone: (509)783-0611
(AAA) [SAVE]
▼▼▼▼
Hotel
$130 All Year

Address: 1101 N Columbia Center Blvd **Location:** SR 240, 0.5 mi s. **Facility:** Smoke free premises. 162 units. 154 one-bedroom standard units. 8 one-bedroom suites, some with whirlpools. 2 stories (no elevator), interior corridors. **Bath:** combo or shower only. **Parking:** on-site. **Terms:** cancellation fee imposed. **Amenities:** video games (fee), voice mail, irons, hair dryers. **Pool(s):** heated outdoor. **Guest Services:** valet laundry, wireless Internet. **Business Services:** conference facilities, business center. **Cards:** AX, CB, DC, DS, MC, VI.

WINGATE BY WYNDHAM   *Book at AAA.com*   Phone: 509/736-3656

Hotel
Rates not provided

Address: 2600 S Quillan Pl **Location:** I-82, exit 113 (US 395), 0.8 mi n. **Facility:** Smoke free premises. 64 units. 62 one-bedroom standard units. 2 one-bedroom suites. 3 stories, interior corridors. *Bath:* combo or shower only. **Parking:** on-site. **Terms:** check-in 4 pm. **Amenities:** high-speed Internet, voice mail, safes, irons, hair dryers. **Pool(s):** heated indoor. **Leisure Activities:** whirlpool, exercise room. **Guest Services:** coin laundry, wireless Internet. **Business Services:** meeting rooms, business center.

───── WHERE TO DINE ─────

CEDARS RESTAURANT   Phone: 509/582-2143

Steak & Seafood
$16-$30

The casual restaurant with sweeping panoramic views of the Columbia River serves a wide variety of fresh seafood and aged beef. Seasonal outdoor dining overlooking the river is available as well as a dock for those arriving by boat. Casual dress. **Bar:** Full bar. **Reservations:** accepted. **Hours:** 5 pm-9:30 pm. Closed: 1/1, 11/26, 12/24, 12/25. **Address:** 355 Clover Island Dr **Location:** US 395, exit Port of Kennewick, 1 mi e on Columbia Dr, then just n. **Parking:** on-site. **Cards:** AX, CB, DC, DS, JC, MC, VI.

───── The following restaurants have not been evaluated by AAA ─────
but are listed for your information only.

BANGKOK RESTAURANT   Phone: 509/735-7631

[fyi]   Not evaluated. Featuring traditional Thai cuisine. **Address:** 8300 Gage Blvd.

CASA MIA   Phone: 509/582-0440

[fyi]   Not evaluated. The family-owned eatery features award-winning pizza and pasta dishes in a casual and comfortable environment. **Address:** 2541 W Kennewick Ave.

KING & I AUTHENTIC THAI CUISINE   Phone: 509/736-5464

[fyi]   Not evaluated. Dishes, including those on the weekday lunch buffet, are seasoned traditionally. **Address:** 6030 Clearwater Ave.

KENT —*See Seattle p. 684.*

KINGSTON —*See Seattle p. 686.*

KIRKLAND —*See Seattle p. 686.*

LACEY pop. 31,226

───── WHERE TO STAY ─────

CANDLEWOOD SUITES OLYMPIA/LACEY   *Book at AAA.com*   Phone: (360)491-1698

Hotel
$150-$186 6/1-2/28
$140-$176 3/1-5/31

Address: 4440 3rd Ave SE **Location:** I-5, exit 108 northbound, just n; exit 109 southbound, just s on Martin Ave E, just e on College Way, then just s. **Facility:** 62 units. 50 one-bedroom standard units with efficiencies. 12 one-bedroom suites with kitchens. 4 stories, interior corridors. *Bath:* combo or shower only. **Parking:** on-site. **Terms:** cancellation fee imposed. **Amenities:** video library, DVD players, CD players, high-speed Internet, dual phone lines, voice mail, irons, hair dryers. **Leisure Activities:** exercise room. **Guest Services:** complimentary and valet laundry, wireless Internet. **Business Services:** meeting rooms, business center. **Cards:** AX, CB, DC, DS, JC, MC, VI.

[ASK] / SOME UNITS FEE

COMFORT INN   *Book great rates at AAA.com*   Phone: (360)456-6300

Hotel
$90-$130 All Year

Address: 4700 Park Center Ave NE **Location:** I-5, exit 109, just sw. **Facility:** Smoke free premises. 69 one-bedroom standard units. 3 stories, interior corridors. *Bath:* combo or shower only. **Parking:** on-site. **Amenities:** high-speed Internet, irons, hair dryers. **Pool(s):** heated indoor. **Leisure Activities:** whirlpool. **Guest Services:** valet laundry, wireless Internet. **Business Services:** meeting rooms, PC. **Cards:** AX, CB, DC, DS, JC, MC, VI. **Free Special Amenities:** expanded continental breakfast and high-speed Internet.

/ SOME UNITS [VCR]

HOLIDAY INN EXPRESS HOTEL & SUITES - LACEY   *Book at AAA.com*   Phone: (360)491-7985

Hotel
$144-$184 6/1-2/28
$139-$179 3/1-5/31

Address: 4460 3rd Ave SE **Location:** I-5, exit 108 northbound, just n; exit 109 southbound, just s on Martin Ave E, just e on College Way, then just s. **Facility:** Smoke free premises. 81 units. 80 one-bedroom standard units. 1 one-bedroom suite. 4 stories, interior corridors. *Bath:* combo or shower only. **Parking:** on-site. **Terms:** 3 day cancellation notice-fee imposed. **Amenities:** high-speed Internet, dual phone lines, voice mail, irons, hair dryers. **Pool(s):** heated indoor. **Leisure Activities:** exercise room. **Guest Services:** valet and coin laundry, wireless Internet. **Business Services:** meeting rooms, PC. **Cards:** AX, DC, DS, MC, VI.

[ASK]

LA QUINTA INN

Hotel
$80-$119 All Year

Phone: (360)412-1200
Address: 4704 Park Center Ave NE **Location:** I-5, exit 109, just sw. **Facility:** 63 one-bedroom standard units. 3 stories, interior corridors. *Bath:* combo or shower only. **Parking:** on-site. **Amenities:** high-speed Internet, dual phone lines, voice mail, irons, hair dryers. **Pool(s):** heated indoor. **Leisure Activities:** whirlpool, limited exercise equipment. **Guest Services:** valet laundry, wireless Internet. **Business Services:** PC. **Cards:** AX, CB, DS, MC, VI. **Free Special Amenities:** expanded continental breakfast and high-speed Internet.

QUALITY INN & SUITES

Hotel
$65-$115 All Year

Phone: (360)493-1991
Address: 120 College St SE **Location:** I-5, exit 109, just sw. **Facility:** 77 one-bedroom standard units, some with whirlpools. 3 stories (no elevator), interior corridors. *Bath:* combo or shower only. **Parking:** on-site. **Terms:** 30 day cancellation notice. **Amenities:** high-speed Internet, voice mail, safes (fee), irons, hair dryers. **Leisure Activities:** saunas, exercise room. **Guest Services:** valet and coin laundry, wireless Internet. **Business Services:** meeting rooms, PC. **Cards:** AX, CB, DC, DS, JC, MC, VI.

─── WHERE TO DINE ───

FARRELLI'S PIZZA AND POOL

Pizza
$8-$24

Phone: 360/493-2090
Classic hand-tossed pizza is cooked in an apple-wood-burning stove and served piping hot to gatherings of friends and softball teams that also take advantage of beers and the billiards tables. Among the few classic Italian dishes are chicken Alfredo and chicken cordon bleu. Casual dress. **Bar:** Full bar. **Reservations:** not accepted. **Hours:** 11 am-1 am, Thurs-Sat to 2 am. Closed: 4/12, 11/26, 12/25. **Address:** 4870 Yelm Hwy SE **Location:** Jct Yelm Hwy SE and College St SE. **Parking:** on-site. **Cards:** AX, DS, MC, VI.

RAMBLIN JACKS' LONESTAR KITCHEN

American
$8-$23

Phone: 360/528-3226
The popular high-energy gathering spot prepares everything from gourmet pizzas and smoked and grilled tri-tips to barbecue pork sandwiches and Southern fried chicken. Casual dress. **Bar:** Full bar. **Reservations:** not accepted. **Hours:** 11 am-9 pm, Fri & Sat-10 pm. Closed major holidays. **Address:** 4441 Pacific Ave **Location:** Jct Pacific Ave and College St. **Parking:** on-site. **Cards:** AX, DS, MC, VI.

RAM RESTAURANT AND BREWERY

American
$8-$22

Phone: 360/923-5900
The enormous restaurant features high ceilings, huge television screens, large sports-themed banners and a brew pub area. The menu is equally enormous, with steaks, poultry, pasta, seafood, salads, sandwiches and pizza. The on-site brewery turns out a large selection of microbrews. Casual dress. **Bar:** Full bar. **Reservations:** not accepted. **Hours:** 11 am-close. Closed: 12/25. **Address:** 8100 Freedom Ln NE, Suite C **Location:** I-5, exit 111 northbound, just ne on SR 512; exit southbound, just se. **Parking:** on-site. **Cards:** AX, MC, VI.

ROUND TABLE PIZZA

Pizza
$10-$17

Phone: 360/438-8844
This casual, family-oriented pizza place features high-quality ingredients and dough rolled fresh daily. Distinctive specialty pizzas are piled high with toppings. Casual dress. **Bar:** Beer & wine. **Reservations:** not accepted. **Hours:** 11 am-9 pm, Fri & Sat-10 pm. Closed major holidays. **Address:** 1401 Marvin Rd, Suite 310 **Location:** I-5, exit 111, just s. **Parking:** on-site. **Cards:** AX, MC, VI.

LA CONNER pop. 761

─── WHERE TO STAY ───

THE HERON INN & WATERGRASS DAY SPA

Bed & Breakfast
Rates not provided

Phone: 360/466-4626
Address: 117 Maple Ave **Location:** At Maple Ave and Morris St; northeast edge of town. **Facility:** Varied room sizes, decor and period furnishings characterize this country inn where three rooms feature gas fireplaces. Smoke free premises. 11 one-bedroom standard units, some with whirlpools. 3 stories (no elevator), interior corridors. **Parking:** on-site. **Terms:** office hours 7 am-7 pm. **Amenities:** video library, DVD players, hair dryers. **Leisure Activities:** whirlpool, spa. **Guest Services:** wireless Internet.

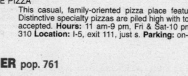

HOTEL PLANTER

Historic Hotel
$99-$159 All Year

Phone: 360/466-4710
Address: 715 1st St **Location:** South end of 1st St at Commercial St; downtown. **Facility:** Custom decorated and furnished guest rooms are located on the second floor of a renovated 1907 building. Smoke free premises. 12 one-bedroom standard units, some with whirlpools. 2 stories (no elevator), interior corridors. *Bath:* shower only. **Parking:** street. **Terms:** office hours 7 am-10 pm, age restrictions may apply, 3 day cancellation notice-fee imposed. **Amenities:** hair dryers. **Leisure Activities:** whirlpool. **Cards:** MC, VI.

LA CONNER CHANNEL LODGE

Hotel
$159-$369 All Year

Phone: 360/466-1500
Address: 205 N 1st St **Location:** Just n of Morris St; downtown. **Facility:** Smoke free premises. 40 units. 38 one-bedroom standard units, some with whirlpools. 2 one-bedroom suites with whirlpools. 3 stories, interior corridors. *Bath:* combo or shower only. **Parking:** on-site. **Terms:** cancellation fee imposed. **Amenities:** DVD players, CD players, high-speed Internet, voice mail, irons, hair dryers. **Leisure Activities:** boat dock. **Guest Services:** wireless Internet. **Business Services:** meeting rooms, PC. **Cards:** AX, DC, DS, MC, VI.

LA CONNER COUNTRY INN

Hotel
$129-$239 All Year

Phone: 360/466-3101
Address: 107 S 2nd St **Location:** 2nd and Morris sts; downtown. **Facility:** Smoke free premises. 28 units. 26 one- and 2 two-bedroom standard units. 2 stories (no elevator), interior/exterior corridors. *Bath:* combo or shower only. **Parking:** on-site. **Terms:** cancellation fee imposed. **Amenities:** DVD players, high-speed Internet, voice mail, hair dryers. **Dining:** Nell Thorn Restaurant & Pub, see separate listing. **Guest Services:** wireless Internet. **Business Services:** meeting rooms, PC. **Cards:** AX, DC, DS, MC, VI.

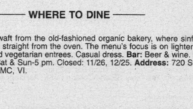

THE WILD IRIS INN

Bed & Breakfast
Rates not provided

Phone: 360/466-1400
Address: 121 Maple Ave **Location:** At Maple Ave and Morris St; northeast edge of town. **Facility:** A deck off each guest room provides panoramic views of the country fields surrounding the property. Smoke free premises. 18 one-bedroom standard units, some with whirlpools. 2 stories (no elevator), interior corridors. **Parking:** on-site. **Terms:** office hours 7:30 am-10 pm. **Amenities:** video library, DVD players, CD players, voice mail, hair dryers. *Some:* irons. **Guest Services:** wireless Internet. **Business Services:** meeting rooms.

─────── **WHERE TO DINE** ───────

CALICO CUPBOARD CAFE & BAKERY

American
$8-$12

Phone: 360/466-4451
Mouthwatering aromas waft from the old-fashioned organic bakery, where sinful cinnamon rolls, soft bread and warm cookies come straight from the oven. The menu's focus is on lighter fare, such as soups, salads, sandwiches, omelets and vegetarian entrees. Casual dress. **Bar:** Beer & wine. **Reservations:** not accepted. **Hours:** 7:30 am-4 pm, Sat & Sun-5 pm. **Closed:** 11/26, 12/25. **Address:** 720 S 1st St **Location:** Downtown. **Parking:** street. **Cards:** MC, VI.

FARMHOUSE RESTAURANT

American
$7-$17

Phone: 360/466-4411
The open dining room of the family restaurant is finished with attractive oak. A good cross-section of dependable comfort foods includes such tasty and neatly presented fare as a hot turkey sandwich with stuffing, mashed potatoes and cranberry sauce. Casual dress. **Bar:** Full bar. **Reservations:** accepted. **Hours:** 7 am-9 pm, Fri & Sat-10 pm. **Address:** 13724 La Conner-Whitney Rd **Location:** I-5, exit 230 (SR 20), 4 mi w. **Parking:** on-site. **Cards:** AX, DC, DS, MC, VI.

LA CONNER BREWING COMPANY

American
$5-$16

Phone: 360/466-1415
The eatery provides a cozy retreat for those tired after a full day of shopping or sightseeing. Patrons can enjoy a good book or a game of cards as they consume lighter dishes or gourmet pizza baked in the open wood-burning oven. In-house microbrews or root beer wash it all down. Casual dress. **Bar:** Beer & wine. **Hours:** 11:30 am-9 pm, Fri & Sat-10 pm; hours vary in winter. **Closed:** 11/26, 12/25. **Address:** 117 S 1st St **Location:** Downtown. **Parking:** street. **Cards:** MC, VI.

LA CONNER SEAFOOD & PRIME RIB HOUSE

Steak & Seafood
$7-$30

Phone: 360/466-4014
Located on the waterfront and surrounded by art galleries and museums, this eatery offers large windows from which to take in a lovely view of the channel while feasting on firecracker prawns; or sample luscious prime rib on the outdoor deck. Casual dress. **Bar:** Full bar. **Reservations:** accepted. **Hours:** 11:30 am-8 pm, Fri & Sat-9 pm. **Closed:** 11/26, 12/25. **Address:** 614 S 1st St **Location:** Downtown. **Parking:** street. **Cards:** AX, CB, DC, DS, MC, VI.

NELL THORN RESTAURANT & PUB

Continental
$10-$29

Phone: 360/466-4261
A charming European country flair envelops the rustic establishment, which serves reasonably priced dishes made from top-quality fresh local ingredients. Two popular items are the braised lamb shank and wild salmon served with seasonal organic vegetables. Each meal starts with crusty organic sourdough bread and should finish with a dessert treat created in house. The seasonally changing hours are listed on the Web site. Casual dress. **Bar:** Full bar. **Reservations:** suggested. **Hours:** noon-3 & 4-9 pm, Tues-Thurs from 4 pm. **Closed:** 1/1, 12/25; also Mon. **Address:** 205 E Washington St **Location:** 2nd and Morris sts; downtown; in La Conner Country Inn. **Parking:** on-site. **Cards:** AX, DS, MC, VI.

PALMER'S ON THE WATERFRONT

Continental
$9-$25

Phone: 360/466-3147
Located on the waterfront, large windows offer a great view of the channel while diners nibble on calamari rings or devour a peppercorn demi-glaced duck breast. Casual dress. **Bar:** Full bar. **Reservations:** accepted. **Hours:** 11:30 am-9 pm, Fri & Sat-10 pm. **Closed:** 12/25. **Address:** 512 S 1st St **Location:** Downtown. **Parking:** on-site. **Cards:** AX, MC, VI.

LAKEWOOD —See Seattle p. 687.

LANGLEY pop. 959

─────── **WHERE TO STAY** ───────

ASHINGDON MANOR

Bed & Breakfast
Rates not provided

Phone: 360/221-2334
Address: 5023 Langley Rd **Location:** 4 mi w on SR 525 from Clinton ferry landing, 2.5 mi n. Located in a quiet rural area. **Facility:** Pine case goods from Europe furnish the guest rooms at this country inn on 10 pastoral acres; available amenities include gas fireplaces and decks. Smoke free premises. 6 units. 5 one-bedroom standard units, some with whirlpools. 1 one-bedroom suite. 2 stories (no elevator), interior corridors. *Bath:* combo or shower only. **Parking:** on-site. **Terms:** age restrictions may apply. **Amenities:** DVD players, hair dryers. *Some:* high-speed Internet. **Guest Services:** wireless Internet.

BOAT YARD INN

▽▽▽▽

Hotel
$140-$250 All Year

Phone: (360)221-5120
Address: 200 Wharf St **Location:** East end of town on the waterfront. **Facility:** Smoke free premises. 10 units. 6 one-bedroom standard units with efficiencies. 4 two-bedroom suites with efficiencies. 2 stories (no elevator), exterior corridors. *Bath:* combo or shower only. **Parking:** on-site. **Terms:** office hours 9 am-6 pm, 2 night minimum stay, 10 day cancellation notice. **Amenities:** video library, DVD players, irons, hair dryers. **Guest Services:** wireless Internet. **Business Services:** meeting rooms. **Cards:** AX, CB, DC, DS, JC, MC, VI.

EAGLES NEST INN

▽▽▽▽

Bed & Breakfast
$125-$200 All Year

Phone: (360)221-5331
Address: 4680 Saratoga Rd **Location:** 1.8 mi n. Located in a quiet rural area. **Facility:** Sweeping views of Mount Baker, Camano Island and Saratoga Passage surround this private country retreat next to 400 acres of public trails. Smoke free premises. 4 one-bedroom standard units, some with whirlpools. 3 stories (no elevator), interior/exterior corridors. *Bath:* combo or shower only. **Parking:** on-site. **Terms:** check-in 4 pm, 2 night minimum stay - seasonal and/or weekends, age restrictions may apply, 7 day cancellation notice-fee imposed. **Amenities:** video library, DVD players, CD players, irons, hair dryers. **Leisure Activities:** whirlpool. **Guest Services:** wireless Internet. **Cards:** MC, VI.

THE INN AT LANGLEY   *Book at AAA.com*

▽▽▽▽

Hotel
Rates not provided

Phone: 360/221-3033
Address: 400 1st St **Location:** Center. **Facility:** Smoke free premises. 28 units. 22 one-bedroom standard units with whirlpools. 3 one- and 1 two-bedroom suites with whirlpools. 4 stories (no elevator), exterior corridors. **Parking:** on-site. **Terms:** office hours 8 am-6 pm, age restrictions may apply. **Amenities:** video library, DVD players, CD players, voice mail, honor bars, irons, hair dryers. **Leisure Activities:** spa. **Guest Services:** wireless Internet. **Business Services:** meeting rooms.

SARATOGA INN

▽▽▽▽

Bed & Breakfast
$180-$300 All Year

Phone: (360)221-5801
Address: 201 Cascade Ave **Location:** Downtown. **Facility:** A full breakfast, evening wine and hors d'oeuvres, and views of the Cascade Mountains and Saratoga Passage are highlights of this inn. Smoke free premises. 16 units. 15 one-bedroom standard units. 1 cottage. 2 stories (no elevator), interior corridors. *Bath:* combo or shower only. **Parking:** on-site. **Terms:** office hours 8 am-8 pm, 7 day cancellation notice-fee imposed. **Amenities:** video library, DVD players, irons, hair dryers. **Leisure Activities:** bicycles. **Guest Services:** wireless Internet. **Business Services:** meeting rooms. **Cards:** AX, DC, DS, MC, VI.

——— **WHERE TO DINE** ———

THE BRAEBURN

▼▼ ▼▼

American
$5-$11

Phone: 360/221-3211
In the center of town, the casual delicatessen/cafe presents a health-conscious menu. Patrons can choose from the menu board or from among the distinctive sandwiches, salads and quiches. Most of the delicious desserts are made on the premises. Casual dress. **Bar:** Beer & wine **Hours:** 9 am-3 pm, Sat & Sun from 7 am. Closed: 12/25. **Address:** 197 D 2nd St **Location:** South end of town center. **Parking:** street. **Cards:** MC, VI.

CAFE LANGLEY

▽▼▽▼

Western
Mediterranean
$7-$22

Phone: 360/221-3090
The menu of the quaint and cozy Mediterranean bistro is swayed by many influences—Greek, Turkish, North African, Armenian and Lebanese among them. Lamb and fish preparations are specialties. The sea theme is appropriate for the seaside town. Casual dress. **Bar:** Full bar. **Reservations:** suggested. **Hours:** 11:30 am-2:30 & 5-9 pm. Closed: 1/1, 11/26, 12/25. **Address:** 113 1st St **Location:** Jct Antes. **Parking:** street. **Cards:** AX, MC, VI.

THE EDGECLIFF BAR & GRILL

▽▼▽▼

American
$8-$28

Phone: 360/221-8899
The casual dining room affords great vistas of Saratoga Passage. Among the entrees are chicken penne Romanesco and beef tenderloin Gorgonzola. Casual dress. **Bar:** Full bar. **Reservations:** suggested. **Hours:** 11:30 am-8:15 pm, Fri & Sat from noon. Closed: 12/25. **Address:** 510 Cascade Ave **Location:** Edge of downtown. **Parking:** on-site. **Cards:** AX, DS, MC, VI.

LEAVENWORTH pop. 2,074

——— **WHERE TO STAY** ———

ALL SEASONS RIVER INN B & B

▽▽▽▽

Bed & Breakfast
$155-$230 All Year

Phone: 509/548-1425
Address: 8751 Icicle Rd **Location:** 1 mi s along Wenatchee River. **Facility:** Built specifically as a bed and breakfast, the inn is situated on the terraced and tree-shaded banks of the river. Smoke free premises. 6 units. 4 one-bedroom standard units with whirlpools. 2 one-bedroom suites with whirlpools. 2 stories (no elevator), interior corridors. **Parking:** on-site. **Terms:** 2-3 night minimum stay - seasonal and/or weekends, 14 day cancellation notice-fee imposed. **Amenities:** irons, hair dryers. **Leisure Activities:** bicycles. **Guest Services:** TV in common area, wireless Internet. **Cards:** MC, VI.

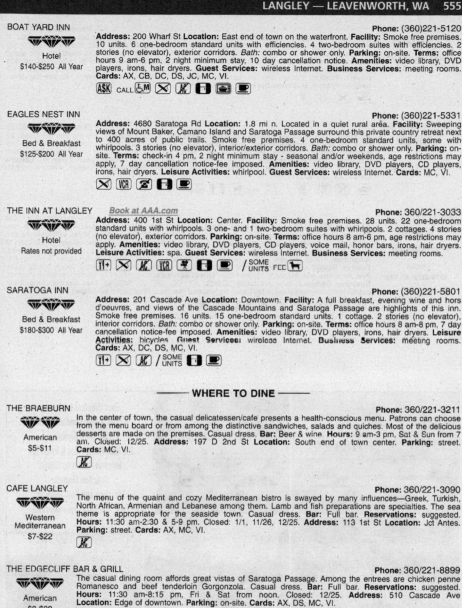

ALPEN ROSE INN

Bed & Breakfast
$105-$205 All Year

Phone: 509/548-3000

Address: 500 Alpine Pl **Location:** West end of town off Icicle Rd. **Facility:** Located just outside of town, but convenient to hiking, cross country skiing and mountain biking trails, this inn offers privacy and an outdoor pool and whirlpool. Designated smoking area. 15 one-bedroom standard units, some with whirlpools. 3 stories, interior corridors. *Bath:* combo or shower only. **Parking:** on-site. **Terms:** age restrictions may apply, 7 day cancellation notice. **Amenities:** video library, hair dryers. *Some:* DVD players. **Pool(s):** heated outdoor. **Leisure Activities:** whirlpool. *Fee:* massage. **Guest Services:** wireless Internet. **Business Services:** meeting rooms, PC. **Cards:** AX, DS, MC, VI.

ALPINE RIVERS INN

Hotel
$89-$119 All Year

Phone: 509/548-8888

Address: 1505 Alpensee Strasse **Location:** East edge of town. **Facility:** Smoke free premises. 27 units. 26 one-bedroom standard units, some with efficiencies. 1 one-bedroom suite. 2 stories (no elevator), exterior corridors. **Parking:** on-site. **Terms:** office hours 8 am-9 pm, 7 day cancellation notice-fee imposed. **Amenities:** DVD players, irons, hair dryers. **Pool(s):** heated outdoor. **Leisure Activities:** whirlpool. **Guest Services:** wireless Internet. **Business Services:** meeting rooms. **Cards:** AX, DS, MC, VI.

ASPEN SUITES

Hotel
$219-$379 All Year

Phone: (509)548-7000

Address: 525 Junction Ln **Location:** West side of town; check-in at Best Western Icicle Inn. **Facility:** Smoke free premises. 19 units. 2 one-, 16 two- and 1 three-bedroom suites with kitchens and whirlpools. 2 stories (no elevator), exterior corridors. **Parking:** on-site. **Terms:** off-site registration, 2 night minimum stay - seasonal and/or weekends, 7 day cancellation notice-fee imposed. **Amenities:** DVD players, CD players, high-speed Internet, voice mail, irons, hair dryers. **Pool(s):** heated outdoor. **Leisure Activities:** whirlpool, movie theatre, exercise room, sports court. *Fee:* miniature golf, massage, game room. **Guest Services:** complimentary laundry, wireless Internet. **Business Services:** business center. **Cards:** AX, DC, DS, JC, MC, VI. **Free Special Amenities:** expanded continental breakfast and high-speed Internet. *(See color ad below)*

BAVARIAN LODGE

AAA SAVE

Hotel
$109-$199 All Year

Phone: (509)548-7878

Address: 810 Hwy 2 **Location:** On US 2; center. **Facility:** Smoke free premises. 54 units. 53 one- and 1 two-bedroom standard units, some with whirlpools. 4 stories, interior corridors. *Bath:* combo or shower only. **Parking:** on-site. **Terms:** 3 day cancellation notice. **Amenities:** video library, DVD players, high-speed Internet, voice mail, irons, hair dryers. **Pool(s):** heated outdoor. **Leisure Activities:** whirlpools. **Guest Services:** wireless Internet. **Business Services:** meeting rooms, PC. **Cards:** AX, DS, MC, VI. **Free Special Amenities:** full breakfast and high-speed Internet. *(See color ad below)*

BAVARIAN RITZ HOTEL

Book great rates at AAA.com

AAA SAVE

Hotel
$89-$269 All Year

Phone: (509)548-5455

Address: 633 Front St **Location:** Center. **Facility:** Smoke free premises. 16 units. 12 one- and 2 two-bedroom standard units, some with kitchens and/or whirlpools. 1 one- and 1 two-bedroom suites with whirlpools. 2 stories (no elevator), interior/exterior corridors. **Parking:** on-site. **Terms:** office hours 8 am-8 pm, 7-9 night minimum stay - seasonal and/or weekends, 3 day cancellation notice-fee imposed. **Amenities:** DVD players, voice mail, irons, hair dryers. **Leisure Activities:** sun deck. **Cards:** AX, DS, MC, VI. **Free Special Amenities:** local telephone calls and early check-in/late check-out. *(See color ad p 550)*

BEST WESTERN ICICLE INN RESORT   *Book great rates at AAA.com*   Phone: (509)548-7000

AAA SAVE

Hotel
$130-$239 All Year

Address: 505 W US 2 **Location:** West side of town. **Facility:** Smoke free premises. 92 one-bedroom standard units, some with whirlpools. 3 stories, interior corridors. *Bath:* combo or shower only. **Parking:** on-site. **Terms:** 2 night minimum stay - seasonal and/or weekends, 7 day cancellation notice-fee imposed. **Amenities:** DVD players, CD players, voice mail, irons, hair dryers. *Some:* high-speed Internet. **Dining:** J. J. Hill's Restaurant & Wine Bar, see separate listing. **Pool(s):** heated outdoor. **Leisure Activities:** whirlpool, movie theater, exercise room, spa, sports court.

AAA Benefit:
Members save up to 20%, plus 10% bonus points with rewards program.

Fee: miniature golf, game room. **Guest Services:** coin laundry, wireless Internet. **Business Services:** meeting rooms, PC. **Cards:** AX, DC, DS, JC, MC, VI. *(See color ad p 556)*

BOSCH GARTEN B&B   Phone: (509)548-6900

Bed & Breakfast
$149-$179 All Year

Address: 9846 Dye Rd **Location:** East end of town via E Leavenworth and Mountain Home rds. **Facility:** A bright home with a living room with soaring cathedral ceiling, floor-to-ceiling windows and a magnificent live 18-foot Norfolk pine tree centerpiece. Smoke free premises. 3 one-bedroom standard units. 2 stories (no elevator), interior corridors. **Parking:** on-site. **Terms:** office hours 7 am-10 pm, 2 night minimum stay - seasonal and/or weekends, age restrictions may apply, 10 day cancellation notice-fee imposed. **Leisure Activities:** whirlpool. **Cards:** DS, MC, VI.

A$K   / SOME UNITS   VCR

DER RITTERHOF MOTOR INN   Phone: (509)548-5845

AAA SAVE

Hotel
$70-$107 All Year

Address: 190 US 2 **Location:** 0.3 mi w. **Facility:** 51 units. 49 one- and 2 two-bedroom standard units, some with efficiencies or kitchens. 2 stories (no elevator), exterior corridors. **Parking:** on-site. **Terms:** office hours 7 am-11 pm, 3 day cancellation notice-fee imposed. **Amenities:** hair dryers. **Pool(s):** heated outdoor. **Leisure Activities:** whirlpool, badminton, barbecue grills, picnic tables, volleyball. **Business Services:** meeting rooms, PC. **Cards:** AX, MC, VI.

CALL   / SOME UNITS   FEE

▼ *See AAA listing p 557* ▼

ENZIAN INN

Hotel
$125-$155 All Year

Phone: 509/548-5269

Address: 590 US 2 **Location:** Downtown. **Facility:** Smoke free premises. 105 units. 97 one-bedroom standard units. 8 one-bedroom suites with whirlpools. 4 stories, interior corridors. **Bath:** combo or shower only. **Parking:** on-site. **Terms:** 7 day cancellation notice-fee imposed. **Amenities:** DVD players, voice mail, irons, hair dryers. **Pool(s):** heated outdoor, heated indoor. **Leisure Activities:** whirlpools, exercise room, sports court. **Guest Services:** wireless Internet. **Business Services:** meeting rooms, PC. **Cards:** AX, DS, MC, VI. *(See color ad below)*

THE EVERGREEN INN

Motel
Rates not provided

Phone: 509/548-5515

Address: 1117 Front St **Location:** US 2, just s. Located in a quiet area. **Facility:** 39 units. 25 one- and 14 two-bedroom standard units, some with kitchens and/or whirlpools. 1-2 stories (no elevator), exterior corridors. **Bath:** combo or shower only. **Parking:** on-site. **Terms:** office hours 7 am-10 pm. **Amenities:** irons, hair dryers. **Leisure Activities:** whirlpools. **Guest Services:** coin laundry.

HOWARD JOHNSON

Motel
Rates not provided

Book at AAA.com

Phone: 509/548-4326

Address: 405 US 2 **Location:** West end of town. **Facility:** 41 one-bedroom standard units, some with whirlpools. 3 stories, exterior corridors. **Parking:** on-site, winter plug-ins. **Terms:** office hours 6 am-11 pm. **Amenities:** high-speed Internet, voice mail, safes, irons, hair dryers. **Pool(s):** heated outdoor. **Guest Services:** wireless Internet. **Business Services:** meeting rooms, PC.

LEAVENWORTH VILLAGE INN

AAA SAVE

Motel
$69-$299 All Year

Phone: (509)548-6620

Address: 1016 Commercial St **Location:** East side of downtown; corner of 10th St. **Facility:** Smoke free premises. 19 units. 15 one-bedroom standard units, some with whirlpools. 4 one-bedroom suites, some with kitchens and/or whirlpools. 3 stories (no elevator), exterior corridors. **Parking:** on-site. **Terms:** office hours 7 am-9 pm, check-in 4 pm, 3 day cancellation notice-fee imposed. **Amenities:** hair dryers. *Some:* irons. **Guest Services:** wireless Internet. **Cards:** AX, DS, MC, VI. **Free Special Amenities:** expanded continental breakfast and high-speed Internet.

LINDERHOF INN

AAA SAVE

Motel
$89-$153 All Year

Phone: (509)548-5283

Address: 690 US 2 **Location:** West end of town. **Facility:** Smoke free premises. 33 units. 22 one-bedroom standard units, some with whirlpools. 10 one- and 1 two-bedroom suites with efficiencies. 2-3 stories (no elevator), interior/exterior corridors. **Bath:** combo or shower only. **Parking:** on-site. **Terms:** office hours 7 am-10 pm, 3 day cancellation notice. **Pool(s):** heated outdoor. **Leisure Activities:** whirlpool, sun deck. **Guest Services:** wireless Internet. **Cards:** AX, DS, MC, VI. **Free Special Amenities:** expanded continental breakfast and high-speed Internet. *(See color ad p 557)*

▼ See AAA listing above ▼

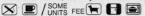

OBERTAL INN

AAA SAVE

Motel
$79-$179 All Year

Phone: 509/548-520

Address: 922 Commercial St **Location:** Off US 2; center. **Facility:** Smoke free premises. 27 on bedroom standard units, some with whirlpools. 3 stories (no elevator), exterior corridors. **Parking:** o site. **Terms:** office hours 8 am-10 pm, 2 night minimum stay - seasonal and/or weekends, cancellatio fee imposed. **Amenities:** hair dryers. **Leisure Activities:** whirlpool. **Guest Services:** wireless Interne **Cards:** AX, DC, DS, MC, VI.

PINE RIVER RANCH

Bed & Breakfast
Rates not provided

Phone: 509/763-395

Address: 19668 Hwy 207 **Location:** 15 mi w, 1.8 mi n on SR 207; off US 2. Located in a quiet rur area. **Facility:** Smoke free premises. 6 units. 5 one-bedroom standard units with whirlpools. 1 on bedroom suite with whirlpool. 1-2 stories (no elevator), interior/exterior corridors. **Parking:** on-sit **Terms:** office hours 9 am-9 pm, age restrictions may apply. **Amenities:** hair dryers. **Leisur Activities:** fishing, cross country skiing, bicycles. **Guest Services:** wireless Internet. **Busines Services:** meeting rooms.

QUALITY INN & SUITES   *Book at AAA.com*

Hotel
Rates not provided

Phone: 509/548-799

Address: 185 US 2 **Location:** 0.3 mi w. **Facility:** Smoke free premises. 78 units. 73 one-bedroo standard units, some with whirlpools. 4 one- and 1 three-bedroom suites. 3 stories, exterior corridor *Bath:* combo or shower only. **Parking:** on-site. **Terms:** check-in 4 pm. **Amenities:** DVD players, voic mail, irons, hair dryers. **Pool(s):** heated indoor. **Leisure Activities:** whirlpool, exercise room. **Gue Services:** coin laundry, wireless Internet. **Business Services:** meeting rooms, PC.

RIVER'S EDGE LODGE

Motel
Rates not provided

Phone: 509/548-761

Address: 8401 US 2 **Location:** 3.5 mi e. **Facility:** 23 one-bedroom standard units, some wit efficiencies. 2 stories (no elevator), exterior corridors. **Parking:** on-site **Terms:** office hours 7 am-10 pm. **Amenities:** voice mail. *Some:* hair dryers. **Pool(s):** heated outdoo **Leisure Activities:** whirlpool. **Guest Services:** wireless Internet. **Business Services:** PC.

RUN OF THE RIVER

▼△▼△▼

Bed & Breakfast
$230-$265 All Year

Phone: 509/548-7171

Address: 9308 E Leavenworth Rd **Location:** 1 mi w; off US 2. Located on the Wenatchee River. **Facility:** A classic log lodge-style building houses luxurious guest units with views of the Cascade Mountains and the adjacent wildlife refuge. Smoke free premises. 7 units. 6 one-bedroom standard units with whirlpools. 1 cabin. 2 stories (no elevator), interior/exterior corridors. **Parking:** on-site. **Terms:** office hours 9 am-8 pm, 2 night minimum stay - weekends, age restrictions may apply, 10 day cancellation notice. **Amenities:** CD players, voice mail, irons, hair dryers. **Leisure Activities:** whirlpool, bicycles, hiking trails. *Fee:* massage. **Guest Services:** wireless Internet. **Cards:** DS, MC, VI.

⊠ ⊠ (VCR) (✦) 🖥 📠

———— *The following lodging was either not evaluated or did not* ————
meet AAA rating requirements but is listed for your information only.

HAUS ROHRBACH PENSION

[fyi]

Phone: 509/548-7024

Not evaluated. **Address:** 12882 Ranger Rd **Location:** US 2, just n, 1.4 mi via Ski Hill Dr. Facilities, services, and decor characterize a mid-scale property.

———— **WHERE TO DINE** ————

THE ALLEY CAFE

▼△▼△▼

Italian
$9-$21

Phone: 509/548-6109

Servers are incredibly friendly in the quietly stylish and comfortable restaurant. Although choices primarily are of Italian fare, diners should keep an eye open for other specials. The tiramisu shouldn't be overlooked. Casual dress. **Bar:** Beer & wine. **Reservations:** accepted. **Hours:** 5 pm-9 pm. **Address:** 214 8th St **Location:** Downtown. **Parking:** street. **Cards:** AX, CB, DC, JC, MC, VI.

ANDREAS KELLER RESTAURANT   *Menu on AAA.com*

(AAA)

▼△▼△▼

German
$10-$22

Phone: 509/548-6000

Specializing in traditional Bavarian dining, music and decor, the restaurant lures guests with live music. On the menu are such savory favorites as wurst, red cabbage and the highlight of any German meal, apple strudel. German is spoken here. Casual dress. **Entertainment. Bar:** Beer & wine. **Hours:** 11 am-close. Closed: 12/25. **Address:** 829 Front St (Lower Level) **Location:** Downtown. **Parking:** street. **Cards:** AX, MC, VI.

CAFE CHRISTA

▼△▼△▼

German
$8-$21

Phone: 509/548-5074

On the second floor of a downtown business, the cafe has an enclosed wraparound porch on which patrons experience the feel of outdoor dining. Friendly servers deliver good German food, such as Wiener schnitzel and sauerbraten. Cordon bleu is another favorite. Casual dress. **Bar:** Beer & wine. **Reservations:** accepted. **Hours:** 11 am-9 pm; hours may vary in winter. Closed: 12/25. **Address:** 801 Front St **Location:** Downtown. **Parking:** street. **Cards:** MC, VI.

J. J. HILL'S RESTAURANT & WINE BAR

(AAA)

▼△▼△▼

American
$12-$24

Phone: 509/548-8000

The dining area features a distinctive railroad theme. The varied menu includes ribs, steak, seafood and some German specialties, which pair with wines from a list that includes several local varieties. Casual dress. **Bar:** Full bar. **Reservations:** suggested. **Hours:** 4:30 pm-9:30 pm. **Address:** 505 W US 2 **Location:** West side of town; in Best Western Icicle Inn Resort. **Parking:** on-site. **Cards:** AX, CB, DC, DS, JC, MC, VI.

KATZENJAMMER

▼△▼△▼

Steak & Seafood
$15-$35

Phone: 509/548-5826

The warm, convivial atmosphere welcomes many tourists at this busy restaurant below street level. A Bavarian theme, with plenty of rich color and dark wood, sets the tone. The menu includes a full range of quality steaks and fresh seafood. Casual dress. **Bar:** Full bar. **Reservations:** suggested. **Hours:** 5 pm-10 pm; to 9 pm 11/1-4/1. Closed: 11/26, 12/25. **Address:** 221 8th St **Location:** Downtown. **Parking:** street. **Cards:** MC, VI.

SANDY'S WAFFLE & DINNER HAUS

(AAA)

▼△▼△▼

American
$6-$8

Phone: 509/548-6779

The small breakfast-and-lunch restaurant serves home cooking with a nod to the Bavarian theme of the town. Homemade hash browns, made-from-scratch soups, sausage specialties and the delicious signature waffles contribute to a pleasing menu. Casual dress. **Hours:** 7 am-3 pm; to 2 pm in winter. Closed: 11/26, 12/25. **Address:** 894 Hwy 2 **Location:** Across from park. **Parking:** on-site. **Cards:** MC, VI.

THE TUMWATER INN RESTAURANT & LOUNGE

(AAA)

▼△▼△▼

American
$6-$22

Phone: 509/548-4232

In addition to a healthy number of German dishes, the menu includes soup, salad and sandwiches to satisfy any appetite. Eggs Benedict is served with a true hollandaise. A kind of "Victorian Bavarian" motif characterizes the comfortable dining room. Casual dress. **Bar:** Full bar. **Reservations:** accepted. **Hours:** 10 am-10 pm, Sat 9 am-11 pm, Sun 9 am-8 pm. Closed: 11/26, 12/25. **Address:** 219 9th St **Location:** Jct Commercial St; downtown. **Parking:** street. **Cards:** AX, DS, MC, VI.

CALL (Ġ.M)

VISCONTI'S

▼△▼△▼

Italian
$8-$28

Phone: 509/548-1213

The quietly elegant restaurant overlooks the downtown area of a quaint Bavarian-style village. Traditional Italian food matches with choices from one of the largest selections of Italian wines in the Northwest. Casual dress. **Bar:** Beer & wine. **Reservations:** suggested, for dinner. **Hours:** 11 am-10 pm, Fri & Sat-11 pm. Closed: 11/26, 12/24, 12/25. **Address:** 636 Front St **Location:** Downtown. **Parking:** street. **Cards:** AX, DS, MC, VI.

LIBERTY LAKE pop. 4,660

──────── WHERE TO STAY ────────

BEST WESTERN PEPPERTREE LIBERTY LAKE INN
Book great rates at AAA.com

Phone: (509)755-111

AAA [SAVE]
▼▼▼▼

Hotel
$64-$219 All Year

Address: 1816 N Pepper Ln **Location:** I-90, exit 296. **Facility:** Smoke free premises. 76 units. 69 one-bedroom standard units. 7 one-bedroom suites. 4 stories, interior corridors. *Bath:* combo or shower only. **Parking:** on-site. **Terms:** check-in 4 pm. **Amenities:** high-speed Internet, dual phone lines, voice mail, irons, hair dryers. **Pool(s):** heated indoor. **Leisure Activities:** whirlpool, exercise room. **Guest Services:** valet and coin laundry, wireless Internet. **Business Services:** meeting rooms, business center. **Cards:** AX, DS, MC, VI. **Free Special Amenities: full breakfast and high-speed Internet.**

AAA Benefit:
Members save up to 20%, plus 10% bonus points with rewards program.

CALL [&M] [≈] [✕] [🎦] [🗄] [🖥] [💻] / SOME UNITS FEE [🐕]

CEDARS INN SPOKANE AT LIBERTY LAKE
Book great rates at AAA.com

Phone: (509)340-3333

AAA [SAVE]
▼▼▼

Hotel
$69-$110 5/31-2/28
$69-$89 3/1-5/30

Address: 2327 N Madson Rd **Location:** I-90, exit 296, 1 mi e on Appleway Ave, then just n. **Facility:** 70 units. 62 one-bedroom standard units, some with whirlpools. 8 one-bedroom suites with efficiencies, some with whirlpools. 3 stories, interior corridors. *Bath:* combo or shower only. **Parking:** on-site. **Amenities:** high-speed Internet, dual phone lines, voice mail, irons, hair dryers. **Pool(s):** heated indoor. **Leisure Activities:** whirlpool, exercise room. **Guest Services:** valet and coin laundry, wireless Internet. **Business Services:** meeting rooms, PC. **Cards:** AX, CB, DC, DS, JC, MC, VI. **Free Special Amenities: expanded continental breakfast and high-speed Internet.** *(See color ad p 725)*

CALL [&M] [≈] [🎦] [💻] / SOME UNITS FEE [🐕] [✕] [🗄] [🖥]

LONG BEACH pop. 1,283

──────── WHERE TO STAY ────────

ANCHORAGE COTTAGES

Phone: 360/642-2351

▼▼▼

Cottage
$70-$128 All Year

Address: 2209 Boulevard N **Location:** Just w of SR 103. **Facility:** Smoke free premises. 10 cottages. 1 story, exterior corridors. *Bath:* combo or shower only. **Parking:** on-site. **Terms:** office hours 9 am-7 pm, 2 night minimum stay - seasonal and/or weekends, 30 day cancellation notice-fee imposed. **Amenities:** video library (fee), DVD players, high-speed Internet. **Leisure Activities:** playground sports court. **Guest Services:** wireless Internet. **Cards:** AX, DS, MC, VI.

[✕] [🅺] [VCR] [🕿] [🗄] [🖥] [💻] / SOME UNITS FEE [🐕]

BOARDWALK COTTAGES

Phone: 360/642-2305

AAA [SAVE]
▼▼▼ ▼▼▼

Cottage
$99-$179 3/1-9/30
$79-$129 10/1-2/28

Address: 800 Ocean Beach Blvd S **Location:** Just w of SR 103. **Facility:** Smoke free premises. 10 cottages. 1-2 stories (no elevator), exterior corridors. *Bath:* combo or shower only. **Parking:** on-site. **Terms:** office hours 9 am-9 pm, 14 day cancellation notice-fee imposed. **Amenities:** DVD players, high-speed Internet. *Some:* CD players. **Leisure Activities:** whirlpool. **Guest Services:** wireless Internet. **Cards:** MC, VI. **Free Special Amenities: continental breakfast and high-speed Internet.**

[✕] [🅺] [VCR] [🕿] [🗄] [🖥] [💻]

THE BREAKERS

Phone: 360/642-4414

AAA [SAVE]
▼▼ ▼▼

Condominium
$119-$298 3/1-10/31
$68-$199 11/1-2/28

Address: 210 26th St NW **Location:** Oceanfront. North end of downtown. **Facility:** 124 units. 34 one- and 30 two-bedroom standard units, some with efficiencies and/or whirlpools. 60 one-bedroom suites with kitchens. 3 stories (no elevator), exterior corridors. *Bath:* combo or shower only. **Terms:** check-in 4 pm, 20 day cancellation notice-fee imposed. **Amenities:** video library (fee), high-speed Internet, hair dryers. *Some:* DVD players. **Pool(s):** heated indoor. **Leisure Activities:** whirlpools, beach access, hiking trails, playground, basketball, horseshoes, volleyball. **Guest Services:** coin laundry, wireless Internet. **Business Services:** meeting rooms. **Cards:** AX, DS, MC, VI. **Free Special Amenities: local telephone calls and high-speed Internet.**

[≈] [✕] [✕] [🅺] [VCR] [💻] / SOME UNITS FFF [🐕] [🗄] [🖥]

OUR PLACE AT THE BEACH
Book at AAA.com

Phone: 360/642-3793

▼

Hotel
Rates not provided

Address: 1309 South Blvd **Location:** Just w of SR 103; south end of town. **Facility:** Smoke free premises. 25 units. 22 one-bedroom standard units, some with kitchens. 1 one- and 2 two-bedroom suites with kitchens. 2 stories (no elevator), exterior corridors. *Bath:* combo or shower only. **Parking:** on-site. **Terms:** office hours 7:30 am-10:30 pm. **Amenities:** video library, high-speed Internet. *Some:* DVD players (fee). **Leisure Activities:** sauna, whirlpools, steamroom, limited exercise equipment. **Guest Services:** wireless Internet.

[✕] [✕] [🅺] [🗄] [🖥] [💻] / SOME UNITS FEE [🐕] FEE [VCR]

RODEWAY INN & SUITES   *Book great rates at AAA.com*   **Phone:** (360)642-3714

AAA SAVE

Hotel
$70-$140 3/1-9/30
$63-$73 10/1-2/28

Address: 115 3rd St SW **Location:** Downtown. **Facility:** 42 units. 41 one-bedroom standard units, some with efficiencies. 1 one-bedroom suite. 2 stories (no elevator), exterior corridors. **Parking:** on-site. **Terms:** office hours 7 am-10 pm, 4 night minimum stay - seasonal and/or weekends, cancellation fee imposed. **Amenities:** high-speed Internet, voice mail, hair dryers. *Some:* DVD players (fee), irons. **Pool(s):** heated outdoor. **Guest Services:** coin laundry, wireless Internet. **Cards:** AX, DS, MC, VI. **Free Special Amenities:** continental breakfast and high-speed Internet.

SUPER 8 MOTEL   *Book great rates at AAA.com*   **Phone:** (360)642-8988

AAA SAVE

Hotel
$89-$199 3/1-8/31
$79-$199 9/1-2/28

Address: 500 Ocean Beach Blvd **Location:** On SR 103; downtown. **Facility:** Smoke free premises. 50 one-bedroom standard units. 3 stories, interior corridors. **Parking:** on-site. **Terms:** check-in 4 pm, 2 night minimum stay - seasonal and/or weekends. **Amenities:** high-speed Internet, irons, hair dryers. *Fee:* video library, safes. **Guest Services:** coin laundry, wireless Internet. **Business Services:** meeting rooms, PC. **Cards:** AX, DC, DS, MC, VI. **Free Special Amenities:** expanded continental breakfast and high-speed Internet.

——— **WHERE TO DINE** ———

CHEN'S CHINESE RESTAURANT   **Phone:** 360/642-8288

Chinese
$7-$10

The restaurant sustains a lively family atmosphere. The staff knows most of the locals, and it's not uncommon for the chef to come out and chat awhile. Traditional dishes are served efficiently. Casual dress. **Bar:** Full bar. **Reservations:** accepted. **Hours:** 11 am-10 pm. Closed: 11/26, 12/25. **Address:** 400 N Pacific Ave **Location:** North end of downtown. **Parking:** on-site. **Cards:** DS, MC, VI.

DEBI'S RESTAURANT   **Phone:** 360/642-3300

American
$4-$13

On the main street downtown, this place serves great eggs Benedict, buttermilk pancakes and other breakfast favorites. Casual dress. **Bar:** Beer & wine. **Hours:** 7 am-3 pm. Closed: 12/25. **Address:** 504 S Pacific Ave **Location:** Downtown. **Parking:** on-site. **Cards:** MC, VI.

DOOGERS SEAFOOD & GRILL   **Phone:** 360/642-4224

Seafood
$5-$22

Popular with families, the comfortable restaurant is rustic in decor with quaint touches. On the menu are traditional preparations of primarily seafood dishes, with a handful of pasta, chicken and beef entrees. Casual dress. **Bar:** Beer & wine. **Reservations:** not accepted. **Hours:** 11 am-9 pm. Closed: 11/26, 12/25. **Address:** 900 S Pacific Ave **Location:** Downtown. **Parking:** on-site. **Cards:** AX, DS, MC, VI.

CALL

EL COMPADRE   **Phone:** 360/642-8280

Mexican
$8-$13

Traditional Mexican food is served by a friendly staff in comfortable surroundings. Casual dress. **Bar:** Full bar. **Hours:** 11 am-9:30 pm, Fri & Sat-10:30 pm, Sun noon-9:30 pm. Closed: 4/12, 11/26, 12/25. **Address:** 1900 Pacific Ave N **Location:** North end of downtown. **Parking:** on-site. **Cards:** MC, VI.

LONG BEACH THAI CUISINE   **Phone:** 360/642-2557

Thai
$7-$15

The simple, clean restaurant focuses on traditional, freshly prepared Thai foods. Casual dress. **Reservations:** not accepted. **Hours:** 11 am-9 pm. Closed: 11/26, 12/25. **Address:** 1003 Pacific Ave N **Location:** North end of downtown. **Parking:** on-site. **Cards:** AX, DS, MC, VI.

LONG BEACH PENINSULA —See ILWACO, LONG BEACH, NAHCOTTA, OCEAN PARK & SEAVIEW.

LONGVIEW pop. 34,660

——— **WHERE TO STAY** ———

HUDSON MANOR INN & SUITES   **Phone:** (360)425-1100

AAA SAVE

Motel
$65-$90 All Year

Address: 1616 Hudson St **Location:** Downtown. **Facility:** 25 one-bedroom standard units, some with efficiencies. 2 stories (no elevator), exterior corridors. *Bath:* combo or shower only. **Parking:** on-site. **Terms:** cancellation fee imposed. **Amenities:** high-speed Internet, irons, hair dryers. **Guest Services:** wireless Internet. **Business Services:** PC. **Cards:** AX, DS, MC, VI. **Free Special Amenities:** expanded continental breakfast and high-speed Internet.

LONGVIEW TRAVELODGE   *Book great rates at AAA.com*   **Phone:** (360)423-6460

AAA SAVE

Motel
$55-$75 All Year

Address: 838 15th Ave **Location:** Downtown; opposite Medical Center. **Facility:** 32 one-bedroom standard units. 2 stories (no elevator), exterior corridors. *Bath:* combo or shower only. **Parking:** on-site. **Terms:** office hours 7:30 am-10 pm, cancellation fee imposed. **Amenities:** high-speed Internet. **Guest Services:** wireless Internet. **Cards:** AX, DC, DS, JC, MC, VI. **Free Special Amenities:** continental breakfast and high-speed Internet.

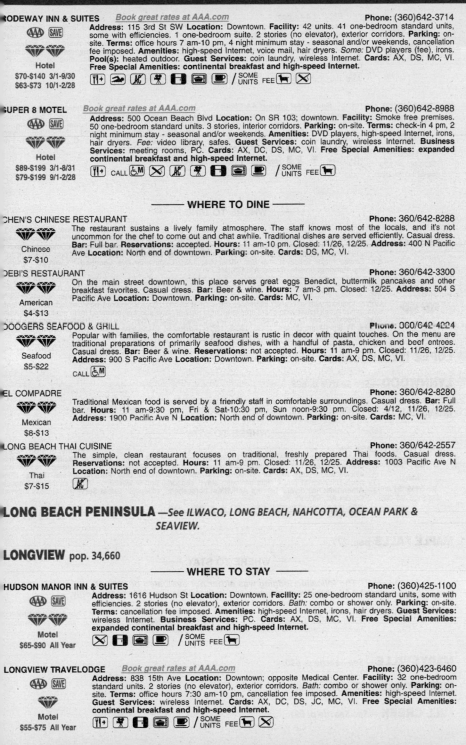

QUALITY INN & SUITES *Book at AAA.com*   **Phone:** (360)414-100

▽▽▽ ▽

Hotel

$80-$190 All Year

Address: 723 7th Ave **Location:** I-5, exit 36, 3 mi w on SR 432. **Facility:** 50 units. 49 one-bedroo standard units. 1 one-bedroom suite with whirlpool. 2 stories (no elevator), interior corridors. *Bat* combo or shower only. **Parking:** on-site. **Terms:** cancellation fee imposed. **Amenities:** high-spee Internet, voice mail, irons, hair dryers. **Pool(s):** heated indoor. **Leisure Activities:** whirlpool. **Gue** **Services:** valet and coin laundry, wireless Internet. **Business Services:** meeting rooms, P(**Cards:** AX, DC, DS, MC, VI.

(ASK) CALL 🔊 ⊠ 🎦 🔲 💻 / SOME UNITS FEE 🐾 🖼

THE TOWNHOUSE MOTEL *Book great rates at AAA.com*   **Phone:** (360)423-720

(AAA) (SAVE)

▽

Motel

$60-$95 3/1-9/30

$55-$75 10/1-2/28

Address: 744 Washington Way **Location:** Downtown. **Facility:** 28 units. 26 one- and 2 two-bedroo standard units. 1-2 stories (no elevator), exterior corridors. *Bath:* combo or shower only. **Parking:** o(site. **Terms:** 3 day cancellation notice. **Amenities:** high-speed Internet. *Some:* hair dryer **Pool(s):** heated outdoor. **Guest Services:** wireless Internet. **Cards:** AX, DC, DS, MC, VI. **Fre** **Special Amenities: continental breakfast and high-speed Internet.**

🎦→ 🔊 🎦 🔲 🖼 💻 / SOME UNITS FEE 🐾 ⊠

------ **WHERE TO DINE** ------

COUNTRY FOLKS DELI   **Phone:** 360/425-283

▽▽ ▽▽

American

$7-$18

The delicatessen, which shares space with a charming antique mall, specializes in fresh, home-cooke foods for lunch and dinner. The daily soup with a garden salad and half of a pineapple-chicken sandwich a good choice. Casual dress. **Bar:** Full bar. **Reservations:** accepted. **Hours:** 8 am-8 pm, Thurs-Sat to pm. Closed major holidays; also Sun. **Address:** 1329 Commerce Ave **Location:** Downtown; in Big Building. **Parking:** on-site. **Cards:** AX, DS, MC, VI.

HENRI'S   **Phone:** 360/425-797

▽▽ ▽▽

American

$6-$22

Lightly touched with a French influence, the casual dining room is relaxed and comfortable. The long established steak house also offers an exceptional rack of lamb and well-prepared fresh seafood. The mult layer chocolate bar is a chocoholic's dream. Dressy casual. **Bar:** Full bar. **Reservations:** accepted **Hours:** 11 am-10 pm. Closed: 11/26, 12/25, 12/26. **Address:** 4545 Ocean Beach Hwy **Location:** SR 4, 5. mi w of downtown. **Parking:** on-site. **Cards:** AX, DS, MC, VI.

LOPEZ ISLAND —See San Juan Islands p. 598.

LYNNWOOD —See Seattle p. 688.

MANSON

------ **WHERE TO STAY** ------

WAPATO POINT VILLAGE INN   **Phone:** 509/687-250(

▽▽ ▽

Motel

$85-$155 3/1-9/6

$85-$105 9/7-2/28

Address: 200 Wapato Point Ct **Location:** Just s of SR 150; downtown. **Facility:** Smoke free premises. 10 units. 4 one-bedroom standard units with efficiencies. 6 one-bedroom suites with efficiencies. 1 story, exterior corridors. *Bath:* combo or shower only. **Parking:** on-site. **Terms:** offic(hours 8:30 am-11 pm, 2 night minimum stay - seasonal and/or weekends, 4 day cancellation notice **Amenities:** hair dryers. **Leisure Activities:** horseshoes, volleyball. **Guest Services:** wireless Interne **Cards:** AX, MC, VI.

(ASK) 🎦→ CALL 🔊 ⊠ (VCR) 🎦 🔲 🖼 💻

MAPLE FALLS pop. 277

------ **WHERE TO STAY** ------

------ *The following lodging was either not evaluated or did not* ------
meet AAA rating requirements but is listed for your information only.

MT. BAKER LODGING   **Phone:** 360/599-245:

(fyi)

Not evaluated. **Location:** Off-site registration on SR 542 (Mt. Baker Hwy), just w of downtown Facilities, services, and decor characterize a mid-scale property.

MARYSVILLE —See Seattle p. 690.

MERCER ISLAND —See Seattle p. 691.

MILL CREEK —See Seattle p. 691.

MOCLIPS pop. 615

——— WHERE TO STAY ———

OCEAN CREST RESORT

AAA SAVE

▽▽▽ ▽▽▽

Hotel

$79-$209 All Year

Phone: (360)276-4465

Address: 4651 SR 109 N **Location:** Oceanfront. South edge of town. **Facility:** Smoke free premises. 45 units. 25 one-bedroom standard units. 12 one- and 8 two-bedroom suites, some with efficiencies or kitchens. 3 stories (no elevator), exterior corridors. *Bath:* combo or shower only. **Parking:** on-site. **Terms:** check-in 4 pm, 2 night minimum stay - weekends, 7 day cancellation notice-fee imposed. **Amenities:** video library (fee), DVD players, hair dryers. **Dining:** Ocean Crest Restaurant, see separate listing. **Pool(s):** heated indoor. **Leisure Activities:** sauna, whirlpool, beach access, playground, exercise room. **Fee:** massage. **Guest Services:** coin laundry, tanning facilities, wireless Internet. **Business Services:** meeting rooms. **Cards:** AX, DS, MC, VI. **Free Special Amenities: local telephone calls and newspaper.**

🍽 ≈ ⊠ ☒ 🅐 🖵 / SOME UNITS FEE 🐾 ▯ 🖵

——— WHERE TO DINE ———

OCEAN CREST RESTAURANT

AAA

▽▽▽▽▽▽

American

$10-$36

Phone: 360/276-4465

Patrons can soak up peaceful sunsets from this clifftop perch overlooking the rolling waves of the Pacific Ocean. Northwest wines pair with memorable meals made from fresh local ingredients. Casual dress. **Bar:** Full bar. **Reservations:** accepted. **Hours:** 8:30 am-2:30 & 5 pm-close. **Address:** 4651 SR 109 N **Location:** South edge of town; in Ocean Crest Resort. **Parking:** on-site. **Cards:** AX, DS, MC, VI.

MONROE —See Seattle p. 691.

MONTESANO pop. 3,312

——— WHERE TO STAY ———

ABEL HOUSE BED & BREAKFAST INN

▽▽▽▽▽

Historic Bed & Breakfast

$130-$170 5/29-2/28

$110-$150 3/1-5/28

Phone: (360)249-6002

Address: 117 Fleet St S **Location:** US 12, exit SR 107, just n on Main St, just w on Pioneer St, then just n. **Facility:** A 1908 Craftsman-style home with shingle siding and a gambrel roof. A wide veranda-style porch becomes very inviting on sunny afternoons. Smoke free premises. 4 one-bedroom standard units. 3 stories (no elevator), interior corridors. *Bath:* some shared or private, combo or shower only. **Parking:** street. **Terms:** check-in 4 pm, cancellation fee imposed. **Amenities:** video library, DVD players. *Some:* high-speed Internet, hair dryers. **Guest Services:** complimentary laundry. **Business Services:** PC. **Cards:** AX, MC, VI.

ASK ☒ 🅐 VCR / SOME UNITS ☎ ▯ 🖵

MORTON pop. 1,045

——— WHERE TO STAY ———

THE SEASONS MOTEL

AAA SAVE

▽▽ ▽▽

Motel

$70-$100 All Year

Phone: 360/496-6835

Address: 200 Westlake Ave **Location:** On US 12; jct SR 7. **Facility:** 49 one-bedroom standard units. 2 stories (no elevator), exterior corridors. *Bath:* combo or shower only. **Parking:** on-site. **Terms:** office hours 7 am-10 pm. **Amenities:** hair dryers. **Guest Services:** wireless Internet. **Business Services:** PC. **Cards:** AX, DC, DS, MC, VI. **Free Special Amenities: expanded continental breakfast and high-speed Internet.**

🍽 🎦 ▯ 🖵 🖵 / SOME UNITS FEE 🐾 ☒

MOSES LAKE pop. 14,953

——— WHERE TO STAY ———

AMERISTAY INN & SUITES   *Book at AAA.com*

▽▽▽▽▽

Hotel

$89-$259 All Year

Phone: (509)764-7500

Address: 1157 N Stratford Rd **Location:** I-90, exit 179, 1 mi n to SR 17, 2.8 mi nw, exit Stratford Rd, just n, then just e. **Facility:** 60 one-bedroom standard units, some with whirlpools. 2 stories (no elevator), interior corridors. *Bath:* combo or shower only. **Parking:** on-site. **Terms:** cancellation fee imposed. **Amenities:** high-speed Internet, voice mail, safes, irons, hair dryers. **Pool(s):** heated indoor. **Leisure Activities:** whirlpool, exercise room. **Guest Services:** valet laundry, wireless Internet. **Business Services:** meeting rooms, PC. **Cards:** AX, DS, MC, VI.

ASK ⊞ 🍽 CALL 🆖 ≈ ▯ 🖵 🖵 / SOME UNITS FEE 🐾 ☒

BEST WESTERN LAKE FRONT HOTEL   *Book great rates at AAA.com*   Phone: (509)765-9211

AAA SAVE
Hotel
$90-$225 3/1-9/30
$80-$225 10/1-2/28

Address: 3000 Marina Dr **Location:** I-90, exit 176, just nw. **Facility:** Smoke free premises. 157 units. 155 one-bedroom standard units, some with whirlpools. 2 one-bedroom suites with whirlpools. 2-3 stories (no elevator), interior corridors. *Bath:* combo or shower only. **Parking:** on-site. **Terms:** check-in 4 pm. **Amenities:** video games (fee), irons, hair dryers. **Pool(s):** heated outdoor. **Leisure Activities:** sauna, whirlpool, boat dock, fishing, jogging, exercise room. **Guest Services:** valet and coin laundry, wireless Internet. **Business Services:** conference facilities, business center. **Cards:** AX, CB, DC, DS, JC, MC, VI. **Free Special Amenities: full breakfast and high-speed Internet.**

AAA Benefit:
Members save up to 20%, plus 10% bonus points with rewards program.

COMFORT SUITES MOSES LAKE   *Book great rates at AAA.com*   Phone: (509)765-3731

AAA SAVE
Hotel
$99-$299 All Year

Address: 1700 E Kittleson Rd **Location:** I-90, exit 179, just nw. **Facility:** Smoke free premises. 60 units. 55 one-bedroom standard units, some with whirlpools. 5 one-bedroom suites with kitchens. 3 stories, interior corridors. *Bath:* combo or shower only. **Parking:** on-site, winter plug-ins. **Terms:** cancellation fee imposed. **Amenities:** high-speed Internet, voice mail, irons, hair dryers. **Pool(s):** heated indoor. **Leisure Activities:** whirlpool, exercise room. **Guest Services:** coin laundry, wireless Internet. **Business Services:** meeting rooms, business center. **Cards:** AX, CB, DC, DS, MC, VI. **Free Special Amenities: full breakfast and high-speed Internet.**
(See color ad p 368, p 586, p 499, p 368, p 752, p 473, p 542, p 299, p 344, p 751, below & p 500)

HOLIDAY INN EXPRESS   *Book at AAA.com*   Phone: (509)766-2000

Hotel
$130-$190 All Year

Address: 1735 E Kittleson Rd **Location:** I-90, exit 179, just n, then just w. **Facility:** Smoke free premises. 80 units. 79 one-bedroom standard units, some with whirlpools. 1 one-bedroom suite with whirlpool. 3 stories, interior corridors. *Bath:* combo or shower only. **Parking:** on-site. **Terms:** 3 night minimum stay - seasonal. **Amenities:** high-speed Internet, dual phone lines, voice mail, irons, hair dryers. **Pool(s):** heated indoor. **Leisure Activities:** whirlpool, exercise room. **Guest Services:** valet and coin laundry, wireless Internet. **Business Services:** meeting rooms, business center. **Cards:** AX, DC, DS, MC, VI.

INN AT MOSES LAKE   *Book at AAA.com*   Phone: (509)766-7000

Hotel
$69-$119 All Year

Address: 1745 E Kittleson Rd **Location:** I-90, exit 179, just n. **Facility:** Smoke free premises. 119 one-bedroom standard units, some with whirlpools. 2-3 stories (no elevator), interior corridors. *Bath:* combo or shower only. **Parking:** on-site. **Amenities:** video library, voice mail, irons, hair dryers. *Some:* DVD players. **Pool(s):** heated indoor/outdoor. **Leisure Activities:** exercise room. **Guest Services:** valet and coin laundry, wireless Internet. **Business Services:** PC. **Cards:** AX, DC, DS, MC, VI.

MOSES LAKE SUPER 8   *Book great rates at AAA.com*   Phone: 509/765-8886

(AAA) (SAVE)

♥♥♥♥

Hotel
Rates not provided

Address: 449 Melva Ln **Location:** I-90, exit 176, just n. **Facility:** 62 one-bedroom standard units. 3 stories (no elevator), interior corridors. **Parking:** on-site. **Amenities:** safes (fee), hair dryers. **Pool(s):** heated indoor. **Guest Services:** coin laundry, wireless Internet.

SHILO INN SUITES-MOSES LAKE   *Book great rates at AAA.com*   Phone: (509)765-9317

(AAA) (SAVE)

♥♥♥♥

Hotel
$75-$170 All Year

Address: 1819 E Kittleson Rd **Location:** I-90, exit 179, just n. **Facility:** 100 one-bedroom standard units, some with efficiencies. 2 stories (no elevator), interior corridors. **Terms:** check-in 4 pm. **Amenities:** video games (fee), voice mail, irons, hair dryers. **Pool(s):** heated indoor. **Leisure Activities:** sauna, whirlpool, steamroom, limited exercise equipment. **Guest Services:** valet and coin laundry, wireless Internet. **Business Services:** meeting rooms, PC. **Cards:** AX, CB, DC, DS, JC, MC, VI. **Free Special Amenities:** continental breakfast and high-speed Internet. *(See color ad below)*

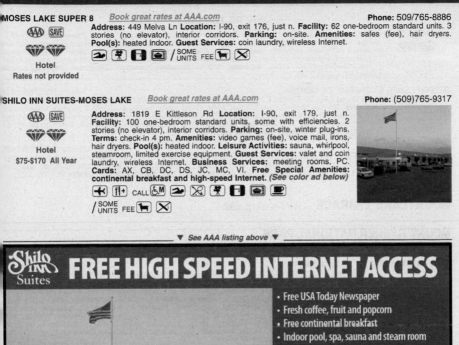
Easy, hassle-free vehicle battery testing or replacement

A battery jump gets you on your way fast … but then what? Another breakdown? A trip to the garage for a new battery? AAA Battery Service provides members on-the-scene battery testing and replacement at competitive prices.

Call **800-AAA-HELP** to find out how it works!*

This service is not available in all areas. Contact your AAA representative for details.

Roadside Assistance

——— WHERE TO DINE ———

MICHAEL'S ON THE LAKE
Phone: 509/765-161?

▼▼▼ ▼▼▼

Steak & Seafood
$10-$30

Michael's on the Lake is a popular steak and seafood restaurant overlooking the waters of Moses Lake and is one of the livelier gathering spots in town. A lounge provides entertainment seven nights per week. Casual dress. Entertainment. **Bar:** Full bar. **Reservations:** suggested. **Hours:** 10:30 am-10 pm, Fri & Sat 11 pm. Closed: 11/26, 12/25. **Address:** 910 W Broadway **Location:** Downtown. **Parking:** on-site. **Cards:** AX, CB, DC, DS, MC, VI.

SERENITY CAFE & CONFERENCE CENTER
Phone: 509/766-141?

▼▼▼ ▼▼▼

American
$10-$21

In the Moses Lake Convention Center, the restaurant is a bit off the beaten path but the food makes the trip worthwhile. The specialty—hickory-smoked prime rib—is served nightly along with a good selection of pork, lamb and seafood dishes. Casual dress. **Bar:** Full bar. **Reservations:** accepted. **Hours:** 11 am-2 & 5-9 pm, Sat from 5 pm. Closed: Sun. **Address:** 1475 Nelson Rd NE **Location:** I-90, exit 179, 1 mi n to SR 17, 0.? mi nw, then just e. **Parking:** on-site. **Cards:** AX, MC, VI.

THAI CUISINE
Phone: 509/766-148?

▼▼▼

Thai
$8-$10

The casual family restaurant prepares a wide selection of traditional Thai dishes and lays out a daily lunch buffet. Casual dress. **Bar:** Beer & wine. **Hours:** 11 am-9:30 pm. Closed major holidays; also Sun. **Address:** 601 S Pioneer Way **Location:** In Grant County Mall. **Parking:** on-site. **Cards:** MC, VI.

MOUNTLAKE TERRACE —See Seattle p. 692.

MOUNT RAINIER NATIONAL PARK

——— WHERE TO STAY ———

ALTA CRYSTAL RESORT AT MT RAINIER
Phone: (360)663-2500

(AAA) (SAVE)

▼▼▼ ▼▼▼

Hotel
$139-$269 All Year

Address: 68317 SR 410 E **Location:** 2 mi outside northeast entrance. **Facility:** Smoke free premises. 24 units. 11 one- and 12 two-bedroom suites with efficiencies. 1 cabin. 2 stories (no elevator), exterior corridors. **Parking:** on-site. **Terms:** office hours 8:30 am-10 pm, check-in 4 pm, 2 night minimum stay - seasonal and/or weekends, 30 day cancellation notice-fee imposed. **Amenities:** video library (fee), DVD players, CD players, voice mail, hair dryers. **Pool(s):** heated outdoor. **Leisure Activities:** whirlpool, cross country skiing, recreation programs in summer, badminton, croquet, foosball, table tennis, charcoal grills, picnic tables, rental bicycles, hiking trails, horseshoes, volleyball. *Fee:* snowshoes, massage. **Guest Services:** wireless Internet. **Business Services:** meeting rooms. **Cards:** AX, MC, VI. *(See color ad below)*

NATIONAL PARK INN
Phone: 360/569-2275

(AAA) (SAVE)

▼▼▼ ▼▼▼

Historic
Country Inn
$112-$150 All Year

Address: Longmire **Location:** 6 mi from southwest entrance. Located within the park. **Facility:** Built in 1926, the lodge is nestled in the forest at Longmire and affords sweeping views of Mount Rainier; some smaller rooms have shared baths. Smoke free premises. 25 units. 23 one- and 2 two-bedroom standard units. 2 stories (no elevator), interior corridors. *Bath:* some shared or private, combo, shower or tub only. **Parking:** on-site. **Terms:** office hours 6 am-10 pm, check-in 4 pm, 7 day cancellation notice-fee imposed. **Amenities:** hair dryers. **Leisure Activities:** cross country skiing, snowshoeing, hiking trails. **Guest Services:** complimentary laundry. **Business Services:** meeting rooms. **Cards:** AX, DC, DS, MC, VI.

——— ▼ See AAA listing above ▼ ———

—— *The following lodging was either not evaluated or did not* ——
meet AAA rating requirements but is listed for your information only.

PARADISE INN
[fyi]
Phone: 360/569-2275
Not evaluated. **Location:** 17.3 mi from southwest entrance; 21 mi from southeast entrance. Located within the park. Facilities, services, and decor characterize an economy property.

—— **WHERE TO DINE** ——

—— *The following restaurant has not been evaluated by AAA* ——
but is listed for your information only.

PARADISE INN DINING ROOM
[fyi]
Phone: 360/569-2275
Not evaluated. Built in 1917 with Alaskan cedar, the old-fashioned lodge is listed on the National Register of Historic Places. While dining, guests can take in spectacular views of Mount Rainier, the Nisqually Glacier and surrounding meadows. **Location:** 17.3 mi from southwest entrance; 21 mi from southeast entrance; in Paradise Inn.

MOUNT VERNON pop. 26,232

—— **WHERE TO STAY** ——

BEST WESTERN COLLEGE WAY INN   *Book great rates at AAA.com*   Phone: (360)424-4287

AAA SAVE
▼▼▼
Hotel
$90-$120 All Year

Address: 300 W College Way **Location:** I-5, exit 227, just w. **Facility:** 66 one-bedroom standard units, some with kitchens. 2 stories (no elevator), exterior corridors. *Bath:* combo or shower only. **Parking:** on-site. **Terms:** 7 day cancellation notice. **Amenities:** high-speed Internet, irons, hair dryers. **Pool(s):** heated outdoor. **Leisure Activities:** whirlpool. **Guest Services:** wireless Internet. **Business Services:** PC. **Cards:** AX, DC, DS, MC, VI. **Free Special Amenities: continental breakfast and high-speed Internet.**

AAA Benefit:
Members save up to 20%, plus 10% bonus points with rewards program.

**BEST WESTERN COTTONTREE INN &
CONVENTION CENTER**   *Book great rates at AAA.com*   Phone: (360)428-5678

AAA SAVE
▼▼▼
Hotel
$99-$180 All Year

Address: 2300 Market St **Location:** I-5, exit 227, 0.3 mi e on College Way, then 0.5 mi n on Riverside Dr. Located in a commercial area. **Facility:** Smoke free premises. 120 one-bedroom standard units, some with whirlpools. 3 stories, interior corridors. *Bath:* combo or shower only. **Parking:** on-site. **Amenities:** video games (fee), high-speed Internet, irons, hair dryers. **Pool(s):** heated outdoor. **Guest Services:** valet and coin laundry, wireless Internet. **Business Services:** conference facilities, PC. **Cards:** AX, DC, DS, JC, MC, VI. **Free Special Amenities: full breakfast and high-speed Internet.**
(See color ad below)

AAA Benefit:
Members save up to 20%, plus 10% bonus points with rewards program.

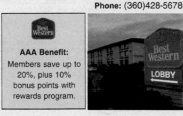

—— ▼ *See AAA listing above* ▼ ——

QUALITY INN-MOUNT VERNON *Book great rates at AAA.com*
Phone: (360)428-7020

AAA SAVE
▼▼ ▼▼
Hotel
$99-$179 6/1-2/28
$90-$170 3/1-5/31

Address: 1910 Freeway Dr **Location:** I-5, exit 227, just w on College Way, then just n. **Facility:** 68 units. 61 one- and 3 two-bedroom standard units, some with efficiencies. 4 one-bedroom suites with efficiencies, some with whirlpools. 3 stories, exterior corridors. **Parking:** on-site. **Terms:** cancellation fee imposed. **Amenities:** high-speed Internet, irons, hair dryers. **Pool(s):** heated indoor. **Leisure Activities:** whirlpool. **Guest Services:** coin laundry, wireless Internet. **Cards:** AX, DS, MC, VI. **Free Special Amenities: expanded continental breakfast and high-speed Internet.**

TULIP INN *Book great rates at AAA.com*
Phone: (360)428-5969

AAA SAVE
▼▼ ▼▼
Motel
$65-$99 All Year

Address: 2200 Freeway Dr **Location:** I-5, exit 227, just w on College Way, then just n. **Facility:** 40 one-bedroom standard units, some with efficiencies. 2 stories (no elevator), exterior corridors. **Bath:** combo or shower only. **Parking:** on-site. **Terms:** office hours 7 am-11 pm, cancellation fee imposed. **Amenities:** high-speed Internet, voice mail, irons, hair dryers. **Guest Services:** wireless Internet. **Cards:** AX, DS, MC, VI. **Free Special Amenities: continental breakfast and high-speed Internet.**

--------- **WHERE TO DINE** ---------

CALICO CUPBOARD CAFE & BAKERY
Phone: 360/336-3107

▼▼ ▼▼
American
$6-$19

This converted granary, with its high, open ceilings, natural brick walls, and antique furnishings, is part of a large book store. Soup, salad, sandwiches, quiche, pasta and vegetarian entrees are offered with bread and desserts baked daily from scratch. Outdoor terrace seating in season. Casual dress. **Bar:** Beer & wine. **Hours:** 7:30 am-3:30 pm. Closed: 11/26, 12/25. **Address:** 121B Freeway Dr **Location:** I-5, exit 226, just w to S 3rd St, then 0.3 mi n. **Parking:** on-site. **Cards:** MC, VI.

MAX DALE'S STEAK AND CHOP HOUSE
Phone: 360/424-7171

▼▼ ▼▼
Steak & Seafood
$7-$29

The restaurant is a longtime favorite of locals in search of a good steak and friendly service. High-back booths and dim lighting contribute to the feel of a period steakhouse. Casual dress. **Bar:** Full bar. **Reservations:** accepted. **Hours:** 11:30 am-9:30 pm, Sat & Sun from 4 pm. Closed: major holidays; also 12/24. **Address:** 2030 Riverside Dr **Location:** I-5, exit 227, 0.5 mi e on E College Way, then just n. **Parking:** on-site. **Cards:** AX, DS, MC, VI.

MEXICO CAFE
Phone: 360/424-1977

▼▼ ▼▼
Mexican
$6-$15

Since 1965, patrons have visited the slightly out-of-the-way cafe for traditional Mexican food and drinks. Casual dress. **Bar:** Full bar. **Reservations:** accepted. **Hours:** 11 am-10 pm, Fri & Sat-11 pm. Closed major holidays. **Address:** 1320 Memorial Hwy **Location:** I-5, exit 226, 1.4 mi w on SR 536. **Parking:** on-site. **Cards:** AX, DS, MC, VI.

PORTO
Phone: 360/428-3699

▼▼ ▼▼
Italian
$17-$24

In an old converted house, the restaurant features the flavors of Italy on its menu and complements them with a strong representation of by-the-glass wines. Several small dining areas allow for a quiet night of good food, wine and conversation. Casual dress. **Bar:** Beer & wine. **Reservations:** accepted. **Hours:** 5 pm-9 pm. Closed major holidays; also Sun. **Address:** 2001 E College Way **Location:** I-5, exit 227, 1 mi e. **Parking:** on-site. **Cards:** AX, CB, DC, DS, JC, MC, VI.

ROUND TABLE PIZZA
Phone: 360/424-7979

▼▼
Pizza
$11-$18

This casual, family-oriented pizza place features high-quality ingredients and dough rolled fresh daily. Distinctive specialty pizzas are piled high with toppings. Casual dress. **Bar:** Beer & wine. **Reservations:** not accepted. **Hours:** 11 am-10 pm, Fri & Sat-11 pm, Sun 11:30 am-10 pm. Closed: 12/25. **Address:** 115 E College Way **Location:** I-5, exit 227, just e. **Parking:** on-site. **Cards:** AX, CB, DC, DS, JC, MC, VI.

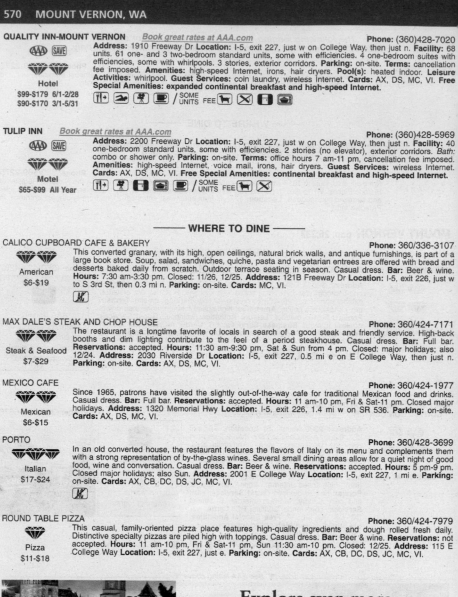

SKAGIT RIVER BREWERY & RESTAURANT

American
$6-$18

Phone: 360/336-2884
Next to the train tracks in what used to be an old grain building, the restaurant now serves microbrews made on site with preparations of good American fare, including pizza and sandwiches. Casual dress. **Bar:** Beer & wine. **Reservations:** accepted. **Hours:** 11 am-10 pm, Sat-11 pm, Sun-9 pm. Closed major holidays. **Address:** 404 S 3rd St **Location:** I-5, exit 226, 0.5 mi nw. **Parking:** on-site and street. **Cards:** AX, MC, VI.

MUKILTEO —See Seattle p. 692.

NAHCOTTA

------- WHERE TO DINE -------

BAILEY'S BAKERY & CAFE
American
$5-$8

Phone: 360/665-4449
Open only for breakfast and lunch, this eatery puts out a limited menu of fresh food, most of which is made in house. Lunch items are surprisingly refined for this remote location in an old post office building. It might start with a mixed greens salad with fresh bread and then progress to grilled chicken breast with chipotle mayonnaise and cilantro pesto. Lines often form Sunday mornings for the chance at a thunder bun, a rich, buttery, sticky baked treat. Casual dress. **Hours:** 8 am-3 pm, Sun from 9 am. Closed major holidays; also Tues & Wed. **Address:** 26910 Sandridge Rd **Location:** 0.5 mi ne of SR 103. **Parking:** on-site.

NORTH BEND —See Seattle p. 693.

NORTH BONNEVILLE pop. 593

------- WHERE TO STAY -------

BONNEVILLE HOT SPRINGS RESORT & SPA
AAA SAVE
Hotel
Rates not provided

Book great rates at AAA.com

Phone: 509/427-7767
Address: 1252 E Cascade Dr **Location:** SR 14 (Evergreen Hwy), exit between MM 38 and 39, just n on Hot Springs Way, then 0.8 mi n. **Facility:** Smoke free premises. 78 one-bedroom standard units, some with whirlpools. 3 stories, interior corridors. **Parking:** on-site **Terms:** check-in 4 pm. **Amenities:** video games (fee), voice mail, irons, hair dryers. **Pool(s):** heated indoor. **Leisure Activities:** sauna, whirlpools, miniature golf, spa. **Guest Services:** wireless Internet. **Business Services:** meeting rooms, PC.

OAK HARBOR pop. 19,795

------- WHERE TO STAY -------

ACORN MOTOR INN
AAA SAVE
Hotel
$46-$109 All Year

Phone: (360)675-6646
Address: 31530 SR 20 **Location:** On SR 20 at 300th Ave W (SE Barrington Dr). **Facility:** 26 one-bedroom standard units. 2 stories (no elevator), interior corridors. **Parking:** on-site. **Terms:** office hours 7 am-11 pm. **Amenities:** high-speed Internet. **Guest Services:** wireless Internet. **Cards:** AX, DC, DS, MC, VI. **Free Special Amenities:** continental breakfast and high-speed Internet.

THE AULD HOLLAND INN
AAA SAVE
Hotel
$49-$168 All Year

Book great rates at AAA.com

Phone: (360)675-2288
Address: 33575 SR 20 **Location:** Just n of town. **Facility:** 34 one-bedroom standard units, some with efficiencies and/or whirlpools. 2 stories (no elevator), interior/exterior corridors. **Parking:** on-site. **Terms:** office hours 7 am-10 pm, check-in 4 pm. **Amenities:** video library (fee), high-speed Internet. Some: hair dryers. **Pool(s):** heated outdoor. **Leisure Activities:** sauna, whirlpool, playground, limited exercise equipment, basketball. **Guest Services:** coin laundry, wireless Internet. **Cards:** AX, DS, MC, VI. **Free Special Amenities:** continental breakfast and high-speed Internet.

BEST WESTERN HARBOR PLAZA
AAA SAVE
Hotel
$99-$189 All Year

Book great rates at AAA.com

Phone: (360)679-4567
Address: 33175 SR 20 **Location:** Just north of town. **Facility:** 80 one-bedroom standard units. 3 stories, interior corridors. **Parking:** on-site. **Terms:** check-in 4 pm. **Amenities:** high-speed Internet, voice mail, irons, hair dryers. **Pool(s):** heated outdoor. **Leisure Activities:** whirlpool, exercise room. **Guest Services:** valet laundry, wireless Internet. **Business Services:** meeting rooms, PC. **Cards:** AX, CB, DC, DS, MC, VI. **Free Special Amenities:** continental breakfast and high-speed Internet. *(See color ad p 572)*

AAA Benefit:
Members save up to 20%, plus 10% bonus points with rewards program.

CANDLEWOOD SUITES   *Book great rates at AAA.com*   **Phone:** (360)279-2222

AAA SAVE

▼▼▼

Hotel

$99-$189 All Year

Address: 33221 SR 20 **Location:** Just n of town. **Facility:** Smoke free premises. 80 units. 68 one-bedroom standard units with efficiencies. 12 one-bedroom suites with efficiencies. 3 stories, interior corridors. *Bath:* combo or shower only. **Parking:** on-site. **Terms:** check-in 4 pm. **Amenities:** video library, DVD players, high-speed Internet, voice mail, irons, hair dryers. **Leisure Activities:** barbecues, exercise room. **Guest Services:** complimentary and valet laundry, wireless Internet. **Business Services:** meeting rooms, PC. **Cards:** AX, CB, DC, DS, JC, MC, VI. **Free Special Amenities: local telephone calls and high-speed Internet.**

COACHMAN INN   *Book great rates at AAA.com*   **Phone:** (360)675-0727

AAA SAVE

▼▼▼

Hotel

$84-$209 All Year

Address: 32959 SR 20 **Location:** Jct Goldie Rd and Midway Blvd. **Facility:** 101 units. 94 one- and 1 two-bedroom standard units, some with efficiencies and/or whirlpools. 3 one- and 3 two-bedroom suites, some with efficiencies, kitchens and/or whirlpools. 2-3 stories (no elevator), exterior corridors. **Parking:** on-site. **Amenities:** video library, voice mail, irons, hair dryers. *Some:* DVD players, high-speed Internet. **Pool(s):** heated outdoor. **Leisure Activities:** whirlpools, playground, exercise room. **Guest Services:** valet and coin laundry, area transportation-within 10 mi, wireless Internet. **Business Services:** meeting rooms, PC. **Cards:** AX, DC, DS, MC, VI. *(See color ad below)*

▼ See AAA listing p 571 ▼

▼ See AAA listing above ▼

——— **WHERE TO DINE** ———

FLYERS RESTAURANT & BREWERY   Phone: 360/675-5858

▼▼▼ Popular with families and military folks, this restaurant features beers crafted in house, perfect for washing
down tasty sandwiches, burgers and fish and chips. Casual dress. **Bar:** Full bar. **Reservations:** accepted.
American **Hours:** 11:30 am-10 pm. Closed major holidays. **Address:** 32295 SR 20 **Location:** Downtown. **Parking:**
$7-$25 on-site. **Cards:** AX, CB, DC, DS, JC, MC, VI.

OCEAN PARK pop. 1,459

——— **WHERE TO STAY** ———

CASWELLS ON THE BAY   Phone: 360/665-6535

▼▼▼ **Address:** 25204 Sandridge Rd **Location:** 0.5 mi e of SR 103. **Facility:** A contemporary Victorian
home situated on a secluded portion of Willapa Bay nestled in the trees with nature encroaching on all
Bed & Breakfast sides. Smoke free premises. 5 one-bedroom standard units. 2 stories (no elevator), interior corridors.
Rates not provided **Parking:** on-site. **Terms:** check-in 3:30 pm. **Amenities:** video library, hair dryers. *Some:* DVD players.
Guest Services: wireless Internet.

[⊠] [AC] [VCR] [☎]

THE DOVESHIRE BED & BREAKFAST   Phone: 360/665-3017

▼▼▼ **Address:** 21914 Pacific Way **Location:** 2 mi s. **Facility:** A contemporary home situated close to the
Pacific Highway but shielded by lots of trees for peace. All rooms have exterior entrance for complete
Bed & Breakfast privacy. Smoke free premises. 4 one-bedroom standard units. 1 story, exterior corridors. *Bath:* shower
$150-$200 All Year only. **Parking:** on-site. **Terms:** age restrictions may apply, 7 day cancellation notice-fee imposed.
Amenities: video library, hair dryers. **Cards:** DS, MC, VI.

[ASK] [⊠] [AC] [VCR] [☎]

OCEAN PARK RESORT   Phone: 360/665-4585

(AAA) [SAVE] **Address:** 25904 R St **Location:** Just e of SR 103; downtown. **Facility:** Smoke free premises. 12 one-
bedroom standard units, some with efficiencies. 2 stories (no elevator), exterior corridors. **Parking:** on-
▼▼▼ site. **Terms:** office hours 8:30 am-11 pm, 10 day cancellation notice. **Amenities:** hair dryers. *Some:*
Motel DVD players. **Pool(s):** heated outdoor. **Leisure Activities:** whirlpool, recreation room, playground,
$65-$168 All Year basketball, volleyball. **Guest Services:** coin laundry, wireless Internet. **Cards:** AX, DS, MC, VI. **Free
Special Amenities: preferred room (subject to availability with advance reservations) and high-
speed Internet.**

[🛶] [⊠] [⊠] [AC] [VCR] [☎] [🛏] [📷] [💻] / SOME UNITS FEE [🐕]

OCEAN SHORES pop. 3,836

——— **WHERE TO STAY** ———

BEST WESTERN LIGHTHOUSE SUITES INN   *Book great rates at AAA.com*   Phone: (360)289-2311

(AAA) [SAVE] **Address:** 491 Damon Rd NW **Location:** Oceanfront. Just w of main entry
arch to town; north end of downtown. **Facility:** Smoke free premises. 94
▼▼▼ units. 92 one-bedroom standard units, some with whirlpools. 2 two-
Hotel bedroom suites. 4 stories, interior corridors. *Bath:* combo or shower only.
$110-$200 All Year **Parking:** on-site. **Terms:** check-in 4 pm, cancellation fee imposed.
Amenities: video library (fee), DVD players, high-speed Internet, irons,
hair dryers. **Pool(s):** heated indoor. **Leisure Activities:** sauna, whirlpool,
exercise room. *Fee:* game room. **Guest Services:** coin laundry, wireless
Internet. **Business Services:** meeting rooms, PC. **Cards:** AX, DS, MC, VI.
**Free Special Amenities: local telephone calls and high-speed
Internet.** *(See color ad p 192)*

[🍴] [🍸] [🛶] [⊠] [⊠] [AC] [VCR] [📷] [🛏] [📷] [💻]

AAA Benefit:
Members save up to
20%, plus 10%
bonus points with
rewards program.

CANTERBURY INN   *Book great rates at AAA.com*   Phone: (360)289-3317

(AAA) [SAVE] **Address:** 643 Ocean Shores Blvd NW **Location:** Oceanfront. 0.3 mi s of
Chance A La Mer Blvd. **Facility:** The property is walking distance from
▼▼▼ the convention center; all guest rooms include a balcony or patio, and
Condominium most have a fireplace and ocean views. Smoke free premises. 45 units.
$82-$198 All Year 12 one-bedroom standard units with efficiencies. 21 one- and 12 two-
bedroom suites with kitchens. 3 stories, interior corridors. *Bath:* combo or
shower only. **Parking:** on-site. **Terms:** check-in 4 pm, 2 night minimum
stay - seasonal and/or weekends, cancellation fee imposed.
Amenities: video library (fee), DVD players, high-speed Internet, irons,
hair dryers. **Pool(s):** heated indoor. **Leisure Activities:** whirlpool,
exercise room. **Guest Services:** coin laundry, wireless Internet.
Business Services: meeting rooms, PC. **Cards:** AX, DC, DS, MC, VI.
Free Special Amenities: newspaper and high-speed Internet.
(See color ad p 192)

[🍴+] [🛶] [⊠] [AC] [VCR] [🛏] [📷] [💻] / SOME UNITS FEE [🐕]

COMFORT INN & SUITES   *Book great rates at AAA.com*   Phone: 360/289-9000

(AAA) [SAVE] **Address:** 829 Ocean Shores Blvd NW **Location:** Oceanfront. Just n of Chance A La Mer Blvd.
Located on the beach. **Facility:** Smoke free premises. 59 one-bedroom standard units, some with
▼▼▼ whirlpools. 4 stories, interior corridors. *Bath:* combo or shower only. **Parking:** on-site. **Terms:** check-in
Hotel 4 pm. **Amenities:** video library (fee), high-speed Internet, irons, hair dryers. *Some:* DVD players (fee).
Rates not provided **Pool(s):** heated indoor. **Leisure Activities:** whirlpool, exercise room. **Guest Services:** coin laundry,
wireless Internet. **Business Services:** meeting rooms, PC. **Free Special Amenities: expanded
continental breakfast and high-speed Internet.**

[🛶] [⊠] [AC] [📷] [🛏] [📷] [💻] / SOME UNITS FEE [VCR]

DAYS INN

Phone: (360)289-9570

(AAA) (SAVE)

▼▼▼ ▼▼▼

Hotel

$69-$169 All Year

Address: 891 Ocean Shores Blvd NW **Location:** North end of downtown. **Facility:** 46 one-bedroom standard units. 2 stories (no elevator), exterior corridors. **Parking:** on-site. **Terms:** 2 night minimum stay - weekends. **Amenities:** high-speed Internet, hair dryers. **Fee:** video library, safes. **Some:** DVD players (fee). **Pool(s):** heated indoor. **Leisure Activities:** whirlpool. **Guest Services:** wireless Internet. **Cards:** AX, DC, DS, MC, VI. **Free Special Amenities: expanded continental breakfast and high-speed Internet.**

🍽️ 🏊 📹 🛗 🖥️ 🖨️ 💻 / SOME UNITS ✕ 🖊️ FEE VCR

FLOATING FEATHER INN "ON THE GRAND CANAL"

Phone: (360)289-2490

(AAA) (SAVE)

▼▼▼ ▼▼▼

Bed & Breakfast

$99-$175 All Year

Address: 982 Point Brown Ave SE **Location:** 4.2 mi s of downtown. **Facility:** A block from the ocean on the "Grand Canal," the inn features large decks for soaking up the sun and watching the fowl play; two rooms have partial ocean views. 5 units. 4 one-bedroom standard units. 1 cottage. 2 stories (no elevator), interior/exterior corridors. **Bath:** combo or shower only. **Parking:** on-site. **Terms:** 2 night minimum stay - seasonal and/or weekends, 5 day cancellation notice-fee imposed. **Amenities:** video library, DVD players, hair dryers. **Some:** irons. **Leisure Activities:** boat dock, fishing, croquet, horseshoes, volleyball. **Guest Services:** wireless Internet. **Cards:** AX, DS, MC, VI. **Free Special Amenities: full breakfast and high-speed Internet.**

✕ ✕ VCR 📹 💻 / SOME UNITS 🛗 🖨️

THE GREY GULL RESORT

Phone: 360/289-3381

▼▼▼ ▼▼▼

Condominium

Rates not provided

Address: 651 Ocean Shores Blvd NW **Location:** Oceanfront. Just s of Chance A La Mer Blvd. Located on the beach. **Facility:** Smoke free premises. 37 units. 10 one-bedroom standard units with efficiencies. 25 one- and 2 two-bedroom suites with kitchens. 3 stories, exterior corridors. **Parking:** on-site. **Terms:** office hours 8 am-10 pm, check-in 4 pm, age restrictions may apply. **Amenities:** video library, high-speed Internet, hair dryers. **Some:** DVD players. **Pool(s):** heated outdoor. **Leisure Activities:** sauna, whirlpool. **Guest Services:** coin laundry, wireless Internet. **Business Services:** meeting rooms, PC.

🍽️ 🏊 ✕ 🖊️ VCR 🛗 🖨️ 💻 / SOME UNITS FEE 🐕

THE POLYNESIAN CONDOMINIUM RESORT

Phone: (360)289-3361

(AAA) (SAVE)

▼▼▼ ▼▼▼

Condominium

$99-$239 All Year

Address: 615 Ocean Shores Blvd NW **Location:** Oceanfront. 0.3 mi s of Chance A La Mer Blvd. **Facility:** Offering mainly suite-type units, the property includes many accommodations with fireplaces and private balconies or patios, most with ocean views. 69 units. 18 one-bedroom standard units, some with efficiencies. 37 one-, 13 two- and 1 three-bedroom suites with kitchens, some with whirlpools. 3-4 stories, interior/exterior corridors. **Parking:** on-site. **Terms:** check-in 4 pm, 2-3 night minimum stay - seasonal and/or weekends, 3 day cancellation notice. **Amenities:** video library (fee), DVD players, high-speed Internet, voice mail, irons, hair dryers. **Dining:** Mariah's Restaurant & Lounge, see separate listing. **Pool(s):** heated indoor. **Leisure Activities:** sauna, whirlpool, playground. **Fee:** game room. **Guest Services:** coin laundry, wireless Internet. **Business Services:** meeting rooms. **Cards:** AX, CB, DC, DS, MC, VI. **Free Special Amenities: continental breakfast and high-speed Internet.**

🍽️ 🏊 ✕ 🖊️ VCR 💻 / SOME UNITS FEE 🐕 ✕ 🛗 🖨️

▼ See AAA listing p 575 ▼

QUALITY INN *Book great rates at AAA.com* Phone: (360)289-2040

AAA SAVE

Hotel
$69-$259 All Year

Address: 773 Ocean Shores Blvd NW **Location:** Oceanfront. Just n of Chance A La Mer Blvd. Located on the beach. **Facility:** Smoke free premises. 62 one-bedroom standard units, some with whirlpools. 1-3 stories, interior corridors. **Parking:** on-site. **Amenities:** video library (fee), high-speed Internet, irons, hair dryers. *Some:* DVD players (fee). **Pool(s):** heated indoor. **Leisure Activities:** whirlpool, miniature golf. **Guest Services:** coin laundry, wireless Internet. **Business Services:** meeting rooms, PC. **Cards:** AX, CB, DC, DS, JC, MC, VI. **Free Special Amenities: continental breakfast and high-speed Internet.**

QUINAULT BEACH RESORT & CASINO *Book great rates at AAA.com* Phone: 360/289-9466

Hotel
Rates not provided

Address: 78 SR 115 **Location:** Oceanfront. 2 mi n of downtown. **Facility:** Large accommodations are tastefully decorated in rich colors; many offer views of the ocean and a gas fireplace. 159 units. 156 one-bedroom standard units, some with whirlpools. 3 one-bedroom suites with whirlpools. 4 stories, interior corridors. *Bath:* combo or shower only. **Parking:** on-site. **Terms:** check-in 4 pm. **Amenities:** video games (fee), high-speed Internet, dual phone lines, voice mail, irons, hair dryers. **Dining:** Emily's, see separate listing. **Pool(s):** heated indoor. **Leisure Activities:** sauna, whirlpool, steamroom, exercise room, spa. *Fee:* game room. **Guest Services:** area transportation, wireless Internet. **Business Services:** meeting rooms.

RAMADA HOTEL & RESORT *Book at AAA.com* Phone: (360)289-7700

Hotel
$89-$225 3/1-9/30
$99-$175 10/1-2/28

Address: 845 Ocean Shores Blvd NW **Location:** Oceanfront. Just n of Chance A La Mer Blvd. **Facility:** Smoke free premises. 54 one-bedroom standard units, some with efficiencies. 3 stories, interior corridors. *Bath:* combo or shower only. **Parking:** on-site. **Amenities:** high-speed Internet, voice mail, irons, hair dryers. **Leisure Activities:** sauna, exercise room, spa. *Fee:* waterslide. **Guest Services:** wireless Internet. **Business Services:** meeting rooms. **Cards:** AX, CB, DC, DS, JC, MC, VI. *(See color ad p 192)*

SHILO INN SUITES OCEANFRONT HOTEL - OCEAN SHORES *Book great rates at AAA.com* Phone: (360)289-4600

AAA SAVE

Hotel
$140-$330 All Year

Address: 707 Ocean Shores Blvd NW **Location:** Oceanfront. Northwest corner of Chance A La Mer and Ocean Shores blvds NW. **Facility:** Smoke free premises. 113 one-bedroom standard units, some with whirlpools. 4 stories, interior corridors. *Bath:* combo or shower only. **Parking:** on-site. **Terms:** check-in 4 pm. **Amenities:** high-speed Internet, voice mail, irons, hair dryers. **Dining:** Shilo Inn Restaurant & Lounge, see separate listing. **Pool(s):** heated indoor. **Leisure Activities:** sauna, whirlpool, steamroom, limited beach access, exercise room. **Guest Services:** coin laundry, wireless Internet. **Business Services:** conference facilities, PC. **Cards:** AX, CB, DC, DS, JC, MC, VI. **Free Special Amenities: newspaper and high-speed Internet.** *(See color ad p 574)*

——— WHERE TO DINE ———

ALEC'S BY THE SEA   *Menu on AAA.com*   Phone: 360/289-4026

Owned and operated by longtime locals, the restaurant is popular with locals and guests alike. Fresh ingredients go into each preparation of beef and seafood. Parties with children in tow are welcomed at this casual spot. Casual dress. **Bar:** Full bar. **Reservations:** accepted. **Hours:** 11 am-8 pm, Fri & Sat-9 pm; to 10 pm 4/12-8/31. Closed: 12/25. **Address:** 131 E Chance A La Mer Blvd **Location:** Downtown. **Parking:** on-site. **Cards:** AX, CB, DC, DS, MC, VI.

Steak & Seafood
$7-$18

EMILY'S   Phone: 360/289-9466

Popular for alder-plank salmon, grilled pork chops and razor clam fritters, the restaurant lures folks for its food and nice view. Also drawing crowds are the Sunday brunch and Friday evening land and seafood buffet. Casual dress. **Bar:** Full bar. **Reservations:** accepted. **Hours:** 7 am-2 & 5-9 pm, Fri & Sat-10 pm. **Address:** 78 SR 115 **Location:** 2 mi n of downtown; in Quinault Beach Resort & Casino. **Parking:** on-site. **Cards:** AX, CB, DC, DS, MC, VI.

American
$6-$45

GALWAY BAY IRISH RESTAURANT & PUB   Phone: 360/289-2300

The bartender addresses locals by name, Celtic music plays, and the smells of fresh clam chowder and dense soda bread fill the air. Traditional fare includes chicken and mushroom pasty, Forfar bridies, limerick sausage roll and shepherd's pie. A full line of Irish beers is on tap. Casual dress. **Bar:** Full bar. **Reservations:** accepted. **Hours:** 11 am-10 pm. Closed: 11/26, 12/25. **Address:** 880 Point Brown Ave NE **Location:** Just s of SR 115; downtown. **Parking:** on-site. **Cards:** AX, DS, MC, VI.

Irish
$8-$25

HOME PORT RESTAURANT   Phone: 360/289-2600

Families enjoy the casual restaurant, which serves well-prepared seafood, steak, burgers and breakfast. Artwork showing scenes of the ocean and ships in port lends to a nautical feel. Homemade blackberry cobbler is a dessert favorite. Casual dress. **Bar:** Full bar. **Reservations:** suggested. **Hours:** 8 am-10 pm. Closed: 12/25. **Address:** 857 Point Brown Ave **Location:** Just n of Chance A La Mer Blvd. **Parking:** on-site. **Cards:** DS, MC, VI.

American
$5-$24

CALL

MARIAH'S RESTAURANT & LOUNGE   Phone: 360/289-3315

Sunday brunch is a popular time at the octagonal restaurant, where locals gather to talk about the weather or fishing conditions in the oceanfront community. Chowder, dinner salad and the house specialty Polynesian shrimp make for a good meal. Casual dress. **Bar:** Full bar. **Hours:** 4 pm-9 pm, Sun 9 am-1 pm. Closed: 12/25. **Address:** 615 Ocean Shores Blvd NW **Location:** 0.3 mi s of Chance A La Mer Blvd; in The Polynesian Condominium Resort. **Parking:** on-site. **Cards:** AX, CB, DC, DS, MC, VI.

American
$8-$20

SHILO INN RESTAURANT & LOUNGE   Phone: 360/289-0567

Tiered seating inside the traditional hotel restaurant allows most tables to offer a panoramic ocean view. Casual dress. **Bar:** Full bar. **Reservations:** accepted. **Hours:** 7 am-9 pm. **Address:** 707 Ocean Shores Blvd NW **Location:** Northwest corner of Chance A La Mer and Ocean Shore blvds NW; in Shilo Inn Suites Oceanfront Hotel-Ocean Shores. **Parking:** on-site.

American
$8-$22

OKANOGAN pop. 2,484

——— WHERE TO STAY ———

OKANOGAN INN & SUITES   Phone: (509)422-6431

Address: 1 Apple Way **Location:** SR 97, exit SR 20, just w. **Facility:** 77 units. 75 one-bedroom standard units, some with efficiencies. 2 one-bedroom suites. 2 stories (no elevator), interior corridors. **Parking:** on-site. **Amenities:** voice mail. **Pool(s):** heated outdoor. **Leisure Activities:** picnic area, limited exercise equipment. **Guest Services:** coin laundry, wireless Internet. **Business Services:** meeting rooms. **Cards:** AX, CB, DC, DS, JC, MC, VI. **Free Special Amenities: continental breakfast and high-speed Internet.**

Hotel
$60-$65 All Year

PONDEROSA MOTOR LODGE   Phone: 509/422-0400

Address: 1034 S 2nd Ave **Location:** 0.3 mi n on SR 215 from jct SR 20. **Facility:** 25 units. 18 one- and 6 two-bedroom standard units, some with efficiencies. 1 one-bedroom suite with kitchen. 1 story, exterior corridors. **Bath:** combo or shower only. **Parking:** on-site, winter plug-ins. **Terms:** office hours 7 am-11:30 pm. **Pool(s):** outdoor. **Guest Services:** coin laundry, wireless Internet. **Business Services:** fax (fee).

Motel
Rates not provided

OLYMPIA pop. 42,514

——— WHERE TO STAY ———

AMERITEL INNS-OLYMPIA   *Book at AAA.com*   Phone: (360)459-8866

Address: 4520 Martin Way E **Location:** I-5, exit 109, just sw. **Facility:** 125 units. 115 one-bedroom standard units. 9 one- and 1 two-bedroom suites, some with efficiencies and/or whirlpools. 4 stories, interior corridors. **Bath:** combo or shower only. **Parking:** on-site. **Terms:** cancellation fee imposed. **Amenities:** video games (fee), high-speed Internet, voice mail, irons, hair dryers. **Pool(s):** heated indoor. **Leisure Activities:** whirlpool, exercise room. **Guest Services:** valet and coin laundry, wireless Internet. **Business Services:** meeting rooms, business center. **Cards:** AX, DC, DS, MC, VI.

Hotel
$109-$149 All Year

CLARION HOTEL

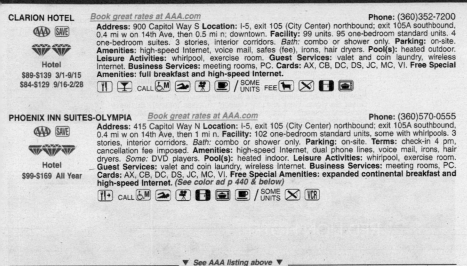

AAA SAVE

◆◆◆

Hotel

$89-$139 3/1-9/15
$84-$129 9/16-2/28

Book great rates at AAA.com   Phone: (360)352-7200

Address: 900 Capitol Way S **Location:** I-5, exit 105 (City Center) northbound; exit 105A southbound, 0.4 mi w on 14th Ave, then 0.5 mi n; downtown. **Facility:** 99 units. 95 one-bedroom standard units. 4 one-bedroom suites. 3 stories, interior corridors. *Bath:* combo or shower only. **Parking:** on-site. **Amenities:** high-speed Internet, voice mail, safes (fee), irons, hair dryers. **Pool(s):** heated outdoor. **Leisure Activities:** whirlpool, exercise room. **Guest Services:** valet and coin laundry, wireless Internet. **Business Services:** meeting rooms, PC. **Cards:** AX, CB, DC, DS, JC, MC, VI. **Free Special Amenities: full breakfast and high-speed Internet.**

PHOENIX INN SUITES-OLYMPIA

AAA SAVE

◆◆◆

Hotel

$99-$169 All Year

Book great rates at AAA.com   Phone: (360)570-0555

Address: 415 Capitol Way N **Location:** I-5, exit 105 (City Center) northbound; exit 105A southbound, 0.4 mi w on 14th Ave, then 1 mi n. **Facility:** 102 one-bedroom standard units, some with whirlpools. 3 stories, interior corridors. *Bath:* combo or shower only. **Parking:** on-site. **Terms:** check-in 4 pm, cancellation fee imposed. **Amenities:** high-speed Internet, dual phone lines, voice mail, irons, hair dryers. *Some:* DVD players. **Pool(s):** heated indoor. **Leisure Activities:** whirlpool, exercise room. **Guest Services:** valet and coin laundry, wireless Internet. **Business Services:** meeting rooms, PC. **Cards:** AX, CB, DC, DS, JC, MC, VI. **Free Special Amenities: expanded continental breakfast and high-speed Internet.** *(See color ad p 440 & below)*

RED LION HOTEL OLYMPIA   *Book great rates at AAA.com*   **Phone:** (360)943-4000

Hotel
$179 All Year

Address: 2300 Evergreen Park Dr SW **Location:** I-5, exit 104, 0.7 mi w on US 101, just n on Cooper Point Rd N, 0.7 mi e on S Evergreen Park Dr SW, then just n on Lakeridge Way SW. Located in Morris Business Park. **Facility:** Smoke free premises. 192 units. 187 one-bedroom standard units, some with whirlpools. 5 one-bedroom suites, some with whirlpools. 3 stories, interior corridors. *Bath:* combo or shower only. **Parking:** on-site. **Terms:** cancellation fee imposed. **Amenities:** video games (fee), high-speed Internet, voice mail, irons, hair dryers. **Pool(s):** heated outdoor. **Leisure Activities:** whirlpool, exercise room. **Guest Services:** valet and coin laundry, wireless Internet. **Business Services:** conference facilities, PC (fee). **Cards:** AX, DC, DS, MC, VI. *(See color ad below)*

▼ *See AAA listing above* ▼

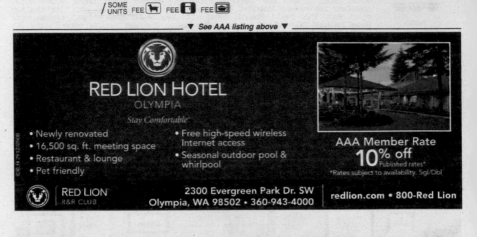

----------- **WHERE TO DINE** -----------

GREAT CUISINE OF INDIA   **Phone:** 360/943-3442

Indian
$7-$15

Diners can savor the exotic flavors of Northern India in dishes such as murgh korma, a chicken dish cooked in saffron and served with a thick, sweet cream sauce and a side of rice. Guests can ask to tour the kitchen to view the tandoor, or clay oven. A lunch buffet is laid out on weekdays. Casual dress. **Bar:** Beer & wine. **Reservations:** accepted. **Hours:** 11 am-2:30 & 5-9:30 pm, Fri & Sat-10 pm. Closed: 11/26, 12/25; also for lunch 1/1. **Address:** 116 4th Ave W **Location:** Downtown. **Parking:** street. **Cards:** AX, DS, MC, VI.

MCMENAMINS   **Phone:** 360/357-6444

American
$5-$20

The casual neighborhood eatery is where friends gather for classic pub and comfort fare, all washed down by pints of locally made beer. Large wooden booths or tables easily accommodate larger groups, and the eclectic, custom-painted walls and varied period light fixtures keep diners' eyes busy should the conversation lag. Casual dress. **Bar:** Full bar. **Reservations:** not accepted. **Hours:** 7 am-midnight, Sun-11 pm. **Address:** 114 4th Ave E **Location:** Between S Capitol Way and Washington St; downtown. **Parking:** street. **Cards:** MC, VI.

MERCATO RESTAURANTE   **Phone:** 360/528-3663

Italian
$10-$25

One of the city's hip gathering spots, the restaurant prepares Italian dishes with a Northwest twist. Among suggestions are prawns caprese, salmon ciabatta and the hazelnut goat cheese appetizer. Casual dress. **Bar:** Full bar. **Reservations:** accepted. **Hours:** 11 am-10 pm, Sun & Mon-9 pm. Closed major holidays; also 12/24. **Address:** 111 Market St NW **Location:** Just n of downtown. **Parking:** on-site (fee). **Cards:** AX, DS, MC, VI.

THE OYSTER HOUSE   **Phone:** 360/753-7000

Seafood
$7-$26

Reputed to be the state's oldest seafood restaurant, the facility started life as an oyster culling house that also housed a small seafood bar where oyster cocktails were served to patrons. Seafood remains the food of choice, and the specialty is Olympia oysters served in varied ways. Diners also can find pasta, chicken and beef dishes. Casual dress. **Bar:** Full bar. **Reservations:** not accepted. **Hours:** 11 am-10 pm, Fri & Sat-11 pm. Closed: 12/25. **Address:** 320 4th Ave W **Location:** Just w of downtown. **Parking:** on-site and street. **Cards:** AX, DS, MC, VI.

CALL ⑤M

RAMBLIN' JACK'S   **Phone:** 360/754-8909

American
$10-$20

Patrons head to the great downtown location for apple-wood-fired pizza, hearty salads and preparations of fish and beef. Many locals come just for the Southern-style smoked meats. Casual dress. **Bar:** Full bar. **Reservations:** not accepted. **Hours:** 11 am-10 pm, Sun & Mon 10 am-9 pm. Closed major holidays; also 12/24. **Address:** 520 E 4th Ave **Location:** Corner of 4th Ave and Cherry St; downtown. **Parking:** street. **Cards:** AX, DS, MC, VI.

OLYMPIC NATIONAL PARK —See also FORKS, PORT ANGELES, SEQUIM & SHELTON.

----------- **WHERE TO STAY** -----------

KALALOCH LODGE   **Phone:** (360)962-2271

AAA SAVE

Cabin
$99-$300 All Year

Book great rates at AAA.com

Address: 157151 Hwy 101 **Location:** Oceanfront. In Kalaloch; at MM 157. **Facility:** 64 units. 19 one-bedroom standard units. 1 one- and 3 two-bedroom suites. 41 cabins. 2 stories (no elevator), interior/exterior corridors. *Bath:* combo or shower only. **Parking:** on-site. **Terms:** check-in 4 pm, 3 day cancellation notice-fee imposed. **Amenities:** CD players, hair dryers. *Some:* DVD players (fee). **Dining:** Creekside Dining Room, see separate listing. **Leisure Activities:** horseshoes, volleyball. **Cards:** AX, DS, MC, VI.

🍽 ✕ 🅰 🅩 💻 /SOME UNITS FEE 🐕 📺 VCR 🔌 🖥

LAKE CRESCENT LODGE   **Phone:** (360)928-3211

AAA SAVE

Classic Historic Hotel
$75-$243 All Year

Address: 416 Lake Crescent Rd **Location:** 22 mi w of Port Angeles on US 101. **Facility:** Situated on the west side of Lake Crescent, this lodge is centrally located for exploring a lot of the popular hiking trails in the Olympic National Park. 52 units. 35 one-bedroom standard units. 17 cottages. 1-2 stories (no elevator), interior/exterior corridors. *Bath:* some shared or private, combo or shower only. **Parking:** on-site. **Terms:** check-in 4 pm, 2 night minimum stay - seasonal and/or weekends, 7 day cancellation notice-fee imposed. **Amenities:** hair dryers. **Dining:** Lake Crescent Lodge Dining Room, see separate listing. **Leisure Activities:** fishing, recreation programs, hiking trails. *Fee:* rowboats, kayaks. **Guest Services:** wireless Internet. **Cards:** AX, DC, DS, MC, VI.
(See color ad p 584)

🍽 ✕ ✕ 🅰 🅦 🅩 💻 /SOME UNITS FEE 🐕 🔌 🖥

LOG CABIN RESORT   **Phone:** 360/928-3325

Cabin
Rates not provided

Address: 3183 E Beach Rd **Location:** 3.3 mi nw of US 101 (MM 232). Located on Lake Crescent Rd, at the Piedmont Recreation Area. **Facility:** 24 units. 4 one-bedroom standard units. 8 cabins and 12 cottages. 1 story, exterior corridors. *Bath:* shower or tub only. **Parking:** on-site. **Terms:** open 5/1-9/30, office hours 8 am-8 pm, check-in 4 pm. **Leisure Activities:** rental boats, rental canoes, rental paddleboats, boat dock, fishing, hiking trails, horseshoes. **Guest Services:** coin laundry, wireless Internet. **Business Services:** meeting rooms.

🍽 ✕ 🅰 🅦 🅩 /SOME UNITS FEE 🐕 ✕ 🔌 🖥 💻

——— WHERE TO DINE ———

CREEKSIDE DINING ROOM   **Phone: 360/962-2271**

American
$6-$30

Like the lodge, this restaurant is a bit more casual and relaxed but still offers dramatic views of the beach and driftwood strewn courtesy of the Pacific's crashing waves. Although menu offerings vary widely, the focus is on the ocean's bounty in items such as sesame-seared Alaskan halibut, saute of scallops and tiger prawns, calamari and crab cakes. Also tempting are the half-pound burger, broiled chicken breast, New York strip, wild mushroom strudel and build-your-own pasta creations. Casual dress. **Bar:** Full bar. **Reservations:** suggested. **Hours:** 7 am-9 pm; 7:30 am-2 & 5-8 pm 10/1-3/1. **Address:** 157151 Hwy 101 **Location:** In Kalaloch; at MM 157; in Kalaloch Lodge. **Parking:** on-site. **Cards:** AX, DS, MC, VI.

LAKE CRESCENT LODGE DINING ROOM   **Phone: 360/928-3211**

American
$8-$30

Although Lake Crescent and the surrounding hills serve as the dramatic backdrop, the menu looks as though it comes straight from one of Seattle's finest restaurants. Sustainable seafood and organic products factor into such choices as wild baked troll-caught salmon and pan-fried local Quilcene oysters. Casual dress. **Bar:** Full bar. **Reservations:** not accepted. **Hours:** Open 5/1-10/15; 7:30-10:30 am, 11:30-2 & 5:30-9 pm. **Address:** 416 Lake Crescent Rd **Location:** 22 mi w of Port Angeles on US 101; in Lake Crescent Lodge. **Parking:** on-site. **Cards:** AX, DC, DS, MC, VI.

THE SPRINGS RESTAURANT   **Phone: 360/327-3583**

American
$10-$30

The charming resort dates back to the turn of the 20th century. Muted hues of mauve and teal decorate the relaxed, comfortable dining room, which has big picture windows overlooking the mountains. Stuffed acorn squash is delicious. Casual dress. **Bar:** Beer & wine. **Hours:** Open 3/25-10/24; 7:30 am-10 & 5:30-9 pm. **Address:** Sol Duc Rd **Location:** In Sol Duc Hot Springs; US 101, 12 mi s. **Parking:** on-site. **Cards:** AX, CB, DS, MC, VI.

CALL &M [AC]

OMAK pop. 4,721

--------- WHERE TO STAY ---------

BEST WESTERN PEPPERTREE INN AT OMAK   *Book great rates at AAA.com*

Phone: (509)422-2088

AAA SAVE
▼▼▼▼
Hotel
$89-$250 All Year

Address: 820 Koala Dr **Location:** US 97, just n of Riverside Dr. **Facility:** Smoke free premises. 77 units. 70 one- and 7 two-bedroom standard units. 4 stories, interior corridors. *Bath:* combo or shower only. **Parking:** on-site. **Terms:** check-in 4 pm. **Amenities:** high-speed Internet, voice mail, irons, hair dryers. **Pool(s):** heated indoor. **Leisure Activities:** whirlpool, exercise room. **Guest Services:** valet and coin laundry, wireless Internet. **Business Services:** meeting rooms, business center. **Cards:** AX, DS, MC, VI. **Free Special Amenities: continental breakfast and high-speed Internet.**

AAA Benefit:
Members save up to 20%, plus 10% bonus points with rewards program.

[icons] CALL M ⊠ ✕ ▣ ▤ ▥ ▦ / SOME UNITS FEE ▧

OMAK INN   *Book great rates at AAA.com*

Phone: (509)826-3822

AAA SAVE
▼▼▼
Hotel
$75-$90 All Year

Address: 912 Koala Dr **Location:** On US 97, just n of Riverside Dr. **Facility:** 66 one-bedroom standard units, some with whirlpools. 2 stories (no elevator), interior corridors. *Bath:* combo or shower only. **Parking:** on-site. **Amenities:** video library, high-speed Internet, voice mail, irons, hair dryers. **Pool(s):** heated indoor. **Leisure Activities:** whirlpool, limited exercise equipment. **Guest Services:** coin laundry, wireless Internet. **Business Services:** meeting rooms, PC. **Cards:** AX, DS, MC, VI. **Free Special Amenities: continental breakfast and high-speed Internet.**

[icons] ▣ ▤ ▥ / SOME UNITS ▧ ✕ FEE VCR ▦ ▨

ORCAS ISLAND —*See San Juan Islands p. 598.*

ORCAS ISLAND —*See San Juan Islands p. 598.*

OTHELLO pop. 5,847

--------- WHERE TO STAY ---------

BEST WESTERN OTHELLO INN   *Book great rates at AAA.com*

Phone: (509)488-5671

AAA SAVE
▼▼▼▼
Hotel
$79-$129 3/1-8/31
$69-$119 9/1-2/28

Address: 1020 E Cedar St **Location:** Just off Main St at 10th and Cedar sts. **Facility:** 50 one-bedroom standard units, some with efficiencies and/or whirlpools. 2 stories (no elevator), interior corridors. **Parking:** on-site. **Amenities:** irons, hair dryers. *Some:* high-speed Internet. **Pool(s):** heated outdoor. **Leisure Activities:** sauna, exercise room. **Guest Services:** coin laundry, wireless Internet. **Business Services:** meeting rooms, business center. **Cards:** AX, DC, DS, MC, VI. **Free Special Amenities: expanded continental breakfast and high-speed Internet.** *(See color ad below)*

AAA Benefit:
Members save up to 20%, plus 10% bonus points with rewards program.

[icons] ▣ ▤ ▥ ▦ ▧ ▨ / SOME UNITS FEE ▩ ✕ VCR

--------- ▼ See AAA listing above ▼ ---------

PACIFIC BEACH

——— WHERE TO STAY ———

SANDPIPER BEACH RESORT

Phone: 360/276-4580

◇
Condominium
Rates not provided

Address: 4159 SR 109 **Location:** Oceanfront. 1.8 mi s. **Facility:** Smoke free premises. 31 units. 9 one-bedroom standard units with efficiencies. 13 one-, 2 two- and 2 three-bedroom suites with efficiencies, some with whirlpools. 5 cottages. 1-4 stories (no elevator), exterior corridors. *Bath:* combo or shower only. **Parking:** on-site. **Terms:** office hours 8 am-6 pm. **Amenities:** hair dryers. **Leisure Activities:** beach access, playground. **Guest Services:** coin laundry.

PACKWOOD

——— WHERE TO STAY ———

COWLITZ RIVER LODGE

Phone: 360/494-4444

◇◇
Motel
Rates not provided

Address: 13069 US 12 **Location:** East end of town. **Facility:** Smoke free premises. 31 one-bedroom standard units. 2 stories (no elevator), exterior corridors. **Parking:** on-site. **Terms:** office hours 7 am-10 pm. **Amenities:** hair dryers. *Some:* irons. **Leisure Activities:** whirlpool. **Guest Services:** coin laundry, wireless Internet. **Business Services:** meeting rooms.

CREST TRAIL LODGE

Phone: 360/494-4944

AAA SAVE
◇◇
Hotel
$70-$100 All Year

Address: 12729 US 12 **Location:** Just w of town. **Facility:** 27 one-bedroom standard units. 2 stories (no elevator), interior corridors. *Bath:* combo or shower only. **Parking:** on-site. **Terms:** office hours 7 am-10 pm. **Leisure Activities:** whirlpool. **Guest Services:** wireless Internet. **Cards:** AX, DS, MC, VI. **Free Special Amenities:** expanded continental breakfast and high-speed Internet.

INN OF PACKWOOD

Phone: (360)494-5500

◇
Motel
$79-$119 All Year

Address: 13032 US 12 **Location:** Center. **Facility:** 34 one-bedroom standard units, some with efficiencies. 1-2 stories (no elevator), exterior corridors. **Parking:** on-site. **Terms:** office hours 7 am-10 pm, cancellation fee imposed. **Pool(s):** heated indoor. **Leisure Activities:** whirlpool. **Guest Services:** wireless Internet. **Cards:** AX, MC, VI.

PASCO pop. 32,066

Map Page	OA	✈ Airport Accommodations TRI-CITIES	Diamond Rated	High Season	Page
N/A	AAA	Best Western Pasco Inn & Suites, 0.5 mi s of terminal	◇◇◇	$120-$160 SAVE	582
N/A	AAA	Red Lion Hotel Pasco, 0.6 mi s of terminal	◇◇◇	Rates not provided SAVE	583

——— WHERE TO STAY ———

BEST WESTERN PASCO INN & SUITES   *Book great rates at AAA.com*

Phone: (509)543-7722

AAA SAVE
◇◇◇
Hotel
$120-$160 All Year

Address: 2811 N 20th Ave **Location:** I-182, exit 12B, just n. **Facility:** Smoke free premises. 110 one-bedroom standard units, some with whirlpools. 3 stories, interior corridors. *Bath:* combo or shower only. **Parking:** on-site. **Amenities:** high-speed Internet, irons, hair dryers. **Pool(s):** heated indoor. **Leisure Activities:** whirlpool, exercise room. **Guest Services:** valet and coin laundry, wireless Internet. **Business Services:** meeting rooms, business center. **Cards:** AX, DC, DS, MC, VI. **Free Special Amenities:** full breakfast and high-speed Internet.

AAA Benefit:
Members save up to 20%, plus 10% bonus points with rewards program.

HOLIDAY INN EXPRESS PASCO AT TRAC   *Book at AAA.com*

Phone: 509/543-7000

◇◇◇
Hotel
Rates not provided

Address: 4525 Convention Pl **Location:** I-182, exit 9 (Rd 68), just n, then just e. **Facility:** Smoke free premises. 85 one-bedroom standard units. 4 stories, interior corridors. *Bath:* combo or shower only. **Parking:** on-site. **Terms:** check-in 4 pm. **Amenities:** DVD players, high-speed Internet, voice mail, irons, hair dryers. *Some:* dual phone lines. **Pool(s):** heated indoor. **Leisure Activities:** whirlpool, exercise room. **Guest Services:** valet and coin laundry, wireless Internet. **Business Services:** meeting rooms, business center.

MOTEL 6-PASCO *Book at AAA.com* **Phone:** 509/546-2010
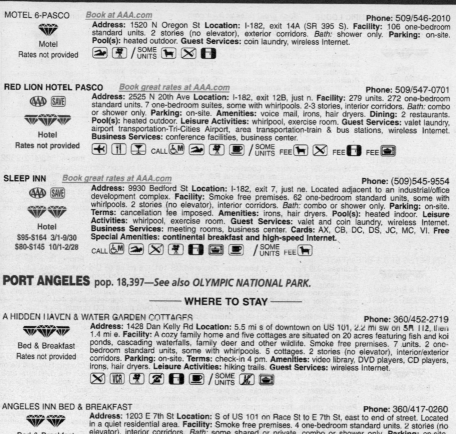
Motel
Rates not provided

Address: 1520 N Oregon St **Location:** I-182, exit 14A (SR 395 S). **Facility:** 106 one-bedroom standard units. 2 stories (no elevator), exterior corridors. *Bath:* shower only. **Parking:** on-site. **Pool(s):** heated outdoor. **Guest Services:** coin laundry, wireless Internet.

RED LION HOTEL PASCO *Book great rates at AAA.com* **Phone:** 509/547-0701

Hotel
Rates not provided

Address: 2525 N 20th Ave **Location:** I-182, exit 12B, just n. **Facility:** 279 units. 272 one-bedroom standard units. 7 one-bedroom suites, some with whirlpools. 2-3 stories, interior corridors. *Bath:* combo or shower only. **Parking:** on-site. **Amenities:** voice mail, irons, hair dryers. **Dining:** 2 restaurants. **Pool(s):** heated outdoor. **Leisure Activities:** whirlpool, exercise room. **Guest Services:** valet laundry, airport transportation-Tri-Cities Airport, area transportation-train & bus stations, wireless Internet. **Business Services:** conference facilities, business center.

SLEEP INN *Book great rates at AAA.com* **Phone:** (509)545-9554

Hotel
$95-$164 3/1-9/30
$80-$145 10/1-2/28

Address: 9930 Bedford St **Location:** I-182, exit 7, just ne. Located adjacent to an industrial/office development complex. **Facility:** Smoke free premises. 62 one-bedroom standard units, some with whirlpools. 2 stories (no elevator), interior corridors. *Bath:* combo or shower only. **Parking:** on-site. **Terms:** cancellation fee imposed. **Amenities:** irons, hair dryers. **Pool(s):** heated indoor. **Leisure Activities:** whirlpool, exercise room. **Guest Services:** valet and coin laundry, wireless Internet. **Business Services:** meeting rooms, business center. **Cards:** AX, CB, DC, DS, JC, MC, VI. **Free Special Amenities:** continental breakfast and high-speed Internet.

PORT ANGELES pop. 18,397—*See also OLYMPIC NATIONAL PARK.*

——— WHERE TO STAY ———

A HIDDEN HAVEN & WATER GARDEN COTTAGES **Phone:** 360/452-2719

Bed & Breakfast
Rates not provided

Address: 1428 Dan Kelly Rd **Location:** 5.5 mi s of downtown on US 101, 2.2 mi sw on SR 112, then 1.4 mi e. **Facility:** A cozy family home and five cottages are situated on 20 acres featuring fish and koi ponds, cascading waterfalls, family deer and other wildlife. Smoke free premises. 7 units. 2 one-bedroom standard units, some with whirlpools. 5 cottages. 2 stories (no elevator), interior/exterior corridors. **Parking:** on-site. **Terms:** check-in 4 pm. **Amenities:** video library, DVD players, CD players, irons, hair dryers. **Leisure Activities:** hiking trails. **Guest Services:** wireless Internet.

ANGELES INN BED & BREAKFAST **Phone:** 360/417-0260

Bed & Breakfast
Rates not provided

Address: 1203 E 7th St **Location:** S of US 101 on Race St to E 7th St, east to end of street. Located in a quiet residential area. **Facility:** Smoke free premises. 4 one-bedroom standard units. 2 stories (no elevator), interior corridors. *Bath:* some shared or private, combo or shower only. **Parking:** on-site. **Terms:** check-in 4 pm, age restrictions may apply. **Amenities:** video library, DVD players, hair dryers. **Guest Services:** wireless Internet. **Business Services:** PC.

BEST WESTERN OLYMPIC LODGE

Book great rates at AAA.com

Phone: (360)452-2993

 AAA SAVE
▼▼▼▼▼
Hotel
$130-$360 3/1-10/31
$130-$260 11/1-2/28

Address: 140 Del Guzzi Dr **Location:** 1.8 mi e of downtown, just off US 101. **Facility:** Smoke free premises. 105 units. 104 one-bedroom standard units. 1 one-bedroom suite with whirlpool. 3 stories, interior corridors. **Parking:** on-site. **Terms:** check-in 4 pm, cancellation fee imposed. **Amenities:** voice mail, irons, hair dryers. **Pool(s):** heated outdoor. **Leisure Activities:** whirlpool, exercise room. **Guest Services:** wireless Internet. **Business Services:** meeting rooms, PC. **Cards:** AX, CB, DC, DS, JC, MC, VI. **Free Special Amenities:** local telephone calls and high-speed Internet. *(See color ad p 583)*

AAA Benefit:
Members save up to 20%, plus 10% bonus points with rewards program.

BJ'S GARDEN GATE

Phone: 360/452-2322

▼▼▼
Bed & Breakfast
$140-$250 All Year

Address: 397 Monterra Dr **Location:** 10 mi e on US 101, 1.5 mi n on Kitchen Dick Rd, 1.5 mi w on Old Olympic Hwy, 0.7 mi n on Gunn Rd, then just w. Located in a quiet rural setting. **Facility:** A waterfront estate, the property features water views, fireplaces and an elaborate English garden. Smoke free premises. 4 one-bedroom standard units, some with whirlpools. 2 stories (no elevator), interior corridors. *Bath:* combo or shower only. **Parking:** on-site. **Terms:** check-in 4 pm, age restrictions may apply, 30 day cancellation notice-fee imposed. **Amenities:** video library, CD players, high-speed Internet. **Guest Services:** wireless Internet. **Cards:** MC, VI.

COLETTE'S BED & BREAKFAST

Phone: 360/457-9197

▼▼▼
Bed & Breakfast
$195-$395 3/1-10/31
$175-$375 11/1-2/28

Address: 339 Finn Hall Rd **Location:** 7 mi e on US 101, 1.5 mi ne on Old Olympic Hwy, just on Wild Current, 0.3 mi n on Gehrke, then just e. Located in a secluded rural area. **Facility:** Featuring professionally designed gardens, this 10-acre waterfront estate offers finely appointed lodgings, all with fireplaces and water views. Smoke free premises. 5 one-bedroom standard units with whirlpools. 1 story, interior corridors. **Parking:** on-site. **Terms:** check-in 4 pm, age restrictions may apply, 14 day cancellation notice-fee imposed. **Amenities:** video library, DVD players, CD players, irons, hair dryers. **Leisure Activities:** *Fee:* massage. **Guest Services:** wireless Internet. **Cards:** MC, VI.

DOMAINE MADELEINE

Phone: 360/457-4174

▼▼▼
Bed & Breakfast
$150-$310 All Year

Address: 146 Wildflower Ln **Location:** 7 mi e on US 101, 1.5 mi ne on Old Olympic Hwy, just on Wild Currant Way, 0.3 mi n on Gehrke Rd, then just e on Finn Hall Rd. Located in a quiet rural area. **Facility:** This contemporary estate features a multi-course gourmet breakfast, a replica Monet garden and waterfront location. Smoke free premises. 5 units. 3 one-bedroom standard units. 1 one-bedroom suite. 1 cottage. 2 stories (no elevator), interior/exterior corridors. *Bath:* combo or shower only. **Parking:** on-site. **Terms:** check-in 4 pm, 2 night minimum stay - seasonal and/or weekends, age restrictions may apply, 14 day cancellation notice-fee imposed. **Amenities:** video library, DVD players, CD players, irons, hair dryers. **Leisure Activities:** horseshoes. **Guest Services:** wireless Internet. **Business Services:** PC. **Cards:** AX, MC, VI.

▼ See AAA listing p 579 ▼

Experience History

In the Heart of Olympic National Park

Comfortable Lodging

Exquisite Dining

Sustainable, Local Seafood

Lake Crescent Lodge
416 Lake Crescent Rd
Port Angeles, WA 98363

LakeCrescentLodge.com
(360) 928-3211

FOREVERRESORTS.COM　Lake Crescent Lodge is managed by Forever Resorts, LLC, an authorized Concessioner of the National Park Service. Forever Resorts is a Committed Equal Opportunity Service Provider.

THE FIVE SEASUNS B&B

Historic Bed & Breakfast
$98-$175 All Year

Phone: (360)452-8248

Address: 1006 S Lincoln St **Location:** Corner of 10th St and US 101. Located in a quiet residential area. **Facility:** A 1920 Dutch Colonial home, this B&B features views of the Straits and Canadian mountains and is just minutes from downtown and the ferry docks. Smoke free premises. 5 one-bedroom standard units, some with whirlpools. 2 stories (no elevator), interior corridors. *Bath:* combo or shower only. **Parking:** on-site. **Terms:** check-in 4 pm, age restrictions may apply, 14 day cancellation notice-fee imposed. **Amenities:** video library, hair dryers. *Some:* CD players. **Guest Services:** area transportation, wireless Internet. **Cards:** AX, DS, MC, VI.

(ASK) ✈ ⊠ ℀ / SOME UNITS 📺 VCR ☎ 🛢 📷 💻

PORT ANGELES INN

AAA SAVE

Motel
$70-$195 3/1-9/30
$60-$125 10/1-2/28

Phone: (360)452-9285

Address: 111 E 2nd St **Location:** Just w of US 101; on bluff. **Facility:** Smoke free premises. 24 one-bedroom standard units. 2-3 stories, exterior corridors. **Parking:** on-site. **Terms:** office hours 7 am-11 pm, cancellation fee imposed. **Amenities:** hair dryers. *Some:* DVD players. **Leisure Activities:** basketball. **Guest Services:** wireless Internet. **Cards:** AX, DS, MC, VI. **Free Special Amenities:** expanded continental breakfast and high-speed Internet. *(See color ad below)*

🍴 ⊠ ℀ 🎥 🛢 📷 💻 / SOME UNITS VCR

PORTSIDE INN

AAA SAVE

Hotel
$59-$119 All Year

Phone: (360)452-4015

Address: 1510 E Front St **Location:** Front St at Alder St; on east side. **Facility:** 109 units. 100 one-bedroom standard units. 9 one-bedroom suites. 3 stories, exterior corridors. **Parking:** on-site. **Terms:** 3 day cancellation notice-fee imposed. **Amenities:** hair dryers. **Pool(s):** heated outdoor. **Leisure Activities:** whirlpool. **Guest Services:** coin laundry, wireless Internet. **Business Services:** meeting rooms. **Cards:** AX, DS, MC, VI.

🍴 🏊 🎥 🛢 📷 💻 / SOME UNITS FEE 🐾 ⊠

───── ▼ *See AAA listing above* ▼ ─────

QUALITY INN-UPTOWN
Book great rates at AAA.com

Phone: 360/457-9434

(AAA) (SAVE)

◆◆◆◆

Motel
Rates not provided

Address: 101 E 2nd St **Location:** At Laurel St, just w of US 101; on bluff. **Facility:** 35 units. 31 one-bedroom standard units. 4 one-bedroom suites with efficiencies. 2-3 stories (no elevator), exterior corridors. **Parking:** on-site. **Terms:** check-in 4 pm. **Amenities:** irons, hair dryers. **Leisure Activities:** whirlpool. **Guest Services:** wireless Internet. **Business Services:** business center. **Free Special Amenities:** expanded continental breakfast and high-speed Internet.
(See color ad p 368, below, p 499, p 368, p 752, p 473, p 542, p 299, p 344, p 751, p 566 & p 500)

⊠ 🄰 🎥 📠 🖥 🖵 / SOME UNITS FEE 🐕

RED LION HOTEL PORT ANGELES
Book great rates at AAA.com

Phone: (360)452-9215

(AAA) (SAVE)

◆◆◆

Hotel
$249 All Year

Address: 221 N Lincoln St **Location:** On US 101 westbound; at ferry landing. **Facility:** 186 units. 185 one-bedroom standard units. 1 one-bedroom suite. 2 stories (no elevator), interior/exterior corridors. *Bath:* combo or shower only. **Parking:** on-site. **Amenities:** voice mail, irons, hair dryers. **Dining:** The Crab House Restaurant, see separate listing. **Pool(s):** heated outdoor. **Leisure Activities:** whirlpool, exercise room. **Guest Services:** valet and coin laundry, wireless Internet. **Business Services:** meeting rooms. **Cards:** AX, DC, DS, MC, VI. **Free Special Amenities:** local telephone calls and high-speed Internet.
(See color ad p 587)

🍴 🏊 ⊠ 🎥 🖵 / SOME UNITS FEE 🐕 📶 🖥

RIVIERA INN

Phone: 360/417-3955

(AAA) (SAVE)

◆◆

Motel
$59-$149 All Year

Address: 535 E Front St **Location:** On US 101 W; downtown. **Facility:** 38 one-bedroom standard units. 2 stories (no elevator), exterior corridors. *Bath:* combo or shower only. **Parking:** on-site. **Terms:** office hours 7 am-11:30 pm, cancellation fee imposed. **Amenities:** *Some:* DVD players. **Guest Services:** wireless Internet. **Cards:** AX, MC, VI. **Free Special Amenities:** continental breakfast and high-speed Internet.

🄰 📶 🖥 / SOME UNITS FEE 🐕 ⊠ [VCR]

ROYAL VICTORIAN MOTEL

Phone: (360)452-8400

(AAA) (SAVE)

◆◆

Motel
$59-$109 3/1-10/10
$49-$99 10/11-2/28

Address: 521 E 1st St **Location:** On US 101 E; between Vine and Albert sts. **Facility:** 20 units. 16 one- and 4 two-bedroom standard units. 2 stories (no elevator), exterior corridors. *Bath:* combo or shower only. **Parking:** on-site. **Terms:** office hours 7 am-11 pm, cancellation fee imposed. **Guest Services:** wireless Internet. **Cards:** AX, DS, MC, VI. **Free Special Amenities:** continental breakfast and high-speed Internet.

⊠ 🎥 📶 🖥 / SOME UNITS 🄰 🖵

SUPER 8 MOTEL   *Book at AAA.com*   Phone: 360/452-8401

Motel
Rates not provided

Address: 2104 E 1st St **Location:** 1.8 mi e of downtown, just s of US 101. **Facility:** 62 units. 61 one-bedroom standard units. 1 one-bedroom suite with kitchen. 3 stories (no elevator), interior corridors. **Parking:** on-site. **Amenities:** safes (fee), hair dryers. **Guest Services:** coin laundry, wireless Internet. **Business Services:** PC.

THE TUDOR INN BED & BREAKFAST   Phone: 360/452-3138

Historic Bed
& Breakfast
Rates not provided

Address: 1108 S Oak St **Location:** At 11th St, just w; 0.9 mi s of ferry terminal. Located in a quiet residential area. **Facility:** This 1910 Tudor-style inn offering flower gardens and antique furnishings is convenient to the ferry docks and downtown. Smoke free premises. 5 one-bedroom standard units. 2 stories (no elevator), interior corridors. *Bath:* combo or shower only. **Parking:** on-site. **Terms:** check-in 4 pm, age restrictions may apply.

▼ See AAA listing p 586 ▼

———— WHERE TO DINE ————

BELLA ITALIA

AAA

WW WW

Italian

$9-$30

Phone: 360/457-5442

Serving Italian cuisine made from fresh ingredients, the eatery presents a menu of all the expected pasta and pizza options. The larger streetfront location offers ample seating and a great selection of wines. Casual dress. **Bar:** Beer & wine. **Reservations:** accepted. **Hours:** 4 pm-close. Closed: 11/26, 12/25; also Super Bowl Sun. **Address:** 118 E 1st St **Location:** Downtown. **Parking:** street. **Cards:** AX, CB, DC, DS, JC, MC, VI.

BUSHWHACKER RESTAURANT

WW WW

Steak & Seafood

$9-$25

Phone: 360/457-4113

The long-established eatery is noted for its prime rib and fresh local seafood. Aromatic bread and desserts are made daily. The dining room has a warm rustic feel with tall, cedar-wood walls. Casual dress. **Bar:** Full bar. **Reservations:** not accepted. **Hours:** 4:30 pm-9:30 pm, Fri & Sat-10 pm. Closed: 11/26, 12/24, 12/25. **Address:** 1527 E 1st St **Location:** East end of downtown. **Parking:** on-site. **Cards:** AX, DS, MC, VI.

CAFE GARDEN

AAA

WW WW

American

$7-$14

Phone: 360/457-4611

When there's a short wait, guests often stroll through the English-style flower garden in front. The warm dining room gives off an airy feeling. The menu has a large offering of fresh local seafood that can be combined with other menu items. The wine list, as well as the nice selection of microbrews, complements the food. Casual dress. **Bar:** Beer & wine. **Reservations:** accepted. **Hours:** 6:30 am-2:30 pm. Closed: 11/26, 12/25. **Address:** 1506 E 1st St **Location:** East end of town on US 101. **Parking:** on-site. **Cards:** DS, MC, VI.

C'EST SI BON

AAA

WW WW WW

French

$27-$32

Phone: 360/452-8888

In a freestanding building surrounded by tall trees, this place is just out of town, but the drive is worth it. There are three dining rooms: one with an outside feel and the others with contemporary styling that incorporates large paintings, all of different style, and musical instruments on the walls. The menu has traditional French trimmings but without the heavy sauces. The complementing wine list includes some French selections. Casual dress. **Bar:** Full bar. **Reservations:** suggested. **Hours:** 5 pm-10 pm. Closed: 1/1; also Mon. **Address:** 23 Cedar Park Rd **Location:** 4 mi e on US 101, n on Buchanan Dr. **Parking:** on-site. **Cards:** AX, DS, MC, VI.

CHESTNUT COTTAGE RESTAURANT

WW WW

American

$10-$13

CALL ⑤M

Phone: 360/452-8344

Served in a warm and airy setting, a creative menu filled with many unique recipes offers house specialties like apricot scones and veggie browns (hash browns with fresh vegetables and cheese topped with tomatoes) as well as items like specialty wraps. Casual dress. **Bar:** Beer & wine. **Hours:** 7 am-3 pm. Closed: 11/26, 12/25. **Address:** 929 E Front St **Location:** Cross street Washington St. **Parking:** on-site. **Cards:** AX, DS, MC, VI.

THE CRAB HOUSE RESTAURANT

WW WW

Seafood

$10-$30

Phone: 360/457-0424

Appealing to families and folks just getting back from a day in Victoria, the more traditional restaurant serves steaks, chicken and fresh seafood. Casual dress. **Bar:** Full bar. **Reservations:** accepted. **Hours:** 5:30 am-11 pm. Closed: 12/25. **Address:** 221 N Lincoln St **Location:** On US 101 westbound; at ferry landing; in Red Lion Hotel Port Angeles. **Parking:** on-site. **Cards:** AX, CB, DC, DS, JC, MC, VI.

DOWNRIGGERS   *Menu on AAA.com*

AAA

WW WW

Steak & Seafood

$7-$25

Phone: 360/452-2700

On the second level of the mall, the casual waterfront restaurant affords great views of the Port Angeles Harbor and the Straits of Juan de Fuca. The large, heated deck is comfortable and inviting. Homemade blackberry cobbler is a delightful treat. Casual dress. **Bar:** Full bar. **Reservations:** accepted. **Hours:** 11:30 am-9 pm. Closed: 1/1. **Address:** 115 E Railroad St **Location:** At ferry landing; in Landing Mall. **Parking:** on-site. **Cards:** AX, DS, MC, VI.

DUPUIS RESTAURANT

WW WW

American

$14-$35

Phone: 360/457-8033

In the same log roadhouse since 1920, the restaurant has welcomed generations of hungry motorists passing through on their way to scenic Olympic National Park. Specialties include prime cuts of beef and seafood. Some folks declare the crab and spaghetti as the best dish, but all agree the fresh blackberry pie is a don't-miss. Casual dress. Entertainment. **Bar:** Full bar. **Reservations:** suggested. **Hours:** 5 pm-close. Closed: 12/25; also Tue in winter. **Address:** 256861 Hwy 101 **Location:** 7.5 mi e on US 101; 7.5 mi w of Sequim. **Parking:** on-site. **Cards:** AX, DS, MC, VI.

FIRST STREET HAVEN

WW WW

American

$8-$11

Phone: 360/457-0352

This eatery draws in guests with the aromas of fresh baked goods. The menu satisfies for breakfast and lunch, as well as dessert for those who arrive early enough to get one. Solo diners can read the on-hand magazines and newspaper. On Sunday, only breakfast is served. Casual dress. **Reservations:** not accepted. **Hours:** 7 am-4 pm, Sun 8 am-2 pm. Closed: 11/26, 12/25. **Address:** 107 E 1st St **Location:** On northeast corner of 1st and Laurel sts; downtown. **Parking:** street. **Cards:** AX, DS, MC, VI.

JOSHUA'S RESTAURANT & LOUNGE

AAA

WW WW

Steak & Seafood

$7-$22

Phone: 360/452-6545

The decor is unfettered and the service relaxed at the comfortable restaurant, which sticks to the basics and delivers a filling meal at a great price. Diners can opt for casual seating at the lunch counter or can settle in at a table in the dining room. Casual dress. **Bar:** Full bar. **Reservations:** accepted. **Hours:** 6 am-10 pm. **Address:** 113 Del Guzzi Dr **Location:** East city limits on US 101. **Parking:** on-site. **Cards:** AX, DC, DS, MC, VI.

MICHAEL'S DIVINE DINING   Phone: 360/417-6929

American
$16-$32

Doesn't the name say it all: divine American dishes with a Northwest focus and Mediterranean influences. The lower-level dining room seems like a cozy wine cellar, which is appropriate considering the great selection of wines. Casual dress. **Bar:** Full bar. **Reservations:** accepted. **Hours:** 4 pm-10 pm, Fri & Sat-midnight. Closed: 1/1, 12/25. **Address:** 117 B E 1st St **Location:** Downtown. **Parking:** on-site. **Cards:** AX, CB, DC, DS, MC, VI.

OLYMPIC BAGEL COMPANY   Phone: 360/452-9100

Deli
$6-$10

All breads are made with the freshest ingredients and no preservatives at the display bakery, and meats are smoked on the premises. Patrons can dine in or get a snack or lunch to go. Casual dress. **Hours:** 6 am-3 pm, Sun from 7 am. Closed: 1/1, 11/26, 12/25. **Address:** 802 E 1st St **Location:** East end of town on US 101. **Parking:** on-site. **Cards:** AX, MC, VI.

THAI PEPPERS RESTAURANT   Phone: 360/452-4995

Thai
$9-$18

Just one block from the ferry terminal, the traditional Thai restaurant is tucked inside a small mall. The small dining room is tastefully decorated in pieces from Thailand, and the aroma of jasmine steamed rice is noticeable upon entry. Those seeking something a little different might like a meal of tom yum, a hot and sour soup with lemongrass; cucumber salad with carrots and ground peanuts; and hot and sour prawns. Casual dress. **Bar:** Full bar. **Hours:** 11 am-2:30 & 4:30-9 pm, Sat from 4:30 pm. Closed major holidays; also Sun. **Address:** 222 N Lincoln St **Location:** Downtown. **Parking:** street. **Cards:** AX, DS, MC, VI.

TRAYLOR'S RESTAURANT   Phone: 360/452-3833

Steak & Seafood
$5-$22

Family-run since 1955, the clean, comfortable restaurant is reliable for standard favorites, such as crab Louie, which are prepared and presented with no surprises. Wine and beer selections are limited. The upbeat wait staff provides friendly service. Casual dress. **Bar:** Full bar. **Reservations:** accepted. **Hours:** 6 am-11 pm, Fri & Sat-midnight. Closed: 1/1, 11/26, 12/25. **Address:** 3256 Hwy 101 E **Location:** 3.3 mi e. **Parking:** on-site. **Cards:** AX, DS, MC, VI.

PORT LUDLOW pop. 1,968

——— WHERE TO STAY ———

THE RESORT AT PORT LUDLOW   *Book at AAA.com*   Phone: (360)437-7000

Resort
Hotel
$199-$799 3/1-9/30
$129-$599 10/1-2/28

Address: 1 Heron Rd **Location:** 8 mi n of Hood Canal Floating Bridge; in town. **Facility:** Many rooms have views of the bay at this waterfront resort, which offers a multitude of leisure activities. 37 units. 35 one-bedroom standard units with whirlpools. 2 one-bedroom suites with whirlpools. 3 stories, interior corridors. **Parking:** on-site. **Terms:** check-in 4 pm, 3 day cancellation notice. **Amenities:** video library, voice mail, irons, hair dryers. **Dining:** Harbormaster Restaurant, see separate listing. **Leisure Activities:** rental boats, tennis court, jogging. *Fee:* marina, charter fishing, golf-27 holes. **Guest Services:** wireless Internet. **Business Services:** meeting rooms, PC. **Cards:** AX, MC, VI.

——— WHERE TO DINE ———

HARBORMASTER RESTAURANT   Phone: 360/437-7400

American
$9-$19

Overlooking Port Ludlow Bay, this restaurant has an attractive nautical decor and bistro style. Boat moorage is available. Casual dress. **Bar:** Full bar. **Reservations:** accepted. **Hours:** 7:30 am-10:30 & 11-8 pm. Closed: 12/25; also Mon & Tues. **Address:** 200 Olympic Pl **Location:** 8 mi n of Hood Canal Floating Bridge; in town; in The Resort at Port Ludlow. **Parking:** on-site. **Cards:** AX, MC, VI.

PORT ORCHARD —*See Seattle p. 693.*

PORT TOWNSEND pop. 8,334

——— WHERE TO STAY ———

ANN STARRETT MANSION   Phone: (360)385-3205

Historic
Hotel
$129-$225 All Year

Address: 744 Clay St **Location:** On the bluff. **Facility:** Frescoed ceilings and a three-tiered spiral staircase leading to a domed ceiling are some of the architectural features of this 1889 Victorian house. Smoke free premises. 11 units. 8 one- and 1 two-bedroom standard units. 2 cottages. 3 stories (no elevator), interior corridors. **Bath:** combo or shower only. **Parking:** street. **Terms:** 14 day cancellation notice-fee imposed. **Amenities:** *Some:* hair dryers. **Cards:** AX, MC, VI.

BISHOP VICTORIAN HOTEL   Phone: (360)385-6122

(AAA) [SAVE]

▼▼▼▼

Historic
Hotel

$135-$225 3/1-10/31
$110-$195 11/1-2/28

Address: 714 Washington St **Location:** Corner of Washington and Quincy sts. Located in the historic district; stairway entry. **Facility:** 1890 vintage hotel with all units furnished in Victorian style. All units with propane fireplace. Smoke free premises. 16 units. 1 two-bedroom standard unit. 13 one- and 2 two-bedroom suites, some with kitchens. 3 stories (no elevator), interior corridors. *Bath:* combo or shower only. **Parking:** on-site. **Terms:** 3 day cancellation notice-fee imposed. **Amenities:** high-speed Internet, voice mail, irons, hair dryers. *Some:* DVD players. **Guest Services:** wireless Internet. **Business Services:** meeting rooms, business center. **Cards:** AX, DS, MC, VI. **Free Special Amenities: expanded continental breakfast and high-speed Internet.**

[符] [符] [X] [AC] [符] [符] / SOME UNITS FEE [符] [符]

HARBORSIDE INN   Phone: 360/385-7909

▼▼▼ ▼▼▼

Hotel

Rates not provided

Address: 330 Benedict St **Location:** Just e of SR 20. **Facility:** Smoke free premises. 63 one-bedroom standard units, some with whirlpools. 3 stories, exterior corridors. **Parking:** on-site. **Terms:** check-in 4 pm. **Amenities:** irons, hair dryers. **Pool(s):** heated outdoor. **Leisure Activities:** whirlpool. **Guest Services:** coin laundry, wireless Internet. **Business Services:** meeting rooms.

[符] [X] [AC] [符] [符] [符] / SOME UNITS FEE [符]

HOLLY HILL HOUSE BED & BREAKFAST   Phone: 360/385-5619

▼▼▼ ▼▼▼ ▼▼▼

Historic Bed
& Breakfast

$99-$190 All Year

Address: 611 Polk St **Location:** On the bluff. **Facility:** This 1872 Victorian has unusual stippled woodwork in the dining room; the upside-down look of a historic camper down elm adds interest to the gardens. Smoke free premises. 5 one-bedroom standard units. 2 stories (no elevator), interior/exterior corridors. *Bath:* combo or shower only. **Parking:** street. **Terms:** age restrictions may apply, 14 day cancellation notice-fee imposed. **Amenities:** video library, CD players, hair dryers. *Some:* DVD players. **Leisure Activities:** *Fee:* massage. **Guest Services:** TV in common area, area transportation, wireless Internet. **Cards:** MC, VI.

[ASK] [符] [符] [X] [AC] [符] [符] / SOME UNITS [VCR]

THE JAMES HOUSE   Phone: 360/385-1238

▼▼▼ ▼▼▼

Historic Bed
& Breakfast

$125-$250 All Year

Address: 1238 Washington St **Location:** On the bluff. **Facility:** Built in 1889, this Victorian mansion overlooks Admiralty Inlet and nearby mountains; a historic downtown is within walking distance. Smoke free premises. 13 units. 12 one-bedroom standard units, some with efficiencies. 1 cottage. 3 stories (no elevator), interior corridors. *Bath:* combo or shower only. **Parking:** street. **Terms:** age restrictions may apply, 7 day cancellation notice. **Amenities:** video library, high-speed Internet, hair dryers. *Some:* CD players. **Guest Services:** wireless Internet. **Cards:** AX, MC, VI.

[X] [AC] / SOME UNITS [符] [VCR] [符] [符] [符]

MANRESA CASTLE   Phone: (360)385-5750

▼▼▼ ▼▼▼

Historic
Country Inn

$109-$229 All Year

Address: 651 Cleveland St **Location:** 1.3 mi s, just w of SR 20 at corner of 7th St and Sheridan Ave. **Facility:** Restored 1892 hilltop Rhine-style castle with city, water and mountain views. Stairway entry. Seven units have private bath down the hall. Smoke free premises. 39 units. 35 one- and 4 two-bedroom standard units, some with whirlpools. 3 stories (no elevator), interior corridors. *Bath:* some combo or shower only. **Parking:** on-site. **Terms:** check-in 4 pm, 3 day cancellation notice-fee imposed. **Dining:** Castle Key Restaurant & Lounge, see separate listing. **Guest Services:** wireless Internet. **Business Services:** meeting rooms. **Cards:** AX, DS, MC, VI.

[ASK] [符] [X] [AC] [符]

OLD CONSULATE INN   Phone: 360/385-6753

▼▼▼ ▼▼▼ ▼▼▼

Historic Bed
& Breakfast

$99-$210 All Year

Address: 313 Walker St **Location:** Cross street Washington St; on the bluff. **Facility:** This 1889 Queen Anne Victorian mansion offers excellent views of Admiralty Inlet and the Olympic Mountains. Smoke free premises. 8 one-bedroom standard units. 3 stories (no elevator), interior corridors. *Bath:* combo, shower or tub only. **Parking:** street. **Terms:** age restrictions may apply, 14 day cancellation notice-fee imposed. **Amenities:** hair dryers. **Leisure Activities:** whirlpool. **Guest Services:** TV in common area, area transportation, wireless Internet. **Cards:** MC, VI.

[符] [X] [AC] [符] [符]

PALACE HOTEL   *Book great rates at AAA.com*   Phone: (360)385-0773

(AAA) [SAVE]

▼▼ ▼▼

Historic
Hotel

$59-$289 All Year

Address: 1004 Water St **Location:** Downtown. Located in the historic district; stairway entry. **Facility:** Restored 1889 building with harmonious Victorian furnishings. Some views. Smoke free premises. 19 one-bedroom standard units, some with whirlpools. 3 stories (no elevator), interior corridors. *Bath:* some shared or private, combo or shower only. **Parking:** on-site. **Terms:** 2 night minimum stay - seasonal and/or weekends. **Amenities:** video library, high-speed Internet. *Some:* DVD players. **Guest Services:** wireless Internet. **Cards:** AX, DS, MC, VI. **Free Special Amenities: room upgrade (subject to availability with advance reservations) and high-speed Internet.**

[符] [X] [AC] [符] [符] [符] / SOME UNITS FEE [符] [VCR] [符]

THE SWAN HOTEL   Phone: (360)385-1718

(AAA) [SAVE]

▼▼ ▼▼

Motel

$110-$510 3/1-10/31
$100-$460 11/1-2/28

Address: 216 Monroe St **Location:** Downtown. Located on the edge of the historic district. **Facility:** Smoke free premises. 13 units. 6 one-bedroom standard units. 2 one- and 1 two-bedroom suites, some with efficiencies or kitchens. 4 cottages. 3 stories (no elevator), interior corridors. *Bath:* combo or shower only. **Parking:** on-site. **Terms:** office hours 9 am-10 pm, 3 day cancellation notice-fee imposed. **Amenities:** high-speed Internet, voice mail, irons, hair dryers. *Some:* DVD players. **Guest Services:** wireless Internet. **Business Services:** PC. **Cards:** AX, DS, MC, VI. **Free Special Amenities: local telephone calls and high-speed Internet.**

[符] [X] [AC] [符] [符] [符] / SOME UNITS FEE [符]

THE WATER STREET HOTEL

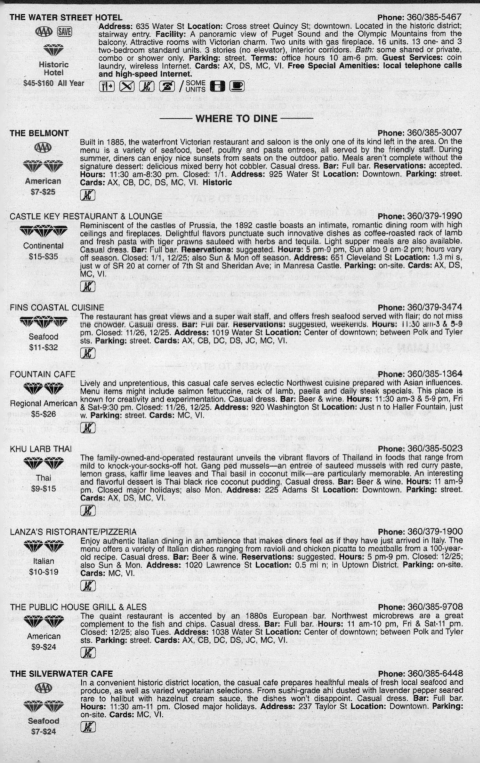

AAA SAVE

Historic
Hotel

$45-$160 All Year

Phone: 360/385-5467

Address: 635 Water St **Location:** Cross street Quincy St; downtown. Located in the historic district; stairway entry. **Facility:** A panoramic view of Puget Sound and the Olympic Mountains from the balcony. Attractive rooms with Victorian charm. Two units with gas fireplace. 16 units. 13 one- and 3 two-bedroom standard units. 3 stories (no elevator), interior corridors. *Bath:* some shared or private, combo or shower only. **Parking:** street. **Terms:** office hours 10 am-6 pm. **Guest Services:** coin laundry, wireless Internet. **Cards:** AX, DS, MC, VI. **Free Special Amenities: local telephone calls and high-speed Internet.**

────── WHERE TO DINE ──────

THE BELMONT

AAA

American
$7-$25

Phone: 360/385-3007

Built in 1885, the waterfront Victorian restaurant and saloon is the only one of its kind left in the area. On the menu is a variety of seafood, beef, poultry and pasta entrees, all served by the friendly staff. During summer, diners can enjoy nice sunsets from seats on the outdoor patio. Meals aren't complete without the signature dessert: delicious mixed berry hot cobbler. Casual dress. **Bar:** Full bar. **Reservations:** accepted. **Hours:** 11:30 am-8:30 pm. Closed: 1/1. **Address:** 925 Water St **Location:** Downtown. **Parking:** street. **Cards:** AX, CB, DC, DS, MC, VI. **Historic**

CASTLE KEY RESTAURANT & LOUNGE

Continental
$15-$35

Phone: 360/379-1990

Reminiscent of the castles of Prussia, the 1892 castle boasts an intimate, romantic dining room with high ceilings and fireplaces. Delightful flavors punctuate such innovative dishes as coffee-roasted rack of lamb and fresh pasta with tiger prawns sauteed with herbs and tequila. Light supper meals are also available. Casual dress. **Bar:** Full bar. **Reservations:** suggested. **Hours:** 5 pm-9 pm, Sun also 9 am-2 pm; hours vary off season. Closed: 1/1, 12/25; also Sun & Mon off season. **Address:** 651 Cleveland St **Location:** 1.3 mi s, just w of SR 20 at corner of 7th St and Sheridan Ave; in Manresa Castle. **Parking:** on-site. **Cards:** AX, DS, MC, VI.

FINS COASTAL CUISINE

Seafood
$11-$32

Phone: 360/379-3474

The restaurant has great views and a super wait staff, and offers fresh seafood served with flair; do not miss the chowder. Casual dress. **Bar:** Full bar. **Reservations:** suggested, weekends. **Hours:** 11:30 am-3 & 5-9 pm. Closed: 11/26, 12/25. **Address:** 1019 Water St **Location:** Center of downtown; between Polk and Tyler sts. **Parking:** street. **Cards:** AX, CB, DC, DS, JC, MC, VI.

FOUNTAIN CAFE

Regional American
$5-$26

Phone: 360/385-1364

Lively and unpretentious, this casual cafe serves eclectic Northwest cuisine prepared with Asian influences. Menu items might include salmon fettuccine, rack of lamb, paella and daily steak specials. This place is known for creativity and experimentation. Casual dress. **Bar:** Beer & wine. **Hours:** 11:30 am-3 & 5-9 pm, Fri & Sat-9:30 pm. Closed: 11/26, 12/25. **Address:** 920 Washington St **Location:** Just n to Haller Fountain, just w. **Parking:** street. **Cards:** MC, VI.

KHU LARB THAI

Thai
$9-$15

Phone: 360/385-5023

The family-owned-and-operated restaurant unveils the vibrant flavors of Thailand in foods that range from mild to knock-your-socks-off hot. Gang ped mussels—an entree of sauteed mussels with red curry paste, lemon grass, kaffir lime leaves and Thai basil in coconut milk—are particularly memorable. An interesting and flavorful dessert is Thai black rice coconut pudding. Casual dress. **Bar:** Beer & wine. **Hours:** 11 am-9 pm. Closed major holidays; also Mon. **Address:** 225 Adams St **Location:** Downtown. **Parking:** street. **Cards:** AX, DS, MC, VI.

LANZA'S RISTORANTE/PIZZERIA

Italian
$10-$19

Phone: 360/379-1900

Enjoy authentic Italian dining in an ambience that makes diners feel as if they have just arrived in Italy. The menu offers a variety of Italian dishes ranging from ravioli and chicken picatta to meatballs from a 100-year-old recipe. Casual dress. **Bar:** Beer & wine. **Reservations:** suggested. **Hours:** 5 pm-9 pm. Closed: 12/25; also Sun & Mon. **Address:** 1020 Lawrence St **Location:** 0.5 mi n; in Uptown District. **Parking:** on-site. **Cards:** MC, VI.

THE PUBLIC HOUSE GRILL & ALES

American
$9-$24

Phone: 360/385-9708

The quaint restaurant is accented by an 1880s European bar. Northwest microbrews are a great complement to the fish and chips. Casual dress. **Bar:** Full bar. **Hours:** 11 am-10 pm, Fri & Sat-11 pm. Closed: 12/25; also Tues. **Address:** 1038 Water St **Location:** Center of downtown; between Polk and Tyler sts. **Parking:** street. **Cards:** AX, CB, DC, DS, JC, MC, VI.

THE SILVERWATER CAFE

AAA

Seafood
$7-$24

Phone: 360/385-6448

In a convenient historic district location, the casual cafe prepares healthful meals of fresh local seafood and produce, as well as varied vegetarian selections. From sushi-grade ahi dusted with lavender pepper seared rare to halibut with hazelnut cream sauce, the dishes won't disappoint. Casual dress. **Bar:** Full bar. **Hours:** 11:30 am-11 pm. Closed major holidays. **Address:** 237 Taylor St **Location:** Downtown. **Parking:** on-site. **Cards:** MC, VI.

T'S RESTAURANT

▼▼▼▼

American
$15-$29

Phone: 360/385-0700

Northwest and Italian influences are reflected in imaginative preparations of local seafood, tasty meats, poultry and limited game. Each meal is individually prepared. Outstanding choices include pork medallions and any of the homemade desserts. The friendly staff enhances the cozy dining experience here. Casual dress. **Bar:** Full bar. **Reservations:** suggested. **Hours:** 4 pm-close. Closed: 12/25; also Tues. **Address:** 2330 Washington St **Location:** Just e of SR 20; at City Boat Haven. **Parking:** on-site. **Cards:** AX, DS, MC, VI.

THE WILD COHO WINE CAFE

▼▼▼▼

Regional American
$15-$22

Phone: 360/379-1030

Using many indredients from local bakers, organic farmers and fisherfolk, the restaurant offers relaxed fine dining and amazing wine selctions. Casual dress. **Bar:** Beer & wine. **Reservations:** not accepted. **Hours:** 5 pm-9 pm; hours may vary. Closed major holidays. **Address:** 1044 Lawrence St **Location:** 0.5 mi n; in the Uptown District. **Parking:** street. **Cards:** MC, VI.

[A̶C̶]

POULSBO —See Seattle p. 693.

PROSSER pop. 4,838

———— **WHERE TO STAY** ————

BEST WESTERN THE INN AT HORSE HEAVEN   *Book great rates at AAA.com*

Phone: (509)786-7977

(AAA) (SAVE)

▼▼▼▼

Hotel
$109-$119 3/1-11/30
$99-$109 12/1-2/28

Address: 259 Merlot Dr **Location:** I-82, exit 80, just s. **Facility:** Smoke free premises. 85 units. 84 one-bedroom standard units, some with kitchens and/or whirlpools. 1 one-bedroom suite with kitchen. 2 stories (no elevator), interior corridors. *Bath:* combo or shower only. **Parking:** on-site. **Amenities:** voice mail, irons, hair dryers. *Some:* high-speed Internet. **Pool(s):** heated outdoor, heated indoor. **Leisure Activities:** whirlpools, exercise room. **Guest Services:** coin laundry, wireless Internet. **Business Services:** meeting rooms, business center. **Cards:** AX, DC, DS, MC, VI. **Free Special Amenities: expanded continental breakfast and high-speed Internet.**

AAA Benefit:
Members save up to 20%, plus 10% bonus points with rewards program.

[⑪↦] CALL [✒M] [⇌] [✕] [🗄] [▣] / SOME UNITS FEE [🐾] [VCR] [▦]

PULLMAN pop. 24,675

———— **WHERE TO STAY** ————

HILLTOP INN   *Book great rates at AAA.com*

(AAA) (SAVE)

▼▼▼▼

Hotel
$70-$199 All Year

Phone: (509)332-0928

Address: 928 NW Olsen St **Location:** 1.6 mi e on SR 270 from US 195. **Facility:** Smoke free premises. 59 units. 58 one-bedroom standard units, some with whirlpools. 1 one-bedroom suite. 3 stories, interior corridors. *Bath:* combo or shower only. **Parking:** on-site. **Terms:** 3 day cancellation notice. **Amenities:** video library (fee), DVD players, irons, hair dryers. **Pool(s):** heated indoor. **Leisure Activities:** sauna, whirlpool, barbecue on patio, exercise room. **Guest Services:** valet and coin laundry, wireless Internet. **Business Services:** meeting rooms, PC. **Cards:** AX, DC, DS, MC, VI. **Free Special Amenities: full breakfast and high-speed Internet.**

[⑪↦] CALL [✒M] [⇌] [✕] [✕] [VCR] [🗄] [▦] [▣] / SOME UNITS FEE [🐾]

HOLIDAY INN EXPRESS HOTEL & SUITES   *Book at AAA.com*

▼▼▼▼

Hotel
$129 All Year

Phone: (509)334-4437

Address: SE 1190 Bishop Blvd **Location:** Jct US 195 business route, 0.5 mi s, 1 mi e on SR 270. **Facility:** Smoke free premises. 130 units. 116 one-bedroom standard units, some with whirlpools. 14 one-bedroom suites. 3 stories, interior corridors. *Bath:* combo or shower only. **Parking:** on-site, winter plug-ins. **Amenities:** video games (fee), dual phone lines, voice mail, irons, hair dryers. **Pool(s):** heated indoor. **Leisure Activities:** whirlpool, exercise room. **Guest Services:** valet and coin laundry, area transportation, wireless Internet. **Business Services:** meeting rooms, business center. **Cards:** AX, CB, DC, DS, JC, MC, VI.

[ASK] [✚] [⑪↦] CALL [✒M] [⇌] [✕] [🎥] [🗄] [▦] [▣] / SOME UNITS [🐾] [▦]

QUALITY INN PARADISE CREEK   *Book great rates at AAA.com*

(AAA) (SAVE)

▼▼▼

Hotel
$85-$160 All Year

Phone: (509)332-0500

Address: 1400 SE Bishop Blvd **Location:** Jct US 195 business route, just s, 1 mi e on SR 270. Located adjacent to Washington State University. **Facility:** Smoke free premises. 66 units. 54 one-bedroom standard units. 12 one-bedroom suites with whirlpools. 2 stories (no elevator), interior corridors. *Bath:* some combo or shower only. **Parking:** on-site, winter plug-ins. **Terms:** 3 day cancellation notice. **Amenities:** safes, irons, hair dryers. *Some:* DVD players. **Pool(s):** heated outdoor. **Leisure Activities:** sauna, whirlpool. **Guest Services:** coin laundry, airport transportation-Pullman/Moscow Regional Airport, area transportation-downtown, wireless Internet. **Business Services:** meeting rooms, PC. **Cards:** AX, CB, DC, DS, JC, MC, VI. **Free Special Amenities: preferred room (subject to availability with advance reservations) and high-speed Internet.**

[✚] [⑪↦] [⇌] [✚] [✕] [🎥] [🗄] [▦] [▣] / SOME UNITS [🐾]

———— **WHERE TO DINE** ————

HILLTOP RESTAURANT

(AAA)

▼▼▼▼

American
$7-$28

Phone: 509/334-2555

As the name implies, the restaurant sits on a hill on the edge of town and affords sweeping views of rolling farmland. Adjacent to a listed lodging, it has occupied the same location since 1950. The menu lists a large selection of Sterling Silver USDA Choice beef dishes, as well as many seafood and pasta selections. All can be enjoyed with a glass from the extensive selection of Washington wines. Casual dress. **Bar:** Full bar. **Reservations:** accepted. **Hours:** 11:30 am-1:30 & 5-10 pm, Sat from 5 pm, Sun 4 pm-9 pm. Closed: 7/4, 12/24, 12/25. **Address:** 900 NW Olsen St **Location:** 1.6 mi e on SR 270 from US 195. **Parking:** on-site. **Cards:** AX, DC, DS, MC, VI.

THE OLD EUROPEAN RESTAURANT

European
$7-$12

Phone: 509/334-6381

European comfort foods include made-from-scratch baked goods along the lines of Swedish cream-filled crepes, Danish aebelskivers (a ball-like pancake), Belgian waffles, German potato pancakes, Hungarian breakfast goulash and Irish shepherd's pie. Homemade soups also are tasty. The breakfast crowd flocks to this place for its large portions. Casual dress. **Hours:** 6 am-1:30 pm, Fri & Sat-2 pm, Sun 7 am-2:30 pm. Closed: 12/25. **Address:** 455 S Grand Ave **Location:** Just s of downtown. **Parking:** on-site. **Cards:** MC, VI.

CALL 🖟M

SUCHADA'S

Thai
$8-$17

Phone: 509/334-1060

Popular with locals, the casual, family-run restaurant prepares dishes from authentic ingredients. Casual dress. **Bar:** Beer & wine. **Hours:** 11 am-3 & 5-9 pm, Sun from 5 pm. Closed: 11/26, 12/25. **Address:** 1020 S Grand St **Location:** Just s of downtown. **Parking:** on-site. **Cards:** MC, VI.

SWILLY'S

Continental
$6-$23

Phone: 509/334-3395

The busy restaurant has the aura of a relaxed bistro. Among beef, seafood and pasta dishes on the seasonal menu is angel hair pasta with creamy garlic sauce and prawns. Homemade desserts are simply sinful. Distressed wood floors and colorful and eclectic multimedia artwork decorate the college hangout. Casual dress. **Bar:** Beer & wine. **Reservations:** accepted. **Hours:** 11 am-3 & 5-9:30 pm, Fri-10 pm, Sat 5 pm-10 pm. Closed major holidays; also Sun. **Address:** 200 NE Kamiaken St **Location:** Downtown. **Parking:** street. **Cards:** AX, CB, DS, JC, MC, VI.

PUYALLUP —See Seattle p. 694.

QUINAULT

——— WHERE TO STAY ———

LAKE QUINAULT LODGE   *Book great rates at AAA.com*

🔺🔺 🅂🅰🅅🄴

Classic Historic
Hotel
$129-$268 All Year

Phone: (360)288-2900

Address: 345 S Shore Rd **Location:** 2 mi off US 101. **Facility:** Located on the south shore of Lake Quinault, this lodge was built in 1926. Most guest rooms have a view of the lake and some have gas fireplaces. Smoke free premises. 91 units. 90 one-bedroom standard units. 1 one-bedroom suite. 3 stories (no elevator), interior/exterior corridors. *Bath:* combo or shower only. **Parking:** on-site. **Terms:** 3 day cancellation notice-fee imposed. **Amenities:** video library, hair dryers. *Some:* CD players. **Dining:** The Roosevelt Dining Room, see separate listing. **Pool(s):** heated indoor. **Leisure Activities:** saunas, rental boats, rental canoes, fishing, spa paddles, kayaks, table tennis, recreation programs, croquet, bocci, hiking trails, horseshoes, game room. **Guest Services:** wireless Internet. **Business Services:** meeting rooms. **Cards:** AX, MC, VI.

🍴 🏊 ⊠ ✕ 🅺 🕿 💻 / SOME UNITS FEE 🐾 📶 🆅🅲🆁 📠 🖨

——— WHERE TO DINE ———

THE ROOSEVELT DINING ROOM

American
$9-$35

Phone: 360/288-2900

Nature and the beauty of the Pacific Northwest seem to rush in from all sides of the dining room, which occupies a glassed-in porch. President Roosevelt was a guest in 1937 while visiting what would become Olympic National Park. Lunch is on the casual side, with delicatessen, French dip and Monte Cristo sandwiches, as well as soups and salads. Dinner is more of an adventure, with duck carnitos tostadas, pesto-seared Alaskan halibut and the house specialty cedar-plank salmon for two. Casual dress. **Bar:** Full bar. **Reservations:** suggested. **Hours:** 7:30 am-3 & 5-9 pm; 8 am-3 & 5:30-8 pm in winter. **Address:** 345 S Shore Rd **Location:** 2 mi off US 101; in Lake Quinault Lodge. **Parking:** on-site. **Cards:** AX, MC, VI.

CALL 🖟M 🅺

QUINCY pop. 5,044

——— WHERE TO STAY ———

TRADITIONAL INNS

Motel
$85-$149 All Year

Phone: (509)787-3525

Address: 500 F St SW **Location:** West end of town on SR 28. **Facility:** Smoke free premises. 30 one-bedroom standard units, some with efficiencies and/or whirlpools. 2 stories (no elevator), exterior corridors. **Parking:** on-site. **Terms:** office hours 6 am-10 pm, 1-3 night minimum stay - seasonal. **Amenities:** DVD players, high-speed Internet, dual phone lines, irons, hair dryers. **Guest Services:** coin laundry, wireless Internet. **Business Services:** PC. **Cards:** AX, CB, DC, DS, MC, VI.

🅰🅂🅺 ✕ 📱 🖨 💻 / SOME UNITS FEE 🐾

——— WHERE TO DINE ———

**THE IDLE HOUR CAFE &
STEAKHOUSE**   *Menu on AAA.com*

🔺🔺🔺

American
$7-$34

Phone: 509/787-3714

Friendly, small-town service and freshly prepared food are hallmarks of this restaurant housed in a 1906 building that was one of the town's original saloons. Worthy of strong consideration is the chef's dinner: a meal of four delightfully surprising courses designed that evening. Casual dress. **Bar:** Beer & wine. **Reservations:** suggested, for dinner. **Hours:** 11 am-2 pm, Thurs & Fri also 6 pm-9 pm, Sat 6 pm-9 pm. Closed major holidays; also Sun & 1st week of July. **Address:** 18 B St SE **Location:** Downtown. **Parking:** street. **Cards:** MC, VI.

REDMOND —See Seattle p. 694.

RENTON —See Seattle p. 696.

REPUBLIC pop. 954

———— WHERE TO STAY ————

PROSPECTOR INN

AAA SAVE

Hotel
$55-$175 All Year

Phone: (509)775-3361

Address: 979 S Clark Ave **Location:** Downtown. **Facility:** Smoke free premises. 28 one-bedroom standard units, some with whirlpools. 3 stories (no elevator), interior corridors. *Bath:* combo or shower only. **Parking:** on-site. **Terms:** office hours 7 am-9:30 pm, cancellation fee imposed. **Amenities:** voice mail. **Leisure Activities:** sauna, whirlpool, exercise room. **Guest Services:** coin laundry, wireless Internet. **Business Services:** meeting rooms. **Cards:** AX, DS, MC, VI. **Free Special Amenities:** expanded continental breakfast and high-speed Internet.

RICHLAND pop. 38,708

———— WHERE TO STAY ————

CLARION HOTEL & CONFERENCE CENTER   *Book at AAA.com*

Hotel
Rates not provided

Phone: 509/946-4121

Address: 1515 George Washington Way **Location:** I-182, exit 5B, 2.5 mi n. **Facility:** 195 units. 194 one-bedroom standard units. 1 one-bedroom suite. 6 stories, interior corridors. *Bath:* combo or shower only. **Parking:** on-site. **Amenities:** voice mail, irons, hair dryers. **Pool(s):** heated indoor. **Leisure Activities:** saunas, whirlpool, exercise room. **Guest Services:** valet and coin laundry, wireless Internet. **Business Services:** conference facilities, business center.

COURTYARD BY MARRIOTT-RICHLAND COLUMBIA POINT   *Book great rates at AAA.com*

AAA SAVE

Hotel
$125-$153 All Year

Phone: (509)942-9400

Address: 480 Columbia Point Dr **Location:** I-182, exit 5B, George Washington Way to Columbia Point Dr, then right. **Facility:** Smoke free premises. 120 units. 112 one-bedroom standard units. 8 one-bedroom suites, some with whirlpools. 3 stories, interior corridors. *Bath:* combo or shower only. **Parking:** on-site. **Terms:** cancellation fee imposed. **Amenities:** video games (fee), high-speed Internet, dual phone lines, voice mail, irons, hair dryers. **Pool(s):** heated indoor. **Leisure Activities:** whirlpool, rental bicycles, exercise room. **Guest Services:** wireless Internet. **Business Services:** meeting rooms, business center. **Cards:** AX, CB, DC, DS, MC, VI. **Free Special Amenities:** newspaper and high-speed Internet.

AAA Benefit:
Members save a minimum 5% off the best available rate.

DAYS INN *Book great rates at AAA.com*   Phone: (509)943-4611

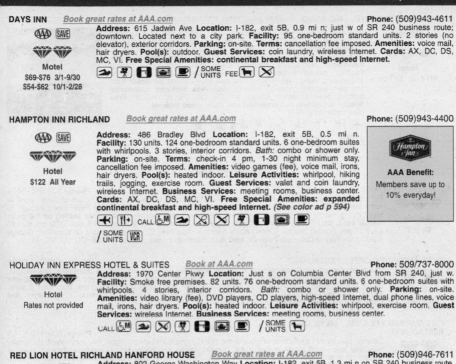

(AAA) (SAVE)

▼▼ ▼▼

Motel
$69-$76 3/1-9/30
$54-$62 10/1-2/28

Address: 615 Jadwin Ave **Location:** I-182, exit 5B, 0.9 mi n; just w of SR 240 business route; downtown. Located next to a city park. **Facility:** 95 one-bedroom standard units. 2 stories (no elevator), exterior corridors. **Parking:** on-site. **Terms:** cancellation fee imposed. **Amenities:** voice mail, hair dryers. **Pool(s):** outdoor. **Guest Services:** coin laundry, wireless Internet. **Cards:** AX, DC, DS, MC, VI. **Free Special Amenities: continental breakfast and high-speed Internet.**

HAMPTON INN RICHLAND   *Book great rates at AAA.com*   Phone: (509)943-4400

(AAA) (SAVE)

▼▼ ▼▼

Hotel
$122 All Year

Address: 486 Bradley Blvd **Location:** I-182, exit 5B, 0.5 mi n. **Facility:** 130 units. 124 one-bedroom standard units. 6 one-bedroom suites with whirlpools. 3 stories, interior corridors. *Bath:* combo or shower only. **Parking:** on-site. **Terms:** check-in 4 pm, 1-30 night minimum stay, cancellation fee imposed. **Amenities:** video games (fee), voice mail, irons, hair dryers. **Pool(s):** heated indoor. **Leisure Activities:** whirlpool, hiking trails, jogging, exercise room. **Guest Services:** valet and coin laundry, wireless Internet. **Business Services:** meeting rooms, business center. **Cards:** AX, DC, DS, MC, VI. **Free Special Amenities: expanded continental breakfast and high-speed Internet.** *(See color ad p 594)*

AAA Benefit:
Members save up to
10% everyday!

HOLIDAY INN EXPRESS HOTEL & SUITES   *Book at AAA.com*   Phone: 509/737-8000

▼▼ ▼▼

Hotel
Rates not provided

Address: 1970 Center Pkwy **Location:** Just s on Columbia Center Blvd from SR 240, just w. **Facility:** Smoke free premises. 82 units. 76 one-bedroom standard units. 6 one-bedroom suites with whirlpools. 4 stories, interior corridors. *Bath:* combo or shower only. **Parking:** on-site. **Amenities:** video library (fee), DVD players, CD players, high-speed Internet, dual phone lines, voice mail, irons, hair dryers. **Pool(s):** heated indoor. **Leisure Activities:** whirlpool, exercise room. **Guest Services:** wireless Internet. **Business Services:** meeting rooms, business center.

RED LION HOTEL RICHLAND HANFORD HOUSE   *Book great rates at AAA.com*   Phone: (509)946-7611

(AAA) (SAVE)

▼▼ ▼▼

Hotel
$139 All Year

Address: 802 George Washington Way **Location:** I-182, exit 5B, 1.3 mi n on SR 240 business route. Located adjacent to a city park. **Facility:** Smoke free premises. 149 units. 148 one-bedroom standard units. 1 one-bedroom suite. 2 stories, interior/exterior corridors. *Bath:* combo or shower only. **Parking:** on-site. **Terms:** cancellation fee imposed. **Amenities:** voice mail, irons, hair dryers. **Pool(s):** heated outdoor. **Leisure Activities:** whirlpool, dock & fishing access adjacent, exercise room, volleyball. **Guest Services:** valet and coin laundry, airport transportation-Tri-Cities Airport, wireless Internet. **Business Services:** meeting rooms, business center. **Cards:** AX, CB, DC, DS, MC, VI.

▼ *See AAA listing p 596* ▼

SHILO INN SUITES HOTEL - RICHLAND

Book great rates at AAA.com

Phone: (509)946-4661

AAA [SAVE]
▽▽▽▽
Hotel
$97-$180 All Year

Address: 50 Comstock St **Location:** I-182, exit 5B, 0.5 mi n. Located next to a city park. **Facility:** 151 one-bedroom standard units, some with kitchens and/or whirlpools. 2 stories (no elevator), exterior corridors. *Bath:* combo or shower only. **Parking:** on-site. **Terms:** check-in 4 pm. **Amenities:** high-speed Internet, voice mail, irons, hair dryers. **Pool(s):** heated outdoor. **Leisure Activities:** sauna, whirlpools, steamroom, hiking trails, jogging, exercise room. **Guest Services:** valet and coin laundry, wireless Internet. **Business Services:** conference facilities, business center. **Cards:** AX, CB, DC, DS, JC, MC, VI. **Free Special Amenities: full breakfast and high-speed Internet.**
(See color ad p 595)

---------- **WHERE TO DINE** ----------

ANTHONY'S RESTAURANT

Phone: 509/946-3474

▽▽▽▽
Seafood
$9-$29

Patrons dine on strictly fresh and always wild-caught Pacific Northwest seafood. Clam chowder alone is worth the trip. The comfortable, modern restaurant affords marina and Columbia River views through its bright dining room's floor-to-ceiling windows. Also available is extensive smoke-free seating on the patio. Casual dress. **Bar:** Full bar. **Reservations:** suggested. **Hours:** 11 am-9:30 pm, Fri & Sat-10:30 pm, Sun 10 am-9:30 pm; Sunday brunch. Closed major holidays. **Address:** 550 Columbia Point Dr **Location:** George Washington Way to Columbia Point Dr, then right. **Parking:** on-site. **Cards:** AX, CB, DC, JC, MC, VI.

APOLLO AUTHENTIC GREEK RESTAURANT

Phone: 509/943-9841

▽▽▽
Greek
$9-$25

The quiet, comfortable family restaurant serves traditional Greek dishes such as moussaka, spanakopita, and the ever-popular gyro sandwiches and plates. The servings here are huge so you might have problems saving enough room for the classic bit of Greek heaven called baklava. Casual dress. **Bar:** Beer & wine. **Hours:** 11 am-9 pm, Fri & Sat-10 pm. Closed major holidays. **Address:** 620 Cullum Ave **Location:** Downtown. **Parking:** on-site. **Cards:** AX, DC, DS, MC, VI.

THREE MARGARITAS FAMILY MEXICAN RESTAURANT

Phone: 509/946-7755

▽▽▽
Mexican
$6-$11

Ceramic parrots add a touch of whimsy to the colorful and festive dining room. The basic menu comprises traditional fare—such as chips and salsa, burritos, fajitas, enchiladas and quesadillas. Prompt, attentive servers do a good job keeping on top of things. Casual dress. **Bar:** Full bar. **Reservations:** accepted. **Hours:** 11 am-10 pm, Fri & Sat-11 pm. Closed: 7/4, 11/26, 12/25. **Address:** 627 Jadwin Ave **Location:** I-182, exit 5B, 0.9 mi n; just w of SR 240 business route; downtown. **Parking:** on-site. **Cards:** AX, DC, DS, MC, VI.

RITZVILLE pop. 1,736

---------- **WHERE TO STAY** ----------

AMERICAS BEST VALUE INN- COLWELL

Book great rates at AAA.com

Phone: (509)659-1620

AAA [SAVE]
▽▽▽▽
Motel
$66-$79 3/1-9/15
$49-$62 9/16-2/28

Address: 501 W 1st Ave **Location:** I-90, exit 220, 0.9 mi n; downtown. **Facility:** 25 units. 22 one- and 3 two-bedroom standard units, some with whirlpools. 1 story, exterior corridors. *Bath:* combo or shower only. **Parking:** on-site, winter plug-ins. **Terms:** office hours 7:30 am-10:30 pm. **Amenities:** high-speed Internet, voice mail, hair dryers. **Pool(s):** heated outdoor. **Leisure Activities:** sauna, croquet, barbecue, horseshoes. **Guest Services:** coin laundry. **Cards:** AX, DC, DS, MC, VI. **Free Special Amenities: continental breakfast and room upgrade (subject to availability with advance reservations).**

BEST WESTERN BRONCO INN

Book great rates at AAA.com

Phone: (509)659-5000

AAA [SAVE]
▽▽▽▽
Hotel
$79-$199 3/1-9/30
$69-$159 10/1-2/28

Address: 105 W Galbreath Way **Location:** I-90, exit 221, cross overpass, then second left. **Facility:** 63 one-bedroom standard units, some with whirlpools. 3 stories, interior corridors. *Bath:* combo or shower only. **Parking:** on-site. **Amenities:** voice mail, irons, hair dryers. *Some:* high-speed Internet. **Pool(s):** heated indoor. **Leisure Activities:** whirlpool, exercise room. **Guest Services:** coin laundry, wireless Internet. **Business Services:** meeting rooms, business center. **Cards:** AX, CB, DC, DS, JC, MC, VI. **Free Special Amenities: continental breakfast and high-speed Internet.**

Best Western

AAA Benefit:
Members save up to 20%, plus 10% bonus points with rewards program.

LA QUINTA INN RITZVILLE

Book great rates at AAA.com

Phone: (509)659-1007

▽▽▽
Hotel
$59-$149 All Year

Address: 1513 Smitty's Blvd **Location:** I-90, exit 221, just n. **Facility:** 54 units. 53 one-bedroom standard units, some with whirlpools. 1 two-bedroom suite with kitchen and whirlpool. 2 stories (no elevator), interior corridors. *Bath:* combo or shower only. **Parking:** on-site, winter plug-ins. **Amenities:** voice mail, irons, hair dryers. *Some:* DVD players. **Pool(s):** heated outdoor. **Leisure Activities:** whirlpool, horseshoes, volleyball. **Guest Services:** wireless Internet. **Business Services:** meeting rooms, business center. **Cards:** AX, CB, DS, MC, VI.

TOP HAT MOTEL

Phone: (509)659-1100

Motel
$38-$64 All Year

Address: 210 E 1st Ave **Location:** I-90, exit 221, 1 mi ne via Division St. **Facility:** 11 one-bedroom standard units. 1 story, exterior corridors. *Bath:* combo or shower only. **Parking:** on-site. **Terms:** office hours 9 am-midnight. **Cards:** AX, DS, MC, VI.

ROCHESTER pop. 1,829

———— WHERE TO DINE ————

PRIME RIB & STEAK HOUSE

Phone: 360/273-2000

Steak & Seafood
$15-$32

Set in a casino, the casual steakhouse features prime rib sliced tableside every night. Casual dress. **Bar:** Full bar. **Reservations:** accepted. **Hours:** 4:30 pm-9 pm, Fri & Sat-10 pm. Closed major holidays. **Address:** 12888 188th Ave SW **Location:** 3 mi w on US 12, 0.8 mi s on Anderson Rd, then just e; in Lucky Eagle Casino. **Parking:** on-site. **Cards:** AX, MC, VI.

SALKUM

———— WHERE TO STAY ————

THE SHEPHERD'S INN BED & BREAKFAST

Phone: 360/985-2434

Bed & Breakfast
$85-$115 All Year

Address: 168 Autumn Heights Dr **Location:** I-5, exit 68, 13.4 mi e on US 12; 0.4 mi s of US 12 via Fischer Rd. Located in a secluded area. **Facility:** Wild huckleberry crepes are the breakfast specialty at this contemporary inn nestled among trees and rolling hills near Mount St. Helens. Smoke free premises. 5 one-bedroom standard units. 2 stories (no elevator), interior corridors. *Bath:* some shared or private, combo or shower only. **Parking:** on-site. **Terms:** 2 night minimum stay - seasonal and/or weekends, 3 day cancellation notice. **Amenities:** irons. *Some:* CD players, hair dryers. **Leisure Activities:** whirlpool. **Cards:** DS, MC, VI.

SAMMAMISH —See Seattle p. 700.

SAN JUAN ISLAND —See San Juan Islands p. 600.

San Juan Islands

LOPEZ ISLAND

———— WHERE TO STAY ————

LOPEZ FARM COTTAGES AND TENT CAMPING

Phone: 360/468-3555

Cottage
Rates not provided

Address: 555 Fisherman Bay Rd **Location:** From ferry landing, 2.6 mi s via Ferry and Fisherman Bay rds. Located in a quiet area. **Facility:** Northwest Scandinavian cottages, each with a gas fireplace, are set amidst a historic family farm; parking is within a short stroll of the units. Smoke free premises. 5 cottages. 1 story, exterior corridors. *Bath:* shower only. **Parking:** on-site. **Terms:** check-in 4 pm, age restrictions may apply. **Amenities:** *Some:* DVD players, CD players. **Leisure Activities:** whirlpool. **Guest Services:** area transportation.

———— WHERE TO DINE ————

BAY CAFE

Phone: 360/468-3700

Ethnic
$19-$32

Guests can watch the sunset either from outdoor deck seating or window seating inside. An impressive selection of wines complements an ever-changing menu consisting of local items. Those who feel like eating early can opt for the three-course tasting menu. The work of local artists decorates the walls. Casual dress. **Bar:** Full bar. **Reservations:** suggested. **Hours:** 5:30 pm-close; hours & days vary fall-spring. **Closed:** 12/25. **Address:** 9 Old Post Rd, Suite C **Location:** From ferry landing, 2 mi s on Ferry Rd, just sw on Fisherman Bay Rd, then just w. **Parking:** on-site. **Cards:** AX, DS, MC, VI.

ORCAS ISLAND

———— WHERE TO STAY ————

BUCK BAY FARM INN & LAVENDER FIELD

Phone: 360/376-2908

Bed & Breakfast
Rates not provided

Address: 716 Point Lawrence Rd **Location:** From Olga community, 0.7 mi e on Point Lawrence Rd; just e of jct Obstruction Pass Rd. Located in a country setting. **Facility:** A century-old farm home on six acres of pasture, the B&B overlooks a forest-edged green lawn where deer sometimes wander. Smoke free premises. 5 units. 4 one- and 1 two-bedroom standard units. 2 stories (no elevator), interior/exterior corridors. **Parking:** on-site. **Amenities:** video library, DVD players, irons, hair dryers. **Leisure Activities:** whirlpool, horseshoes. **Guest Services:** wireless Internet.

DEER HARBOR INN

Phone: 360/376-4110

Country Inn
Rates not provided

Address: 33 Inn Ln **Location:** In Deer Harbor; 7 mi sw of ferry landing; 3.5 mi sw of Westsound. **Facility:** Smoke free premises. 11 units. 8 one-bedroom standard units. 3 cottages. 2 stories (no elevator), interior/exterior corridors. *Bath:* combo or shower only. **Parking:** on-site. **Terms:** office hours 8 am-8 pm. **Amenities:** hair dryers. *Some:* DVD players, irons. **Dining:** restaurant, see separate listing. **Leisure Activities:** whirlpool. *Fee:* massage. **Guest Services:** wireless Internet. **Business Services:** PC.

EASTSOUND LANDMARK INN

Phone: 360/376-2423

Condominium
$170-$229 6/15-2/28
$100-$209 3/1-6/14

Address: 67 Main St **Location:** In Eastsound; downtown. **Facility:** 15 condominiums. 3 stories (no elevator), interior corridors. **Parking:** on-site. **Terms:** office hours 9 am-9 pm, 2 night minimum stay - seasonal and/or weekends, 7 day cancellation notice-fee imposed. **Amenities:** DVD players, irons, hair dryers. *Some:* CD players. **Guest Services:** wireless Internet. **Cards:** AX, DS, MC, VI. **Free Special Amenities:** local telephone calls and high-speed Internet.

THE INN ON ORCAS ISLAND

Phone: 360/376-5227

Bed & Breakfast
$145-$315 All Year

Address: 114 Channel Rd **Location:** 7 mi sw of ferry landing; 3.5 mi sw of Westsound. **Facility:** This contemporary home situated on six acres features walking trails that border the tip of peaceful Deer Harbor lagoon, home to varied wildlife. Smoke free premises. 8 units. 6 one-bedroom standard units, some with whirlpools. 1 one-bedroom suite with kitchen. 1 cottage. 2 stories (no elevator), interior/exterior corridors. *Bath:* combo or shower only. **Parking:** on-site. **Terms:** 2 night minimum stay - seasonal and/or weekends, age restrictions may apply, 21 day cancellation notice-fee imposed. **Amenities:** video library, hair dryers. *Some:* CD players, irons. **Leisure Activities:** canoeing, bicycles. *Fee:* massage. **Guest Services:** wireless Internet. **Cards:** AX, MC, VI.

KANGAROO HOUSE BED & BREAKFAST
Phone: 360/376-2175

▼▼▼▼
Historic Bed
& Breakfast
Rates not provided

Address: 1459 N Beach Rd **Location:** 1 mi n of Eastsound via Prune Alley and N Beach Rd. **Facility:** A centrally located 1907 Craftsman home with a turn-of-the-20th-century feel, this family-oriented property includes 1.5 acres of lawn and gardens. Smoke free premises. 5 units. 3 one-bedroom standard units. 2 one-bedroom suites. 2 stories (no elevator), interior corridors. *Bath:* combo or shower only. **Parking:** on-site. **Terms:** age restrictions may apply. **Amenities:** video library, hair dryers. *Some:* DVD players, CD players, irons. **Leisure Activities:** whirlpool. **Guest Services:** wireless Internet. **Business Services:** meeting rooms.

OTTERS POND BED & BREAKFAST OF ORCAS ISLAND
Phone: (360)376-8844

▼▼▼▼
Bed & Breakfast
$115-$245 All Year

Address: 100 Tomihi Dr **Location:** From Eastsound, just se; just w of Rosario Resort and Moran State Park. **Facility:** A modern home situated on a serene otter pond that abounds with wildlife. Situated in close proximity to both Eastsound and Moran State Park. Smoke free premises. 5 units. 5 one-bedroom standard units. 2 stories (no elevator), interior/exterior corridors. *Bath:* combo or shower only. **Parking:** on-site. **Terms:** 2 night minimum stay, age restrictions may apply, 30 day cancellation notice-fee imposed. **Amenities:** video library, CD players, hair dryers. *Some:* DVD players. **Leisure Activities:** whirlpool. **Guest Services:** wireless Internet. **Cards:** DS, MC, VI.

OUTLOOK INN ON ORCAS ISLAND
Phone: 360/376-2200

▼▼▼
Historic
Hotel
Rates not provided

Address: 171 Main St **Location:** In Eastsound; downtown. **Facility:** Turn-of-the-20th-century Victorian inn; also offers a contemporary wing with suites. Some shared showers and shared half-baths in the original building. Smoke free premises. 40 one-bedroom standard units, some with whirlpools. 3 stories (no elevator), interior/exterior corridors. *Bath:* some shared or private, combo or shower only. **Parking:** on-site. **Terms:** office hours 8 am-9 pm. **Amenities:** voice mail. *Some:* hair dryers. **Guest Services:** wireless Internet. **Business Services:** meeting rooms.

SPRING BAY INN ON ORCAS ISLAND
Phone: 360/376-5531

▼▼▼
Bed & Breakfast
$240-$280 All Year

Address: 464 Spring Bay Tr **Location:** From Olga community, 0.6 mi e on Point Lawrence Rd, 0.8 mi s on Obstruction Pass Rd, then 0.8 mi sw on dirt road, follow signs. Located in a quiet rural area. **Facility:** Nestled between steep ravines and surrounded by 57 acres of forest, this inn features comfortable rooms with wood stoves and views of Spring Bay. Smoke free premises. 5 one-bedroom standard units, some with whirlpools. 2 stories (no elevator), interior/exterior corridors. **Parking:** on-site. **Terms:** check-in 3:30 pm, 30 day cancellation notice-fee imposed. **Amenities:** CD players, irons, hair dryers. **Leisure Activities:** whirlpool, recreation programs, hiking trails. **Guest Services:** wireless Internet. **Business Services:** PC. **Cards:** DS, MC, VI.

TURTLEBACK FARM INN
Phone: (360)376-4914

AAA SAVE
▼▼▼
Historic Bed
& Breakfast
$100-$260 All Year

Address: 1981 Crow Valley Rd **Location:** 4 mi sw of Eastsound; 6 mi n of ferry landing; 2.5 mi n of Westsound Marina. **Facility:** This property on 80 acres of forest and farmland includes an 1890s restored farmhouse and a recently built home with four luxury rooms. Smoke free premises. 11 one-bedroom standard units. 2 stories (no elevator), interior corridors. *Bath:* combo or shower only. **Parking:** on-site. **Terms:** 2 night minimum stay - seasonal and/or weekends, age restrictions may apply, 15 day cancellation notice-fee imposed. **Amenities:** hair dryers. *Some:* CD players, irons. **Leisure Activities:** hiking trails. **Guest Services:** wireless Internet. **Cards:** DS, MC, VI. **Free Special Amenities:** full breakfast and high-speed Internet.

The following lodging was either not evaluated or did not meet AAA rating requirements but is listed for your information only.

CASCADE HARBOR INN
Phone: 360/376-6350

fyi

Not evaluated. **Address:** 1800 Rosario Rd **Location:** 5 mi se of Eastsound; just e of Rosario Harbor. Facilities, services, and decor characterize an economy property.

——— WHERE TO DINE ———

BILBO'S FESTIVO
Phone: 360/376-4728

▼▼
Mexican
$4-$20

Mexican items as well as American-prepared beef, seafood and chicken make up the menu at the charming restaurant. Grapes grow overhead on trellises that surround the airy courtyard. Freshly squeezed lime juice margaritas are a house specialty. Casual dress. **Bar:** Full bar. **Reservations:** accepted. **Hours:** 5 pm-close; Sat & Sun also 11:30 am-3 pm 4/1-5/31; 11:30 am-3 & 5-close 6/1-9/30. Closed: 11/26, 12/24, 12/25. **Address:** 310 A St **Location:** In Eastsound; downtown. **Parking:** street. **Cards:** MC, VI.

CAFE OLGA
Phone: 360/376-5098

▼▼
American
$8-$28

In Orcas Island Artworks Cooperative Gallery, the cafe is near Moran State Park. Built in 1938 as a strawberry barreling plant, the building has been beautifully restored. The restaurant remains popular among the locals. Casual dress. **Bar:** Beer & wine. **Reservations:** not accepted. **Hours:** Open 3/1-1/1 & 2/15-2/28; 9 am-8 pm; seasonal hours may vary. Closed: 11/26, 12/25; also Wed in winter. **Address:** 11 Point Lawrence Rd **Location:** In Olga community; jct Olga and Point Lawrence rds. **Parking:** on-site. **Cards:** MC, VI.

CHRISTINA'S

▼▼▼

Regional American
$13-$35

Phone: 360/376-4904

Great presentation and garnishes punctuate steak and seafood dishes. The porch and terrace offer great views, while the elegant dining room exudes cozy ambience. Dressy casual. **Bar:** Full bar. **Hours:** 5 pm-9 pm; to 10 pm 7/1-9/15. Closed: 12/25; also 11/1-11/25; Tues & Wed 9/16-6/30. **Address:** 310 Main St **Location:** In Eastsound; downtown. **Parking:** on-site. **Cards:** MC, VI.

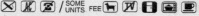

DEER HARBOR INN RESTAURANT

▼▼

Regional Steak & Seafood
$15-$38

Phone: 360/376-1040

Enjoy country cooking at this turn-of-the-20th-century farmhouse with an outdoor deck overlooking the harbor and hillside. The menu specializes in local seafood and some beef items. Casual dress. **Bar:** Full bar. **Reservations:** suggested. **Hours:** 4 pm-9 pm. Closed: 2 days per week 11/1-4/30; call for days. **Address:** 33 Inn Ln **Location:** In Deer Harbor; 7 mi sw of ferry landing; 3.5 mi sw of Westsound; in Deer Harbor Inn. **Parking:** on-site. **Cards:** AX, DS, MC, VI.

OCTAVIA'S BISTRO

▼▼

American
$15-$24

Phone: 360/376-4300

In the Orcas Hotel, Octavia's affords a view of the San Juans. Service is relaxed, and the food is good. Casual dress. **Bar:** Full bar. **Reservations:** suggested. **Hours:** 5 pm-8:30 pm, Sun also 7 am-11 am. Closed: 12/25. **Address:** 18 Orcas Hill Rd **Location:** Overlooking Orcas Island ferry landing. **Parking:** on-site. **Cards:** AX, MC, VI.

SAN JUAN ISLAND

——— WHERE TO STAY ———

ARGYLE HOUSE BED & BREAKFAST

▼▼ ▼▼

Historic Bed
& Breakfast
$100-$250 All Year

Phone: 360/378-4084

Address: 685 Argyle Ave **Location:** In Friday Harbor; 0.3 mi e of jct Spring St. **Facility:** Charming 1910 home with a comfortable, old-fashioned appeal. Convenient to shops, restaurants and ferry. TV/VCR available upon request. Smoke free premises. 5 units. 4 one-bedroom standard units. 1 one-bedroom suite. 1-2 stories (no elevator), interior/exterior corridors. *Bath:* combo or shower only. **Parking:** on-site. **Terms:** 14 day cancellation notice-fee imposed. **Amenities:** video library, hair dryers. **Leisure Activities:** whirlpool. **Guest Services:** TV in common area, wireless Internet. **Cards:** AX, DS, MC, VI.

BEST WESTERN FRIDAY HARBOR SUITES   *Book great rates at AAA.com*

(AAA) (SAVE)

▼▼ ▼▼

Hotel
$165-$330 3/1-9/30
$135-$215 10/1-2/28

Phone: (360)378-3031

Address: 680 Spring St **Location:** In Friday Harbor; 0.7 mi w of ferry dock. **Facility:** Designated smoking area. 62 units. 5 one-bedroom standard units with efficiencies. 51 one- and 6 two-bedroom suites, some with efficiencies. 2 stories, interior corridors. **Parking:** on-site. **Terms:** check-in 4 pm, 7 day cancellation notice. **Amenities:** high-speed Internet, voice mail, irons, hair dryers. **Dining:** Peppermill Seafood & Steakhouse, see separate listing. **Leisure Activities:** whirlpool, exercise room. **Guest Services:** airport transportation-Friday Harbor Airport, area transportation-ferry terminal, wireless Internet. **Business Services:** meeting rooms, PC. **Cards:** AX, DC, DS, MC, VI. *(See color ad below)*

AAA Benefit:
Members save up to 20%, plus 10% bonus points with rewards program.

▼ See AAA listing above ▼

Relax in the comfort of our elegant all-suites hotel nestled in the waterfront village of Friday Harbor, on San Juan Island, Washington.

fridayharborsuites.com • 800.752.5752

THE DRAGONFLY INN

(AAA) (SAVE)
▼▼ ▼▼ ▼▼

Bed & Breakfast
$195-$250 All Year

Phone: (360)378-4280

Address: 4770 Roche Harbor Rd **Location:** 4.6 mi n of Friday Harbor via Tucker Ave. **Facility:** The Asian inspired decor and authentic Far Eastern foods provide for a unique lodging experience; each guest room includes a deep whirlpool tub. 4 one-bedroom standard units with whirlpools. 1 story, interior corridors. **Parking:** on-site. **Terms:** 2 night minimum stay - seasonal and/or weekends, 7 day cancellation notice-fee imposed. **Amenities:** video library, DVD players, hair dryers. **Guest Services:** wireless Internet. **Business Services:** meeting rooms. **Cards:** AX, DS, MC, VI. **Free Special Amenities: full breakfast and high-speed Internet.**

⊠ 🐾 🛎 🖥

ELEMENTS HOTEL & SPA   *Book at AAA.com*

▼▼ ▼▼
Hotel
$147-$407 All Year

Phone: (360)378-4000

Address: 410 Spring St **Location:** In Friday Harbor; 0.5 mi w of ferry dock. **Facility:** Designated smoking area. 73 units. 72 one-bedroom standard units, some with kitchens and/or whirlpools. 1 house. 2 stories (no elevator), exterior corridors. *Bath:* combo or shower only. **Parking:** on-site. **Terms:** office hours 8 am-11 pm, 10 day cancellation notice-fee imposed. **Amenities:** hair dryers. **Pool(s):** heated indoor. **Leisure Activities:** sauna, whirlpool, bicycles, exercise room. *Fee:* massage. **Guest Services:** coin laundry, area transportation, wireless Internet. **Business Services:** meeting rooms, PC. **Cards:** AX, MC, VI.

(ASK) 🌙 🐾 ⊠ ⊠ 🛎 🖥 / SOME UNITS FEE 🐾 (K)

FRIDAY HARBOR HOUSE   *Book at AAA.com*

▼▼ ▼▼ ▼▼
Hotel
Rates not provided

Phone: 360/378-8455

Address: 130 West St **Location:** In Friday Harbor; just w of Spring St; at the waterfront. **Facility:** Smoke free premises. 23 units. 22 one-bedroom standard units with whirlpools. 1 one-bedroom suite with whirlpool. 2-3 stories, interior/exterior corridors. **Parking:** on-site. **Terms:** office hours 7 am-11 pm, check-in 4 pm. **Amenities:** video library, DVD players, voice mail, irons, hair dryers. *Some:* CD players. **Dining:** restaurant, see separate listing. **Guest Services:** valet laundry, wireless Internet. **Business Services:** meeting rooms, PC.

🍴 ⊠ 🛎 🖥 / SOME UNITS (K) 🖥

HILLSIDE HOUSE BED & BREAKFAST   *Book great rates at AAA.com*

(AAA) (SAVE)
▼▼ ▼▼ ▼▼

Bed & Breakfast
$75-$275 All Year

Phone: (360)378-4730

Address: 365 Carter Ave **Location:** In Friday Harbor; just off Guard St. **Facility:** Situated on a small hill overlooking Friday Harbor. Some of the rooms in this contemporary B&B have views of the harbor. Smoke free premises. 7 one-bedroom standard units, some with whirlpools. 3 stories (no elevator), interior corridors. *Bath:* combo or shower only. **Parking:** on-site. **Terms:** age restrictions may apply, 15 day cancellation notice-fee imposed. **Amenities:** video library, hair dryers. *Some:* DVD players, CD players, irons. **Guest Services:** wireless Internet. **Cards:** AX, DS, MC, VI. **Free Special Amenities: full breakfast and high-speed Internet.**

⊠ (K) (VCR) 🖥

LAKEDALE RESORT   *Book great rates at AAA.com*

(AAA) (SAVE)
▼▼ ▼▼ ▼▼

Resort
Hotel
$179-$489 All Year

Phone: (360)378-2350

Address: 4313 Roche Harbor Rd **Location:** 4 mi n of Friday Harbor via Tucker Ave. **Facility:** A rustic log structure set lakeside; many guest rooms provide direct access to the deck with views of the lake. Smoke free premises. 17 units. 9 one-bedroom standard units with whirlpools. 1 two-bedroom suite with whirlpool. 1 house and 6 cottages. 2 stories (no elevator), interior/exterior corridors. **Parking:** on-site. **Terms:** office hours 8 am-6 pm, check-in 4 pm, 2 night minimum stay - weekends, 7 day cancellation notice. **Amenities:** video library, DVD players, voice mail, irons, hair dryers. *Some:* CD players. **Leisure Activities:** whirlpool, rental boats, rental canoes, rental paddleboats, boat dock, badminton, horseshoes, volleyball. *Fee:* fishing, massage. **Guest Services:** wireless Internet. **Cards:** AX, DS, MC, VI. **Free Special Amenities: continental breakfast and local telephone calls.**

⊠ ⊠ (K) 🖥 / SOME UNITS FEE 🐾 🕅 🛎 🖥

STATES INN & RANCH
Phone: (360)378-6240

(AAA) (SAVE)

▼▼▼ ▼▼▼
Historic Bed
& Breakfast
$122-$210 All Year

Address: 2687 W Valley Rd **Location:** 7 mi nw of Friday Harbor via 2nd St, Guard St and Beaverton Valley Rd. Located in a rural area. **Facility:** This converted turn-of-the-20th-century schoolhouse is on 60 pastoral acres next to the English Camp section of the national park. Smoke free premises. 10 units. 8 one-bedroom standard units. 1 two-bedroom suite. 1 cabin. 2 stories (no elevator), interior corridors. *Bath:* combo or shower only. **Parking:** on-site. **Terms:** 7 day cancellation notice. **Amenities:** hair dryers. *Some:* DVD players, irons. **Leisure Activities:** farm tour, hiking trails. **Guest Services:** airport transportation-Friday Harbor Airport, area transportation-ferry terminal, wireless Internet. **Business Services:** PC. **Cards:** AX, DS, JC, MC, VI. **Free Special Amenities: full breakfast and high-speed Internet.**

⊞ ⊠ 📶 🐾 ☎ / SOME UNITS 📺 VCR 🔌 🖥 💳

TRUMPETER INN BED & BREAKFAST
Phone: (360)378-3884

▼▼▼ ▼▼▼
Bed & Breakfast
$125-$195 4/1-10/31

Address: 318 Trumpeter Way **Location:** 1.5 mi w of Friday Harbor via Spring St and San Juan Valley Rd. Located in a quiet rural area. **Facility:** Rooms in this B&B nestled in a farmland setting are decorated with contemporary furnishings and offer views of the countryside and trout pond. Smoke free premises. 6 one-bedroom standard units. 2 stories (no elevator), interior corridors. *Bath:* combo or shower only. **Parking:** on-site. **Terms:** open 4/1-10/31, age restrictions may apply, 7 day cancellation notice-fee imposed. **Amenities:** video library, hair dryers. *Some:* CD players, irons. **Leisure Activities:** whirlpool. *Fee:* massage. **Guest Services:** TV in common area, area transportation, VCR in common area, wireless Internet. **Cards:** DS, MC, VI.

ASK ⊞ ⊠ 📶 📺 ☎

The following lodgings were either not evaluated or did not meet AAA rating requirements but are listed for your information only.

BIRD ROCK HOTEL
Phone: 360/378-5848

(fyi)

Not evaluated. **Address:** 35 1st St **Location:** In Friday Harbor; just n of Spring St. Facilities, services, and decor characterize a mid-scale property.

ROCHE HARBOR VILLAGE
Phone: 360/378-2155

(fyi)

Not evaluated. **Address:** 248 Reuben Memorial Dr **Location:** In Roche Harbor; on north end of island. Facilities, services, and decor characterize a mid-scale property.

WHERE TO DINE

DOWNRIGGER
Phone: 360/378-2700

▼▼ ▼▼
Seafood
$7-$33

Overlooking the busy harbor, the laid-back restaurant lets diners unwind while enjoying fresh seafood, burgers, fish 'n chips and salads. Seating on the outdoor deck is hard to come by when the weather is nice. Casual dress. **Bar:** Full bar. **Reservations:** suggested. **Hours:** 11 am-9 pm, Sat & Sun from 9 am; hours may vary in summer. Closed: 11/26, 12/25. **Address:** 10 Front St **Location:** In Friday Harbor; at ferry landing; downtown. **Parking:** on-site. **Cards:** AX, MC, VI.

📶

DUCK SOUP INN
Menu on AAA.com
Phone: 360/378-4878

(AAA)

▼▼▼ ▼▼▼
Regional
American
$25-$35

Fresh, high-quality ingredients go into seasonal dishes of seafood, chicken, beef and pasta. Fresh flowers, sprigs of spices and leaves garnish attractive plates. Casual dress. **Bar:** Full bar. **Reservations:** required. **Hours:** Open 4/1-10/31; 5 pm-close. Closed: Mon. **Address:** 50 Duck Soup Ln **Location:** 4.5 mi n of Friday Harbor via Tucker Ave. **Parking:** on-site. **Cards:** MC, VI.

📶

FRIDAY HARBOR HOUSE RESTAURANT
Phone: 360/378-8455

▼▼▼ ▼▼▼
New American
$24-$35

The harborside restaurant offers great views of Puget Sound. Sophisticated preparations feature ingredients from the local islands. Casual dress. **Bar:** Full bar. **Reservations:** suggested. **Hours:** 5:30 pm-9:30 pm. Closed: Tues, Wed 10/15-6/15. **Address:** 130 West St **Location:** In Friday Harbor; just w of Spring St; at the waterfront; in Friday Harbor House. **Parking:** street. **Cards:** AX, DC, DS, MC, VI.

📶

FRONT STREET ALE HOUSE
Phone: 360/378-2337

▼▼ ▼▼
American
$8-$20

The two-story building is in the heart of town, where one can walk just about anywhere including the ferry terminal. Some windows have great views of the harbor and boats sailing lazily about. The fairly traditional menu offers burgers, fish and chips, pasta, chicken and sandwiches, all of which can be enjoyed with a pint of craft beer made on the premises. Casual dress. **Bar:** Full bar. **Reservations:** not accepted. **Hours:** 11 am-11 pm. Closed major holidays. **Address:** 1 Front St **Location:** In Friday Harbor; downtown. **Parking:** street. **Cards:** AX, DS, MC, VI.

LIME KILN CAFE
Phone: 360/378-2155

▼▼
American
$5-$13

Visitors to the light and airy place can choose to eat inside or on the pier, where boat owners parade past on their way to market and dry land. After guests order with the cashier, items are quickly prepared and delivered to the table. Mornings find a real rush for the freshly made doughnuts. Casual dress. **Reservations:** not accepted. **Hours:** 7 am-9 pm; to 2 pm 10/1-5/1. Closed: 11/26, 12/25. **Address:** 248 Reuben Memorial Dr **Location:** In Roche Harbor; on north end of island. **Parking:** on-site. **Cards:** AX, MC, VI.

📶

MADRONA BAR & GRILL　　　　　　　　　　　　　　　　**Phone: 360/378-2155**

American
$10-$20

The pace is a bit slower than in the Lime Kiln Cafe, but the restaurant offers the same great views of Roche Harbor and the boats at moor. Entrees show a small degree of complexity, and service is attentive. Sandwiches and burgers are popular, as are the chowder and desserts. Casual dress. **Bar:** Full bar. **Reservations:** not accepted. **Hours:** Open 5/15-9/30; 11 am-10 pm. Closed: 11/26, 12/25. **Address:** 248 Reuben Memorial Dr **Location:** In Roche Harbor; on north end of island. **Parking:** on-site. **Cards:** AX, MC, VI.

MALOULA　　*Menu on AAA.com*　　　　　　　　　　　　**Phone: 360/378-8485**

Mediterranean
$8-$36

On a lovely rooftop, the casual eatery affords views of the harbor from both its inside and outside seats. The Mediterranean menu, which ranges from East to West, features fresh seafood, lamb, beef and chicken dishes. Homemade baklavas are offered daily. Casual dress. **Bar:** Full bar. **Reservations:** suggested, in summer. **Hours:** Open 4/1-9/30; 11 am-3 & 5:30-9 pm. Closed: Mon. **Address:** 1 Front St **Location:** In Friday Harbor; downtown. **Parking:** street. **Cards:** MC, VI.

MCMILLIN'S DINING ROOM　　　　　　　　　　　　　　**Phone: 360/378-5757**

American
$22-$42

Originally the home of Roche Harbor's founder, the dining room is perched on a second floor and affords perfect views of the marina and boats at rest. Guests plan to be present at sunset, when the colors are officially lowered for the evening and the cannon fired. Tradition is the norm here, as beef and seafood dishes are carefully prepared. Look to the evening specials for something distinctive and seasonal. Casual dress. **Bar:** Full bar. **Reservations:** suggested. **Hours:** 5 pm-10 pm. Closed: 9/7, 11/26, 12/25; also Tues & Wed 10/29-5/9. **Address:** 248 Reuben Memorial Dr **Location:** In Roche Harbor; on north end of island. **Parking:** on-site. **Cards:** AX, MC, VI.

PEPPERMILL SEAFOOD & STEAKHOUSE　　　　　　　　**Phone: 360/378-7060**

Steak & Seafood
$23-$45

Guests sit indoors or on the garden patio to dine on selections of seafood, steak and pasta. Casual dress. **Bar:** Full bar. **Reservations:** accepted. **Hours:** 4 pm-10 pm. Closed: 1/1, 12/25. **Address:** 680 Spring St **Location:** In Friday Harbor; 0.7 mi w of ferry dock; in Best Western Friday Harbor Suites. **Parking:** on-site. **Cards:** AX, CB, DC, DS, JC, MC, VI.

STEPS WINE BAR & CAFE　　　　　　　　　　　　　　**Phone: 360/378-5050**

American
$16-$28

A well-chosen wine list complements the tapas-type dishes, served in both small- and large-plate varieties, at the casual waterfront cafe. Fresh local ingredients enhance the interesting menu. Casual dress. **Bar:** Full bar. **Reservations:** suggested. **Hours:** 5 pm-9 pm; 11 am-2 pm 5/25-9/7. Closed: 1/1, 12/25; also Mon & Tues in winter. **Address:** 140 A 1st St **Location:** In Friday Harbor; at the waterfront. **Parking:** street. **Cards:** MC, VI.

VINNY'S RISTORANTE　　　　　　　　　　　　　　　**Phone: 360/378-1934**

Italian
$15-$40

Perched on a hill, this Italian restaurant presents a seafood-oriented menu. Casual dress. **Bar:** Full bar. **Reservations:** accepted. **Hours:** 4:30 pm-9:30 pm. Closed major holidays; also Sun; Mon in winter. **Address:** 165 West St **Location:** In Friday Harbor; just w of Spring St. **Parking:** street. **Cards:** AX, DS, MC, VI.

The previous listings were for the San Juan Islands.
This page resumes the alphabetical listings of cities in Washington.

SEABECK

──────── **WHERE TO STAY** ────────

WILLCOX HOUSE　　　　　　　　　　　　　　　　　**Phone: (360)830-4492**

Historic Bed
& Breakfast
$189-$279　All Year

Address: 2390 Tekiu Rd NW **Location:** US 3, exit Newberry Hill Rd, 3 mi w to Seabeck Hwy, 13.5 mi nw to Old Holly Hill Rd, just n to Tekiu Rd, then 1.2 mi n to end of road. Located in a quiet secluded area. **Facility:** A drive down a gently winding, tree-lined road leads to this B&B with views of the Olympic Mountains and Hoods Canal. Smoke free premises. 5 units. 4 one- and 1 two-bedroom standard units, some with whirlpools. 2 stories (no elevator), interior corridors. *Bath:* combo or shower only. **Parking:** on-site. **Terms:** 2 night minimum stay - seasonal and/or weekends, age restrictions may apply, 7 day cancellation notice. **Amenities:** hair dryers. **Leisure Activities:** boat dock, fishing. **Guest Services:** TV in common area, wireless Internet. **Business Services:** meeting rooms. **Cards:** MC, VI.

SEATAC —*See Seattle p. 700.*

Destination Seattle
pop. 563,374

Nestled between the Olympic Mountains to the west and the Cascade Range on the east, Seattle is perfectly situated to take advantage of the gifts Mother Nature has bestowed upon the region.

Water seems to be everywhere—the city is practically surrounded by Elliott Bay, Puget Sound and lakes Washington and Union. Miles of bicycle and jogging routes, lakes made for sailing and the nearby promise of downhill skiing make outdoors the place to be.

Seattle's CVB

Seattle skyline. High-rise office buildings are nothing new to Seattle, which boasted the tallest skyscraper west of the Mississippi for nearly 50 years.

See Vicinity map page 624

Tacoma Regional CVB

Old City Hall, Tacoma. This view of the landmark Old City Hall, built in 1893, reveals the lovely Italian Renaissance-style details of the building's clock tower.

Kingston •

Poulsbo •

Suquamish •

Silverdale •

Bainbridge Island

Bremerton •
• Port Orchard

(16)

Gig Harbor •

University • Place

Lakewood •

(5)

• Dupont

Places included in this AAA Destination City:

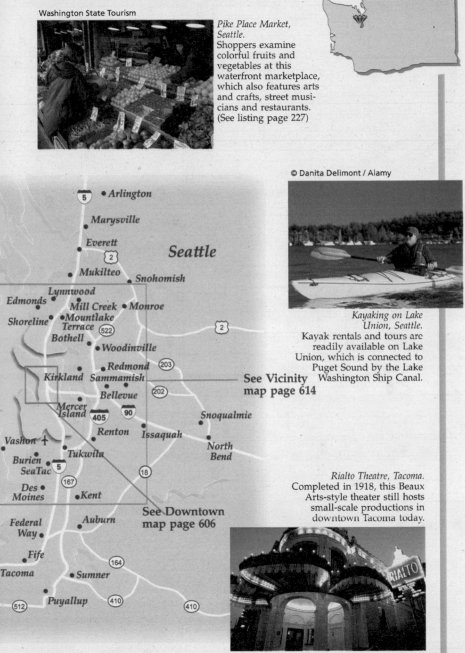

Washington State Tourism

Pike Place Market, Seattle.
Shoppers examine colorful fruits and vegetables at this waterfront marketplace, which also features arts and crafts, street musicians and restaurants. (See listing page 227)

© Danita Delimont / Alamy

Kayaking on Lake Union, Seattle.
Kayak rentals and tours are readily available on Lake Union, which is connected to Puget Sound by the Lake Washington Ship Canal.

See Vicinity map page 614

See Downtown map page 606

Rialto Theatre, Tacoma.
Completed in 1918, this Beaux Arts-style theater still hosts small-scale productions in downtown Tacoma today.

Tacoma Regional CVB

Seattle

Arlington
Marysville
Everett
Mukilteo   Snohomish
Lynnwood
Edmonds   Mill Creek   Monroe
Shoreline   Mountlake
Terrace
Bothell   Woodinville
Redmond
Kirkland   Sammamish
Bellevue
Mercer
Island
Renton   Issaquah
Vashon
Burien   Tukwila
SeaTac
Des
Moines   Kent
Federal   Auburn
Way
Fife
Tacoma   Sumner
Puyallup
Snoqualmie
North
Bend

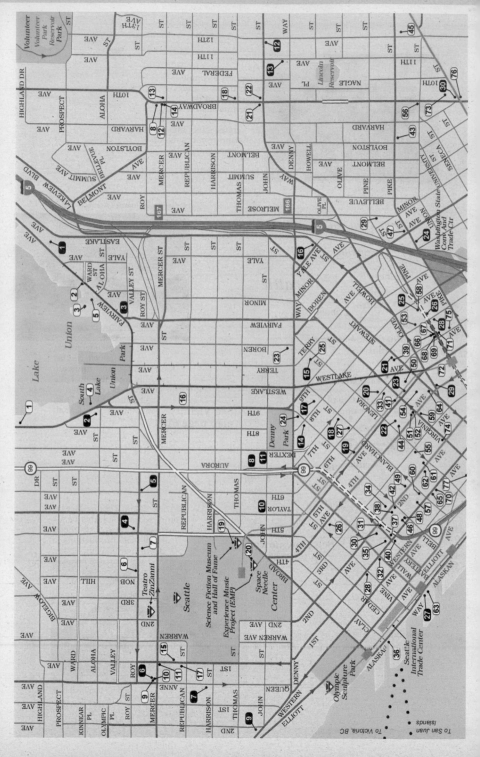

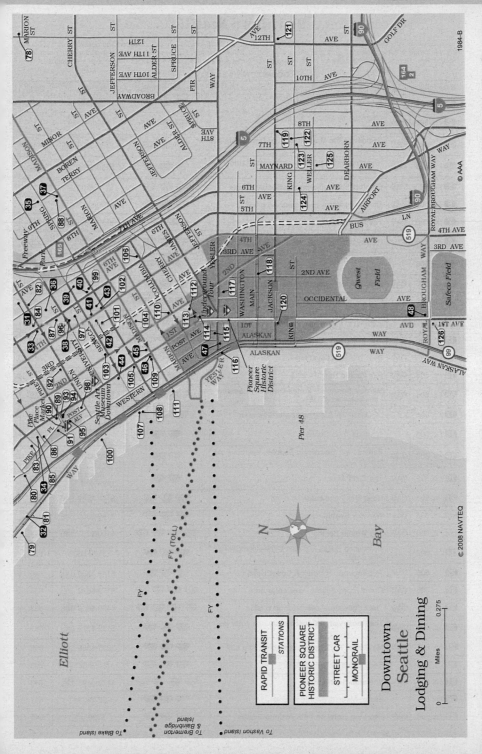

Downtown
Seattle
Lodging & Dining

RAPID TRANSIT
STATIONS
PIONEER SQUARE
HISTORIC DISTRICT
STREET CAR
MONORAIL

1984-B

© AAA

© 2008 NAVTEQ

Downtown Seattle

This index helps you "spot" where approved lodgings and restaurants are located on the corresponding detailed maps. Lodging daily rate range is for comparison only and show the property's high season. Restaurant rate range is a combination of lunch and/or dinner. Turn to the listing page for more detailed rate information and consult display ads for special promotions.

DOWNTOWN SEATTLE

Map Page	OA	Lodgings	Diamond Rated	High Season	Page
1 / p. 606		Silver Cloud Inn Lake Union	◈◈◈	$199-$279	643
2 / p. 606		Courtyard by Marriott Seattle Downtown/Lake Union	◈◈◈	$209-$249	632
3 / p. 606	AAA	**Residence Inn Marriott Seattle Downtown/Lake Union**	◈◈◈	$239-$299 SAVE	641
4 / p. 606	AAA	**Hampton Inn & Suites-Downtown/Seattle Center**	◈◈◈	$139-$259 SAVE	634
5 / p. 606	AAA	**Comfort Suites-Downtown/Seattle Center**	◈◈◈	$119-$209 SAVE	631
6 / p. 606	AAA	**MarQueen Hotel - see color ad p 638**	◈◈◈	$149-$400 SAVE	638
7 / p. 606	AAA	**The Mediterranean Inn**	◈◈	$119-$169 SAVE	640
8 / p. 606		Holiday Inn Express-Downtown Seattle	◈◈◈	Rates not provided	635
9 / p. 606		Homewood Suites by Hilton-Seattle Downtown - see color ad p 636	◈◈◈	$159-$299	636
10 / p. 606	AAA	**Best Western Executive Inn/Seattle**	◈◈◈	$124-$209 SAVE	629
11 / p. 606		Holiday Inn Seattle Center	◈◈◈	$169-$224	635
12 / p. 606		Seattle Hill House Bed & Breakfast	◈◈◈	Rates not provided	641
13 / p. 606		11th Avenue Inn Bed and Breakfast	◈◈◈	$69-$169	629
14 / p. 606	AAA	**Best Western Loyal Inn**	◈◈	$114-$199 SAVE	629
15 / p. 606	AAA	**Pan Pacific Hotel Seattle**	◈◈◈◈	$195-$425 SAVE	640
16 / p. 606	AAA	**Marriott SpringHill Suites-Downtown Seattle - see color ad p 639**	◈◈◈	$189-$259 SAVE	638
17 / p. 606		La Quinta Inn & Suites Seattle Downtown	◈◈◈	$79-$169	637
18 / p. 606		Days Inn Town Center	◈◈	Rates not provided	632
19 / p. 606	AAA	**Ramada Inn Downtown Seattle - see color ad p 640**	◈◈	$139-$169 SAVE	640
20 / p. 606	AAA	**The Sixth Avenue Inn**	◈◈	Rates not provided SAVE	643
21 / p. 606	AAA	**Hotel Max - see color ad p 637**	◈◈◈	$149-$269 SAVE	636
22 / p. 606	AAA	**Warwick Seattle Hotel**	◈◈◈	$199-$350 SAVE	643
23 / p. 606	AAA	**The Westin Seattle**	◈◈◈	$190-$399 SAVE	644
24 / p. 606		Homewood Suites by Hilton Convention Center/Pike Street	◈◈◈	$179-$309	635
25 / p. 606	AAA	**The Paramount Hotel, A Coast Hotel**	◈◈◈	$149-$300 SAVE	640
26 / p. 606	AAA	**Grand Hyatt Seattle - see color ad p 634**	◈◈◈◈	$179-$529 SAVE	634
27 / p. 606	AAA	**The Edgewater - see color ad p 633**	◈◈◈◈	$459-$659 SAVE	633
28 / p. 606	AAA	**The Roosevelt, A Coast Hotel - see color ad p 641**	◈◈◈	$159-$279 SAVE	641
29 / p. 606	AAA	**Mayflower Park Hotel - see color ad p 609**	◈◈◈	$205-$365 SAVE	638
30 / p. 606		Silver Cloud Hotel-Broadway	◈◈◈	$189-$279	643
31 / p. 606	AAA	**Sheraton Seattle Hotel**	◈◈◈◈	$179-$399 SAVE	643
32 / p. 606		Seattle Marriott Waterfront Hotel	◈◈◈	$278-$340	641
33 / p. 606	AAA	**Red Lion Hotel on Fifth Avenue-Seattle**	◈◈◈	$329 SAVE	640

DOWNTOWN SEATTLE (cont'd)

Map Page	OA	Lodgings (cont'd)	Diamond Rated	High Season	Page
34 / p. 606		Inn at the Market	◆◆◆◆	$245-$625	637
35 / p. 606	AAA	The Inn at Virginia Mason	◆◆	$135-$324 SAVE	637
36 / p. 606	AAA	Hilton Seattle - see color ad p 635	◆◆◆	$189-$575 SAVE	634
37 / p. 606	AAA	Sorrento Hotel	◆◆◆◆	Rates not provided SAVE	643
38 / p. 606	AAA	The Fairmont Olympic Hotel	◆◆◆◆◆	$299-$469 SAVE	633
39 / p. 606	AAA	Crowne Plaza Seattle-Downtown - see color ad p 632	◆◆◆	$169-$329 SAVE	632
40 / p. 606	AAA	Hotel Vintage Park	◆◆◆	$139-$309 SAVE	637
41 / p. 606	AAA	W Seattle	◆◆◆◆	$239-$509 SAVE	644
42 / p. 606	AAA	Hotel Monaco	◆◆◆◆	$139-$349 SAVE	636
43 / p. 606		Executive Hotel Pacific	◆◆	$169-$249	633
44 / p. 606		Inn at Harbor Steps	◆◆◆	$175-$250	637
45 / p. 606		Hotel 1000	◆◆◆◆	$219-$439	636
46 / p. 606	AAA	Alexis Hotel	◆◆◆◆	$139-$349 SAVE	629
47 / p. 606	AAA	Best Western Pioneer Square Hotel - see color ad p 631	◆◆◆	$150-$399 SAVE	631
48 / p. 606		Silver Cloud Hotel Seattle-Stadium	◆◆◆	$229-$399	643

Map Page	OA	Restaurants	Diamond Rated	Cuisine	Meal Range	Page
1 / p. 606		Rock Salt Steak & Seafood	◆◆	Steak & Seafood	$10-$39	654
2 / p. 606		BluWater Bistro	◆◆◆	American	$9-$26	646
3 / p. 606		Duke's Chowder House	◆◆	Seafood	$10-$25	648
4 / p. 606		McCormick & Schmick's	◆◆◆	Seafood	$6-$25	652
5 / p. 606		Chandlers Crabhouse	◆◆◆	Seafood	$12-$40	647
6 / p. 606		Bamboo Garden	◆◆	Vegetarian	$8-$21	646
7 / p. 606		Bahn Thai Restaurant	◆◆	Thai	$6-$14	645
8 / p. 606		Galerias	◆◆	Mexican	$6-$19	649
9 / p. 606		Ten Mercer	◆◆◆	Regional American	$13-$28	656
10 / p. 606		Caffe Ladro	◆	Coffee/Tea	$2-$9	647
11 / p. 606		Racha Noodles and Thai Cuisine	◆◆	Thai	$8-$27	653
12 / p. 606		Aoki Japanese Grill & Sushi Bar	◆◆	Japanese	$6-$18	645
13 / p. 606		Siam on Broadway	◆◆	Thai	$7-$15	655
14 / p. 606		The Byzantion	◆◆	Greek	$6-$22	646
15 / p. 606		Moxie	◆◆◆	Western American	$16-$29	652
16 / p. 606		Blue Moon Burgers	◆	American	$8-$12	646
17 / p. 606		Chutney's	◆◆	Indian	$8-$16	647
18 / p. 606		Broadway Grill	◆◆	American	$9-$19	646
19 / p. 606		Revolution Bar & Grill	◆◆◆	American	$9-$25	654
20 / p. 606	AAA	The Space Needle-Sky City Restaurant - see color ad p 232	◆◆◆	American	$25-$56	655
21 / p. 606		table 219	◆◆	Mediterranean	$5-$19	655
22 / p. 606		Cafe Septieme	◆◆	Mediterranean	$5-$24	647

Map Page	OA	Restaurants (cont'd)	Diamond Rated	Cuisine	Meal Range	Page
㉓ / p. 606		13 Coins Restaurant	◈◈◈	American	$8-$35	645
㉔ / p. 606		Restaurant Shilla	◈◈	Korean	$6-$19	654
㉕ / p. 606		Marazul	◈◈◈	Latin American	$8-$17	651
㉖ / p. 606		Shallots Asian Bistro	◈◈	Asian	$7-$17	654
㉗ / p. 606	AAA	Tillicum Village NW Indian Coast Cultural Center and Restaurant	◈◈	Seafood	$80	656
㉘ / p. 606		CJ's Eatery	◈◈	American	$5-$11	648
㉙ / p. 606		Ristorante Machiavelli	◈◈	Italian	$8-$16	654
㉚ / p. 606		La Vita E'Bella	◈◈	Italian	$10-$20	651
㉛ / p. 606		Shiro's	◈◈	Japanese	$17-$27	655
㉜ / p. 606		El Gaucho	◈◈◈	Steak & Seafood	$23-$74	649
㉝ / p. 606		Dimitriou's Jazz Alley Restaurant & Nightclub	◈◈	International	$22-$36	648
㉞ / p. 606		Marrakesh Moroccan Restaurant	◈◈	Moroccan	$19-$29	652
㉟ / p. 606		Macrina Bakery & Cafe	◈◈	Breads/Pastries	$6-$11	651
㊱ / p. 606		Waterfront Seafood Grill	◈◈◈	Seafood	$20-$65	656
㊲ / p. 606		Lampreia	◈◈◈	New Italian	$30-$45	651
㊳ / p. 606		Marjorie	◈◈	International	$8-$22	651
㊴ / p. 606		Red Fin Restaurant	◈◈	New Asian	$8-$28	653
㊵ / p. 606		Cyclops	◈◈	American	$8-$16	648
㊶ / p. 606		Palace Kitchen	◈◈	American	$15-$30	653
㊷ / p. 606		Wasabi Bistro	◈◈◈	Japanese	$8-$32	656
㊸ / p. 606		Ayutthaya	◈◈	Thai	$6-$11	645
㊹ / p. 606	AAA	**Brasserie Margaux**	◈◈◈	French	$9-$26	646
㊺ / p. 606		Elysian Brewing	◈◈	American	$8-$13	649
㊻ / p. 606		Cascadia	◈◈◈	Regional American	$20-$48	647
㊼ / p. 606		Tango	◈◈◈	Latin American	$8-$17	655
㊽ / p. 606		Belltown Bistro	◈◈◈	American	$10-$25	646
㊾ / p. 606		Noodle Ranch	◈	Asian	$7-$12	653
㊿ / p. 606		Coldwater Bar & Grill	◈◈◈	Seafood	$12-$42	648
51 / p. 606		Assaggio Ristorante	◈◈◈	Italian	$12-$30	645
52 / p. 606		Lola	◈◈◈	New Greek	$11-$38	651
53 / p. 606		Oceanaire	◈◈◈	Seafood	$10-$35	653
54 / p. 606		Icon Grill	◈◈◈	American	$8-$35	650
55 / p. 606		Brasa	◈◈◈	Mediterranean	$17-$30	646
56 / p. 606		Osteria La Spiga	◈◈◈	Italian	$9-$23	653
57 / p. 606		Flying Fish	◈◈◈	Seafood	$16-$26	649
58 / p. 606		Dragonfish Asian Cafe	◈◈◈	Asian	$6-$19	648
59 / p. 606		Dahlia Lounge	◈◈◈	American	$10-$40	648
60 / p. 606		La Fontana Siciliana	◈◈◈	Italian	$10-$35	651
61 / p. 606		Saito's Japanese Cafe & Bar	◈◈	Japanese	$6-$22	654

Map Page	OA	Restaurants (cont'd)	Diamond Rated	Cuisine	Meal Range	Page
62 / p. 606		Restaurant Zoe	◆◆◆	American	$18-$33	654
63 / p. 606		Six Seven - see color ad p 633	◆◆◆	Seafood	$12-$65	655
64 / p. 606		Toi	◆◆	Thai	$5-$25	656
65 / p. 606		Frontier Room	◆◆	Barbecue	$5-$28	649
66 / p. 606		Gordon Biersch Brewery Restaurant	◆◆◆	American	$7-$25	650
67 / p. 606		Mexico Cantina Y Veracruz Cooking	◆◆	Regional Mexican	$9-$20	652
68 / p. 606		Il Fornaio Panetteria & Caffe	◆◆	Italian	$7-$32	650
69 / p. 606		Il Fornaio	◆◆◆	Italian	$10-$20	650
70 / p. 606		Queen City Grill	◆◆	American	$11-$34	653
71 / p. 606		Von's Grand City Cafe - see color ad p 641	◆◆	American	$8-$40	656
72 / p. 606	AAA	**Andaluca**	◆◆◆	Mediterranean	$5-$42	645
73 / p. 606		Garage	◆◆	American	$8-$15	649
74 / p. 606		Buenos Aires Grill	◆◆	Argentine	$20-$35	646
75 / p. 606		Fox Sports Grill	◆◆	American	$8-$22	649
76 / p. 606		Cayenne Bar & Grill	◆◆	American	$7-$20	647
77 / p. 606		Etta's	◆◆◆	Seafood	$14-$35	649
78 / p. 606		Lark	◆◆◆	American	$10-$16	651
79 / p. 606		Anthony's Restaurant	◆◆◆	Seafood	$19-$39	645
80 / p. 606		Cutter's Bayhouse	◆◆◆	Seafood	$9-$45	648
81 / p. 606	AAA	**Fish Club**	◆◆◆	Mediterranean	$10-$28	649
82 / p. 606		Union Square Grill	◆◆◆	Steak	$8-$45	656
83 / p. 606		The Pink Door	◆◆	Italian	$10-$25	653
84 / p. 606		Palomino Restaurant	◆◆◆	American	$9-$32	653
85 / p. 606		Campagne	◆◆◆	French	$28-$39	647
86 / p. 606		Cafe Campagne	◆◆	French	$11-$21	647
87 / p. 606		Crepe de Paris	◆◆	French	$10-$28	648
88 / p. 606	AAA	**The Hunt Club**	◆◆◆	American	$10-$40	650
89 / p. 606		Chez Shea	◆◆◆	Regional American	$25-$37	647
90 / p. 606		Matt's in the Market	◆◆	Regional American	$8-$22	652
91 / p. 606		Athenian Inn	◆◆	Seafood	$6-$16	645
92 / p. 606		Wild Ginger Asian Restaurant & Satay Bar	◆◆◆	Asian	$9-$30	657
93 / p. 606		Place Pigalle	◆◆◆	French	$15-$25	653
94 / p. 606		Il Bistro	◆◆◆	Italian	$17-$44	650
95 / p. 606		Soundview Cafe	◆	American	$6-$10	655
96 / p. 606		The Georgian	◆◆◆◆	Regional American	$12-$49	650
97 / p. 606		Shuckers	◆◆◆	Seafood	$10-$28	655
98 / p. 606		The Pike Pub and Brewery	◆◆	American	$8-$18	653
99 / p. 606	AAA	**Tulio Ristorante**	◆◆◆	Regional Italian	$8-$32	656
100 / p. 606		Steamer's Seafood Cafe	◆	Seafood	$7-$12	655

Map Page	OA	Restaurants (cont'd)	Diamond Rated	Cuisine	Meal Range	Page
101 / p. 606	AAA	Saze Rac	▽▽▽	Southern Pacific Rim	$12-$30	654
102 / p. 606		Earth & Ocean	▽▽▽	American	$10-$30	648
103 / p. 606	AAA	The Brooklyn Seafood, Steak & Oyster House	▽▽▽	Steak & Seafood	$10-$40	646
104 / p. 606		Troiani	▽▽▽	Italian	$16-$60	656
105 / p. 606		McCormick & Schmick's	▽▽▽	Seafood	$7-$40	652
106 / p. 606		Ruth's Chris Steak House	▽▽▽	Steak	$10-$37	654
107 / p. 606	AAA	Royal Argosy Dining Cruises	▽▽	American	$50-$120	654
108 / p. 606		Elliott's Oyster House	▽▽▽	Seafood	$10-$36	649
109 / p. 606	AAA	The Library Bistro	▽▽▽	American	$8-$19	651
110 / p. 606		Metropolitan Grill	▽▽▽	Steak	$8-$65	652
111 / p. 606		Ivar's Acres of Clams	▽▽	Seafood	$9-$35	651
112 / p. 606		Bakeman's Restaurant	▽	American	$4-$7	645
113 / p. 606		Zaina	▽	Middle Eastern	$5-$15	657
114 / p. 606		Cafe Bengodi	▽▽	Italian	$7-$13	647
115 / p. 606	AAA	Mitchelli's	▽▽	Italian	$6-$18	652
116 / p. 606		Al Boccalino Ristorante	▽▽	Italian	$10-$25	645
117 / p. 606		Soup Daddy Soups	▽	American	$5-$7	655
118 / p. 606		Cafe Hue	▽▽	Vietnamese	$7-$30	647
119 / p. 606		House of Hong	▽▽	Chinese	$5-$28	650
120 / p. 606		Il Terrazzo Carmine	▽▽▽	Italian	$11-$35	650
121 / p. 606		Huong Binh	▽▽	Vietnamese	$5-$8	650
122 / p. 606		Four Seas Restaurant	▽▽	Chinese	$8-$28	649
123 / p. 606		The China Gate	▽▽	Chinese	$7-$16	647
124 / p. 606		Shanghi Gardens	▽▽	Chinese	$5-$23	654
125 / p. 606		Bush Garden	▽▽	Japanese	$8-$16	646
126 / p. 606		Pyramid Alehouse-Brewery & Restaurant	▽▽	American	$8-$15	653

AAA Diamond Ratings for the *Perfect Fit*

Comfortable and basic – One Diamond lodgings and restaurants meet our cleanliness requirements and can be ideal for the budget-minded traveler.

A little more style – Two Diamond hotels and restaurants offer modest enhancements, often at a moderate price.

Goes more places – for vacation or business, to relax or impress, Three Diamond properties offer a range of style and facilities.

Time to make an impression – only **3%** of our inspections result in a Four Diamond Rating, with hospitality, service and attention to detail.

It's a black-tie event – or luxury, sophistication and service with a relaxed feel. With only 100 Five Diamond lodgings and 60 restaurants, expect the best.

• Each year, AAA conducts professional evaluations at more than 58,000 hotels and restaurants throughout North America.

• More information can be found on pages 20-21 and at AAA.com/Diamonds.

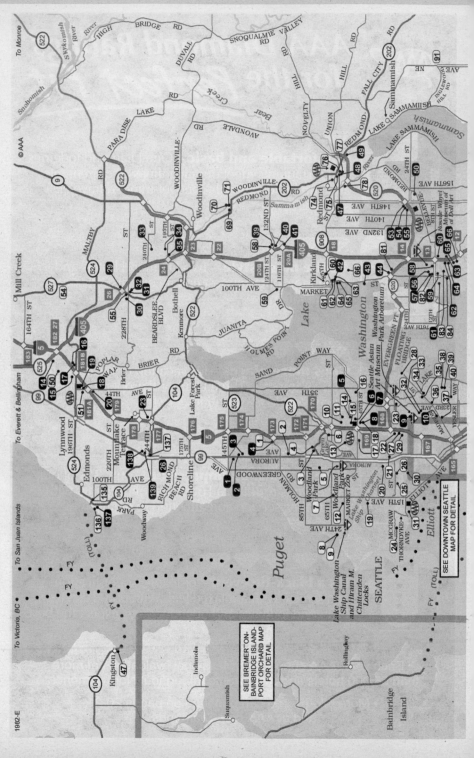

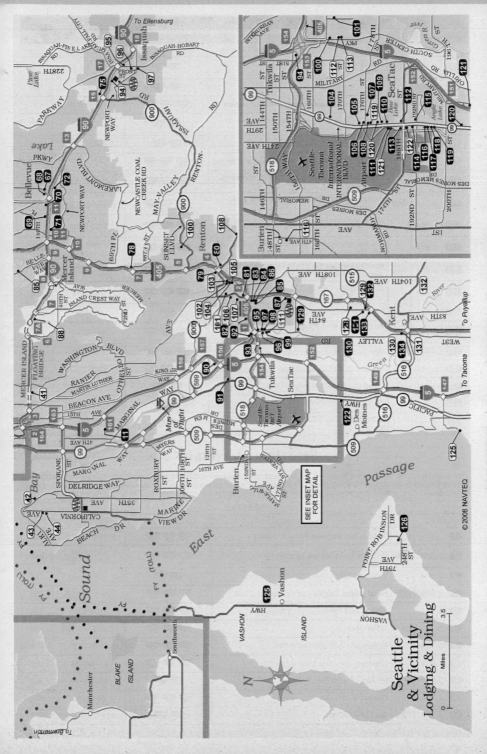

Seattle
& Vicinity
Lodging & Dining

✈ Airport Accommodations

Map Page	OA	SEATTLE-TACOMA INTERNATIONAL	Diamond Rated	High Season	Page
122 / p. 614	AAA	Best Western Airport Executel, 1.6 mi s of airport	▽▽	$89-$139 SAVE	700
106 / p. 614		Clarion Hotel, 0.3 mi ne of airport	▽▽	$109-$119	700
111 / p. 614	AAA	The Coast Gateway Hotel, just s of airport	▽▽▽	$140-$158 SAVE	700
116 / p. 614		Comfort Inn & Suites-Sea Tac Airport, 0.7 mi s of airport	▽▽	$99-$275	700
114 / p. 614	AAA	Days Inn SeaTac, 0.4 mi s of airport	▽▽	$95-$115 SAVE	701
112 / p. 614		Doubletree Hotel Seattle Airport, just s of airport	▽▽▽	$119-$289	701
119 / p. 614		Fairfield Inn by Marriott Seattle-Seatac/Airport, 0.9 mi s of airport	▽▽▽	$119-$149	701
117 / p. 614	AAA	Hampton Inn Seattle Airport, 0.8 mi s of airport	▽▽▽	$145-$165 SAVE	701
108 / p. 614		Hilton Seattle Airport & Conference Center, just n of airport	▽▽▽	$129-$299	702
118 / p. 614		Holiday Inn Express Hotel & Suites-Seattle Sea-Tac Airport, 0.9 mi s of airport	▽▽▽	Rates not provided	702
105 / p. 614	AAA	Holiday Inn Seattle SeaTac International Airport, 0.4 mi n of airport	▽▽▽	Rates not provided SAVE	702
113 / p. 614		La Quinta Inn Seattle (Sea-Tac International), 0.3 mi s of airport	▽▽	$69-$169	702
104 / p. 614		Motel 6 - 1332, 1 mi n of airport	▽	$59-$69	702
109 / p. 614		Radisson Hotel Gateway Seattle-Tacoma Airport, opposite airport	▽▽▽	$98-$229	703
110 / p. 614		Red Lion Hotel Seattle Airport, opposite airport	▽▽▽	$99-$279	704
107 / p. 614		Seattle Airport Marriott, 0.4 mi ne of airport	▽▽▽	$229-$249	704
120 / p. 614	AAA	Sleep Inn SeaTac Airport, 1.4 mi s of airport	▽▽	$80-$150 SAVE	704
115 / p. 614		Super 8 Motel Sea-Tac, 0.5 mi s of airport	▽▽	$77-$97	705
91 / p. 614		Ramada Limited Sea-Tac Airport, 2.5 mi n of airport	▽▽	$90-$100	714

Seattle and Vicinity

This index helps you "spot" where approved lodgings and restaurants are located on the corresponding detailed maps. Lodging daily rate range is for comparison only and show the property's high season. Restaurant rate range is a combination of lunch and/or dinner. Turn to the listing page for more detailed rate information and consult display ads for special promotions.

SEATTLE

Map Page	OA	Lodgings	Diamond Rated	High Season	Page
1 / p. 614	AAA	Holiday Inn Express Hotel & Suites	▽▽▽	$129-$179 SAVE	657
2 / p. 614	AAA	Comfort Inn & Suites Seattle	▽▽▽	Rates not provided SAVE	657
3 / p. 614		Extended StayAmerica-Seattle-Northgate	▽▽	$90-$110	657
4 / p. 614	AAA	Hotel Nexus Seattle - see color ad p 658	▽▽▽	$99-$159 SAVE	658
5 / p. 614		Silver Cloud Inn-University Village	▽▽▽	$179-$249	658
6 / p. 614	AAA	Hotel Deca	▽▽▽	$249-$399 SAVE	658
7 / p. 614		Watertown - see color ad p 620	▽▽▽	$179-$229	659
8 / p. 614		University Inn - see color ad p 659	▽▽▽	$145-$185	659
9 / p. 614		Mildred's Bed & Breakfast	▽▽	$165-$195	658
10 / p. 614		Gaslight Inn	▽▽▽	$88-$158	657
11 / p. 614	AAA	Georgetown Inn	▽▽	$94-$173 SAVE	657

Map Page	OA	Restaurants	Diamond Rated	Cuisine	Meal Range	Page
① / p. 614		Saffron Bar & Grill - see color ad p 658	▽▽	American	$7-$27	660
② / p. 614		Aurora Burgermaster	▽	American	$5-$9	660
③ / p. 614		Duke's Chowder House	▽▽	Seafood	$8-$25	661
④ / p. 614		BluWater Bistro	▽▽▽	American	$8-$22	660
⑤ / p. 614		Carmelita	▽▽▽	Vegetarian	$16-$18	661
⑥ / p. 614		Nell's	▽▽▽	Continental	$19-$30	662
⑦ / p. 614		Zesto's	▽	American	$5-$14	664
⑧ / p. 614		Ray's Boathouse	▽▽▽	Seafood	$18-$45	663
⑨ / p. 614		Ray's Cafe	▽▽	Seafood	$8-$20	663
⑩ / p. 614		Blue Onion Bistro	▽▽	American	$14-$22	660
⑪ / p. 614		Tempero do Brasil	▽▽	Brazilian	$11-$20	663
⑫ / p. 614		Market Street Grill	▽▽▽	American	$15-$29	662
⑬ / p. 614		Tangletown	▽▽	American	$7-$15	663
⑭ / p. 614		Mandarin Chef Restaurant	▽▽	Chinese	$6-$12	662
⑮ / p. 614		Bombay Grill	▽▽	Indian	$7-$15	660
⑯ / p. 614		Burgermaster	▽	American	$3-$7	660
⑰ / p. 614	AAA	**Kabul Afghan Cuisine**	▽▽	Afghan	$9-$28	661
⑱ / p. 614		Portage Bay Cafe	▽▽	Regional American	$8-$12	662
⑲ / p. 614		Chinook's at Salmon Bay	▽▽	Seafood	$6-$22	661
⑳ / p. 614		Ponti Seafood Grill	▽▽▽	Seafood	$16-$40	662
㉑ / p. 614		Canlis	▽▽▽▽	Regional American	$34-$70	661
㉒ / p. 614		Terry's 14 Carrot Cafe'	▽▽	American	$8-$10	664
㉓ / p. 614		Cafe Lago	▽▽	Italian	$15-$21	660
㉔ / p. 614		Szmania's	▽▽▽	Regional Continental	$6-$24	663
㉕ / p. 614		Macrina Bakery & Cafe	▽▽	Breads/Pastries	$7-$11	662
㉖ / p. 614		Orrapin Thai Cuisine	▽▽	Thai	$8-$15	662
㉗ / p. 614		Serafina	▽▽▽	Italian	$10-$28	663
㉘ / p. 614		Cactus Madison Park	▽▽	Mexican	$7-$19	660
㉙ / p. 614		Siam on Lake Union	▽▽	Thai	$7-$17	663
㉚ / p. 614		5 Spot	▽▽	American	$6-$28	660
㉛ / p. 614		Palisade	▽▽▽	Steak & Seafood	$12-$50	662
㉜ / p. 614		Monsoon	▽▽	Vietnamese	$8-$18	662
㉝ / p. 614		Kingfish Cafe	▽▽	Southern Soul Food	$7-$19	661
㉞ / p. 614		Cafe Flora	▽▽▽	Vegetarian	$10-$19	660
㉟ / p. 614		Rover's Restaurant	▽▽▽▽	French	$35-$130	663
㊱ / p. 614		Crush	▽▽▽	American	$22-$38	661
㊲ / p. 614		Piecora's Pizza	▽	Italian	$7-$12	662
㊳ / p. 614		Dulces Latin Bistro	▽▽▽	Latin American	$18-$32	661
㊴ / p. 614		St. Clouds	▽▽	International	$10-$24	663

Map Page	OA	Restaurants (cont'd)	Diamond Rated	Cuisine	Meal Range	Page
㊵ / p. 614		Catfish Corner	♦	Seafood	$6-$13	661
㊶ / p. 614		That's Amore! Italian Cafe	♦♦	Italian	$8-$19	664
㊷ / p. 614		Salty's on Alki	♦♦♦	Seafood	$12-$70	663
㊸ / p. 614		Angelina's Trattoria	♦♦	Italian	$8-$20	660
㊹ / p. 614		Circa	♦♦	American	$8-$20	661

LYNNWOOD

Map Page	OA	Lodgings	Diamond Rated	High Season	Page
⓮ / p. 614		Residence Inn by Marriott-Seattle North/ Lynnwood	♦♦♦	$233-$285	689
⓯ / p. 614	AAA	**Best Western Alderwood**	♦♦♦	$119-$169 SAVE	688
⓰ / p. 614	AAA	**Hampton Inn & Suites**	♦♦♦	$124-$169 SAVE	689
⓱ / p. 614		Extended StayAmerica-Seattle-Lynnwood	♦♦	$95-$110	689
⓲ / p. 614	AAA	**La Quinta Inn Lynnwood**	♦♦♦	$59-$169 SAVE	689
⓳ / p. 614		Courtyard By Marriott-Lynnwood	♦♦♦	$144-$159	689
⓴ / p. 614		Embassy Suites Hotel Seattle North/Lynnwood	♦♦♦	$119-$249	689

Map Page	OA	Restaurants	Diamond Rated	Cuisine	Meal Range	Page
㊿ / p. 614		Billy McHale's	♦♦	American	$7-$20	690
(51) / p. 614		Talay Thai Restaurant	♦♦	Thai	$5-$9	690

MOUNTLAKE TERRACE

Map Page	OA	Lodging	Diamond Rated	High Season	Page
㉓ / p. 614		Studio 6 #6042	♦♦	$81-$91	692

SHORELINE

Map Page	OA	Lodging	Diamond Rated	High Season	Page
㉖ / p. 614		Days Inn-North Seattle	♦♦	Rates not provided	705

BOTHELL

Map Page	OA	Lodgings	Diamond Rated	High Season	Page
㉙ / p. 614		Extended Stay Deluxe Seattle-Bothell	♦♦♦	$125-$140	673
㉚ / p. 614		Extended StayAmerica-Seattle-Bothell	♦♦	$110-$125	672
㉛ / p. 614	AAA	**Comfort Inn & Suites**	♦♦♦	$105-$125 SAVE	672
㉜ / p. 614	AAA	**Holiday Inn Express Canyon Park**	♦♦♦	$110-$139 SAVE	673
㉝ / p. 614		SpringHill Suites by Marriott	♦♦♦	$159-$189	673
㉞ / p. 614		Residence Inn by Marriott Seattle NE	♦♦♦	$188-$230	673
㉟ / p. 614		Country Inn & Suites by Carlson	♦♦♦	$79-$179	672

Map Page	OA	Restaurants	Diamond Rated	Cuisine	Meal Range	Page
(54) / p. 614		Burgermaster	♦	American	$4-$10	673
(55) / p. 614		Bonefish Grill	♦♦♦	Seafood	$13-$20	673

KIRKLAND

Map Page	OA	Lodgings	Diamond Rated	High Season	Page
㊴ / p. 614	AAA	**Comfort Inn-Kirkland**	♦♦	$129 SAVE	686
㊵ / p. 614		Motel 6 - 687	♦	$75-$85	686
㊶ / p. 614	AAA	**Baymont Inn & Suites**	♦♦	$94-$275 SAVE	686
㊷ / p. 614	AAA	**The Heathman Hotel**	♦♦♦♦	$219-$399 SAVE	686
㊸ / p. 614	AAA	**Woodmark Hotel, Yacht Club & Spa**	♦♦♦♦	$279-$1800 SAVE	686

KIRKLAND (cont'd)

Map Page	OA	Lodgings (cont'd)	Diamond Rated	High Season	Page
44 / p. 614		La Quinta Inn & Suites Seattle (Bellevue/Kirkland)	▽▽▽	$69-$169	686

Map Page	OA	Restaurants	Diamond Rated	Cuisine	Meal Range	Page
58 / p. 614		Cafe Veloce	▽▽	Italian	$8-$16	687
59 / p. 614		Cafe Juanita	▽▽▽	Northern Italian	$14-$36	687
60 / p. 614		The Crab Cracker	▽▽▽	Seafood	$9-$35	687
61 / p. 614		Ristorante Paradiso	▽▽▽	Regional Italian	$8-$27	687
62 / p. 614		Cactus Kirkland	▽▽	Mexican	$7-$18	687
63 / p. 614		trellis	▽▽▽	American	$9-$29	687
64 / p. 614		21 Central Prime Steakhouse	▽▽▽	Steak	$20-$48	686
65 / p. 614		The Third Floor Fish Cafe	▽▽▽	Continental	$24-$45	687
66 / p. 614		Shamiana	▽▽	Indian	$7-$18	687

REDMOND

Map Page	OA	Lodgings	Diamond Rated	High Season	Page
47 / p. 614		Residence Inn by Marriott Redmond Town Center	▽▽▽	$259-$269	695
48 / p. 614		Redmond Marriott Town Center	▽▽▽	$249-$259	695
49 / p. 614	ⒶⒶⒶ	**Redmond Inn**	▽▽▽	$109-$199 [SAVE]	694
50 / p. 614		Silver Cloud Inn Redmond	▽▽▽	$179-$239	695

Map Page	OA	Restaurants	Diamond Rated	Cuisine	Meal Range	Page
74 / p. 614		Tropea	▽▽	Southern Italian	$11-$20	696
75 / p. 614		El Toreador	▽▽	Mexican	$5-$12	696
76 / p. 614		Nara Japanese Restaurant	▽▽	Japanese	$8-$19	696
77 / p. 614		Spazzo Italian Grill & Wine Bar	▽▽▽	Italian	$12-$30	696
78 / p. 614		Celtic Bayou-Irish Pub & Cajun Cafe	▽▽	Cajun	$6-$15	696

BELLEVUE

Map Page	OA	Lodgings	Diamond Rated	High Season	Page
53 / p. 614		Courtyard by Marriott	▽▽▽	$209-$219	668
54 / p. 614		Fairfield Inn	▽▽▽	$199-$209	668
55 / p. 614		Residence Inn by Marriott, Bellevue-Redmond	▽▽▽	$215-$263	670
56 / p. 614		Silver Cloud Inn-Bellevue	▽▽▽	$179-$239	671
57 / p. 614	ⒶⒶⒶ	**Hyatt Regency Bellevue**	▽▽▽▽	$129-$419 [SAVE]	669
58 / p. 614		Courtyard by Marriott	▽▽▽	$229-$249	667
59 / p. 614	ⒶⒶⒶ	**The Westin Bellevue**	▽▽▽▽	$149-$419 [SAVE]	671
60 / p. 614	ⒶⒶⒶ	**Coast Bellevue Hotel**	▽▽▽	Rates not provided [SAVE]	667
61 / p. 614	ⒶⒶⒶ	**La Residence Suite Hotel**	▽▽	$125-$199 [SAVE]	669
62 / p. 614	ⒶⒶⒶ	**Sheraton Bellevue Hotel**	▽▽▽	$119-$419 [SAVE]	671
63 / p. 614		Extended StayAmerica-Seattle-Bellevue	▽▽	$125-$143	668
64 / p. 614	ⒶⒶⒶ	**Red Lion Hotel Bellevue**	▽▽▽	Rates not provided [SAVE]	670
65 / p. 614		Hilton Bellevue	▽▽▽	$149-$389	668
66 / p. 614	ⒶⒶⒶ	**Bellevue Club Hotel**	▽▽▽▽	$285-$655 [SAVE]	667

BELLEVUE (cont'd)

Map Page	OA	Lodgings (cont'd)	Diamond Rated	High Season	Page
67 / p. 614		Embassy Suites Hotel Bellevue	◆◆◆	$119-$279	668
68 / p. 614	AAA	**Days Inn Bellevue**	◆◆	$75-$120 SAVE	668
69 / p. 614	AAA	**Hotel Sierra Bellevue**	◆◆◆	$109-$249 SAVE	669
70 / p. 614		Silver Cloud Inn-Bellevue Eastgate	◆◆◆	$189-$239	671
71 / p. 614		Homestead Studio Suites Hotel-Seattle-Bellevue	◆◆	$125-$143	669
72 / p. 614	AAA	**Larkspur Landing Bellevue/Seattle - see color ad p 670**	◆◆◆	$169-$219 SAVE	670

Map Page	OA	Restaurants	Diamond Rated	Cuisine	Meal Range	Page
81 / p. 614		Burgermaster	◆	American	$6-$12	671
82 / p. 614		Daniel's Broiler, Bellevue Place	◆◆◆	Steak	$13-$50	671
83 / p. 614		Seastar Restaurant & Raw Bar	◆◆◆	Seafood	$10-$50	672
84 / p. 614		The Orexi	◆◆	Greek	$6-$15	671
85 / p. 614		Chace's - Pancake Corral	◆◆	American	$6-$10	671

ISSAQUAH

Map Page	OA	Lodging	Diamond Rated	High Season	Page
75 / p. 614		Holiday Inn Seattle Issaquah	◆◆◆	Rates not provided	683

Map Page	OA	Restaurants	Diamond Rated	Cuisine	Meal Range	Page
94 / p. 614		Lombardi's Cucina of Issaquah	◆◆	Italian	$7-$22	684
95 / p. 614		Triple XXX Rootbeer Drive-In	◆◆	American	$6-$12	684
96 / p. 614		Fins Bistro	◆◆	Seafood	$9-$35	683
97 / p. 614		Issaquah Brewhouse	◆◆	American	$8-$15	684

RENTON

Map Page	OA	Lodgings	Diamond Rated	High Season	Page
78 / p. 614	AAA	**Guest House Inn & Suites**	◆◆	$100-$110 SAVE	697
79 / p. 614		Renton Inn	◆◆	Rates not provided	698
80 / p. 614		Quality Inn Renton	◆◆◆	$99-$119	698
81 / p. 614	AAA	**Holiday Inn Seattle-Renton**	◆◆◆	$79-$169 SAVE	697
82 / p. 614		Extended Stay Deluxe-Seattle	◆◆	$121-$136	697
83 / p. 614	AAA	**Larkspur Landing Renton/Seattle - see color ad p 698**	◆◆◆	$149-$179 SAVE	698
84 / p. 614		Hilton Garden Inn Seattle/Renton	◆◆◆	$89-$209	697
85 / p. 614		TownePlace Suites Seattle South/Renton	◆◆◆	$169-$179	699
86 / p. 614		SpringHill Suites by Marriott	◆◆◆	$169-$189	698
87 / p. 614	AAA	**Clarion Hotel**	◆◆	Rates not provided SAVE	696

Map Page	OA	Restaurants	Diamond Rated	Cuisine	Meal Range	Page
100 / p. 614		Plum Delicious	◆◆	American	$6-$19	699
101 / p. 614		Vino Ristorante Italiano	◆◆	Italian	$0-$20	700
102 / p. 614		Armondo's Cafe Italiano	◆◆	Italian	$6-$16	699
103 / p. 614		Fin N Bone	◆◆◆	Steak	$9-$34	699
104 / p. 614		Melrose Grill	◆◆	Steak	$17-$37	699
105 / p. 614		Whistle Stop Ale House	◆◆	American	$7-$16	700
106 / p. 614		Torero's	◆◆	Mexican	$5-$15	699

Map Page	OA	Restaurants (cont'd)	Diamond Rated	Cuisine	Meal Range	Page
107 / p. 614		Billy McHale's	◆◆	American	$7-$22	699
108 / p. 614		River Rock Grill & Ale House	◆◆	American	$9-$21	699

TUKWILA

Map Page	OA	Lodgings	Diamond Rated	High Season	Page
90 / p. 614	AAA	**Days Inn-Seattle South**	◆◆	$59-$110 SAVE	712
91 / p. 614		Ramada Limited Sea-Tac Airport	◆◆	$90-$100	714
92 / p. 614		Homewood Suites by Hilton	◆◆◆	$99-$209	714
93 / p. 614	AAA	**Comfort Suites Airport-Tukwila**	◆◆◆	$108-$190 SAVE	712
94 / p. 614		Extended StayAmerica-Seattle-Tukwila	◆◆	$85-$100	713
95 / p. 614	AAA	**Hampton Inn Seattle Southcenter - see color ad p 713**	◆◆◆	$90-$125 SAVE	713
96 / p. 614	AAA	**Best Western River's Edge**	◆◆◆	$110-$140 SAVE	712
97 / p. 614		Embassy Suites Hotel	◆◆◆	$129-$359	713
98 / p. 614		Courtyard by Marriott/Sea Tac Area	◆◆◆	$194-$214	712
99 / p. 614		Residence Inn by Marriott-Seattle South	◆◆◆	$188-$230	714
100 / p. 614		DoubleTree Guest Suites Seattle Airport-Southcenter	◆◆◆	$99-$229	713
101 / p. 614		Courtyard by Marriott-Seattle/Southcenter	◆◆◆	$199-$219	712

Map Page	OA	Restaurants	Diamond Rated	Cuisine	Meal Range	Page
111 / p. 614		Barnaby's	◆◆	Traditional Steak	$10-$30	714
112 / p. 614		Miyabi Restaurant	◆◆	Japanese	$6-$17	714
113 / p. 614		Bai Tong Thai Restaurant	◆◆	Thai	$7-$14	714

SEATAC

Map Page	OA	Lodgings	Diamond Rated	High Season	Page
104 / p. 614		Motel 6 - 1332	◆	$59-$69	702
105 / p. 614	AAA	**Holiday Inn Seattle SeaTac International Airport - see color ad p 702**	◆◆◆	Rates not provided SAVE	702
106 / p. 614		Clarion Hotel	◆◆	$109-$119	700
107 / p. 614		Seattle Airport Marriott	◆◆◆	$229-$249	704
108 / p. 614		Hilton Seattle Airport & Conference Center	◆◆◆	$129-$299	702
109 / p. 614		Radisson Hotel Gateway Seattle-Tacoma Airport - see color ad p 703	◆◆◆	$98-$229	703
110 / p. 614		Red Lion Hotel Seattle Airport - see color ad p 703	◆◆◆	$99-$279	704
111 / p. 614	AAA	**The Coast Gateway Hotel**	◆◆◆	$140-$158 SAVE	700
112 / p. 614		Doubletree Hotel Seattle Airport	◆◆◆	$119-$289	701
113 / p. 614		La Quinta Inn Seattle (Sea-Tac International)	◆◆◆	$69-$169	702
114 / p. 614	AAA	**Days Inn SeaTac**	◆◆	$95-$115 SAVE	701
115 / p. 614		Super 8 Motel Sea-Tac	◆◆	$77-$97	705
116 / p. 614		Comfort Inn & Suites-Sea Tac Airport - see color ad p 701	◆◆	$99-$275	700
117 / p. 614	AAA	**Hampton Inn Seattle Airport**	◆◆◆	$145-$165 SAVE	701
118 / p. 614		Holiday Inn Express Hotel & Suites-Seattle Sea-Tac Airport	◆◆◆	Rates not provided	702
119 / p. 614		Fairfield Inn by Marriott Seattle-Seatac/Airport	◆◆◆	$119-$149	701
120 / p. 614	AAA	**Sleep Inn SeaTac Airport**	◆◆	$80-$150 SAVE	704

SEATAC (cont'd)

Map Page	OA	Lodgings (cont'd)	Diamond Rated	High Season	Page
121 / p. 614		Motel 6 - 736	▽	$55-$65	702
122 / p. 614	AAA	**Best Western Airport Executel**	▽ ▽	$89-$139 SAVE	700

Map Page	OA	Restaurants	Diamond Rated	Cuisine	Meal Range	Page
119 / p. 614		Spencer's for Steaks and Chops	▽ ▽ ▽	Steak	$9-$60	705
120 / p. 614		13 Coins Restaurant	▽ ▽ ▽	American	$10-$30	705
121 / p. 614		Sharps Roaster & Ale House	▽ ▽	American	$8-$30	705
122 / p. 614		Dave's Diner & Brew	▽ ▽	American	$6-$16	705

VASHON

Map Page	OA	Lodgings	Diamond Rated	High Season	Page
125 / p. 614		Artist's Studio Loft B&B	▽ ▽ ▽	$119-$215	715
126 / p. 614		The Swallow's Nest Guest Cottages	▽	Rates not provided	715

KENT

Map Page	OA	Lodgings	Diamond Rated	High Season	Page
129 / p. 614		TownePlace Suites by Marriott-Seattle Southcenter	▽ ▽ ▽	$170-$208	685
130 / p. 614		Hawthorn Suites	▽ ▽	$129-$199	684
131 / p. 614		Comfort Inn Kent	▽ ▽	$99-$130	684
132 / p. 614	AAA	**Holiday Inn Hotel & Suites**	▽ ▽ ▽	$99-$149 SAVE	685
133 / p. 614		Extended StayAmerica-Seattle-Kent	▽ ▽	$90-$105	684
134 / p. 614	AAA	**Best Western Plaza By The Green**	▽ ▽ ▽	$99-$159 SAVE	684

Map Page	OA	Restaurants	Diamond Rated	Cuisine	Meal Range	Page
128 / p. 614		Chao Praya Restaurant	▽ ▽	Thai	$4-$11	685
129 / p. 614		Mitzel's American Kitchen	▽ ▽	American	$7-$15	685
130 / p. 614		Cave Man Kitchens	▽	Barbecue	$4-$10	685
131 / p. 614		Thai Chili Restaurant	▽ ▽	Thai	$7-$13	685
132 / p. 614		Velvet Goose	▽ ▽	American	$7-$9	685

EDMONDS

Map Page	OA	Lodgings	Diamond Rated	High Season	Page
137 / p. 614	AAA	**Best Western Edmonds Harbor Inn - see color ad p 676**	▽ ▽ ▽	$109-$140 SAVE	676
138 / p. 614	AAA	**Travelodge Seattle/Edmonds**	▽ ▽	$69-$109 SAVE	676
139 / p. 614	AAA	**K & E Motor Inn**	▽	$60-$89 SAVE	676

Map Page	OA	Restaurants	Diamond Rated	Cuisine	Meal Range	Page
135 / p. 614	AAA	**Chanterelle**	▽ ▽ ▽	American	$6-$19	677
136 / p. 614		Arnies at Edmonds	▽ ▽	American	$7-$27	676
137 / p. 614		Scott's Bar & Grill	▽ ▽	American	$8-$28	677

KINGSTON

Map Page	OA	Restaurant	Diamond Rated	Cuisine	Meal Range	Page
47 / p. 614		Main Street Ale House	▽ ▽ ▽	American	$10-$25	686

WOODINVILLE

Map Page	OA	Restaurants	Diamond Rated	Cuisine	Meal Range	Page
69 / p. 614		Red Hook Brewery & Forecasters Pub	▽ ▽	American	$7-$20	716
70 / p. 614	AAA	**The Herbfarm Restaurant**	▽ ▽ ▽ ▽ ▽	Continental	$179-$195	716

WOODINVILLE (cont'd)

Map Page	OA	Restaurant	Diamond Rated	Cuisine	Meal Range	Page
㉛ / p. 614		Barking Frog at Willows Lodge	◈ ◈ ◈	Pacific Rim	$14-$49	716

MERCER ISLAND

Map Page	OA	Restaurant	Diamond Rated	Cuisine	Meal Range	Page
㊻ / p. 614		Thai on Mercer	◈ ◈	Thai	$8-$15	691

SAMMAMISH

Map Page	OA	Restaurant	Diamond Rated	Cuisine	Meal Range	Page
㉛ / p. 614		DC's Grill	◈ ◈	Steak & Seafood	$9-$42	700

BURIEN

Map Page	OA	Restaurant	Diamond Rated	Cuisine	Meal Range	Page
⑯ / p. 614		Mick Kelly's Irish Pub	◈ ◈	Irish	$8-$30	675

DES MOINES

Map Page	OA	Restaurant	Diamond Rated	Cuisine	Meal Range	Page
⑫⑤ / p. 614		Salty's at Redondo Beach	◈ ◈ ◈	Seafood	$9-$30	675

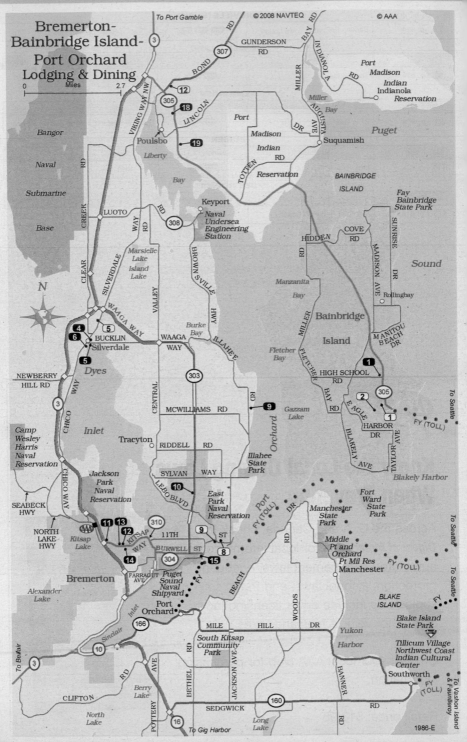

Bremerton-
Bainbridge Island-
Port Orchard
Lodging & Dining

0 Miles 2.7

Bremerton-Bainbridge Island-Port Orchard

This index helps you "spot" where approved lodgings and restaurants are located on the corresponding detailed maps. Lodging daily rate range is for comparison only and show the property's high season. Restaurant rate range is a combination of lunch and/or dinner. Turn to the listing page for more detailed rate information and consult display ads for special promotions.

BAINBRIDGE ISLAND

Map Page	OA	Lodging	Diamond Rated	High Season	Page
1 / p. 624	AAA	**Best Western Bainbridge Island Suites**	◇◇◇	$119-$169 SAVE	666

Map Page	OA	Restaurants	Diamond Rated	Cuisine	Meal Range	Page
① / p. 624		The Streamliner Diner	◇◇	American	$8-$12	666
② / p. 624		Doc's Marina Grill	◇◇	American	$6-$30	666

SILVERDALE

Map Page	OA	Lodgings	Diamond Rated	High Season	Page
4 / p. 624		Oxford Inn	◇◇	$89	705
5 / p. 624	AAA	**Silverdale Beach Hotel**	◇◇◇	$115-$160 SAVE	706
6 / p. 624		Oxford Suites Silverdale	◇◇◇	$129-$189	705

Map Page	OA	Restaurant	Diamond Rated	Cuisine	Meal Range	Page
⑤ / p. 624		Silver City Restaurant & Brewery	◇◇	American	$9-$30	706

BREMERTON

Map Page	OA	Lodgings	Diamond Rated	High Season	Page
9 / p. 624	AAA	**Illahee Manor Bed & Breakfast**	◇◇◇	$130-$255 SAVE	674
10 / p. 624		Midway Inn	◇◇	Rates not provided	674
11 / p. 624		Super 8 Motel	◇◇	Rates not provided	675
12 / p. 624	AAA	**Flagship Inn - see color ad p 674**	◇◇	$75-$115 SAVE	674
13 / p. 624	AAA	**Oyster Bay Inn**	◇◇	$89-$99 SAVE	675
14 / p. 624	AAA	**Bremerton Inn & Suites**	◇◇◇	$100-$170 SAVE	674
15 / p. 624		Hampton Inn & Suites	◇◇◇	$79-$129	674

Map Page	OA	Restaurants	Diamond Rated	Cuisine	Meal Range	Page
⑧ / p. 624		La Fermata Ristorante	◇◇◇	Italian	$20-$37	675
⑨ / p. 624		Boat Shed	◇◇	American	$8-$22	675

POULSBO

Map Page	OA	Lodgings	Diamond Rated	High Season	Page
18 / p. 624		Holiday Inn Express	◇◇◇	$99-$199	693
19 / p. 624	AAA	**Poulsbo Inn & Suites**	◇◇◇	$110-$130 SAVE	693

Map Page	OA	Restaurant	Diamond Rated	Cuisine	Meal Range	Page
⑫ / p. 624		Molly Ward Gardens	◇◇	Regional Continental	$6-$42	693

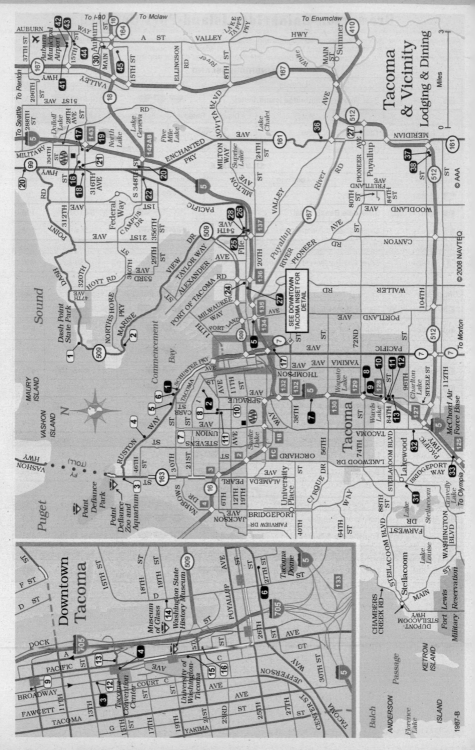

Tacoma & Vicinity
Lodging & Dining

Downtown Tacoma

© 2008 NAVTEQ

© AAA

1987-B

Tacoma and Vicinity

This index helps you "spot" where approved lodgings and restaurants are located on the corresponding detailed maps. Lodging daily rate range is for comparison only and show the property's high season. Restaurant rate range is a combination of lunch and/or dinner. Turn to the listing page for more detailed rate information and consult display ads for special promotions.

TACOMA

Map Page	OA	Lodgings	Diamond Rated	High Season	Page
❶ / p. 626		Silver Cloud Inn Tacoma	▽▽▽	$179-$329	709
❷ / p. 626		A Plum Duff House	▽▽▽	$110-$150	707
❸ / p. 626	AAA	**Hotel Murano**	▽▽▽	$189-$469 SAVE	708
❹ / p. 626		Courtyard by Marriott-Tacoma Downtown	▽▽▽	$219-$229	708
❺ / p. 626		La Quinta Inn & Suites Tacoma (Conference Center)	▽▽▽	$79-$169	709
❻ / p. 626	AAA	**Best Western Tacoma Dome Hotel**	▽▽▽	$79-$149 SAVE	707
❼ / p. 626		Extended StayAmerica-Tacoma-South	▽▽	$105-$115	708
❽ / p. 626	AAA	**Shilo Inn & Suites -Tacoma - see color ad p 709**	▽▽	$112-$200 SAVE	709
❾ / p. 626		Hampton Inn & Suites Tacoma - South	▽▽▽	$129-$179	708
❿ / p. 626	AAA	**Red Lion Hotel Tacoma**	▽▽▽	$109-$149 SAVE	709
⓫ / p. 626		Holiday Inn Express Hotel & Suites	▽▽▽	$159-$199	708
⓬ / p. 626		Comfort Inn	▽▽▽	$100-$135	707
⓭ / p. 626		Crossland Studios-Tacoma-Hosmer	▽	$74-$89	708

Map Page	OA	Restaurants	Diamond Rated	Cuisine	Meal Range	Page
① / p. 626	AAA	**The Dash Point Lobster Shop**	▽▽▽	Seafood	$18-$30	710
② / p. 626	AAA	**The Cliff House**	▽▽▽	Continental	$12-$38	710
③ / p. 626		Antique Sandwich Company	▽	American	$5-$8	710
④ / p. 626	AAA	**The Ruston Way Lobster Shop**	▽▽▽	Western Seafood	$9-$35	711
⑤ / p. 626		CI Shenanigans Chophouse-Tacoma	▽▽▽	American	$10-$40	710
⑥ / p. 626		Harbor Lights	▽▽	Steak & Seafood	$10-$40	710
⑦ / p. 626	AAA	**The Old House Cafe**	▽▽▽	Regional Seafood	$10-$33	711
⑧ / p. 626		Engine House #9	▽▽	American	$7-$15	710
⑨ / p. 626		Ravenous Restaurant	▽▽	American	$7-$25	711
⑩ / p. 626		Il Fiasco	▽▽	Italian	$14-$30	711
⑪ / p. 626		Primo Grill	▽▽▽	American	$8-$27	711
⑫ / p. 626		Bite	▽▽	American	$12-$32	710
⑬ / p. 626		Sea Grill	▽▽▽	Seafood	$27-$69	711
⑭ / p. 626		Johnny's Dock	▽▽	Steak & Seafood	$7-$30	711
⑮ / p. 626		Harmon Restaurant & Brewery	▽▽	American	$8-$16	710
⑯ / p. 626		El Gaucho	▽▽▽	Steak & Seafood	$21-$63	710
⑰ / p. 626		Stanley & Seaforts	▽▽▽	Steak & Seafood	$10-$38	711

FEDERAL WAY

Map Page	OA	Lodgings	Diamond Rated	High Season	Page
⓰ / p. 626	AAA	**Clarion Hotel Federal Way**	▽▽▽	$75-$169 SAVE	681
⓱ / p. 626		Courtyard by Marriott Seattle/Federal Way	▽▽▽	$199-$219	681
⓲ / p. 626		Extended StayAmerica-Seattle-Federal Way	▽▽	$90-$115	681

FEDERAL WAY (cont'd)

Map Page	OA	Lodgings (cont'd)	Diamond Rated	High Season	Page
19 / p. 626	AAA	Best Western Evergreen Inn & Suites	▽▽▽	$79-$169 SAVE	680
20 / p. 626		Federal Way Super 8	▽▽	$74-$100	681
22 / p. 626	AAA	Days Inn Federal Way	▽▽	Rates not provided SAVE	681

Map Page	OA	Restaurants	Diamond Rated	Cuisine	Meal Range	Page
20 / p. 626		Verrazano's Ristorante Italiano	▽▽▽	Italian	$9-$27	682
21 / p. 626		Billy McHale's	▽▽	American	$8-$22	681

FIFE

Map Page	OA	Lodgings	Diamond Rated	High Season	Page
25 / p. 626	AAA	Quality Inn	▽▽	$86-$110 SAVE	682
26 / p. 626	AAA	GuestHouse Royal Coachman, Fife	▽▽	Rates not provided SAVE	682
27 / p. 626		Extended StayAmerica-Tacoma-Fife	▽▽	$100-$115	682
28 / p. 626	AAA	Emerald Queen Hotel & Casino	▽▽▽	$89-$119 SAVE	682

Map Page	OA	Restaurant	Diamond Rated	Cuisine	Meal Range	Page
24 / p. 626		Fife City Bar & Grill	▽▽	American	$9-$20	682

LAKEWOOD

Map Page	OA	Lodgings	Diamond Rated	High Season	Page
31 / p. 626	AAA	Best Western Lakewood Motor Inn	▽▽▽	$115-$125 SAVE	687
32 / p. 626	AAA	Western Inn	▽▽	$59-$78 SAVE	688
33 / p. 626		La Quinta - Lakewood Inn & Suites	▽▽▽	$119-$139	688

PUYALLUP

Map Page	OA	Lodgings	Diamond Rated	High Season	Page
36 / p. 626		Crossland Economy Suites-Tacoma-Puyallup	▽	$74-$89	694
37 / p. 626	AAA	Best Western Park Plaza	▽▽▽	$159-$169 SAVE	694
38 / p. 626		Holiday Inn Express Hotel & Suites Puyallup	▽▽▽	$189-$239	694

Map Page	OA	Restaurant	Diamond Rated	Cuisine	Meal Range	Page
27 / p. 626		Powerhouse Restaurant & Brewery	▽▽	American	$7-$13	694

AUBURN

Map Page	OA	Lodgings	Diamond Rated	High Season	Page
41 / p. 626	AAA	Travelodge Suites	▽▽	Rates not provided SAVE	666
42 / p. 626		Comfort Inn-Auburn	▽▽▽	$109-$189	666
43 / p. 626	AAA	Cedars Inn Auburn	▽	$55-$109 SAVE	665
44 / p. 626		Auburn GuestHouse Inn	▽▽	$89-$99	665
45 / p. 626	AAA	Best Western Peppertree Auburn Inn	▽▽▽	$90-$220 SAVE	665

Map Page	OA	Restaurant	Diamond Rated	Cuisine	Meal Range	Page
30 / p. 626		Sun Break Cafe	▽▽	American	$6-$10	666

DOWNTOWN SEATTLE (See map and index starting on p. 606-609)

——— WHERE TO STAY ———

11TH AVENUE INN BED AND BREAKFAST

Phone: 206/720-7161 🔟③

Historic Bed & Breakfast
$69-$169 All Year

Address: 121 11th Ave E **Location:** I-5, exit 166 northbound, Olive Way to John St, then just s; exit southbound via Roanoke to 10th Ave, 1 mi e. **Facility:** The renovated, 1906 Craftsman-style home is situated on a peaceful tree-lined side street a block from Broadway and its many shops and restaurants. Smoke free premises. 8 one-bedroom standard units, some with whirlpools. 3 stories (no elevator), interior corridors. *Bath:* some shared or private, combo or shower only. **Parking:** on-site. **Terms:** age restrictions may apply, 14 day cancellation notice-fee imposed. **Amenities:** video library, high-speed Internet, voice mail, hair dryers. **Guest Services:** wireless Internet. **Business Services:** PC. **Cards:** AX, MC, VI.

ALEXIS HOTEL

Phone: 206/624-4844 🔟④⑥

Historic Hotel
$139-$349 All Year

Address: 1007 1st Ave **Location:** Corner of Madison St and 1st Ave. **Facility:** The hotel combines two turn-of-the-20th-century-style buildings near the waterfront, where works by local artists are the focal point of public areas. Smoke free premises. 121 units. 111 one-bedroom standard units, some with kitchens and/or whirlpools. 10 one-bedroom suites. 6 stories, interior corridors. *Bath:* combo or shower only. **Parking:** valet. **Terms:** cancellation fee imposed. **Amenities:** video games (fee), high-speed Internet, dual phone lines, voice mail, safes, honor bars, irons, hair dryers. **Dining:** The Library Bistro, see separate listing. **Leisure Activities:** steamroom, exercise room, spa. **Guest Services:** valet laundry, wireless Internet. **Business Services:** meeting rooms, business center. **Cards:** AX, CB, DC, DS, JC, MC, VI. **Free Special Amenities:** newspaper and early check-in/late check-out.

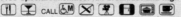

BEST WESTERN EXECUTIVE INN/SEATTLE

Book great rates at AAA.com

Phone: (206)448-9444 🔟⓪

Hotel
$124-$209 3/1-10/15
$109-$139 10/16-2/28

Address: 200 Taylor Ave N **Location:** I-5, exit 166, 1 mi w; near Seattle Center; just w of SR 99. Located in a commercial area. **Facility:** 123 one-bedroom standard units. 5 stories, interior corridors. *Bath:* combo or shower only. **Parking:** on-site (fee). **Terms:** check-in 4 pm, cancellation fee imposed. **Amenities:** video games (fee), high-speed Internet, voice mail, irons, hair dryers. *Some:* CD players. **Leisure Activities:** whirlpool, exercise room. **Guest Services:** valet laundry, wireless Internet. **Business Services:** conference facilities, PC. **Cards:** AX, CB, DC, DS, JC, MC, VI. **Free Special Amenities:** full breakfast and high-speed Internet.

AAA Benefit:
Members save up to 20%, plus 10% bonus points with rewards program.

BEST WESTERN LOYAL INN

Book great rates at AAA.com

Phone: (206)682-0200 🔟④

Hotel
$114-$199 3/1-10/15
$99-$129 10/16-2/28

Address: 2301 8th Ave **Location:** Corner of 8th Ave and Denny Way. Located in a commercial area. **Facility:** 91 one-bedroom standard units. 4 stories, interior corridors. **Parking:** on-site (fee). **Terms:** check-in 4 pm, cancellation fee imposed. **Amenities:** high-speed Internet, voice mail, safes, irons, hair dryers. **Leisure Activities:** sauna, whirlpool, limited exercise equipment. **Guest Services:** valet and coin laundry, wireless Internet. **Business Services:** PC. **Cards:** AX, CB, DC, DS, JC, MC, VI. **Free Special Amenities:** expanded continental breakfast and high-speed Internet.

AAA Benefit:
Members save up to 20%, plus 10% bonus points with rewards program.

▼ See AAA listing p 659 ▼

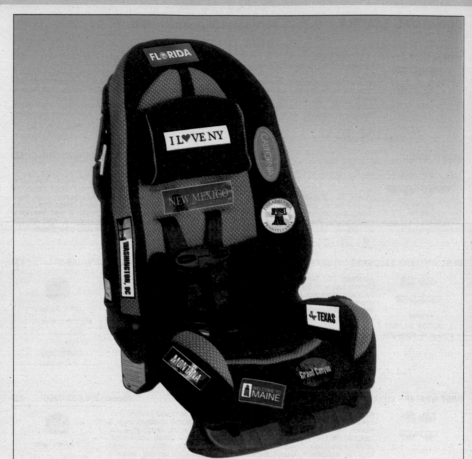

(See map and index starting on p. 606)

BEST WESTERN PIONEER SQUARE HOTEL

Book great rates at AAA.com   **Phone:** (206)340-1234   **47**

(AAA) **(SAVE)**

▼▼▼▼▼

Historic
Hotel

$150-$399 All Year

Address: 77 Yesler Way **Location:** Just w of 1st Ave. Located in historic Pioneer Square. **Facility:** Located near several sports venues, the waterfront and historic Pioneer Square; parking is available one block from the hotel for a nominal fee. Smoke free premises. 75 one-bedroom standard units. 4 stories, interior corridors. *Bath:* combo or shower only. **Parking:** street. **Terms:** 2-7 night minimum stay - seasonal and/or weekends, 7 day cancellation notice-fee imposed. **Amenities:** high-speed Internet, voice mail, irons, hair dryers. **Guest Services:** valet laundry, wireless Internet. **Business Services:** meeting rooms, PC. **Cards:** AX, CB, DC, DS, JC, MC, VI. **Free Special Amenities: local telephone calls and high-speed Internet.** *(See color ad below)*

AAA Benefit:
Members save up to
20%, plus 10%
bonus points with
rewards program.

[II→] FEE [♿] [✕] [▣] / [SOME UNITS] [⊞]

COMFORT SUITES-DOWNTOWN/SEATTLE CENTER

Book great rates at AAA.com **Phone:** (206)282-2600   **5**

(AAA) **(SAVE)**

▼▼▼▼▼

Hotel

$119-$209 3/1-10/31
$99-$139 11/1-2/28

Address: 601 Roy St **Location:** I-5, exit 166 northbound, just ne, just w on Denny Way, just n on 5th Ave N, then just e; exit southbound, just sw on Stewart St, just w on Denny Way, just n on 5th Ave N, then just e. **Facility:** Smoke free premises. 158 units. 147 one-bedroom standard units. 8 one- and 3 two-bedroom suites. 4 stories, interior corridors. *Bath:* combo or shower only. **Parking:** on-site. **Terms:** cancellation fee imposed. **Amenities:** high-speed Internet, dual phone lines, voice mail, irons, hair dryers. **Fee:** video games, safes. **Leisure Activities:** exercise room. **Guest Services:** valet and coin laundry, wireless Internet. **Business Services:** meeting rooms, PC. **Cards:** AX, CB, DC, DS, JC, MC, VI. **Free Special Amenities: expanded continental breakfast and high-speed Internet.**

[II→] [✕] [🎥] [⊞] [▤] [▣]

──────── ▼ See AAA listing above ▼ ────────

(See map and index starting on p. 606)

COURTYARD BY MARRIOTT SEATTLE
DOWNTOWN/LAKE UNION *Book great rates at AAA.com*

Phone: (206)213-0100 **2**

Hotel
$209-$249 All Year

Address: 925 Westlake Ave N **Location:** I-5, exit 167 (Mercer St), just n on Fairview Ave, just w on Valley St, then just n. **Facility:** Smoke free premises. 250 units. 248 one-bedroom standard units. 2 one-bedroom suites. 7 stories, interior corridors. *Bath:* combo or shower only. **Parking:** on-site (fee). **Terms:** cancellation fee imposed. **Amenities:** high-speed Internet, voice mail, irons, hair dryers. *Some:* CD players. **Pool(s):** heated indoor. **Leisure Activities:** whirlpool, exercise room. **Guest Services:** valet and coin laundry, wireless Internet. **Business Services:** meeting rooms, business center. **Cards:** AX, CB, DC, DS, JC, MC, VI.

AAA Benefit:
Members save a minimum 5% off the best available rate.

CROWNE PLAZA SEATTLE-DOWNTOWN *Book great rates at AAA.com*

Phone: (206)464-1980 **39**

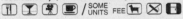

Hotel
$169-$329 All Year

Address: 1113 6th Ave **Location:** Corner of 6th Ave and Seneca St. Located in a commercial area. **Facility:** 415 units. 389 one-bedroom standard units. 26 one-bedroom suites. 34 stories, interior corridors. *Bath:* combo or shower only. **Parking:** valet. **Terms:** check-in 4 pm, cancellation fee imposed. **Amenities:** video games (fee), CD players, high-speed Internet, voice mail, irons, hair dryers. *Some:* safes. **Leisure Activities:** exercise room. **Guest Services:** valet laundry, wireless Internet. **Business Services:** conference facilities, business center. **Cards:** AX, CB, DC, DS, JC, MC, VI. **Free Special Amenities: newspaper and room upgrade (subject to availability with advance reservations).** *(See color ad below)*

DAYS INN TOWN CENTER *Book at AAA.com*

Phone: 206/448-3434 **18**

Hotel
Rates not provided

Address: 2205 7th Ave **Location:** Between Bell and Blanchard sts. **Facility:** 92 one-bedroom standard units, some with kitchens. 4 stories, interior corridors. *Bath:* combo or shower only. **Parking:** on-site (fee). **Amenities:** high-speed Internet (fee), voice mail, irons, hair dryers. **Guest Services:** valet laundry, wireless Internet.

▼ *See AAA listing above* ▼

Downtown Location - Superb Value!

- Located in Downtown Seattle, within one mile to: Pikes Place Market, Space Needle, Safeco Field, Pioneer Square, Convention Center, Experience Music Project, Seattle Art Museum, theaters, hospitals, universities and waterfront activities
- Just 15 miles to wine country
- Guest rooms feature city views, Space Needle and mountain views, Crowne Plaza Sleep Advantage™ bed, CD player and wireless Internet access
- Regatta Grille Restaurant and Bar, 24-hour Fitness Center, and Wi-Fi access in all public areas

Approved

CROWNE PLAZA
SEATTLE - DOWNTOWN AREA
cphotelseattle.com • 1.800.521.2762

Crowne Plaza Seattle-Downtown Area
1113 6th Avenue, Seattle, WA 98101 • 206-464-1980

(See map and index starting on p. 606)

THE EDGEWATER

Book great rates at AAA.com

Phone: (206)728-7000 **27**

[AAA] [SAVE]

▼▼▼ ▼▼▼

Hotel

$459-$659 All Year

Address: 2411 Alaskan Way, Pier 67 **Location:** On waterfront at Pier 67; at base of Wall St. **Facility:** Units include a gas fireplace, many overlook Elliott Bay and Olympic Mountains; located on pier extending over the water. Smoke free premises. 223 units. 220 one-bedroom standard units, some with whirlpools. 3 one-bedroom suites. 4 stories, interior corridors. *Bath:* combo or shower only. **Parking:** valet. **Terms:** check-in 4 pm, cancellation fee imposed. **Amenities:** high-speed Internet (fee), voice mail, honor bars, irons, hair dryers. **Dining:** Six Seven, see separate listing. **Leisure Activities:** exercise room. **Guest Services:** valet laundry, area transportation-within 2 mi, wireless Internet. **Business Services:** meeting rooms, business center. **Cards:** AX, CB, DC, DS, JC, MC, VI. **Free Special Amenities:** newspaper and early check-in/late check-out. *(See color ad below)*

[icons]

EXECUTIVE HOTEL PACIFIC

Book at AAA.com

Phone: (206)623-3900 **43**

▼▼ ▼▼

Historic Hotel

$169-$249 5/2-2/28
$159-$219 3/1-5/1

Address: 400 Spring St **Location:** Between 4th and 5th aves. **Facility:** 1928 vintage hotel. Smoke free premises. 153 units. 152 one-bedroom standard units. 1 one-bedroom suite. 8 stories, interior corridors. **Parking:** on-site (fee) and valet. **Terms:** check-in 4 pm, cancellation fee imposed. **Amenities:** CD players, high-speed Internet, voice mail, safes, irons, hair dryers. **Leisure Activities:** exercise room. **Guest Services:** valet laundry, wireless Internet. **Business Services:** meeting rooms, PC. **Cards:** AX, CB, DC, DS, JC, MC, VI.

[icons]

THE FAIRMONT OLYMPIC HOTEL

Book great rates at AAA.com

Phone: (206)621-1700 **38**

[AAA] [SAVE]

▼▼▼ ▼▼▼

Historic Hotel

$299-$469 All Year

Address: 411 University St **Location:** Corner of 4th Ave and University St. Located in the financial and retail districts. **Facility:** A historic icon, the Italian Renaissance-style hotel is in the heart of the city; it reflects the grandeur of the past but with modern conveniences. 450 units. 251 one-bedroom standard units. 199 one-bedroom suites. 12 stories, interior corridors. *Bath:* combo or shower only. **Parking:** on-site (fee) and valet. **Terms:** cancellation fee imposed. **Amenities:** CD players, high-speed Internet, dual phone lines, voice mail, safes, honor bars, irons, hair dryers. *Some:* DVD players, fax. **Dining:** The Georgian, Shuckers, see separate listings, entertainment. **Pool(s):** heated indoor. **Leisure Activities:** saunas, whirlpool, spa. **Guest Services:** valet laundry, area transportation-downtown, wireless Internet. **Business Services:** conference facilities, business center. **Cards:** AX, DC, DS, MC, VI. **Free Special Amenities:** newspaper and high-speed Internet.

[icons]

FOUR SEASONS HOTEL SEATTLE

Phone: 206/749-7000

[fyi]

Hotel

$375-$445 11/1-2/28
$365-$435 3/1-10/31

Too new to rate, opening scheduled for November 2008. **Address:** 99 Union St **Location:** Southwest corner of 1st Ave and Union St. **Amenities:** 147 units, pets, restaurant, pool. **Terms:** cancellation fee imposed. **Cards:** AX, CB, DC, DS, JC, MC, VI.

(See map and index starting on p. 606)

GRAND HYATT SEATTLE *Book great rates at AAA.com*

Phone: (206)774-1234 **26**

Hotel
$179-$529 All Year

Address: 721 Pine St **Location:** Corner of 7th Ave and Pine St. **Facility:** Guest units provide panoramic views of the city, some offer views of Elliott Bay; modern amenities and an elegant ambiance combine for a luxurious feel. 425 units. 312 one-bedroom standard units. 113 one-bedroom suites, some with whirlpools. 30 stories, interior corridors. *Bath:* combo or shower only. **Parking:** on-site (fee) and valet. **Terms:** 3 day cancellation notice-fee imposed. **Amenities:** high-speed Internet (fee), dual phone lines, voice mail, safes, honor bars, irons, hair dryers. *Some:* DVD players (fee), CD players. **Dining:** Ruth's Chris Steak House, see separate listing. **Leisure Activities:** sauna, whirlpool, steamroom. *Fee:* massage. **Guest Services:** valet laundry, wireless Internet. **Business Services:** conference facilities, business center. **Cards:** AX, CB, DC, DS, JC, MC, VI. *(See color ad below)*

AAA Benefit:
Ask for the AAA rate
and save 10%.

HAMPTON INN & SUITES-DOWNTOWN/SEATTLE CENTER *Book great rates at AAA.com*

Phone: (206)282-7700 **4**

Hotel
$139-$259 All Year

Address: 700 5th Ave N **Location:** I-5, exit 166 northbound, just ne, then just w on Denny Way, just n; exit southbound, just sw on Stewart St, just w on Denny Way, then just n. Located across from the Seattle Center. **Facility:** 199 units. 144 one-bedroom standard units. 47 one- and 8 two-bedroom suites. 6 stories, interior corridors. *Bath:* combo or shower only. **Parking:** on-site (fee). **Terms:** 1-30 night minimum stay, cancellation fee imposed. **Amenities:** video games (fee), high-speed Internet, voice mail, safes, irons, hair dryers. *Some:* dual phone lines. **Leisure Activities:** exercise room. **Guest Services:** valet and coin laundry, wireless Internet. **Business Services:** meeting rooms, business center. **Cards:** AX, DC, DS, JC, MC, VI.

AAA Benefit:
Members save up to
10% everyday!

HILTON SEATTLE *Book great rates at AAA.com*

Phone: (206)624-0500 **36**

Hotel
$189-$575 All Year

Address: 1301 6th Ave **Location:** Corner of 6th Ave and University St. Located in a business area. **Facility:** Smoke free premises. 236 one-bedroom standard units. 29 stories, interior corridors. **Parking:** on-site (fee). **Terms:** 1-30 night minimum stay, cancellation fee imposed. **Amenities:** dual phone lines, voice mail, safes, honor bars, irons, hair dryers. *Fee:* video games, high-speed Internet. **Leisure Activities:** exercise room. **Guest Services:** valet laundry, wireless Internet. **Business Services:** meeting rooms, business center. **Cards:** AX, CB, DC, DS, JC, MC, VI. **Free Special Amenities:** newspaper. *(See color ad p 635)*

Hilton

AAA Benefit:
Members save 5%
or more everyday!

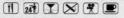

▼ *See AAA listing above* ▼

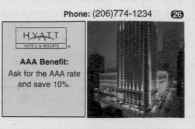

GRAND HYATT SEATTLE. A PERFECT GETAWAY.

Enjoy superior accommodations with significant savings exclusively for AAA members. Located in the heart of downtown, the Grand Hyatt Seattle is walking distance to prime shopping and dining. Simply request the AAA member rate at the time of booking and present your card at check-in. Feel the Hyatt Touch. For Reservations call 800-532 1496 or visit **www.grandseattle.hyatt.com**.

(See map and index starting on p. 606)

HOLIDAY INN EXPRESS-DOWNTOWN SEATTLE   *Book at AAA.com*   Phone: 206/441-7222   **8**

Hotel
Rates not provided

Address: 226 Aurora Ave N **Location:** I-5, exit 167 (Mercer St), 0.3 mi w, 0.5 mi s on Fairview Ave, 0.5 mi w on Denny Way, then just n. Located in a commercial area. **Facility:** 195 units. 185 one-bedroom standard units, some with whirlpools. 10 one-bedroom suites, some with whirlpools. 6 stories, interior corridors. **Bath:** combo or shower only. **Parking:** on-site (fee). **Amenities:** video games (fee), high-speed Internet, dual phone lines, voice mail, irons, hair dryers. **Pool(s):** heated indoor. **Leisure Activities:** exercise room. **Guest Services:** valet and coin laundry, wireless Internet. **Business Services:** meeting rooms, business center.

HOLIDAY INN SEATTLE CENTER   *Book at AAA.com*   Phone: (206)728-8123   **11**

Hotel
$169-$224 3/1-8/31
$139-$199 9/1-2/28

Address: 211 Dexter Ave N **Location:** I-5, exit 167 (Mercer St), 0.3 mi w, 0.5 mi s on Fairview Ave, 0.5 mi w on Denny Way, then just n. **Facility:** 196 units. 171 one- and 5 two-bedroom standard units. 20 one-bedroom suites. 6 stories, interior corridors. **Bath:** combo or shower only. **Parking:** on-site (fee). **Terms:** cancellation fee imposed. **Amenities:** video games (fee), high-speed Internet, dual phone lines, voice mail, irons, hair dryers. **Leisure Activities:** exercise room. **Guest Services:** valet and coin laundry, wireless Internet. **Business Services:** meeting rooms, business center. **Cards:** AX, CB, DC, DS, JC, MC, VI.

HOMEWOOD SUITES BY HILTON CONVENTION
CENTER/PIKE STREET   *Book great rates at AAA.com*   Phone: (206)682-8282   **24**

Hotel
$179-$309 All Year

Address: 1011 Pike St **Location:** I-5, exit 165 northbound to Pike St via 6th Ave; exit Union St southbound to Pike St. Next to Convention Center. **Facility:** 195 units. 17 one-bedroom standard units. 178 one-bedroom suites with efficiencies, some with whirlpools. 9 stories, interior corridors. **Bath:** combo or shower only. **Parking:** valet. **Terms:** 1-30 night minimum stay, cancellation fee imposed. **Amenities:** voice mail, irons, hair dryers. **Pool(s):** heated outdoor. **Leisure Activities:** whirlpools, exercise room. **Guest Services:** valet and coin laundry, area transportation, wireless Internet. **Business Services:** business center. **Cards:** AX, CB, DC, DS, JC, MC, VI.

AAA Benefit:
Members save 5% or more everyday!

▼ See AAA listing p 634 ▼

(See map and index starting on p. 606)

HOMEWOOD SUITES BY HILTON-SEATTLE
DOWNTOWN   *Book great rates at AAA.com*

Phone: (206)281-9393   **9**

Hotel
$159-$299 All Year

Address: 206 Western Ave W **Location:** I-5, exit 167 (Mercer St), 0.3 mi w, 0.5 mi s on Fairview Ave, 1.2 mi w on Denny Way, then just n. **Facility:** 161 units. 156 one- and 5 two-bedroom suites with efficiencies. 6 stories, interior corridors. **Parking:** on-site (fee). **Terms:** 1-30 night minimum stay, cancellation fee imposed. **Amenities:** video games (fee), dual phone lines, voice mail, irons, hair dryers. **Leisure Activities:** exercise room. **Guest Services:** complimentary and valet laundry, wireless Internet. **Business Services:** meeting rooms, business center. **Cards:** AX, CB, DC, DS, JC, MC, VI. *(See color ad below)*

AAA Benefit:
Members save 5%
or more everyday!

(VCR) (🎮) (📶) (🛏) (💻) / SOME UNITS FEE (🐕) (✖)

HOTEL 1000   *Book at AAA.com*

Phone: (206)957-1000   **45**

Hotel
$219-$439 All Year

Address: 1000 1st Ave **Location:** Northeast corner of 1st Ave and Madison St. **Facility:** Ultra modern guest rooms at this high-rise hotel provide panoramic views of the city and water. Smoke free premises. 120 units. 102 one-bedroom standard units. 18 one-bedroom suites. 24 stories, interior corridors. *Bath:* combo or shower only. **Parking:** valet. **Terms:** check-in 4 pm, cancellation fee imposed. **Amenities:** high-speed Internet, dual phone lines, voice mail, safes, honor bars, irons, hair dryers. *Some:* DVD players, CD players. **Leisure Activities:** exercise room, spa. **Guest Services:** valet laundry, wireless Internet. **Business Services:** meeting rooms, business center. **Cards:** AX, MC, VI.

(ASK) (🍴) (24) (🍸) (✖) (🎮) (💻) / SOME UNITS FEE (🐕)

HOTEL MAX   *Book great rates at AAA.com*

Phone: (206)728-6299   **21**

(AAA) (SAVE)

Hotel
$149-$269 All Year

Address: 620 Stewart St **Location:** Corner of 7th Ave and Stewart St. Located in a business area. **Facility:** 163 one-bedroom standard units. 10 stories, interior corridors. *Bath:* combo or shower only. **Parking:** valet. **Terms:** check-in 4 pm, cancellation fee imposed. **Amenities:** CD players, dual phone lines, voice mail, safes, honor bars, irons, hair dryers. **Dining:** Red Fin Restaurant, see separate listing. **Leisure Activities:** exercise room. **Guest Services:** valet laundry, wireless Internet. **Business Services:** meeting rooms, business center. **Cards:** AX, CB, DC, DS, MC, VI. **Free Special Amenities:** newspaper. *(See color ad p 637)*

(🍴) (🍸) CALL (♿M) (🎮) (📶) (💻) / SOME UNITS FEE (🐕) (✖)

HOTEL MONACO   *Book great rates at AAA.com*

Phone: (206)621-1770   **42**

(AAA) (SAVE)

Hotel
$139-$349 All Year

Address: 1101 4th Ave **Location:** Corner of 4th Ave and Spring St. **Facility:** In the center of downtown, this hotel offers upscale accommodations with distinctive decor in a renovated building. 189 units. 187 one-bedroom standard units, some with whirlpools. 2 one-bedroom suites, some with whirlpools. 11 stories, interior corridors. *Bath:* combo or shower only. **Parking:** valet. **Terms:** cancellation fee imposed. **Amenities:** DVD players, video games (fee), CD players, high-speed Internet, dual phone lines, voice mail, safes, honor bars, irons, hair dryers. **Dining:** Saze Rac, see separate listing. **Leisure Activities:** exercise room. *Fee:* massage. **Guest Services:** valet laundry, wireless Internet. **Business Services:** conference facilities, business center. **Cards:** AX, CB, DC, DS, JC, MC, VI. **Free Special Amenities:** newspaper and early check-in/late check-out.

(🍴) (24) (🍸) (💻) / SOME UNITS (🐕) (✖) (VCR)

———— ▼ *See AAA listing above* ▼ ————

(See map and index starting on p. 606)

HOTEL VINTAGE PARK   *Book great rates at AAA.com*   Phone: (206)624-8000   **40**

AAA SAVE

▼▼▼ ▼▼▼

Historic
Hotel

$139-$309 All Year

Address: 1100 5th Ave **Location:** Corner of Spring St and 5th Ave. **Facility:** A wood-burning fireplace graces the lobby of this hotel, and the rooms are decorated with rich fabrics. Smoke free premises. 125 units. 124 one-bedroom standard units. 1 one-bedroom suite with whirlpool. 11 stories, interior corridors. **Parking:** valet. **Terms:** cancellation fee imposed. **Amenities:** DVD players, video games (fee), CD players, dual phone lines, voice mail, safes, honor bars, irons, hair dryers. **Dining:** Tulio Ristorante, see separate listing. **Leisure Activities:** exercise room. *Fee:* massage. **Guest Services:** valet laundry, wireless Internet. **Business Services:** meeting rooms, PC. **Cards:** AX, CB, DC, DS, JC, MC, VI. **Free Special Amenities: newspaper and early check-in/late check-out.**

INN AT HARBOR STEPS   *Book at AAA.com*   Phone: (206)748-0973   **44**

▼▼▼ ▼▼▼

Hotel

$175-$250 All Year

Address: 1221 1st Ave **Location:** Corner of Seneca St and 1st Ave. **Facility:** Smoke free premises. 28 one-bedroom standard units, some with whirlpools. 25 stories, interior corridors. **Parking:** on-site (fee). **Terms:** cancellation fee imposed. **Amenities:** video library, CD players, high-speed Internet, voice mail, irons, hair dryers. *Some:* DVD players. **Pool(s):** heated indoor. **Leisure Activities:** saunas, whirlpools, exercise room, basketball. *Fee:* massage. **Guest Services:** complimentary and valet laundry, wireless Internet. **Business Services:** meeting rooms, PC. **Cards:** AX, DC, DS, MC, VI.

INN AT THE MARKET   *Book at AAA.com*   Phone: (206)443-3600   **34**

▼▼▼ ▼▼▼

Boutique
Hotel

$245-$625 All Year

Address: 86 Pine St **Location:** Northwest corner of 1st Ave and Pine St. **Facility:** This charming luxury boutique hotel is located amidst the cobblestones of Pike Place Market, entered through a quiet, intimate courtyard. Smoke free premises. 70 units. 63 one-bedroom standard units. 7 one-bedroom suites. 4-8 stories, interior/exterior corridors. *Bath:* combo or shower only. **Parking:** valet. **Terms:** check-in 4 pm. **Amenities:** video games (fee), dual phone lines, voice mail, safes, irons, hair dryers. **Dining:** Cafe Campagne, Campagne, see separate listings. **Guest Services:** valet laundry, area transportation, beauty salon, wireless Internet. **Business Services:** meeting rooms. **Cards:** AX, DC, DS, MC, VI.

THE INN AT VIRGINIA MASON   Phone: (206)583-6453   **35**

AAA SAVE

▼▼▼

Historic
Hotel

$135-$324 All Year

Address: 1006 Spring St **Location:** I-5, exit Madison St, just ne at Terry Ave and Spring St. Attached to the Virginia Mason Hospital. **Facility:** This intimate European-style hotel with a smaller lobby and a variety of room sizes has a rooftop patio that provides great views of Seattle. Smoke free premises. 79 units. 78 one-bedroom standard units, some with whirlpools. 1 one-bedroom suite with whirlpool. 9 stories, interior corridors. **Parking:** on-site (fee). **Guest Services:** valet and coin laundry, wireless Internet. **Business Services:** PC. **Cards:** AX, DS, MC, VI. **Free Special Amenities: local telephone calls and high-speed Internet.**

LA QUINTA INN & SUITES SEATTLE DOWNTOWN   *Book great rates at AAA.com*   Phone: (206)624-6820   **17**

▼▼▼

Hotel

$79-$169 All Year

Address: 2224 8th Ave **Location:** Corner of 8th Ave and Blanchard St. Located in a commercial area. **Facility:** Smoke free premises. 72 units. 60 one-bedroom standard units. 12 one-bedroom suites. 7 stories, interior corridors. *Bath:* combo or shower only. **Parking:** on-site. **Amenities:** dual phone lines, voice mail, irons, hair dryers. **Leisure Activities:** sauna, whirlpool, exercise room. **Guest Services:** valet and coin laundry, wireless Internet. **Business Services:** PC. **Cards:** AX, CB, DS, MC, VI.

▼ *See AAA listing p 636* ▼

(See map and index starting on p. 606)

MARQUEEN HOTEL *Book great rates at AAA.com* Phone: (206)282-7407 **6**

AAA SAVE

Historic
Hotel
$149-$400 5/1-2/28
$149-$210 3/1-4/30

Address: 600 Queen Anne Ave N **Location:** I-5, exit 167 (Mercer St), just w via Valley and Roy sts, then just s; just w of Seattle Center. **Facility:** Newly restored facility with large suite-style rooms in a 1918 building; located near Seattle Center. Smoke free premises. 59 units. 55 one-bedroom standard units with efficiencies. 4 one-bedroom suites with efficiencies, some with whirlpools. 3 stories (no elevator), interior corridors. **Bath:** combo or shower only. **Parking:** valet. **Terms:** cancellation fee imposed. **Amenities:** voice mail, honor bars, irons, hair dryers. *Some:* DVD players, CD players. **Leisure Activities:** exercise room, spa. **Guest Services:** valet laundry, area transportation-within 5 mi, wireless Internet. **Business Services:** meeting rooms. **Cards:** AX, DC, DS, JC, MC, VI. **Free Special Amenities:** newspaper and high-speed Internet. *(See color ad below)*

**MARRIOTT SPRINGHILL SUITES-DOWNTOWN
SEATTLE** *Book great rates at AAA.com* Phone: (206)254-0500 **16**

AAA SAVE

Hotel
$189-$259 All Year

Address: 1800 Yale Ave **Location:** I-5, exit 165 northbound, just sw, just nw on 4th Ave, just ne on Olive Way, then just ne on Howell; exit 166 southbound, just sw. **Facility:** Smoke free premises. 234 one-bedroom standard units. 10 stories, interior corridors. **Bath:** combo or shower only. **Parking:** valet. **Terms:** cancellation fee imposed. **Amenities:** video games (fee), high-speed Internet, dual phone lines, voice mail, irons, hair dryers. **Pool(s):** heated indoor. **Leisure Activities:** whirlpool, exercise room. **Guest Services:** valet and coin laundry, area transportation-convention center, Westlake Center & Seattle Center, wireless Internet. **Business Services:** meeting rooms, business center. **Cards:** AX, CB, DC, DS, MC, VI. **Free Special Amenities:** full breakfast and high-speed Internet. *(See color ad p 639)*

AAA Benefit:
Members save a minimum 5% off the best available rate.

MAYFLOWER PARK HOTEL *Book great rates at AAA.com* Phone: (206)623-8700 **29**

AAA SAVE

Historic
Hotel
$235-$365 All Year

Address: 405 Olive Way **Location:** Corner of 4th Ave and Olive Way. **Facility:** This property has the Old World charm of a small European hotel; guests can choose from rooms of various sizes. Smoke free premises. 161 units. 141 one-bedroom standard units, some with whirlpools. 20 one-bedroom suites. 12 stories, interior corridors. **Bath:** combo or shower only. **Parking:** valet. **Terms:** check-in 4 pm, cancellation fee imposed. **Amenities:** video games (fee), voice mail, safes, irons, hair dryers. *Some:* DVD players, CD players. **Dining:** Andaluca, see separate listing. **Leisure Activities:** exercise room. **Guest Services:** valet laundry, wireless Internet. **Business Services:** meeting rooms, PC. **Cards:** AX, CB, DC, DS, JC, MC, VI. **Free Special Amenities:** newspaper and high-speed Internet. *(See color ad p 639)*

▼ See AAA listing p 638 ▼

▼ See AAA listing p 638 ▼

(See map and index starting on p. 606)

THE MEDITERRANEAN INN   *Book great rates at AAA.com*   Phone: (206)428-4700
(AAA) (SAVE)   **Address:** 425 Queen Anne Ave N **Location:** I-5, exit 167 (Mercer St), just w via Valley and Roy s
▼▼▼ ▼▼▼   then just s; just w of Seattle Center; jct Republican St. **Facility:** Smoke free premises. 180 on
Hotel   bedroom standard units. 6 stories, interior corridors. *Bath:* combo or shower only. **Parking:** on-si
$119-$169 All Year   (fee). **Terms:** check-in 4 pm. **Amenities:** video library, high-speed Internet (fee), voice mail, irons, ha
dryers. *Some:* DVD players. **Leisure Activities:** rooftop deck & atrium courtyard, exercise roor
Guest Services: coin laundry. **Business Services:** meeting rooms, business center. **Cards:** AX, DS
JC, MC, VI. **Free Special Amenities: local telephone calls.**

PAN PACIFIC HOTEL SEATTLE   *Book great rates at AAA.com*   Phone: (206)264-8111
(AAA) (SAVE)   **Address:** 2125 Terry Ave **Location:** Just s of jct E Denny Way. **Facility:** Luxury units, situated on th
▼▼▼ ▼▼▼   edge of the downtown area, feature unique zebra wood walls and cabinets as well as plasma TV
Hotel   Smoke free premises. 160 units. 159 one-bedroom standard units. 1 one-bedroom suite. 11 storie
interior corridors. **Parking:** on-site (fee) and valet. **Terms:** check-in 4 pm. **Amenities:** video game
$195-$425 3/1-10/31   (fee), high-speed Internet, dual phone lines, voice mail, safes, honor bars, irons, hair dryers. *Som*
$169-$425 11/1-2/28   DVD players, CD players. **Dining:** Marazul, see separate listing. **Leisure Activities:** saunas, whirlpoo
exercise room, spa. **Guest Services:** valet laundry, wireless Internet. **Business Services:** meetir
rooms, business center. **Cards:** AX, DC, DS, JC, MC, VI. **Free Special Amenities: local telephor**
calls and high-speed Internet.

THE PARAMOUNT HOTEL, A COAST HOTEL   *Book great rates at AAA.com*   Phone: (206)292-9500
(AAA) (SAVE)   **Address:** 724 Pine St **Location:** Corner of 8th Ave and Pine St. **Facility:** Smoke free premises. 14
▼▼▼ ▼▼   units. 144 one-bedroom standard units. 2 one-bedroom suites. 11 stories, interior corridors. *Bath*
Hotel   combo or shower only. **Parking:** valet. **Terms:** cancellation fee imposed. **Amenities:** video game
(fee), dual phone lines, voice mail, irons, hair dryers. **Dining:** Dragonfish Asian Cafe, see separa
$149-$300 All Year   listing. **Leisure Activities:** exercise room. **Guest Services:** valet laundry, wireless Internet. **Busines**
Services: meeting rooms, PC. **Cards:** AX, DC, DS, MC, VI. **Free Special Amenities: newspaper an**
early check-in/late check-out.

RAMADA INN DOWNTOWN SEATTLE   Phone: (206)441-9785
(AAA) (SAVE)   **Address:** 2200 5th Ave **Location:** Corner of Blanchard St and 5th Ave. Located in a commercial are
▼▼▼ ▼▼   **Facility:** Smoke free premises. 120 one-bedroom standard units. 5 stories, interior corridors. *Bath*
Hotel   combo or shower only. **Parking:** on-site (fee). **Terms:** cancellation fee imposed. **Amenities:** high
speed Internet, voice mail, irons, hair dryers. *Fee:* video games, safes. **Leisure Activities:** exercis
$139-$169 All Year   room. **Guest Services:** valet laundry, wireless Internet. **Business Services:** meeting rooms, PC
Cards: AX, CB, DC, DS, JC, MC, VI. **Free Special Amenities: local telephone calls and high**
speed Internet. *(See color ad below)*

RED LION HOTEL ON FIFTH AVENUE-SEATTLE   *Book great rates at AAA.com*   Phone: (206)971-8000
(AAA) (SAVE)   **Address:** 1415 5th Ave **Location:** Between Pike and Union sts. **Facility:** 297 units. 291 one-bedroor
▼▼▼ ▼▼▼   standard units. 6 one-bedroom suites. 20 stories, interior corridors. *Bath:* combo or shower onl
Hotel   **Parking:** on-site (fee). **Terms:** cancellation fee imposed. **Amenities:** video games (fee), dual phon
lines, voice mail, irons, hair dryers. **Leisure Activities:** exercise room. **Guest Services:** valet laundr
$329 All Year   wireless Internet. **Business Services:** conference facilities, business center. **Cards:** AX, CB, DC, DS
JC, MC, VI. **Free Special Amenities: newspaper and high-speed Internet.**

ee map and index starting on p. 606)

**ESIDENCE INN MARRIOTT SEATTLE
DOWNTOWN/LAKE UNION** *Book great rates at AAA.com* **Phone:** (206)624-6000 **3**

(AAA) (SAVE)
▼▼▼

Hotel
$239-$299 All Year

Address: 800 Fairview Ave N **Location:** I-5, exit 167 (Mercer St); south end of Lake Union. **Facility:** Smoke free premises. 234 units. 25 one-bedroom standard units with kitchens. 155 one- and 54 two-bedroom suites with kitchens. 7 stories, interior corridors. **Parking:** on-site (fee). **Terms:** check-in 4 pm, cancellation fee imposed. **Amenities:** high-speed Internet, dual phone lines, voice mail, irons, hair dryers. *Some:* DVD players. **Pool(s):** heated indoor. **Leisure Activities:** sauna, whirlpool, exercise room. **Guest Services:** valet and coin laundry, wireless Internet. **Business Services:** meeting rooms, PC. **Cards:** AX, CB, DC, DS, JC, MC, VI. **Free Special Amenities: expanded continental breakfast and high-speed Internet.**

AAA Benefit:
Members save a minimum 5% off the best available rate.

[icons] / SOME UNITS FEE

HE ROOSEVELT, A COAST HOTEL *Book great rates at AAA.com* **Phone:** (206)621-1200 **28**

(AAA) (SAVE)
▼▼▼

Hotel
$159-$279 All Year

Address: 1531 7th Ave **Location:** Corner of 7th Ave and Pine St. **Facility:** Smoke free premises. 151 units. 121 one-bedroom standard units, some with whirlpools. 30 one-bedroom suites. 20 stories, interior corridors. *Bath:* combo or shower only. **Parking:** valet. **Terms:** check-in 4 pm, cancellation fee imposed. **Amenities:** video games (fee), voice mail, irons, hair dryers. **Dining:** Von's Grand City Cafe, see separate listing. **Leisure Activities:** exercise room. **Guest Services:** valet laundry, wireless Internet. **Business Services:** meeting rooms, PC. **Cards:** AX, DC, DS, MC, VI.

(See color ad below)

[icons] / SOME UNITS FEE FEE

EATTLE HILL HOUSE BED & BREAKFAST **Phone:** 206/323-4455 **12**

▼▼▼

Historic Bed
& Breakfast
Rates not provided

Address: 1113 E John St **Location:** I-5, exit 166 (Olive Way) northbound, to John St; exit 166 southbound via Roanoke to 10th Ave, 1 mi e. **Facility:** This restored 1903 Victorian home in the historic Capitol Hill District features picturesque urban floral gardens. Smoke free premises. 8 units. 6 one-bedroom standard units. 2 one-bedroom suites. 2 stories (no elevator), interior/exterior corridors. *Bath:* some shared or private, combo or shower only. **Parking:** on-site. **Terms:** age restrictions may apply. **Amenities:** hair dryers. *Some:* DVD players. **Guest Services:** wireless Internet. **Business Services:** PC.

[icons] / SOME UNITS

EATTLE MARRIOTT WATERFRONT HOTEL *Book great rates at AAA.com* **Phone:** (206)443-5000 **32**

▼▼▼

Hotel
$278-$340 All Year

Address: 2100 Alaskan Way **Location:** Between Wall and Vine sts. **Facility:** Smoke free premises. 358 units. 345 one-bedroom standard units. 13 one-bedroom suites. 8 stories, interior corridors. *Bath:* combo or shower only. **Parking:** valet. **Terms:** check-in 4 pm, cancellation fee imposed. **Amenities:** dual phone lines, voice mail, irons, hair dryers. *Fee:* video games, high-speed Internet. *Some:* safes. **Dining:** Fish Club, see separate listing. **Pool(s):** heated indoor/outdoor. **Leisure Activities:** whirlpool, exercise room. **Guest Services:** complimentary and valet laundry, wireless Internet. **Business Services:** conference facilities, business center. **Cards:** AX, CB, DC, DS, MC, VI.

Marriott
HOTELS & RESORTS

AAA Benefit:
Members save a minimum 5% off the best available rate.

[icons] / SOME UNITS

▼ *See AAA listing above* ▼

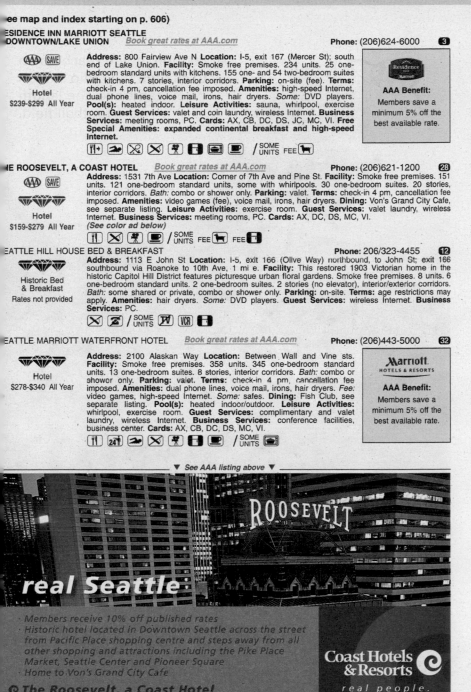

At 60 mph, if you reach down to change the radio station you can travel the length of a football field.

Stay Focused

Keep your mind on the road.

(See map and index starting on p. 606)

SHERATON SEATTLE HOTEL   *Book great rates at AAA.com*   Phone: (206)621-9000   **31**

AAA [SAVE]
▼▼▼▼
Hotel
$179-$399 All Year

Address: 1400 6th Ave **Location:** Corner of 6th Ave and Pike St. **Facility:** Offering great views from its upper rooms, this large metropolitan hotel is within walking distance of the convention center and major shopping areas. Smoke free premises. 1258 units. 1240 one-bedroom standard units. 18 one-bedroom suites. 35 stories, interior corridors. *Bath:* combo or shower only. **Parking:** valet. **Terms:** cancellation fee imposed. **Amenities:** dual phone lines, voice mail, safes, honor bars, irons, hair dryers. *Fee:* video games, high-speed Internet. *Some:* fax. **Pool(s):** heated indoor. **Leisure Activities:** sauna, whirlpool, exercise room. **Guest Services:** valet laundry, wireless Internet. **Business Services:** conference facilities, business center. **Cards:** AX, CB, DC, DS, JC, MC, VI.

> **⑤ Sheraton**
> HOTELS & RESORTS
> **AAA Benefit:**
> Members get up to 15% off, plus Starwood Preferred Guest® bonuses.

🍴 🍸 🏊 ⊠ ⊠ 🎥 💻 / SOME UNITS 🐾 VCR 🔌

SILVER CLOUD HOTEL-BROADWAY   *Book at AAA.com*   Phone: (206)325-1400   **30**

▼▼▼
Hotel
$189-$279 All Year

Address: 1100 Broadway **Location:** Corner of Madison St and Broadway; on Capitol Hill. **Facility:** Smoke free premises. 179 units. 175 one-bedroom standard units, some with whirlpools. 4 one-bedroom suites. 6 stories, interior corridors. *Bath:* combo or shower only. **Parking:** on-site (fee). **Amenities:** video games (fee), high-speed Internet, dual phone lines, voice mail, irons, hair dryers. **Dining:** Cayenne Bar & Grill, see separate listing. **Pool(s):** heated indoor. **Leisure Activities:** whirlpool, exercise room. **Guest Services:** complimentary and valet laundry, area transportation, wireless Internet. **Business Services:** meeting rooms, business center. **Cards:** AX, DC, DS, JC, MC, VI.

🍴 🏊 ⊠ 🎥 🔌 🖥 💻

SILVER CLOUD HOTEL SEATTLE-STADIUM   *Book at AAA.com*   Phone: (206)204-9800   **48**

▼▼▼
Hotel
$229-$399 All Year

Address: 1046 1st Ave S **Location:** Northeast corner of Royal Brougham Way and 1st Ave S. **Facility:** Smoke free premises. 211 units. 185 one-bedroom standard units, some with whirlpools. 26 one-bedroom suites. 9 stories, interior corridors. *Bath:* combo or shower only. **Parking:** valet. **Amenities:** high-speed Internet, dual phone lines, voice mail, irons, hair dryers. **Pool(s):** heated outdoor. **Leisure Activities:** whirlpool, exercise room. **Guest Services:** complimentary and valet laundry, area transportation, wireless Internet. **Business Services:** meeting rooms, business center. **Cards:** AX, DC, DC, JC, MC, VI.

🍴 🍸 CALL [M] 🏊 ⊠ 🎥 🔌 🖥 💻

SILVER CLOUD INN LAKE UNION   *Book at AAA.com*   Phone: (206)447-9500   **1**

▼▼▼
Hotel
$199-$279 All Year

Address: 1150 Fairview Ave N **Location:** I-5, exit 167 (Mercer St); south end of Lake Union. **Facility:** Smoke free premises. 184 units. 150 one-bedroom standard units, some with whirlpools. 34 one-bedroom suites. 7 stories, interior corridors. *Bath:* combo or shower only. **Parking:** on-site. **Amenities:** video games (fee), high-speed Internet, voice mail, irons, hair dryers. **Pool(s):** heated indoor. **Leisure Activities:** whirlpool, exercise room. **Guest Services:** complimentary and valet laundry, area transportation, wireless Internet. **Business Services:** meeting rooms, business center. **Cards:** AX, DC, DS, JC, MC, VI.

🍴 🏊 ⊠ 🎥 🔌 🖥 💻

THE SIXTH AVENUE INN   Phone: 206/441-8300   **20**

AAA [SAVE]
▼▼
Hotel
Rates not provided

Address: 2000 6th Ave **Location:** Jct Virginia St. **Facility:** 167 units. 166 one-bedroom standard units. 1 one-bedroom suite with kitchen. 5 stories, interior corridors. *Bath:* combo or shower only. **Parking:** on-site (fee). **Amenities:** voice mail, irons, hair dryers. *Fee:* video games, high-speed Internet. **Leisure Activities:** exercise room. **Guest Services:** valet and coin laundry, wireless Internet. **Business Services:** meeting rooms, PC.

🍴 🍸 🎥 💻 / SOME UNITS 🐾 ⊠ VCR FEE🔌 FEE🖥

SORRENTO HOTEL   *Book great rates at AAA.com*   Phone: 206/622-6400   **37**

AAA [SAVE]
▼▼▼
Historic
Hotel
Rates not provided

Address: 900 Madison St **Location:** I-5, exit Madison St, just e; at 9th Ave and Madison St. **Facility:** Fronted by wrought-iron gates, this European-style hotel built in 1908 features Old World elegance with modern conveniences. Smoke free premises. 76 units. 53 one-bedroom standard units. 23 one-bedroom suites, some with whirlpools. 7 stories, interior corridors. *Bath:* combo or shower only. **Parking:** valet. **Terms:** check-in 4 pm. **Amenities:** CD players, high-speed Internet, dual phone lines, voice mail, honor bars, irons, hair dryers. *Some:* DVD players. **Dining:** The Hunt Club, see separate listing. **Leisure Activities:** exercise room. *Fee:* massage. **Guest Services:** valet laundry, area transportation-downtown, wireless Internet. **Business Services:** meeting rooms, business center. **Free Special Amenities:** local telephone calls and newspaper. Affiliated with A Preferred Hotel.

🍴 24️ ⊠ 🎥 💻 / SOME UNITS FEE🐾 VCR

WARWICK SEATTLE HOTEL   *Book great rates at AAA.com*   Phone: (206)443-4300   **22**

AAA [SAVE]
▼▼▼
Hotel
$199-$350 3/1-10/31
$149-$290 11/1-2/28

Address: 401 Lenora St **Location:** Corner of 4th Ave and Lenora St. Located in a commercial area. **Facility:** 230 units. 226 one-bedroom standard units. 4 one-bedroom suites with whirlpools. 19 stories, interior corridors. *Bath:* combo or shower only. **Parking:** on-site (fee) and valet. **Terms:** cancellation fee imposed. **Amenities:** video games (fee), dual phone lines, voice mail, safes, irons, hair dryers. *Some:* CD players, honor bars. **Dining:** Brasserie Margaux, see separate listing. **Pool(s):** heated indoor. **Leisure Activities:** sauna, whirlpool, exercise room. **Guest Services:** valet laundry, wireless Internet. **Business Services:** meeting rooms, business center. **Cards:** AX, CB, DC, DS, JC, MC, VI.

🍴 24️ 🏊 ⊠ 🎥 💻 / SOME UNITS ⊠ 🔌

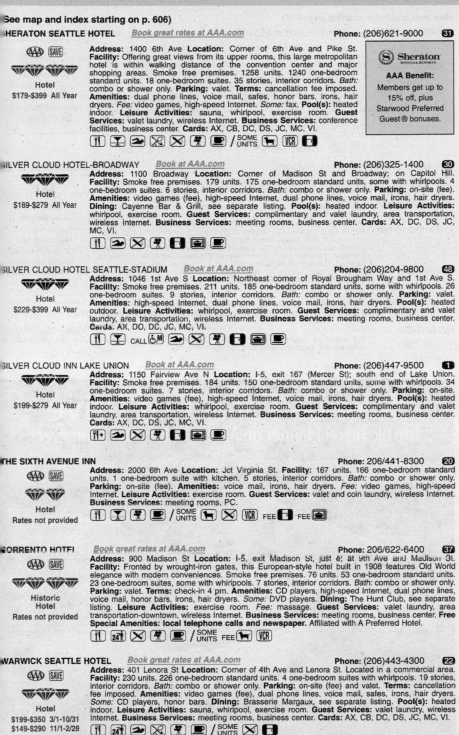

(See map and index starting on p. 606)

THE WESTIN SEATTLE   *Book great rates at AAA.com*   Phone: (206)728-1000

Hotel
$190-$399 All Year

Address: 1900 5th Ave **Location:** Corner of 5th Ave and Stewart St. **Facility:** The Westin's two cylindrical towers stand out on the Seattle skyline; guest rooms have sweeping views of the city and Elliott Bay. Smoke free premises. 891 units. 889 one-bedroom standard units. 2 one-bedroom suites. 47 stories, interior corridors. *Bath:* some combo or shower only. **Parking:** on-site (fee) and valet. **Amenities:** high-speed Internet (fee), dual phone lines, voice mail, safes, honor bars, irons, hair dryers. *Some:* DVD players (fee). **Dining:** Coldwater Bar & Grill, see separate listing. **Pool(s):** heated indoor. **Leisure Activities:** whirlpool, exercise room. **Guest Services:** valet laundry, wireless Internet. **Business Services:** conference facilities, business center. **Cards:** AX, CB, DC, DS, JC, MC, VI.

WESTIN
HOTELS & RESORTS

AAA Benefit:
Enjoy up to 15% off your next stay, plus Starwood Preferred Guest® bonuses.

W SEATTLE . *Book great rates at AAA.com*   Phone: (206)264-6000

Hotel
$239-$509 All Year

Address: 1112 4th Ave **Location:** Corner of 4th Ave and Seneca St. **Facility:** The sleek tower sports polished chrome, bright colors and well-appointed units; a CD, video and board game library is available. 426 units. 425 one-bedroom standard units, some with whirlpools. 1 one-bedroom suite with whirlpool. 26 stories, interior corridors. *Bath:* combo or shower only. **Parking:** valet. **Terms:** cancellation fee imposed. **Amenities:** video library, DVD players, CD players, high-speed Internet (fee), dual phone lines, voice mail, safes, honor bars, irons, hair dryers. **Dining:** Earth & Ocean, see separate listing. **Leisure Activities:** exercise room. **Guest Services:** valet laundry, wireless Internet. **Business Services:** conference facilities, business center. **Cards:** AX, CB, DC, DS, JC, MC, VI.

W
HOTELS

AAA Benefit:
Special member room rates, plus Starwood Preferred Guest® bonuses.

———— *The following lodging was either not evaluated or did not* ————
meet AAA rating requirements but is listed for your information only.

HOTEL ANDRA   Phone: 206/448-8600

(fyi)

Not evaluated. **Address:** 2000 4th Ave **Location:** Corner of Virginia St and 4th Ave. Facilities services, and decor characterize a mid-scale property.

See map and index starting on p. 606)

WHERE TO DINE

3 COINS RESTAURANT — **Phone:** 206/682-2513 ㉓

◆◆◆
American
$8-$35

Diners can look forward to a unique Seattle experience at a diner that's been serving good food since 1967. Chicken parmigiana and fried ice cream are house specialties on a menu that focuses on American fare. Seats at the dining counter offer a view of the cooks in busy mode. Casual dress. **Bar:** Full bar. **Hours:** 24 hours. **Address:** 125 Boren Ave N **Location:** Corner of Boren Ave and John St. **Parking:** on-site. **Cards:** AX, DC, DS, MC, VI.

CALL ♿M

L BOCCALINO RISTORANTE — **Phone:** 206/622-7688 (116)

◆◆
Italian
$10-$25

In a rustic brick building just down from Pioneer Square, this restaurant brings award-winning Italian creations—including a wide array of pasta and seafood offerings, as well as the decadent chocolate terrina dessert—to its hungry guests. The lively interior incorporates linoleum floors, brick walls and wood accents. Casual dress. **Bar:** Beer & wine. **Reservations:** suggested, weekends. **Hours:** 11:30 am-2:30 & 5-10 pm. Closed major holidays; also Sun. **Address:** 1 Yesler Way **Location:** Just w of 1st Ave. **Parking:** street. **Cards:** AX, MC, VI.

ANDALUCA *Menu on AAA.com* — **Phone:** 206/382-6999 (72)

AAA
◆◆◆
Mediterranean
$5-$42

Mediterranean influences punctuate preparations of fresh Northwestern ingredients. Casual dress. **Bar:** Full bar. **Reservations:** suggested. **Hours:** 6-10:30 am, 11:30-2:30 & 5-10 pm, Fri & Sat 6 am-10:30 & 5-11 pm. **Address:** 407 Olive Way **Location:** Corner of 4th Ave and Olive Way; in Mayflower Park Hotel. **Parking:** valet. **Cards:** AX, CB, DC, DS, MC, VI.

ANTHONY'S RESTAURANT — **Phone:** 206/448-6688 (79)

◆◆◆
Seafood
$19-$39

On the waterfront, the nautically contemporary restaurant offers views of Elliott Bay and the surrounding mountains, which are as pleasing as the selection of fresh seafood. This place is well suited for tourists, businesspeople and special-occasion diners. Casual dress. **Bar:** Full bar. **Reservations:** suggested. **Hours:** 5 pm-10 pm, Fri & Sat-10:30 pm. Closed: 11/26, 12/25. **Address:** 2201 Alaskan Way **Location:** At Pier 66. **Parking:** valet and street. **Cards:** AX, DC, DS, MC, VI.

CALL ♿M

AOKI JAPANESE GRILL & SUSHI BAR — **Phone:** 206/324-3633 ⑫

◆◆
Japanese
$6-$18

Choices and combinations range from steak, chicken and vegetables to an extensive array of seafood. This location is popular with the local community. Casual dress. **Bar:** Beer & wine. **Hours:** 11:30 am-3 & 5-10 pm, Fri & Sat-11 pm, Sun 5 pm-10 pm. Closed major holidays; also Mon. **Address:** 621 Broadway E **Location:** Between Roy and Mercer sts; in Capitol Hill District. **Parking:** street. **Cards:** AX, DC, MC, VI.

ASSAGGIO RISTORANTE — **Phone:** 206/441-1399 (51)

◆◆◆
Italian
$12-$30

The restaurant features Central and Northern Italian cuisine as well as award-winning Italian vintage wines, all served in an upscale dining room with sculptures and soft lighting. Casual dress. **Bar:** Full bar. **Reservations:** suggested. **Hours:** 11 am-2 & 5-10 pm, Sat from 5 pm. Closed major holidays; also Sun. **Address:** 2010 4th Ave **Location:** Jct Virginia St; adjacent to Hotel Andra; in Belltown area. **Parking:** valet and street. **Cards:** AX, DC, DS, MC, VI.

CALL ♿M

ATHENIAN INN — **Phone:** 206/624-7166 (91)

◆◆
Seafood
$6-$16

An American institution, the restaurant has been serving fresh seafood overlooking the water in Pike Place Market since 1909. Casual dress. **Bar:** Full bar. **Hours:** 6:30 am-6:30 pm, Sun 4 pm. Closed major holidays; also Sun 10/1-4/30. **Address:** 1517 Pike Pl **Location:** In Pike Place Market. **Parking:** street. **Cards:** AX, DS, MC, VI.

AYUTTHAYA — **Phone:** 206/324-8833 ㊸

◆◆
Thai
$6-$11

Many chef's recommendations are among Thai selections at the casual storefront restaurant. Casual dress. **Bar:** Beer & wine. **Reservations:** accepted. **Hours:** 11:30 am-2:30 & 5-9:30 pm, Fri-10 pm, Sat 5 pm-10 pm, Sun 5 pm-9:30 pm. Closed major holidays. **Address:** 727 E Pike St **Location:** Between Boylston and Harvard aves; in Capitol Hill District. **Parking:** street. **Cards:** AX, MC, VI.

BAHN THAI RESTAURANT — **Phone:** 206/283-0444 ⑦

◆◆
Thai
$6-$14

One of the city's first authentic Thai restaurants, the establishment has been in operation since 1984. On the menu are preparations of seafood, chicken and beef, as well as curry and several vegetarian dishes, all prepared without monosodium glutamate. In a former house in the lower Queen Anne area, this place draws many opera, ballet and other nearby event attendees. Patrons may request a table by the aquarium to watch the fish while dining. Casual dress. **Bar:** Beer & wine. **Reservations:** suggested. **Hours:** 11:30 am-3 & 4:30-9:30 pm, Fri-10 pm, Sat 4 pm-10 pm, Sun 4 pm-9:30 pm. Closed major holidays. **Address:** 409 Roy St **Location:** I-5, exit 167 (Mercer St), Valley St to 5th Ave, then just n; near Seattle Center. **Parking:** on-site and street. **Cards:** AX, DS, MC, VI.

BAKEMAN'S RESTAURANT — **Phone:** 206/622-3375 (112)

◆
American
$4-$7

The basement lunch counter harks back to an era when the working masses came down from their office buildings for a quick bite. On the menu are custom-made sandwiches, hot soup and fresh pie. Casual dress. **Reservations:** not accepted. **Hours:** 10 am-3 pm. Closed major holidays; also Sat, Sun & weeks of 7/4 & 12/25. **Address:** 122 Cherry St **Location:** Between 1st and 2nd aves; in Pioneer Square District. **Parking:** street.

(See map and index starting on p. 606)

BAMBOO GARDEN
▼▼ ▼▼▼
Vegetarian
$8-$21
Phone: 206/282-6616 6

This family-run, all-vegetarian restaurant offers traditional-tasting Chinese food using faux meats and seafood and no dairy products. Parking is a premium in Seattle; this restaurant has onsite parking. Casual dress. **Bar:** Full bar. **Reservations:** suggested. **Hours:** 11 am-10 pm. **Address:** 364 Roy St **Location:** Near jct Summit Ave E; in South Lake Union area. **Parking:** on-site. **Cards:** AX, DC, DS, MC, VI.

BELLTOWN BISTRO
▼▼▼▼▼
American
$10-$25
Phone: 206/728-2000 48

An intimate gathering spot for couples or groups of friends looking for a great meal after bar-hopping in the city's trendy Belltown area, the bistro features soft lighting and soothing music. Dungeness crab macaroni and cheese won't disappoint. Casual dress. **Bar:** Full bar. **Reservations:** accepted. **Hours:** 4 pm-2 am. Closed: 11/26, 12/25. **Address:** 2322 1st Ave **Location:** Between Bell and Battery sts; in Belltown area. **Parking:** street. **Cards:** AX, DC, MC, VI.

BLUE MOON BURGERS
▼▼▼
American
$8-$12
Phone: 206/652-0400 16

Patrons walk up to order traditional burgers or maybe wild king salmon burgers for a fun change. Also on the menu are chicken sandwiches and a few salads. Casual dress. **Bar:** Beer only. **Reservations:** not accepted. **Hours:** 11 am-9 pm, Sat noon-6 pm, Sun noon-5 pm. Closed: 11/26, 12/25. **Address:** 920 Republican St **Location:** Between Westlake and Terry aves; in South Lake Union area. **Parking:** street **Cards:** AX, MC, VI.

BLUWATER BISTRO
▼▼ ▼▼▼
American
$9-$26
Phone: 206/447-0769 2

The high-energy bistro offers picturesque deck seating in season. Choices range from pork chop with whipped potatoes to cheese-filled ravioli and hearty cups of clam chowder. Chocolate fondue is worth a splurge. Casual dress. **Bar:** Full bar. **Reservations:** accepted. **Hours:** 11:30 am-1 am. Closed: 11/26, 12/25. **Address:** 1001 Fairview Ave N **Location:** I-5, exit 167 (Mercer St); southeast end of Lake Union. **Parking:** on-site (fee). **Cards:** AX, DC, MC, VI.

BRASA
▼▼ ▼▼▼
Mediterranean
$17-$30
Phone: 206/728-4220 55

In trendy Belltown, the bistro presents a menu of Seattle-style dishes infused with Mediterranean flavor. Memorable courses might include squid ink risotto with sauteed calamari or roasted suckling pig with garlic mashed potatoes. Casual dress. **Bar:** Full bar. **Reservations:** accepted. **Hours:** 5 pm-10:30 pm, Fri & Sat-11 pm. Closed major holidays. **Address:** 2107 3rd Ave **Location:** Corner of 3rd Ave and Lenora St. **Parking:** street. **Cards:** AX, CB, DC, DS, MC, VI.

BRASSERIE MARGAUX
ⒶⒶⒶ
▼▼▼▼▼
French
$9-$26
Phone: 206/777-1990 44

A warm, intimate ambience pervades the casual yet tony dining room, which reflects a dignified Old World charm. The restaurant spotlights culinary offerings influenced by Mediterranean, Caribbean, South American, French and Northwest cuisines. Casual dress. **Bar:** Full bar. **Reservations:** suggested. **Hours:** 6:30 am-2 & 5-10 pm. **Address:** 401 Lenora St **Location:** Corner of 4th Ave and Lenora St; in Warwick Seattle Hotel. **Parking:** on-site. **Cards:** AX, CB, DC, DS, JC, MC, VI.

BROADWAY GRILL
▼▼ ▼▼ ▼▼
American
$9-$19
Phone: 206/328-7000 18

The open-grill kitchen offers creative twists on grill items; intimate dining is available in the evening. Casual dress. **Bar:** Full bar. **Reservations:** not accepted. **Hours:** 9 am-2 am, Sat & Sun from 8 am. Closed: 12/25. **Address:** 314 Broadway E **Location:** Jct E Olive Way; in Capitol Hill area. **Parking:** street. **Cards:** AX, DC, MC, VI.

THE BROOKLYN SEAFOOD, STEAK & OYSTER HOUSE
ⒶⒶⒶ
▼▼▼▼▼
Steak & Seafood
$10-$40
Phone: 206/224-7000 103

This is the place to go for raw oysters, quality seafood and steaks. Nine distinctive varieties of the mollusks entice adventurous palates, while presentations inform about the history and art of harvesting and eating the cold-water creatures. Guests can reserve one of the oversize chairs at the exhibition table to watch the chefs prepare the tasty food. Dressy casual. **Bar:** Full bar. **Reservations:** suggested. **Hours:** 11 am-3 & 5-10 pm, Fri-10:30 pm, Sat 4:30 pm-10:30 pm, Sun 4 pm-10 pm. Closed: 1/1, 11/26, 12/25. **Address:** 1212 2nd Ave **Location:** Corner of 2nd Ave and University St. **Parking:** valet and street. **Cards:** AX, CB, DC, DS, JC, MC, VI.

CALL

BUENOS AIRES GRILL
▼▼ ▼▼
Argentine
$20-$35
Phone: 206/441-7076 74

Patrons can relax in the festive dining room and watch as the busy chefs create Argentinean selections. Choices on the extensive menu include preparations of steak, pork, sausage and shortbreads, as well as desserts made on site. Noise levels often rise as diners enjoy the upbeat experience, which is enhanced by skilled, attentive service. A tango show entertains guests on Friday and Saturday evenings. Casual dress. **Bar:** Full bar. **Reservations:** suggested. **Hours:** 5 pm-10:30 pm, Fri & Sat-midnight. Closed: 9/7. **Address:** 220 Virginia St **Location:** Jct Virginia St and 2nd Ave. **Parking:** street. **Cards:** DC, MC, VI.

BUSH GARDEN
▼▼ ▼▼
Japanese
$8-$16
Phone: 206/682-6830 125

A very popular spot, the eatery features Japanese decor complete with a small waterfall, private tatami rooms, karaoke and a sushi bar. Great meals like gyoza pot stickers, and shrimp wrapped in bacon and white rice come with green tea and soup. Casual dress. **Bar:** Full bar. **Reservations:** suggested. **Hours:** 11:30 am-2 & 5-10 pm, Sun 5 pm-9 pm. Closed major holidays. **Address:** 614 Maynard Ave S **Location:** On Maynard Ave S; between S Lane and S Weller sts; in International District. **Parking:** on-site. **Cards:** AX, DC, DS, MC, VI.

THE BYZANTION
▼▼ ▼▼
Greek
$6-$22
Phone: 206/325-7580 14

The intimate, family-run restaurant offers authentic Greek cuisine in a very casual setting. Casual dress. **Bar:** Full bar. **Reservations:** accepted. **Hours:** 5 pm-10 pm, Fri-Sun from 11:30 am. **Address:** 601 Broadway E **Location:** Just s of jct E Roy St; in Capitol Hill area. **Parking:** street. **Cards:** MC, VI.

See map and index starting on p. 606)

AFE BENGODI **Phone:** 206/381-0705 (114)

Italian
$7-$13

The casual family-run corner trattoria features homemade sausage; limited seating. Casual dress. **Bar:** Beer & wine. **Reservations:** accepted. **Hours:** 11 am-9 pm, Fri & Sat-9:30 pm. Closed: 1/1, 11/26, 12/25. **Address:** 700 1st Ave **Location:** Jct Cherry St; in Pioneer Square. **Parking:** street. **Cards:** AX, DS, MC, VI.

AFE CAMPAGNE **Phone:** 206/728-2233 (86)

French
$11-$21

Just above Pike Place Market in Post Alley, the quaint French cafe prepares bistro-style lunches. The separate dessert menu is loaded with temptations. Alley cobblestones and cafe drapes evoke France. Casual dress. **Bar:** Full bar. **Reservations:** accepted. **Hours:** 11 am-10 pm, Fri-11 pm, Sat 8 am-11 pm, Sun 8 am-10 pm. Closed: 1/1, 11/26, 12/25. **Address:** 1600 Post Alley at Pine **Location:** Northwest corner of 1st Ave and Pine St; at historic Pike Place Market; in Inn at the Market. **Parking:** street. **Cards:** AX, CB, DC, DS, MC, VI.

AFE HUE **Phone:** 206/625-9833 (118)

Vietnamese
$7-$30

Located in a historic building, the casual family-run eatery serves authentic cuisine and is busy at lunch. Casual dress. **Bar:** Beer & wine. **Reservations:** accepted. **Hours:** 11 am-9 pm, Sun-3 pm. Closed: 12/24, 12/25. **Address:** 314 2nd Ave S **Location:** Between Main and Jackson sts; in Pioneer Square Historic District. **Parking:** street. **Cards:** MC, VI.

AFE SEPTIEME **Phone:** 206/860-8858 (22)

Mediterranean
$5-$24

The eatery serves casual, European bistro-style fare at lunch and a bit more sophisticated offerings at dinner. Regional seafood is featured in the cafe's menu, which focuses on French cuisine. Casual dress. **Bar:** Full bar. **Reservations:** accepted. **Hours:** 9 am-midnight. Closed: 11/26. **Address:** 214 Broadway E **Location:** Just n of jct E Olive Way; in Capitol Hill area. **Parking:** street. **Cards:** AX, DC, DS, JC, MC, VI.

AFFE LADRO **Phone:** 206/282-1549 (10)

Coffee/Tea
$2-$9

With many locations, the eatery features an espresso bar and bakery and is good for people-watching. Casual dress. **Hours:** 5:30 am-11 pm; hours may vary holidays. **Address:** 600 Queen Ave N **Location:** Jct Mercer St; in Queen Anne area. **Parking:** street. **Cards:** AX, MC, VI.

AMPAGNE **Phone:** 206/728-2800 (85)

French
$28-$39

The intimate French dining room offers romantic courtyard seating or window seating with a view of Elliott Bay and Pike Place Market. The menu, which changes every two months, might include such items as cold lobster salad in a citrus/caviar cream dressing or foie gras and rack of lamb. Casual dress. **Bar:** Full bar. **Reservations:** suggested. **Hours:** 5:30 pm-10 pm. Closed: 1/1, 11/26, 12/25. **Address:** 86 Pine St **Location:** Northwest corner of 1st Ave and Pine St; at historic Pike Place Market; in Inn at the Market. **Parking:** street. **Cards:** AX, CB, DC, DS, MC, VI.

CASCADIA **Phone:** 206/448-8884 (46)

Regional American
$20-$48

In the trendy Belltown section, the restaurant offers fine dining with an urban flair. The Northwest menu highlights the best available in local fresh produce, meats and seafood. Patrons can choose to order a la carte or from the prix fixe tasting menu. Dressy casual. **Reservations:** suggested. **Hours:** 5 pm-10 pm, Fri & Sat-10:30 pm. Closed: 1/1, 7/4, 12/25; also Sun. **Address:** 2328 1st Ave **Location:** Between Bell and Battery sts; in Belltown area. **Parking:** street. **Cards:** AX, MC, VI.

CAYENNE BAR & GRILL **Phone:** 206/204-1188 (76)

American
$7-$20

The eatery offers an American menu with sandwiches and burgers along with many southwest choices like a steak burrito, marinated skirt steak and fish tacos. Casual dress. **Bar:** Full bar. **Reservations:** accepted. **Hours:** 11:30 am-10 pm. **Address:** 1100 Broadway **Location:** Corner of Madison St and Broadway; on Capitol Hill; in Silver Cloud Hotel-Broadway. **Parking:** on-site. **Cards:** AX, CB, DC, DS, JC, MC, VI.

CHANDLERS CRABHOUSE **Phone:** 206/223-2722 (5)

Seafood
$12-$40

Menu offerings include a variety of seafood, steak and chicken entrees as well as a few signature dishes like mahi-mahi, lightly breaded and served with a sweet mango chutney, or the clam chowder, served thick with lots of clams and potatoes. Spectacular views of the lake and marina enhance the dining experience. Casual dress. **Bar:** Full bar. **Reservations:** suggested. **Hours:** 11 am-9 pm, Fri-10 pm, Sat 10 am-10 pm, Sun 10 am-9 pm. Closed: 12/25. **Address:** 901 Fairview Ave N **Location:** I-5, exit 167 (Mercer St); southeast end of Lake Union. **Parking:** valet and street. **Cards:** AX, CB, DC, DS, JC, MC, VI.

CHEZ SHEA **Phone:** 206/467-9990 (89)

Regional American
$25-$37

Enjoy an intimate four-course prix fixe meal made from the freshest local ingredients while relaxing in this romantic upstairs hideaway, where the sun sets over Elliott Bay and the distant Olympic Mountains. If you are looking for a more casual meal, try the Mediterranean-infused bistro menu in the lounge. Dressy casual. **Bar:** Full bar. **Reservations:** required. **Hours:** 5 pm-10 pm. Closed: 1/1, 11/26, 12/25; also Mon. **Address:** 94 Pike St, Suite 34 **Location:** Corner of Market Building, top floor; in Pike Place Market. **Parking:** street. **Cards:** AX, MC, VI.

THE CHINA GATE **Phone:** 206/624-1730 (123)

Chinese
$7-$16

Featuring a very large dining room decorated with golden dragons and red accents, the restaurant offers an extensive menu of authentic cuisine and excellent dim sum. Casual dress. **Bar:** Full bar. **Reservations:** accepted. **Hours:** 9 am-1 am. **Address:** 516 7th Ave S **Location:** Jct King St S; in International District. **Parking:** street. **Cards:** AX, MC, VI.

CHUTNEY'S **Phone:** 206/284-6799 (17)

Indian
$8-$16

Featuring authentic Indian cuisine and friendly service, the restaurant has more than one location. Casual dress. **Bar:** Full bar. **Reservations:** accepted. **Hours:** 11:30 am-2:30 & 5-10 pm, Fri & Sat-10:30 pm, Sun 5 pm-10 pm. Closed: 11/26, 12/25. **Address:** 519 1st Ave N **Location:** Just s of Mercer St; in Queen Anne area. **Parking:** street. **Cards:** AX, DC, MC, VI.

(See map and index starting on p. 606)

CJ'S EATERY
▽▽ ▽▽
American
$5-$11

Phone: 206/728-1648 ②■

Experience breakfast and lunch in a New York deli-style. Friendly and informative servers dish up a goo selection of deli favorites including a latke that's a potato pancake served with applesauce and sour crea or perhaps the tofu veggie saute. Also try one of the outstanding burgers. Casual dress. **Bar:** Beer & win **Hours:** 7 am-3 pm. Closed: 11/26, 12/25. **Address:** 2619 1st Ave **Location:** Cross street Cedar; in Belltow area. **Parking:** street. **Cards:** AX, DS, MC, VI.

COLDWATER BAR & GRILL
▽▽▽▽▽▽
Seafood
$12-$42

Phone: 206/256-7697 ⑤(

Fresh Northwestern seafood, including raw-bar items, is central to the hotel restaurant's offering of Seatt food. Casual dress. **Bar:** Full bar. **Reservations:** suggested. **Hours:** 6-10 am, 11:30-2 & 5:30-9:30 pm, F & Sat-10 pm. **Address:** 1900 5th Ave **Location:** Corner of 5th Ave and Stewart St; in The Westin Seattle **Parking:** valet. **Cards:** AX, CB, DC, DS, JC, MC, VI.

CREPE DE PARIS
▽▽ ▽▽
French
$10-$28

Phone: 206/623-4111 ⑧

Crepes any way you like them, from a delicate seafood crepe to a decadent chocolate crepe for desser cabaret shows in the evening. Casual dress. **Bar:** Full bar. **Reservations:** suggested. **Hours:** 11 am-3 & 5 10 pm. Closed major holidays; also Sun. **Address:** 1333 5th Ave **Location:** Jct Union St; in Rainier Square **Parking:** street. **Cards:** AX, DC, DS, MC, VI.

CUTTER'S BAYHOUSE
▽▽ ▽▽
Seafood
$9-$45

Phone: 206/448-4884 ⑧(

Next to bustling Pike Place Market, the fantastic waterfront location overlooks Elliot Bay. Eight-foot window all around the dining area enable patrons to enjoy fabulous views of the city skyline. Fresh fish and othe seafood dominate the menu, which also lists prime steaks, pasta and sushi. Beautifully presented dishe are excellently prepared. Dressy casual. **Bar:** Full bar. **Reservations:** accepted. **Hours:** 9:30 am-10 pm Sun-9:30 pm. Closed: 12/25. **Address:** 2001 Western Ave **Location:** Between Virginia and Lenora sts; jus n of Pike Place Market. **Parking:** on-site and street. **Cards:** AX, DC, DS, MC, VI.

CYCLOPS
▽▽ ▽▽
American
$8-$16

Phone: 206/441-1677 ④(

A huge eye is the sign pointing you to the restaurant's location. The decor is retro, but the cuisine is now Mexican cuisine is the highlight of the weekend breakfasts. Casual dress. **Bar:** Full ba **Reservations:** accepted. **Hours:** 3 pm-midnight, Sat from 9 am, Sun 9 am-10 pm. Closed: 11/26, 12/25 **Address:** 2421 1st Ave **Location:** Jct Wall St; in Belltown area. **Parking:** street. **Cards:** MC, VI.

ᴀᴄ

DAHLIA LOUNGE
▽▽▽▽▽▽
American
$10-$40

Phone: 206/682-4142 ⑤⑤

Imaginative Northwest cuisine is served in a warm, romantic atmosphere where both business associate and couples enjoy a pleasing experience. Friends can meet in the small bar before sitting down to a dinne of crispy roasted duck or maybe the house specialty crab cakes. Among enticing desserts are the pear tar with almond cream or coconut cream pie with white chocolate. Dressy casual. **Bar:** Full ba **Reservations:** suggested. **Hours:** 11:30 am-2:30 & 5-10 pm, Fri-11 pm, Sat 5 pm-11 pm, Sun 5 pm-9 pm Closed major holidays. **Address:** 2001 4th Ave **Location:** Corner of 4th Ave and Virginia St. **Parking:** vale and street. **Cards:** AX, CB, DC, DS, MC, VI.

DIMITRIOU'S JAZZ ALLEY RESTAURANT &
   NIGHTCLUB
▽▽ ▽▽
International
$22-$36

Phone: 206/441-9729 ③③

The well-known, award-winning jazz club recently was renovated and expanded. Although the dress code i casual, patrons typically don dressy casual attire. All tables in the tiered, two-story dining room afford views of the stage. The menu centers on Northwest cuisine. The ticket price does not include cost of dinner, and the purchase of a show ticket is required for entry. Casual dress. **Bar:** Full bar. **Reservations:** suggested **Hours:** 5:30 pm-11 pm, Tues, Wed & Sun 7:30 pm seating, Thurs-Sat 7:30 pm & 9:30 pm seating. Closed 1/1, 11/26, 12/24, 12/25; also Mon. **Address:** 2033 6th Ave **Location:** Corner of 6th Ave and Lenora S **Parking:** on-site. **Cards:** AX, MC, VI.

DRAGONFISH ASIAN CAFE
▽▽▽▽▽▽
Asian
$6-$19

Phone: 206/467-7777 ⑤⑧

The pop-culture-themed Asian bistro provides a lively environment. Guests sample twists on popular dishe of China, Japan, Korea, Thailand, Vietnam and Singapore. Wok preparations of meat, seafood, vegetables and fried rice delight the eyes and taste buds. Casual dress. **Bar:** Full bar. **Reservations:** suggested **Hours:** 7 am-1 am. Closed: 11/26, 12/25. **Address:** 722 Pine St **Location:** Corner of 8th Ave and Pine St in The Paramount Hotel, A Coast Hotel. **Parking:** street. **Cards:** AX, DS, MC, VI.

CALL Ⓛ Ⓜ

DUKE'S CHOWDER HOUSE
▽▽▽▽ ▽▽
Seafood
$10-$25

Phone: 206/382-9963 ③

The name says it all. Guests can expect excellent chowder in an impressive number of varieties, in additio to fresh seafood and meat dishes. Nautical decor lends character to the dining room. Casual dress. **Bar** Full bar. **Reservations:** accepted. **Hours:** 11:30 am-midnight. Closed: 11/26, 12/24, 12/25. **Address:** 90 Fairview Ave N **Location:** I-5, exit 167 (Mercer St); southeast end of Lake Union. **Parking:** on-site (fee) and valet. **Cards:** AX, DS, MC, VI.

EARTH & OCEAN
▽▽▽▽▽▽
American
$10-$30

Phone: 206-264-6060 ⑩②

A dark ambiance blends with a hip menu at this stylish and trendy restaurant. Offerings include such favorites as carrot soup with lobster and lime, wild boar ravioli, shepherd's pie with braised oxtail, spring rabbit stew and grilled lamb. Don't leave without trying any of their specialty desserts that boast catchy names like coco la te da and cherry pop tart. Dressy casual. **Bar:** Full bar. **Reservations:** suggested **Hours:** 6:30-10:30 am, 11:30-2 & 5-10 pm, Fri-10:30 pm, Sat 7:30 am-1:30 & 5-10:30 pm, Sun 7:30 am 1:30 pm. **Address:** 1112 4th Ave **Location:** Corner of 4th Ave and Seneca St; in W Seattle. **Parking:** vale and street. **Cards:** AX, CB, DC, DS, JC, MC, VI.

(See map and index starting on p. 606)

EL GAUCHO
Phone: 206/728-1337 (32)
Steak & Seafood
$23-$74
A remake of the classic metropolitan steak house, the restaurant features comfortable banquettes in a theater-in-the-round-style dining room. Jazz music entertains the bar crowd as diners enjoy table-side preparations of vodka-flamed lamb tenderloin. Dressy casual. Entertainment. **Bar:** Full bar. **Reservations:** suggested. **Hours:** 5 pm-1 am, Sun-11 pm. Closed major holidays. **Address:** 2505 1st Ave **Location:** Between Wall and Vine sts; in Belltown area. **Parking:** valet and street. **Cards:** AX, CB, DC, JC, MC, VI.

ELLIOTT'S OYSTER HOUSE
Phone: 206/623-4340 (108)
Seafood
$10-$36
The oyster bar is the big draw at the noisy, energetic restaurant, which sits on Elliott Bay. Enjoy thoughtfully prepared entrees of fresh seafood as well as the pastry chef's sweet creations. Outside deck seating is popular during the summer. Casual dress. **Bar:** Full bar. **Reservations:** suggested. **Hours:** 11 am-10 pm, Fri & Sat-11 pm. Closed: 11/26, 12/25. **Address:** Pier 56-Alaskan Way, Suite 100 **Location:** On waterfront; at Pier 56. **Parking:** valet and street. **Cards:** AX, CB, DC, DS, JC, MC, VI.

ELYSIAN BREWING
Phone: 206/860-1920 (45)
American
$8-$13
On Capitol Hill, the neighborhood fixture has been brewing beer and serving great-tasting food for years. Casual dress. **Bar:** Full bar. **Reservations:** not accepted. **Hours:** 11:30 am-11 pm, Sat from noon. Closed: 1/1, 11/26, 12/25. **Address:** 1221 E Pike St **Location:** Southeast corner of Pike and 13th sts; in Capitol Hill area. **Parking:** street. **Cards:** AX, DS, MC, VI.

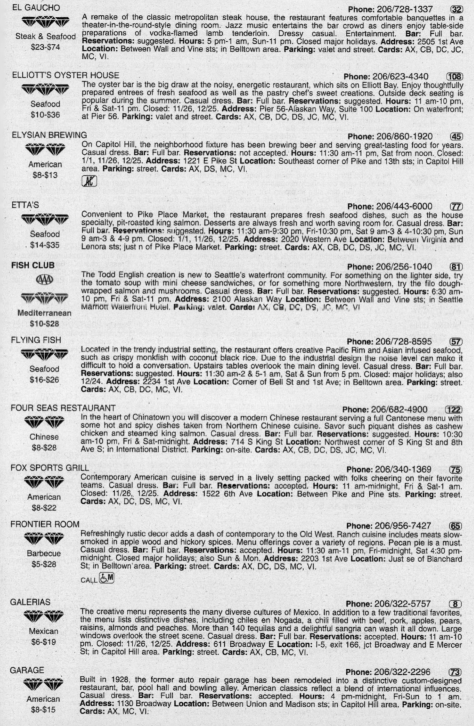

ETTA'S
Phone: 206/443-6000 (77)
Seafood
$14-$35
Convenient to Pike Place Market, the restaurant prepares fresh seafood dishes, such as the house specialty, pit-roasted king salmon. Desserts are always fresh and worth saving room for. Casual dress. **Bar:** Full bar. **Reservations:** suggested. **Hours:** 11:30 am-9:30 pm, Fri-10:30 pm, Sat 9 am-3 & 4-10:30 pm, Sun 9 am-3 & 4-9 pm. Closed: 1/1, 11/26, 12/25. **Address:** 2020 Western Ave **Location:** Between Virginia and Lenora sts; just n of Pike Place Market. **Parking:** street. **Cards:** AX, CB, DC, DS, JC, MC, VI.

FISH CLUB
Phone: 206/256-1040 (81)
(AAA)
Mediterranean
$10-$28
The Todd English creation is new to Seattle's waterfront community. For something on the lighter side, try the tomato soup with mini cheese sandwiches, or for something more Northwestern, try the filo dough-wrapped salmon and mushrooms. Casual dress. **Bar:** Full bar. **Reservations:** suggested. **Hours:** 6:30 am-10 pm, Fri & Sat-11 pm. **Address:** 2100 Alaskan Way **Location:** Between Wall and Vine sts; in Seattle Marriott Waterfront Hotel. **Parking:** valet. **Cards:** AX, CB, DC, DS, JC, MC, VI.

FLYING FISH
Phone: 206/728-8595 (57)
Seafood
$16-$26
Located in the trendy industrial setting, the restaurant offers creative Pacific Rim and Asian infused seafood, such as crispy monkfish with coconut black rice. Due to the industrial design the noise level can make it difficult to hold a conversation. Upstairs tables overlook the main dining level. Casual dress. **Bar:** Full bar. **Reservations:** suggested. **Hours:** 11:30 am-2 & 5-1 am, Sat & Sun from 5 pm. Closed: major holidays; also 12/24. **Address:** 2234 1st Ave **Location:** Corner of Bell St and 1st Ave; in Belltown area. **Parking:** street. **Cards:** AX, CB, DC, MC, VI.

FOUR SEAS RESTAURANT
Phone: 206/682-4900 (122)
Chinese
$8-$28
In the heart of Chinatown you will discover a modern Chinese restaurant serving a full Cantonese menu with some hot and spicy dishes taken from Northern Chinese cuisine. Savor such piquant dishes as cashew chicken and steamed king salmon. Casual dress. **Bar:** Full bar. **Reservations:** suggested. **Hours:** 10:30 am-10 pm, Fri & Sat-midnight. **Address:** 714 S King St **Location:** Northwest corner of S King St and 8th Ave S; in International District. **Parking:** on-site. **Cards:** AX, CB, DC, DS, JC, MC, VI.

FOX SPORTS GRILL
Phone: 206/340-1369 (75)
American
$8-$22
Contemporary American cuisine is served in a lively setting packed with folks cheering on their favorite teams. Casual dress. **Bar:** Full bar. **Reservations:** accepted. **Hours:** 11 am-midnight, Fri & Sat-1 am. Closed: 11/26, 12/25. **Address:** 1522 6th Ave **Location:** Between Pike and Pine sts. **Parking:** street. **Cards:** AX, DC, DS, MC, VI.

FRONTIER ROOM
Phone: 206/956-7427 (65)
Barbecue
$5-$28
Refreshingly rustic decor adds a dash of contemporary to the Old West. Ranch cuisine includes meats slow-smoked in apple wood and hickory spices. Menu offerings cover a variety of regions. Pecan pie is a must. Casual dress. **Bar:** Full bar. **Reservations:** accepted. **Hours:** 11:30 am-11 pm, Fri-midnight, Sat 4:30 pm-midnight. Closed major holidays; also Sun & Mon. **Address:** 2203 1st Ave **Location:** Just se of Blanchard St; in Belltown area. **Parking:** street. **Cards:** AX, DC, DS, MC, VI.
CALL [M]

GALERIAS
Phone: 206/322-5757 (8)
Mexican
$6-$19
The creative menu represents the many diverse cultures of Mexico. In addition to a few traditional favorites, the menu lists distinctive dishes, including chiles en Nogada, a chili filled with beef, pork, apples, pears, raisins, almonds and peaches. More than 140 tequilas and a delightful sangria can wash it all down. Large windows overlook the street scene. Casual dress. **Bar:** Full bar. **Reservations:** accepted. **Hours:** 11 am-10 pm. Closed: 11/26, 12/25. **Address:** 611 Broadway E **Location:** I-5, exit 166, jct Broadway and E Mercer St; in Capitol Hill area. **Parking:** street. **Cards:** AX, CB, MC, VI.

GARAGE
Phone: 206/322-2296 (73)
American
$8-$15
Built in 1928, the former auto repair garage has been remodeled into a distinctive custom-designed restaurant, bar, pool hall and bowling alley. American classics reflect a blend of international influences. Casual dress. **Bar:** Full bar. **Reservations:** accepted. **Hours:** 4 pm-midnight, Fri-Sun to 1 am. **Address:** 1130 Broadway **Location:** Between Union and Madison sts; in Capitol Hill area. **Parking:** on-site. **Cards:** AX, MC, VI.

(See map and index starting on p. 606)

THE GEORGIAN
Phone: 206/621-1700 [96]

Regional American
$12-$49

The grand, elegant dining room is adorned with formal Renaissance appointments and gilded trims. Carefully prepared and creatively presented dishes on the Continental menu are created from fresh, local ingredients. Seafood is always a solid choice in the Northwest, so a good meal might include the trio of cakes, Canadian lobster and a souffle for dessert. Dressy casual. Entertainment. **Bar:** Full bar. **Reservations:** suggested. **Hours:** 6:30 am-2:30 & 5:30-10 pm, Fri-10:30 pm, Sat 7 am-2:30 & 5:30-10:30 pm, Sun 7 am-2:30 & 5:30-10 pm. **Address:** 411 University St **Location:** Corner of 4th Ave and University St; in The Fairmont Olympic Hotel. **Parking:** valet and street. **Cards:** AX, CB, DC, DS, JC, MC, VI. **Historic**

GORDON BIERSCH BREWERY RESTAURANT
Phone: 206/405-4205 [66]

American
$7-$25

As the name implies this restaurant features fresh, brewed-on-site beer which is crafted in a German tradition. What may not be evident is the wide variety of foods like meal-sized salads, burgers and sandwiches, pizza, pastas, steaks and seafood that is also a huge draw for an upscale, casual dining experience. Casual dress. **Bar:** Full bar. **Reservations:** accepted. **Hours:** 11:30 am-10 pm, Fri & Sat-11 pm. Closed: 11/26, 12/25. **Address:** 600 Pine St, Suite 401 **Location:** On 4th floor of Pacific Place Mall. **Parking:** on-site (fee). **Cards:** AX, CB, DC, DS, MC, VI.

HOUSE OF HONG
Phone: 206/622-7997 [119]

Chinese
$5-$28

It's a good thing the dining room is huge, as the cuisine brings in crowds. Guests may choose either dim sum from carts continually circulating the room or mark a choice from the order sheet. Served from bamboo steamers, the dim sum is piping hot, aromatic and delicious. Traditional dishes also are offered. Casual dress. **Bar:** Full bar. **Hours:** 9 am-2 am, Sun-midnight. **Address:** 409 8th Ave S **Location:** Between Jackson and King sts; in International District. **Parking:** on-site and street. **Cards:** AX, MC, VI.

CALL 🔲M

THE HUNT CLUB
Phone: 206/343-6156 [88]

American
$10-$40

Artistically presented Northwest and Mediterranean cuisine is the focus at the intimate restaurant. Attentive, knowledgeable staff members serve beautifully arranged dishes. Dressy casual. **Bar:** Full bar. **Reservations:** suggested. **Hours:** 7-10:30 am, 11-2 & 5-9 pm, Fri & Sat-10 pm. **Address:** 900 Madison St **Location:** I-5, exit Madison St, just e; at 9th Ave and Madison St; in Sorrento Hotel. **Parking:** valet. **Cards:** AX, CB, DC, DS, JC, MC, VI.

HUONG BINH
Phone: 206/720-4907 [121]

Vietnamese
$5-$8

In a strip mall, the small neighborhood restaurant is a prudent choice for steaming bowls of rice noodles served with charbroiled pork or shrimp. Portions are generous and the prices reasonable, but service can be erratic. Casual dress. **Hours:** 9 am-8 pm. Closed major holidays. **Address:** 1207 Jackson St, Suite 104 **Location:** Between 12th and 13th aves; in International District. **Parking:** street. **Cards:** MC, VI.

ICON GRILL
Phone: 206/441-6330 [54]

American
$8-$35

The bustling, eclectic restaurant specializes in American comfort foods. The decor is incredibly whimsical and the atmosphere fun. Casual dress. **Bar:** Full bar. **Reservations:** suggested. **Hours:** 11:30 am-2 & 5-10 pm, Fri-11 pm, Sat 5 pm-11 pm, Sun 5 pm-10 pm. Closed: 11/26, 12/24. **Address:** 1933 5th Ave **Location:** Corner of Virginia St and 5th Ave. **Parking:** street. **Cards:** AX, MC, VI.

IL BISTRO
Phone: 206/682-3049 [94]

Italian
$17-$44

Located literally under the Pike Place Market, the bistro is a popular dining choice of locals where the staff is friendly and the rack of lamb is remembered by all who taste it. Fresh ingredients are acquired in the market and then carefully prepared into the evening specials. Save room for the sinful desserts, made in-house. Dressy casual. **Bar:** Full bar. **Reservations:** suggested. **Hours:** 5:30 pm-10 pm, Fri & Sat-11 pm. Closed: 1/1, 7/4, 11/26, 12/24. **Address:** 93A Pike St **Location:** Corner of 1st Ave and Pike St. **Parking:** street. **Cards:** AX, DC, DS, MC, VI.

IL FORNAIO
Phone: 206/264-0994 [69]

Italian
$10-$20

Accomplished servers begin guests' experiences with crisp, crusty bread hot from the oven. Pasta and flavorful sauces enhance the roasted meats and vegetables. The spacious restaurant thoughtfully replicates the trattorias of Italy. Dressy casual. **Bar:** Full bar. **Reservations:** suggested. **Hours:** 11 am-10 pm, Fri & Sat-11 pm, Sun 10:30 am-10 pm. **Address:** 600 Pine St **Location:** Jct 6th St; in Pacific Place Shopping Mall, 2nd level. **Parking:** on-site (fee). **Cards:** AX, DS, MC, VI.

CALL 🔲M

IL FORNAIO PANETTERIA & CAFFE
Phone: 206/264-0993 [68]

Italian
$7-$32

Accomplished servers begin guests' experiences with crisp, crusty bread hot from the oven. Pasta and flavorful sauces enhance the roasted meats and vegetables. The spacious restaurant thoughtfully replicates the trattorias of Italy. Casual dress. **Bar:** Full bar. **Reservations:** suggested. **Hours:** 11:30 am-10 pm, Fri & Sat-11 pm. Closed: 11/26, 12/25. **Address:** 600 Pine St **Location:** Jct 6th St; in Pacific Place Shopping Mall, 1st level. **Parking:** on-site (fee). **Cards:** AX, DC, DS, MC, VI.

IL TERRAZZO CARMINE
Phone: 206/467-7797 [120]

Italian
$11-$35

On the south end of the Pioneer Square Historic District, the restaurant has a dining room with an outdoor feel. With a large open room and red tile floor, the terrace beckons diners to relax on sunny days. Dressy casual. **Bar:** Full bar. **Reservations:** suggested. **Hours:** 11:30 am-2:30 & 5:30-10:30 pm, Sat from 5:30 pm. Closed major holidays; also Sun. **Address:** 411 1st Ave S **Location:** Corner of 1st Ave and King St; in Merrill Place Building. **Parking:** on-site and valet. **Cards:** AX, CB, DC, DS, MC, VI.

(See map and index starting on p. 606)

IVAR'S ACRES OF CLAMS
▼▼ ▼▼
Seafood
$9-$35
Phone: 206/624-6852   111
A virtual landmark, the Seattle tradition has served the waterfront area since 1938. Among good choices are the renowned "acre of clams," fresh steamers and other fresh fish items. New England-style clam chowder comes from a creamy, delicious recipe known the world over. Casual dress. **Bar:** Full bar. **Reservations:** accepted. **Hours:** 11 am-10 pm, Fri & Sat-11 pm, Sun 9 am-2 & 3:30-10 pm; Sunday brunch. Closed: 11/26, 12/25. **Address:** 1001 Alaskan Way **Location:** On waterfront of Pier 54. **Parking:** street. **Cards:** AX, MC, VI.

LA FONTANA SICILIANA
▼▼▼▼
Italian
$10-$35
Phone: 206/441-1045   60
A delightful courtyard entry, cozy atmosphere and traditional Sicilian and Italian fare combine to offer a satisfying dining experience. The setting is intimate. Dressy casual. **Bar:** Beer & wine. **Reservations:** suggested. **Hours:** 5 pm-10 pm, Thurs & Fri also 10:30 am-2 pm. Closed: 1/1, 12/25. **Address:** 120 Blanchard St **Location:** Between 1st and 2nd aves, just nw; in Belltown area. **Parking:** street. **Cards:** AX, DC, MC, VI.
CALL ⑤M

LAMPREIA
▼▼▼▼
New Italian
$30-$45
Phone: 206/443-3301   37
The intimate Belltown restaurant treats patrons to an elegant dining experience. Continental cuisine is prepared with creative flair. Dressy casual. **Bar:** Full bar. **Reservations:** suggested. **Hours:** 5 pm-close. Closed: 1/1, 11/26, 12/25; also Sun & Mon. **Address:** 2400 1st Ave **Location:** Corner of 1st Ave and Battery St; in Belltown area. **Parking:** street. **Cards:** AX, MC, VI.

LARK
▼▼▼▼
American
$10-$16
Phone: 206/323-5275   78
While seating can be a bit crowded in this small hot spot, the tasting dishes are worth the elbow wars. A good meal might include two or three small plates per person at the table, and passing them around allows for a wide selection of nibbles. Dressy casual. **Bar:** Full bar. **Reservations:** not accepted. **Hours:** 5 pm-10:30 pm. Closed major holidays; also Mon. **Address:** 926 12th Ave **Location:** Between E Spring and E Marion sts; in Capitol Hill District. **Parking:** street. **Cards:** MC, VI.

LA VITA E'BELLA
▼▼ ▼▼
Italian
$10-$20
Phone: 206/441-5322   30
Not the traditional red-and-white-linen Italian place, the more relaxed Belltown hangout serves fresh pasta dishes, panini, bruschetta and crepes filled with prosciutto di Parma or spinach and bechamel sauce. Casual dress. **Bar:** Full bar. **Reservations:** accepted. **Hours:** 11 am-3 & 5-10 pm, Fri & Sat-11 pm, Sun 5 pm-10 pm. Closed: 1/1, 11/26, 12/25. **Address:** 2411 2nd Ave **Location:** Between Battery and Wall sts; in Belltown area. **Parking:** street. **Cards:** AX, DS, MC, VI.

THE LIBRARY BISTRO
🆎🆎🆎
▼▼▼▼
American
$8-$19
Phone: 206/624-3646   109
Book-lined walls lend an instant feeling of warmth. Diners slip into cozy, fabric-covered seats to browse a menu of comfort food and fresh, local, organic produce. Menu items change on a regular basis, but the s'more dessert remains a popular choice. Casual dress. **Bar:** Full bar. **Reservations:** suggested. **Hours:** 7 am-10 & 11:30-2 pm, Sat & Sun 7:30 am-2:30 pm. **Address:** 1007 1st Ave **Location:** Corner of Madison St and 1st Ave; in Alexis Hotel. **Parking:** valet and street. **Cards:** AX, CB, DC, DS, JC, MC, VI.

LOLA
▼▼▼▼
New Greek
$11-$38
Phone: 206/441-1430   52
Another brainchild of Tom Douglas, the restaurant tickles guests' taste buds with creative dishes such as prawn kebabs with curried Muscat glaze, smoked leg of lamb with preserved lemon and maybe Greek salad. Freshly griddled pita bread is a good starter, while fresh miniature doughnuts end the meal sweetly. The trendy hot spot can be a bit loud, but it's otherwise comfortable. Casual dress. **Bar:** Full bar. **Reservations:** suggested. **Hours:** 6 am-11 & 11:30-10 pm, Fri-11 pm, Sat 7 am-3 & 4-11 pm, Sun 7 am-3 & 4-10 pm. Closed: 12/25. **Address:** 2000-B 4th Ave **Location:** Corner of Virginia St and 4th Ave; in Hotel Andra. **Parking:** street. **Cards:** AX, DS, MC, VI.

MACRINA BAKERY & CAFE
▼▼ ▼▼
Breads/Pastries
$6-$11
Phone: 206/448-4032   35
The quaint bakery and cafe prepares exquisite baked goods throughout the day. Cafe seating is available. Casual dress. **Bar:** Beer & wine. **Reservations:** not accepted. **Hours:** 7 am-7 pm, Sun 8 am-6 pm. Closed major holidays. **Address:** 2408 1st Ave **Location:** Between Wall and Battery sts; in Belltown area. **Parking:** street. **Cards:** MC, VI.

MARAZUL
▼▼▼▼
Latin American
$8-$17
Phone: 206/654-8170   25
Cuisine and decor are influenced by the Caribbean islands, Cuba and Indo-Asian territories. The menu features a variety of such well-known ingredients as black cod, scallops, ahi tuna and striped bass. The preparation and spices, however, provide a flavorful, exciting twist to these favorites. A large selection of tropical beverages is available from the Rhum bar, and the overall experience is unique and fun. Casual dress. **Bar:** Full bar. **Hours:** 6:30-10:30 am, 11:30-2 & 5-midnight. **Address:** 2125 Terry Ave **Location:** Just s of jct E Denny Way; in Pan Pacific Hotel Seattle. **Parking:** on-site and valet. **Cards:** AX, CB, DC, DS, JC, MC, VI.
🅐🅒

MARJORIE
▼▼▼▼
International
$8-$22
Phone: 206/441-9842   38
The intimate venue prepares New American cuisine. Guests walk into a candlelit dining room then sink into overstuffed chairs covered in soft fabric. A glass of wine gets the meal started as menu options of Thai beef, Max's noodles, beet salad and beef short ribs are considered. Casual dress. **Bar:** Full bar. **Reservations:** accepted. **Hours:** 5 pm-11 pm, Fri & Sat-midnight. Closed: 7/4, 11/26, 12/25; also Sun & Mon. **Address:** 2331 2nd Ave **Location:** Southwest corner of 2nd Ave and SW Battery St; in Belltown area. **Parking:** street. **Cards:** AX, MC, VI.

(See map and index starting on p. 606)

MARRAKESH MOROCCAN RESTAURANT
Phone: 206/956-0500   (34)

▼▼▼ ▼▼▼
Moroccan
$19-$29

Inside a nondescript building is an oasis harboring a traditional Moroccan atmosphere. The five-course prix fixe menu includes soup, salad Marrakesh, b'stilla royale (phyllo dough filled with ground chicken and spices), a choice of entree, dessert and mint tea. Among interesting dishes is lamb m'rouzia with onions, raisins and honey sauce. Menu items also can be ordered a la carte. Moroccan wines and beers are served. Belly dancing provides entertainment Wednesday through Sunday nights. Casual dress. Entertainment. **Bar:** Beer & wine. **Reservations:** suggested. **Hours:** 5 pm-10 pm. **Address:** 2334 2nd Ave **Location:** Between Bell and Battery sts. **Parking:** street. **Cards:** AX, CB, DC, DS, JC, MC, VI.

MATT'S IN THE MARKET
Phone: 206/467-7909   (90)

▼▼▼ ▼▼▼
Regional American
$8-$22

The dining room accommodates a limited amount of diners, so reservations are a must. A table near the window affords a view of the water and bustling Pike Place Market below. Those who choose a stool at the counter are entertained by watching the chef create their meal. Only the freshest ingredients go into the preparations. A wonderful complement to any food choice is a glass of wine from the extensive list. Casual dress. **Bar:** Beer & wine. **Reservations:** suggested. **Hours:** 11:30 am-2:30 & 5:30-10 pm. Closed major holidays; also Sun. **Address:** 94 Pike St, #32 **Location:** Corner of Pike St and 1st Ave; at Pike Place Market; in Corner Market Building, 2nd floor. **Parking:** street. **Cards:** MC, VI.

MCCORMICK & SCHMICK'S
Phone: 206/270-9052   (4)

▼▼▼▼▼▼
Seafood
$6-$25

This place is all about seafood, which is imported from all over the world. Among good choices are Washington state oysters, Maine clams, delicate Hawaiian escolar and tuna from Ecuador. The clublike decor is cozy, and expert staff provide able assistance. Casual dress. **Bar:** Full bar. **Reservations:** suggested. **Hours:** 11:30 am-10 pm, Fri-11 pm, Sat 10 am-11 pm, Sun 10 am-10 pm. **Address:** 1200 Westlake Ave N **Location:** I-5, exit 167 (Mercer St); on southwest end of Lake Union. **Parking:** on-site (fee). **Cards:** AX, MC, VI.

MCCORMICK & SCHMICK'S
Phone: 206/623-5500   (105)

▼▼▼▼▼▼
Seafood
$7-$40

This place is all about seafood, which is imported from all over the world. Among good choices are Washington state oysters, Maine clams, delicate Hawaiian escolar and tuna from Ecuador. The clublike decor is cozy, and expert staff provide able assistance. Casual dress. **Bar:** Full bar. **Reservations:** suggested. **Hours:** 11:30 am-11 pm, Sun-10 pm. Closed: 12/25. **Address:** 1103 1st Ave **Location:** Corner of 1st Ave and Spring St. **Parking:** valet and street. **Cards:** AX, DC, DS, MC, VI.

MCMENAMINS
Phone: 206/223-1698

▼▼▼ ▼▼▼
American
$5-$20

The casual neighborhood eatery is where friends gather for classic pub and comfort fare, all washed down by pints of locally made beer. Large wooden booths or tables easily accommodate larger groups, and the eclectic, custom-painted walls and varied period light fixtures keep diners' eyes busy should the conversation lag. Casual dress. **Bar:** Full bar. **Reservations:** not accepted. **Hours:** 11 am-1 am, Fri & Sat-2 am, Sun noon-midnight. Closed: 11/26, 12/25. **Address:** 300 E Pike St **Location:** Just e of downtown at Pike St and Melrose Ave. **Parking:** street. **Cards:** MC, VI.

MCMENAMINS
Phone: 206/285-4722

▼▼▼ ▼▼▼
American
$5-$20

The casual neighborhood eatery is where friends gather for classic pub and comfort fare, all washed down by pints of locally made beer. Large wooden booths or tables easily accommodate larger groups, and the eclectic, custom-painted walls and varied period light fixtures keep diners' eyes busy should the conversation lag. Casual dress. **Bar:** Full bar. **Reservations:** not accepted. **Hours:** 11 am-1 am, Sun noon-midnight, Mon 11 am-midnight. Closed: 11/26, 12/25. **Address:** 200 Roy St, Suite 105 **Location:** Just n of Seattle Center at Roy St and 2nd Ave. **Parking:** street. **Cards:** MC, VI.

METROPOLITAN GRILL
Phone: 206/624-3287   (110)

▼▼▼▼▼▼
Steak
$8-$65

Hand-selected cuts of 28-day dry-aged prime beef are carefully prepared and well presented. The cellar houses many red wines. High ceilings, mahogany tables and dark green booths accented with brass add to the dining room's Old World charm. Dressy casual. **Bar:** Full bar. **Reservations:** suggested. **Hours:** 11 am-3 & 4:30-10:30 pm, Fri-11 pm, Sat 4 pm-11 pm, Sun 4 pm-10 pm. Closed: 11/26, 12/25. **Address:** 820 2nd Ave **Location:** 2nd Ave and Marion St. **Parking:** valet. **Cards:** AX, CB, DC, DS, JC, MC, VI. **Historic**

MEXICO CANTINA Y VERACRUZ COOKING
Phone: 206/405-3400   (67)

▼▼▼ ▼▼▼
Regional Mexican
$9-$20

Intriguing Veracruz-style preparation is applied to the abundant seafood dishes in the brightly colored cantina-style restaurant. Lively salsa music lends to the upbeat atmosphere. Casual dress. **Bar:** Full bar. **Reservations:** accepted. **Hours:** 11:30 am-10 pm, Fri & Sat-11 pm. Closed: 11/26, 12/25. **Address:** 600 Pine St, Suite 402 **Location:** 4th floor of Pacific Place Mall. **Parking:** on-site (fee). **Cards:** AX, CB, DC, DS, MC, VI.

MITCHELLI'S
Phone: 206/623-3883   (115)

ⒶⒶ

▼▼▼ ▼▼▼
Italian
$6-$18

Just down from Pioneer Square Park, the lively, fun restaurant rocks until 4 am on weekends. Classic, creative entrees are delightfully complete with a big serving of tiramisu. Casual dress. **Bar:** Full bar. **Reservations:** accepted. **Hours:** 11:30 am-10 pm, Fri-2 am, Sat 9 am-2 am, Sun 9 am-10 pm. Closed: 11/26, 12/24, 12/25. **Address:** 84 Yesler Way **Location:** Just w of 1st Ave; in Pioneer Square. **Parking:** street. **Cards:** AX, MC, VI.

MOXIE
Phone: 206/283-6614   (15)

▼▼▼▼▼▼
Western American
$16-$29

Locals gather at the casual neighborhood spot, within blocks of busy Seattle Center, for after-work socializing and the late-evening happy hour. Locally grown and naturally raised ingredients, such as salmon and halibut, anchor dishes along the lines of curried fish cakes with mint yogurt sauce or an herb crepe pouch stuffed with seasonal mushrooms, grilled onions and sherried tomato vinaigrette. Sidewalk tables allow for great people-watching. Casual dress. **Bar:** Full bar. **Reservations:** suggested. **Hours:** 5 pm-11 pm, Fri-11 pm, Sat 10 am-2 & 5-11 pm, Sun 10 am-2 & 5-10 pm. Closed: 7/4, 11/26, 12/25; also Mon. **Address:** 530 First Ave N **Location:** Between Mercer and Republic sts; just w of Seattle Center. **Parking:** street. **Cards:** AX, MC, VI.

(See map and index starting on p. 606)

NOODLE RANCH
Asian
$7-$12

Phone: 206/728-0463 (49)

The busy eatery serves Pan-Asian dishes and noodle bowls amid bright and simple contemporary decor. Portions are generous. Guests should arrive early for quicker seating. Sidewalk seating is offered seasonally. Casual dress. **Bar:** Beer & wine. **Hours:** 11 am-10 pm, Sat from noon. Closed major holidays; also Sun. **Address:** 2228 2nd Ave **Location:** Between Bell and Blanchard sts; in Belltown area. **Parking:** street. **Cards:** AX, MC, VI.

OCEANAIRE
Seafood
$10-$35

Phone: 206/267-2277 (53)

Fresh fish and shellfish are flown in daily from around the globe. The sleek, handsomely designed dining room has a raw bar and is tastefully appointed in an art deco/nautical theme. The menu notes the seafood available daily and the varied preparation styles, such as broiled, grilled and blackened. Casual dress. **Bar:** Full bar. **Reservations:** suggested. **Hours:** 11:30 am-10 pm, Fri-11 pm, Sat 5 pm-11 pm, Sun 5 pm-10 pm. Closed major holidays. **Address:** 1700 7th Ave **Location:** Corner of 7th Ave and Olive St. **Parking:** valet and street. **Cards:** AX, DC, DS, MC, VI.

OSTERIA LA SPIGA
Italian
$9-$23

Phone: 206/323-8881 (56)

Popular with the locals, well-prepared Italian favorites include ravioli stuffed with butternut squash, lasagna Verdi and hand-made potato dumplings. The desserts are delectable and wrap up a perfect meal. Casual dress. **Bar:** Full bar. **Reservations:** suggested. **Hours:** 5 pm-midnight, Thurs-Sat to 1:30 am. Closed major holidays. **Address:** 1429 12th Ave **Location:** Between Union St and Broadway; in Capitol Hill District. **Parking:** street. **Cards:** AX, MC, VI.

PALACE KITCHEN
American
$15-$30

Phone: 206/448-2001 (41)

Under the monorail, the restaurant presents specialties of pork loin, chicken and rib-eye, which are prepared over an apple-wood grill. Fresh creme brulee merits the indulgence. Casual dress. **Bar:** Full bar. **Hours:** 5 pm-1 am. Closed major holidays. **Address:** 2030 5th Ave **Location:** Corner of Lenora St and 5th Ave. **Parking:** street. **Cards:** AX, CB, DC, DS, MC, VI.

PALOMINO RESTAURANT
American
$9-$32

Phone: 206/623-1300 (84)

This national chain restaurant offers patrons an impressive assortment of dishes including seafood, pasta and steak. Rounding out the menu are pizzas, salads and Tuscan-style rotisserie roasted chicken all served up in a trendy, casual upscale atmosphere. Casual dress. **Bar:** Full bar. **Reservations:** suggested. **Hours:** 11 am-3 & 5-9:30 pm, Fri & Sat-10:30 pm, Sun 11 am-3 & 4-9 pm. Closed: 12/25. **Address:** 1420 5th Ave **Location:** Jct 5th Ave and Pike St; in US Bank Center, 3rd floor. **Parking:** on-site (fee). **Cards:** AX, CB, DC, DS, MC, VI.

THE PIKE PUB AND BREWERY
American
$8-$18

Phone: 206/622-6044 (98)

The casual pub isn't easy to find, but people seek it out for great beers made in house and a lively, high-energy crowd. On the menu are traditional pub foods, as well as creative seafood dishes along the lines of stuffed king salmon. Casual dress. **Bar:** Full bar. **Reservations:** accepted. **Hours:** 11 am-9 pm, Fri & Sat-10 pm. Closed major holidays. **Address:** 1415 1st Ave **Location:** Northwest corner of 1st Ave and Union St. **Parking:** street. **Cards:** AX, DC, DS, MC, VI.

THE PINK DOOR
Italian
$10-$25

Phone: 206/443-3241 (83)

The decor, with wall murals and an indoor fountain, contributes to the feeling of an eclectic, rustic courtyard. Classic dishes, such as Mama's meatballs and daily risotto specials, are served piping hot. Desserts are temptingly interesting. Dressy casual. **Bar:** Full bar. **Reservations:** suggested. **Hours:** 11:30 am-10 pm, Sun from 4 pm. Closed major holidays. **Address:** 1919 Post Alley **Location:** Just nw of jct 1st Ave and Stewart St. **Parking:** on-site (fee). **Cards:** AX, DS, MC, VI.

PLACE PIGALLE
French
$15-$25

Phone: 206/624-1756 (93)

Nestled in the market, this intimate cafe affords an amazing view of the harbor. Fresh local ingredients are prepared with a French flair. Casual dress. **Bar:** Full bar. **Reservations:** accepted. **Hours:** 11:30 am-10 pm, Fri & Sat-10:30 pm. Closed major holidays; also Sun. **Address:** 81 Pike St **Location:** In Pike Place Market. **Parking:** on-site (fee). **Cards:** AX, DC, DS, MC, VI.

PYRAMID ALEHOUSE-BREWERY & RESTAURANT
American
$8-$15

Phone: 206/682-3377 (126)

Locals frequent the brewery and restaurant for American grill favorites along the lines of three bean chicken chili, slabs of baby back ribs, pub pizzas and cherry-berry cobbler, not to mention fresh Thomas Kemper sodas and Pyramid beers, many of which are made in house. This spot is convenient to venues for both the Mariners and the Seahawks. Casual dress. **Bar:** Beer & wine. **Reservations:** accepted. **Hours:** 11 am-10 pm, Fri & Sat-11 pm, Sun-9 pm. Closed: 1/1, 11/26, 12/25. **Address:** 1201 1st Ave S **Location:** Southeast corner of Royal Brougham Way and 1st Ave S. **Parking:** on-site. **Cards:** AX, CB, DC, MC, VI.

CALL (LM)

QUEEN CITY GRILL
American
$11-$34

Phone: 206/443-0975 (70)

Seafood dishes are served in a high-energy, Euro-bistro atmosphere. A wall of windows allows for great people-watching. Casual dress. **Bar:** Full bar. **Reservations:** accepted. **Hours:** 11:30 am-2:30 & 4:30-11 pm, Fri & Sat-midnight. Closed major holidays. **Address:** 2201 1st Ave **Location:** Corner of 1st Ave and Blanchard St; in Belltown area. **Parking:** street. **Cards:** AX, CB, DC, DS, MC, VI.

RACHA NOODLES AND THAI CUISINE
Thai
$8-$27

Phone: 206/281-8883 (11)

Diners can escape to Thailand for the evening, even if they are still within walking distance of Seattle Center and Queen Anne Hill. Warm, friendly staff members serve traditional Thai favorites. Casual dress. **Bar:** Full bar. **Reservations:** accepted. **Hours:** 11 am-3 & 4:30-10:30 pm, Fri-midnight, Sat 4:30 pm-midnight, Sun 4:30 pm-10:30 pm. Closed: 11/26. **Address:** 23 Mercer St **Location:** Southwest corner of Mercer St and 1st Ave; just w of Seattle Center. **Parking:** street. **Cards:** AX, MC, VI.

RED FIN RESTAURANT
New Asian
$8-$28

Phone: 206/441-4340 (39)

The sushi bar, where experts hand-roll made-to-order sushi creations, takes center stage. A full menu of contemporary Asian specialties features small and large plates. Casual dress. **Bar:** Full bar. **Reservations:** suggested. **Hours:** 6:30-10:30 am, 11-2:30 & 4-11 pm, Sat & Sun 8 am-3 & 4-11 pm. Closed: 11/26, 12/25. **Address:** 612 Stewart St **Location:** Corner of 7th Ave and Stewart St; in Hotel Max. **Parking:** street. **Cards:** AX, MC, VI.

(See map and index starting on p. 606)

RESTAURANT SHILLA
Phone: 206/623-9996   (24)
Korean
$6-$19
Convenient to many hotels around Seattle Center, the restaurant caters to foreign tourists seeking authentic Korean dishes. Food can be cooked by the chef or on the small grill placed in the center of each table. Casual dress. **Bar:** Full bar. **Reservations:** accepted. **Hours:** 11 am-2:30 & 4:30-10 pm. Closed: 1/1, 11/26, 12/25. **Address:** 2300 8th Ave **Location:** Corner of 8th Ave and Denny Way. **Parking:** on-site. **Cards:** AX, CB, DC, DS, JC, MC, VI.

RESTAURANT ZOE
Phone: 206/256-2060   (62)
American
$18-$33
Taking up a small corner location in Belltown, this trendy eatery keeps diners coming back for new and creatively prepared seasonal specials featured on the bistro-style menu. Offerings might include a pork cheek confit, spice-crusted pork tenderloin served with orange-cinnamon couscous or maybe a basil-crusted Copper River salmon. Casual dress. **Bar:** Full bar. **Reservations:** suggested. **Hours:** 5 pm-10 pm, Fri & Sat-10:45 pm. Closed major holidays. **Address:** 2137 2nd Ave **Location:** Corner of 2nd Ave and Blanchard St; in Belltown area. **Parking:** street. **Cards:** AX, MC, VI.

REVOLUTION BAR & GRILL
Phone: 206/770-2777   (19)
American
$9-$25
Select from 50 hand-crafted draft beers from regional microbreweries. The menu focuses on casual, contemporary Pacific Northwest cuisine. Casual dress. **Bar:** Full bar. **Reservations:** suggested. **Hours:** 11:30 am-5:30 pm. Closed major holidays. **Address:** 325 5th Ave N **Location:** In Experience Music Project; at Seattle Center. **Parking:** on-site (fee). **Cards:** AX, CB, DC, DS, JC, MC, VI.

CALL (&M)

RISTORANTE MACHIAVELLI
Phone: 206/621-7941   (29)
Italian
$8-$16
Truly a prince of a restaurant, the casual, friendly neighborhood location is noted for its spinach ravioli filled with mushrooms and ricotta, as well as for its gnocchi al sugo. Casual dress. **Bar:** Full bar. **Reservations:** not accepted. **Hours:** 5 pm-11 pm. Closed: Sun, 12/22-1/2, 3 days for Memorial & Labor days. **Address:** 1215 Pine St **Location:** Corner of Pine St and Melrose Ave; in Capitol Hill area. **Parking:** street. **Cards:** MC, VI.

ROCK SALT STEAK & SEAFOOD
Phone: 206/284-1047   (1)
Steak & Seafood
$10-$39
Established in 1973, the family-owned restaurant is known for excellent steaks but also serves dishes of seafood, chicken and pasta. The dining room overlooks the marinas of Lake Union. Casual dress. **Bar:** Full bar. **Reservations:** suggested. **Hours:** 11 am-3 & 4-11 pm; seasonal hours may vary. Closed: 1/1, 12/25. **Address:** 1232 Westlake Ave N **Location:** On southwest shore of Lake Union. **Parking:** on-site. **Cards:** AX, MC, VI.

ROYAL ARGOSY DINING CRUISES
Phone: 206/623-1445   (107)
American
$50-$120
The elegant cruise affords striking views of city lights, the harbor and the islands. Live music rounds out the experience. Dressy casual. **Bar:** Full bar. **Reservations:** required. **Hours:** call for hours. Closed: 12/25. **Address:** Pier 56, 1201 Alaskan Way **Location:** Sails from Pier 56. **Parking:** on-site (fee). **Cards:** AX, CB, DC, DS, JC, MC, VI.

RUTH'S CHRIS STEAK HOUSE
Phone: 206/624-8524   (106)
Steak
$10-$37
The main fare is steak, which is prepared from several cuts of prime beef and cooked to perfection, but the menu also lists lamb, chicken and seafood dishes. Guests should come hungry because the side dishes, which are among the a la carte offerings, could make a meal in themselves. Dressy casual. **Bar:** Full bar. **Reservations:** suggested. **Hours:** 6:30 am-10 pm. **Address:** 727 Pine St **Location:** Corner 7th Ave and Pine St; in Grand Hyatt Seattle. **Parking:** on-site (fee) and valet. **Cards:** AX, DC, DS, MC, VI.

SAITO'S JAPANESE CAFE & BAR
Phone: 206/728-1333   (61)
Japanese
$6-$22
The comfortable cafe prepares a range of sushi offerings and other dishes, including many with fresh seafood. Casual dress. **Bar:** Full bar. **Reservations:** suggested. **Hours:** 11:30 am-2 & 5:30-10 pm, Fri & Sat 5:30 pm-11 pm. Closed: 11/26, 12/25; also Sun & Mon. **Address:** 2122 2nd Ave **Location:** Just nw of jct Lenora St; in Belltown area. **Parking:** street. **Cards:** AX, DS, MC, VI.

SAZE RAC
Phone: 206/624-7755   (101)
Southern Pacific Rim
$12-$30
The trendy, high energy restaurant is popular for its Southern-inspired American dishes like cedar-plank-smoked salmon with a down-home side such as collard greens. Casual dress. **Bar:** Full bar. **Reservations:** suggested. **Hours:** 7-10 am, 11:30-2:30 & 5-10 pm. Closed major holidays. **Address:** 1101 4th Ave **Location:** Corner of 4th Ave and Spring St; in Hotel Monaco. **Parking:** valet and street. **Cards:** AX, DC, DS, MC, VI.

SHALLOTS ASIAN BISTRO
Phone: 206/728-1888   (26)
Asian
$7-$17
The handsome bistro's sleek, contemporary design incorporates mirrors, light-colored woodwork, soft lighting, an open kitchen and a wall of windows permitting guests to view the activity on the street outside. Fresh ingredients go into varied Asian dishes. Several satays share menu space with fresh seafood, beef, pork and chicken dishes. Also offered is a good selection of wines, drafts and microbrews. Casual dress. **Bar:** Full bar. **Reservations:** accepted. **Hours:** 11 am-3 & 5-10 pm, Fri-10:30 pm, Sat 5 pm-10:30 pm, Sun 5 pm-10 pm. Closed major holidays. **Address:** 2525 4th Ave **Location:** Jct Vine St; in Belltown area. **Parking:** street. **Cards:** AX, DS, MC, VI.

SHANGHI GARDENS
Phone: 206/625-1689   (124)
Chinese
$5-$23
The menu comprises a good variety of traditional fare, ranging from shredded rolls and lemon chicken to Mongolian barbecue and noodles. The portion sizes are generous, and the seasonings are flavorful. An aquarium adds to the dining room's ambience. Casual dress. **Bar:** Beer & wine. **Reservations:** accepted. **Hours:** 11 am-9:30 pm, Fri & Sat-10:30 pm. **Address:** 524 6th Ave S **Location:** Corner of 6th Ave S and Weller St; in International District. **Parking:** street. **Cards:** MC, VI.

(See map and index starting on p. 606)

SHIRO'S
◆◆◆
Japanese
$17-$27

Phone: 206/443-9844 **31**

The intimate sushi bar offers tempura, sukiyaki and teriyaki in a clean, brightly lit streetside cafe environment. Casual dress. **Bar:** Full bar. **Reservations:** accepted. **Hours:** 5 pm-10 pm. Closed major holidays. **Address:** 2401 2nd Ave **Location:** Corner of 2nd Ave and Battery St; in Belltown area. **Parking:** street. **Cards:** AX, JC, MC, VI.

SHUCKERS
◆◆◆◆
Seafood
$10-$28

Phone: 206/621-1984 **97**

Locally inspired cuisine adorn the menu at the sophisticated pub-style restaurant. An extensive selection of seafood include Shuckers' signature fresh oysters, which are prepared in a number of ways. **Bar:** Full bar. **Reservations:** suggested. **Hours:** 11:30 am-10 pm, Fri & Sat-11 pm, Sun 5 pm-10 pm. **Address:** 411 University St **Location:** Corner of 4th Ave and University St; in The Fairmont Olympic Hotel. **Parking:** on-site (fee) and valet. **Cards:** AX, CB, DC, DS, JC, MC, VI.

SIAM ON BROADWAY
◆◆◆
Thai
$7-$15

Phone: 206/324-0892 **13**

Locals drop in to the small eatery for take-out or a quick meal at the counter, where they can watch the chefs at work. Groups prefer to gather at the larger tables in back, where they can chat about their day and watch the fish swim about. Casual dress. **Bar:** Beer & wine. **Reservations:** accepted. **Hours:** 11:30 am-10 pm, Fri-11 pm, Sat 5 pm-11 pm, Sun 5 pm-10 pm. Closed: major holidays; also 12/24. **Address:** 616 Broadway E **Location:** Between Roy and Mercer sts; in Capitol Hill District. **Parking:** street. **Cards:** AX, DC, MC, VI.

SIX SEVEN
◆◆◆
Seafood
$12-$65

Phone: 206/269-4575 **63**

Boats nearly hit the windows as they pass by the spot on Pier 67. When the weather is too nasty to take advantage of the seasonal deck seating, diners can watch the fish circle lazily in the bright tanks. Creative seafood dishes are served with artful flair. Casual dress. **Bar:** Full bar. **Reservations:** suggested. **Hours:** 6:30 am-3 & 5:30-9:30 pm. **Address:** 2411 Alaskan Way, Pier 67 **Location:** On waterfront at Pier 67; at base of Wall St; in The Edgewater. **Parking:** valet. **Cards:** AX, CB, DC, DS, JC, MC, VI.
(See color ad p 633)

SOUNDVIEW CAFE
◆
American
$6-$10

Phone: 206/623-5700 **95**

The popular restaurant affords expansive views of Puget Sound. Shoppers can take a break and watch the fish "tossers" while eating a casual lunch. Casual dress. **Bar:** Beer & wine. **Hours:** 8 am-6 pm, Fri & Sat-8 pm. Closed: 12/26. **Address:** 1501 Pike Place Market **Location:** In Pike Place Market. **Parking:** street. **Cards:** AX, CB, DC, DS, JC, MC, VI.

SOUP DADDY SOUPS
◆
American
$5-$7

Phone: 206/682-7202 **117**

Exuding charm courtesy of its historic location, the establishment satisfies appetites for soups, sandwiches, salads and morning bagels in a timely manner without compromising quality or flavor. Homemade desserts vary daily. Casual dress. **Reservations:** not accepted. **Hours:** 9 am-4 pm. Closed major holidays; also Sat & Sun. **Address:** 106 Occidental Ave **Location:** In Pioneer Square. **Parking:** street. **Cards:** MC, VI.
CALL &M

THE SPACE NEEDLE-SKY CITY RESTAURANT
AAA
◆◆◆
American
$25-$56

Phone: 206/905-2100 **20**

It's hard to beat the 360-degree view at the revolving restaurant atop the Space Needle, Seattle's 600-foot-tall symbol. Innovative Pacific Northwest cuisine makes up the menu. The elevator ride and Observation Deck visit are complimentary with dinner. Casual dress. **Reservations:** suggested. **Hours:** 11 am-3:30 & 5-10 pm, Sat & Sun from 10 am; Saturday & Sunday brunch. **Address:** 400 Broad St **Location:** In Seattle Center. **Parking:** valet. **Cards:** AX, CB, DC, DS, JC, MC, VI. *(See color ad p 232)*
CALL &M

STEAMER'S SEAFOOD CAFE
◆
Seafood
$7-$12

Phone: 206/623-2066 **100**

On the harborfront, the cafe serves fish and chips, fried clams and oysters, and (for landlubber types) burgers with fries. Guests order at the counter and then savor one of the fine local microbrewed beers while the meal is prepared. For dessert, it's hard to beat a simple ice cream cone. Patio seating allows diners to enjoy the sometimes bracing Seattle climate. Casual dress. **Bar:** Beer & wine. **Hours:** 10 am-9 pm, Fri & Sat-10 pm. Closed: 11/26, 12/25. **Address:** 1201 Alaskan Way **Location:** Jct Seneca St and Alaskan Way; at Pier 56. **Parking:** street. **Cards:** DC, DS, MC, VI.
AC

TABLE 219
◆◆
Mediterranean
$5-$19

Phone: 206/328-4604 **21**

The Mediterranean restaurant serves salads, pasta dishes, lamb and a daily risotto. A favorite appetizer is the hummus and pita. Greek salad brims with feta cheese and kalamata olives. A popular pasta dish is sauteed crispy penne with eggplant, tomato, kalamata olives and caper sauce. Dessert choices are limited. Casual dress. **Bar:** Beer & wine. **Reservations:** accepted. **Hours:** 4:30 pm-10 pm, Fri & Sat from 9 am; Sunday brunch. Closed: 11/26, 12/25; also Mon. **Address:** 219 Broadway E **Location:** Between John and Thomas sts; in Capitol Hill area. **Parking:** street. **Cards:** MC, VI.

TANGO
◆◆◆
Latin American
$8-$17

Phone: 206/583-0382 **47**

Described as Pan-Latin, the restaurant's cuisine includes choices such as tapas, paella and seviche, all of which can be washed down with tasty sangria or a mojito. For dessert, chocolate lovers must try el diablo. Casual dress. **Bar:** Full bar. **Reservations:** accepted. **Hours:** 5 pm-10:30 pm, Fri & Sat-11 pm. Closed major holidays. **Address:** 1100 Pike St **Location:** Corner of Pike St and Boren Ave. **Parking:** street. **Cards:** AX, MC, VI.

(See map and index starting on p. 606)

TEN MERCER
▼▼▼
Regional American
$13-$28

Phone: 206/691-3723   ⑨

The hip, contemporary location is popular with the locals who return for the seasonally changing menu. Couples tend to prefer the more romantic upstairs loft, with vantage points of the upscale bar and bistro below. The dramatic back bar rises to the second level, with access granted via a rolling library ladder to fine liquors and wines. Dressy casual. **Bar:** Full bar. **Reservations:** suggested. **Hours:** 4:30 pm-midnight. Closed: 1/1, 11/26, 12/24, 12/25. **Address:** 10 Mercer St **Location:** Between Queen Anne and 1st aves N; just w of Seattle Center. **Parking:** valet. **Cards:** AX, DS, MC, VI.

TILLICUM VILLAGE NW INDIAN
COAST CULTURAL CENTER AND RESTAURANT
AAA
▼▼ ▼▼
Seafood
$80

Phone: 206/933-8600   ㉗

The distinctive experience starts with a narrated boat tour of Elliott Bay and ends at the Indian Cultural Center on Blake Island, where alder-smoked salmon is awaiting. After the meal, there is a half-hour native dance program followed by some free time to discover the island before boarding the boat for the ride back to Seattle. Guests can take advantage of great photography opportunities of the Seattle skyline, Mount Rainier and Puget Sound. Casual dress. **Entertainment.** **Bar:** Beer & wine. **Reservations:** suggested. **Hours:** Open 3/1-11/30; departure times 11:30 am & 4:30 pm, Sun 11:30 am. Closed: boat weekdays from 10/1-4/30, call for schedule. **Address:** Pier 55 Alaskan Way **Location:** Blake Island Marine State Park via charter vessel from Pier 55; Seattle central waterfront. **Parking:** street. **Cards:** AX, DS, MC, VI.

TOI
▼▼ ▼▼
Thai
$5-$25

Phone: 206/267-1017   ㉔

The downtown favorite's decor, which includes subdued lighting and a quieting ambience, is intimate and appealing in the evening. The menu lists selections ranging from fish and other seafood to chicken and beef preparations, with some vegetarian dishes also included. Accompanying sauces are a must. Save room for one of the scrumptious desserts. Dressy casual. **Bar:** Full bar. **Reservations:** accepted. **Hours:** 4 pm-10:30 pm. Closed: 1/1, 11/26, 12/25; also Sun. **Address:** 1904 4th Ave **Location:** Corner of Stewart St and 4th Ave. **Parking:** street. **Cards:** AX, MC, VI.

TROIANI
▼▼▼
Italian
$16-$60

Phone: 206/624-4060   ⑩④

In the heart of Seattle, this upscale Italian grill is where pasta dishes take on a whole new flair. For those not looking for innovative pasta, there are traditional American dishes such as salmon, steak and chops served in large portions. Sides are ordered separately and can be shared by the whole table. Dressy casual. **Bar:** Full bar. **Reservations:** suggested. **Hours:** 11 am-9 pm, Sat from 5 pm. Closed major holidays. **Address:** 1001 3rd Ave **Location:** Corner of 3rd Ave and Madison St. **Parking:** valet. **Cards:** AX, MC, VI.

TULIO RISTORANTE
AAA
▼▼ ▼▼
Regional Italian
$8-$32

Phone: 206/624-5500   ⑨⑨

A great meal starter at the casual Italian restaurant is their mozzarella appetizer of layered cheese, tomato and grilled eggplant that's soaked in soy sauce. Fresh, local seafood is used during preparation of several entrees. Casual dress. **Bar:** Full bar. **Reservations:** suggested. **Hours:** 7-10 am, 11:30-2:30 & 5-10 pm, Fri-11 pm, Sat 8 am-2:30 & 5-11 pm, Sun 8 am-2:30 & 5-10 pm. Closed major holidays. **Address:** 1100 5th Ave **Location:** Corner of Spring St and 5th Ave; in Hotel Vintage Park. **Parking:** valet and street. **Cards:** AX, CB, DC, DS, JC, MC, VI.

TYPHOON!
▼▼▼ ▼▼▼
Thai
$8-$19

Phone: 206/262-9797

The artful, contemporary Thai restaurant features classic entrees and new twists on old favorites. The extensive beverage menu lists an impressive tea selection from China, Japan and Thailand, as well as Thai beers and microbrews. Casual dress. **Bar:** Full bar. **Reservations:** suggested. **Hours:** 11 am-2 & 5-10 pm. **Address:** 1400 Western Ave **Location:** Corner of Western Ave and Union St. **Parking:** street. **Cards:** AX, DS, MC, VI.

UNION SQUARE GRILL
▼▼ ▼▼
Steak
$8-$45

Phone: 206/224-4321   ㉒

Crisp, polished, art deco lines decorate the casually elegant dining room, where patrons enjoy such specialties as halibut with cherry pine nut glaze; spicy, dry-rubbed pork loin; and homemade baked Alaska. Dressy casual. **Bar:** Full bar. **Reservations:** suggested. **Hours:** 11 am-3 & 5-10 pm, Fri-11 pm, Sat 5 pm-11 pm, Sun 4 pm-9 pm. Closed major holidays. **Address:** 621 Union St **Location:** Jct 7th Ave and Union St. **Parking:** on-site (fee). **Cards:** AX, DC, DS, JC, MC, VI.

VON'S GRAND CITY CAFE
▼▼▼ ▼▼▼
American
$8-$40

Phone: 206/621-8667   ㉒①

Prime rib is the favorite entree—although barbecue's a close second—at the jovial, lively restaurant. The memorabilia of local merchants and businesses decorates the upbeat dining room. For dessert, check out the made-in-house SoftCream. Casual dress. **Bar:** Full bar. **Reservations:** suggested. **Hours:** 7:30 am-10 pm, Fri & Sat-11 pm. Closed: 1/1, 12/25. **Address:** 619 Pine St **Location:** Corner of 7th Ave and Pine St; in The Roosevelt, A Coast Hotel. **Parking:** on-site (fee). **Cards:** AX, MC, VI. *(See color ad p 641)*

WASABI BISTRO
▼▼▼
Japanese
$8-$32

Phone: 206/441-6044   ㊷

Modern Japanese dishes are served in a trendy dining room and high-energy bar with exposed beams and soft lighting. Dominating the menu are more than 25 sushi rolls, but such items as rice bowls, noodles, soups and grilled rib-eye also are available. Dressy casual. **Entertainment.** **Bar:** Full bar. **Reservations:** suggested. **Hours:** 11:30 am-2:30 & 4-1 am, Sat & Sun from 4 pm. Closed: 1/1, 11/26, 12/25. **Address:** 2311 2nd Ave **Location:** Between Bell and Battery sts; in Belltown area. **Parking:** street. **Cards:** AX, DS, MC, VI.

WATERFRONT SEAFOOD GRILL
▼▼▼
Seafood
$20-$65

Phone: 206/956-9171   ㊱

Waterfront views don't get much better than the ones afforded from the floor-to-ceiling windows that wrap around three walls of the restaurant, which is perched on the end of the pier. Seafood tastes so fresh that guests might think the chefs pluck it from the cold waters of Elliott Bay, which flow beneath this place. On the menu are such dishes as Penn Cove mussels in saffron cream, Hawaiian swordfish with a choice of sauces, lobster risotto and steamed Dungeness crab. Dressy casual. **Bar:** Full bar. **Reservations:** suggested. **Hours:** 4 pm-10 pm, Fri & Sat-11 pm. Closed major holidays. **Address:** 2801 Alaskan Way, Pier 70 **Location:** Jct Alaskan Way and Broad St; at Pier 70. **Parking:** valet. **Cards:** AX, MC, VI.

(See map and index starting on p. 606)

WILD GINGER ASIAN RESTAURANT & SATAY BAR   Phone: 206/623-4450   [92]

▼▼▼
Asian
$9-$30

Select from an array of ethnic cuisines from Malaysia, Burma, Vietnam, Indonesia, China, Korea, Thailand and Singapore. The sea bass with peanuts and herbs and wild ginger duck with steamed buns are a nice menu selection. Jazz musicians perform Monday nights. Casual dress. **Bar:** Full bar. **Reservations:** suggested. **Hours:** 11:30 am-3 & 5-11 pm, Fri-midnight, Sat 11:30 am-3 & 4:30-midnight, Sun 4 pm-11 pm. Closed: 7/4, 11/26, 12/25. **Address:** 1401 3rd Ave **Location:** Corner of 3rd Ave and Union St. **Parking:** valet. **Cards:** AX, CB, DC, DS, MC, VI.

ZAINA   Phone: 206/624-5687   [113]

▼▼
Middle Eastern
$5-$15

The casual Middle Eastern restaurant is tucked just off of Pioneer Square. Offerings include falafel, baklava and Turkish coffee. Counter service is standard. Casual dress. **Hours:** 10 am-9 pm, Sat from 11 am. Closed: Sun. **Address:** 108 Cherry St **Location:** Between 1st and 2nd aves; in Pioneer Square District. **Parking:** street. **Cards:** AX, DS, MC, VI.

SEATTLE pop. 563,374 (See map and index starting on p. 614)

──── WHERE TO STAY ────

ARTIC CLUB HOTEL   Phone: 206/340-0340

[fyi]
Historic Boutique
Hotel
$305-$675 All Year

Too new to rate. **Address:** 700 3rd Ave **Location:** Corner of 3rd Ave and Cherry St. **Amenities:** 120 units, pets, restaurant, coffeemakers, refrigerators. **Terms:** check-in 4 pm, cancellation fee imposed. **Cards:** AX, CB, DC, DS, JC, MC, VI.

COMFORT INN & SUITES SEATTLE   *Book great rates at AAA.com*   Phone: 206/361-3700   [2]

AAA [SAVE]
▼▼▼▼
Hotel
Rates not provided

Address: 13700 Aurora Ave N **Location:** I-5, exit 175, 1.1 mi w on NE 145th St, then 0.3 mi s. **Facility:** 72 units. 59 one-bedroom standard units, some with kitchens. 13 one-bedroom suites with kitchens. 4 stories, interior corridors. **Parking:** on-site. **Amenities:** DVD players, high-speed Internet, voice mail, irons, hair dryers. **Leisure Activities:** sauna, whirlpool, exercise room. **Guest Services:** valet and coin laundry, wireless Internet **Business Services:** PC. **Free Special Amenities: continental breakfast and high-speed Internet.**

[X] [✦] [▣] / SOME UNITS FEE [🐾] [X] [🔳] [📷]

EXTENDED STAYAMERICA-SEATTLE-NORTHGATE   *Book at AAA.com*   Phone: (206)365-8100   [3]

▼▼▼
Hotel
$90-$110 All Year

Address: 13300 Stone Ave N **Location:** I-5, exit 175, 1 mi w on n 145th St, 0.5 mi s on Aurora Ave, then just e on 135th St. **Facility:** 131 one-bedroom standard units. 3 stories, interior corridors. *Bath:* combo or shower only. **Parking:** on-site. **Terms:** office hours 7 am-11 pm, cancellation fee imposed. **Amenities:** high-speed Internet (fee), voice mail, irons. **Guest Services:** coin laundry, wireless Internet. **Cards:** AX, CB, DC, DS, JC, MC, VI.

[ASK] [✦] [🔳] [📷] [▣] / SOME UNITS FEE [🐾] [X]

GASLIGHT INN   Phone: 206/325-3654   [10]

▼▼▼
Historic Bed
& Breakfast
$88-$158 All Year

Address: 1727 15th Ave **Location:** I-5, exit 164A northbound, 0.9 mi e via Madison St, then just n; exit 166 southbound, 0.5 mi e via Denny Way and Olive St to 15th Ave. **Facility:** Two adjacent, turn-of-the-20th-century homes offer some rooms with fireplaces and views of the cityscape; the main house is Craftsman in style. Smoke free premises. 8 one-bedroom standard units. 3 stories (no elevator), interior corridors. *Bath:* some shared or private, combo or shower only. **Parking:** street. **Terms:** office hours 8 am-6 pm, age restrictions may apply, 7 day cancellation notice-fee imposed. **Amenities:** voice mail, irons, hair dryers. **Pool(s):** heated outdoor. **Guest Services:** wireless Internet. **Business Services:** PC. **Cards:** AX, MC, VI.

[⇆] [X] / SOME UNITS [XC] [🔳]

GEORGETOWN INN   Phone: (206)762-2233   [11]

AAA [SAVE]
▼▼
Hotel
$94-$173 All Year

Address: 6100 Corson Ave S **Location:** I-5, exit 162, just sw. Located in a commercial area. **Facility:** Smoke free premises. 52 units. 50 one-bedroom standard units, some with efficiencies (no utensils) and/or whirlpools. 2 one-bedroom suites with kitchens (no utensils) and whirlpools. 3 stories, interior corridors. **Parking:** on-site. **Terms:** cancellation fee imposed. **Amenities:** high-speed Internet, voice mail. **Leisure Activities:** sauna, exercise room. **Guest Services:** complimentary laundry, wireless Internet. **Cards:** AX, DC, DS, JC, MC, VI. **Free Special Amenities: continental breakfast.**

[❙✚] [X] [✦] [🔳] / SOME UNITS [📷]

HOLIDAY INN EXPRESS HOTEL & SUITES   *Book great rates at AAA.com* Phone: (206)365-7777   [1]

AAA [SAVE]
▼▼▼
Hotel
$129-$179 All Year

Address: 14115 Aurora Ave N **Location:** I-5, exit 175, 1.1 mi w on NE 145th St, then just s. Located in a commerical area. **Facility:** 102 one-bedroom standard units. 4 stories, interior corridors. *Bath:* combo or shower only. **Parking:** on-site. **Terms:** cancellation fee imposed. **Amenities:** high-speed Internet, dual phone lines, voice mail, irons, hair dryers. **Pool(s):** heated indoor. **Leisure Activities:** whirlpool, exercise room. **Guest Services:** valet and coin laundry, wireless Internet. **Business Services:** meeting rooms, PC. **Cards:** AX, CB, DC, DS, JC, MC, VI. **Free Special Amenities: full breakfast and high-speed Internet.**

CALL [♿M] [⇆] [✦] [▣] / SOME UNITS [X] [🔳] [📷]

(See map and index starting on p. 614)

HOTEL DECA   *Book great rates at AAA.com*   **Phone:** (206)634-2000   **6**

Hotel
$249-$399 All Year

Address: 4507 Brooklyn Ave NE **Location:** I-5, exit 169, 0.3 mi e. **Facility:** Smoke free premises. 158 units. 157 one-bedroom standard units. 1 one-bedroom suite. 16 stories, interior corridors. *Bath:* combo or shower only. **Parking:** on-site (fee). **Terms:** cancellation fee imposed. **Amenities:** DVD players, high-speed Internet, voice mail, safes, irons, hair dryers. **Leisure Activities:** exercise room. **Guest Services:** valet laundry, area transportation-within 4 mi, wireless Internet. **Business Services:** meeting rooms, PC. **Cards:** AX, DC, DS, JC, MC, VI. **Free Special Amenities:** newspaper and high-speed Internet.

HOTEL NEXUS SEATTLE   *Book great rates at AAA.com*   **Phone:** (206)365-0700   **4**

Hotel
$99-$159 All Year

Address: 2140 N Northgate Way **Location:** I-5, exit 173, just nw. **Facility:** Smoke free premises. 169 units. 157 one-bedroom standard units, some with whirlpools. 12 one-bedroom suites, some with efficiencies. 4 stories, exterior corridors. *Bath:* combo or shower only. **Parking:** on-site. **Terms:** check-in 4 pm, cancellation fee imposed. **Amenities:** video games (fee), voice mail, irons, hair dryers. *Some:* DVD players, high-speed Internet, dual phone lines. **Dining:** Saffron Bar & Grill, see separate listing. **Pool(s):** heated outdoor. **Leisure Activities:** whirlpools, exercise room. **Guest Services:** valet and coin laundry, area transportation, wireless Internet. **Business Services:** meeting rooms, PC. **Cards:** AX, CB, DC, DS, JC, MC, VI. **Free Special Amenities:** expanded continental breakfast and high-speed Internet.
(See color ad below)

MILDRED'S BED & BREAKFAST   **Phone:** 206/325-6072   **9**

Bed & Breakfast
$165-$195 3/1-10/1
$145-$175 10/2-2/28

Address: 1202 15th Ave E **Location:** I-5, exit 166 northbound, 0.8 mi e on Olive Way, then 0.7 mi n; exit 168A southbound, just e on Roanoke St, 0.3 mi s on 10th Ave, just w on Boston St, then 0.5 mi e. Located across from Volunteer Park. **Facility:** Smoke free premises. 4 one-bedroom standard units. 3 stories (no elevator), interior corridors. *Bath:* combo or shower only. **Parking:** street. **Terms:** check-in 4 pm, 2-3 night minimum stay - seasonal and/or weekends, 7 day cancellation notice-fee imposed. **Amenities:** video library, hair dryers. *Some:* DVD players. **Leisure Activities:** putting green. **Guest Services:** wireless Internet. **Business Services:** PC. **Cards:** AX, MC, VI.

SILVER CLOUD INN-UNIVERSITY VILLAGE   *Book at AAA.com*   **Phone:** (206)526-5200   **5**

Hotel
$179-$249 All Year

Address: 5036 25th Ave NE **Location:** I-5, exit 169, 1 mi e on NE 45th St, then just n. **Facility:** Smoke free premises. 179 units. 163 one-bedroom standard units. 16 one-bedroom suites. 4 stories, interior corridors. *Bath:* combo or shower only. **Parking:** on-site. **Amenities:** high-speed Internet, voice mail, irons, hair dryers. **Pool(s):** heated indoor. **Leisure Activities:** whirlpool, exercise room. **Guest Services:** complimentary and valet laundry, area transportation, wireless Internet. **Business Services:** meeting rooms, PC. **Cards:** AX, DC, DS, JC, MC, VI.

(See map and index starting on p. 614)

UNIVERSITY INN   *Book great rates at AAA.com*   Phone: (206)632-5055   **8**

Hotel
$145-$185 All Year

Address: 4140 Roosevelt Way NE **Location:** I-5, exit 169, 0.5 mi e, then just s. **Facility:** Smoke free premises. 102 one-bedroom standard units. 4 stories, interior corridors. *Bath:* combo or shower only. **Parking:** on-site. **Terms:** cancellation fee imposed. **Amenities:** video games (fee), voice mail, safes, irons, hair dryers. *Some:* CD players. **Dining:** Portage Bay Cafe, see separate listing. **Pool(s):** heated outdoor. **Leisure Activities:** whirlpool, exercise room. **Guest Services:** complimentary and valet laundry, area transportation, wireless Internet. **Business Services:** meeting rooms, PC. **Cards:** AX, DC, DS, MC, VI. *(See color ad below)*

ASK ⊕ ⊕ ⊠ ⊕ ⊕ / SOME UNITS FEE ⊕ ⊕ ⊕

WATERTOWN   *Book great rates at AAA.com*   Phone: (206)826-4242   **7**

Hotel
$179-$229 3/1-10/31
$159-$209 11/1-2/28

Address: 4242 Roosevelt Way NE **Location:** I-5, exit 169, just e, then just s. **Facility:** Smoke free premises. 100 one-bedroom standard units, some with whirlpools. 6 stories, interior corridors. *Bath:* combo or shower only. **Parking:** on-site. **Amenities:** high-speed Internet, voice mail, safes, irons, hair dryers. **Leisure Activities:** bicycles, exercise room. **Guest Services:** complimentary and valet laundry, area transportation, wireless Internet. **Business Services:** meeting rooms, PC. **Cards:** AX, CB, DC, DS, JC, MC, VI. *(See color ad p 629)*

ASK CALL ⊕ ⊠ ⊕ ⊕ ⊕ ⊕

(See map and index starting on p. 614)

———— WHERE TO DINE ————

5 SPOT
Phone: 206/285-7768 ㉚
♦♦ ♦♦
American
$6-$28
Though a diner, the eatery does not serve your typical diner food; heaping portions of everything from salmon scramble at breakfast to house-made brisket for dinner are featured at the very busy location. Casual dress. **Bar:** Full bar. **Hours:** 8:30 am-midnight, Sat & Sun 8:30 am-3 & 5-midnight. Closed: 11/26, 12/24, 12/25. **Address:** 1502 Queen Anne Ave N **Location:** Jct Gater St; in Queen Anne District. **Parking:** street. **Cards:** MC, VI.

ANGELINA'S TRATTORIA
Phone: 206/932-7311 ㊸
♦♦ ♦♦
Italian
$8-$20
The casual eatery on the west side of town offers friendly service and tasty food. Casual dress. **Bar:** Beer & wine. **Reservations:** accepted. **Hours:** 11:30 am-9 pm, Fri-10 pm, Sat 8 am-10 pm, Sun 8 am-9 pm. Closed major holidays. **Address:** 2311 California Ave SW **Location:** W on W Seattle Bridge, exit SW Admiral Way, 1 mi n, then just n; in West Seattle. **Parking:** on-site. **Cards:** AX, DS, MC, VI.

AURORA BURGERMASTER
Phone: 206/522-2044 ②
♦♦
American
$5-$9
This is the drive-up eatery that you remember from your childhood, where once your car headlights have been turned on, a staff person comes straight to your car window to take your order of burger, onion rings and a malt. Don't forget to leave your window up about 3 inches as that is where your tray will hang when the food is delivered. Casual dress. **Reservations:** not accepted. **Hours:** 11 am-11 pm, Fri & Sat-midnight. Closed: 11/26, 12/25. **Address:** 9820 Aurora Ave **Location:** Jct SR 99 (Aurora Ave) and 100th St. **Parking:** on-site. **Cards:** MC, VI.
🅰

BLUE ONION BISTRO
Phone: 206/729-0579 ⑩
♦♦ ♦♦
American
$14-$22
The converted 1930s filling station is a local favorite, serving freshly baked bread and featuring vintage art on the walls. Casual dress. **Bar:** Full bar. **Reservations:** accepted. **Hours:** 5 pm-9 pm, Sat & Sun from 8 am. Closed: Mon. **Address:** 5801 Roosevelt Way NE **Location:** I-5, exit 170, 0.5 mi e on NE Ravenna Blvd, then just s; jct 58th St; in Green Lake area. **Parking:** on-site. **Cards:** MC, VI.
🅰

BLUWATER BISTRO
Phone: 206/524-3985 ④
♦♦ ♦♦
American
$8-$22
Friends gather at the trendy neighborhood place, and there is always a wait on weekends. A starter of classic spinach salad primes the palate for the roasted, stuffed pork chop or prime sirloin meatloaf. Casual dress. **Bar:** Full bar. **Reservations:** accepted. **Hours:** 4 pm-1 am, Sat & Sun from 9 am. Closed: 12/25. **Address:** 7900 E Green Lake Dr N **Location:** I-5, exit 172 (N 85th St), 0.3 mi w, then 0.3 mi s on Wallingford Ave; in Green Lake area. **Parking:** on-site. **Cards:** AX, DC, MC, VI.

BOMBAY GRILL
Phone: 206/632-5072 ⑮
♦♦ ♦♦
Indian
$7-$15
Featuring exotic villa decor taken from various regions in India, this restaurant has been serving Indian cuisine for more than 30 years. Dishes such as tandoori chicken and items on the all-you-can-eat luncheon buffet make this a must for lovers of Indian fare. Casual dress. **Bar:** Full bar. **Reservations:** suggested, weekends. **Hours:** 11:30 am-2:30 & 5-10 pm. **Address:** 4737 Roosevelt Way NE **Location:** I-5, exit 169, 0.5 mi e, then just s; in University District. **Parking:** on-site. **Cards:** AX, CB, DC, DS, MC, VI.
CALL 🚹♿

BURGERMASTER
Phone: 206/525-7100 ⑯
♦♦ ♦♦
American
$3-$7
The eatery offers an indoor spin on the old drive-up. Guests come in to order their burgers, onion rings and milk shakes, then pick a table, where they set out their assigned number so the staff can easily determine where to deliver the food. The dining room bustles with activity. Warm apple pie with cinnamon sauce is a sure way to top off a filling belly. Casual dress. **Reservations:** not accepted. **Hours:** 6:30 am-10 pm, Sun from 7:30 am. Closed: 4/12, 11/26, 12/25. **Address:** 3040 NE 45th St **Location:** I-5, exit 169, 1.2 mi e; in University District. **Parking:** on-site. **Cards:** AX, DC, DS, MC, VI.

CACTUS MADISON PARK
Phone: 206/324-4140 ㉘
♦♦ ♦♦
Mexican
$7-$19
Traditional Mexican food is served in a Southwestern atmosphere. The restaurant's location in a trendy walking area is ideal for diners who want to stroll after their meal. Casual dress. **Bar:** Full bar. **Hours:** 11:30 am-3 & 5-10 pm, Fri & Sat-11 pm, Sun 4 pm-10 pm. Closed: major holidays; also 12/24. **Address:** 4220 E Madison St **Location:** I-5, exit Madison St, 3 mi ne. **Parking:** street. **Cards:** AX, CB, DC, DS, MC, VI.

CAFE FLORA
Phone: 206/325-9100 ㉞
♦♦ ♦♦ ♦♦
Vegetarian
$10-$10
An upscale vegetarian cafe, it offers three eating areas: an open, airy dining room, an area for private parties, and a garden room with a fountain and lots of live plants and trees. Imaginative and healthy, the cuisine features fresh, homemade dishes. Casual dress. **Bar:** Beer & wine. **Hours:** 11:30 am-10 pm, Sat & Sun 9 am-2 & 5-10 pm. Closed: 7/4, 12/25. **Address:** 2901 E Madison St **Location:** Just e of jct Madison St and Martin Luther King Jr Way. **Parking:** on-site. **Cards:** MC, VI.
CALL 🚹♿

CAFE LAGO
Phone: 206/329-8005 ㉓
♦♦ ♦♦
Italian
$15-$21
Locals congregate over fresh pasta and hearty wine at the bright and open streetside cafe. On the menu are wood-fired pizzas, antipasti and pasta specialties, such as homemade lasagna and ravioli all'aquilana. Casual dress. **Bar:** Full bar. **Reservations:** accepted. **Hours:** 5 pm-9:30 pm, Fri & Sat-10 pm, Sun & Mon-9 pm. Closed major holidays. **Address:** 2305 24th Ave E **Location:** Jct E Lynn St; in northeast Seattle. **Parking:** street. **Cards:** AX, CB, DC, DS, MC, VI.

(See map and index starting on p. 614)

CANLIS
Phone: 206/283-3313 [21]

Regional American
$34-$70

In the relaxed, upscale atmosphere, a pianist plays as guests take in breathtaking views of the Cascade Mountains and serene Lake Union. A Pacific Northwest-focused menu offers such choices as fresh king salmon or Kobe-style Washington steaks, served with fresh market vegetables. The food can be accompanied by a bottle of wine from the award-winning cellar. Save room for dark chocolate lava cake. Semi-formal attire. Entertainment. **Bar:** Full bar. **Reservations:** suggested. **Hours:** 5:30 pm-9 pm, Fri & Sat 5 pm-10 pm. Closed major holidays; also Sun. **Address:** 2576 Aurora Ave N **Location:** Cross street Halladay St; 1.5 mi n of Space Needle. **Parking:** valet. **Cards:** AX, CB, DC, DS, MC, VI.

CALL [&M]

CARMELITA
Phone: 206/706-7703 [5]

Vegetarian
$16-$18

Offering intimate dining in an artsy setting, the restaurant features a seasonal menu influenced by foods and flavors from around the Mediterranean, including haute vegetarian cuisine. During summer months, guests can enjoy their dining experience on the garden patio. Dressy casual. **Bar:** Beer & wine. **Reservations:** suggested. **Hours:** 5 pm-9 pm, Fri & Sat-10 pm. Closed: 1/1, 7/4, 12/24, 12/25; also Mon. **Address:** 7314 Greenwood Ave N **Location:** Jct 73rd St; in Phinney Ridge area. **Parking:** street. **Cards:** MC, VI.

[K]

CATFISH CORNER
Phone: 206/323-4330 [40]

Seafood
$6-$13

When folks crave catfish, red beans and rice or prawns, they head to the quaint little diner, which serves them fresh and quickly. Casual dress. **Hours:** 11 am-10 pm, Sat from noon. Closed major holidays; also Sun. **Address:** 2726 E Cherry St **Location:** Jct Martin Luther King Jr Way. **Parking:** street. **Cards:** MC, VI.

CHINOOK'S AT SALMON BAY
Phone: 206/283-4665 [19]

Seafood
$6-$22

On Fisherman's Wharf, the restaurant offers fresh seafood and views of the marina. Reservations aren't accepted, so short waits are common. Casual dress. **Bar:** Full bar. **Reservations:** not accepted. **Hours:** 11 am-10 pm, Fri-11 pm, Sat 7:30 am-11 pm, Sun 7:30 am-10 pm. Closed: 11/26, 12/25. **Address:** 1900 W Nickerson St, Suite 103 **Location:** At Fisherman's Terminal. **Parking:** on-site. **Cards:** AX, MC, VI.

CIRCA
Phone: 206/923-1102 [44]

American
$8-$20

Popular for locals at lunch, the casual eatery on the west side of town serves up comfort food. Casual dress. **Bar:** Beer & wine. **Reservations:** not accepted. **Hours:** 11:30 am-2:30 & 5-9 pm, Sat & Sun 9 am-2 & 5-9 pm. Closed major holidays. **Address:** 2605 California Ave SW **Location:** West on W Seattle Bridge, exit SW Admiral Way, 1 mi n, then just s; in West Seattle. **Parking:** on-site. **Cards:** AX, DC, DS, MC, VI.

CRUSH
Phone: 206/302-7874 [36]

American
$22-$38

The trendy little home is all about wine and great food. Reservations are recommended at the intimate venue, where diners tend to linger and order s'mores for dessert. Dressy casual. **Bar:** Full bar. **Reservations:** suggested. **Hours:** 5:30 pm-10:30 pm. Closed: 7/4, 11/26, 12/24, 12/25; also Mon. **Address:** 2319 E Madison St **Location:** Just e of 23rd St; in Madison Valley. **Parking:** street. **Cards:** AX, DC, DS, MC, VI.

[K]

DUKE'S CHOWDER HOUSE
Phone: 206/522-4908 [3]

Seafood
$8-$25

The name says it all: expect excellent chowder and fresh seafood and meats served in a nautical decor. Casual dress. **Bar:** Full bar. **Reservations:** accepted. **Hours:** 11 am-11 pm, Fri & Sat-midnight. Closed: 11/26, 12/25. **Address:** 7850 Greenlake Dr N **Location:** I-5, exit 172, 2 mi w on 85th St, 0.5 mi s on Aurora Ave, then just sw; across from lake; in Green Lake area. **Parking:** on-site. **Cards:** AX, DS, MC, VI.

DULCES LATIN BISTRO
Phone: 206/322-5453 [38]

Latin American
$18-$32

In the upscale residential neighborhood of Madrona, the polished restaurant presents a menu that fuses Latin, French, Italian, Spanish and regional Mexican cuisine. Among offerings are interesting appetizers, classic paella, hand-made pasta and well-prepared desserts. Most entrees are available in half portions. The extensive wine list lists more than 1,200 labels. A separate cigar room is on the premises. Casual dress. **Bar:** Full bar. **Reservations:** suggested. **Hours:** 5 pm-10 pm. Closed major holidays; also Sun & Mon. **Address:** 1430 34th Ave **Location:** Between E Union and E Pike sts. **Parking:** street. **Cards:** AX, DS, MC, VI.

CALL [&M]

KABUL AFGHAN CUISINE   _Menu on AAA.com_
Phone: 206/545-9000 [17]

(AAA)

Afghan
$9-$28

A unique culinary experience, this eatery features kabobs and vegetarian dishes served in a large dining room that is decorated with a collection of hats from Afghanistan. Try the savory Ashak, fresh pasta topped with seasoned ground beef and yogurt/garlic sauce. Dressy casual. **Bar:** Beer & wine. **Hours:** 5 pm-9:30 pm, Fri & Sat-10 pm. Closed major holidays. **Address:** 2301 N 45th St **Location:** I-5, exit 169, 0.5 mi w. **Parking:** street. **Cards:** AX, DC, DS, MC, VI.

KINGFISH CAFE
Phone: 206/320-8757 [33]

Southern Soul Food
$7-$19

The intimate diner serves ample portions of Southern soul food. Down-home macaroni and cheese with two cheeses and bits of onion and mushroom is a favorite, as are buttermilk fried chicken and barbecue ribs. Diners lucky enough to visit during the summer can splurge on the enormous strawberry shortcake. Casual dress. **Bar:** Full bar. **Reservations:** not accepted. **Hours:** 11:30 am-2 & 5:30-9:30 pm, Fri-10:30 pm; Saturday & Sunday brunch 10 am-2 pm. Closed: 11/26, 12/25. **Address:** 602 19th Ave E **Location:** At 19th Ave and Mercer St; Northeast Seattle. **Parking:** street. **Cards:** MC, VI.

[K]

(See map and index starting on p. 614)

MACRINA BAKERY & CAFE
Phone: 206/283-5900   (25)

♦♦♦ ♦♦♦

Breads/Pastries

$7-$11

In the Queen Anne neighborhood, the quaint bakery and cafe prepares exquisite baked goods throughout the day. Cafe seating is available. Casual dress. **Reservations:** not accepted. **Hours:** 7 am-7 pm, Sun 8 am-6 pm. Closed major holidays. **Address:** 615 W McGraw St **Location:** At 6th Ave; at top of Queen Anne Hill. **Parking:** street. **Cards:** MC, VI.

MANDARIN CHEF RESTAURANT
Phone: 206/528-7596   (14)

♦♦♦ ♦♦♦

Chinese

$6-$12

Traditional dishes, such as hot and sour soup and kung pao chicken, are prepared in Hunan, Szechuan and Mandarin styles. Homemade hand-shaved noodles and dumplings lend freshness to the preparations. Attractive oil paintings and silk plants decorate the cozy dining room. Casual dress. **Bar:** Beer & wine. **Reservations:** accepted. **Hours:** 11 am-10 pm. Closed: 11/26, 12/25; also Sun. **Address:** 5022 University Way NE **Location:** I-5, exit 169, 0.3 mi e on 45th St, then 0.3 mi n; 3 mi ne of downtown; in University District. **Parking:** street. **Cards:** MC, VI.

MARKET STREET GRILL
Phone: 206/789-6766   (12)

♦♦♦ ♦♦♦

American

$15-$29

The urban grill offers meals that reflect a spin on Eurocentric cuisine. Casual dress. **Bar:** Full bar. **Reservations:** suggested. **Hours:** 5 pm-10 pm, Fri & Sat-11 pm. Closed major holidays. **Address:** 1744 NW Market St **Location:** In Ballard District. **Parking:** on-site. **Cards:** AX, DS, MC, VI.

MCMENAMINS
Phone: 206/632-6505

♦♦♦ ♦♦♦

American

$5-$20

The casual neighborhood eatery is where friends gather for classic pub and comfort fare, all washed down by pints of locally made beer. Large wooden booths or tables easily accommodate larger groups, and the eclectic, custom-painted walls and varied period light fixtures keep diners' eyes busy should the conversation lag. Casual dress. **Bar:** Full bar. **Hours:** 11:30 am-1 am, Fri & Sat-2 am, Sun-midnight. Closed: 11/26, 12/25. **Address:** 3601 Fremont Ave N **Location:** Jct N 36th St; in Fremont District. **Parking:** street. **Cards:** MC, VI.

MONSOON
Phone: 206/325-2111   (32)

♦♦♦ ♦♦♦

Vietnamese

$8-$18

Impressively prepared Vietnamese cuisine is the feature at the intimate neighborhood restaurant. The freshest vegetables are united with fresh seafood, duck, steak, wild boar, pork loin, chicken or vegetarian ingredients to create a variety of interesting flavors. Food is prepared in an open kitchen, where guests can see and hear the busy staff at work. Outside patio seating is available in season. Dressy casual. **Bar:** Beer & wine. **Reservations:** accepted. **Hours:** 5 pm-10 pm; Saturday & Sunday brunch 10 am-2:30 pm. Closed major holidays. **Address:** 615 19th Ave E **Location:** Just n of jct E Mercer St. **Parking:** street. **Cards:** AX, DS, MC, VI.

NELL'S
Phone: 206/524-4044   (6)

♦♦♦♦♦♦

Continental

$19-$30

Located across a busy boulevard from Green Lake, the large picture windows allow diners to observe the hustling street life while enjoying a Northwest spin on European dishes like Columbia River salmon with salsify braised in veal jus and asparagus. Dressy casual. **Bar:** Full bar. **Reservations:** accepted. **Hours:** 5:30 pm-10 pm. Closed major holidays. **Address:** 6804 E Green Lake Way N **Location:** I-5, exit 170, 0.4 mi w on Ravenna Blvd, then just s. **Parking:** on-site. **Cards:** AX, MC, VI.

ORRAPIN THAI CUISINE
Phone: 206/283-7118   (26)

♦♦♦ ♦♦♦

Thai

$8-$15

Down a quiet side street, the quaint, family-run restaurant dishes up friendly service and traditional Thai dishes. Casual dress. **Bar:** Full bar. **Reservations:** accepted. **Hours:** 11 am-10 pm. Closed: 11/26, 12/25. **Address:** 10 Boston St **Location:** Just e of jct Queen Anne Ave and Boston St; on Queen Anne Hill. **Parking:** street. **Cards:** MC, VI.

[JC]

PALISADE
Phone: 206/285-1000   (31)

♦♦♦♦♦♦

Steak & Seafood

$12-$50

Guests cross the bridge over an attractive indoor tide pool to get to the large, upscale dining room, which looks out at Elliott Bay, the downtown skyline and striking Mount Rainier. Specialties include plank-roasted salmon and wood-fire rotisserie dishes. Casual dress. **Bar:** Full bar. **Reservations:** suggested. **Hours:** 11:15 am-2 & 5-9 pm, Fri 5 pm-10 pm, Sat 4 pm-10 pm, Sun 9:30 am-2 & 4-9 pm. Closed: 12/25. **Address:** 2601 W Marina Pl **Location:** In Elliott Bay Marina. **Parking:** on-site and valet. **Cards:** AX, DC, DS, MC, VI.

PIECORA'S PIZZA
Phone: 206/322-9411   (37)

♦♦♦

Italian

$7-$12

A great place to enjoy a slice, this New York-style pizzeria makes fantastic pies, as well as many other tasty selections. For friendly service and great food, this place is hard to beat. Casual dress. **Bar:** Full bar. **Reservations:** not accepted. **Hours:** 11:30 am-11 pm, Fri-midnight, Sat noon-midnight, Sun noon-10 pm. Closed: 12/25. **Address:** 1401 E Madison St **Location:** Southwest corner of E Madison St and 14th Ave; in Capital Hill area. **Parking:** on-site. **Cards:** AX, DS, MC, VI.

PONTI SEAFOOD GRILL
Phone: 206/284-3000   (20)

♦♦♦ ♦♦♦

Seafood

$16-$40

A view of the ship canal entertains diners who relax on the patio of the seafood restaurant. Pan-Asian influences are evident in some entree preparations. Casual dress. **Bar:** Full bar. **Reservations:** accepted. **Hours:** 5 pm-9:30 pm, Fri & Sat-10 pm; 11 am-10 pm, Sat from 5 pm, Sun 5 pm-9:30 pm 12/1-12/31; hours vary in winter. Closed: 12/25. **Address:** 3014 3rd Ave N **Location:** Just w of Fremont Bridge at Nickerson St. **Parking:** valet. **Cards:** AX, CB, DC, DS, MC, VI.

CALL [&M]

PORTAGE BAY CAFE
Phone: 206/547-8230   (18)

♦♦♦ ♦♦♦

Regional American

$8-$12

This lighthearted cafe serves up fresh, nourishing cuisine with a homey charm. Brightly painted walls create a cheery mood as a racing scull suspended from the ceiling appears to glide overhead. A noteworthy item is the unique bananas Foster French toast. Casual dress. **Bar:** Beer & wine. **Hours:** 7:30 am-3 pm. Closed: 11/26, 12/25. **Address:** 4130 Roosevelt Way NE **Location:** I-5, exit 169, 0.5 mi e, then just s; in University Inn. **Parking:** on-site. **Cards:** AX, DC, MC, VI.

(See map and index starting on p. 614)

RAM RESTAURANT AND BREWERY
Phone: 206/525-3565

▼▼ ▼▼
American
$8-$22

The enormous restaurant features high ceilings, huge television screens, large sports-themed banners and a brew pub area. The menu is equally enormous, with steaks, poultry, pasta, seafood, salads, sandwiches and pizza. The on-site brewery turns out a large selection of microbrews. Casual dress. **Bar:** Full bar. **Reservations:** not accepted. **Hours:** 11 am-close. Closed: 12/25. **Address:** 2650 University Village **Location:** I-5, exit 169, 1.1 mi e on NE 45th St, then just n; northeast corner of University Village. **Parking:** on-site. **Cards:** AX, MC, VI.

RAY'S BOATHOUSE
Phone: 206/789-3770   ⑧

▼▼▼▼
Seafood
$18-$45

Offering lovely views of Puget Sound, the upscale eatery is known for its elegant presentation and careful preparation of Northwest cuisine. Simple cooking methods preserve all the natural flavors and textures of the local ingredients used during preparation. Casual dress. **Bar:** Full bar. **Reservations:** suggested. **Hours:** 5 pm-9:30 pm, Sat & Sun from 4:30 pm. Closed: 12/25. **Address:** 6049 Seaview Ave NW **Location:** I-5, exit 169, 4.5 mi w via N 45th and NW Market sts. **Parking:** valet. **Cards:** AX, CB, DC, DS, MC, VI.

RAY'S CAFE
Phone: 206/782-0094   ⑨

▼▼ ▼▼
Seafood
$8-$20

Upstairs from the more upscale Ray's Boathouse, the casual bistro-style dining room features the same carefully prepared Northwest cuisine as its downstairs neighbor but with a more relaxed attitude and more fun menu items such as lunchtime burgers. Casual dress. **Bar:** Full bar. **Reservations:** accepted. **Hours:** 11:30 am-10 pm, Fri & Sat-10:30 pm. Closed: 12/25. **Address:** 6049 Seaview Ave NW **Location:** I-5, exit 169, 4.5 mi w via N 45th and NW Market sts. **Parking:** on-site. **Cards:** AX, CB, DC, DS, MC, VI.

ROVER'S RESTAURANT
Phone: 206/325-7442   ㉟

▼▼▼▼ ▼▼▼▼
French
$35-$130

Innovative French creations by the chef/owner are the primary focus of the intimate eatery. Dining options are a la carte or from five- or eight-course menus, with which the staff is happy to suggest wines from the extensive list. Hungry diners leave totally satisfied. Dressy casual. **Bar:** Full bar. **Reservations:** required. **Hours:** 5:30 pm-9:30 pm, Tues-Thurs from 6 pm, Fri noon-1:30 pm. Closed: Sun & Mon. **Address:** 2808 E Madison St **Location:** I-5, exit Madison St, 2 mi e. **Parking:** street. **Cards:** AX, MC, VI.

SAFFRON BAR & GRILL
Phone: 206/417-0707   ①

▼▼ ▼▼
American
$7-$27

The casual restaurant serves standard American fare with beef, chicken and seafood choices, as well as some lighter dishes. Casual dress. **Bar:** Full bar. **Reservations:** accepted. **Hours:** 11 am-10:30 pm, Fri-11:30 pm, Sat 8 am-11:30 pm, Sun 8 am-10:30 pm. **Address:** 2132 N Northgate Way **Location:** I-5, exit 173, just nw; adjacent to Hotel Nexus Seattle. **Parking:** on-site. **Cards:** AX, CB, DC, DS, MC, VI.
(See color ad p 658)

ST. CLOUDS
Phone: 206/726-1522   ㊴

▼▼ ▼▼
International
$10-$24

The restaurant's distinctive feature is the menu, which centers on home-style dishes jazzed up with gourmet flair, spice, sauces and tempting ingredients. Casual dress. **Bar:** Full bar. **Reservations:** suggested. **Hours:** 5 pm-midnight, Saturday & Sunday brunch 9 am-2:30 pm. Closed: 7/4, 11/26, 12/25. **Address:** 1131 34th Ave **Location:** Just s of jct Union St. **Parking:** street. **Cards:** AX, DS, MC, VI.

SALTY'S ON ALKI
Phone: 206/937-1600   ㊷

▼▼▼▼
Seafood
$12-$70

From the waterfront restaurant's open patio and the windowed dining room, diners appreciate spectacular views of the city skyline and Elliott Bay. Flavors from around the world meld in such dishes as blackened salmon on Caesar salad. The Sunday brunch is especially popular, as are the in-house desserts. Casual dress. **Bar:** Full bar. **Reservations:** suggested. **Hours:** 11 am-3 & 5-9 pm, Fri-9:30 pm, Sat 9 am-1:30 & 4-9:30 pm, Sun 9 am-1:30 & 4-9 pm; Saturday and Sunday brunch; extended hours in summer. Closed: 12/25. **Address:** 1936 Harbor Ave SW **Location:** I-3, exit 163 via W Seattle Frwy and Harbor Ave; in West Seattle. **Parking:** on-site. **Cards:** AX, CB, DC, DS, JC, MC, VI.

SERAFINA
Phone: 206/323-0807   ㉗

▼▼▼▼
Italian
$10-$28

Amazing Italian cuisine such as the signature melanzana alla Serafina, which consists of eggplant rolled with ricotta and fresh basil, is the trademark of the romantic restaurant. Garden dining in the European courtyard is inviting. Casual dress. Entertainment. **Bar:** Full bar. **Reservations:** suggested. **Hours:** 11:30 am-2:30 & 5:30-10 pm, Fri-11 pm, Sat 5:30 pm-11 pm, Sun 10 am-2:30 & 5:30-10 pm. Closed: 1/1, 11/26, 12/24, 12/25. **Address:** 2043 Eastlake Ave E **Location:** Corner of Boston St and Eastlake Ave. **Parking:** street. **Cards:** AX, MC, VI.

Ⓚ

SIAM ON LAKE UNION
Phone: 206/323-8101   ㉙

▼▼ ▼▼
Thai
$7-$17

The popular Thai hangout can be a little difficult to find; the old freight car, converted caboose and old English telephone booth give visual cues. Those who like to feel the heat in their food should request four chili peppers for some of the hottest, nose-dripping, mouth-burning action. Casual dress. **Bar:** Full bar. **Reservations:** accepted. **Hours:** 11:30 am-10 pm, Fri-11 pm, Sat 5 pm-11 pm, Sun 5 pm-10 pm. Closed: major holidays; also 12/24. **Address:** 1880 Fairview Ave E **Location:** Southeast end of Lake Union. **Parking:** on-site. **Cards:** AX, MC, VI.

SZMANIA'S
Phone: 206/284-7305   ㉔

▼▼▼▼
Regional
Continental
$6-$24

The owner-chef's creativity is demonstrated in such dishes as Chilean sea bass with steamed vegetables and creme brulee trio. Hanging fabrics, soft lighting, candles and a fossil stone fireplace contribute to an intimate, romantic ambiance. Casual dress. **Bar:** Full bar. **Reservations:** suggested. **Hours:** 11:30 am-2 & 5-10 pm, Sat & Sun from 5 pm. Closed major holidays; also Mon. **Address:** 3321 W McGraw St **Location:** 3.5 mi nw of Space Needle via Elliott Way; over Magnolia Bridge. **Parking:** on-site. **Cards:** AX, MC, VI.

TANGLETOWN
Phone: 206/547-5929   ⑬

▼▼ ▼▼
American
$7-$15

The food is good and the beers made in house at the local neighborhood kind of place. Casual dress. **Bar:** Full bar. **Reservations:** not accepted. **Hours:** 11:30 am-10 pm, Sat 10 am-11 pm, Sun 10 am-10 pm. Closed: 1/1, 11/26, 12/25. **Address:** 2106 N 55th St **Location:** I-5, exit 169, 0.5 mi w on NE 50th St, then 0.5 mi n. **Parking:** street. **Cards:** AX, MC, VI.

(See map and index starting on p. 614)

TEMPERO DO BRASIL
Brazilian
$11-$20

Phone: 206/523-6229   (11)

Patrons enjoy the traditional flavors and musical sounds of Brazil at this vibrant restaurant while unwinding indoors or on the patio. Musicians perform Thursday through Saturday. Casual dress. **Bar:** Full bar. **Reservations:** suggested. **Hours:** 5 pm-10 pm; from 6 pm 6/30-9/30. Closed: 11/26, 12/25; also Mon. **Address:** 5628 University Way NE **Location:** Just s of NE 56th St. **Parking:** street. **Cards:** AX, DC, DS, MC, VI.

TERRY'S 14 CARROT CAFE'
American
$8-$10

Phone: 206/324-1442   (22)

An institution in this quiet neighborhood since 1977, the locally popular breakfast and lunch restaurant prides itself on the fresh ingredients used and the fact that the food is prepared from scratch on site. Some Greek influence shows in such fine offerings as the Athenian omelet with feta cheese, black olives, artichokes, tomatoes, onions and gyro. Making the casual dining room distinctive is the lovely, colorful decor, including the many paintings and art pieces on display. Casual dress. **Reservations:** accepted. **Hours:** 7 am-3 pm, Sat & Sun-4 pm. Closed: 12/25. **Address:** 2305 Eastlake Ave E **Location:** Jct E Lynn St, just n. **Parking:** street. **Cards:** AX, MC, VI.

THAT'S AMORE! ITALIAN CAFE
Italian
$8-$19

Phone: 206/322-3677   (41)

Pizza and delightful pasta dishes are prepared at the neighborhood eatery, which sits atop the Mount Baker tunnel over Interstate 90. Large windows take in the wonderful view of downtown. Casual dress. **Bar:** Beer & wine. **Reservations:** accepted. **Hours:** 11:30 am-9 pm, Fri-10 pm, Sat 4 pm-10 pm, Sun 10 am-9 pm; Sunday brunch. Closed major holidays. **Address:** 1425 31st Ave S **Location:** I-90, exit Rainier Ave S, just s to S Massachusetts St, 1.3 mi, then just n. **Parking:** street. **Cards:** AX, MC, VI.

ZESTO'S
American
$5-$14

Phone: 206/783-3350   (7)

At the traditional burger place, patrons order freshly made burgers from a young staffer at the counter and then dig in to enormous creations that wash down nicely with a malt. Casual dress. **Hours:** 10 am-10 pm. Closed: 11/26, 12/25. **Address:** 6416 15th Ave NW **Location:** Corner of 15th Ave NW and NW 65th St. **Parking:** on-site. **Cards:** AX, DS, MC, VI.

The following restaurants have not been evaluated by AAA but are listed for your information only.

JAK'S GRILL
(fyi)

Phone: 206/937-7809

Not evaluated. Because reservations are not accepted, diners should arrive early or plan to wait. After an entree of 28-day wet- and dry-aged corn-fed Nebraska beef, which can be prepared in varied ways, a sinful treat awaits in chocolate cake, which is more like a huge piece of fudge. **Address:** 4548 California Ave SW **Location:** In West Seattle.

JAK'S GRILL
(fyi)

Phone: 206/985-8545

Not evaluated. Because reservations are not accepted, diners should arrive early or plan to wait. After an entree of 28-day wet- and dry-aged corn-fed Nebraska beef, which can be prepared in varied ways, a sinful treat awaits in chocolate cake, which is more like a huge piece of fudge. **Address:** 3701 NE 45th **Location:** Just n of University Village.

LE GOURMAND
(fyi)

Phone: 206/784-3463

Not evaluated. The prix fixe menu centers on classic French cuisine prepared with local ingredients. **Address:** 425 NW Market St.

(See map and index starting on p. 614)

The Seattle Vicinity

ARLINGTON pop. 11,713

──── WHERE TO STAY ────

ARLINGTON'S RIVER ROCK INN
Phone: 360/403-7014

Bed & Breakfast
$195-$225 All Year

Address: 15425 133rd Ave NE **Location:** I-5, exit 208 (SR 530), 3.8 mi e on SR 530, 1.2 mi s on SR 9, 0.6 mi e on 204th St NE, 4.6 mi se on Burn Rd, 0.5 mi e on Jordan Trails Rd, then 0.4 mi s. **Facility:** Situated on three acres, all units features a handcrafted, peeled log bed and private deck; two rooms include an electric fireplace. Smoke free premises. 5 one-bedroom standard units, some with whirlpools. 2 stories (no elevator), interior corridors. **Parking:** on-site. **Terms:** check-in 4 pm, 2 night minimum stay - seasonal and/or weekends, age restrictions may apply, 21 day cancellation notice-fee imposed. **Amenities:** CD players, high-speed Internet, hair dryers. *Some:* irons. **Leisure Activities:** whirlpool, hiking trails, spa, horseshoes, volleyball. **Guest Services:** TV in common area, wireless Internet. **Business Services:** PC. **Cards:** AX, DS, MC, VI.

MEDALLION HOTEL
Phone: (360)657-0500

Hotel
$109-$119 All Year

Address: 16710 Smokey Point Blvd **Location:** I-5, exit 206, just e on 172nd St NE, then just s. **Facility:** Smoke free premises. 97 one-bedroom standard units, some with efficiencies and/or whirlpools. 4 stories, interior corridors. *Bath:* combo or shower only. **Parking:** on-site. **Terms:** cancellation fee imposed. **Amenities:** DVD players, CD players, high-speed Internet, dual phone lines, voice mail, irons, hair dryers. **Pool(s):** heated indoor. **Leisure Activities:** whirlpool, exercise room, spa. **Guest Services:** valet and coin laundry, wireless Internet. **Business Services:** meeting rooms, business center. **Cards:** AX, CB, DC, DS, JC, MC, VI. **Free Special Amenities:** full breakfast and high-speed Internet.

AUBURN pop. 40,314   (See map and index starting on p. 626)

──── WHERE TO STAY ────

AUBURN GUESTHOUSE INN   *Book at AAA.com*
Phone: (253)735-9600   **44**

Hotel
$89-$99 All Year

Address: 9 14th Ave NW **Location:** SR 167, exit 15th St NW, 0.8 mi e, just s on A St NE, then just w. Located in a commercial area. **Facility:** 96 one-bedroom standard units. 3 stories, interior corridors. *Bath:* combo or shower only. **Parking:** on-site. **Amenities:** high-speed Internet, voice mail, irons, hair dryers. **Leisure Activities:** whirlpool. **Guest Services:** valet and coin laundry, area transportation, wireless Internet. **Business Services:** PC. **Cards:** AX, DC, DS, MC, VI.

BEST WESTERN PEPPERTREE AUBURN INN   *Book great rates at AAA.com*
Phone: (253)887-7600   **45**

Hotel
$90-$220 All Year

Address: 401 8th St SW **Location:** SR 18, exit C St, just s, then just w. **Facility:** Smoke free premises. 124 units. 114 one-bedroom standard units. 10 one-bedroom suites, some with whirlpools. 4 stories, interior corridors. *Bath:* combo or shower only. **Parking:** on-site. **Amenities:** high-speed Internet, dual phone lines, voice mail, irons, hair dryers. **Pool(s):** heated indoor. **Leisure Activities:** whirlpool, exercise room. **Guest Services:** valet and coin laundry, wireless Internet. **Business Services:** meeting rooms, business center. **Cards:** AX, DS, MC, VI. **Free Special Amenities:** continental breakfast and high-speed Internet.

Best Western
AAA Benefit:
Members save up to 20%, plus 10% bonus points with rewards program.

CEDARS INN AUBURN   *Book great rates at AAA.com*
Phone: (253)833-8007   **43**

Hotel
$55-$109 All Year

Address: 102 15th St NE **Location:** SR 167, exit 15th St NW, 0.8 mi e. **Facility:** 34 one-bedroom standard units. 2 stories (no elevator), interior corridors. **Parking:** on-site. **Terms:** office hours 7 am-10 pm, cancellation fee imposed. **Amenities:** high-speed Internet. **Guest Services:** wireless Internet. **Cards:** AX, DS, JC, MC, VI. **Free Special Amenities:** continental breakfast and high-speed Internet.

(See map and index starting on p. 626)

COMFORT INN-AUBURN   *Book at AAA.com*   Phone: (253)333-8888   42

Hotel
$109-$189 All Year

Address: 1 16th St NE **Location:** SR 167, exit 15th St NW, 0.8 mi e, then just n on A St NE. Located in a commercial area. **Facility:** 53 one-bedroom standard units. 3 stories, interior corridors. *Bath:* combo or shower only. **Parking:** on-site. **Amenities:** voice mail, safes (fee), irons, hair dryers. **Pool(s):** heated indoor. **Leisure Activities:** whirlpool, exercise room. **Guest Services:** valet laundry, wireless Internet. **Business Services:** meeting rooms, PC. **Cards:** AX, CB, DC, DS, JC, MC, VI.

TRAVELODGE SUITES   *Book great rates at AAA.com*   Phone: 253/833-7171   41

Hotel
Rates not provided

Address: 9 16th St NW **Location:** SR 167, exit 15th St NW, 0.8 mi e, then just n on A St NE. Located in a commercial area. **Facility:** 95 one-bedroom standard units. 3 stories, interior corridors. *Bath:* combo or shower only. **Parking:** on-site. **Amenities:** video games (fee), high-speed Internet, hair dryers. **Guest Services:** valet laundry, wireless Internet. **Business Services:** meeting rooms, PC. **Free Special Amenities:** expanded continental breakfast.

——— WHERE TO DINE ———

ROUND TABLE PIZZA   Phone: 253/735-4000

Pizza
$5-$20

This casual, family-oriented pizza place features high-quality ingredients and dough rolled fresh daily. Distinctive specialty pizzas are piled high with toppings. Casual dress. **Bar:** Beer & wine. **Reservations:** not accepted. **Hours:** 11 am-9 pm. Closed major holidays. **Address:** 4002 A St SE **Location:** Corner of A St and Ellingson Rd. **Parking:** on-site. **Cards:** AX, DS, MC, VI.

SUN BREAK CAFE   Phone: 253/939-5225   30

American
$6-$10

Dishing up down-home cooking for close to 25 years, the cafe is open for breakfast and lunch. Helpings are generous, and food is prepared fresh in front of guests' eyes as they order straight from the cook. There can be a sizeable line at lunchtime. Casual dress. **Hours:** 5:30 am-3 pm, Sat & Sun 6 am-1:30 pm. Closed: 11/26, 12/25; also Mon. **Address:** 22 A St SW **Location:** SR 18, exit C St, just n, just e on W Main St, then just s. **Parking:** on-site. **Cards:** MC, VI.

CALL

BAINBRIDGE ISLAND pop. 20,308   (See map and index starting on p. 624)

——— WHERE TO STAY ———

BEST WESTERN BAINBRIDGE ISLAND SUITES   *Book great rates at AAA.com*   Phone: (206)855-9666   1

Hotel
$119-$169 All Year

Address: 350 NE High School Rd **Location:** 0.8 mi n of ferry dock on SR 305, then just w. **Facility:** Smoke free premises. 51 units. 45 one-bedroom standard units, some with efficiencies. 6 one-bedroom suites. 4 stories, interior corridors. *Bath:* combo or shower only. **Parking:** on-site. **Terms:** check-in 4 pm, cancellation fee imposed. **Amenities:** high-speed Internet, voice mail, irons, hair dryers. **Leisure Activities:** exercise room. **Guest Services:** valet and coin laundry, wireless Internet. **Business Services:** PC. **Cards:** AX, DS, JC, MC, VI. **Free Special Amenities:** continental breakfast and high-speed Internet.

Best Western

AAA Benefit:
Members save up to 20%, plus 10% bonus points with rewards program.

——— WHERE TO DINE ———

DOC'S MARINA GRILL   Phone: 206/842-8339   2

American
$6-$30

The high-energy cafe's tri-level dining room affords great views of Puget Sound. Casual dress. **Bar:** Full bar. **Reservations:** suggested. **Hours:** 8 am-10 pm. Closed: 11/26, 12/25. **Address:** 403 Madison Ave S **Location:** Jct Parfitt Way. **Parking:** on-site. **Cards:** AX, DS, MC, VI.

THE STREAMLINER DINER   Phone: 206/842-8595   1

American
$8-$12

A casual diner decor includes vintage tablecloths, an open kitchen, local artwork and Mr. Potatoheads to occupy the kids. Breakfast is served all day and features luscious buttermilk waffles in rich maple syrup. For lunch, try the savory potatoes deluxe. Casual dress. **Hours:** 7 am-2:30 pm, Sun from 7:30 am. Closed: 7/4, 11/26, 12/25. **Address:** 397 Winslow Way E **Location:** Just nw of ferry dock; downtown. **Parking:** on-site.

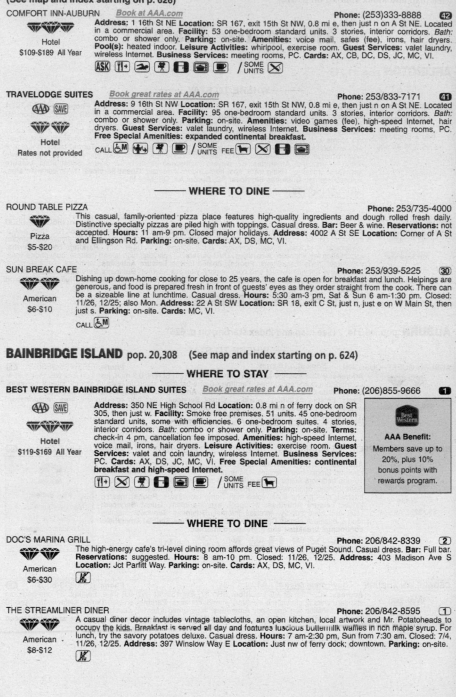

BELLEVUE pop. 109,569   (See map and index starting on p. 614)

——— WHERE TO STAY ———

BELLEVUE CLUB HOTEL

Book great rates at AAA.com

Phone: (425)454-4424   **66**

🔺🔺🔺 (SAVE)
🔻🔻🔻 🔻🔻🔻

Hotel
$285-$655 All Year

Address: 11200 SE 6th St **Location:** I-405, exit 12, 0.4 mi nw. **Facility:** A doorman greets guests at this elegant hotel decorated with hand-crafted cherry wood furniture and artwork by international and local artists. Smoke free premises. 67 units. 64 one-bedroom standard units. 3 one-bedroom suites with whirlpools. 4 stories, interior corridors. *Bath:* combo or shower only. **Parking:** on-site (fee) and valet. **Terms:** cancellation fee imposed. **Amenities:** video games (fee), high-speed Internet, dual phone lines, voice mail, safes, honor bars, irons, hair dryers. *Some:* DVD players, CD players. **Dining:** 3 restaurants. **Pool(s):** heated outdoor, 2 heated indoor. **Leisure Activities:** saunas, whirlpools, steamrooms, lifeguard on duty, 10 tennis courts (6 indoor, 10 lighted), racquetball courts, aerobics studio, running track, gymnasium, kids activity room, jogging, spa, sports court. **Guest Services:** valet laundry, area transportation-within 5 mi, tanning facilities, wireless Internet. **Business Services:** meeting rooms, business center. **Cards:** AX, DC, DS, MC, VI.

🍴 24🕐 🍸 📶 CALL 🆑M 🏊 🐾 ⊠ ✕ 📽 / SOME UNITS FEE 🐾 VCR 📇 🖥

COAST BELLEVUE HOTEL

Book great rates at AAA.com

Phone: 425/455-9444   **60**

🔺🔺🔺 (SAVE)
🔻🔻🔻

Hotel
Rates not provided

Address: 625 116th Ave NE **Location:** I-405, exit 13B, 0.3 mi se. **Facility:** 176 units. 160 one-bedroom standard units. 16 one-bedroom suites. 3-6 stories, interior/exterior corridors. *Bath:* combo or shower only. **Parking:** on-site. **Amenities:** video games (fee), high-speed Internet, voice mail, irons, hair dryers. **Pool(s):** heated outdoor. **Leisure Activities:** exercise room. **Guest Services:** valet and coin laundry, area transportation-within 5 mi, wireless Internet. **Business Services:** conference facilities, PC.

🍴 🍸 CALL 🆑M 🏊 📽 📇 🖥 / SOME UNITS ⊠ 🖥

COURTYARD BY MARRIOTT

Book great rates at AAA.com

Phone: (425)454-5888   **58**

🔻🔻🔻

Hotel
$229-$249 All Year

Address: 11010 NE 8th St **Location:** I-405, exit 13B, just w. **Facility:** Smoke free premises. 253 units. 245 one-bedroom standard units, some with whirlpools. 8 one-bedroom suites. 5 stories, interior corridors. *Bath:* combo or shower only. **Parking:** on-site (fee) and valet. **Terms:** cancellation fee imposed. **Amenities:** CD players, high-speed Internet, dual phone lines, voice mail, irons, hair dryers. **Pool(s):** heated indoor. **Leisure Activities:** whirlpool, exercise room. **Guest Services:** valet and coin laundry, wireless Internet. **Business Services:** meeting rooms, PC. **Cards:** AX, CB, DC, DS, MC, VI.

🍴 🍸 CALL 🆑M 🏊 ✕ 📽 📇 🖥 / SOME UNITS 🖥

COURTYARD *Marriott*

AAA Benefit:
Members save a minimum 5% off the best available rate.

(See map and index starting on p. 614)

COURTYARD BY MARRIOTT   *Book great rates at AAA.com*   Phone: (425)869-5300   **53**

▼▼▼
Hotel
$209-$219 All Year

Address: 14615 NE 29th Pl **Location:** I-405, exit 14 (SR 520), 2.3 mi e to 148th Ave NE (north exit), then just nw. **Facility:** Smoke free premises. 152 units. 144 one-bedroom standard units. 8 one-bedroom suites. 2 stories (no elevator), interior corridors. *Bath:* combo or shower only. **Parking:** on-site. **Terms:** check-in 4 pm, cancellation fee imposed. **Amenities:** high-speed Internet, voice mail, irons, hair dryers. **Pool(s):** indoor. **Leisure Activities:** whirlpool, exercise room. **Guest Services:** valet and coin laundry, wireless Internet. **Business Services:** meeting rooms, business center. **Cards:** AX, CB, DC, DS, JC, MC, VI.

AAA Benefit:
Members save a minimum 5% off the best available rate.

🍴 🍸 CALL 🅜 🏊 ✖ 🎥 🛄 💻 / SOME UNITS 🖨

DAYS INN BELLEVUE   *Book great rates at AAA.com*   Phone: (425)643-6644   **68**

Ⓐ SAVE
▼▼ ▼▼
Hotel
$75-$120 All Year

Address: 3241 156th Ave SE **Location:** I-90, exit 11 westbound; just ne. **Facility:** 106 one-bedroom standard units. 2-3 stories, exterior corridors. **Parking:** on-site. **Amenities:** high-speed Internet, safes (fee), irons, hair dryers. **Leisure Activities:** whirlpool. **Guest Services:** coin laundry, wireless Internet. **Business Services:** meeting rooms, PC. **Cards:** AX, CB, DC, DS, JC, MC, VI. **Free Special Amenities: continental breakfast and high-speed Internet.**

🍴 🛄 🎥 🛄 💻 / SOME UNITS FEE 🐾 ✖ 🖨

EMBASSY SUITES HOTEL BELLEVUE   *Book great rates at AAA.com*   Phone: (425)644-2500   **67**

▼▼▼
Hotel
$119-$279 All Year

Address: 3225 158th Ave SE **Location:** I-90, exit 11 westbound; exit 11A (156th Ave SE) eastbound, just ne. **Facility:** 240 one-bedroom suites, some with whirlpools. 5 stories, interior corridors. **Parking:** on-site. **Terms:** check-in 4 pm, 1-30 night minimum stay, cancellation fee imposed. **Amenities:** voice mail, irons, hair dryers. *Fee:* video games, high-speed Internet. **Pool(s):** heated indoor. **Leisure Activities:** sauna, whirlpool, exercise room. **Guest Services:** valet and coin laundry, area transportation, wireless Internet. **Business Services:** conference facilities, business center. **Cards:** AX, CB, DC, DS, JC, MC, VI.

EMBASSY SUITES
HOTELS'
AAA Benefit:
Members save 5% or more everyday!

🍴 🍸 🏊 ✖ 🎥 🛄 🖨 💻 / SOME UNITS ✖ VCR

EXTENDED STAYAMERICA-SEATTLE-BELLEVUE   *Book at AAA.com*   Phone: (425)453-8186   **63**

▼▼
Hotel
$125-$143 All Year

Address: 11400 Main St **Location:** I-405, exit 13A, just se. **Facility:** 148 one-bedroom standard units with efficiencies. 5 stories, interior corridors. **Parking:** on-site. **Terms:** office hours 7 am-11 pm, cancellation fee imposed. **Amenities:** high-speed Internet (fee), voice mail, irons. **Guest Services:** coin laundry, wireless Internet. **Cards:** AX, CB, DC, DS, JC, MC, VI.

ASK 🎥 🛄 🖨 💻 / SOME UNITS FEE 🐾 ✖

FAIRFIELD INN   *Book great rates at AAA.com*   Phone: (425)869-6548   **54**

▼▼▼
Hotel
$199-$209 All Year

Address: 14595 NE 29th Pl **Location:** I-405, exit 14 (SR 520), 2.3 mi e to 148th Ave NE (north exit), then just nw. **Facility:** Smoke free premises. 144 one-bedroom standard units, some with whirlpools. 3 stories, interior corridors. *Bath:* combo or shower only. **Parking:** on-site. **Terms:** cancellation fee imposed. **Amenities:** video games (fee), high-speed Internet, voice mail, irons, hair dryers. **Pool(s):** heated indoor. **Leisure Activities:** whirlpool, exercise room. **Guest Services:** valet and coin laundry, wireless Internet. **Business Services:** meeting rooms, PC. **Cards:** AX, CB, DC, DS, MC, VI.

AAA Benefit:
Members save a minimum 5% off the best available rate.

🍴 CALL 🅜 🏊 ✖ 🎥 💻 / SOME UNITS 🛄 🖨

HILTON BELLEVUE   *Book great rates at AAA.com*   Phone: (425)455-1300   **65**

▼▼▼
Hotel
$149-$389 All Year

Address: 300 112th Ave SE **Location:** I-405, exit 12, just nw. **Facility:** 360 units. 348 one-bedroom standard units. 5 one-bedroom suites, some with whirlpools. 10 stories, interior corridors. *Bath:* combo or shower only. **Parking:** on-site (fee) and valet. **Terms:** 1-30 night minimum stay, cancellation fee imposed. **Amenities:** high-speed Internet (fee), dual phone lines, voice mail, irons, hair dryers. **Pool(s):** heated outdoor. **Leisure Activities:** whirlpool, exercise room. **Guest Services:** valet laundry, area transportation, wireless Internet. **Business Services:** conference facilities, business center. **Cards:** AX, CB, DC, DS, JC, MC, VI.

Ⓗ
Hilton
AAA Benefit:
Members save 5% or more everyday!

🍴 🍸 🏊 🎥 💻 / SOME UNITS ✖ 🛄

(See map and index starting on p. 614)

HOMESTEAD STUDIO SUITES HOTEL-SEATTLE-BELLEVUE   *Book at AAA.com*   Phone: (425)865-8680   **71**

Motel
$125-$143 All Year

Address: 3700 132nd Ave SE **Location:** I-90, exit 11A (156th Ave SE) westbound; exit 10B eastbound, 0.5 mi se. **Facility:** 150 one-bedroom standard units with efficiencies. 2 stories (no elevator), exterior corridors. *Bath:* combo or shower only. **Parking:** on-site. **Terms:** cancellation fee imposed. **Amenities:** high-speed Internet (fee), voice mail, irons, hair dryers. **Guest Services:** coin laundry, wireless Internet. **Cards:** AX, CB, DC, DS, JC, MC, VI.

HOTEL SIERRA BELLEVUE   *Book great rates at AAA.com*   Phone: (425)747-2705   **69**

Hotel
$109-$249 All Year

Address: 3244 139th Ave SE **Location:** I-90, exit 11 westbound, 0.9 mi w, just n; exit 10B eastbound, just n, 0.7 mi e, then just n. **Facility:** Smoke free premises. 160 units. 128 one-bedroom standard units, some with efficiencies. 32 one-bedroom suites with kitchens. 5 stories, interior corridors. *Bath:* combo or shower only. **Parking:** on-site. **Amenities:** high-speed Internet, irons, hair dryers. **Pool(s):** heated indoor. **Leisure Activities:** whirlpool, sun deck, exercise room. **Guest Services:** valet and coin laundry, area transportation-within 5 mi, wireless Internet. **Business Services:** meeting rooms, PC. **Cards:** AX, CB, DC, DS, JC, MC, VI. **Free Special Amenities: full breakfast and high-speed Internet.**

HYATT REGENCY BELLEVUE   *Book great rates at AAA.com*   Phone: (425)462-1234   **57**

Hotel
$129-$419 All Year

Address: 900 Bellevue Way NE **Location:** I-405, exit 13B, 1.5 mi w on NE 8th St. **Facility:** Located in downtown Bellevue, this property connects to the Wintergarden retail shops and is a short stroll from the Bellevue Square Mall and convention center. 382 units. 360 one-bedroom standard units. 22 one-bedroom suites, some with kitchens and/or whirlpools. 24 stories, interior corridors. *Bath:* combo or shower only. **Parking:** on-site (fee) and valet. **Terms:** cancellation fee imposed. **Amenities:** high-speed Internet (fee), voice mail, safes, irons, hair dryers. *Some:* DVD players, CD players, dual phone lines. **Dining:** 2 restaurants. **Leisure Activities:** exercise room. **Guest Services:** valet laundry, wireless Internet. **Business Services:** conference facilities, business center. **Cards:** AX, CB, DC, DS, JC, MC, VI.

HYATT
HOTELS & RESORTS

AAA Benefit:
Ask for the AAA rate
and save 10%.

LA RESIDENCE SUITE HOTEL   Phone: 425/455-1475   **61**

Hotel
$125-$199 All Year

Address: 475 100th Ave NE **Location:** I-405, exit 13B, 0.9 mi w on NE 8th St, then just s. **Facility:** 24 units. 22 one- and 2 two-bedroom suites with kitchens. 4 stories, interior corridors. **Parking:** on-site. **Terms:** office hours 7 am-10 pm, cancellation fee imposed. **Amenities:** DVD players, high-speed Internet, irons, hair dryers. **Leisure Activities:** limited exercise equipment. **Guest Services:** coin laundry, wireless Internet. **Business Services:** meeting rooms, PC. **Cards:** AX, MC, VI. **Free Special Amenities: local telephone calls and early check-in/late check-out.**

(See map and index starting on p. 614)

LARKSPUR LANDING BELLEVUE/SEATTLE

Book great rates at AAA.com   Phase — **Phone: (425)373-1212**

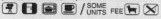

AAA [SAVE]

▽▽▽▽

Hotel
$169-$219 All Year

Address: 15805 SE 37th St **Location:** I-90, exit 11 westbound; exit 11A (156th Ave SE) eastbound, 0.9 mi se on south frontage road. **Facility:** 126 units. 83 one-bedroom standard units with efficiencies. 43 one-bedroom suites with efficiencies. 5 stories, interior corridors. *Bath:* combo or shower only. **Parking:** on-site. **Terms:** cancellation fee imposed. **Amenities:** video library, DVD players, video games (fee), CD players, high-speed Internet, dual phone lines, voice mail, irons, hair dryers. **Leisure Activities:** whirlpool, exercise room. **Guest Services:** complimentary and valet laundry, area transportation-within 5 mi, wireless Internet. **Business Services:** meeting rooms, business center. **Cards:** AX, CB, DC, DS, JC, MC, VI. **Free Special Amenities:** expanded continental breakfast and high-speed Internet. *(See color ad below)*

🎦 🖥 🛎 💻 / SOME UNITS FEE 🐕 ✕

RED LION HOTEL BELLEVUE

Book great rates at AAA.com   **Phone: 425/455-5240**

AAA [SAVE]

▽▽▽▽

Hotel
Rates not provided

Address: 11211 Main St **Location:** I-405, exit 12, 0.4 mi n on 114th St. **Facility:** 181 one-bedroom standard units. 2 stories (no elevator), interior corridors. *Bath:* combo or shower only. **Parking:** on-site. **Terms:** check-in 4 pm. **Amenities:** video games (fee), high-speed Internet, dual phone lines, voice mail, irons, hair dryers. **Pool(s):** heated outdoor. **Leisure Activities:** exercise room. **Guest Services:** valet laundry, area transportation-within 3 mi, wireless Internet. **Business Services:** conference facilities, PC (fee). **Free Special Amenities:** newspaper and high-speed Internet.

🍴 🍸 🏊 🎦 🖥 💻 / SOME UNITS FEE 🐕 ✕

RESIDENCE INN BY MARRIOTT, BELLEVUE-REDMOND

Book great rates at AAA.com   **Phone: (425)882-1222**

▽▽▽▽

Hotel
$215-$263 All Year

Address: 14455 NE 29th Pl **Location:** I-405, exit 14 (SR 520), 2.3 mi e to 148th Ave NE (north exit), then just nw. **Facility:** Smoke free premises. 120 units. 79 one-bedroom standard units with kitchens. 11 one- and 30 two-bedroom suites with kitchens. 2 stories (no elevator), exterior corridors. *Bath:* combo or shower only. **Parking:** on-site. **Terms:** check-in 4 pm, cancellation fee imposed. **Amenities:** high-speed Internet, dual phone lines, voice mail, irons, hair dryers. **Pool(s):** heated outdoor. **Leisure Activities:** whirlpools, exercise room, sports court. **Guest Services:** valet and coin laundry, area transportation, wireless Internet. **Cards:** AX, CB, DC, DS, JC, MC, VI.

🍴 🏊 🚫 ✕ 🎦 🖥 🛎 💻 / SOME UNITS FEE 🐕

AAA Benefit:
Members save a minimum 5% off the best available rate.

RESIDENCE INN BY MARRIOTT SEATTLE-BELLEVUE/DOWNTOWN

Phone: 425/637-8500

[fyi]

Extended Stay Hotel
$233-$285 All Year

Too new to rate, opening scheduled for September 2008. **Address:** 605 114th Ave SE **Location:** I-405, exit 12, just sw. **Amenities:** 231 units, pets, coffeemakers, microwaves, refrigerators, pool. **Terms:** cancellation fee imposed. **Cards:** AX, DS, MC, VI.

AAA Benefit:
Members save a minimum 5% off the best available rate.

▼ *See AAA listing above* ▼

(See map and index starting on p. 614)

SHERATON BELLEVUE HOTEL   *Book great rates at AAA.com*   Phone: (425)455-3330   62

AAA SAVE
▼▼◆▼▼
Hotel
$119-$419 All Year

Address: 100 112th Ave NE **Location:** I-405, exit 12 northbound; exit 13 southbound, just s. **Facility:** Smoke free premises. 178 one-bedroom standard units. 7 stories, interior corridors. *Bath:* combo or shower only. **Parking:** on-site. **Terms:** cancellation fee imposed. **Amenities:** high-speed Internet (fee), dual phone lines, voice mail, irons, hair dress. **Leisure Activities:** exercise room. **Guest Services:** valet laundry, area transportation-within 5 mi, wireless Internet. **Business Services:** conference facilities, business center. **Cards:** AX, CB, DC, DS, JC, MC, VI. **Free Special Amenities:** local telephone calls and newspaper.

⊘ Sheraton
HOTELS & RESORTS

AAA Benefit:
Members get up to 15% off, plus Starwood Preferred Guest® bonuses.

🍽 🍸 CALL 📠M ✕ 🐾 💻 / SOME UNITS 🐾 FEE 🛗

SILVER CLOUD INN-BELLEVUE   *Book at AAA.com*   Phone: (425)637-7000   56

▼◆▼▼
Hotel
$179-$239 All Year

Address: 10621 NE 12th St **Location:** I-405, exit 13B, 0.5 mi nw via NE 8th St W and 106th St. **Facility:** Smoke free premises. 98 units. 95 one-bedroom standard units, some with kitchens and/or whirlpools. 3 one-bedroom suites. 4 stories, interior corridors. *Bath:* combo or shower only. **Parking:** on-site. **Amenities:** high-speed Internet, voice mail, irons, hair dryers. **Pool(s):** heated outdoor. **Leisure Activities:** whirlpool, exercise room. **Guest Services:** complimentary and valet laundry, wireless Internet. **Business Services:** meeting rooms, PC. **Cards:** AX, DC, DS, JC, MC, VI.

🏊 ✕ 🐾 🛗 🖨 💻

SILVER CLOUD INN-BELLEVUE EASTGATE   *Book at AAA.com*   Phone: (425)957-9100   70

▼◆▼▼
Hotel
$189-$239 All Year

Address: 14632 SE Eastgate Way **Location:** I-90, exit 11 westbound; exit 11A (156th Ave SE) eastbound, just ne. **Facility:** Smoke free premises. 152 units. 118 one-bedroom standard units, some with efficiencies and/or whirlpools. 34 one-bedroom suites, some with efficiencies. 6 stories, interior corridors. *Bath:* combo or shower only. **Parking:** on-site. **Amenities:** video games (fee), high-speed Internet, dual phone lines, voice mail, irons, hair dryers. **Leisure Activities:** exercise room. **Guest Services:** complimentary and valet laundry, area transportation, wireless Internet. **Business Services:** meeting rooms, business center. **Cards:** AX, DC, DS, JC, MC, VI.

CALL 📠M ✕ 🐾 🛗 🖨 💻

THE WESTIN BELLEVUE   *Book great rates at AAA.com*   Phone: (425)638-1000   59

AAA SAVE
▼▼◆▼▼
Hotel
$149-$419 All Year

Address: 600 Bellevue Way NE **Location:** I-405, exit 13B, 1.5 mi w on NE 8th St. **Facility:** Featuring luxury linens and pampering service, this downtown hotel is located in Lincoln Square, a shopping, entertainment and business hub. Smoke free premises. 337 units. 319 one-bedroom standard units, some with whirlpools. 18 one-bedroom suites, some with whirlpools. 42 stories, interior corridors. *Bath:* combo or shower only. **Terms:** cancellation fee imposed. **Amenities:** high-speed Internet (fee), dual phone lines, voice mail, safes, honor bars, irons, hair dryers. *Some:* DVD players. **Dining:** 2 restaurants. **Pool(s):** heated indoor. **Leisure Activities:** whirlpool, exercise room. **Guest Services:** valet laundry, wireless Internet. **Business Services:** meeting rooms, business center. **Cards:** AX, CB, DC, DS, JC, MC, VI. **Free Special Amenities:** newspaper.

WESTIN
HOTELS & RESORTS

AAA Benefit:
Enjoy up to 15% off your next stay, plus Starwood Preferred Guest® bonuses.

🍽 🍸 🏊 ✕ 🐾 💻 / SOME UNITS 🐾

——— WHERE TO DINE ———

BURGERMASTER   Phone: 425/827-9566   81

◆▼▼
American
$6-$12

The restaurant evokes memories of the drive-ups guests patronized as children. Once the headlights are turned on, a staff person comes straight to the vehicle's window to take orders, which typically consist of a burger, onion rings and malt. Food is delivered on a tray that hangs on the vehicle's window. Casual dress. **Reservations:** not accepted. **Hours:** 10 am-midnight, Fri & Sat-1 am. **Closed:** 11/26, 12/25. **Address:** 10606 Northup Way **Location:** I-405, exit 14 (SR 520), via 108th Ave exit, s on 108th St, then just w. **Parking:** on-site. **Cards:** AX, CB, DC, DS, MC, VI.

🍴

CHACE'S - PANCAKE CORRAL   Phone: 425/454-8888   85

◆▼◆▼
American
$6-$10

Locals are treated like family at the small eatery, where hearty portions of classic breakfast favorites are delivered piping hot. Casual dress. **Hours:** 5:45 am-2:30 pm, Sat & Sun 6:30 am-3 pm. **Closed:** 12/25. **Address:** 1606 Bellevue Way SE **Location:** I-90, exit 9, 1 mi nw. **Parking:** on-site. **Cards:** MC, VI.

DANIEL'S BROILER, BELLEVUE PLACE   Phone: 425/462-4662   82

▼◆▼◆▼
Steak
$13-$50

The casually elegant restaurant offers sweeping views of the Seattle skyline and the majestic Olympic Mountains. Prime cuts of steak and delectable desserts made in house are menu favorites. Off to the side, the large piano bar is energetic and fun. Casual dress. **Entertainment. Bar:** Full bar. **Reservations:** suggested. **Hours:** 11:30 am-2:30 & 5-10 pm, Fri & Sat-11 pm, Sat & Sun 5 pm-10 pm. **Closed:** 12/25. **Address:** 10500 NE 8th St, Suite 2100 **Location:** I-405, exit 13, 0.5 mi w; 21st floor of high-rise over Bellevue Place public parking. **Parking:** on-site. **Cards:** AX, CB, DC, DS, JC, MC, VI.

THE OREXI   Phone: 425/455-5344   84

▼◆▼
Greek
$6-$15

The relaxed restaurant's authentic Greek menu offers specialties such as avgolemono soup, dolmades and the delicious galactoboureko dessert—orange and lemon custard served hot. The walls are decorated with attractive and subtle fresco paintings. Casual dress. **Bar:** Beer & wine. **Reservations:** accepted. **Hours:** 11 am-9 pm. **Closed:** 11/26, 12/24, 12/25. **Address:** 31 Bellevue Way NE **Location:** Just n of jct Main St and Bellevue Way; downtown. **Parking:** on-site. **Cards:** AX, MC, VI.

(See map and index starting on p. 614)

SEASTAR RESTAURANT & RAW BAR   Phone: 425/456-0010   83

Seafood
$10-$50

One of the hipper new restaurants in town brings friends together for fresh seafood. Those who really want to see it prepared fresh can sit at the raw bar. To enjoy salmon the traditional way, order it prepared on a cedar plank. Casual dress. **Bar:** Full bar. **Reservations:** suggested. **Hours:** 11:30 am-2:30 & 5-10 pm, Sat from 5 pm, Sun 5 pm-9 pm. Closed major holidays. **Address:** 205 108th Ave NE, Suite 100 **Location:** I-405, exit 13A, 0.3 mi w, then just s. **Parking:** on-site and valet. **Cards:** AX, CB, DC, DS, JC, MC, VI.

CALL

——— *The following restaurant has not been evaluated by AAA* ———
but is listed for your information only.

POLARIS   Phone: 425/454-4424

fyi

Not evaluated. On the Continental menu are specialties of lamb, pasta and seafood. **Address:** 11200 SE 6th St **Location:** I-405, exit 12, 0.4 mi nw; in Bellevue Club Hotel.

BOTHELL pop. 30,150   (See map and index starting on p. 614)

——— WHERE TO STAY ———

COMFORT INN & SUITES   *Book great rates at AAA.com*   Phone: (425)402-0900   31

Hotel
$105-$125 All Year

Address: 1414 228th St SE **Location:** I-405, exit 26, just sw on Bothell Everett Hwy, then just e. **Facility:** 61 one-bedroom standard units. 3 stories, interior corridors. *Bath:* combo or shower only. **Parking:** on-site. **Amenities:** DVD players, high-speed Internet, dual phone lines, voice mail, irons, hair dryers. **Pool(s):** heated indoor. **Leisure Activities:** whirlpool. **Guest Services:** valet and coin laundry, wireless Internet. **Business Services:** business center. **Cards:** AX, CB, DC, DS, JC, MC, VI. **Free Special Amenities:** expanded continental breakfast and high-speed Internet.

COUNTRY INN & SUITES BY CARLSON   *Book great rates at AAA.com*   Phone: (425)485-5557   35

Hotel
$79-$179 3/1-9/30
$79-$159 10/1-2/28

Address: 19333 N Creek Pkwy **Location:** I-405, exit 24, just e. **Facility:** 166 units. 140 one-bedroom standard units. 26 one-bedroom suites. 2 stories, interior corridors. *Bath:* combo or shower only. **Parking:** on-site. **Terms:** cancellation fee imposed. **Amenities:** video games (fee), high-speed Internet, voice mail, irons, hair dryers. **Pool(s):** heated outdoor. **Leisure Activities:** whirlpool, exercise room. **Guest Services:** valet and coin laundry, area transportation, wireless Internet. **Business Services:** meeting rooms, PC. **Cards:** AX, CB, DC, DS, JC, MC, VI.

EXTENDED STAYAMERICA-SEATTLE-BOTHELL   *Book at AAA.com*   Phone: (425)402-4252   30

Hotel
$110-$125 All Year

Address: 923 228th St SE **Location:** I-405, exit 26, just sw. **Facility:** 101 one-bedroom standard units. 4 stories, interior corridors. *Bath:* combo or shower only. **Parking:** on-site. **Terms:** office hours 7 am-11 pm, cancellation fee imposed. **Amenities:** high-speed Internet (fee), voice mail, irons. **Guest Services:** coin laundry, wireless Internet. **Cards:** AX, CB, DC, DS, JC, MC, VI.

(See map and index starting on p. 614)

EXTENDED STAY DELUXE SEATTLE-BOTHELL   *Book at AAA.com*   Phone: (425)482-2900   **29**

Hotel
$125-$140 All Year

Address: 22122 17th Ave SE **Location:** I-405, exit 26, just n on Bothell Everett Hwy, just e on Canyon Park Blvd SE, then just s. Located on the edge of a corporate business park. **Facility:** 123 one-bedroom standard units with efficiéncies. 3 stories, interior corridors. *Bath:* combo or shower only. **Parking:** on-site. **Terms:** cancellation fee imposed. **Amenities:** DVD players, CD players, high-speed Internet (fee), dual phone lines, voice mail, irons, hair dryers. **Pool(s):** heated outdoor. **Leisure Activities:** exercise room. **Guest Services:** valet and coin laundry, area transportation, wireless Internet. **Cards:** AX, CB, DC, DS, JC, MC, VI.

HOLIDAY INN EXPRESS CANYON PARK   *Book great rates at AAA.com*   Phone: (425)483-8100   **32**

Hotel
$110-$139 All Year

Address: 22922 15th Ave SE **Location:** I-405, exit 26, just sw on Bothell Everett Hwy, then just e. **Facility:** 62 one-bedroom standard units. 3 stories, interior corridors. *Bath:* combo or shower only. **Parking:** on-site. **Terms:** cancellation fee imposed. **Amenities:** video library, DVD players, high-speed Internet, dual phone lines, voice mail, irons, hair dryers. **Pool(s):** heated indoor. **Leisure Activities:** whirlpool, exercise room. **Guest Services:** valet and coin laundry, wireless Internet. **Business Services:** business center. **Cards:** AX, CB, DC, DS, JC, MC, VI.

RESIDENCE INN BY MARRIOTT SEATTLE NE   *Book great rates at AAA.com*   Phone: (425)485-3030   **34**

Hotel
$188-$230 All Year

Address: 11920 NE 195th St **Location:** I-405, exit 24, 0.4 mi ne. **Facility:** Smoke free premises. 120 units. 50 one-bedroom standard units with kitchens. 41 one- and 29 two-bedroom suites with kitchens. 2 stories (no elevator), exterior corridors. **Parking:** check-in 4 pm, cancellation fee imposed. **Amenities:** high-speed Internet, dual phone lines, voice mail, irons, hair dryers. **Pool(s):** heated outdoor. **Leisure Activities:** whirlpools, exercise room, sports court. **Guest Services:** valet and coin laundry, area transportation, wireless Internet. **Business Services:** meeting rooms, PC. **Cards:** AX, CB, DC, DS, JC, MC, VI.

AAA Benefit:
Members save a minimum 5% off the best available rate.

SPRINGHILL SUITES BY MARRIOTT   *Book great rates at AAA.com*   Phone: (425)398-9700   **33**

Hotel
$159-$189 All Year

Address: 3850 Monte Villa Pkwy **Location:** I-405. exit 24, 0.4 mi e on NE 195th St, 0.7 mi n on 120th Ave NE, then just s. Located on the edge of a business park. **Facility:** Smoke free premises. 84 one-bedroom standard units. 4 stories, interior corridors. *Bath:* combo or shower only. **Parking:** on-site. **Terms:** cancellation fee imposed. **Amenities:** high-speed Internet, dual phone lines, voice mail, irons, hair dryers. **Pool(s):** heated indoor. **Leisure Activities:** whirlpool, exercise room. **Guest Services:** valet and coin laundry, wireless Internet. **Business Services:** meeting rooms, business center. **Cards:** AX, CB, DC, DS, MC, VI.

AAA Benefit:
Members save a minimum 5% off the best available rate.

──────── **WHERE TO DINE** ────────

BONEFISH GRILL   Phone: 425/485-0305   **55**

Seafood
$13-$20

Fish is the house specialty, and the menu and nightly specials offer a variety of choices. Well-prepared food is cooked to perfection. Service is casual in nature, and the staff is skilled and attentive. Casual dress. **Bar:** Full bar. **Reservations:** accepted. **Hours:** 4 pm-close. Closed: 11/26, 12/25. **Address:** 22616 Bothell Everett Hwy **Location:** I-405, exit 26, just sw. **Parking:** on-site. **Cards:** AX, DC, DS, MC, VI.

BURGERMASTER   Phone: 425/486-8980   **54**

American
$4-$10

The restaurant evokes memories of the drive-ups guests patronized as children. Once the headlights are turned on, a staff person comes straight to the vehicle's window to take orders, which typically consist of a burger, onion rings and malt. Food is delivered on a tray that hangs on the vehicle's window. Casual dress. **Reservations:** not accepted. **Hours:** 10 am-10 pm, Fri & Sat-11 pm. Closed: 11/26, 12/25. **Address:** 18626 Bothell Everett Hwy **Location:** I-405, exit 26, 2.3 mi n. **Parking:** on-site. **Cards:** AX, DS, MC, VI.

CANYONS RESTAURANT   Phone: 425/485-3288

American
$8-$19

Diners can experience a small taste of the Southwest in the colorful, festive restaurant. Hand paintings that resemble lithographs of buffalo decorate the stucco-finished walls and tell a story of early man. Casual dress. **Bar:** Full bar. **Reservations:** accepted. **Hours:** 11 am-10 pm, Fri & Sat-11 pm, Sun 9 am-9 pm. Closed: 11/26, 12/25. **Address:** 22010 17th Ave SE **Location:** I-405, exit 26, just ne. **Parking:** on-site. **Cards:** AX, DC, MC, VI.

BREMERTON pop. 37,259 (See map and index starting on p. 624)

─── WHERE TO STAY ───

BREMERTON INN & SUITES *Book great rates at AAA.com*

(AAA) (SAVE)
◆◆◆◆
Hotel
$100-$170 All Year

Phone: (360)405-1111 **14**

Address: 4303 Kitsap Way **Location:** 3.5 mi w of ferry terminal; SR 3, exit Kitsap Way, 0.5 mi e. **Facility:** 103 units. 91 one-bedroom standard units, some with efficiencies. 9 one-, 2 two- and 1 three-bedroom suites, some with efficiencies or kitchens. 1-3 stories (no elevator), exterior corridors. *Bath:* combo or shower only. **Parking:** on-site. **Terms:** cancellation fee imposed. **Amenities:** high-speed Internet, voice mail, irons. *Some:* hair dryers. **Pool(s):** heated outdoor. **Leisure Activities:** playground, exercise room. **Guest Services:** coin laundry. **Business Services:** meeting rooms, PC. **Cards:** AX, CB, DC, DS, JC, MC, VI. **Free Special Amenities: continental breakfast and high-speed Internet.**

🍽️➕ 🏊 🎬 🖥️ 🖨️ 💻 / SOME UNITS ❌

FLAGSHIP INN *Book great rates at AAA.com*

(AAA) (SAVE)
◆◆◆◆
Hotel
$75-$115 All Year

Phone: (360)479-6566 **12**

Address: 4320 Kitsap Way **Location:** 3.5 mi w of ferry terminal; SR 3, exit Kitsap Way, 0.5 mi e. **Facility:** 29 one-bedroom standard units. 2 stories (no elevator), interior corridors. **Parking:** on-site. **Amenities:** video library, DVD players, high-speed Internet, irons, hair dryers. **Pool(s):** heated outdoor. **Guest Services:** coin laundry, wireless Internet. **Business Services:** PC. **Cards:** AX, CB, DC, DS, MC, VI. **Free Special Amenities: expanded continental breakfast and high-speed Internet.** *(See color ad below)*

🍽️➕ 🏊 (VCR) 🎬 🖥️ 🖨️ 💻 / SOME UNITS FEE 🐾 ❌

HAMPTON INN & SUITES *Book great rates at AAA.com*

◆◆◆◆
Hotel
$79-$129 All Year

Phone: (360)405-0200 **15**

Address: 150 Washington Ave **Location:** Downtown; at ferry terminal. **Facility:** 105 units. 99 one-bedroom standard units. 6 one-bedroom suites. 4 stories, interior corridors. *Bath:* combo or shower only. **Parking:** on-site (fee). **Terms:** 1-30 night minimum stay, cancellation fee imposed. **Amenities:** video games (fee), high-speed Internet, voice mail, irons, hair dryers. **Pool(s):** heated indoor. **Leisure Activities:** exercise room. **Guest Services:** valet· and coin laundry, wireless Internet. **Business Services:** meeting rooms, PC. **Cards:** AX, CB, DC, DS, MC, VI.

🍽️➕ CALL 📞M 🏊 🎥 🖥️ 🖨️ 💻 / SOME UNITS ❌

Hampton Inn & Suites

AAA Benefit:

Members save up to 10% everyday!

ILLAHEE MANOR BED & BREAKFAST *Book great rates at AAA.com*

(AAA) (SAVE)
◆◆◆◆
Bed & Breakfast
$130-$255 3/1-10/14
$120-$230 10/15-2/28

Phone: (360)698-7555 **9**

Address: 6680 Illahee Rd NE **Location:** Downtown/ferry terminal, just n on Washington Ave, across Manette Bridge, 0.7 mi e on 11th St, then 3.9 mi n via Trenton Ave and Illahee Rd. **Facility:** Located along the shores of Kitsap Peninsula, the B&B offers elegantly appointed guest rooms, a honeymoon cabin and a family beach house. Smoke free premises. 5 one-bedroom standard units, some with whirlpools. 1-3 stories (no elevator), interior/exterior corridors. **Parking:** on-site. **Terms:** check-in 4 pm, age restrictions may apply, 10 day cancellation notice. **Amenities:** video library, hair dryers. *Some:* DVD players. **Leisure Activities:** fishing, clamming, spa. **Guest Services:** wireless Internet. **Business Services:** meeting rooms. **Cards:** AX, CB, DC, DS, JC, MC, VI. **Free Special Amenities: full breakfast and high-speed Internet.**

🍽️➕ ❌ ❌ 🎿 🛁 🖥️ / SOME UNITS (VCR) 🖨️ 💻

MIDWAY INN *Book at AAA.com*

◆◆ ◆◆
Hotel
Rates not provided

Phone: 360/479-2909 **10**

Address: 2909 Wheaton Way **Location:** SR 303, 2 mi n. Located in East Bremerton. **Facility:** 60 one-bedroom standard units, some with efficiencies. 3 stories, interior corridors. *Bath:* combo or shower only. **Parking:** on-site. **Amenities:** DVD players, CD players, high-speed Internet, irons, hair dryers. **Guest Services:** valet and coin laundry, wireless Internet. **Business Services:** meeting rooms, PC.

🍽️➕ 🎬 🖥️ 🖨️ 💻 / SOME UNITS FEE 🐾 ❌

─── ▼ See AAA listing above ▼ ───

(See map and index starting on p. 624)

OYSTER BAY INN   *Book great rates at AAA.com*   Phone: (360)377-5510   🔟③

AAA SAVE

▼▼▼ ▼▼▼

Hotel
$89-$99 3/1-9/30
$84-$94 10/1-2/28

Address: 4412 Kitsap Way **Location:** 3.8 mi w of ferry terminal; SR 3, exit Kitsap Way, 0.5 mi e. **Facility:** 78 units. 73 one-bedroom standard units. 1 one-, 1 two- and 2 three-bedroom suites with kitchens. 1 cabin. 3 stories (no elevator), interior corridors. *Bath:* combo or shower only. **Parking:** on-site. **Amenities:** high-speed Internet, dual phone lines, voice mail, irons, hair dryers. **Leisure Activities:** limited exercise equipment. **Guest Services:** wireless Internet. **Business Services:** meeting rooms, PC. **Cards:** AX, DC, DS, MC, VI. **Free Special Amenities:** continental breakfast and high-speed Internet.

🍴 🍸 🎦 📠 🖨 / SOME UNITS FEE 🐕 ☒ 🖵

SUPER 8 MOTEL   *Book at AAA.com*   Phone: 360/377-8881   🔟①

▼▼▼ ▼▼▼

Hotel
Rates not provided

Address: 5068 Kitsap Way **Location:** 4.2 mi w of ferry terminal; SR 3, exit Kitsap Way, just ne. **Facility:** 77 one-bedroom standard units. 3 stories (no elevator), interior corridors. **Parking:** on-site. **Amenities:** high-speed Internet, hair dryers. **Guest Services:** coin laundry, wireless Internet. **Business Services:** meeting rooms.

🍴 CALL 🔊M 🎦 🖵 / SOME UNITS FEE 🐕 ☒ 📠 🖨

--------- WHERE TO DINE ---------

BOAT SHED   Phone: 360/377-2600   ⑨

▼▼▼ ▼▼▼

American
$8-$22

Casual waterfront dining can be found in a rustic "warehouse" setting featuring a large outdoor deck and a western exposure perfect for watching sunsets. Seafood is the focus with prime rib offered on weekends. Also try the homemade blackberry cobbler. Casual dress. **Bar:** Full bar. **Reservations:** accepted. **Hours:** 11 am-10 pm. Closed: 7/4, 11/26, 12/25. **Address:** 101 Shore Dr **Location:** East side of Manette Bridge. **Parking:** on-site. **Cards:** AX, MC, VI.

LA FERMATA RISTORANTE   Phone: 360/373-5927   ⑧

▼▼▼ ▼▼▼

Italian
$20-$37

The quiet street-side bistro serves dishes such as tortellini with pork and prosciutto in herb-chicken broth, tuna tartare in caper vinaigrette with garlic bruschetta and hominy custard topped with fresh Dungeness crab and roasted peppers puree. Casual dress. **Bar:** Beer & wine. **Reservations:** accepted. **Hours:** 5 pm-10 pm. Closed: 7/4, 11/26, 12/24, 12/25; also Sun & Mon. **Address:** 2204 E 11th St **Location:** East side of Manette Bridge at 11th St and Scott Ave. **Parking:** street. **Cards:** AX, MC, VI.

🅰🅲

BURIEN pop. 31,881   (See map and index starting on p. 614)

--------- WHERE TO DINE ---------

MICK KELLY'S IRISH PUB   Phone: 206/246-2473   ⑪⑥

▼▼▼ ▼▼▼

Irish
$8-$30

Friendly staff members go out of their way to be accommodating at the Irish pub, which turns out classic shepherd's pie that really hits the spot. Patrons can grab a seat at the bar or at a table to take advantage of the tasty food, friendly crowds and lively atmosphere. Casual dress. **Bar:** Full bar. **Reservations:** accepted. **Hours:** 11 am-10 pm, Sat & Sun from 7 am. Closed: 12/25. **Address:** 435 SW 152 Ave **Location:** Between 4th and 6th aves SW; downtown. **Parking:** street. **Cards:** MC, VI.

ROUND TABLE PIZZA   Phone: 206/431-8600

▼▼▼

Pizza
$4-$19

This casual, family-oriented pizza place features high-quality ingredients and dough rolled fresh daily. Distinctive specialty pizzas are piled high with toppings. Casual dress. **Bar:** Beer & wine. **Reservations:** not accepted. **Hours:** 11 am-10 pm, Fri & Sat-11 pm. Closed major holidays. **Address:** 15730 1st Ave S **Location:** Downtown. **Parking:** on-site. **Cards:** AX, MC, VI.

DES MOINES pop. 29,267   (See map and index starting on p. 614)

--------- WHERE TO DINE ---------

SALTY'S AT REDONDO BEACH   Phone: 253/946-0636   ⑫⑤

▼▼▼ ▼▼▼

Seafood
$9-$30

This place is a bit harder to find than its sister location in Seattle, but the views across Elliott Bay of the magnificent Olympic Mountains and Maury Island are just as spectacular and the seafood just as fresh. Sunday brunch is always a popular event. Guests can enjoy a full meal or maybe just a starter of crab cakes and a cup of creamy seafood chowder. Casual dress. **Bar:** Full bar. **Reservations:** accepted. **Hours:** 11 am-3 & 4:30-9 pm, Fri & Sat-9:30 pm, Sun 9 am-1:30 & 4:30-9 pm; extended hours in summer; Sunday brunch. Closed: 12/25. **Address:** 28201 Redondo Beach Dr S **Location:** I-5, exit 147, 1.8 mi sw via 272nd St and Redondo Beach Dr. **Parking:** on-site. **Cards:** AX, CB, DS, MC, VI.

DUPONT pop. 2,452

--------- WHERE TO STAY ---------

LIBERTY INN   Phone: 253/912-8777

AAA SAVE

▼▼▼ ▼▼▼

Hotel
$125-$185 All Year

Address: 1400 Wilmington Dr **Location:** I-5, exit 118, just nw on Center Dr, then just ne. **Facility:** 72 one-bedroom standard units, some with whirlpools. 3 stories, interior corridors. *Bath:* combo or shower only. **Parking:** on-site. **Terms:** check-in 4 pm, cancellation fee imposed. **Amenities:** video library (fee), DVD players, high-speed Internet, voice mail, irons, hair dryers. **Pool(s):** heated indoor. **Leisure Activities:** whirlpool, exercise room. **Guest Services:** coin laundry, wireless Internet. **Business Services:** meeting rooms, PC. **Cards:** AX, DS, MC, VI. **Free Special Amenities:** expanded continental breakfast and high-speed Internet.

CALL 🔊M 🛋 ☒ 🎦 📠 🖨 🖵

*———— The following lodging was either not evaluated or did not ————
meet AAA rating requirements but is listed for your information only.*

GUESTHOUSE INN & SUITES   Phone: 253/912-8900

[fyi]   Not evaluated. **Address:** 1609 McNeil St **Location:** I-5, exit 118, just nw on Center Dr, then just w.
Facilities, services, and decor characterize a mid-scale property.

———— **WHERE TO DINE** ————

FARRELLI'S WOOD FIRE PIZZA   Phone: 253/912-5200

▼▼ ▼▼   As the name suggests, this place is all about the hand-tossed, wood-fired pizzas. An order of breadsticks
made from sliced pizza dough serves to temporarily calm cravings as the pizza is created and cooked.
Pizza   Casual dress. **Bar:** Full bar. **Hours:** 11 am-midnight, Wed-Sat to 2 am. Closed major holidays.
$10-$20   **Address:** 1590 Wilmington **Location:** I-5, exit 118, 0.5 mi nw. **Parking:** on-site. **Cards:** AX, DS, MC, VI.

EDMONDS pop. 39,515   (See map and index starting on p. 614)

———— **WHERE TO STAY** ————

BEST WESTERN EDMONDS HARBOR INN   *Book great rates at AAA.com*   Phone: (425)771-5021   [137]

(AAA) [SAVE]   **Address:** 130 W Dayton St **Location:** Just s at Port of Edmonds. Located
in Harbor Square Business Park. **Facility:** 91 units. 79 one-bedroom
▼▼ ▼▼ ▼▼   standard units, some with whirlpools. 12 one-bedroom suites. 3 stories.
interior/exterior corridors. **Bath:** combo or shower only. **Parking:** on-site.   **AAA Benefit:**
Hotel   **Amenities:** high-speed Internet, voice mail, irons, hair dryers. *Some:* DVD   Members save up to
$109-$140 All Year players, dual phone lines. **Leisure Activities:** *Fee:* massage. **Guest**   20%, plus 10%
Services: valet and coin laundry, wireless Internet. **Business Services:**   bonus points with
meeting rooms, PC. **Cards:** AX, CB, DC, DS, JC, MC, VI. **Free Special**   rewards program.
Amenities: expanded continental breakfast and preferred room
(subject to availability with advance reservations).
(See color ad below)

[🍽] FEE[👕] [✕] [🎬] [🔒] [💻] / SOME UNITS FEE[🐕] [VCR] [🛜]

K & E MOTOR INN   Phone: 425/778-2181   [139]

(AAA) [SAVE]   **Address:** 23921 Hwy 99 **Location:** I-5, exit 177, 1 mi w on SR 104, exit SR 99 (Aurora Ave), then just
n. **Facility:** 32 one-bedroom standard units, some with kitchens. 2 stories (no elevator), exterior
▼   corridors. **Parking:** on-site. **Terms:** 3 day cancellation notice-fee imposed. **Guest Services:** coin
Motel   laundry. **Cards:** AX, DC, DS, MC, VI. **Free Special Amenities: local telephone calls and**
$60-$89 All Year **newspaper.**

[🍽] [🎬] / SOME UNITS FEE[🐕] [✕] [🔒] [🛜]

TRAVELODGE SEATTLE/EDMONDS   *Book great rates at AAA.com*   Phone: (425)771-8008   [138]

(AAA) [SAVE]   **Address:** 23825 Hwy 99 **Location:** I-5, exit 177, 1 mi w on SR 104, exit SR 99 (Aurora Ave), then just
n. Located in a commercial area. **Facility:** 58 one-bedroom standard units, some with whirlpools. 3
▼▼ ▼▼   stories (no elevator), exterior corridors. **Parking:** on-site. **Terms:** cancellation fee imposed.
Hotel   **Amenities:** voice mail, hair dryers. **Leisure Activities:** whirlpool. **Guest Services:** coin laundry,
$69-$109 All Year wireless Internet. **Business Services:** PC. **Cards:** AX, CB, DC, DS, JC, MC, VI. **Free Special**
Amenities: continental breakfast and high-speed Internet.

[🍽] [🎬] [🔒] [📷] [💻] / SOME UNITS FEE[🐕] [✕]

———— **WHERE TO DINE** ————

ARNIES AT EDMONDS   Phone: 425/771-5688   [136]

▼▼ ▼▼   Cooked-to-order steaks and fresh Northwest seafood along the lines of the excellent poached halibut and
tasty, clam- and potato-thick chowder make up the core of the menu, which also tempts with a tasty
American   seasonal fruit cobbler. Patrons are treated to a picturesque view of Edmonds Bay. Servers are pleasant.
$7-$27   Casual dress. **Bar:** Full bar. **Reservations:** accepted. **Hours:** 11:30 am-9 pm, Sat-10 pm, Sun 10 am-2 &
4-9 pm; seasonal hours vary. Closed: 12/25. **Address:** 300 Admiral Way **Location:** I-5, exit 177, 6 mi w via
SR 1, then just s of ferry terminal. **Parking:** on-site. **Cards:** AX, DS, MC, VI.

_____ ▼ *See AAA listing above* ▼ _____

(See map and index starting on p. 614)

CHANTERELLE

American
$6-$19

Phone: 425/774-0650   135

The great downtown location is convenient to shopping and the ferry. Locals gather for friendly banter and dishes such as Italian fisherman's stew, citrus halibut, Main Street meatloaf and chicken Brie. It's worth saving room for the decadent paradiso chocolate dessert. Casual dress. **Bar:** Beer & wine. **Reservations:** accepted, for dinner. **Hours:** 8 am-9 pm, Sun-1 pm. Closed major holidays. **Address:** 316 Main St **Location:** Between 3rd and 4th sts; downtown. **Parking:** street. **Cards:** AX, MC, VI.

SCOTT'S BAR & GRILL

American
$8-$28

Phone: 425/775-2561   137

Near shopping and highways, the spot is popular with locals for its friendly service and good food. Prime rib is the specialty on a menu of mostly Northwest meats and fresh seafood. Key lime pie shouldn't be missed. Casual dress. **Bar:** Full bar. **Reservations:** accepted. **Hours:** 11 am-9:30 pm, Fri & Sat-10:30 pm, Sun 10 am-2:30 & 3-9:30 pm; Saturday & Sunday brunch. Closed: 7/4, 12/25. **Address:** 8115 Lake Ballinger Way **Location:** I-5, exit 177, 1 mi w via SR 104 and 99 S (Aurora Ave). **Parking:** on-site. **Cards:** AX, DC, DS, MC, VI.

EVERETT pop. 91,488

──────── WHERE TO STAY ────────

BEST WESTERN CASCADIA INN   *Book great rates at AAA.com*

Hotel
$87-$120 All Year

Phone: (425)258-4141

Address: 2800 Pacific Ave **Location:** I-5, exit 193 northbound; exit 194 southbound, just w. **Facility:** 134 units. 133 one-bedroom standard units. 1 one-bedroom suite. 3 stories, interior corridors. *Bath:* combo or shower only. **Parking:** on-site. **Terms:** 3 day cancellation notice. **Amenities:** video games (fee), high-speed Internet, voice mail, safes, irons, hair dryers. **Pool(s):** heated outdoor. **Leisure Activities:** whirlpool. **Guest Services:** valet and coin laundry, area transportation-within 6 mi, wireless Internet. **Business Services:** conference facilities, business center. **Cards:** AX, CB, DC, DS, JC, MC, VI. **Free Special Amenities:** full breakfast and high-speed Internet.

AAA Benefit:
Members save up to 20%, plus 10% bonus points with rewards program.

BEST WESTERN NAVIGATOR INN & SUITES   *Book great rates at AAA.com*

Hotel
$99-$139 All Year

Phone: (425)347-2555

Address: 10210 Evergreen Way **Location:** I-5, exit 189, 1 mi w on SR 526 to Evergreen Way, then 1.6 mi s. **Facility:** Smoke free premises. 103 units. 79 one-bedroom standard units, some with efficiencies. 24 one-bedroom suites with kitchens, some with whirlpools. 3 stories, interior corridors. *Bath:* combo or shower only. **Parking:** on-site. **Amenities:** video games (fee), high-speed Internet, dual phone lines, voice mail, irons, hair dryers. **Pool(s):** heated indoor. **Leisure Activities:** whirlpool. **Guest Services:** valet and coin laundry, area transportation-within 10 mi, wireless Internet. **Business Services:** PC. **Cards:** AX, DC, DS, MC, VI.

AAA Benefit:
Members save up to 20%, plus 10% bonus points with rewards program.

DAYS INN SEATTLE/EVERETT   *Book great rates at AAA.com*   Phone: (425)355-1570

Hotel
$80-$121 All Year

Address: 1602 SE Everett Mall Way **Location:** I-5, exit 189 northbound, 0.5 mi w on SR 527, then 0.5 mi s; exit southbound, 0.7 mi s. Located adjacent to the Everett Mall. **Facility:** 76 units. 75 one-bedroom standard units, some with whirlpools. 1 two-bedroom suite with kitchen. 2 stories (no elevator), exterior corridors. **Parking:** on-site. **Amenities:** high-speed Internet, hair dryers. *Some:* DVD players. **Pool(s):** heated outdoor. **Guest Services:** coin laundry, wireless Internet. **Business Services:** meeting rooms, PC. **Cards:** AX, DS, MC, VI. *(See color ad below)*

ASK ❐ ⚲ ❐ 🖥 / SOME UNITS FEE 🐾 ⊠

EXTENDED STAYAMERICA-SEATTLE-EVERETT   *Book at AAA.com*   Phone: (425)355-1923

Hotel
$110-$125 All Year

Address: 8410 Broadway **Location:** I-5, exit 189, follow signs to Broadway, just nw. **Facility:** 104 one-bedroom standard units. 4 stories, interior corridors. *Bath:* combo or shower only. **Parking:** on-site. **Terms:** cancellation fee imposed. **Amenities:** high-speed Internet (fee), voice mail, irons. **Guest Services:** coin laundry, wireless Internet. **Cards:** AX, CB, DC, DS, JC, MC, VI.

ASK ❐ 🖥 / SOME UNITS FEE 🐾 ⊠

EXTENDED STAY DELUXE-SEATTLE-EVERETT   *Book at AAA.com*   Phone: (425)337-1341

Hotel
$131-$146 All Year

Address: 1431 112th St SE **Location:** I-5, exit 189, 1.5 mi se on 19th Ave SE, then 0.3 mi w. **Facility:** 88 units. 87 one-bedroom standard units with kitchens. 1 one-bedroom suite with kitchen. 3 stories, interior corridors. *Bath:* combo or shower only. **Parking:** on-site. **Terms:** office hours 7 am-11 pm, cancellation fee imposed. **Amenities:** DVD players, CD players, high-speed Internet (fee), voice mail, irons, hair dryers. **Leisure Activities:** exercise room. **Guest Services:** coin laundry, wireless Internet. **Cards:** AX, CB, DC, DS, JC, MC, VI.

ASK ❐ 🖥 / SOME UNITS FEE 🐾 ⊠

GAYLORD HOUSE   Phone: 425/339-9153

Bed & Breakfast
$100-$135 All Year

Address: 3301 Grand Ave **Location:** I-5, exit 193 northbound, 1 mi w on Pacific Ave, then just s; exit 194 southbound, 1 mi w on Everett Ave, then 0.5 mi s. Located in a residential area. **Facility:** This 1910 Craftsman home on a maple-tree-lined avenue is walking distance from downtown. Smoke free premises. 5 one-bedroom standard units, some with whirlpools. 2 stories (no elevator), interior corridors. *Bath:* combo, shower or tub only. **Parking:** on-site. **Terms:** office hours 7 am-11 pm, check-in 4 pm, age restrictions may apply, 3 day cancellation notice-fee imposed. **Amenities:** video library, high-speed Internet, hair dryers. *Some:* DVD players, irons. **Guest Services:** wireless Internet. **Cards:** DS, MC, VI.

ASK ⊠ ⌻ / SOME UNITS VCR

HOLIDAY INN DOWNTOWN EVERETT   *Book great rates at AAA.com*   Phone: 425/339-2000

(AAA) SAVE

Hotel
Rates not provided

Address: 3105 Pine St **Location:** I-5, exit 193 northbound; exit 194 southbound, just sw. **Facility:** 243 units. 236 one-bedroom standard units. 7 one-bedroom suites. 7 stories, interior corridors. *Bath:* combo or shower only. **Parking:** on-site. **Terms:** check-in 4 pm. **Amenities:** video games (fee), high-speed Internet, dual phone lines, voice mail, safes, irons, hair dryers. **Pool(s):** heated indoor. **Leisure Activities:** whirlpool, exercise room. **Guest Services:** valet and coin laundry, area transportation-within 10 mi, wireless Internet. **Business Services:** conference facilities. **Free Special Amenities:** full breakfast and high-speed Internet.

❐ 🍴 🍸 ⚲ ❐ 🖥 / SOME UNITS FEE 🐾 ⊠ 🖥 🖳

▼ *See AAA listing above* ▼

HOLIDAY INN EXPRESS HOTEL & SUITES
Book great rates at AAA.com
Phone: (425)609-4000

Hotel
$109-$199 All Year

Address: 131 128th St SW **Location:** I-5, exit 186, just nw. **Facility:** Smoke free premises. 99 units. 74 one-bedroom standard units. 25 one-bedroom suites, some with whirlpools. 3 stories, interior corridors. *Bath:* combo or shower only. **Parking:** on-site. **Terms:** check-in 4 pm. **Amenities:** video library (fee), DVD players, high-speed Internet, dual phone lines, voice mail, irons, hair dryers. **Pool(s):** heated indoor. **Leisure Activities:** whirlpool, exercise room. **Guest Services:** valet and coin laundry, wireless Internet. **Business Services:** meeting rooms, business center. **Cards:** AX, CB, DC, DS, MC, VI.

INN AT PORT GARDNER
Book great rates at AAA.com
Phone: (425)252-6779

Hotel
$139-$289 All Year

Address: 1700 W Marine View Dr **Location:** I-5, exit 193 northbound, 1.2 mi w on Pacific Ave, then 1.2 mi n; exit 194 southbound, 1.2 mi w on Everett Ave, then 1 mi n; in Everett Marina Village. **Facility:** Smoke free premises. 33 units. 27 one-bedroom standard units. 6 one-bedroom suites, some with whirlpools. 3 stories, interior corridors. **Parking:** on-site. **Amenities:** video library (fee), DVD players, high-speed Internet, dual phone lines, voice mail, irons, hair dryers. **Guest Services:** valet laundry, wireless Internet. **Business Services:** meeting rooms. **Cards:** AX, CB, DC, DS, JC, MC, VI. **Free Special Amenities:** expanded continental breakfast and high-speed Internet.

LA QUINTA INN EVERETT
Book great rates at AAA.com
Phone: 425/347-9099

Hotel
Rates not provided

Address: 12619 4th Ave W **Location:** I-5, exit 186, just w. **Facility:** 73 one-bedroom standard units. 3 stories, interior corridors. **Parking:** on-site. **Terms:** age restrictions may apply. **Amenities:** voice mail, irons, hair dryers. **Pool(s):** heated outdoor. **Guest Services:** valet laundry, wireless Internet. **Business Services:** business center. **Free Special Amenities:** expanded continental breakfast and high-speed Internet.

QUALITY INN & SUITES
Book great rates at AAA.com
Phone: (425)609-4550

Hotel
$99-$129 All Year

Address: 101 128th St SE **Location:** I-5, exit 186, just e. **Facility:** Smoke free premises. 82 units. 76 one-bedroom standard units. 6 one-bedroom suites. 4 stories, interior corridors. **Parking:** on-site. **Terms:** cancellation fee imposed. **Amenities:** high-speed Internet, voice mail, safes (fee), irons, hair dryers. **Leisure Activities:** exercise room. **Guest Services:** valet and coin laundry, wireless Internet. **Business Services:** meeting rooms, PC. **Cards:** AX, DS, MC, VI.

TRAVELODGE EVERETT MALL
Book at AAA.com
Phone: (425)337-9090

Motel
$54-$89 All Year

Address: 9602 19th Ave SE **Location:** I-5, exit 189, just e. **Facility:** Smoke free premises. 116 one-bedroom standard units, some with efficiencies. 2 stories (no elevator), exterior corridors. **Parking:** on-site. **Amenities:** high-speed Internet. **Pool(s):** heated outdoor. **Leisure Activities:** whirlpool. **Guest Services:** coin laundry, wireless Internet. **Business Services:** meeting rooms. **Cards:** AX, CB, DC, DS, JC, MC, VI.

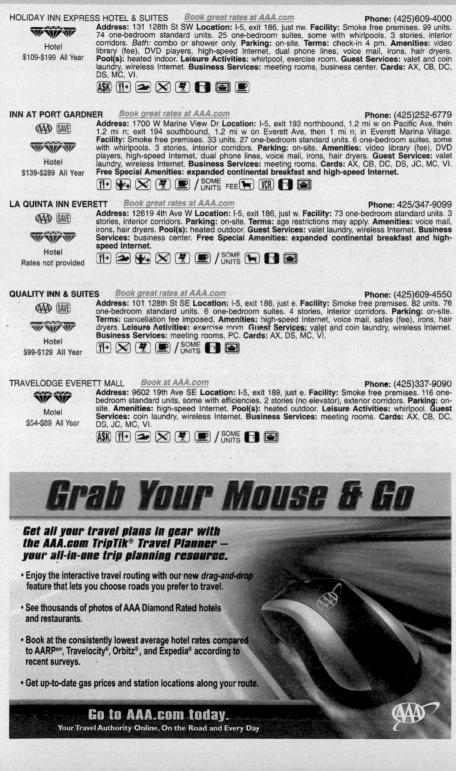

——— WHERE TO DINE ———

ALLIGATOR SOUL

Creole
$7-$22

Phone: 425/259-6311

Creole and Cajun cooking, with such dishes as seafood gumbo, is the restaurant's trademark. Several nights a week, the bluesy, jazzy sounds of Louisiana echo through the upbeat and raucous dining room. Casual dress. Entertainment. **Bar:** Full bar. **Reservations:** accepted. **Hours:** 11 am-3 & 4-9 pm, Fri & Sat-10 pm. Closed major holidays; also Sun & Mon. **Address:** 3121 Broadway **Location:** Just w of Broadway; downtown. **Parking:** on-site. **Cards:** DS, MC, VI.

ANTHONY'S RESTAURANT

Steak & Seafood
$10-$25

Phone: 425/258-4000

Specializing in wood-fired rotisserie and oven-baked items, this dockside eatery offers slow-roasted prime rib finished on the rotisserie for added flavor. Guests can savor spicy chicken wings while watching boats dock in the huge marina. Casual dress. **Bar:** Full bar. **Reservations:** accepted. **Hours:** 11:30 am-10 pm, Fri & Sat-10:30 pm, Sun 10 am-9:30 pm; Sunday brunch. Closed: 11/26, 12/25. **Address:** 1722 W Marine View Dr **Location:** I-5, exit 193 northbound, 1.2 mi w on Pacific Ave, then 1.4 mi n; exit 194 southbound, 1.2 mi w on Everett Ave, then 1 mi n; in Everett Marina Village. **Parking:** on-site. **Cards:** AX, DS, MC, VI.

EMORY'S ON SILVER LAKE

American
$10-$30

Phone: 425/337-7772

A light, airy dining room and open-air summer terrace overlook sparkling Silver Lake. Innovative preparations of seafood, steaks and pasta show a Mediterranean touch. The wine list is comprehensive. Save room for one of the homemade desserts. Casual dress. **Bar:** Full bar. **Reservations:** suggested. **Hours:** 11:30 am-9 pm, Fri-10 pm, Sat 4 pm-10 pm, Sun 10 am-8 pm. Closed: 7/4, 12/25. **Address:** 11830 19th Ave SE **Location:** I-5, exit 186, 1.3 mi e on SR 96, then 0.8 mi n on SR 527 (19th Ave SE). **Parking:** on-site. **Cards:** AX, DS, MC, VI.

CALL

THE FLYING PIG RESTAURANT & BAR

American
$9-$24

Phone: 425/339-1393

Guests can get not only some of the freshest beer in town but also gourmet pizzas with Sicilian-style crusts, hearty pasta dishes, fresh salads and Angus beef. Well-known to the locals are the filling breakfast-style scrambles, which are served with fresh hash browns (or, as this place calls it, "pig style"). Casual dress. **Bar:** Full bar. **Hours:** 11 am-10 pm, Fri & Sat-midnight. Closed: 4/12, 11/26, 12/25. **Address:** 2929 Colby Ave **Location:** On Colby Ave; between Hewitt Ave and Wall St; downtown. **Parking:** street. **Cards:** AX, MC, VI.

LOMBARDI'S

Italian
$6-$21

Phone: 425/252-1886

Treating patrons to a spectacular view of the marina, the restaurant serves creative Italian dishes. The mood in the dining room is upbeat and friendly. Casual dress. **Bar:** Full bar. **Reservations:** accepted. **Hours:** 11:30 am-9 pm, Fri & Sat-9:30 pm; to 9:30 pm, Fri & Sat-10 pm, Sun-9 pm 6/20-9/1. Closed: 1/1, 12/25. **Address:** 1620 W Marine View Dr **Location:** I-5, exit 193 northbound, 1.2 mi w on Pacific Ave, then 1.4 mi n; exit 194 southbound, 1.2 mi w on Everett Ave, then 1.1 mi n; in Everett Marina Village. **Parking:** on-site. **Cards:** AX, DS, MC, VI.

MITZEL'S AMERICAN KITCHEN

American
$7-$15

Phone: 425/355-3383

The local chain is where families gather for traditional small-town fare and to get caught up on life. The spot is popular all day long, but it's the freshly made pies and muffins that bring patrons back. Thick chowders are comfort food on a cold winter's night, and hot turkey sandwiches are reminiscent of home. Casual dress. **Bar:** Beer & wine. **Hours:** 6 am-11 pm, Sun 7 am-10 pm; seasonal hours may vary. **Address:** 303 128th St SW **Location:** I-5, exit 186, just nw. **Parking:** on-site. **Cards:** AX, DS, MC, VI.

SCUTTLEBUTT BREWING CO.

American
$7-$12

Phone: 425/257-9316

The small family-owned-and-run brewery has a simple dining room that's ideal for a quick bite. Patrons can watch the brewing process through large plate-glass windows while playing one of the many available board games. This place is serious about its beer, root beer and beer-battered fish and chips. Casual dress. **Bar:** Beer & wine. **Reservations:** not accepted. **Hours:** 11:30 am-8 pm, Fri & Sat-9 pm. Closed major holidays; also Sun. **Address:** 1524 W Marine View Dr **Location:** I-5, exit 193 northbound, 1.2 mi w on Pacific Ave, then 1.4 mi n; exit 194 southbound, 1.2 mi w on Everett Ave, then 1.2 mi n. **Parking:** on-site. **Cards:** MC, VI.

FEDERAL WAY pop. 83,259 (See map and index starting on p. 626)

——— WHERE TO STAY ———

BEST WESTERN EVERGREEN INN & SUITES *Book great rates at AAA.com* Phone: (253)529-4000 **19**

Hotel
$79-$169 All Year

Address: 32124 25th Ave S **Location:** I-5, exit 143, just sw. **Facility:** Smoke free premises. 165 units. 135 one-bedroom standard units. 16 one- and 14 two-bedroom suites, some with whirlpools. 8 stories, interior corridors. *Bath:* combo or shower only. **Parking:** on-site. **Amenities:** video games (fee), high-speed Internet, dual phone lines, voice mail, irons, hair dryers. **Pool(s):** heated indoor. **Leisure Activities:** whirlpool, exercise room. **Guest Services:** valet and coin laundry, area transportation-within 5 mi, wireless Internet. **Business Services:** meeting rooms, business center. **Cards:** AX, CB, DS, MC, VI. **Free Special Amenities:** full breakfast and high-speed Internet.

AAA Benefit:
Members save up to 20%, plus 10% bonus points with rewards program.

(See map and index starting on p. 626)

CLARION HOTEL FEDERAL WAY   *Book great rates at AAA.com*   Phone: (253)941-6000   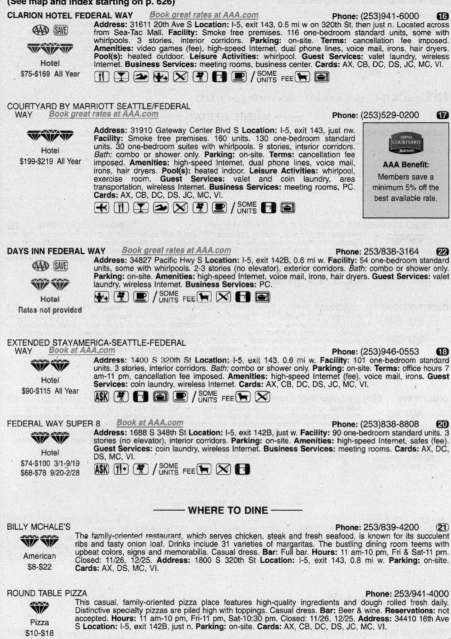 🔟6️⃣

AAA SAVE
▼▼▼
Hotel
$75-$169 All Year

Address: 31611 20th Ave S **Location:** I-5, exit 143, 0.5 mi w on 320th St, then just n. Located across from Sea-Tac Mall. **Facility:** Smoke free premises. 116 one-bedroom standard units, some with whirlpools. 3 stories, interior corridors. **Parking:** on-site. **Terms:** cancellation fee imposed. **Amenities:** video games (fee), high-speed Internet, dual phone lines, voice mail, irons, hair dryers. **Pool(s):** heated outdoor. **Leisure Activities:** whirlpool. **Guest Services:** valet laundry, wireless Internet. **Business Services:** meeting rooms, business center. **Cards:** AX, CB, DC, DS, JC, MC, VI.

COURTYARD BY MARRIOTT SEATTLE/FEDERAL WAY   *Book great rates at AAA.com*   Phone: (253)529-0200   1️⃣7️⃣

▼▼▼
Hotel
$199-$219 All Year

Address: 31910 Gateway Center Blvd S **Location:** I-5, exit 143, just nw. **Facility:** Smoke free premises. 160 units. 130 one-bedroom standard units. 30 one-bedroom suites with whirlpools. 9 stories, interior corridors. *Bath:* combo or shower only. **Parking:** on-site. **Terms:** cancellation fee imposed. **Amenities:** high-speed Internet, dual phone lines, voice mail, irons, hair dryers. **Pool(s):** heated indoor. **Leisure Activities:** whirlpool, exercise room. **Guest Services:** valet and coin laundry, area transportation, wireless Internet. **Business Services:** meeting rooms, PC. **Cards:** AX, CB, DC, DS, JC, MC, VI.

COURTYARD Marriott

AAA Benefit:

Members save a minimum 5% off the best available rate.

DAYS INN FEDERAL WAY   *Book great rates at AAA.com*   Phone: 253-838-3164   2️⃣2️⃣

AAA SAVE
▼▼
Hotel
Rates not provided

Address: 34827 Pacific Hwy S **Location:** I-5, exit 142B, 0.6 mi w. **Facility:** 54 one-bedroom standard units, some with whirlpools. 2-3 stories (no elevator), exterior corridors. *Bath:* combo or shower only. **Parking:** on-site. **Amenities:** high-speed Internet, voice mail, irons, hair dryers. **Guest Services:** valet laundry, wireless Internet. **Business Services:** PC.

EXTENDED STAYAMERICA-SEATTLE-FEDERAL WAY   *Book at AAA.com*   Phone: (253)946-0553   1️⃣8️⃣

▼▼
Hotel
$90-$115 All Year

Address: 1400 S 320th St **Location:** I-5, exit 143, 0.6 mi w. **Facility:** 101 one-bedroom standard units. 3 stories, interior corridors. *Bath:* combo or shower only. **Parking:** on-site. **Terms:** office hours 7 am-11 pm, cancellation fee imposed. **Amenities:** high-speed Internet (fee), voice mail, irons. **Guest Services:** coin laundry, wireless Internet. **Cards:** AX, CB, DC, DS, JC, MC, VI.

FEDERAL WAY SUPER 8   *Book at AAA.com*   Phone: (253)838-8808   2️⃣0️⃣

▼▼
Hotel
$74-$100 3/1-9/19
$68-$78 9/20-2/28

Address: 1688 S 348th St **Location:** I-5, exit 142B, just w. **Facility:** 90 one-bedroom standard units. 3 stories (no elevator), interior corridors. **Parking:** on-site. **Amenities:** high-speed Internet, safes (fee). **Guest Services:** coin laundry, wireless Internet. **Business Services:** meeting rooms. **Cards:** AX, DC, DS, MC, VI.

——— **WHERE TO DINE** ———

BILLY MCHALE'S   Phone: 253/839-4200   2️⃣1️⃣

▼▼
American
$8-$22

The family-oriented restaurant, which serves chicken, steak and fresh seafood, is known for its succulent ribs and tasty onion loaf. Drinks include 31 varieties of margaritas. The bustling dining room teems with upbeat colors, signs and memorabilia. Casual dress. **Bar:** Full bar. **Hours:** 11 am-10 pm, Fri & Sat-11 pm. Closed: 11/26, 12/25. **Address:** 1800 S 320th St **Location:** I-5, exit 143, 0.8 mi w. **Parking:** on-site. **Cards:** AX, DS, MC, VI.

ROUND TABLE PIZZA   Phone: 253/941-4000

▼
Pizza
$10-$18

This casual, family-oriented pizza place features high-quality ingredients and dough rolled fresh daily. Distinctive specialty pizzas are piled high with toppings. Casual dress. **Bar:** Beer & wine. **Reservations:** not accepted. **Hours:** 11 am-10 pm, Fri-11 pm, Sat-10:30 pm. Closed: 11/26, 12/25. **Address:** 34410 16th Ave S **Location:** I-5, exit 142B, just n. **Parking:** on-site. **Cards:** AX, CB, DC, DS, JC, MC, VI.

(See map and index starting on p. 626)

VERRAZANO'S RISTORANTE ITALIANO   Phone: 253/946-4122   ⓴

Italian
$9-$27

A solid Italian menu lists several choices of steak and seafood, and hand-tossed gourmet pizzas, calzones and pastas are always a good choice. Live jazz plays every Wednesday evening. A large outdoor deck open in the summer is a great spot for soaking up the rays while gazing at sweeping views of the Puget Sound and distant mountains. Casual dress. **Bar:** Full bar. **Reservations:** accepted. **Hours:** 11 am-9 pm, Wed & Fri-10 pm, Sat 1 pm-11 pm, Sun 1 pm-9 pm. Closed: 7/4, 11/26. **Address:** 28835 Pacific Hwy S **Location:** I-5, exit 147, 0.5 mi w on S 272nd St, then 1 mi s. **Parking:** on-site. **Cards:** AX, CB, DC, DS, JC, MC, VI.

FIFE pop. 4,784   (See map and index starting on p. 626)

———— WHERE TO STAY ————

EMERALD QUEEN HOTEL & CASINO   Phone: (253)922-2000   ㉘

Hotel
$89-$119 All Year

Address: 5700 Pacific Hwy E **Location:** I-5, exit 137, just ne. **Facility:** Contemporary guest rooms and a full-service slots casino. 124 units. 121 one-bedroom standard units. 3 one-bedroom suites. 4 stories, interior corridors. *Bath:* combo or shower only. **Parking:** on-site. **Amenities:** high-speed Internet, dual phone lines, voice mail, safes, irons, hair dryers. **Guest Services:** valet laundry, area transportation-Emerald Queen Casino. **Cards:** AX, DS, MC, VI.

EXTENDED STAYAMERICA-TACOMA-FIFE   *Book at AAA.com*   Phone: (253)926-6316   ㉗

Hotel
$100-$115 All Year

Address: 2820 Pacific Hwy E **Location:** I-5, exit 136B northbound; exit 136 southbound, just nw. **Facility:** 104 one-bedroom standard units with efficiencies. 3 stories, interior corridors. *Bath:* combo or shower only. **Parking:** on-site. **Terms:** office hours 7 am-11 pm, cancellation fee imposed. **Amenities:** high-speed Internet (fee), voice mail, irons. **Guest Services:** coin laundry, wireless Internet. **Cards:** AX, CB, DC, DS, JC, MC, VI.

GUESTHOUSE ROYAL COACHMAN, FIFE   *Book great rates at AAA.com*   Phone: 253/922-2500   ㉖

Hotel
Rates not provided

Address: 5805 Pacific Hwy E **Location:** I-5, exit 137, just ne. **Facility:** 96 units. 94 one-bedroom standard units, some with whirlpools. 2 one-bedroom suites with kitchens. 2 stories (no elevator), exterior corridors. **Parking:** on-site. **Amenities:** high-speed Internet, hair dryers. **Leisure Activities:** exercise room. **Guest Services:** coin laundry, wireless Internet. **Business Services:** meeting rooms, PC. **Free Special Amenities:** full breakfast and high-speed Internet.

QUALITY INN   *Book great rates at AAA.com*   Phone: (253)926-2301   ㉕

Motel
$86-$110 3/1-9/30
$75-$90 10/1-2/28

Address: 5601 Pacific Hwy E **Location:** I-5, exit 137, just ne. **Facility:** 68 one-bedroom standard units, some with whirlpools. 2 stories (no elevator), exterior corridors. *Bath:* combo or shower only. **Parking:** on-site. **Terms:** cancellation fee imposed. **Amenities:** high-speed Internet, voice mail, irons, hair dryers. **Guest Services:** coin laundry, wireless Internet. **Business Services:** meeting rooms, PC. **Free Special Amenities:** continental breakfast and high-speed Internet.

———— WHERE TO DINE ————

FIFE CITY BAR & GRILL   Phone: 253/922-9555   ㉔

American
$9-$20

Have a taste for the homemade? Everything on the menu is made from scratch including ice cream and desserts like chocolate-espresso flan. Other specialties include chicken smoked in-house and tossed with penne pasta in a tasty lemon and white wine sauce. Casual dress. **Bar:** Full bar. **Reservations:** accepted. **Hours:** 11 am-9 pm, Sat from 8 am, Sun 8 am-8 pm. Closed major holidays. **Address:** 3025 Pacific Hwy E **Location:** I-5, exit 136 southbound; exit 136B northbound, just nw. **Parking:** on-site. **Cards:** AX, DS, MC, VI.

GIG HARBOR pop. 6,465

———— WHERE TO STAY ————

BEAR'S LAIR BED & BREAKFAST   Phone: 253/857 8877

Bed & Breakfast
$105-$205 All Year

Address: 13706 92nd Ave Ct NW **Location:** SR 16, exit SR 302 (Purdy Dr/Gig Harbor-Longbranch Hwy), 2.7 mi nw, 0.4 mi s on Danforth Dr NW, then just w. **Facility:** A Swiss Chalet-style home just north of town on the Key Peninsula, the B&B is in a peaceful setting on six acres of gardens and woodland. Smoke free premises. 4 units. 3 one-bedroom standard units. 1 cottage. 1-2 stories (no elevator), interior/exterior corridors. *Bath:* combo or shower only. **Parking:** on-site. **Terms:** age restrictions may apply, 14 day cancellation notice. **Amenities:** video library, DVD players, hair dryers. *Some:* CD players, irons. **Cards:** MC, VI.

BEST WESTERN WESLEY INN
Book great rates at AAA.com

Phone: (253)858-9690

AAA SAVE
▽▽▽▽

Hotel
$159-$279 All Year

Address: 6575 Kimball Dr **Location:** SR 16, exit City Center, just e on Pioneer Way, then 0.3 mi s. **Facility:** Smoke free premises. 81 units. 67 one-bedroom standard units, some with whirlpools. 14 one-bedroom suites, some with whirlpools. 2 stories (no elevator), interior corridors. *Bath:* combo or shower only. **Parking:** on-site. **Terms:** 3 day cancellation notice-fee imposed. **Amenities:** high-speed Internet, dual phone lines, irons, hair dryers. *Some:* DVD players. **Pool(s):** heated outdoor. **Leisure Activities:** whirlpool. **Guest Services:** valet and coin laundry, wireless Internet. **Business Services:** meeting rooms, PC. **Cards:** AX, CB, DC, DS, JC, MC, VI. **Free Special Amenities: expanded continental breakfast and high-speed Internet.**

> **AAA Benefit:**
> Members save up to 20%, plus 10% bonus points with rewards program.

THE INN AT GIG HARBOR
Book great rates at AAA.com

Phone: (253)858-1111

AAA SAVE
▽▽▽

Hotel
$171-$220 All Year

Address: 3211 56th St NW **Location:** SR 16, exit Olympic Dr, just w, then 0.4 mi n. **Facility:** Smoke free premises. 64 units. 56 one- and 3 two-bedroom standard units, some with whirlpools. 5 one-bedroom suites, some with whirlpools. 4 stories, interior corridors. *Bath:* combo or shower only. **Parking:** on-site. **Terms:** 3 day cancellation notice-fee imposed. **Amenities:** high-speed Internet, voice mail, irons, hair dryers. *Some:* DVD players. **Leisure Activities:** whirlpool, exercise room. **Fee:** massage. **Guest Services:** coin laundry, wireless Internet. **Business Services:** conference facilities, business center. **Cards:** AX, DC, DS, MC, VI. **Free Special Amenities: expanded continental breakfast and high-speed Internet.**

THE MARITIME INN

Phone: (253)858-1818

AAA SAVE
▽▽▽

Hotel
$139-$198 All Year

Address: 3212 Harborview Dr **Location:** SR 16, exit City Center, 0.7 mi e on Pioneer Way, then just n. **Facility:** Smoke free premises. 15 one-bedroom standard units. 1-2 stories (no elevator), interior/exterior corridors. **Parking:** on-site. **Terms:** office hours 8 am-10 pm, 3 day cancellation notice-fee imposed. **Amenities:** high-speed Internet, voice mail, irons, hair dryers. **Guest Services:** wireless Internet. **Cards:** AX, DC, DS, MC, VI. **Free Special Amenities: expanded continental breakfast and high-speed Internet.**

──── **WHERE TO DINE** ────

THE GREEN TURTLE

Phone: 253/851-3167

▽▽ ▽▽
Pacific Rim
$7-$32

This restaurant offers more than just great food and service. During summer months, enjoy outdoor patio dining with breathtaking views of Mount Rainier as the sun sets. For dinner, try the Hawaiian ono topped with a fresh fruit salsa and for dessert, you can't leave without tasting the incredible fresh strawberry cake. Casual dress. **Bar:** Beer & wine. **Reservations:** suggested. **Hours:** 11 am-2:30 & 4:30-9 pm, Fri-10 pm, Sat 4:30 pm-10 pm, Sun 4:30 pm-9 pm. Closed major holidays; also Mon; Sun in winter. **Address:** 2905 Harborview Dr **Location:** South end of town; next to marina. **Parking:** on-site. **Cards:** AX, DS, MC, VI.

ROUND TABLE PIZZA

Phone: 253/851-6250

▽▽
Pizza
$6-$12

This casual, family-oriented pizza place features high-quality ingredients and dough rolled fresh daily. Distinctive specialty pizzas are piled high with toppings. Casual dress. **Bar:** Beer & wine. **Reservations:** not accepted. **Hours:** 11 am-10 pm. Closed: 11/26, 12/25. **Address:** 5500 Olympic Dr, #H101 **Location:** SR 16, exit Olympic Dr, just ne. **Parking:** on-site. **Cards:** MC, VI.

ISSAQUAH pop. 11,212   (See map and index starting on p. 614)

──── **WHERE TO STAY** ────

HOLIDAY INN SEATTLE ISSAQUAH
Book at AAA.com

Phone: 425/392-6421   **75**

▽▽▽
Hotel
Rates not provided

Address: 1801 12th Ave NW **Location:** I-90, exit 15, 0.3 mi n on 17th Ave NW, then just e. **Facility:** Smoke free premises. 100 one-bedroom standard units. 2 stories (no elevator), interior corridors. *Bath:* combo or shower only. **Parking:** on-site. **Amenities:** video games (fee), CD players, high-speed Internet, voice mail, irons, hair dryers. **Pool(s):** heated outdoor. **Leisure Activities:** whirlpool. **Guest Services:** valet and coin laundry, wireless Internet. **Business Services:** conference facilities, business center.

──── **WHERE TO DINE** ────

EXTREME PIZZA

Phone: 425/837-1700

▽▽
Pizza
$4-$30

This casual, family-oriented pizza place features high-quality ingredients and dough rolled fresh daily. Distinctive specialty pizzas are piled high with toppings. Casual dress. **Bar:** Beer & wine. **Reservations:** not accepted. **Hours:** 11 am-10 pm, Fri & Sat-11 pm. Closed major holidays. **Address:** 660 Front St N **Location:** I-90, exit 17, just s. **Parking:** on-site. **Cards:** AX, DS, MC, VI.

FINS BISTRO

Phone: 425/392-0109   **96**

▽▽ ▽▽
Seafood
$9-$35

With brightly painted walls and a bistro decor, the bustling restaurant offers fresh seafood and is popular for weekend brunch. Dressy casual. **Bar:** Full bar. **Reservations:** suggested. **Hours:** 11 am-10 pm, Sat & Sun from 9 am. Closed major holidays; also Mon. **Address:** 301 Front St N **Location:** I-90, exit 17, 0.5 mi s. **Parking:** on-site. **Cards:** AX, DS, MC, VI.

CALL

(See map and index starting on p. 614)

ISSAQUAH BREWHOUSE
Phase: 425/557-1911 [97]

American
$8-$15

In historic downtown, the brewhouse is the type of place folks might hope to stumble across on a cold, wet night. Everyone is family, and the atmosphere is warm and inviting. Part of the Rogue family of breweries, the establishment employs people who know how to craft such distinctive beers as Bullfrog Ale. Comfort foods are served hot and fresh. Outdoor seating is a summer option. Casual dress. **Bar:** Full bar. **Hours:** 11:30 am-midnight, Fri & Sat-2 am. **Address:** 35 W Sunset Way **Location:** I-90, exit 17, 0.7 mi s on Front St E, then just w. **Parking:** street. **Cards:** AX, DS, MC, VI.

JAK'S GRILL
Phone: 425/837-8834

Steak
$9-$42

Because reservations are not accepted, diners should arrive early or plan to wait. After an entree of 28-day wet- and dry-aged corn-fed Nebraska beef, which can be prepared in varied ways, a sinful treat awaits in chocolate cake, which is more like a huge piece of fudge. Casual dress. **Bar:** Full bar. **Hours:** 11 am-2 & 4-10 pm, Fri-11 pm, Sat 4 pm-11 pm, Sun 9 am-2 & 4-9 pm, Mon 4 pm-9 pm. Closed major holidays. **Address:** 14 Front St N **Location:** I-90, exit 17, 0.7 mi s. **Parking:** street. **Cards:** AX, MC, VI.

LOMBARDI'S CUCINA OF ISSAQUAH
Phone: 425/391-9097 [94]

Italian
$7-$22

Creative Italian dishes keep diners satisfied in the upbeat and friendly dining room. Casual dress. **Bar:** Full bar. **Reservations:** accepted. **Hours:** 11:30 am-9 pm, Fri & Sat-10 pm. Closed: 11/26, 12/25. **Address:** 695 NW Gilman Blvd **Location:** I-90, exit 17, just s on Front St, then 0.5 mi w. **Parking:** on-site. **Cards:** AX, DS, MC, VI.

ROUND TABLE PIZZA
Phone: 425/391-7117

Pizza
$10-$16

This casual, family-oriented pizza place features high-quality ingredients and dough rolled fresh daily. Distinctive specialty pizzas are piled high with toppings. Casual dress. **Bar:** Beer & wine. **Reservations:** not accepted. **Hours:** 10:30 am-10 pm, Sat & Sun 10 am-11 pm. **Address:** 730 NW Gilman Blvd **Location:** I-90, exit 17, just sw. **Parking:** on-site. **Cards:** AX, DS, MC, VI.

TRIPLE XXX ROOTBEER DRIVE-IN
Phone: 425/392-1266 [95]

American
$6-$12

A real throwback, the drive-in brings a gathering of classic cars on the weekends, and a cruise-in is held every Saturday night. Burgers are messy, shakes super-thick and onion rings hearty. Casual dress. **Reservations:** accepted. **Hours:** 11 am-8 pm; to 10 pm 5/1/08-9/30/08. Closed: 11/26, 12/25. **Address:** 98 NE Gilman Blvd **Location:** I-90, exit 17, just s on Front St, then just e. **Parking:** on-site.

KENT pop. 79,524   (See map and index starting on p. 614)

— WHERE TO STAY —

BEST WESTERN PLAZA BY THE GREEN   *Book great rates at AAA.com*
Phone: (253)854-8767 [134]

Hotel
$99-$159 3/1-10/31
$79-$129 11/1-2/28

Address: 24415 Russell Rd **Location:** I-5, exit 149 southbound; exit 149A northbound, 2 mi ne via Kent Des Moines Rd (SR 516) and Meeker St. Located adjacent to golf course. **Facility:** Smoke free premises. 97 units. 95 one-bedroom standard units. 2 one-bedroom suites, some with whirlpools. 2 stories, interior corridors. *Bath:* combo or shower only. **Parking:** on-site. **Terms:** 3 day cancellation notice. **Amenities:** high-speed Internet, irons, hair dryers. *Some:* dual phone lines. **Leisure Activities:** sauna, whirlpool, exercise room. **Guest Services:** valet laundry, wireless Internet. **Business Services:** PC. **Cards:** AX, CB, DC, DS, JC, MC, VI.

AAA Benefit:
Members save up to 20%, plus 10% bonus points with rewards program.

COMFORT INN KENT   *Book at AAA.com*
Phone: (253)872-2211 [131]

Hotel
$99-$130 All Year

Address: 22311 84th Ave S **Location:** SR 167, exit 84th Ave S, just n. **Facility:** 102 units. 99 one-bedroom standard units. 3 one-bedroom suites with whirlpools. 3 stories, interior corridors. *Bath:* combo or shower only. **Parking:** on-site. **Amenities:** high-speed Internet, voice mail, irons, hair dryers. **Pool(s):** heated indoor. **Leisure Activities:** whirlpool, exercise room. **Guest Services:** valet and coin laundry, wireless Internet. **Business Services:** meeting rooms, PC. **Cards:** AX, DC, DS, JC, MC, VI.

EXTENDED STAYAMERICA-SEATTLE-KENT   *Book at AAA.com*
Phone: (253)872-6514 [133]

Hotel
$90-$105 All Year

Address: 22520 83rd Ave S **Location:** SR 167, exit 84th Ave S, just nw. **Facility:** 120 one-bedroom standard units with efficiencies. 4 stories, interior corridors. *Bath:* combo or shower only. **Parking:** on-site. **Terms:** office hours 7 am-11 pm, cancellation fee imposed. **Amenities:** high-speed Internet (fee), voice mail, irons. **Guest Services:** coin laundry, wireless Internet. **Cards:** AX, CB, DC, DS, JC, MC, VI.

HAWTHORN SUITES   *Book at AAA.com*
Phone: (253)395-3800 [130]

Hotel
$129-$199 All Year

Address: 6329 S 212th St **Location:** I-5, exit 152, 2.6 mi se via Orilla Rd and 212th St. Located in a business park. **Facility:** 152 units. 76 one-bedroom standard units with kitchens, some with whirlpools. 2 one- and 74 two-bedroom suites with kitchens, some with whirlpools. 2 stories (no elevator), exterior corridors. **Parking:** on-site. **Amenities:** video games (fee), high-speed Internet, dual phone lines, voice mail, irons, hair dryers. **Pool(s):** heated outdoor. **Leisure Activities:** whirlpool, tennis court, exercise room. **Guest Services:** valet and coin laundry, area transportation, wireless Internet. **Business Services:** meeting rooms, PC. **Cards:** AX, CB, DC, DS, JC, MC, VI.

(See map and index starting on p. 614)

HOLIDAY INN HOTEL & SUITES   *Book great rates at AAA.com*   Phone: (253)395-4300   132

Hotel
$99-$149 3/1-10/1
$79-$119 10/2-2/28

Address: 22318 84th Ave S. **Location:** SR 167, exit 84th Ave S, just n. **Facility:** 125 units. 101 one-bedroom standard units, some with whirlpools. 24 one-bedroom suites. 2 stories, interior/exterior corridors. *Bath:* combo or shower only. **Parking:** on-site. **Terms:** cancellation fee imposed. **Amenities:** video games (fee), high-speed Internet, voice mail, irons, hair dryers. **Pool(s):** outdoor. **Leisure Activities:** whirlpool, exercise room. **Guest Services:** valet and coin laundry, area transportation-within 5 mi, wireless Internet. **Business Services:** meeting rooms, PC. **Cards:** AX, DC, DS, MC, VI.

TOWNEPLACE SUITES BY MARRIOTT-SEATTLE
SOUTHCENTER   *Book great rates at AAA.com*   Phone: (253)796-6000   129

Hotel
$170-$208 All Year

Address: 18123 72nd Ave S **Location:** I-405, exit 1 (SR 181), 1.6 mi s on W Valley Hwy, just e on S 180th St, then just s. **Facility:** Smoke free premises. 152 one-bedroom standard units, some with efficiencies or kitchens. 2 stories (no elevator), exterior corridors. *Bath:* combo or shower only. **Parking:** on-site. **Terms:** check-in 4 pm, cancellation fee imposed. **Amenities:** high-speed Internet, voice mail, irons, hair dryers. **Pool(s):** heated outdoor. **Leisure Activities:** whirlpool, exercise room, basketball. **Guest Services:** valet and coin laundry, area transportation, wireless Internet. **Business Services:** meeting rooms, PC. **Cards:** AX, CB, DC, DS, JC, MC, VI.

AAA Benefit:
Members save a minimum 5% off the best available rate.

--------- **WHERE TO DINE** ---------

CAVE MAN KITCHENS   Phone: 253/854-1210   130

Barbecue
$4-$10

Guests shouldn't let the building's simple exterior fool them, as this place is plenty worthy of a visit. Generations of family recipes are used along with alder hardwood to create dishes with a Northwestern smoked flavor. Casual dress. **Hours:** 9 am-9 pm, Sun-8 pm. Closed major holidays. **Address:** 807 W Valley Hwy **Location:** SR 516, exit Willis St/Kent Des Moines Rd, just w on Willis St, 0.8 mi n via Washington Ave and W Valley Hwy, then just w on W Morton St. **Parking:** on-site. **Cards:** MC, VI.

CHAO PRAYA RESTAURANT   Phone: 253/395-7777   128

Thai
$4-$11

The restaurant's simple exterior belies what has made this place a local hot spot: its authentic Thai food. Service here is basic. Casual dress. **Bar:** Beer & wine. **Reservations:** accepted. **Hours:** 11 am-9 pm. Closed major holidays; also Sun. **Address:** 21222 84th Ave S **Location:** SR 167, exit 84th Ave S, 1 mi n. **Parking:** on-site. **Cards:** AX, DS, MC, VI.

MITZEL'S AMERICAN KITCHEN   Phone: 253/395-3635   129

American
$7-$15

The local chain is where families gather for traditional small-town fare and to get caught up on life. The spot is popular all day long, but it's the freshly made pies and muffins that bring patrons back. Thick chowders are comfort food on a cold winter's night, and hot turkey sandwiches are reminiscent of home. Casual dress. **Bar:** Full bar. **Reservations:** not accepted. **Hours:** 6 am-11 pm, Sun 7 am-10 pm. **Address:** 22330 84th Ave S **Location:** SR 167, exit 84th Ave S, just n. **Parking:** on-site. **Cards:** AX, DS, MC, VI.

RAM RESTAURANT AND BREWERY   Phone: 253/520-3881

American
$8-$22

The enormous restaurant features high ceilings, huge television screens, large sports-themed banners and a brew pub area. The menu is equally enormous, with steaks, poultry, pasta, seafood, salads, sandwiches and pizza. The on-site brewery turns out a large selection of microbrews. Casual dress. **Bar:** Full bar. **Reservations:** not accepted. **Hours:** 11 am-close. Closed: 12/25. **Address:** 512 Ramsay Way, Suite 4-103 **Location:** In Kent Station complex. **Parking:** on-site. **Cards:** AX, MC, VI.

ROUND TABLE PIZZA   Phone: 253/630-6900

Pizza
$9-$16

This casual, family-oriented pizza place features high-quality ingredients and dough rolled fresh daily. Distinctive specialty pizzas are piled high with toppings. Casual dress. **Bar:** Beer & wine. **Reservations:** not accepted. **Hours:** 11 am-9 pm, Fri & Sat-10 pm. Closed major holidays. **Address:** 13036 Kent Kangley Rd **Location:** Jct SE Kent Kangley Rd and 132nd Ave SE. **Parking:** on-site. **Cards:** MC, VI.

THAI CHILI RESTAURANT   Phone: 253/850-5887   131

Thai
$7-$13

From mild to palate-shocking spicy, traditional Thai cuisine comes in an extensive array of tasty lunch and dinner dishes. Affordable prices make it easy to indulge in all courses. This place is as good for a night on the town as it is for a business lunch. Good-size portions mean no one leaves hungry. Casual dress. **Bar:** Beer & wine. **Reservations:** accepted. **Hours:** 11 am-9 pm, Sat from noon. Closed major holidays; also Sun. **Address:** 120 Washington Ave N **Location:** SR 167, exit Kent Des Moines Rd, just w, then just n. **Parking:** on-site. **Cards:** DS, MC, VI.

VELVET GOOSE   Phone: 253/854-7706   132

American
$7-$9

Enchanting and intimate, the decor features all antique furnishings and artwork from the '20s and '30s. Enjoy a breakfast of real European pancakes like crepes and ebelskievers, or a lunch of fresh chicken noodle soup with a hot Monte Cristo sandwich. Casual dress. **Reservations:** accepted. **Hours:** 9 am-3 pm. Closed: 1/1, 11/26, 12/25; also Mon. **Address:** 25748 101st Ave SE **Location:** Jct SE 256th St, just s; in Mad Hatter's Antique Mall. **Parking:** on-site. **Cards:** MC, VI.

KINGSTON pop. 1,611 (See map and index starting on p. 614)

—— WHERE TO DINE ——

MAIN STREET ALE HOUSE
Phone: 360/297-0440 **[47]**

▼▼▼

· American
$10-$25

Patrons have a choice of two dining rooms: the streetside room with a full-service bar, wainscoting and local art or the back room with lots of large windows and cozy booths. In the summer, a third seating option opens in the form of the outdoor deck. Casual dress. **Bar:** Full bar. **Reservations:** accepted. **Hours:** 11 am-9:30 pm. Closed: 11/26, 12/25. **Address:** 11225 Main St (SR 104) **Location:** 1 blk from Ferry Landing; downtown. **Parking:** on-site. **Cards:** AX, DS, MC, VI.

🄰🄲

KIRKLAND pop. 45,054 (See map and index starting on p. 614)

—— WHERE TO STAY ——

BAYMONT INN & SUITES *Book great rates at AAA.com*
Phone: (425)822-2300 **[41]**

AAA SAVE
▼▼▼
Hotel
$94-$275 All Year

Address: 12223 NE 116th St **Location:** I-405, exit 20A northbound; exit 20 southbound, just e; in Totem Lake area. **Facility:** 105 units. 102 one-bedroom standard units. 3 one-bedroom suites, some with whirlpools. 3 stories, exterior corridors. *Bath:* combo or shower only. **Parking:** on-site. **Amenities:** high-speed Internet, voice mail, irons, hair dryers. **Pool(s):** heated outdoor. **Leisure Activities:** whirlpool. **Guest Services:** valet and coin laundry, wireless Internet. **Business Services:** meeting rooms. **Cards:** AX, CB, DC, DS, JC, MC, VI. **Free Special Amenities:** expanded continental breakfast and high-speed Internet.

🍽️➕ 🛢️ 📷 🖥️ 🖨️ 💻 / SOME UNITS FEE 🐕 ❌

COMFORT INN-KIRKLAND *Book great rates at AAA.com*
Phone: (425)821-8300 **[39]**

AAA SAVE
▼▼▼
Hotel
$129 All Year

Address: 12204 NE 124th St **Location:** I-405, exit 20B northbound; exit 20 southbound, just e. **Facility:** 97 units. 95 one-bedroom standard units. 2 one-bedroom suites, some with kitchens. 3 stories (no elevator), interior corridors. *Bath:* combo or shower only. **Parking:** on-site. **Terms:** 2 night minimum stay - seasonal, cancellation fee imposed. **Amenities:** video games (fee), high-speed Internet, voice mail, irons, hair dryers. **Pool(s):** heated outdoor. **Leisure Activities:** whirlpool, exercise room. **Guest Services:** valet and coin laundry, area transportation-within 5 mi, wireless Internet. **Business Services:** PC. **Cards:** AX, DC, DS, JC, MC, VI. **Free Special Amenities:** continental breakfast and high-speed Internet.

🍽️➕ 🛢️ 📷 🖥️ 💻 / SOME UNITS ❌ 🖨️

THE HEATHMAN HOTEL *Book great rates at AAA.com*
Phone: (425)284-5800 **[42]**

AAA SAVE
▼▼▼▼
Contemporary Hotel
$219-$399 All Year

Address: 220 Kirkland Ave **Location:** I-405, exit 18 (NE 85th St), 1 mi w, then just s on 3rd St. **Facility:** Select from three different mattress styles at this boutique-style hotel; an onsite spa features both organic and natural treatments. Smoke free premises. 91 units. 86 one-bedroom standard units. 5 one-bedroom suites, some with whirlpools. 4 stories, interior corridors. *Bath:* combo or shower only. **Parking:** valet. **Terms:** check-in 3:30 pm, cancellation fee imposed. **Amenities:** high-speed Internet, dual phone lines, voice mail, safes, honor bars, irons, hair dryers. **Leisure Activities:** exercise room, spa. **Guest Services:** valet laundry, wireless Internet. **Business Services:** meeting rooms. **Cards:** AX, MC, VI. **Free Special Amenities:** local telephone calls and high-speed Internet.

🍽️ 24🍽️ 🍸 CALL 🅰️M ❌ 🎾 💻 / SOME UNITS FEE 🐕

LA QUINTA INN & SUITES SEATTLE (BELLEVUE/KIRKLAND) *Book great rates at AAA.com*
Phone: (425)828-6585 **[44]**

▼▼▼▼
Hotel
$69-$169 All Year

Address: 10530 NE Northup Way **Location:** I-405, exit 14 (SR 520) via 108th Ave exit, n on 108th Ave, then just w. **Facility:** 121 units. 116 one-bedroom standard units. 5 one-bedroom suites. 5 stories, interior corridors. *Bath:* combo or shower only. **Parking:** on-site. **Amenities:** video games (fee), high-speed Internet, voice mail, irons, hair dryers. **Pool(s):** heated outdoor. **Leisure Activities:** exercise room. **Guest Services:** valet and coin laundry, wireless Internet. **Business Services:** meeting rooms. **Cards:** AX, DS, MC, VI.

ASK 🍽️➕ 🛢️ 🎾 🖥️ 🖨️ 💻 / SOME UNITS 🐕 ❌

MOTEL 6 - 687 *Book at AAA.com*
Phone: (425)821-5618 **[40]**

▼
Motel
$75-$85 All Year

Address: 12010 120th Pl NE **Location:** I-405, exit 20B northbound; exit 20 southbound, just se. Located in a commercial area. **Facility:** 123 one-bedroom standard units. 3 stories, exterior corridors. *Bath:* shower only. **Parking:** on-site. **Amenities:** high-speed Internet. **Pool(s):** heated outdoor. **Guest Services:** coin laundry, wireless Internet. **Cards:** AX, CB, DC, DS, MC, VI.

🍽️➕ 🛢️ 📷 / SOME UNITS 🐕 ❌

WOODMARK HOTEL, YACHT CLUB & SPA *Book great rates at AAA.com*
Phone: (425)822-3700 **[43]**

AAA SAVE
▼▼▼▼
Hotel
$279-$1800 All Year

Address: 1200 Carillon Point **Location:** On Lake Washington Blvd, 1 mi n of SR 520. **Facility:** A cross between an upscale lodge and an urban hotel, this property on the east shore of Lake Washington offers many guest rooms with water views. 100 units. 79 one-bedroom standard units. 21 one-bedroom suites, some with whirlpools. 4 stories, interior corridors. **Parking:** on-site (fee) and valet. **Terms:** check-in 4 pm, cancellation fee imposed. **Amenities:** video games (fee), CD players, dual phone lines, voice mail, safes, honor bars, irons, hair dryers. **Leisure Activities:** rental boats, kayak, yacht cruises, jogging, exercise room, spa. **Guest Services:** valet laundry, wireless Internet. **Business Services:** conference facilities, PC. **Cards:** AX, DC, JC, MC, VI. **Free Special Amenities:** newspaper and high-speed Internet. Affiliated with A Preferred Hotel.

🍽️ 24🍽️ 🍸 ❌ ❌ 🎾 💻 / SOME UNITS 🐕

—— WHERE TO DINE ——

21 CENTRAL PRIME STEAKHOUSE
Phone: 425/822-1515 **[64]**

▼▼▼
Steak
$20-$48

This place is truly a steakhouse from the past, with comfy booths, soft candle lighting and thick, juicy steaks served with baked potatoes. Guests might start the meal with a salad or seafood chowder and end it with creme brulee. Dressy casual. **Bar:** Full bar. **Reservations:** suggested. **Hours:** 5 pm-10 pm. Closed: major holidays; also 12/24, Sun. **Address:** 21 Central Way **Location:** I-405, exit 18 (NE 85th St), 1 mi w. **Parking:** on-site. **Cards:** AX, CB, DC, DS, MC, VI.

(See map and index starting on p. 614)

CACTUS KIRKLAND

Mexican
$7-$18

Phone: 425/893-9799 62

Traditional Mexican food is served in a Southwestern atmosphere. The restaurant's location in a trendy walking area is ideal for diners who want to stroll after their meal. Casual dress. **Bar:** Full bar. **Reservations:** not accepted. **Hours:** 11:30 am-10 pm, Fri & Sat-11 pm. Closed major holidays. **Address:** 121 Park Ln **Location:** I-405, exit 18 (NE 85th St), 1.2 mi w, just s on Lake St, then just e. **Parking:** street. **Cards:** AX, DC, DS, MC, VI.

CAFE JUANITA

Northern Italian
$14-$36

Phone: 425/823-1505 59

The seasonal menu incorporates plenty of fresh pasta as well as many seafood choices. In addition to an extensive list of Italian wines, the popular, unassuming restaurant boasts a flavorful house wine, which is produced right on the premises. Casual dress. **Bar:** Full bar. **Reservations:** suggested. **Hours:** 5 pm-10 pm, Sun & Mon-9 pm. Closed: 7/4, 11/26, 12/25. **Address:** 9702 NE 120th Pl **Location:** I-405, exit 20 southbound, 1.5 mi via 124th St to 100th Ave, then s; exit 20A northbound, 1.5 mi via 116th to 97th Ave, then n. **Parking:** on-site. **Cards:** AX, MC, VI.

CAFE VELOCE

Italian
$8-$16

Phone: 425/814-2972 58

The restaurant features motorcycle racing decor, including a checkerboard floor, and serves casual Italian cuisine including gourmet pastas and pizza. Ride your motorcycle to the restaurant and receive 10% off your meal. Casual dress. **Bar:** Beer & wine. **Reservations:** accepted. **Hours:** 11 am-10 pm, Sat from 4 pm, Sun 4 pm-9:30 pm. Closed: 7/4, 11/26, 12/25. **Address:** 12514 120th Ave NE **Location:** I-405, exit 20B, just s; adjacent to Totem Lake Cinemas. **Parking:** on-site. **Cards:** AX, DS, MC, VI.

THE CRAB CRACKER

Seafood
$9-$35

Phone: 425/827-8700 60

The restaurant offers fresh regional seafood expertly prepared amidst a nautical decor; bustling at lunchtime and reservations at dinner are a must. Casual dress. **Bar:** Full bar. **Reservations:** suggested. **Hours:** 11 am-10 pm, Fri & Sat-11 pm. Closed: 11/26, 12/25. **Address:** 452 Central Way **Location:** I-405, exit 18, (NE 85th St), 1 mi w. **Parking:** on-site. **Cards:** AX, DC, DS, MC, VI.

NEWPORT BAY RESTAURANT

Seafood
$8-$25

Phone: 425/827-2722

This restaurant is for those seeking a casual, relaxing time. A menu favorite is New England clam chowder, which is available nightly. Fresh Northwest salmon and Alaskan halibut prepared several ways share menu space with pasta, chicken and salads. Casual dress. **Bar:** Full bar. **Reservations:** accepted. **Hours:** 11 am-10 pm, Fri & Sat-11 pm, Sun 9 am-10 pm. Closed: 11/26, 12/25. **Address:** 10426 NE Northup Way **Location:** I-405, exit 14 (SR 520 W) via 108th St, just s, then just w. **Parking:** on-site. **Cards:** AX, DS, MC, VI.

CALL ♿️

RISTORANTE PARADISO

Regional Italian
$8-$27

Phone: 425/889-8601 61

The small, romantic restaurant experiments in nouvelle cuisine, such as chicken with spinach mozzarella and seafood garlic toast. Lemon cheesecake and chocolate decadence are delightful indulgences. Casual dress. **Bar:** Beer & wine. **Reservations:** suggested. **Hours:** 11:30 am-10 pm, Fri & Sat 3 pm-10:30 pm. Closed: 1/1, 11/26, 12/25. **Address:** 120 A Park Ln **Location:** I-405, exit 18 (NE 85th St), 1.2 mi w, just s on Lake St, then just e. **Parking:** on-site. **Cards:** AX, DC, DS, MC, VI.

SHAMIANA

Indian
$7-$18

Phone: 425/827-4902 66

The family-run Indian restaurant serves naan, a wide selection of vegetarian dishes and Pakistani barbecue with items such as coriander ginger chicken served with pulao (basmati rice seasoned with turmeric, cinnamon and cumin). Casual dress. **Bar:** Beer & wine. **Reservations:** not accepted. **Hours:** 11 am-2:30 & 5-9:30 pm, Fri-10 pm, Sat 5 pm-10 pm, Sun 5 pm-9:30 pm. Closed major holidays. **Address:** 10724 NE 68th St **Location:** I-405, exit 17, 0.5 mi sw; in Houghton Village Shopping Center. **Parking:** on-site. **Cards:** AX, CB, DC, DS, MC, VI.

THE THIRD FLOOR FISH CAFE

Continental
$24-$45

Phone: 425/822-3553 65

Fresh fish specials are always a hit at this spectacular location on Lake Washington. Offerings include late-night bites in the ever-popular piano bar and an array of decadent desserts. Dressy casual. **Bar:** Full bar. **Reservations:** accepted. **Hours:** 5 pm-9 pm. Closed: 1/1, 7/4, 12/25. **Address:** 205 Lake St S **Location:** I-405, exit 18 (NE 85th St), 1.2 mi w, then just s. **Parking:** valet. **Cards:** AX, CB, DC, DS, MC, VI.

TRELLIS

American
$9-$29

Phone: 425/284-5800 63

Fresh ingredients are the name of the game, and the chef grows the fruit and vegetables used in many of the dishes. Fresh seafood and hand-raised meats accompany these garden treats. Dressy casual. **Bar:** Full bar. **Reservations:** suggested. **Hours:** 7 am-9 pm, Fri & Sat-10 pm. **Address:** 220 Kirkland Ave **Location:** I-405, exit 18 (NE 85th St), 1 mi w, then just s on 3rd St; in the Heathman Hotel. **Parking:** valet. **Cards:** AX, JC, MC, VI.

LAKEWOOD pop. 58,211 (See map and index starting on p. 626)

— WHERE TO STAY —

BEST WESTERN LAKEWOOD MOTOR INN *Book great rates at AAA.com* **Phone: (253)584-2212** 31

Hotel
$115-$125 3/1-9/30
$105-$115 10/1-2/28

Address: 6125 Motor Ave SW **Location:** I-5, exit 125, 2 mi nw on Bridgeport Way SW, then just left on Gravelly Lake Dr, then first right. **Facility:** 78 one-bedroom standard units. 2 stories (no elevator), exterior corridors. *Bath:* combo or shower only. **Parking:** on-site. **Amenities:** high-speed Internet, voice mail, irons, hair dryers. **Pool(s):** heated outdoor. **Guest Services:** coin laundry. **Business Services:** meeting rooms, PC. **Cards:** AX, CB, DC, DS, JC, MC, VI.

CALL  / SOME UNITS

Best Western

AAA Benefit:
Members save up to 20%, plus 10% bonus points with rewards program.

(See map and index starting on p. 626)

LA QUINTA - LAKEWOOD INN & SUITES   *Book at AAA.com*   Phone: (253)582-7000 **33**

▼▼▼▼▼
Hotel
$119-$139 All Year

Address: 11751 Pacific Hwy SW **Location:** I-5, exit 125, just nw. **Facility:** Smoke free premises. 120 one-bedroom standard units, some with whirlpools. 4 stories, interior corridors. **Parking:** on-site. **Amenities:** high-speed Internet, voice mail, irons, hair dryers. **Pool(s):** heated indoor. **Leisure Activities:** whirlpool, exercise room. **Guest Services:** coin laundry, wireless Internet. **Business Services:** meeting rooms, business center. **Cards:** AX, DS, MC, VI.

🏊 ⊗ 🐾 🖥 📠 💻 / SOME UNITS 🐕

WESTERN INN   Phone: 253/588-5241 **32**

AAA SAVE
▼▼▼ ▼▼
Hotel
$59-$78 All Year

Address: 9920 S Tacoma Way **Location:** I-5, exit 127 (S Tacoma Way), just w on SR 512, then just n. **Facility:** 104 units. 84 one-bedroom standard units. 20 one-bedroom suites, some with efficiencies. 2 stories (no elevator), exterior corridors. **Parking:** on-site. **Terms:** cancellation fee imposed. **Amenities:** high-speed Internet, irons, hair dryers. **Guest Services:** coin laundry, wireless Internet. **Business Services:** meeting rooms, PC. **Cards:** AX, DS, MC, VI. **Free Special Amenities:** continental breakfast and high-speed Internet.

🍴 🎥 🖥 📠 💻 / SOME UNITS FEE 🐕 ⊗

------- **WHERE TO DINE** -------

RAM RESTAURANT AND BREWERY   Phone: 253/584-3191

▼▼▼ ▼▼▼
American
$8-$22

The enormous restaurant features high ceilings, huge television screens, large sports-themed banners and a brew pub area. The menu is equally enormous, with steaks, poultry, pasta, seafood, salads, sandwiches and pizza. The on-site brewery turns out a large selection of microbrews. Casual dress. **Bar:** Full bar. **Reservations:** not accepted. **Hours:** 11 am-close. **Closed:** 12/25. **Address:** 10019 59th Ave **Location:** I-5, exit 125, 1.8 mi nw on Bridgeport Way SW, then just s. **Parking:** on-site. **Cards:** AX, MC, VI.

LYNNWOOD pop. 33,847   (See map and index starting on p. 614)

------- **WHERE TO STAY** -------

BEST WESTERN ALDERWOOD   *Book great rates at AAA.com*   Phone: (425)775-7600 **15**

AAA SAVE
▼▼▼▼▼
Hotel
$119-$169 3/1-11/30
$109-$159 12/1-2/28

Address: 19332 36th Ave W **Location:** I-5, exit 181B northbound, just n on Poplar Way, just w on 196th St SW, then just n; exit 181 (SR 524 W) southbound, just nw. **Facility:** 141 units. 120 one-bedroom standard units, some with whirlpools. 21 one-bedroom suites, some with kitchens. 4 stories, interior corridors. *Bath:* combo or shower only. **Parking:** on-site. **Terms:** cancellation fee imposed. **Amenities:** high-speed Internet, voice mail, irons, hair dryers. **Pool(s):** heated outdoor. **Leisure Activities:** whirlpool, exercise room. **Guest Services:** complimentary and valet laundry, wireless Internet. **Business Services:** meeting rooms, PC. **Cards:** AX, DC, DS, MC, VI. **Free Special Amenities:** continental breakfast and high-speed Internet.

Best Western

AAA Benefit:
Members save up to 20%, plus 10% bonus points with rewards program.

🍴 🏊 🎥 🖥 💻 / SOME UNITS 🐕 ⊗ 📠

(See map and index starting on p. 614)

COURTYARD BY MARRIOTT-LYNNWOOD   *Book great rates at AAA.com*   Phone: (425)670-0500

Hotel
$144-$159 All Year

Address: 4220 Alderwood Mall Blvd **Location:** I-5, exit 181A northbound, just w on 44th Ave W, then just n; exit 181 (SR 524 W) southbound, 0.5 mi w on 196th SW, just s on 44th Ave W, then just e. **Facility:** Smoke free premises. 164 units. 156 one-bedroom standard units, some with whirlpools. 8 one-bedroom suites. 4 stories, interior corridors. *Bath:* combo or shower only. **Parking:** on-site. **Terms:** cancellation fee imposed. **Amenities:** high-speed Internet, dual phone lines, voice mail, irons, hair dryers. **Pool(s):** heated indoor. **Leisure Activities:** whirlpool, exercise room. **Guest Services:** valet and coin laundry, area transportation, wireless Internet. **Business Services:** meeting rooms, PC. **Cards:** AX, CB, DC, DS, JC, MC, VI.

AAA Benefit:
Members save a minimum 5% off the best available rate.

EMBASSY SUITES HOTEL SEATTLE NORTH/LYNNWOOD   *Book great rates at AAA.com*   Phone: (425)775-2500   ⑳

Hotel
$119-$249 All Year

Address: 20610 44th Ave W **Location:** I-5, exit 181A northbound, just se; exit 181 (SR 524 W) southbound, 0.5 w on 196th St SW, then 0.6 mi s. **Facility:** 240 one-bedroom suites, some with whirlpools. 5 stories, interior corridors. *Bath:* combo or shower only. **Parking:** on-site. **Terms:** check-in 4 pm, 1-30 night minimum stay, cancellation fee imposed. **Amenities:** voice mail, irons, hair dryers. *Fee:* video games, high-speed Internet. **Pool(s):** heated indoor. **Leisure Activities:** sauna, whirlpool, exercise room. **Guest Services:** valet and coin laundry, area transportation, wireless Internet. **Business Services:** conference facilities, business center. **Cards:** AX, CB, DC, DS, JC, MC, VI.

EMBASSY SUITES HOTELS·
AAA Benefit:
Members save 5% or more everyday!

EXTENDED STAYAMERICA-SEATTLE-LYNNWOOD   *Book at AAA.com*   Phone: (425)670-2520   ⑰

Hotel
$95-$110 All Year

Address: 3021 196th St SW **Location:** I-5, exit 181E southbound; exit 181B northbound, just ne. **Facility:** 109 one-bedroom standard units. 4 stories, interior corridors. *Bath:* combo or shower only. **Parking:** on-site. **Terms:** office hours 7 am-11 pm, cancellation fee imposed. **Amenities:** high-speed Internet (fee), voice mail, irons. **Guest Services:** coin laundry, wireless Internet. **Cards:** AX, CD, DO, DS, JC, MC, VI.

HAMPTON INN & SUITES   *Book great rates at AAA.com*   Phone: (425)771-1888   ⑯

Hotel
$124-$169 All Year

Address: 19324 Alderwood Mall Pkwy **Location:** I-5, exit 181B northbound, 0.6 mi n; exit 181 (SR 524 E) southbound, 0.5 mi e on 196th St SE, then just n. **Facility:** Smoke free premises. 152 units. 111 one-bedroom standard units, some with efficiencies. 41 one-bedroom suites with efficiencies, some with whirlpools. 4 stories, interior corridors. *Bath:* combo or shower only. **Parking:** on-site. **Terms:** check-in 4 pm, 1-30 night minimum stay, cancellation fee imposed. **Amenities:** video games (fee), high-speed Internet, dual phone lines, voice mail, safes, irons, hair dryers. *Some:* DVD players. **Pool(s):** heated indoor. **Leisure Activities:** whirlpool, exercise room. **Guest Services:** valet and coin laundry, area transportation-within 10 mi, wireless Internet. **Business Services:** meeting rooms, business center. **Cards:** AX, CB, DC, DS, JC, MC, VI. **Free Special Amenities: expanded continental breakfast and high-speed Internet.**

AAA Benefit:
Members save up to 10% everyday!

LA QUINTA INN LYNNWOOD   *Book great rates at AAA.com*   Phone: (425)775-7447   ⑱

Hotel
$59-$169 All Year

Address: 4300 Alderwood Mall Blvd **Location:** I-5, exit 181A northbound, just w; exit 181 (SR 524 W) southbound, 0.5 mi w on 196th St SW, just s on 44th Ave SW, then just e. **Facility:** 101 one-bedroom standard units. 5 stories, interior corridors. **Parking:** on-site. **Amenities:** video games (fee), high-speed Internet, voice mail, irons, hair dryers. **Pool(s):** heated indoor. **Leisure Activities:** whirlpool, exercise room. **Guest Services:** valet laundry, wireless Internet. **Business Services:** meeting rooms, PC. **Cards:** AX, CB, DS, MC, VI. **Free Special Amenities: continental breakfast and high-speed Internet.**

RESIDENCE INN BY MARRIOTT-SEATTLE NORTH/LYNNWOOD   *Book great rates at AAA.com*   Phone: (425)771-1100   ⑭

Hotel
$233-$285 All Year

Address: 18200 Alderwood Mall Pkwy **Location:** I-5, exit 183 southbound, just w on 164th St SW, then 1.5 mi se on 28th St W; exit 182 northbound on SR 525, exit 1, then just s; just n of Alderwood Mall Shopping Center. **Facility:** Smoke free premises. 120 units. 79 one-bedroom standard units with kitchens. 11 one- and 30 two-bedroom suites with kitchens. 2 stories (no elevator), exterior corridors. *Bath:* combo or shower only. **Parking:** on-site. **Terms:** check-in 4 pm, cancellation fee imposed. **Amenities:** CD players, high-speed Internet, dual phone lines, voice mail, irons, hair dryers. *Some:* DVD players. **Pool(s):** heated outdoor. **Leisure Activities:** whirlpools, exercise room, sports court. **Guest Services:** valet and coin laundry, area transportation, wireless Internet. **Business Services:** meeting rooms, business center. **Cards:** AX, CB, DC, DS, JC, MC, VI.

AAA Benefit:
Members save a minimum 5% off the best available rate.

(See map and index starting on p. 614)

——— WHERE TO DINE ———

BILLY MCHALE'S

Phone: 425/775-8500   (50)

▼▼▼

American
$7-$20

The family-oriented restaurant, which serves chicken, steak and fresh seafood, is known for its succulent ribs and tasty onion loaf. Drinks include 31 varieties of margaritas. The bustling dining room teems with upbeat colors, signs and memorabilia. Casual dress. **Bar:** Full bar. **Reservations:** accepted. **Hours:** 11 am-10 pm, Fri & Sat-11 pm, Sun & Mon-9:30 pm. Closed: 11/26, 12/25. **Address:** 18430 33rd Ave W **Location:** I-5, exit 181B northbound; exit 181 (SR 524 W) southbound, just w; across from Alderwood Mall Shopping Center. **Parking:** on-site. **Cards:** AX, CB, DC, DS, MC, VI.

CLAIM JUMPER

Phone: 425/778-5700

▼▼▼

American
$9-$24

Great menu variety makes this place a good stop for parties with diverse tastes. Choices include specialty appetizers, salads, rotisserie chicken and barbecue items, not to mention good comfort foods, such as traditional pot pie. Hearty portions satisfy big appetites. The atmosphere is fun and lively. Casual dress. **Bar:** Full bar. **Hours:** 11 am-10 pm, Fri & Sat-11 pm. Closed: 7/4, 11/26, 12/25. **Address:** 3000 184th St **Location:** Just w of Alderwood Mall Pkwy; at Alderwood Mall. **Parking:** on-site. **Cards:** AX, CB, DC, DS, JC, MC, VI.

CALL 🛗♿

MCGRATH'S FISH HOUSE

Phone: 425/670-9050

▼▼

Seafood
$9-$19

The popular chain specializes in fresh Pacific Northwest seafood, including dishes grilled over a wood fire and items from the daily fresh sheet. Also on the menu are steaks, chicken, pasta and gourmet burgers. Casual dress. **Bar:** Full bar. **Reservations:** not accepted. **Hours:** 11 am-10 pm. Closed: 11/26, 12/25. **Address:** 3000 184th St SW **Location:** Adjacent to Alderwood Mall. **Parking:** on-site. **Cards:** AX, DC, DS, MC, VI.

TALAY THAI RESTAURANT

Phone: 425/670-1340   (51)

▼▼▼

Thai
$5-$9

A cozy setting awaits inside the restaurant's nondescript exterior. Many representations of Thai fare can be customized to the patron's taste for spiciness. A starter of tum yum soup takes off the edge before a meal of pad thai noodles and panang beef with steamed rice. Casual dress. **Bar:** Beer & wine. **Hours:** 11 am-9 pm, Fri-10 pm, Sat noon-10 pm, Sun 4 pm-9 pm. Closed major holidays. **Address:** 4520 200th St SW, #208 **Location:** I-5, exit 181A northbound, just nw on 44th Ave SW, then just s; exit 181 (SR 524 W) southbound, just w on 196th SW, just s on 44th Ave SW, then just s. **Parking:** on-site. **Cards:** AX, MC, VI.

MARYSVILLE pop. 25,315

——— WHERE TO STAY ———

BEST WESTERN TULALIP INN

Book great rates at AAA.com

Phone: (360)659-4488

AAA SAVE
▼▼▼
Hotel
$110-$160 All Year

Address: 3228 Marine Dr NE **Location:** I-5, exit 199, just w. **Facility:** 69 units. 67 one-bedroom standard units, some with whirlpools. 2 one-bedroom suites. 3 stories, interior corridors. *Bath:* combo or shower only. **Parking:** on-site. **Terms:** cancellation fee imposed. **Amenities:** high-speed Internet, voice mail, irons, hair dryers. **Pool(s):** heated indoor. **Leisure Activities:** whirlpool. **Guest Services:** valet laundry, wireless Internet. **Business Services:** meeting rooms, PC. **Cards:** AX, CB, DC, DS, JC, MC, VI. **Free Special Amenities: expanded continental breakfast and high-speed Internet.**

CALL 🛗♿ 🏊 📷 🛗 🖥 / SOME UNITS 🚫

AAA Benefit:
Members save up to 20%, plus 10% bonus points with rewards program.

COMFORT INN EVERETT-MARYSVILLE

Book great rates at AAA.com

Phone: (360)658-1339

AAA SAVE
▼▼▼
Hotel
$99-$199 All Year

Address: 6311 33rd Ave NE **Location:** I-5, exit 199, just nw. **Facility:** 59 one-bedroom standard units, some with whirlpools. 2 stories (no elevator), interior corridors. **Parking:** on-site. **Amenities:** high-speed Internet, voice mail, irons, hair dryers. **Leisure Activities:** exercise room. **Guest Services:** valet and coin laundry, wireless Internet. **Cards:** AX, DC, DS, MC, VI. **Free Special Amenities: expanded continental breakfast and high-speed Internet.**

🍴 CALL 🛗♿ 📷 🖥 / SOME UNITS 🚫

HOLIDAY INN EXPRESS HOTEL & SUITES-MARYSVILLE

Book at AAA.com

Phone: 360/530-1234

▼▼▼
Hotel
Rates not provided

Address: 8606 36th Ave NE **Location:** I-5, exit 200, just se. **Facility:** Smoke free premises. 100 one-bedroom standard units, some with whirlpools. 4 stories, interior corridors. *Bath:* combo or shower only. **Parking:** on-site. **Terms:** check-in 4 pm. **Amenities:** high-speed Internet, voice mail, irons, hair dryers. **Pool(s):** heated indoor. **Leisure Activities:** whirlpool, exercise room. **Guest Services:** valet and coin laundry, wireless Internet. **Business Services:** meeting rooms, business center.

🍴 🏊 🚫 📷 🛗 🖥

——— WHERE TO DINE ———

BOONDOCKERS CAFE

Menu on AAA.com

Phone: 360/653-7545

AAA
▼▼
American
$8-$20

This casual diner serves breakfast, lunch and dinner dishes, such as the satisfying classic burger, fries and shake. Service is friendly. Casual dress. **Bar:** Beer & wine. **Reservations:** accepted. **Hours:** 8 am-9 pm, Fri & Sat-10 pm. **Address:** 1008 Cedar Ave **Location:** I-5, exit 199, just e, then just n. **Parking:** on-site. **Cards:** MC, VI.

G. A. MAXWELL'S RESTAURANT   *Menu on AAA.com*   Phone: 360/659-1000

The attractive log lodge boasts high ceilings and a cozy, classy ambience. Prime rib, steak and seafood make up a traditional menu. Blackberry cobbler with burnt cream is outstanding. Casual dress. **Bar:** Full bar. **Hours:** 8 am-9 pm, Fri & Sat 7 am-10 pm, Sun 7 am-9 pm. Closed: 12/25. **Address:** 1204 3rd St **Location:** I-5, exit 199, just se. **Parking:** on-site. **Cards:** DS, MC, VI.

American
$9-$22

MERCER ISLAND pop. 22,036   (See map and index starting on p. 614)

───── WHERE TO DINE ─────

THAI ON MERCER   Phone: 206/236-9990   88

Piquant flavors mingle in such entrees as Thai halibut. A strong emphasis is placed on healthful food, with many low-fat dishes and only lean beef. The open dining room is colored with fresh flowers. Work by local artists is changed often. Casual dress. **Bar:** Beer & wine. **Reservations:** suggested, weekends. **Hours:** 11 am-9 pm, Sat & Sun from 4 pm. **Address:** 7691 27th St SE **Location:** I-90, exit 7, just s. **Parking:** on-site. **Cards:** AX, MC, VI.

Thai
$8-$15

MILL CREEK pop. 11,525

───── WHERE TO DINE ─────

MCMENAMINS   Phone: 425/316-0520

The casual neighborhood eatery is where friends gather for classic pub and comfort fare, all washed down by pints of locally made beer. Large wooden booths or tables easily accommodate larger groups, and the coloctic, custom-painted walls and varied period light fixtures keep diners' eyes busy should the conversation lag. Casual dress. **Bar:** Full bar. **Reservations:** not accepted. **Hours:** 11 am-midnight, Thurs-Sat to 1 am, Sun noon-midnight. Closed: 11/26, 12/25. **Address:** 13300 Bothell Everett Hwy, Suite 304 **Location:** I-5, exit 186, 1 mi e, then just s. **Parking:** on-site. **Cards:** MC, VI.

American
$5-$20

ROUND TABLE PIZZA   Phone: 425/745-4561

This casual, family-oriented pizza place features high-quality ingredients and dough rolled fresh daily. Distinctive specialty pizzas are piled high with toppings. Casual dress. **Bar:** Beer & wine. **Reservations:** not accepted. **Hours:** 11 am-9 pm, Fri & Sat-10 pm. **Address:** 16314 Bothell Everett Hwy **Location:** Jct Bothell Everett Hwy and 164th St SW. **Parking:** on-site. **Cards:** AX, DS, MC, VI.

Pizza
$10-$16

MONROE pop. 13,795

───── WHERE TO STAY ─────

BEST WESTERN SKY VALLEY INN   *Book great rates at AAA.com*   Phone: (360)794-3111

Hotel
$109-$159 3/1-10/31
$99-$149 11/1-2/28

Address: 19233 US 2 **Location:** West end of town. **Facility:** Smoke free premises. 58 units. 57 one-bedroom standard units, some with whirlpools. 1 one-bedroom suite with kitchen and whirlpool. 3 stories, interior corridors. *Bath:* combo or shower only. **Parking:** on-site. **Amenities:** high-speed Internet, voice mail, irons, hair dryers. **Pool(s):** heated outdoor. **Leisure Activities:** whirlpool, exercise room. **Guest Services:** valet and coin laundry, wireless Internet. **Business Services:** meeting rooms, PC. **Free Special Amenities:** continental breakfast and high-speed Internet.

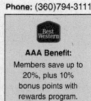

AAA Benefit:
Members save up to 20%, plus 10% bonus points with rewards program.

GUESTHOUSE INTERNATIONAL INN & SUITES   *Book great rates at AAA.com*   Phone: (360)863-1900

Hotel
$114-$144 All Year

Address: 19103 US 2 **Location:** West end of town. **Facility:** Smoke free premises. 66 one-bedroom standard units. 3 stories, interior corridors. *Bath:* combo or shower only. **Parking:** on-site. **Terms:** cancellation fee imposed. **Amenities:** high-speed Internet, dual phone lines, voice mail, irons, hair dryers. **Pool(s):** whirlpool, exercise room. **Guest Services:** valet and coin laundry, wireless Internet. **Business Services:** meeting rooms, PC. **Cards:** AX, CB, DC, DS, JC, MC, VI. **Free Special Amenities:** expanded continental breakfast and high-speed Internet.

───── WHERE TO DINE ─────

CANYONS RESTAURANT   Phone: 360/805-5453

Diners can experience a small taste of the Southwest in the colorful, festive restaurant. Hand paintings that resemble lithographs of buffalo decorate the stucco-finished walls and tell a story of early man. Casual dress. **Bar:** Full bar. **Reservations:** accepted. **Hours:** 11 am-10 pm, Fri & Sat-11 pm, Sun 9 am-9 pm. Closed: 11/26, 12/25. **Address:** 14919 N Kelsey St **Location:** West end of town. **Parking:** on-site. **Cards:** AX, DC, MC, VI.

American
$8-$19

SAILFISH BAR & GRILL   Phone: 360/794-4056

No need to go into Seattle for great food. This local eatery offers a great selection of beef and seafood dishes with a little duck, chicken and pasta tossed in for variety. Specials tend to focus around seafood, including salmon or marlin to go with a microbrew from the adjoining Twin Rivers Brewery. Casual dress. **Bar:** Full bar. **Hours:** 5 pm-10 pm. Closed major holidays; also Sun & Mon. **Address:** 104 N Lewis St **Location:** Jct Main and Lewis sts; downtown. **Parking:** street. **Cards:** MC, VI.

American
$12-$26

MOUNTLAKE TERRACE pop. 20,362   (See map and index starting on p. 614)

──────── WHERE TO STAY ────────

STUDIO 6 #6042   *Book at AAA.com*   Phone: (425)771-3139   23
▽▽▽ ▽▽▽▽
Motel
$81-$91 All Year
Address: 6017 244th St SW **Location:** I-5, exit 177, just ne. **Facility:** 119 one-bedroom standard units with efficiencies. 2 stories (no elevator), exterior corridors. *Bath:* combo or shower only. **Parking:** on-site. **Terms:** office hours 7 am-8 pm. **Amenities:** high-speed Internet (fee), voice mail, irons. **Guest Services:** coin laundry, wireless Internet. **Cards:** AX, CB, DC, DS, MC, VI.

──────── WHERE TO DINE ────────

CANYONS RESTAURANT   Phone: 425/744-1525
▽▽▽ ▽▽
American
$8-$19
Diners can experience a small taste of the Southwest in the colorful, festive restaurant. Hand paintings that resemble lithographs of buffalo decorate the stucco-finished walls and tell a story of early man. Casual dress. **Bar:** Full bar. **Reservations:** accepted. **Hours:** 11 am-10 pm, Fri & Sat-11 pm, Sun 9 am-9 pm. Closed: 11/26, 12/25. **Address:** 6003 244th St SW **Location:** I-5, exit 177, just ne. **Parking:** on-site. **Cards:** AX, DC, MC, VI.

MUKILTEO pop. 18,019

──────── WHERE TO STAY ────────

EXTENDED STAYAMERICA-SEATTLE-MUKILTEO   *Book at AAA.com*   Phone: (425)493-1561
▽▽ ▽▽
Hotel
$121-$136 All Year
Address: 3917 Harbour Pointe Blvd SW **Location:** Jct SR 526 and 525 (Mukilteo Speedway), 1.5 mi s, then just w. **Facility:** 107 one-bedroom standard units. 3 stories, interior corridors. *Bath:* combo or shower only. **Parking:** on-site. **Terms:** office hours 7 am-11 pm, cancellation fee imposed. **Amenities:** high-speed Internet (fee), voice mail, irons. **Guest Services:** coin laundry, wireless Internet. **Cards:** AX, CB, DC, DS, JC, MC, VI.

HILTON GARDEN INN SEATTLE NORTH/EVERETT   *Book great rates at AAA.com*   Phone: (425)423-9000
▽▽▽ ▽▽▽
Hotel
$99-$219 All Year
Address: 8401 Paine Field Blvd **Location:** I-5, exit 189 (SR 526 W), 4.1 mi w. **Facility:** 99 one-bedroom standard units, some with whirlpools. 3 one-bedroom suites with whirlpools. 4 stories, interior corridors. *Bath:* combo or shower only. **Parking:** on-site. **Terms:** 1-30 night minimum stay, cancellation fee imposed. **Amenities:** video games (fee), high-speed Internet, dual phone lines, voice mail, irons, hair dryers. **Pool(s):** heated indoor. **Leisure Activities:** whirlpool, exercise room. **Guest Services:** valet and coin laundry, area transportation, wireless Internet. **Business Services:** meeting rooms, business center. **Cards:** AX, CB, DC, DS, JC, MC, VI.

Hilton Garden Inn

AAA Benefit:
Members save 5% or more everyday!

SILVER CLOUD INN MUKILTEO   *Book at AAA.com*   Phone: (425)423-8600
▽▽ ▽▽▽
Hotel
$169-$289 All Year
Address: 718 Front St **Location:** Just n of Mukilteo Ferry Landing; downtown. **Facility:** Smoke free premises. 70 units. 56 one-bedroom standard units, some with whirlpools. 14 one-bedroom suites. 3 stories, interior corridors. *Bath:* combo or shower only. **Parking:** on-site. **Amenities:** video games (fee), high-speed Internet, dual phone lines, voice mail, irons, hair dryers. **Guest Services:** complimentary and valet laundry, wireless Internet. **Business Services:** meeting rooms, PC. **Cards:** AX, DC, DS, JC, MC, VI.

TOWNEPLACE SUITES BY MARRIOTT-MUKILTEO   *Book great rates at AAA.com*   Phone: (425)551-5900
▽▽▽ ▽▽▽
Hotel
$143-$175 All Year
Address: 8521 Mukilteo Speedway **Location:** Just se of jct 84th St SW and SR 525 (Mukilteo Speedway). **Facility:** Smoke free premises. 128 one-bedroom standard units, some with efficiencies. 2 stories (no elevator), exterior corridors. *Bath:* combo or shower only. **Parking:** on-site. **Terms:** check-in 4 pm, cancellation fee imposed. **Amenities:** high-speed Internet, dual phone lines, voice mail, irons, hair dryers. **Pool(s):** heated outdoor. **Leisure Activities:** whirlpool, exercise room, sports court. **Guest Services:** valet and coin laundry, area transportation, wireless Internet. **Business Services:** meeting rooms, PC. **Cards:** AX, CB, DC, DS, JC, MC, VI.

TownePlace Marriott

AAA Benefit:
Members save a minimum 5% off the best available rate.

──────── WHERE TO DINE ────────

ARNIES RESTAURANT   Phone: 425/355-2181
▽▽▽ ▽▽
Seafood
$8-$31
Standouts on a menu of mostly Northwest seafood include hearty clam chowder and halibut selections. The restaurant also delivers with friendly service and lovely views of Puget Sound and the distant Olympic Mountains. Casual dress. **Bar:** Full bar. **Reservations:** suggested, weekends. **Hours:** 11 am-2 & 4-9 pm, Sat 4 pm-9:30 pm, Sun 10 am-2 & 4-9 pm. Closed: 12/25. **Address:** 714 2nd St **Location:** Downtown. **Parking:** on-site. **Cards:** AX, MC, VI.

NORTH BEND pop. 4,746

─── WHERE TO STAY ───

NORTH BEND MOTEL
AAA SAVE
Motel
$60-$84 All Year

Phone: 425/888-1121
Address: 322 E North Bend Way **Location:** I-90, exit 31, 0.7 mi n on Bendigo Blvd (SR 202), then just e. **Facility:** 17 one-bedroom standard units. 1 story, exterior corridors. *Bath:* shower only. **Parking:** on-site. **Terms:** office hours 7 am-11 pm, 3 day cancellation notice. **Amenities:** *Some:* irons. **Cards:** AX, DS, MC, VI. **Free Special Amenities: early check-in/late check-out and preferred room (subject to availability with advance reservations).**

ROARING RIVER BED & BREAKFAST
Bed & Breakfast
$109-$195 All Year

Phone: 425/888-4834
Address: 46715 SE 129th St **Location:** I-90, exit 31, 0.7 mi n on Bendigo Blvd (SR 202), 1.3 mi e on North Bend Way, 2.5 mi ne on Mt. Si Rd, just s on 464th St, then just e. Located in a quiet rural area. **Facility:** On 2.6 forested acres, the property offers views of the Snoqualmie River and distant mountain peaks; popular Mount Si Park is within walking distance. Smoke free premises. 5 units. 4 one-bedroom standard units, some with whirlpools. 1 cabin. 2 stories (no elevator), exterior corridors. *Bath:* combo or shower only. **Parking:** on-site. **Terms:** check-in 4 pm, age restrictions may apply, 14 day cancellation notice-fee imposed. **Amenities:** *Some:* hair dryers. **Leisure Activities:** fishing, hiking trails. **Guest Services:** wireless Internet. **Cards:** AX, DS, MC, VI.

PORT ORCHARD pop. 7,693

─── WHERE TO STAY ───

─── *The following lodging was either not evaluated or did not* ───
meet AAA rating requirements but is listed for your information only.

COMFORT INN PORT ORCHARD
fyi

Phone: 360/895-2666
Not evaluated. **Address:** 1121 Bay St **Location:** SR 16, exit Tremont St, 0.9 mi e to Sidney Ave, 1.2 mi n to Bay St, then just e. Facilities, services, and decor characterize an economy property.

POULSBO pop. 6,813   (See map and index starting on p. 624)

─── WHERE TO STAY ───

HOLIDAY INN EXPRESS   *Book at AAA.com*
Hotel
$99-$199 All Year

Phone: (360)697-4400   **18**
Address: 19801 NE 7th Ave **Location:** On SR 305. Located in commercial area at Poulsbo Village. **Facility:** 63 one-bedroom standard units, some with whirlpools. 2 stories (no elevator), interior corridors. *Bath:* combo or shower only. **Parking:** on-site. **Terms:** cancellation fee imposed. **Amenities:** video games (fee), high-speed Internet, dual phone lines, voice mail, irons, hair dryers. **Leisure Activities:** whirlpool. **Guest Services:** valet and coin laundry, wireless Internet. **Business Services:** PC. **Cards:** AX, CB, DC, DS, JC, MC, VI.

POULSBO INN & SUITES   *Book great rates at AAA.com*
AAA SAVE
Hotel
$110-$130 3/1-10/1
$99-$116 10/2-2/28

Phone: (360)779-3921   **19**
Address: 18680 SR 305 **Location:** SR 3, 2.3 mi e. Located in a commercial area. **Facility:** 83 units. 68 one-bedroom standard units. 15 one-bedroom suites, some with efficiencies. 1-2 stories (no elevator), exterior corridors. *Bath:* combo or shower only. **Parking:** on-site. **Terms:** 7 day cancellation notice-fee imposed. **Amenities:** high-speed Internet, voice mail, irons. *Some:* DVD players, CD players. **Pool(s):** heated outdoor. **Leisure Activities:** whirlpool, playground, exercise room. **Guest Services:** coin laundry. **Business Services:** PC. **Cards:** AX, CB, DC, DS, MC, VI. **Free Special Amenities: expanded continental breakfast and high-speed Internet.**

─── WHERE TO DINE ───

MOLLY WARD GARDENS
Regional
Continental
$6-$42

Phone: 360/779-4471   **12**
Patrons can dine indoors in an eclectic country setting or outdoors among the fragrant, colorful flower and herb gardens. Organic vegetables grown on the premises are served fresh. Prime filet mignon and the creations of the in-house baker are menu favorites. Casual dress. **Bar:** Full bar. **Reservations:** suggested. **Hours:** 11 am-2 & 6-9 pm, Sun 10:30 am-2:30 & 6-9 pm, Tues from 6 pm; Sunday brunch. Closed major holidays; also Mon. **Address:** 27462 Big Valley Rd **Location:** SR 3, 5 mi n, s of Hood Canal Bridge to Big Valley Rd, then 0.3 mi e. **Parking:** on-site. **Cards:** MC, VI.

PUYALLUP pop. 33,011   (See map and index starting on p. 626)

——— WHERE TO STAY ———

BEST WESTERN PARK PLAZA   *Book great rates at AAA.com*   Phone: (253)848-1500   37

(AAA) (SAVE)
▼▼▼▼
Hotel
$159-$169 All Year

Address: 620 S Hill Park Dr **Location:** SR 512, exit S Hill Park Dr southbound, just w; exit 9th St SW northbound, just w. **Facility:** 100 units. 94 one-bedroom standard units. 6 one-bedroom suites with whirlpools. 3 stories, interior corridors. *Bath:* combo or shower only. **Parking:** on-site. **Terms:** 2-4 night minimum stay - weekends, 7 day cancellation notice. **Amenities:** high-speed Internet, dual phone lines, voice mail, irons, hair dryers. *Some:* DVD players (fee). **Pool(s):** heated outdoor. **Leisure Activities:** whirlpool. **Guest Services:** valet and coin laundry, wireless Internet. **Business Services:** meeting rooms, business center. **Cards:** AX, CB, DC, DS, JC, MC, VI. **Free Special Amenities: expanded continental breakfast and high-speed Internet.**

Best Western
AAA Benefit:
Members save up to 20%, plus 10% bonus points with rewards program.

[icons] CALL ▥ ⊠ ... / SOME UNITS FEE ⊠ FEE VCR ⊡ ⊞

CROSSLAND ECONOMY SUITES-TACOMA-PUYALLUP   *Book at AAA.com*   Phone: (253)445-5945   36

▼
Motel
$74-$89 All Year

Address: 2101 N Meridian **Location:** SR 512, exit Milton/Tacoma, just w on SR 167, then just n. **Facility:** 133 one-bedroom standard units with efficiencies. 3 stories, exterior corridors. *Bath:* combo or shower only. **Parking:** on-site. **Terms:** office hours 7 am-11 pm, cancellation fee imposed. **Amenities:** high-speed Internet (fee), voice mail, irons. **Guest Services:** coin laundry, wireless Internet. **Cards:** AX, CB, DC, DS, JC, MC, VI.

(ASK) CALL ▥ ⊠ ... ⊡ ⊞ ⊡ / SOME UNITS FEE ⊠

HOLIDAY INN EXPRESS HOTEL & SUITES PUYALLUP   *Book at AAA.com*   Phone: (253)848-4900   38

▼▼▼
Hotel
$189-$239 All Year

Address: 812 S Hill Park Dr **Location:** SR 512, exit S Hill Park Dr southbound, just w; exit 9th St SW northbound, just w. **Facility:** Smoke free premises. 96 units. 93 one-bedroom standard units. 3 one-bedroom suites. 4 stories, interior' corridors. *Bath:* combo or shower only. **Parking:** on-site. **Amenities:** video library, DVD players, CD players, high-speed Internet, dual phone lines, voice mail, irons, hair dryers. **Pool(s):** heated indoor. **Leisure Activities:** whirlpool. **Guest Services:** valet and coin laundry, wireless Internet. **Business Services:** meeting rooms, business center. **Cards:** AX, CB, DC, DS, JC, MC, VI.

(ASK) [icons] / SOME UNITS FEE ⊠

——— WHERE TO DINE ———

POWERHOUSE RESTAURANT & BREWERY   Phone: 253/845-1370   27

▼▼▼
American
$7-$13

Serving pasta, pizza, burgers and craft beer, the restaurant is in a building that once provided power to the old Puget Sound Electric Railway. As freight trains rumble past the building during meals, guests can see electric currents rising in a glass tube mounted to a brick wall. Casual dress. **Bar:** Full bar. **Reservations:** not accepted. **Hours:** 11 am-10 pm, Fri & Sat-11 pm. Closed: 11/26, 12/25. **Address:** 454 E Main Ave **Location:** SR 512, exit Pioneer Ave, just w, just n on 5th St SE, then just nw. **Parking:** on-site. **Cards:** MC, VI.

RAM RESTAURANT AND BREWERY   Phone: 253/841-3317

▼▼ ▼▼
American
$8-$22

The enormous restaurant features high ceilings, huge television screens, large sports-themed banners and a brew pub area. The menu is equally enormous, with steaks, poultry, pasta, seafood, salads, sandwiches and pizza. The on-site brewery turns out a large selection of microbrews. Casual dress. **Bar:** Full bar. **Reservations:** not accepted. **Hours:** 11 am-close. Closed: 12/25. **Address:** 103 35th Ave SE **Location:** SR 512, exit S Hill Park Dr, just e on S Meridian, then just n. **Parking:** on-site. **Cards:** AX, MC, VI.

ROUND TABLE PIZZA   Phone: 253/840-5500

▼▼
Pizza
$4-$8

This casual, family-oriented pizza place features high-quality ingredients and dough rolled fresh daily. Distinctive specialty pizzas are piled high with toppings. Casual dress. **Bar:** Beer & wine. **Reservations:** not accepted. **Hours:** 11 am-10 pm, Fri & Sat-11 pm. Closed major holidays. **Address:** 16016 Meridian E **Location:** Jct Meridian E and 160th St E. **Parking:** on-site.

REDMOND pop. 45,256   (See map and index starting on p. 614)

——— WHERE TO STAY ———

REDMOND INN   *Book great rates at AAA.com*   Phone: (425)883-4900   49

(AAA) (SAVE)
▼▼▼
Hotel
$109-$199 All Year

Address: 17601 Redmond Way **Location:** I-405, exit 14 (SR 520), 5.5 mi e to Redmond Way, then just s. **Facility:** Smoke free premises. 137 units. 136 one-bedroom standard units, some with whirlpools. 1 one-bedroom suite. 3 stories, interior corridors. **Parking:** on-site. **Terms:** cancellation fee imposed. **Amenities:** high-speed Internet, voice mail, irons, hair dryers. *Some:* DVD players. **Pool(s):** heated outdoor. **Leisure Activities:** whirlpool, exercise room. **Guest Services:** valet and coin laundry, area transportation-within 5 mi, wireless Internet. **Business Services:** meeting rooms, PC. **Cards:** AX, DC, DS, MC, VI. **Free Special Amenities: continental breakfast and high-speed Internet.**

[icons] ⊠ ... ⊡ / SOME UNITS VCR ⊡ ⊞

(See map and index starting on p. 614)

REDMOND MARRIOTT TOWN CENTER    *Book great rates at AAA.com*   Phone: (425)498-4000   **48**

Hotel
$249-$259 All Year

Address: 7401 164th Ave NE **Location:** I-405, exit 14 (SR 520), 4.5 mi e to W Lake Sammamish Pkwy, just n to Leary Way, just e to Bear Creek Pkwy, just s to NE 74th Ave, then just w. **Facility:** Smoke free premises. 262 units. 259 one-bedroom standard units. 3 one-bedroom suites. 7 stories, interior corridors. *Bath:* combo or shower only. **Parking:** on-site (fee) and valet. **Terms:** cancellation fee imposed. **Amenities:** CD players, high-speed Internet (fee), voice mail, irons, hair dryers. **Pool(s):** heated outdoor. **Leisure Activities:** whirlpool, exercise room. **Guest Services:** valet and coin laundry, wireless Internet. **Business Services:** conference facilities, business center. **Cards:** AX, CB, DC, DS, JC, MC, VI.

AAA Benefit:
Members save a minimum 5% off the best available rate.

RESIDENCE INN BY MARRIOTT REDMOND TOWN CENTER   *Book great rates at AAA.com*   Phone: (425)497-9226   **47**

Hotel
$259-$269 All Year

Address: 7575 164th Ave NE **Location:** I-405, exit 14 (SR 520), 4.5 mi e to W Lake Sammamish Pkwy, just n to Leary Way, just e to Bear Creek Pkwy, just s to NE 74th Ave, just w to 164th Ave NE, then just n; center. **Facility:** Smoke free premises. 180 units. 159 one-bedroom standard units, some with efficiencies or kitchens. 21 two-bedroom suites with kitchens. 6 stories, interior corridors. *Bath:* combo or shower only. **Parking:** on-site. **Terms:** check-in 4 pm, cancellation fee imposed. **Amenities:** high-speed Internet, voice mail, irons, hair dryers. *Some:* DVD players. **Pool(s):** heated outdoor. **Leisure Activities:** whirlpool, exercise room. **Guest Services:** valet and coin laundry, wireless Internet. **Business Services:** meeting rooms, PC. **Cards:** AX, CB, DC, DS, JC, MC, VI.

AAA Benefit:
Members save a minimum 5% off the best available rate.

SILVER CLOUD INN REDMOND   *Book at AAA.com*   Phone: (425)746-8200   **50**

Hotel
$179-$239 All Year

Address: 2122 152nd Ave NE **Location:** I-405, exit 14 (SR 520), 3.3 mi e, exit 148th Ave NE, just e on 24th St, then just s. **Facility:** 144 units. 127 one-bedroom standard units, some with whirlpools. 17 one-bedroom suites, some with whirlpools. 4 stories, interior corridors. *Bath:* combo or shower only. **Parking:** on-site. **Amenities:** high-speed Internet, dual phone lines, voice mail, irons, hair dryers. **Pool(s):** heated indoor. **Leisure Activities:** whirlpool, exercise room. **Guest Services:** complimentary and valet laundry, wireless Internet. **Business Services:** meeting rooms, business center. **Cards:** AX, DC, DS, JC, MC, VI.

(See map and index starting on p. 614)

———— WHERE TO DINE ————

CANYONS RESTAURANT

WWW WWW
American
$8-$19

Phone: 425/556-1390

Diners can experience a small taste of the Southwest in the colorful, festive restaurant. Hand paintings that resemble lithographs of buffalo decorate the stucco-finished walls and tell a story of early man. Casual dress. **Bar:** Full bar. **Reservations:** accepted. **Hours:** 11 am-10 pm, Fri & Sat-11 pm, Sun 9 am-9 pm. Closed: 11/26, 12/25. **Address:** 15740 Redmond Way **Location:** I-405, exit 14 (SR 520), 5.5 mi e to Redmond Way, then 1.1 mi n. **Parking:** on-site. **Cards:** AX, DC, MC, VI.

CALL &M

CELTIC BAYOU-IRISH PUB & CAJUN CAFE

WWW WWW
Cajun
$6-$15

Phone: 425/869-5933   78

Diners can come in for a little touch of the bayou, in choices such as gumbo, etouffee or jambalaya, or maybe black pool Irish stew, which pairs nicely with the many Irish craft beers made in house. Casual dress. **Bar:** Full bar. **Reservations:** not accepted. **Hours:** 11 am-11 pm, Thurs-midnight, Fri & Sat-1 am, Sun-10 pm. Closed: 1/1, 11/26, 12/25. **Address:** 7281 W Lake Sammamish Pkwy NE **Location:** I-405, exit 14 (SR 520), 4.5 mi e to W Lake Sammamish Pkwy NE, then just n. **Parking:** on-site. **Cards:** AX, MC, VI.

CLAIM JUMPER

WWW WWW
American
$10-$24

Phone: 425/885-1273

Great menu variety makes this place a good stop for parties with diverse tastes. Choices include specialty appetizers, salads, rotisserie chicken and barbecue items, not to mention good comfort foods, such as traditional pot pie. Hearty portions satisfy big appetites. The atmosphere is fun and lively. Casual dress. **Bar:** Full bar. **Reservations:** accepted. **Hours:** 11 am-10 pm, Fri & Sat-11 pm. Closed: 7/4, 11/26, 12/25. **Address:** 7210 164th Ave NE **Location:** SR 520, exit Redmond Way W, then s. **Parking:** on-site. **Cards:** AX, CB, DC, DS, JC, MC, VI.

CALL &M

EL TOREADOR

WWW WWW
Mexican
$5-$12

Phone: 425/883-7570   75

Old Mexican movie posters, pinatas, porcelain bulls and sombreros contribute to the fun, colorful decor. The menu comprises traditional fare, as well as new takes on some old favorites. Casual dress. **Bar:** Full bar. **Reservations:** accepted. **Hours:** 11 am-9:30 pm, Fri & Sat-10:30 pm. Closed major holidays. **Address:** 7845 Leary Way NE **Location:** I-405, exit 14 (SR 520), 5.5 mi e to Redmond Way, 0.8 mi n, then just w. **Parking:** on-site. **Cards:** AX, CB, DC, DS, MC, VI.

NARA JAPANESE RESTAURANT

WWW WWW
Japanese
$8-$19

Phone: 425/885-0703   76

Comfortable, friendly Japanese dining features a sushi counter, several types of sake and Japanese beer. A recommended meal includes ground beef wrapped in a skin of rice noodle and served with a side of plum sauce, crab legs, and traditional green tea. Casual dress. **Bar:** Beer & wine. **Reservations:** accepted. **Hours:** 11:30 am-9:30 pm, Sat from 4:30 pm. Closed major holidays; also Sun. **Address:** 16564 Cleveland St, Suite M **Location:** Downtown. **Parking:** on-site. **Cards:** MC, VI.

ROUND TABLE PIZZA

WWW
American
$4-$25

Phone: 425/644-7117

This casual, family-oriented pizza place features high-quality ingredients and dough rolled fresh daily. Distinctive specialty pizzas are piled high with toppings. Casual dress. **Bar:** Beer & wine. **Reservations:** not accepted. **Hours:** 11 am-9:30 pm, Fri & Sat-10 pm, Sun noon-9 pm. Closed major holidays. **Address:** 148th NE 24th St **Location:** Just e of jct NE 24th St and 148th Ave NE. **Parking:** on-site. **Cards:** AX, DS, MC, VI.

SPAZZO ITALIAN GRILL & WINE BAR

WWWW
Italian
$12-$30

Phone: 425/881-4400   77

For good Italian food with great wine, it's hard to beat this comfortable spot. A broad selection of traditional Italian dishes pairs with an extensive wine list that includes both bottles and by-the-glass choices. As much a hot spot for a night on the town as it is for a romantic dinner, the restaurant also exudes charm on its seasonal patio. Casual dress. **Bar:** Full bar. **Reservations:** accepted. **Hours:** 11 am-9 pm, Fri & Sat-10 pm. Closed: 11/26, 12/25. **Address:** 16499 NE 74th St, Suite E255 **Location:** I-405, exit 14 (SR 520), 5 mi e to W Lake Sammamish Pkwy, just n to Leary Way, just e to Bear Creek Pkwy, then just s to NE 74th Ave. **Parking:** on-site. **Cards:** AX, MC, VI.

TROPEA

WWW WWW
Southern Italian
$11-$20

Phone: 425/867-1082   74

Among freshly made entrees are preparations of seafood, veal, chicken and pasta. Murals decorate many walls, and a wine display lines another. A favorite lunch spot with the locals, the casual restaurant is often busy. Casual dress. **Bar:** Beer & wine. **Reservations:** not accepted. **Hours:** 11 am-2 & 4:30-9:30 pm, Fri-10 pm, Sat 4:30 pm-10 pm, Sun 4:30 pm-9:30 pm. Closed major holidays. **Address:** 8042 161st Ave NE **Location:** Just n of SR 202 (Redmond Way). **Parking:** on-site. **Cards:** AX, DS, MC, VI.

TYPHOON!

WWW WWW
Thai
$8-$19

Phone: 425/558-7666

The artful, contemporary Thai restaurant features classic entrees and new twists on old favorites. The extensive beverage menu lists an impressive tea selection from China, Japan and Thailand, as well as Thai beers and microbrews. Casual dress. **Bar:** Full bar. **Reservations:** suggested. **Hours:** 11 am-2 & 5-10 pm. **Address:** 8936 161st Ave NE, Bella Bottega Center **Location:** I-405, exit 14 (SR 520), 5.5 mi e to Redmond Way, 0.9 mi n, then 0.4 mi e. **Parking:** on-site. **Cards:** AX, DS, MC, VI.

RENTON pop. 50,052   (See map and index starting on p. 614)

———— WHERE TO STAY ————

CLARION HOTEL

AAA SAVE

WWW WWW
Hotel
Rates not provided

Book great rates at AAA.com

Phone: 425/251-9591   87

Address: 3700 E Valley Rd **Location:** SR 167, exit E Valley Rd, just nw. Located in commercial area. **Facility:** Smoke free premises. 111 one-bedroom standard units. 4 stories, interior corridors. *Bath:* combo or shower only. **Parking:** on-site. **Amenities:** DVD players, voice mail, irons, hair dryers. **Leisure Activities:** exercise room. **Guest Services:** coin laundry, airport transportation-Seattle-Tacoma International Airport, area transportation-within 3 mi, wireless Internet. **Business Services:** PC. **Free Special Amenities:** full breakfast and high-speed Internet.

(See map and index starting on p. 614)

EXTENDED STAY DELUXE-SEATTLE   *Book at AAA.com*   Phone: (425)228-2454   [82]

Hotel
$121-$136 All Year

Address: 1150 Oakesdale Ave SW **Location:** I-405, exit 1 southbound, just s; exit Renton northbound, just n on Interurban Ave, 0.6 mi e on SW Grady Way, then just n. **Facility:** 110 units. 109 one-bedroom standard units with kitchens. 1 one-bedroom suite with kitchen. 3 stories, interior corridors. *Bath:* combo or shower only. **Parking:** on-site. **Terms:** cancellation fee imposed. **Amenities:** DVD players, high-speed Internet (fee), voice mail, irons, hair dryers. **Pool(s):** heated outdoor. **Leisure Activities:** exercise room. **Guest Services:** coin laundry, wireless Internet. **Cards:** AX, CB, DC, DS, JC, MC, VI.

(ASK) (icons) / SOME UNITS FEE (icons)

GUEST HOUSE INN & SUITES   *Book great rates at AAA.com*   Phone: (425)228-2858   [78]

(AAA) (SAVE)

Motel
$100-$110 10/1-2/28
$90-$100 3/1-9/30

Address: 4710 Lake Washington Blvd NE **Location:** I-405, exit 7, just ne. Located in a commercial area. **Facility:** Smoke free premises. 116 units. 115 one-bedroom standard units. 1 one-bedroom suite. 2-3 stories (no elevator), exterior corridors. **Parking:** on-site. **Terms:** cancellation fee imposed. **Amenities:** high-speed Internet. **Pool(s):** heated outdoor. **Guest Services:** coin laundry, wireless Internet. **Business Services:** PC. **Cards:** AX, DS, MC, VI. **Free Special Amenities:** continental breakfast and local telephone calls.

(icons) FEE (icons) / SOME UNITS FEE (icons)

HILTON GARDEN INN SEATTLE/RENTON   *Book great rates at AAA.com*   Phone: (425)430-1414   [84]

Hotel
$89-$209 All Year

Address: 1801 E Valley Rd **Location:** SR 167, exit E Valley Rd, 1 mi nw. **Facility:** 150 one-bedroom standard units. 4 stories, interior corridors. *Bath:* combo or shower only. **Parking:** on-site. **Terms:** 1-30 night minimum stay, cancellation fee imposed. **Amenities:** high-speed Internet, dual phone lines, voice mail, irons, hair dryers. **Pool(s):** heated indoor. **Leisure Activities:** whirlpool, exercise room. **Guest Services:** valet and coin laundry, area transportation, wireless Internet. **Business Services:** meeting rooms, business center. **Cards:** AX, CB, DC, DS, JC, MC, VI.

Hilton Garden Inn

AAA Benefit:
Members save 5% or more everyday!

(icons) / SOME UNITS (icon)

HOLIDAY INN SEATTLE-RENTON   *Book great rates at AAA.com*   Phone: (425)226-7700   [81]

(AAA) (SAVE)

Hotel
$79-$169 All Year

Address: One S Grady Way **Location:** I-405, exit 2 (SR 167/Rainier Ave), jct SR 167 N. Located in a commercial area. **Facility:** 226 units. 221 one-bedroom standard units. 5 one-bedroom suites. 3-6 stories, interior corridors. *Bath:* combo or shower only. **Parking:** on-site. **Amenities:** video games (fee), high-speed Internet, voice mail, irons, hair dryers. **Pool(s):** heated outdoor. **Leisure Activities:** whirlpool, exercise room. **Guest Services:** valet and coin laundry, area transportation-within 5 mi, wireless Internet. **Business Services:** meeting rooms, PC, fax. **Cards:** AX, CB, DC, DS, JC, MC, VI. **Free Special Amenities:** local telephone calls and high-speed Internet.

(icons) / SOME UNITS FEE (icons) FEE (icons) FEE (icon)

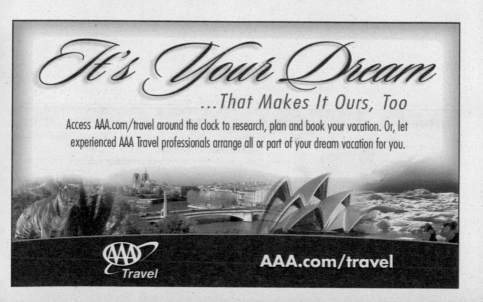

(See map and index starting on p. 614)

LARKSPUR LANDING RENTON/SEATTLE   *Book great rates at AAA.com*   Phone: (425)235-1212   [83]

AAA **SAVE**
▼▼▼▼
Hotel
$149-$179 All Year

Address: 1701 E Valley Rd **Location:** SR 167, exit E Valley Rd, 1 mi nw. **Facility:** 127 units. 74 one-bedroom standard units with efficiencies. 53 one-bedroom suites with efficiencies. 4 stories, interior corridors. *Bath:* combo or shower only. **Parking:** on-site. **Terms:** cancellation fee imposed. **Amenities:** video library, DVD players, video games (fee), CD players, high-speed Internet, dual phone lines, voice mail, irons, hair dryers. **Leisure Activities:** whirlpool, exercise room. **Guest Services:** complimentary and valet laundry, area transportation-within 5 mi, wireless Internet. **Business Services:** meeting rooms, business center. **Cards:** AX, CB, DC, DS, JC, MC, VI. **Free Special Amenities:** expanded continental breakfast and high-speed Internet. *(See color ad below)*

QUALITY INN RENTON   *Book at AAA.com*   Phone: (425)226-7600   [80]

▼▼▼▼
Hotel
$99-$119 All Year

Address: 1850 Maple Valley Hwy **Location:** I-405, exit 4 (Bronson Way) northbound, follow Maple Valley Hwy; exit southbound, 0.6 mi s to 2nd light, then just e. Located in a commercial area. **Facility:** 105 units. 104 one-bedroom standard units, some with whirlpools. 1 one-bedroom suite with kitchen (no utensils). 4 stories, interior corridors. **Parking:** on-site. **Terms:** cancellation fee imposed. **Amenities:** voice mail, irons, hair dryers. *Some:* high-speed Internet. **Leisure Activities:** exercise room. **Guest Services:** valet and coin laundry, wireless Internet. **Business Services:** meeting rooms, PC. **Cards:** AX, DS, MC, VI.

RENTON INN   Phone: 425/687-9846   [79]

▼▼
Hotel
Rates not provided

Address: 219 Sunset Blvd N **Location:** I-405, exit 4 (Bronson Way) northbound, just nw; exit southbound, 0.5 mi sw. **Facility:** 33 units. 31 one- and 2 two-bedroom standard units. 3 stories, interior corridors. **Parking:** on-site. **Terms:** office hours 8 am-midnight. **Amenities:** irons, hair dryers. *Some:* high-speed Internet. **Guest Services:** coin laundry.

SPRINGHILL SUITES BY MARRIOTT   *Book great rates at AAA.com*   Phone: (425)226-4100   [86]

▼▼▼
Hotel
$169-$189 All Year

Address: 200 SW 19th St **Location:** SR 167, exit E Valley Rd, 1 mi nw, then just w. **Facility:** Smoke free premises. 114 one-bedroom standard units, some with whirlpools. 4 stories, interior corridors. *Bath:* combo or shower only. **Parking:** on-site. **Terms:** cancellation fee imposed. **Amenities:** high-speed Internet, dual phone lines, voice mail, irons, hair dryers. **Pool(s):** heated indoor. **Leisure Activities:** whirlpool, exercise room. **Guest Services:** valet and coin laundry, area transportation, wireless Internet. **Business Services:** meeting rooms, PC. **Cards:** AX, CB, DC, DS, JC, MC, VI.

AAA Benefit:
Members save a minimum 5% off the best available rate.

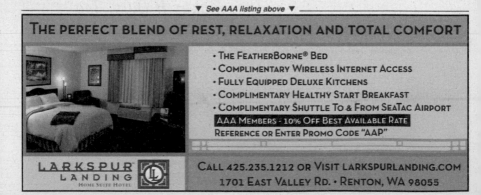

(See map and index starting on p. 614)

TOWNEPLACE SUITES SEATTLE SOUTH/RENTON   *Book great rates at AAA.com*   Phone: (425)917-2000

▼▼▼
Extended Stay
Hotel
$169-$179 All Year

Address: 300 SW 19th St **Location:** SR 167, exit E Valley Rd, 1 mi nw, then just w. **Facility:** The extended-stay property is close to freeways. Smoke free premises. 137 units. 99 one-bedroom standard units with kitchens. 6 one- and 32 two-bedroom suites with kitchens. 4 stories, interior corridors. *Bath:* combo or shower only. **Parking:** on-site. **Terms:** cancellation fee imposed. **Amenities:** high-speed Internet, voice mail, irons, hair dryers. **Pool(s):** heated outdoor. **Leisure Activities:** exercise room. **Guest Services:** valet and coin laundry, area transportation, wireless Internet. **Business Services:** PC. **Cards:** AX, CB, DC, DS, JC, MC, VI.

AAA Benefit:
Members save a
minimum 5% off the
best available rate.

🔁 CALL Ⓜ 🏊 ✕ 🐾 🖥 🖨 💻 / SOME UNITS FEE 🐕

─── WHERE TO DINE ───

ARMONDO'S CAFE ITALIANO   Phone: 425/228-0759   (102)

▼▼▼ ▼▼▼
Italian
$6-$16

In the city's heart, where shopping is fun and foot traffic common, the restaurant dishes up a variety of dishes—from traditional pizza and pasta to veal parmigiana. Casual dress. **Bar:** Full bar. **Reservations:** not accepted. **Hours:** 11 am-9 pm, Fri-10 pm, Sat 4 pm-10 pm, Sun 4 pm-9 pm. Closed major holidays. **Address:** 310 Wells Ave S **Location:** I-405, exit 2 (SR 167/Rainier Ave); corner of Wells Ave and Houser Way; downtown. **Parking:** street. **Cards:** AX, MC, VI.

BILLY MCHALE'S   Phone: 425/271-7427   (107)

▼▼▼ ▼▼▼
American
$7-$22

The family-oriented restaurant, which serves chicken, steak and fresh seafood, is known for its succulent ribs and tasty onion loaf. Drinks include 31 varieties of margaritas. The bustling dining room teems with upbeat colors, signs and memorabilia. Casual dress. **Bar:** Full bar. **Reservations:** accepted. **Hours:** 11 am-10 pm, Fri & Sat-11 pm. Closed: 12/25. **Address:** 241 SW 7th **Location:** I-405, exit 2 (SR 167/Rainier Ave), 0.5 mi n, then just w. **Parking:** on-site. **Cards:** AX, MC, VI.

FIN N BONE   Phone: 425/271-6644   (103)

▼▼▼▼
Steak
$9-$34

Convenient to the antique shops in the heart of town, the stylish restaurant presents a great wine menu of choices that pair with strong selections of seafood, steak and chops. Live jazz music enhances the atmosphere every Thursday evening. Casual dress. **Bar:** Full bar. **Reservations:** accepted. **Hours:** 11 am-3 & 4:30-9:30 pm, Fri-10:30 pm, Sat 4:30 pm-10:30 pm, Sun 4:30 pm-9:30 pm. Closed major holidays. **Address:** 317 Main Ave S **Location:** I-405, exit 2 (SR 167/Rainier Ave), just n, then 1 mi ne via S Grady Way and Main Ave S. **Parking:** on-site. **Cards:** AX, DC, DS, MC, VI.

MELROSE GRILL   Phone: 425/254-0759   (104)

▼▼▼ ▼▼
Steak
$17-$37

Operating as a tavern since the days of horse and buggy, the establishment has been given a fresh look. However, the original back bar, with its rich dark wood, is still the focus as diners enter. Locals keep coming back for dishes such as porterhouse steak, herb-rubbed free-range chicken and pan-seared Northwest salmon. Casual dress. **Bar:** Full bar. **Hours:** 5 pm-close. **Address:** 819 Houser Way S **Location:** I-405, exit 2 (SR 167/Rainier Ave), just n, 1 mi ne via S Grady Way and Main Ave S, then just w. **Parking:** street. **Cards:** AX, MC, VI.

PLUM DELICIOUS   Phone: 425/255-8510   (100)

▼▼▼ ▼▼▼
American
$6-$19

At this nice family-oriented diner, the staff knows the regulars by name and good old-fashioned home-style cooking is simply presented and a good value. Casual dress. **Bar:** Full bar. **Reservations:** accepted. **Hours:** 6 am-9 pm, Sat 7 am-10 pm, Sun 7 am-9 pm. Closed: 12/25. **Address:** 3212 NE Sunset Blvd **Location:** I-405, exit 5, 1.3 mi e. **Parking:** on-site. **Cards:** AX, MC, VI.

RIVER ROCK GRILL & ALE HOUSE   Phone: 425/430-0311   (108)

▼▼▼ ▼▼
American
$9-$21

The clubby restaurant affords great views of the adjoining golf course. Among lunch offerings are sandwiches and salads, while the dinner menu lists such selections as salmon Caesar salad, the River Rock Reuben, chicken linguine, baby back ribs, saffron sea scallops and Northwest pot pie. Casual dress. **Bar:** Full bar. **Hours:** 6:30 am-10 pm, Fri & Sat-11 pm; hours vary in winter. Closed: 12/25. **Address:** 4050 Maple Valley Hwy **Location:** I-405, exit 4 (Bronson Way) northbound, follow Maple Valley Hwy, 1.8 mi e; exit southbound to 2nd light, then 1.8 mi e. **Parking:** on-site. **Cards:** AX, CB, DC, DS, MC, VI.

ROUND TABLE PIZZA   Phone: 425/277-2100

▼▼▼
Pizza
$9-$15

This casual, family-oriented pizza place features high-quality ingredients and dough rolled fresh daily. Distinctive specialty pizzas are piled high with toppings. Casual dress. **Bar:** Beer & wine. **Reservations:** not accepted. **Hours:** 11 am-10 pm. Closed major holidays. **Address:** 14020 SE Petrovitsky Rd **Location:** Jct SE Petrovitsky Rd and 140th Ave SE. **Parking:** on-site. **Cards:** AX, MC, VI.

ROUND TABLE PIZZA   Phone: 425/251-0606

▼▼▼
Pizza
$10-$16

This casual, family-oriented pizza place features high-quality ingredients and dough rolled fresh daily. Distinctive specialty pizzas are piled high with toppings. Casual dress. **Bar:** Beer & wine. **Hours:** 11 am-10 pm, Sun from noon. Closed: 4/12, 11/26, 12/25. **Address:** 302 SW 43rd St **Location:** Just w of SR 167; at jct SW 43rd St and E Valley Hwy. **Parking:** on-site. **Cards:** AX, DS, MC, VI.

TORERO'S   Phone: 425/228-6180   (106)

▼▼▼ ▼▼
Mexican
$5-$15

Portion sizes are ample and the taste is great in such standard fare as tacos, enchiladas, fajitas and burritos. The familiar neighborhood restaurant is decorated in rich shades of green. Casual dress. **Bar:** Full bar. **Reservations:** accepted. **Hours:** 11 am-10:30 pm, Fri & Sat-11:30 pm. Closed major holidays. **Address:** 431-B Rainier Ave S **Location:** I-405, exit 2 (SR 167/Rainier Ave), 0.7 mi n. **Parking:** on-site. **Cards:** AX, CB, DC, DS, MC, VI.

(See map and index starting on p. 614)

VINO RISTORANTE ITALIANO

Italian
$6-$20

Phone: 425/271-7042   101

Ravioli rolled from scratch, lasagna, fresh baked bread and homemade apple pie make mouths water at the established restaurant. Colorful flowering vines wrap around the deck of the restored house, giving the place the feel of a European cafe. Casual dress. **Bar:** Full bar. **Reservations:** accepted. **Hours:** 11 am-2 & 5-10 pm, Sat & Sun from 5 pm. Closed: 4/12, 11/26, 12/25. **Address:** 212 S 3rd St **Location:** I-405, exit 2 (SR 167/Rainier Ave), 1 mi n, then just e. **Parking:** on-site. **Cards:** AX, MC, VI.

WHISTLE STOP ALE HOUSE

American
$7-$16

Phone: 425/277-3039   105

For more than a century, the popular gathering spot has served satisfied customers. Friends and families meet here for its high-energy atmosphere and friendly staff. The menu features traditional American cuisine and varied global dishes, which can be paired with choices from a wide selection of Northwest microbrews on tap. Casual dress. **Bar:** Full bar. **Reservations:** accepted. **Hours:** 11 am-10 pm, Fri–midnight, Sat 9 am-midnight, Sun 9 am-3 pm. Closed: major holidays; also 12/24. **Address:** 809 S 4th St **Location:** I-405, exit 2 (SR 167/Rainier Ave), just n, 1 mi ne via Grady Way and Main Ave S, then just e. **Parking:** on-site. **Cards:** AX, MC, VI.

SAMMAMISH pop. 34,104   (See map and index starting on p. 614)

──── **WHERE TO DINE** ────

DC'S GRILL

Steak & Seafood
$9-$42

Phone: 425/898-1231   91

Steaks are the specialty here. Diners also can choose from plenty of other dishes like chicken, pork, pasta and fish. Wines by the glass are plentiful, and the staff is happy to make suggestions. Casual dress. **Bar:** Full bar. **Reservations:** accepted. **Hours:** 4 pm-10 pm, Fri & Sat-11 pm. Closed: 11/26, 12/25. **Address:** 22850 NE 8th St **Location:** Jct 228th Ave NE and NE 8th St. **Parking:** on-site. **Cards:** AX, DS, MC, VI.

CALL 🔲M

SEATAC pop. 25,496   (See map and index starting on p. 614)

──── **WHERE TO STAY** ────

BEST WESTERN AIRPORT EXECUTEL   *Book great rates at AAA.com*

Hotel
$89-$139 3/1-9/30
$79-$119 10/1-2/28

Phone: (206)878-3300   122

Address: 20717 International Blvd **Location:** On SR 99. **Facility:** Smoke free premises. 140 one-bedroom standard units, some with whirlpools. 3 stories, interior corridors. **Parking:** on-site. **Amenities:** high-speed Internet, irons, hair dryers. **Pool(s):** heated indoor. **Leisure Activities:** sauna, whirlpool, exercise room. **Guest Services:** area transportation-within 5 mi, wireless Internet. **Business Services:** meeting rooms, PC. **Cards:** AX, DC, DS, JC, MC, VI. **Free Special Amenities:** expanded continental breakfast.

AAA Benefit:
Members save up to 20%, plus 10% bonus points with rewards program.

CLARION HOTEL   *Book at AAA.com*

Hotel
$109-$119 6/1-2/28
$99-$109 3/1-5/31

Phone: (206)242-0200   106

Address: 3000 S 176th St **Location:** Just e of SR 99. **Facility:** Smoke free premises. 214 one-bedroom standard units, some with whirlpools. 3 stories, interior corridors. **Parking:** on-site. **Amenities:** voice mail, safes (fee), irons, hair dryers. *Some:* high-speed Internet. **Pool(s):** heated indoor. **Leisure Activities:** whirlpool, exercise room. **Guest Services:** valet and coin laundry, area transportation, wireless Internet. **Business Services:** meeting rooms, business center. **Cards:** AX, CB, DC, DS, JC, MC, VI.

THE COAST GATEWAY HOTEL   *Book great rates at AAA.com*

Hotel
$140-$158 All Year

Phone: (206)248-8200   111

Address: 18415 International Blvd **Location:** On SR 99. **Facility:** 143 units. 142 one-bedroom standard units. 1 one-bedroom suite. 6 stories, interior corridors. **Parking:** on-site. **Amenities:** video games (fee), voice mail, irons, hair dryers. **Leisure Activities:** exercise room. **Guest Services:** complimentary and valet laundry, airport transportation-Seattle-Tacoma International Airport, area transportation-within 2 mi, wireless Internet. **Business Services:** meeting rooms, PC. **Cards:** AX, DC, DS, MC, VI. **Free Special Amenities:** continental breakfast and newspaper.

COMFORT INN & SUITES-SEA TAC AIRPORT   *Book great rates at AAA.com*

Hotel
$99-$275 All Year

Phone: (206)878-1100   116

Address: 19333 International Blvd **Location:** On SR 99. **Facility:** 176 units. 153 one-bedroom standard units, some with whirlpools. 23 one-bedroom suites, some with whirlpools. 4 stories, interior corridors. *Bath:* combo or shower only. **Parking:** on-site. **Amenities:** video games (fee), high-speed Internet, voice mail, irons, hair dryers. *Some:* dual phone lines. **Leisure Activities:** whirlpool, exercise room. **Guest Services:** valet and coin laundry, area transportation, wireless Internet. **Business Services:** meeting rooms, PC. **Cards:** AX, CB, DC, DS, JC, MC, VI. *(See color ad p 701)*

(See map and index starting on p. 614)

DAYS INN SEATAC

Book great rates at AAA.com   **Phone:** (206)244-3600 **114**

Address: 19015 International Blvd S **Location:** On SR 99. **Facility:** 86 units. 80 one-bedroom standard units, some with whirlpools. 6 one-bedroom suites, some with whirlpools. 4 stories, interior corridors. **Parking:** on-site. **Terms:** cancellation fee imposed. **Amenities:** high-speed Internet, hair dryers. **Leisure Activities:** exercise room. **Guest Services:** coin laundry, area transportation-within 2 mi, wireless Internet. **Business Services:** PC. **Cards:** AX, DC, DS, MC, VI. **Free Special Amenities: expanded continental breakfast and high-speed Internet.**

AAA SAVE
Hotel
$95-$115 5/31-2/28
$80-$95 3/1-5/30

DOUBLETREE HOTEL SEATTLE AIRPORT

Book great rates at AAA.com   **Phone:** (206)246-8600 **112**

Address: 18740 International Blvd **Location:** On SR 99. Located in a commercial area. **Facility:** 850 units. 838 one-bedroom standard units. 12 one-bedroom suites. 3-13 stories, interior corridors. *Bath:* combo or shower only. **Parking:** on-site (fee) and valet. **Terms:** 1-30 night minimum stay, cancellation fee imposed. **Amenities:** video games, high-speed Internet. *Some:* CD players. **Pool(s):** heated outdoor. **Leisure Activities:** whirlpool, exercise room. **Guest Services:** valet and coin laundry, area transportation, wireless Internet. **Business Services:** conference facilities, business center. **Cards:** AX, CB, DC, DS, MC, VI.

Hotel
$119-$289 All Year

DOUBLETREE
HOTELS·SUITES·RESORTS·CLUBS

AAA Benefit:
Members save 5% or
more everyday!

FAIRFIELD INN BY MARRIOTT SEATTLE-SEATAC/AIRPORT

Book great rates at AAA.com   **Phone:** (206)824-9909 **119**

Address: 19631 International Blvd **Location:** On SR 99. **Facility:** Smoke free premises. 146 one-bedroom standard units, some with whirlpools. 4 stories, interior corridors. *Bath:* combo or shower only. **Terms:** cancellation fee imposed. **Amenities:** high-speed Internet, voice mail, irons, hair dryers. **Pool(s):** heated indoor. **Leisure Activities:** whirlpool, exercise room. **Guest Services:** valet and coin laundry, area transportation, wireless Internet. **Business Services:** PC. **Cards:** AX, CB, DC, DS, MC, VI.

Hotel
$119-$149 All Year

FAIRFIELD INN Marriott

AAA Benefit:
Members save a
minimum 5% off the
best available rate.

HAMPTON INN SEATTLE AIRPORT

Book great rates at AAA.com   **Phone:** (206)878-1700 **117**

Address: 19445 International Blvd **Location:** On SR 99. **Facility:** 130 one-bedroom standard units. 4 stories, interior corridors. **Parking:** on-site. **Terms:** 1-30 night minimum stay, cancellation fee imposed. **Amenities:** high-speed Internet, voice mail, irons, hair dryers. **Pool(s):** heated outdoor. **Leisure Activities:** exercise room. **Guest Services:** valet laundry, area transportation-within 1 mi, wireless Internet. **Business Services:** meeting rooms, PC. **Cards:** AX, CB, DC, DS, MC, VI. **Free Special Amenities: continental breakfast and high-speed Internet.**

AAA SAVE
Hotel
$145-$165 All Year

Hampton Inn

AAA Benefit:
Members save up to
10% everyday!

▼ See AAA listing p 700 ▼

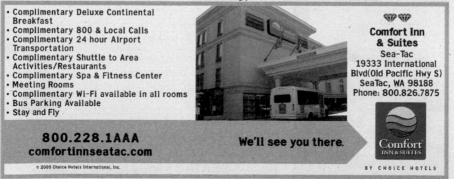

(See map and index starting on p. 614)

HILTON SEATTLE AIRPORT & CONFERENCE CENTER   *Book great rates at AAA.com*

Phone: (206)244-4800   **108**

▼▼▼
Hotel
$129-$299 All Year

Address: 17620 International Blvd **Location:** On SR 99. **Facility:** 396 one-bedroom standard units. 4 stories, interior corridors. *Bath:* combo or shower only. **Parking:** on-site (fee) and valet. **Terms:** 1-30 night minimum stay, cancellation fee imposed. **Amenities:** dual phone lines, voice mail, irons, hair dryers. *Fee:* video games, high-speed Internet. **Dining:** Spencer's for Steaks and Chops, see separate listing. **Pool(s):** heated outdoor. **Leisure Activities:** whirlpool, exercise room. **Guest Services:** valet and coin laundry, area transportation, wireless Internet. **Business Services:** conference facilities, business center. **Cards:** AX, DC, DS, JC, MC, VI.

🅷 **Hilton**
AAA Benefit:
Members save 5% or more everyday!

✈ 🍴 ▽ 🐾 ✕ 🎦 🖥 / SOME UNITS FEE 🛏

HOLIDAY INN EXPRESS HOTEL & SUITES-SEATTLE SEA-TAC AIRPORT   *Book at AAA.com*

Phone: 206/824-3200   **118**

▼▼▼
Hotel
Rates not provided

Address: 19621 International Blvd **Location:** On SR 99. **Facility:** 171 units. 118 one-bedroom standard units. 53 one-bedroom suites with efficiencies. 5 stories, interior corridors. *Bath:* combo or shower only. **Parking:** on-site. **Amenities:** video games (fee), high-speed Internet, dual phone lines, voice mail, irons, hair dryers. **Leisure Activities:** exercise room. **Guest Services:** valet and coin laundry, area transportation, wireless Internet. **Business Services:** meeting rooms, PC.

✈ 🎦 🖥 🖥 / SOME UNITS FEE 🛏 ✕

HOLIDAY INN SEATTLE SEATAC INTERNATIONAL AIRPORT   *Book great rates at AAA.com*

Phone: 206/248-1000   **105**

AAA SAVE
▼▼▼
Hotel
Rates not provided

Address: 17338 International Blvd **Location:** On SR 99. **Facility:** 260 one-bedroom standard units. 12 stories, interior corridors. *Bath:* combo or shower only. **Parking:** on-site (fee). **Amenities:** high-speed Internet, voice mail, irons, hair dryers. *Some:* safes. **Pool(s):** heated indoor. **Leisure Activities:** whirlpool, exercise room. **Guest Services:** valet and coin laundry, wireless Internet. **Business Services:** conference facilities, business center. *(See color ad below)*

✈ 🍴 ▽ CALL 🔊M 🐾 🎦 🖥 / SOME UNITS FEE 🛏 ✕ 🖥 🖥

LA QUINTA INN SEATTLE (SEA-TAC INTERNATIONAL)   *Book great rates at AAA.com*

Phone: (206)241-5211   **113**

▼▼▼
Hotel
$69-$169 All Year

Address: 2824 S 188th St **Location:** On SR 99. **Facility:** 143 units. 142 one-bedroom standard units. 1 one-bedroom suite. 6 stories, interior corridors. *Bath:* combo or shower only. **Parking:** on-site. **Amenities:** video games (fee), high-speed Internet, voice mail, irons, hair dryers. **Pool(s):** heated outdoor. **Leisure Activities:** whirlpool, exercise room. **Guest Services:** valet and coin laundry. **Business Services:** meeting rooms, PC. **Cards:** AX, CB, DS, MC, VI.

ASK ✈ 🍴 🐾 🎦 🖥 / SOME UNITS 🛏 ✕ 🖥 🖥

MOTEL 6 - 1332   *Book at AAA.com*

Phone: (206)246-4101   **104**

▼
Motel
$59-$69 All Year

Address: 16500 International Blvd **Location:** On SR 99. Located in a commercial area. **Facility:** 109 one-bedroom standard units. 2 stories (no elevator), exterior corridors. *Bath:* combo or shower only. **Parking:** on-site. **Cards:** AX, CB, DC, DS, MC, VI.

🎦 / SOME UNITS 🛏 ✕

MOTEL 6 - 736   *Book at AAA.com*

Phone: (206)824-9902   **121**

▼
Motel
$55-$65 All Year

Address: 20651 Military Rd **Location:** I-5, exit 151, just se. **Facility:** 124 one-bedroom standard units. 2 stories (no elevator), exterior corridors. *Bath:* combo or shower only. **Parking:** on-site. **Amenities:** high-speed Internet (fee). **Pool(s):** heated outdoor. **Leisure Activities:** whirlpool. **Guest Services:** coin laundry, wireless Internet. **Cards:** CB, DC, DS, MC, VI.

🐾 🎦 / SOME UNITS 🛏 ✕ FEE 🖥 FEE 🖥

(See map and index starting on p. 614)

RADISSON HOTEL GATEWAY SEATTLE-TACOMA
AIRPORT   *Book great rates at AAA.com*

Phone: (206)244-6666   [109]

Hotel
$98-$229 All Year

Address: 18118 International Blvd **Location:** On SR 99. **Facility:** 204 units. 180 one-bedroom standard units. 24 one-bedroom suites. 7 stories, interior corridors. *Bath:* combo or shower only. **Parking:** on-site. **Terms:** cancellation fee imposed. **Amenities:** video games (fee), high-speed Internet, dual phone lines, voice mail, irons, hair dryers. **Pool(s):** heated indoor. **Leisure Activities:** whirlpool, exercise room. **Guest Services:** valet and coin laundry, wireless Internet. **Business Services:** conference facilities, PC. **Cards:** AX, CB, DC, DS, JC, MC, VI. *(See color ad below)*

▼ See AAA listing above ▼

Radisson Hotel Gateway Seattle-Tacoma Airport

18118 International Blvd • Seattle, WA 98188
206-244-6666

- Located directly across from Seattle Tacoma Int'l Airport
- Free parking with each paid night
- Indoor pool and whirlpool
- AAA member discounts

Radisson

800-333-3333
radisson.com

▼ See AAA listing p 704 ▼

(See map and index starting on p. 614)

RED LION HOTEL SEATTLE AIRPORT   *Book great rates at AAA.com*   **Phone:** (206)246-5535   110

Hotel
$99-$279 All Year

Address: 18220 International Blvd **Location:** On SR 99. **Facility:** 144 one-bedroom standard units. 5 stories, interior corridors. **Parking:** on-site and valet. **Terms:** cancellation fee imposed. **Amenities:** video games (fee), high-speed Internet, voice mail, irons, hair dryers. **Pool(s):** heated outdoor. **Leisure Activities:** whirlpool, exercise room. **Guest Services:** valet laundry, wireless Internet. **Business Services:** meeting rooms, PC (fee). **Cards:** AX, DC, DS, MC, VI.
(See color ad p 703)

SEATTLE AIRPORT MARRIOTT   *Book great rates at AAA.com*   **Phone:** (206)241-2000   107

Hotel
$229-$249 All Year

Address: 3201 S 176th St **Location:** Just e of SR 99. Located in a commercial area. **Facility:** Smoke free premises. 459 units. 454 one-bedroom standard units. 5 one-bedroom suites. 5-9 stories, interior corridors. *Bath:* combo or shower only. **Parking:** on-site (fee) and valet. **Terms:** cancellation fee imposed. **Amenities:** high-speed Internet (fee), dual phone lines, voice mail, irons, hair dryers. **Pool(s):** heated indoor. **Leisure Activities:** saunas, whirlpools, exercise room. **Guest Services:** valet laundry, wireless Internet. **Business Services:** conference facilities, PC. **Cards:** AX, CB, DC, DS, JC, MC, VI.

Marriott
HOTELS & RESORTS

AAA Benefit:
Members save a minimum 5% off the best available rate.

SLEEP INN SEATAC AIRPORT   *Book great rates at AAA.com*   **Phone:** (206)878-3600   120

Hotel
$80-$150 All Year

Address: 20406 International Blvd **Location:** On SR 99. **Facility:** 105 one-bedroom standard units. 4 stories, interior corridors. *Bath:* combo or shower only. **Parking:** on-site. **Amenities:** high-speed Internet, voice mail, irons, hair dryers. **Leisure Activities:** exercise room. **Guest Services:** coin laundry, area transportation-within 3 mi, wireless Internet. **Business Services:** meeting rooms, PC. **Cards:** AX, DC, DS, JC, MC, VI. **Free Special Amenities:** expanded continental breakfast and local telephone calls.

(See map and index starting on p. 614)

SUPER 8 MOTEL SEA-TAC *Book at AAA.com* Phone: (206)433-8188 **115**
▼▼
Hotel
$77-$97 All Year
Address: 3100 S 192nd St **Location:** Just e of SR 99. **Facility:** 119 one-bedroom standard units. 3 stories, interior corridors. **Parking:** on-site. **Amenities:** high-speed Internet, voice mail, safes (fee); hair dryers. **Guest Services:** coin laundry, area transportation, wireless Internet. **Business Services:** meeting rooms. **Cards:** AX, CB, DC, DS, JC, MC, VI.

─── *The following lodging was either not evaluated or did not* ───
meet AAA rating requirements but is listed for your information only.

RED ROOF INN Phone: 206/248-0901
[fyi]
Not evaluated. **Address:** 16838 International Blvd **Location:** On SR 99. Facilities, services, and decor characterize an economy property.

─────── **WHERE TO DINE** ───────

13 COINS RESTAURANT Phone: 206/243-9500 **120**
▼▲▲▲
American
$10-$30
Established in 1967, the energetic restaurant offers such specialties as chicken parmigiana, seafood fettuccine and luscious cheesecake. Seating at the counter is popular, as it allows diners to supervise exhibition cooking. Casual dress. Entertainment. **Bar:** Full bar. **Hours:** 24 hours. **Address:** 18000 International Blvd **Location:** Across from Sea-Tac International Airport. **Parking:** on-site. **Cards:** AX, CB, DC, DS, MC, VI.

DAVE'S DINER & BREW Phone: 206/277-7196 **122**
▼▼
American
$6-$16
Convenient to the airport, the laid-back spot plies guests with good diner food and friendly service. Casual dress. **Bar:** Full bar. **Reservations:** accepted. **Hours:** 6 am-10 pm. **Closed:** 11/26, 12/25. **Address:** 2825 S 188th St **Location:** Just w of jct International Blvd. **Parking:** on-site. **Cards:** AX, DS, MC, VI.

SHARPS ROASTER & ALE HOUSE Phone: 206/241-5744 **121**
▼▼
American
$8-$30
A festive ambience is achieved with colorful, eclectic framed art that covers the walls and the unusual touch of beer coasters blanketing the ceiling. All meats are smoked and roasted on the premises, including prime rib that's simply fantastic. Casual dress. **Bar:** Full bar. **Reservations:** required. **Hours:** 10 am-11 pm, Fri & Sat-midnight. **Closed:** 1/1, 12/25. **Address:** 18427 International Blvd **Location:** On SR 99; adjacent to Sea-Tac International Airport. **Parking:** on-site. **Cards:** AX, CB, DC, MC, VI.

SPENCER'S FOR STEAKS AND CHOPS Phone: 206/248-7153 **119**
▼▼▼
Steak
$9-$60
The traditional steakhouse offers a sophisticated dining alternative, with an a la carte menu of classic favorites. Casual dress. **Bar:** Full bar. **Reservations:** suggested. **Hours:** 6 am-2 & 5-11 pm, Sun from 7 am. **Address:** 17620 International Blvd **Location:** On SR 99; in Hilton Seattle Airport & Conference Center. **Parking:** on-site and valet. **Cards:** AX, CB, DC, DS, JC, MC, VI.

SHORELINE pop. 53,025 (See map and index starting on p. 614)

─────── **WHERE TO STAY** ───────

DAYS INN-NORTH SEATTLE *Book at AAA.com* Phone: 206/542-6300 **26**
▲▲▲
Hotel
Rates not provided
Address: 19527 Aurora Ave N **Location:** I-5, exit 176 northbound, 2 mi nw via 175th St and Aurora Ave; exit 177 southbound, 2 mi sw via 205th St and Aurora Ave. **Facility:** 56 units. 55 one-bedroom standard units, some with whirlpools. 1 one-bedroom suite. 3 stories, interior corridors. **Parking:** on-site. **Terms:** check-in 4 pm. **Amenities:** voice mail, irons, hair dryers. **Guest Services:** coin laundry, wireless Internet. **Business Services:** PC.

SILVERDALE pop. 15,816 (See map and index starting on p. 624)

─────── **WHERE TO STAY** ───────

OXFORD INN *Book at AAA.com* Phone: (360)692-7777 **4**
▼▼
Hotel
$89 All Year
Address: 9734 NW Silverdale Way **Location:** SR 3, exit Newberry Hill Rd, just e, then 1.2 mi n. **Facility:** 63 one-bedroom standard units, some with efficiencies. 3 stories (no elevator), interior corridors. **Bath:** combo or shower only. **Parking:** on-site. **Terms:** cancellation fee imposed. **Amenities:** video library (fee), high-speed Internet, irons, hair dryers. **Business Services:** PC. **Cards:** AX, DC, DS, MC, VI.

OXFORD SUITES SILVERDALE *Book at AAA.com* Phone: (360)698-9550 **6**
▼▼▼
Hotel
$129-$189 All Year
Address: 9550 SW Silverdale Way **Location:** SR 3, exit Newberry Hill Rd, 1.5 mi. **Facility:** Smoke free premises. 104 units. 101 one-bedroom standard units. 1 one- and 2 two-bedroom suites. 5 stories, interior corridors. **Parking:** on-site. **Amenities:** high-speed Internet, voice mail, irons, hair dryers. **Pool(s):** heated indoor. **Leisure Activities:** sauna, whirlpool, steamroom, exercise room. **Guest Services:** valet and coin laundry, wireless Internet. **Business Services:** meeting rooms, PC. **Cards:** AX, CB, DC, DS, MC, VI.

(See map and index starting on p. 624)

SILVERDALE BEACH HOTEL   *Book great rates at AAA.com*   Phone: (360)698-1000   **5**

AAA SAVE

Hotel
$115-$160 All Year

Address: 3073 NW Bucklin Hill Dr **Location:** SR 3, exit Newberry Hill Rd, just e, 1 mi n on Silverdale Way, then just e. **Facility:** Smoke free premises. 151 one-bedroom standard units. 3 stories, interior corridors. *Bath:* combo or shower only. **Parking:** on-site. **Terms:** cancellation fee imposed. **Amenities:** video games (fee), high-speed Internet, dual phone lines, voice mail, irons, hair dryers. **Pool(s):** heated indoor. **Leisure Activities:** whirlpool, 2 lighted tennis courts, exercise room. *Fee:* game room. **Guest Services:** valet laundry, wireless Internet. **Business Services:** conference facilities, business center. **Cards:** AX, CB, DC, DS, MC, VI. **Free Special Amenities:** local telephone calls and high-speed Internet.

[icons]

──────── WHERE TO DINE ────────

ROUND TABLE PIZZA   Phone: 360/698-4040

Pizza
$9-$15

This casual, family-oriented pizza place features high-quality ingredients and dough rolled fresh daily. Distinctive specialty pizzas are piled high with toppings. Casual dress. **Bar:** Beer & wine. **Reservations:** not accepted. **Hours:** 11 am-9 pm, Fri & Sat-10 pm, Sun noon-9 pm. Closed: 4/12, 11/26, 12/25. **Address:** 3276 NW Plaza Rd, Suite 101 **Location:** Just w of Kitsap Mall. **Parking:** on-site. **Cards:** MC, VI.

SILVER CITY RESTAURANT & BREWERY   Phone: 360/698-5879   **5**

American
$9-$30

Pan-Pacific influences mingle with standard pub fare, resulting in innovative and tasty creations such as Hawaiian chicken salad and Santa Fe quesadillas. Diners can watch the brewing of six hand-crafted ales and lagers through a glass wall. Casual dress. **Bar:** Full bar. **Reservations:** accepted, weekdays. **Hours:** 11 am-10 pm, Fri & Sat-11 pm, Sun-9 pm. Closed: 12/25. **Address:** 2799 NW Myhre Rd **Location:** SR 3, exit Wagga Way, just e, just s on Silverdale Way, then just w. **Parking:** on-site. **Cards:** AX, DC, DS, MC, VI.

SNOHOMISH pop. 8,494

──────── WHERE TO STAY ────────

INN AT SNOHOMISH   Phone: (360)568-2208

AAA SAVE

Motel
$65-$130 All Year

Address: 323 2nd St **Location:** East end of town. **Facility:** 22 one-bedroom standard units, some with whirlpools. 2 stories (no elevator), exterior corridors. **Parking:** on-site. **Terms:** office hours 9 am-10 pm, cancellation fee imposed. **Amenities:** high-speed Internet, voice mail, hair dryers. *Fee:* video library. **Guest Services:** wireless Internet. **Business Services:** meeting rooms. **Cards:** AX, DS, MC, VI. **Free Special Amenities:** local telephone calls and high-speed Internet.

 [icons]

──────── WHERE TO DINE ────────

COLLECTOR'S CHOICE   Phone: 360/568-1277

AAA

American
$7-$23

In the heart of downtown's antiques district, this restaurant shares space with a collectors' mall. Choices might include seasonal fresh halibut or salmon, as well as seafood pasta or a center-cut sirloin steak. The garden patio opens from May through September. Casual dress. **Bar:** Full bar. **Reservations:** accepted. **Hours:** 7 am-9 pm, Fri & Sat-10 pm. Closed: 12/25. **Address:** 120 Glen Ave **Location:** In Star Center Mall. **Parking:** on-site. **Cards:** AX, DS, MC, VI.

MARDINI'S RESTAURANT   Phone: 360/568-8080

Mediterranean
$8-$23

Lunch at the family-owned and -operated spot is popular with tourists, who come to stroll the streets and hunt for antique bargains. Evenings get rolling with more of a local crowd. Mediterranean dishes here mean Northwest offerings with exotic spices and fruits, like papaya crab cakes or perhaps ginger chicken. Casual dress. **Bar:** Full bar. **Reservations:** accepted. **Hours:** 10 am-10 pm. **Address:** 101 Union Ave **Location:** Corner of Union Ave and First St; downtown. **Parking:** street. **Cards:** AX, CB, DC, DS, MC, VI.

SNOQUALMIE pop. 1,631

──────── WHERE TO STAY ────────

SALISH LODGE & SPA   *Book great rates at AAA.com*   Phone: (425)888-2556

AAA SAVE

Hotel
$329-$429 All Year

Address: 6501 Railroad Ave SE **Location:** I-90, exit 27 eastbound, 5 mi ne via North Bend Way, Meadowbrook Way and SR 202; exit 01 westbound, 7 mi nw via SR 202. **Facility:** This lodge, situated on the cliff above Snoqualmie Falls, features a full-service spa and all rooms come with a wood burning fireplace. 89 one-bedroom standard units with whirlpools. 4 stories, interior corridors. *Bath:* combo or shower only. **Parking:** valet. **Terms:** check-in 4 pm, 7 day cancellation notice-fee imposed. **Amenities:** video games (fee), CD players, dual phone lines, voice mail, safes, honor bars, irons, hair dryers. *Some:* DVD players. **Dining:** restaurant, see separate listing. **Leisure Activities:** sauna, whirlpools, steamroom, fishing, guided fishing tour, bicycles, hiking trails, exercise room, spa. **Guest Services:** valet laundry, wireless Internet. **Business Services:** conference facilities, PC, fax. **Cards:** AX, CB, DC, DS, JC, MC, VI. **Free Special Amenities:** high-speed Internet.

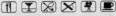 [icons]

---------- WHERE TO DINE ----------

SALISH LODGE DINING ROOM   Phone: 425/888-2556
▼▼▼▼ ▼▼▼▼
Regional American
$28-$60
The elegant country dining room is a quick hour's drive from Seattle. On the lodge's outer wall, the room sits on the crest of 268-foot Snoqualmie Falls. Maine diver sea scallops with black summer truffle are served with a nest of Yukon potatoes, red endives and a watercress broth. The evening's dessert of choice may be a chocolate pot prepared tableside and served with fresh beignets. Dressy casual. **Bar:** Full bar. **Reservations:** suggested. **Hours:** 7 am-11 & 5:30-9:30 pm, Fri-10 pm, Sat 7 am-2 & 5:30-10 pm, Sun 7 am-2 & 5:30-9:30 pm. Closed: Mon. **Address:** 6501 Railroad Ave SE **Location:** I-90, exit 27 eastbound, 5 mi ne via North Bend Way, Meadowbrook Way and SR 202; exit 31 westbound, 7 mi nw via SR 202; in Salish Lodge & Spa. **Parking:** valet. **Cards:** AX, CB, DC, DS, JC, MC, VI.

SUMNER pop. 8,504

---------- WHERE TO STAY ----------

HOLIDAY INN EXPRESS SUMNER   Phone: 253/200-7260
[fyi]
Hotel
Rates not provided
Too new to rate, opening scheduled for September 2008. **Address:** 2500 136th Ave Ct E **Location:** SR 167, exit 24th St. **Amenities:** 112 units, coffeemakers, microwaves, refrigerators, pool.

---------- WHERE TO DINE ----------

AL LAGO RISTORANTE ITALIANO   Phone: 253/863-8636
▼▼▼
Italian
$8-$23
The solid Italian menu lists several choices of seafood and steak, in addition to pasta dishes and hand-tossed gourmet pizza and calzones. Jazz musicians perform every Wednesday evening. In the summer, the patio opens to enable patrons to catch some sun and watch the boating fun on distant Lake Tapps. Casual dress. **Bar:** Full bar. **Reservations:** accepted. **Hours:** 11 am-10 pm, Fri & Sat-11 pm, Sun 3 pm-10 pm. Closed: 11/26. **Address:** 3110 Sumner Tapps Hwy E **Location:** Jct W Tapps Dr E. **Parking:** on-site. **Cards:** AX, CB, DC, DS, JC, MC, VI.

SUQUAMISH pop. 3,510

---------- WHERE TO STAY ----------

---------- The following lodging was either not evaluated or did not meet AAA rating requirements but is listed for your information only. ----------

SUQUAMISH CLEARWATER CASINO RESORT   Phone: 360/598-8700
[fyi]
Not evaluated. **Address:** 15347 Suquamish Way. Facilities, services, and decor characterize a mid-scale property.

TACOMA pop. 193,556   (See map and index starting on p. 626)

---------- WHERE TO STAY ----------

A PLUM DUFF HOUSE   Phone: 253/627-6916   ❷
▼▼▼
Historic Bed
& Breakfast
$110-$150 3/1-9/30
$100-$140 10/1-2/28
Address: 619 N K St **Location:** Between 6th and 7th sts; 0.3 mi n of Division Ave. **Facility:** Built in 1901, this home is filled with a blend of antiques and oriental furnishings. Smoke free premises. 4 one-bedroom standard units, some with whirlpools. 3 stories (no elevator), interior corridors. **Bath:** combo or shower only. **Parking:** street. **Terms:** age restrictions may apply, 7 day cancellation notice-fee imposed. **Amenities:** video library, hair dryers. *Some:* high-speed Internet. **Guest Services:** wireless Internet. **Cards:** AX, DS, MC, VI.
[ASK] [X] [AC] [VCR] / SOME UNITS [▯]

BEST WESTERN TACOMA DOME HOTEL   *Book great rates at AAA.com*   Phone: (253)272-7737   ❻
(AAA) [SAVE]
▼▼▼
Hotel
$79-$149 All Year
Address: 2611 East E St **Location:** I-5, exit 133 (City Center), follow E 26th St/Tacoma Dome lanes, just n on E 26th St, then just e. **Facility:** 162 one-bedroom standard units, some with whirlpools. 6 stories, interior corridors. **Bath:** combo or shower only. **Parking:** on-site. **Terms:** 3 day cancellation notice. **Amenities:** high-speed Internet, dual phone lines, voice mail, irons, hair dryers. **Leisure Activities:** sauna, exercise room. **Guest Services:** valet laundry, wireless Internet. **Business Services:** meeting rooms, PC. **Cards:** AX, DC, DS, MC, VI. **Free Special Amenities:** full breakfast and high-speed Internet.

AAA Benefit:
Members save up to 20%, plus 10% bonus points with rewards program.
[▯▯] [Y] CALL [M] [X] [▯] [▯] [▯] [▯]

COMFORT INN   *Book at AAA.com*   Phone: (253)538-7998   ⓬
▼▼▼
Hotel
$100-$135 All Year
Address: 8620 S Hosmer St **Location:** I-5, exit 128 northbound; exit 129 southbound, follow signs to 84th St, e to Hosmer St, then just s. **Facility:** 90 units. 89 one-bedroom standard units. 1 one-bedroom suite. 3 stories, interior corridors. **Bath:** combo or shower only. **Parking:** on-site. **Terms:** cancellation fee imposed. **Amenities:** high-speed Internet, voice mail, safes (fee), irons, hair dryers. *Some:* dual phone lines. **Pool(s):** heated indoor. **Leisure Activities:** exercise room. **Guest Services:** coin laundry, wireless Internet. **Business Services:** meeting rooms, PC. **Cards:** AX, CB, DC, DS, JC, MC, VI.
[ASK] [▯▯] [⟲] [X] [▯] [▯] / SOME UNITS [▯] [▯]

(See map and index starting on p. 626)

COURTYARD BY MARRIOTT-TACOMA DOWNTOWN   *Book great rates at AAA.com*   **Phone:** (253)591-9100   **4**

▼▼▼▼
Hotel
$219-$229 All Year

Address: 1515 Commerce St **Location:** I-5, exit 133 (City Center) to I-705 N, exit S 15th St, just s; downtown. Located across from Tacoma Convention and Trade Center. **Facility:** Smoke free premises. 162 units. 158 one-bedroom standard units, some with whirlpools. 4 one-bedroom suites. 5 stories, interior corridors. *Bath:* combo or shower only. **Parking:** on-site (fee) and valet. **Terms:** cancellation fee imposed. **Amenities:** high-speed Internet, dual phone lines, voice mail, irons, hair dryers. **Pool(s):** heated indoor. **Leisure Activities:** whirlpool, exercise room, spa. **Guest Services:** valet and coin laundry, wireless Internet. **Business Services:** meeting rooms, PC. **Cards:** AX, DS, MC, VI.

AAA Benefit:
Members save a minimum 5% off the best available rate.

CROSSLAND STUDIOS-TACOMA-HOSMER   *Book at AAA.com*   **Phone:** (253)538-9448   **13**

▼
Motel
$74-$89 All Year

Address: 8801 S Hosmer St **Location:** I-5, exit 128 northbound, just se; exit 129 southbound, just e on 72nd St, then 1.0 mi s. **Facility:** 129 one-bedroom standard units. 3 stories, exterior corridors. *Bath:* combo or shower only. **Parking:** on-site. **Terms:** office hours 7 am-11 pm, cancellation fee imposed. **Amenities:** voice mail, irons. **Guest Services:** coin laundry, wireless Internet. **Cards:** AX, CB, DC, DS, JC, MC, VI.

DEVOE MANSION BED & BREAKFAST   **Phone:** (253)539-3991

▼▼▼
Bed & Breakfast
$125-$155 All Year

Address: 208 133rd St E **Location:** I-5, exit 127 (SR 512), 2 mi e, exit 7 (Pacific Ave), 1.5 mi s, then just e. **Facility:** This mansion traces its origins to the 1800s, when it was built as a modest farm house and later enlarged in the early 1900s. The individually decorated guest rooms feature luxurious appointments. Smoke free premises. 4 one-bedroom standard units. 2 stories (no elevator), interior corridors. *Bath:* combo, shower or tub only. **Parking:** on-site. **Terms:** check-in 4 pm, 2 night minimum stay - seasonal and/or weekends, age restrictions may apply, 10 day cancellation notice-fee imposed. **Amenities:** video library, CD players, high-speed Internet, irons, hair dryers. **Guest Services:** wireless Internet. **Cards:** MC, VI.

EXTENDED STAYAMERICA-TACOMA-SOUTH   *Book at AAA.com*   **Phone:** (253)475-6565   **7**

▼▼▼
Hotel
$105-$115 All Year

Address: 2120 S 48th St **Location:** I-5, exit 130, 0.4 mi nw. **Facility:** Smoke free premises. 109 one-bedroom standard units. 4 stories, interior corridors. *Bath:* combo or shower only. **Parking:** on-site. **Terms:** office hours 7 am-11 pm, cancellation fee imposed. **Amenities:** high-speed Internet (fee), voice mail, irons. **Guest Services:** coin laundry, wireless Internet. **Cards:** AX, CB, DC, DS, JC, MC, VI.

HAMPTON INN & SUITES TACOMA - SOUTH   *Book great rates at AAA.com*   **Phone:** (253)539-2288   **9**

▼▼▼
Hotel
$129-$179 All Year

Address: 8203 S Hosmer St **Location:** I-5, exit 128 northbound, just ne; exit 129 southbend, just e on 72nd St, then 1 mi s. **Facility:** Smoke free premises. 146 one-bedroom standard units. *Bath:* combo or shower only. **Parking:** on-site. **Terms:** 1-30 night minimum stay, cancellation fee imposed. **Amenities:** high-speed Internet, voice mail, irons, hair dryers. **Leisure Activities:** exercise room. **Guest Services:** valet and coin laundry, wireless Internet. **Business Services:** meeting rooms, business center. **Cards:** AX, CB, DC, DS, MC, VI.

AAA Benefit:
Members save up to 10% everyday!

HOLIDAY INN EXPRESS HOTEL & SUITES   *Book at AAA.com*   **Phone:** (253)539-2020   **11**

▼▼▼
Hotel
$159-$199 All Year

Address: 8601 S Hosmer St **Location:** I-5, exit 128 northbound, just e; exit 129 southbound, just e on 72nd St, then 0.9 mi s. **Facility:** 78 one-bedroom standard units, some with whirlpools. 4 stories, interior corridors. *Bath:* combo or shower only. **Parking:** on-site. **Terms:** cancellation fee imposed. **Amenities:** high-speed Internet, dual phone lines, voice mail, irons, hair dryers. **Pool(s):** heated indoor. **Leisure Activities:** sauna, whirlpool, exercise room. **Guest Services:** valet and coin laundry, wireless Internet. **Business Services:** PC. **Cards:** AX, DS, MC, VI.

HOTEL MURANO   *Book great rates at AAA.com*   **Phone:** (253)238-8000   **3**

ⒶⒶⒶ [SAVE]
▼▼▼
Hotel
$189-$469 All Year

Address: 1320 Broadway Plaza **Location:** I-5, exit 133 (City Center) to I-705 N, exit A St, left on 11th St, then left; downtown. Located adjacent to Tacoma Convention & Trade Center. **Facility:** Smoke free premises. 319 units. 309 one-bedroom standard units. 10 one-bedroom suites, some with whirlpools. 26 stories, interior corridors. **Parking:** on-site (fee) and valet. **Terms:** cancellation fee imposed. **Amenities:** high-speed Internet, dual phone lines, voice mail, safes, honor bars, irons, hair dryers. *Some:* CD players, fax. **Leisure Activities:** whirlpool, exercise room, spa. **Guest Services:** valet laundry, wireless Internet. **Business Services:** conference facilities, business center. **Cards:** AX, DS, MC, VI. **Free Special Amenities:** newspaper.

(See map and index starting on p. 626)

LA QUINTA INN & SUITES TACOMA (CONFERENCE CENTER) *Book great rates at AAA.com*

Phone: (253)383-0146 **5**

▼▼▼

Hotel
$79-$169 All Year

Address: 1425 E 27th St **Location:** I-5, exit 135 southbound; exit 134 northbound, just n. **Facility:** 155 units. 149 one-bedroom standard units. 6 one-bedroom suites. 7 stories, interior corridors. *Bath:* combo or shower only. **Parking:** on-site. **Amenities:** video games (fee), high-speed Internet, voice mail, irons, hair dryers. **Pool(s):** heated outdoor. **Leisure Activities:** whirlpool, exercise room. **Guest Services:** valet and coin laundry, wireless Internet. **Business Services:** conference facilities, business center. **Cards:** AX, DS, MC, VI.

ASK ▥ ▤ ▧ ▨ ▦ / SOME UNITS ▨ ✕ ▤ ▦

RED LION HOTEL TACOMA *Book great rates at AAA.com*

Phone: (253)548-1212 **10**

AAA SAVE

▼▼▼

Hotel
$109-$149 All Year

Address: 8402 S Hosmer St **Location:** I-5, exit 128 northbound, just ne; exit 129 southbound, just e on 72nd St, then 1 mi s. **Facility:** 119 one-bedroom standard units, some with whirlpools. 4 stories, interior corridors. *Bath:* combo or shower only. **Parking:** on-site. **Terms:** cancellation fee imposed. **Amenities:** high-speed Internet, voice mail, irons, hair dryers. **Pool(s):** heated indoor. **Leisure Activities:** whirlpool, exercise room. **Guest Services:** valet and coin laundry, wireless Internet. **Business Services:** meeting rooms, PC. **Cards:** AX, DC, DS, MC, VI. **Free Special Amenities: expanded continental breakfast and high-speed Internet.**

▨ ▧ ▤ ▦ ▨ / SOME UNITS FEE ▨ ✕

SHILO INN & SUITES -TACOMA *Book great rates at AAA.com*

Phone: (253)475-4020 **8**

AAA SAVE

▼▼▼

Hotel
$112-$200 All Year

Address: 7414 S Hosmer St **Location:** I-5, exit 129, just se. **Facility:** 132 one-bedroom standard units, some with efficiencies (no utensils). 4 stories, interior corridors. *Bath:* combo or shower only. **Parking:** on-site. **Amenities:** video games (fee), high-speed Internet, voice mail, irons, hair dryers. **Pool(s):** heated indoor. **Leisure Activities:** sauna, whirlpool, steamroom, exercise room. **Guest Services:** valet and coin laundry, wireless Internet. **Business Services:** meeting rooms, PC. **Cards:** AX, CB, DC, DS, JC, MC, VI. **Free Special Amenities: continental breakfast and high-speed Internet.** *(See color ad below)*

▥ ▧ ✕ ✕ ▨ ▤ ▦ ▨ / SOME UNITS FEE ▨

SILVER CLOUD INN TACOMA *Book at AAA.com*

Phone: (253)272-1300 **1**

▼▼▼

Hotel
$179-$329 All Year

Address: 2317 N Ruston Way **Location:** I-5, exit 133 (City Center) to I-705 N and Schuster Pkwy, 2.4 mi to Ruston Way/Waterfront, then 0.6 mi nw. **Facility:** Smoke free premises. 90 units. 76 one-bedroom standard units, some with whirlpools. 14 one-bedroom suites. 3 stories, interior corridors. *Bath:* combo or shower only. **Parking:** on-site. **Amenities:** video games (fee), high-speed Internet, voice mail, irons, hair dryers. **Leisure Activities:** exercise room. **Guest Services:** complimentary and valet laundry, area transportation, wireless Internet. **Business Services:** meeting rooms, business center. **Cards:** AX, DC, DS, JC, MC, VI.

▥ CALL ▧ ✕ ▧ ▤ ▦ ▨

▼ *See AAA listing above* ▼

(See map and index starting on p. 626)

The following lodging was either not evaluated or did not meet AAA rating requirements but is listed for your information only.

THE VILLA

Phone: 253/572-1157

[fyi]

Not evaluated. **Address:** 705 N 5th St **Location:** I-5, exit 133 (City Center) to I-705 N and Schuster Pkwy, exit Stadium Way, 0.8 mi nw on Stadium Way/1st St N, 0.3 mi w on Tacoma Way, then 0.3 mi s. Facilities, services, and decor characterize an economy property.

WHERE TO DINE

ANTIQUE SANDWICH COMPANY

Phone: 253/752-4069   ③

American
$5-$8

Basic, wholesome fare—such as delicatessen-style sandwiches and ethnic selections of hummus, spanakopita and lasagna—is the no-frills restaurant's bread and butter. Among homemade desserts are cheesecake and pies. Casual dress. **Hours:** 7 am-7:30 pm, Sun from 8 am, Tues 7 am-10 pm. Closed major holidays. **Address:** 5102 N Pearl St **Location:** Jct N Pearl and 51st sts; just s of Point Defiance Park. **Parking:** on-site. **Cards:** AX, DS, MC, VI.

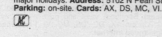

BITE

Phone: 253/572-3200   ⑫

American
$12-$32

The modern restaurant prepares a good mixture of traditional food with an upscale touch. Casual dress. **Bar:** Full bar. **Reservations:** accepted. **Hours:** 6 am-10 pm, Fri-11 pm, Sat 7 am-11 pm, Sun 7 am-10 pm. **Address:** 1320 Broadway Plaza **Location:** I-5, exit 133 (City Center) to I-705 N, exit A St, just w on 11th St, then just s; downtown; in Hotel Murano. **Parking:** on-site (fee) and valet. **Cards:** AX, DS, MC, VI.

CALL 🅕🅜

CI SHENANIGANS CHOPHOUSE-TACOMA

Phone: 253/752-8811   ⑤

American
$10-$40

A great location on the edge of Puget Sound, the restaurant affords water views from most tables. Speed is the guarantee at lunch, where the longest guests wait from order to eating is 15 minutes. Characterizing the comfortable dining room are rich dark woods, soft lighting and comfortable booths. Offerings on a menu that combines the best of the land and ocean are potato-crusted halibut, cooked-to-order steak and chops. Casual dress. **Bar:** Full bar. **Reservations:** accepted. **Hours:** 11 am-9 pm, Fri & Sat-10 pm, Sun 9:30 am-9 pm. **Address:** 3017 N Ruston Way **Location:** I-5, exit 133 (City Center), 2.3 mi nw via Schuster Pkwy and Ruston Way. **Parking:** on-site. **Cards:** AX, DS, MC, VI.

THE CLIFF HOUSE

Phone: 253/927-0400   ②

Continental
$12-$38

Guests in all dining areas are treated to scenic views of Mount Rainier and Commencement Bay. Northwestern influences punctuate the excellent food. The downstairs area, known as Guido's, is casual and lively while the main floor offers a more upscale experience. Casual dress. **Bar:** Full bar. **Reservations:** suggested. **Hours:** 11:30 am-9 pm, Fri-10 pm, Sat 5 pm-10 pm, Sun 4 pm-9 pm. Closed: 1/1, 12/25. **Address:** 6300 Marine View Dr NE **Location:** I-5, exit 142B, 6.7 mi w via 348th St/Campus Dr/SW 340th St/Northshore Pkwy and Slayden Rd; all roads merge into the next. **Parking:** on-site. **Cards:** AX, DC, DS, MC, VI.

THE DASH POINT LOBSTER SHOP

Phone: 253/927-1513   ①

Seafood
$18-$30

Set in a residential neighborhood, the renovated house is quaintly appointed with linen-covered tables and romantic candles. Simple, but attractively prepared dishes of fresh seafood include sea bass garnished with colorful diced peppers. Casual dress. **Bar:** Full bar. **Reservations:** suggested. **Hours:** 4:30 pm-9 pm, Fri & Sat-10 pm. Closed: 12/25. **Address:** 6912 Soundview Dr NE **Location:** I-5, exit 143, 4.4 mi w on 320th St, 0.3 mi n on 47th Ave, 1.5 mi w on Dash Point Rd, then 0.3 mi w on Markham Ave. **Parking:** on-site. **Cards:** AX, DC, DS, MC, VI.

EL GAUCHO

Phone: 253/272-1510   ⑯

Steak & Seafood
$21-$63

Friends gather to enjoy Angus beef, which is dry-aged for 28 days, and attentive, friendly service. Classic piano tunes emanate from a corner of the lounge. Menu items include all the tradition cuts of beef, along with double-thick venison chops, baby back ribs, Australian lobster and pan-seared oysters. Dressy casual. **Bar:** Full bar. **Reservations:** suggested. **Hours:** 5 pm-1 am, Sun-11 pm. Closed: 7/4, 12/25. **Address:** 2119 Pacific Ave **Location:** Downtown. **Parking:** valet and street. **Cards:** AX, CB, DC, DS, JC, MC, VI.

ENGINE HOUSE #9

Phone: 253/272-3435   ⑧

American
$7-$15

As the name would suggest, this eatery and brewery is located in a historic firehouse that served to protect the community for many years. Guests might select the barbecue pork sandwich with a pint of whatever to wash it down. Outdoor seating is available in season. Casual dress. **Bar:** Full bar. **Reservations:** accepted. **Hours:** 11 am-1 am, Fri & Sat-2 am. Closed: 7/4, 11/26, 12/25. **Address:** 611 N Pine St **Location:** Jct 6th and N Pine sts. **Parking:** on-site. **Cards:** DS, MC, VI.

HARBOR LIGHTS

Phone: 253/752-8600   ⑥

Steak & Seafood
$10-$40

With a lovely view of Commencement Bay and Puget Sound and a classic menu of seafood, steak, chops and shellfish, it is no wonder that this is such a bustling and popular eatery. Generous portions are the rule, as seen in the four-pound buckets of clams. Casual dress. **Bar:** Full bar. **Reservations:** suggested. **Hours:** 11 am-9:30 pm, Fri & Sat-10:30 pm, Sun noon-9 pm. Closed: 11/26, 12/25. **Address:** 2761 Ruston Way **Location:** I-5, exit 133 (City Center), 2 mi on Schuster Pkwy. **Parking:** on-site. **Cards:** AX, DC, MC, VI.

HARMON RESTAURANT & BREWERY

Phone: 253/383-2739   ⑮

American
$8-$16

Known as "Tacoma's favorite gathering place," the downtown restaurant is on the main floor of a historic landmark building. On any given night, diners might catch a bunch of co-workers devouring pizza or chicken Caesar wraps or maybe a softball team tackling piles of fries and freshly made hamburgers. As the name might suggest, made-in-house beer is a favorite beverage. Casual dress. **Bar:** Full bar. **Reservations:** accepted. **Hours:** 11 am-11 pm, Fri & Sat-midnight, Sun-8 pm. Closed: 11/26, 12/25; also for dinner 7/4. **Address:** 1938 Pacific Ave **Location:** Downtown. **Parking:** on-site. **Cards:** AX, CB, DC, DS, MC, VI.

(See map and index starting on p. 626)

IL FIASCO
Italian
$14-$30
Phone: 253/272-6688 ⑩
Family and friends gather in the quaint, bustling dining room. On Wednesdays, guests can enjoy a half-price bottle of wine with their choice of excellent Italian fare. Those who want to start off with an appetizer should try asparago arrostitio; it's delicioso! Casual dress. **Bar:** Full bar. **Reservations:** accepted. **Hours:** 11 am-2 & 5-9 pm, Fri-10:30 pm, Sat 4 pm-10:30 pm, Sun 5 pm-9 pm. Closed major holidays. **Address:** 2717 6th Ave **Location:** SR 16, exit Sprague Ave, 1.4 mi n on S Sprague Ave, then 0.4 mi w. **Parking:** street. **Cards:** AX, DS, MC, VI.

JOHNNY'S DOCK
Steak & Seafood
$7-$30
Phone: 253/627-3186 ⑭
Since 1953, this waterfront restaurant with views of the marina and the Glass Art museum has been a part of the Tacoma dining scene. Offerings of fresh seafood and steak include Hood Canal oysters and blue mussels. The deck opens seasonally. Casual dress. **Bar:** Full bar. **Reservations:** suggested. **Hours:** 11 am-3 & 4-8 pm, Fri-9:30 pm, Sat 1 pm-10 pm, Sun 1 pm-8 pm. Closed: 12/25. **Address:** 1900 E D St **Location:** I-5, exit 133 (City Center), follow signs to Tacoma Dome, just n on 26th St, then 0.3 mi w. **Parking:** on-site. **Cards:** AX, DS, MC, VI.

THE OLD HOUSE CAFE   _Menu on AAA.com_
Regional Seafood
$10-$33
Phone: 253/759-7336 ⑦
Patrons experience relaxed fine dining in a historic 1907 house decorated with many antique fixtures from local establishments. Large salads, fresh pasta dishes and raspberry king salmon are some of the delicious house specialties. Casual dress. **Bar:** Full bar. **Reservations:** suggested. **Hours:** 11:30 am-3 & 5-8 pm, Fri & Sat-9 pm, Sun 10:30 am-2 pm. Closed major holidays; also Mon. **Address:** 2717 N Proctor **Location:** 3 mi nw; between 27th and 28th sts. **Parking:** on-site. **Cards:** AX, CB, DC, MC, VI.

PRIMO GRILL
American
$8-$27
Phone: 253/383-7000 ⑪
Menu offerings include grilled fennel spiced prawn with citrus salad, homemade gnocchi with Bolognese sauce, grilled Tuscan chicken with arugula, rosemary butter and roasted garlic mash and fresh creme brulee. Casual dress. **Bar:** Full bar. **Reservations:** accepted. **Hours:** 11:30 am-2:30 & 4-9:30 pm, Fri-10:30 pm, Sat 5 pm-10:30 pm, Sun 4:30 pm-9 pm. Closed major holidays. **Address:** 601 S Pine St **Location:** I-5, exit 132 (SR 16 W), just nw on SR 16, exit Sprague Ave, 1.4 mi n, 0.4 mi w on S 6th St, then just s. **Parking:** on-site. **Cards:** AX, DC, MC, VI.

RAM RESTAURANT AND BREWERY
American
$8-$22
Phone: 253/756-7886
The enormous restaurant features high ceilings, huge television screens, large sports-themed banners and a brew pub area. The menu is equally enormous, with steaks, poultry, pasta, seafood, salads, sandwiches and pizza. The on-site brewery turns out a large selection of microbrews. Casual dress. **Bar:** Full bar. **Reservations:** not accepted. **Hours:** 11 am-close. Closed: 12/25. **Address:** 3001 Ruston Way **Location:** I-5, exit 133 (City Center), 2.3 mi nw via Schuster Pkwy and Ruston Way. **Parking:** on-site. **Cards:** AX, MC, VI.

RAVENOUS RESTAURANT
American
$7-$25
Phone: 253/572-6374 ⑨
Across the street from the theater, the downtown restaurant is known for everything from soups, salads and pasta to prawns, salmon, and steak, depending on what time of day you visit. Small lights and colorful tablecloths decorate the casual dining room. Casual dress. **Bar:** Beer & wine. **Reservations:** suggested, evenings. **Hours:** 11:30 am-2 & 5:30-9 pm, Sat from 5:30 pm. Closed: 11/26, 12/25; also Sun & for dinner Mon. **Address:** 785 Broadway **Location:** I-5, exit 133 (City Center); 9th St and Broadway. **Parking:** street. **Cards:** AX, DS, MC, VI.

ROUND TABLE PIZZA
Pizza
$4-$8
Phone: 253/756-5313
This casual, family-oriented pizza place features high-quality ingredients and dough rolled fresh daily. Distinctive specialty pizzas are piled high with toppings. Casual dress. **Bar:** Beer & wine. **Reservations:** not accepted. **Hours:** 11 am-10 pm. Closed major holidays. **Address:** 2601 N Pearl St **Location:** Jct N Pearl St (SR 163) and N 26th St. **Parking:** on-site.

THE RUSTON WAY LOBSTER SHOP   _Menu on AAA.com_
Western Seafood
$9-$35
Phone: 253/759-2165 ④
Classic Northwest seafood dishes are the emphasis, with selections such as fresh wild salmon and blackened tuna. Take advantage of outdoor deck dining in season for a spectacular view of the Olympic Mountains rising high above Commencement Bay. Dressy casual. **Bar:** Full bar. **Reservations:** suggested. **Hours:** 11:30 am-2:30 & 4:30-9:30 pm, Fri-10:30 pm, Sat 11:30 am-3:45 & 4:30-10:30 pm, Sun 9:30 am-1:30 & 4:30-9:30 pm; Sunday brunch. Closed: 7/4, 12/25. **Address:** 4015 Ruston Way **Location:** I-5, exit 133 (City Center), 5 mi nw via Schuster Pkwy and Ruston Way. **Parking:** on-site. **Cards:** AX, DC, DS, MC, VI.
CALL

SEA GRILL
Seafood
$27-$69
Phone: 253/272-5656 ⑬
This sophisticated restaurant features seafood from around the world; try the Mount Ranier Volcano dessert, a flaming concoction prepared tableside. Casual dress. **Bar:** Full bar. **Reservations:** suggested. **Hours:** 5 pm-10 pm, Fri & Sat-11 pm, Sun 4 pm-9 pm. Closed: 1/1, 11/26, 12/25. **Address:** 1498 Pacific Ave, Suite 300 **Location:** Corner of 15th St; downtown. **Parking:** on-site (fee). **Cards:** AX, DC, MC, VI.

STANLEY & SEAFORTS
Steak & Seafood
$10-$38
Phone: 253/473-7300 ⑰
Rock salt-roasted prime rib, applewood-smoked fish and steak and dessert made on the premises are among tasty offerings at the romantic restaurant, which overlooks the city and Commencement Bay. Rich, dark wood and plants decorate the three-tier dining room. Early-bird specials can be ordered during the first hour of dinner seating every night except Saturday. Casual dress. **Bar:** Full bar. **Reservations:** suggested. **Hours:** 11:15 am-3 & 4-9:30 pm, Sat 4 pm-10:30 pm, Sun 3:30 pm-9 pm. Closed: 11/26, 12/25. **Address:** 115 E 34th **Location:** I-5, exit 133 (City Center), s to 38th St, w to Pacific St, then n to 34th St. **Parking:** on-site. **Cards:** AX, DC, DS, MC, VI.
CALL

TUKWILA pop. 17,181   (See map and index starting on p. 614)

─────── WHERE TO STAY ───────

BEST WESTERN RIVER'S EDGE   *Book great rates at AAA.com*   Phone: (425)226-1812   96

(AAA) (SAVE)
▼▼▼

Hotel
$110-$140 All Year

Address: 15901 W Valley Hwy **Location:** I-405, exit 1 (SR 181), just s. Located across from Boeing Longacres Park. **Facility:** 146 one-bedroom standard units, some with whirlpools. 3 stories, interior corridors. **Parking:** on-site. **Terms:** cancellation fee imposed. **Amenities:** video games (fee), high-speed Internet, voice mail, irons, hair dryers. **Pool(s):** heated outdoor. **Leisure Activities:** sauna, whirlpool, exercise room. **Guest Services:** valet and coin laundry, area transportation-within 5 mi, wireless Internet. **Business Services:** meeting rooms, PC. **Cards:** AX, DC, DS, MC, VI. **Free Special Amenities: expanded continental breakfast and high-speed Internet.**

AAA Benefit:
Members save up to 20%, plus 10% bonus points with rewards program.

COMFORT SUITES AIRPORT-TUKWILA   *Book great rates at AAA.com*   Phone: (425)227-7200   93

(AAA) (SAVE)
▼▼▼

Hotel
$108-$190 All Year

Address: 7200 Fun Center Way **Location:** I-405, exit 1 (SR 181), just n on Interurban Ave, then just e. Located adjacent to Bull Winkle's Amusement Park. **Facility:** Smoke free premises. 138 units. 129 one- and 5 two-bedroom standard units, some with whirlpools. 4 one-bedroom suites. 4 stories, interior corridors. *Bath:* combo or shower only. **Amenities:** high-speed Internet, dual phone lines, voice mail, irons, hair dryers. *Some:* DVD players (fee). **Pool(s):** heated indoor. **Leisure Activities:** whirlpool, jogging, exercise room. **Guest Services:** valet and coin laundry, area transportation-Southcenter Mall, wireless Internet. **Business Services:** meeting rooms, business center. **Cards:** AX, CB, DC, DS, JC, MC, VI. **Free Special Amenities: expanded continental breakfast and high-speed Internet.**

COURTYARD BY MARRIOTT/SEA TAC AREA   *Book great rates at AAA.com*   Phone: (425)255-0300   98

▼▼▼

Hotel
$194-$214 All Year

Address: 16038 W Valley Hwy **Location:** I-405, exit 1 (SR 181), just s. **Facility:** Smoke free premises. 211 units. 204 one-bedroom standard units, some with whirlpools. 7 one-bedroom suites. 8 stories, interior corridors. *Bath:* combo or shower only. **Parking:** on-site. **Terms:** cancellation fee imposed. **Amenities:** video games (fee), high-speed Internet, dual phone lines, voice mail, irons, hair dryers. **Pool(s):** heated indoor. **Leisure Activities:** whirlpool, exercise room. **Guest Services:** valet and coin laundry, area transportation, wireless Internet. **Business Services:** meeting rooms, PC. **Cards:** AX, CB, DC, DS, JC, MC, VI.

AAA Benefit:
Members save a minimum 5% off the best available rate.

COURTYARD BY MARRIOTT-SEATTLE/SOUTHCENTER   *Book great rates at AAA.com*   Phone: (206)575-2500   101

▼▼▼

Hotel
$199-$219 All Year

Address: 400 Andover Park W **Location:** I-5, exit 153 northbound, s on Southcenter Pkwy, e on Strander Blvd, then s; exit 154B southbound, 0.5 mi s on Southcenter Blvd, just s on 61st Ave, just e on Tukwila Pkwy, then just s. Located in a commercial area. **Facility:** Smoke free premises. 149 units. 137 one-bedroom standard units. 12 one-bedroom suites. 3 stories, interior corridors. *Bath:* combo or shower only. **Parking:** on-site. **Terms:** cancellation fee imposed. **Amenities:** video games (fee), high-speed Internet, dual phone lines, voice mail, irons, hair dryers. **Pool(s):** heated indoor. **Leisure Activities:** whirlpool, exercise room. **Guest Services:** valet and coin laundry, area transportation, wireless Internet. **Business Services:** meeting rooms, PC. **Cards:** AX, CB, DC, DS, MC, VI.

AAA Benefit:
Members save a minimum 5% off the best available rate.

DAYS INN-SEATTLE SOUTH   *Book great rates at AAA.com*   Phone: (206)241-2200   90

(AAA) (SAVE)
▼▼▼

Motel
$59-$110 All Year

Address: 13050 48th Ave S **Location:** I-5, exit 156, just e on Interurban Ave, then just n. Located in an industrial area. **Facility:** 119 one-bedroom standard units. 2 stories (no elevator), exterior corridors. *Bath:* combo or shower only. **Parking:** on-site. **Terms:** cancellation fee imposed. **Amenities:** high-speed Internet, voice mail, irons, hair dryers. **Pool(s):** heated outdoor. **Leisure Activities:** whirlpool. **Guest Services:** coin laundry, wireless Internet. **Business Services:** PC. **Cards:** AX, DS, MC, VI. **Free Special Amenities: continental breakfast and high-speed Internet.**

(See map and index starting on p. 614)

DOUBLETREE GUEST SUITES SEATTLE AIRPORT-SOUTHCENTER   *Book great rates at AAA.com*

Phone: (206)575-8220   100

▼▼▼▼
Hotel
$99-$229 All Year

Address: 16500 Southcenter Pkwy **Location:** I-5, exit 153 northbound just s; exit 154B southbound, 0.5 mi e on Southcenter Blvd, just s on 61st Ave, then 0.6 mi w on Tukwila Pkwy. **Facility:** 219 one-bedroom suites. 8 stories, interior corridors. *Bath:* combo or shower only. **Parking:** on-site. **Terms:** 1-30 night minimum stay, cancellation fee imposed. **Amenities:** dual phone lines, voice mail, irons, hair dryers. *Fee:* video games, high-speed Internet. *Some:* CD players. **Pool(s):** heated indoor. **Leisure Activities:** sauna, whirlpool, racquetball courts, exercise room. **Guest Services:** valet laundry, area transportation, wireless Internet. **Business Services:** conference facilities, business center. **Cards:** AX, CB, DC, DS, JC, MC, VI.

DOUBLETREE
HOTELS•SUITES•RESORTS•CLUBS

AAA Benefit:
Members save 5% or
more everyday!

EMBASSY SUITES HOTEL   *Book great rates at AAA.com*

Phone: (425)227-8844   97

▼▼▼▼
Hotel
$129-$359 All Year

Address: 15920 W Valley Hwy **Location:** I-405, exit 1 (SR 181), just s. Located next to Boeing Longacres Park. **Facility:** 239 units. 238 one- and 1 two-bedroom suites. 8 stories, interior corridors. *Bath:* combo or shower only. **Parking:** on-site. **Terms:** check-in 4 pm, 1-30 night minimum stay, cancellation fee imposed. **Amenities:** dual phone lines, voice mail, irons, hair dryers. *Fee:* video games, high-speed Internet. **Pool(s):** heated indoor. **Leisure Activities:** sauna, whirlpool, exercise room. **Guest Services:** valet and coin laundry, area transportation, wireless Internet. **Business Services:** conference facilities, business center. **Cards:** AX, CB, DC, DS, JC, MC, VI.

E
EMBASSY SUITES
HOTELS•

AAA Benefit:
Members save 5% or
more everyday!

EXTENDED STAYAMERICA-SEATTLE-TUKWILA   *Book at AAA.com*

Phone: (206)244-2537   94

▼▼
Hotel
$85-$100 All Year

Address: 15451 53rd Ave S **Location:** I-5, exit 153 northbound, just n on Southcenter Pkwy, just n on 61st St, just w on Southcenter Blvd, then just sw; exit 154D (Southcenter Mall) southbound, just sw. **Facility:** 96 one-bedroom standard units. 3 stories, exterior corridors. *Bath:* combo or shower only. **Parking:** on-site. **Terms:** office hours 7 am-11 pm, cancellation fee imposed. **Amenities:** high-speed Internet (fee), voice mail, irons. **Guest Services:** coin laundry, wireless Internet. **Cards:** AX, CB, DC, DS, JC, MC, VI.

HAMPTON INN SEATTLE SOUTHCENTER   *Book great rates at AAA.com*

Phone: (425)228-5800   95

AAA SAVE
▼▼▼▼
Hotel
$90-$125 All Year

Address: 7200 S 156th St **Location:** I-405, exit 1 (SR 181), just s. **Facility:** 153 one-bedroom standard units. 4 stories, interior corridors. *Bath:* combo or shower only. **Parking:** on-site. **Terms:** 1-30 night minimum stay, cancellation fee imposed. **Amenities:** voice mail, safes, irons, hair dryers. **Pool(s):** heated outdoor. **Leisure Activities:** whirlpool, exercise room. **Guest Services:** valet and coin laundry, airport transportation-Seattle-Tacoma International Airport, area transportation-within 5 mi, wireless Internet. **Business Services:** meeting rooms, PC. **Cards:** AX, CB, DC, DS, MC, VI. **Free Special Amenities:** expanded continental breakfast and high-speed Internet. *(See color ad below)*

Hampton Inn

AAA Benefit:
Members save up to
10% everyday!

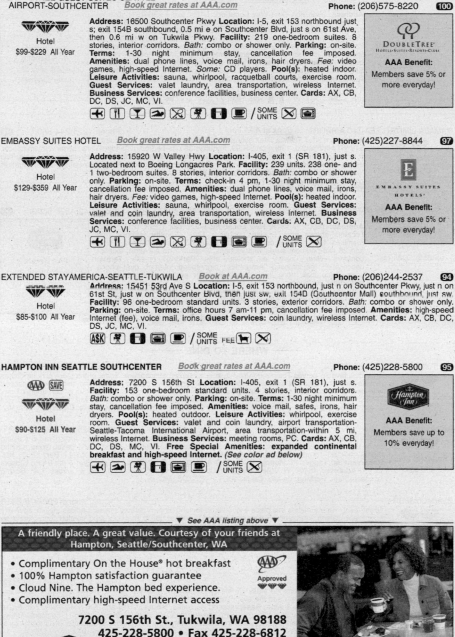

(See map and index starting on p. 614)

HOMEWOOD SUITES BY HILTON   *Book great rates at AAA.com*   Phone: (206)433-8000   **92**

Hotel
$99-$209 All Year

Address: 6955 Fort Dent Way **Location:** I-405, exit 1 (SR 181), just ne. Located in a commercial area. **Facility:** 106 units. 98 one- and 8 two-bedroom suites with efficiencies. 2-3 stories, interior/exterior corridors. **Parking:** on-site. **Terms:** 1-30 night minimum stay, cancellation fee imposed. **Amenities:** video games (fee), high-speed Internet, dual phone lines, voice mail, irons, hair dryers. *Some:* DVD players. **Pool(s):** heated outdoor. **Leisure Activities:** whirlpool, exercise room, sports court. **Guest Services:** valet and coin laundry, area transportation, wireless Internet. **Business Services:** meeting rooms, business center. **Cards:** AX, DC, DS, JC, MC, VI.

AAA Benefit:
Members save 5% or
more everyday!

 / SOME UNITS FEE

RAMADA LIMITED SEA-TAC AIRPORT   *Book at AAA.com*   Phone: (206)244-8800   **91**

Hotel
$90-$100 All Year

Address: 13900 Tukwila International Blvd **Location:** I-5, exit 158 southbound, 2 mi s; exit 154A (SR 518 W) northbound, 1 mi n on SR 99. **Facility:** 38 one-bedroom standard units, some with whirlpools. 2 stories, interior corridors. **Parking:** on-site. **Amenities:** high-speed Internet, voice mail, irons, hair dryers. **Leisure Activities:** exercise room. **Guest Services:** coin laundry, area transportation, wireless Internet. **Business Services:** PC. **Cards:** AX, DS, MC, VI.

ASK / SOME UNITS FEE

RESIDENCE INN BY MARRIOTT-SEATTLE SOUTH   *Book great rates at AAA.com*   Phone: (425)226-5500   **99**

Hotel
$188-$230 All Year

Address: 16201 W Valley Hwy **Location:** I-405, exit 1 (SR 181), just s. Located across from Boeing Longacre Park. **Facility:** Smoke free premises. 144 units. 108 one-bedroom standard units with kitchens. 8 one- and 28 two-bedroom suites with kitchens. 2 stories (no elevator), exterior corridors. *Bath:* combo or shower only. **Parking:** on-site. **Terms:** cancellation fee imposed. **Amenities:** high-speed Internet, dual phone lines, voice mail, irons, hair dryers. **Pool(s):** heated outdoor. **Leisure Activities:** whirlpools, exercise room, sports court, horseshoes. **Guest Services:** valet and coin laundry, area transportation, wireless Internet. **Business Services:** meeting rooms, PC. **Cards:** AX, CB, DC, DS, JC, MC, VI.

AAA Benefit:
Members save a
minimum 5% off the
best available rate.

CALL / SOME UNITS FEE

——— WHERE TO DINE ———

BAI TONG THAI RESTAURANT   Phone: 206/575-3366   **113**

Thai
$7-$14

This local favorite serves Thai food family style in a relaxed atmosphere. Some of the more popular dishes include pad thai (a noodle dish with prawns, chicken and pork), curried chicken and chicken satay topped with peanut sauce. Casual dress. **Bar:** Beer & wine. **Hours:** 11 am-3 & 5-9 pm, Sat & Sun noon-10 pm. Closed: 1/1, 12/25; also 12/31. **Address:** 16876 Southcenter Pkwy **Location:** I-5, exit 153 northbound, just s; exit 154B southbound, 0.5 mi e on Southcenter Blvd, then 1 mi s. **Parking:** on-site. **Cards:** AX, MC, VI.

BARNABY'S   Phone: 425/251-8341   **111**

Traditional Steak
$10-$30

USDA prime beef cuts, including porterhouse, filet mignon and New York strip steaks, are served in a dining room replete with wood, leather and stained-glass accents. Seafood, chicken and pasta round out the menu, as do preparations from the well-stocked salad bar. Casual dress. **Bar:** Full bar. **Reservations:** suggested. **Hours:** 11 am-2:30 & 5-10 pm, Fri & Sat-10:30 pm, Sun 4 pm-9 pm. Closed: 12/25. **Address:** 16401 W Valley Hwy **Location:** I-405, exit 1 (SR 181), just s; across from Boeing Longacre Park. **Parking:** on-site. **Cards:** AX, CB, DC, DS, MC, VI.

CLAIM JUMPER   Phone: 206/575-3918

American
$8-$30

Great menu variety makes this place a good stop for parties with diverse tastes. Choices include specialty appetizers, salads, rotisserie chicken and barbecue items, not to mention good comfort foods, such as traditional pot pie. Hearty portions satisfy big appetites. The atmosphere is fun and lively. Casual dress. **Bar:** Full bar. **Hours:** 11 am-10 pm, Fri & Sat-11 pm. Closed: 7/4, 11/26, 12/25. **Address:** 5901 S 180th St **Location:** At Southcenter Pkwy. **Parking:** on-site. **Cards:** AX, CB, DC, DS, JC, MC, VI.

CALL

MIYABI RESTAURANT   Phone: 206/575-6815   **112**

Japanese
$6-$17

Stenciled rice-paper adorn the walls of this casual eatery and add to the overall ambiance. Staff are attentive and friendly. Visitors to the sushi bar can watch their food being prepared right before their eyes. Casual dress. **Bar:** Beer & wine. **Reservations:** accepted. **Hours:** 11:15 am-2:30 & 4:30-9:30 pm, Fri-10 pm, Sat 4:30 pm-10 pm, Sun 4:30 pm-9 pm. Closed major holidays. **Address:** 16820 Southcenter Pkwy **Location:** I-5, exit 153 northbound, just s; exit 154B southbound, 0.5 mi e on Southcenter Blvd, then 1 mi s. **Parking:** on-site. **Cards:** AX, DS, MC, VI.

NEWPORT BAY RESTAURANT   Phone: 206/575-0446

Seafood
$8-$25

This restaurant is for those seeking a casual, relaxing time. A menu favorite is New England clam chowder, which is available nightly. Fresh Northwest salmon and Alaskan halibut prepared several ways share menu space with pasta, chicken and salads. Casual dress. **Bar:** Full bar. **Hours:** 11 am-11 pm, Fri & Sat-midnight, Sun 9 am-3 pm. Closed: 11/26, 12/25. **Address:** 17920 Southcenter Pkwy **Location:** I-5, exit 153 northbound, just s; exit 154B southbound, 0.5 mi e on Southcenter Blvd, then 1.5 mi s. **Parking:** on-site. **Cards:** AX, DS, MC, VI.

(See map and index starting on p. 614)

STANFORD'S RESTAURANT & BAR

Phone: 206/575-7454

American
$8-$38

Noted for the way it prepares meats—by wood-fire grilling—the eatery sustains an upbeat, high-energy atmosphere. Baby back ribs and seasonal nightly dinner features stand out. Site of a popular happy hour, the full-service lounge lines up extensive beer selections. The location is convenient to Southcenter Mall and movie theaters. Casual dress. **Bar:** Full bar. **Hours:** 11 am-11 pm, Fri & Sat-midnight. Closed: 11/26, 12/25. **Address:** 17380 Southcenter Pkwy **Location:** I-5, exit 153 northbound, just s; exit 154B southbound, 0.5 mi e on Southcenter Blvd, then 1 mi s. **Parking:** on-site. **Cards:** AX, CB, DC, DS, MC, VI.

UNIVERSITY PLACE pop. 29,933

-------- WHERE TO DINE --------

ROUND TABLE PIZZA

Phone: 253/565-3000

Pizza
$4-$8

This casual, family-oriented pizza place features high-quality ingredients and dough rolled fresh daily. Distinctive specialty pizzas are piled high with toppings. Casual dress. **Bar:** Beer & wine. **Reservations:** not accepted. **Hours:** 11 am-10 pm. Closed major holidays. **Address:** 7011 27th St W **Location:** Jct 27th St W and 70th Ave W. **Parking:** on-site.

VASHON pop. 10,123   (See map and index starting on p. 614)

-------- WHERE TO STAY --------

ARTIST'S STUDIO LOFT B&B

Phone: 206/463-2583   125

Bed & Breakfast
$119-$215 All Year

Address: 16529 91st Ave SW **Location:** North end Ferry Landing, 4.2 mi s on Vashon Hwy; south end (Tahlequah) Ferry Landing, 9.4 mi n on Vashon Hwy, 0.5 mi e on Gorsuch Rd, then just n. Located in a country area. **Facility:** Gardens, ponds and meandering paths enhance the five-acre grounds at this nature-oriented B&B; original artwork decorates guest rooms. 5 units. 2 one-bedroom standard units. 3 cottages. 1-2 stories (no elevator), exterior corridors. *Bath:* combo or shower only. **Parking:** on-site. **Terms:** check-in 4 pm, 2 night minimum stay - seasonal and/or weekends, age restrictions may apply, 30 day cancellation notice-fee imposed. **Amenities:** video library, CD players, irons, hair dryers. *Some:* DVD players. **Leisure Activities:** whirlpool. **Cards:** AX, DS, MC, VI.

⊠ 🐾 📺 (VCR) ☎ 🖥 💻 / SOME UNITS 🖨

THE SWALLOW'S NEST GUEST COTTAGES

Phone: 206/463-2646   126

Cottage
Rates not provided

Address: 6030 SW 248th St **Location:** North end Ferry Landing, 7.8 mi s on Vashon Hwy; south end (Tahlequah) Ferry Landing, 5.8 mi n on Vashon Hwy, 1.4 mi e on Quartermaster Dr, 1.5 mi s on Dockton Rd, 0.4 mi s on 75th Ave, then 1 mi e. **Facility:** Smoke free premises. 7 cottages. 1-2 stories, exterior corridors. *Bath:* combo, shower or tub only. **Parking:** on-site. **Terms:** check-in 4 pm. **Amenities:** DVD players. *Some:* CD players, irons, hair dryers. **Leisure Activities:** *Fee:* whirlpool, massage.

⊠ 🐾 📺 (VCR) 🖥 💻 / SOME UNITS FEE 🐾 🖨

WOODINVILLE pop. 9,194   (See map and index starting on p. 614)

-------- WHERE TO STAY --------

-------- *The following lodging was either not evaluated or did not* --------
meet AAA rating requirements but is listed for your information only.

WILLOWS LODGE

Phone: 425/424-3900

fyi

Not evaluated. **Address:** 14580 NE 145th St **Location:** I-405, exit 20B (NE 124th St), 0.9 mi e, 1.3 mi n on 132nd Ave NE, 0.6 mi e on NE 143rd Pl, then just e. Facilities, services, and decor characterize an upscale property.

(See map and index starting on p. 614)

———— WHERE TO DINE ————

BARKING FROG AT WILLOWS LODGE   Phone: 425/424-2999   71

▼▼▼▼
Pacific Rim
$14-$49

Although the food here is delicious, many visit this place primarily for its great setting: a casually elegant, nicely decorated and delightfully laid-back hangout. Casual dress. **Bar:** Full bar. **Reservations:** accepted. **Hours:** 6-10 am, 11:30-2:30 & 5-10 pm, Sat & Sun 6 am-2:30 & 5-10 pm; Saturday & Sunday brunch. **Address:** 14580 NE 145th St **Location:** I-405, exit 20B (NE 124th St), 0.9 mi e, 1.3 mi n on 132nd Ave NE, 0.6 mi e on NE 143rd Pl, then just e; in Willows Lodge. **Parking:** on-site. **Cards:** AX, CB, DC, DS, JC, MC, VI.

THE HERBFARM RESTAURANT   Phone: 425/485-5300   70

AAA
▼▼▼▼▼
Continental
$179-$195

Chefs rely on the freshest, best-available ingredients in the Northwest to create nine-course meals accompanied by five to six paired wines. Meals are given a general theme in advance, but specific menu items are not finalized until a few hours before preparation. Guests should plan to arrive early and join a walking tour of the herb gardens while sipping a glass of lavender lemonade; advance reservations are required for this 4.5- to 5-hour experience. Dressy casual. Entertainment. **Bar:** Wine only. **Reservations:** required. **Hours:** 7 pm seating, Sun 4:30 pm. Closed: Mon-Wed. **Address:** 14590 NE 145th St **Location:** I-405, exit 20B (NE 124th St), 0.9 mi e, 1.3 mi n on 132nd Ave, 0.6 mi e on NE 143rd Pl, then just e. **Parking:** on-site. **Cards:** AX, MC, VI.

RED HOOK BREWERY & FORECASTERS PUB   Phone: 425/483-3232   69

▼▼▼ ▼▼▼
American
$7-$20

A great gathering place to consume comfort food and get re-acquainted with old friends. A large open room with movable tables makes for a high energy venue, and is a hit with larger parties. Foods include clam chowder, burgers, chicken satay and lots of salads. The drink of choice is beer, and at this place it's anything "Red Hook". Casual dress. **Bar:** Beer & wine. **Hours:** 11 am-10 pm, Tues & Thurs-11 pm, Fri & Sat-midnight. Closed: 1/1, 11/26, 12/25. **Address:** 14300 NE 145th St **Location:** I-405, exit 20B (NE 124th St), 0.9 mi e, 1.3 mi n on 132nd Ave, 0.6 mi e on NE 143rd Pl, then just e. **Parking:** on-site. **Cards:** AX, DC, MC, VI.

ROUND TABLE PIZZA   Phone: 425/481-7117

▼▼▼
Pizza
$10-$16

This casual, family-oriented pizza place features high-quality ingredients and dough rolled fresh daily. Distinctive specialty pizzas are piled high with toppings. Casual dress. **Bar:** Beer & wine. **Reservations:** not accepted. **Hours:** 11 am-9:30 pm, Fri & Sat-10 pm, Sun noon-9:30 pm, Mon 11 am-9 pm. Closed major holidays. **Address:** 17600 140th Ave NE **Location:** Just n of NE 175th St. **Parking:** on-site. **Cards:** AX, CB, DC, DS, JC, MC, VI.

Museum of Glass / Tacoma Regional Convention & Visitor Bureau

This ends listings for the Seattle Vicinity.
The following page resumes the alphabetical listings of cities in Washington.

SEAVIEW

—— WHERE TO STAY ——

THE SHELBURNE INN & CHINA BEACH RETREAT
Phone: 360/642-2442

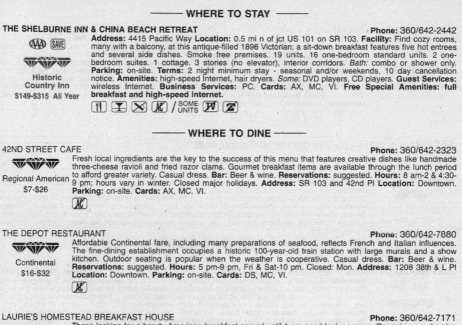

AAA **SAVE**

▼▼▼▼▼

Historic
Country Inn

$149-$315 All Year

Address: 4415 Pacific Way **Location:** 0.5 mi n of jct US 101 on SR 103. **Facility:** Find cozy rooms, many with a balcony, at this antique-filled 1896 Victorian; a sit-down breakfast features five hot entrees and several side dishes. Smoke free premises. 19 units. 16 one-bedroom standard units. 2 one-bedroom suites. 1 cottage. 3 stories (no elevator), interior corridors. *Bath:* combo or shower only. **Parking:** on-site. **Terms:** 2 night minimum stay - seasonal and/or weekends, 10 day cancellation notice. **Amenities:** high-speed Internet, hair dryers. *Some:* DVD players, CD players. **Guest Services:** wireless Internet. **Business Services:** PC. **Cards:** AX, MC, VI. **Free Special Amenities: full breakfast and high-speed Internet.**

🍴 🍸 ⊠ 🅺 / SOME UNITS 🅿 🆉

—— WHERE TO DINE ——

42ND STREET CAFE
Phone: 360/642-2323

▼▼▼

Regional American

$7-$26

Fresh local ingredients are the key to the success of this menu that features creative dishes like handmade three-cheese ravioli and fried razor clams. Gourmet breakfast items are available through the lunch period to afford greater variety. Casual dress. **Bar:** Beer & wine. **Reservations:** suggested. **Hours:** 8 am-2 & 4:30-9 pm; hours vary in winter. Closed major holidays. **Address:** SR 103 and 42nd Pl **Location:** Downtown. **Parking:** on-site. **Cards:** AX, MC, VI.

🅺

THE DEPOT RESTAURANT
Phone: 360/642-7880

▼▼▼

Continental

$16-$32

Affordable Continental fare, including many preparations of seafood, reflects French and Italian influences. The fine-dining establishment occupies a historic 100-year-old train station with large murals and a show kitchen. Outdoor seating is popular when the weather is cooperative. Casual dress. **Bar:** Beer & wine. **Reservations:** suggested. **Hours:** 5 pm-9 pm, Fri & Sat-10 pm. Closed: Mon. **Address:** 1208 38th & L Pl **Location:** Downtown. **Parking:** on-site. **Cards:** DS, MC, VI.

🅺

LAURIE'S HOMESTEAD BREAKFAST HOUSE
Phone: 360/642-7171

▼▼ ▼▼

American

$5-$9

Those looking for a hearty American breakfast served until 1 pm need look no more. Pancakes are the size of dinner plates, hash browns are dished up with a shovel, eggs don't come just in pairs, and most meals require at least two plates just to reach the table. The comfortable spot feels more like grandma's house than a restaurant. Casual dress. **Hours:** 6:30 am-12:45 pm. Closed: 11/26, 12/25. **Address:** 43rd & Pacific Hwy **Location:** Downtown. **Parking:** on-site. **Cards:** MC, VI.

🅺

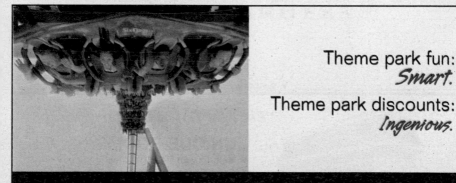

SEDRO-WOOLLEY pop. 8,658

──────── WHERE TO STAY ────────

SOUTH BAY BED AND BREAKFAST @ LAKE WHATCOM

AAA **SAVE**

▼▼▼▼▼

Bed & Breakfast
$165-$185 All Year

Phone: 360/595-2086

Address: 4095 S Bay Dr **Location:** I-5, exit 240, 5.5 mi ne via Lake Samish and Cain Lake rds, then 3.2 mi e. **Facility:** Constructed originally on another site, this B&B was relocated to its present perch on a steep hill overlooking Lake Whatcom. Smoke free premises. 6 one-bedroom standard units, some with whirlpools. 2 stories (no elevator), interior corridors. *Bath:* combo or shower only. **Parking:** on-site. **Terms:** check-in 4 pm, 2 night minimum stay - seasonal and/or weekends, age restrictions may apply, 14 day cancellation notice-fee imposed. **Amenities:** CD players, hair dryers. **Leisure Activities:** canoeing. **Guest Services:** wireless Internet. **Cards:** AX, DS, MC, VI. **Free Special Amenities: continental breakfast and high-speed Internet.**

⊠ 🄿 🅩 / SOME UNITS FEE 🐕 🄰🄲

SEQUIM pop. 4,334—See also OLYMPIC NATIONAL PARK.

──────── WHERE TO STAY ────────

DIAMOND POINT INN BED & BREAKFAST

◈◈ ◈◈

Bed & Breakfast
$114-$149 All Year

Phone: (360)797-7720

Address: 241 Sunshine Rd **Location:** Jct US 101 and SR 20, 8 mi nw on US 101, 0.8 mi n on Diamond Point Rd to Eagle Creek Rd, then just se. **Facility:** Smoke free premises. 4 one-bedroom standard units. 1 story, interior/exterior corridors. *Bath:* combo or shower only. **Parking:** on-site. **Terms:** check-in 4 pm, 14 day cancellation notice-fee imposed. **Amenities:** video library, hair dryers. **Leisure Activities:** whirlpool, bicycles, hiking trails, horseshoes. **Guest Services:** wireless Internet. **Cards:** MC, VI.

🄰🅂🄺 ⊠ ⊠ 🄰🄲 🅩 / SOME UNITS 🄿 🅅🄲🅁 🄸 🄳

JUAN DE FUCA COTTAGES   *Book great rates at AAA.com*

AAA **SAVE**

▼▼▼▼▼

Cottage
$145-$275 6/16-2/28
$99-$235 3/1-6/15

Phone: (360)683-4433

Address: 182 Marine Dr **Location:** From downtown, 7 mi n via Sequim Ave and E Anderson Rd. **Facility:** These fully equipped housekeeping cottages include robes for blustery nights; the property overlooks Dungeness Spit and the Strait of Juan de Fuca. 9 units. 3 one-bedroom standard units. 1 one-bedroom suite with kitchen. 5 cottages. 1 story, exterior corridors. *Bath:* combo or shower only. **Parking:** on-site. **Terms:** office hours 10 am-5 pm, 14 day cancellation notice-fee imposed. **Amenities:** video library, CD players, high-speed Internet, irons, hair dryers. **Leisure Activities:** beach access. *Fee:* kayaks. **Guest Services:** wireless Internet. **Business Services:** meeting rooms. **Cards:** DS, MC, VI. **Free Special Amenities: room upgrade (subject to availability with advance reservations) and high-speed Internet.**

⊠ 🄰🄲 🅅🄲🅁 🅩 🄸 🖥 🄳 / SOME UNITS FEE 🐕

QUALITY INN & SUITES - SEQUIM   *Book great rates at AAA.com*

AAA **SAVE**

▼▼▼▼▼

Hotel
$80-$180 All Year

Phone: (360)683-2800

Address: 134 River Rd **Location:** US 101, exit River Rd, just nw. **Facility:** 60 one-bedroom standard units, some with whirlpools. 3 stories, interior corridors. *Bath:* combo or shower only. **Parking:** on-site. **Terms:** check-in 4 pm, 2 night minimum stay - seasonal and/or weekends, cancellation fee imposed. **Amenities:** high-speed Internet, voice mail, irons, hair dryers. **Pool(s):** heated indoor. **Leisure Activities:** whirlpool, limited exercise equipment. **Guest Services:** coin laundry, wireless Internet. **Business Services:** meeting rooms, business center. **Cards:** AX, CB, DC, DS, JC, MC, VI. **Free Special Amenities: expanded continental breakfast and high-speed Internet.**

🍴 🏊 ⊠ 🄿 🄸 🖥 🄳 / SOME UNITS FEE 🐕

────── ▼ See AAA listing p 719 ▼ ──────

SEQUIM WEST INN

AAA SAVE

◈◈◈
◈◈◈

Motel

$54-$125 All Year

Phone: 360/683-4144

Address: 740 W Washington St **Location:** US 101, exit River Rd, 0.9 mi ne via River Rd and W Washington St. **Facility:** 36 units. 21 one- and 4 two-bedroom standard units. 11 cottages. 2 stories (no elevator), exterior corridors. **Parking:** on-site. **Terms:** office hours 7 am-11 pm, 3 day cancellation notice. **Amenities:** hair dryers. **Guest Services:** coin laundry. **Cards:** AX, DS, MC, VI. *(See color ad p 718)*

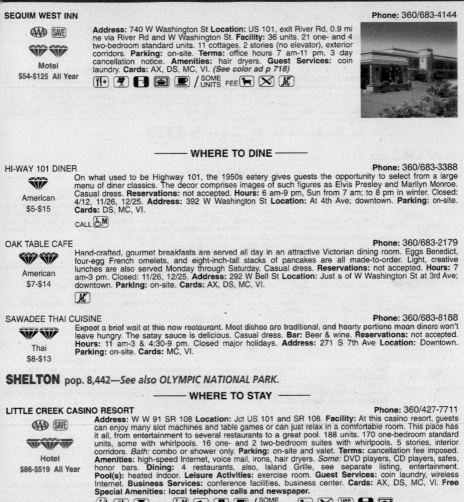

--------- **WHERE TO DINE** ---------

HI-WAY 101 DINER

◈◈◈

American

$5-$15

Phone: 360/683-3388

On what used to be Highway 101, the 1950s eatery gives guests the opportunity to select from a large menu of diner classics. The decor comprises images of such figures as Elvis Presley and Marilyn Monroe. Casual dress. **Reservations:** not accepted. **Hours:** 6 am-9 pm, Sun from 7 am; to 8 pm in winter. Closed: 4/12, 11/26, 12/25. **Address:** 392 W Washington St **Location:** At 4th Ave; downtown. **Parking:** on-site. **Cards:** DS, MC, VI.

OAK TABLE CAFE

◈◈◈

American

$7-$14

Phone: 360/683-2179

Hand-crafted, gourmet breakfasts are served all day in an attractive Victorian dining room. Eggs Benedict, four-egg French omelets, and eight-inch-tall stacks of pancakes are all made-to-order. Light, creative lunches are also served Monday through Saturday. Casual dress. **Reservations:** not accepted. **Hours:** 7 am-3 pm. Closed: 11/26, 12/25. **Address:** 292 W Bell St **Location:** Just s of W Washington St at 3rd Ave; downtown. **Parking:** on-site. **Cards:** AX, DS, MC, VI.

SAWADEE THAI CUISINE

◈◈◈

Thai

$8-$13

Phone: 360/683-8188

Expect a brief wait at this new restaurant. Most dishes are traditional, and hearty portions mean diners won't leave hungry. The satay sauce is delicious. Casual dress. **Bar:** Beer & wine. **Reservations:** not accepted. **Hours:** 11 am-3 & 4:30-9 pm. Closed major holidays. **Address:** 271 S 7th Ave **Location:** Downtown. **Parking:** on-site. **Cards:** MC, VI.

SHELTON pop. 8,442—See also OLYMPIC NATIONAL PARK.

--------- **WHERE TO STAY** ---------

LITTLE CREEK CASINO RESORT

AAA SAVE

◈◈◈

Hotel

$86-$519 All Year

Phone: 360/427-7711

Address: W W 91 SR 108 **Location:** Jct US 101 and SR 108. **Facility:** At this casino resort, guests can enjoy many slot machines and table games or can just relax in a comfortable room. This place has it all, from entertainment to several restaurants to a great pool. 188 units. 170 one-bedroom standard units, some with whirlpools. 16 one- and 2 two-bedroom suites with whirlpools. 5 stories, interior corridors. *Bath:* combo or shower only. **Parking:** on-site and valet. **Terms:** cancellation fee imposed. **Amenities:** high-speed Internet, voice mail, irons, hair dryers. *Some:* DVD players, CD players, safes, honor bars. **Dining:** 4 restaurants, also, Island Grille, see separate listing, entertainment. **Pool(s):** heated indoor. **Leisure Activities:** exercise room. **Guest Services:** coin laundry, wireless Internet. **Business Services:** conference facilities, business center. **Cards:** AX, DS, MC, VI. **Free Special Amenities: local telephone calls and newspaper.**

SUPER 8 MOTEL OF SHELTON   *Book at AAA.com.*

◈◈◈

Hotel

Rates not provided

Phone: 360/426-1654

Address: 2943 Northview Cir **Location:** US 101, exit Wallace-Kneeland Blvd, just se. **Facility:** 39 one-bedroom standard units. 2 stories (no elevator), interior corridors. **Parking:** on-site. **Amenities:** high-speed Internet, voice mail, hair dryers. **Guest Services:** wireless Internet.

--------- **WHERE TO DINE** ---------

ISLAND GRILLE

◈◈◈

American

$6-$25

Phone: 360/427-7711

A nice quiet place to come and sit after a hectic run of playing the slots or gaming tables of the adjoining casino, the restaurant plies patrons with breaded crab cakes or maybe a nice steak and a slice of chocolate cake. Casual dress. **Bar:** Full bar. **Reservations:** not accepted. **Hours:** 6:30 am-10 pm. **Address:** W 91 SR 108 **Location:** Jct US 101 and SR 108; in Little Creek Casino Resort. **Parking:** on-site and valet. **Cards:** AX, DS, MC, VI.

SHORELINE —See Seattle p. 705.

SILVERDALE —See Seattle p. 705.

SNOHOMISH —See Seattle p. 706.

SNOQUALMIE —See Seattle p. 706.

SNOQUALMIE PASS

──────── WHERE TO STAY ────────

SUMMIT LODGE AT SNOQUALMIE PASS   *Book at AAA.com*   **Phone:** (425)434-6300
▽▽ ▽▽
Hotel
$119-$279 All Year
Address: 603 SR 906 **Location:** I-90, exit 52 eastbound, 0.3 mi e; exit 53 westbound, 0.3 mi w. Located in a rural area. **Facility:** Smoke free premises. 81 units. 79 one-bedroom standard units. 2 one-bedroom suites, some with kitchens. 2 stories, interior corridors. **Parking:** on-site. **Terms:** check-in 5 pm, 3 day cancellation notice-fee imposed. **Amenities:** irons, hair dryers. **Pool(s):** heated outdoor. **Leisure Activities:** sauna, whirlpool. **Guest Services:** coin laundry, wireless Internet. **Business Services:** meeting rooms, PC. **Cards:** AX, MC, VI.

ASK ❙❙ ⬛ 🏊 ✕ 🖥 / SOME UNITS FEE 🛏 📱 🖨

SOAP LAKE pop. 1,733

──────── WHERE TO STAY ────────

INN AT SOAP LAKE   **Phone:** 509/246-1132
▽▽▽▽
Motel
$59-$125 All Year
Address: 226 E Main Ave **Location:** Just w of SR 17. **Facility:** Smoke free premises. 29 units. 25 one-bedroom standard units, some with efficiencies and/or whirlpools. 4 one-bedroom suites with kitchens, some with whirlpools. 1-3 stories (no elevator), interior/exterior corridors. *Bath:* combo or shower only. **Parking:** on-site. **Terms:** office hours 8 am-10 pm. **Amenities:** video library, voice mail, hair dryers. *Some:* DVD players. **Leisure Activities:** exercise room, horseshoes, volleyball. **Guest Services:** wireless Internet. **Business Services:** PC. **Cards:** AX, DS, MC, VI.

❙❙+ ✕ ✕ 🖥 / SOME UNITS 🛏 FEE VCR 📱 🖨

NOTARAS LODGE   **Phone:** 509/246-0462
▽▽▽▽
Motel
$65-$135 All Year
Address: 236 E Main Ave **Location:** Just w of SR 17. **Facility:** 15 units. 13 one- and 1 two-bedroom standard units, some with efficiencies and/or whirlpools. 1 two-bedroom suite with kitchen and whirlpool. 1-2 stories (no elevator), exterior corridors. **Parking:** on-site. **Terms:** office hours 7:30 am-5 pm, check-in 4 pm. **Amenities:** irons, hair dryers. **Leisure Activities:** *Fee:* massage. **Guest Services:** wireless Internet. **Cards:** DS, MC, VI.

❙❙+ 📱 🖨 🖥 / SOME UNITS FEE 🛏 ✕ VCR

──────── WHERE TO DINE ────────

DON'S RESTAURANT   **Phone:** 509/246-1217
▽▽ ▽▽
Steak & Seafood
$6-$24
Family owned-and -operated for three generations, this restaurant sits a block from Soap Lake. The menu features lamb chops, prime rib, seafood, pasta and a special Greek cuisine served Monday evening and Friday for lunch. Casual dress. **Bar:** Full bar. **Hours:** 11 am-9:30 pm, Sat 4 pm-10 pm, Sun noon-9 pm. Closed: 12/25; also Tues off season. **Address:** 14 Canna St N **Location:** Just w of SR 17 off Main St. **Parking:** on-site. **Cards:** DS, MC, VI.

SOUTH BEND pop. 1,807

──────── WHERE TO STAY ────────

THE RUSSELL HOUSE   **Phone:** 360/875-6487
▽▽▽▽
Historic Bed
& Breakfast
$100-$250 All Year
Address: 902 E Water St **Location:** 0.5 mi s on Harrison St. **Facility:** Fully restored guest rooms and bathrooms with such period fixtures as claw foot tubs are characteristics of this 1891 Queen Anne home. Smoke free premises. 7 one-bedroom standard units. 3 stories (no elevator), interior corridors. *Bath:* some shared or private, combo or shower only. **Parking:** on-site. **Terms:** check-in 4 pm, 5 day cancellation notice-fee imposed. **Amenities:** *Some:* hair dryers. **Guest Services:** wireless Internet. **Cards:** AX, DS, MC, VI.

ASK ✕ 🎿 / SOME UNITS 📺 🆓

SOUTH CLE ELUM pop. 500

──────── WHERE TO STAY ────────

IRON HORSE INN B & B   **Phone:** 509/674-5939
▽▽▽▽
Bed & Breakfast
$80-$145 All Year
Address: 526 Marie Ave **Location:** I-90, exit 84, 1.5 mi s; exit 1st St onto S Cle Elum Way via Madison Ave and 6th St. **Facility:** Designated smoking area. 11 units. 10 one-bedroom standard units, some with whirlpools. 1 one-bedroom suite with whirlpool. 1-2 stories (no elevator), interior/exterior corridors. *Bath:* some shared or private, combo, shower or tub only. **Parking:** on-site. **Terms:** check-in 4 pm, 7 day cancellation notice-fee imposed. **Leisure Activities:** whirlpool, cross country skiing, bicycles, hiking trails, jogging, horseshoes. **Cards:** MC, VI.

ASK CALL &M ✕ ✕ 🆓 / SOME UNITS 🎿 📺 📱 🖨

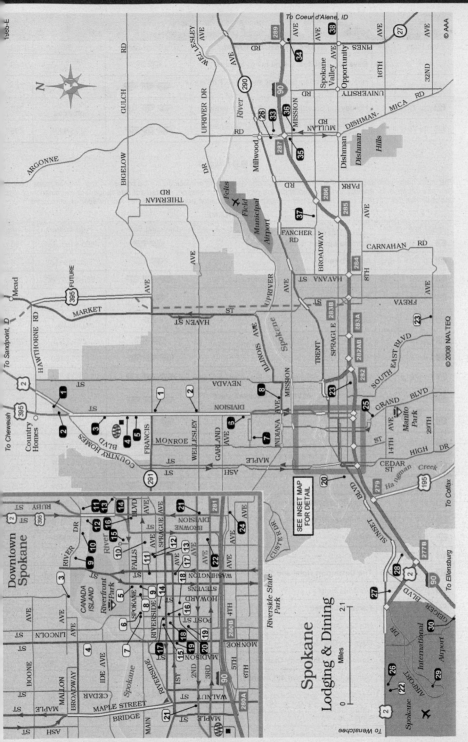

✈ Airport Accommodations

Map Page	OA	SPOKANE INTERNATIONAL	Diamond Rated	High Season	Page
N/A	AAA	Days Inn & Suites, 2.4 mi nw of terminal	◈◈	Rates not provided SAVE	520
26 / p. 721	AAA	Hilton Garden Inn Spokane Airport, 0.7 mi n of terminal	◈◈◈	$129-$209 SAVE	727
27 / p. 721		Holiday Inn Spokane Airport, 3 mi e of terminal	◈◈◈	Rates not provided	728
29 / p. 721		Ramada Spokane Airport & Indoor Waterpark, at airport	◈◈◈	$125-$130	730

Spokane

This index helps you "spot" where approved lodgings and restaurants are located on the corresponding detailed maps. Lodging daily rate range is for comparison only and show the property's high season. Restaurant rate range is a combination of lunch and/or dinner. Turn to the listing page for more detailed rate information and consult display ads for special promotions.

SPOKANE

Map Page	OA	Lodgings	Diamond Rated	High Season	Page
1 / p. 721	AAA	Ramada Limited Suites	◈◈	$80-$150 SAVE	730
2 / p. 721	AAA	Apple Tree Inn	◈◈	$59-$69 SAVE	724
3 / p. 721	AAA	Quality Inn Oakwood - see color ad p 730	◈◈◈	$89-$159 SAVE	730
4 / p. 721		Comfort Inn North	◈◈	Rates not provided	724
5 / p. 721		Liberty Motel	◈	Rates not provided	728
6 / p. 721		Howard Johnson Inn North	◈◈	$61-$275	728
7 / p. 721		Waverly Place Bed & Breakfast	◈◈◈	$105-$150	732
8 / p. 721		Marianna Stoltz House Bed & Breakfast	◈◈◈	Rates not provided	729
9 / p. 721	AAA	Red Lion Hotel at the Park-Spokane - see color ad p 731	◈◈◈	$199 SAVE	731
10 / p. 721		Oxford Suites-Downtown Spokane	◈◈◈	Rates not provided	729
11 / p. 721	AAA	Red Lion River Inn-Spokane - see color ad p 731	◈◈◈	$175 SAVE	731
12 / p. 721		Holiday Inn Express-Downtown	◈◈◈	Rates not provided	728
13 / p. 721		Courtyard by Marriott	◈◈◈	$139-$159	725
14 / p. 721		Fairfield Inn by Marriott	◈◈◈	$119-$129	726
15 / p. 721	AAA	Doubletree Hotel Spokane City Center	◈◈◈	$124-$234 SAVE	726
16 / p. 721		Travelodge	◈◈	$89-$109	732
17 / p. 721		Hotel Lusso	◈◈◈	$159-$300	728
18 / p. 721	AAA	The Davenport Hotel and Tower	◈◈◈◈	$169-$319 SAVE	725
19 / p. 721		Montvale Hotel	◈◈◈	$139-$179	729
20 / p. 721	AAA	Ramada Limited	◈◈	$65-$150 SAVE	730
21 / p. 721		Howard Johnson Inn	◈◈	$119-$199	728
22 / p. 721		Days Inn City Center	◈◈	$59-$99	725
23 / p. 721	AAA	Comfort Inn University District/Downtown	◈◈	$89-$130 SAVE	724
24 / p. 721	AAA	Quality Inn Downtown 4th Avenue	◈◈	$79-$199 SAVE	730
25 / p. 721	AAA	Madison Inn - see color ad p 728	◈◈	$75-$90 SAVE	729
26 / p. 721	AAA	Hilton Garden Inn Spokane Airport - see color ad p 727	◈◈◈	$129-$209 SAVE	727

SPOKANE (cont'd)

Map Page	OA	Lodgings (cont'd)	Diamond Rated	High Season	Page
27 / p. 721		Holiday Inn Spokane Airport	◇◇◇	Rates not provided	728
28 / p. 721	AAA	**Hampton Inn Spokane - see color ad p 727**	◇◇◇	$69-$179 SAVE	727
29 / p. 721		Ramada Spokane Airport & Indoor Waterpark	◇◇◇	$125-$130	730
30 / p. 721	AAA	**Best Western Peppertree Airport Inn**	◇◇◇	$89-$219 SAVE	724

Map Page	OA	Restaurants	Diamond Rated	Cuisine	Meal Range	Page
1 / p. 721		Tomato Street	◇◇	Italian	$8-$18	735
2 / p. 721		The Mustard Seed Asian Cafe	◇◇	International	$7-$12	734
3 / p. 721		Clinkerdagger	◇◇◇	American	$8-$25	733
4 / p. 721	AAA	**Milford's Fish House**	◇◇◇	Seafood	$22-$30	733
5 / p. 721		O'Doherty's Irish Grill	◇◇	Irish	$5-$12	734
6 / p. 721		Rock City Grill	◇◇	International	$6-$20	734
7 / p. 721		Sawtooth Grill	◇◇	American	$9-$20	734
8 / p. 721		Mizuna Restaurant & Wine Bar	◇◇	International	$7-$30	734
9 / p. 721		Cyrus O'Leary's	◇◇	American	$9-$19	733
10 / p. 721		Luigi's	◇◇◇	Italian	$6-$20	733
11 / p. 721		Herbal Essence Cafe	◇◇	American	$6-$25	733
12 / p. 721		The Onion	◇◇	American	$6-$20	734
13 / p. 721		Italian Kitchen	◇◇	Italian	$7-$24	733
14 / p. 721		Niko's Greek Restaurant & Wine Bar	◇◇	Greek	$16-$30	734
15 / p. 721		Moxie	◇◇◇	American	$7-$35	734
16 / p. 721		Fugazzi	◇◇	International	$18-$29	733
17 / p. 721		Thai on 1st	◇◇	Thai	$8-$14	734
18 / p. 721		Europa Pizzaria & Bakery	◇◇◇	Italian	$7-$18	733
19 / p. 721		Steam Plant Grill	◇◇◇	American	$6-$30	734
20 / p. 721		Elk Public House	◇◇	American	$7-$12	733
21 / p. 721		Frank's Diner	◇	American	$7-$12	733
22 / p. 721		The Rusty Moose Bar & Grill	◇◇	American	$9-$22	734
23 / p. 721		Vin Rouge	◇◇◇	American	$7-$26	735

SPOKANE VALLEY

Map Page	OA	Lodgings	Diamond Rated	High Season	Page
33 / p. 721		Super 8 Motel	◇◇	$70-$92	737
34 / p. 721	AAA	**Pheasant Hill Inn & Suites - see color ad p 729**	◇◇◇	$80-$190 SAVE	736
35 / p. 721		Quality Inn Valley Suites	◇◇◇	$89-$129	736
36 / p. 721		Holiday Inn Express-Valley	◇◇◇	$129-$209	735
37 / p. 721	AAA	**Rodeway Inn & Suites**	◇◇	$49-$129 SAVE	737
38 / p. 721		Crossland Studios-Spokane Valley	◇	$59-$74	735

Map Page	OA	Restaurant	Diamond Rated	Cuisine	Meal Range	Page
26 / p. 721		Longhorn Barbecue	◇	American	$5-$15	737

SPOKANE pop. 195,629 (See map and index starting on p. 721)

─── WHERE TO STAY ───

APPLE TREE INN

(AAA) **[SAVE]**
♦♦♦ ♦♦♦
Motel
$59-$69 3/1-9/30
$49-$59 10/1-2/28

Book great rates at AAA.com

Phone: (509)466-3020 **2**

Address: 9508 N Division St **Location:** Jct US 2 and 395, just n. **Facility:** 71 units. 53 one- and 18 two-bedroom standard units, some with kitchens. 2 stories (no elevator), interior/exterior corridors. **Parking:** on-site, winter plug-ins. **Amenities:** hair dryers. *Some:* high-speed Internet. **Pool(s):** heated outdoor. **Guest Services:** coin laundry, wireless Internet. **Business Services:** PC. **Cards:** AX, DS, MC, VI. **Free Special Amenities: continental breakfast and high-speed Internet.**

BEST WESTERN PEPPERTREE AIRPORT INN

(AAA) **[SAVE]**
♦♦♦ ♦♦♦
Hotel
$89-$219 All Year

Book great rates at AAA.com

Phone: (509)624-4655 **30**

Address: 3711 S Geiger Blvd **Location:** I-90, exit 276, just n. **Facility:** Smoke free premises. 100 one-bedroom standard units, some with whirlpools. 3 stories, interior corridors. *Bath:* combo or shower only. **Parking:** on-site. **Amenities:** high-speed Internet, voice mail, irons, hair dryers. **Pool(s):** heated indoor. **Leisure Activities:** whirlpool, exercise room. *Fee:* massage. **Guest Services:** coin laundry, airport transportation-Spokane International Airport, wireless Internet. **Business Services:** business center. **Cards:** AX, DS, MC, VI. **Free Special Amenities: continental breakfast and high-speed Internet.**

AAA Benefit:
Members save up to 20%, plus 10% bonus points with rewards program.

COMFORT INN NORTH

♦♦♦ ♦♦♦
Hotel
Rates not provided

Book at AAA.com

Phone: 509/467-7111 **4**

Address: 7111 N Division St **Location:** I-90, exit 281 (Division St), 4.6 mi n. Located in a busy commercial area. **Facility:** 96 one-bedroom standard units, some with efficiencies and/or whirlpools. 3 stories (no elevator), interior corridors. **Parking:** on-site. **Terms:** check-in 4 pm. **Amenities:** irons, hair dryers. **Pool(s):** heated outdoor. **Leisure Activities:** sauna, whirlpool, exercise room. *Fee:* game room. **Guest Services:** valet and coin laundry, wireless Internet. **Business Services:** PC.

COMFORT INN UNIVERSITY DISTRICT/DOWNTOWN

(AAA) **[SAVE]**
♦♦♦ ♦♦♦
Hotel
$89-$130 All Year

Book great rates at AAA.com **Phone:** (509)535-9000 **23**

Address: 923 E 3rd Ave **Location:** I-90, exit 281 (Division St), just n to E 3rd Ave, then 0.7 mi e. **Facility:** 105 one-bedroom standard units. 5 stories, interior corridors. *Bath:* combo or shower only. **Parking:** on-site. **Amenities:** voice mail, irons, hair dryers. **Pool(s):** heated indoor. **Leisure Activities:** exercise room. **Guest Services:** valet and coin laundry, area transportation-Amtrak station, bus depot, hospitals, wireless Internet. **Business Services:** meeting rooms, business center. **Cards:** AX, DC, DS, JC, MC, VI. **Free Special Amenities: continental breakfast and high-speed Internet.**

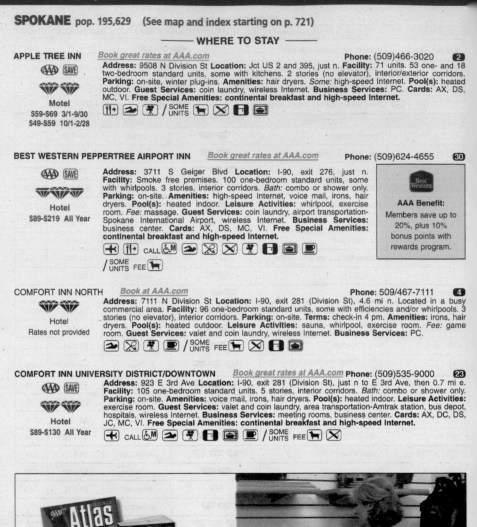

See map and index starting on p. 721)

COURTYARD BY MARRIOTT *Book great rates at AAA.com* **Phone:** (509)456-7600 **13**

Hotel
$139-$159 All Year

Address: 401 N Riverpoint Blvd **Location:** I-90, exit 281 (Division St), 0.6 mi n. **Facility:** Smoke free premises. 149 units. 137 one-bedroom standard units. 12 one-bedroom suites. 3 stories, interior corridors. *Bath:* combo or shower only. **Parking:** on-site. **Terms:** cancellation fee imposed. **Amenities:** high-speed Internet, voice mail, irons, hair dryers. **Pool(s):** heated indoor. **Leisure Activities:** whirlpool, exercise room. **Guest Services:** valet and coin laundry, wireless Internet. **Business Services:** meeting rooms, business center. **Cards:** AX, CB, DC, DS, MC, VI.

CALL

AAA Benefit:
Members save a minimum 5% off the best available rate.

THE DAVENPORT HOTEL AND TOWER *Book great rates at AAA.com* **Phone:** (509)455-8888 **18**

AAA SAVE

Classic Historic Hotel
$169-$319 All Year

Address: 10 S Post St **Location:** Downtown. **Facility:** Known as "The Grand Old Lady" of historic hotels, The Davenport, built in 1914, has been restored to all its original and impressive glory. Smoke free premises. 611 units. 564 one-bedroom standard units. 44 one-, 1 two- and 2 three-bedroom suites, some with whirlpools. 13-21 stories, interior corridors. *Bath:* combo or shower only. **Parking:** on-site (fee) and valet. **Terms:** check-in 4 pm, cancellation fee imposed. **Amenities:** high-speed Internet, dual phone lines, voice mail, safes, irons, hair dryers. *Some:* DVD players, CD players. **Dining:** 4 restaurants. **Pool(s):** 2 heated indoor. **Leisure Activities:** sauna, whirlpools, spa. **Guest Services:** valet laundry, airport transportation (fee)-Spokane International Airport, area transportation-within 2 mi, wireless Internet. **Business Services:** conference facilities, business center. **Cards:** AX, CB, DC, DS, JC, MC, VI. **Free Special Amenities: newspaper and high-speed Internet.**

FEE 24 CALL / SOME UNITS

DAYS INN CITY CENTER *Book at AAA.com* **Phone:** (509)747-2011 **22**

Hotel
$59-$99 5/1-2/28
$54-$79 3/1-4/30

Address: 120 W 3rd Ave **Location:** I-90, exit 281 (Division St), just n, then just w on 2nd Ave. **Facility:** 89 one-bedroom standard units. 2 stories (no elevator), exterior corridors. **Parking:** on-site. **Amenities:** irons, hair dryers. **Pool(s):** heated outdoor. **Guest Services:** wireless Internet. **Business Services:** PC. **Cards:** AX, DC, DS, MC, VI.

ASK / SOME UNITS FEE

▼ See AAA listing p 562 ▼

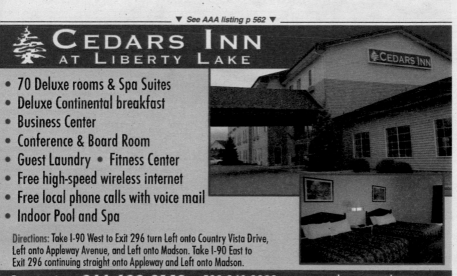

(See map and index starting on p. 721)

DOUBLETREE HOTEL SPOKANE CITY CENTER *Book great rates at AAA.com* Phone: (509)455-9600

Hotel
$124-$234 All Year

Address: 322 N Spokane Falls Ct **Location:** I-90, exit 281 (Division St), just n; downtown. Adjacent to the Ag Trade Center and Opera House. **Facility:** 375 units. 369 one-bedroom standard units. 6 one-bedroom suites, some with whirlpools. 12 stories, interior corridors. *Bath:* combo or shower only. **Parking:** on-site (fee) and valet. **Terms:** 1-30 night minimum stay, cancellation fee imposed. **Amenities:** video games (fee), voice mail, irons, hair dryers. *Some:* dual phone lines. **Dining:** 2 restaurants. **Pool(s):** heated outdoor. **Leisure Activities:** sauna, whirlpool, exercise room. **Guest Services:** valet laundry, wireless Internet. **Business Services:** conference facilities, business center. **Cards:** AX, CB, DC, DS, JC, MC, VI.

DOUBLETREE
HOTELS·SUITES·RESORTS·CLUBS

AAA Benefit:
Members save 5% or
more everyday!

FAIRFIELD INN BY MARRIOTT *Book great rates at AAA.com* Phone: (509)747-9131

Hotel
$119-$129 All Year

Address: 311 N Riverpoint Blvd **Location:** I-90, exit 281 (Division St), 0.6 mi n; downtown. **Facility:** Smoke free premises. 86 one-bedroom standard units. 4 stories, interior corridors. *Bath:* combo or shower only. **Parking:** on-site. **Terms:** cancellation fee imposed. **Amenities:** voice mail, irons, hair dryers. **Pool(s):** heated indoor. **Leisure Activities:** whirlpool, exercise room. **Guest Services:** valet and coin laundry, wireless Internet. **Business Services:** business center. **Cards:** AX, CB, DC, DS, JC, MC, VI.

FAIRFIELD
INN
Marriott

AAA Benefit:
Members save a
minimum 5% off the
best available rate.

(See map and index starting on p. 721)

HAMPTON INN SPOKANE   *Book great rates at AAA.com*   Phone: (509)747-1100   28

Hotel
$69-$179 All Year

Address: 2010 S Assembly Rd **Location:** I-90, exit 277A eastbound, 1 mi ne to Sunset Hwy, just w to Assembly Rd, then just s; exit 277 westbound, just e to Rustle St, just n to Sunset Hwy, just w to Assembly Rd, then just s. **Facility:** 129 units. 123 one-bedroom standard units. 6 one-bedroom suites with whirlpools. 3 stories, interior corridors. **Parking:** on-site, winter plug-ins. **Terms:** check-in 4 pm, 1-30 night minimum stay, cancellation fee imposed. **Amenities:** video games (fee), high-speed Internet, voice mail, irons, hair dryers. **Pool(s):** heated indoor. **Leisure Activities:** whirlpool, exercise room. **Guest Services:** valet and coin laundry, airport transportation-Spokane International Airport, wireless Internet. **Business Services:** meeting rooms, business center. **Cards:** AX, CB, DC, DS, MC, VI. **Free Special Amenities: expanded continental breakfast and high-speed Internet.** *(See color ad below)*

AAA Benefit:
Members save up to 10% everyday!

HILTON GARDEN INN SPOKANE AIRPORT   *Book great rates at AAA.com*   Phone: (509)244-5866   26

Hotel
$129-$209 All Year

Address: 9015 W US 2 **Location:** I-90, exit 277B eastbound; exit 277 westbound, 3 mi w. **Facility:** 120 one-bedroom standard units. 3 stories, interior corridors. *Bath:* combo or shower only. **Parking:** on-site. **Terms:** check-in 4 pm, 1-30 night minimum stay, cancellation fee imposed. **Amenities:** video games (fee), high-speed Internet, dual phone lines, voice mail, irons, hair dryers. **Pool(s):** heated indoor. **Leisure Activities:** whirlpool, exercise room. **Guest Services:** valet and coin laundry, wireless Internet. **Business Services:** meeting rooms, business center. **Cards:** AX, CB, DC, DS, JC, MC, VI. **Free Special Amenities: full breakfast and high-speed Internet.** *(See color ad below)*

AAA Benefit:
Members save 5% or more everyday!

▼ See AAA listing above ▼

(See map and index starting on p. 721)

HOLIDAY INN EXPRESS-DOWNTOWN *Book at AAA.com*
Hotel
Rates not provided

Phone: 509/328-8505 **12**

Address: 801 N Division St **Location:** I-90, exit 281 (Division St), 0.8 mi n. **Facility:** Smoke free premises. 119 units. 116 one-bedroom standard units, some with whirlpools. 3 one-bedroom suites with whirlpools. 4 stories, interior/exterior corridors. *Bath:* combo or shower only. **Parking:** on-site, winter plug-ins. **Amenities:** high-speed Internet, voice mail, irons, hair dryers. **Leisure Activities:** exercise room. **Guest Services:** valet laundry, wireless Internet. **Business Services:** business center.

CALL 🚹Ⓜ ✕ 🛢 🖼 💻 / SOME UNITS 🐕

HOLIDAY INN SPOKANE AIRPORT *Book at AAA.com*
Hotel
Rates not provided

Phone: 509/838-1170 **27**

Address: 1616 S Windsor Dr **Location:** I-90, exit 277 westbound; exit 277B eastbound, just w on US 2, then just s. **Facility:** Smoke free premises. 122 one-bedroom standard units. 4 stories, interior corridors. *Bath:* combo or shower only. **Parking:** on-site. **Amenities:** video games (fee), high-speed Internet, dual phone lines, voice mail, irons, hair dryers. **Pool(s):** heated indoor. **Leisure Activities:** whirlpool, exercise room. **Guest Services:** coin laundry, area transportation, wireless Internet. **Business Services:** conference facilities, business center.

✈ 🍽 🍸 CALL 🚹Ⓜ 🛁 ✕ 🎦 🛢 🖼 💻 / SOME UNITS FEE 🐕

HOTEL LUSSO *Book at AAA.com*
Historic Boutique Hotel
$159-$300 All Year

Phone: (509)747-9750 **17**

Address: North One Post **Location:** Downtown. **Facility:** The unique and quietly elegant boutique-style hotel in the heart of the downtown area is a favorite of business travelers and tourists alike. Smoke free premises. 48 one-bedroom standard units, some with whirlpools. 5 stories, interior corridors. **Parking:** valet. **Terms:** cancellation fee imposed. **Amenities:** voice mail, honor bars, irons, hair dryers. *Some:* CD players, dual phone lines. **Dining:** Fugazzi, see separate listing. **Leisure Activities:** massage. **Guest Services:** valet laundry, area transportation, wireless Internet. **Business Services:** meeting rooms, PC. **Cards:** AX, DC, DS, MC, VI.

ASK 🍽 🍸 FEE 🛁 ✕ 🎦 💻 / SOME UNITS 🛢

HOWARD JOHNSON INN *Book at AAA.com*
Hotel
$119-$199 All Year

Phone: (509)838-6630 **21**

Address: 211 S Division St **Location:** I-90, exit 281 (Division St), just n. **Facility:** 79 one-bedroom standard units. 4 stories, interior corridors. *Bath:* combo or shower only. **Parking:** on-site, winter plug-ins. **Amenities:** high-speed Internet, voice mail, safes (fee), irons, hair dryers. **Leisure Activities:** exercise room. **Guest Services:** valet and coin laundry, wireless Internet. **Business Services:** meeting rooms. **Cards:** AX, DC, DS, MC, VI.

ASK 🍽 🎦 💻 / SOME UNITS FEE 🐕 ✕ 🛢 🖼

HOWARD JOHNSON INN NORTH *Book great rates at AAA.com*
Motel
$61-$275 3/1-9/7
$61-$130 9/8-2/28

Phone: (509)326-5500 **6**

Address: 3033 N Division St **Location:** I-90, exit 281 (Division St), 2.3 mi n on US 2 and 395. **Facility:** Smoke free premises. 61 one-bedroom standard units. 2 stories (no elevator), interior corridors. **Parking:** on-site. **Terms:** cancellation fee imposed. **Amenities:** voice mail, irons, hair dryers. *Some:* DVD players. **Pool(s):** heated indoor. **Leisure Activities:** whirlpool, exercise room. **Guest Services:** coin laundry, wireless Internet. **Business Services:** meeting rooms, PC. **Cards:** AX, CB, DC, DS, JC, MC, VI.

ASK 🍽 🚲 ✕ 🎦 🛢 🖼 💻 / SOME UNITS 🐕 VCR

LIBERTY MOTEL
Motel
Rates not provided

Phone: 509/467-6000 **5**

Address: 6801 N Division St **Location:** I-90, exit 281 (Division St), 4.4 mi n. **Facility:** 19 one-bedroom standard units. 1 story, exterior corridors. *Bath:* combo or shower only. **Parking:** on-site, winter plug-ins. **Terms:** office hours 8 am-10 pm.

🎦 / SOME UNITS ✕ 🛢 🖼

▼ See AAA listing p 729 ▼

(See map and index starting on p. 721)

MADISON INN *Book great rates at AAA.com*   Phone: (509)474-4200 **25**

[AAA] [SAVE]
◆◆◆◆
Hotel
$75-$90 All Year

Address: 15 W Rockwood Blvd **Location:** I-90, exit 281 (Division St) eastbound, just e to Cowley St, 0.4 mi s, then just w; exit westbound, just n to 2nd Ave, just w to Browne St, 0.5 mi s to 9th Ave, then just e. Located across from main entrance of Sacred Heart Medical Center. **Facility:** Smoke free premises. 80 one-bedroom standard units. 4 stories, interior corridors. *Bath:* combo or shower only. **Parking:** on-site. **Terms:** cancellation fee imposed. **Amenities:** irons, hair dryers. *Some:* high-speed Internet, dual phone lines. **Leisure Activities:** exercise room. **Guest Services:** valet and coin laundry, wireless Internet. **Business Services:** fax (fee). **Cards:** DS, MC, VI. **Free Special Amenities: continental breakfast and high-speed Internet.**
(See color ad p 728)

CALL [⚒M] [✕] [🛏] [📶] [🖥] [📺] / SOME UNITS FEE [🐾] FEE [VCR]

MARIANNA STOLTZ HOUSE BED & BREAKFAST   Phone: 509/483-4316 **8**

◆◆◆
Historic Bed
& Breakfast
Rates not provided

Address: 427 E Indiana Ave **Location:** I-90, exit 282 and 282A, 1.5 mi n on Hamilton St, then 0.4 mi w. Located in a quiet neighborhood. **Facility:** This 1908 American foursquare home, on a quiet, tree-lined street near Gonzaga University, is decorated with authentic period furnishings. Smoke free premises. 4 one-bedroom standard units. 2 stories (no elevator), interior corridors. *Bath:* some combo or shower only. **Parking:** on-site. **Terms:** office hours 8 am-9 pm, age restrictions may apply. **Guest Services:** wireless Internet.

[✕] [☎] / SOME UNITS [VCR]

MONTVALE HOTEL   *Book at AAA.com*   Phone: (509)747-1919 **19**

◆◆◆
Hotel
$139-$179 All Year

Address: 1005 W First Ave **Location:** Downtown; at Monroe St. **Facility:** Smoke free premises. 36 units. 32 one-bedroom standard units. 4 one-bedroom suites with whirlpools. 3 stories, interior corridors. *Bath:* combo or shower only. **Parking:** valet and street. **Terms:** cancellation fee imposed. **Amenities:** CD players, high-speed Internet, voice mail, irons, hair dryers. **Guest Services:** valet laundry, wireless Internet. **Business Services:** meeting rooms, fax (fee). **Cards:** AX, DC, DS, MC, VI.

[ASK] [🍴] [🍸] CALL [⚒M] FEE [📶] [✕] [🛏]

OXFORD SUITES-DOWNTOWN SPOKANE   *Book at AAA.com*   Phone: 509/353-9000 **10**

◆◆◆
Hotel
Rates not provided

Address: 115 W North River Dr **Location:** I-90, exit 281 (Division St), 1 mi n, then just n. **Facility:** Smoke free premises. 125 units. 95 one- and 5 two-bedroom standard units. 25 one-bedroom suites. 5 stories, interior corridors. *Bath:* combo or shower only. **Parking:** on-site. **Amenities:** high-speed Internet, voice mail, irons, hair dryers. **Pool(s):** heated indoor. **Leisure Activities:** sauna, whirlpool, steamroom, hiking trails, jogging, exercise room, adjacent to Centennial Trail. *Fee:* game room. **Guest Services:** valet and coin laundry, wireless Internet. **Business Services:** meeting rooms, business center.

[🏋] [🏊] [✕] [✕] [🛏] [📶] [🖥] [📺] / SOME UNITS FEE [🐾]

▼ See AAA listing p 736 ▼

(See map and index starting on p. 721)

QUALITY INN DOWNTOWN 4TH AVENUE   *Book great rates at AAA.com*   Phone: (509)838-6101   24

AAA (SAVE)
▼▼▼
Hotel
$79-$199 All Year

Address: 110 E 4th Ave **Location:** I-90, exit 281 (Division St), just n to 2nd Ave, just w to Browne St, just s to 4th Ave W, then just e. **Facility:** 151 one-bedroom standard units. 6 stories, interior corridors. **Parking:** on-site. **Terms:** cancellation fee imposed. **Amenities:** irons, hair dryers. **Pool(s):** heated outdoor. **Leisure Activities:** limited exercise equipment. **Guest Services:** valet and coin laundry, area transportation (fee), wireless Internet. **Business Services:** meeting rooms, business center. **Cards:** AX, CB, DC, DS, MC, VI. **Free Special Amenities: expanded continental breakfast and room upgrade (subject to availability with advance reservations).**

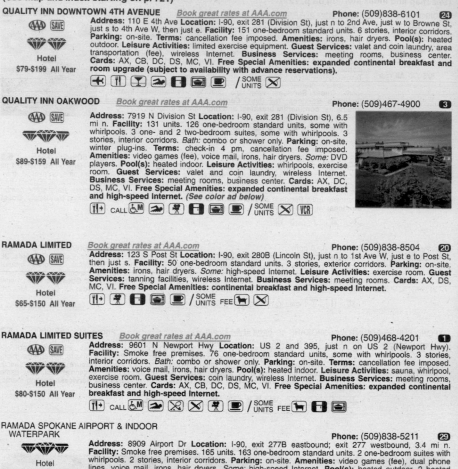

QUALITY INN OAKWOOD   *Book great rates at AAA.com*   Phone: (509)467-4900   3

AAA (SAVE)
▼▼▼
Hotel
$89-$159 All Year

Address: 7919 N Division St **Location:** I-90, exit 281 (Division St), 6.5 mi n. **Facility:** 131 units. 126 one-bedroom standard units, some with whirlpools. 3 one- and 2 two-bedroom suites, some with whirlpools. 3 stories, interior corridors. **Bath:** combo or shower only. **Parking:** on-site, winter plug-ins. **Terms:** check-in 4 pm, cancellation fee imposed. **Amenities:** video games (fee), voice mail, irons, hair dryers. *Some:* DVD players. **Pool(s):** heated indoor. **Leisure Activities:** whirlpools, exercise room. **Guest Services:** valet and coin laundry, wireless Internet. **Business Services:** meeting rooms, business center. **Cards:** AX, DC, DS, MC, VI. **Free Special Amenities: expanded continental breakfast and high-speed Internet.** *(See color ad below)*

RAMADA LIMITED   *Book great rates at AAA.com*   Phone: (509)838-8504   20

AAA (SAVE)
▼▼▼
Hotel
$65-$150 All Year

Address: 123 S Post St **Location:** I-90, exit 280B (Lincoln St), just n to 1st Ave W, just e to Post St, then just s. **Facility:** 50 one-bedroom standard units. 3 stories, exterior corridors. **Parking:** on-site. **Amenities:** irons, hair dryers. *Some:* high-speed Internet. **Leisure Activities:** exercise room. **Guest Services:** tanning facilities, wireless Internet. **Business Services:** meeting rooms. **Cards:** AX, DS, MC, VI. **Free Special Amenities: continental breakfast and high-speed Internet.**

RAMADA LIMITED SUITES   *Book great rates at AAA.com*   Phone: (509)468-4201   1

AAA (SAVE)
▼▼▼
Hotel
$80-$150 All Year

Address: 9601 N Newport Hwy **Location:** US 2 and 395, just n on US 2 (Newport Hwy). **Facility:** Smoke free premises. 76 one-bedroom standard units, some with whirlpools. 3 stories, interior corridors. **Bath:** combo or shower only. **Parking:** on-site. **Terms:** cancellation fee imposed. **Amenities:** voice mail, irons, hair dryers. **Pool(s):** heated indoor. **Leisure Activities:** sauna, whirlpool, exercise room. **Guest Services:** coin laundry, wireless Internet. **Business Services:** meeting rooms, business center. **Cards:** AX, CB, DC, DS, MC, VI. **Free Special Amenities: expanded continental breakfast and high-speed Internet.**

RAMADA SPOKANE AIRPORT & INDOOR WATERPARK   Phone: (509)838-5211   29

▼▼▼
Hotel
$125-$130 All Year

Address: 8909 Airport Dr **Location:** I-90, exit 277B eastbound; exit 277 westbound, 3.4 mi n. **Facility:** Smoke free premises. 165 units. 163 one-bedroom standard units. 2 one-bedroom suites with whirlpools. 2 stories, interior corridors. **Parking:** on-site. **Amenities:** video games (fee), dual phone lines, voice mail, irons, hair dryers. *Some:* high-speed Internet. **Pool(s):** heated outdoor, 2 heated indoor. **Leisure Activities:** whirlpool, waterslide, exercise room. **Guest Services:** valet and coin laundry, wireless Internet. **Business Services:** meeting rooms, business center. **Cards:** AX, CB, DC, DS, JC, MC, VI.

▼ *See AAA listing above* ▼

(See map and index starting on p. 721)

RED LION HOTEL AT THE PARK-SPOKANE   *Book great rates at AAA.com*   Phone: (509)326-8000   **9**

Hotel
$199 All Year

Address: 303 W North River Dr **Location:** I-90, exit 281 (Division St), 1.5 mi n on US 195, then just w. **Facility:** Smoke free premises. 400 units. 375 one-bedroom standard units. 25 one-bedroom suites, some with whirlpools. 5-12 stories, interior corridors. *Bath:* combo or shower only. **Parking:** on-site and valet. **Terms:** cancellation fee imposed. **Amenities:** video games (fee), voice mail, irons, hair dryers. *Some:* dual phone lines. **Dining:** 2 restaurants. **Pool(s):** heated outdoor, heated indoor. **Leisure Activities:** sauna, whirlpool, exercise room. *Fee:* massage. **Guest Services:** valet laundry, airport transportation-Spokane Interantional Airport, wireless Internet. **Business Services:** conference facilities, PC (fee). **Cards:** AX, CB, DC, DS, MC, VI. **Free Special Amenities: high-speed Internet.** *(See color ad below)*

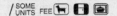

RED LION RIVER INN-SPOKANE   *Book great rates at AAA.com*   Phone: (509)326-5577   **11**

Hotel
$175 All Year

Address: 700 N Division St **Location:** I-90, exit 281 (Division St), 0.8 mi n; downtown. Located adjacent to Gonzaga University. **Facility:** Smoke free premises. 245 units. 244 one-bedroom standard units. 1 one-bedroom suite. 2 stories (no elevator), interior corridors. *Bath:* combo or shower only. **Parking:** on-site. **Terms:** cancellation fee imposed. **Amenities:** video games (fee), voice mail, irons, hair dryers. **Pool(s):** 2 heated outdoor. **Leisure Activities:** whirlpool, tennis court, jogging, exercise room, basketball, volleyball. **Guest Services:** valet and coin laundry, area transportation-downtown, within 3 mi, wireless Internet. **Business Services:** meeting rooms. **Cards:** AX, DC, DS, MC, VI. **Free Special Amenities: high-speed Internet.** *(See color ad below)*

(See map and index starting on p. 721)

SUPER 8 AIRPORT WEST   *Book great rates at AAA.com*   Phone: (509)838-8800

AAA **SAVE**

▽▽▽

Hotel
$60-$150 All Year

Address: 11102 W Westbow Blvd **Location:** I-90, exit 272 (Medical Lake Rd), just s. **Facility:** 81 one-bedroom standard units. 3 stories, interior corridors. **Parking:** on-site, winter plug-ins. **Amenities:** hair dryers. **Pool(s):** heated indoor. **Leisure Activities:** whirlpool, exercise room. **Guest Services:** coin laundry, wireless Internet. **Business Services:** PC. **Cards:** AX, CB, DC, DS, MC, VI. **Free Special Amenities:** expanded continental breakfast and high-speed Internet.

CALL 🔊M 🛄 🖥 💻 / SOME UNITS FEE 🐾 ✕ 🔋 🖳

TRAVELODGE   *Book at AAA.com*   Phone: (509)623-9727   **16**

▽▽ ▽▽

Hotel
$89-$109 All Year

Address: W 33 Spokane Falls Blvd **Location:** I-90, exit 281 (Division St), 0.5 mi n, then just w. **Facility:** 80 units. 75 one-bedroom standard units, some with whirlpools. 5 one-bedroom suites, some with whirlpools. 4 stories, interior corridors. *Bath:* combo or shower only. **Parking:** on-site. **Amenities:** high-speed Internet, voice mail, irons, hair dryers. **Leisure Activities:** exercise room. **Guest Services:** coin laundry, wireless Internet. **Business Services:** meeting rooms, business center. **Cards:** AX, DC, DS, MC, VI.

(A$K) 📶 CALL 🔊M 🖥 💻 / SOME UNITS FEE 🐾 ✕ 🔋 🖳

WAVERLY PLACE BED & BREAKFAST   Phone: (509)328-1856   **7**

▽▽▽

Historic Bed
& Breakfast
$105-$150 All Year

Address: 709 W Waverly Pl **Location:** I-90, exit 281 (Division St), 2.3 mi n, 0.3 mi w on N Foothills Dr, just n on Wall St. Located in a quiet residential area, across from Corbin Park. **Facility:** This turn-of-the-20th-century Victorian home is just five minutes away from shopping, theaters and events in the downtown area. Smoke free premises. 4 units. 3 one-bedroom standard units. 1 one-bedroom suite. 3 stories (no elevator), interior corridors. *Bath:* some shared or private, combo or shower only. **Parking:** street. **Terms:** office hours 7 am-9 pm, 2 night minimum stay - seasonal and/or weekends, 7 day cancellation notice. **Pool(s):** outdoor. **Cards:** MC, VI.

🛥 ✕ 🅦 🄯

────────── WHERE TO DINE ──────────

98 TWENTY BISTRO LOUNGE   Phone: 509/468-9820

▽▽▽

International
$9-$25

The stylish, intimate bistro's eclectic and interesting menu has something for every taste. The dinner menu includes creative entrees such as wild cider salmon, short ribs braised in root beer and apple-wood smoked Kurobuta pork loin with Japanese butterscotch sauce. Casual dress. **Bar:** Full bar. **Reservations:** accepted. **Hours:** 11 am-10 pm, Fri & Sat-11 pm, Sun 4 pm-9 pm. Closed: 11/26, 12/25. **Address:** 9820 N Nevada St **Location:** US 2 and 395, just n on US 2 (Newport Hwy) to Holland Ave, just e, then just n. **Parking:** on-site. **Cards:** AX, MC, VI.

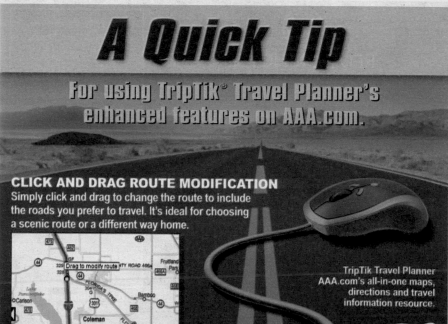

(See map and index starting on p. 721)

CLINKERDAGGER

Phone: 509/328-5965   ③

▼△▼△▼△

American

$8-$25

Some river view seating is available at the warm, intimate restaurant, a favorite spot for celebrating special occasions. The varied menu lists meat, fish, poultry and pasta dishes, most notably a succulent prime rib. Give into your cravings for dessert. Casual dress. **Bar:** Full bar. **Reservations:** suggested. **Hours:** 11:15 am-2:30 & 5-9:30 pm, Fri-10:30 pm, Sat 11:15 am-2:30 & 4:30-10:30 pm, Sun 3 pm-8 pm. Closed: 7/4, 12/25. **Address:** 621 W Mallon St **Location:** Downtown; in Flour Mill. **Parking:** on-site. **Cards:** AX, DC, DS, MC, VI.

CYRUS O'LEARY'S

Phone: 509/624-9000   ⑨

▼△▼△ ▼△▼△

American

$9-$19

Boundless energy overflows from the fun, colorful restaurant. On weekends, costumed servers become sports referees and jumpsuited Elvis Presleys. Tasty food is served in ample portions with an inventive selection of specialty drinks, juices and coffees. Casual dress. **Bar:** Full bar. **Hours:** 11:30 am-10 pm, Fri & Sat-11 pm; hours may vary in summer. Closed: 11/26, 12/25. **Address:** 516 W Main Ave. **Location:** Downtown. **Parking:** street. **Cards:** AX, DS, MC, VI.

ELK PUBLIC HOUSE

Phone: 509/363-1973   ⑳

▼△▼△ ▼△▼△

American

$7-$12

In a building of 1950s vintage that operated for many years as a drugstore and classic soda fountain, the casual and lively eatery/brew pub is in the historic Brown's Addition neighborhood. Casual dress. **Bar:** Full bar. **Hours:** 11 am-midnight. Closed: 11/26, 12/25. **Address:** 1931 W Pacific Ave **Location:** I-90, exit 280, just n on Lincoln St to 2nd Ave W, 0.8 mi w to Cannon St, then just n. **Parking:** street. **Cards:** MC, VI.

EUROPA PIZZARIA & BAKERY

Phone: 509/455-4051   ⑱

▼△▼△▼△

Italian

$7-$18

A Mediterranean mood settles over the casual, somewhat rustic restaurant. The specialties are Italian dishes, homemade pizza and the breads and many tempting desserts made at the in-house bakery. Casual dress. **Bar:** Full bar. **Reservations:** accepted. **Hours:** 11 am-11 pm, Fri & Sat-midnight. Closed: 1/1, 12/25. **Address:** 125 S Wall St **Location:** Downtown. **Parking:** street. **Cards:** AX, DS, MC, VI.

FRANK'S DINER

Phone: 509/747-8798   ㉑

▼△▼△

American

$7-$12

The original 1906 Barney-Smith observation railroad car is decorated in rich woods, stained-glass windows and brass and glass light fixtures. Basic diner fare includes all-day breakfast items, huge burgers, old-fashioned milkshakes and homemade desserts. Casual dress. **Bar:** Beer & wine. **Hours:** 6 am-8 pm. Closed: 11/26, 12/25. **Address:** 1516 W 2nd Ave **Location:** At 2nd Ave and Maple St; downtown. **Parking:** on-site. **Cards:** DS, MC, VI.

FUGAZZI

Phone: 509/624-1133   ⑯

▼△▼△ ▼△▼△

International

$18-$29

The sleek and trendy restaurant nurtures a European feel. Some foods are traditional, and some are prepared with a twist, such as the interesting orange chicken soup. Dessert lovers should leave room for the outstanding creme caramel. Casual dress. **Bar:** Full bar. **Reservations:** suggested. **Hours:** 5 pm-11 pm. Closed major holidays; also Sun. **Address:** North One Post **Location:** Downtown; in Hotel Lusso. **Parking:** valet and street. **Cards:** AX, CB, DC, DS, JC, MC, VI.

HERBAL ESSENCE CAFE

Phone: 509/838-4600   ⑪

▼△▼△ ▼△▼△

American

$6-$25

The restaurant serves contemporary Northwest cuisine in an intimate bistro-style setting. Casual dress. **Bar:** Full bar. **Reservations:** suggested. **Hours:** 11 am-2 & 5-9 pm, Sat from 5 pm. Closed major holidays; also Sun. **Address:** 115 N Washington St **Location:** Downtown. **Parking:** street. **Cards:** AX, DS, MC, VI.

ITALIAN KITCHEN

Phone: 509/363-1210   ⑬

▼△▼△ ▼△▼△

Italian

$7-$24

The quaint, casual restaurant features traditional Italian pasta dishes as well as daily specials and offers some sidewalk dining in the summer. Casual dress. **Bar:** Full bar. **Reservations:** accepted. **Hours:** 11 am-9 pm, Fri & Sat-10 pm. **Address:** 113 N Bernard St **Location:** Downtown. **Parking:** street. **Cards:** AX, DS, MC, VI.

LUIGI'S

Phone: 509/624-5226   ⑩

▼△▼△ ▼△▼△

Italian

$6-$20

The time-honored downtown favorite has garnered many awards and accolades over the years for its traditional Italian food. Casual dress. **Bar:** Full bar. **Reservations:** accepted. **Hours:** 11:30 am-10 pm, Fri-11 pm, Sat 4 pm-11 pm, Sun & Mon 4 pm-9 pm. Closed: 11/26, 12/25. **Address:** 245 W Main Ave **Location:** Downtown. **Parking:** street. **Cards:** AX, DC, DS, MC, VI.

LUNA

Phone: 509/448-2383

▼△▼△▼△

American

$5-$28

This South Hill neighborhood, casual dining restaurant features Northwest cuisine in a trendy, upscale atmosphere. Marble tables, light wood floors and large windows set a bright and airy scene. Saturday and Sunday feature full breakfast and lunch menus. Outdoor seating in season on the terrace. Casual dress. **Bar:** Full bar. **Reservations:** suggested. **Hours:** 11 am-close, Sun 9 am-2 & 5-10 pm. Closed major holidays. **Address:** 5620 S Perry St **Location:** I-90, exit 280, 1.7 mi s on Maple St, 1 mi e on 29th Ave, then 1.9 mi s. **Parking:** on-site. **Cards:** AX, DC, DS, MC, VI.

CALL Ⓛ Ⓜ

MILFORD'S FISH HOUSE

Phone: 509/326-7251   ④

▼△▼△▼△

Seafood

$22-$30

In a 1925 building originally constructed to house three businesses, the near-downtown restaurant is the city's original seafood restaurant. A cigar store occupied what is now the main dining room. Following Prohibition, the store became the Pastime Tavern, receiving the city's second liquor license, which in 1979 was transferred to Milford's. The menu is a showcase for a broad array of local, regional and international fish entrees. Casual dress. **Bar:** Full bar. **Reservations:** accepted. **Hours:** 5 pm-10 pm, Sun & Mon 4 pm-9 pm. Closed major holidays. **Address:** 719 N Monroe St **Location:** I-90, exit 280B, just n to Spokane Falls Blvd, just w to Monroe St, then just n. **Parking:** on-site. **Cards:** DS, MC, VI.

(See map and index starting on p. 721)

MIZUNA RESTAURANT & WINE BAR
Phone: 509/747-2004 ⑧

International
$7-$30

Interesting and inventive International and Northwest cuisine make up a menu that changes at least seasonally. Patrons can savor cumin-scented ahi tuna or the Indian tandoori bowl in stylish and artistically eclectic surroundings. Save room for one of the excellent desserts, which are made in house. Casual dress. **Bar:** Full bar. **Reservations:** suggested, weekends. **Hours:** 11:30 am-2:30 & 5-10 pm, Fri-midnight, Sat & Sun 5 pm-10 pm. Closed major holidays. **Address:** 214 N Howard St **Location:** Downtown. **Parking:** street. **Cards:** AX, CB, DC, DS, JC, MC, VI.

MOXIE
Phone: 509/456-3594 ⑮

American
$7-$35

Both the decor and the food of this busy downtown restaurant combines elements of both the traditional and the ultra-modern. The chef/owner melds his training in classical French cooking with his Hawaiian upbringing to create flavorful and fanciful dishes. Good examples include the Kobe beef hamburger for lunch or the Hawaiian-style ahi poke for dinner. Casual dress. **Bar:** Full bar. **Reservations:** suggested. **Hours:** 11 am-2 & 5-9 pm, Fri-10 pm, Sat 5 pm-10 pm. Closed major holidays. **Address:** 816 W Sprague Ave **Location:** Downtown. **Parking:** street. **Cards:** AX, DS, MC, VI.

THE MUSTARD SEED ASIAN CAFE
Phone: 509/483-1500 ②

International
$7-$12

The Mustard Seed is a wildly popular restaurant serving "Asian food for the American palate" in an artistically decorated and convenient shopping mall setting. Their private entrance makes dining and take-out pick-up more convenient than most mall restaurants. Casual dress. **Bar:** Full bar. **Hours:** 11 am-9 pm, Fri & Sat-10 pm, Sun noon-8 pm. Closed: 11/26, 12/25. **Address:** 4750 N Division St **Location:** I-90, exit 281 (Division St), 3.4 mi n; in Northtown Mall. **Parking:** on-site. **Cards:** AX, CB, DC, DS, JC, MC, VI.

CALL

NIKO'S GREEK RESTAURANT & WINE BAR
Phone: 509/624-7444 ⑭

Greek
$16-$30

Greek, Mediterranean and inventive fusion dishes are served under stylized grape arbors. The restaurant boasts an intimate and dramatic wine bar with more than 800 bottles from which to choose. Casual dress. **Bar:** Beer & wine. **Reservations:** suggested, weekends. **Hours:** 4 pm-10 pm, Thurs-Sat to 11 pm. **Address:** 725 W Riverside Ave **Location:** Jct Post St; downtown. **Parking:** valet and street. **Cards:** AX, DC, MC, VI.

O'DOHERTY'S IRISH GRILL
Phone: 509/747-0322 ⑤

Irish
$5-$12

The classic Irish pub atmosphere incorporates fiddle music, Guinness stout on tap and such tried-and-true dishes as corned beef and cabbage. The pastie—a traditional miner's lunch made from a beef, potato, onion and carrot mixture that's wrapped in pie crust, baked and served with gravy—is difficult to find outside of Ireland, Wales and Butte, Montana. Sidewalk tables, which are available when the weather permits, overlook Riverside Park and the antique carousel across the street. Casual dress. **Bar:** Full bar. **Reservations:** accepted. **Hours:** 11:30 am-10 pm, Fri & Sat-midnight. Closed major holidays. **Address:** 525 W Spokane Falls Blvd **Location:** Downtown. **Parking:** street. **Cards:** AX, MC, VI.

THE ONION
Phone: 509/747-3852 ⑫

American
$6-$20

Antique stylings and accents of wood, brass and glass give the popular laid-back restaurant the aura of a Chicago-style saloon. Sandwiches, salads, ethnic foods, steaks and seafood—not to mention the signature onion ring—make up the menu. Casual dress. **Bar:** Full bar. **Reservations:** accepted. **Hours:** 11 am-11 pm, Fri & Sat-1 am. Closed: 11/26, 12/25. **Address:** 302 W Riverside Ave **Location:** Downtown. **Parking:** street. **Cards:** AX, DS, MC, VI.

ROCK CITY GRILL
Phone: 509/455-4400 ⑥

International
$6-$20

The lively, trendy restaurant is in an urban mall. The menu lists pasta dishes, pizza and calzones, as well as chicken, fish and steaks. Signature drinks by the pitcher round out the experience. Casual dress. **Bar:** Full bar. **Reservations:** accepted. **Hours:** 11 am-9:30 pm, Fri & Sat-10:30 pm. Closed: 11/26, 12/25. **Address:** 808 W Main Ave **Location:** Downtown; in River Park Square. **Parking:** on-site (fee). **Cards:** AX, CB, DC, DS, JC, MC, VI.

THE RUSTY MOOSE BAR & GRILL
Phone: 509/747-5579 ㉒

American
$9-$22

The vast menu of the rustic, Western-themed family restaurant encompasses steaks, seafood, pasta, pizza and "American regional comfort food with a twist." The in-house bakery turns out delicious desserts, including a dozen varieties of cheesecake. Hearty appetites are needed to handle the huge portions. Casual dress. **Bar:** Full bar. **Reservations:** accepted. **Hours:** 11 am-9 pm, Fri-10 pm, Sat 7 am-10 pm, Sun 7 am-9 pm. Closed: 1/1, 12/25. **Address:** W 9105 US 2 **Location:** I-90, exit 277B eastbound; exit 277 westbound, 3 mi w. **Parking:** on-site. **Cards:** AX, DS, MC, VI.

SAWTOOTH GRILL
Phone: 509/363-1100 ⑦

American
$9-$20

Burgers are the specialty, but also on the menu is a wide array of appetizers, finger foods, sandwiches, salads and even a steak or two. The comfortable, rustic-themed restaurant is in a downtown urban mall. Casual dress. **Bar:** Full bar. **Reservations:** accepted. **Hours:** 11 am-9 pm, Fri & Sat-10 pm. Closed: 4/12, 12/25. **Address:** 808 W Main Ave **Location:** Downtown; in River Park Sqaure. **Parking:** on-site (fee). **Cards:** AX, DS, MC, VI.

STEAM PLANT GRILL
Phone: 509/777-3900 ⑲

American
$6-$30

Built in 1916 and listed on the National Register of Historic Places, the Steam Plant is a three-story, steel-reinforced concrete and brick structure that for 70 years provided steam heat to more than 350 downtown buildings. The industrial interior has been preserved, and two huge boilers are in the dining room. The setting is a distinctive one in which to experience "new American" cuisine and hand-crafted micro-brews. Casual dress. **Bar:** Full bar. **Reservations:** suggested. **Hours:** 11 am-9:30 pm, Fri & Sat-11 pm. Closed major holidays. **Address:** 159 S Lincoln St **Location:** I-90, exit 280 eastbound; exit 280B (Lincoln St) westbound, just n. **Parking:** on-site. **Cards:** AX, DS, MC, VI.

THAI ON 1ST
Phone: 509/455-4288 ⑰

Thai
$8-$14

A wide selection of traditional Thai dishes is served in a casual location close to shopping, hotels and offices. Casual dress. **Bar:** Beer & wine. **Hours:** 11:30 am-2 & 5-9 pm, Sat from 5 pm. Closed major holidays; also Sun. **Address:** 411 W 1st Ave **Location:** Downtown. **Parking:** street. **Cards:** MC, VI.

(See map and index starting on p. 721)

TOMATO STREET

Italian
$8-$18

Phone: 509/484-4500 ①

The family-oriented, market-style eatery features brick-oven pizzas, Italian specialties and a few American dishes. Canopied tables in the center of the dining room give off the feel of a sidewalk spot. The restaurant is almost always busy. Casually dressed servers with interesting hats and headgear provide energetic, upbeat service. Casual dress. **Bar:** Full bar. **Reservations:** accepted, Mon-Thurs. **Hours:** 11 am-10 pm, Fri & Sat-11 pm. Closed: 11/26, 12/25. **Address:** 6220 N Division St **Location:** I-90, exit 281 (Division St), 4.3 mi n. **Parking:** on-site. **Cards:** AX, DS, MC, VI.

TWIGS BISTRO & MARTINI BAR

International
$10-$22

Phone: 509/232-3377

In an urban mall, the convenient restaurant is part food court, part trendy bistro. Quality food is served with a minimum of fuss. Casual dress. **Bar:** Full bar. **Reservations:** accepted, Sun-Thurs. **Hours:** 11 am-10 pm, Fri & Sat-11 pm, Sun-9 pm. Closed: 11/26, 12/25. **Address:** 808 W Main Ave **Location:** Downtown; in River Park Square. **Parking:** on-site (fee). **Cards:** AX, CB, JC, MC, VI.

VIN ROUGE

American
$7-$26

Phone: 509/535-8800 ㉓

The sleek and stylish bistro incorporates minimalist lines and dramatic indirect lighting. Myriad options on the interesting and creative menu make decisions difficult, but the choices are never disappointing. Casual dress. **Bar:** Full bar. **Reservations:** suggested. **Hours:** 11 am-close, Sat & Sun from 9 am. **Address:** 3029 E 29th Ave **Location:** I-90, exit 283, 2.5 mi s, then just w. **Parking:** on-site. **Cards:** AX, DC, MC, VI.

———— *The following restaurants have not been evaluated by AAA* ————
but are listed for your information only.

CATACOMBS PUB

[fyi]

Phone: 509/838-4610

Not evaluated. The near-Byzantine-style restaurant, located below ground level with rockwork walls and vaulted brick archways, is a cool, quiet, and interesting place to enjoy a hand-made personal pizza or any number of other entrees. **Address:** 110 S Monroe St.

CATHAY INN

[fyi]

Phone: 509/326-2226

Not evaluated. Native Chinese and Szechuan dishes are at the heart of the expansive menu. The family-owned restaurant has operated from the same location for more than 50 years. **Address:** 3714 N Division St.

SHOGUN SUSHI PALACE

[fyi]

Phone: 509/534-7777

Not evaluated. Guests enjoy themselves at the sushi bar or seated around hibachi grills as highly trained chefs put on a flamboyant show while wielding knives and other utensils. Kimono-clad waitresses complete the experience. **Address:** 821 E 3rd Ave.

TOP OF CHINA BUFFET

[fyi]

Phone: 509/468-9988

Not evaluated. The popular buffet restaurant lines up incredibly extensive selections of Chinese dishes, as well as some American foods. Every member of the family can find something to like. **Address:** 21 E Lincoln Rd.

SPOKANE VALLEY pop. 80,700 (See map and index starting on p. 721)

———— **WHERE TO STAY** ————

COMFORT INN VALLEY

Hotel
Rates not provided

Phone: 509/924-3838

Address: 905 N Sullivan Rd **Location:** I-90, exit 291B, just s. **Facility:** 76 units. 64 one-bedroom standard units, some with whirlpools. 6 one- and 6 two-bedroom suites with kitchens. 2 stories (no elevator), interior corridors. **Parking:** on-site. **Terms:** check-in 4 pm. **Amenities:** irons, hair dryers. **Pool(s):** heated outdoor. **Leisure Activities:** sauna, whirlpool. **Guest Services:** valet and coin laundry, wireless Internet. **Business Services:** meeting rooms, PC.

CROSSLAND STUDIOS-SPOKANE VALLEY *Book at AAA.com*

Hotel
$59-$74 All Year

Phone: (509)928-5948 ㊳

Address: 12803 E Sprague Ave **Location:** I-90, exit 289, 1.1 mi s, just e. **Facility:** 115 one-bedroom standard units with efficiencies. 3 stories, exterior corridors. *Bath:* combo or shower only. **Parking:** on-site. **Terms:** office hours 7 am-11 pm, cancellation fee imposed. **Amenities:** voice mail. **Guest Services:** coin laundry, wireless Internet. **Cards:** AX, CB, DC, DS, JC, MC, VI.

HOLIDAY INN EXPRESS-VALLEY *Book at AAA.com*

Hotel
$129-$209 5/1-2/28
$109-$209 3/1-4/30

Phone: (509)927-7100 ㊱

Address: 9220 E Mission Ave **Location:** I-90, exit 287, just s. **Facility:** 103 units. 92 one-bedroom standard units, some with whirlpools. 11 one-bedroom suites. 4 stories, interior/exterior corridors. *Bath:* combo or shower only. **Parking:** on-site, winter plug-ins. **Amenities:** voice mail, irons, hair dryers. **Pool(s):** heated indoor. **Leisure Activities:** whirlpool, exercise room. **Guest Services:** valet and coin laundry, wireless Internet. **Business Services:** meeting rooms, business center. **Cards:** AX, DC, DS, MC, VI.

LA QUINTA INN & SUITES SPOKANE *Book great rates at AAA.com*

Hotel
$89-$159 All Year

Phone: (509)893-0955

Address: 3808 N Sullivan Rd **Location:** I-90, exit 291B, 1.3 mi n. **Facility:** 59 units. 58 one-bedroom standard units, some with efficiencies and/or whirlpools. 1 one-bedroom suite. 3 stories, interior corridors. *Bath:* combo or shower only. **Parking:** on-site. **Amenities:** video library (fee), dual phone lines, voice mail, irons, hair dryers. *Some:* high-speed Internet. **Pool(s):** heated indoor. **Leisure Activities:** whirlpool, exercise room. **Guest Services:** valet and coin laundry, wireless Internet. **Business Services:** meeting rooms, business center. **Cards:** AX, CB, DS, JC, MC, VI.

(See map and index starting on p. 721)

MIRABEAU PARK HOTEL AND CONVENTION
CENTER   *Book great rates at AAA.com*

Phone: (509)924-9000

AAA SAVE
WWWW
Hotel
$96-$169 All Year

Address: 1100 N Sullivan Rd **Location:** I-90, exit 291B, just s. **Facility:** 236 units. 230 one-bedroom standard units, some with whirlpools. 6 one-bedroom suites. 2-3 stories, interior corridors. **Parking:** on-site. **Amenities:** video games (fee), irons, hair dryers. *Some:* high-speed Internet. **Pool(s):** heated outdoor. **Leisure Activities:** whirlpool, exercise room, basketball. **Guest Services:** valet laundry, airport transportation (fee)-Spokane International Airport, area transportation-within Spokane Valley, wireless Internet. **Business Services:** conference facilities, business center. **Cards:** AX, DC, DS, MC, VI. **Free Special Amenities:** local telephone calls and high-speed Internet. *(See color ad below)*

OXFORD SUITES SPOKANE VALLEY   *Book great rates at AAA.com*

Phone: (509)847-1000

AAA SAVE
WWWW
Hotel
$115-$199 All Year

Address: 15015 E Indiana Ave **Location:** I-90, exit 291A eastbound; exit 291B westbound, just nw. Located across from Spokane Valley Mall. **Facility:** 127 units. 119 one-bedroom standard units. 8 one-bedroom suites. 4 stories, interior corridors. **Bath:** combo or shower only. **Parking:** on-site. **Amenities:** high-speed Internet, voice mail, irons, hair dryers. **Pool(s):** heated indoor. **Leisure Activities:** sauna, whirlpool, steamroom, jogging, exercise room. **Guest Services:** valet and coin laundry, airport transportation-Spokane International Airport, wireless Internet. **Business Services:** meeting rooms, business center. **Cards:** AX, DS, MC, VI. **Free Special Amenities:** full breakfast and high-speed Internet.

PHEASANT HILL INN & SUITES   *Book great rates at AAA.com*

Phone: (509)926-7432   34

AAA SAVE
WWWW
Hotel
$80-$190 All Year

Address: 12415 E Mission Ave **Location:** I-90, exit 289, just se. **Facility:** 104 units. 100 one-bedroom standard units. 4 one-bedroom suites with whirlpools. 4 stories, interior corridors. **Bath:** combo or shower only. **Parking:** on-site. **Terms:** check-in 4 pm, cancellation fee imposed. **Amenities:** high-speed Internet, dual phone lines, voice mail, irons, hair dryers. *Fee:* video games, safes. **Pool(s):** heated indoor. **Leisure Activities:** whirlpool. **Guest Services:** valet and coin laundry, wireless Internet. **Business Services:** meeting rooms, business center. **Cards:** AX, CB, DS, MC, VI. **Free Special Amenities:** full breakfast and high-speed Internet. *(See color ad p 729)*

QUALITY INN VALLEY SUITES   *Book at AAA.com*

Phone: (509)928-5218   35

WWWW
Hotel
$89-$129 All Year

Address: 8923 E Mission Ave **Location:** I-90, exit 287. **Facility:** 128 units. 94 one-bedroom standard units. 34 one-bedroom suites, some with kitchens. 4 stories, interior corridors. **Bath:** combo or shower only. **Parking:** on-site. **Amenities:** voice mail, irons, hair dryers. **Pool(s):** heated indoor. **Leisure Activities:** whirlpool, exercise room. *Fee:* game room. **Guest Services:** valet and coin laundry, tanning facility, wireless Internet. **Business Services:** meeting rooms, business center. **Cards:** AX, CB, DC, DS, JC, MC, VI.

RESIDENCE INN BY MARRIOTT   *Book great rates at AAA.com*

Phone: (509)892-9300

WWWW
Hotel
$139-$149 All Year

Address: 15915 E Indiana Ave **Location:** I-90, exit 291 westbound, just e; exit 291B eastbound, just n, then just e. **Facility:** Smoke free premises. 84 units. 33 one-bedroom standard units, some with efficiencies or kitchens. 39 one- and 12 two-bedroom suites, some with efficiencies or kitchens. 3 stories, interior corridors. **Bath:** combo or shower only. **Parking:** on-site. **Terms:** cancellation fee imposed. **Amenities:** high-speed Internet, dual phone lines, voice mail, irons, hair dryers. **Pool(s):** heated indoor. **Leisure Activities:** whirlpool, bicycles, exercise room, sports court. **Guest Services:** valet and coin laundry, wireless Internet. **Business Services:** PC. **Cards:** AX, DS, MC, VI.

AAA Benefit: Members save a minimum 5% off the best available rate.

(See map and index starting on p. 721)

RODEWAY INN & SUITES   *Book great rates at AAA.com*   Phone: (509)535-7185   **37**

(AAA) (SAVE)

▼▼ ▼▼
Hotel
$49-$129 7/1-2/28
$49-$99 3/1-6/30

Address: 6309 E Broadway **Location:** I-90, exit 286, just w. Located in a commercial area. **Facility:** 72 one-bedroom standard units, some with efficiencies and/or whirlpools. 2 stories (no elevator), interior/exterior corridors. *Bath:* combo or shower only. **Parking:** on-site, winter plug-ins. **Terms:** 7 day cancellation notice-fee imposed. **Pool(s):** heated outdoor. **Leisure Activities:** whirlpool, exercise room. **Guest Services:** coin laundry, wireless Internet. **Business Services:** meeting rooms, PC. **Cards:** AX, DC, DS, MC, VI. **Free Special Amenities: continental breakfast and high-speed Internet.**

[⊤⊦] [≈] / SOME UNITS FEE [🐕] [✕] [⬛] [🖥] [▭]

SUPER 8 MOTEL   *Book at AAA.com*   Phone: (509)928-4888   **33**

▼▼ ▼▼
Hotel
$70-$92 6/1-2/28
$62-$80 3/1-5/31

Address: N 2020 Argonne Rd **Location:** I-90, exit 287, just n. **Facility:** 180 one-bedroom standard units. 3 stories, interior corridors. **Parking:** on-site, winter plug-ins. **Amenities:** hair dryers. **Pool(s):** heated indoor. **Leisure Activities:** whirlpool, exercise room. **Guest Services:** coin laundry, wireless Internet. **Business Services:** meeting rooms, PC. **Cards:** AX, DC, DS, MC, VI.

[ASK] [⊤⊦] [≈] [🐾] / SOME UNITS FEE [🐕] [✕] [⬛] [🖥] [▭]

——— WHERE TO DINE ———

LONGHORN BARBECUE   Phone: 509/924-9600   **26**

▼▼
American
$5-$15

With its claims of "tendin' the pits since '56," the restaurant is a favorite for real Texas barbecue. In addition to full dinners, the menu includes barbecue and smoked meat sandwiches, cool and fresh offerings from the salad bar and hot and spicy Texas chili. Casual dress. **Bar:** Full bar. **Hours:** 10:30 am-9 pm, Fri & Sat-10 pm, Sun 11 am-8 pm. Closed major holidays. **Address:** 2315 N Argonne Rd **Location:** I-90, exit 287, just n. **Parking:** on-site. **Cards:** AX, DS, MC, VI.

CALL [&M]

STEVENSON pop. 1,200

——— WHERE TO STAY ———

SKAMANIA LODGE   *Book great rates at AAA.com*   Phone: (509)427-7700

(AAA) (SAVE)

▼▼ ▼▼
Hotel
$129-$269 All Year

Address: 1131 SW Skamania Lodge Way **Location:** 1 mi w on SR 14, just n on Rock Creek Dr, then just w. **Facility:** Smoke free premises. 254 units. 248 one-bedroom standard units. 6 one-bedroom suites. 4 stories, interior corridors. *Bath:* combo or shower only. **Parking:** on-site. **Terms:** check-in 4 pm, 5 day cancellation notice-fee imposed. **Amenities:** video games (fee), high-speed Internet, dual phone lines, voice mail, irons, hair dryers. *Some:* CD players, honor bars. **Dining:** 2 restaurants, also, The Cascade Room, see separate listing. **Pool(s):** heated indoor. **Leisure Activities:** saunas, whirlpools, sailboats, windsurfing, fishing, 2 tennis courts, recreation programs, concert series in summer, bicycles, hiking trails, playground, exercise room, spa. *Fee:* golf-18 holes. **Guest Services:** airport transportation (fee)-Portland International Airport, wireless Internet. **Business Services:** conference facilities, business center. **Cards:** AX, DC, DS, MC, VI. **Free Special Amenities: local telephone calls and newspaper.** *(See color ad below & p 59)*

FEE [✈] [⊤⊦] [≈] [✕] [✕] [🐾] [▭] / SOME UNITS FEE [🐕] FEE [⬛] FEE [🖥]

——— WHERE TO DINE ———

BIG RIVER GRILL   Phone: 509/427-4888

▼▼ ▼▼
American
$7-$19

After a busy day of exploring the Columbia River Gorge or sailboarding, hungry diners can retreat into the welcoming restaurant for filling hamburgers, slow-braised barbecue country pork ribs and some mom's-cooking-variety items, including spaghetti with meatballs and home-style meatloaf. Local Northwest wines and microbrews complement the meals. Casual dress. **Bar:** Beer & wine. **Reservations:** not accepted. **Hours:** 11:30 am-9 pm. Closed: 1/1, 11/26, 12/25. **Address:** 192 SW 2nd St **Location:** Downtown. **Parking:** street. **Cards:** DS, MC, VI.

▼ *See AAA listing above* ▼

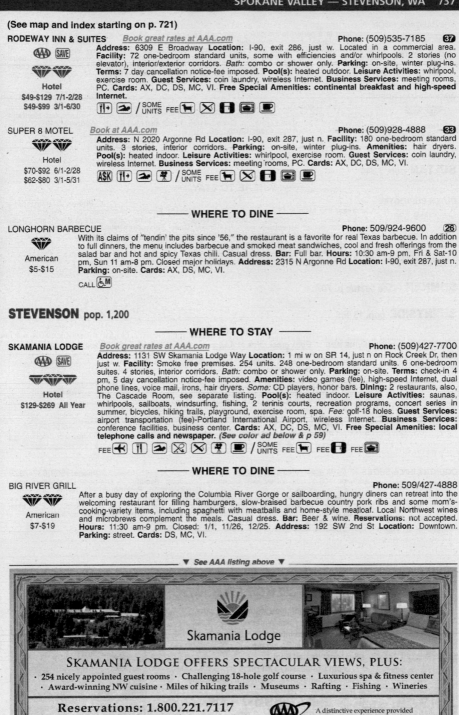

THE CASCADE ROOM

Phone: 509/427-7700

Northern American
$11-$34

The restaurant is a perfect lodge dining room with its wood-fired oven, panoramic views of the Columbia Gorge and a northwest-inspired menu that includes Potlatch salmon cooked on an alder plank, Washington prime grade roast beef and an oat crusted Idaho trout. Reservations are always encouraged but are especially recommended on Friday nights for the Gorge Harvest Buffet and the Sunday Brunch. Casual dress. **Bar:** Full bar. **Reservations:** suggested. **Hours:** 7 am-10 pm. **Address:** 1131 SW Skamania Lodge Way **Location:** 1 mi w on SR 14, just n on Rock Creek Dr, then just w; in Skamania Lodge. **Parking:** on-site. **Cards:** AX, CB, DC, DS, MC, VI.

WALKING MAN BREWING

Phone: 509/427-5520

American
$7-$10

The casual eatery specializes in pizza, beer and soda, all made on the premises. The patio is a fine spot for unwinding with a pint of craft beer. Casual dress. **Bar:** Beer only. **Reservations:** not accepted. **Hours:** 4 pm-9 pm, Sat from 3 pm, Sun 3 pm-8 pm. Closed: 11/26, 12/25; also Mon & Tues. **Address:** 240 SW 1st St **Location:** Downtown. **Parking:** street. **Cards:** MC, VI.

SULTAN pop. 3,344

─── WHERE TO STAY ───

DUTCH CUP MOTEL

Phone: 360/793-2215

Motel
$77-$96 All Year

Address: 819 Main St **Location:** Jct US 2 and Main St. **Facility:** 20 one-bedroom standard units. 2 stories (no elevator), exterior corridors. **Parking:** on-site. **Terms:** office hours 6 am-11 pm, 3 day cancellation notice. **Amenities:** irons, hair dryers. **Guest Services:** wireless Internet. **Cards:** AX, DS, MC, VI. **Free Special Amenities: local telephone calls and high-speed Internet.**

SUMNER —See Seattle p. 707.

SUNNYSIDE pop. 13,905

─── WHERE TO STAY ───

BEST WESTERN GRAPEVINE INN   *Book great rates at AAA.com*

Phone: (509)839-6070

Hotel
$110-$210 3/1-11/1
$100-$210 11/2-2/28

Address: 1849 Quail Ln **Location:** I-82, exit 69, just n, then just w. **Facility:** Smoke free premises. 54 units. 52 one-bedroom standard units. 2 one-bedroom suites with kitchens and whirlpools. 2 stories (no elevator), interior corridors. **Bath:** combo or shower only. **Parking:** on-site, winter plug-ins. **Terms:** 3 day cancellation notice. **Amenities:** high-speed Internet, dual phone lines, voice mail, irons, hair dryers. **Pool(s):** heated indoor. **Leisure Activities:** whirlpool, exercise room. **Guest Services:** coin laundry, wireless Internet. **Business Services:** meeting rooms, business center. **Cards:** AX, CB, DC, DS, MC, VI. **Free Special Amenities: full breakfast and high-speed Internet.**

AAA Benefit:
Members save up to 20%, plus 10% bonus points with rewards program.

COUNTRY INN & SUITES   *Book great rates at AAA.com*

Phone: (509)837-7878

Motel
$45-$60 All Year

Address: 408 Yakima Valley Hwy **Location:** Downtown. **Facility:** 45 one-bedroom standard units, some with whirlpools. 2 stories (no elevator), exterior corridors. **Parking:** on-site. **Terms:** cancellation fee imposed. **Amenities:** high-speed Internet. *Some:* DVD players (fee), hair dryers. **Pool(s):** heated outdoor. **Guest Services:** coin laundry, wireless Internet. **Cards:** AX, CB, DC, DS, JC, MC, VI. **Free Special Amenities: continental breakfast and high-speed Internet.** *(See color ad below)*

▼ *See AAA listing above* ▼

In the Heart of the Wine Country

- Award Winning Snipes Mountain Brewery Restaurant and Apex Winery
- Free high Speed Internet
- Free Continental Breakfast
- Seasonal Heated Pool
- In-room Coffee, Micro + Fridge
- Pets Welcome w/fee • On-site Restaurant

Country Inn & Suites

1-877-896-7878
Phone: 509-837-7878
www.sunnysidecountryinn.com
408 Yakima Valley Highway • Sunnyside, WA 98944

$40 - $55
1 person
*$5 for extra person

$45 - $60
2 persons
*$5 for extra person

──────── **WHERE TO DINE** ────────

SNIPES MOUNTAIN MICROBREWERY &
RESTAURANT

Phone: 509/837-2739

▼▼ ▼▼
American
$8-$27

The impressive lodge-style log restaurant has a large rock fireplace in its center. For lunch, patrons can check out huge entree salads, burgers, sandwiches and pizzas cooked in a wood-fired oven. Dinner offerings include a wide array of steaks, seafood and pasta. Casual dress. **Bar:** Beer & wine. **Reservations:** accepted. **Hours:** 10 am-10 pm, Fri & Sat 11 am-11 pm. Closed: 1/1, 7/4, 12/25. **Address:** 905 Yakima Valley Hwy **Location:** Downtown. **Parking:** on-site. **Cards:** AX, DS, MC, VI.

SUQUAMISH —*See Seattle p. 707.*

TACOMA —*See Seattle p. 707.*

TOPPENISH pop. 8,946

──────── **WHERE TO STAY** ────────

BEST WESTERN TOPPENISH INN   *Book great rates at AAA.com*

Phone: (509)865-7444

(AAA) (SAVE)
▼▼ ▼▼ ▼▼
Hotel
$100-$140 3/1-10/31
$90-$110 11/1-2/28

Address: 515 S Elm St **Location:** I-82, exit 50, 3.1 mi e. **Facility:** Smoke free premises. 40 units. 37 one-bedroom standard units, some with whirlpools. 3 one-bedroom suites, some with efficiencies or kitchens. 2 stories (no elevator), interior corridors. **Parking:** on-site. **Amenities:** high-speed Internet, voice mail, irons, hair dryers. **Pool(s):** heated indoor. **Leisure Activities:** whirlpool, limited exercise equipment. **Guest Services:** coin laundry, wireless Internet. **Business Services:** business center. **Cards:** AX, DS, MC, VI. **Free Special Amenities:** expanded continental breakfast and high-speed Internet. *(See color ad p 752)*

CALL (&M) (≈) (✕) (✦) (🖥) (📠) (💻) / SOME UNITS FEE (🐾)

AAA Benefit:
Members save up to 20%, plus 10% bonus points with rewards program.

QUALITY INN & SUITES   *Book great rates at AAA.com*

Phone: (509)865-5800

(AAA) (SAVE)
▼▼ ▼▼
Hotel
$80-$120 3/1-9/30
$72-$110 10/1-2/28

Address: 511 S Elm St **Location:** I-82, exit 50, 3.2 mi e. **Facility:** 44 one-bedroom standard units, some with efficiencies and/or whirlpools. 2 stories, interior corridors. **Parking:** on-site. **Terms:** cancellation fee imposed. **Amenities:** voice mail, irons, hair dryers. *Some:* DVD players. **Guest Services:** wireless Internet. **Cards:** AX, DS, MC, VI. **Free Special Amenities:** expanded continental breakfast and early check-in/late check-out. *(See color ad below)*

(🍽→) CALL (&M) (✦) (🖥) (📠) (💻) / SOME UNITS FEE (🐾) (✕) (VCR)

──────── ▼ *See AAA listing above* ▼ ────────

——— WHERE TO DINE ———

VILLASENOR

Mexican
$6-$12

Phone: 509/865-4707

The popular Mexican restaurant, which occupies a festive, comfortable setting, presents an expansive menu of traditional dishes as well as American offerings. Casual dress. **Bar:** Full bar. **Reservations:** accepted **Hours:** 11 am-9 pm, Fri & Sat-10 pm. Closed: 4/12, 11/26, 12/25. **Address:** 225 S Toppenish Ave **Location:** Downtown. **Parking:** street. **Cards:** AX, DS, MC, VI.

TROUT LAKE pop. 494

——— WHERE TO STAY ———

SERENITY'S

Cabin
$89-$149 All Year

Phone: (509)395-2500

Address: 2291 SR 141 S **Location:** On SR 141, 1 mi s. **Facility:** Modern chalet-style cabins in wooded area. Some with loft, all with gas fireplace and most with view of Mount Adams. Smoke free premises. 4 cabins. 1 story, exterior corridors. **Parking:** on-site. **Terms:** office hours 9 am-10 pm, 2 night minimum stay - weekends, 14 day cancellation notice. **Amenities:** video library, DVD players, CD players, high-speed Internet. **Leisure Activities:** whirlpool, barbecue grills, picnic tables. *Fee:* massage. **Guest Services:** wireless Internet. **Cards:** AX, DS, MC, VI. **Free Special Amenities:** early check-in/late check-out and high-speed Internet.

TUKWILA —See Seattle p. 712.

TULALIP

——— WHERE TO STAY ———

TULALIP RESORT CASINO

[fyi]
Hotel
Rates not provided

Phone: 360/651-1111

Too new to rate. **Address:** 10200 Quil Ceda Blvd **Location:** I-5, exit 200, just w, then 0.9 mi n. **Amenities:** 370 units, restaurant, coffeemakers, refrigerators, pool. **Terms:** check-in 4 pm.

TUMWATER pop. 12,698

——— WHERE TO STAY ———

BEST WESTERN TUMWATER INN   *Book great rates at AAA.com*

Hotel
$103-$120 All Year

Phone: (360)956-1235

Address: 5188 Capitol Blvd **Location:** I-5, exit 102, just e. **Facility:** 90 one-bedroom standard units. 2 stories (no elevator), interior corridors. *Bath:* combo or shower only. **Parking:** on-site. **Amenities:** high-speed Internet, voice mail, hair dryers. **Guest Services:** valet and coin laundry, wireless Internet. **Business Services:** meeting rooms, PC. **Cards:** AX, DC, DS, MC, VI. **Free Special Amenities:** expanded continental breakfast and high-speed Internet.

AAA Benefit:
Members save up to 20%, plus 10% bonus points with rewards program.

COMFORT INN AND CONFERENCE CENTER   *Book at AAA.com*

Hotel
$89-$120 All Year

Phone: (360)352-0691

Address: 1620 74th Ave SW **Location:** I-5, exit 101, just se. **Facility:** Smoke free premises. 58 units. 51 one-bedroom standard units, some with whirlpools. 7 one-bedroom suites with efficiencies. 3 stories, interior corridors. *Bath:* combo or shower only. **Parking:** on-site. **Amenities:** high-speed Internet, voice mail, irons, hair dryers. **Pool(s):** heated indoor. **Leisure Activities:** whirlpool, exercise room. **Guest Services:** valet and coin laundry, wireless Internet. **Business Services:** meeting rooms, PC. **Cards:** AX, DC, DS, MC, VI.

EXTENDED STAYAMERICA-OLYMPIA-TUMWATER   *Book at AAA.com*

Hotel
$90-$105 All Year

Phone: (360)754-6063

Address: 1675 Mottman Rd SW **Location:** I-5, exit 104, 0.4 mi nw on US 101, just s on Crosby Blvd, then just se. **Facility:** 107 one-bedroom standard units. 3 stories, interior corridors. *Bath:* combo or shower only. **Parking:** on-site. **Terms:** office hours 7 am-11 pm, cancellation fee imposed. **Amenities:** high-speed Internet, voice mail, irons. **Guest Services:** coin laundry, wireless Internet. **Cards:** AX, CB, DC, DS, JC, MC, VI.

GUESTHOUSE INN & SUITES   *Book at AAA.com*

Hotel
$89-$120 All Year

Phone: (360)943-5040

Address: 1600 74th Ave SW **Location:** I-5, exit 101, just se. **Facility:** 59 units. 57 one-bedroom standard units, some with whirlpools. 2 one-bedroom suites with efficiencies. 3 stories, interior corridors. *Bath:* combo or shower only. **Parking:** on-site. **Terms:** cancellation fee imposed. **Amenities:** video library (fee), high-speed Internet, voice mail, irons, hair dryers. **Pool(s):** heated indoor. **Leisure Activities:** whirlpool, exercise room. **Guest Services:** coin laundry, wireless Internet. **Business Services:** meeting rooms, PC. **Cards:** AX, DC, DS, MC, VI.

------ **WHERE TO DINE** ------

FALLS TERRACE RESTAURANT   Phone: 360/943-7830

AAA
▼▼▼
American
$9-$20

A two-tiered dining area affords every seat an unobstructed view of Tumwater Falls. Fresh salmon is served year round. Famous for mud pie and baker's cream, the eatery goes out of its way to satisfy your sweet tooth. Casual dress. **Bar:** Full bar. **Reservations:** accepted. **Hours:** 11 am-8:30 pm, Fri-9 pm, Sat 11:30 am-9 pm, Sun 11:30 am-8 pm. Closed: 1/1, 7/4, 12/25. **Address:** 106 Deschutes Way SW **Location:** I-5, exit 103, 0.4 mi n. **Parking:** on-site. **Cards:** AX, CB, DS, MC, VI.

TWISP pop. 938

------ **WHERE TO STAY** ------

IDLE-A-WHILE MOTEL   Phone: 509/997-3222

▼▼▼
Motel
$50-$130 All Year

Address: 505 N SR 20 **Location:** Just n of town. **Facility:** 25 units. 16 one-bedroom standard units, some with kitchens. 9 cottages. 1 story, exterior corridors. *Bath:* combo or shower only. **Parking:** on-site. **Terms:** office hours 7 am-9 pm. **Amenities:** video library. **Leisure Activities:** sauna, whirlpool, tennis court, basketball. **Guest Services:** wireless Internet. **Cards:** AX, DS, MC, VI.

[ASK] [✕] [📺] / SOME UNITS FEE [🐕] [✕] FEE [VCR] [🖥] [📠]

------ **WHERE TO DINE** ------

TWISP RIVER PUB   Phone: 509/997-6822

▼▼▼
American
$6-$17

A comfortable resting place after a fast-paced day in the Methow Valley, the restaurant lets guests settle into a chair on the expansive deck overlooking the Twisp River or maybe slide into a booth to get a bird's-eye view of the bar patrons. At least 10 taps flow with fresh beers made on site. Casual foods might include burgers, sandwiches, Thai peanut stir-fry or brats. Those looking for a bigger meal might opt for sirloin steak or pork tenderloin. Casual dress. **Bar:** Full bar. **Hours:** 11:30 am-8:30 pm, Fri-9 pm, Sat 10 am-9 pm, Sun 10 am-8:30 pm. Closed: 11/26, 12/24, 12/25; also Mon & Tues. **Address:** 201 N Methow Valley Hwy (US 20) **Location:** West end of town. **Parking:** on-site. **Cards:** AX, DS, MC, VI.

UNION

------ **WHERE TO STAY** ------

ALDERBROOK RESORT & SPA   *Book at AAA.com*   Phone: (360)898-2200

▼▼▼
Resort
Hotel
$139-$529 All Year

Address: 7101 E SR 106 **Location:** Just e of town. **Facility:** Located on the shores of the Hood Canal, lush green lawns, a full-service spa and a few rental cottages add to the property's charm. Smoke free premises. 93 units. 75 one-bedroom standard units. 2 one-bedroom suites. 16 cottages. 1-3 stories, interior/exterior corridors. *Bath:* combo or shower only. **Parking:** on-site. **Terms:** check-in 4 pm, 7 day cancellation notice-fee imposed. **Amenities:** video library, DVD players, CD players, high-speed Internet, dual phone lines, voice mail, safes, honor bars, irons, hair dryers. **Pool(s):** heated indoor. **Leisure Activities:** sauna, whirlpool, steamroom, rental canoes, rental paddleboats, fishing, 2 tennis courts, recreation programs in summer, playground, exercise room, spa, shuffleboard, volleyball. *Fee:* boat dock, golf-18 holes. **Guest Services:** valet laundry, area transportation, wireless Internet. **Business Services:** conference facilities, business center. **Cards:** AX, MC, VI.

[ASK] [🍴] [🍸] [🏊] [✕] [✕] [🖥] [📠] / SOME UNITS FEE [🐕] [📠]

UNION GAP pop. 5,621

------ **WHERE TO STAY** ------

BEST WESTERN AHTANUM INN   *Book great rates at AAA.com*   Phone: (509)248-9700

AAA [SAVE]
▼▼▼
Hotel
$89-$209 All Year

Address: 2408 Rudkin Rd **Location:** I-82, exit 36, just n. **Facility:** 118 units. 106 one-bedroom standard units, some with whirlpools. 12 one-bedroom suites with efficiencies. 2 stories (no elevator), interior corridors. **Parking:** on-site. **Terms:** 3 night minimum stay - weekends, cancellation fee imposed. **Amenities:** high-speed Internet, voice mail, irons, hair dryers. *Some:* DVD players. **Pool(s):** heated outdoor. **Leisure Activities:** croquet, soccer, barbecue area, exercise room, horseshoes, volleyball. **Guest Services:** valet and coin laundry, wireless Internet. **Business Services:** meeting rooms, business center. **Cards:** AX, DC, DS, MC, VI. **Free Special Amenities:** expanded continental breakfast and high-speed Internet.

AAA Benefit:
Members save up to 20%, plus 10% bonus points with rewards program.

[🍴+] CALL [📶M] [🏊] [✕] [🖥] [📠] [📠] / SOME UNITS FEE [🐕] [✕]

QUALITY INN-YAKIMA VALLEY   *Book great rates at AAA.com*   Phone: (509)248-6924

AAA [SAVE]
▼▼▼
Motel
$69-$169 All Year

Address: 12 E Valley Mall Blvd **Location:** I-82, exit 36, just s. Located adjacent to Valley Mall. **Facility:** 85 one-bedroom standard units. 2 stories (no elevator), exterior corridors. *Bath:* combo or shower only. **Parking:** on-site. **Terms:** cancellation fee imposed. **Amenities:** high-speed Internet, voice mail, irons, hair dryers. **Pool(s):** heated outdoor. **Guest Services:** valet and coin laundry, wireless Internet. **Business Services:** meeting rooms, business center. **Cards:** AX, CB, DC, DS, MC, VI. **Free Special Amenities:** expanded continental breakfast and high-speed Internet.

[🍴+] CALL [📶M] [🏊] [📺] [🖥] [📠] [📠] / SOME UNITS FEE [🐕] [✕]

SUPER 8 MOTEL YAKIMA   *Book at AAA.com*   Phone: (509)248-8880

▼▼▼
Hotel
$83-$110 3/1-10/11
$76-$110 10/12-2/28

Address: 2605 Rudkin Rd **Location:** I-82, exit 36, just s. **Facility:** 96 units. 95 one-bedroom standard units. 1 one-bedroom suite. 3 stories (no elevator), interior corridors. **Parking:** on-site. **Amenities:** high-speed Internet, hair dryers. **Pool(s):** heated indoor. **Guest Services:** coin laundry, wireless Internet. **Cards:** AX, CB, DC, DS, MC, VI.

[ASK] CALL [📶M] [🏊] [📺] [📠] / SOME UNITS FEE [🐕] [✕] [🖥] [📠]

UNIVERSITY PLACE —See Seattle p. 715.

VANCOUVER —See Nearby Portland, OR p. 476.

VASHON —See Seattle p. 715.

WALLA WALLA pop. 29,686

—————— WHERE TO STAY ——————

BEST WESTERN WALLA WALLA SUITES INN Book great rates at AAA.com
Phone: (509)525-4700

(AAA) (SAVE)

Hotel
$110-$150 All Year

Address: 7 E Oak St **Location:** US 12, exit 2nd Ave, just s. **Facility:** Smoke free premises. 78 one-bedroom standard units, some with whirlpools. 3 stories, interior corridors. *Bath:* combo or shower only. **Parking:** on-site. **Amenities:** voice mail, irons, hair dryers. *Some:* high-speed Internet. **Pool(s):** heated indoor. **Leisure Activities:** whirlpool, exercise room. **Guest Services:** valet and coin laundry, wireless Internet. **Business Services:** meeting rooms, business center. **Cards:** AX, CB, DC, DS, JC, MC, VI. **Free Special Amenities: expanded continental breakfast and local telephone calls.**

Best Western
AAA Benefit:
Members save up to 20%, plus 10% bonus points with rewards program.

BUDGET INN Book great rates at AAA.com
Phone: (509)529-4410

(AAA) (SAVE)

Motel
$55-$99 All Year

Address: 305 N 2nd Ave **Location:** US 12, exit 2nd Ave, 0.3 mi s. **Facility:** 58 units. 56 one- and 2 two-bedroom standard units, some with kitchens. 2 stories (no elevator), exterior corridors. *Bath:* combo or shower only. **Parking:** on-site. **Terms:** office hours 7 am-11 pm. **Amenities:** irons, hair dryers. **Pool(s):** heated outdoor. **Guest Services:** coin laundry, wireless Internet. **Cards:** AX, DS, MC, VI. **Free Special Amenities: continental breakfast and newspaper.**

COMFORT INN & SUITES Book at AAA.com
Phone: 509/522-3500

Hotel
Rates not provided

Address: 1419 W Pine St **Location:** US 12, exit Pendleton/Prescott. **Facility:** 76 units. 73 one- and 1 two-bedroom standard units. 2 one-bedroom suites. 4 stories, interior corridors. *Bath:* combo or shower only. **Parking:** on-site. **Amenities:** high-speed Internet, voice mail, irons, hair dryers. **Pool(s):** heated indoor. **Leisure Activities:** whirlpool, exercise room. **Guest Services:** coin laundry, wireless Internet. **Business Services:** business center.

GREEN GABLES INN
Phone: 509/525-5501

Bed & Breakfast
$165-$225 All Year

Address: 922 Bonsella St **Location:** US 12, exit Clinton St, just s, then just w. Located in a quiet residential area. **Facility:** A turn-of-the-20th-century Craftsman-style house with tastefully furnished rooms, this inn is close to Whitman College. Smoke free premises. 5 one-bedroom standard units, some with whirlpools. 2 stories (no elevator), interior corridors. **Parking:** on-site. **Terms:** office hours 9 am-5 pm, 2-3 night minimum stay - seasonal and/or weekends, age restrictions may apply, 30 day cancellation notice-fee imposed. **Amenities:** video library, hair dryers. **Cards:** AX, DS, MC, VI.

HOLIDAY INN EXPRESS Book at AAA.com
Phone: (509)525-6200

Hotel
$129 3/1-10/1
$119 10/2-2/28

Address: 1433 W Pine St **Location:** US 12, exit Pendleton/Prescott. **Facility:** Smoke free premises. 81 one-bedroom standard units, some with whirlpools. 3 stories, interior corridors. **Parking:** on-site. **Terms:** check-in 4 pm. **Amenities:** high-speed Internet, dual phone lines, voice mail, irons, hair dryers. **Pool(s):** heated indoor. **Leisure Activities:** whirlpool, hiking trails, jogging, exercise room. **Guest Services:** valet and coin laundry, wireless Internet. **Business Services:** meeting rooms, business center. **Cards:** AX, DC, DS, MC, VI.

LA QUINTA INN WALLA WALLA Book great rates at AAA.com
Phone: (509)525-2522

(AAA) (SAVE)

Hotel
$69-$139 All Year

Address: 520 N 2nd Ave **Location:** US 12, exit 2nd Ave, just s. Located adjacent to the historic railroad passenger depot. **Facility:** Smoke free premises. 61 units. 60 one-bedroom standard units, some with efficiencies and/or whirlpools. 1 one-bedroom suite with kitchen. 3 stories (no elevator), interior corridors. **Parking:** on-site. **Amenities:** irons, hair dryers. **Pool(s):** heated indoor. **Leisure Activities:** sauna, whirlpool, exercise room. **Guest Services:** valet and coin laundry, wireless Internet. **Business Services:** meeting rooms, business center. **Cards:** AX, CB, DS, MC, VI. **Free Special Amenities: expanded continental breakfast and high-speed Internet.**

MARCUS WHITMAN HOTEL & CONFERENCE CENTER
Book great rates at AAA.com

Phone: (509)525-2200

AAA SAVE

♦♦♦♦

Hotel
$129-$349 3/1-10/31
$119-$325 11/1-2/28

Address: 6 W Rose St **Location:** Downtown. **Facility:** Smoke free premises. 127 units. 105 one-bedroom standard units, some with whirlpools. 22 one-bedroom suites. 4-7 stories, interior corridors. *Bath:* combo or shower only. **Parking:** on-site. **Amenities:** high-speed Internet, dual phone lines, voice mail, irons, hair dryers. *Some:* DVD players, safes. **Dining:** The Marc, see separate listing. **Leisure Activities:** exercise room. **Guest Services:** valet laundry, airport transportation-Walla Walla Regional Airport, wireless Internet. **Business Services:** conference facilities, business center. **Cards:** AX, DC, DS, MC, VI. **Free Special Amenities:** full breakfast and high-speed Internet.
(See color ad below)

🛬 🍴 ✖ 🐾 🛢 💻 / SOME UNITS FEE 🐾

WALLA WALLA SUPER 8
Book at AAA.com

Phone: 509/525-8800

♦♦ ♦

Hotel
Rates not provided

Address: 2315 Eastgate St N **Location:** US 12, exit Wilbur Ave, just s. **Facility:** 101 units. 99 one-bedroom standard units. 2 one-bedroom suites, some with kitchens (no utensils). 3 stories, interior corridors. *Bath:* combo or shower only. **Parking:** on-site. **Amenities:** safes (fee), hair dryers. **Pool(s):** heated indoor. **Leisure Activities:** whirlpool. **Guest Services:** coin laundry, wireless Internet.

CALL 🔊 🏊 🎬 / SOME UNITS FEE 🐾 ✖ 🛢 🖥

WALLA WALLA TRAVELODGE
Book great rates at AAA.com

Phone: (509)529-4940

AAA SAVE

♦♦♦ ♦

Motel
$55-$99 All Year

Address: 421 E Main St **Location:** US 12, exit 2nd Ave, 0.5 mi s, then just e. **Facility:** 39 one-bedroom standard units. 2 stories (no elevator), interior/exterior corridors. *Bath:* combo or shower only. **Parking:** on-site. **Terms:** 2 night minimum stay. **Amenities:** safes (fee), irons, hair dryers. **Pool(s):** heated outdoor. **Guest Services:** wireless Internet. **Cards:** AX, DS, MC, VI. **Free Special Amenities:** continental breakfast and high-speed Internet.

🍴 🏊 🎬 🛢 🖥 💻 / SOME UNITS FEE 🐾 ✖ VCR

WALLA WALLA VINEYARD INN
Book great rates at AAA.com

Phone: (509)529-4360

AAA SAVE

♦♦ ♦

Hotel
$69-$149 3/1-10/31
$59-$99 11/1-2/28

Address: 325 E Main St **Location:** US 12, exit 2nd Ave, 0.5 mi s, then just e. **Facility:** 85 one-bedroom standard units, some with efficiencies and/or whirlpools. 2 stories (no elevator), interior/exterior corridors. **Parking:** on-site. **Pool(s):** heated outdoor. **Leisure Activities:** sauna, whirlpool, exercise room. **Guest Services:** valet and coin laundry. **Cards:** AX, DC, DS, MC, VI. **Free Special Amenities:** continental breakfast and high-speed Internet.

🍴 🏊 ✖ 🎬 💻 / SOME UNITS FEE 🐾 ✖ 🛢 🖥

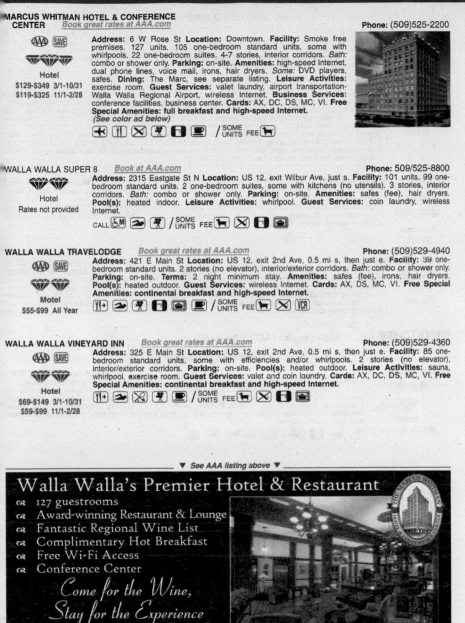

——— WHERE TO DINE ———

DESTINATION GRILL AT THE DEPOT

American
$11-$42

Phone: 509/526-0100

In a remodeled historic train depot, this restaurant features smoked prime rib, seafood, pasta and vegetarian dishes. Casual dress. **Bar:** Full bar. **Reservations:** accepted. **Hours:** 11 am-9 pm, Sun & Mon 5 pm-8 pm. Closed: 12/25; also Super Bowl Sun. **Address:** 416 N 2nd Ave **Location:** US 12, exit 2nd Ave, just s. **Parking:** on-site. **Cards:** AX, DS, MC, VI.

THE HOMESTEAD RESTAURANT

American
$6-$25

Phone: 509/522-0345

Reproduced antiques and other decorative touches support the Early West theme of this homey restaurant, which is tucked well off the street in a commercial strip area near shopping and Whitman College. Oak dividers with decorative stained-glass panels separate the comfortable booths. The menu comprises specialties of fresh seafood, aged beef, pasta and vegetarian entrees, as well as home cooking along the lines of cornbread with honey or macaroni and cheese. The desserts are homemade. Casual dress. **Bar:** Full bar. **Reservations:** accepted. **Hours:** 11:30 am-2 & 5-8 pm, Fri-9 pm, Sat 8 am-2 & 5-9 pm, Sun 8 am-2 pm. Closed: 12/25; also Mon. **Address:** 1528 E Isaacs Ave **Location:** US 12, exit Wilbur Ave, 0.4 mi s, then 0.5 mi w. **Parking:** on-site. **Cards:** AX, DS, MC, VI.

THE MARC   *Menu on AAA.com*

AAA
American
$9-$30

Phone: 509/525-2200

The Marc features regional seasonal fun with Pacific Northwest Cuisine, serving Certified Angus Beef, Seasonal Wild Pacific Seafood and the freshest local produce. Casual dress. **Bar:** Full bar. **Reservations:** accepted. **Hours:** 11:30 am-1:30 & 6-8:30 pm, Sat 6 pm-9 pm, Sun 6 pm-8:30 pm; seasonal hours may vary. **Address:** 6 W Rose St **Location:** Downtown; in Marcus Whitman Hotel & Conference Center. **Parking:** on-site. **Cards:** AX, DC, DS, MC, VI. *(See color ad p 743)*

WHITEHOUSE-CRAWFORD

American
$12-$40

Phone: 509/525-2222

In a former warehouse, the large dining room has a spare, uncluttered yet elegant appeal. The interesting, and sometimes even challenging, menu comes together with amazingly satisfying results. All desserts, even the ice creams, are made on site, and although the breads are not, they are imported daily from Seattle by, of all things, the bus. Casual dress. **Bar:** Full bar. **Reservations:** accepted. **Hours:** 4 pm-10 pm. Closed: major holidays; also 12/24, 12/31, Tues & Super Bowl Sun. **Address:** 55 W Cherry St **Location:** Downtown. **Parking:** street. **Cards:** AX, MC, VI.

WENATCHEE pop. 27,856—See also *EAST WENATCHEE*.

——— WHERE TO STA ———

AVENUE MOTEL

AAA SAVE

Motel
$50-$76 All Year

Phone: 509/663-7161

Address: 720 N Wenatchee Ave **Location:** On US 2 business loop; just nw of downtown. **Facility:** 38 units. 36 one-bedroom standard units, some with efficiencies. 2 one-bedroom suites. 1-2 stories (no elevator), interior/exterior corridors. **Bath:** combo or shower only. **Parking:** on-site. **Terms:** office hours 7 am-11 pm, cancellation fee imposed. **Pool(s):** heated outdoor. **Leisure Activities:** whirlpool. **Guest Services:** wireless Internet. **Cards:** AX, DS, MC, VI. **Free Special Amenities:** continental breakfast and high-speed Internet.

▮▸ 🏊 🖥 🖨 / SOME UNITS FEE 🐾 ✕ ▭

▼ See AAA listing p 745 ▼

BEST WESTERN CHIEFTAIN INN
Book great rates at AAA.com

Phone: (509)665-8585

AAA SAVE

Hotel
$110-$120 3/1-10/15
$90-$100 10/16-2/28

Address: 1017 N Wenatchee Ave **Location:** Downtown. **Facility:** Smoke free premises. 77 one-bedroom standard units. 2 stories (no elevator), interior corridors. *Bath:* combo or shower only. **Parking:** on-site. **Amenities:** irons, hair dryers. *Some:* high-speed Internet. **Pool(s):** heated outdoor. **Leisure Activities:** whirlpool, exercise room. **Guest Services:** valet and coin laundry, wireless Internet. **Business Services:** meeting rooms, business center. **Cards:** AX, DC, DS, MC, VI. **Free Special Amenities: full breakfast and high-speed Internet.** *(See color ad p 744)*

AAA Benefit:
Members save up to 20%, plus 10% bonus points with rewards program.

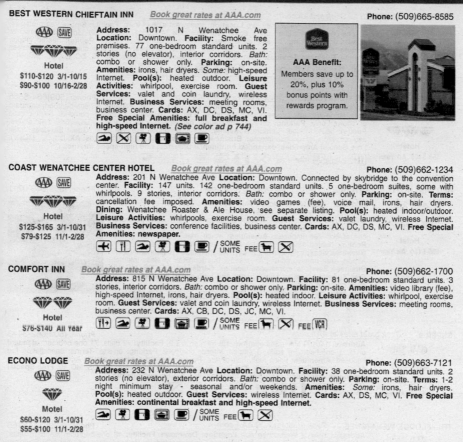

COAST WENATCHEE CENTER HOTEL
Book great rates at AAA.com

Phone: (509)662-1234

AAA SAVE

Hotel
$125-$165 3/1-10/31
$79-$125 11/1-2/28

Address: 201 N Wenatchee Ave **Location:** Downtown. Connected by skybridge to the convention center. **Facility:** 147 units. 142 one-bedroom standard units. 5 one-bedroom suites, some with whirlpools. 9 stories, interior corridors. *Bath:* combo or shower only. **Parking:** on-site. **Terms:** cancellation fee imposed. **Amenities:** video games (fee), voice mail, irons, hair dryers. **Dining:** Wenatchee Roaster & Ale House, see separate listing. **Pool(s):** heated indoor/outdoor. **Leisure Activities:** whirlpools, exercise room. **Guest Services:** valet laundry, wireless Internet. **Business Services:** conference facilities, business center. **Cards:** AX, DC, DS, MC, VI. **Free Special Amenities: newspaper.**

COMFORT INN
Book great rates at AAA.com

Phone: (509)662-1700

AAA SAVE

Hotel
$76-$140 All Year

Address: 815 N Wenatchee Ave **Location:** Downtown. **Facility:** 81 one-bedroom standard units. 3 stories, interior corridors. *Bath:* combo or shower only. **Parking:** on-site. **Amenities:** video games (fee), high-speed Internet, irons, hair dryers. **Pool(s):** heated indoor. **Leisure Activities:** whirlpool, exercise room. **Guest Services:** valet and coin laundry, wireless Internet. **Business Services:** meeting rooms, business center. **Cards:** AX, CB, DC, DS, JC, MC, VI.

ECONO LODGE
Book great rates at AAA.com

Phone: (509)663-7121

AAA SAVE

Motel
$60-$120 3/1-10/31
$55-$100 11/1-2/28

Address: 232 N Wenatchee Ave **Location:** Downtown. **Facility:** 38 one-bedroom standard units. 2 stories (no elevator), exterior corridors. *Bath:* combo or shower only. **Parking:** on-site. **Terms:** 1-2 night minimum stay - seasonal and/or weekends. **Amenities:** *Some:* irons, hair dryers. **Pool(s):** heated outdoor. **Guest Services:** wireless Internet. **Cards:** AX, DS, MC, VI. **Free Special Amenities: continental breakfast and high-speed Internet.**

HOLIDAY INN EXPRESS *Book at AAA.com*   **Phone:** (509)663-6355

Hotel

$119-$189 3/1-10/31
$99-$169 11/1-2/28

Address: 1921 N Wenatchee Ave **Location:** Northwest side of town. **Facility:** Smoke free premises. 90 one-bedroom standard units, some with whirlpools. 4 stories, interior corridors. *Bath:* combo or shower only. **Parking:** on-site. **Amenities:** voice mail, irons, hair dryers. **Pool(s):** heated indoor. **Leisure Activities:** whirlpool, exercise room. **Guest Services:** valet and coin laundry, wireless Internet. **Business Services:** meeting rooms, business center. **Cards:** AX, CB, DC, DS, JC, MC, VI.

LA QUINTA INN & SUITES WENATCHEE *Book great rates at AAA.com*   **Phone:** (509)664-6565

Hotel

$69-$139 All Year

Address: 1905 N Wenatchee Ave **Location:** West end of town. **Facility:** 65 one-bedroom standard units, some with efficiencies and/or whirlpools. 3 stories (no elevator), interior corridors. *Bath:* combo or shower only. **Parking:** on-site. **Amenities:** high-speed Internet, voice mail, irons, hair dryers. **Pool(s):** heated indoor. **Leisure Activities:** sauna, whirlpool, exercise room. **Guest Services:** valet and coin laundry, wireless Internet. **Business Services:** business center. **Cards:** AX, DS, JC, MC, VI. **Free Special Amenities: expanded continental breakfast and high-speed Internet.**

RED LION HOTEL WENATCHEE *Book great rates at AAA.com*   **Phone:** (509)663-0711

Hotel

$99-$180 All Year

Address: 1225 N Wenatchee Ave **Location:** Just nw of downtown. **Facility:** Smoke free premises. 149 units. 148 one-bedroom standard units. 1 one-bedroom suite. 3 stories, interior corridors. *Bath:* combo or shower only. **Parking:** on-site. **Terms:** 2-3 night minimum stay, cancellation fee imposed. **Amenities:** voice mail, irons, hair dryers. **Pool(s):** heated outdoor. **Leisure Activities:** whirlpool, exercise room. **Guest Services:** valet laundry, airport transportation-Pangborn Memorial Airport, area transportation-train station, bus terminal, wireless Internet. **Business Services:** conference facilities. **Cards:** AX, DC, DS, MC, VI. **Free Special Amenities: newspaper and high-speed Internet.** *(See color ad below)*

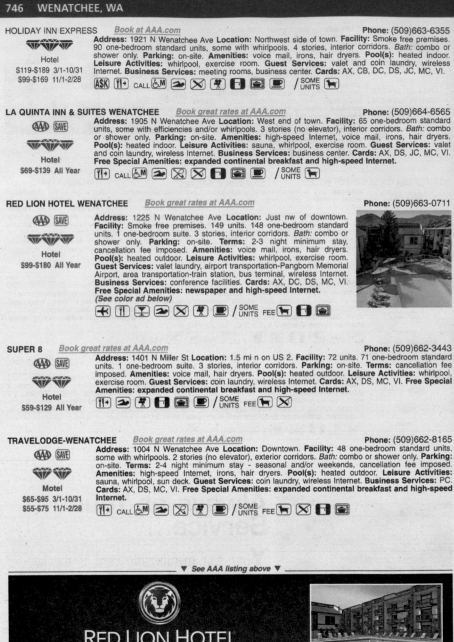

SUPER 8 *Book great rates at AAA.com*   **Phone:** (509)662-3443

Hotel

$59-$129 All Year

Address: 1401 N Miller St **Location:** 1.5 mi n on US 2. **Facility:** 72 units. 71 one-bedroom standard units. 1 one-bedroom suite. 3 stories, interior corridors. **Parking:** on-site. **Terms:** cancellation fee imposed. **Amenities:** voice mail, hair dryers. **Pool(s):** heated outdoor. **Leisure Activities:** whirlpool, exercise room. **Guest Services:** coin laundry, wireless Internet. **Cards:** AX, DS, MC, VI. **Free Special Amenities: expanded continental breakfast and high-speed Internet.**

TRAVELODGE-WENATCHEE *Book great rates at AAA.com*   **Phone:** (509)662-8165

Motel

$65-$95 3/1-10/31
$55-$75 11/1-2/28

Address: 1004 N Wenatchee Ave **Location:** Downtown. **Facility:** 48 one-bedroom standard units, some with whirlpools. 2 stories (no elevator), exterior corridors. *Bath:* combo or shower only. **Parking:** on-site. **Terms:** 2-4 night minimum stay - seasonal and/or weekends, cancellation fee imposed. **Amenities:** high-speed Internet, irons, hair dryers. **Pool(s):** heated outdoor. **Leisure Activities:** sauna, whirlpool, sun deck. **Guest Services:** coin laundry, wireless Internet. **Business Services:** PC. **Cards:** AX, DS, MC, VI. **Free Special Amenities: expanded continental breakfast and high-speed Internet.**

▼ *See AAA listing above* ▼

WARM SPRINGS INN

(AAA) [SAVE]

▽▽▽▽

Historic Bed
& Breakfast

$105-$150 All Year

Address: 1611 Love Ln **Location:** Northwest of town; just s of US 2 via Lower Sunny Slope Rd. Located in a quiet area. **Facility:** Located on a 10-acre, park-like setting next to the Wenatchee River, this 1917 home offers a retreat and an expansive deck to view the scenery. Designated smoking area. 6 one-bedroom standard units. 2 stories (no elevator), interior/exterior corridors. *Bath:* combo or shower only. **Parking:** on-site. **Terms:** 7 day cancellation notice-fee imposed. **Amenities:** video library, DVD players, irons, hair dryers. **Leisure Activities:** whirlpool, fishing, gazebo, bicycles, hiking trails. **Guest Services:** wireless Internet. **Business Services:** meeting rooms. **Cards:** AX, CB, DC, DS, JC, MC, VI.

Phone: (509)662-8365

[🖾] [⊠] [📷] [☎] / SOME UNITS [🛢] [💻]

——— WHERE TO DINE ———

THE COTTAGE INN

▽▽ ▽▽

Steak & Seafood
$6-$26

Steak, seafood and pan-fried chicken are house specialties at the cozy, casual restaurant, but lunch is also interesting, with pasta dishes and such entree salads as crab Louis or shrimp with bleu cheese, apples and almonds. Distinctive sandwiches, such as salmon burgers and turkey pitas, also tempt the taste buds. Save room for a slice of homemade pie; the coconut cream with nut crust is nearly a religious experience. Casual dress. **Bar:** Full bar. **Hours:** 11 am-2 & 4:30-9 pm, Sat 4 pm-9 pm, Sun 9 am-2 & 4-8 pm. Closed: 11/26, 12/25; also Mon. **Address:** 134 Easy St **Location:** Northwest edge of town via Wenatchee Ave and Easy St. **Parking:** on-site. **Cards:** MC, VI.

Phone: 509/663-4435

EL ABUELO

▽▽ ▽▽

Mexican
$6-$14

A traditional Mexican restaurant located in a business setting, El Abuelo serves a hearty fare of enchiladas, fajitas and quesadillas. Colorful interior and relaxed service. Casual dress. **Bar:** Full bar. **Reservations:** suggested, Mon-Thurs. **Hours:** 11 am-10 pm, Fri & Sat-11 pm. Closed: 11/26, 12/25. **Address:** 601 S Mission St **Location:** Downtown. **Parking:** on-site. **Cards:** AX, DS, MC, VI.

Phone: 509/662-7331

INNA'S CUISINE

(AAA)

▽▽▽▽

International
$8-$23

Menu on AAA.com

Well suited to business lunches and romantic dinners, the tasteful downtown retreat exudes Old World charm and ambience. Strong Russian beers complement made-from-scratch dishes, including many pasta and puff pastry choices. Freshly prepared desserts merit consideration. Indecisive diners might try a food "visit," which compiles smaller portions of a particular style. The Russian visit, for example, comes with a cabbage roll, beef stroganoff with egg noodles and fried pirozhki. Casual dress. **Bar:** Beer & wine. **Reservations:** suggested. **Hours:** 11 am-9 pm. Closed: 11/26, 12/25; also Sun. **Address:** 26 N Wenatchee Ave **Location:** Downtown. **Parking:** street. **Cards:** MC, VI.

Phone: 509/888-4662

MISSION STREET BISTRO & WINE BAR

▽▽▽▽

French
$6-$11

The beautifully decorated, intimate bistro offers seasonal outdoor seating at classic umbrella tables. Crepes and fondue are specialties. Among homemade desserts are yummy crepes. Casual dress. **Bar:** Beer & wine. **Reservations:** accepted. **Hours:** 11 am-10 pm, Sat from 5 pm. Closed major holidays; also Sun. **Address:** 202 N Mission St **Location:** Downtown. **Parking:** on-site. **Cards:** MC, VI.

Phone: 509/665-2406

SHAKTI'S

▽▽▽▽

Northern Italian
$15-$28

A Mediterranean influence punctuates offerings of Northern Italian cuisine. The intimate, softly illuminated dining room is infused with the sounds of jazz. The dining patio is open seasonally. Casual dress. **Bar:** Full bar. **Reservations:** suggested. **Hours:** 5:30 pm-8:30 pm. Closed: 1/1, 11/26, 12/24, 12/25; also 1st weeks of Jan & July. **Address:** 218 N Mission St **Location:** Downtown. **Parking:** on-site. **Cards:** AX, MC, VI.

Phone: 509/662-3321

THE THAI RESTAURANT

▽▽▽▽

Thai
$6-$15

A friendly, informative staff attends to the family restaurant, where fresh dishes including chicken sa te, won ton soup and spicy prawns are well-prepared and flavorful. The lunch buffet is a quick alternative to a full-service meal. **Bar:** Beer & wine. **Reservations:** accepted. **Hours:** 11 am-2 & 5-9 pm. Closed major holidays; also Sun. **Address:** 1211 N Mission St **Location:** Downtown. **Parking:** on-site. **Cards:** MC, VI.

Phone: 509/662-8077

VISCONTI'S ITALIAN RESTAURANT

▽▽▽▽

Italian
$6-$28

Try the locals favorite Italian restaurant that serves fresh items like spaghetti with broccoli and prawns or fresh tortellini. Don't forget to save room for the tiramisu. **Bar:** Beer & wine. **Reservations:** suggested. **Hours:** 11 am-9:30 pm, Fri-10 pm, Sat 5 pm-10 pm, Sun 5 pm-9 pm. Closed: 11/26, 12/25. **Address:** 1737 N Wenatchee Ave **Location:** Downtown. **Parking:** on-site. **Cards:** AX, DS, MC, VI.

Phone: 509/662-5013

WENATCHEE ROASTER & ALE HOUSE

▽▽▽▽

American
$6-$20

From the ninth-floor location, diners enjoy views of the river and mountains. Herbs and spices flavor meats and poultry that roast over a horizontal spit until they're tender enough to slice with a fork. Live music and dancing create an upbeat atmosphere. Casual dress. Entertainment. **Bar:** Full bar. **Reservations:** suggested, weekends. **Hours:** 6:30 am-9 pm, Fri-10 pm, Sat 7 am-10 pm, Sun 7 am-9 pm. **Address:** 201 N Wenatchee Ave **Location:** Downtown; in Coast Wenatchee Center Hotel. **Parking:** on-site. **Cards:** AX, CB, DC, DS, JC, MC, VI.

Phone: 509/662-1234

CALL [🔊M]

WILD HUCKLEBERRY

▽▽ ▽▽

American
$6-$20

In a 1919 vintage house with extensive woodwork and many windows, the bright and charming restaurant serves a broad menu with many comfort foods. The freshest of ingredients are used, and all meats are roasted in house. Casual dress. **Bar:** Beer & wine. **Reservations:** accepted. **Hours:** 7 am-3 & 5-9 pm, Sat from 8 am, Sun & Mon 8 am-3 pm. Closed: 1/1, 11/26, 12/25. **Address:** 302 S Mission St **Location:** Downtown. **Parking:** on-site. **Cards:** AX, MC, VI.

Phone: 509/663-1013

THE WINDMILL

AAA

Steak & Seafood
$13-$35

Phone: 509/665-9529

This windmill-shaped structure was built in 1931. The personable staff has worked for years to build a loyal clientele who return for the friendly service, hand-cut steak, fresh seafood and from-scratch dessert. Casual dress. **Bar:** Beer & wine. **Reservations:** accepted. **Hours:** 5 pm-close. Closed major holidays **Address:** 1501 N Wenatchee Ave **Location:** Downtown. **Parking:** on-site. **Cards:** AX, DS, MC, VI.

WESTPORT pop. 2,137

──────── WHERE TO STAY ────────

ALBATROSS MOTEL

Motel
$49-$89 All Year

Phone: 360/268-9233

Address: 200 E Dock St **Location:** Just s from boat basin. **Facility:** Smoke free premises. 13 units 12 one-bedroom standard units, some with efficiencies. 1 one-bedroom suite with efficiency. 2 stories (no elevator), exterior corridors. *Bath:* combo or shower only. **Parking:** street. **Terms:** office hours am-11 pm, 3 day cancellation notice. **Cards:** CB, DC, DS, MC, VI.

 / SOME UNITS FEE

CHATEAU WESTPORT

AAA SAVE

Hotel
$89-$388 All Year

Phone: 360/268-9101

Address: 710 W Hancock St **Location:** Just w of SR 105 Spur N; 1.5 mi n of Twin Harbors State Park. **Facility:** Smoke free premises. 104 units. 102 one-bedroom standard units, some with efficiencies. 2 two-bedroom suites with kitchens. 4 stories, interior corridors. **Parking:** on-site. **Terms:** cancellation fee imposed. **Amenities:** hair dryers. **Pool(s):** heated indoor. **Leisure Activities:** whirlpool, playground, basketball, horseshoes, volleyball. **Guest Services:** wireless Internet. **Business Services:** meeting rooms. **Cards:** AX, DS, MC, VI. **Free Special Amenities:** expanded continental breakfast and high-speed Internet.

CALL / SOME UNITS FEE FEE

PACIFIC MOTEL & RV

Motel
$19-$25 All Year

Phone: 360/268-9325

Address: 330 S Forrest St **Location:** 1.7 mi n of Twin Harbors State Park. **Facility:** Smoke free premises. 12 units. 11 one-bedroom standard units. 1 two-bedroom suite with kitchen. 1 story, exterior corridors. *Bath:* combo or shower only. **Parking:** on-site. **Terms:** office hours 9 am-11 pm. **Pool(s):** heated outdoor. **Leisure Activities:** horseshoes. **Guest Services:** coin laundry, wireless Internet. **Cards:** DS, MC, VI.

──────── *The following lodging was either not evaluated or did not* ────────
meet AAA rating requirements but is listed for your information only.

WINDJAMMER MOTEL

fyi

Phone: 360/268-9351

Not evaluated. **Address:** 461 E Pacific Ave **Location:** Downtown. Facilities, services, and decor characterize an economy property.

WINTHROP pop. 349

──────── WHERE TO STAY ────────

AMERICAS BEST VALUE CASCADE INN

AAA SAVE

Motel
$80-$150 3/1-10/20
$70-$120 10/21-2/28

Book great rates at AAA.com

Phone: (509)996-3100

Address: 1006 SR 20 **Location:** 1 mi e. **Facility:** 63 one-bedroom standard units. 2 stories (no elevator), exterior corridors. **Parking:** on-site. **Terms:** office hours 7 am-10 pm, 2 night minimum stay - weekends, 3 day cancellation notice-fee imposed. **Amenities:** voice mail, irons, hair dryers. *Some:* high-speed Internet. **Pool(s):** heated outdoor. **Leisure Activities:** whirlpool, fishing, picnic & barbecue area at river. **Guest Services:** coin laundry, wireless Internet. **Cards:** AX, DS, MC, VI. **Free Special Amenities:** continental breakfast and high-speed Internet.

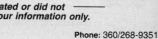 / SOME UNITS FEE

THE CHEWUCH INN & CABINS

Bed & Breakfast
$80-$195 All Year

Phone: (509)996-3107

Address: 223 White Ave **Location:** Just s of jct SR 20. **Facility:** Nestled in a pine grove by a Nordic ski trail system, this inn includes a billiard room, a whirlpool and six deluxe cabins with kitchenettes. Smoke free premises. 17 units. 10 one- and 1 two-bedroom standard units. 6 cabins. 1-3 stories (no elevator), interior/exterior corridors. **Parking:** on-site, winter plug-ins. **Terms:** office hours 8 am-8 pm, 2-3 night minimum stay - seasonal and/or weekends, 30 day cancellation notice-fee imposed. **Amenities:** video library, hair dryers. *Some:* DVD players, CD players. **Leisure Activities:** whirlpool. **Guest Services:** wireless Internet. **Business Services:** meeting rooms, PC. **Cards:** AX, DS, MC, VI.

/ SOME UNITS

HOTEL RIO VISTA

Motel
$75-$115 All Year

Phone: 509/996-3535

Address: 285 Riverside Ave **Location:** Downtown. **Facility:** Smoke free premises. 29 one-bedroom standard units. 2 stories (no elevator), interior/exterior corridors. **Parking:** on-site, winter plug-ins. **Terms:** office hours 7 am-11 pm, 2 night minimum stay - seasonal and/or weekends, 14 day cancellation notice-fee imposed. **Amenities:** hair dryers. *Some:* DVD players, irons. **Leisure Activities:** fishing, cross country skiing. **Guest Services:** wireless Internet. **Cards:** MC, VI.

/ SOME UNITS

RIVER RUN INN

AAA [SAVE]

◆◆◆

Motel
$75-$145 All Year

Phone: (509)996-2173
Address: 27 Rader Rd **Location:** 0.5 mi w on SR 20. Located in a quiet mountain setting on the river. **Facility:** Smoke free premises. 15 units. 9 one- and 1 two-bedroom standard units. 1 house, 3 cabins and 1 cottage. 1-2 stories (no elevator), exterior corridors. **Parking:** on-site. **Terms:** office hours 8:30 am-10 pm, 2 night minimum stay - seasonal and/or weekends, 10 day cancellation notice. **Amenities:** video library, DVD players. **Pool(s):** heated indoor. **Leisure Activities:** fishing, hot tub, picnic area with charcoal barbecues, hammocks, croquet, horseshoes. **Guest Services:** wireless Internet. **Cards:** MC, VI.

🛥️ ⊠ ✕ 🕏 🗄️ 🖵 🖵 / SOME UNITS FEE 🐾

SUN MOUNTAIN LODGE

AAA [SAVE]

◆◆◆◆

Resort
Hotel

$220-$435 6/13-2/28
$160-$350 3/1-6/12

Book great rates at AAA.com

Phone: (509)996-2211
Address: 604 Patterson Lake Rd **Location:** SR 20, 1.8 mi w on Twin Lakes Rd, 6.2 mi sw, follow signs. Located in a quiet rural area. **Facility:** Mountain-top serenity, sweeping panoramic views and a myriad of activities are the hallmarks of this luxurious and casually elegant resort. Smoke free premises. 96 units. 90 one-bedroom standard units, some with whirlpools. 6 one-bedroom suites, some with whirlpools. 2-3 stories (no elevator), interior/exterior corridors. **Parking:** on-site. **Terms:** check-in 4 pm, 2 night minimum stay - weekends, 30 day cancellation notice. **Amenities:** CD players, voice mail, irons, hair dryers. *Some:* honor bars. **Dining:** 2 restaurants, restaurant, see separate listing. **Pool(s):** 2 heated outdoor. **Leisure Activities:** whirlpools, rental boats, rental canoes, rental paddleboats, fishing, 4 tennis courts, cross country skiing, snowshoeing, sleigh rides, recreation programs, badminton, wagon rides, rental bicycles, hiking trails, jogging, playground, exercise room, spa, horseshoes, volleyball. *Fee:* ice skating, horseback riding. **Guest Services:** wireless Internet. **Business Services:** conference facilities, PC. **Cards:** AX, DC, MC, VI. *(See color ad below)*

🍴 🛥️ ⊠ ✕ 🕏 🖵 / SOME UNITS 🗄️

WINTHROP INN

AAA [SAVE]

◆◆

Motel

$75-$125 3/1-10/15
$70-$95 10/16-2/28

Phone: (509)996-2217
Address: 960 SR 20 **Location:** 0.9 mi e. **Facility:** Smoke free premises. 30 one-bedroom standard units. 2 stories (no elevator), interior corridors. *Bath:* shower only. **Parking:** on-site, winter plug-ins. **Terms:** office hours 7 am-11 pm, 3 day cancellation notice. **Amenities:** video library. *Some:* DVD players. **Pool(s):** heated outdoor. **Leisure Activities:** whirlpool, fishing, cross country skiing, barbecue, picnic area on river, basketball, volleyball. **Guest Services:** wireless Internet. **Business Services:** PC. **Cards:** DS, MC, VI.

🛥️ ⊠ ✕ 🗄️ 🖵 / SOME UNITS FEE 🐾 [VCR]

Navigate Life's Roads Safely

AAA Roadwise Review helps older drivers keep tabs on the driving abilities associated with crash risk. Perfect for the home computer, the easy, self-paced sessions provide feedback on important safety measures. Available at local AAA offices.

For more information, visit www.AAA.com/seniors.

AAA   LIFELONG SAFE MOBILITY

WINTHROP MTN VIEW CHALETS

Phone: (509)996-3113

Cabin
$75-$125 All Year

Address: 1120 SR 20 **Location:** South end of town. **Facility:** Deluxe cabins, modern amenities. Smoke free premises. 6 cabins. 1 story, exterior corridors. **Parking:** on-site. **Terms:** office hours 9 am-9 pm, check-in 3:30 pm, 7 day cancellation notice. **Amenities:** video library. **Guest Services:** wireless Internet. **Cards:** MC, VI. **Free Special Amenities: local telephone calls and high-speed Internet.**

──────── WHERE TO DINE ────────

DUCK BRAND RESTAURANT

Phone: 509/996-2192

American
$8-$23

This restaurant is a casual dining experience in the heart of downtown where a wide variety of foods and baked goods are served indoors or on the outdoor deck. Save room for fresh cheesecake. Casual dress. **Bar:** Full bar. **Hours:** 7 am-9:30 pm; seasonal hours vary. Closed: 11/26, 12/25. **Address:** 248 Riverside Ave **Location:** Center. **Parking:** on-site. **Cards:** AX, CB, DC, DS, MC, VI.

SUN MOUNTAIN LODGE DINING ROOM

Phone: 509/996-4707

Continental
$9-$50

This dining room is perched in a mountain retreat above the Methow Valley. The restaurant encourages diners to savor a thoughtfully prepared meal with a bottle of fine wine as they sit back and enjoy the panoramic view of the North Cascade Mountains. Casual dress. **Bar:** Full bar. **Reservations:** suggested. **Hours:** 7-11 am, 11:30-2 & 5:30-9 pm; seasonal hours may vary. **Address:** 604 Patterson Lake Rd **Location:** SR 20, 1.8 mi w on Twin Lakes Rd, 6.2 mi sw, follow signs; in Sun Mountain Lodge. **Parking:** on-site. **Cards:** AX, DC, MC, VI. *(See color ad p 749)*

CALL

WOODINVILLE —See Seattle p. 715.

WOODLAND pop. 3,780

──────── WHERE TO STAY ────────

BEST WESTERN WOODLAND INN & SUITES

Phone: (360)225-1000

Hotel
$70-$100 All Year

Address: 1380 Atlantic Ave **Location:** I-5, exit 21, just ne. **Facility:** 51 one-bedroom standard units, some with whirlpools. 2 stories (no elevator), interior corridors. **Parking:** on-site. **Terms:** cancellation fee imposed. **Amenities:** high-speed Internet, irons, hair dryers. **Pool(s):** heated indoor. **Leisure Activities:** whirlpool, exercise room. **Guest Services:** coin laundry, wireless Internet. **Business Services:** meeting rooms, PC. **Cards:** AX, DS, MC, VI. **Free Special Amenities: expanded continental breakfast and high-speed Internet.**

CEDARS INN WOODLAND

Phone: 360/225-6548

Hotel
Rates not provided

Address: 1500 Atlantic Ave **Location:** I-5, exit 21, just ne. **Facility:** 60 one-bedroom standard units. 2 stories (no elevator), exterior corridors. **Parking:** on-site. **Terms:** office hours 6 am-3 am. **Amenities:** high-speed Internet, hair dryers. **Pool(s):** heated indoor. **Leisure Activities:** whirlpool, exercise room. **Guest Services:** coin laundry, wireless Internet.

LEWIS RIVER INN

Phone: (360)225-6257

Motel
$64-$110 All Year

Address: 1100 Lewis River Rd **Location:** I-5, exit 21, just e. **Facility:** 49 one-bedroom standard units. 2 stories (no elevator), exterior corridors. **Parking:** on-site. **Terms:** office hours 6 am-11 pm. **Amenities:** high-speed Internet, voice mail, hair dryers. *Some:* irons. **Guest Services:** wireless Internet. **Cards:** AX, DS, MC, VI. **Free Special Amenities: continental breakfast and high-speed Internet.**

──────── WHERE TO DINE ────────

BURGERVILLE

Phone: 360/225-7965

American
$2-$8

First timers shouldn't let the fast food exterior fool them, as the burgers and chicken here adhere to a higher standard. Northwest ingredients come into play in the sandwiches. Casual dress. **Hours:** 7 am-10 pm. Closed: 11/26, 12/25. **Address:** 1120 Lewis River Rd **Location:** I-5, exit 21, just ne. **Parking:** on-site. **Cards:** DS, MC, VI.

OAK TREE RESTAURANT

Phone: 360/225-8446

American
$7-$15

Interstate travelers will find this a great break from the road. Traditional items share menu space with bakery-fresh foods, including cinnamon rolls. Prime rib is fresh and hot Friday, Saturday and Sunday. Casual dress. **Bar:** Full bar. **Reservations:** accepted. **Hours:** 7 am-10 pm, Fri & Sat-11 pm. Closed: 12/25. **Address:** 1020 Atlantic Ave **Location:** I-5, exit 21, just ne. **Parking:** on-site. **Cards:** AX, DS, MC, VI.

YAKIMA pop. 71,845

———— **WHERE TO STAY** ————

BEST WESTERN LINCOLN INN   *Book great rates at AAA.com*   Phone: (509)453-8898

Hotel
$99-$299 All Year

Address: 1614 N 1st St **Location:** I-82, exit 31, just s. **Facility:** Smoke free premises. 75 units. 74 one-bedroom standard units. 1 two-bedroom suite. 3 stories, interior corridors. *Bath:* combo or shower only. **Parking:** on-site. **Terms:** cancellation fee imposed. **Amenities:** high-speed Internet, voice mail, irons, hair dryers. **Pool(s):** heated indoor. **Leisure Activities:** whirlpool, exercise room. **Guest Services:** valet and coin laundry, wireless Internet. **Business Services:** business center. **Cards:** AX, CB, DC, DS, MC, VI. **Free Special Amenities: full breakfast and high-speed Internet.**
(See color ad p 368, p 586, p 499, p 368, p 753, p 473, p 542, p 299, p 344, below, p 566 & p 500)

AAA Benefit:
Members save up to 20%, plus 10% bonus points with rewards program.

BIRCHFIELD MANOR COUNTRY INN   Phone: (509)452-1960

Country Inn
$119-$219 All Year

Address: 2018 Birchfield Rd **Location:** I-82, exit 34, 2 mi e to Birchfield Rd, then just s. Located in a secluded area. **Facility:** Lots of antiques, Victorian bric-a-brac and lace give this conveniently located house a 19th-century flavor. Designated smoking area. 11 one-bedroom standard units, some with whirlpools. 2 stories (no elevator), interior corridors. *Bath:* combo or shower only. **Parking:** on-site. **Terms:** office hours 2 pm-10 pm, 14 day cancellation notice-fee imposed. **Amenities:** DVD players, high-speed Internet, irons, hair dryers. **Dining:** restaurant, see separate listing. **Pool(s):** heated outdoor. **Guest Services:** wireless Internet. **Cards:** AX, DC, DS, MC, VI.

CEDARS SUITES YAKIMA DOWNTOWN   *Book great rates at AAA.com*   Phone: (509)452-8101

Motel
$55-$110 All Year

Address: 1010 E A St **Location:** I-82, exit 33B eastbound; exit 33 westbound, just w to 9th St, just n to A St, then just e. **Facility:** 47 one-bedroom standard units. 2 stories (no elevator), exterior corridors. **Parking:** on-site. **Terms:** office hours 6 am-11 pm, cancellation fee imposed. **Amenities:** high-speed Internet, irons, hair dryers. **Guest Services:** coin laundry, wireless Internet. **Cards:** AX, CB, DC, DS, MC, VI. **Free Special Amenities: continental breakfast and local telephone calls.**
(See color ad p 752)

LINCOLN INN YAKIMA

Free Deluxe Hot Breakfast
Fresh Baked Cookies Every Night
Free High Speed Internet
24 Hour Pool & Spa · Fitness Center
100% Non Smoking Rooms
Business Center & Meeting Rooms
Microwave & Refrigerator · HBO

800-834-1649 or 509.453.8898
1614 N 1st Street, Yakima, WA, 98901
www.BestWesternYakima.com

LINCOLN ASSET MANAGEMENT

STAY WITH US WHEN VISITING THESE LOCATIONS:

OREGON	WASHINGTON
Astoria · Forest Grove · Lincoln City	Ellensburg · Moses Lake
Seaside · Tualatin (Portland)	Port Angeles · Yakima

COMFORT SUITES

AAA SAVE

Hotel
Rates not provided

Book great rates at AAA.com

Phone: 509/249-1900

Address: 3702 Fruitvale Blvd **Location:** US 12, exit 40th Ave, just s. **Facility:** Smoke free premises. 59 units. 57 one-bedroom standard units, some with whirlpools. 2 one-bedroom suites with efficiencies. 3 stories, interior corridors. *Bath:* combo or shower only. **Parking:** on-site. **Amenities:** high-speed Internet, voice mail, irons, hair dryers. **Pool(s):** heated indoor. **Leisure Activities:** whirlpool, exercise room. **Guest Services:** valet and coin laundry, wireless Internet. **Business Services:** meeting rooms, business center. *(See color ad p 368, p 586, p 499, p 368, p 753, p 473, p 542, p 299, p 344, p 751, p 566 & p 500)*

CALL 🔻M 🐬 ✕ 🎥 ▯ 🖥 ▯ / SOME UNITS 🐾

DAYS INN YAKIMA

Hotel
$70-$130 All Year

Book at AAA.com

Phone: (509)248-3393

Address: 1504 N 1st St **Location:** I-82, exit 31, 0.6 mi s. **Facility:** 61 units. 58 one-bedroom standard units. 3 one-bedroom suites. 2 stories (no elevator), interior corridors. **Parking:** on-site. **Amenities:** high-speed Internet, hair dryers. **Pool(s):** heated outdoor. **Guest Services:** wireless Internet. **Cards:** AX, DS, MC, VI.

ASK CALL 🔻M 🐬 🎥 ▯ 🖥 ▯ / SOME UNITS FEE 🐾 ✕

▼ See AAA listing p 739 ▼

▼ See AAA listing p 751 ▼

FAIRFIELD INN & SUITES BY MARRIOTT   *Book great rates at AAA.com*

Hotel
$112-$136 All Year

Phone: (509)452-3100

Address: 137 N Fair Ave **Location:** I-82, exit 33A eastbound, just s; exit 33 westbound, just w to 9th St, just n to B St, then just e. **Facility:** Smoke free premises. 81 units. 61 one-bedroom standard units, some with whirlpools. 20 one-bedroom suites. 3 stories, interior corridors. *Bath:* combo or shower only. **Parking:** on-site. **Terms:** cancellation fee imposed. **Amenities:** high-speed Internet, voice mail, irons, hair dryers. *Some:* DVD players. **Pool(s):** heated indoor. **Leisure Activities:** whirlpool, exercise room. **Guest Services:** valet and coin laundry, wireless Internet. **Business Services:** meeting rooms, business center. **Cards:** AX, CB, DC, DS, MC, VI.

CALL

AAA Benefit:
Members save a minimum 5% off the best available rate.

HILTON GARDEN INN   *Book great rates at AAA.com*

Hotel
$99-$199 All Year

Phone: (509)454-1111

Address: 401 E Yakima Ave **Location:** Downtown. **Facility:** Smoke free premises. 111 units. 108 one-bedroom standard units. 3 one-bedroom suites with whirlpools. 5 stories, interior corridors. **Parking:** on-site. **Terms:** 1-30 night minimum stay, cancellation fee imposed. **Amenities:** video games (fee), high-speed Internet, voice mail, irons, hair dryers. **Pool(s):** heated indoor. **Leisure Activities:** whirlpool, exercise room, spa. **Guest Services:** valet and coin laundry, wireless Internet. **Business Services:** meeting rooms, business center. **Cards:** AX, CB, DC, DS, JC, MC, VI.

CALL

AAA Benefit:
Members save 5% or more everyday!

HOLIDAY INN EXPRESS YAKIMA   *Book great rates at AAA.com*

Hotel
$139-$169 All Year

Phone: (509)249-1000

Address: 1001 E A St **Location:** I-82, exit 33B eastbound; exit 33 westbound, just w to 9th St, just n to A St, then just e. **Facility:** Smoke free premises. 87 units. 86 one-bedroom standard units, some with whirlpools. 1 one-bedroom suite with kitchen and whirlpool. 4 stories, interior corridors. *Bath:* combo or shower only. **Parking:** on-site. **Amenities:** voice mail, irons, hair dryers. *Some:* high-speed Internet. **Pool(s):** heated indoor. **Leisure Activities:** whirlpool, exercise room. **Guest Services:** valet and coin laundry, wireless Internet. **Business Services:** business center. **Cards:** AX, DC, DS, MC, VI. **Free Special Amenities:** expanded continental breakfast and high-speed Internet.

CALL

HOWARD JOHNSON PLAZA YAKIMA GATEWAY   *Book at AAA.com*

Hotel
$89-$129 All Year

Phone: (509)452-6511

Address: 9 N 9th St **Location:** I-82, exit 33 westbound; exit 33B eastbound, just s. **Facility:** Smoke free premises. 172 one-bedroom standard units, some with efficiencies and/or whirlpools. 2-3 stories, interior corridors. *Bath:* combo or shower only. **Parking:** on-site. **Terms:** cancellation fee imposed. **Amenities:** high-speed Internet, voice mail, safes, irons, hair dryers. **Pool(s):** heated outdoor. **Leisure Activities:** whirlpool, exercise room. **Guest Services:** valet and coin laundry, wireless Internet. **Business Services:** conference facilities, PC. **Cards:** AX, DS, MC, VI.

ASK   CALL

OXFORD INN *Book at AAA.com*

Hotel
$86-$96 All Year
Phone: (509)457-4444
Address: 1603 E Yakima Ave **Location:** I-82, exit 33 westbound, just e; exit 33B eastbound. **Facility:** 95 one-bedroom standard units, some with efficiencies. 4 stories, interior corridors. *Bath:* combo or shower only. **Parking:** on-site. **Terms:** cancellation fee imposed. **Amenities:** video library (fee), high-speed Internet, voice mail, irons, hair dryers. **Pool(s):** heated outdoor. **Leisure Activities:** whirlpool, fishing, exercise room. **Guest Services:** valet and coin laundry, area transportation, wireless Internet. **Business Services:** business center. **Cards:** AX, DS, MC, VI.

OXFORD SUITES *Book at AAA.com*
Hotel
$105-$165 All Year
Phone: (509)457-9000
Address: 1701 E Yakima Ave **Location:** I-82, exit 33 westbound; exit 33B eastbound. **Facility:** 107 units. 68 one-bedroom standard units. 39 one-bedroom suites, some with whirlpools. 4 stories, interior corridors. *Bath:* combo or shower only. **Parking:** on-site. **Terms:** 1-20 night minimum stay, cancellation fee imposed. **Amenities:** video library, DVD players, high-speed Internet, voice mail, irons, hair dryers. **Pool(s):** heated indoor. **Leisure Activities:** whirlpool, hiking trails, jogging, exercise room. **Guest Services:** valet and coin laundry, area transportation, wireless Internet. **Business Services:** meeting rooms, business center. **Cards:** AX, DC, DS, MC, VI.

RAMADA LIMITED *Book at AAA.com*
Motel
$70-$301 3/1-8/31
$60-$250 9/1-2/28
Phone: (509)453-0391
Address: 818 N 1st St **Location:** I-82, exit 31, 1.2 mi s. **Facility:** 58 units. 56 one- and 2 two-bedroom standard units. 2 stories (no elevator), exterior corridors. *Bath:* combo or shower only. **Parking:** on-site. **Terms:** cancellation fee imposed. **Amenities:** high-speed Internet, irons, hair dryers. **Pool(s):** heated outdoor. **Leisure Activities:** sauna, exercise room. **Guest Services:** coin laundry, wireless Internet. **Business Services:** business center. **Cards:** AX, DC, DS, MC, VI.

RED LION HOTEL YAKIMA CENTER *Book at AAA.com*
Hotel
$85-$169 All Year
Phone: (509)248-5900
Address: 607 E Yakima Ave **Location:** I-82, exit 33 westbound; exit 33B eastbound, 0.8 mi w. **Facility:** Smoke free premises. 156 units. 152 one-bedroom standard units. 4 one-bedroom suites, some with whirlpools. 2 stories (no elevator); interior/exterior corridors. *Bath:* combo or shower only. **Parking:** on-site. **Amenities:** video games (fee), high-speed Internet, voice mail, irons, hair dryers. **Pool(s):** 2 heated outdoor. **Guest Services:** valet laundry, wireless Internet. **Business Services:** conference facilities, business center. **Cards:** AX, DC, DS, MC, VI.

SUN COUNTRY INN *Book at AAA.com*
Motel
$58-$70 All Year
Phone: (509)248-5650
Address: 1700 N 1st St **Location:** I-82, exit 31, just s. **Facility:** 71 units. 70 one-bedroom standard units, some with efficiencies. 1 one-bedroom suite with kitchen. 2 stories (no elevator), exterior corridors. **Parking:** on-site. **Terms:** 3 day cancellation notice-fee imposed. **Amenities:** high-speed Internet, hair dryers. **Pool(s):** heated outdoor. **Leisure Activities:** sauna, exercise room. **Guest Services:** coin laundry, wireless Internet. **Business Services:** PC. **Cards:** AX, DC, DS, MC, VI.

WHERE TO DINE

BIRCHFIELD MANOR COUNTRY INN
French
$29-$49
Phone: 509/452-1960
Patrons can savor French cuisine with a Northwest American influence in a gracious turn-of-the-20th-century Victorian mansion. Casual dress. **Bar:** Beer & wine. **Reservations:** required. **Hours:** 7 pm seating, Sat 6 pm & 8:45 pm seatings. Closed major holidays; also Sun-Wed. **Address:** 2018 Birchfield Rd **Location:** I-82, exit 34, 2 mi e to Birchfield Rd, then just s; in Birchfield Manor Country Inn. **Parking:** on-site. **Cards:** AX, DS, MC, VI.

CAFE MELANGE
Italian
$6-$35
Phone: 509/453-0571
The intimate restaurant serves primarily Italian food but with menu surprises of other cuisines. All pasta is made in-house, and the bread here is absolutely heavenly. Casual dress. **Bar:** Full bar. **Reservations:** suggested. **Hours:** 11:30 am-8:30 pm, Fri & Sat-9:30 pm. Closed major holidays; also Sun & Mon. **Address:** 7 N Front St **Location:** Downtown. **Parking:** on-site. **Cards:** AX, CB, DC, DS, JC, MC, VI.

GASPERETTI'S
Northern Italian
$6-$35
Phone: 509/248-0628
The award-winning restaurant features Northern Italian and American Northwest cuisine, including traditional antipasti and interesting selections such as roasted filet mignon with Gorgonzola and pecan sauce. The comfortable, casually upscale surroundings are reminiscent of a Tuscan villa. Casual dress. **Bar:** Full bar. **Reservations:** suggested. **Hours:** 11 am-close. Closed major holidays; also Sun. **Address:** 1013 N 1st St **Location:** 1 mi n of jct Yakima Ave and N 1st St. **Parking:** on-site. **Cards:** AX, DS, MC, VI.

GREYSTONE RESTAURANT
Steak & Seafood
$35
Phone: 509/248-9801
The historic stone building exudes a turn-of-the-20th-century feel, with a pressed-tin ceiling, metal pedestals and many antiques. Specialties of fresh seafood, beef and lamb are served in hearty portions, with a limited selection of wines. Casual dress. **Bar:** Full bar. **Reservations:** suggested. **Hours:** 11:30 am-10 pm, Sat from 5 pm, Sun 3 pm-7 pm. Closed major holidays. **Address:** 5 N Front St **Location:** Corner of Front St and Yakima Ave; downtown. **Parking:** on-site. **Cards:** AX, DS, MC, VI.

SANTIAGO'S GOURMET MEXICAN COOKING
Mexican
$7-$20
Phone: 509/453-1644
A Southwestern scheme, including 1900s brickwork and what is said to be the state's largest mural, sets the stage for a feast of Mexican favorites with gourmet twists. Diners can savor taco Santiago, the popular fish tacos and chicken fajita salad, saving room for sweet fried ice cream. Casual dress. **Bar:** Full bar. **Hours:** 11:30 am-2 & 5-10 pm, Sat from 5 pm. Closed major holidays; also Sun. **Address:** 111 E Yakima Ave **Location:** I-82, exit 33 westbound; exit 33B eastbound, 1 mi s. **Parking:** on-site. **Cards:** MC, VI.

──────── *The following restaurants have not been evaluated by AAA* ────────
but are listed for your information only.

EL PORTON

fyi

Phone: 509/965-5422

Not evaluated. In an area with many Mexican restaurants from which to choose, El Porton is a standout with several locations serving traditional Mexican favorites. **Address:** 420 S 48th Ave.

PAPA BAIRD'S RESTAURANT

fyi

Phone: 509/453-5103

Not evaluated. The no-frills family restaurant specializing in good old-fashioned home cooking with large portions is a favorite of locals and tourists alike. **Address:** 4108 Terrace Heights Dr.

ZILLAH pop. 2,198

──────── **WHERE TO STAY** ────────

COMFORT INN

Hotel
$104-$160 All Year

Book at AAA.com

Phone: (509)829-3399

Address: 911 Vintage Valley Pkwy **Location:** I-82, exit 52, just n. **Facility:** 40 one-bedroom standard units, some with whirlpools. 2 stories (no elevator), interior corridors. *Bath:* combo or shower only. **Parking:** on-site. **Terms:** cancellation fee imposed. **Amenities:** video library (fee), high-speed Internet, irons, hair dryers. *Some:* DVD players. **Pool(s):** heated indoor. **Leisure Activities:** whirlpool, exercise room. **Guest Services:** coin laundry, wireless Internet. **Business Services:** meeting rooms, business center. **Cards:** AX, DC, DS, MC, VI.

(A$K) (T]→) CALL (&M) (➡) (🛁) (🖥) / SOME UNITS FEE (🛏) (✕) (VCR) (🔌) (📷)

──────── **WHERE TO DINE** ────────

EL PORTON

Mexican
$6-$12

Phone: 509/829-9100

In an area with many Mexican restaurants from which to choose, El Porton is a standout with several locations serving traditional favorites. Casual dress. **Bar:** Full bar. **Hours:** 11 am-9 pm, Fri & Sat-10 pm. Closed major holidays. **Address:** 905 Vintage Valley Pkwy **Location:** I-82, exit 52, just n, then just w. **Parking:** on-site. **Cards:** AX, MC, VI.

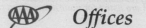 *Offices*

Cities with main offices are listed in **BOLD TYPE** and toll-free member service numbers in *ITALIC TYPE*.
All are closed Saturdays, Sundays and holidays unless otherwise indicated.
The addresses, phone numbers and hours for any AAA/CAA office are subject to change.
The type of service provided is designated below the name of the city where the office is located:

✛ Auto travel services, including books and maps, and on-demand TripTik ® routings.
● Auto travel services, including selected books and maps, and on-demand TripTik ® routings.
■ Books/maps only, no marked maps or on-demand TripTik ® routings.
▲ Travel Agency Services, cruise, tour, air, car and rail reservations; domestic and international hotel reservations;
passport photo services; international and domestic travel guides and maps; travel money products; and International Driving Permits. In addition, assistance with travel related insurance products including trip cancellation, travel accident, lost luggage, trip delay and assistance products.
❂ Insurance services provided.
✖ Car Care Plus Facility provides car care services.

AAA NATIONAL OFFICE: 1000 AAA DRIVE, HEATHROW, FLORIDA 32746-5063, (407) 444-7000

OREGON

BEAVERTON—AAA OREGON/IDAHO, 8555 SW APPLE WAY, 97225. WEEKDAYS (M-F) 8:00-5:30. (503) 243-6444, *(800) 633-8400.*. ✛ ▲ ❂

BEND—AAA OREGON/IDAHO, 20350 EMPIRE BLVD #5, 97701. WEEKDAYS (M-F) 8:00-5:30. (541) 382-1303, *(800) 464-1303.*
✛ ▲ ❂

CLACKAMAS—AAA OREGON/IDAHO, 10365 SE SUNNYSIDE RD-100, 97015. WEEKDAYS (M-F) 8:00-5:30. (503) 241-6800, *(800) 950-7800.* ✛ ▲ ❂

COOS BAY—AAA OREGON/IDAHO, 1705 OCEAN BLVD SE STE A, 97420. WEEKDAYS (M-F) 8:30-5:30. (541) 269-7432, *(800) 222-6636.* ✛ ❂

CORVALLIS—AAA OREGON/IDAHO, 1318 NW 9TH ST #A, 97330. WEEKDAYS (M-F) 8:00-5:30. (541) 757-2535, *(800) 764-4222.* ✛ ▲ ❂

EUGENE—AAA OREGON/IDAHO, 983 WILLAGILLESPIE RD, 97401. WEEKDAYS (M-F) 8:00-5:30. (541) 484-0661, *(800) 248-5540.* ✛ ▲ ❂

GRANTS PASS—AAA OREGON/IDAHO, 1883 NE 7TH ST, 97526. WEEKDAYS (M-F) 8:00-5:30. (541) 479-7829, *(800) 999-6007.*
✛ ▲ ❂

HILLSBORO—AAA OREGON/IDAHO, 7162 NE CORNELL RD, 97124. WEEKDAYS (M-F) 8:30-5:30. (503) 726-5900. ■ ▲ ❂

KLAMATH FALLS—AAA OREGON/IDAHO, 1745 WASHBURN WAY, 97603. WEEKDAYS (M-F) 8:30-5:30. (541) 882-3439. ■ ❂

LAKE OSWEGO—AAA OREGON/IDAHO, 6 CENTERPOINTE DR #100, 97035. WEEKDAYS (M-F) 8:00-5:30. (503) 973-6555, *(800) 361-9482.* ✛ ▲ ❂

MEDFORD—AAA OREGON/IDAHO, 1777 E BARNETT RD, 97504. WEEKDAYS (M-F) 8:00-5:30. (541) 779-7170, *(800) 325-3089.*
✛ ▲ ❂

PENDLETON—AAA OREGON/IDAHO, 1729 SW COURT PLACE, 97801. WEEKDAYS (M-F) 8:30-5:30. (541) 276-2243, *(800) 646-2243.* ✛ ❂

PORTLAND—**AAA OREGON/IDAHO,** 600 SW MARKET ST, 97201. WEEKDAYS (M-F) 8:00-5:30. (503) 222-6734. ✛ ▲ ❂

ROSEBURG—AAA OREGON/IDAHO, 3019 NW STEWART PKY #303, 97470. WEEKDAYS (M-F) 8:30-5:30. (541) 673-7453, *(866) 467-7467.* ■ ▲ ❂

SALEM—AAA OREGON/IDAHO, 2909 RYAN DR SE, 97301. WEEKDAYS (M-F) 8:00-5:30. (503) 584-5200, *(800) 962-5855.*
✛ ▲ ❂

SPRINGFIELD—AAA OREGON/IDAHO, 939 HARLOW RD STE 100, 97477. WEEKDAYS (M-F) 8:30-5:30. (541) 741-8200, *(866) 808-7199.* ✛ ▲ ❂

WARRENTON—AAA OREGON/IDAHO, 135 S HWY 101, 97146. WEEKDAYS (M-F) 8:00-5:30. (503) 861-3118, *(800) 281-3118.*
✛ ❂

WOOD VILLAGE—AAA OREGON/IDAHO, 22741 NE PARK LN STE G, 97060. WEEKDAYS (M-F) 8:30-5:30. (503) 489-2842. ❂

WASHINGTON

BELLEVUE—AAA WASHINGTON, 14404 NE 20TH ST #150, 98007. WEEKDAYS (M-F) 8:30-5:30. (425) 455-3933, *(877) 477-4221.* ✛ ▲ ❂

BELLINGHAM—AAA WASHINGTON, 4280 MERIDIAN ST STE 106, 98226. WEEKDAYS (M-F) 8:30-5:30. (360) 733-2740, *(877) 477-4222.* ✛ ▲ ❂

BREMERTON—AAA WASHINGTON, 5700 KITSAP WAY, 98312. WEEKDAYS (M-F) 8:30-5:30. (360) 377-0081, *(877) 802-6894.*
✛ ▲ ❂

EVERETT—AAA WASHINGTON, 909 SE EVERETT MALL #E520, 98208. WEEKDAYS (M-F) 8:30-5:30. (425) 353-7222, *(877) 802-6895.* ✛ ▲ ❂

FEDERAL WAY—AAA WASHINGTON, 2122 S 314TH ST, 98003. WEEKDAYS (M-F) 8:30-5:30. (253) 945-8700, *(800) 430-8997.*

ISSAQUAH—AAA WASHINGTON, 405 NW GILMAN BLVD #102, 98027. WEEKDAYS (M-F) 8:30-5:00. (425) 557-0222. ✛ ▲ ❂

KENNEWICK—AAA WASHINGTON, 6501 W GRANDRIDGE BLVD #G, 99336. WEEKDAYS (M-F) 8:30-5:30. (509) 735-6351, *(877) 802-6907.* ✛ ▲ ❂

LYNNWOOD—AAA WASHINGTON, 4100 ALDERWOOD MALL BLVD, 98036. WEEKDAYS (M-F) 8:30-5:30. (425) 775-3571, *(877) 802-6896.* ✛ ▲ ❂

MOUNT VERNON—AAA WASHINGTON, 1600 E COLLEGE WAY #A, 98273. WEEKDAYS (M-F) 8:30-5:30. (360) 428-5800, *(800) 743-1703.* ✛ ▲ ❂

OLYMPIA—AAA WASHINGTON, 2415 CAPITAL MALL DR SW, 98502. WEEKDAYS (M-F) 8:30-5:30. (360) 357-5561, *(877) 802-6897.* ✛ ▲ ❂

PUYALLUP—AAA WASHINGTON, 10210 123RD ST CT E #B, 98374. WEEKDAYS (M-F) 8:30-5:30. (253) 841-5684, *(866) 715-4496.* ● ▲ ❂

REDMOND—AAA WASHINGTON, 7950 164TH AVE NE #102, 98052. WEEKDAYS (M-F) 8:30-5:30. (425) 869-9222, *(800) 430-1090.* ✛ ▲ ❂

RENTON—AAA WASHINGTON, 3900 E VALLEY RD #105, 98055. WEEKDAYS (M-F) 8:30-5:30. (425) 251-6040, *(877) 802-6898.*
✛ ▲ ❂

SEATTLE—AAA WASHINGTON, 4701 42ND AVE SW, 98116. WEEKDAYS (M-F) 8:30-5:30. (206) 937-8222, *(866) 660-0832.*
✛ ▲ ❂

SEATTLE—AAA WASHINGTON, 4554 9TH AVE NE STE 120, 98105. WEEKDAYS (M-F) 8:30-5:30. (206) 633-4222, *(800) 303-2465.* ✛ ▲ ❂

SEATTLE—AAA WASHINGTON, 1523 15TH AVE W, 98119. WEEKDAYS (M-F) 8:30-5:30. (206) 218-1222, *(800) 420-0513.*
✛ ▲

SPOKANE—AAA WASHINGTON, 1717 W 4TH AVE, 99201. WEEKDAYS (M-F) 8:30-5:30. (509) 358-6900, *(800) 456-3222.*
✛ ▲ ❂

SPOKANE—AAA WASHINGTON, 7307 N DIVISION ST #103, 99208. WEEKDAYS (M-F) 8:30-5:30. (509) 358-7050, *(800) 439-9290.* ✛ ▲ ❂

SPOKANE VALLEY—AAA WASHINGTON, 13817 E SPRAGUE AVE STE 6, 99216. WEEKDAYS (M-F) 8:30-5:30. (509) 358-7040, *(800) 439-9267.* ✛ ▲ ❂

TACOMA—AAA WASHINGTON, 1801 S UNION AVE, 98405. WEEKDAYS (M-F) 8:30-5:30. (253) 756-3050, *(877) 802-6906.*
✛ ▲ ❂

VANCOUVER—AAA WASHINGTON, 4301 E 4TH PLAIN BLVD, 98661. WEEKDAYS (M-F) 8:30-5:30. (360) 696-4081, *(877) 802-6908.* ✛ ▲ ❂

WALLA WALLA—AAA WASHINGTON, 1361 DALLES MILITARY RD, 99362. WEEKDAYS (M-F) 8:30-5:30. (509) 525-9213, *(800) 439-9293.* ✛ ▲ ❂

WENATCHEE—AAA WASHINGTON, 221 N MISSION ST, 98801. WEEKDAYS (M-F) 8:30-5:30. (509) 662-8550, *(800) 487-3273.*
✛ ▲ ❂

YAKIMA—AAA WASHINGTON, 2301 W NOB HILL BLVD #1, 98902. WEEKDAYS (M-F) 8:30-5:30. (509) 248-6520, *(800) 898-6524.* ✛ ▲ ❂

Metric Equivalents Chart

TEMPERATURE

To convert Fahrenheit to Celsius, subtract 32 from the Fahrenheit temperature, multiply by 5 and divide by 9.
To convert Celsius to Fahrenheit, multipy by 9, divide by 5 and add 32.

ACRES

1 acre = 0.4 hectare (ha)   1 hectare = 2.47 acres

MILES AND KILOMETRES

Note: A kilometre is approximately 5/8 or 0.6 of a mile.
To convert kilometres to miles multiply by 0.6.

Miles/Kilometres		Kilometres/Miles	
15	24.1	30	18.6
20	32.2	35	21.7
25	40.2	40	24.8
30	48.3	45	27.9
35	56.3	50	31.0
40	64.4	55	34.1
45	72.4	60	37.2
50	80.5	65	40.3
55	88.5	70	43.4
60	96.6	75	46.6
65	104.6	80	49.7
70	112.7	85	52.8
75	120.7	90	55.9
80	128.7	95	59.0
85	136.8	100	62.1
90	144.8	105	65.2
95	152.9	110	68.3
100	160.9	115	71.4

Celsius °		Fahrenheit °
100	BOILING	212
37		100
35		95
32		90
29		85
27		80
24		75
21		70
18		65
16		60
13		55
10		50
7		45
4		40
2		35
0	FREEZING	32
-4		25
-7		20
-9		15
-12		10
-15		5
-18		0
-21		-5
-24		-10
-27		-15

LINEAR MEASURE

Customary	Metric
1 inch = 2.54 centimetres	1 centimetre = 0.4 inches
1 foot = 30 centimetres	1 metre = 3.3 feet
1 yard = 0.91 metres	1 metre = 1.09 yards
1 mile = 1.6 kilometres	1 kilometre = .62 miles

LIQUID MEASURE

Customary	Metric
1 fluid ounce = 30 millilitres	1 millilitre = .03 fluid ounces
1 cup = .24 litres	1 litre = 2.1 pints
1 pint = .47 litres	1 litre = 1.06 quarts
1 quart = .95 litres	1 litre = .26 gallons
1 gallon = 3.8 litres	

WEIGHT

If You Know:	Multiply By:	To Find:
Ounces	28.000	Grams
Pounds	0.450	Kilograms
Grams	0.035	Ounces
Kilograms	2.200	Pounds

PRESSURE

Air pressure in automobile tires is expressed in kilopascals. Multiply pound-force per square inch (psi) by 6.89 to find kilopascals (kPa).

24 psi = 165 kPa   28 psi = 193 kPa
26 psi = 179 kPa   30 psi = 207 kPa

GALLON AND LITRES

Gallons/Litres				Litres/Gallons			
5	19.0	12	45.6	10	2.6	40	10.4
6	22.8	14	53.2	15	3.9	50	13.0
7	26.6	16	60.8	20	5.2	60	15.6
8	30.4	18	68.4	25	6.5	70	18.2
9	34.2	20	76.0	30	7.8	80	20.8
10	38.0	25	95.0	35	9.1	90	23.4

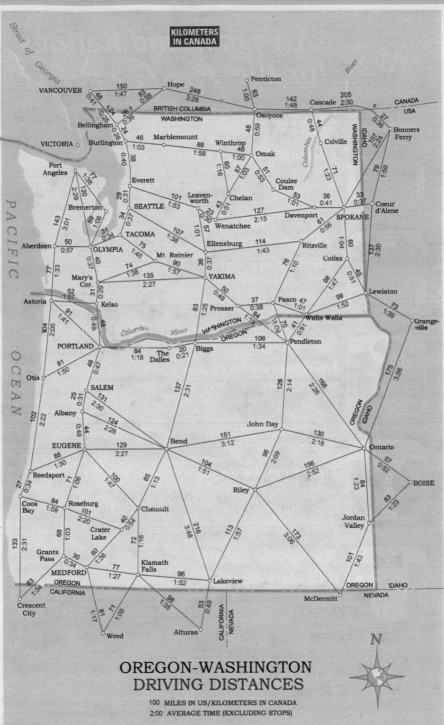

OREGON-WASHINGTON DRIVING DISTANCES

100 MILES IN US/KILOMETERS IN CANADA
2:00 AVERAGE TIME (EXCLUDING STOPS)

© AAA

3681-E

AAA Diamond Ratings
for the *Perfect Fit*

Comfortable and basic – One Diamond lodgings and restaurants meet our cleanliness requirements and can be ideal for the budget-minded traveler.

A little more style – Two Diamond hotels and restaurants offer modest enhancements, often at a moderate price.

Goes more places – for vacation or business, to relax or impress, Three Diamond properties offer a range of style and facilities.

Time to make an impression – only **3%** of our inspections result in a Four Diamond Rating, with hospitality, service and attention to detail.

It's a black-tie event – or luxury, sophistication and service with a relaxed feel. With only 100 Five Diamond lodgings and 60 restaurants, expect the best.

• Each year, AAA conducts professional evaluations at more than 58,000 hotels and restaurants throughout North America.

• More information can be found on pages 20-21 and at AAA.com/Diamonds.

Border Information

U.S. – Canada Border Information

For United States Residents Traveling to Canada

Passports for air travel are now required for travel to Canada. It is expected that at some point in 2009, U.S. citizens traveling between the U.S. and Canada, Mexico, the Caribbean, and Bermuda by land or sea (including ferries), will be required to present a valid U.S. passport. Please refer to the U.S. Department of State's Web site travel.state.gov for the most current information on these requirements.

Native-born citizens of the United States:
- Passport not required (but is recommended)
- Proof of citizenship required (a birth certificate and photo ID)
- Proof of residence may be required

Naturalized citizens: naturalization certificate required

U.S. resident aliens: Alien Registration Receipt Card (Green Card) required

Single parents, grandparents or guardians traveling with a minor must show documentation of legal custody and provide proof of citizenship for each child (the minor's passport or a parent's passport that includes the child).

When a child is traveling with only 1 parent that parent should have a notarized letter of consent from the other parent or legal custody documents.

When a child is traveling alone or with an individual other than a parent the minor should have a notarized letter of consent with phone number(s) from both parents or a custody document.

Legal Issues: Persons with felony convictions, driving while intoxicated records or other offenses may be denied admittance into Canada. Contact the Canadian embassy or nearest consulate before travel.

Firearms: Canada has strict laws regarding the importing, exporting, possession, use, storage, display and transportation of firearms. These are federal laws that apply across the country.

Classes of Firearms:
- Non-restricted (most ordinary rifles and shotguns)
- Restricted (mainly handguns)
- Prohibited (full automatics, converted automatics, handguns with a barrel length of 105 m ($\approx$4 inches) or less, and .25 or .32 caliber handguns among others)

Certain handguns used in International Shooting Union sporting competition are classified as restricted even though they meet the prohibited handgun definition.

Yes: To bring a non-restricted or restricted firearm into Canada you must:
- Be 18 years of age or older
- Declare firearm(s) at first point of entry
- Get an Authorization to Transport (ATT) from a provincial or territorial Chief Firearms Officer before arriving at point of entry (Note: ATT not issued for hunting or self-protection purposes)

No: You may not bring into Canada a prohibited firearm or replica firearm, except replicas of firearms classified as antiques (a replica that looks exactly, or almost exactly, like a firearm but is not a firearm; it cannot discharge projectiles or discharges only harmless projectiles).

The Canada Border Services Agency is responsible for all customs procedures.

Yes:
- You may import non-restricted firearms for legitimate purposes: sporting or hunting; use in competitions; transit movement; or personal protection against wildlife in remote areas (customs officer must agree that circumstances warrant firearm possession)
- Register weapons with U.S. Customs before departure
- Upon return you must show proof that you had the weapon before departure
- Under certain circumstances individuals and businesses may import firearms

No: Non-residents may not import prohibited items.

Fees (in Canadian funds):
- Non-Resident Firearm Declaration – $25 covers all firearms listed on declaration
- Possession and acquisition license – $60 for nonrestricted firearms; valid for 5 years
- Temporary Firearms Borrowing License (for non-residents) – $30; may renew once in a 12-month period at no extra cost; $30 thereafter (800-731-4000)
- Imported firearm registration fee – No fee to register or transfer a firearm

Prohibited: Any large capacity cartridge magazine

(limited to 5 rounds for semiautomatic rifles or shotguns, 10 rounds for handguns), any device designed to stop the sound of a firearm, any knife with a blade opened by spring pressure (e.g., switchblade), martial arts weapons (e.g., shuriken (shooting stars), nunchaku sticks), mace, blowguns, hand-held compact crossbows and any other weapons declared prohibited by regulation.

Yes: Hunters may bring in, duty-free, 200 rounds of ammunition; competition participants 1,500 rounds. Must show valid license or declaration to purchase ammunition. If planning to hunt in multiple provinces or territories, you must obtain a hunting license from each one.

No: Firearms forbidden in many of Canada's national and provincial parks, game reserves and adjacent areas.

Parks and Hunting Regulation Information: Newfoundland and Labrador 800-563-6353 or 709-729-2830; Prince Edward Island 888-734-7529 or 902-629-2400; Nova Scotia 800-565-0000 ext 998 or 902-425-5781; New Brunswick 800-561-0123 or 506-789-4982; Quebec 800-363-7777 or 514-873-2015; Ontario 800-668-2746 or 416-314-0944; Manitoba 800-665-0040 or 204-945-3777; Saskatchewan 877-237-2273 or 306-787-2300; Alberta 800-661-8888 or 780-427-4321; British Columbia 800-663-6000 or 250-387-1642; Northwest Territories (Western NWT) 800-661-0788 or 867-873-4059; Nunavut (Eastern NWT) 800-491-7910 or 867-979-1261; Yukon 867-667-5340.

Note: Provinces and territories also have their own laws regulating the transportation of firearms through their areas, usually in connection with their hunting regulations. For further information on the entry of firearms, applying for a license or to obtain authorization to transport a firearm, contact: Canadian Firearms Centre at 800-731-4000.

Personal Baggage:
- Admissible into Canada on a temporary basis without payment of duty and taxes
- Customs may require a refundable security deposit at time of entry
- Deposits not normally required for health- or pleasure-related visits as long as all items are exported at trip's end

Personal baggage that may be taken into Canada on a duty- and tax-free basis includes

clothing and personal items, sporting goods, automobiles, vessels, aircraft, snowmobiles, cameras, personal computers, food products and other items appropriate for the purpose and duration of the visit.

Tobacco products – Those meeting age requirements (18 years in Alberta, Manitoba, Northwest Territories and Nunavut, Saskatchewan, Quebec and Yukon Territory; 19 years in other provinces) may bring in 50 cigars, 200 cigarettes, 200 grams of tobacco and 200 tobacco sticks.

Alcohol – Those meeting age requirements (18 years in Alberta, Manitoba and Quebec; 19 years in other provinces and territories) may bring in limited alcoholic beverages: 40 ounces (1.14 L) of liquor, 1.6 quarts (1.5 L) of wine or 9 quarts (8.5 L) of beer or ale (equivalent to 24 12-ounce bottles or cans).

- Generally, a minimum 48-hour stay is required to transport any liquor or tobacco into Canada
- Amounts exceeding the allowable quantities noted above are subject to federal duty and taxes, and provincial/territorial liquor fees
- Pay provincial fees at customs at the time of entry in all provinces and the Yukon Territory
- Illegal to bring more than the allowable alcohol quantity into the Northwest Territories and Nunavut

Articles purchased at Canadian duty-free shops are subject to U.S. Customs exemptions and restrictions; those purchased at U.S. duty-free shops before entering Canada are subject to duty if brought back into the United States.

Prescription Drugs: Persons requiring medication while visiting Canada are permitted to bring it for their own use. Clearly identify and carry in original packaging with a label listing the drug and its intended use. Have a copy of the prescription and prescribing doctor's phone number.

Gifts: Items not exceeding $60 (CAN) in value, excluding tobacco, alcoholic beverages and advertising matter, taken into or mailed to Canada are allowed free entry. Gifts valued at more than $60 are subject to regular duty and taxes on the excess amount.

Pets and Plants: You must have a certificate for a dog or cat age 3 months and older. It must clearly describe the animal, declare that the animal has been vaccinated against rabies within the past 36 months, and have a licensed veterinarian signature.

- Collar tags are not sufficient proof of immunization
- Be sure the vaccination does not expire while traveling in Canada
- The certificate is also required to bring the animal back into the United States

Exempt From These Rules: Assist dogs; healthy puppies and kittens under 3 months old with a health certificate, signed by a licensed veterinarian, indicating that the animal is too young to vaccinate.

Plants or plant material must be declared. For information, contact: Canadian Food Inspection Agency (CFIA), 59 Camelot Dr., Ottawa, ON K1A 0Y9; 613-225-2342.

Radio Communication Equipment
- Cell phone, PCS phone, citizens band (CB) or Family Radio Service radio allowed without prior registration
- Use of aircraft, marine or amateur radio allowed without prior authorization
- All other types of radio transmitting stations allowed with authorization letter from Industry Canada's Radiocommunication and Broadcasting Regulatory Branch

Special Permits: A CITIES (Convention on International Trade in Endangered Species) permit is required for any endangered species brought into Canada, including those kept as pets, and for any items made from them (e.g., coats, handbags, shoes). For information contact: Environment Canada, Canadian Wildlife Service at 819-997-1840.

An Export Permit may be required to take out of Canada objects more than 50 years old (e.g., fossils, archaeological artifacts, fine and decorative art, technological objects or books and archival material). Contact: Movable Cultural Property Program of Canadian Heritage, 15 Eddy St., 3rd Floor, Hull, Quebec, Canada K1A 0M5; 819-997-7761.

An Import Permit may be required for the importation of clothing, textiles, steel and certain agricultural products in excess of minimum quantities. For information contact: Department of Foreign Affairs and Int'l Trade, Export and Import Controls Bureau, Tower C, 4th Floor, LB Pearson Bldg, 125 Sussex Dr., Ottawa, ON K1A 0G2.

Vehicles
- Vehicles entering Canada for touring, including trailers not exceeding 8 feet 6 inches (2.6 m) in width are generally subject to quick and routine entry procedures.
- To leave or store a car, trailer or other goods in Canada while you leave the country you must pay import duty and taxes or present a valid permit. Canadian Customs officials issue permits at point of entry.
- You may not store a vacation trailer in Canada during the off-season.
- Vehicle registration cards required for Canadian travel.
- If driving a car other than your own, you must have written permission from the owner to use it.
- If driving a rented car, you must possess a copy of the contract.
- A valid U.S. driver's license is valid in Canada for time period specified by the individual provinces and territories.
- In all Canadian provinces and territories it is illegal to use radar detectors.
- Seat belts required for the driver and all passengers throughout Canada.

Headlights: Driving with daytime running lights is required for all car models after 1990.
- In Alberta, British Columbia, New Brunswick, Nova Scotia and Prince Edward Island, lights must be turned on when light conditions restrict visibility to 500 feet (150 m).
- In Manitoba, lights must be turned on when light conditions restrict visibility to 200 feet (60 m).
- In Yukon Territory and Northwest Territories and Nunavut, headlights must remain on at all times.
- Elsewhere in Canada, driving with headlights on during all hours of the day is advised.

FINANCIAL RESPONSIBILITY LAWS IN CANADA
When an accident involves death, injury or property damage, Canadian provinces and territories require evidence of financial responsibility. You may be asked to show this evidence at any time.

U.S. motorists should obtain from their own U.S. insurance companies a yellow Non-Resident Inter-Province Motor Vehicle Liability Insurance Card (accepted as evidence of financial responsibility throughout Canada). Those not carrying proper proof may be subject to a substantial fine (minimum $575). Fine varies in each province. If renting a vehicle, check with the rental car company.

The minimum liability insurance requirement is $200,000 in all provinces and territories except Quebec, which requires $50,000. Should the courts' judgments exceed these figures, motorists held accountable are responsible for paying the full amount.

If traveling in Quebec, discuss your collision, disability and bodily injury coverages with your insurance agent. Since Quebec's minimum requirement does not include bodily injury, coverage of $200,000 or more is recommended. Consider additional coverage (i.e., trip accident policy).

For United States Residents Returning to the United States

Everyone who seeks entry into the United States – whether foreign visitors, U.S. citizens, or U.S. lawful permanent residents – must be inspected at the point of entry. Random searches may be conducted by U.S. Customs and Border Protection agents.

U.S. Exemptions for a Stay in Canada No Less Than 48 hours

- You may bring back tax- and duty-free articles not exceeding $800 in retail value
- Any amount over the $800 exemption is subject to duty
- The exemption is allowed once every 30 days
- A family (related persons living in the same household) may combine its exemptions (a family of 6 is entitled to $4,800 worth of goods duty-free on 1 declaration, even if articles claimed by 1 member exceed that individual's $800 amount)
- Exemptions based on fair retail value (keep receipts of all purchases as proof of fair retail value)
- Exemptions apply to articles acquired only for personal or household use or as gifts, but not intended for sale
- The exemption may include 100 cigars, 200 cigarettes and 1 liter of liquor per person over age 21 (customs enforces state liquor laws)
- All articles claimed under this exemption must accompany you on your return

U.S. Exemptions for a Stay in Canada Less Than 48 hours

- You may bring back tax- and duty-free articles not exceeding $200 in retail value
- The exemption may include no more than 50 cigarettes, 10 cigars, 5 fluid ounces (150 milliliters) of alcoholic beverage or 150 milliliters of perfume containing alcohol
- A family may not combine purchases
- If purchases exceed the $200 exemption, you lose the exemption and all purchases become subject to duty
- All goods must be declared
  - All articles claimed under this exemption must accompany you on your return

Gifts

- Gifts up to $100 fair retail value may be sent to friends or relatives in the United States provided no recipient receives more than 1 gift per day (need not be included in the $800 exemption)
- Gifts containing tobacco products, alcoholic beverages or perfume containing alcohol valued at more than $5 retail are excluded from this provision
- Write on outside of package the contents, retail value and "Unsolicited Gift"

Prohibited: Articles considered detrimental to the general welfare of the United States are prohibited entry: narcotics and dangerous drugs, drug paraphernalia, obscene articles and publications, seditious or treasonable matter, lottery tickets, hazardous items (fireworks, dangerous toys, toxic or poisonous substances) and switchblade knives. Any goods originating in the following countries are prohibited: Balkans, Burma, Cuba, Iran, Iraq, Liberia, Libya, North Korea, Sudan, Syria and Zimbabwe. Please note embargoes are not limited to these countries.

Restricted items include automobiles, biological materials (disease organisms and vectors for research), ceramic tableware, cultural treasures, firearms and ammunition, articles bearing marks or names copying or simulating trademarked articles or trade names (watches, cameras, perfumes), pirated copies of copyrighted articles (books, CDs, DVDs, audio- and video-tapes, computer programs), agricultural goods (plants and animal products) and pets, wildlife and fish.

You may bring into or take out of the United States an unlimited amount of money, however, if you transport more than $10,000 you must file a FinCen 105 with U.S. Customs. Failure to comply can result in civil, criminal and/or forfeiture penalties. Monies include currency, traveler's checks, U.S. or foreign coins in circulation, money orders and negotiable instruments or investment securities in bearer form. For a currency reporting flier contact: U.S. Customs, P.O. Box 7407, Washington, D.C. 20044.

While some agricultural products of Canadian origin (fruits, some plants with phyto-sanitary certificates, meats, etc.) may be brought into the United States, many are restricted to prevent the introduction of plant and animal pests and diseases. All must be declared at the U.S. border. Write to APHIS, Dept. of Agriculture, Room 1147-S, Wash., DC 20205, www.aphis.usda.gov, for a free copy of *Traveler's Tips*. Write to U.S. Customs, P.O. Box 7407, Washington, D.C. 20044 for other helpful leaflets: *Visiting the U.S.: Requirements for Non-Residents, Know Before You Go, Importing a Car*, and *Pets, Wildlife and U.S. Customs*.

For Canada Residents Traveling to the United States

Passports for air travel are now required for travel to the U.S. It is expected that at some point in 2009, Canada residents traveling between the U.S. and Canada, Mexico, the Caribbean, and Bermuda by land or sea (including ferries), will be required to present a valid passport. Please refer to the U.S. Department of State's Web site travel.state.gov for the most current information on these requirements.

Native-born citizens of Canada:
- Passport not required (but is recommended)
- Proof of citizenship required (a birth certificate and photo ID)
- Proof of residence may be required

If traveling to the United States with a child, carry documentation proving your custodial rights. A person under age 18 traveling to the United States alone or with only 1 parent or another adult, must have certified documentation proving that the trip is permitted by both parents.

United States Customs permits Canadian residents to bring, free of duty, for personal use and not intended for sale: clothing, personal items and equipment appropriate to the trip, including 200 cigarettes, 50 cigars or 2 kilograms of tobacco, or proportionate amounts of each, and 1 liter of alcoholic beverage.

Visitors in the United States for at least 72 hours who have not claimed this exemption in the preceding 6 months may bring gifts totaling $100 (US) retail value. Perfume containing alcohol and valued at more than $5 retail, tobacco products and alcoholic beverages excluded from the gift provision.

Use of cell phones and General Radio Service Station (CB) is unrestricted.

For Canada Residents Returning to Canada

The Canada Border Services Agency allows Canadian residents to bring, free of duty and taxes, goods valued up to $400 (CAN) any number of times a year, provided the visit to the United States is 48 hours or more and all goods accompany the purchaser (written declaration may be required).

You may claim a $50 (CAN) exemption on goods, excluding alcoholic beverages and tobacco products, if returning after an absence of 24 hours or more and are not using any other exemption. If bringing back more than $50 worth of goods, the regular duty and tax rate is levied on the entire value. This exemption may apply any number of times in a year.

If returning after 7 days or more in the United States (not counting departure day from Canada) you may claim up to a $750 (CAN) exemption on goods. Goods, other than alcohol and tobacco products, need not accompany you (written declaration may be required).

Permitted within the $200 and $750 exemptions: up to 50 cigars, 200 cigarettes, 200 tobacco sticks and 200 grams (6.4 oz) of tobacco, and up to 1.14 liters (40 oz) of liquor or 1.5 liters (1.6 qts) of wine or 8.5 liters (9 qts) of beer or ale (or its equivalent of 24 12-ounce bottles or cans). You must meet the minimum age requirement of the province or territory entered to claim alcohol or tobacco products.

Special Tariff: When exceeding the $200 or $750 exemption, a special rate of 7 percent combined duty and taxes is levied on the next $300 value in goods (except tobacco and alcohol) exceeding the maximum exemptible amounts, provided goods are of U.S origin. Regular duties apply on any additional amount. A 15 percent Harmonized Sales Tax (HST) (7 percent Goods and Services Tax (GST) and 8 percent provincial component) is charged on most goods and services supplied in Nova Scotia, New Brunswick and Newfoundland and Labrador. For information contact the Canada Border Services Agency before departing Canada. All extra goods must accompany you.

All exemptions are individual and may not be combined with those of other people. You may be asked to verify the length of your visit. Dated receipts normally constitute proof. Gifts (excluding alcoholic beverages, tobacco products and advertising matter) up to $60 (CAN) retail may be sent from abroad free of duty or taxes. For gifts valued at more than $60 (CAN), duty and taxes apply to amount exceeding $60. Gifts sent from abroad do not count against personal exemptions; gifts brought back must be included in exemptions.

While AAA makes every effort to provide accurate and complete information, AAA makes no warranty, express or implied, and assumes no legal liability or responsibility for the accuracy or completeness of any information contained herein.

NATIONAL PARKS ENTRANCE FEES

At Canada's national parks, the basic per person or per family entry fee gives visitors access to the park, scenic outlooks, picnic areas and a variety of facilities. Additional fees are charged for visitors who choose to use other recreational services such as campgrounds, special interpretation programs and golf courses.

To receive a free Parks Canada vacation planner, phone (888) 773-8888. Detailed information about the services, benefits, entry fees and discounts at all national parks and historic sites is available by calling the following numbers:

(800) 748-7275 for Alberta;

(902) 426-3436 for Atlantic provinces (Newfoundland and Labrador, New Brunswick, Nova Scotia and Prince Edward Island);

(604) 513-4777 for British Columbia;

(888)748-2928 for Manitoba;

(800) 748-7275 for Saskatchewan;

(800) 463-6769 for Québec;

(800) 661-0186 for Yukon Territory.

Points of Interest Index

Index Legend

NB...................................national battlefield	NR...national river
NBP..........................national battlefield park	NS.....................................national seashore
NC....................................national cemetery	NWR............................national wildlife refuge
NF.......................................national forest	PHP..........................provincial historic(al) park
NHM.......................national historic(al) monument	PHS...........................provincial historic(al) site
NHP...........................national historic(al) park	PP.......................................provincial park
NHS............................national historic(al) site	SF...state forest
NL....................................national lakeshore	SHM..........................state historic(al) monument
NME...................................national memorial	SHP...............................state historic(al) park
NMO...................................national monument	SHS................................state historic(al) site
NMP...............................national military park	SME.....................................state memorial
NP.......................................national park	SP..state park
NRA.............................national recreation area	SRA.............................state recreation area

⚜ GEM: Points of Interest Offering a *Great Experience for Members*®

MURALS & MOSAICS

MUSEUMS

PARKS, NATIONAL

RECREATION-WINTER ACTIVITIES

RESEARCH ORGANIZATIONS

RESTORED VILLAGES & SETTLEMENTS

RIVERS

SHOPS, FIRMS & STORES

TRAILS-WINTER RECREATION

TREES

TUNNELS

VIEWS

[SAVE] *Attraction Admission Discount Index*

Bed & Breakfast Lodgings Index

Some bed and breakfasts listed below might have historical significance.
Those properties are also referenced in the Historical index.

Country Inns Index

Some of the following country inns can also be considered as bed-and-breakfast operations.

Historical Lodgings & Restaurants Index

Some of the following historical lodgings can also be considered as bed-and-breakfast operations.

Resorts Index

Many establishments are located in resort areas; however, the following places have extensive on-premises recreational facilities:

Comprehensive City Index

Here is an alphabetical list of all cities appearing in this TourBook® guide. Cities are presented by state/province. Page numbers under the POI column indicate where points of interest text begins. Page numbers under the L&R column indicate where lodging and restaurant listings begin.

Comprehensive City Index (cont'd)

Comprehensive City Index (cont'd)

Are You Making the Most of Your Membership?

You know about AAA's famous roadside assistance and its popular TourBook® guides.

But are you using all of your membership benefits?

- **Travel services** including personalized TripTik® routings and free maps, as well as exclusive savings on cruises, tours, member-exclusive vacation packages, and more.

- **Exclusive money-saving discounts** at more than 150,000 Show Your Card & Save® partner locations worldwide.

- **Insurance and financial services**, often at discounted rates. Check your local club for availability.

And so many more! To find out more about all the benefits AAA offers you, visit **AAA.com**.